Baedeker's
GREAT BRITAIN

Cover picture: Big Ben, Houses of Parliament, London

168 colour photographs
71 maps, plans and sketches
1 large road map

Text:
Dr Inge Ingus (Country, Population, Government and Society, Education and Science, Literature, Music, Economy; Britain from A to Z, except London)
Gerald Sawade (Climate)
Christine Wessely (Art)

Editorial work:
Baedeker Stuttgart
English language: Alec Court

Cartography:
Ingenieurbüro für Kartographie,
Huber & Oberländer, Munich
David L. Fryer and Co.,
Henley-on-Thames

Design and layout:
HF Ottmann,
Atelier für Buchgestaltung
und Grafik-Design, Leonberg

Conception and general direction:
Dr Peter Baumgarten,
Baedeker Stuttgart

English translation:
James Hogarth

© Baedeker Stuttgart
Original German edition

© The Automobile Association
United Kingdom and Ireland 57406

© Jarrold and Sons Ltd
English Language edition Worldwide

Licensed user:
Mairs Geographischer Verlag GmbH & Co.,
Ostfildern-Kemnat bei Stuttgart

Reproductions:
Golz Repro-Service GmbH,
Ludwigsburg

The name *Baedeker* is a registered trademark

Source of illustrations:

Most of the coloured photographs were provided by the British Tourist Authority.

Others:
Automobile Association (pp. 296, 303, 306, 333, 352, 356, 375, 380, 391).
Giselher Ernst, Stuttgart (pp. 150, right; 151, 184, 271, 272).
Jarrold Colour Publications, Norwich (pp. 89, 299, 309, 313, 316, 319, 322, 325, 329, 336, 339, 342, 345, 349, 358, 361, 364, 368, 371, 378, 383, 386, 390, 393, 396, 399, 402, 405, 409).
Gerald Sawade, Stuttgart (pp. 74, 178, 181, 185, 224, 227).
Woodmansterne Ltd, Watford (pp. 75, 91, 110, 176, 208, bottom; 232, 276, 282).
Zentrale Farbbild Agentur GmbH (ZEFA), Düsseldorf (cover picture).

The drawing of the City skyline (pp. 174–175) is by Monika Dostler, Schwäbisch Hall.

The panorama of Snowdonia (pp. 212–213) was redrawn by Georg Schiffner, Lahr/Schwarzwald, on the basis of the panorama in Baedeker's "Great Britain".

The imaginary drawing of the Loch Ness monster (p. 205) is by Katja Ungerer, Stuttgart.

Printed in Great Britain by Jarrold and Sons Ltd, Norwich

0-13-055855-9 US & Canada
0-86145-059-0 UK

How to Use this Guide

Europe uses the metric system of measurement. Since this is the only system you will encounter in your travels, many of the measurements in this guide are expressed in metric terms. Conversion is easy. Multiply metres by 3·3 to get the approximate dimension in feet. A kilometre (1000 m) is approximately 0·62 mile.

The principal towns and areas of tourist interest are described in alphabetical order. The names of other places referred to under these general headings can be found in the very full index.

Following the tradition established by Karl Baedeker in 1844, sights of outstanding interest are distinguished by either one or two asterisks.

In the lists of hotels b.=beds and r.=rooms.

The symbol ⓘ at the beginning of an entry or on a town plan indicates the local tourist office or other organisation from which further information can be obtained. The post-horn symbol on a town plan indicates a post office.

Only a selection of hotels and restaurants can be given: no reflection is implied on establishments not included.

This guidebook forms part of a completely new series of the world-famous Baedeker Guides to Europe.

Each volume is the result of long and careful preparation and, true to the traditions of Baedeker, is designed in every respect to meet the needs and expectations of the modern traveller.

The name of Baedeker has long been identified in the field of guidebooks with reliable, comprehensive and up-to-date information, prepared by expert writers who work from detailed, first-hand knowledge of the country concerned. Following a tradition that goes back over 150 years to the date when Karl Baedeker published the first of his handbooks for travellers, these guides have been planned to give the tourist all the essential information about the country and its inhabitants: where to go, how to get there and what to see. Baedeker's account of a country was always based on his personal observation and experience during his travels in that country. This tradition of writing a guidebook in the field rather than at an office desk has been maintained by Baedeker ever since.

Lavishly illustrated with superb colour photographs and numerous specially drawn maps and street plans of the major towns, the new Baedeker Guides concentrate on making available to the modern traveller all the information he needs in a format that is both attractive and easy to follow. For every place that appears in the gazetteer, the principal features of architectural, artistic and historic interest are described, as are its main areas of scenic beauty. Selected hotels and restaurants are also included. Features of exceptional merit are indicated by either one or two asterisks.

A special section at the end of each book contains practical information, details of leisure activities and useful addresses. The separate road map will prove an invaluable aid to planning your route and your travel within the country.

Contents

Introduction to Great Britain

England
Wales
Scotland
Northern Ireland

Cliffs at Yasnaby (Orkney Islands)

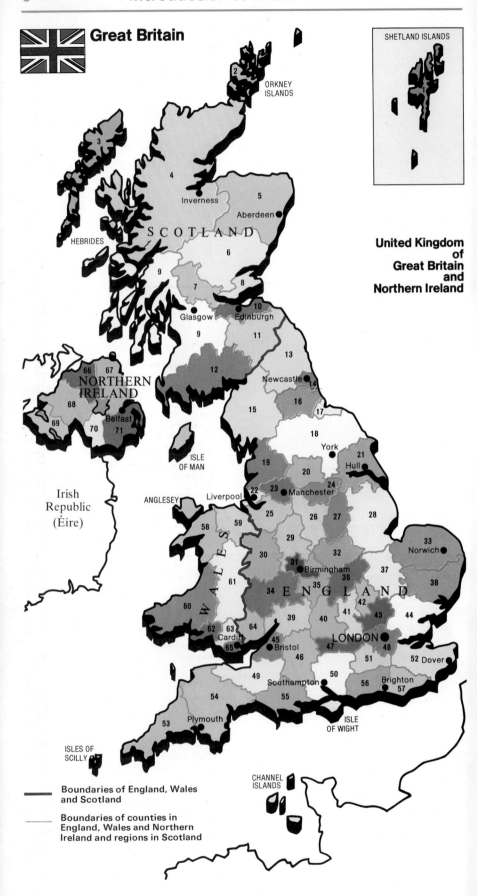

Great Britain

SHETLAND ISLANDS

ORKNEY ISLANDS

United Kingdom
of
Great Britain
and
Northern Ireland

Inverness
Aberdeen
SCOTLAND
HEBRIDES
Glasgow
Edinburgh
NORTHERN IRELAND
Belfast
Newcastle
ISLE OF MAN
Irish Republic (Éire)
ANGLESEY
Liverpool
Manchester
York
Hull
WALES
ENGLAND
Birmingham
Norwich
Cardiff
Bristol
LONDON
Dover
Southampton
Brighton
Plymouth
ISLE OF WIGHT
ISLES OF SCILLY
CHANNEL ISLANDS

Boundaries of England, Wales
and Scotland

Boundaries of counties in
England, Wales and Northern
Ireland and regions in Scotland

Scotland (Areas, Regions)

1	Shetland Islands Area	Borders Region	11
2	Orkney Islands Area	Central Region	7
3	Western Isles Area	Dumfries and Galloway Region	12
4	Highland Region	Fife Region	8
5	Grampian Region	Grampian Region	5
6	Tayside Region	Highland Region	4
7	Central Region	Lothian Region	10
8	Fife Region	Orkney Islands Area	2
9	Strathclyde Region	Shetland Islands Area	1
10	Lothian Region	Strathclyde Region	9
11	Borders Region	Tayside Region	6
12	Dumfries and Galloway Region	Western Isles Area	3

England (Counties)

13	Northumberland	Avon	45
14	Tyne and Wear	Bedfordshire	42
15	Cumbria	Berkshire	47
16	Durham	Buckinghamshire	41
17	Cleveland	Cambridgeshire	37
18	North Yorkshire	Cheshire	25
19	Lancashire	Cleveland	17
20	West Yorkshire	Cornwall	53
21	Humberside	Cumbria	15
22	Merseyside	Derbyshire	26
23	Greater Manchester	Devon	54
24	South Yorkshire	Dorset	55
25	Cheshire	Durham	16
26	Derbyshire	East Sussex	57
27	Nottinghamshire	Essex	44
28	Lincolnshire	Gloucestershire	39
29	Staffordshire	Hampshire	50
30	Shropshire	Hereford and Worcester	34
31	West Midlands	Hertfordshire	43
32	Leicestershire	Humberside	21
33	Norfolk	Kent	52
34	Hereford and Worcester	Lancashire	19
35	Warwickshire	Leicestershire	32
36	Northamptonshire	Lincolnshire	28
37	Cambridgeshire	London (Greater)	48
38	Suffolk	Manchester (Greater)	23
39	Gloucestershire	Merseyside	22
40	Oxfordshire	Norfolk	33
41	Buckinghamshire	Northamptonshire	36
42	Bedfordshire	Northumberland	13
43	Hertfordshire	North Yorkshire	18
44	Essex	Nottinghamshire	27
45	Avon	Oxfordshire	40
46	Wiltshire	Shropshire	30
47	Berkshire	Somerset	49
48	Greater London	South Yorkshire	24
49	Somerset	Staffordshire	29
50	Hampshire	Suffolk	38
51	Surrey	Surrey	51
52	Kent	Tyne and Wear	14
53	Cornwall	Warwickshire	35
54	Devon	West Midlands	31
55	Dorset	West Sussex	56
56	West Sussex	West Yorkshire	20
57	East Sussex	Wiltshire	46

Wales (Counties)

58	Gwynedd	Clwyd	59
59	Clwyd	Dyfed	60
60	Dyfed	Gwent	64
61	Powys	Gwynedd	58
62	West Glamorgan	Mid Glamorgan	63
63	Mid Glamorgan	Powys	61
64	Gwent	South Glamorgan	65
65	South Glamorgan	West Glamorgan	62

Northern Ireland (Counties)

66	Londonderry	Armagh	70
67	Antrim	Antrim	67
68	Tyrone	Down	71
69	Fermanagh	Fermanagh	69
70	Armagh	Londonderry	66
71	Down	Tyrone	68

Throughout recorded history Britain has attracted a fair share of overseas visitors — conquerors such as the Romans and Vikings, traders from continental Europe, refugees, colonial residents and tourists from all corners of the globe. Still today the number of visitors to Britain continues to increase — tourists and businessmen alike drawn by the country's commercial opportunities, cultural heritage and a great wealth of scenic attractions, ranging from many thousands of miles of varied coastline to the mountains, lakes and fell-sides of the north and west, and the gentler slopes, woodlands and arable lands of the south. More even than the "swinging London", which erupted in a blaze of publicity in the 1960s, it is rural Britain, with its tranquil and uniquely pretty villages, its historic castles, cathedrals and museums, which continues to beckon the visitor from overseas.

Finchingfield (Essex)

But to think of Britain merely as what has been described as the "offshore island" — close to the European continent but physically separate from it — is misleading. For Britain is in fact a whole archipelago of islands, extending from the Channel Islands, a few miles off the coast of France, all the way to the Shetland Islands, which lie in the same latitude as Bergen in Norway. The term **British Isles** is applied to the whole complex, often including the independent Republic of Ireland which constitutes the major part of the Emerald Isle. The "Britain" with which this guide is concerned is the country officially known as the **United Kingdom** of Great Britain: England, Wales, Scotland and Northern Ireland.

The British Isles lie on the continental shelf of the European landmass, to which they were connected by a land bridge until the Mesolithic period (c. 6000–5000 B.C.). In consequence many features in British topography represent a continuation of continental land-forms. The post-glacial vegetation is similar to that of the European continent and the prehistoric inhabitants of Britain belonged to the same cultural systems as those of the Continent.

Britain has been physically separated from Europe for long enough, however, for its inhabitants to have developed a sense of standing apart. For many centuries this feeling of isolation from Europe was reinforced by Britain's links with the rest of the world, particularly with its widespread colonies and with the United States. It is only quite recently that political and economic events have turned Britain's attention slowly in the direction of Europe.

The United Kingdom (England, Wales, Scotland and Northern Ireland) has a total area of some 95,000 sq. miles, including 1200 sq. miles of inland waters. In length, the mainland extends more than 600 miles from north to south; at its broadest point, in the south, it spans some 300 miles. Because of its shape, and the many estuaries and inlets which penetrate inland, all Britain's large towns (and many smaller ones) are located no more than an hour's journey-time from the sea — an accident of geography which has proved advantageous both to trade and transport and to holidaymakers from Britain and overseas.

The British landscape is a patchwork of different elements, all relatively small, and is therefore notable for its rich variety. Two main regions can be distinguished: in the north and west the *highland zone*; in the east the *lowland zone*, based on more recent geological formations. The two zones are roughly defined by an imaginary line from the mouth of the River Exe in the SW and the mouth of the Tees in the NE.

The highland areas of Scotland, Northern Ireland, the north of England and North Wales, which attain a height of 4406 ft in Scotland (Ben Nevis, Britain's highest peak) and 3560 ft in Wales (Snowdon), have a geological structure which represents the westward continuation (but at a lower level) of the Scandinavian highlands. Their surface topography is strongly marked by glacial action.

The coastline of the British Isles ranks among the most beautiful in the world by virtue of its extraordinary variety of form – long fjord-like inlets in the NW of Scotland, rias (drowned valleys) in SW England and Wales, sheer cliffs of many different rocks, low-lying beaches of shingle or sand, sometimes backed by dunes, great areas of fenland along the East Anglian coasts.

More than half of Scotland's land area, north of a line between the Clyde estuary and Stonehaven, consists of the Highlands, where rugged peaks rise out of vast expanses of moorland and heath. The southern half of the country has gentler hills, the Southern Uplands, running in a great swathe from SW to NE. Most of the mountains in Britain, even in the Highlands, have rounded rather than craggy forms; Ben Nevis has a rounded top.

Between the Highlands and the Southern Uplands lies the rift valley of the Central Lowlands, occupying only a fifth of Scotland's total area but containing three-quarters of its population. Even here, however, the lower ground is interrupted by hills.

The Southern Uplands are linked by the Cheviot Hills with the mountain backbone of northern England, the Pennines. To the west are the beautiful hills of Cumbria and the Lake District.

The Welsh mountains, composed of older rocks, have foothills extending into the English counties of Shropshire and Herefordshire. The highest summits are in North Wales, clustered round Snowdon in the magnificent Snowdonia National Park. In Mid and South Wales there are extensive areas of moorland.

The rock masses of the south-western peninsula (Devon and Cornwall) have been levelled down into a plateau out of which rise areas of higher ground, notably Dartmoor and Exmoor.

Even the British lowland zone is by no means monotonously flat. Here low-lying plains are interrupted by ranges of sandstone or limestone hills, usually with their steeper scarps on the west or north side. Long valleys extend between the hills, sometimes opening out into basins such as the Wash on the east coast and the Ouse basin in Yorkshire. Between these "scarpland" areas and the Scottish

Loch Leven, near Ballachulish (Scottish Highlands)

Britain's Principal Mountains and Hills

hills lies the large Midland plain, roughly triangular in shape.

To the south and east of the scarplands are a variety of land-forms. East Anglia is an undulating region of relatively low-lying country, mostly under 1000 ft. The lower course of the Thames turns east to run through the London basin to the sea; and the Hampshire basin is similar, extending around Southampton.

To the SE, beyond the Thames, are ridges of higher ground running from east to west. Main features are the North Downs and South Downs, chalk ridges which end in the famous white cliffs of the south coast.

Climate

The British Isles, lying between the Atlantic and the North Sea, have an oceànic climate – cool summers and mild winters, with only a relatively limited range of temperature variation over the year. On the side facing the Atlantic the air is also warmed in winter by the benign currents of the Gulf Stream. The prevailing SW winds, continuing even during winter, favour south-western England, where sub-tropical vegetation such as dwarf palms can flourish. In summer the prevailing W and NW winds have a cooling effect. A more markedly continental climate is found only in SE England, lying closer to the Continent and sheltered from the open sea by hills.

Given the great length of the British Isles from north to south, **temperatures** primarily depend on latitude. Since most of the places mentioned below lie at least than 300 ft, the effect of altitude on temperature can usually be left out of account (exceptions are noted below).

The *mean annual temperature* falls from south to north: 13·1 °C (56 °F) on Jersey, off the French coast; 11·5° (53°) in the Scilly Isles and at Penzance (Cornwall); 11° (52°) at Plymouth, Torquay and Westminster (London); 10·1° (50°) at Cardiff and Oxford; 9·6° (49°) at Liverpool, Sheffield and York; 9·1° (48°) at Belfast and Tynemouth; 8·6° (47°) at Edinburgh (400 ft) and Perth; 8·4° (47°) at Aberdeen; 8·2° (47°) at Cape Wrath (370 ft), at the NW tip of Scotland; 7·7° (46°) at Wick, just south of the NE tip of Scotland; 7·4° (45°) at Deerness in the Orkneys; 7·1° (45°) at Lerwick in the Shetlands.

The *January mean* (in some cases February) also falls markedly from the west to the more continental east: 7·5 °C (46 °F) in the Scilly Isles and at Penzance (Jersey only 6·2° (43°)); 6·3° (43°) at St Ann's Head, near the SW tip of Wales; 5·5° (42°) at Westminster (London) and Margate; 5° (41°) at Cardiff, Portsmouth, Douglas (Isle of Man) and Dover; 4° (39°) at Belfast, Canterbury, Yarmouth and Cape Wrath; 3·2° (38°) at Lerwick; 2·6° (37°) at Princetown (1350 ft) on Dartmoor; 1·2° (34°) at Dalwhinnie (1180 ft), south of Inverness.

The *July mean* (in some cases August) also tends to fall from west to east as well as from south to north:

18·8 °C (66 °F) on Jersey; 17·5° (64°) at Dover, Westminster (London) and Margate; 17° (63°) at Canterbury; 16·5° (62°) at Birmingham, Norwich and Hull; 16° (61°) in the Scilly Isles; 15° (59°) at Haverfordwest in SW Wales and Armagh in Northern Ireland; 14·5° (58°) at Belfast; 14° (57°) at Edinburgh (400 ft); 13·9° (57°) at Aberdeen; 12·9° (55°) at Balmoral (900 ft) in NE Scotland; 12° (54°) at Lerwick; 11·7° (53°) at Deerness in the Orkneys.

The *Temperature range* falls from 13·7 °C (57 °F) at Shoeburyness (on the north side of the Thames estuary) in the more continental east to 13·3° (56°) at Cambridge; 12·8° (55°) at Birmingham (420 ft); 12·5° (55°) at Dover and Liverpool; 11·3° (52°) at Cardiff and Balmoral; 10·5° (51°) at Belfast; 9·5° (49°) at Haverfordwest; 8·7° (48°) at Penzance and St Ann's Head; 8·5° (47°) in the Scillies and at Cape Wrath; 8·2° (47°) at Stornoway in the Outer Hebrides; and 8·1° (47°) at Deerness. Particularly striking is the difference between the last named places, lying directly on the Atlantic, and places such as Liverpool which are buffered from the full effects of the ocean by Ireland.

The figures for Oxford can be taken as typical of a more continental climatic pattern – annual mean 10·1 °C (50 °F), January mean 3·8° (39°), July mean 17° (63°), annual range 13·2° (56°). An entirely oceanic climate is shown in the south by the Scillies (annual mean 11·4° (53°), February, 7·5° (46°), July and August 16° (61°), range 8·5° (47°)) and in the north by Deerness in the Orkneys (annual mean 7·4° (45°), February 3·6° (38°), July and August 11·7° (53°), range 8·1° (47°)).

The oceanic character of the climate is also shown in the distribution of **rainfall**. Moving in from the Atlantic, the rain-bearing west winds cause the air to rise against the hills along the west coasts of England and Scotland and produce considerable falls of rain, frequently accompanied in autumn and winter (under the influence of heavy depressions over Iceland) by violent storms. The areas, in Northern Ireland as well as England and Scotland, lying in the rain-shadow to the east of the hills are much drier, though here rain is scarcely less frequent, even if less heavy, and the sky is overcast for considerable periods Only in the mountainous areas does snow lie for any length of time. The high humidity of the air throughout the country (in winter often over 90%, in summer usually over 75%) means that large areas are subject to fog, particularly in winter.

Most of the rain usually falls between October and January. In Northern Ireland the wettest periods are in August and from October to December; in SE Scotland and certain areas in the lee of the hills in July and August. The period with least rainfall is between March and June, when Britain often enjoys considerable spells of fine weather. In a region subject to the passage of cyclones, however, the weather can vary considerably from year to year – hence its constant fascination for the British as a topic of conversation. Some idea of the rainfall pattern can be gained from the following figures, arranged in groups going from south to north, with the places in each group listed from west to east. The figures given are of mean annual rainfall, with minimum and maximum in certain characteristic cases:

1. (Maximum almost always in November, minimum in June; exceptions noted): Scilly Isles 831 mm (33 in.), (92 mm (4 in.), 44 mm (2 in.)), Penzance 1058 mm (42 in.) (max. January 130 mm (5 in.)), Plymouth 958 mm (38 in.), Princetown (1350 ft; on windward side of Dartmoor) 2154 mm (85 in.) (January 268 mm (11 in.), April and July each 135 mm (5 in.)), Torquay

Britain's Principal Rivers and Lakes*

SHETLAND ISLANDS

ORKNEY ISLANDS

Inverness
Loch Ness
Spey
Aberdeen
Dee
Tay
HEBRIDES
Firth of Forth
Glasgow
Edinburgh
Clyde
Tweed
Firth of Clyde
Nith
Newcastle
Tyne
Tees
Ure
Bann
Lough Neagh
Lough Erne
Belfast
Wharfe
York
Hull
ISLE OF MAN
Humber
ANGLESEY
Liverpool
Manchester
The Wash
Trent
Witham
Nene
Norwich
Birmingham
Severn
Ouse
Wye
Avon
Usk
LONDON
Cardiff
Severn
Bristol
Thames
Dover
Southampton
Brighton
Plymouth
ISLE OF WIGHT
ISLES OF SCILLY
CHANNEL ISLANDS

*Lochs in Scotland, loughs in Northern Ireland

889 mm (35 in.), Bournemouth 794 mm (31 in.), Portsmouth 705 mm (28 in.), Eastbourne 783 mm (31 in.), Dover 848 mm (33 in.) (115 mm (5 in.), 44 mm (2 in.)).
2. Cardiff 1043 mm (41 in.) (max. October to January each 118 mm (5 in.), min. July 58 mm (2 in.)), Bath 785 mm (31 in.), Oxford 652 mm (26 in.), Westminster (London) 595 mm (23 in.), Shoeburyness (north side of Thames estuary) 515 mm (20 in.) (November 57 mm (2 in.), June 30 mm (1 in.) – lowest of all the places listed).
3. Aberystwyth (west coast of Wales) 1254 mm (49 in.) (October 115 mm (5 in.), March and April each 57 mm (2 in.)), Birmingham 757 mm (30 in.), Cambridge 551 mm (22 in.), Great Yarmouth 598 mm (24 in.).
4. Snowdon (3560 ft) 2500 mm (98 in.), Liverpool 737 mm (29 in.) (August 78 mm (3 in), March 42 mm (2 in.)), Buxton 1233 mm (49 in.) (January 130 mm (5 in.), May 74 mm (3 in.)), Skegness (east coast) 567 mm (22 in.) (November 60 mm (2 in.), March 34 mm (1 in.)).
5. Belfast 879 mm (35 in.) (August and December each 93 mm (4 in.), April 57 mm (2 in.)), Douglas (Isle of Man) 1145 mm (45 in.), Keswick (Lake District) 1476 mm (58 in.) (November and January each 165 mm (6 in.), May 82 mm (3 in.)), Eskdalemuir (780 ft, in Cheviot Hills) 1581 mm (62 in.), Durham 668 mm (26 in.) (July 70 mm (3 in.), March 42 mm (2 in.)).
6. Tiree (a flat island off the west coast of Scotland) 1204 mm (47 in.), Glenbranter (120 ft, near Loch Fyne) 2394 mm (94 in.) (January 300 mm (12 in.), October 290 mm (11 in.), May 120 mm (5 in.)), Stirling 978 mm (39 in.), Edinburgh 699 mm (28 in.) (August 79 mm (3 in.), March 42 mm (2 in.)).
7. Fort William 2067 mm (81 in.) (December 235 mm (9 in.), May 80 mm (3 in.)), Ben Nevis (4406 ft) 4000 mm (157 in.), Dalwhinnie 1251 mm (49 in.), Aberdeen 836 mm (33 in.) (November 85 mm (3 in.), July 55 mm (2 in.)).
8. Stornoway (Outer Hebrides) 1002 mm (39 in.) (October 120 mm (5 in.), March 58 mm (2 in.)), Cape Wrath 1203 mm (47 in.), Wick 761 mm (30 in.), Deerness (Orkney) 900 mm (35 in.), Lerwick (Shetland) 1028 mm (40 in.) (November, December and January each 135 mm (5 in.), June 53 mm (2 in.)).

Population

The United Kingdom (England, Wales, Scotland and Northern Ireland) has a population of some 56 million, distributed at an average density of 590 to the square mile – a little less than West Germany but almost two and a half times as high as in France. Since about half the UK population lives in the 60 largest towns, however, there are considerable tracts of territory which are only sparsely populated.

The largest single entity within the United Kingdom is *England*, with a population of more than 46 million. The people of Scotland, Northern Ireland and Wales, though they regard themselves as British

and part of the United Kingdom, tend to cherish their own separate histories and traditions, and different characters. In addition, the Welsh have preserved their own Celtic language – still the living tongue of a considerable proportion of the population.

Scotland has a population of 5·1 million, spread over an area of more than 30,000 square miles – almost a third of the whole United Kingdom – at a density of only 180 to the square mile. It has its own historic capital in Edinburgh, its own Church and legal system, its own educational traditions and pattern of local government. Most Scottish domestic matters (health services, education, police, agriculture, etc.) are the responsibility of separate Scottish government departments based in Scotland and subject to a Scottish minister, the Secretary of State for Scotland, who is a member of the British Cabinet. But, after much discussion of the possibility of further devolution of government responsibility from the United Kingdom Parliament to some kind of parliamentary body based in Scotland, government proposals for the establishment of a Scottish Assembly were rejected following a national referendum in 1979.

Scottish bagpiper

At the last census (1971) only some 88,000 people in Scotland, mainly in the north-western Highlands and islands, were able to speak Gaelic, the Scottish form of Celtic. One of the most potent factors in the growth of Scottish Nationalist feeling has been economic backwardness and the low standard of living which this produces in many parts of the country. In the 1960s Scotsmen were leaving their homeland at the rate of between 20,000 and 40,000 a year.

Wales, with a population of 2·8 million, has been joined to England since 1536. Like Scotland, it feels economically disadvantaged, with a high rate of unemployment following the closure of many of the coalmines. But Welsh nationalism also has a large cultural element. Almost a quarter of the population speak Welsh, and a movement to promote the spread and official recognition of the language has been active since 1962. Welsh writers, dramatists and musicians have been encouraged to develop their creative talents, and the traditional Welsh festival of music and poetry, the Eisteddfod, has been revived. Since 1967 Welsh has shared equal status with English in the administration of justice and the conduct of government business. Welsh is used as the medium of instruction in some schools; there is a Welsh-language newspaper; and Welsh is used in some radio and television programmes. In 1972 bilingual street names and road signs were introduced.

Northern Ireland, the former province of Ulster, which remained part of the United Kingdom after the establishment of the Irish Free State in 1921, has a population of 1½ million, mainly Protestants of Scottish and English descent, with some 35% Roman Catholics.

More than half the UK population nominally belongs to the established Anglican Church, the Church of England, of which the Queen is the Head. The number of Roman Catholics has almost tripled during the 20th c. and now amounts to some 5 million. The Church of Scotland is Presbyterian, but Scotland also has a substantial minority of Roman Catholics. In England there are also active Nonconformist groups (dissenting from the established church), mainly Methodists and various Presbyterian denominations; there are also some smaller sects, notably the Baptists and Quakers. There are more than half a million Jews in Britain, as well as some 300,000 Moslems

Government and Society

The **United Kingdom of Great Britain and Northern Ireland** is made up of the four countries of England, Wales, Scotland and Northern Ireland. The main local government units in England, Wales and Northern Ireland are the *counties*, of which, following reorganisation of local government structure in 1974, there are 45 in England, 8 in Wales and 6 in Northern Ireland. In Scotland the former counties and burghs were reorganised in 1975 into 9 *regions*, subdivided into 51 *districts*, and 3 island areas, many of the new units retaining the names of the old counties.

As the oldest of the great democracies, Britain has no written constitution. This is a defect more apparent than real, for the principles of the constitution are firmly established in the consciousness of the British public and the politicians they elect. The lack of any basic or fundamental law of the constitution is the consequence of the country's gradual development from a feudal to a liberal and democratic state, achieved by a process of reform over centuries rather than revolution. One important written document, however, is honoured as the cornerstone of the constitution: Magna Carta, which King John was compelled by his nobles to sign in 1215, is a charter representing a synthesis of old Anglo-Saxon and Norman law and giving guarantees of civil rights, liberties and property.

In the course of centuries, however, some elements in the constitution have been

Carrick-a-Rede, Northern Ireland

laid down in writing, on the basis of the "common law" determined by a succession of legal judgments which have elaborated the law and modified previous judgments in accordance with the prevailing climate of opinion. In modern times there has been a great proliferation of statutory law – incorporated in Acts of Parliament. Nevertheless the unwritten "laws and customs of the constitution" have continued to regulate the behaviour of the Crown and Cabinet and the government and opposition.

The British **monarchy** is a hereditary institution in which the right of succession rests with the monarch's eldest son, or with a daughter if there is no son. The sovereign must be a member of the Church of England. In modern times the monarch's parliamentary role is almost entirely ritual – the opening and closing of the sessions of Parliament, the dissolution of Parliament, the formal appointment of the prime minister and members of the government, the granting of the royal assent to laws passed by Parliament. In practice the monarch must act on ministerial advice. He or she also has formal and representational functions as Head of the Commonwealth.

Parliament consists of the *House of Lords* or Upper House and the *House of Commons* or Lower House. In fact the final decision always rests with the House of Commons: the House of Lords has no say in financial legislation, and other measures of which it disapproves can only be delayed but not finally countermanded. The House of Commons has 630 members directly elected by majority vote for the life of a Parliament (maximum 5 years). The first woman MP was admitted in 1928. The House of Lords, with something over 900 members, is predominantly composed of hereditary peers, together with 9 senior judges and 26 bishops. Recent years, however, have seen an increasing number of nonhereditary "life peers" appointed by the government of the day. Reform of the House of Lords has been the subject of debate for many years.

The *government*, which is responsible to Parliament, consists of the Prime Minister, normally the leader of the majority party, and ministers selected by him or her. The House of Commons is presided over by the Speaker, who, on election to an office with traditions going back to medieval times, withdraws from party political activity. He seeks to maintain strict neutrality, in order to promote orderly debate and to ensure that the rights of the opposition are safeguarded. An important tradition in the Commons is "Questiontime" – an hour of Parliamentary time on four days every week during which members can put questions to ministers on any matters within their field of responsibility. Much Parliamentary work, particularly in the framing of legislation, is done in committee.

The two-party system has a long tradition in Britain, and during most of this century there has been a fairly regular alternation between Labour and Conservative governments. More recently there has been an upsurge of the smaller parties, the Liberals and the Scottish and Welsh nationalist parties, but these have not succeeded in undermining the predominance of the two main parties. Except in the special circumstances of strife-torn Northern Ireland, religion plays practically no part in determining party allegiance.

The *legal system* of Britain differs in many respects from those of other European countries. In England and Wales the most important source is the common law, the origins of which go back to the time of the Norman kings. In Scotland the system is based on Roman law. In modern times the common law has been supplemented or superseded by a great volume of statute law. Since 1965 two Law Commissions, one for England and Wales and one for Scotland, have been responsible for keeping the law under review and recommending measures for its reform, simplification and codification. The lower courts in England and Wales are the magistrates' courts (for criminal and civil matters), with crown courts (criminal) and county courts (civil) at the next higher level. There are appeals to the High Court, which sits in London, and there is also a right of appeal to the House of Lords. In Scotland the lower courts are the district courts (minor criminal cases) and the sheriff courts (criminal and civil), with appeals to the supreme courts, sitting in Edinburgh, and a final appeal (civil cases only) to the House of Lords. The magistrates' courts in England and Wales and district courts in Scotland are chaired by lay "justices of the peace", who deal outright with most cases of petty crime. High-court judges still wear the traditional robes and wigs. They are appointed by the Crown. In criminal cases the accused person is deemed to be innocent until he is proved guilty. The death sentence was abolished in 1966.

Conscription – formerly two years' national service – was abolished in Britain in 1960, and the armed forces now consist solely of volunteers. Recruitment varies, but a period of recession tends to boost enlistment to the armed forces, as it does to the essential civilian services – the police, fire and ambulance brigades. Fundamental defence matters are considered by the Defence Council, whose membership includes the ministers concerned, the chiefs of staff and other senior advisers and officials. Britain produces its own atomic weapons.

Britain is famed for its system of *health and social services* – the "welfare state". A major element in the system is the National Health Service, to which practically all doctors contribute, though still retaining the right to engage also in private practice if they wish. All British residents are entitled to receive a full range of medical care, subject only to the payment of modest charges for medicines, appliances and certain other services; visitors to Britain who fall ill or have an accident during their stay are permitted to receive care on the same basis. The major part of the spiralling costs of the health services is met by the taxpayer.

Other services provided by the welfare state include sickness and unemployment benefit, family allowances and retirement and invalidity pensions. Large-scale public housing developments have been carried out, particularly in the larger towns and cities, but have barely been able to keep pace with the demand. Almost a quarter of the population lives in a "council house" (a house built by a local authority); another quarter of the population lives in privately owned rented houses; and half own their houses. Home-ownership is made easier by the availability of mortgages and loans from building societies and local authorities, requiring only a small deposit (sometimes as little as 5%) against the purchase price. Present high interest rates make these facilities less attractive than in the past, but in spite of this many young couples are anxious to achieve the traditional British ideal of a house, preferably with a garden, of their own.

Television and radio, until 1955 the sole responsibility of the British Broadcasting Corporation (BBC), are now also served by a number of commercial companies. The BBC, which has two television channels and a nation-wide radio network, is financed by licence fees paid by television viewers; the commercial companies (two television channels with regional programmes) and the more recently established local radio stations get their revenue from advertising. It is hard to say whether competition from the commercial companies has improved or lowered the standard of BBC programmes. But, despite criticisms, outside observers seem agreed that British television is the best in the world.

Education

The British *school system* differs considerably from that of other European countries, a notable feature being the coexistence of a public educational system, in which the schools are run by local government authorities, and a private sector consisting of the confusingly named "public schools" and other privately run establishments. Education is compulsory from the ages of 5 to 16.

In 1964 the Labour government introduced a new system doing away with the "11-plus" examination and making the transition from primary to secondary education more flexible. The "comprehensive school" system was introduced, which in effect combined the functions of the earlier grammar, technical and modern schools. Comprehensives were seen as ensuring equality of opportunity for all pupils. Grammar Schools still exist in a few places, but the majority of local authorities have now adopted a comprehensive system. In some areas Sixth-Form Colleges have been established to cater for pupils over the age of 16, and vocational as well as general education is also available in Colleges of Further Education.

In Scotland, with different educational traditions, the controversy is less acute, since public secondary education is almost completely organised on the comprehensive principle.

In the final years of their school career most pupils sit examinations controlled by various examining boards, on the basis of which they obtain certificates in chosen subjects, either at O (ordinary) or A (advanced) level or a Certificate of Secondary Education. Performance in these exams is an important factor in determining choice of career and job prospects.

Outside the state system, the "public schools" are primarily an English institution, though there are also some elsewhere in the United Kingdom. Catering for only 5% of the school population, at very high fees, they have been criticised as being socially divisive.

Britain has a total of 45 *universities*: 33 in England, 8 in Scotland, 2 in Northern Ireland and the federated University of Wales, with 5 colleges, a medical school and an institute of science and technology. Included in the total is the Open University, which provides instruction by television and radio for students (usually older people) who have not had an opportunity of going to a conventional university.

The two ancient English universities, Oxford and Cambridge, are traditional rivals, Cambridge being regarded as pre-eminent in the sciences, Oxford in the arts. The largest of the other English universities, all of which date from the 19th and 20th centuries, is London. The oldest Scottish university is St Andrews, founded in 1412; the other three senior Scottish universities were founded in the 15th and 16th centuries, the four most recent in the 20th. Undergraduate clubs cater for a great variety of leisure interests, and sport also plays an important role in university life.

Much attention is also paid to *adult education*, provided by education authorities, residential colleges, the extra-mural departments of universities and a variety of other bodies.

History

Prehistory and the early historical period (before 60000 to 1st c. B.C.). – The territory of the British Isles was occupied from a very early period by peoples belonging to the Western European cultural movement.

Before 60000 B.C. **Palaeolithic period** (Old Stone Age). The earliest implements of flaked stone belonged to the **Acheulian culture**. The Swanscombe skull indicates that the Acheulian people belonged to the pre-*sapiens* group.
An important cultural phase in Britain is the **Clactonian** (after a site at Clacton-on-Sea in Essex), with a fire-hardened wooden spear-tip as well as stone implements.

About 8000 to 1800 B.C. **Neolithic period** (New Stone Age). During the Mesolithic period (Middle Stone Age) incomers from northern and western Europe reach the British Isles. After 3000 B.C. these immigrants belong to a Neolithic farming culture, the Windmill Hill culture, established on the chalk soils of southern England. These peoples, mostly of Iberian origin, develop the **megalithic culture** with its imposing chambered tombs and standing stones.
At the beginning of the 2nd millennium B.C. several waves of the Beaker peoples from the Low Countries begin to arrive in Britain. Recent research suggests that these peoples were responsible for the erection of the great stone circles of Stonehenge (*c.* 19th–15th c. B.C.) and the first mining of copper in England.

About 1660 B.C. Beginning of the **Bronze Age**. After further waves of newcomers the **Wessex culture** is established, owing its wealth to the trade in gold and tin.

In the 14th c. B.C. the **Urnfield culture** develops. Accompanied by the growing of wheat and barley, it spreads from England into Scotland and Ireland, persisting in many areas until the beginning of the Christian era.

About 600 B.C. In the late Bronze Age the first group of **Celts**, the GOIDELS (hence, perhaps, the term "Gaelic"), arrives in Britain.

About 500 B.C. Beginning of the **Iron Age**, with a new influx of Celts from the N coast of France. Another group of Celts, the BRYTHONS ("Britons"), arrive about 300 B.C.

55 B.C. to A.D. 412 **Roman period.** Following two invasions by *Julius Caesar* in 55 and 54 B.C., which leave no mark on the country, SE England becomes a Roman province in A.D. 43. After repressing a rising by the Iceni, led by their queen Boudica or Boadicea, the Romans advance westward and northward. In 78 *Julius Agricola* begins a campaign of conquest which ends with his victory at Mons Graupius in 84, bringing the whole of England and part of Scotland (Caledonia) under Roman control.

After 122 **Hadrian's Wall** is built between Wallsend-on-Tyne and Bowness, on the Solent, as a defence against the warlike peoples of the north. 290 onwards: defences built against the Saxons on the SE coast of England (the "Saxon shore"). About 360: raids by Picts and Scots from Ireland.

The Romans in Britain

1 Bellie
2 Inchtuthil
3 Eboracum (York)
4 Deva (Chester)
5 Lindum (Lincoln)
6 Viroconium (Wroxeter)
7 Pennocrucium (Water Eaton)
8 Ratae (Leicester)
9 Durobrivae (Water Newton)
10 Venta (Caistor St. Edmund)
11 Moridunum (Carmarthen)
12 Burrium (Usk)
13 Isca (Caerleon)
14 Venta (Caerwent)
15 Glevum (Gloucester)
16 Corinium (Cirencester)
17 Verulamium (St. Albans)
18 Camulodunum (Colchester)
19 Calleva (Silchester)
20 Londinium Augusta (London)
21 Durovernum (Canterbury)
22 Isca Dumnoniorum (Exeter)
23 Durnovaria (Dorchester)
24 Venta (Winchester)
25 Noviomagus (Chichester)

CORNOVII
CARNONACAE
DECANTAE
CALEDONII
VACOMAGI
TAEXALI
VENICONES
Oceanus
Germanicus
Vallum Antonini
DUMNONII
VOTADINI
SELGOVAE
NOVANTA
Vallum Hadriani
BRIGANTES
DECEANGLI
ORDOVICES
CORITANI
ICENI
DEMETAE
CATUVELLAUNI
TRINOVANTES
SILURES
DOBUNNI
CANTIACI
BELGAE
DUROTRIGES
DUMNONII
Oceanus   *Britannicus*
Fretum Gallicum

Permanent frontier fortifications
Most northerly known fort
Colonia and legionary fort
Legionary fort
Fort for Standard bearers
Tribal capitals
BELGAE   Latin names of tribes

367 Hadrian's Wall is breached but is later rebuilt.

412 Final withdrawal of the Roman legions from Britain. The Britons, unable to withstand Pictish attacks without Roman help, appeal to the Angles and Saxons for aid.

449–1066 **Anglo-Saxon period.** The ANGLES, SAXONS and JUTES land in Britain and defeat the Britons, some of whom withdraw to the mountainous W coast of Wales, while others emigrate to Armorica (Brittany).
The Anglo-Saxon conquerors found seven kingdoms in England – Kent, Sussex, Essex, East Anglia, Wessex, Mercia and Northumbria. About 516 a British general named *Arthur* is believed to have defeated the invaders at a place called Mons Badonicus. This is the origin of the legend of King Arthur and the knights of the Round Table.

596 The monk *Augustine* is sent from Rome to convert the Anglo-Saxons. Christianity is also spread in the north by the Iro-Scottish church, which is independent of Rome.

About 800 Raids by the Norsemen. King *Egbert of Wessex* unites the ANGLO-SAXONS in a single kingdom.

871–899 King *Alfred the Great* defeats the Danes and in 885 signs a treaty under which England NE of a line from London to Chester remains in Danish hands. He creates an army and a navy, promulgates a new legal code and promotes learning.

Around 1000 During the reign of *Ethelred the Unready* (978–1016) there are renewed Danish raids. In order to raise money for the Danish tribute he introduces the first general tax to be levied by a medieval kingdom (Danegeld).

1016–42 England, a *Danish kingdom* under *Canute (Knut) the Great* and his sons.

1042–66 *Edward the Confessor* rebuilds and enlarges Westminster Abbey.

1066 Duke *William of Normandy* lands with an army and defeats King Harold in the **battle of Hastings** on 14 October.

1066–1138 The **Norman kings.** By 1071 *William I, the Conqueror* (1066–87) has established control over the whole of England. He introduces the Norman feudal system. The Anglo-Saxon landowners are replaced by Norman barons, and Norman bishops are appointed. This ruling class speaks French and writes Latin, while Anglo-Saxon remains the language of the uneducated. English does not reappear in documents until the 13th c. – *Henry I*, having no son, names his daughter *Matilda* heiress to the throne and marries her to a count of Anjou (family name Plantagenet) Stephen. Seventeen years of civil war followed his succession to the crown. Their son Henry becomes king and founds a new dynasty.

1138–1399 **House of Plantagenet.** *Henry II* (1154–89) comes into conflict with *Thomas Becket*, archbishop of Canterbury, over the respective powers of church and state. Becket excommunicates the king's supporters, and is murdered in Canterbury Cathedral in 1170 by four of the king's knights. *Richard I, Cœur-de-Lion* takes a prominent part in the third Crusade and is taken prisoner on his way home from the Holy Land. He becomes involved in war with Philip II of France. He is succeeded by his brother, King *John* (1199–1216), known as Lackland, who loses Normandy.

1215 The English barons compel John to sign **Magna Carta**, the foundation stone of the English constitution.
Henry III (1216–72) makes war on the rebellious barons led by *Simon de Montfort*. After winning some initial victories de Montfort is defeated and killed by Henry's son Edward at the battle of Evesham.
Edward I (1272–1302) completes the conquest of Wales, and the heir to the throne takes the title of Prince of Wales. In the contest for the Scottish throne between *Robert the Bruce* and *John Balliol*, Edward supports Balliol, who swears an oath of allegiance to him, and defeats Bruce.

1295 **Parliament** is established in its modern form. *Edward II* is defeated at Bannockburn by a Scottish army led by Robert the Bruce. Returning to London, he is deposed and murdered.
Edward III (1327–77) defeats the Scots in several battles. He advances his claim to the French throne, thereby provoking the *Hundred Years War*. The English are victorious in a naval battle at Sluys and in the land battles of Crécy (1346) and Poitiers (1356). At Poitiers the French king is taken prisoner by Edward's son, the Black Prince. After the death of the Black Prince all the English possessions in France except Calais and Gascony are lost. – The Lower House of Parliament breaks away from the Upper House.
Richard II (1377–99) suffers several defeats at the hands of the Scots. Henry Bolingbroke, duke of Lancaster, leads a rising against the king and takes him prisoner.

1399–1461 **House of Lancaster.** Bolingbroke, as *Henry IV*, establishes his possession of the crown and defeats a rising by the nobility.
Henry V (1413–22) renews the English claim to the French throne and conquers northern France.
Henry VI has himself proclaimed king of France, but the French, inspired by Joan of Arc, recover their territory.
Outbreak of the *Wars of the Roses*, a conflict between the House of Lancaster (the red rose) and the House of York (the white rose). Richard, duke of York, Edward III's great-grandson, claims the throne and allies himself with the "King-maker", the earl of Warwick. Although Richard is defeated and killed at Wakefield, his son Edward becomes king.

1461–85 **House of York.** After a series of battles and temporary flight to Holland, *Edward IV* (1461–83) establishes himself on the throne. Henry VI dies in the Tower.
The boy *Edward V* is declared illegitimate and, along with his brother, murdered in the Tower. The duke of Gloucester ascends the throne as *Richard III* (1483–85). He in turn is defeated by Henry Tudor, earl of Richmond, a scion of the House of Lancaster.

1485–1603 **House of Tudor.** *Henry VII* (1485–1509) marries Elizabeth, daughter of Edward IV, and thus brings the Wars of the Roses to an end.

Henry VIII (1509–47), married six times, breaks with the Church of Rome in order to legitimise divorce. Dissolution of the Monasteries.
Edward VI (1547–53) supports the Reformed church. His successor *Mary I* (1553–58) marries

Philip of Spain, restores Catholicism as the established religion and initiates a bloody persecution of Protestants.
Under **Elizabeth I** (1558–1603) the Reformed church is re-established. Economic upsurge. Privateering war against Spain. Execution of Mary Queen of Scots.

1588 Destruction of the *Spanish Armada*. Foundation of the East India Company.

Around 1600 Flowering of literature: **Shakespeare**.

1603–1714 House of Stuart. *James I* (James VI of Scotland), son of Mary Queen of Scots, unites England and Scotland under his rule (1603–25). Persecution of Puritans and Roman Catholics.
Charles I (1625–49) attempts to rule on his own against the will of Parliament. The "Long Parliament". Outbreak of the Civil War between the "Cavaliers", who support the king, and the "Roundheads" who support Parliament. Roundhead leader **Oliver Cromwell** and his "Ironsides" defeat the Royalists. The king flees to the Scottish camp but is handed over to the Parliamentary forces, tried and executed.

1653 Cromwell becomes Lord Protector, but has difficulty in securing Parliamentary agreement to his policies. He is succeeded in 1658 by his son Richard, who soon withdraws, allowing *Charles II* (1660–85) to return to the throne with the help of General Monk. War with Holland. Persecution of Catholics. **Habeas Corpus Act.** The names of Whigs and Tories begin to be applied to the opposing parties in Parliament.
James II (1685–88) loses the confidence of the population by his preference for Catholicism, is unable to prevent the landing of William of Orange, and flees to France.
William III (1689–1702) rules jointly with his wife *Mary II*, James II's daughter. Declaration of Rights.
Anne (1702–14), James II's younger daughter, completes the incorporation of Scotland into the United Kingdom by the union of the English and Scottish Parliaments (1707).
Victories by Marlborough in the War of the Spanish Succession. Capture of Gibraltar.

1714–1901 House of Hanover. *George I* (1714–27) succeeds to the throne by virtue of his descent from James I. Abortive rising in Scotland in support of the Stuarts (1715).
In the reign of *George II* (1727–60) a further Stuart rising in Scotland, led by "Bonnie Prince Charlie", is finally crushed at the battle of Culloden (1746).
Under *George III* (1760–1820) Britain loses its American colonies in the *War of American Independence*. In the Napoleonic wars Nelson is victorious at Trafalgar and Wellington at Waterloo. During the last ten years of George III's reign his son rules as Regent – the *Regency* period – and then succeeds him as *George IV* (1820–30).
In the reign of *William IV* (1830–37) the Parliamentary franchise is extended (1832) and slavery is abolished (1834).

1837–1901 During the long reign of Queen **Victoria**, who married her cousin, Prince Albert of Saxe Coburg in 1840, Britain enjoys a period of industrial expansion and great prosperity, leading to the Industrial Revolution and making the transition to a modern state.

During the reign of *Edward VII* (1901–10), of the house of **Saxe-Coburg-Gotha**, old-age pensions are introduced; the *Boer War* gives rise to much political controversy; the Liberals come to power.

1914–18 First World War. Britain declares war on Germany. At first relying largely on its naval blockade, Britain later shows that its land forces, following army reform, are stronger than had been supposed. The coalition government replaces the traditional liberal economy by a planned economy. Easter Rising in Dublin (1916).
The royal family takes the name of **Windsor** (1917).

1922 Establishment of Irish Free State; the province (six counties) of Ulster (Northern Ireland) remain part of the United Kingdom.
Although, after the war, the British Empire reaches its fullest extent, Britain itself emerges from the war economically weakened. The end of the colonial regime is foreshadowed by the Indian independence movement led by *Mahatma Gandhi*. The British Empire develops into the **British Commonwealth of Nations**.

1936 *Edward VIII* abdicates in favour of his brother, *George VI*.

1939–45 Second World War, provoked by the German attack on Poland. *Winston Churchill* becomes Prime Minister, at the head of an all-party government.

1946 The Labour Party wins the first post-war election. Economic and social reforms.

1949 Britain joins Western European Union, the Council of Europe and the North Atlantic Treaty Organisation (NATO).

1952 Accession of Queen **Elizabeth II**.

1958 The House of Lords is reinforced by the introduction of life peers and the admission of women.

1966 The Labour government of *Harold Wilson* begins the withdrawal (completed by 1971) from all British bases east of Suez.

1969 Outbreak of religious and social disturbances in Northern Ireland.

1970 Conservative government led by *Edward Heath*. A new Industrial Relations Act fails to solve the country's industrial and economic problems.

1973 Britain becomes a member of the European Economic Community.

1974 The Labour Party wins a narrow victory in a general election, but is unable to solve the continuing economic problems.

1975 A national referendum shows a majority in favour of remaining in the European Economic Community.

1976 *James Callaghan* succeeds Harold Wilson as Prime Minister. "Social contract" between the government and the trade unions on wage and price limitation, in an attempt to improve the country's economic situation.
Growth of nationalist feeling in Scotland and Wales.

National referenda in Scotland and Wales show only limited support for the establishment of semi-independent National Assemblies.

1978 The Liberals withdraw from a pact with the Labour Party designed to bolster up the government's tiny majority.

1979 After a Conservative election victory **Margaret Thatcher** becomes the first woman Prime Minister of Britain.

1980 Great Britain grants independence to Rhodesia, renamed Zimbabwe, and to the New Hebrides as Vanuatu.

1981 Social-Democrat Party (SDP) founded by former Labour ministers.
Prince Charles marries Lady Diana Spencer. The colony of Belize becomes independent.

1982 Raising of the Argentinian flag on the British Crown Colony of the Falkland Islands sparks off the Falkland conflict. After ten weeks the Argentinians capitulate.

1983 The Conservatives win an absolute majority in the parliamentary elections.

1984 The EEC summit conference in Brussels reaches no agreement on the question of repayment of contributions to Great Britain.
After a policewoman is killed by a shot fired from the Libyan "People's Bureau", Great Britain breaks off diplomatic relations with Libya.
Inflation, unemployment, etc., are discussed at the World Economic Conference in London (June). At the summit meeting of heads of government in Fontainebleau it is agreed that Great Britain is to be repaid part of its contribution to the Community funds (June).

Kings and Queens of England (before 1603) and the United Kingdom (since 1603)

Anglo-Saxon and Danish kings

Alfred the Great	871–899
Edward the Elder	899–924
Athelstan	924–939
Edmund	939–946
Edred	946–955
Edwy	955–959
Edgar	959–975
Edward the Martyr	975–978
Ethelred	978–1016
Edmund Ironside	1016
Knut (Canute)	1016–1035
Harold Harefoot	1035–1040
Harthaknut	1040–1042
Edward the Confessor	1042–1066
Harold Godwinson	1066

Norman kings

William I, the Conqueror	1066–1087
William II	1087–1100
Henry I	1100–1135
Stephen	1135–1154

House of Anjou-Plantagenet

Henry II	1154–1189
Richard I, Cœur-de-Lion	1189–1199
John	1199–1216
Henry III	1216–1272
Edward I	1272–1307
Edward II	1307–1327
Edward III	1327–1377
Richard II	1377–1399

House of Lancaster

Henry IV	1399–1413
Henry V	1413–1422
Henry VI	1422–1461

House of York

Edward IV	1461–1483
Edward V	1483
Richard III	1483–1485

House of Tudor

Henry VII	1485–1509
Henry VIII	1509–1547
Edward VI	1547–1553
Mary I	1553–1558
Elizabeth I	1558–1603

House of Stuart

James I	1603–1625
Charles I	1625–1649

Commonwealth (1649–1659)

Oliver Cromwell, Lord Protector	1653–1658
Richard Cromwell, Lord Protector	1658–1659

House of Stuart (restored)

Charles II	1660–1685
James II	1685–1688
William III, and Mary II	1689–1702
Anne	1702–1714

House of Hanover

George I	1714–1727
George II	1727–1760
George III	1760–1820
George IV	1820–1830
William IV	1830–1837
Victoria	1837–1901
Edward VII	1901–1910

House of Windsor

George V	1910–1936
Edward VIII	1936
George VI	1936–1952
Elizabeth II	since 1952

Art

During the **Neolithic period** Britain was occupied by a pre-Indo-European people of Iberian origin. The dates assigned to this period vary with different authorities, but it seems to have lasted in Britain until about 1800 B.C. The characteristic features of this *megalithic culture*, found also in Italy, France and Ireland, are its chambered tombs, consisting of a massive capstone borne on upright slabs and originally covered by a mound of earth, and, in a later phase, its domed tombs with corbelled vaults and its standing stones or menhirs (huge slabs of undressed stone, occasionally carved with anthropomorphic figures). Often numbers of standing stones are set in avenues or circles, usually with a single great stone in the centre of the circle. The most famous example of a stone circle is Stonehenge, near Salisbury, which has the remains of two outer circles of stones surrounding two smaller horseshoe formations, the whole structure being enclosed within a circular earthwork 320 ft in diameter and approached by an "avenue". Stonehenge is now recognised as a solar temple and dated to different periods of construction between the 19th and 15th centuries B.C.

Some of the "Beaker people" (characterised by beaker-like cups, reddish in colour, with patterned bands) also arrived in Britain during the period of transition from the Neolithic to the Bronze Age.

The **Clactonian**, a Palaeolithic culture named after the site discovered in Essex, is represented by flaked stone implements.

During the **Bronze Age** (1700–800 B.C.) representatives of the *Urnfield culture* reached SE England.

After the impressive achievements of the megalithic culture, however, Britain remained culturally backward until the *La Tène* culture of the **Late Iron Age** (from about 450 B.C.) brought powerful new impulses. These Celtic newcomers, under the leadership of a warlike aristocracy and an influential priestly caste (the Druids), mingled with the indigenous Iberian population. While continental La Tène art fell into decline after about 100 B.C., a vigorous **British La Tène style** developed between 50 B.C. and A.D. 150. In this art the patterns, based on Roman plant ornament, evolve in the most fascinating way from the vegetable into the animal world (worked bronze mirrors from Birdlip and Desborough) and make striking use of inlaid enamel to produce a colourful effect (Battersea bronze shield). Among the last creations of British La Tène art was the trumpet spiral which is still found in the neo-Celtic art of Ireland and Scotland.

Although at this time Britain lay on the edge of the known world, its deposits of tin aroused trading interest. In A.D. 43 Roman forces landed in the south of England and soon brought the whole country, with the exception of northern Scotland, under their control. The major vestiges of the **Roman period** in Britain are works of military engineering rather than architecture. The most striking Roman structure is in the north of England – *Hadrian's Wall*, built between A.D. 122 and 128 between the Solway in the west and the mouth of the Tyne in the east, as a defence against the Picts and Scots (remnants of the indigenous Iberian population) to the north. There are numerous remains of Roman villas in the southern half of England, like the one excavated at Brading on the Isle of Wight. Many of the early British and Anglo-Saxon Christian buildings were built in the Roman style, though these have mostly been incorporated in later work. Examples can be seen at Brixworth, Bradford-on-Avon, Escomb, Jarrow, Monkwearmouth and Worth.

During the **Dark Ages**, the period of the great migrations, the country was occupied by Angles, Saxons and Jutes, who brought with them the Germanic technique of *timber construction* but soon learned Roman masonry techniques. In the areas of Saxon settlement, however, timber buildings were still being erected until about the year 1000, and stone buildings imitating timber ones continued for some centuries.

A typically Anglo-Saxon feature is the tall slender *tower* with small round-headed windows which is found in Britain at a much earlier date than in Italy or Germany (Sompting; Lincoln; Lindsey; Earls Barton, with stone "half-timbering"; Barton-on-Humber). This primitive Anglo-Saxon **Early Romanesque** is markedly different from the later Norman or High Romanesque style (1070–1170).

The *ship burial* (probably of the East Anglian king Aethelhere, d. 655), an oared vessel some 85 ft long, found at Sutton Hoo in Suffolk in 1939, contained one of the richest collections of Germanic burial artefacts ever discovered – a gilt bronze helmet, a harp, drinking horns, silver dishes, Merovingian coins, etc. The high quality of the East Anglian goldsmiths' work, using both pagan decorative themes and Christian symbols, points to connections with the eastern Mediterranean, Gaul, Ireland and Sweden.

The *book illumination* of the Irish and Anglo-Saxon period is of outstanding quality. Its principal achievements date from the 8th c. The decorated initials reflect a religious intensity (developed to its ornamental utmost in neo-Celtic art), combined with Anglo-Saxon animal ornament, itself derived from the animal style of Germanic art, and with motifs from the Eastern Church (already showing figure representations of a kind not found in contemporary continental art). A number of different schools can be distinguished – Lindisfarne (the Lindisfarne Gospels, a Northumbrian counterpart of the Irish Book of Kells which is now in the British Museum), Canterbury (the Codex Aureus, in the Royal Library, Stockholm), Winchester (the Benedictional of St Aethelwold, *c.* 975, now at Chatsworth); the Caedmon manuscript of *c.* 1000 (in the Bodleian Library, Oxford). The Cutbercht Gospel Book (*c.* 770; National Library, Vienna) comes from southern England. The Utrecht Psalter (early 9th century), with its freely sketched outline drawings, became a model for English artists, who exercised a strong influence on Irish art and the scriptoria of continental Europe (Echternach, St Gall, Salzburg).

In *stone sculpture*, the most notable works are the early medieval crosses, richly ornamented and sometimes adorned with figures. The earlier crosses from the north of England (650–680) have vine ornamentation (Otley, Bewcastle and Ruthwell crosses). The later ones (800–1050) are strongly influenced by Viking art (Collingham, Ilkley, Walton, Middleton). The Scottish crosses (Hilton of Cadboll, Thornhill, Abercorn) also have vine ornamentation, but are stylistically different. The Isle of Man crosses (700–1000) mostly have interlaced ornament.

In Britain Romanesque style of architecture is usually known as **Norman**. The earliest Romanesque minsters are of massive, simple structure and enormous size; they were originally modelled on the cathedrals of Normandy (Caen, Jumièges). St Albans (begun *c.* 1080) is the oldest and largest, partly built with bricks from nearby Roman Verulamium. Ely Cathedral (begun 1083) has an enormously long nave (521 ft) with a painted timber roof. Durham Cathedral (1093–1133), the work of Norman builders, is notable for its vaulting; its sturdy, square-built west front is reminiscent of the twin-towered façade of St Etienne in Caen. The Galilee porch of 1150 – a feature which has no counterpart on the Continent – is particularly attractive.

Other major cathedrals of the 11th and 12th centuries include Lincoln (begun 1072), Gloucester (begun 1089), Norwich (1096), Peterborough (1118) and Oxford (12th c.).

Among surviving *secular buildings* of the period are the oldest part of the Tower of London, the White Tower, as well as Norwich Castle and Oakham Castle (Rutland).

Monumental sculpture is represented mainly by the magnificent sculptural decoration of the church façades, such as the relief carving on Chichester Cathedral (11th c.), the south doorway of Ely Cathedral, the doorways of the little church of Kilpeck in Herefordshire with their fantastic mingling of human and animal figures and monsters (second half of 12th c.), the sculpture in the south porch of Malmesbury Abbey (*c.* 1160), the west front of Lincoln Cathedral (after 1150) and the west doorway of Rochester Cathedral (1140–80).

Irish and Anglo-Saxon book illumination with its linear style developed further under Norman influence (Bayeux Tapestry: see below), and it is almost possible to speak of a "Channel school" in the 11th and 12th centuries. The characteristic English delicacy of line, however, is still preserved, as can be seen in the works produced by the St Albans scriptorium. This feeling for line, combined with great subtlety of colour, became known throughout Europe, particularly during the 13th and 14th centuries, as *opus anglicanum*. There were also renowned centres of illumination at Bury St Edmunds, Winchester and York.

The *wall paintings* in St Anselm's Chapel in Canterbury Cathedral (12th c.) are a fine example of Romanesque monumental painting.

A special form of narrative painting is represented by the embroidery known as the Bayeux Tapestry (Bayeux Museum, Normandy), which depicts the Norman Conquest of England in 1066 and is said to have been worked by William the Conqueror's wife, Matilda, about 1080.

Gothic architecture in Britain is seen less as a unified style than as a sequence of three phases – *Early English* (1180–1250), *Decorated* (1250–1350) and *Perpendicular* (1350–1550), corresponding very roughly to the Early Gothic, High Gothic and Late Gothic phases recognised in the architecture of continental Europe.

In *church architecture* the **Early English** style begins about 1180 by adopting the French technique of ribbed vaulting. The chancel is frequently lengthened by the addition of a Lady Chapel, replacing the apse. The arches are lancet-shaped: hence the phrase Pointed style, sometimes used instead of Early English. The west front is often of great breadth, and the whole building is dominated by the massive tower over the crossing. The elaborate development of the chapterhouse is an English characteristic. The first example of the new style was the choir of Canterbury Cathedral (1175–84), begun by Guillaume de Sens, and this was followed by the cathedrals of Ripon (begun between 1153 and 1181), Chichester (rebuilt after 1186), Lincoln (rebuilding begun 1192), Wells (nave and transepts 1180–1239), Peterborough (west transepts and west front 1193–1214), Worcester (choir begun in the early 13th c., nave and transepts 1317–77), Salisbury (1220–70), central tower 14th c.) and Southwell (choir, second quarter of 13th c.).

In *secular architecture* the finest example of Early English is Winchester Castle (mid-13th c.).

Fine examples of Early English *sculpture* are to be seen in Peterborough Cathedral (abbots' tombs, *c.* 1200), Wells (west front, 1220 onwards) and Westminster Abbey (architectural sculpture in transepts, *c.* 1250).

Among the finest examples of the *book illumination* of the period are those produced in the famous school at St Albans, directed from 1236 to 1259 by an English monk, Matthew Paris. In his "Virgin and Child" of about 1260 he depicts himself kneeling at the Virgin's feet.

A life of St Edward (*c.* 1250), the Ormesby Psalter, Queen Mary's Psalter, the Peterborough Psalter and the Luttrell Psalter (*c.* 1340) – all products of the East Anglian school – together with Queen Isabella's Psalter, produced in Nottinghamshire, may be taken as examples of the profusion of beautiful illuminated manuscripts of this period.

Early English *stained glass* is notable for its brilliance of colour, as in the choir of Canterbury Cathedral. There are *wall paintings* of this period in the Chapel of the Holy Sepulchre in Winchester Cathedral (*c.* 1250).

The **Decorated** style in *church architecture* is notable for the rich tracery of the windows and wall surfaces. The finest examples of Decorated architecture are Westminster Abbey (choir begun 1245), the Angel Choir of Lincoln Cathedral (1256–1320, with magnificent architectural sculpture), the nave, Lady Chapel, west front and chapterhouse of Lichfield Cathedral (*c.* 1250–1330), the nave and chapterhouse of York Minster (*c.* 1290–1340), the west front and the rebuilt part of the choir of Wells Cathedral (*c.* 1285–1318), the choir of Bristol Cathedral (1298–1332) and the choir of Gloucester Cathedral (1329–37).

Notable *secular buildings* of the period are Caernarvon Castle (begun 1283), a fortified manor-house in Warwick (13th–14th c.), St Mary's Hospital in Chichester (end of 13th c.) and Penshurst Place in Kent (*c.* 1341).

Among fine examples of *sculpture* of the Decorated period are the Lady Chapel of Ely Cathedral (1321–49), the Virgin and Child in Winchester Cathedral (*c.* 1340) and a number of remarkable tombs (for example in the Temple church in London, *c.* 1230–1300, Westminster Abbey and Hereford and Gloucester Cathedrals).

Fine *wall paintings* of the Decorated period can be seen in the transept of Westminster Abbey (*c.* 1300). *Panel painting* for the most part reflects French influences: altar, Westminster Abbey, *c.* 1260; reredos, Thornham Parva, Suffolk, *c.* 1320.

In *church architecture* the **Perpendicular** style breaks up wall surfaces and windows with an elaborate lattice-work of tracery and develops with ever greater richness the characteristic decorative form of fan vaulting. The three great masterpieces of the Perpendicular style are the nave of Winchester Cathedral (begun 1394), King's College Chapel in Cambridge (begun 1446) and the Henry VII Chapel in Westminster Abbey (1503–19). Other fine examples of Perpendicular architecture are the rebuilding of Gloucester Cathedral (cloisters, 1351–1407), the chapel of New College in Oxford (1383), the choir of Tewkesbury Abbey (*c.* 1350) and St George's Chapel in Windsor Castle (1460–83).

Numerous *secular buildings* have survived from this period, including many half-timbered houses and larger structures like Westminster Hall in London (1393–99), Christ Church in Oxford and the great palace of Hampton Court, begun in 1510 for Cardinal Wolsey and later acquired by Henry VIII. The transition to the Renaissance is evident.

Sculpture is represented by some fine monumental sculpture (west front of Exeter Cathedral) and a number of tombs of outstanding beauty (Black Prince, d. 1376, and Henry IV, d. 1405, both in Canterbury Cathedral; Henry VII and his queen, by Torrigiano, *c.* 1550, in Westminster Abbey). There are remains of fine *wall paintings* in St Stephen's Chapel in Westminster Abbey (1350–63). *Panel painting* is mainly represented by altarpieces. *Book illumination* achieves a final period of brilliance.

The **Renaissance** style in Britain took over many features from the Perpendicular style, which persisted into the 18th century. Combined with influences brought into the country by Italian artists during the reign of Henry VIII, this produced, in the **Tudor** and **Elizabethan** styles, new and typically English forms (Hampton Court; Longleat House, by Giovanni da Padova, 1567–79; Kirby Hall, *c.* 1572; Hatfield House, Hertfordshire. 1607–11).

The greatest *painter* of the Tudor period was Hans Holbein the Younger (1497–1543), who became court painter to Henry VIII in 1536 (portraits of Henry VIII, Sir Thomas More, Anne of Cleves). His portrait drawings (in Windsor Castle) achieve the most accurate representation of character with great economy of line, and are often superior to the pictures painted from them. Holbein was to influence English painting for almost a century.

Nicholas Hilliard (1547–1619) worked as a miniaturist, recording the spirit of the Elizabethan period in his intimate portraits. Isaac Oliver, a French Huguenot, continued Hilliard's style in a grander and more realistic but less poetic form.

The **Baroque** developed in Britain and on the Continent in rather different ways. In *architecture* a neo-Classical style influenced by Palladio came to the fore, its principal exponents being Inigo Jones and Christopher Wren. Inigo Jones (1573–1652) studied in Italy and in 1615 became Surveyor of the Royal Works, erecting elegantly simple and substantial buildings in a strict classical and Palladian style (Banqueting House, London).

Sir Christopher Wren (1632–1723) was presented after the Fire of London in 1666 with an opportunity such as few architects have enjoyed. In London alone he is said to have built no fewer than 55 churches, not all of which have survived. His greatest achievement was St Paul's Cathedral (1672–1700), modelled on St Peter's in Rome, combining a domed central area with a long nave. Among his secular buildings were the Monument in London, which commemorates the Great Fire (1671–77), and Greenwich Hospital.

Other noted architects of the period were James Gibbs (1682–1754: St Martin-in-the-Fields, London), Nicholas Hawksmoor (1661–1736) and John Vanbrugh (1664–1726: Blenheim Palace).

From the middle of the 18th century there developed a **neo-Classical architecture** which increasingly looked back to ancient models. Exponents of this style, which spread from Britain to the Continent, were Sir William Chambers, the two George Dances, father and son, the two John Woods, also father and son (Royal Crescent, Bath) and above all Robert and James Adam. The **Adam style** is notable particularly for its interiors.

The *decorative arts* were promoted as a result of the new middle-class concern with the elegance and comfort of their houses. Thomas Chippendale (1707–79), George Hepplewhite (d. 1788) and Thomas Sheraton (1751–1806) produced high-quality furniture, while Josiah Wedgwood (1730–95) created his famous *ceramics*, including the cream Queen's ware and his jasperware, which was coloured by metallic oxides, and was used particularly in relief work (white on a blue ground), medallions and vases.

The new English-style *landscaped garden*, created by William Kent (1684–1748), among others, now displaced the French-style Baroque garden. The object was to achieve a "natural" effect, but an artificial element reflecting the taste of the times was introduced by the carefully contrived siting of miniature temples, artificial ruins, cottages, Chinese pavilions and so on.

Almost simultaneously with the neo-Classical style there developed a neo-Gothic or **Gothic Revival**, the earliest example being Horace Walpole's Strawberry Hill (*c.* 1750). This remained influential into the 19th century (Houses of Parliament by Sir Charles Barry, 1837–67). The 18th and 19th centuries were the great age of the country house. A distinctive example towards the end of the period was Philip Webb's Red House at Bexleyheath, Kent (1859–60).

British *sculpture* of the 17th, 18th and 19th centuries cannot compare with work produced on the Continent, and British Baroque *painting* was largely the legacy of foreign artists like Anthony Van Dyck (1599–1641), whose approach to portraiture remained influential in Britain until the end of the 18th century. Among Van Dyck's contemporaries were Paul van Somer (1576–1621), a native of Antwerp, and Daniel Mytens (1590–1642), who came from The Hague. William Dobson (1610–46), Sir Peter Lely (1618–80) and Sir Godfrey Kneller (1646–1723), a native of Lübeck, painted excellent portraits, while Sir James Thornhill (1675–1734) is chiefly noted for his grandiose ceiling paintings (scenes from the life of St Paul in St Paul's Cathedral, London, 1717).

Mezzotint engraving reached its zenith in Britain in the 18th c. Richard Earlom (1743–1822) was a leading exponent of the art. The *coloured print* also flourished during this period.

William Hogarth (1697–1764), originally an engraver, became one of the leading painters of the 18th century ("A Harlot's Progress" and "Marriage à la Mode", each a series of six scenes; "Shrimp Girl") and an unsparing commentator on contemporary manners and morals. With the 18th century began the *great age of British painting*. In the second half of the century portrait painting reached its peak of achievement in the work of Sir Joshua Reynolds (1723–92), who dominated the artistic life of London and produced a large number of fine portraits ("Lady Crosbie", "Mrs Siddons as the Tragic Muse", "Lord Heathfield with the Keys of Gibraltar").

Thomas Gainsborough (1727–88) was a fashionable portrait painter who was also a considerable landscapist ("The Blue Boy", "Mrs Siddons", "The Watering Place"). Other portraitists of the period were George Romney (1734–1802), John Zoffany (1735–1810), a native of Frankfurt, and the Scottish artist Sir Henry Raeburn (1756–1823). Among noted painters of country life and sport were George Morland (1763–1804) and George Stubbs (1724–1806), famous for his paintings of horses. Other painters of the period included John Opie (1761–1807 the "Cornish wonder"), the landscapist John Crome (1768–1821) and Sir Thomas Lawrence (1769–1830). Thomas Rowlandson (1756–1827) is noted mainly for his drawings and caricatures. Leading watercolour painters were John Sell Cotman (1782–1842),

Thomas Girtin (1775–1802), David Wilkie (1785–1841) and William Etty (1787–1849).

John Constable (1776–1837) was a master of realistic landscape painting based on the direct observation of nature (principal works in the National Gallery, London). J. M. W. Turner (1775–1851) carried landscape painting to further heights of achievement. Influenced by Claude Lorrain, he painted landscapes which were sometimes a true depiction of nature and sometimes peopled with mythological figures; and in the end the representational aspect became totally dissolved in fantasies of light and colour. His attempts to reproduce the effect of light filtering through the atmosphere, the play of colours and reflections in water have led him to be regarded, probably in error, as a forerunner of Impressionism (principal works in the Tate Gallery).

Alongside the realistic portrait and landscape painting which appealed so strongly to the public there also developed an imaginative and romantic trend, a reaction against the rationalism of the 18th century, which looked to the Middle Ages for its models and became known as the Gothic school. The poet and artist William Blake (1757–1827), with his fantastic and mystical illustrations to his own and other writers' works (Book of Job, Virgil, Dante, Chaucer; "Songs of Innocence"), derived from the Classical school, while the Swiss-born John Fuseli (Johann Heinrich Füssli, 1741–1825), who became President of the Royal Academy in 1779, specialised in the grotesque and the horrific ("The Nightmare"), with a strongly literary element (illustrations to Homer, Dante, Shakespeare, Milton, and others).

Sculpture – never a field favoured by British artists – was represented by John Flaxman (1755–1826), Francis Leggatt Chantrey (1781–1841) and John Gibson (1790–1866).

The *architecture* of the end of the 18th century and the first half of the 19th was characterised by the continuing juxtaposition of Classical and Gothic revival styles together with influences from the Far East (John Nash, 1752–1835, Royal Pavilion in Brighton; Regent Street, London; Sir John Soane, 1753–1837, Bank of England, London; Sir Robert Smirke, 1781–1864, British Museum, London).

But Britain also produced the *beginnings of modern architecture*. The buildings and engineering works of the Industrial Revolution (bridges, canals, factories, glasshouses, railway stations) and above all the Crystal Palace, a structure of cast-iron and glass built by Sir Joseph Paxton (1803–65) for the Great Exhibition of 1851, contain all the essential elements of 20th century architecture. Leading architects of the **Victorian period**, in addition to Sir Charles Barry and Paxton, were Sir George Gilbert Scott (1811–78: Albert Memorial, London), Philip S. Webb (1831–1915; Red House, Bexleyheath) and Norman Shaw (1831–1912: town mansions, country houses). Sir George Gilbert Scott's sons, George Gilbert Scott (1839–97) and John Oldrid Scott (1842–1913), and his grandson, Sir Giles Gilbert Scott (1880–1960), were active both in the restoration of old buildings (mainly churches) and the design of new ones.

The imaginative art of Blake and Fuseli prepared the way for the **Pre-Raphaelites**, the "Pre-Raphaelite Brotherhood" established by a group of young artists in 1848 which was directed against the Royal Academy and the pretentious or trivial attitude to art of such painters as Sir Lawrence Alma-Tadema and Sir Edwin Landseer. The leaders of the movement, who sought to return to the period before Raphael (before, that is, the High Renaissance), were the painter and poet Dante Gabriel Rossetti (1828–82), William Holman Hunt (1827–1910) and Sir John Everett Millais (1829–96), together with Ford Madox Brown (1821–93) and Edward Burne-Jones (1833–98). William Morris (1834–96) aimed at a renewal of the decorative arts as opposed to industrialisation. His work (particularly in the printing of books) was at the origin of the new interest throughout Europe in the applied and decorative arts, reflected in the **Art Nouveau** which came to the fore at the turn of the 19th and 20th centuries.

The American-born painter James McNeill Whistler (1834–1903), who spent most of his life in Britain, was one of the first European artists to discover the beauty of the Japanese coloured woodcut. His pictures were conceived wholly in terms of colour, like the famous portrait of his mother in grey, black and white. The typical representative of the *fin de siècle* in British art was Aubrey Beardsley (1872–98), with his decadently decorative and fantastic illustrations (for example to Wilde's "Salome").

After its promising upsurge in the earlier part of the 19th century, *architecture* now fell back into a traditional mould. An exception was the conception of the "garden city" put forward in 1898 by Ebenezer Howard, who advocated the development of suburbs with a lower building density, even though this meant an extension of the total built-up area (Sir Raymond Unwin, 1863–1940: Letchworth Garden City).

It was not until 1931, with the formation of the *Mars group*, that British architecture again linked up with international developments. Thereafter British architects soon established themselves as leaders in the field of town planning and development, with a whole series of *new towns* like Harlow (1947), though the architecture was rarely up to the level of the planning. School buildings in particular were frequently of high quality (such as those built by the London County Council). Alison and Peter Smithson were prominent exponents of the **New Brutalism** (a term introduced by Le Corbusier about 1950 to describe the use of *béton brut*, concrete exposed at its roughest, with the structures prominently visible). This trend is represented by housing on Ham Common, London, by J. Stirling and J. Gowan (1959), and the flats at Roehampton (1952–59), also built by the London City Architect's Department, which continues to produce fine modern buildings.

Early 20th century *painting* in Britain lacked the unity of approach shown by contemporary French painting. Among artists of this period, caught between the claims of tradition and change, were Augustus John (1878–1961), his sister Gwen John (1876–1939), and Stanley Spencer (1891–1959).

The various trends of modern paintings are represented by Vanessa Bell (1880–1961), Matthew Smith (1879–1959), Paul Nash (1889–1946), Ben Nicholson (b. 1895, a member of the Paris "Abstraction-Création" group), Graham Sutherland (1903–80), Francis Bacon (b. 1910) and John Piper (b. 1903).

John Hoyland (b. 1934) and Jack Smith (b. 1928) belong to the geometrical and abstract school. Pop art is represented by Peter Blake (b. 1931), Peter Phillips (b. 1939) and Derek Boshier (b. 1939).

The *sculpture* of the first half of the 20th century is represented by the American-born Jacob Epstein (1880–1959), who lived in London from 1905, Barbara Hepworth (1903–75) and above all by Henry Moore (b. 1898). Influenced by archaic and exotic sculpture, Moore creates figures of massive solidity, with a preference for reclining figures, mother-and-child groups and seated couples. He achieves great expressive force by carrying abstraction to its extreme, striving in his later works to achieve an interaction between the sculptured forms and the space surrounding them, reflected in the use of hollows and openings in the structure of his works. Moore is now the recognised "old master" of modern sculpture, giving Britain a leading position in the field. He has been followed by a number of other notable sculptors, all with very characteristic and individual styles. Prominent among them are Kenneth Armitage (b. 1916), who forms a kind of sculptural screen out of groups of his highly abstract, idol-like bronze figures with thin, insect-like limbs, R. Butler, L. Chadwick, B. Meadows, L. Thornton, R. Adams, H. Dalwood and Paolozzi. To the youngest generation belong G. Evans (b. 1934), L. Gibson (b. 1945), Katherine Gili (b. 1948), N. Hall (b. 1943), J. Hawkes (b. 1944), P. Hide (b. 1944), J. Lowe (b. 1952), J. Maine (b. 1942), D. Nash (b. 1945), Emma Park (b. 1950), N, Pope (b. 1949), T. Scott (b. 1937), D. Seaton (b. 1943), A. Smart (b. 1949) and B. Thompson (b. 1950).

Literature

The earliest works of literature of the Anglo-Saxon period, before the Norman Conquest, are the poems of *Caedmon* (7th c.) and *Cynewulf* (8th c.). *Beowulf*, a heroic poem in alliterative verse, dates from the middle of the 9th century. At the end of the 9th century Alfred the Great ordered various theological and historical works to be translated, and the Abbot Aelfric produced a translation of the Old Testament.

After the Norman Conquest in 1066 the Old English written language fell into disuse, and it was only in the 13th century that Middle English took its place as a literary language alongside French and Latin; there was a great flowering of romances on Arthurian themes. The 14th century, was the great period which produced *Geoffrey Chaucer*'s "Canterbury Tales" (*c.* 1387) and William Langland's "Piers Plowman". Wycliffe's *translation of the Bible* (1383) and *Mandeville*'s "Travels" are both notable examples of the prose writing of the period.

Outstanding personalities of the 15th and 16th centuries were *Sir Thomas More* (1448–1535), Lord Chancellor in the reign of Henry VIII and a friend of Erasmus, with his humanist writings, particularly "Utopia", and *Edmund Spenser* (1552–99), author of "The Faerie Queene" and the pastoral "Shepheards Calender". At the end of the 16th century came the greatest English poet and dramatist, **William Shakespeare** (1564–1616). Although his verse tales, "Venus and Adonis" and "The Rape of Lucrece", and even his sonnets are relatively little read, his plays have lost nothing of their dramatic effectiveness on the modern stage, and his historical plays, his great tragic creations like "Hamlet", "Macbeth" and "King Lear", comedies like "Twelfth Night" and "As You Like It", "The Tempest" and many more are still popular items of the theatrical repertoire.

Forerunners of Shakespeare were dramatists such as *Robert Greene* (1558–92) and *Christopher Marlowe* (1564–93: translations of Ovid, tragedies). Among his contemporaries was *Ben Jonson* (1573–1637: dramas, poems).

Notable prose writers of the period were *John Lyly* (1554–1606), author of the didactic romance "Euphues", and *Thomas Nash* (1567–1601), who wrote the first English adventure story and introduced the picaresque novel into English literature.

Shakespeare's successors in the field of drama included *Francis Beaumont* (1584–1616) and *John Fletcher* (1579–1625), who jointly wrote some 50 plays and had more success with the contemporary public than Shakespeare; *John Webster* (1580–1625), with his horror tragedies; and *Philip Massinger* (1584–1640), author of serious and romantic dramas and a fine comedy. In 1642 all theatres were closed by the Puritans, bringing Renaissance drama to a sudden end. A characteristic representative of Puritanism was **John Milton** (1608–74), with his great epic "Paradise Lost". Almost at the same time *John Bunyan* (1628–88) wrote "The Pilgrim's Progress".

After Charles II's return to the throne in 1660 art and drama revived, and French literature began to make an impact on Britain's intellectual life. *John Dryden* (1631–1700) sought to imitate the French heroic play. *William Congreve* (1670–1729) wrote witty comedies of manners in the French style ("The Way of the World"). *Alexander Pope* (1688–1744) introduced the rationalism of the Enlightenment into English literature ("The Rape of the Lock"). **Jonathan Swift** (1667–1745) became world-famed with his satirical "Gulliver's Travels", **Daniel Defoe** (1660–1731) with "Robinson Crusoe".

First Folio of Shakespeare (1623)

The second half of the 18th century was the great age of realism and sensibility. Leading representatives of these trends were *Samuel Johnson* (1709–84), an influential critic and compiler of the great "Dictionary of the English Language", *Laurence Sterne* (1713–68), author of "Tristram Shandy", and *Oliver Goldsmith* (1728–74), with the "Vicar of Wakefield". The tone of the novel during this period was set by the realistic and humorous novels of *Henry Fielding* (1707–54) and *Tobias Smollett* (1721–71). At the beginning of the 19th century came the witty and psychologically perceptive novels of *Jane Austen* (1775–1817). The plays of *Richard Sheridan* (1751–1816) were comedies of manners ("The School for Scandal"). *Thomas Percy* (1729–1811), an Anglican bishop, published "Reliques of Ancient English Poetry", which led to a wave of interest in the old English ballads. The "Lyrical Ballads" of *William Wordsworth* (1771–1850) and *Samuel Taylor Coleridge* (1772–1834) brought English literature into the mainstream of the great European Romantic movement. In deliberately simple language Wordsworth observed and described the divine element which he saw in nature, and wrote more than 500 sonnets, a form of which he was a master.

The second generation of Romantic poets tended to die young – Lord **Byron** (1788–1824), **Percy Bysshe Shelley** (1792–1822) and **John Keats** (1795–1821). Byron's principal works ("Childe Harold's Pilgrimage", "Manfred") reflect his world-weariness, melancholy and passion. The central theme of Shelley's poems ("Ode to the West Wind", "Prometheus Unbound") is his quest for harmony and union with nature.

Sir **Walter Scott** (1771–1832) collected and composed ballads and verse romances, translated many German poems and Goethe's play "Götz von Berlichingen", and wrote more than forty historical novels, vivid re-creations of life in earlier centuries, particularly Scotland in the 17th and 18th centuries. His work laid the foundations of the historical novel of the 19th and 20th centuries. The best of a number of historical novels written by *Edward Bulwer-Lytton* (1803–73), "The Last Days of Pompeii", remains popular to this day.

The Victorian period was an age of realism. Its great poets were *Alfred Lord Tennyson* (1809–92), Poet Laureate, who had a remarkable feeling for rhythm and the music of words ("Poems by Two Brothers" and other collections), and *Robert Browning* (1812–99), author of eight plays ("Pippa Passes", "Men and Women") and numerous poems. Browning's adored wife, *Elizabeth Barrett Browning* (1806–61), was renowned as a sensitive poet. **Charles Dickens**. (1812–70) introduced the novel of social criticism, pillorying the social abuses of the new industrial society, but covered a wide range of mood: "David Copperfield" (with a strong autobiographical element), "Pickwick Papers", "A Christmas Carol". The second most important novelist of the period after Dickens was *William Makepeace Thackeray* (1811–63), whose strength lies in social satire: "Vanity Fair", "The Newcomers", "Henry Esmond". Three sisters, *Charlotte, Emily* and *Anne Brontë* wrote novels of life on the Yorkshire moors, depicting finely drawn female characters ("Jane Eyre", 1847; "Wuthering Heights").

One of the Pre-Raphaelite group of artists, *Dante Gabriel Rossetti* (1828–82), was also a writer of prose ("Hand and Soul"), ballads ("Sister Helen") and other poems. The greatest poet of this generation was *Algernon Charles Swinburne* (1837–1909), who was influenced by ancient literature and French poetry. He wrote plays (including a trilogy on Mary Queen of Scots), poems and ballads which gave rise to some criticism in the strictly moral world of Victorian Britain, novels and lyrical dramas ("Atalanta in Calydon"). *George Eliot*, the pseudonym of Mary Ann Evans (1819–80), an unusually emacipated woman for her time, wrote psychological novels of social concern ("Adam Bede", "Silas Marner") and others which are convincing portrayals of simple people and their problems. *Benjamin Disraeli* (1804–81), Chancellor of the Exchequer and Prime Minister, who is regarded as the father of British imperialism, was also a novelist, writing political, social and romantic novels "Sybil", "Coningsby", "Tancred"). The best known novel dealing with life in the schools of the day – the model for a whole succession of other works – was "Tom Brown's Schooldays", by the Christian social reformer *Thomas Hughes* (1822–96).

At the end of the century *George Meredith* (1828–1909) was the most famous representative of the psychological and philosophical novel ("The Egotist", "Diana of the Crossways"). *Thomas Hardy* (1840–1928) wrote mostly tragic novels, in which pastoral descriptions played a considerable part ("Tess of the D'Urbervilles", "Under the Greenwood Tree", "Jude the Obscure"). *Samuel Butler* (1835–1902) described a satirical utopia in his "Erewhon" and "Erewhon Revisited" and wrote a fine autobiographical novel ("The Way of All Flesh"). *Robert Louis Stevenson* (1850–94) wrote a novel of adventure, "Treasure Island", which is still popular, and others with a Scottish setting ("Kidnapped"). *Rudyard Kipling* (1865–1936), wrote stories with an Indian background and a number of books which are still popular with children ("Kim", "The Jungle Book"). *Oscar Wilde* (1856–1900) gave expression to an aestheticism allied to the French decadent movement in his novel, "The Picture of Dorian Gray". While in prison following his trial on homosexual charges, he wrote "The Ballad of Reading Gaol", perhaps his finest poem. He is principally remembered today for his pungent comedies ("The Importance of Being Earnest", "Lady Windermere's Fan", "A Woman of No Importance"). Plays with a content based on social realism were written by Sir *Arthur Wing Pinero* (1855–1934), for thirty years London's most successful dramatist ("The Second Mrs Tanqueray", "The Notorious Mrs Ebbsmith"), the briefly very popular *Thomas William Robertson* (1829–71: "Caste", "David Garrick", "Society") and *Henry Arthur Jones* (1851–1929), author of some 60 plays ("Saints and Sinners").

A leading critic of the art and manners of the day was *Thomas Carlyle* (1795–1881), who attacked the materialism of his time ("Past and Present", "Chartism" and a number of historical works). *John Ruskin* (1819–1900) began as an art critic but later turned to social criticism ("Modern Painters", "A Joy for Ever").

Arthur Symons (1865–1945), a critic and writer, was a representative of Symbolism ("The Symbolist Movement in Literature"). *Thomas Babington Macaulay*, a leading historian of the Victorian period, wrote brilliant essays and an unfinished "History of England". Two writers rather outside the mainstream of literature but with a niche of their own were Edward Lear and Lewis Carroll. *Edward Lear* (1812–88), the landscape painter who created the genre of nonsense literature (limericks, nonsense poems and ballads), has had many imitators. *Lewis Carroll*, the pseudonym of Charles L. Dodgson (1832–98), professor of mathematics at Oxford, is best known for "Alice's Adventures in Wonderland" and other books and poems in the same vein.

The literature of the 20th century shows a variety of conflicting trends. Lyric poetry was strongly influenced by the newly awakened Celtic consciousness. The leading representative of this school, and the most important lyric poet of the first half of the 20th century, was **William Butler Yeats** (1865–1939), author of essays as well as numerous poems. His contemporary, *George William Russell* (1867–1935), was inspired by ancient Irish mythology ("Voices of the Stones", "Midsummer Eve"). A major modern lyric poet, and also a dramatist, was *Thomas Stearns Eliot* (1888–1965), who, in 1948, won the Nobel prize for literature ("The Waste Land", "The Hollow Men", "Four Quartets"). Another outstanding lyric poet was Dame *Edith Sitwell* (1887–1964), whose later poems were principally concerned with the insoluble problem of human existence. She also wrote critical essays and novels.

Wystan Hugh Auden (1907–73) was the leader of a group of young left-wing Oxford students known as the "Pylon poets". His work shows a mingling of old heroic songs and psychoanalysis, mystery plays and Symbolism. Other members of his circle were *Stephen Spender* (b. 1909), author of works of social criticism as well as poems, Louis MacNeice and Cecil Day Lewis.

The *Imagist* school was launched in London in 1912 with a manifesto written by *Ezra Pound* (1885–1972). Other members of his group were *T. E. Hulme* (1883–1917), regarded as the father of Imagism, *Richard Aldington* (1892–1962), T. S. Eliot, Frank Stewart Flint and Sir Herbert Read, who was mainly active as an art critic.

There was also a *neo-Romantic* trend in lyric poetry, a leading representative of which was *John Masefield* (1878–1967), author of "Salt Water Ballads", inspired by the old sea-shanties. Masefield was also known for his dramatic work. Neo-Romantic poetry, much of it written by poets of Welsh or Irish origin, largely prevailed over the more intellectual trend of T. S. Eliot's followers. The most famous of the neo-Romantics was the Welsh poet *Dylan Thomas* (1915–53), whose "Under Milk Wood" was a very successful television play. His most important lyrical work was "Deaths and Entrances". Other neo-Romantic poets were *Walter de la Mare* (1873–1956), the Anglo-Welsh writer *W. H. Davies* (1871–1940: "Autobiography of a Supertramp"), *Laurie Lee* (b. 1914), *George Granville Barker* (b. 1913), Lawrence Durrell, Vernon Watkins, a friend of Dylan Thomas and a fellow Welshman who also sang of Wales in his poems, and *Kathleen Raine* (b. 1908), a successor to the metaphysical poets of the 17th century, who glorifies the wonders of Creation.

In the 20th century the novel turns from the descriptive to harsh realism; psychoanalysis plays an increasingly important role; and society's outsiders become the heroes of the novel. The subconscious, the world of dreams and science fiction come to the fore. The mode of expression becomes sparer; humour is replaced by the grotesque; description gives way to allusion; and flashbacks and the recollection of characters and events are favourite techniques. It becomes almost impossible to assign particular writers to this or that group. One of the best-known novelists of the early decades of the century was *John Galsworthy* (1867–1933), who received the Nobel prize for literature in 1932; his fame was founded on the sequence of novels which he called the "Forsyte Saga". Another popular author was *Sir Hugh Walpole* (1884–1941), author of the Jeremy books and "The Dark Forest", but even he was exceeded in popularity by *A. J. Cronin* (1896–1981), whose novels ("The Citadel", "The Stars Look Down") became international best-sellers. A very versatile writer is *J. B. Priestley* (b. 1894), novelist ("The Good Companions"), dramatist, essayist and critic. *W. Somerset Maugham* (1874–1965) deals with psychological problems in his novels and his brilliant short stories ("Liza of Lambeth", "The Moon and Sixpence",

"Cakes and Ale"). An intelligent critic of his time, who inspired many successors, was *Aldous Huxley* (1894–1963), grandson of the famous scientist T. H. Huxley, whose "Brave New World" and "Brave New World Revisited" were the *reductio ad absurdum* of society's belief in progress. Another sharply satirical writer was *Evelyn Waugh* (1903–66), author of "Decline and Fall", "Vile Bodies", "The Loved One."

One of the most brilliant English storytellers was *Joseph Conrad* (1857–1924), born in the Ukraine of Polish parents, who learned English only in adult years. He was a sailor for many years, and the sea, adventure, the irresistible force of the elements and the longing for distant places are the most important features of his novels ("Lord Jim", "An Outcast of the Islands").

Impressions gained from travel also play an important part in the work of *Edward Morgan Forster* (1879–1970). Among his best novels are "Howards End" and "A Passage to India". In the novels of *Joyce Cary* (1888–1957) events are frequently seen through the eyes of a narrator – a device employed in modern fiction – and the central characters are often children ("The House of Children", "The Horse's Mouth").

Among the numerous women novelists of the early 20th century are *Victoria Sackville-West* (1892–1962: "The Edwardians"), *Elizabeth Bowen* (1899–1973: "The House in Paris" and many short stories) and *Katherine Mansfield* (1888–1923: "The Garden Party").

A distinctive category of modern writing is the "stream of consciousness" novel – concerned not with action but with what goes on in the characters' minds. Leading representatives of this genre are **James Joyce** (1882–1941), who had a great influence on the European novel ("Ulysses", "Finnegans Wake"), and *Virginia Woolf* (1882–1941: "Mrs Dalloway", "Orlando").

World-famous authors of Utopian novels were *H. G. Wells* (1886–1946: "The Time Machine", "The Invisible Man") and *George Orwell*, the pseudonym of Eric Blair (1903–50), who wrote "Animal Farm" and "Nineteen Eighty Four". Religious themes are common in the novels of *Graham Greene* (b. 1904), who has also written books for children and light fiction ("The Power and the Glory"), and *Bruce Marshall* (b. 1899: "All Glorious Within", "To Every Man a Penny").

A distinguished author between the wars was *Charles Morgan* (1894–1958), author of rather insightful philosophical novels ("The Fountain", "Sparkenbroke").

An advocate of natural healthy sensuality was *David Herbert Lawrence* (1855–1930), who wrote essays, plays and poems as well as novels. His best work, "Sons and Lovers", has many autobiographical elements. His explicitly sexual novel, "Lady Chatterley's Lover" banned until 1960, was the subject of a celebrated court case.

Irish writers have made a considerable contribution to the modern novel, most notably perhaps *Liam O'Flaherty* (b. 1897), who is also an excellent short story writer. The English regional novel is represented by *Mary Webb* (1881–1927: "Precious Bane", "Gone to Earth"), and the humorous novels by *Gilbert Keith Chesterton* (1874–1936).

In the special genre of the detective novel a leading place has long been occupied by English writers, from Sir *Arthur Conan Doyle* (1859–1930), author of the Sherlock Holmes stories, through *Edgar Wallace* (1875–1932) to Dame *Agatha Christie* (1890–1976).

Contemporary women novelists include *Iris Murdoch* (b. 1919), *Doris Lessing* (b. 1919), *Rumer Godden* (b. 1907), *Muriel Spark* (b. 1918) and *Daphne du Maurier* (b. 1907).

In recent decades the influence of British playwrights has been a predominant one on the theatre throughout the Western World. One of the earliest was **George Bernard Shaw** (1856–1950), who received the Nobel prize for literature in 1925 ("Arms and the Man", "Candida", "Man and Superman", "Mrs Warren's Profession", "St Joan"). Other successful dramatists have been *W. Somerset Maugham*, Noël Coward (1899–1973: "Fallen Angels", "Private Lives"), *Sean O'Casey* (1884–1964: "Juno and the Paycock", "The Star Turns Red"), the Irish writer *Brendan Behan* (1923–64), and *Austin Clarke* (1896–1974). T. S. *Eliot* (1888–1965) achieved international fame with

"Murder in the Cathedral" (conceived as a kind of mystery play like "Everyman"), *Christopher Fry* (b. 1907) with "The Lady's not for Burning", "The Dark is Light Enough".

The "angry young men" of the 1950s also left their mark on the theatre, with their vigorous criticisms of society which, often in their plays, was expressed in language designed to shock. These were people who also wrote novels, but it was their stage plays that generated most publicity – and heat. Now, however, across a distance of 20 years or more, their forthrightness seems relatively tame. The original angry young man was John Osborne (b. 1929), with his "Look Back in Anger"; others were *Arnold Wesker* (b. 1932), *Shelagh Delaney* (b. 1938) and *John Mortimer* (b. 1923). In the plays of *Harold Pinter* (b. 1930) and *Norman F. Simpson* (b. 1919) the influence of English naturalism is combined with influences from the "théâtre de l'absurde" of *Samuel Beckett* (b. 1906), an Irishman who lives in France and has written many of his plays in French and then translated them into English ("Waiting for Godot"). Other popular dramatists are *Terence Rattigan* (1911–77: "The Deep Blue Sea"), *Peter Ustinov* (b. 1920), *Emlyn Williams*, *William Douglas-Home* and *John van Druten*.

Music

In the early days of Christianity in Ireland the monasteries devoted much attention to *plainsong*, and their influence spread to the Continent of Europe. As early as the 10th century Winchester Cathedral had an organ with more than 400 pipes. Settings for several voices are found in Church and secular music from the 11th century onwards ("Sumer is icumen in", early 13th c.). Fauxbourdon (a simple form of harmonisation) occurs from the first half of the 15th century onwards, but was probably used earlier as a harmonic technique in improvisation. Musical theorists like John Cotton (*c.* 1100) and Lionel Power had great influence.

The leading European master in the 15th century was John Dunstable (d. 1453), but after him other nations began to come to the fore musically. An important contribution was made during the Elizabethan period by English *music for virginals*, which influenced instrumental music in general. Hugh Aston (d. 1522) and Thomas Tallis (d. 1585) were followed at the end of the 16th century by composers of *madrigals* like William Byrd and Orlando Gibbons and the great lutenist John Dowland. They were particularly fond of variations and used many folk tunes. The madrigal rose to great heights in the work of John Blow (1649–1708), still more in that of his pupil **Henry Purcell** (1658–95), the best known English composer, who also wrote vocal and instrumental music and operas.

With *Handel* (George Frederick Handel), who became director of the Haymarket Opera House in London in 1719, the Germanic influence reached Britain. Even the music for "The Beggar's Opera" was written by a German composer, Pepusch. In the second half of the 18th century Johann Christian Bach, Johann Sebastian's son, became music master to the family of George III and founded the Bach-Abel concerts. In the last decade of the century Haydn was enthusiastically feted in London before achieving full recognition in Vienna. The catch and the glee, two typically English musical genres, flourished, as did the carol (originally danced as well as sung). Until modern times the English round-dance or country dance had considerable influence in Europe.

During the 19th century there was another great flowering of music in Britain. Arthur Sullivan (1842–1900) composed the music for the ever-popular light operas including "The Mikado", with libretti by W. S. Gilbert. Sidney Jones was another successful composer of light operas. Around 1880 a number of notable musicians came to the fore – Hubert Parry (1848–1914), Charles Villiers Stanford (1852–1924) and Alexander Mackenzie (1847–1935). One of the most important British composers since Purcell was Sir Edward Elgar (1857–1934), whose music has a strongly national emphasis. Frederick Delius (1863–1934) composed operas and orchestral and choral works characterised by rich tonal colour; at first his music tended to be more readily accepted abroad than in Britain. Another composer who achieved international success was Cyril Scott. One of the leading musical personalities of recent times was Ralph Vaughan Williams (1872–1958), who composed symphonic music and operas; he was also a leader of the folk-song movement. Other important composers were Gustav Holst (1874–1935) and Frank Bridge (1879–1941). Among composers born around the turn of the century, some, like Sir Arthur Bliss (1891–1975), have achieved international reputation. These include William Walton (1902–83), Michael Tippett (b. 1905), Edmund Rubbra (b. 1901) and Constant Lambert (1905–51). An outstanding composer of the 20th century was **Benjamin Britten** (1913–76), remembered particularly for his operas. Born slightly later (1920), Peter Racine Fricker is noted as a composer of symphonies.

Britain has made relatively little contribution to the most recent developments in music. Practitioners of *dodecaphonic music* include Elizabeth Lutyens (b. 1906) and H. Searle (b. 1926), a pupil of Webern's, also respected as a theorist. A more moderate trend is represented by F. Burt (b. 1926) and A. Goehr (b. 1932); C. Cardew (b. 1936), on the other hand, belongs to the *avant-garde*.

However, Britain has been well represented in the phenomenal growth of the pop-music scene of the last few decades. Particularly memorable was the rise of the Beatles in the early 1960s. From playing in cellar-bars, these four young men from Liverpool rocketed to fame almost overnight. The earlier rock-and-roll sound seemed almost lethargic in comparison, and the Beatles – more than any other single group – were responsible for extending the scope of pop music worldwide. They and other British groups used mainly electric guitars and percussion to accompany the vocalists.

"Folk rock" was a development from Anglo-Irish folk music. In the early 1970s elements from non-European cultures (Asian and Black) began to influence pop music. Major pop festivals, often spanning several days and held in the open-air, attract hundreds of thousands of young people both from the host country and from overseas.

Sunset in the western Highlands: view from Kyle of Lochalsh towards the islands of Scalpay and Skye

Economy

In the mid-19th century Britain was, by a considerable margin, the world's leading industrial nation. It produced more than half the world's industrial output and half the world's iron and possessed the largest merchant fleet. A century later, with the break-up of the Empire which once covered a quarter of the earth's surface and contained a quarter of its population, Britain gradually lost its sources of cheap raw materials and its world-wide markets. The former colonies, by now independent members of the Commonwealth, began seeking aid from the mother country. To this extent the Empire had become a liability rather than an asset. In addition Britain was now faced with stiff competition in world markets from the United States, Japan, India and many other countries, and its difficulties were aggravated by the need to re-equip industry with updated technology and by shortage of investment capital.

In 1900 Britain still accounted for 18% of world industrial production; by 1937 the figure had fallen to 13%; today it is only 7%. Another considerable factor in this decline has been the fall in the demand for Britain's main form of mineral wealth — coal. This is not least because it is now cheaper to import coal from the United States, where it is mined by open-cast methods, than to exploit its own deeper supplies in Wales. This has led within the past 15 years or so to the closing down of many pits, although two-thirds of Britain's power requirements are still met by coal (the rest coming mainly from oil, now available from the offshore oilfields in the North Sea and the Irish Sea).

Possessing few raw materials apart from coal and iron-ore, Britain now occupies fifth place in the world trade league, behind the United States, West Germany, Japan and France. It still retains a leading industrial role as a processor of imported raw materials, and the pound sterling holds its position as the leading currency of the Commonwealth, with a quarter of the world's population living within the sterling area.

Britain produces a sixth of the world output of manufactured goods. Major contributions are made by its mechanical engineering, textile, chemical, electrical engineering and computer industries. It imports a fifth of world output of raw materials. The huge oil import bill which in the past proved so damaging to the balance of trade has been mitigated to a very great extent by North Sea oil. However, in view of probable continuing difficulties in world fuel supply, Britain has made a large investment – of expertise as well as capital – in the development of atomic energy. It is now the leading nation in Europe in the use of nuclear energy for peaceful purposes. A considerable portion of the country's power is now produced in nuclear stations, at a unit cost lower than that of electricity produced from coal. Britain is also a considerable exporter of atomic fuels.

Britain's most highly industrialised regions are in the Midlands and northern England. Great efforts are being made to establish new industry in depressed areas and to check the steady drift of young people to other parts of the country.

As an important means of helping the economy and the country's balance of trade considerable efforts are being made, both by central and regional organisations, to promote the growth of tourism. Tourism has always been an important currency-earner for Britain: 1983 brought about $12\frac{1}{2}$ million foreign visitors to the UK and the revenue from tourism was estimated at more than £3000 million. But, in a time of world recession, it is one figure which Britain is uniquely equipped to improve.

Great Britain
A to Z

A Beefeater on guard at the Tower of London

Aberdeen

Scotland. – Region: Grampian.
Altitude: 869 ft. – Population: 203,900.
Telephone dialling code: 0224.
ⓘ **Corporation of the City of Aberdeen**,
St Nicholas House, Broad Street;
tel. 23456.
Information Caravan (May to October),
Stonehaven Road;
tel. 873030.

HOTELS. – *Tree Tops Crest*, 161 Springfield Road, C,
108 r.; *Caledonian Thistle*, Union Terrace, C, 79 r.;
Gloucester, 102 Union Street, C, 73 r.; *Station*, 78
Guild Street, C, 59 r. – AT THE AIRPORT: *Holiday Inn*, B,
154 r.

YOUTH HOSTEL. – *King George VI Memorial Hostel*,
8 Queens Road, 128 b.

Two CAMPING SITES.

RESTAURANTS. – *Chivas*, 387 Union Street; *Pol-
dino's*, 7 Little Belmont Street; *Dickens*, 347 Union
Street; *Fidlers*, 1 Portland Street.

EVENTS. – *Aberdeen Festival* (end July–beginning of
Aug.), with concerts, parades, fireworks; *International
Festival of Youth Orchestras and Performing Arts*
(Aug.).

SPORT and RECREATION. – Golf, fishing, swimming, tennis, pony trekking. Centre for model ship
enthusiasts.

**Aberdeen, Scotland's third largest
city and an important fishing harbour, is picturesquely situated on
the North Sea between the rivers
Dee and Don. With a rich cultural
tradition as well as modern industry,
it is an important tourist centre with
interesting old buildings and beautiful parks. The city has several times
won the "Britain in Bloom" competition.**

The traditional building material of the
Aberdeen area is granite, and the Cathedral is said to be the oldest granite cathedral
in the world. Most of the University is in
Old Aberdeen. The port has acquired
increased importance thanks to North Sea
oil. There are ferry services from here to
the Orkney and Shetland Islands.

HISTORY. – The origins of the Celtic chapel of St
Machar (who probably died in 594) can be traced
back to the 6th c. The cathedral which succeeded it
was founded in 1136, although the earliest work in the
present building dates only from the 14th c. The
building of the famous bridge which spans the Don in
a steep Gothic arch, the Brig o' Balgownie, was begun
in 1285 but not completed until 1320. The municipal
records have been preserved almost without a break
since 1398. Mary Queen of Scots is said to have
watched the execution in 1562 of her cousin and
admirer, John Gordon, from the town house of the
Earl Marischal. Marischal College was founded in
1593 by George Keith, fifth Earl Marischal.

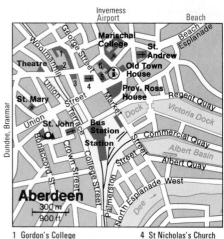

Inverness
Airport   Beach

1 Gordon's College   4 St Nicholas's Church
2 Art Gallery   5 Provost Skene's House
3 Museum   6 St Nicholas House

SIGHTS. – *Castlegate*, now Castle Street,
was the old main street of the town, and
most of the municipal buildings are still
here. The castle itself has disappeared,
and the oldest building is the tower of the
Tolbooth, formerly a prison. Nearby is the
Mercat Cross or City Cross (1668), with
carved portraits of the Stuart kings. Also in
Castlegate is the *Lead Man*, a statue
(1706) commemorating the first public
water supply in Aberdeen. A short distance away are *Provost Ross's House*
(1593, now a marine museum) and
Provost Skene's House (first mentioned
1545), which belonged to Sir George
Skene, provost of Aberdeen 1676–85.
*Marischal College, said to be the
largest and most imposing granite building in the world, was begun in 1840 and
enlarged between 1890 and 1906;
notable features are the *Mitchell Tower*
(235 ft) and the *Mitchell Hall*. In 1840
Marischal College was united with
King's College (founded 1494–95),
which lies a mile to the N. King's College
has preserved its original chapel with a
beautiful dome, carved stalls and a
remarkable timber roof.

N of King's College is *St Machar's
Cathedral, which is believed to have
been built on the site of a small chapel
erected by St Machar in 581. The present
building was begun in 1378 and completed in 1552. The striking W towers with
sandstone spires date from 1518–30.
There is a notable *ceiling* decorated with
coats of arms.

St Nicholas's Church, better known as
the East and West Churches, is Scotland's
largest parish church, divided into two at

the Reformation. The West Church contains four fine 17th c. *tapestries*. – Other features of interest in the city are the *Fish Market*, the *Docks* and the *parks*.

SURROUNDINGS. – On the coast N and S of Aberdeen are a number of seaside resorts and other places of interest. **Stonehaven** (pop. 7880), 15 miles S, is a fishing port but also a popular holiday resort with beautiful walks along the cliffs. 1½ miles S, on a crag jutting out into the sea, is **Dunnottar Castle**, an imposing stronghold protected on three sides by water and on the landward side by a cleft in the rock. The rectangular keep is well preserved, and some idea of Donnottar's past magnificence can be gained from the remains of the castle and its chapels – ranges of roofless buildings, towers and turrets, arched doorways and halls. The castle was the scene of many bloody events. During a siege of the castle in 1652 the regalia of Scotland, which were in safe keeping here, were smuggled out by the wife of the minister of Kinnef church (6½ miles S), as a monument erected in her honour records.

Dunnottar Castle

To the N, at the mouth of the River Ythan, is the fishing village of **Newburgh**. A pearl from one of the mussels which are found in abundance here is set in the Scottish crown. Beyond Newburgh is the seaside resort of **Cruden Bay** (pop. 1443), with a sandy beach and a golf-course. The *Bullers of Buchan*, a rocky chasm near here, impressed Dr Johnson as did **Slains Castle**, now a ruin, which Johnson declared was the finest he had ever seen. 11 miles NW are the ruins of the 13th c. *Deer Abbey*. – On the Hill of Fare, 18 miles W of Aberdeen on A 974, is **Midmar Castle**, a picturesque early 17th c. castle, complete with towers and turrets. 8 miles farther W along the same road and then SE on A 980 (3 miles) is **Lumphanan**, where Macbeth is supposed to have died. 4 miles N is **Craigievar Castle** (1696), with a seven-storey keep (17th c.) and a magnificent Renaissance ceiling. **Crathes Castle**, 23 miles SW of Aberdeen, has valuable furniture and a painted wooden ceiling.

Pitmedden House, 18 miles N, near A 981, has delightful old-world gardens, with pavilions, sundials and fountains in 17th c. style. 1 mile NW are the remains of the 16th c. **Tolquhon Castle**, with the even earlier Preston's Tower.

Anglesey

North Wales. – County: Gwynedd.

ⓘ **Wales Tourist Office,**
Marine Square, Salt Island Approach,
Holyhead;
tel. 2622.

The Isle of Anglesey, separated from the mainland by the ¾-mile-wide Menai Strait, is spanned by two imposing bridges; the Menai Suspension Bridge (1818–26), built by Telford and a two-level bridge, opened in 1970 which has the roadway above the railway and which rests on the pillars of a former structure (magnificent view from the Anglesey Column). Along the coast are a series of small seaside resorts which have grown out of fishing villages. Apart from five market towns there are only tiny villages, linked by narrow roads.

The coasts of Anglesey are very attractive, the cliffs being interrupted at intervals by picturesque sandy bays. The interior – fertile pastureland with huge flocks of sheep – is of less interest to the tourist.

The principal place is **Holyhead**, on the neighbouring **Holy Island** to the W, from which there are ferry services to Dublin. Holy Island, which is linked with Anglesey by two bridges, is an increasingly popular holiday resort. Two promenades, one on the 1½-mile-long breakwater, and Salt Island afford interesting views of the rugged coast and Holyhead Mountain (710 ft), on the top of which are a fort and the remains of a small chapel (the only survivor of the six or seven that originally stood here).

Menai Suspension Bridge

These chapels are said to have earned the island its name of "Holy"; but this interpretation is open to doubt, since in earlier times the local people were predominantly Welsh-speaking, as many of them still are. There is, similarly, doubt about the interpretation of Anglesey as the "Island of Angels". Also of historical interest are the *Cytiau'r Gwyddelod* on Holy Island, remains of stone dwellings dating from pre-Christian times.

Trearddur Bay (pop. 1300; hotels – Trearddur Bay, D, 28 r.; Fairway, E, 7 r.), 2½ miles from Holyhead, is a well-known seaside resort with a good golf-course. The direct road across the island to Holyhead from Bangor via Menai Bridge (pop. 2730; Wales Tourist Information Centre, Menai Bridge, Isle of Anglesey, Coed Cyrnol, tel. 712626) is not of great interest, and it is preferable to take the road round the coast.

Beaumaris Castle

10 miles NE of Bangor is **Beaumaris** (pop. 2500; hotel – Plas Llanfaes, Country House; E, 8 r.), a popular seaside resort and yachting centre (regatta in August). Beaumaris Castle (1295), an imposing structure with strong walls and towers surrounded by a moat, was one of the numerous castles built in Wales by Edward I. From the castle there is a magnificent *view of Snowdonia. The finest room in the castle is the chapel. Other features of interest in the town are the parish church (14th c. nave), County Hall (1614) and the Old Gaol. – 5 miles away is *Penmon Priory* (early Norman). The little offshore island of *Priestholm* or *Puffin Island* is the nesting-place of countless seabirds.

The route continues via **Pentreath** (pop. 740), with a beautiful sandy beach, and the little seaside resort of *Benllech* in Red Wharf Bay. 1 mile away is the quiet and unspoiled fishing village of *Moelfre*.

Within easy reach are the little market towns of *Llanerchymedd* and **Llangefni**, the administrative centre of Anglesey, and *Lligwy*, with a fortified village of the late Roman period. **Amlwch** (pop. 4000), another little market town and a seaside resort, was of some importance in the early 19th c. as the port of shipment for copper from the Parys mines, which were already being worked in Roman times. *Bull Bay* offers excellent bathing and fishing. *Llaneilian* has an interesting parish church, with parts dating from the 5th and the 12th c.

W of Bull Bay the coast becomes higher and more rugged. There are good bathing beaches between the rocks in *Cemaes Bay*. The coast is particularly wild at *Carmel Head*, the NW tip of the island. The next seaside resort of any size is **Rhosneigr**, with sand dunes and rocky bays (boating, fishing, golf). Llangwyfan Old Church can be reached on foot at low tide. Farther along the coast there is good bathing at *Aberffraw* and *Malltraeth Bay*. *Newborough Warren* is an interesting nature reserve with sand dunes and maritime plants in abundance.

Anglesey has the village (half a mile from Menai Bridge) with the longest name in Britain (58 letters):
Llanfairpwllgwyngyllgogerychwyrndrobwl-llantysiliogogogoch.

Antonine Wall

Central Scotland. – Regions: Strathclyde and Central.

The Antonine Wall, traditionally known as Grim's Dyke or Graham's Dyke, was a Roman fortification extending from Bo'ness on the Firth of Forth to Dunglass Castle on Dunglass Point (near Clydebank) on the Firth of Clyde, a total distance of 39 miles. The wall was built of turf and earth on a stone base, and was originally about 12 ft high and 14 ft wide. To the N was a ditch 20 ft deep and 40 ft across, and there were 19 forts situated at intervals along the wall. A paved road ran along the S side.

The wall was built by Roman legionaries in A.D. 142, and in the Hunterian Museum

Antonine Wall

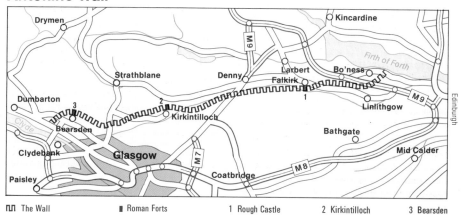

| ⊓⊓ The Wall | ▌ Roman Forts | 1 Rough Castle | 2 Kirkintilloch | 3 Bearsden |

in Glasgow can be seen a model showing which sections were built by each unit. The wall was designed to afford protection against attacks from the N.

Scotland, unlike England, was never firmly under Roman control, but was partly occupied on a temporary basis to protect the province of Britannia. Agricola advanced into Scotland in A.D. 80, and in 84 inflicted a crushing defeat on the natives at Mons Graupius, a site which has not been identified with certainty (Perthshire, or possibly farther N?). Agricola built a number of forts, and the wall was erected by his successor Quintus Lollius Urbicus and named after the reigning Emperor, Titus Aurelius Antoninus. – The forts along the wall were occupied by Gauls and Belgians, Syrians and Thracians. Only 40 years after the building of the wall, about 185, it was abandoned, and thereafter the Romans confined themselves to occasional punitive expeditions into Scotland.

Little is left of the wall itself, though the ditch is well preserved in some places. Six of the forts have been excavated; the material recovered is mainly in Glasgow. The best preserved of the forts are at **Kirkintilloch** (pop. 34,900) and *Rough Castle* near the industrial town of **Falkirk** (pop. 36,900; hotel – Stakis Park, C, 55 r.). Remains of the wall can be seen at *Callendar Park*, just E of Falkirk, and to the NW and NE of **Bearsden** (pop. 27,000; hotel – Stakis Burnbrae, C, 16 r.), NW of Glasgow.

Arran

South-western Scotland. – Region: Strathclyde.

Arran is the largest and scenically most attractive of the islands in the Clyde. Together with the neighbouring islands of Bute (pop. 14,400) and the Cumbraes, it formed the old county of Bute. Arran itself has a population of only 3600, the rugged northern part of the island being almost uninhabited. The island, lying 12 miles from the Ayrshire coast, is 20 miles long by 11 miles across. Often called "Scotland in miniature", it is of great interest to geologists, with almost every kind of rock found in Britain. For the archaeologically inclined there are numerous burial cairns, standing stones and Iron Age and medieval remains. Many rare species of plant are to be found in the mountains.

Brodick Bay, Arran

There are regular boat services to Arran from *Ardrossan*. From a distance the island looks like a single solid mass of rock, but from closer in it takes on a less rugged aspect, with fields and patches of forest. The ferry lands at **Brodick** (pop. 816), in Brodick Bay. *Brodick Castle* is mostly modern, but incorporates parts of an earlier 14th c. structure. Fine collection of furniture, silver and pictures; beautiful grounds. From Brodick the island's highest mountain, *Goatfell* (2866 ft), can be climbed; in good weather there are magnificent panoramic views from the top. The climb takes about 5 hours there and back; the return can also be to *Corrie*. It is possible also to go round by the very beautiful *Glen Rosa* (4 miles).

Holy Island (1 mile long) lies on the seaward side of Lamlash Bay, 5 miles S of Brodick. It is an island of varied scenery, rising to a height of 1030 ft. Its name reflects the tradition that St Molaise, a disciple of St Columba, lived here. The cave which the saint is said to have occupied can be seen; its walls are covered with inscriptions of various dates, including large runic signs. A large block of sandstone surrounded by artificial depressions in the rock is known as the Saint's Chair. For many centuries a spring on the island was credited with healing powers.

Lamlash (pop. 4100; hotel – Glenisle, E, 22 r.) is a popular seaside resort with a sailing school and a beautiful bay which offers good bathing. The parish church is a prominent feature of the village. At the S end of the bay is Kingscross, beyond which is *Whiting Bay* (golf-course, youth hostel). Immediately S is *Glenashdale*, with two waterfalls. *Kildonan Castle* was a royal hunting lodge in the days when Arran was Crown property and the Scottish kings came here to hunt; the red deer which were then introduced into Arran can still be seen on the island. The castle is now a picturesque ruin, situated in an exposed position on the coast. On *Brennan Head*, the most southerly point on the island, are the *Struey Rocks*, which are well worth a visit. Here too is the *Black Cave*, 80 ft deep and extending into the cliffs for some 50 yards.

The road continues by way of the restful little holiday place of **Lagg** to beautiful *Glen Monarmore* and *Sliddery*, on the coast, with remains of a watch-tower on Castle Hill.

On the SW coast, looking out on to the Kilbrennan Sound, is the seaside resort of **Blackwaterfoot** (hotels – Kinloch, D, 46 r.; Rock, E, 9 r.), with a golf-course and good fishing. On King's Hill, at the N end of Drumadoon Bay, are a number of caves in which Robert the Bruce (1274–1329), who defeated Edward II of England at Bannockburn in 1314, is said to have hidden along with his men. The largest of the caves is known as the *King's Cave*.

The most interesting of Arran's prehistoric remains are the **Standing Stones of Tormore**, $2\frac{1}{2}$ miles N of Blackwaterfoot. – The road continues N by way of the little villages of Auchencar and Catacol to Lochranza, in a very beautiful bay, with the remains of the 17th c. *Lochranza Castle*. The most northerly point on the island is the *Cock of Arran*, 2 miles from Lochranza. The road runs SE from Lochranza through Glen Chalmadale and Glen Sannox, the wildest of Arran's glens, to Corrie and Brodick (6 miles).

Avebury

Southern England. – County: Wiltshire.
Altitude: 500 ft. – Population: 540.
Telephone dialling code: 06723.
ⓘ **Tourist Information Centre**,
32 The Arcade, Brunel Centre,
Swindon, Wilts.;
tel. 0793 30328.

HOTELS. – IN LAYCOCK (10 miles away): *The Sign of the Angel*, A, 6 r. – IN DEVIZES (5 miles away): *The Bear*, Market Place, D, 26 r.

The Avebury *stone circles are the largest megalithic monument in England – larger and older than Stonehenge, though less celebrated. The present village is situated partly within and partly outside the outermost circle. Built during the Neolithic period, the Avebury Circles originally consisted of some 700 rough-hewn stones set in three rings. They are surrounded by an earth rampart and a ditch almost 50 ft deep, probably dating from the same period.**

The rampart has a total perimeter of some 1300 yards. Many of the stones have been

Avebury

re-erected by the Department of the Environment, in whose care the monument now is; many of them were removed during the 18th c. for use in building. The circles undoubtedly served cult purposes and had no defensive function.

The imposing *Kennet Avenue*, lined by some 200 stones set in pairs, links Avebury with the *Sanctuary* on **Overton Hill** (1 mile). The ceremonial circles here, using two different types of stone, are attributed to the Beaker People who came to England from the Lower Rhineland and Holland.

In the immediate neighbourhood of Avebury there is a great concentration of prehistoric sites, on a scale scarcely equalled anywhere else. 1½ miles away is *Windmill Hill, now owned by the National Trust, which gave its name to the earliest farming and stock-rearing culture (2950–2570 B.C.). Finds from the site are in the interesting *Avebury Museum*.

Nearby, too, is **Silbury Hill**, a man-made conical hill 50 ft high and 130 ft in diameter which is the largest prehistoric construction in Europe. Built up of the local limestone, it is probably of Neolithic date. Excavation yielded no evidence pointing to its use for burial, and the assumption is that it was a cult site or perhaps served some calendrical purpose.

West Kennet Long Barrow, the largest chambered tomb in England (350 ft long, 8 ft high), contained 30 burials in five chambers. It dates from the early Stone Age.

There is an attractive walk over the downs from Avebury to Marlborough, passing the *Grey Wethers* (erratic sandstone boulders) and the large megalithic burial chamber known as the *Devil's Den*. – Near Avebury are *Beckhampton* and *Manton*, both noted for their training stables.

SURROUNDINGS. – 7 miles SE of Avebury is **Marlborough** (pop. 7000), on the River Kennet, a pretty little town with a fine arcaded High Street, wide enough to accommodate the weekly market. A 17th c. building regulation required main streets to be broad enough to allow a horse and cart to turn in them, and this is certainly true of the High Street of Marlborough. Marlborough College is a leading public school (800 pupils). – *Savernake Forest* and the *Marlborough Downs* offer much attractive scenery.

8 miles W of Avebury is **Lacock**, one of the most beautiful villages in Britain. The village of some 100 houses, mostly built of grey sandstone and dating back to the 14th c., and the splendidly preserved remains of Lacock Abbey belong to the National Trust. *Lacock Abbey*, founded 1232 and largely in Tudor style, was occupied by Augustinian nuns until 1538 and then converted into a country house. Here William Henry Fox Talbot invented photography, and there is now an interesting museum of photography in the house, with the earliest photograph (1835). Talbot is buried in the village churchyard.

A beautiful road runs over the *Marlborough Downs*, passing through the little town of *Wootton Bassett*, with a half-timbered town hall of around 1700, to **Malmesbury** (pop. 2600; hotel – Mayfield House, D, 21 r.), a charming township with many old houses and a late medieval market cross (c. 1500). St John's Hospital dates from the mid 13th c. Of particular interest is the Abbey, which has a long history. The first church on the site was probably built at the end of the 7th c.: it is established, at any rate, that St Aldhelm, who died in 709, was the first abbot. The abbey was rebuilt by King Athelstan (d. 940), whose reputed tomb is in the church. Six of the original nine bays of the nave of the old Benedictine abbey church still remain; the style is Norman and Early English (c. 1150). The finest feature of the church is the Norman S doorway, with magnificent sculpture and eightfold columns. The central tower collapsed in the 16th c., the W tower rather later, destroying the eastern end of the church. Notable features of the interior are a font (partly Saxon), an organ of 1714, the porter's lodge and the stone choir screen.

Every tourist should see the famous *White Horse, cut in the turf of a hillside near Uffington in the *Vale of the White Horse*, amid beautiful chalk hills. The date of the horse, which is 374 ft long, is uncertain. One suggestion is that it was a tribal totem figure of the Iceni (1st or 2nd c. B.C.) – a theory supported by the presence of the Iron Age fort (probably 2nd c. B.C.) known as *Uffington Castle* on the top of the hill. The figure shows some resemblance to the horses depicted on late Iron Age coins.

The valley to the W is known as the *Manger*. In it is *Dragon Hill*, where St George is supposed to have slain the dragon. Visitors with enough time at their disposal will find it well worth while to follow the beautiful footpath along the prehistoric Ridgeway to *Wayland's Smithy*, a Neolithic chamber tomb 185 ft long situated in a wood. Eight burials were found in the three chambers (c. 2500–2000 B.C.).

The village of *Uffington*, 2 miles N of the White Horse, has a fine Early English church of about 1200.

Bath

Southern England. – County: Avon.
Population: 80,000.
Telephone dialling code: 0225.
ⓘ **Tourist Information Centre,**
8 Abbey Churchyard;
tel. 62831 (information),
60521 (accommodation).

HOTELS. – *Ladbroke Beaufort*, Walcot Street, B, 123 r.; *Francis*, Queen Square, B, 90 r.; *Pratt's*, South Parade, C, 47 r.; *Lansdown Grove*, Lansdown Road, C, 41 r.; *Royal York*, George Street, D, 54 r.

YOUTH HOSTEL. – Bathwick Hill, 100 b.

RESTAURANTS. – *Hole in the Wall*, 16 George Street; *Popjoys*, Beau Nash House; *Ainslie's*, 12 Pierrepont Street.

EVENTS. – *Bath Festival of the Arts* (May); *Mid Somerset Festival* (Mar.).

SPORT and RECREATION. – Golf, riding, tennis, swimming, rowing.

*Bath was, and still is, the most celebrated spa in England, the only resort with hot springs (49°C–120°F) and is one of England's most elegant and attractive towns. It lies in a sheltered situation in the valley of the Avon and on the slopes of the adjoining hills. With its Georgian houses the town plays a leading role in the cultural life of the country.

With its elegant crescents and terraces, squares and circuses, and the well-proportioned façades of its houses, Bath has a very distinctive townscape of its own, imitated though it was by many other towns during the Georgian period. Some 500 buildings are statutorily protected as being of historical or architectural importance, and innumerable houses have tablets recording the celebrities, particularly of the 18th and 19th c., who lived in them. With its agreeable climate, the town still attracts large numbers of visitors.

Bath is a masterpiece of town planning, thanks to its architects John Wood and his son. A great benefactor of the town in the 18th c. was Ralph Allen, owner of the quarries of Bath stone which provided the building material for its houses.

HISTORY. – Tradition has it that the healing power of the springs was discovered by a British prince named Bladud who suffered from leprosy. What is certain, however, is that in A.D. 53 the Romans built an extensive bath establishment in the town, which they called *Aquae Sulis*, with an elaborate system of hot and cold water pipes, a large pool and a promenade. Remains of the Roman baths, with the original lead facing, can still be seen. In the 12th c. the town was the see of a bishop. It was noted for its clothing industry, which is referred to in Chaucer's "Wife of Bath's Tale". It did not become widely known as a spa until 1701, when Queen Anne visited the town. Its heyday was in the 18th c., thanks mainly to Beau Nash, master of ceremonies and the uncrowned "king of Bath". Nash laid down how the polite world must behave, and the whole of the aristocracy meekly followed his lead. Gainsborough, Sheridan, Fielding and many other artists and writers were among notabilities who came to Bath, and the town provided a setting for many English novels.

The Roman Baths and Abbey, Bath

SIGHTS. – The remains of the *Roman baths are of great interest, and the *Cross Bath*, famous in the 17th c., is also worth seeing. The *Pump Room*, a large building in classical style (designed by Thomas Baldwin, completed by John Palmer in 1796), contains a statue of Beau Nash and a Tompion clock. From one of the windows can be seen the *King's Bath*, with large numbers of brass rings presented by grateful patients.

Bath Abbey, the last of the great pre-Reformation churches, is in Perpendicular style (16th c.). The number and size of its windows have earned it the name of "Lantern of the West". It has magnificent *fan vaulting*. The sculpture on the W front, with angels on ladders, depicts the dream

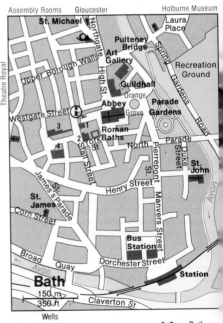

1 Pump Room
2 King's and Queen's Baths
3 Cross Bath
4 Old Royal Bath

of Bishop Oliver King, who rebuilt the church at the turn of the 15th and 16th c. There are numerous tablets and monuments commemorating famous residents of Bath, including the economist Thomas Robert Malthus (1766–1834).

The Georgian architecture for which Bath is famed is mostly in the NW of the town. *Queen Square* (1729–36), *Gay Street* and the *Circus were built by the elder Wood, while his son's masterpiece was **Royal Crescent**, a 200-yard-long sweep of 30 houses designed as a single whole. The *Assembly Rooms* (1769–71; damaged during the last war and later rebuilt) were also by the younger Wood; they now house a magnificent *Museum of Costume. St James's Square* and *Lansdown Crescent* were built by John Palmer (completed 1790), *Camden Crescent* (1788) by John Eveleigh. Also of interest are *Somersetshire Buildings*, by Baldwin (1782), and the *Theatre Royal*. The *Holburne of Menstrie Museum* contains pictures, *miniatures, silver, glass, furniture and rare books. The old *Guildhall*, the *Victoria Art Gallery* and the *Public Reference Library* also deserve a visit. In Royal Victoria Park is a *Botanical Garden*. The charming *Pulteney Bridge* (by Robert Adam, 1770) spans the Avon with three arches; there are shops on both sides of the bridge.

SURROUNDINGS. – On one of the surrounding hills, from which there are good views of the town, is the imposing **Sham Castle** built by Ralph Allen in 1762, a battlemented wall, towers and gate with nothing behind them. – In *Lansdown*, 2 miles NW, are Kingswood School and Beckford's Tower.

2½ miles E, in **Claverton Manor** (by Wyatville, 1820), is the *American Museum in Britain*. – 2 miles SE is *Prior Park* (by John Wood, 1735–50), one of the finest Palladian mansions in England, the home of Ralph Allen.

Battle

Southern England. – County: East Sussex.
Population: 5000.
Telephone dialling code: 04246.
ⓘ **Tourist Information Centre,**
88 High Street;
tel. 3721.

HOTELS. – *George*, High Street, D, 22 r.; *Netherfield Place Country House* (1¾ miles NW), D, 11 r.

CAMPING SITE.

RESTAURANT. – *The Pilgrim's Rest*.

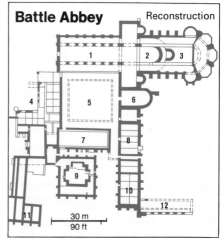

Battle Abbey   Reconstruction

1 Nave	5 Cloisters	9 Kitchen
2 Choir	6 Chapterhouse	10 Novices' quarters
3 Presbytery	7 Refectory	11 Guest-house
4 Abbot's lodging	8 Warming room	12 Latrines

Battle Abbey

Although the school-books say that William the Conqueror defeated the Saxon king Harold at Hastings in 1066, the battle actually took place at the little town now called Battle, 6 miles from Hastings.

This charming market town owes its existence to a vow made by William that if he were victorious in the battle he would found an abbey. The high altar of the **Benedictine abbey** built in fulfilment of this vow was set up on the spot where Harold was killed. After the Dissolution of the Monasteries Henry VIII presented the abbey to his Master of the Horse, Sir Anthony Browne, who converted it into a country house. Particularly fine are the beautiful *gateway* (1338) and the ruined *dormitory* (1120). The house is now a girls' school. In the parish church is the magnificent Renaissance *tomb of Sir Anthony Browne*.

Herstmonceux Castle

SURROUNDINGS. – 10 miles S is *Herstmonceux Castle, a magnificent brick-built Renaissance manor-house (1440), fortified and moated. It now houses the Royal Observatory, formerly at Greenwich – so that Greenwich Mean Time now comes from Herstmonceux.

In the opinion of many visitors *Bodiam Castle is the most romantic ruined castle in England: at any rate it is undoubtedly one of the best preserved medieval moated castles (1386–89). The moat is so wide that the castle with its towers and battlements appears to rise out of the middle of a lake. From the castle there are extensive views of the Rother valley.

Bodiam Castle

Bedford

Central England. – County: Bedfordshire.
Altitude: 93 ft. – Population: 75,000.
Telephone dialling code: 0234
ⓘ Tourist Information Centre,
    St Paul's Square;
    tel. 215226.

HOTELS. – Bedford Moat House, St Mary's, B, 117 r.;
Bedford Swan, The Embankment, D, 99 r.

RESTAURANT. – De Parys, 45 Parys Avenue.

SPORT and RECREATION. – Rowing, canoeing, fishing.

Bedford, on the River Ouse, is the county town of Bedfordshire, a quiet residential town in spite of its various industries. It now has one of the largest Italian colonies in Britain. The Ouse offers excellent fishing and boating. The town is noted for its schools and its associations with John Bunyan.

HISTORY. – In 1552 Sir William Harpur (1496–1573), a cloth merchant who became Lord Mayor of London (1561–62), founded a school in his native town of Bedford. The Harpur Trust now runs four schools with a total of some 3500 pupils.

John Bunyan (1628–88), author of "The Pilgrim's Progress", was born in the neighbouring village of Elstow, the son of a tinker. After marrying a pious woman, he became an itinerant preacher of a Nonconformist sect. Although prohibited from preaching he continued to do so, and was thereupon confined in the county gaol from 1660 to 1672, preaching to his warders and fellow prisoners. In 1675 he was again arrested and committed to the town prison, where he wrote most of "The Pilgrim's Progress".

SIGHTS. – Near the bridge over the Ouse is St Paul's Church, which has a 14th c. pulpit. In St Paul's Square is a statue of John Howard (1726–90), the great prison reformer. At the end of High Street, looking towards the site of the old county gaol, is a statue of John Bunyan. In Castle Close stands the Cecil Higgins Art Gallery, with a notable collection of porcelain, glass, furniture and water-colours. Nearby is the Bedford Museum (local history). St Peter's Church has a Norman tower containing some Saxon work.

In Mill Street is the Howard Congregational Church, founded by John Howard in 1772. In this street too is the Bunyan Meeting, on the site of the barn in which Bunyan used to preach. On the bronze doors (1876) are ten scenes from "The Pilgrim's Progress". The library and museum contain many mementoes of Bunyan and editions of his works. The adjoining Howard House belonged to John Howard, who in 1858 moved to Cardington, 3 miles SW.

SURROUNDINGS. – 2 miles S is Elstow, Bunyan's birthplace, which has many associations with him, from the font in which he was baptised to the church bells which he used to ring.

Luton (pop. 164,200; hotels – Strathmore, C, 151 r.; Crest Motel, C, 137 r.; Luton Eurocrest, C, 96 r.), an industrial town with an airport, has an interesting church, St Mary's, mainly in Decorated style, with the

Wenlock Chapel (1461: William Wenlock was a prebendary in St Paul's Cathedral in London) and a beautiful canopied *font. – 2½ miles S is **Luton Hoo**, a handsome country house begun by Robert Adam in 1767 which now houses the magnificent *art collection assembled by Sir Harold Wernher (jewellery, 18th c. furniture and carpets, pictures by Rembrandt, Memling, Constable, Reynolds and many other artists).

Belfast

Northern Ireland. – County: Antrim.
Population: 297,800.
Telephone dialling code: 0232.
(i) **River House**,
   48 High Street;
   tel. 246609.

HOTELS. – *Forum*, Great Victoria Street, B, 200 r.; *Stormont*, 587 Upper Newtownwards Road, C, 67 r.; *Wellington Park*, 21 Malone Road, C, 54 r.; *Drumkeen*, Upper Galwally, C, 26 r.

YOUTH HOSTEL. – 11 Saintfield Road, 60 b.

RESTAURANTS. – *Chimes*, 78–80 Botanic Avenue; *Skandia*, 46 Howard Street; *Windsor*, Knocknagoney Road.

SPORT and RECREATION. – Golf, tennis, riding, sailing, fishing, swimming, shooting.

Belfast, capital of Northern Ireland since 1920, is also an important port and industrial city. It is beautifully situated on Belfast Lough, at the mouth of the River Lagan, which forms the boundary between the counties of Down and Antrim. The Belfast shipyards are among the largest in Europe. The city has numerous fine buildings and about 170 churches. The scenery in the surrounding area, along the coast and round Lough Neagh (Northern Ireland's largest lake), is very fine.

HISTORY. – Belfast (*Beal feirste*, the fjord on the coast) already possessed a fort in the early Middle Ages, but this was destroyed in 1177. Thereafter a castle was built, the possession of which was often stubbornly contested between the native Irish and the English conquerors. In 1613 the town which had grown up around the castle was granted a charter by James I. The manufacture of linen had long been an important industry in Belfast, and it received additional impetus in the latter part of the 17th c., when Huguenots fleeing from France introduced improved industrial methods. The newcomers gave the life of the town a French stamp and contributed to the development of its intellectual life, so that it became known as the "Athens of the North". This led to a considerable influx of both Irish and British settlers, who built their own churches, giving Belfast its present multiplicity of religious denominations and sects. Industry continued to develop, making Belfast the most important industrial city in the whole of Ireland. In 1941, during the Second World War, the

Dome of City Hall, Belfast

city suffered considerable damage. It has also suffered much damage during the recent troubles, which have severely reduced the city's tourist trade.

SIGHTS. – The central feature is **City Hall** in *Donegall Square*, a huge Renaissance palazzo (by Sir Brumwell Thomas, 1898–1906) with four towers and a massive dome. In front of it are statues of Queen Victoria and prominent citizens of Belfast, and on the W side is the War Memorial in a *Garden of Remembrance*. There is also a sculptured group commemorating the sinking of the *Titanic* (which was built in a Belfast shipyard) in 1912. Donegall Place and the adjoining streets, particularly **Royal Avenue**, are Belfast's main shopping streets, with large department stores.

To the N, by way of Royal Avenue, is **St Anne's Cathedral** (by Sir Thomas Drew, begun 1898), the principal church of the (Anglican) Church of Ireland. Of basilican type, it has three fine W doorways decorated with sculpture. The baptismal chapel has a *mosaic ceiling* made of hundreds of thousands of tiny pieces of glass. In the chapel is the tomb of Lord Duncairn (Sir Edward Carson, d. 1935), leader of the Ulster Unionists.

Other churches are *St Patrick's Pro-Cathedral* (R.C.) in Upper Donegall Street, the *Unitarian Church* in Elmwood Avenue and the *Carlisle Memorial Church* in Carlisle Circle.

About ¾ mile from Donegall Square, reached by way of University Road, is the

red-brick Tudor-style *Queen's University*
(built 1845–94), which has been an
independent University since 1909. There
is a *historical museum.*

The *Museum and Art Gallery*, in the large
and well-tended *Botanic Gardens*, has
much material of the Celtic and early
Christian periods, with fine examples of

Viking and Celtic ornament. The gallery is
particularly strong in European painting of
the 17th and 18th c. and Irish art from
early times to the progressive Ulster
school.

Evidence of the scale of Irish emigration through the
centuries, particularly to the United States, is given by
the portraits of prominent people of Northern Ireland
origin, including ten American Presidents.

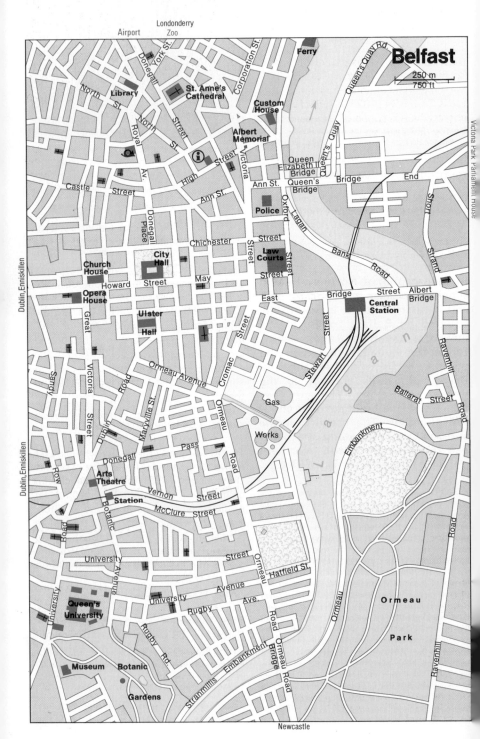

Near the River Lagan are the *Custom House* (1854–57) and the **Albert Memorial Clock Tower**, popularly known as the Big Ben of Belfast. It was built in 1869 to commemorate the Prince Consort.

$3\frac{1}{2}$ miles outside the city, at **Stormont**, is the imposing building erected in 1928–32 to house the Parliament of Northern Ireland. In front of it is a monument to Sir Edward Carson.

To the N of the city are the *Zoological Gardens*, parks, sports grounds and golf-courses, as well as *Belfast Castle* (1870), once the home of Lord Shaftesbury. Here too is *Cave Hill* (1182 ft), a hill of volcanic origin which is supposed to resemble the profile of Napoleon. It is worth climbing the hill for the fine views which it affords in good weather of the city and Lough Neagh, the coast and, in the distance, the Isle of Man.

Other features of interest are the *Transport Museum* (Witham Street) and the Harland and Wolff shipyard. In a park about $7\frac{1}{2}$ miles E of the town lies the **Ulster Folk Museum*, an open-air architectural museum, and the castle of Cultra Manor which houses a transport museum.

SURROUNDINGS. – There are a number of roads leading to **Lough Neagh**, the largest lake in Northern Ireland, 18 miles long and 11 miles wide. Ten rivers flow into the lough, which is well stocked with fish. There is no road running round the lough, nor even a good footpath, for the shores of the lough are low and overgrown with vegetation. The best view of the lough is from *Glenavy*, where boats can be hired in summer. 5 miles W of Glenavy is the beautiful *Ram's Island*.

There is another route to Lough Neagh via **Antrim** (pop. 8500), which gave its name to the county and the coastal area. The town is situated at the outflow of the Six Mile Water into the lough. *Antrim Castle* (1622) has been burned down and rebuilt several times. The gardens were designed by Le Nôtre, who laid out the gardens of Versailles. One of the best preserved round towers in Ireland stands in the grounds of Steeple House, $\frac{3}{4}$ mile NE of the town. It is over 90 ft high and of massive girth.

On the N and S shores of Belfast Lough, the wide inlet in which the city lies, are a series of popular seaside resorts. The coast immediately N of the lough is particularly beautiful. Half-way along the N side of the lough is **Carrickfergus** (pop. 19,000; hotels – Coast Road, D, 24 r.; Dobbin's Inn, D, 14 r.), a considerable port before its displacement by Belfast. It is noted for its excellently preserved *Norman castle, one of the finest in Northern Ireland, situated on a rocky peninsula. Begun between 1180 and 1205, it was taken by King John in 1210 after a year's siege. Its finest features are the splendid Great Hall (one of the best examples extant of a Norman hall), the massive keep, the well and the prison. From the roof of the castle there are fine views.

10th c. round tower, Antrim

From Carrickfergus a particularly beautiful section of the coast road runs NE to **Whitehead** (hotel – Dolphin, D, 19 r.), a popular seaside resort at the mouth of Belfast Lough, and the peninsula of **Island Magee* (7 miles long by 2 miles wide). A striking feature on the E side of the peninsula is the Gobbins, a stretch of basalt cliffs 250 ft high containing a number of caves. There are numerous legends associated with the cliffs and the caves. At the end of the peninsula is a megalithic chambered tomb. – A series of quarries and cement works disfigure the coast road to **Larne** (pop. 18,600; hotels – King's Arms, D, 48 r.; Magheramorne House, D, 23 r.), from which there are ferry services to Stranraer in Scotland. Larne, situated at the mouth of Lough Larne, is a busy industrial town as well as a seaside resort (ferry to Island Magee). There are notable remains of Olderfleet Castle (three-storied defence tower).

From Larne there is a romantic and beautiful stretch of coast road to *Cushendun*. After passing through the Black Cave Tunnel it rounds *Ballygalley Head* with its great basalt crags. *Ballygalley* is a popular seaside resort, and the old castle is now a hotel (D, 30 r.). From here to *Glenarm*, a little port at the mouth of the River Glenarm, the road is lined by white limestone cliffs. The next seaside resort is *Carnlough*, with a small harbour and a good sandy beach.

Waterfoot, at the near end of Red Bay, is delightfully situated in a kind of amphitheatre of sandstone cliffs, at the mouth of **Glenariff*, one of the most beautiful of the Glens of Antrim. Just beyond Waterfoot are the little resort of *Cushendall* and the better known *Cushendun*.

The road along the S side of Belfast Lough and down the coast also has beautiful scenery and a number of attractive little towns and villages. *Holywood*, a suburb of Belfast, has remains of the 12th c. Franciscan friary of Sanctus Boscus. From here the road continues via Crawfordsburn to **Bangor** (pop. 39,300; hotels – Tedworth, D, 13 r.; The Sands, D, 12 r.; Winston, E, 47 r.), the most popular of Northern Ireland's seaside resorts, with wide sandy beaches, beautiful promenades and plentiful facilities for sport and entertainment. Features of interest are the Castle and Castle Park, and the Abbey Church, on the site of a monastery founded in 555 which had a notable monastic school. – On the way to Bangor, Helen's Tower, near Crawfordsburn, should not be missed.

The coast road continues to *Donaghadee*, with Copeland Island lying just offshore on the left.

Beyond this extends the 20-mile-long **Ards Peninsula**. The route follows the coast of the Irish Sea or North Channel to *Ballywalter* (beautiful beach), *Ballyhalbert* and *Cloughey*, from which it runs inland to Portaferry, on the S tip of the peninsula.

From the little port of **Portaferry** there is a ferry service to Strangford, on the other side of Strangford Lough. – It is also possible to return up the W side of the Ards Peninsula along the shores of the lough (A 20). After passing through Ardkeen (ruined castle) and Kircubbin the road comes to **Greyabbey**, with remains of a Cistercian abbey founded in 1193, one of the best preserved in Ireland. Notable features are the fine Perpendicular windows and the magnificent W doorway.

The road continues via *Mountstewart House* (beautiful park with many dwarf trees) to **Newtownards**, a noted linen-making centre and a good base from which to explore the coastal region and the Mourne Mountains. It has a Town Hall of 1770 and a ruined Dominican church (1244). The Old Cross in the High Street has been several times restored.

From here it is possible to return direct to Belfast (6 miles), or alternatively to turn S via the whiskey-distilling town of *Comber* and continue down the W side of Strangford Lough to *Downpatrick* (21 miles). Garden-lovers will prefer the road which runs away from the lough via the little town of *Saintfield and enables them to see the beautiful *Rowallane Gardens* (National Trust), with many rare flowers and plants.

On the W shore of the lough is **Killyleagh** (birthplace of Sir Hans Sloane, founder of the British Museum), with Hilltop Castle overlooking the town. The parish church dates from the Jacobean period. The scenery is very beautiful, with the Mourne Mountains shimmering blue in the distance.

Downpatrick (pop. 7400) is the county town of Co. Down. Here St Patrick began the conversion of Ireland in 432. 2 miles N is Saul, where he landed, built his first church and is said to have died – although the granite stone in the churchyard does not appear to date from his period. The Cathedral was built in 1790 on the remains of an earlier church; the font and some of the capitals came from the older church.

More interesting than the direct road to Clough is the road round the coast by **Strangford**, an old Viking settlement in a beautiful situation on Strangford Lough. The strategic importance of this area is shown by the fact that there are four Anglo-Norman castles of the 16th c. in the immediate vicinity. *Audley Castle* is open to visitors.

No fewer than seven castles protect the little village of *Ardglass*, formerly an important harbour but now mainly a fishing village. One of these, Jordan Castle, has considerable remains, including a square keep. W of *Killough* is a very beautiful beach.

At *St John's Point* begins a magnificent *panoramic road along what is perhaps the most beautiful stretch of coast in Northern Ireland to Newry (39 miles). It runs round the wide bay of Dundrum, large areas of which are exposed at low tide, to Newcastle. **Dundrum** is a picturesque fishing village with sandy bays which offer excellent bathing, and an old tower surrounded by a moat, all that is left of the former castle.

The Mourne Mountains

Newcastle (4600; hotels – Slieve Donard, D, 118 r.; Brook Cottage, E, 11 r.) has all the amenities of a seaside resort, including a golf-course. It lies at the W end of Dundrum, at the foot of *Slieve Donard* (2796 ft), the highest of the **Mourne Mountains** and the second highest point in Ireland. The climb takes some 2 hours, and is rewarded by a magnificent *view from the top, extending as far as the Scottish coast.

From Newcastle the road begins to climb, with the sea on the left and the ever-changing backdrop of the Mourne Mountains (the home of many rare plants) on the right. It passes through a number of quiet little fishing and farming villages like *Glasdrumman* and *Annalong*, from which a number of peaks between 1700 and 2450 ft (Rocky Mountain, Slieve Bignian, etc.) can be climbed.

Kilkeel is a favourite resort with anglers, since there are good catches to be had both in the sea and in the River Kilkeel and nearby Carlingford Lough. Round Kilkeel are a number of prehistoric chambered tombs.

Between *Greencastle* in the N and *Greenore* in the S **Carlingford Lough** cuts deep inland, with a road running along each side. From Kilkeel a road runs N through the Mourne Mountains, with steep climbs and descents, to *Hilltown*, a good base for climbs and walks in the hills, richly coloured with the changing hues of their granites and schists.

On the N shore of Carlingford Lough, surrounded by woodland (mainly oaks), is **Rostrevor**, a pretty and peaceful little holiday resort (boating, pony trekking, fishing, walking).

At the head of the lough is **Newry** (pop. 28,000), a port and industrial town on the River Newry and a canal, between the Mourne Mountains to the E and Camlough Mountains to the W. The tower of St Patrick's Church, the first Protestant church in Ireland, dates from 1578; the nearby Cathedral (R.C.) is neo-Gothic. Near the town are the picturesque village of Bessbrook and Derrymore House, an 18th c. thatched villa in Georgian style.

The road continues via *Markethill*, with Gosford Castle, one of the largest in Ireland, to **Armagh** (pop. 13,000), named after a fortress built here in the 3rd c. by Queen Macha, remains of which can be seen 2 miles W. St Patrick built a cathedral here, but thereafter the town was several times burned down and rebuilt. The site of St Patrick's cathedral is now occupied by the Cathedral of the Church of Ireland, a medieval building restored in the 19th c. The neo-Gothic Roman Catholic Cathedral (1840–73) is also dedicated to St Patrick. The Protestant Cathedral has a number of notable monuments and an old crypt, the Roman Catholic one interesting mosaics. Nearby are the fine Georgian Archbishop's Palace and the Diocesan College. Also worth seeing are the Royal School, founded by Charles I, the Observatory (1791), the Court House (by Francis Johnston, 1761–1829), numerous Georgian houses and the County Museum.

Birmingham

Central England. – County: West Midlands.
Altitude: 250–750 ft. – Population: 1,006,900.
Telephone dialling code: 021.

(i) **Tourist Information Centre,**
110 Colmore Row;
tel. 235 3411.
Convention and Visitors Information Bureau,
National Exhibition Centre;
tel. 780 4141.

HOTELS. – *Holiday Inn*, Holliday Street (ATV Centre), B, 304 r.; *Albany*, Smallbrook, Queensway, B, 254 r.; *Plough and Harrow*, Hagley Road, Edgbaston, B, 44 r.; *Post House*, Chapel Lane, Great Barr, C, 204 r.; *Strathallan Thistle*, Hagley Road, Edgbaston, C, 171 r.; *Grand*, Colmore Row, C, 145 r.; *Royal Angus Thistle*, St Chads, Queensway, C, 139 r. – AT THE NATIONAL EXHIBITION CENTRE (about 6 miles E): *Birmingham Metropole and Warwick*, B, 709 r. – AT THE AIRPORT: *Excelsior*, Coventry Road, B, 141 r.

RESTAURANTS. – *Lorenzo*, 3 Park Street; *Pinocchio*, 8 Chad Square, Harborne Road.

SPORT and RECREATION. – Golf, tennis, riding, boating.

Birmingham is Britain's second largest city and one of the largest industrial centres in the world, with a modern Exhibition Centre for trade fairs, etc. Apart from a number of crowded and unattractive older housing areas it is a well-planned modern city, with pleasant residential suburbs and open spaces. It has few historic old buildings but is rich in art treasures. The University is one of the largest in the country. Birmingham is a good base from which to explore the Cotswolds, the Malvern Hills and the Vale of Evesham. Its numerous canals, formerly used for the transport of goods, are now mainly used for pleasure boating.

HISTORY. – The name probably means "settlement of Beormund's people". As early as 1538 the town appears in the records as the place of manufacture of knives, tools and nails, and in 1689 an arms manufactory was established here. Birmingham's rise to economic importance, however, really began after Boulton and Watt perfected the steam engine here between 1774 and 1800. The nearby iron and coal mines also contributed to its prosperity.

SIGHTS. – Since the last war Birmingham has undergone massive redevelopment,

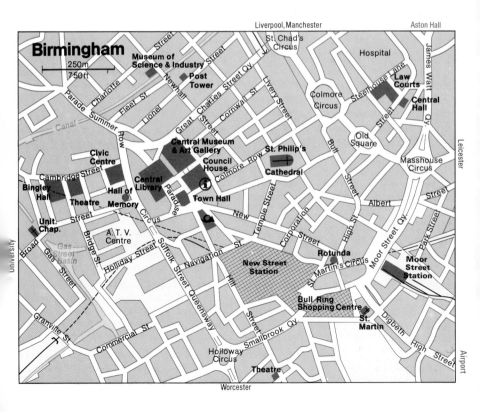

and this process is still continuing, so that the city is changing all the time. The older public buildings are round Victoria Park. The **Town Hall** (1832–50), a masterpiece of Victorian architecture, is in the form of a Roman temple with Corinthian columns; the large hall can seat 2000. It has been the centre of the city's musical life since the first performance of Mendelssohn's "Elijah" here in 1847, and has one of the finest organs in the country. The large hall is decorated with paintings illustrating the history of the city.

In *Chamberlain Square*, N of the Town Hall, is a *fountain* commemorating Joseph Chamberlain, Lord Mayor of Birmingham in 1873–75. There is also a statue of Joseph Priestley, the discoverer of oxygen, who was minister of the Unitarian church in 1680–91. On the N side of Victoria Square is the Renaissance-style **Council House** (1874–81), with a clock-tower popularly known as "Big Brum". To the W is the *Hall of Memory*, built in 1925 to commemorate the 14,000 Birmingham men who fell in the First World War. Nearby is the new *Civic Centre*.

The *Central Museum and Art Gallery*, opened in 1925, is one of the finest in the country outside London, with a rich collection of famous pictures, including many works by the Brimingham landscape painter David Cox and a good representation of the Pre-Raphaelites.

The *Central Library* has what is probably the largest Shakespeare collection in the world (37,000 volumes in 79 languages). There is also a large *collection of stamps and coins* and a well-stocked archaeological section. The *Museum of Science and Industry* illustrates Birmingham's industrial history and has a fine collection of machinery and motor cars.

The Palladian-style **Cathedral** (1711–15) was until 1905 the parish church of St Philip; the pulpit was added in 1897. It has four stained-glass windows designed by Burne-Jones and made by William Morris. *St Martin's Church*, founded in the 13th c., was rebuilt in Decorated style in 1872–75; it too has windows by Burne-Jones and Morris. The Roman Catholic **St Chad's Cathedral** (by Pugin, 1839–41), the see of an archbishop, has a 16th c. oak *pulpit*

The Bull Ring shopping centre, Birmingham

and 15th c. *choir-stalls* and *lectern* from Cologne.

The *University* was founded in 1900. The *Chamberlain Tower*, 325 ft high, commemorates its first Chancellor. To the E of the University is *King Edward VI's School*, founded in 1552. Also near the University is the **Barber Institute of Fine Arts**, founded in 1932, which contains the rich University *art collection*, with works by Botticelli, Bellini, Tintoretto, Rubens, Rembrandt, Watteau, Manet, Monet, Gainsborough, Constable and many other artists.

Birmingham has now a second university – Aston University, previously a College of Advanced Technology, which received its charter in 1966.

Also of interest are the *Selly Oak Colleges*, with the large Rendel Harris Library (1903). 2 miles away, in Alwold Street, is *Weoley Castle*, a moated house of the 12th–14th c. which now contains a local museum.

To the S is *Bournville*, headquarters of a famous chocolate and cocoa firm established in 1831. From 1879 onwards a fine *garden city was built for the workers.

In **Aston Park**, 2½ miles N of the Civic Centre, stands *Aston Hall*, a red-brick Jacobean mansion built by Sir Thomas Holte between 1617 and 1635 which now houses a *museum* and *art gallery*. Notable features are the oak staircase, the furniture and the chimneypieces.

The busiest shopping streets are *Corporation Street* and the streets around *St Martin's Circus*, the old market square. There are also many imposing new shopping centres in the city. – The *Botanical Garden* in Harborne is also worth a visit. On the E edge of the city lies the National Exhibition Centre.

SURROUNDINGS. – In Walsall (pop. 265,000), 12 miles NW, is a *Museum of Locks (locks from many countries).

Bradford-on-Avon

Southern England. – County: Wiltshire.
Altitude: 200 ft. – Population: 8310.
Telephone dialling code: 02216.
ⓘ **Tourist Information Centre,**
    1 Church Street;
    tel. 2224.

HOTEL. – *Leigh Park*, D, 20 r.

The little town of Bradford-on-Avon, picturesquely situated on the river, has an almost Italian aspect, with its narrow lanes and terraces. Huddled closely on the banks of the river, it has many stepped lanes. The houses are built of grey stone, as is the bridge over the Avon. Two of the nine arches of the bridge date from the 13th c., the others from the 17th c.

An unusual feature is the chapel in the middle of the bridge – formerly frequented by pilgrims, later used as a lockup, now merely a viewpoint. The town's great tourist attraction, however, is *St Laurence's Church, one of the finest of the few Anglo-Saxon churches which have been preserved more or less unchanged.

HISTORY. – The church is believed to have been founded by Abbot Aldhelm (d. 709), and is first referred to in a document of 705. In the 10th c. it was increased in height. Later it ceased to be used as a church, and was enclosed by other buildings and used for a variety of purposes, until the very existence of the church was forgotten. It was rediscovered in 1856, when the local vicar is said to have recognised the cross of the old church when looking from a window over the huddle of roofs. Thereafter the adjoining buildings were removed, revealing the church as it can now be seen.

SIGHTS. – *St Laurence's Church** impresses the spectator with the powerful simplicity of its architecture and its lack of decoration. It is a high, long and narrow building notable for its clarity of structure, with an aisleless nave and a rectangular chancel. In both the nave and the chancel,

which are linked by a narrow round-headed doorway, the height is greater than the length. The small round-arched windows admit little light. High above the chancel doorway are two sculptured angels, probably fragments of a larger group. – Among the most attractive of the numerous fine old houses in the town are the *Hall*, built for a local clothier in 1610, and the *Almshouses* of 1700. On Barton Farm is a large 14th c. *tithe barn*.

SURROUNDINGS. – 1½ miles SW is *Westwood Manor*, a 15th c. house which was enlarged in the 16th c. – 2½ miles NE is **Great Chalfield**, which has a church, with fine wall paintings, attached to a 15th c. manor-house.

11 miles S is **Longleat House**, seat of the Marquess of Bath, a splendid early Renaissance country house built in 1559–78 and restored by Wyatville in 1801–11. The beautiful park was landscaped by Capability Brown. Pets' cemetery. Safari Park, with many lions, through which visitors can drive in their own cars.

Bristol

Southern England. – County: Avon.
Altitude: 355 ft. – Population: 405,500.
Telephone dialling code: 0272.
ⓘ **Information Centre,**
    Colston House, Colston Street;
    tel. 293891.

HOTELS. – *Holiday Inn*, Lower Castle Street, B, 285 r.; *Ladbroke Dragonara*, Redcliffe Way, B, 198 r.; *Unicorn*, Prince Street, C, 193 r.; *Grand*, Broad Street, C, 179 r.; *Crest*, Filton Road, Hambrook, C, 151 r.; *Avon Gorge*, Sion Hill, Clifton, C, 76 r.; *Redwood Lodge*, Begger Bush Lane, Failand, C, 72 r.; *St Vincent Rocks*, Sion Hill, C, 46 r.; *Hawthorns*, Woodland Road, *Clifton*, D, 165 r.

RESTAURANTS. – *Harvey's*, 12 Denmark Street; *Floyds Bistro*, 112 Princess Victoria Street; *Rajdoot*, 83 Park Street; *Restaurant du Gourmet*, 43 Whiteladies Road; *Rossi Nr.10*, 10 The Mall; *La Taverna Dell'Artista*, 33 King Street (Italian); *Trattoria da Renato*, 19 King Street (Italian).

EVENTS. – Commemoration service in St Mary Redcliffe (Whit Sunday).

SPORT and RECREATION. – Sailing, rowing, swimming, golf, tennis.

Although the old town centre suffered severe destruction during the last war, Bristol still ranks as one of the most beautiful of England's larger cities. It is a port and an industrial town, but also a town of churches and of seamen's taverns, with a great past and rich traditions. Between the 15th and the 18th c.

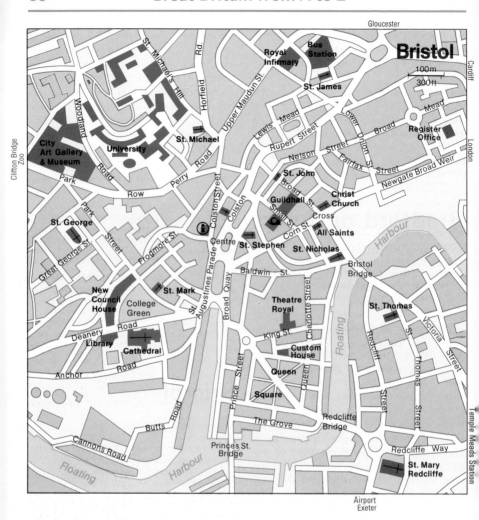

Bristol was the second most important town in England, surpassed only by London.

Bristol has two notable churches, the Cathedral and St Mary Redcliffe, as well as the oldest theatre in the country, still in use, and a fine modern University. The Avon gorge is spanned by Brunel's impressive Clifton Bridge.

Another of Brunel's great creations, the *Great Britain*, the first iron-built ship, can be seen in the Bristol shipyard in which it was originally built. Many emigrants sailed to the New World from Bristol, following in the wake of John Cabot, who set out from here in 1497 on the expedition which discovered North America. He is commemorated by the Cabot Tower. In addition to shipping and shipbuilding, the city's industries now include aircraft construction, engineering, chocolate and tobacco.

HISTORY. – From the 12th c. onwards Bristol was a considerable trading town. Its later rise to prosperity was based on the slave trade: its ships sailed to West Africa with English goods, carried slaves from there to the West Indies (70,000 a year by the end of the 18th c.) and loaded up with sugar, rum and tobacco for the return voyage. As early as the 14th c. Edward III recognised the importance of Bristol by granting it the status of a county. – In 1643–45 the town was the main Royalist base in the West Country. The *Great Western*, the first steamship to make regular crossings of the Atlantic, was built in Bristol by Brunel in 1838. In 1940–41 great destruction was caused by German air raids.

SIGHTS. – As in any large port, there is always a lot to see around the harbour, particularly in a town like Bristol where the city and the port are closely bound up together. In the harbour area there are, of course, typical bars and taverns. The most famous of these is the *Llandoger Trow* in King Street, a half-timbered 17th c. inn in which Defoe is said to have heard from Alexander Selkirk the story which he immortalised as "Robinson Crusoe"; it is believed also to have been the model for the inn frequented by Long John Silver in Stevenson's "Treasure Island". There is a tunnel from the Llandoger Trow which leads to the *Theatre Royal on the other side of the street. This is the oldest English theatre (1766), now the home of the Bristol Old Vic company. Old, too, is the area round *High Street*, which runs from Bristol Bridge to the Cross. The old *High Cross* is no longer here but in Stourhead; there is a reproduction on College Green. The Cross is the meeting-place of four short streets, High Street and Broad Street intersecting with Corn Street and Wine Street. This was the *heart of the old town*, which suffered very severe destruction during the last war. The **Old Council House**, a building in classical style by Sir Robert Smirke (1781–1867), has been extensively renovated. *Broad Street* runs past the *Guildhall* (1843–46) to the old town walls, with a tower surmounted by the spire of *St John's Church*, the remains of which are of the same height as the walls.

Through the arch of St John's Gate, with its figures of Brennus and Belinus, the legendary founders of Bristol, are *Christmas Street* and *Christmas Steps*, which lead to an attractive quarter of the town, with old *almshouses*, a chapel of 1504 and, in nearby Broad Mead, the oldest Methodist church in the world, Wesley's *"New Room"* (1739).

Corn Street leads to the *Exchange*, in front of which are the "Nails" – four bronze tables on which the Bristol merchants used to settle their accounts. Farther on, in St Stephen's Street, is the large mid 16th c. *St Stephen's Church*.

*St Mary Redcliffe ranks as the finest parish church in England, and was described by Elizabeth I as "the fairest, the goodliest and the most famous" in her kingdom. Its name comes from the red cliffs on which the church was built in the 13th c. at the expense of wealthy merchants. The spire is 290 ft high. The interior, primarily in 15th c. Perpendicular style, is of enchanting elegance with its tall arches, slender pillars and reticulated vaulting. The beauty of the church is enhanced by some work in Decorated style. Particularly fine is the hexagonal *N porch*, with a richly decorated doorway.

The wealth and splendour of the church is due to one of the richest merchants of the day, William Canynge, whose likeness can be seen in the S transept. He is commemorated at a special service on Whit Sunday.

It was in the muniment room of St Mary Redcliffe that Thomas Chatterton (1752–70) claimed to have found the poems by a monk named Rowley which he had in fact written himself. Chatterton was born nearby in Redcliffe Way; there is a monument to him NE of the church.

Bristol's other famous church is the *Cathedral, originally the church of an Augustinian house founded by Robert Fitzharding in 1140, which was raised to cathedral status on the establishment of the diocese by Henry VIII in 1542. The E end was splendidly remodelled in Decorated style by Abbot Knowle between 1298 and 1330. The *central tower* was rebuilt about 1450. The Cathedral is a hall-church, with aisles of the same height as the nave and no clerestory or triforium. The Decorated style is seen at its most typical in the piers and ribs and the stellate and fan vaulting.

View from Cabot Tower, Bristol

The most splendid feature of the church is the **choir (rebuilt 1298), a structure of inspired lightness and an entirely new feeling for space. The choir-stalls are modern but have misericords of about 1520. There are two *Lady Chapels*, one in Early English style (1210–20) adjoining the N transept and a later one (1298–1330) at the E end, still with its original altarpiece and 14th c. windows. In the S aisle are unusual stellate tomb recesses containing the remains of abbots. The *Berkeley Chapel* contains a rare 15th c. brass chandelier.

Notable also is the rectangular *chapterhouse (late Norman, c. 1150–70). *College Gate* (Perpendicular, with Norman archways) is the gateway to the old abbey.

Clifton Suspension Bridge

Another fine church is *St Mark's Chapel*
or the *Lord Mayor's Chapel*, originally the
chapel of a hospital founded by the
Fitzharding family in 1220. The aisle is
Early English (late 13th c.), the rest
Perpendicular (15th and late 16th c.).
The imposing pile of the *University*
(founded 1909), largely financed by the
munificence of the Wills tobacco family, is
in CLIFTON, a favourite residential district
of Bristol, with a number of streets mainly
composed of Georgian houses. The tower
of the University, which contains a bell
weighing 10 tons, is a prominent landmark. A short distance away, in Queen's
Road, is the **Museum and Art Gallery**,
with Hogarth's great *altarpiece* from St
Mary Redcliffe. Also in this area is the *Red
Lodge*, with beautiful furniture and a
particularly fine *Elizabethan room*. There
is also an interesting *Georgian House*. To
the W of the limestone plateau of *Clifton
Down* and *Durdham Down* is the Avon
Gorge, spanned by the famous * **Suspension Bridge**. To the E is Bristol Zoo,
notable particularly for its monkeys'
enclosure and its aquaria. – The *Merchants' House*, headquarters of the Society of Merchant Venturers of Bristol,
founded in 1532, contains interesting
furniture. – In *Henbury*, 4 miles NNW, is
Blaise Hamlet, with charming thatched
almshouses (now a museum) designed
by John Nash (1811).

SURROUNDINGS. – **Clevedon** (pop. 17,900) is a
quiet seaside resort in a small bay, with the old
mansion of Clevedon Court. Thackeray (1811–63)
lived in the town for some time. There are boat services
between Bristol and Clevedon.

Farther down the Severn estuary, on the Bristol
Channel, is the seaside resort of **Weston-super-
Mare** (pop. 58,400; hotels – Grand Atlantic, B, 77 r.;
Royal Pier, D, 47 r.), which can also be reached by
boat from Bristol. It has a 2-mile-long bathing beach,

beautiful parks, excellent sports and recreation
facilities and a boating lake. In *Yatton* and *Con-
gressbury*, between Clevedon and Weston-super-
Mare, are interesting Perpendicular churches. Of
interest to bird-watchers are the uninhabited islands
of *Steep Holm* and *Flat Holm* in the Bristol Channel,
the haunt of countless seabirds. 9½ miles NE of Bristol
in *Dodington House* is a coach museum.

Cambridge

Eastern England. – County: Cambridgeshire.
Altitude: 34 ft. – Population: 101,000.
Telephone dialling code: 0223.
ⓘ **Tourist Information Centre,**
Wheeler Street;
tel. 358977.

HOTELS. – *Post House*, Bridge Road, B, 121 r.;
Garden House, Granta Place, C, 117 r.; *University
Arms*, Regent Street, C, 115; *Blue Boar*, Trinity Street,
C, 48 r. – AT BARR HILL (about 4 miles NW): *Cunard
Cambridgeshire*, Huntingdon Road, C, 100 r.

YOUTH HOSTEL. – 97 Tenison Road, 84 b.

RESTAURANTS. – *Pentagon and Roof Garden*, 6 St
Edward's Passage; *Cambridge Lodge*, 139 Huntingdon Road.

EVENTS. – *May Week* (college boat races: June).

SPORT and RECREATION. – Golf, riding, tennis,
cricket, hockey, rowing, punting.

**Cambridge and Oxford are perhaps
the best known, if not the oldest,
universities in Europe – the oldest in
Britain and for nearly six hundred
years the only universities in England. Both were founded in the mid
13th c., Cambridge slightly later
than Oxford, and both have some
10,000 students.**

Cambridge, situated on the little River
Cam, is the county town of Cambridgeshire. Scarcely anywhere else in England is so much of historical, architectural
and artistic interest to be found con-
centrated in such a small area. The
University has 22 colleges, almost every
one of which has some distinctive quality
of its own. Along the banks of the Cam are
the Backs, the beautiful riverside parks
and gardens.

HISTORY. – In Roman times there was a small town
on the N bank of the Cam, which beyond the Silver
Street bridge is known as the Granta; and in Saxon
times this was called *Grantebrycg*, later (c. 1125)
Cantebruge. The form *Chambrugge* appears in
Chaucer. The first teaching establishments, then
attached to monasteries, were probably founded in
the 12th c., and the earliest reference to them appears
in a writ of Henry III (1231). The first college,
Peterhouse, was founded in 1284. In 1318 the
University was recognised by Pope John XXII. King's
College was founded by Henry VI in 1441.

In the reign of Elizabeth I (1558–1603) Cambridge was widely known, as far afield as Germany and Holland, for its trade fair, held annually in autumn.

SIGHTS. – The architecture of the colleges was based on the traditions of church architecture, and the colleges originally had a monastic atmosphere, which has not yet entirely disappeared. As in fortified castles and religious houses, they usually have a gatehouse giving access to a central courtyard.

The oldest college in Cambridge, **Peterhouse**, was founded by Hugh de Balsam, Bishop of Ely, in 1284. It is one of the smallest colleges. A notable feature is the *Laudian Chapel* (1628–32). Its most famous student was the poet Thomas Gray (1716–71), whose room looked out on to the church of *St Mary the Less* ("Little Mary"), which has a beautiful E window.

Across Trumpington Street from Peterhouse is **Pembroke College**, founded in 1347 by the Countess of Pembroke but much altered since then. The *chapel* (1663–65) was Wren's first work; it was lengthened by George Gilbert Scott in 1881. Pembroke produced many bishops and poets, the most celebrated of whom was Edmund Spenser (c. 1552–1599). Thomas Gray, having left Peterhouse, lived here until his death.

In Silver Street is *Queens' College**, founded in 1448 by Andrew Dockett under the patronage of Margaret of Anjou, wife of Henry VI, which has the most complete and most picturesque complex of medieval buildings of all the colleges. In the red-brick **First Court**, which dates from the period of foundation, are the Hall (decorated by William Morris), the Library and the Old Chapel. On the wall is a sundial of 1733. The *Cloister Court* (c. 1460) has the *President's Lodge*, a handsome half-timbered building (1460–95), on its N side. To the S is the small *Pump Court*, with the *Erasmus Tower*, above the rooms occupied by Erasmus as professor of Greek (1510–15). To the N is the *Walnut Tree Court* (1618), with the *Erasmus Building* (by Sir Basil Spence, 1961) and the Chapel.

From the Cloister Court the wooden *Mathematical Bridge* leads over the Cam to the beautiful College Gardens. The bridge is called "mathematical" because it was built without nails, on the basis of careful mathematical calculations.

Farther along Silver Street is **Darwin College**, founded in 1943. – Almost opposite Silver Street, on the far side of Trumpington Street, is **Corpus Christi College**, founded in 1352. The Old Court dates from the period of foundation, though much restored. The *Library* contains valuable *manuscripts and incunabula collected by Matthew Parker, Archbishop of Canterbury, c. 1550. The adjoining *St Bene't's Church* was formerly the college chapel. Christopher Marlowe was a notable member of Corpus Christi.

Trumpington Streets runs into King's Parade, on the left-hand side of which is **King's College**, founded in 1441 by Henry VI. ****King's College Chapel** (1446–1515), built of white limestone, is Cambridge's finest building, a masterpiece of late Gothic architecture.

King's College, Cambridge

The INTERIOR is famed for its beautiful *fan vaulting* (by John Wastell of Canterbury). Other notable features are the *choir-stalls* and the *organ screen* (1531–36). Behind the altar is a painting by Rubens. The 25 ****stained-glass windows** of 1515–31 depict scenes from the Old and New Testaments. The W window is modern. A service in the chapel is an impressive experience.

The other college buildings date from the 18th–20th c. Behind the college a great expanse of lawn extends down to the river. From *King's Bridge* there is a beautiful view of the Backs. Among distinguished members of the college was Horace Walpole (1717–97).

Beyond King's is the *Senate House*, a Palladian building by James Gibbs (1722–30), with delicate plasterwork and woodwork and numerous statues. The Senate House is used for great academic occasions such as the award of degrees. Other buildings in the square, like the *Old Schools* (14th–15th and 18th–19th c.), are occupied by university offices.

Great St Mary's, opposite the Senate House, is both a parish church and the University church. Built between 1478 and 1608, it has a very fine interior (organ by Father Smith). The adjoining bookshop is believed to be the oldest in Britain (1581).

Trinity Hall, founded in 1350 by William Bateman, Bishop of Norwich, has an old *Library, a gabled Elizabethan house which has preserved the original interior. It has a beautiful little garden.

***Clare College**, in Trinity Lane, between Trinity Hall and King's College Chapel, is the second oldest college in Cambridge, founded in 1326 as University Hall and re-founded in 1338 by Lady Elizabeth de Clare. The magnificent Renaissance buildings were erected between 1638 and 1715. The beautiful *Clare Bridge* (1640) leads over the Cam to the *Fellows' Garden* and the new college buildings beyond Queen's Road. Notable members of the college include Chaucer.

***Caius College** (pronounced "Keys"), officially Gonville and Caius, in Trinity Street, the continuation of King's Parade, was founded in 1348 by Edward Gonville and enlarged from 1558 onwards by Dr John Caius, personal physician to Edward VI and Queen Mary. It is favoured by medical students.

Caius has three gates symbolising the student's academic career. The *Gate of Humility* gives access from Trinity Street to Tree Court (1868–70), from which the *Gate of Virtue* leads into Caius Court (completed 1567), from which in turn the *Gate of Honour* (1575) leads into Senate House Passage and the Old Schools. In the Chapel is the tomb of Dr Caius.

***Trinity College** is the largest of all the Oxford and Cambridge colleges, founded in 1546 by Henry VIII. It incorporates some even older building, including the *Great Gate* (1490–1535: statue of Henry VIII).

The *Great Court*, built in the time of Thomas Nevile (Master 1593–1615), is 334 ft long and 228 ft wide. Newton, Thackeray and Macaulay had rooms here. In the centre is a fine *fountain* of about 1610. The *Chapel* was built in 1555–64; the interior is 18th and 19th c. In the ante-chapel are statues of Newton, Bacon, Tennyson and others. The asymmetric *King Edward III's Gate* W of the Chapel, with a statue of Edward III, is a relic of the older *King's Hall*. The college Hall (1605) is the largest in Cambridge, and exactly the same size as the Hall of the Middle Temple in London. *Queen's Gate*, on the S side of the court, has a statue of Elizabeth I. A passage leads into *Nevile's Court*, completed in 1614.

The **Library** was built by Wren (1676–90). The old oak bookcases have fine *limewood carving by Grinling Gibbons. It also contains white marble busts of eminent members of the college, including one of Byron by Thorwaldsen.

Trinity can claim more distinguished former members than any other college, including statesmen like Balfour, Austen Chamberlain, Baldwin and Nehru, poets and writers, among them George Herbert, Abraham Cowley, Dryden, Edward Fitzgerald, A. E. Housman and G. M. Trevelyan, the philosopher Bertrand Russell, and scientists such as Galton, Clerk-Maxwell, Thomson, Gowland Hopkins, Rutherford, Rayleigh, Eddington and – most famous of all – Isaac Newton. Edward VII and George VI were also members of Trinity.

From New Court or King's Court (1823–25) there is a bridge over the Cam, with a beautiful view of the Backs. A magnificent *avenue of lime-trees* leads to the College Grounds.

The adjoining **St John's College**, in St John's Street, was founded in 1511 by Lady Margaret Beaufort, mother of Henry VII.

A decorated *Gateway* leads into the red-brick First Court (1511–20); the passage under the gatehouse is the finest in Cambridge. The *Chapel*, built by Sir George Gilbert Scott (1836–39), contains stalls and monuments from the earlier chapel. The *Hall*, which was enlarged by Scott, has a fine hammer-beam roof, beautiful panelling and some good portraits. The *Combination Room* has a splendid plaster ceiling.

The Second Court, built by Ralph Symons in 1598–1602, is very attractive with its

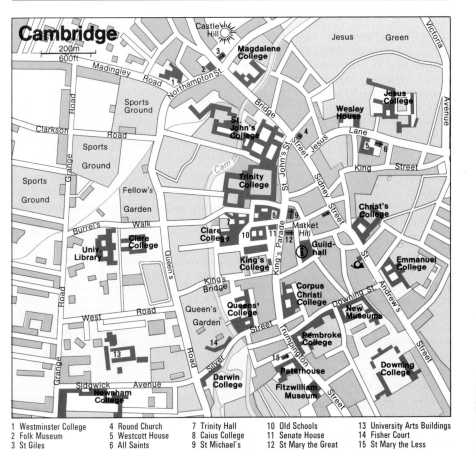

1	Westminster College	4	Round Church	7	Trinity Hall	
2	Folk Museum	5	Westcott House	8	Caius College	
3	St Giles	6	All Saints	9	St Michael's	

10	Old Schools	13	University Arts Buildings
11	Senate House	14	Fisher Court
12	St Mary the Great	15	St Mary the Less

mellow brickwork. The Third Court dates from 1669–71, and has the *Library* (1623–24) on its N side. From here the *Bridge of Sighs* (by Henry Hutchinson, 1831) leads over the Cam into the *College Grounds, which include an artificial "wilderness". It is possible to return across the Cam by the *Old Bridge* (1709–12).

Famous members of St John's were Ben Jonson and Wordsworth.

The *Round Church or Church of the Holy Sepulchre in Bridge Street is one of the few Norman round churches in England (c. 1131), with a rectangular 15th c. chancel; it was drastically restored in 1841. Bridge Street leads to the Great Bridge, an iron structure of 1823. From the far side of the Cam there is a good view of the picturesque *Fisher's Lane.*

Magdalene College (pronounced "Maudlen"), the only one of the old colleges on the W side of the Cam, was founded in 1542 by Lord Audley on the site of an earlier hostel for Benedictine monks. The Hall and Chapel are relics of

this older building, but were altered in the 18th c. The Pepysian Library in the Second Court, a handsome building dating from the second half of the 17th c., contains the *library* (over 3000 volumes and valuable manuscripts) which Samuel Pepys (1633–1703) bequeathed to his old college. – On the other side of Magdalene Street is a row of old *half-timbered houses*, behind which are *Mallory Court* and *Benson Court* (by Sir Edwin Lutyens, 1931.–32).

E of the Round Church, in Jesus Lane, is *Jesus College**, founded in 1496, on a site then outside the town walls, by John Alcock, Bishop of Ely. It contains parts of the old Benedictine nunnery of St Radegund, founded in the early 12th c. The entrance is by a fine gateway built by Alcock. The *Chapel*, formerly the conventual church, is Early English (mid 13th c.). The *stained-glass windows* are by Ford Madox Brown and Burne-Jones. On the E side of the court is the façade of the former *chapterhouse* (c. 1230). Among famous members of the college were John Eliot, Sterne, Malthus and Coleridge.

S of Jesus, in St Andrew's Street, is **Christ's College**, founded, like St John's, by Lady Margaret Beaufort (1505). This foundation marked a step on the way towards the modern university, for students were allowed to attend lectures at Christ's without being members of the college. The buildings have been drastically modernised. The *Chapel* (dedicated in 1510) has panelling of 1703 and old stained glass. The *Fellows' Building* (1640–43) is very fine. Notable members of Christ's include Milton, who is supposed to have planted a mulberry tree in the garden, and Darwin.

Emmanuel College, farther along St Andrew's Street, was founded in 1584 by Sir Walter Mildmay, and incorporates parts of a former Dominican priory. The college produced numbers of Protestant ministers, many of whom emigrated to America, including some of the Pilgrim Fathers. The Chapel and cloister are by Wren (1668–74). A window in the Chapel commemorates John Harvard, the principal founder of Harvard University in Massachusetts.

The *New Museums*, or "Labs", are a large group of museums, laboratories, etc., in Downing and Pembroke Streets. They include the famous Cavendish Physical Laboratory, the Archaeological and Ethnological Museum, the Museum of Geology, etc.

The most famous museum in Cambridge, which should be included in every visitor's programme, is the *Fitzwilliam Museum* in Trumpington Street, a neoclassical building of Portland stone which was the masterpiece of George Basevi (1837–48). The original collection was bequeathed to the University by the 7th Viscount Fitzwilliam (d. 1816). The Museum contains a magnificent collection of coins and medals, pottery and china, objets d'art from Greece, Rome, Egypt and China, weapons, textiles, pictures (Constable, Turner, Reynolds, many Impressionists, Titian, Tintoretto, Rubens, Van Dyck, Frans Hals, etc.) and valuable manuscripts.

Visitors can also see the **University Library** in Burrell's Walk, with more than 1½ million volumes.

SURROUNDINGS. – There are very pleasant walks along the Backs, through the beautiful college grounds on the W bank of the Cam, and also a river path to **Grantchester** (2½ miles), a favourite haunt of Byron and of Rupert Brooke, and a popular outing by boat. Not far away is *Trumpington*, which has a war memorial by Eric Gill (1922) and a 14th c. church with the second oldest memorial brass in England (for Sir Roger de Trumpington, 1289).

3½ miles N of Cambridge is **Impington**, with Impington Hall, once the residence of the Pepys family. There is now a college here (by Walter Gropius and Maxwell Fry, 1936–39). In **Newmarket**, about 10 miles NW of Cambridge, are the National Stud and the National Racing Museum.

On the *Gogmagog Hills* (4 miles SE) are Wandlebury Camp and remains of a Roman road (the Via Devana).

Huntingdon 18 miles NW of Cambridge (pop. 17,500; hotels – George, C, 25 r.; Old Bridge, C, 22 r.), a pleasant old town on the Ouse, is famous as the birthplace of Oliver Cromwell, who went to the local grammar school (as did Samuel Pepys); the Norman front of the school has survived. Huntingdon has two fine churches, St Mary's (17th c.) and All Saints (15th c., in late Perpendicular style). All Saints preserves the parish registers of St John's Church (destroyed), with a record of Cromwell's birth and baptism. Only foundations remain of a former Norman castle. Huntingdon is linked with **Godmanchester** by a 14th c. bridge, near which is a house in which the poet William Cowper lived with the Unwins (1765–67).

1 mile SW of Huntingdon is *Hinchingbrooke House*, which now houses a grammar school. The site was originally occupied by a nunnery founded in the 11th c. which at the Dissolution of the Monasteries passed into the hands of the Cromwell family. In 1560 they converted the old building into a splendid mansion, incorporating parts of the church and the chapterhouse. In 1644 the house was sold to the Montagu family, and terraced gardens were laid out by Edward Montagu after his elevation to the Earldom of Sandwich. – 15 miles away is the pretty little town of **Saffron Walden**, in a beautiful setting. The name comes from the saffron obtained from the yellow crocuses which were grown here. The town (pop. 10,370) has a long history, evidenced by the discovery of a large Saxon cemetery. There are only scanty remains of the old Norman castle. Some of the old houses offer well-preserved examples of the technique known as pargeting (timber framing with a plaster facing, often patterned); the best example is the *Sun Inn*. There is an interesting museum and a fine church, *St Mary's* (c. 1450–1525). Near the museum, on Castle Hill, is the largest turf-cut maze in Britain, with four round "bastions"; its origin is unknown.

1½ miles from Saffron Walden is **Audley End**, a splendid Jacobean mansion built by Thomas Howard, Earl of Suffolk, in 1603–16.

Within easy reach of Saffron Walden is *Finchingfield*, one of the most picturesque and attractive little towns in England (photograph, p. 10), with many old houses, a sturdy Norman church tower and an old windmill. 1 mile N is *Spain's Hall*, a magnificent example of Tudor architecture with its red-brick façade, mullioned windows and curved gables.

Bury St Edmunds (pop. 31,000), 27 miles NE of Cambridge, is the burial place of King Edmund. The Abbey (11th c.) with massive gatehouses, the *Cathedral of St James* (c. 1500) and the *Church of St Mary* (15th c.) with many monuments are all worth seeing.

Canterbury

Southern England. – County: Kent.
Population: 36,300.
Telephone dialling code: 0227.

ⓘ Tourist Information Centre,
22 St Peter's Street;
tel. 66567.

HOTELS. – *Chaucer*, Ivy Lane, C, 51 r.; *Canterbury*, 71 New Dover Road, D, 30 r.; *Statters*, Margaret's Street, D, 30 r.

YOUTH HOSTEL. – 54 New Dover Road, 56 b.

RESTAURANT. – *Castle Restaurant & Adelaide Silver Grill*, 71 Castle Street.

SPORT and RECREATION. – Rowing, swimming; theatre.

*Canterbury is one of England's most beautiful cathedral cities, picturesquely situated on the River Stour, and a busy market town, the centre of a predominantly agricultural region. It is a city with a long history and a rich past, the birthplace of Christianity in England and the scene of Thomas Becket's murder. The Cathedral contains Becket's tomb, which began to draw pilgrims soon after his death, and also the tomb of the Black Prince, son of Edward III.

Canterbury also has the ancient King's School, whose pupils have included Christopher Marlowe (1564–95), a native of the town, William Harvey (1578–1657), who discovered the circulation of the blood, and the famous novelist W. Somerset Maugham (1874–1965). Maugham gives a picture of life in the school in his novel "Of Human Bondage". In very different fields of interest, Canterbury has a late Norman tower (near the East railway station) and – for railway-lovers – a steam locomotive built by Stephenson. Joseph Conrad (1857–1924) is buried in the cemetery. Canterbury is also acquiring increasing importance as a university town.

HISTORY. – In Roman times Canterbury was known as *Darovernon* or *Durovernum*. The Saxons called it *Cantwaraburg* (the town of the people of Kent). There was probably a Christian church here before King Ethelbert of Kent (560–616) married Bertha, daughter of the Frankish king Haribert. In 597 St Augustine came here from Rome with a mission to convert the pagan Saxons, and Ethelbert became a Christian along with many of his subjects. Augustine was appointed bishop and later archbishop of Canterbury.

After the Norman Conquest the old Saxon church was burned down, and Lanfranc, appointed archbishop by William the Conqueror, built a new cathedral, of which only the crypt survives. In the reign of Henry II (1154–89) Thomas Becket, who as Chancellor had promoted the king's policies even when these ran counter to the Church, was appointed by Henry to the archbishopric and thereupon defended the interests of the Church against the king. After a period of voluntary exile in France Becket returned to Canterbury in 1170, and in December of that year was murdered by four of the king's knights in the NW transept of the Cathedral. A small square stone in the floor marks the spot where he was killed. Thereafter, for many centuries, pilgrims flocked to Canterbury to the martyr's shrine, and hostels (like the late 12th c. Eastbridge Hospital) were built to accommodate them, together with a number of religious houses. The Franciscans established their first English friary in Canterbury. Chaucer's "Canterbury Tales" give a lively and amusing picture of the pilgrims. – During the Second World War Canterbury suffered considerable damage, but the Cathedral remained unscathed. In the course of post-war reconstruction remains of a Roman theatre, town walls, houses and streets were discovered.

SIGHTS. – The **Cathedral** represents the architecture of five centuries. The new church begun by the Norman archbishop Lanfranc (1070–89) was continued by St Anselm (1093–1109), Prior Ernulf (1096–1107) and Prior Conrad (1108–26), and was consecrated in 1130.

Canterbury Cathedral

Four years after Becket's death the splendid *choir* was destroyed by fire and rebuilt by a French master mason, Guillaume de Sens, as we see it today, a typical example of the Transitional style between Norman and Early English. Between 1375 and 1421 the Norman nave and transepts were pulled down and rebuilt in Perpendicular style. The *Bell Harry Tower* over the crossing was built between 1495 and 1503. The bell in this tower, presented by Prior Henry de Eastry, is rung every night. The tower can be climbed. The *gatehouse* dates from 1517; the Baroque oak *doorway* was added in the second half of the 17th c.

Canterbury Cathedral

N ⟵

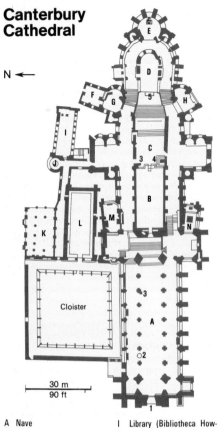

30 m
90 ft

Cloister

A Nave	I Library (Bibliotheca How-
B Choir	leiana)
C Presbytery	J Water Tower
D Trinity Chapel	K Library
E Corona	L Chapterhouse
F Treasury	M Lady Chapel
G St Andrew's Chapel	N St Michael's Chapel
H St Anselm's Chapel	

1 West doorway	3 Pulpits	5 High altar
2 Font	4 Archbishop's throne	6 St Augustine's Chair

In the NW transept, with the stone marking the spot of Becket's murder, is the magnificent **Edward IV Window**. The other transepts contain fine late 12th c. stained glass, numerous monuments and war memorials of the Royal East Kent Regiment (the Buffs) and the Queen's Own Rifles of Canada.

The splendid *screen between the nave and the choir dates from 1304. The choir, which is considerably higher than the nave, is the longest in the country and one of the earliest major Gothic structures in England. On both sides of the choir are the *tombs of archbishops,* notable among them the tomb which Archbishop Chichele (1414–43), founder of All Souls College in Oxford, designed for himself. In the **Trinity Chapel** (built by William the Englishman in 1178–80) there formerly stood the shrine of St Thomas Becket (archbishop 1162–70), the most popular of the English saints. The marble paving is worn away by the passage of many pilgrims. Here too are the tombs of Henry IV and Edward the Black Prince. Some of the *windows* in the Trinity Chapel are masterpieces of medieval glass-painting (1213–20); others are modern reproductions. – At the E end of the Cathedral is a small round chapel known as the *Corona* or "Becket's Crown", with St Augustine's Chair, still used in the enthronement of archbishops.

The large **Crypt** is the oldest part of the Cathedral, a relic of the Norman church. The pillars have beautiful carved capitals (some of them unfinished). *St Gabriel's Chapel* contains old wall paintings, and the paintings in *St Anselm's Chapel* are among the finest of the period. – In the spacious Cloister (1397–1411) are over 800 painted roof-bosses. The first performance of T. S. Eliot's "Murder in the Cathedral" was given in the *Chapterhouse* in 1935.

There are numerous other features of interest within the precincts of the Cathedral. The **Chapter Library** contains a fine collection of old manuscripts. The building N of the Corona was formerly a guest-house for distinguished visitors; it is now part of the King's School.

The *Brick Walk* leads to the *Infirmary Cloister* and through the Dark Entry to *Prior Sellinge's Gate* and the **Green Court**, with the *Norman staircase* giving access to the King's School. The open *arcades* round the court are unique in England. The **King's School** was founded by Henry VIII but has traditions going back to about 600, when Canterbury was a centre of Anglo-Saxon culture.

Close to the Cathedral is **St Augustine's College** (1846–48), which contains remains of the abbey founded by St Augustine in 604. *St Augustine's Gate* and the *Cemetery Gate* date from the 13th c., but are partly destroyed. The foundations of the old abbey and the *graves of St Augustine, King Ethelbert, Queen Bertha* and nine of Augustine's successors have been revealed by excavation. There are also the excavated remains of the early Saxon *St Pancras's Church*, incorporating much Roman material.

*St Martin's Church, the "mother church of England", is one of the oldest surviving English churches, probably originally built for Queen Bertha before the coming of Augustine. Many Roman bricks are built into the walls.

Of the old 11th c. *Castle* only a late Norman tower survives. Near it is a tumulus known as *Dane John*. Here, too, round the gardens, are remains of the old *town walls*. In the **Poor Priest's Hospital** stands the "*Invicta*", a locomotive built by Robert Stephenson which ran on the second oldest railway line in Europe, from Canterbury to Whitstable (opened in 1830).

SURROUNDINGS. – 2 miles W is **Bigbury**, with an Iron Age fort on a hill from which there is a good view of Canterbury. The British settlement here was taken by the Romans in 54 B.C.

2 miles NE is **Fordwich**, once the port for Canterbury, with a tiny town hall and a ducking stool on which nagging wives were dipped into the River Stour. **Chilham**, 5 miles SW of Canterbury, has a *Battle of Britain Museum.*

Cardiff (Caerdydd)

South Wales. – County: South Glamorgan.
Population: 281,300.
Telephone dialling code: 0222.
(i) **Wales Tourist Board,**
   3 Castle Street;
   tel. 27281.

HOTELS. – *Crest*, Westgate Street, C, 160 r.; *Post House*, Church Road, Pentwyn, C, 150 r.; *Park*, Park Place, C, 108 r.; *Angel*, Castle Street, C, 100 r.

Cardiff, capital of Wales, lies on the wide estuary of the Severn and is traversed by two much smaller rivers, the Taff and the Rhymmey. An important port, it is also a university town and the cultural as well as the economic centre of Wales.

SIGHTS. – The imposing **Civic Centre** was the first of its kind in Britain. Among the public buildings ranged round Cathays Park are the *City Hall* (1904), with a bell-tower and a dome crowned by the Welsh dragon. The Marble Hall is decorated with historical figures from the story of Wales. In the centre of the complex is a *War Memorial.* Other buildings in the Civic Centre include the University College of South Wales, the Law Courts, government offices and the *National Museum of Wales*.

Caerphilly Castle

The Museum was founded in 1907 to "tell the world about Wales, and the Welsh about their own country". It contains important early Christian material, archaeological collections, exhibits illustrating the development of industry, pre-industrial crafts and implements, domestic utensils and furnishings of the past, and musical instruments. The *Art Gallery* gives an excellent survey of the work of Welsh artists but also includes pictures by English painters (Gainsborough, Constable, etc.) and works by foreign artists.

Llandaff Cathedral was founded in the time of Bishop Urban (1107–34). It is one of the oldest episcopal sees in Britain. The main part of the Cathedral dates from the 13th c.; the NW tower was rebuilt in the 15th. Later the whole Cathedral fell into a dilapidated state, and in 1734 an "Italian temple" was built within its walls by John Wood of Bath. The Cathedral was severely damaged during the last war (1941), but has since been restored. It contains a notable figure of "Christ in Majesty" by Epstein.

Cardiff Castle, in the centre of the city, stands on a site once occupied by a Roman fort; and part of the Roman walls, the polygonal bastions (4th c.) and the N gate have been preserved and partially restored. Cardiff Castle is really three castles in one, for in 1090 a new fortress was built on an artificial motte by Robert Fitzhammon. His successor, finding it too small, built on a new range of richly decorated buildings. In 1404 the castle was burned down by Owen Glendower. Between 1865 and 1920 the whole complex was rebuilt at great expense but with a great deal of skill and understanding. The *State Apartments*, decorated in

City Hall, Cardiff

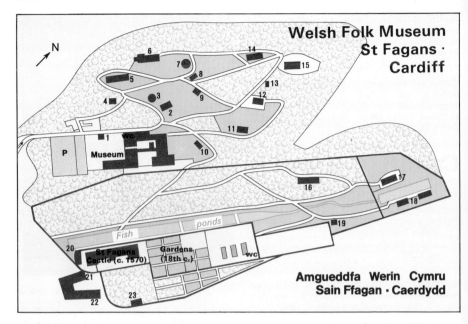

Welsh Folk Museum · St Fagans · Cardiff

Amgueddfa Werin Cymru Sain Ffagan · Caerdydd

1 Ticket office
2 Kennixton: cottage from Llangennydd, Gower, West Glamorgan (c. 1630)
3 Hendre Ifan Prosser: round pigstye from Mid Glamorgan (18th c.)
4 Melin Bompren: water-driven grain-mill from Cross Inn, Dyfed (1852–53)
5 Hendre'r-ywydd Uchaf: cottage from Llangynhafal, Clwyd (end of 15th c.)
6 Tannery from Rhayader, Powys
7 Cockpit from the Hawk and Buckle Inn, Denbigh, Clwyd (beginning of 18th c.)
8 Tollhouse from Pemparcau, Aberystwyth, Dyfed (1771)
9 Llanifadyn: cottage from Rhostryfan, Gwynedd (1762)
10 Gipsy caravan
11 Capel Pen-rhiw: Unitarian chapel from Dre-fach, Felindre, Dyfed (18th c.)
12 Abernodwydd: half-timbered cottage from Llangadfan, Powys (16th c.)
13 Hay-shed from Maentwrog, Gwynedd (19th c.)

14 Smithy from Llawr-y-Glyn, Llanidloes, Powys (18th c.)
15 Cilewent: cottage from Dyffryn Claerwen, Powys (originally 16th c.)
16 Stryt Llydan: barn from Penley, Clwyd (c. 1550)
17 Esgair Moel: wool factory from Llanwrtyd, Powys (c. 1760)
18 Boat-house and net-house, with nets and other fishing equipment
19 Kiosk
20 Demonstrations of cooper's work
21 Demonstrations of wood-turning
22 Coach-house
23 Entrance to Castle (ticket office)

MUSEUM

Gallery of Material Culture
Costume Gallery
Agricultural Gallery
Agricultural Vehicles Gallery

Pre-Raphaelite style, include the Library and various other interesting rooms. – In Greyfriars Road can be seen the foundations of *Greyfriars Church* (1280) and the ruins of a mansion built on the site of the old friary after the Reformation.

Cardiff is well supplied with good shops. *Queen Street* is the busiest street in Wales; here is situated the congress building, *St David's Centre*. Cardiff has a municipal theatre, the *New Theatre*, as well as the *Sherman Theatre* in Senghenydd Road and a puppet theatre, the *Caricature Theatre*, in Station Terrace. The city also offers a wide range of entertainments and sports facilities of all kinds, including a golf-course and a riding centre. Below Castle Bridge, on the river, is the new Cardiff Arms Park Rugby Stadium.

The *Welsh Folk Museum, a branch of the National Museum of Wales, is in a beautiful park in St Fagans, 4 miles W. The

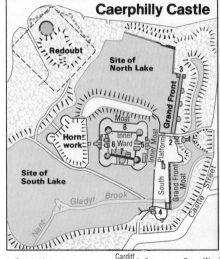

Caerphilly Castle

1 Drawbridge
2 Gateway to Grand Front
3 North Postern
4 South Postern
5 Gateway to Outer Ward
6 Gateway to Inner Ward
7 Great Hall and Kitchen
8 Outer Ward

Museum contains furniture of various periods and illustrates the life and work of earlier days in Wales. At certain times visitors can see Welsh craftsmen at work.

SURROUNDINGS. – 7½ miles N of Cardiff is the industrial town of **Caerphilly** (pop. 29,000), with another mighty castle, also excellently restored. The town itself, which is also known for its excellent Caerphilly cheese, offers little else of interest. The *Castle*, first established in 1268, has the most elaborate defensive system of any British castle. It was enlarged several times and presents a formidable and imposing aspect, with its two drawbridges, massive walls, round towers and moat.

Along the coast between Cardiff and Swansea are a number of small seaside resorts. Nearest to Cardiff (5 miles S) – indeed almost a suburb of the city – is **Penarth** (pop. 23,600), which has a shingle beach and offers excellent facilities for water skiing, sailing and fishing, as well as wide scope for attractive cliff walks. One such walk leads S to secluded Ranny Bay, St Mary's Well Bay at *Lavernock* and on to *Sully* with its offshore island, which can be reached on foot at low tide. Lavernock is a popular resort, with a sandy beach and cliffs.

Carlisle

Northern England. – County: Cumbria.
Population: 71,500.
Telephone dialling code: 0228.
ⓘ **Old Town Hall**, Greenmarket;
tel. 25517 and 25396.

HOTELS. – *Crest*, Kingstown, C, 100 r.; *Crown and Mitre*, English Street, C, 94 r.; *The Cumbrian Thistle*, Court Square, C, 70 r.; *Swallow Hilltop*, London Road, D, 115 r.

YOUTH HOSTEL. – *Etterby House*, Etterby, 73 b.

RESTAURANTS. – *Belowstairs*, English Street; *Pinegrove*, 262 London Road.

EVENTS. – *Carlisle Great Fair* (last Saturday in Aug.).

SPORT and RECREATION. – Sailing, rowing, swimming, walking.

Carlisle, an old frontier town on the River Eden and now county town of Cumbria, is mainly an industrial centre and a road and rail junction. The Cathedral and the Castle are the chief points of interest in the town which lies in an attractive area, within easy reach of the Scottish border country to the N and the Lake District to the S.

HISTORY. – Hadrian's Wall ran just N of Carlisle, through what is now the suburb of Stanwix, where the Roman fortifications crossed the river. The fort later developed into the Romano-British town of *Luguvalium*. In the 11th and 12th c. the Scots claimed the town, but after it was fortified by William Rufus had little chance of taking it. In 1645 the town surrendered to a Scottish army under General Leslie after an eight months' siege during which the Cathedral was damaged.

SIGHTS. – The *Cathedral was originally the church of an Augustinian priory founded in 1102, and was made the see of a bishop by Henry I in 1133. The *S transept* and two bays of the nave are Norman (1123). The beautiful *choir* was rebuilt in Decorated style after a fire in 1292, but was not completed until 1362. The *N transept* and *central tower*, destroyed in a later fire, were rebuilt between 1400 and 1419.

The choir has a large and very fine *E window*, with beautiful Decorated tracery and old glass (1380), with a representation of the Last Judgment. The delicately carved *capitals* of the pillars show the labours of the months. The *choir-stalls*, with 46 misericords, date from 1400 to 1433; they are carved with scenes from the lives of saints. – The Cathedral is one of the smallest in England.

In the precincts of the Cathedral are a *gatehouse* of 1527, a *tower* of 1510, several Georgian houses and the *Chapter Library*, housed in the *refectory*, a fine building of the early 14th c. remodelled about 1500.

On the way to the **Castle**, in Castle Street and Abbey Street, are many fine Georgian houses. Also in Castle Street is *Tullie House* (1689), now part of the local *museum* (Roman finds, modern painting).

The Castle has a fine Norman* **keep**, built about 1092 by William Rufus to provide protection against Scottish raids; it now houses a *regimental museum*. The *Ireby Tower* (13th c.) and *Captain's Tower* (14th c.) are also imposing. Visitors can see the dungeons in which more than 300 Scottish prisoners were confined in 1745, and also various mementoes of Mary Queen of Scots' two months' imprisonment in Queen Mary's Tower in 1568. From the Castle there is a good view of the town, which still preserves part of its old *town walls*.

SURROUNDINGS. – Since Carlisle is only 8 miles from the Scottish border, it is easy to visit **Gretna Green** (9 miles NW: pop. 2200; hotels – Gretna Chase, D, 8 r.; Royal Steward Motel, E, 18 r.), formerly famous for its runaway marriages. The road crosses the River Eden, on which Carlisle lies, and then the Esk and the little border stream, the Sark; but it is by no means so romantic as it may have seemed to young couples on their way to be married, without their parents' consent, by the Gretna blacksmith. In the past Scottish law, unlike English law, provided for marriage by declaration before witnesses, and this led many eloping couples to make for Gretna, sometimes hotly pursued by their parents. Following changes in the law hasty marriages of this kind are no longer possible, and the place has lost its attraction for those in a hurry to get married, though it still exerts a fascination on visitors – and has more accommodation for them than would normally be expected in a village of some 2000 inhabitants.

12 miles NE of Carlisle is *Lanercost Priory, a former Augustinian house founded in 1166. The choir (1175) and transepts (1220) of the church are roofless, but the nave, which dates from the first third of the 13th c., is still used as the parish church. The W end is very fine, and the church contains a number of interesting monuments. Nearby, beyond the attractive medieval bridge over the Irthing, is the entrance to **Naworth Castle**, the magnificent seat of the Earl of Carlisle, which dates from 1335. Particularly fine are the Great Hall and the Library, which has a Burne-Jones chimneypiece. The tower (c. 1350) is named after Lord William Howard, son of the Duke of Norfolk, who converted the castle into a country house (seen only by prior arrangement).

Channel Islands

The *Channel Islands, which attract over half a million British holidaymakers every year, belong geographically to France. They lie in the Gulf of St-Malo, at distances of between 10 and 30 miles from the French coast, whereas even the island nearest Britain, Alderney, is 50 miles from the English coast. The largest of the islands is Jersey, followed in order of size by Guernsey, Alderney, Sark, Herm, Jethou and a number of tiny uninhabited islets and clusters of rocks.

Although each of the islands has its own character, they all have one thing in common, the mildness of their climate. Jersey is famed for its early potatoes and tomatoes, Guernsey for grapes, tomatoes and flowers. They all share, too, the advantage of having lower taxes and duties than the mainland of Britain, so that alcohol, cigarettes and many luxury articles are very reasonably priced – one of the reasons for the islands' popularity. In more than a geographical sense they are half way between Britain and France: their language is English but full of French expressions, their cuisine is largely French, and their whole way of life, particularly in summer, has a lively southern quality about it. Strolling through one of the larger places, with the shops open until late in the evening, a visitor might well imagine himself in Italy or southern France. With all these attractions, it is not surprising that the Channel Islands are as crowded with visitors during the summer

months and that the streets are as busy as those of a large city. The high point of the season is the Battle of Flowers in Jersey at the end of July, and holiday accommodation for this period must be booked a year in advance.

HISTORY. – Excavations have shown that the Channel Islands were inhabited three thousand years before the Christian era. The Romans certainly occupied some of the islands, and Jersey appears in the records under the name of *Caesarea*. In the 6th c. Christianity was brought to the islands by St Helier (after whom the chief town of Jersey is named) and St Sampson. The islands became part of the Duchy of Normandy, and from 1154 onwards they belonged to England. During the Second World War they were occupied by German forces from June 1940 to May 1945, and mementoes of this period are to be seen in many small museums in the islands. Although belonging to the Crown, the Channel Islands have extensive powers of self-government, issue their own coins and banknotes.

Visitors who want to get to know the islands properly, and do not go only for the golf or the bathing, should allow at least a week, and preferably longer.

A good programme for a week's visit (which unfortunately does not leave time for the very attractive island of Herm) would be as follows: 2 days on Guernsey, with St Peter Port and the E and N coasts on the first day and the W and SW coasts on the second; on the 3rd day Sark (by boat); on the 4th day Alderney (though if necessary this could be omitted, particularly since it is the most distant of the islands); on the 5th, 6th and 7th days Jersey, covering at least St Helier, Gorey and Mont Orgueil, La Hougue Bie and the N and SW coasts.

There are excellent *air services* from London and other English airports to Jersey and Guernsey, and less frequent services to Alderney. There are *ferry services* (daily in summer) from Weymouth and Portsmouth and also from St-Malo. There are frequent boat and air connections between the various islands.

Jersey has a population of 63,300, and extends over 11 miles from E to W and 7 miles from N to S. The N coast has the more striking scenery, with a chain of high cliffs, rocky creeks and caves; the other coasts are flatter and more densely populated. Few visitors find their way along very narrow roads into the interior, an area of intensive vegetable-growing and farming.

The chief town, **St Helier** (hotels – Hotel de la Plage, C, 96 r.; Apollo, C, 53 r.; Beaufort, C, 50 r.; Pomme d'Or, D, 151 r.; Angleterre, D, 92 r.; Uplands, E, 28 r., etc.), is magnificently situated on the wide St Aubin's Bay. It is a town full of life and charm which has largely preserved its Victorian character. The streets and the very picturesque harbour are the scene of almost constant bustle and activity. On a small rocky island outside the harbour, reached by ferry or by a causeway, stands *Elizabeth Castle*, which was built during the reign of Elizabeth I and afforded shelter to Charles II on several occasions. On an adjoining rock St Helier, the 6th c. apostle of Christianity, is said to have had his hermitage. In Royal Square, in the centre of the town, are the *Town Church* (originally 10th c.), the *Royal Court House*, the *States' Chamber*, the Library and a gilded statue of George II. There is also an interesting museum. – From St Helier to Gorey it is between 5 and 7 miles according to the route chosen. The coastal road is the more beautiful; the inland road runs through *Grouville*, a pretty little holiday resort with a splendidly situated golf-course.

Bouley Bay, Jersey

Gorey is a charming little town with a row of picturesque houses along the harbour (hotels – Old Court House, C, 27 r.; Trafalgar Bay, D, 37 r.). It is dominated by the formidable castle of * *Mont Orgueil*, a magnificent example of medieval military engineering, founded in the reign of King John. Inland from Gorey are Jersey's main tourist sights – **La Hougue Bie**, a large burial mound topped by two chapels, the Norman chapel of *Notre Dame de Clarté* and the 16th c. *Jerusalem Chapel*. Excavations in 1924 revealed one of the largest passage graves in Europe, probably dating from the late Iron Age and the Bronze Age (2000 B.C. or earlier), built of stones weighing from 25 to 30 tons. It consists of a passage 46 ft long, an oval chamber 6 ft high and three side chambers, all constructed of undressed granite slabs.

Beyond Gorey the coast road runs past the pretty bay of Anne Port, the wide sweep of St Catherine's Bay and the secluded and very beautiful Rozel Bay. Farther W is the large *Bouley Bay*, just inland from which at Les Augrès, is the excellent Jersey Zoo. The *N coast* is romantic and much indented, with small sandy bays nestling between the rocks, but to the W of Bouley Bay the road no longer runs close to the coast, passing through a region of lonely and unspoiled scenery. A little way inland is the highest point on the island, Les Platons (485 ft). Other features along this attractive stretch of the N coast are Bonne Nuit Bay, with its shingle beach and the Mont Mado quarries; St John's Bay; La Houle cave; Sorel Point, the most northerly point on the island; the waterfalls of Les Mouriers; and a number of caves.

On the S coast is the very popular holiday resort of **St Aubin**, in the sandy St Aubin's Bay, with a small harbour and a *castle* built on a crag. To the W is St Brelade's Bay, with the little town of **St Brelade**, which has one of the oldest churches on the island, dating in part from 1042. – The whole of the W coast is occupied by St Ouen's Bay.

Guernsey is only about half the size of Jersey but, with a population of just over 53,300, is even more densely populated. The cliffs on the S coast rise to 270 ft, but the land falls gradually away towards the N. Inland stands the tiny *Chapel of Les Vauxbelets* (1923–25) which is covered with shells.

The chief town of Guernsey, **St Peter Port**, is beautifully situated (hotels – The St Pierre Park, B, 135 r.; Old Government House, C, 92 r.; Royal, C, 79 r., etc.). The streets climb uphill from the sea, narrow and often steep. There are many houses in Regency style, giving the town a pleasant old-world air. On a small island connected with the mainland by the Castle Pier stands *Castle Cornet*, founded in 1150 but in its present form largely Elizabethan. The castle, originally the governor's residence, was later used as a prison and is now a museum. The *Town Church* dates from the 12th–15th c. *Hauteville House* was the home of the French poet Victor Hugo (1802–85) while a political refugee from France (1852–55 and 1856–70); it contains mementoes of the poet and furniture of his period. – On the E coast of the island are a number of Martello towers, the ruins of Vale Castle, the early Norman Vale church and a large passage grave.

The *S coast is interesting and attractive, with cliffs and caves. The largest of the caves is Creux Mahie, 200 ft long. Corbière Point is of interest to geologists, with green veins in the pink and grey granite. – On the W coast is the very beautiful Rocquaine Bay; the island of Lihou, linked with the mainland by a causeway, has remains of a 12th c. priory.

Three miles NE of St Peter Port is the little island of **Herm**, which has a resident population of only 40 but may attract up to 3000 visitors a day during the summer. It has a number of old stone-built houses converted into holiday homes and a camping site. The inhabitants live by tourism and farming. Unusual wild flowers can be found here, and 200 different kinds of shells can be collected on the N coast.

Between Herm and Guernsey is the island of Jethou, which is private property but can be visited.

*ic**Alderney** is the least visited of the islands – a consequence of its relative remoteness. It is 4 miles long by 1 mile wide, with a population of 1900. Its economy is based on vegetable and flower growing as well as on tourism. The island, which is almost treeless, has beautiful sandy bays between much indented cliffs and rugged crags. The little town of **St Anne**, with something of a French air, is a mile from the harbour and dates from the 15th c. (hotels – Belle Vue, D, 23 r.; Royal Connaught, D, 17 r.; Grand Islands, E, 32 r.). It has cobbled streets and many shops and inns. In Telegraph Bay are two interestingly coloured rocks known as the Two Sisters. – The uninhabited island of Burhou, 1 mile N, is a bird reserve; it can be visited by boat (but not in the nesting season).

** **Sark**, the jewel of the Channel Islands, is the smallest of the main islands with a population of 611 (hotels – Stocks, C, 25 r.; Petit Champ, D, 16 r. There are boat services (daily in summer) from Guernsey, and less frequently from Jersey, with return the same evening. The boats come into La Maseline harbour, on the E side of the island, from which a steep road winds up the cliffs to the little settlement of La Collinette, the chief place on the island, with a school, a church, an old manor-house, a windmill on the highest point and, of course, inns. There are a number of small guest-houses scattered about on the island. There are few roads and no cars, but the main features of interest can easily be reached on foot.

The most rewarding walk is along La Coupée, a rugged isthmus of rock, to the part of the island known as Little Sark. After the last war a new track was constructed along this ridge, which falls steeply down to the sea, a distance of over 250 ft. It leads to Port Gorey, with the Venus Pool and Adonis Pool, which offer good bathing at low tide.

Farther S are bizarrely shaped cliffs and the Gouliot Caves, accessible only at low tide, with interesting sea anemones, etc. Offshore is the privately owned island of Brechou. A path on the left leads to the fishing harbour of Havre Gosselin; but little fishing is now done on Sark. Another picturesque spot is Dixcart Bay, where most of the island's holiday accommodation is to be found. Creux Derrible, a natural cleft in the rock 180 ft deep, can be reached only at low tide, through two rock arches. There are also a number of small caves and interesting rock scenery, best seen by boat.

The Seigneurie (1565), the residence of the Seigneur or feudal lord of Sark, can be reached from the church. Only Sark has preserved the feudal system which once prevailed on all the islands.

Chester

Western England. – County: Cheshire.
Population: 114,000.
Telephone dialling code: 0244.
ⓘ **Publicity Department**,
Town Hall, Northgate Street;
tel. 40144/318356.

HOTELS. – Ladbroke, Backford Cross, B, 121 r.; Grosvenor, Eastgate Street, B, 100 r.; Abbots Well, Whitchurch Road, C, 127 r.; Queen, City Road, C, 91 r.; Post House, Wrexham Road, C, 62 r.

YOUTH HOSTEL. – 40 Hough Green, 120 b.

CAMPING SITE.

RESTAURANTS. – Courtyard, St Werburgh Street; Chester Curzon, Wrexham Road; Oaklands, 93 Hoole Road; Ye Olde Kings Head, Lower Bridge Street.

SPORT and RECREATION. – Rowing, fishing, walking.

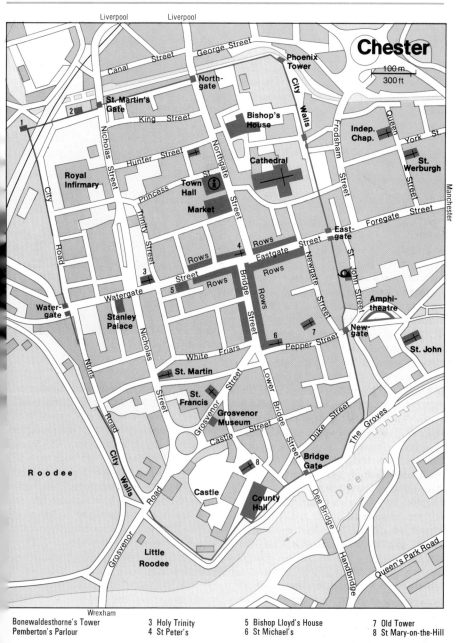

Chester

100 m
300 ft

Liverpool   Liverpool

George Street

Canal Street

Phoenix Tower

North-gate

City Walls

St. Martin's Gate

King Street

Bishop's House

Frodsham Street

Indep. Chap.

Queen Street

York St.

Nicholas Street

Hunter Street

Northgate Street

Cathedral

St. Werburgh Street

Royal Infirmary

Town Hall

Market

Eastgate Street

East-gate

Foregate Street

Manchester

Princess Street

Trinity Street

Rows

Rows

Eastgate

Rows

Newgate Street

St. John Street

City Road

Watergate

Bridge Street

Rows

Amphi-theatre

New-gate

St. John

Water-gate

Stanley Palace

Nicholas Street

White Friars

Lower Bridge Street

Pepper Street

Old Tower

St. Martin

Grosvenor Street

St. Francis

Grosvenor Museum

Castle Street

Duke Street

The Groves

Roodee

City Walls

Grosvenor Road

Castle

County Hall

Bridge Gate

Dee Bridge

Dee

Little Roodee

Handbridge

Queen's Park Road

Wrexham

Bonewaldesthorne's Tower	3 Holy Trinity	5 Bishop Lloyd's House	7 Old Tower
Pemberton's Parlour	4 St Peter's	6 St Michael's	8 St Mary-on-the-Hill

Chester, the county town of Cheshire, situated on the N bank of the River Dee 7 miles from its mouth, is of all English towns the one which has most completely preserved its medieval aspect. It still has its old town walls, large numbers of well-preserved half-timbered houses and its characteristic "Rows", the arcades or galleries which run along the house fronts at first-floor level; and with its attractive bridges, its beautiful parks and riverside promenades, its old gates and towers and its fine Cathedral Chester is a jewel among English cities.

HISTORY. – For four centuries, from A.D. 78 onwards, Chester (*Deva*) was the headquarters of the famous XXth Legion, and excavations have revealed an amphitheatre, houses and other remains. The town was known to the Britons as *Caerleon* (*Castra legionis*), to the Anglo-Saxons as *Legacaestir*. Ethelred of Northumbria defeated the Welsh near the town in 613. Chester was the last place of any consequence to surrender to William the Conqueror. During the Civil War the town declared for Charles I, but was starved into surrender in 1646. – During the Middle Ages Chester was famous for its mystery and miracle plays, performed by the town's guilds, but in the 16th c. these were superseded by performances of Shakespeare.

SIGHTS. – A first impression of the town can be gained from a walk round the ****town walls**. Built mostly of red sandstone, they follow the line of the Roman walls except in the S and W, where they extend down to the banks of the river to take in the *Castle*. The complete circuit is about 2 miles. The four gates – the North and East Gates, the Bridge Gate and the Water Gate – were rebuilt in the 18th and 19th c.

From the *East Gate* the walls run N, affording a good view of the *Cathedral*. The *Phoenix Tower* or *King Charles's Tower* (1658) is the most interesting of the surviving towers; it now contains a small museum. Charles I is said to have watched the defeat of his troops from here. Along the N walls traces of the Roman foundations can be seen. Beyond the *North Gate* are a watch-tower known as *Morgan's Mount* (good view) and the semicircular *Pemberton's Parlour* or *Goblin Tower*. From the *Water Tower* (early 14th c.) there is also a good view. In the garden below it there are some Roman remains. Beyond the *Water Gate* is the Roodee, a racecourse on which there has been horse-racing at least since 1609. The walls are then interrupted by Grosvenor Road, leading to *Grosvenor Bridge* (1827–32), which when it was built had the greatest span of any single-arched stone bridge. In the SW corner of the walls is the **Castle**, which is entered by way of a Doric pillared hall. The buildings, now occupied by the assize court, the county gaol, etc., date from the 19th c. The only old part is the *Agricola Tower*, which now houses the Museum of the Cheshire Regiment.

Farther round the walls, on the S side, is the *Bridge Gate*, leading to the *Old Dee Bridge* (13th c.). At the point where the walls turn N are the *Wishing Steps*: it is said that anyone who runs twice up and down the steps without drawing breath will have his wish fulfilled. The walls then continue to the *New Gate* and return to the East Gate.

A striking and distinctive feature of Chester is the ****Rows**, which date from the early 13th c. They are found in the town's four main streets, which, following the Roman town plan, meet at right angles at the market cross. In *Eastgate Street*, *Bridge Street* and *Watergate Street* they run along at first-floor level in the form of pedestrian galleries or arcades in half-timbered construction, supported on timber posts, with staircases leading up to

Half-timbered houses, Chester

them. With shops, cafés and houses on two levels, the Rows offer pedestrians shelter from the weather and safety from the traffic while doing their shopping or simply strolling about the town. The many unexpected nooks and crannies add to their charm. The Rows are seen at their best in Eastgate Street, and the finest half-timbered houses are in Watergate Street. There are more half-timbered buildings in Chester than in any other English town – though some of them are 19th or 20th c. imitations, barely distinguishable from the genuine article.

Bishop Lloyd's House (*c.* 1600), with rich carving, is open to visitors. *Stanley Palace*, though much restored, still has its original three gables. Many houses have vaulted cellars, and at 39 Bridge Street remains of a Roman bath can be seen. *Abbey Gate* (14th c.) leads into *Abbey Square*, with houses dating from about 1760.

Northgate Street, in which the Rows are at street level, leads to the **Cathedral*, built of the same red sandstone as the town walls, which shows the whole range of styles from Norman to Jacobean. It was originally the church of an abbey dedicated to St Werburgh (*c.* 700), daughter of King Wulfhere of Mercia, which in 1093 became a Benedictine house. There is some Norman work on the N side of the church. The *Lady Chapel* and *Chapterhouse* are Early English (after 1240); most of the *Choir* dates from the early Decorated period (1280–1300); while the tower, the W front and the upper parts of the nave are late Perpendicular (1485–90). The whole building was restored by George Gilbert Scott between 1868 and 1899. The *tracery* of the windows is very varied. From the *central tower* there are wide views.

The INTERIOR has *fan vaulting* by George Gilbert Scott. The *baptistery*, a relic of the Norman church, contains a Venetian **font**, which probably came from a village near Venice in the 6th c. The *Consistory Court*, in Jacobean style (1635), is unique in England. The *S transept* is four times the size of the N transept, which was cramped by the existing conventual buildings.

The *Choir*, in early Decorated style, is the finest part of the Cathedral. The *choir-stalls* are magnificently carved, with 48 misericords; stalls of comparable perfection are found perhaps only in Lincoln and Beverley. The *Lady Chapel* is in pure Early English style. Behind the high altar is the 14th c. shrine of St Werburgh.

The conventual buildings are, unusually, on the N side of the church. The rectangular *Chapterhouse* and vestibule are Early English, rather earlier than the Lady Chapel but equally beautiful. Above the Norman crypt is the guest-house. From here steps lead up to *St Anselm's Chapel*, with a Jacobean ceiling and panelling. A fine doorway leads into the *refectory*, which has an Early English reader's pulpit approached by a flight of steps in the wall.

Just outside the New Gate are the *Amphitheatre Gardens*, on the site of the largest Roman amphitheatre in England. Nearby is **St John's Church**, the remnant of a late 12th c. Norman church. The *nave* is still impressive, but the choir and Lady Chapel are mere picturesque ruins, destroyed by the collapse of the central tower. The *triforium* is in Transitional style. Parts of the church were built in the latter part of the 19th c.

The **Grosvenor Museum** has a very fine collection of Roman antiquities, with special displays illustrating the life of the legionaries and the defence of Britain. – Chester has an excellent *Zoo* (in Upton, 1½ miles N). In summer it is possible to go by boat to *Eaton Hall*, a former residence of the Duke of Westminster, now almost completely destroyed.

Chichester

Southern England. – County: West Sussex.
Population: 24,100.
Telephone dialling code: 0243.
(i) **Tourist Information Centre,**
    The Council House, North Street;
    tel. 775888.

HOTELS. – *Dolphin & Anchor*, West Street, B, 54 r.; *Chichester Lodge*, Westhampnett, C, 43 r.; *Ship*, North Street, D, 27 r.

RESTAURANTS. – *Christopher's*, 140 St Pancras; *Little London*, 38 Little London; *Woodpecker*, 117 St Pancras; *Ship Hotel*, North Street (Georgian House with maritime tradition).

EVENTS. – *Chichester Festival Theatre Season* (beginning of Aug. to mid Sept.).

SPORT and RECREATION. – Sailing, boating, golf.

Chichester, county town of West Sussex, situated between the South Downs and the coast, is an attractive cathedral city of Roman origin. The four main streets – North, East, South and West Streets – meet at right angles at the late Gothic Market Cross, an octagonal market hall open on all sides, surmounted by a superstructure reminiscent of a church.

The Cathedral is the only one in England with a separate belfry; the spire is a landmark which can be seen from some distance out at sea. The town was one of the earliest to have walls of which considerable portions remain. Outside the

Chichester Cathedral

walls the foundations of a Roman amphitheatre have been excavated. The Festival Theatre in Oaklands Park is an interesting modern building (1962); it was at one time directed by Sir Laurence Olivier and enjoys a considerable reputation. – Chichester Harbour, sheltered by a sandbank and by Hayling Island, offers ideal conditions for sailing in its many inlets and attractive little bays.

HISTORY. – The Romans founded the town of *Regnum* or *Noviomagus Regnensium* at the intersection of two important roads. Later it became known as *Cissas Castrum*. After the Norman Conquest it became the see of a bishop, and the Cathedral was consecrated in 1108. The town's heyday was in the 14th and 15th c., when it was an important port for the shipment of wool. In 1804 the poet and painter William Blake (1757–1827) was put on trial in the Guildhall, now the Museum, accused of high treason as an anarchist and defender of the French Revolution, but was acquitted.

SIGHTS. – The **Cathedral** is one of the finest and also one of the most attractive cathedrals in England. The first church on the site, a late Norman building consecrated in 1080, was burned down in 1114; rebuilt nine years later, it was again destroyed by fire in 1186. The arcades and gallery of the nave date from the original Norman building. The irregularly shaped 14th c. cloister encloses the S transept. The 15th c. *belfry* is the only surviving detached cathedral belfry in England. The nave is flanked by double aisles, with various chapels in the outer aisles. After the second fire the Norman walls were decorated in Early English style. The *central tower* and *windows* are recent, the tower having collapsed in 1861 and the windows having been destroyed by Puritan troops in 1642.

INTERIOR. – In the S choir aisle are two 12th c. Romanesque carvings (sandstone) of particular interest, depicting the resurrection of Lazarus, and Christ being received by Martha and Mary. There are a number of monuments by Flaxman, including one to William Collins, the 18th c. poet (b. in Chichester 1721 and d. there, insane, in 1759). *St George's Chapel* is a memorial to the Royal Sussex Regiment; in the *SE chapel* is a modern altarpiece by Graham Sutherland ("Noli me tangere", 1962).

SW of the Cathedral is the **Bishop's Palace**, with a medieval kitchen and in the private chapel one of the finest *wall paintings* of the Winchester school (12th c.), depicting the Virgin and Child with angels. Around the Cathedral, particularly in the *Pallant*, are a number of fine old houses. In St Martin's Square is *St Mary's Hospital* (13th c.), an almshouse for eight women or married couples; adjoining the living accommodation is a *refectory*, with an interesting chapel. In Priory Park is the *Guildhall Museum* (excavated material, mainly Roman).

SURROUNDINGS. – W of Chichester is *Chichester Harbour*, with an attractive and distinctive landscape of its own – an area of waterways and marshland with large numbers of waterfowl, thatched cottages, little sandy bays and reed-fringed shores. On one of the arms of the sea is the village of **Bosham** (4 miles W of Chichester; pop. 3800; Millstream Hotel C, 16 r.), with a church dating from Saxon times. The tower and pulpit are Saxon, other parts 13th c. The church is depicted on the Bayeux Tapestry: it was from here that Harold set sail in 1064 on his unsuccessful visit to Normandy. – Between Bosham and Chichester is the **Roman palace of Fishbourne** (c. A.D. 75), discovered in 1960. The palace of unusual size and magnificence, with some 100 rooms paved with mosaics, may have belonged to the tribal ruler Cogidubnus. Some of the mosaics are excellently preserved.

3½ miles NE is **Goodwood**, seat of the Duke of Richmond. The house was built between 1790 and 1800, mainly by James Wyatt, and contains fine furniture and pictures including works by Canaletto and Van Dyck. In the large park is a racecourse, on which the well-known Goodwood Races are held at the end of July.

12 miles N is **Midhurst** (hotel – Spread Eagle, D, 27 r.), an attractively situated little town on the Rother, with the imposing ruins of a Tudor mansion. Nearby is *Cowdray Park*, with beautiful trees, a polo ground and a golf-course.

7 miles E of Midhurst is **Petworth**, a tiny village adjoining a large country house – *Petworth House*, with a typically English landscaped park and one of the largest privately owned art collections in the country. There are many pictures by Turner in the Turner Room, but also works by Titian, Rogier van der Weyden, Van Dyck, Gainsborough, Reynolds and other artists. In one of the many handsome rooms shown to visitors is magnificent carved limewood decoration by Grinling Gibbons (1692). The collection of ancient sculpture is one of the best in England.

Chiltern Hills

Southern England. – Counties: Oxfordshire, Buckinghamshire and Hertfordshire.

The Chilterns are a range of chalk hills, mainly in Buckinghamshire and Oxfordshire, rising to heights of up to 850 ft. Unlike similar hills elsewhere in England, they are well wooded, with some of the finest stands of beeches in the country, and offer excellent walking. The abundant supplies of good timber led to the establishment of the furniture-making industry in this area.

Although they are of no great height, the Chilterns were in earlier centuries a considerable barrier to communications between London and the NW. A road ran along the northern fringes of the hills, but on the S side much of the traffic was carried by the Thames.

The main traffic routes followed – and still follow – the valleys. One of the earliest roads from London led by way of *Watford* into the hills and then continued by *Berkhamsted* and *Tring* to *Aylesbury*, situated at the lowest point in the hills. A second road ran from *Amersham* into the pretty *Misbourne* valley, by way of *Little* and *Great Missenden*, still charming little villages. The third cut across the hills and followed the Wye valley from *Bradenham* by way of *Princes Risborough* to *Bledlow* and *Whiteleaf*. At Bledlow and Whiteleaf are crosses of unknown origin carved in the chalk crags.

A 7th c. manuscript bewails the solitude and desolation of the Chiltern Hills. The situation has considerably changed since then, with the continuing expansion of London and the desire of wealthy Londoners for a house in the country; but there are still parts of the Chilterns which show little change, and many charming little towns and villages.

A good centre from which to explore the Chilterns is **Aylesbury** (pop. 46,100; Bell Hotel, C, 17 r.), county town of Buckinghamshire, with a large Market Square and attractive old half-timbered houses. St Mary's Church (13th c.) has an unusual spire and a fine Lady Chapel and misericords.

6 miles N is **Waddesdon Manor**, built for Baron Ferdinand de Rothschild, which contains a magnificent ****collection** of French art and furniture surpassed only by the Wallace Collection in London. It also has fine tapestries and porcelain, notable manuscripts and a library, as well as a very beautiful garden. *Claydon House* (1752–68), 8 miles NW, has splendid Rococo state apartments.

6 miles SE is **Wendover** (pop. 6400; hotel – Red Lion, D, 18 r.), with many fine half-timbered houses. 1½ miles W of the town is *Coombe Hill*, the highest point in the Chilterns (852 ft), with fine views of the Thames, Aylesbury and the magnificent woods round Chequers. *Chequers Court*, 2 miles SW, is a historic Tudor mansion (1566), which was presented to the nation in 1917 by Lord Lee of Fareham as a country residence for the Prime Minister of the day.

Amersham (pop. 17,500; hotels – Crown, C, 19 r.; Ken House, D, 24 r.) is a favourite residential town at the foot of the Chilterns, in the Misbourne valley. The wide *High Street* has many handsome 17th and 18th c. houses. Other features of interest are the market hall (1682), the Drake Almshouses (1657) and the Town Hall.

West Wycombe (pop., with High Wycombe, 60,000; Falcon Hotel, 12 r. in nearby High Wycombe), in a narrow valley in the Chilterns, has many furniture factories. The large parish church of *All Saints*, in the centre of the town, dates from the 13th c. but has been much rebuilt and restored. There are two handsome 18th c. buildings, the Guildhall (1757) and the Market Hall, renovated by Robert Adam in 1761. The Art Gallery and Museum contains an interesting collection of furniture and tools. Wycombe Abbey, built in 1795, is now occupied by a girls' school. – The whole town which dates from the 15th to the 18th c. belongs to the National Trust, which has undertaken to preserve its distinctive character. West Wycombe Park, an Adam-style country house (1765–80), has beautiful grounds, with a lake, a pavilion and small temples. On the hill above the town is a huge mausoleum built by the eccentric Sir Francis Dashwood.

Hughenden Manor, 1½ miles N, belonged to Benjamin Disraeli (1804–81), the great 19th c. statesman and novelist, and contains much of his furniture, books and other mementoes. He died in the house and is buried in the churchyard.

Fingest is a charming little village in a fold in the Chilterns, with beautiful views of the hills. It has a notable church with a Norman tower.

Another good base from which to discover the Chilterns is **Berkhamsted** (pop. 16,900; Swan Hotel, D, 14 r.), an attractive town in a lush green valley in the hills. Little is left of the castle in which William the Conqueror received the homage of the Saxon dukes and bishops before his coronation in Westminster. Berkhamsted School, founded in 1541, has some fine Tudor buildings. William Cowper (1731–1800) was born in the town.

Ashridge Park, 3 miles N, is a large mansion designed by James Wyatt which is now a management training college. It

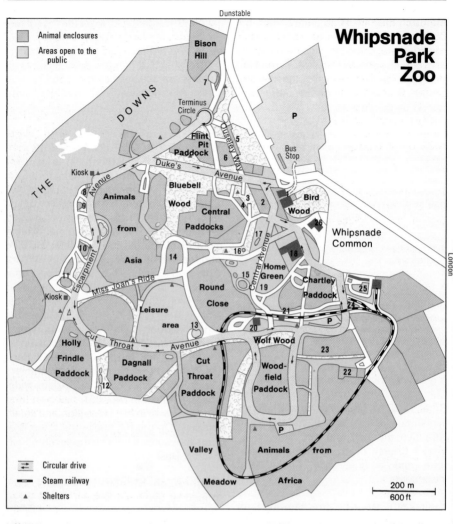

Whipsnade Park Zoo

Animal enclosures

Areas open to the public

Dunstable

Bison Hill

Terminus Circle

Flint Pit Paddock

Kiosk

Duke's Avenue

Bluebell Wood

Animals

Central Paddocks

from

Asia

Bird Wood

Whipsnade Common

Bus Stop

Kiosk

Miss Joan's Ride

Round Close

Home Green

Chartley Paddock

Leisure area

Holly

Frindle Paddock

Dagnall Paddock

Cut Throat Avenue

Cut Throat Paddock

Wolf Wood

Wood-field Paddock

Valley Meadow

Animals   from   Africa

⇄ Circular drive

▬ Steam railway

▲ Shelters

200 m
600 ft

1 Main entrance	7 Penguins	14 Giraffes	20 Avenue Café
2 Elephants	8 Polar bears	15 Sealions	21 Railway station
3 Monkeys	9 Kodiak bears	16 Aviary	22 Rhinoceroses
4 Cheetahs	10 Lions	17 Riding animals	23 Birds
5 Small felines	11 Tigers	18 Cloisters Cafeteria	24 Steam engines
6 Bears	12 Hippopotamuses	19 Marine mammals	25 Children's Zoo
	13 Flamingoes		26 Administration

has a beautiful park with a magnificent avenue of beeches.

Ivinghoe, the village which suggested to Scott the name of his novel "Ivanhoe", has an interesting church with fine woodcarving. From *Ivinghoe Beacon* (904 ft) there are wide views of the Chilterns, the historic old Ivinghoe windmill (1627), the oldest post mill in the country, and the lion cut out of the chalk which acts as a signpost to Whipsnade Zoo.

*Whipsnade Zoo, the largest of its kind (500 acres), is part of the London Zoo, established in 1927–31. It is not only well stocked with animals but is of great scenic beauty. The outline of a lion was cut out of

the hillside on the N side of the park as a warning to aircraft. A narrow-gauge railway runs through part of the park.

It is well worth while making an excursion to **Dunstable** (pop. 31,200; hotels – Old Palace Lodge, C, 34 r.; Highwayman, D, 25 r.), at the foot of Dunstable Downs 3½ miles from Whipsnade. The church of *St Peter and St Paul,* originally belonging to an abbey founded in 1131, has a Norman nave. 9 miles NW is **Woburn Abbey,* which draws many thousands of visitors every year, most of them attracted by the varied range of entertainments it offers – a zoo-park and an aquarium, sports facilities and playgrounds, boating, cafés, an antique market, etc. The house itself, seat of the Duke of Bedford, is a huge mansion, mainly dating from 1746–47, built on the site of an earlier Cistercian abbey. The interior decoration of the state apartments was the work of Henry Holland (1802). The mansion is a treasure-house of art, with valuable furniture of the 18th c., silver and porcelain and a richly stocked picture gallery (works by Holbein, Van Dyck, Rembrandt, Gainsborough, Reynolds, Canaletto and Velazquez, etc.).

In the southern foothills of the Chilterns lies **Goring**, where vines were formerly grown, as the place-name "Vineyards" indicates. Here, at the Goring Gap, the Thames has cut its way through the chalk. The *Icknield Way*, the old strategic Roman highway along the northern slopes of the Chilterns, is crossed just N of Goring by the massive earthworks known as Grim's Dyke or Grim's Ditch, the purpose of which has not been established. Here too is a hill named after St Birinus, the apostle of Wessex, who converted its king Cynegils in 634.

Colchester

Eastern England. – County: Essex.
Altitude: 107 ft. – Population: 84,000.
Telephone dialling code: 0206.
   Tourist Information Centre,
(i) 4 Trinity Street;
   tel. 46379.

HOTELS. – *Red Lion*, High Street, C, 20 r.; *George*, High Street, D, 47 r.; *Rose and Crown*, East Gates, D, 28 r.; *Peveril*, 51 North Hill, E, 16 r.

RESTAURANT. – *Wm Scragg's*, 2 North Hill.

YOUTH HOSTEL. – *East Bay House*, 18 East Bay, 50 b.

EVENT. – *Oyster Feast* (Oct.).

SPORT and RECREATION. – Golf, tennis.

Colchester, a Celtic capital even before the Romans came, can claim to be the oldest town in Britain. It is now famous for its fields of roses and its excellent oysters. It is an attractive town with many old buildings of different periods.

Colchester Castle, with a massive Norman keep, houses a very fine museum containing the main finds of Romano-British material; and the town has other impressive Roman remains, including the best preserved Roman town walls in the country.

In the Castle Museum, Colchester

HISTORY. – Some time before 43 B.C. Cunobelin (Shakespeare's Cymbeline), chief of the Catuvellauni, moved his capital from what is now St Albans to Colchester (*Camulodunum*). In A.D. 44, during the reign of Claudius, the Romans captured the town, but in 61–62 it was sacked by the Iceni under Boudica or Boadicea. When the Normans arrived Colchester had a population of some 2000 and several churches, and still preserved parts of its Roman walls. In modern times excavation has revealed the British town, the Roman camp and the later Roman city. – In 1648 the town surrendered to Fairfax after a 76 days' siege. Later it became an important centre of the wool and cloth trade.

SIGHTS. – The *Roman walls*, the best preserved in Britain, are some 9 ft thick and enclose an area 1000 yards by 500. The imposing *Balkerne Gate, the W gate of the Roman town, is still partly preserved. The walls and the gate date from about A.D. 140.

In the wide, well-built *High Street* is the Town Hall (by Sir John Belcher, 1898–1902). On the tower is a bronze figure of St Helen, who according to local tradition was the daughter of "Old King Cole" of Colchester. The king himself is said to be buried in a mound in the Dykes area on the outskirts of the town.

St Martin's Church in West Stockwell Street dates mainly from the 14th c.; the tower, now destroyed, was constructed partly of Roman bricks. The **Castle**, N of the High Street, built by William the Conqueror about 1080, also contains Roman bricks. It has the largest Norman *keep* in England, and now contains a notable *Museum* with a fine collection of Roman material.

Nearby is *Holly Trees*, a Georgian mansion which now houses a museum (medieval material). In the Castle Park, through which the River Colne flows, can be seen a section of the Roman town walls.

Queen Street leads to *St Botolph's Priory*, the first Augustinian house in England, founded after 1093; the church, built of Roman material, is now destroyed. In Stanwell Street are remains of a *Benedictine abbey* founded by Eudo in 1096 and restored in the 15th c.

On the way back to the High Street the line of the Roman walls is crossed at *Scheregate Steps*. In Trinity Street is **Holy Trinity Church**, which has a Saxon tower incorporating Roman bricks. *Siege House*, an old half-timbered house, shows traces of the 1648 siege. *Bourne Mill*, 1 mile S, is very picturesque.

Cornwall

South-western England. – County: Cornwall.

**Cornwall is one of the most popular holiday areas in England. Its attraction lies partly in its climate – southern Cornwall being known as the English Riviera, with subtropical plants growing in its parks and gardens – and partly in the great variety of its scenery, with beautiful beaches in modern seaside resorts, picturesque cliffs which offer walks along the sea (Cornwall Coast Path) with constantly changing views, fjord-like estuaries, small fishing villages and, in the interior, wide expanses of moorland. No part of Cornwall is more than 12 or 13 miles from the sea. Many artists, including Kokoschka, who found asylum here, and many writers, among them Daphne du Maurier, have been attracted by Cornwall and have come to live and to work in the county.

The people of Cornwall are still proud of their Celtic descent. Although the Cornish language died out at the end of the 18th c. many expressions and many elements in place-names – in particular *tre* (farm), *lan* (church) and *pen* (head or end) – still recall the older language. The churches are dedicated to saints who are often quite

Bedruthan Steps, Cornwall

unknown in the rest of England – a result of the Christianisation of Cornwall by Irish and Welsh monks.

Cornwall is rich in remains of the past, with many prehistoric burial mounds and stone circles, standing stones with enigmatic inscriptions, stone and earth ramparts, Iron Age settlements, Celtic stone crosses and, from more recent times, the engine-houses of abandoned tin-mines of the 18th and early 19th c. For long Cornwall occupied a leading position in the production of tin, and later was a major producer of copper. It is said that in the middle of the 19th c. there were more than 600 mines in production: now there are only two. The others, abandoned and neglected, often look from a distance like little churches. With their windows and doorways, frequently round-headed like those of a Norman church, and their ivy-covered chimneys.

Cornwall's mineral wealth, now of little significance, gave it prosperity in the past, and it became a royal duchy. The revenue from tin and copper was supplemented by fishing. Nowadays the main sources of income are the tourist trade, vegetable and flower growing, stone-quarrying and the working of kaolin for use in the manufacture of china. Thousands of Cornish miners have emigrated to other countries.

On the map Cornwall has the shape of a topboot, complete with heel and toe. This region in the most westerly tip of England, beyond the River Tamar, is best reached from Plymouth, over a bridge built in 1859. A car ferry joins Plymouth with Roscoff in France.

The first place of interest on the coast road is **Antony House**, a 17th and 18th c. mansion with beautiful gardens.

Looe (pop. 4100; hotels – Hannafore Point, C, 40 r.; Rock Towers, D, 23 r.), situated on both sides of the mouth of the River Looe, is a popular seaside resort with a sandy beach. – *Polperro*, an old fishing village shut in between two steep and rocky tongues of land, is crowded with visitors during the season.

Fowey (pop. 22,000 (with St Austell); hotels – Fowey, C, 25 r.; Riverside, D, 14 r.), formerly a considerable port, is very picturesque but tends to be crowded. It has many old houses and a church (St Nicholas) which dates in part from the 12th c.

Between Fowey and Truro is a stretch of coast, still relatively untouched by tourism, with picturesque little fishing villages like *Mevagissey*. **St Mawes** (hotels – Idle Rocks, C, 22 r.; Rising Sun, D, 17 r.) is a pleasant modern seaside resort, connected by ferry with Falmouth.

Truro (pop. 16,500; hotels – Brookdale, D, 54 r.; Carlton, D, 20 r.), county town of Cornwall, lies at the head of the many-branched fjord-like mouth of the River Truro. The town is dominated by the Cathedral, built between 1880 and 1910 in Early English style. The County Museum has a fine collection of minerals.

Falmouth (pop. 18,000; hotels – Falmouth, C, 97 r.; Green Bank, C, 40 r.; Penmere Manor, C, 29 r.; St Michael's, D, 75 r.; Melville, D, 22 r.; Somerdale, D, 19 r.) has a fine natural harbour, but has lost its earlier importance as a seaport and now caters mainly for yachts and boating for holidaymakers. Falmouth has the mildest winter climate in England. The bay is commanded by two castles dating from the time of Henry VIII, *Pendennis Castle* and *St Mawes Castle*, from which there are very fine views.

Beyond Falmouth Cornwall is split up into the heel and the toe of the boot. The heel is the Lizard peninsula, which many people consider the finest part of Cornwall, the most southerly point on the mainland of Britain. It is a windswept region edged by steep and rugged coasts and covered with heather and broom. The clifftop walks afford magnificent views. An obelisk commemorates Guglielmo Marconi (1874–1937), the inventor of wireless telegraphy. The village of *Lizard* is a popular seaside resort, where souvenirs made of serpentine, the green local rock, are popular. On Lizard Point is a tall lighthouse. At Mullion, to the N, are interesting caves.

Between the heel and the toe of the Cornish boot is the wide sweep of Mount's Bay, the beautiful and sheltered stretch of coast known as the Cornish Riviera, with the offshore island of *St Michael's Mount*, which can be reached on foot at low tide on a narrow causeway 500 yards long.

St Michael's Mount

The chief town of the Cornish Riviera is ***Penzance** (pop. 19,100; hotels – Mount Prospect, C, 26 r.; Queen's, D, 71 r.; Marine, D, 35 r.; Penmorvah, E, 10 r.; youth hostel, Horneck Castle, Alverton, 78 b.), a lively resort and shopping centre which attracts visitors in both summer and winter. Subtropical plants grow in the Morrab Gardens. Near Penzance are *Lanyon Quoit* (a Neolithic chambered tomb), the *Nine Maidens* (a line of standing stones), the Iron Age village of *Chysauster* and other remains of the past. From Penzance there are ferry (3 hrs) and helicopter ($\frac{1}{2}$ hr) services to the Scilly Isles.

St Michael's Mount was a fortified Benedictine house (14th c.). The castle seems to grow out of the 200-ft-high crag, with the village and a small harbour clinging to the rock at the foot. From the castle, later converted into a private house (open to visitors), there are fine views of the bay.

* **Land's End** is the most westerly point of England apart from the Scilly Isles (which can be seen from here in clear weather). It offers beautiful clifftop walks. During the summer months it draws large numbers of visitors.

Land's End

St Ives at low tide

On the way to St Ives is the most westerly town in England, *St Just*, with an amphitheatre known as the St Just Round and a 15th c. church. St Just was a tin and copper mining centre and still preserves an old engine-house.

St Ives (pop. 6000; hotels – Tregenna Castle, D, 83 r.; Pedn-Olva, D, 34 r.; Chy-an-Dour, D, 29 r.; Garrack, D, 18 r.; Ocean Breezes, E, 20 r.) was much favoured by artists at the end of the 19th c., and still has many studios, craft workshops and galleries. It is a very popular holiday resort, with sandy bays and cliffs. There is a fine 14th c. church.

Portreath is an attractive little resort with a sandy bay and good clifftop walks. *Perranporth*, with large numbers of caravans, tends to be overcrowded. The beach, some 3 miles long, is fringed with cliffs, with small secluded bays nestling between the rocks.

Newquay (pop. 12,400; hotels – Bristol, C, 100 r.; Atlantic, C, 80 r.; Riviera, C, 50 r.; Porth Veor Manor, D, 14 r.; Windsor, E, 47 r.; Corisande Manor, E, 21 r.; Wheal Treasure E, 11 r.; youth hostel, Alexandra Court, Narrowcliff, 70 b.) is one of the most popular seaside resorts in Cornwall, attracting large numbers of holidaymakers. The town, formerly an important fishing port, is beautifully situated, and offers a variety of interesting excursions in the surrounding area. Of particular interest are the remains of a Celtic village of the 9th–11th c. at Mawgan Porth.

Padstow, at the mouth of the River Camel, has an interesting church (13th and 14th c.) and an Elizabethan manor-house. 2 miles away is the resort of *Trevone Bay*. There is a ferry over the river to *Rock*, with dunes and a sandy beach. At Wadebridge is a bridge of 17 arches over the Camel, built in 1485.

Tintagel is probably the best known village in Cornwall, thanks to its association with the story of King Arthur and the Holy Grail. The link with the Arthurian legend first appears in Geoffrey of Monmouth in the 12th c. A few scanty remains of walls provide little for the imagination to work on.

Perhaps the most interesting feature of Tintagel is the old Post Office with its Victorian interior restored by the National Trust. The village itself, which attracts very many visitors in summer, lies half a mile from the sea, but the parish church (mainly Norman) stands directly on the coast. There is a beautiful clifftop path to *Boscastle*, caught between cliffs which are constantly lashed by the waves. In one of the old grey houses with high slated roofs is a Museum of Witchcraft.

Bude (pop. 6800; hotels – Strand, C, 40 r.; Grenville, D, 71 r.; Penarvot, E, 14 r.) is a lively modern resort with a long beach.

In *Morwenstow*, the most northerly village in Cornwall, hemmed in by cliffs, is a lonely church with a fine Norman doorway. The vicarage has unusual chimney-stacks in the form of church towers, built by Robert Stephen Hawker, a writer of Cornish ballads who was vicar here for some 40 years (d. 1875).

In the interior of the peninsula is *Bodmin Moor*, good walking country. The highest point is *Brown Willy*, from which there are wide views. The moor is dotted with standing stones and other monuments of various periods. In the little village of Bolventor is the *Jamaica Inn* made famous by Daphne du Maurier's novel.

Bodmin, which succeeded *Launceston* (early Tudor church, remains of a medieval church, handsome 18th c. houses) as county town in the 19th c., has the largest parish church in Cornwall, St Petrock's, with a Norman tower; the church was rebuilt in 1469–91.

S of Bodmin is *Lanhydrock House* (originally Jacobean), with magnificent plaster ceilings and a handsome avenue of sycamores in the park.

Cotswolds

Southern England. – County: Oxfordshire.

The Cotswolds, a range of low limestone hills which forms the watershed between the Thames and Severn basins, lie between the M 4 (London to Bristol) and A 40 (Oxford to Gloucester) and are bounded on the W by the M 5. Extending from Chipping Camden in the N to Bath in the S, a distance of some 55 miles, the Cotswolds have an E–W width of

24 miles and reach a maximum height of 1070 ft. Their designation as an "area of outstanding natural beauty" is well earned, and they provide splendid walking country, in which beech woods alternate with pastureland grazed by immense flocks of sheep renowned for the quality of their wool.

Sheep-farming has a long tradition in the Cotswolds; it was originated in the 12th c. by the monastic houses. Wool brought prosperity to the region, a prosperity still reflected today in the splendid churches built by wealthy wool-merchants and in the trim villages and little towns, usually built of the weather-resistant local oolitic limestone, as are the low walls dividing the fields – though many of these have been removed with the expansion of wheat-growing at the expense of sheep-farming.

A good starting point for a tour through an interesting part of the Cotswolds is **Cirencester** (pop. 15,500; hotels – King's Head, C, 66 r.; Fleece, D, 22 r.), an ancient city at the meeting-place of five Roman roads. Much Roman material recovered by excavation can be seen in the excellent Corinium Museum. In medieval times Cirencester was the largest

Market Place and parish church, Cirencester

wool market in England, and in consequence has one of the richest and finest parish churches in the country, with an imposing tower (c. 1400). Particularly notable is the beautifully carved three-storeyed S porch; there is also fine fan vaulting in St Catherine's Chapel and some good stained glass. *Cirencester Park*, seat of Earl Bathurst, has beautiful grounds, with a 5-mile-long avenue of chestnut-trees.

From Cirencester A 419 runs W through *Oakley Woods*, passes close to *Sap-*

perton, with Daneway House, a manor-house of the 14th–17th c., and then enters the *"**Golden Valley**" of the Stroud-water, with many cloth factories. 12 miles from Cirencester is **Stroud** (pop. 20,900), a lively modern town which was formerly a prominent centre of the textile trade. 2 miles S is *Woodchester*, with an old Dominican abbey and a large Roman villa (beautiful mosaics), which has been excavated but covered over again for protection; the mosaics are uncovered at rare intervals.

4 miles N of Stroud on A 46 is **Painswick** (pop. 3100; Painswick Hotel, D, 16 r.), with many handsome stone-built houses dating from the great days of the wool trade. In the churchyard are 99 fine yews.

6 miles beyond Painswick on A 46 a short detour can be made to **Birdlip** on A 417, from which there is a beautiful view of the Severn valley. Here the Cotswolds have their steepest westerly scarp.

A 46 continues NE through *Cheltenham* (see p. 112) to **Winchcombe** (13 miles; pop. 4700; hotel – George, C, 17 r.); an attractive old Cotswold town built of grey sandstone. The church, in late Perpendicular style (1490), contains carving from the earlier Benedictine abbey (founded c. 800), of which nothing now remains. Close by is *Sudeley Castle*, once the home of Catherine Parr (d. 1548), Henry VIII's widow, who married Lord Seymour of Sudeley; it stands in very beautiful gardens. On a hilltop S of Winchcombe, almost 1000 ft high, is a Neolithic chambered cairn, *Belas Knap*. 2 miles NE is *Hailes Abbey*, once a great Cistercian house but now represented only by a few scanty remains. Adjoining is a small archaeological museum.

3 miles farther along A 46 in the direction of Broadway a visit can be made to two picturesque little villages, *Stanton*, with a street lined by 16th–17th c. houses, many of them lovingly restored, and the equally attractive *Stanway*. Both villages have Tudor manor-houses.

Broadway (pop. 2400; hotels – Lygon Arms, A, 67 r.; Dormy House, C, 50 r.; Broadway, D, 23 r.), at the foot of the Cotswolds, is a good centre from which to explore the surrounding area on foot, with the additional attractions provided by its picturesque old inns and numerous antique shops. With its wide, busy main street and its many Elizabethan houses, Broadway is one of the most attractive of the Cotswold towns. Among the finest houses are *Abbot's Grange*, the *Tudor House* and the *Lygon Arms*. Just outside Broadway on the road which climbs up in the direction of Stow-on-the-Wold is *Fish Hill* (1024 ft), with the *Beacon Tower*, from which there are wide views. It is said that in good weather thirteen counties can be seen from here.

From A 44, here following a fairly winding course, a side road goes off on the left to Chipping Campden, the most northerly point in the Cotswolds and one of the prettiest and most appealing little towns in England.

Chipping Campden (pop. 1960; hotels – Cotswold House, D, 25 r.; Noel Arms, D, 19 r.; King's Arms, D, 14 r.) was once the centre of the wool trade and the residence of many wealthy wool-merchants of the 14th and 15th c., who built themselves magnificent houses in the town. The finest of these houses (late 14th c.), is the one which belonged to William Grevil who is commemorated by a brass in the 15th c. church as "the flower of the merchants of all England". Other outstanding buildings are the *Town Hall*, the *Woolstaplers' Hall* (partly 14th c.), the old *Grammar School* (1628), the *Market Hall* (1625) and late 14th c. almshouses. 3 miles NE is *Hidcote Manor*, with a beautiful garden.

The road continues by way of **Chastleton House**, a large Jacobean mansion built about 1610 by a wool merchant, with beautiful old furniture and other items of interest, set in a magnificent garden, to *Chipping Norton*, another old wool town. Some 3 miles outside the town are the *Rollright Stones, a famous Bronze Age stone circle, less impressive than the larger monuments at Avebury and Stonehenge, but in a very beautiful setting. There are about 70 stones in the main circle, known as the *King's Men*, together with a burial chamber called the *Whispering Knights* and the isolated *King Stone*.

W of Chipping Norton is **Stow-on-the-Wold** (pop. 1700; hotels – Unicorn Crest, C, 20 r.; Stow Lodge, D, 22 r.; Fosse Manor, E, 21 r.; Parkdene, E, 12 r.; youth hostel, 60 b.), a small town, situated at the meeting-place of eight roads, with an extensive market square in which large sheep markets are held every year. 1 mile W is *Abbotswood*, famous for its beautiful

park. The return to Cirencester (10 miles) is by way of *Northleach* (beautiful church) on the River Leach and *Chedworth Roman villa* ($4\frac{1}{4}$ miles S), one of the best preserved in the country (A.D. 180–350), with mosaic floors, baths, hypocausts and a museum containing finds from the site. – Visitors with more time at their disposal can visit many other interesting little towns, among them *Bourton-on-the-Water* (several windmills), *Evenlode, Upper Slaughter* and *Lower Slaughter*.

Coventry

Central England. – County: West Midlands.
Population: 314,000.
Telephone dialling code: 0203.
Ⓘ **Tourist Information Centre,**
36 Broadgate;
tel. 20084.

HOTELS. – *De Vere*, Cathedral Square, B, 215 r.; *Post House*, Rye Hill, Allesley, C, 196 r.; *Crest*, Hinckley Road, C, 161 r.; *Leofric*, Broadgate, C, 101 r.; *Novotel*, Wilson Lane, Longford, C, 100 r.; *The Chace Crest*, London Road, Willenhall, C, 66 r.; *Royal Court*, Tamworth Road, Keresley, D, 99 r.; *Allesley*, Birmingham Old Road, Allesley, D, 45 r.; *Beechwood*, Sandpits Lane, Keresley, E, 28 r.

RESTAURANTS. – *Allesley*, Birmingham Old Road; *Falcon*, 16 Manor Road; *Post House*, Rye Hill; *Grandstand*, King Richard Street.

SPORT and RECREATION. – Tennis, golf.

Coventry, as the centre of the British car industry, suffered one of the most devastating air raids of the Second World War in November 1940, when the old town centre was almost completely destroyed. Of the old Cathedral nothing is left but a few fragments, which have been incorporated into the new Cathedral built after the war, a masterpiece of modern architecture. The rebuilding of the town itself, with fine open squares, wide streets and pedestrian zones, is an excellent example of contemporary town planning.

HISTORY. – Coventry grew up in the 7th c. under the protection of a monastic house. Between the 14th and the 17th c. the textile industry made it one of the leading towns in England. In the 20th c. it developed as a great centre of car and motorcycle manufacture and acquired other modern industries. – The town became the see of a bishop in 1102, but thereafter Coventry and Lichfield vied with one another for centuries over the right to elect the bishop.

SIGHTS. – The traditional centre of the city, **Broadgate**, has been replanned as a spacious square, with a *statue of Lady Godiva* (by W. Reid Dick) in the middle.

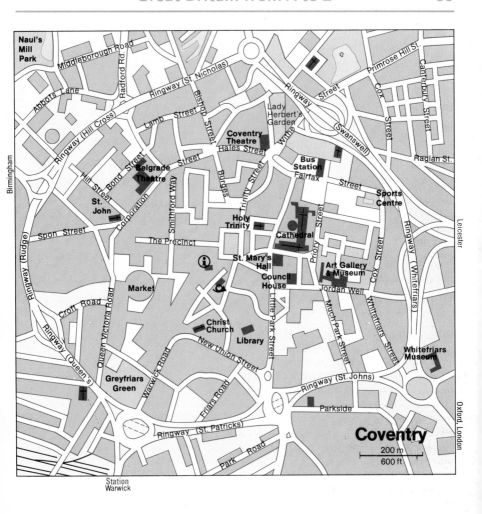

Coventry

200 m
600 ft

Station
Warwick

The well-known story relates that Lady Godiva, wife of Earl Leofric of Mercia, sought to protect the people of Coventry from the exactions of her hard-hearted husband, who agreed to reduce his demands if she rode naked through the streets of the town; none of the grateful citizens looked out of their windows while she was doing so with the single exception of "Peeping Tom". Thereupon Leofric founded a Benedictine priory in her honour (1043). On *Broadgate House*, at the SW end of the square, is a clock on which Lady Godiva appears on the stroke of the hour, with Peeping Tom at a window above her.

Holy Trinity Church, at the NE corner of Broadgate, has one of the three slender *spires* which are Coventry's best known landmarks. The spire of Holy Trinity, rebuilt in 1166, is 327 ft high. The church, in Perpendicular style, has very beautiful *windows*, a stone *pulpit* of about 1470 and interesting *tapestries* woven for the coronation of Queen Elizabeth II.

Behind Holy Trinity Church are the ruins of the old Cathedral and the new Cathedral. The *old Cathedral*, originally one of the largest parish churches in England (Perpendicular, 1373–1433), was raised to cathedral status only in 1918. After the bombing there survived only parts of the external walls and the slender *spire*, 303 ft high, which is the third tallest in the country and is regarded as the most beautiful. The *vestries* were rebuilt after the war with the help of young German volunteer workers. The remains of the first cathedral built by Leofric and Godiva were excavated in 1965.

The ****new Cathedral** was designed to serve Christians of all denominations and promote Christian unity. It was built between 1956 and 1962 to the design of Sir Basil Spence. From the outside the Cathedral has an almost fortress-like aspect. On the outer wall by the entrance, at the SE end, is a figure of *St Michael* subduing Lucifer, Epstein's last work. The *nave*, 420 ft long and oriented N–S, can

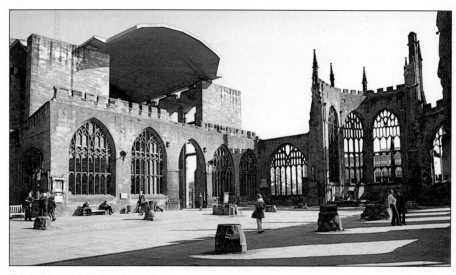

Ruins of the old Cathedral, Coventry

seat a congregation of 2000. The side walls are made up of offset panels of concrete alternating with windows facing towards the altar. The concrete ceiling is broken up by the diamond pattern of its ribs.

Coventry Cathedral

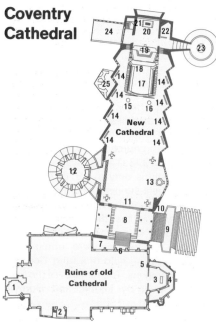

1 Tower
2 Haigh Chapel
3 Cross made
  from charred beams
4 International Centre
5 Figure of Christ
6 Queen's Staircase
7 Entrances to Crypt
8 Porch
9 St Michael's Steps
10 St Michael and Lucifer
11 Engraved glass screen
12 Chapel of Unity
13 Baptistry
14 Tablets of the Word
15 Pulpit
16 Reading-desk
17 Choir
18 Bishop's throne
19 High altar
20 Lady Chapel
21 Tapestry
22 Chapel of
   Christ in Gethsemane
23 Chapel of
   Christ the Servant
   (Chapel of Industry)
24 Refectory
25 Remains of
   Benedictine priory

A particularly impressive feature of the INTERIOR is the great *stained glass window* by John Piper in the *baptistery*, centred on the radiant sun which symbolises the Holy Spirit. The ten *stained glass panels* in the walls of the nave are set at an angle so that they are seen only from the N end (where the high altar stands). In their spectrum of colours, from yellow through red to blue and violet, they are intended to symbolise the life of man, from birth through death to resurrection. They were designed by Lawrence Lee, Geoffrey Clark and Keith New. Also very beautiful is the great glass screen at the S end of the nave, with incised figures of angels by John Hutton. At the N end hangs a huge **tapestry* (75 by 38 ft) in glowing colour showing Christ in Glory surrounded by four beasts mentioned in the Revelation. Designed by Graham Sutherland, it was woven near Aubusson in France.

The *Chapel of Unity* is intended to symbolise concord between the Church of England and the Free Churches. The *mosaic floor* was a gift from the Church of Sweden; the *stained glass windows* came from Germany. There are very beautiful details to be seen in the **Gethsemane Chapel**, adjoining the *Lady Chapel*, and in the *Chapel of Industry*. The windows in the Chapel of Industry, which is intended to bridge the gap between workers and the Church, depict the industries of Coventry.

St Mary's Hall, immediately S of the Cathedral, survived the bombing. The adjoining *Caesar's Tower* (13th c.) was rebuilt after war damage. The Great Hall (1394–1414), with a fine oak roof, was the meeting-place of the guilds; it contains an Arras tapestry thought to depict Henry VII's visit to Coventry in 1500.

The most interesting of the surviving half-timbered buildings is **Ford's Hospital** in Greyfriars Lane, an almshouse for five poor married couples founded in 1509 (restored 1953). Of the *monastery of the Grey Friars*, destroyed in 1539, there survives the beautiful steeple, now incorporated in *Christ Church*. The dormitory and cloister of the *monastery of the White Friars* have been restored and now house a local museum. Two other interesting old buildings are *Bablake School* (1560) and the picturesque *Bond's Hospital*, a half-timbered almshouse for old men, founded in 1506. A small section of the *town walls* of 1356 has been preserved between *Cook Street Gate* and *Swanswell Gate*, the only two of the town's original twelve gates which still survive. – The *Herbert Art Gallery and Museum* contains material illustrating early industrial developments in Coventry and the history of the town.

SURROUNDINGS. – 5 miles SW is *Kenilworth Castle, built in 1120 by Geoffrey de Clinton, Treasurer of England in the reign of Henry I, and enlarged by Elizabeth I's favourite Robert Dudley, Earl of Leicester. The castle, built of red sandstone, was formerly surrounded by a lake. Elizabeth often stayed here, and on one occasion Leicester provided for her the three weeks' entertainment which is described in Scott's "Kenilworth". The friendship lasted until his death in 1588; his tomb is in St Mary's Church in Warwick. Even in ruin the castle is highly impressive, with its walls and towers surrounding the bailey, the old half-timbered stables and the Norman keep. From the period when the castle belonged to the Earls and Dukes of Lancaster date the Great Hall, the White Hall, the private apartments and the Audience Chamber. – The *parish church* of Kenilworth, with a Norman doorway, adjoins the remains of *Kenilworth Priory*, founded in 1126 by Geoffrey de Clinton.

Just off the road from Kenilworth to Warwick is **Royal Leamington Spa** (pop. 43,000; hotels – Regent, C, 80 r.; Manor House, C, 53 r.; Falstaff, C, 50 r.; Berni Inn, D, 32 r.; Angel, D, 17 r.; Park, D, 16 r.), which is worth visiting not so much for its mineral springs as for its beautiful parks (Jephson Gardens, Pump Room Gardens).

Dartmoor

South-western England. – County: Devon.

When Dartmoor is mentioned most people think of the prison, but in fact the prison is merely one small feature in a vast expanse of moorland which occupies almost the whole of the western part of Devon. Dartmoor is a great mass of granite covered by moorland, heath and large areas of bog, with a higher rainfall than most other parts of England. It has now been designated as a national park, extending for 23 miles from Okehampton in the N to Ivybridge in the S and for 18 miles

from Bovey Tracey in the E to Tavistock in the W. Its highest point is High Willhays (2038 ft).

Much of Dartmoor is bleak and inhospitable: its charm lies in the numerous little streams, which have earned it the name of "mother of rivers", and their beautiful valleys. The rivers Dart, Avon, Tavy, Taw and Teign – to name only a few – are clear and clean, and well stocked with trout. The famous Dartmoor ponies are shaggy, tough and half-wild.

An interesting feature of Dartmoor is the "tors", the granite crags, often eroded into bizarre shapes, which jut up out of the moorland. Many of these stones were used in prehistoric times to make the chamber tombs, cairns and stone circles which are so numerous on Dartmoor. The origin of some of these structures is unknown, and some thought to be prehistoric have been shown to be relatively recent. There is similar uncertainty about the date of the "clapper bridges" made of slabs of stone which are found on some of the rivers.

One of the best preserved Bronze Age settlements is *Grimspound*, near Manaton, with some 24 huts. Remains of an early village were found at Great Tor. At *Merrivale*, near Princetown, are three stone rows, a stone circle and numerous cairns. *Green Hill Row*, 4½ miles NW of South Brent, is probably the longest series of burials, with more than 70 stones.

These mysterious remains of the past have combined with the desolate and impenetrable character of the moor itself and the frequent blankets of mist to give Dartmoor its rather sinister reputation, and as in many moorland regions the stories of ghosts and apparitions are legion. At any rate visitors should pay heed to the warnings by the National Park authorities about the dangers of getting lost on the moor, for it is easy to go astray in its pathless wastes.

There are only two major roads on Dartmoor – one from Tavistock to Ashburton, the other from Yelverton by way of Princetown and Two Bridges (where it crosses the first road) to Moretonhampstead.

Moretonhampstead (pop. 1600; Manor House Hotel, B, 68 r.) and *Chagford* (pop. 1250; hotels – Mill End, C, 16 r.; Easton Court, D, 8 r.) are good bases from which to explore the surrounding country on foot. Moretonhampstead is a little market town with 17th c. houses and a market hall of the same period. Chagford, 4 miles W, is on the Teign, in the shadow of high granite tors. E of Moretonhampstead is *Bovey Tracey* (pop. 4000; hotels – Edgemoor, D, 28 r.; Willmead Farm, D, 3 r.), a popular holiday place in the Bovey valley, with potters' and hand weavers' workshops.

Buckland-in-the-Moor

Postbridge, 8 miles SW, has one of the best known clapper bridges. **Buckland-in-the-Moor**, 8 miles S, is one of the most charming villages in Devon. *Two Bridges*, 7 miles SW of Postbridge, is at the crossing of the two roads over Dartmoor. From here there is a very pleasant walk to *Wistman's Wood*, a nature reserve which extends for half a mile along the River Dart.

Another, easier, walk is up the beautiful *Cowsic valley* to *Lydford*, with a ruined 12th c. castle. This was the first prison on Dartmoor, preceding the better known one at *Princetown* which was originally built by French prisoners of war in 1806, and only later became a convict prison. Further details about the prison can be obtained from the information bureau in the Town Hall in Princetown.

8 miles SW, beyond Yelverton, is **Buckland Abbey**, a former Cistercian house (founded 1278) which was presented in 1541 to Sir Richard Grenville, whose grandson made it into a country house. In 1581 it was bought by Sir Francis Drake (d. 1596). It is now a museum.

Those who want to see more of the moor or to return to Moretonhampstead should take the road via *Tavistock*, once a very prosperous wool and tin town, or alternatively make for Two Bridges and turn E towards the pretty little town of Ashburton, on a road which runs for part of the way alongside the River Dart. On this road it is worth making a detour to *Widecombe-in-the-Moor*, well known from the song "Widdicombe Fair". The fair is still held every year in September. The village has a beautiful church (*c.* 1500) with a fine tower.

Ashburton (pop. 3600; Dartmoor Motel, D, 22 r.) lies on the outskirts of Dartmoor. A place of some consequence during the tin-mining period, it has preserved a number of interesting buildings, including some handsome 17th and 18th c. houses and a granite church (14th–15th c.) with a very beautiful tower; it also has a museum.

From Ashburton a trip can be made to *Totnes*, off Dartmoor, on a road which passes close to *Buckfastleigh* (pop. 2870) and **Buckfast Abbey**, on the banks of the Dart. Originally a Benedictine foundation (1018), it was taken over by the Cistercians in 1148. In 1882 the Benedictines re-established themselves in the abbey and built a large new church (1907–37). They now sell their products – honey, fruit wine and stained glass – to the numerous visitors who flock to the abbey.

Farther down the Dart valley is **Totnes** (pop. 5600; hotels – Seymour, D, 30 r.; Royal Seven Stars, D, 18 r.), an interesting old town of narrow winding streets and gabled houses. Parts of the old town walls have been preserved, including the East and North Gates. The Guildhall (rebuilt 1611) is a relic of a Norman abbey. St Mary's Church (mid 15th c.) has a notable W tower and a very beautiful rood-screen. The main surviving feature of the castle is the Norman keep, from which there is a fine view. The town was formerly an important wool town and is still a busy shopping centre for the whole surrounding area. There are boats from Totnes to Dartmouth.

Derby

Central England. – County: Derbyshire.
Population: 216,900.
Telephone dialling code: 0332.
ⓘ **Tourist Information Centre,**
Central Library, The Strand;
tel. 31111 ext 2185–6.

HOTELS. – *Crest*, Pasture Hill, Littleover, C, 66 r.; *International*, 288 Burton Road, C, 50 r.; *Midland*, Midland Road, D, 63 r.

RESTAURANTS. – *Golden Pheasant*, 221 Chellaston Road; *La Goldola*, 220 Osmaston Road; *Palm Court*, Duffield Road.

SPORT and RECREATION. – Golf, tennis.

Derby is an industrial city noted mainly for the Rolls-Royce works and its large china manufactories. It lies on the W bank of the Derwent not far from its junction with the Trent. The town flourished during the Industrial Revolution of the

18th c., and preserves many buildings of that period, particularly in the centre. It has a notable Cathedral. Derby is a good centre from which to explore the Peak District, now a national park with an area of over 500 sq. miles.

HISTORY. – The Roman fort of *Derventio* lay on the other bank of the Derwent at Little Chester. During the Middle Ages the town was several times ravaged by plague. In 1715 John Lombe established the first silk-mill in England here, and in 1756 William Duesbury founded the first porcelain manufactory. Thereafter silk and porcelain brought the town prosperity, and it grew rapidly. In 1877 the Royal Crown Derby Porcelain Company was established, and revived the manufacture of porcelain. The Rolls-Royce firm was founded by Frederick Henry Royce in 1906.

SIGHTS. – The church of All Saints became the **Cathedral** in 1927. The tower, built 1508–27, is 210 ft high; the church itself was remodelled by James Gibbs in 1722–25. It contains the *tombs* of *"Bess of Hardwick"* (Elizabeth, Countess of Shrewsbury, d. 1608) and *Henry Cavendish*. The *Museum and Art Gallery* contains 25 pictures by Joseph Wright (1734–97), "Wright of Derby", and valuable porcelain. There is fine *wrought-iron work* in the Cathedral and at the entrance to the old silk-works. There are some handsome 18th c. buildings in *Market Place, Irongate* and *Friargate*.

Other notable buildings are the **County Hall** (1660) and *Assembly Rooms* (1764; façade rebuilt after fire damage). Not far NW in a former silk mill is the Industrial Museum, including Rolls-Royce aero engines.

SURROUNDINGS. – The church at *Littleover*, 1 mile W, has a Norman porch with 14th c. windows. – *Kedleston Hall, 4½ miles NW near Quarndon, is probably the finest Adam house in England, built about 1760 by Robert and James Adam. Its principal feature is the great marble hall, with 20 pink alabaster pillars; fine furniture by Chippendale and other leading cabinet-makers of the day. The N front, with six Corinthian columns, was built by James Paine in 1757–61.

Melbourne, 6 miles S, is a charming little town (pop. 3600), which has a very beautiful early Norman church, reminiscent of Southwell, with three Norman towers. Melbourne Hall, a seat of the Marquess of Lothian, dates from the 16th c., with an 18th c. extension. It stands in a beautiful park with fine old trees.

Repton (pop. 2200), 8 miles SW of Derby, is noted for its public school, founded in 1557. Remains of a 12th c. priory are incorporated in the school complex; of particular interest is Prior Overton's Tower. The little late Saxon crypt (10th c.) of St Wystan's Church should not be missed.

Foremark Hall, 2 miles E, is a Palladian mansion built in 1760. In the church (17th c. Perpendicular) the wrought-iron choir screens from Bakewell are notable.

Burton-upon-Trent (pop. 47,900; hotels – Newton Park, C, 27 r.; Edgecote, E, 12 r.; 4 miles SW, is a famous brewing town. The monks of Burton Abbey (founded 1002, now almost completely destroyed) were the first to discover that the local water was particularly suitable for making beer, and in later centuries numerous breweries were built here.

Stoke-on-Trent (15 miles NW; pop. 257,200) is the centre of the British Potteries (museum of ceramics).

Dorchester

Southern England. – County: Dorset.
Altitude: 250 ft. – Population: 14,000.
Telephone dialling code: 0305.

ⓘ **Tourist Information Centre,**
Antelope Yard, South Street;
tel. 67992.

HOTELS. – *King's Arms*, D, 27 r.; *Owermoigne Moor Country House*, D, 7 r.

CAMPING SITE.

RESTAURANTS. – *Judge Jeffreys*, High Street; *Smith's Arms*, Godmanston (5 miles N).

EVENTS. – *Thomas Hardy Festival* (Aug.).

SPORT and RECREATION. – Tennis.

Dorchester, the county town, is an ideal centre from which to explore the beauties of Dorset. Although now a small place it has a rich past. It has close associations with Thomas Hardy (1840–1928), who lived in the town and described the surrounding area in his novels and poems. There are many features of historical interest in Dorchester and its neighbourhood.

Thomas Hardy's birthplace, Brockhampton, Nr. Dorchester

HISTORY. – The town was founded by the Romans, under the name of *Durnovaria*; but excavations in the area have shown that there was a settlement here at a much earlier period.

SIGHTS. – In the High Street is the house occupied by *Judge Jeffreys* during the "Bloody Assize" of 1685, in which more than 60 of Monmouth's supporters were condemned to death, after the battle of Sedgemoor.

Other interesting old buildings are the *Grammar School* and the **Old Crown Court** in which the "Tolpuddle martyrs" were tried in 1834. (The martyrs were six farm workers from the little neighbouring village of Tolpuddle who had banded together in an attempt to secure higher wages. Since it was government policy to keep wages fixed they were accused of conspiracy and sentenced to deportation for seven years – although in fact they returned after two years. The incident is regarded as a milestone in British trade union history.)

The *County Museum* has much Roman and pre-Roman material, and a Hardy Memorial Room. Thomas Hardy lived and died in Max Gate, a house on the Wareham road, a mile away. In his novels he depicts with loving accuracy the landscapes of Dorset, the hills and the heathland, the beautiful countryside and the little villages, many of them little changed since his day. Dorchester appears in his novels as Casterbridge. There is a *statue of Hardy* by Eric Kennington on the N side of the town, on the Dorchester road.

SURROUNDINGS. – On the S side of the town are **Maumbury Rings**, the best preserved Roman amphitheatre in England. – 2 miles SW is **Maiden Castle**, one of the most imposing prehistoric sites in the country. The main feature is a huge hill-fort of the Early Iron Age, a 900 yards long oval surrounded by four massive earth ramparts, originally topped by palisades, which in places still stand 80 ft high. The site also includes Neolithic burials and a Romano-Celtic temple dating from A.D. 350–370.

8 miles N of Dorchester, at Cerne Abbas, is another interesting relic of the past – the **Cerne Giant**, a huge male figure 180 ft in length hewn out of the chalk hillside. The origin and significance of the figure are unknown: it may possibly have been associated with fertility rites.

The village of Cerne Abbas has a fine *gatehouse* which belonged to a Benedictine abbey, a *tithe barn* and a number of Tudor cottages. Flower-lovers will want to visit the gardens at *Mintern*, 2 miles away, which specialise in rhododendrons.

Milton Abbas, 10 miles N, is a picturesque village built in 1786 by Lord Milton, an eccentric landowner who objected to having the villagers too near his country house, a converted abbey, and therefore moved them to this picturesque new village of thatched houses. His house, *Milton Abbey*, is now a school. Of the old Benedictine monastic buildings the Abbot's Hall (1490) has survived intact; the 12th c. church has a number of features of interest.

It is well worth making the trip from Dorchester to the *Isle of Purbeck*, a peninsula renowned for its "Purbeck marble" (not real marble but a kind of sandstone), found in many English churches. 12 miles from Dorchester is the village of *Wool*, with a 15th c. bridge over the River Frome. Just outside the village is Woolbridge Manor, which appears in "Tess of the D'Urbervilles" as Wellbridge House. 5 miles S is **Lulworth**, with a ruined castle, situated in Lulworth Cove, an almost exactly circular bay, with an interesting petrified forest extending for half a mile. At *Bovington*, in the large military training area around Wool and Lulworth, is a museum of military vehicles. A mile N of Bovington, at Clouds Hill, is Lawrence of Arabia's cottage (National Trust).

The next place of interest, visible from miles away, is *Corfe Castle, the gigantic ruin of a Norman stronghold (12th and 13th c.). King Edward the Martyr was murdered here in 978, probably at the instigation of his stepmother Elfrida. The castle was defended by Lady Bankes against Parliamentary forces in 1643 and again in 1645, but was taken by treachery and blown up. The village, which is older than the castle, is charming.

Corfe Castle

5 miles SE of Corfe Castle is the seaside resort of **Swanage** (pop. 8100; hotels – Grosvenor, C, 105 r.; Pines, D, 51 r.; Clifftop, E, 17 r.; Sefton, E, 11 r.; youth hostel, Cluny Crescent, 93 b.), situated on a sandy bay in gently rolling country. A remarkable feature of the town is a stone terrestrial globe weighing some 40 tons, and there are also a variety of columns, house-fronts and towers from demolished London buildings. Although mainly modern, the town has a number of attractive old houses, particularly round the mill-pond. There is a good yachting harbour.

From Swanage continue via *Studland*, with beautiful bays and a Norman church, and Corfe Castle to **Wareham** (pop. 7600; hotel – Springfield Country,

C, 34 r.), an ancient little town near the mouth of the River Frome. Round the town are pre-Roman earthworks. The little Saxon church of St Martin (restored) contains a figure of T. E. Lawrence in Arab dress by Eric Kennington. In St Mary's Church are a hexagonal lead font (1100) and the marble sarcophagus of Edward the Martyr.

6 miles NW of Wareham is *Bere Regis*, a royal residence in Saxon times, with an interesting parish church (15th c. timber ceiling with 12 large oak figures of the Apostles).

In *Puddletown*, 6 miles W, is a fine 15th c. manor-house in Perpendicular style, **Athelhampton Hall**. From here it is 5 miles back to Dorchester.

Durham

Northern England. – County: Durham.
Population: 24,800.
Telephone dialling code: 0385.
(i) **Tourist Information Centre,**
13 Claypath;
tel. 43720.

HOTELS. – *Royal County*, Old Elvet, C, 118 r.; *Three Tuns*, New Elvet, D, 51 r.; *Kylesku*, 6–7 Crossgate Path, D, 10 r.

YOUTH HOSTEL. – *Gilesgate Secondary School*, Providence Row, 40 b.

RESTAURANTS. – *Duke of Wellington*; *Waterloo*.

EVENTS. – *Miners' Gala* (July).

SPORT and RECREATION. – Sailing, rowing, fishing, skating.

The *situation of Durham is strikingly impressive. The old part of the town – the Cathedral, the Castle and some fine old houses – lies on a steeply scarped crag encircled on three sides by the River Wear; the houses have been taken over by the University; on the campus outside the town are modern concrete buildings. Scott's description of Durham is both brief and apt: "half church of God, half castle 'gainst the Scot".

Historically and architecturally the Cathedral is one of the most interesting in England. Although it ranks as the country's finest Norman building, it already shows the transition towards Gothic, and its ribbed vaulting is among the earliest in Europe. – Durham is the county town and centre of the important Durham coalfield.

HISTORY. – In 995 Bishop Aldhun, attracted by the situation and its defensive possibilities, built on

Durham Cathedral

Dunholm ("island on a hill") a church to house the remains of St Cuthbert, who had lived for eight years as a hermit on Holy Island. Tradition has it that he was given help in finding a suitable site by a cow; and as a mark of gratitude the cow is depicted on the outer wall of the N transept. The first bishop appointed by the Normans was Walcher (1071–80), a native of Lorraine. In view of the constant frontier fighting with the Scots he was given an army of his own, together with the right to dispense justice, coin money and levy

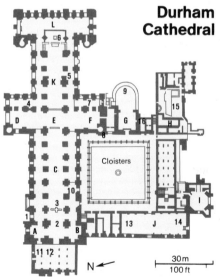

Durham Cathedral

A North-West Tower
B South-West Tower
C Nave
D North Transept
E Central Tower
F South Transept

G Chapterhouse
H Crypt
I Kitchen
J Dormitory
K Choir
L Chapel of Nine Altars

1 Sanctuary door-knocker
2 Font
3 Black marble cross
4 Gregory Chapel
5 Bishop's throne
6 Tomb of St Cuthbert
7 Light Infantry Memorial Chapel
8 Stairs up Central Tower
9 Prior's chair
10 Miners' Memorial

11 12th c. painting of
   St Cuthbert and
   King Oswald
12 Crucifixion (13th c.)
13 Treasury
14 Restaurant and book-
   shop
15 Deanery
16 Prison

taxes – rights which no other ecclesiastic but the Bishop of Ely possessed and which were not done away with until 1836. In 1074 Walcher was created Earl of Northumberland.

SIGHTS. – The present**Cathedral was begun by the second bishop after the Norman Conquest, William of St Carilef (1081–96), who brought monks from Jarrow and Monkwearmouth to Durham. The choir and transepts were probably completed and the nave begun during his episcopate. His successor Ranulf Flambard (1099–1128) completed the nave and chapterhouse, still in Norman style. The Galilee Porch at the W end was built by Bishop Hugh of Puiset or Pudsey (1153–95). The W towers were completed in 1226, the upper part of the central tower (Perpendicular) in 1490. The E transept or Chapel of the Nine Altars was begun in 1242 and completed in 1280. Considerable damage was done to both the exterior and the interior by James Wyatt's "restoration" of 1778–1800.

Visitors entering the Cathedral by the *NW doorway* (with a fine sanctuary knocker of 1133) are at once impressed by the size of the INTERIOR, which is seen in its full length. No less impressive is the abundance of ornament on the pillars. The *ribbed vaulting* (1128–35) represented a turning point in the development of church architecture. A marble cross in the floor of the nave marks the point beyond which women were not allowed to go. The alabaster *font* with its high tabernacle dates from the time of Bishop John Cosin (1660–72), who was also responsible for the Cathedral's magnificent Renaissance woodwork. The W window is 14th c. There are notable *monuments* to John, Lord Neville (d. 1331), and his son Ralph (d. 1367).

The *Lady Chapel, unusually situated at the W end of the nave, is a good example of the transition from Norman to Early English. The pillars, of Purbeck marble, support arches of decidedly Moorish effect. The *wall paintings* probably represent St Oswald and St Cuthbert. The window on the W side contains the surviving medieval glass. The Venerable Bede (673–735), who lived in Jarrow monastery and wrote almost 80 books, was buried in the Lady Chapel.

The large *transepts* of the Cathedral were built between 1093 and 1104, rather earlier than the nave, which they resemble in style. Among the many notable features in the **Choir** is the *altar screen* (1372–80). The *choir-stalls* date from 1665. The *bishop's throne*, the "highest in Christendom", was made for Thomas of Hatfield (bishop 1345–81) and also serves as his monument. Behind the high altar is the *shrine* containing the remains of *St Cuthbert* (d. 687). The *Chapel of the Nine Altars shows the transition from Early English to Decorated: a magnificent piece of architecture which harmonises well with the Norman choir. The beautiful carving, particularly the figures of the Evangelists, should be examined in detail.

The Benedictine *monastic buildings* have been preserved almost in their original condition. The late Norman *Prior's Door* leads into the cloister, with arcades of 1418. On the W side of the cloister is the *monks' dormitory* (1398–1404), which now contains a magnificent collection of early manuscripts (8th c. onwards), Saxon crosses, Roman altars, remains of St Cuthbert's tomb and fragments of textiles and clothing, the oldest material of the kind found in England. The *refectory* was converted into a library in 1648. The octagonal *kitchen*, with fine vaulting, dates from 1366–70, and remained in use without interruption until 1940.

In front of the Cathedral is *Palace Green*, flanked by a number of picturesque Georgian houses. On the far side is Durham's second major historic building, the *Castle, built in 1072. The most interesting rooms in the Castle are the *kitchen* with its huge fireplace and larder (1499) and the large *dining room*.

The Castle has been part of the University since the 19th c.; 1½ miles S on Elvet Hill in a university building is the Gulbenkian Museum, with a collection of art and archaeology of the Near and Far East (including China, Japan and Egypt).

East and South-East Coasts

South-eastern England. – Counties: Kent, Essex, Suffolk, Norfolk and Lincolnshire.

The E and SE coasts of England extend from the Thames estuary by way of the Wash to the S side of the Humber, and have along their length many well-known and popular seaside resorts as well as a number of important ports. The topographical pattern of this long stretch of coastline is very varied – sometimes rocky, elsewhere fringed by sandy beaches, often fertile fenland reclaimed from the sea. Many hundred miles of embankments and dykes protect this land, lying only just above sea level. The level of the coast is sinking all the time: over the last 2000 years it has fallen by something like 40 ft. In spite of the length of the coast there are only a few harbours deep enough to take tankers and other large vessels.

Margate (pop. 50,300; hotels – Grosvenor, E, 64 r.; Haven, E, 27 r.), with

Cliftonville, a popular seaside resort which has many miles of clean fine sand, good entertainment facilities, a theatre, a concert hall and an amusement park. A beautiful path runs along the cliffs to *Broadstairs*, a quieter resort (5 miles), with Bleak House, where Dickens stayed several times.

Westgate-on-Sea and **Birchington** are two relatively quiet seaside resorts which have preserved something of their earlier charm. There are some stretches of cliff between the sandy beaches.

Clacton-on-Sea

Herne Bay is a resort like many others, with a promenade and a beach of sand and shingle. There is an interesting walk to *Reculver*, site of the Roman fort of *Regulbium*, built to protect the wide *Wantsum Channel* which then separated the *Isle of Thanet* from the mainland. The former channel is now an area of marshland.

Whitstable (pop. 25,500) is a name well known to gourmets for its excellent oysters. There is evidence of the existence of oyster-beds here for at least 2000 years. The former railway line from here to Canterbury, built by George Stephenson in 1830, was one of the first passenger-carrying lines in the world. The town has some attractive old houses. There is a shingle beach and a small harbour.

On the **Isle of Sheppey**, which is separated from the mainland by the Swale, are *Minster-on-Sea, Queensborough, Sheerness* and *Leysdown-on-Sea*. There are numerous camping sites, holiday camps and chalets on the Isle. Minster has an abbey church founded in 673 and rebuilt in the 12th c. The beach is largely of shingle.

Southend-on-Sea (pop. 155,800; hotels – Roslin, D, 44 r.; Balmoral, D, 19 r.; West Park, D, 17 r.), which with *Leigh-on-Sea, Prittlewell* and *Westcliff* now forms a considerable town. It is a large and very popular seaside resort with a pier 1½ miles long, the future of which is in doubt. Although the beach is over 6 miles long it is often very crowded at weekends. At low tide the sea retreats for almost a mile. – A former Cluniac priory in Prittlewell (*c.* 100) now houses a museum.

Clacton-on-Sea (pop. 43,600; hotels – Waverley Hall, D, 52 r.; Royal, D, 46 r.; Kings Cliff, E, 13 r.; York House, E, 6 r.), with a gently sloping beach 7 miles long, s particularly suitable for families with children. It has everything a modern seaside resort ought to have – a pier, a promenade, beautiful parks and gardens, a golf-course and a wide range of entertainments. *Frinton-on-Sea* and *Walton-on-the-Naze* are quieter resorts a few miles farther up the coast.

Harwich (pop., with Dovercourt, 15,000; Cliff Hotel, Dovercourt, D, 34 r.) is a busy port which handles a large part of the ferry traffic to and from the Continent. The old town, situated at the mouths of the Stour and the Orwell, bears the marks of its long seafaring tradition. Nelson was a frequent visitor to the old Three Cups Inn. The town has many fine Georgian houses, including the red-brick Guildhall (1769). *Dovercourt* is a smart Victorian suburb and seaside resort.

Felixstowe (pop. 20,900; hotels – Orwell Moat House, C, 70 r.; Marlborough, D, 60 r.) is increasing in importance as a ferry terminal, and is also a popular seaside resort, with a beautiful promenade, public gardens and entertainment facilities. The town is built on the cliffs in an almost island-like position between the River Deben and the wide estuary of the Orwell, which must be crossed by ferry, since there is no bridge. On the N side of the Deben is the little resort of *Bawdsey* where the first radar station was set up in 1936.

On *Orford Ness* is the old port of **Orford**, now a sleepy little village (pop. 670) on the Ore, which flows parallel to the coast for more than 12 miles. The castle (1165–76) has a polygonal keep and is surrounded by a moat. The church has a ruined Norman tower and choir. Orford Ness is a nature reserve, the nesting-place of many seabirds.

Aldeburgh (pop. 2900; hotels – Brudenell, C, 47 r.; Wentworth, C, 47 r.) was a considerable port from the 15th to the 17th c. From this period date the *Moot Hall* (1520–40) and a number of picturesque old houses. Aldeburgh is now a popular seaside resort, internationally known for the Festival held here in June, which features the works of Benjamin Britten (1913–76), a former resident of Aldeburgh. The town is also a favourite resort of anglers, as is *Thorpeness*, 2 miles N, which has fishing in a large fresh-water lagoon as well as in the sea.

Southwold (pop. 6500) is a typical old-world English town, situated on a hill amid extensive areas of green. The church, rebuilt in 1430 after a fire, is a fine example of the flint and stone masonry frequently found in Suffolk. The town is becoming increasingly popular as a holiday resort.

Lowestoft (pop. 58,000; hotels – Victoria, C, 55 r.; Windsor, D, 11 r.), the most easterly town in England, is a seaside resort, a fishing port and a centre of the fish-processing industry. It has a very dry climate and an excellent sandy beach. It was formerly noted for the Lowestoft porcelain produced between 1756 and 1803. The fish market and the comings and goings of the fishing boats add life and colour to the town, and the narrow lanes in the old part of the town are also very picturesque. The harbour is connected with *Oulton Broad* and with the River *Waveney*, which offers excellent fishing. Oulton Broad is popular with sailing enthusiasts. N of Lowestoft lies the Pleasurewood Hills American Theme Park (entertainment, technical demonstrations).

Great Yarmouth (pop. 52,000; hotels – Carlton, C, 90 r.; Star, D, 34 r.) is situated on a narrow tongue of land between the

sea and the River Yare, from which the town takes its name. It is a pleasant modern seaside resort, with a 6-mile-long sandy beach, an attractive promenade, three piers and a wide range of entertainments. The Yare is navigable by seagoing vessels right up to the town, and the harbour is a busy scene. Great Yarmouth is also a good centre from which to visit the beautiful *Norfolk Broads*. There are regular race meetings during the summer.

The characteristic feature of the older part of the town, which suffered considerable destruction during the last war, is the "Rows", the very narrow lanes of which there were 120 before the bombing. The narrowest of them all is Kitty Witches Row. The old *Tollhouse* and the 17th c. *Old Merchant's House* are now museums. On *South Quay* are a number of fine old houses; No. 4 contains an attractive Elizabethan museum. At the end of the street is the *Town Hall* (1883). The Maritime Museum for East Anglia in Marine Parade has a fine collection of ship models.

St Nicholas's Church is the second largest parish church in the country, coming after Holy Trinity Church in Hull. It was destroyed during the last war but was later rebuilt. The churchyard is enclosed by parts of the old town walls; nearby are King Henry's Tower and the Blackfriars Tower. Close to the church is the interesting old *Fishermen's Hospital* (1702).

From Great Yarmouth there are many possible trips to interesting places in the surrounding area – for example to Burgh Castle, 3 miles from *Gorleston-on-Sea*, a seaside resort adjoining Great Yarmouth.

Burgh Castle stands above Breydon Water, formed by the junction of the Yare, the Waveney and the Bure. As *Gariannonum* it was one of the Roman forts on the "Saxon shore", with four massive round towers. – N of the little coastal towns of *Caister*, which boasts the remains of a Roman villa, Hemsby, *Winterton* and *Sea Palling*, is **Happisburgh**, a picturesque village with a Perpendicular church. 3 miles NW is *Bacton*, with the ruins of Bromholm Priory (1113).

Mundesley-on-Sea (pop. 1600; Continental Hotel, D, 55 r.) is a select seaside resort, with a beautiful clean beach. Inland from the town are a number of interesting churches, for example at *Knapton, Trunch* and *Paston*.

Cromer (pop. 6200; hotels – Paris, D, 55 r.; Cliftonville, D, 46 r.; Colne House, D, 30 r.) is the best known seaside resort on the North Norfolk coast, with every amenity and facility required for an enjoyable holiday – a long beach, cliffs, a

Bascule bridge, Great Yarmouth

golf-course, a variety of entertainments and, inland, the beautiful *Norfolk Broads*. The cliffs are part of the Cromer Forest Bed rocks and are a happy hunting ground for fossil-collectors at low tide. The parish church (Perpendicular) has a tower 160 ft high. There are interesting excursions to *Blickling Hall* (10 miles SW), a Jacobean manor-house with stucco work (staircase and gallery ceiling) and beautiful gardens, and the church at *Felbrigg* (3 miles SW), with old brasses and monuments.

W of Cromer, still on the long stretch of cliffs which extends for some 30 miles S to Happisburgh, is *Sheringham* (pop. 5500; hotels – Burlington, D, 33 r.; Beaumaris, D, 28 r.; Two Lifeboats, D, 22 r.; youth hostel, 1 Cremer's Drift, 96 b.), with a famous golf-course. The country inland from her is beautifully wooded, with the ruins of *Beeston Priory* on the edge of the woods. W of Sheringham, where the coastline forms a wide arc, is an expanse of flat marshland.

Blakeney Point is a narrow tongue of land covered with grass and sand-dunes which is the nesting-place of countless water birds and a port of call for many migrants. It is now a nature reserve in which wildlife and rare plants are protected. Salthouse Broad, to the E, is also a nature reserve. Permission for bird-watching can be obtained on application to Point House, Morston.

Hunstanton (pop. 4000; hotels – Golden Lion, D, 31 r.; Le Strange Arms and Golf Links, D, 27 r.; Lodge, D, 15 r.), which consists of Old Hunstanton and New Hunstanton, offers a magnificent view of the Wash such as can be had from scarcely anywhere else. This huge shallow bay is the remnant of an even larger one which took in what are now the Fens. Hunstanton is a quiet modern seaside resort with a good sandy beach. The cliffs are of interest to geologists for their variegated colouring. The church in Old Hunstanton (Decorated) contains some fine monuments.

There are no seaside resorts on the Wash, large areas of which are abandoned by the sea at low tide. Measurements show that it is steadily silting up. The next seaside resort of any consequence is **Skegness** (pop. 13,600; hotels – County, D, 46 r.; Links, D, 21 r.), which has attracted holidaymakers since 1785. It has a pier 615 yards long and a wide range of entertainments. S of the town, on *Gibraltar Point*, is a bird reserve with a bird-watching station.

Mablethorpe and **Sutton-on-Sea** (joint pop. 6200) are little seaside towns, with good beaches. Tennyson (1809–92) spent his childhood here, when Sutton was a mere village amid lonely sand-dunes.

Cleethorpes (pop. 35,500; Kingsway Hotel, C, 59 r.) has grown from a small fishing village into a popular seaside resort with a beach of fine sand, a promenade and a swimming pool. The church has a Saxon tower, a Norman nave and an Early English choir. – Immediately adjoining Cleethorpes is **Grimsby** (pop. 92,600; hotels – Crest Motel, C, 132 r.; Humber Royal, C, 52 r.), a world-famous fishing port at the mouth of the Humber. It is also an important industrial town with extensive docks, largely involved in the import of timber. The fish market and fish auctions offer a lively and interesting spectacle. According to the 14th c. "Lay of Havelock the Dane", Grimsby is so called because a fisherman named Grim saved the king's son here.

Edinburgh

South-eastern Scotland. – Region: Lothian.
Population: 446,400.
Telephone dialling code: 031.

Tourist Information Centre,
5 Waverley Bridge;
ⓘ tel. 226 6591.
Edinburgh Airport;
tel. 333 2167.

HOTELS. – *Ladbroke Dragonara*, 69 Belford Road, A, 142 r.; *Caledonian*, Princes Street, B, 262 r.; *Post House*, Corstorphine Road, B, 208 r.; *King James Thistle*, St James Centre, B, 160 r.; *Crest*, Queensferry Road, B, 120 r.; *Carlton*, North Bridge, B, 97 r.; *Royal Scott*, 111 Glasgow Road, C, 250 r.; *George*, George Street, C, 196 r.; *North British*, Princes Street, C, 193 r.; *Mount Royal*, 53 Princes Street, C, 153 r.; *Grosvenor Crest*, 7 Grosvenor Road, C, 159 r.; *Roxburghe*, 38 Charlotte Square, C, 76 r.; *Old Waverley*, 43 Princes Street, C, 66 r.; *Ellersly House*, Ellersly Road, D, 57 r.

YOUTH HOSTELS. – 7 Bruntsfield Crescent, 170 b.; 18 Eglinton Crescent, 233 b.

Three CAMP SITES.

RESTAURANTS. – *Chez Julie*, 110 Reaburn Place; *Cosmo*, 58A North Castle Street; *Denzler's*, 80 Queen Street; *Howtowdie*, 27A Stafford Street; *Lightbody's*, 23 Glasgow Road; *Pompadour*, Princes Street (in Caledonian Hotel); *Prestonfield House*, Priestfield Road.

EVENTS. – *Edinburgh International Festival of Music and Drama* (Aug.–Sept.), with "Festival Fringe" (an extensive programme of events supplementing the main Festival) and Film Festival; *Highland Games* (three weeks in Aug.–Sept.); *Edinburgh Folk Festival* (Mar.–Apr.).

SPORT and RECREATION. – All kinds of water sports, golf, tennis, riding.

Edinburgh, capital and cultural centre of Scotland since the 15th c., is one of the most beautifully situated cities in the world. It has been called the "Athens of the North" by virtue of its rich cultural tradition, and it was also known in the past as "Auld Reekie" from the smoke of its many chimneys: the latter designation at any rate is no longer apt. Edinburgh is really two towns in one – or three, if the vast spread of modern suburbs is included. To the S is the Old Town, a maze of narrow lanes flanking the "Royal Mile" which runs down the long ridge linking the Castle perched on its crag at the top with the Palace of Holyroodhouse at the foot; to the N is the New Town, a masterpiece of 18th c. town planning. In both parts of the city there are numerous museums, galleries and fine old buildings.

HISTORY. – Nothing is known of Edinburgh during the Roman occupation and earlier periods, though there are remains of a Roman fort at Cramond, within the modern city limits. It became a place of some consequence when the Angles from Northumbria moved into Lothian, and its name is thought to be derived from that of King Edwin of Northumbria (617–633). The town was probably retaken by the Scoto-Picts when they advanced S in the mid 10th c. Malcolm Canmore (1057–93) built a castle on the castle rock and his wife (St Margaret) a chapel. By 1329, when Robert the Bruce granted Edinburgh its first charter, together with the port of Leith, there was quite a large settlement on the ridge below the castle. After the loss of Berwick in 1482 Edinburgh – by then an important centre of trade and craft industry – became capital of Scotland, although the Scottish kings still frequently resided elsewhere. After the Union of the Parliaments in 1707 Edinburgh's political importance declined, but it remained a town of considerable consequence, particularly in the intellectual and cultural field. In the last third of the 18th c. the New Town began to draw population away from the cramped conditions of the Old Town, and the Nor' Loch between the two, now drained, was laid out as gardens.

SIGHTS. – The dominant feature of Edinburgh's skyline is the **Castle**, visible from many points in the city and also offering a magnificent viewpoint from which to see the rest of Edinburgh. After crossing the spacious *Esplanade*, the scene of military parades and, in earlier days, of executions, the visitor enters the Castle by a *drawbridge* over the waterless moat. At the entrance are bronze figures of two Scottish national heroes, Robert the Bruce (1274–1329), crowned king in 1306, who won a decisive victory over Edward II of England at Bannockburn in 1314, and William Wallace (*c.* 1270–1305), who led the struggle against Edward I and was captured and executed by him. From here the roadway runs up to the *Portcullis Gate*, under the state prison, better known as *Argyll's Prison* because the Marquess of Argyll was confined there in the 17th c. The highest point on the Castle Rock is known as the *Citadel* or *King's Bastion* (443 ft). From here, in front of a huge 15th c. cannon called *Mons Meg*, there is a magnificent view of the city. Here too is *St Margaret's Chapel*, the oldest building in Edinburgh (1090). Although very small (17 by 11 ft), it is an interesting example of early Norman architecture; it was restored on Queen Victoria's orders in 1853. Nearby are the Fore Well and the Half Moon Battery. Adjoining the tearoom is the modern gun which is fired at one o'clock every day – Edinburgh's famous "One O'Clock Gun".

To the S of St Margaret's Chapel is the old Palace Yard or *Crown Square*, around which are the main historic apartments and the Scottish National War Memorial. The **National War Memorial** (by Sir Robert Lorimer, 1927) is an impressive and moving building with memorials to all the Scottish regiments, and even to the animals who also played their part. In the central shrine is a silver casket containing the roll of honour of the 100,000 Scots who fell in the First World War. Round the other sides of Crown Square are Mary Queen of Scots' bedroom, in which the future James VI of Scotland and I of England was born in 1566, and other historic apartments; the room in which the *regalia of Scotland* are displayed; the *Banqueting Hall*; and the *Scottish United Services Museum*, containing uniforms and war relics of various kinds. On a lower level are casemates, which were used as prisons.

The OLD TOWN huddles closely on either side of the **Royal Mile** (comprising the Lawnmarket, the High Street and Canongate), which runs down the ridge from the Castle to Holyrood Palace. On both sides are tall tenement blocks, historic old

Edinburgh Castle from Princes Street Gardens

buildings, some of them rather dilapidated but mostly now restored or rebuilt. At No. 352 is *Boswell's Court* (17th c.), named after the uncle of Dr Johnson's biographer. *Tolbooth St John's Church* contains a chair which belonged to the great Scottish Reformer John Knox (*c.* 1505–72). *Gladstone's Land* (*c.* 1620) has fine painted ceilings. *Lady Stair's House* (1622), in Lady Stair's Close, contains a museum with mementoes of Burns and other Scottish writers. Other interesting old houses are to be seen in *Riddle's Court* and *Brodie's Close*. Beside St Giles' Cathedral studs in the roadway mark the site of the Old Tolbooth, the town prison which features in Scott's "Heart of Midlothian"; a heart formed of cobblestones marks the position of the entrance.

***St Giles' Cathedral** Edinburgh's principal church (though not in fact a cathedral), was probably begun in 1387, after the destruction of an earlier church during a raid by Richard II of England. Of this earlier church there survive only a *doorway* and part of the *choir*. The *central tower* (161 ft), completed in 1495, is topped by a crown spire which can be seen from all over the city. During the 16th c. the church was divided into two, and parts of it were used for other purposes. The *Thistle Chapel* is a fine example of modern Gothic. W of the chapel is the

Preston Aisle, with the royal pew. In the S aisle is the pre-Reformation *Vesper Bell*. The church contains numerous monuments commemorating eminent Scots. The four octagonal *piers* supporting the tower are believed to date from the Norman church of 1120. – Although St Giles is usually referred to as a cathedral, it was actually a cathedral only for a short period in the 17th c. – Behind the church is Parliament Square, on the site of the old churchyard in which John Knox was buried in 1572. The lead *equestrian statue of Charles II* (1685) in the square is probably the oldest of the kind in Britain.

Parliament Hall, in which the Scottish Parliament met from 1639 until the Union in 1707, was built in 1632–40 but considerably altered in 1808. The *Hall*, 122 ft long, has a fine hammerbeam roof. The buildings are now occupied by the High Court of Justiciary and the Court of Session, the principal criminal and civil courts of Scotland. Adjoining is the *Signet Library*.

E of St Giles is the *Mercat Cross*, from which the accession of a new monarch is still proclaimed by a herald. On the other side of the High Street are the City Chambers, the headquarters of municipal administration, with a cenotaph commemorating the dead of the two world wars.

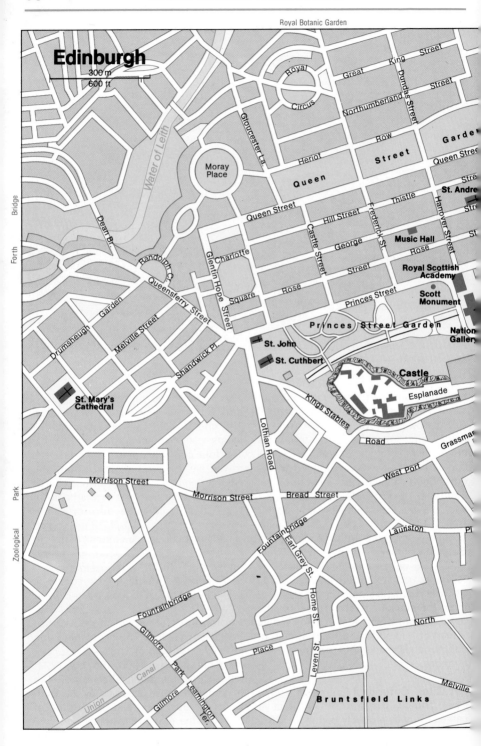

Royal Botanic Garden

Edinburgh

300 m
600 ft

Water of Leith

Bridge

Forth

Gloucester La.

Moray
Place

Royal
Circus

Great

King   Street

Street

Dundas Street

Northumberland Street

Row

Garde

Street

Queen Stree

Heriot

Street

Dean Br.

Queen

Randolph C.

Queensferry Street

Queen Street

Castle   Street

Hill Street

George

Street

Frederick St.

Thistle

St. Andre

Str

Music Hall

Hanover Street

St

Rose

Royal Scottish
Academy

Stre

St. Andre

Glentin Hope Street

Charlotte

Square

Rose

Princes Street

Scott
Monument

Melville Street

Shandwick Pl.

Drumsheugh

Garden

St. Mary's
Cathedral

St. John

St. Cuthbert

Princes Street Garden

Nation
Gallery

Castle

Esplanade

Kings Stables

Park

Zoological

Lothian Road

Kings Stables   Road

West Port

Grassman

Morrison Street

Morrison Street

Bread Street

Laurstion

Pl

Fountainbridge

Earl Grey St.

Home St.

North

Fountainbridge

Gilmore

Park

Leamington Ter.

Place

Leven St.

Melville

Gilmore

Canal

Union

Bruntsfield Links

By the 17th c. *Tron Church* (closed) the High Street cuts across the South Bridge. Along this to the S, at the foot of Chambers Street, is the Old Quad of the *University*, founded in 1583, a traditional Scottish university. The Old Quad, built in the late 18th and early 19th c., is now mainly used for administrative purposes; the newer parts of the University are mostly around *George Square*, a short distance SW, and at King's Buildings on the southern outskirts of the city. In Guthrie Street, on the opposite side of Chambers Street, is a tablet marking the position of the house in which Walter Scott was born in 1771. Higher up Chambers Street is the **Royal Scottish Museum**, with a particularly fine exhibi-

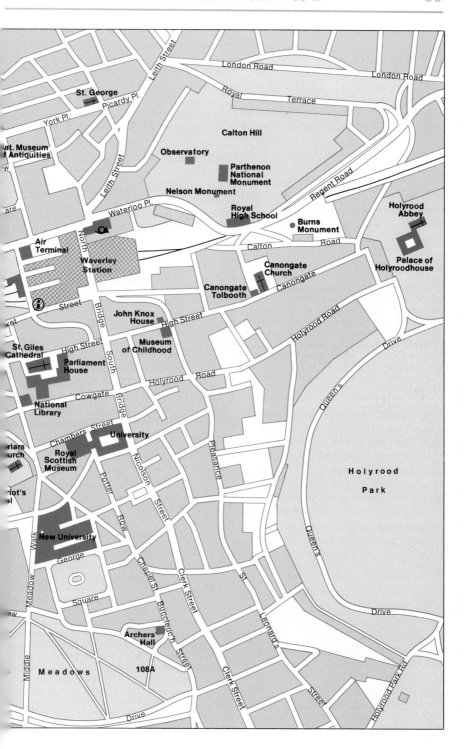

on of primitive art. At the top of Chambers Street is *Greyfriars Church* (1620) with a churchyard containing the graves of many noted Scots, which also played a part in Scottish history. Adjoining is *George Heriot's School*, founded in 1563.

The lowest section of the Royal Mile is CANONGATE, formerly the most aristo-

cratic part of the town but now somewhat less so, though recently much improved by restoration. In St John's Street is the *Canongate Kilwinning Lodge of Freemasons*, of which Burns was a member. Lower down, on the left, are *Canongate Tolbooth* (1591; formerly the City Hall and now a museum), with a turreted steeple and a projecting clock, and

Canongate Church (1688), with the graves of many distinguished Scots. Opposite is Huntly House (1570), containing the City Museum (local history).

At the foot of the Royal Mile is *Holyrood Palace (officially the Palace of Holyroodhouse), a royal residence which was originally an abbey. The building of the palace was begun by James IV. Most of it was burned down in 1544, and after being rebuilt it was again devastated by fire in 1630. The present building was mostly erected between 1670 and 1679; the architect was Sir William Bruce of Kinross.

The oldest part of the palace contains Queen Mary's Apartments. Visitors are also taken through a series of state apartments containing valuable furniture, tapestries and pictures. The Picture Gallery contains a mass-produced series of portraits of Scottish kings, both real and mythical, painted by a 17th c. Dutch artist. – The Chapel Royal adjoining the palace, in which many Scottish monarchs were married, is now a ruin, the only relic of the original abbey. The roof of the chapel collapsed in the 18th c., and the E end was rebuilt from the ruins, revealing a number of old gravestones.

In the gardens behind the palace is a curious 17th c. sundial. To the W, at the foot of Abbeyhill, is a little building with a pyramidal roof known as Queen Mary's Bath, in which tradition has it that Mary bathed in wine to preserve her beauty. Beyond the palace is Holyrood Park, in which is Arthur's Seat, an extinct volcano with two main craters, from which there are magnificent views of the city. Below the hill are the precipitous Salisbury Crags.

The best known street in the New Town is Princes Street, with shops, hotels and restaurants on the N side and the beautiful Princes Street Gardens below it to the S. At the E end is the beautifully proportioned Palladian façade of the Register House (by Robert and James Adam, 1774). A short distance W, in the gardens, is the Scott Monument, a 200-ft-high Gothic spire completed in 1844. Farther W again are the two classical buildings occupied by the Royal Scottish Academy and the *National Gallery. The National Gallery has a very fine collection, including works by Rubens and Rembrandt, many French Impressionists, and pictures by Scottish artists (fine portraits by Raeburn).

Little is left of the original 18th c. houses of Princes Street, but to the N are many streets (George Street, Queen Street), squares (particularly Charlotte Square, at the W end of George Street, and Moray Place, below it to the N) and crescents of fine Georgian houses.

At the W end of Princes Street is St John's Episcopal Church (1817), in part an imitation of Westminster Abbey. Below it is St Cuthbert's Church (the West Kirk), the seventh of a series of churches on this site dating back to the 8th c. Nearby, in Princes Street Gardens, are an ornate fountain, originally made for the Paris Exhibition of 1867, and the remains of the 14th c. Wellhouse Tower below the Castle.

Excellent views of the city can be had from Calton Hill, at the E end of Princes Street. At the foot of the hill are the classical buildings of the old Royal High School, originally founded in the 13th c., at which Walter Scott was a pupil. Opposite the school are the modern government buildings of St Andrew's House and a monument to Burns (1832). On the hill itself are the National Monument (1822), an unfinished imitation of the Parthenon, the telescope-shaped Nelson Monument, the former City Observatory (1776) and its successor of 1818.

On the N side of the city is the *Royal Botanic Garden, with an extensive arboretum, a celebrated rock garden and numerous glasshouses. In the grounds are the Scottish National Gallery of Modern Art. – On the southern outskirts of the city is Craigmillar Castle (14th c.), a favourite resort of Mary Queen of Scots.

SURROUNDINGS. – About 5 miles S of Edinburgh lies Roslin with a chapel notable for its sculpture. Another attractive excursion is to Haddington and the Lammermuir Hills. Much of the old counties of Midlothian and West Lothian is industrialised, but East Lothian is still almost entirely agricultural, with fertile red soil and red sandstone houses. Haddington can be reached from Edinburgh by the direct route on A 1, but a more attractive route is the longer one by the little coast towns on the Firth of Forth – Prestonpans, with a fine Mercat Cross, and Aberlady (pop. 1200), with a sandy beach and the Aberlady Bay nature reserve (many sea-birds). From here it is 6 miles S to Haddington, but it is possible to continue along the coast by way of Gullane, with a famous golf-course, the pretty little village of Dirleton, with remains of a large 13th c. castle, and North Berwick (pop. 5200; hotels – Marine, C, 85 r.; Point Garry, D, 15 r.; Blenheim House, D, 12 r.), a trim seaside resort with two popular golf-courses. From here there are boat trips to the little offshore islands, in particular the Bass Rock (350 ft high), the nesting-place of countless sea-birds (including gannets). 3 miles E of the town is

The Forth Railway Bridge

the magnificently situated *Tantallon Castle* (1374), with ramparts and a moat, corner towers and a central gatehouse.

From Tantallon the road continues S, running inland, to *Whitekirk*, with a 15th c. church (rebuilt after severe destruction), and **East Linton** (pop. 1400), a picturesque little town on the Tyne, which here flows through a small gorge and is crossed by a 16th c. bridge. 2 miles SW is *Hailes Castle* (13th c.), with a massive keep. Behind it is *Traprain Law*, where a hoard of Roman silver coins (4th c.) was found in 1919.

Haddington (pop. 6500; hotel – Browns, D, 9 r.), formerly county town of East Lothian, is attractively situated on the Tyne, here spanned by two fine 16th c. bridges. It is a town of fine old houses, well preserved and well cared for. The 14th c. parish church, known as the "Lamp of Lothian", still has the original central tower, nave and W front. There are three notable 17th c. mansions – Haddington House, Bothwell Castle and Moat House.

To the S of Haddington are the *Lammermuir Hills*, rounded hills of no great height, with some good trout streams. The little town of **Gifford** is a good base from which to explore the hills. Near the village are the remains of *Yester Castle*, which features in Scott's "Marmion". In the hills is *Nunraw Castle* (17th c.), which plays a part in his novel "The Bride of Lammermoor"; it is now incorporated in a Cistercian abbey.

Another interesting trip is a circuit of the Firth of Forth, returning by way of the fine modern road bridge. The first place of interest on the route is *Dalmeny*, with one of the finest Norman churches in Scotland (second half of 12th c.); it has fine woodwork. To the N, on the shores of the Firth of Forth, is *Barnbougle Castle* (restored).

South Queensferry (pop. 5000; hotel – Forth Bridges Moat House, C, 108 r.) lies in the shadow of the two great bridges over the Forth, the famous *Forth Railway Bridge*, 2765 yards long, a masterpiece of 19th c. engineering, and the *Forth Road Bridge*, one of the longest suspension bridges in

Europe, opened in 1964. Between the two bridges is the Hawes Inn, which features in Stevenson's "Kidnapped". St Mary's Church (founded 1330), the only Carmelite church in Britain which is still in use, has a 16th c. tower. 3 miles E is *Hopetoun House*, a magnificent Adam mansion (originally built 1699, rebuilt by the Adams 1721–54), with fine paintings and furniture and a museum. 6½ miles farther on is the old town of *Linlithgow* (pop. 9520), which has two important and historic buildings. The first is the famous *Linlithgow Palace*, picturesquely situated on a small loch, in which Mary Queen of Scots was born in 1542. The Palace dates from the 15th c. In the courtyard is a fountain erected by James V, a copy of which stands in the forecourt of Holyrood Palace in Edinburgh. The Great Hall or "Lyon Chalmer", 100 ft long, has a magnificent fireplace with three compartments, reputedly the finest in Scotland. Another interesting room is "Queen Margaret's Bower", at the top of the NW tower. – Adjoining the Palace is the parish church, *St Michael's*, one of Scotland's finest churches, begun in the 15th c. and completed in the mid 16th. The nave and choir are particularly fine; notable also is the tracery of the windows in St Catherine's Aisle. There are a number of well-preserved 16th c. houses in the town.

From Linlithgow the route continues to *Falkirk* (pop. 36,900; hotel – Stakis Park, C, 55 r.), a town with much heavy industry, close to the end of the Antonine Wall (see p. 44). The Forth is crossed by the

The Forth Road Bridge

Kincardine Bridge, and the return route eastward is on A 985 before following the side road to Culross.

Culross is the very picture of an old Scottish burgh, much of it in the ownership of the National Trust for Scotland and accordingly well restored and maintained. It has many 17th c. houses with outside staircases, a Mercat Cross, a Town House of 1626 and a fine mansion known as the Palace (1597–1611), with painted walls and terraced gardens. The present church consists of the choir and central tower of an abbey church founded in 1217.

The coastal road from Culross to the Forth Road Bridge is very attractive. The bridge offers the quickest way back to Edinburgh, but if time permits it is well worth continuing along the N shore of the Firth of Forth to see the historic town of *St Andrews*, a favourite seaside resort with an ancient university and many fine old buildings, but even more widely known, perhaps, as the home of golf. The route continues via *Inverkeithing*, with an old Mercat Cross, a number of fine old houses and the 14th c. Greyfriars Hospice, and *Burntisland* to Kirkcaldy.

Kirkcaldy (pop. 51,200) is an industrial town and coal-shipping port, which apart from the group of 17th c. houses known as Sailors' Walk near the harbour has no particular features of interest. It was the birthplace of the architect Robert Adam (1728–92), who along with his brother created the neo-classical style associated with their name, and of Adam Smith (1723–90), founder of the classical school of political economy.

The road continues round a wide sweep of bay (for those in a hurry there is a shorter but less interesting inland road) to the little town of *Dysart*, with a large 16th c. tower, and East and West *Wemyss*, pleasant little seaside resorts with good bathing, splendid views and the scanty remains of Wemyss Castle. *Coaltown*, *Buckhaven* and the trim seaside resort of *Leven* offer nothing to detain the tourist. *Elie* (pop. with Earlsferry, 820) is an attractive little place, with its picturesque harbour, its gabled houses and its pleasant beach. It is a popular holiday resort. Then come two other pretty little fishing villages which are also holiday resorts – *St Monance*, with a fine 17th c. church, now the home of a number of painters, and *Pittenweem*, which has a church with a medieval tower (1592) and a group of picturesque houses round the harbour. Offshore is the *Isle of May*, a nature reserve. The next town, *Anstruther* (pop. 3100; Craws Nest Hotel, C, 31 r.), is an important fishing port with a Fisheries Museum. The manse, the oldest manse in Scotland still occupied, bears the date 1590. *Crail* (pop. 11,200), a very popular holiday resort, has remains of an old castle and a 13th c. monastic school (restored).

****St Andrews** (pop. 13,500; hotels – Old Course, A, 128 r.; Rusacks Marine, C, 50 r.; St Andrew's Golf Hotel, C, 25 r.; Argley House, E, 18 r.) is known to golfers as the home of the Royal and Ancient Club, guardian of the rules of golf, whose Old Course takes a leading place, if not *the* leading place, among the world's golf-courses. It is an attractive town situated on higher ground above long sandy beaches, and has many churches and other monuments to bear witness to the important part it has played in Scottish Church history. It was once the seat of an archbishop, and its cathedral, founded in 1160, was the largest in Scotland, though today nothing is left but a gatehouse and parts of the gables and walls. Close by is the little 12th c. church of *St Rule*, with a square tower and an unusually narrow choir. On the Kirk Hill are remains of

another church, St Mary on the Rock. The *Blackfriars Chapel* is a relic of a Dominican abbey founded in the 16th c.

St Andrews is notable not only for its churches but for its University, the oldest in Scotland, founded in 1411 (about 3600 students; Department of Arabic Studies). St Mary's College was founded in 1538, St Leonard's in 1512; both are housed in handsome old buildings. The University Chapel, formerly St Salvator's Church, contains John Knox's pulpit, removed from the town church where he preached his first sermons. In the quadrangle of St Mary's College a thorn-tree said to have been planted by Mary Queen of Scots still flowers. – The Martyrs' Monument commemorates four Reformers who were burnt at the stake in St Andrews in the 16th c.

St Andrews Castle

The remains of *St Andrews Castle* stand on a crag above the sea. Notable features are the "Bottle Dungeon" and the Subterranean Passage (a 16th c. mine dug during a siege of the castle). – 2 miles SE are the remarkable basalt crags known as the Rock and Spindle.

The return to Edinburgh is by way of A 91 and then M 90, with a short stop at **Kinross**, close to Loch Leven, famous for its pink trout. On one of the two islands in the loch is a castle in which Mary Queen of Scots was imprisoned for almost a year before making her escape with the help of William Douglas. On the other island are the remains of St Serf's Priory. – From Kinross it is a straight run back to Edinburgh by way of the road bridge.

Eton

Southern England. – County: Berkshire.
Population: 4500.
Telephone dialling code: 07535.
ⓘ **Tourist Information Centre,**
Civic Centre, Reading, Berkshire;
    tel. 0734–55911.
Thames and Chilterns Tourist Board,
8 Market Place, Abingdon, Oxfordshire;
    tel. 0235–22711.

HOTELS. (See also Windsor entry on page 278) – *Crest*, Manor Lane, Maidenhead, C, 190 r.; *Frederick's*, Shoppenhangers Road, Maidenhead, C, 30 r.; *Bear*, High Street, Maidenhead, C, 12 r.; *Christopher*, 110 High Street, D, 16 r.; *Kingswood*, Boyn Hill Avenue, Maidenhead, D, 10 r.

RESTAURANT. – *House on the Bridge*, 71 High Street.

EVENTS. – *Fourth of June* celebrations; *Wall Game* on St Andrew's Day (30 November).

SPORT and RECREATION. – Rowing, sailing, swimming.

**Eton College, the most famous of the great English public schools, has a long tradition behind it, having been founded by Henry VI in 1440. The school has produced 20 British prime ministers and countless other prominent and influential people.

The life of the little town of Eton, attractively situated on the Thames, revolves round the school, with which almost all the inhabitants are involved either directly or indirectly. There are some 1200 pupils, living in the masters' houses, of whom 70 are "collegers" with scholarships and the remainder are "oppidans". The boys still wear the traditional dormal dress.

SIGHTS. – The old red-brick buildings date from the time of the school's foundation, but most of the school buildings (on the opposite side of the road) are modern. The oldest classroom is *Lower School*. The walls of *Upper School* are covered with the names of former pupils cut in the panelling. The **Chapel**, founded by Henry VI, is merely the choir of the church, almost twice the size of that which was originally planned. It contains old brasses and splendid late 15th c. ***wall paintings** (scenes from the life of the Virgin), which were painted over the second half of the 16th c., rediscovered in the 19th c. and restored from 1928 onwards. In School Yard stands a *bronze statue of Henry VI* by Francis Bird (1719). A passage under *Lupton's Tower* (1520) gives access to the Cloisters, in which are the *Dining Hall* (1450) and *Library* (1729).

Exeter

Southern England. – County: Devon.
Altitude: 165 ft. – Population: 98,900.
Telephone dialling code: 0392.
(i) **Civic Centre**,
   Dix's Field;
   tel. 72434

HOTELS. – *Rougemont*, Queen Street, C, 63 r.; *Ladbroke, Kennford Services*, Kennford, C, 61 r.; *Royal Clarence*, Cathedral Yard, C, 60 r.; *Buckerell Lodge*, Topsham Road, C, 54 r.; *Exeter Moat House*, Topsham Road, C, 44 r.; *Imperial*, New North Road, D, 28 r.; *Bystock*, 6–8 Bystock Terrace, D, 24 r.; *St Andrews*, 28 Alphington Road, D, 16 r.; *Edgerton Park*, Pennsylvania Road, E, 17 r.; *Park View*, 8 Howell Road, E, 15 r.; *Red House*, 2 Whipton Village Road, E, 13 r.

YOUTH HOSTEL. – 47 Countess Road, 90 b.

RESTAURANTS. – *Gipsy Hill*, Blackhorse Lane, Pinhoe; *Great Western*, St David's Station Approach; *Imperial*, New North Road; *White Hart*, 66 South Street; *St Andrews*, 28 Alphington Road; *Ship Inn*, St Martin's Lane.

SPORT and RECREATION. – Water sports of all kinds, golf, tennis.

Exeter, county town of Devon and a university and cathedral city, has preserved its charm in spite of its growth in size and importance. The predominant colours of Exeter are red and green – the red of its buildings, in brick or the reddish local sandstone, and the green of its many parks and gardens and the fertile plain country which surrounds it. Devon is one of England's richest areas of pastureland, famous for its thick cream and its cream cheese.

Exeter is a good base from which to explore the West Country. The town itself has many old Tudor and Jacobean houses and Georgian crescents, and the Guildhall

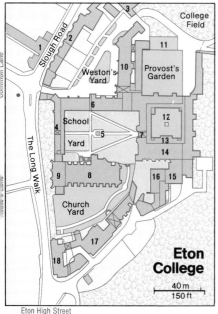

Eton High Street

1 New Schools (1861)
2 Saville House (18th c.)
3 Westons
4 Upper School (1694)
5 Statue of Henry VI
6 College (1443) and Lower School
7 Lupton's Tower (1520)
8 College Chapel (1448–82)
9 Ante Chapel (1479–82)
10 New Buildings (1844)
11 King of Siam's Garden
12 Cloisters
13 Library (1729)
14 College Hall (1450)
15 Kitchen (1507)
16 Brewhouse Gallery (1714)
17 Baldwin's Bec
18 Corner House

is believed to be the oldest municipal building in the country. Although Exeter suffered severe destruction in 1942, most of the old town walls have been preserved.

HISTORY. – Exeter is the only town in England which has been continuously populated since pre-Roman times; it was the only town to fall into the hands of the Saxons after their conversion to Christianity. The British town of *Caerwisc* became the Roman *Isca Dumnoniorum*, a cantonal capital. The present name comes from the Saxon *Exanceaster*, the Roman camp on the River Exe. The town was granted its motto of "Semper Fidelis" by Elizabeth I. It has been the see of a bishop since 1050. At the beginning of the 18th c. Exeter was the fourth largest seaport in the country.

SIGHTS. – Exeter's most notable building is the *Cathedral (St Mary and St Peter), which was begun in 1257 and is almost entirely in Decorated style, with only its two massive *towers* surviving from the earlier Norman church. Of particular interest is the *W front*, with 88 figures of kings and apostles, angels and prophets arranged in three rows.

The INTERIOR is remarkable for its symmetry and uniformity. Notable features are the *fan vaulting* and the pillars of Purbeck marble. There is no crossing tower, and the long stretch of continuous vaulting over the nave and chancel is extremely impressive. The *Minstrels' Gallery*, built by Bishop Grandison (1327–69), has figures of angels playing musical instruments; much of the original colouring has been preserved. Other particularly fine features are the *misericords*, some 50 in number, dating from 1230–70, and the old *bishop's throne*, 50 ft high.

Exeter Cathedral

The *tracery* of the windows is particularly intricate in the Perpendicular W window and the rose in the E window, which contains some 14th c. glass. The *Lady Chapel*, with a 15th c. Assumption, contains the tombs of Bishop Bronescombe and Bishop Peter of Quivil (1280–91), who renovated the towers. The *Chapterhouse* has a fine ceiling of 1465–78. Among the treasures in the Library are the 10th c. Exeter

Codex, with poems by Cynewulf and other Anglo-Saxon writers, and a copy of the Bible printed by John Eliot in the 17th c. in Massachusetts for the use of the Indians. In the former library are the *archives* of the Cathedral, going back to the 10th c.

In the *Cathedral close* are a number of old houses, including *Mol's Coffee House* (16th c.), now occupied by an art dealer. A few steps away is the Ship Inn, an ancient tavern which is referred to with approval by Sir Francis Drake. In front of the Cathedral is a *statue* of the Anglican theologian Richard Hooker (*c.* 1554–1600), who was born in a suburb of Exeter. – The *Guildhall*, originally 12th c., was rebuilt in 1330 and again in 1466; the façade was added in 1592.

In Waterbeer Street can be seen *Roman mosaics* brought to light by wartime bombing. Of the Norman stronghold of **Rougemont Castle** there remain only the moat, Athelstan's Tower (mentioned in Shakespeare's "Richard III") and the gatehouse. *Rougemont Gardens* and the adjoining *Northernhay Gardens* are attractive parks. The *Royal Albert Memorial Museum and Art Gallery* in Queen Street has a collection which includes clothing of the past, pottery, some good watercolours and fine products by local craftsmen.

From the bridge over the Exe, by following New Bridge Street and Fore Street, one reaches *Tucker's Hall* (1471) which has fine oak panelling and a fireplace of 1638; a short distance NW is *St Nicholas Priory*, founded in 1080 (fine rooms). E of the bridge are the *Custom House* (1681) and the *Maritime Museum*.

In many streets – for example in Southernhay, Barnfield Crescent, Colleton Crescent, Cowick Street, St David's Hill and Pennsylvania – there are attractive old houses in Georgian, Regency and early Victorian style.

SURROUNDINGS. – 7 miles NE are *Killerton Gardens*, which are particularly attractive in spring and summer. – 8 miles SE is **Powderham Castle**, home of the Courtenay family, with a beautiful deer park. The house, originally built in 1390 and later modernised, has beautiful staircases and plaster decoration. In the nearby village of *Kenton* is a Perpendicular church (*c.* 1360–70) in the style typical of Devon.

The Fens

Eastern England. – Counties: Cambridgeshire, Lincolnshire and Norfolk.

The Fens are an area of some 1400 sq. miles round the Wash, a dead flat expanse of alluvial land watered by the rivers Ouse, Nene, Welland and Witham. In the time of Hadrian there were large Roman settlements here, engaged in growing corn and winning salt, and the process of draining the fenland was begun by the Romans. Large-scale drainage works were carried out between 1622 and 1656 by a Dutch engineer, Sir Cornelius Vermuyden, thus reclaiming large areas of land for agriculture; in consequence the Fens are now a fertile wheat-growing region.

In addition to this drained land there are large areas of marshland reclaimed from the sea, mostly used for the grazing of stock. These areas mainly lie between the Lincoln Wolds and the sea. The whole of the Fen district is crisscrossed by a network of waterways. The water was formerly pumped by windmills, as in Holland, and a few windmills can still be seen, for example at Waltham, Heckington, Alford and Burgh-le-Marsh. Later came steam-driven pumps, and these in turn have now been superseded by electric power.

To nature-lovers this tranquil green landscape stretching endlessly away to the horizon offers great attractions, with its rare birds, dragonflies and insects, its many wild flowers, its grazing cattle and sheep, its wide fields and handsome farmhouses. Also of great interest are the still undrained areas, many of which have been left in their original state and are now nature reserves, like *Holme Fen* and *Woodwalton Fen* (with rare butterflies found nowhere else in England). Special permission is required to enter these areas. In the *Wicken Fen* nature reserve S of Ely an area of marshland has been preserved, with the oldest form of drainage using wind-power. At *Stretham* an old steam pump can be seen.

One of the best bases from which to explore the Fens is the charming cathedral city of **Ely** (pop. 10,300; Lamb Hotel, D, 32 r.; youth hostel, Bedford House, City of Ely College, 28 St Mary's Street, 35 b.), in Cambridgeshire. It has been called the "little town with the large cathedral", for the ****Cathedral** is the third largest in England. Rising out of the flat fenland, it looks even larger – a landmark visible from far and wide.

The Octagon, Ely Cathedral

Before the drainage of the Fens, Ely was an island in the midst of the marshland. In the 7th c. St Etheldreda, queen of Northumbria, founded an abbey here, later occupied by the Benedictines. The present building was begun by Simeon, the first Norman abbot, in 1083, and by 1109, when the bishopric of Ely was founded, the eastern part was complete. The western half was completed in 1180–90. In 1322 the Norman crossing tower collapsed. Unlike other churches where this happened – as it did not infrequently – the Cathedral was not given a new spire but a unique stone octagon surmounted by an octagonal timber lantern. The new structure, completed in 1342, is of remarkable harmony and beauty.

On entering the Cathedral through the beautiful W doorway the visitor's first impression is of the astonishing lightness of the 248 ft long *nave*, typically Norman in style though it is. This is due to the elaborate articulation of the twelve bays, and also perhaps to the painted ceiling, a 19th c. addition. The **Octagon*, the only structure of its kind in England, is as impressive from inside as from the exterior. The Norman SW transept serves as the *baptistery*. *St Edmund's Chapel* contains a wall painting of about 1200 and a beautiful 15th c. *screen*, both restored.

The *choir* has three elegant Decorated bays at the W end. The 59 misericords of the *choir-stalls* (1342) have mostly been renewed. The *Lady Chapel*, an admirable example of the Decorated style, contains sculptured scenes from the life of the Virgin, with hundreds of now headless statuettes. In the north cloister is a *museum of stained glass*. The surviving *conventual buildings* are occupied by the King's School, among them the beautiful *Prior Crauden's Chapel*, the *Queen's Hall* and a number of others. – The vicarage of *St Mary's Church* was occupied by Oliver Cromwell and his family from 1636 to 1647. From Stuntney (1 mile SE), where Cromwell had a farm, there is the finest view of the Cathedral.

Two other places of interest in the Fens are Spalding and Crowland.

Spalding (pop. 18,200; White Hart Hotel, Market Place, C, 28 r.) lies in the centre of a bulb-growing area. In spring the fields are full of daffodils and tulips in bloom, attracting crowds of visitors in

April and May. The trim little town with its brick-built houses is reminiscent of Holland. Ayscoughfee Hall, built in 1429 but much altered since then, has a good ornithological collection.

Crowland (pop. 2900), 10 miles S, is famous for the Benedictine abbey which King Ethelbald of Mercia built over the grave of a hermit in the 8th c. Of the church there survive the beautiful 12th c. W front (begun 1170 in Early English style and completed in the early Perpendicular period), with old statues; a Norman arch from the crossing; the bell-tower (1427), from which there are extensive views; and the N aisle, now used as the parish church.

Crowland's *Trinity Bridge* dates from the time when the waterways were the main traffic routes of the Fens. It was built in the mid 14th c. over the junction of two canals, but these have since been diverted and the bridge is now stranded on dry land in the centre of the town. On it is an effigy of Christ.

Another interesting town is **Boston** (pop. 22,500; hotel – New England, D, 25 r.), which gave its name (originally "Botolph's Town") to Boston in Massachusetts. Lying 6 miles from the Witham, it was at one time England's second largest seaport. It is the administrative centre of the Fen district known as South Holland.

*St Boptolph's Church is one of the largest parish churches in the country and one of the best known, at any rate for its tower, "Boston Stump" (view from top), a landmark visible from miles around. It has a carillon of 36 bells. There are 64 choir-stalls with fine misericords.

Other buildings of interest are the *Guildhall* (15th c., altered) and *Fydell House*.

Boston has maintained its contacts with the United States, and the SW chapel of St Botolph's was restored in the 19th c. by the people of Boston, Mass., in memory of John Cotton, who was vicar here before emigrating to America.

Glasgow

Central Scotland. – Region: Strathclyde.
Population: 763,200.
Telephone dialling code: 041.
(i) **Information Bureau,**
George Square;
tel. 221 7371, 221 6136.

HOTELS. – *Holiday Inn,* Argyle Street, Anderston, A, 296 r.; *Albany,* Bothwell Street, B, 251 r.; *Stakis Grosvenor,* Grosvenor Terrace, Great Western Road, B, 93 r.; *White House,* 12 Cleveland Crescent, B, 35 r.; *Stakis Pond,* Great Western Road, C, 137 r.; *Stakis Ingram,* 201 Ingram Street, C, 90 r.; *Central,* Gordon Street, D, 213 r.; *North British,* George Square, D, 125 r.; *Bellahouston,* 517 Paisley Road West, D, 122 r. – AT THE AIRPORT: (7 miles W in Abbotsinch) *Excelsior,* B, 316 r.

YOUTH HOSTEL. – 11 Woodlands Terrace, 120 b.

RESTAURANTS. – *Ambassador,* 19 Blythswood Square; *Colonial,* 25 High Street; *Malmaison,* Gordon Street; *Kensingtons,* 164 Darnley Street; *Poacher's,* Ruthven Lane.

SPORT and RECREATION. – Sailing, fishing, golf, tennis, riding.

Glasgow, situated in the Scottish Lowlands, on both banks of the River Clyde and some 18 miles from its estuary, is Scotland's largest town and its industrial and commercial metropolis with large shipyards. It is also an excellent base from which to tour the West of Scotland. Apart from a few buildings, especially the Cathedral, the aspect of the city bears the stamp of the last 200 years. A decisive factor in its earlier development was the dredging of a channel in the Clyde to enable the largest vessels to sail up the river; 200 years ago it was possible to cross the river on foot at low tide. Within the city boundaries 11 bridges and a tunnel link the two sides of the Clyde.

HISTORY. – Glasgow lacks the long historical tradition of Edinburgh and other Scottish towns, and no traces of early settlement have been found within the city. The town became the seat of a bishop in 561, and the beginnings of the Cathedral date back to the 12th c. Wealthy citizens built churches, hospitals and other buildings, but little of all this has survived. The character of the present-day city is entirely Victorian. The University was founded in 1451.

Glasgow Cathedral

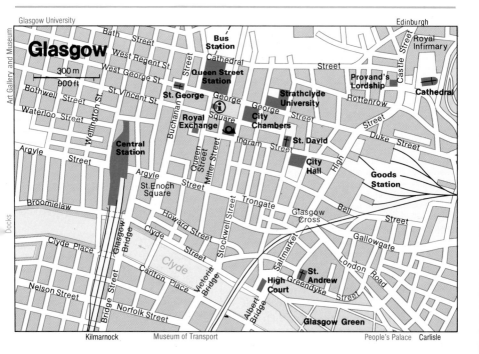

SIGHTS. – Among the old buildings of Glasgow pride of place is taken by the *Cathedral in Castle Street, Scotland's finest Gothic building. The *crypt* dates from the 12th c., the *choir* and *nave* from the early 13th c., the *Lady Chapel* and *tower* from the 15th. Both externally and internally, however, the Cathedral, with its clear lines and absence of superfluous decoration, has the appearance of a single whole. The finest part of the building is the *Crypt* or *Lower Church*, with the tomb of St Mungo, who is believed to have founded the church in the mid 6th c., and St Mungo's Well. Other notable features are the *fan vaulting* and a fine *rood-screen* depicting the seven deadly sins. The glass is mainly modern.

Behind the Cathedral, reached by the "Bridge of Sighs" over the little Molendinar stream, is *Glasgow Necropolis*, in which wealthy Victorian merchants were buried. It contains a monument to John Knox and many handsome tombs. Opposite the Cathedral, on the W side of Castle Street, is Glasgow's oldest house, *Provand's Lordship*, built in 1471 for the priest of a nearby hospital; it now houses a *museum* (old furniture and domestic equipment).

In the centre of the city is **George Square**, with 12 *statues* of famous people, including Queen Victoria, Sir Walter Scott (the first monument erected in his honour), Robert Burns and Sir Robert Peel (1788–1850), Prime Minister and Rector of the University. Around the square are the *Merchants' House* (1877), home of the oldest Chamber of Commerce in Britain (founded 1605), the *Bank of Scotland*, the *Head Post Office* and the *City Chambers* – all late 19th c. buildings – and the *Cenotaph* (1924). In the vicinity of the square are some of Glasgow's most popular shopping streets, including the Buchanan Street pedestrian precinct.

Every visitor to Glasgow should see the *Art Gallery and Museum in *Kelvingrove Park*, which has one of the finest collections in Britain of pictures by both British and foreign masters. The French Impressionists are strongly represented, as are the leading Scottish artists. There is also a good collection in *Pollok House* (pictures by El Greco, Goya and Murillo, silver, porcelain, furniture); the house (by William Adam, 1752) stands in a beautiful park. In *Haggs Castle* is a museum for children, while the *Museum of Transport* in Albert Drive displays famous locomotives and other means of transport since the beginnings of motorisation. Glasgow's oldest museum is the *Hunterian Museum* (archaeology, geology) at the University. – Here a new building houses the fabulous *Burrell Collection* presented to the city by Sir William Burrell in 1944.

Glasgow is also an important university city, with two universities – the old-established *Glasgow University* and the

The Old Bridge and Wallace Monument, Stirling

recently founded *Strathclyde University* (previously a college of technology). It has over 20,000 students – more than any other city in Britain in proportion to population. The main part of Glasgow University is in Kelvingrove Park; Strathclyde University is in George Street, in the city centre.

Glasgow is well supplied with *parks and open spaces*, among the finest of which are the *Zoo*, the *Botanic Gardens* and the *Victoria Park*. It offers a wide range of entertainments, including the *Glasgow Citizens' Theatre* (founded by James Bridie in 1942), the *Scottish Opera* and the *Scottish Theatre Ballet*, all of which enjoy high reputations.

SURROUNDINGS. – There is wide scope for day trips or longer excursions from Glasgow, either in the lowland regions to the E and S or in the highland areas to the N and W. From **Gourock** (pop. 11,100; Stakis Gantock Hotel, Cloch Road, C, 63 r.), lower down the Clyde estuary, there are ferry services to *Dunoon* on the Cowal peninsula; from **Ardrossan** (pop. 11,300; Howard Park Hotel, D, 45 r.) on the Ayrshire coast, reached by a beautiful coastal road, there are boats to *Arran* (see p. 45). Only 15 miles from the city is *Loch Lomond*, the "queen of lochs", and it is not much farther to the beautiful *Trossachs*.

28 miles NE of Glasgow is **Stirling** (pop. 29,800); hotels – Park Lodge, C, 9 r.; Stakis Station, C, 25 r.). The Stirling Festival takes place annually in May.

The earliest inhabitants of the site were perhaps Britons, since the name Stirling appears to be a corruption of a Celtic word meaning "place of strife". However this may be, it is an established historical fact that King Alexander I died in Stirling Castle in 1124. In 1296 the town was surrendered to the English, but was retaken by the Scots in the following year after Wallace's victory in the battle of Stirling Bridge. The castle was the last to surrender to Edward I. Under the Stuarts Stirling became an important royal residence, and James III was born here in 1451. Mary Queen of Scots lived in Stirling until she went to France.

*Stirling Castle, dominating the town on its high crag, dates in its present form mainly from the 15th and 16th c. It is approached by way of the Esplanade (Statue of Bruce after the battle of Bannockburn) and the outer moat, with outworks dating from the reign of Queen Anne. Beyond this is the Gatehouse, flanked by 15th c. round towers, which gives access to the Lower Square, with *Parliament Hall* and the *Palace* (decorated façade, with figures). On the N side of the Upper Square is the *Chapel Royal* (1594), with 17th c. frescoes. In the *King's Old Buildings* is a museum. – From the NW part of the ramparts there are fine views.

S of the castle, separated from it by a small depression, is the *Church of the Holy Rude*, with a nave originally built in Transitional style (*c.* 1270) and altered in the 15th c. Here Mary was crowned Queen of Scots in 1542 at the age of eight months.

On the N side of the town is the Old Bridge or *Auld Brig* over the Forth (*c.* 1400). Some distance beyond the river is a prominent landmark, the sturdy square tower of the *Wallace Monument* (220 ft high), erected in 1869 to commemorate the victor of Stirling Bridge; in the interior are marble busts of distinguished Scotsmen.

Glastonbury

Southern England. – County: Somerset.
Population: 6800.
Telephone dialling code: 0458.
    Tourist Information Centre,
    7 Northload Street;
(i) tel. 32954
    (open only May–Sept.).

HOTELS. – *George and Pilgrims Hotel* (15th c., formerly a pilgrims' hostel), 1 High Street, 15 r.; *Hawthorn House*, 8–10 Northload Street, 12 r.

RESTAURANTS. – *Beckets Inn*, 43 High Street; *Market House Inn*, Magdalene Street.

The *abbey church of Glastonbury, still bearing witness to the splendour and beauty of the church as it once was, is England's most famous ruin. Many visitors are attracted to the site by the legends associated with it. All that is known with certainty, however, is that the town was an island until the surrounding moorland was drained.

It is said that St Joseph of Arimathea stuck his staff into the ground here and that it took root and grew into a thorn-tree, which still blooms every year at Christmas. The legend also relates that Joseph founded the first Christian church in the country here and that he buried the Holy Grail, the chalice of the Last Supper containing Christ's blood, at the foot of Glastonbury Tor, a hill 526 ft high, whereupon the Blood Spring burst forth. There is still a spring of that name at the foot of the hill. Glastonbury is also reputed to be the Isle of Avalon of the Arthurian legend.

HISTORY. – The hills of Glastonbury, known to the Celts as *Yniswitrin* or *Avalon*, were occupied by man in prehistoric times, as the remains of prehistoric and Iron Age settlements in the museum demonstrate. The material discovered included boats which would provide links between the various hill settlements, probably occupied from the 3rd c. B.C. until the coming of the Romans. Coins of the Celtic period were found here, but no Roman coins. There are references to the foundation of an abbey in the year 601, with a church which was preserved from ruin by Bishop Paulinus about 630. About 700 the abbey was re-founded by Ine, king of the West Saxons. The first stone church was built by St Dunstan (924–988), who was a monk and later abbot here. He himself and the Saxon kings Edmund (d. 946), Edgar (d. 975) and Edmund Ironside (d. 1016) were buried in the abbey. The first Norman church was completed in 1120 but destroyed by fire in 1184. Thereafter the church was rebuilt on a vast scale, beginning in 1186 and continuing into the 16th c. In 1539, on Henry VIII's orders, the last abbot, Richard Whiting, was hanged on Glastonbury Tor and the abbey was destroyed. The remains changed hands several times and were used as a quarry of building material, until finally the site was purchased for the Church of England at the beginning of the 20th c.

SIGHTS. – Little is left of the once gigantic **abbey church**, 580 ft long. The late Norman *Lady Chapel* or *St Joseph's Chapel* is of interest, with interlacing arcades and two corner towers (1184–86). The two *doorways*, with figures in the archivolts, are other reminders of past splendour. The plan of the church has been revealed by excavation. Of the conventual buildings only the *Abbot's Kitchen*, with four fireplaces, remains intact (1435–40). Also preserved are the *George Inn*, formerly a hostel for pilgrims (1456–83), the *Abbot's Tribunal* and the 14th c. *Abbot's Barn*.

The early 16th c. *Almshouses* have a chapel dated to 1512. Two other churches are worth seeing – the early 16th c. *St Benignus* and the church of *St John the Baptist*, which has one of the finest towers in the region. Glastonbury Tor, crowned by the (Perpendicular) tower of a chapel, affords magnificent views of the surrounding area.

SURROUNDINGS. – 2 miles SW is *Sharpham Manor*, birthplace of the novelist Henry Fielding (1707–54) with elaborate wrought-iron ornament on the door.

Ruin of the church, Glastonbury Abbey

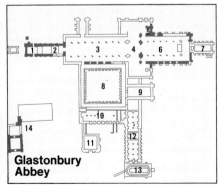

Glastonbury Abbey

1 Lady Chapel
2 Galilee Chapel
3 Nave
4 Central tower
5 Chapel of St Thomas Becket
6 Choir
7 Edgar Chapel
8 Cloisters
9 Chapterhouse
10 Refectory
11 Abbot's Kitchen
12 Dormitory
13 Lavatory
14 Abbot's Lodging

Gloucester

Central England. – County: Gloucestershire.
Population: 93,000.
Telephone dialling code: 0452.
Tourist Information Centre,
ⓘ 6 College Street;
tel. 421188.

HOTELS. – *Crest*, Crest Way, Barnwood, C, 100 r.; *Gloucester Hotel and Country Club*, Robinswood Hill, C, 77 r.; *New Inn*, Northgate Street, D, 31 r.

RESTAURANTS. – *Don Pasquale*, 19 Worcester Street; *Fleece*, Westgate Street.

EVENTS. – *Three Choirs Festival* in Cathedral (Sept.: alternating with Worcester and Hereford).

SPORT and RECREATION. – Rowing, swimming, fishing.

Gloucester, situated on the E bank of the Severn, is the county town of Gloucestershire, an individual town which has considerably developed in recent years and also a port, connected with the River Severn by a canal. It is also a good base from which to explore the beautiful surrounding country – the Cotswolds, the Forest of Dean and the picturesque Wye valley.

Gloucester Cathedral

An interesting natural phenomenon is the Severn "bore", a wave of water driven up the river by the incoming tide, particularly violent at the spring-tides and when the wind is in the SW. It can be watched from Telford's Over Bridge (1826–28) just W of the city, or, better still, from Stonebench, Elmore, 4 miles downstream.

HISTORY. – In Roman times Gloucester (*Glevum*) was an important fortified town at a ford on the Severn, guarding the road into Wales. It was one of four *coloniae* with special privileges (as were Colchester, Lincoln and York). The ending "-cester" comes from the Roman *castra*, and the town's four main streets, meeting at right angles in the centre, reflect Roman planning. After the Norman Conquest Gloucester became a favourite residence of the Plantagenet kings, and Henry III was crowned here in 1216. In 1643 the town held out for a month against the Royalists, and by way of punishment its fortifications were demolished after the Restoration.

SIGHTS.– The *Cathedral was originally the church of an abbey founded by King Osric of Northumbria (d. 729). In 1022 it became a Benedictine house. The present church, begun in 1089 and consecrated in 1100, was raised to the status of a cathedral by Henry VIII in 1542.

The Norman origin of the church can still be seen in its massive cylindrical pillars, but the exterior, dating from a rebuilding in the 14th c., is in early Perpendicular style. The church benefited from the fact that the murdered Edward II (1307–27) was buried here and that his son Edward

Gloucester Cathedral

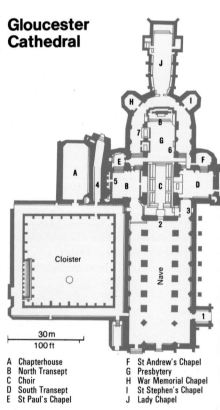

30 m
100 ft

A	Chapterhouse	F St Andrew's Chapel
B	North Transept	G Presbytery
C	Choir	H War Memorial Chapel
D	South Transept	I St Stephen's Chapel
E	St Paul's Chapel	J Lady Chapel

1	South Doorway	5 Shrine
2	Altar	6 Tomb of Robert Curthose
3	Tomb of Sir John Bridges	7 Tomb of Edward II
	(14th c.)	8 High altar
4	Parlour	

III (1327–77) encouraged pilgrimages to his tomb; the income which this brought in enabled the monks to embellish their church. The *tower* over the crossing was built in the 15th c.; the *Lady Chapel* dates from 1457–98. The *transepts* show most clearly how the early Perpendicular style was grafted on to the Norman structure.

The ***Choir** is one of the most beautiful in Britain, and since the destruction of St Paul's in the Great Fire of London has been the country's oldest Perpendicular choir. Like the transepts, it is an insertion within the Norman structure. The *vaulting* over the choir has no structural function and the ribs are merely ornamental, their intersections being richly decorated; the bosses have figures of angels playing musical instruments.

The *E window has the largest area of glass in England. The *stained glass*, still mainly original, dates from the 14th c. and depicts the coronation of the Virgin. The *choir-stalls*, some 60 in number, have beautiful *misericords* (restored). The individual features and details are beautiful in themselves but gain added effect when seen as a whole. In the presbytery is the *tomb of Robert Curthose*, Duke of Normandy, William the Conqueror's son, with an effigy of Irish bog-oak (13th c.). Nearby is the tomb of the murdered Edward II.

On either side of the **Lady Chapel**, the last part of the Cathedral to be built (1457–98) are small chapels with fan vaulting. Other notable features are the *triforium*, with the Whispering Gallery, and the impressive Norman *crypt*, with an apse and five chapels.

The *Cloister, with its fine fan vaulting, can stand comparison with any in Britain. It was built between 1351 and 1412; the fan vaulting is probably the earliest in the country. It measures 150 ft each way; the N side, with recesses for desks, was the monks' *scriptorium*, the S side was the *lavatory*. – The *Chapterhouse* is Norman apart from the large Perpendicular window. A staircase leads up to the *Library*. In the *tower* (which can be climbed) hangs the 15th c. bell known as *Great Peter*. Adjoining the Cathedral is the *Abbot's House* (11th–13th c.).

Opposite the *W gate* of the abbey precincts (12th c.), on the site of a Roman villa, is the church of *St Mary-de-Lode*, with a Norman tower. In front of it is a *monument to John Hooper*, bishop of Gloucester and Worcester, who was burned at the stake here in 1555 during the reign of Queen Mary. Tradition has it that he spent his last night in a late 15th c. house in Westgate Street which now houses a *Folk Museum*. In Northgate Street is the *New Inn*, built in 1450 for the accommodation of pilgrims.

In the SW of the town are the ***Docks**, the construction of which was begun at the turn of the 18th and 19th c. They lie at the end of the *Gloucester and Sharpness Canal*, originally intended to go as far as Berkeley, which runs parallel to the Severn but at a rather higher level in order to obviate the river's considerable variations in level. The various installations,

Port of Gloucester

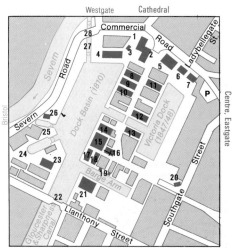

19th c. dock installations

1 Main entrance
2 Dock Office (c. 1830)
3 Tap and drinking fountain (1863)
4 North (Telford) Warehouse (1826)
5 City Flour Mills (c. 1850)
6 Custom House
7 Early 19th c. houses
8 Robinson and Philpotts
9 Warehouses
10 Warehouses (second half of 19th c.)
11 Victoria, Britannia and Albert
12 Associated Warehouses
13 Warehouses (second half of 19th c.)
14 Albert and Reynolds Mills
15 Flour mills (c. 1840)
16 Mariners' Chapel (1849)
17 Biddles' Warehouses
18 Warehouses (first half of 19th c.)
19 Old bollards (perhaps a crane base)
20 Weighbridge
21 Llanthony Warehouse (c. 1870)
22 Llanthony Bridge
23 Alexandra Warehouse (mid 19th c.)
24 Dry dock (1853)
25 Dry dock (before 1843)
26 Pumping house
27 Lock
28 Swing-bridge

still largely preserved in their original state, are well worth a visit (apply to the Dock Office of the British Waterways Board in Commercial Road); but good views can also be had from the neighbouring streets. See plan above.

SURROUNDINGS. – 13 miles SW is ***Berkeley Castle**, a 12th c. stronghold which is still in the hands of the Berkeley family. An imposing structure built in stone of different colours, it stands commandingly above the Severn, surrounded by beautiful grounds. Visitors are shown the cell in which Edward II was murdered in 1327, a large 14th c. hall, the old kitchens and the state apartments, with beautiful tapestries, silver, furniture and pictures. In the fine Early English parish church are Berkeley family monuments. Dr Edward Jenner (1749–1823), the pioneer of vaccination, who practised in Berkeley, is buried in the churchyard. Near Berkeley, in the Severn plain, is an atomic power station.

Also near here, 1½ miles NW of *Slimbridge*, are the grounds of the *Severn Wildfowl Trust* (founded by Sir Peter Scott), with the largest collection of waterfowl in the world.

Walkers and nature-lovers will find ample scope in the *Forest of Dean*, a wooded area of more than 40 sq. miles lying between the Severn and the Wye. Formerly a royal hunting reserve, it now contains little in the way of game. Part of the forest is designated as a national park. Though it contains few trees of great age, it still offers considerable tracts of unspoiled woodland (mostly oaks and beeches). In some areas there are iron and coal workings, particularly round the tiny industrial towns of *Coleford* and *Cinderford*, which offer no particular tourist attractions. The pits, all small, were worked by "free miners", but most of them are now closed down. At Coleford in the heart of the forest is the *Speech House Hotel* (14 r.), where the Verderer's Court formerly met.

One attractive place in the Forest of Dean is *St Briavels*, with a 12th c. castle which is now a youth hostel, offering fine views of the surrounding area.

Within easy reach of Gloucester are two attractive and typically English towns, *Tewkesbury* and *Cheltenham*. On the way to Tewkesbury it is well worth looking in at Deerhurst.

Deerhurst, 9 miles N of Gloucester, is a charming little village in the heart of the countryside, with one of the best preserved Saxon churches in the country. *St Mary's Church originally belonged to a monastery which is first recorded in 804. The chancel is entirely Saxon; the aisles, arches, roof and clerestory are Norman. The lower half of the tower is Saxon with later long-and-short work, and in the E wall is a two-light triangular-headed window. The cylindrical font, with spiral ornament, is also Saxon, dating from the 8th or 9th c. Nearby, adjoining a half-timbered house, is Odda's Chapel; a stone found here bears the date 1056, making this the oldest dated chapel in England.

Tewkesbury (pop. 9600; hotels – Tewkesbury Park Hotel Golf and Country Club, C, 52 r.; Royal Hop Pole Crest, C, 29 r.). A charming old-world town with half-timbered houses and ancient inns it lies near the junction of the Severn and Avon, with scope for boating on both rivers. A monument commemorates the battle of Tewkesbury (1471), fought in the "Bloody Meadow" during the Wars of the Roses.

The pride of Tewkesbury is *Tewkesbury Abbey, one of the finest Norman buildings in the country. Building began in 1092, on the site of an earlier Benedictine house, and was completed in 1121. The church is of very similar size and plan to Westminster Abbey. Some of the stone used was imported from France. Particularly impressive features are the massive Norman tower (which can be climbed) and the W front with its recessed arches. In the 14th c. new

lierne vaulting was built over the old cylindrical pillars, the new Decorated work harmonising well with the older structure. The transepts are Norman, with 14th c. windows. The choir has Norman pillars, seven splendid windows with stained glass dated before 1430, and choir-stalls with misericords. The finest of the many tombs and monuments is the Beauchamp Chantry (c. 1425), built by Isabel le Despenser over the tomb of her first husband Richard Beauchamp, Earl of Worcester. Also notable is the tomb of Hugh le Despenser (d. 1326).

10 miles NE of Gloucester is **Cheltenham** (pop. 85,000; hotels – *Golden Valley Thistle*, B, 103 r.; *Queen's*, B, 77 r.; *Greenway*, B, 12 r.; *Carlton*, C, 49 r.; *Wyastone*, C, 13 r.; *Savoy*, D, 57 r.; *Park Place*, D, 55 r.), formerly a spa and now a much favoured residential town, particularly for retired people. George III and Wellington made the town a fashionable spa. Its many trees give it the aspect of a garden city. There is no finer shopping street in England than the *Promenade, and there are numerous other handsome streets of the Regency period. The town has two famous schools, Cheltenham College (founded 1841) and Cheltenham Ladies' College (1853). St Mary's Church has a beautiful rose window. The Art Gallery and Museum in Clarence Street has a good collection of Dutch masters.

Cheltenham's many parks include Pittville Park, which contains a lake, and Prestbury Park, to the N of the town. National Hunt steeplechases are run in Prestbury Park. The Cheltenham Festival of Contemporary Music is held in July.

The Grampians

Central Scotland. – Regions: Grampian, Highland, Tayside, Strathclyde.

The Grampians are a range of mountains extending across Scotland between the Caledonian Canal in the N and the Clyde valley in the S, with large expanses of heath and moorland. Within the Grampian range are Britain's highest peak, Ben Nevis (4406 ft), Ben Macdhui (4296 ft) and numerous other notable heights which offer good climbing and mountain walking. Grampian Region, with Aberdeen as its chief town, is a new administrative unit created by the recent local government reform which takes in the old counties of Aberdeen, Kincardine and Banff and part of Moray; but the Grampian range extends westward across most of Scotland.

Within the Grampian Highlands is the Cairngorm range, the largest high plateau area in Britain, over 60 sq. miles in extent. The whole of the Cairngorm plateau lies over 900 ft, and it has several peaks of over 4000 ft. The predominant vegetation is heather and bracken, with scattered birches and rowans, but there

Municipal Offices, Cheltenham

are also considerable areas of pine forest planted by the Forestry Commission. The wild life includes red deer, hares and rabbits, as well as large numbers of birds. The region is famous for its beef cattle (Aberdeen-Angus), and thousands of sheep find pasture on the hills. The barley grown here is mainly used for the manufacture of whisky. One of the most famous whisky distilleries is in the Spey valley, and there is a particular concentration of distilleries producing malt whisky within a radius of 25 miles of Elgin. There is a special signposted Whisky Trail for tourists. The rivers of the Grampian region – the Dee, Don, Ythan, Ugie, Deveron and Spey – are well stocked with fish, and the Spey in particular is famous for its salmon. The finding of oil in the North Sea (some 130 miles E of Aberdeen) has led to a considerable development of industry in the region, fortunately without spoiling the tourist attractions of the area.

The chief town in the western part of the Grampian area is **Oban** (pop. 7000; hotels – Regent, C, 75 r.; Great Western, C, 72 r.; Alexandra, C, 56 r.; Royal, D, 118 r.; Park, D, 81 r.; Kelvin Guest House, E, 19 r.; youth hostel, Esplanade, 130 b.), a popular holiday resort situated in a bay sheltered by the offshore island of Kerrera. From here there are boat trips to Mull and the Hebridean islands and abundant scope for excursions into the surrounding hills and lochs.

Oban has a harbour and is the headquarters of the Royal Highland Yacht Club. There is good bathing on Ganavan Sands. The best view of the town is from McCaig's Folly, a circular structure built by a 19th c. banker on a hill above the town. *Dunstaffnage Castle*, 3 miles N, on a crag at the entrance to Loch Etive has three round towers, the 10 ft thick walls dating from the 15th c. On the ramparts is an old cannon from a Spanish galleon belonging to the Armada which sank in Tobermory Bay (Mull). Flora Macdonald was a prisoner here for a short time. It is said that some of the early Scottish kings were buried in the 13th c. chapel, and it is also claimed – with some improbability – that Dunstaffnage was once capital of Scotland. Tradition also asserts that the Stone of Destiny on which the Scottish kings were crowned for many centuries was kept here, having been brought from Ireland to Iona and from there to Dunstaffnage.

Other interesting castles within easy reach of Oban are *Dunollie Castle*, 1 mile N on Loch Linnhe, of which only the ivy-covered keep survives, and *Castle Stalker* (13 miles N), on a small island in beautiful Loch Creran, with a tower which has been restored. A visit to *Carnasserie Castle* (mid 16th c.), the seat of John

Carswell, last bishop of the Isles and abbot of Iona, can be combined with a tour of *Loch Awe*, one of the largest and most beautiful lochs in Scotland, surrounded by wooded hills and dotted with islands and islets. There is a beautiful road down the W side of the loch to *Ford*, beyond which, on the E side, is Kilneuair church, which appears in the records in 1394 and is said to be haunted. Farther up the E side are the ruins of Fincharn and Ardconnel castles. Beyond Portsonachan the loch becomes wider, and the road runs past Priests' Isle and Inisbail, which once had a Cistercian priory. There is a monument commemorating Duncan Ban McIntyre (1724–1812), one of the Highland bards.

One of the finest and most popular sea trips from Oban is to *Iona* and *Staffa*, skirting the island of *Mull*. This offers magnificent views, with Duart Castle and a tower commemorating the novelist William Black (1841–98) straight ahead, to the E *Ben Nevis*, the Glencoe peaks and *Loch Linnhe*, with countless islands and islets. The route continues past *Loch Aline*, with Kinlochaline Tower, followed by *Manse of Fiunary*, *Salen* and *Aros Castle*, with a fine view of *Ben More*, Mull's highest peak (3169 ft). For Iona and Staffa, see pp. 120, 121.

A quiet little town which makes a good base for exploration of the southern and western Highlands is **Inveraray** (pop. 450; youth hostel, 40 b.), a trim 18th c. planned village on Loch Fyne which replaced an earlier village in the grounds of Inveraray Castle. Inveraray features in novels by Scott (who was a great admirer of the castle), R. L. Stevenson and the local writer Neil Munro. *Inveraray Castle*, set in a beautiful park, is the seat of the duke of Argyll, an imposing mansion with much of interest in the interior (recently damaged by fire but since restored). *Loch Fyne* is surrounded by wooded hills. A beautiful road leads to *Essachosan Glen* or Lovers' Glen. Also very beautiful is Glen Shira, with the ruins of *Rob Roy's House*, 7 miles NE. The River Shira, a good trout stream, rises on Beinn Bhuidhe (3106 ft). Just before it flows into Loch Fyne it widens to form the Dubh Loch.

From the head of Loch Fyne a road climbs up to the highest point on the pass, *Rest and be Thankful*, and then descends to Loch Long through picturesque *Glen Croe*, with a view of the *Cobbler* or Ben Arthur (2891 ft). The old road, with awkward bends and steep gradients, can be seen in the valley below the modern road. At the head of Loch Long is *Arrochar*, a good starting point for the climb of the Cobbler. From here a road bears left to Loch Lomond, 2 miles away, with a very beautiful (though narrow) lochside road.

Loch Lomond

There is a very attractive trip from Loch Lomond to the *Trossachs, a beautiful valley between *Loch Katrine* and *Loch Vennachar*. The standard tour, strongly recommended, is by boat from *Balloch Pier* at the S end of *Loch Lomond, with magnificent views, past *Rowardennan* (from which *Ben Lomond*, 3192 ft, can be climbed) and Tarbet to *Inversnaid*; from there by bus to the very beautiful **Loch Katrine**, passing Loch Arklet on the way; and then by boat along Loch Katrine to the Trossachs Pier. From here there are pleasant walks in all directions, with views of the hills and other lochs, some large, some quite small.

Another popular holiday centre in the heart of the Grampian Highlands is **Pitlochry** (pop. 2500; hotels – Atholl Palace, B, 92 r.; Pitlochry Hydro, C, 62 r.; Fisher's, D, 77 r.; Green Park, D, 37 r.; Pine Trees, D, 29 r.; Burnside, D, 24 r.; Birchwood, D, 16 r.; Craigvrack, E, 19 r.; Tigh-na-Cloich, E, 14 r.; Port-an-Eilean, E, 12 r.), with the Pitlochry Festival Theatre, the "Theatre in the Hills".

Pitlochry, in the Tummel valley, is said to be the geographical centre of Scotland. Just beside the town is the artificial *Loch Faskally*, formed in the 1950s by a dam built to provide hydroelectric power. One of the popular sights is the salmon-ladder, with glass walls through which the salmon making their way upstream can be observed.

Pitlochry's central situation makes it a good starting point for excursions in all directions. 8 miles NW is **Blair Castle**, on a beautiful road which runs past the approach to the Queen's View (with a particularly fine view of Loch Tummel) and through the famous Pass of Killie-crankie. The 13th c. castle, beside the little town of Blair Atholl, is the seat of the duke of Atholl, the only citizen in Britain with the right to maintain a private army, the Atholl Highlanders. The interior of the castle gives a picture of life in Scotland over the past four centuries.

A few miles SW of Pitlochry is **Aberfeldy**, on the Urlar Burn near its junction with the Tay, with the three Falls of Moness and an interesting nature trail, the Birks. 12 miles SE is **Dunkeld**, with one of Scotland's oldest cathedrals, beautifully situated on the banks of the Tay. The church was founded in 1107; the nave (15th c.) is roofless, but the choir (14th c.) is still used, after restoration, as the parish church. Near the Cathedral are a number of fine 18th c. houses. The Hermitage nature trail is notable for its tall and handsome trees.

Farther S is **Perth** (pop. 41,700; hotels – Stakis City Mills, C, 78 r.; Isle of Skye, C, 44 r.; Royal George, C, 43 r.; Salutation, D, 62 r.; Station, D, 55 r.; youth hostel, 107 Glasgow Road, 64 b.), once capital of Scotland and the scene of many historic events. The town, known as the "Fair City", lies on the Tay, between the North and South Inches, areas of level grassland along the banks of the river. In the parish church, St John's, which dates from the 15th c., Knox preached a fiery sermon against idolatory in 1559, setting off a destructive wave of iconoclasm in which many works of art perished.

Although Perth was capital of Scotland until the 15th c., it has few old buildings. The Fair Maid's House, which features in Scott's "Fair Maid of Perth", is in Curfew Row; it is now a craft shop. There is an excellent nature trail on Kinnoull Hill (729 ft), from which there are magnificent views.

View of Ben Lawers from Killin

2 miles W of Perth is *Huntingtower Castle*, formerly known as Ruthven Castle. Its two 15th c. towers are linked by a later building, with a hall containing fine wall and ceiling paintings. Tradition has it that a daughter of the earl leapt from one tower to the other in order to avoid being caught in the company of a lover: hence the name Maiden's Leap given to the space between the two towers.

2 miles N of Perth is *Scone Palace*, a Victorian country house near the site of the old Scone Abbey, in which Scottish kings from Kenneth II to James VI were crowned. The famous Stone of Scone or Coronation Stone is now in Westminster Abbey.

In Glamis Castle

NE of Perth, on the road (A 94) to the coastal town of Montrose, is one of the finest castles in Scotland, ***Glamis Castle**, in which Princess Margaret was born. The present castle, in baronial style, dates mainly from the 17th c., but there was a castle on the site a thousand years before that. Glamis is the seat of the earls of Strathmore, the family of the present Queen Mother. Tradition has it that Macbeth murdered King Duncan here. The castle contains fine furniture, tapestries, pictures and weapons. In the village of Glamis is the interesting *Angus Folk Museum*.

A 94 continues to **Forfar** (pop. 10,200), a historic old town in Strathmore, now a historic old town in Strathmore, now a centre of the jute-milling industry. $1\frac{1}{2}$ miles E is Restenneth Priory, with an 18th c. spire set on the remains of a 9th c. tower, the upper part of which dates from the 12th c. – SE of Forfar, on the coast, is **Arbroath** (pop. 23,500), a popular holiday resort with remains of *Arbroath Abbey* (12th and 13th c.), built of red sandstone.

In the S transept is a round window known as the "O" of Arbroath, in which a beacon used to be lighted to guide ships at sea. The *Abbot's House* has a fine kitchen; the hall (restored) is now a museum. Just outside Arbroath is *St Vigeans*, with an 11th c. church (much restored) and a *museum* containing a collection of Early Christian (Pictish and Celtic) sculptured stones; among them is the Drosten Stone, with an inscription in the Pictish language written in Roman script.

SE of Arbroath, at the mouth of the Firth of Tay, is the city of **Dundee** (pop. 192,000; Angus Hotel, 58 r.), chief town of Tayside Region, an industrial centre with extensive docks. The University was founded in 1881 as a college of St Andrews University, but became independent in 1967. It has an interesting City Museum and Art Gallery but has preserved few old buildings, having been extensively redeveloped since the last war.

A beautiful coastal road, with fine cliff scenery, runs N from Arbroath to **Montrose** (pop. 10,500; hotel – Park, C, 59 r.), a holiday resort with a mile-long sandy beach. To the S is a stretch of fine cliffs, the nesting-place of countless seabirds.

In the northern Grampians, E of Aberdeen, is one of the most popular holiday centres in the region, **Braemar** (pop. 400; hotels – Fife Arms, D, 90 r.; Invercauld Arms, D, 55 r.; youth hostel, Corrie Feragie, 80 b.), situated at an altitude of 1100 ft. It is both a summer and a winter sports resort, and one of the great events in its year is the Braemar Gathering (Highland games), at which members of the royal family are usually present. It is a good base for walks and climbs in the *Cairngorms*. The Dee valley is very beautiful, particularly at the Linn of Dee. Braemar Castle is an imposing complex dating from the first half of the 17th c.

7 miles NE of Braemar is ***Balmoral Castle**, the Queen's Highland residence, a Victorian mansion in the Scottish Baronial style. The estate was bought by Queen Victoria in 1852. The castle itself is not open to the public, but visitors are admitted to the grounds at certain times when the royal family are not in residence. The best view of this storybook castle, set

amid tall trees, is from the Strathdon road. Nearby is *Crathie Church*, which is attended by members of the royal family when they are at Balmoral. The foundation stone was laid by Queen Victoria in 1893, and the church contains many mementoes of the old queen. The highest point in the Balmoral Forest is *Lochnagar* (3786 ft), which is often snow-covered.

The most popular skiing area in Scotland is NW of Braemar, in the *Cairngorms*, now a large nature reserve. The highest point is *Ben Macdhui* (4296 ft), from which there is a magnificent walk to Cairn Gorm, and from there down to Glenmore Lodge (6½ miles from Aviemore), another good base for climbers and hill walkers. *Cairn Gorm* (4084 ft), which gives its name to the whole range, is only fourth in order of height, coming after Ben Macdhui, *Braeriach* (4248 ft) and *Cairn Toul* (4241 ft). The easiest way to reach the summits is by way of the White Lady chair-lift.

Between the red granite mountains are a number of lochs, including *Loch Avon* and *Loch an Eilean*. The most impressive views are of *Braeriach*, *Cairn Toul* and the *Devil's Point*. There is an endless range of fine mountain walks, sometimes strenuous; the finest of all, offering splendid views, is the 30 miles (with no overnight accommodation on the way) from Aviemore over the *Lairig Ghru* pass to Braemar. There is another walk of about the same length from Braemar to Blair Atholl, and a shorter but very attractive one from Aviemore over the Revoan pass and past Loch Avon to the pretty little town of **Nethy Bridge**, with good skiing and fishing and a golf-course. In this area, too, are *Loch Garten* (bird reserve) and the popular holiday town *Boat of Garten*. Other holiday places are *Dufftown*, famous for its whisky, *Grantown* and *Ballindalloch*, with a handsome castle, at the junction of the Avon and the Spey.

The leading winter sports resort is **Aviemore** (pop. 1300; hotels – Stakis Coylumbridge, C, 157 r.; Post House, C, 103 r.; Strathspey Thistle, C, 90 r.; youth hostel, Aviemore, Inverness-shire, 92 b.; Aviemore Leisure Centre), between the Cairngorms and the Monadhliath Mountains, with many attractive excursions in the area. Trips by steam train to Boat of Garten. 3 miles S is one of the best known of the smaller lochs, *Loch an Eilean* (nature trail). Also in the area are interesting stone circles.

Grantham

Central England. – County: Lincolnshire.
Altitude: 200 ft. – Population: 30,100.
Telephone dialling code: 0476.
ⓘ **Tourist Information Centre,**
The Guildhall;
tel. 66444.

HOTELS. – *Angel & Royal*, High Street, C, 32 r.; *George*, High Street, D, 32 r.

YOUTH HOSTEL. – 6 Dudley Road, 40 b.

RESTAURANT. – **Angel Inn* (15th c. façade).

Grantham is a busy market town in a rich agricultural region, surrounded by areas of pastureland which are reputed to produce some of the best meat, especially sausages, in England. The town is also noted for its gingerbread. The tall spire of St Wulfram's Church is a prominent landmark, seen well before the town is reached. Opposite the Guildhall stands a statue of Isaac Newton (1642–1727), who was a pupil at the local grammar school, and the Museum on St Peter's Hill contains many mementoes of the famous philosopher and scientist.

SIGHTS. – The parish church, **St Wulfram's**, has a *spire* 281 ft high, beautiful *tracery* in the windows, a 14th c. *crypt* and a 15th c. *font*. Above the S doorway is a valuable *library* presented to the church in 1598, with many chained books. Adjoining the church is King's School, where Newton was a pupil, and where he carved his name on a window-ledge. – The **Angel Inn* (originally 13th c.) in High Street is one of the finest old inns in England.

In **Grantham House** (not open) is a 14th c. room occupied by Princess Margaret, daughter of Henry VII, during her journey north in 1503 to marry King James IV of Scotland.

SURROUNDINGS. – 7 miles W is the imposing **Belvoir Castle*, seat of the duke of Rutland, rebuilt by James Wyatt in 1808–16. The castle contains an outstanding collection of pictures (including works by Rembrandt and Rubens), tapestries and furniture.

2 miles N is Belton Park (1685), seat of Lord Brownlow. Wren was partly responsible for the house, which contains fine carving by Grinling Gibbons, as well as pictures and old silver. The park, beautifully landscaped, is sometimes open to the public. The village church has a Norman font.

7 miles S, at Colsterworth, is *Woolsthorpe Manor*, birthplace of Isaac Newton, with the orchard in which he is supposed to have seen the famous apple falling which gave him the idea of the law of gravity.

Hadrian's Wall

Hadrian's Wall at Cuddy's Crag

Northern England. – Counties: Cumbria, Northumberland and Tyne & Wear.

Two large works of fortification were built by the Romans against the "barbarians" of the north. The more northerly of the two was the Antonine Wall from the Firth of Forth to the Firth of Clyde; the other was **Hadrian's Wall, which extended from Wallsend in the E to the Solway Firth in the W, a total distance of 73½ miles. It was begun in A.D. 122 by Aulus Platorius Nepos, legate of the Emperor Hadrian, who visited Britain in that year, and completed in 132. The wall was built primarily for defence, but was provided with gates for N–S traffic.

The Wall runs from sea to sea, adapting itself to the hilly landscape in wide curves and gentle gradients. It was faced on both sides with small, regularly coursed stones, with a core of rubble and mortar. It was reinforced by a wide ditch, the *vallum*, on the N side and a rather smaller ditch to the S. The wall was up to 10 ft thick and 20 ft high; now its height is nowhere greater than 6 ft. Along its length there was a series of *forts* (17–19 in number) accommodating 500 or 1000 men, with barracks and headquarters buildings, storerooms and workshops; and at regular intervals of a Roman mile between the forts were *milecastles* which no doubt served as lookout posts. Between every two milecastles were two turrets or watch-towers to provide continuous surveillance of the whole frontier and raise the alarm if danger threatened. Along the rear of the Wall ran a military road. The total garrison of the Wall probably amounted to some 10,000 men, who came from all parts of the Roman Empire, including Britain. Small settlements, with shops, inns and temples grew up in the vicinity of the forts.

It is established that the Wall was overrun by the northern tribes on more than one occasion. It was several times renovated and improved, the last occasion being in 369, but in the end it had to be abandoned. In subsequent centuries the Wall was used as a convenient quarry of building material, and Roman stones can be seen in churches and private houses in the area. A walk along the Wall is now a very popular form of recreation, although no one but a specialist or a particularly enthusiastic amateur archaeologist would want to traverse its whole length, since for long stretches there is not much to see. The better preserved forts, however, are well worth visiting, and there are considerable sections of the Wall which are still extremely impressive. The most rewarding part is between Chollerford and Greenhead, within the Northumberland National Park.

At *Chollerford*, near a handsome 18th c. country house, is the best preserved fort, *Chesters (*Cilurnum*), designed for a cavalry unit of 500 men. The surviving remains include gates, barrack blocks, the headquarters building, stables, bathhouses and hypocausts (under-floor heating installations). In the entrance hall of Chesters House is an excellent collection of Roman material from the site. On the opposite bank of the North Tyne are considerable remains of a *bridge abutment*. The church at Chollerton (2½ miles E) has monolithic Roman columns in the S arcade (*c.* 1150) and a Roman altar used as a font.

Hadrian's Wall

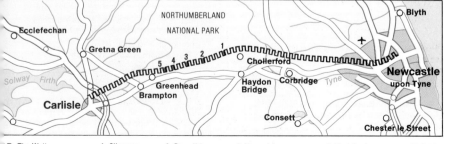

Ecclefechan • Gretna Green • NORTHUMBERLAND NATIONAL PARK • Chollerford • Blyth • Newcastle upon Tyne • Solway Firth • Greenhead • Brampton • Carlisle • Haydon Bridge • Corbridge • Tyne • Consett • Chester le Street

| ᒣᒥ The Wall Forts | 1 Cilurnum | 2 Brocolitia | 3 Vercovicium | 4 Vindolanda | 5 Aesica |

Excavations at Vindolanda

Going W from Housesteads, beyond *Limestone Corner*, the Wall runs along the Great Whin Sill, a ridge of higher ground which rises to 1230 ft. The best preserved stretch begins here. At *Carrawburgh* was the fort of *Brocolitia*, where a *shrine of Mithras* (3rd or early 4th c.) was excavated. (This mystical cult was carried into Germany and Britain by the Roman army from about A.D. 70.) There is a reproduction of the shrine in the Museum of Antiquities in Newcastle.

At *Shield-on-the-Wall* (the suffix "on-the-Wall" being found in the names of a number of small places near the Wall, like Heddon-on-the-Wall, which has a largely Norman church), at Milecastle 33, the

military way (followed by the modern road) leaves the Wall and runs roughly a mile to the S. Those who want to follow the Wall further, therefore, must continue on foot – an effort which is well rewarded by the magnificent scenery.

***Housesteads** (*Vercovicium*) is the fort on the Wall which attracts most visitors. Here there has been considerable excavation of the civilian settlement outside the fort. There are remains of four gates, the headquarters building, granaries, barrack blocks, bath-houses, and infirmary, stables, latrines, workshops and water tanks. The fort was designed for an infantry unit of 1000 men. There is a small museum on the site (which belongs to the National Trust).

2 miles S, at *Chesterholm*, is the fort of ***Vindolanda**, with one of the most interesting headquarters buildings and a Roman milestone.

The Wall, with a well-preserved milecastle (No. 37) runs close to *Crag Lough*. Then comes one of the best preserved stretches, at *Steel Rig*. At **Greatchesters**, 5 miles from Housesteads, is the much overgrown fort of *Aesica*. Beyond this point the Wall, in places much dilapidated, follows the line of the crags known as the *Nine Nicks of Thirlwall* to *Walltown*, with a well-preserved section, and *Carvoran*, near Greenhead, the site of the fort of *Banna* or *Magna*. 1 mile N is the ruined *Thirlwall Castle*, largely built with material from the Wall.

Another site worth seeing is **Birdoswald**, the site of one of the largest forts, *Camboglanna*. Here there are very well-preserved stretches of the wall and magnificent views.

Roman fort at

Vindolanda

30 m / 100 ft

(4th c. A.D.)

1 Commanding officer's house
2 Commanding officer's baths
3 Headquarters building
4 Hospital
5 Granary
6 Stables(?)
7 Baths
8 Cistern
9 Latrines
10 Civilian settlement
11 Workshops
12 Barracks

Harrogate

Northern England. – County: North Yorkshire.
Altitude: 350–600 ft. – Population: 65,000.
Telephone dialling code: 0423.
(i) **Royal Bath Assembly Rooms**,
Crescent Road;
tel. 65912.

HOTELS. – *Crown*, Crown Place, B, 120 r.; *Granby*, Granby Road, B, 114 r.; *St George*, 1 Ripon Road, B, 82 r.; *Majestic*, Ripon Road, C, 151 r.; *Hospitality Inn* West Park, C, 66 r.; *Studley*, Swan Road, C, 40 r.

CAMP SITE.

RESTAURANTS. – *Number Six*, 6 Ripon Road; *Oliver*, 24 King's Road; *Shabab*, 1 John Street.

SPORT and RECREATION. – Golf, tennis, swimming.

Harrogate, situated in the foothills of the Pennines, was formerly the leading spa in the North of England, with 88 mineral springs, mostly sulphurous and chalybeate. The springs were already being used for curative purposes in the 16th c. but are no longer so used. Harrogate today is primarily a holiday and conference centre with many trade shows and exhibitions.

The town prides itself on being "Britain's floral resort", by virtue of its many parks and public gardens and the extensive Harlow Car Gardens of the Northern Horticultural Society. It is also a favoured residential town. It has little industry, but a number of large firms have their administrative headquarters here. Harrogate is an excellent shopping centre, with many elegant shops and antique dealers.

SIGHTS. – The *Royal Pump Room*, built over the largest sulphur spring, is now a museum. The numerous *parks* offer pleasant walking, among them the famous *Stray*, claimed to be the largest stretch of turf in the world. In the centre of the town are the beautiful **Valley Gardens**. The *Fountain Court*, with its fountain and flowerbeds, is also very attractive. From *Harlow Hill* there is a good view of the town, with wider views extending to York and the Humber. A visit to *Harlow Car Gardens*, just off Otley Road, should not be missed by flower-lovers. The modern *Conference and Exhibition Centre* is situated in King's Road.

SURROUNDINGS. – 14 miles NE is **Newby Hall**, a beautifully situated country house rebuilt by Robert Adam in 1770. It is famed for its Gobelin tapestries and its sculpture. The grounds are also very beautiful.

◀The Hebrides

Western Scotland. – Regions: Highland, Western Isles, Strathclyde.

The Hebrides are a large group of islands lying off the W coast of Scotland. There are really in fact two groups – the long chain of the Outer Hebrides or Western Isles, the main islands in which are Lewis and Harris (the "Long Island"), North Uist, Benbecula, South Uist, Eriskay and Barra, and the Inner Hebrides, the largest islands in which are Skye, Mull, Islay, Jura, Rhum, Eigg, Coll and Colonsay. Between the Outer and Inner Hebrides are the Minch, the Little Minch and the Sea of the Hebrides.

There is a ferry service from Mallaig to Skye, and boats from there to some of the other islands. From Uig, on Skye, there is a boat service to Lewis; there are also boats from Oban and Kyle of Lochalsh, on the mainland, to the Outer Hebrides. Additional information can be obtained from the relevant ferry services.

INNER HEBRIDES

Skye (pop. 11,700) is known as the "misty isle", though it is not, perhaps, any mistier or wetter than some other parts of Scotland. It is an island of romantic aspect, with a chain of rugged hills, green

View from Kyle of Lochalsh towards Skye

valleys and glens, caves, waterfalls and sandy beaches. It is some 50 miles long and between 4 and 15 miles across, irregularly shaped, with many arms of the sea cutting deep into the land. The main places on the island are Portree, Broadford, Kyleakin and Dunvegan.

The ferry from Kyle of Lochalsh runs to *Kyleakin* (pop. 250), a pretty village with the ruins of Castle Moil. From here there is a road W via *Lusa* to **Broadford** (pop. 800), the second largest place on the island (8 miles from Kyleakin), a good centre from which to explore the surrounding area. One of the finest trips from here is to *Loch Scavaig* (15 miles), with magnificent views of *Blaven* (3042 ft) and *Loch Slapin*, and *Elgol*, a little village with a steep descent to the coast; from the

Castle Moil, Kyleakin, Skye

been built in the 9th c.; the tower dates from the 14th. From here a road, offering splendid views, runs E to Broadford, via Sligachan and the three basalt columns known as Macleod's Maidens.

Mull (pop. 2420) is one of the largest islands in the Hebrides. The S and E are hilly, with peaks rising to over 3000 ft; the hills on the N side are lower. The capital of the island is **Tobermory** (pop. 800), an

Tobermory, Mull

village there is one of the grandest views in the country. The incomparably beautiful *Loch Coruisk* must be approached by boat. Linked with Loch Scavaig by a river, it lies at the foot of the *Cuillins* or Coolins, one of the finest climbing areas in Britain, not so much on account of their elevation (the highest point being only 3251 ft) as of their harmonious proportions. The Cuillins are for experienced climbers only, not for beginners. The iron content of the rocks makes compasses unreliable, and a number of climbers have lost their lives here. The best known peak is *Sgurr nan Gillean*. At *Glenbrittle* there is a climbing centre (training courses).

Portree (pop. 1800; hotels – Coolin Hills, D, 29 r.; Royal, D, 26 r.) is the largest place on Skye. To the N are *Prince Charlie's Cave* and the black crag known as the *Old Man of Storr*. At the northern tip of Skye is the *Quiraing*, an extraordinary group of bizarrely shaped basalt towers, pinnacles and ledges.

Dunvegan (pop. 250), on *Loch Dunvegan* in western Skye, is famous for its *castle*, the home of the chief of the Clan Macleod, which is reputed to be the oldest castle of the Macleods. It is said to have

important fishing port and tourist centre. The wreck of the "Florencia", one of the galleons of the Spanish Armada, laden with treasure, lies under the waters of the bay. There are a number of ruined castles (Aros, Mingary) in the surrounding area.

Just off the SW coast of Mull is the little island of **Iona**, with a great historical past. The Christianisation of Scotland began in Iona, where St Columba landed in 563 with 12 companions and founded a monastery; but long before then the island had been a druidical shrine. Its original name was *Hy*. Many visitors, including Wordsworth and Dr Johnson, have been roused to enthusiasm by Iona.

The *monastery* was destroyed several times by the Norsemen but always rebuilt (in the 11th c. by Queen Margaret). About 1200 it became a Benedictine house, and from this period survive the 13th c Norman choir and parts of the chapel. To the W is the "Street of the Dead" leading to *St Oran's Cemetery*, in which many Scottish kings were buried, and McLean's Cross (11 ft high). Among the more than 60 kings who are said to have been buried here were Macbeth and King Duncan, whom he murdered; the gravestones were thrown into the sea at the Reformation.

St Oran's Chapel, in the cemetery, is the oldest building on the island, erected in the late 11th c. by St Margaret, Malcolm Canmore's queen, probably on the spot where St Columba's first church stood. On the

Loch Ainort, Skye

Iona Cathedral

"musical cave", referring to the echo of the waves which is heard inside. A visit to the cave inspired Mendelssohn to compose his famous overture. Here too there is a *basalt causeway* like the Giant's Causeway in Northern Ireland. W of Fingal's Cave is the *Boat Cave*, which can be reached only by boat; and there are a number of other inaccessible caves on the island.

way to the Cathedral, just outside the W door, is *St Martin's Cross* (14 ft high), with rich sculptured decoration (figures of the Holy Family).

The Cathedral, dedicated to St Mary, is a red granite building begun in the 12th c. and mainly Norman in style; but it was enlarged several times and shows a mingling of different styles. The square tower over the crossing, 70 ft high, is borne on four Norman arches. The former nunnery and other buildings associated with the Cathedral have been restored by the Iona Community, members of which live and work on the island during the summer.

The normal population of the island is about 100, living in *Baile Mor* ("big town"). There are two small hotels. There are fine views from *Dun-I*, a hill behind the Cathedral (332 ft), from which over 30 islands can be seen.

6 miles N of Iona is the uninhabited island of **Staffa**, on which it is possible to land in good weather. The main feature of Staffa is *Fingal's Cave, 227 ft long, with bizarre rock formations, beautiful colouring and handsome basalt columns. It is named after the Celtic hero Fingal. The Gaelic name, Uaimh Binn, means

Islay and Jura, separated only by the narrow Sound of Islay, can be reached from West Tarbert. **Islay** is an unspoiled island with rugged rocks, many bays and sandy beaches. It has two ruined castles and a number of ancient Celtic crosses. The bathing and the fishing are excellent. The unofficial capital of the island is **Bowmore**, the largest place, with wide streets and the *Kilarrow* parish church, built in 1769, the only round church of that period. There are numerous hotels and guest-houses. – The island of **Jura** (pop. 420, with Colonsay), is rugged and little visited by tourists. Its highest points are the *Paps of Jura* (2571 ft), best climbed from *Feolin*, where the ferry puts in. – **Colonsay** and **Oronsay** are two smaller islands, also separated only by a narrow channel. The mailboat calls several times weekly at *Scalasaig*, where there is a hotel. At low tide it is possible to walk across to *Oronsay*, which has the ruins of a 14th c. priory and a fine 16th c. cross. A Viking grave was found here, with a man and his horse buried in his ship. Oronsay is of interest to botanists for the very rare species of orchis found on the island.

South of Skye is a group of four islands – **Eigg, Muck, Rhum** and **Canna** – each inhabited by a few dozen families. The most attractive of the four is Canna, with large numbers of sea-birds. At the NE corner of Canna is the notorious Compass Hill, whose iron-bearing basalt rocks used to deflect ships' compasses and drive them off their course. On Eigg is an interesting geological feature, the Sgurr of Eigg, a towering crag of black pitchstone.

OUTER HEBRIDES

The Outer Hebrides are linked with the mainland of Scotland by a variety of boat services – Ullapool to *Stornoway* on Lewis (mail-boat, also carrying cars); Uig

ingal's Cave, Staffa

on Skye to *Tarbert*, Harris, and *Loch-maddy*, North Uist (car ferry); Oban via Coll and Tiree to *Lochboisdale*, South Uist, and *Castlebay*, Barra; less frequent services from Glasgow. There are also air services from Glasgow and Inverness. – The Outer Hebrides are formed of some of the oldest rocks in the world, Pre-Cambrian gneiss. The country is fairly featureless, with great expanses of heath and moorland, few trees, numerous little lochs and simple stone-built houses. The inhabitants live by crofting (small-scale farming, combined with some fishing), and on Harris also by the weaving of Harris tweed. Many still speak Gaelic. The islands are mainly of interest to anglers and the archaeologically inclined, who will find here many remains of different periods of the past.

On the most northerly island, **Lewis** (pop. 16,700), there is only one town – **Stornoway** (pop. 6000; hotels – Sea-forth, D, 72 r.; Royal, D, 22 r.), with a good natural harbour which has made it an important fishing port. There are bus services from Stornoway to places all over the island. *Stornoway Castle* now houses a technical college. The most notable features of archaeological interest on the island are the *Standing Stones of Callanish* (15 miles W), the finest stone circle in Scotland, and the *broch of Carloway*, also on the W coast.

Harris is the southern part of the "Long Island", the northern part of which consists of Lewis. The principal place is *Tarbert*, and the highest summit is *Clisham* (2622 ft), which can be conveniently climbed from Tarbert. The rest of Harris is also mountainous, with beautiful bays and good bathing beaches. It is famous for Harris tweed, formerly almost all hand-woven but now made in small factories – though there are still many hand-weavers. The most southerly point on the island is *Rodel*, with St Clement's Church (15th–16th c.), which has fine carving and monuments.

To the S of the Sound of Harris is the third largest island, **North Uist** (pop. 3230), a much indented area of land with numerous lochs, both salt- and fresh-water, a number of hills and a fringe of many tiny islets. The principal township on the island is **Lochmaddy** (Lochmaddy Hotel, D, 20 r.), the largest place in the southern Outer Hebrides. A road runs across the island to *Carinish* at its southern tip and then by way of a causeway (built 1960) over the North Ford on to the neighbouring island of **Benbecula**. North Uist is well stocked with wildlife – deer, wild cats, otters, seals – and also offers good fishing. The inhabitants are all crofters, supplementing their income by spinning and gathering seaweed, from which a local factory makes cattle feed.

The island of **Benbecula** lies between North and South Uist and is now connected to both by road. **South Uist** is the second largest of the Outer Hebrides, with a population of 4850. The principal place is **Lochboisdale** (pop. 700), which has a harbour. An excellent road runs from N to S of the island, which also has an airfield. Its second highest peak, *Hecla* (1988 ft) offers a rewarding climb. Near *Askernish* is one of the island's tourist attractions, the birthplace of Flora Macdonald (1727–90), daughter of a local crofter, who helped Bonnie Prince Charlie on his flight in 1746. After his defeat at Culloden the Prince, with a high price on his head, wandered for months about the Highlands before escaping on a French ship, having eluded his pursuers by travelling in disguise as Flora Macdonald's servant girl. Flora herself was sent to the Tower but was later pardoned. There are many old songs and ballads about Prince Charles Edward and many places in the Highlands associated with his adventures. Among them is the little island of Eriskay, to the S of South Uist, where he first set foot on Scottish soil.

Barra is the most southerly of the larger Outer Hebrides, 8 miles long and 5 miles across. Many of the inhabitants – crofters and fishermen – still speak Gaelic as well as English. There are many trout in the lochs which surround the only hill on the island, *Ben Heaval* (1260 ft). The principal place, **Castlebay** (hotels – Isle of Barra, C, 14 r.; Castlebay, D, 10 r.), is a herring port. Picturesquely situated on a rocky islet in the bay is the medieval *Kisimul Castle*.

Similar in character are the smaller islands to the S, with solitary beaches and often bizarrely shaped cliffs – e.g. *Vatersay*, *Mingulay* and *Berneray*, with Barra Head, the most southerly point in the Outer Hebrides.

Hereford

Central England. – County: Hereford and Worcester.
Population: 47,800.
Telephone dialling code: 0432.

ⓘ **Shirehall,**
1A St Owen Street:
tel. 268430.

HOTELS. – *Green Dragon*, Broad Street, C, 88 r.;
Hereford Moat House, Belmont Road, D, 32 r.; *Castle
Pool*, Castle Street, D, 27 r.

RESTAURANTS. – *Greyfriars Garden*, Greyfriars
Avenue; *Graftonbury*, Grafton Lane.

EVENTS. – *Three Choirs Festival* in the Cathedral
(Sept.; in rotation with Gloucester and Worcester).

SPORT and RECREATION. – Rowing, canoeing,
swimming, fishing.

Hereford Cathedral

**Hereford, on the Wye, is the centre
of a large and prosperous farming
region. Hereford cattle are world-
famous, and farmers from all over
Europe come to the livestock auctions here. It is also noted for its
cider, more than half the total English output of cider coming from the
district. The city is surrounded by
extensive apple orchards and hop-
fields. – To the art-lover Hereford's
main attractions are its Cathedral
and its "Mappa Mundi", one of
the oldest maps of the world in
existence.**

SIGHTS. – The town has many handsome
old houses and remains of its *town walls*.
The principal shopping street, **High
Town**, is the scene of great activity on
market days. At its E end is the *Old House*,
a half-timbered building of 1621 which is
now a museum. The *City Museum and Art
Gallery* contains Roman material and
pictures. The parish church of *All Saints*
has 15th c. choir-stalls and a 15th c. wall
painting of the Annunciation; the library
(1715) contains 313 chained books. The
Coningsby Hospital or *Black Cross Hospital* is an early 17th c. building designed
to accommodate old soldiers and sailors;
in the garden is a *preaching cross* of 1370.
David Garrick (1717–79), the famous
actor who was manager of Drury Lane
Theatre in London from 1747 to 1776,
was born in the Angel Inn. Hereford has
other connections with the theatre: Nell
Gwynne is said to have been born in the
town, and the famous actress Sarah
Siddons (1755–1831) and the Kemble
family also lived here. Mementoes of them
can be seen in the Old House.

The great tourist attraction of Hereford,
however, is the *Cathedral, which is
dedicated to St Mary and St Ethelbert. It
was founded about 672, and was the
burial place of St Ethelbert, king of East
Anglia, who was beheaded by King Offa
of Mercia in 794. The present church,
begun either in the time of the first
Norman bishop Robert de Losinga
(1079–95) or of Bishop Reynelm
(1107–15), displays outstanding examples of the various styles of the pre-
Reformation period. The *arches*, the *piers*
supporting the tower, most of the S
transept and the arches and triforium of
the *Choir* are Norman. The *Lady Chapel*
and the *Crypt* are Early English (after
1200), and the N transept was rebuilt
between 1250 and 1288 in a style
transitional between Early English and
Decorated. The *tower* is Decorated (early
14th c.). The W front collapsed in 1786
and was rebuilt, in rather unsatisfactory
style, by James Wyatt and again by John
Oldrid Scott in 1902–08.

INTERIOR. – The *N transept* is notable for its tall
narrow windows and unusual vaulting. It contains
the tombs of Peter of Aigueblanche or Aquablanca
(bishop 1240–68) and Thomas de Cantelupe. The *S
transept* is Norman, with Perpendicular windows. In
the *Choir* are the *bishop's throne* and fine *choir-stalls*
with 60 misericords (14th c.). To the left of the high
altar is a *chair* which is said to have been used by King
Stephen but is probably later. In the Choir is the
famous *Mappa Mundi, a large map of the world

(c. 1290) representing the world as a circle with Jerusalem at the centre, surrounded by figures of animals and historical and mythological characters. The *Crypt* (Early English) is the only medieval crypt in England under a Lady Chapel of the same period.

The Cathedral is also noted for its *chained library* of over 1440 volumes, including 266 volumes of manuscripts: it also has blocks and printing-presses of 1611. It is housed partly above the N transept and partly above the *Bishop's Cloisters*, which have very fine tracery.

SURROUNDINGS. – 13 miles SW is the beautiful parish church of **Abbey Dore**, set among fruit orchards at the end of the "Golden Valley" of the little River Dor. The church was founded in 1147 as the church of a Cistercian abbey and is in the latest Transitional style. It was restored in the early 17th c. by Viscount Scudamore.

7 miles SW is the small but very beautiful Norman church of **Kilpeck**, built about 1120–70, with magnificent carving and a Norman font. The carving shows Scandinavian affinities, which may be attributed to settlers brought here from Kent by Harold (who became Earl of Hereford in 1058).

Ledbury (pop. 3900; Feathers Hotel, D, 13 r.) is a pretty little town which makes a good base for the exploration of the *Malvern Hills*. It has many "black and white" half-timbered houses. The *Market House* (1633) stands on 16 oak pillars, still those of the original structure. From here a narrow street lined with attractive old houses leads to the large parish church with its separate tower. The church shows a variety of different styles. John Masefield (1878–1967) was born in the town, and Elizabeth Barrett Browning (1806–61) spent part of her childhood here.

Eastnor Castle (1½ miles E), built 1812–17, contains a good collection of pictures, weapons and tapestries. It stands in a beautiful park with many rare trees.

Birtsmorton Court (5 miles E) is a beautiful moated manor-house.

Leominster (pronounced Lemster; pop. 9100; hotels – Talbot, D, 31 r.; Royal Oak, D, 16 r.) is a beautiful old wool town on the River Lugg, situated among orchards and hop-fields. It has a number of "black and white" half-timbered houses and a church dating from the 12th, 13th and 14th c. Originally belonging to a priory, the church has a Perpendicular tower over the Norman W doorway and windows with fine ballflower ornament in the S choir aisle. In the N choir aisle is a ducking-stool, last used in 1809, on which nagging wives were dipped into the river. The E end of the church has been demolished.

5 miles NW is **Croft Castle** (14th–15th c.), on land which has been held for 900 years, since the Norman conquest, by the Croft family (fine 17th and 18th c. furniture). It has four round corner towers. There are beautiful avenues of trees in the park.

9 miles SW is the pretty little village of **Weobley** (pop. 1100; hotels – Red Lion, C, 7 r.; Unicorn, D, 10 r.), which has an unusually large number of half-timbered houses. The Red Lion dates from the 13th c. The church, which is mainly 14th c., has a beautiful tower and fine monuments.

Hexham

Northern England. – County: Northumberland.
Altitude: 198 ft. – Population: 10,000.
Telephone dialling code: 0434.
ⓘ **Manor Office**,
Hallgates;
tel. 605225.

HOTELS. – *Royal*, Priestpopple, D, 25 r.; *County*, Priestpopple, D, 10 r.

SPORT and RECREATION. – Swimming, fishing, rowing, walking.

Hexham, situated on the S bank of the Tyne, is one of the most romantic places in the North of England, without any of the industry which leaves its mark on so many of the towns in Northumberland. It lies half way across the narrowest part of England, at roughly the same distance from the North Sea to the E and the Irish Sea or the Solway to the W. It is a good base from which to see Hadrian's Wall. With its narrow streets, handsome old houses, picturesque market place and famous Priory Church, it has preserved much of its medieval aspect.

SIGHTS. – The *Priory Church, also known as the Abbey, is a classic example of Early English architecture (c. 1180–1250). The original church on this site was founded by St Wilfrid of York in

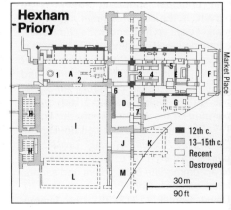

Hexham Priory

■ 12th c.
▨ 13–15th c.
☐ Recent
⌑ Destroyed

| 30 m |
| 90 ft |

A	Nave	G	Chapel
B	Central Tower	H	Cellars
C	North Transept	I	Cloister
D	South Transept	J	Vestibule
E	Choir	K	Chapterhouse
F	Chapel of	L	Refectory
	Five Altars	M	Dormitory

1	Font	3	St Wilfrid's Chair	5	Pulpit
2	Entrance to	4	Position of 7th and	6	Roman monument
	Crypt		12th c. apses	7	Roman altar

674 and partly built of stone from Hadrian's Wall. The *crypt* of this first church has been preserved. Over this crypt the present church, which originally belonged to an Augustinian priory, was built between 1180 and 1250. The *nave* is modern (1907–09), and the E end was rebuilt in 1858.

The INTERIOR contains more medieval features than any other church in the country. They include the old *pulpit* and fragments of sculpture. The basin of the *font* is of Roman origin. In the S transept is a massive "night stair" which led up to the monks' dormitory, now destroyed. At the foot of the stairs are the *Acca Cross* (*c.* 740) and the tombstone of a Roman cavalryman named Flavinus. In the **Choir** the *triforium* is particularly notable. The church contains many portraits of bishops of *c.* 1500 on the old rood-screen and pulpit. The Saxon *bishop's chair* probably belonged to St Wilfrid. On the S side of the choir is the *chantry of Prior Ogle* (d. 1410), on the N side the chantry of Prior Leschman (d. 1491).

The most notable part of the church is the **Crypt* or "Confessio", in which sacred relics were housed. It incorporates stones from Hadrian's Wall, some of them with inscriptions. Under the choir are the foundations of the apse of St Peter's Chapel. Of the priory buildings only a few parts are preserved, among them the *lavatory* (*c.* 1300), the *chapterhouse vestibule* (13th c.) and the *Priory Gate* (*c.* 1160).

Other features of interest in the town are the *Market Place* with its pillars, which has an almost southern aspect; the *Moot Hall* of *c.* 1400, now housing a library, which once belonged to the Archbishops of York; the *Manor Office* (1330–32), a medieval prison; the *Grammar School* (1684); the *Shambles* (market hall) of 1766; a number of Tudor and many Georgian houses.

SURROUNDINGS. – 10½ miles S is a charming little village of barely 200 inhabitants, **Blanchland** (Lord Crewe Arms Hotel, D, 14 r.), reached by a road which runs over high moorland and heath, passing *Dukesfield Fell* (1170 ft). Blanchland is a sleepy little place of stone-built houses dating from the second half of the 18th c., with remains of a Premonstratensian abbey of the 12th c., parts of the church and a gatehouse of *c.* 1500.

Highlands
See North of Scotland

Hull (Kingston upon Hull)

Northern England. – County: Humberside.
Population: 270,000.
Telephone dialling code: 0482.
ⓘ **Central Library**, Albion Street;
tel. 223344.

HOTELS. – *Crest Hull City*, Paragon Street, C, 125 r.; *Royal Station*, Ferensway, C, 121 r.; *Crest Humber Bridge*, Ferriby High Road, C, 102 r.

RESTAURANT. – *Cerutti's* (fish and seafood a speciality), 10 Nelson Street.

The city of Kingston upon Hull, usually known simply as Hull, lies on the N bank of the Humber, which flows into the North Sea 22 miles to the SE. Its economy is centred on its docks, its deep-sea fisheries and its industry. The town suffered extensive destruction during the last war. The University was founded in 1954.

HISTORY. – Kingston upon Hull was founded in 1292 by Edward I and built on both banks of the little River Hull, which here flows into the Humber. The refusal by the governor of the town, Sir John Hotham, to admit Charles I in 1642 was an early act of defiance to royal authority which played a part in bringing on the Civil War. During the war the town was several times unsuccessfully besieged by Royalist forces.

SIGHTS. – In Victoria Square are the *City Hall* and the *Ferens Art Gallery*, which contains many old masters (Frans Hals, Constable, Hogarth, etc.). From here *Whitefriar Gate* runs E to the oldest part of the town and leads by way of Trinity House Lane to *Trinity House*, founded in 1369 for the care of sick or distressed seamen and from 1456 it was their guild house. ****Holy Trinity Church**, which can accommodate a congregation of more than 2200, is said to be the largest parish church in the country. It is in Decorated and Perpendicular style, and has a very fine tower. It is notable for the lightness of its pillars and for its front.

The *Old Grammar School*, SW of the church, was founded in 1486; the present buildings date from 1583. William Wilberforce (1759–1833), M.P. for Hull and Yorkshire for many years and one of the most vigorous opponents of the slave trade, was a pupil of the school. His

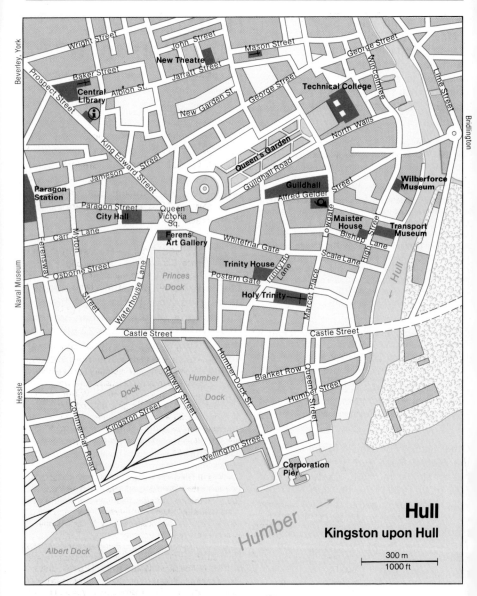

Hull

Kingston upon Hull

300 m
1000 ft

birthplace at 25 High Street, a short distance away, is now a museum, with exhibits concerning the slave trade and local history. In the same street, at Nos. 23 and 24, are two Georgian houses containing a *Transport Museum* (old coaches and motor-cars) and an *Archaeological Museum*.

King's Lynn

Eastern England. – County: Norfolk.
Population: 33,300.
Telephone dialling code: 0553.
ⓘ **Town Hall,**
Saturday Market Place;
tel. 63044.

HOTELS. – *Duke's Head*, C, 72 r. (a handsome 17th c. house); *Stuart House*, Goodwins Road, D, 15 r.; *Runcton House*, 53 Goodwins Road, E, 8 r.

RESTAURANT. – *Globe*, Tuesday Market Place.

YOUTH HOSTEL. – *Thoresby College*, College Lane, 40 b.

SPORT and RECREATION. – Sailing, rowing, swimming.

King's Lynn is a charming and typically English small town which in the past was a place of considerable importance. It lies on the E bank of the Ouse $2\frac{1}{2}$ miles from its outflow into the Wash. It was once the fourth largest town in England and a member of the Hanseatic League. This period of prosperity is still recalled by a 15th c. Hanseatic warehouse. Today King's Lynn is a thriving market town with light industry and a not inconsiderable port.

Lynn's heyday as a fishing port from which ships sailed as far as the waters of Greenland is represented by the Greenland Fishery House, an old timber building of about 1600 which was severely damaged by bombing during the last war but has since been restored and now houses a fishery museum. With its many other historic old buildings, King's Lynn is a jewel among English towns; but it is also a good base from which to see the "seven churches of Marshland". The original name of the town was Lynn: the prefix "King's" was added when Henry VIII granted it the right to hold an additional market. Hence there are two market places in the town, the Tuesday Market and the Saturday Market, round which the older houses are clustered.

SIGHTS. – In *Saturday Market*, near the river, is the town's principal church, **St Margaret's**, with massive W towers which give it almost the air of a cathedral. It was built by the bishop of Norwich in the 12th c., when the town was known as Bishop's Lynn. The W front is particularly fine. It contains two very fine *brasses (probably of Flemish workmanship) which are among the most notable in the whole of England. Both date from the 14th c.; one represents a vintage scene, the other (the "Peacock Brass") a feast centred on a peacock given by the commemorated man. Opposite the church is the **Guildhall of the Holy Trinity** (1421), in a striking flint-chequered pattern. It contains a fine collection of *regalia*, including a valuable cup and sword which are said to have belonged to King John. They recall the famous occasion when John lost his crown jewels and treasure in an unexpectedly early high tide in the Wash; he died of dysentery a few days later (1216).

In Queen Street are *Thoresby College*, founded in 1500, with a 17th c. front, and *Clifton House* (Georgian, with an Elizabethan watch-tower). The *Custom House* (by Henry Bell, 1683) has a statue of Charles II above the entrance. From here King Street runs N, past *St George's Guildhall* (1406), now used as a theatre, to *Tuesday Market*. A short distance away is *St Nicholas's Church*, rebuilt in Perpendicular style in 1419, which has interesting window tracery, a late 15th c. brass lectern and numerous monuments. The octagonal late 14th c. *Greyfriars*

Tower, reached by way of High Street, is a relic of a former priory. In Market Street is the *Museum and Art Gallery*. The *Red Mount Chapel* is an octagonal red-brick building, once frequented by pilgrims on their way to the shrine of Our Lady of Walsingham.

There are numerous handsome *Tudor and Georgian houses*, in the area around King Street. One of the most picturesque spots is where the old ship canal flows into the Ouse, beside the ancient Custom House. The town's 15th c. *South Gate* is still preserved.

SURROUNDINGS. – 8 miles NE is **Sandringham House**, a neo-Elizabethan mansion belonging to the queen. The park is open to the public and the house itself can be visited when the royal family are not in residence. The church has a silver altar and many royal mementoes. Queen Alexandra and the kings George V and VI died at Sandringham.

On the way to *Sandringham*, a small village (pop. 260) which was formerly a harbour town, is **Castle Rising**. Of this once mighty stronghold there remain a Norman keep and massive defensive earthworks. The parish church, with a very beautiful W front, is late Norman. Opposite the church is the Bede House, an almshouse with a small chapel, for 12 poor elderly women founded in 1614. The old ladies who still live there dress in high-domed hats and livery coats on special occasions.

Visitors interested in churches should see at least some of the "**Seven Churches of Marshland**", built on the fenland reclaimed from the sea. They lie between King's Lynn and *Wisbech*, 13 miles away, and are mostly built of silvery-grey Ancaster stone, in Perpendicular style (*Clenchwarton, Terrington St Clement, Walpole St Peter*), Perpendicular and Early English (*Emneth*), Early English (*West Walton*) and Norman (*Walsoken*). *Walpole St Peter* is the "cathedral" of the Marshland churches, with a separate tower and 81 very beautiful windows. Nearby is a charming manor-house, *Lovell's Hall*.

Wisbech (pop. 17,300; White Lion Hotel, C, 14 r.) is an attractive town which was formerly only 4 miles from the sea but is now 11 miles away. It has a harbour on the Nene and is surrounded by orchards, bulb-fields and green fenland. In spring, when the trees are in blossom, and also when the tulips are out it attracts large numbers of visitors. The canals, with houses built along their banks, are reminiscent of Holland. On both banks of the river (North Brink and South Brink) are handsome Georgian houses. Peckover House, with beautiful plasterwork and woodwork, belongs to the National Trust and is open to the public. Near the bridge is a monument to Thomas Clarkson, an active opponent of the slave trade. Also of interest are the two market-places and the parish church, which has a fine 16th c. tower. The Norman castle has long since disappeared, but there is a house built from its stone by Thomas Thurloe, Cromwell's secretary of state. Adjoining it is a museum, one of the oldest in the county. Wisbech is a busy little town and is a centre of the flower and fruit trades.

Kingston upon Hull

See Hull

The Lake District

Northern England. – Cumbria.

The **Lake District is a region of incomparable beauty and great variety, a paradise for fishermen and yachtsmen, covering parts of Cumbria (formerly Cumberland and Westmorland). With its 16 lakes and numerous small reservoirs it fully justifies its name. Between the lakes are innumerable fells, including 180 over 2000 ft; the highest of them all is Scafell Pike (3210 ft). The Lake District covers a distance of some 30 miles from N to S and 25 miles from E to W. At its centre is the little town of Grasmere.

Millions of years have contributed to the shaping of the Lake District. Its landscape bears the marks of volcanic eruptions, the Caledonian folding movements, the subsequent submersion by the sea and the resultant deposition of limestone, and finally the glaciers of the Ice Age. From the centre of the area erosion valleys radiate in all directions, and up in the high valleys the water is collected in round basins which feed the lakes lower down through a series of mountain streams, waterfalls and rivers. There is much more rain here than in the rest of England, and this makes the grass greener and the flowers brighter than elsewhere. The Lake District has an abundance of wild plants and large numbers of waterfowl: herons are a common sight, though less abundant than the sheep which roam over the hills. It is magnificent walking country, particularly outside the main holiday season when there are fewer people about, but it also offers good fishing and is full of interest for the geologically inclined.

The Lake District was "discovered" by the poet Thomas Gray (1716–71), who visited the area in 1769 and wrote a book entitled "A Tour in the Lakes". Thereafter many writers and poets sang the praises of the Lakes, in particular William Wordsworth (1770–1850) and his sister Dorothy (1771–1855), Robert Southey (1774–1843) and Samuel Taylor Coleridge (1772–1834), who became known as the Lake Poets.

The lakes differ considerably in size and character, and their aspect changes from season to season. Much of the Lake District is a national park. Five main areas can be distinguished – the southern or Windermere area, the northern or Keswick area, the eastern or Ullswater area, the western area and the passes.

During the summer there are regular boat services on Lake Windermere, Ullswater and Derwentwater. Sailing and rowing, fishing and swimming are possible in most lakes (permit required for fishing). Climbing is a popular sport on many of the crags (some of which are by no means easy to conquer), and there is an abundance of very attractive footpaths, either going round the lakes (Windermere, 27 miles) or radiating from the towns and villages.

*Lake Windermere, a glacier lake formed during the Ice Age, is England's largest lake, 10 miles in length and over 230 ft deep. At its northern end it is enclosed by rocks; at the S end it is drained by the River Leven, which flows into Morecambe Bay. Its shores are beautifully wooded, and in some places lined by houses. The largest island, *Belle Isle*, and some of the smaller ones can be reached by regular boat services. On *Ladyholme* are the remains of a 13th c. chapel.

The town of **Windermere** (pop. 8100; hotels – Miller Howe, A, 13 r.; Old England, B, 82 r.; Windermere Hydro, C, 76 r.; Belsfield, C, 64 r.; Wild Boar, C, 38 r.; youth hostel, High Cross, Troutbeck, 76 b.) consists of the older part, Bowness-on-Windermere, and the more modern part higher up the hill. The parish church, *St Martin's* (consecrated 1843), has some old glass. The National Park Information Centre has its headquarters in High Street, Windermere.

A particularly fine *view of the southern part of the Lake District and of Morecambe Bay is to be had from **Orrest Head**, reached on a track which runs through Elleray Woods.

Buttermere

A few miles W of Lake Windermere is the charming little village of **Hawkshead** (pop. 700; hotels – Tarn Hows, C, 30 r.; Highfield House, D, 11 r.; youth hostel, Esthwaite Lodge, 78 b.), which has picturesque old stone houses nestling amid gardens and trees, a modest 16th c. church and a grammar school at which Wordsworth was a pupil in 1778–79. To the S of the village is *Grizedale Forest*, with the Treetops look-out tower.

Coniston (pop. 1100; hotel – Sun, D, 9 r.; youth hostel, Holly How, Far End, 70 b.) is beautifully situated half a mile from Coniston Water under the jagged *Yewdale Crags*. In the churchyard is the grave of John Ruskin (1819–1900), writer and social reformer, whose books, collections, drawings and other possessions are in the *Ruskin Museum* to the N of the church. His house was at *Brantwood*, $2\frac{1}{2}$ miles away on the E side of the lake.

Coniston Water is a smaller version of Windermere. Donald Campbell lost his life here in 1967 in an attempt to break the water speed record. The most impressive part of the lake is the N end, with Coniston Fells, but the wooded shores are also very attractive. The **Old Man of Coniston** (2631 ft: magnificent views of surrounding hills) can be climbed in $1\frac{1}{2}$–2 hours.

A popular walk is to the very beautiful **Tarn Hows**, $2\frac{1}{2}$ miles NE. The *Duddon valley*, celebrated by Wordsworth, can be reached by a footpath which runs over the Walna Scar pass (2000 ft: good views) or by a road (narrow in places) via Broughton-in-Furness.

The best centre for the southern part of the Lake District is **Ambleside**, 5 miles from Windermere (pop. 2600; hotels – Rothay Manor, B, 16 r.; Kirkstone Foot County House, C, 12 r.; Vale View, D, 20 r.; youth hostel, Waterhead, 240 b.), a typical tourist resort which apart from the Bridge House has no features of special interest. It does, however, offer a magnificent range of walks and excursions – into *Little Langdale*, to *Loughrigg Terrace* (view), up *Wansfell Pike* and *Loughrigg Fell*, etc. The ascent of the *Langdale Pikes* takes $1\frac{1}{2}$–2 hours. *Dungeon Ghyll* is a popular climbing centre.

Rydal (pop. 530; Lodge Hotel, E, 8 r.) is a quiet little village on the River Rothay at the E end of Rydal Water, 1 mile NW of Ambleside. The very beautiful *Rydal Water* lies in a sheltered situation under *Rydal Fell* (2000 ft). Rydal Mount was Wordsworth's home from 1813 until his death in 1850. In the grounds of Rydal Hall are the Rydal Falls. Rydal Water, the first lake to freeze in winter, is popular with skaters.

Grasmere is a small lake, almost circular in shape, with a lonely green island in the middle. The village of **Grasmere** (pop. 1000; hotels – Michaels Nook Country House, A, 10 r.; Swan, C, 41 r.; Wordsworth, C, 35 r.; youth hostel, Butharlyp How, 89 b.) was a great favourite with the Lake poets. Wordsworth lived in Dove Cottage (now a museum) and is buried in the churchyard. In the little church of St Oswald (14th–17th c.), which has a beautiful interior, are memorials to him and other poets. – There are excellent walks from here, e.g. into *Easedale* and *Borrowdale*. *Helvellyn, only the third highest of the Lakeland hills (3118 ft) but the most impressive in aspect, can be climbed in 3–$3\frac{1}{2}$ hours.

Ullswater

At the foot of Helvellyn is *Thirlmere*, a reservoir belonging to the city of Manchester. On its E side is **Ullswater**, the second largest of the lakes, which offers ideal conditions for sailing and fishing. On the shores of the lake is *Gowbarrow Park* (National Trust), the scene of Wordsworth's best known poem, "Daffodils". **Glenridding** (pop. 600; Glenridding Hotel, D, 43 r.), at the mouth of a gorge-like valley, and **Patterdale** are beautifully situated on the shores of Ullswater and make excellent centres for walkers. Unfortunately there is a good deal of rain in this area.

Haweswater, in a lonely setting fringed by fir forests and flanked by gently rounded hills, has lost much of its beauty

Derwentwater

since it became a reservoir for Manchester.

From Patterdale a very attractive road runs N past *Great Mell Fell* (1760 ft) and then W to **Keswick**, one of the most popular Lake District centres (pop. 4900; hotels – Keswick, C, 64 r.; Derwentwater, D, 42 r.; King's Arms, D, 20 r.; George, D, 17 r.; Chaucer House, E, 32 r.; youth hostel, Station Road, 99 b.). The town, which is crowded with visitors during the holiday season, lies on the River Greta, close to Derwentwater, in the middle of a beautiful range of hills. It has an interesting Moot Hall. Greta Hall, now part of the local school, was the home of Coleridge and later of Southey.

*Derwentwater is generally agreed to be the most beautiful of the lakes, with its grandiose backdrop of hills and the wooded crags and green fells which rise from its shores. A number of pretty little islands in the lake add to the charm of the scene. The River Derwent flows in at one end and out at the other, and the lake is famed for its trout and salmon. A fine view of the lake can be had from *Castle Head*. There are pleasant trips into *Borrowdale*, one of the most beautiful valleys in the Lake District, or round the lake (10 miles), passing the *Falls of Lodore*, made famous by Southey's poem. Particular beauty spots in Borrowdale, which is famed for its fine birch-trees and its good-quality slate, are *Grange-in-Borrowdale* and *Rosthwaite*. The village of **Buttermere** lies between *Buttermere* and *Crummock Water*, two small lakes belonging to the

National Trust, linked by a stream ¾ mile long. *Scale Force, on a stream which flows into Crummock Water, is acknowledged to be the most beautiful waterfall in the Lake District (156 ft high).

From *Keswick* there are good walks to *Wasdale Head* over the *Sty Head pass* (5–6 hours) or by way of *Scarth Gap* and *Black Sail*; but all over the Lake District there are innumerable opportunities for walkers, each offering its own particular scenic beauty, while the fells offer ample scope for climbers. Good maps and guidebooks are readily available.

No visitor to the Lake District should omit the excursion to *Furness Abbey, in the "Vale of Deadly Nightshade", 6 miles from the busy old town of *Ulverston*. The abbey was founded by King Stephen in 1127 for Benedictine monks, who later adopted the Cistercian rule. It was a rich and powerful house, since the abbots held feudal superiority over Furness. At one time it was the second richest Cistercian house in England, surpassed only by Fountains Abbey. There are extensive ruins of the red sandstone buildings. The transepts, choir and W tower of the church still stand to their full height, but the nave is in ruins. The round-headed arches of the cloister, the Early English chapterhouse, the dormitories and the infirmary are also preserved. The chapel contains two effigies of knights, believed to be the oldest of their kind (12th c.). Large parts of the church also date from the 12th c.; the E end and the W tower were added about 1500.

Lancaster

Northern England. – County: Lancashire.
Population: 45,100.
Telephone dialling code: 0524.
ⓘ **Tourist Information Centre**,
    7 Dalton Square;
    tel. 32878.

HOTELS. – *Post House*, Waterside Park, Caton Road, B, 120 r.; *Hampson House*, Hampson Green, D, 13 r.

RESTAURANT. – *Portofino*, 23 Castle Hill.

SPORT and RECREATION. – Water sports of all kinds, fishing, tennis.

A visitor to Lancaster has difficulty in realising that this town was once a more important port than Liverpool and gave its name to the royal dynasty of Lancaster; even its former status as county town has been lost to Preston. What remains is a town with many fine old buildings

which is half old and half modern, the centre of a fertile farming region. Lancaster, a university town since the 1960s, also has some industry. It is attractively situated on the River Lune.

HISTORY. – The town was originally a Roman foundation, *Luncastrum*, the fort on the River Lune. Later the Saxons built a wooden tower here, the Normans a massive keep. George Fox (1624–91), founder of the Society of Friends (Quakers), spent some time in prison in the town.

SIGHTS. – The **Castle**, towering above the river on the site of the original Roman fort, now houses the law courts and a prison. It has preserved its Norman *keep*, the Lungess Tower, with a turret known as *John o' Gaunt's Chair*, and the round *Hadrian's Tower* (1209, much altered). A notable feature is the *porter's lodge*. The *Shire Hall* (1798) has fine woodwork.

St Mary's Church, close by, is mostly Perpendicular in style (1431). The *tower* dates from 1754; the canopied *choir-stalls*, dating from 1340, rank among the finest work of their period. The church has a Saxon doorway. The *Old Town Hall* in Market Square is now a museum (Roman material, history of local industry).

The *Town Hall* in Dalton Square was built in 1909. Other notable buildings are *St John's Church* (1734) and the *Custom House*. *Skerton Bridge* over the Lune (by

Thomas Harrison, 1783–88) was the first road bridge in England to be built without piers. There are good views from the *Ashton Memorial*, which stands on high ground to the E of the town.

SURROUNDINGS. – 7½ miles SW, near the mouth of the Lune, is **Cockersand Abbey**, a Premonstratensian house founded in 1190. It has an octagonal chapterhouse. Nearby, on the river, is a bird reserve for wild geese and other waterfowl.

28 miles SE is the **Forest of Bowland**, which is designated as an area of outstanding natural beauty. This is an area of moorland at heights ranging between 1000 and 1836 ft (highest point *Ward's Stone*), which offers excellent walking and beautiful scenery. The area is traversed by a number of roads, often steep and narrow, which are convenient for walkers and are also used by motor traffic. The Trough of Bowland is a pass at a height of 1000 ft. There are a number of particularly attractive places in this area, such as *Whitewell* in the pretty Hodder valley (trout fishing in the river). **Browsholme Hall**, is a beautiful old Tudor house (1507) with a notable art collection. *Stonyhurst*, a famous boys' school run by the Jesuits, has some fine old buildings.

Leeds

Northern England. – County: West Yorkshire.
Altitude: 150 ft. – Population: 448,600.
Telephone dialling code: 0532.
ⓘ **Central Library**,
    Calverley Street;
    tel. 462454.

HOTELS. – *Ladbroke Dragonara*, Neville Street, B, 237 r.; *Queen's*, City Square, C, 193 r.; *Ladbroke*, Wakefield Road, Garforth, C, 149 r.; *Metropole*, King Street, C, 110 r.; *Wellesley*, Wellington Street, C, 54 r.; *Crest*, The Grove, Oulton, C, 40 r.; *Staki's Windmil* , Ring Road, C, 40 r.; *Merrion*, Merrion Centre, D, 120 r.

RESTAURANTS. – *Embassy*, 333 Roundhay Road; *Gardini's Terrazza*, 16 Greek Street; *Mandalay*, 8 Harrison Street; *Rules*, 188 Selby Road.

EVENTS. – *Leeds Musical Festival* (every 3 years in April: 1985, 1988, etc.).

SPORT and RECREATION. – Water sports, golf, tennis, riding.

Leeds, situated on the River Aire, is an industrial city (textiles, furniture, paper, leather, electrical equipment) with a university which is particularly notable for its departments of science and technology. It is a good shopping centre and has a number of interesting museums, as well as an active musical life. It also has attractive parks and gardens.

SIGHTS. – The hub of Leeds is **City Square**, outside the City Station. In the square are numerous *statues*, including

Ashton Memorial, Lancaster

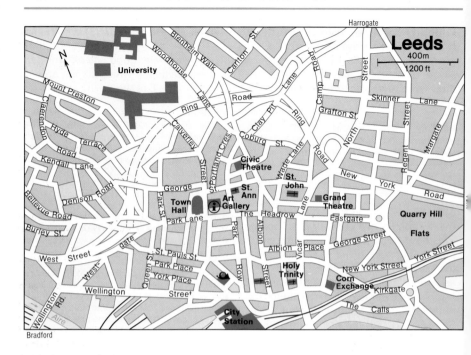

figures of the Black Prince (son of Edward III) and James Watt. Park Row, a shopping and business street, leads to *Victoria Square*, in which stands the **Town Hall** (1853–58), a building in Palladian style with a Corinthian colonnade along the main front and a high clock-tower. Its ornate *Victoria Hall* is used for concerts and the Leeds Musical Festival. On the E side of the square is the *City Art Gallery*, opened in 1888, which has a fine collection of works by British artists, with particular emphasis on the 20th c. English watercolour painting is also well represented, with 750 pictures by J. S. Cotman (1782–1842), one of the leading members of the Norwich School, mainly East Anglian landscapes. There are also works by Italian and French painters, including Courbet, Corot, Renoir and Signac.

Adjoining the Art Gallery is the *City Museum*, which has departments of geology, zoology, ethnology and archaeology, including particularly material from Yorkshire.

Near the Town Hall is the **Civic Hall**, an imposing building opened by King George V in 1933. Adjoining it are the *General Infirmary* and various colleges.

The best shopping area is to be found in the side streets off the **Headrow**, the main through route across the city, laid out in 1924–33. The finest of the city's churches is *St John's* in New Briggate,

built 1632–34. The exterior is in Perpendicular style; the interior is notable for having two naves. The church has been preserved almost completely in the style in which it was built and still has the original *rood-screen*, *pulpit* and *stalls*. The Roman Catholic **Cathedral** in Cookridge Street, dedicated to St Anne, was built in 1902–04. *Holy Trinity* in Boar Lane (1721–27) has a very fine tower added by Chantrell in 1831. It stands close to the Aire. Between the river and the railway is the city's oldest parish church, *St Peter's*, a medieval church rebuilt in 1839–41 in a mixture of Decorated and Perpendicular styles.

Other interesting buildings of a later date are the *Corn Exchange*, a functional building, oval in plan, erected in 1861–63, and the *Quarry Hill Flats*, a fine example of local authority housing of the late 1930s.

SURROUNDINGS. – 3½ miles NW, in the Aire valley, is **Kirkstall Abbey**, a Cistercian house founded in 1151. The picturesque remains include a roofless church with a narrow choir and a ruined Perpendicular tower, an almost completely preserved chapterhouse, the refectory, the kitchen and various other buildings. The gatehouse is now part of the Abbey House Museum, with reproductions of houses, shops and workshops illustrating Yorkshire life in earlier days. It belongs to the city of Leeds.

4½ miles E is **Temple Newsam**, a 17th c. mansion (also belonging to the city of Leeds) mainly in Tudor and Jacobean style, on the site of a preceptory of the Knights Templar. It contains valuable furniture (by Chippendale among others), porcelain, ceramics and silver. The house stands in beautiful grounds, notable particularly for their roses.

3 miles S is the *oldest railway in Britain* (now belonging to the National Trust), built in 1758 to carry coal from the Middleton mine to Leeds. Trains are run on the line during the summer.

8 miles N is *Harewood House, seat of the Earl of Harewood. This magnificent mansion (by Robert Adam, 1759–71) has interior decoration by Adam, magnificent plasterwork, fine wall and ceiling paintings by Angelica Kauffman and other artists, and furniture by Thomas Chippendale. It has an outstanding collection of porcelain and a large number of valuable pictures, including works by Reynolds, Gainsborough and El Greco. The house is open to visitors from Easter to September (11 a.m. to 6 p.m.). There is a beautiful park designed by Capability Brown, with a large lake and remains of a 12th c. castle. The church contains a number of notable monuments.

Leicester

Central England. – County. Leicestershire.
Population: 279,800.
Telephone dialling code: 0533.
(i) **Tourist Information Centre,**
12 Bishop Street;
tel. 556699.

HOTELS. – *Leicester International*, Humberstone Road, C, 220 r.; *Holiday Inn*, St Nicholas Circle, C, 190 r.; *Post House*, Braunstone Lane East, C, 179 r.; *Grand*, Granby Street, C, 93 r.; *Eaton Bray*, Abbey Street, C, 73 r.; *Belmont*, De Montfort Street, C, 62 r.

RESTAURANTS. – *Europa Lodge*, Hinckley Road; *Old Vicarage*, 123 Enderby Road, Whetstone.

Leicester, county town of Leicestershire, situated on the River Soar in a region of great scenic attraction, is a modern commercial and industrial centre with a long history. Its traditional industries – hosiery, knitwear and shoe manufacture – have been supplemented in recent years by engineering. It has a variety of churches and other old buildings of many different periods, mostly built in red brick; and cultural interests are well catered for by its museums and art galleries, two theatres and a large concert hall.

Leicester can claim to be the birthplace of modern mass tourism – if the medieval pilgrimages are excluded – since it was here that Thomas Cook organised his first package tour in 1841, a round trip of 30 miles to Loughborough.

HISTORY. – Leicester occupies the site of the Roman city of *Ratae Coritanorum*, of which a number of interesting remains have survived. From 780 to 869 it was the see of a bishop, and during the period of Danish rule one of the five boroughs of the Danelaw. The town was fortified by the Normans, and in 1239 passed into the hands of Simon de Montfort, Earl of Leicester. As the father of the English Parliament his main aim was to strengthen the influence of the English nobility against the French court, but he also succeeded in arousing the country's national consciousness. Three Parliaments were held in Leicester. Richard III (1483–85) spent the night before the battle of Bosworth in the town, and after the battle his body was brought back and buried in Leicester Abbey; after the Dissolution of the Monasteries, however, his remains were thrown into the River Soar. Thomas Wolsey (1472–1530), Henry VIII's Lord Chancellor but later dismissed, was also buried here.

SIGHTS. – In the centre of the city is the Victorian *Clock-Tower*, with figures of Leicester's four principal benefactors. From here the High Street runs W to *St Nicholas's Church*, the oldest in the city, with a Norman tower, a Saxon nave and re-used Roman bricks in the masonry. Close to its W end is the *Jewry Wall* (79 ft long by 18 ft high), Leicester's most impressive relic of Roman times, originally part of a basilica. Adjoining this are the excavations of the *Roman forum*, which have revealed the remains of baths, beautiful mosaic pavements and other features. Material from this and other Roman sites can be seen in the *Jewry Wall Museum*.

Little is left of *Leicester Castle*, except parts of the Great Hall and the cellars which are incorporated in the 18th c. *County Hall*. Close by is the church of *St Mary de Castro* (1107), partly in Norman and partly in Early English style, with a late Norman choir and a fine Early English baptistery. The ruined Turret Gateway (1423) leads to *Trinity Hospital*, an almshouse founded in 1331 and rebuilt in 1901, and *Newarke*, with a museum devoted to the historical development of industry in Leicester.

The fine *Newarke Gateway* leads to the **Cathedral** (St Martin's), a church in Early English and Perpendicular styles which was raised to cathedral status in 1919. Nearby is the *Old Guildhall*, a 14th c. half-timbered building which is now a museum, with a valuable library. Other features of interest are the *Market Place*, the *Corn Exchange*, with a handsome external staircase, and the Victorian *Town Hall* with its clock-tower. *New Walk* (pedestrians only) runs SE to the *Museum and Art Gallery*, and beyond this joins Victoria Road, in which are the *De Montfort Hall* (1913) and the *War Memorial Arch* (by Lutyens, 1925).

On the N side of the city is the beautiful *Abbey Park*, with the remains of *Leicester Abbey*, an Augustinian house founded in 1143 of which only the foundations have been preserved. On its site was built an Elizabethan mansion, *Cavendish House*, now also a ruin.

SURROUNDINGS. – 6 miles NW is the very beautiful **Bradgate Park**, with the ruins of the mansion in which Lady Jane Grey (1537–54), the "nine days' queen", was born. In the 12th c. this was a hunting preserve, and it has preserved much of its original character. "Going out to Bradgate" is a popular recreation with the people of Leicester.

N of Bradgate extends **Charnwood Forest**, an area of rocky and rugged country which offers excellent walking. From *Bardon Hill* (912 ft) there are good views of the forest, towards Derbyshire and the Welsh Marches. There was a Bronze Age settlement here, but stone-quarrying has destroyed all traces. In the midst of this region of scrub, bracken and heather lie the remains of two abbeys.

17 miles NW of Leicester is **Ashby-de-la-Zouch** (pop. 11,500; hotel – Royal Crest, C, 31 r.), an attractive little town in a fertile valley, in spite of its situation in the middle of a coalfield. It has the ruins of the castle which features in Scott's "Ivanhoe" (built by Lord Hastings in 1460, destroyed by Parliamentary forces in 1648). The parish church, in late Perpendicular style, contains an effigy of a pilgrim (15th c.), a number of monuments, and finger-stocks for those who misbehaved in church. About 9 miles NE in *Castle Donington* can be found the *Donington Carriage Collection*.

Lichfield

Central England. – County: Staffordshire.
Altitude: 266 ft. – Population: 25,600.
Telephone dialling code: 05432.
ⓘ **Tourist Information Centre**,
   9 Breadmarket Street;
   tel. 52109.

HOTELS. – *George*, Bird Street, C, 40 r.; *Swan*, Bird Street, C, 31 r.; *Little Barrow*, Beacon Street, C, 26 r.

RESTAURANT. – *Champs Elysées*, Minster Pool Walk.

EVENTS. – *Dr Johnson's Birthday* (18 September).

Lichfield is a quiet and attractive little town whose main tourist attractions are its magnificent Cathedral and its associations with Dr Samuel Johnson (1709–84), author of the famous Dictionary. The son of a Lichfield bookseller, he wrote of the people of Lichfield in glowing terms, saying that they were "the most sober, decent people in England, the genteelest in proportion to their wealth, and spoke the purest English" – a eulogy in which the inhabitants still take no small pride.

Lichfield Cathedral

SIGHTS. – Lichfield offers little of tourist interest apart from the ****Cathedral** (St Mary and St Chad), one of the most beautiful in England. Built of red sandstone, it is mainly Early English and Decorated (1200–1370). Its exquisite symmetry and fine proportions have earned it the title of "queen of English minsters". The oldest part is the lower section of the W end of the *choir* (c. 1198); the *transepts* date from 1220–40, the *nave* from about 1250, the W front from 1280, the *Lady Chapel* and *presbytery* from the first half of the 14th c. The church received severe damage during two sieges in 1643 and 1646, and suffered even more severely from drastic restoration, particularly by Wyatt at the end of the 18th c. The worst damage was done to the exterior, which preserves little original work.

The three elegant spires – a feature unique in England – are known as the "Ladies of the Vale". The *W front*, notable for the splendid harmony of its composition, is particularly beautiful, with niches containing 113 *statues* (modern, with only one or two exceptions). The central door has intricate *wrought-iron work* by Thomas of Leighton. The entrance to the N transept, a delicate piece of Early English work, is also very fine.

The INTERIOR is notable for its beautiful proportions and the play of colour. The *capitals* in the nave have, fortunately, survived without restoration. In the aisles and transepts are numerous monuments, including a

Lichfield Cathedral

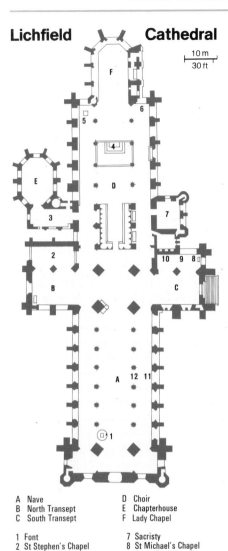

```
10 m
30 ft
```

A Nave
B North Transept
C South Transept

D Choir
E Chapterhouse
F Lady Chapel

1 Font
2 St Stephen's Chapel
3 Vestibule
4 High altar
5 Monument of Bishop Ryder
6 Sleeping Children

7 Sacristy
8 St Michael's Chapel
9 David Garrick
10 Samuel Johnson
11 Col. Anson
12 Earl of Lichfield

tablet commemorating Lady Mary Wortley Montagu (1689–1762), a pioneer of smallpox inoculation, and a bust of Dr Johnson.

The *Choir* was built in the Early English period but partly rebuilt in Decorated style in 1325. The stalls were carved c. 1860 by Samuel Evans of Ellastone, a cousin of George Eliot. In the S aisle is the famous monument of the *Sleeping Children*, by Sir Francis Chantrey (1817). A *medallion* commemorates Erasmus Darwin (1731–1802), the botanist, grandfather of Charles Darwin.

The *Lady Chapel*, in Decorated style, was built in 1324. The beautiful stained glass windows (1532–39), with scenes from the Passion, were brought to Lichfield from Herkenrode Abbey, near Liège, in 1802. The two most westerly windows are also Flemish work. Above the elegant Chapterhouse of c. 1240 is the *Library*, whose greatest treasures are an Irish manuscript Gospel (St Chad's Gospel) of 721 and a manuscript of Chaucer's "Canterbury Tales".

Lincoln

Central England. – County: Lincolnshire.
Altitude: 299 ft. – Population: 76,600.
Telephone dialling code: 0522.

(i) **Tourist Information Centre,**
City Hall,
Beaumont Fee;
tel. 32151, ext. 515.

HOTELS. – *Eastgate Post House*, Eastgate, B, 71 r.; *White Hart*, Bailgate, C, 68 r.; *Grand*, St Mary's Street, D, 49 r.

YOUTH HOSTEL. – 77 South Park, 40 b.

RESTAURANTS. – *Harvey's*, Castle Square; *White's*, 15 The Strait.

*Lincoln, county town of Lincoln-
shire, is one of the finest of
England's historic old cities. It lies
on the River Witham, which at this
point has carved out its course
through a ridge of limestone. Lincoln consists of an upper and a lower
town, linked by a number of exceedingly steep streets. It is dominated
by its Cathedral, one of the largest in
England, and also has many handsome old houses, medieval streets,
stepped lanes and gates, as well as
remains of Roman town gates and
a medieval castle. Lincoln is also
famed for its "Lincoln cakes", made
with curds, raisins, currants and
saffron.*

HISTORY. – The British settlement of *Lindun* (the hill fort by the pond) became one of the few Roman colonies in Britain, under the name of *Lindum Colonia*; and it is the only one to preserve the Latin word for colony in its name. Excavations have shown that the town had a very fine water supply system in Roman times. In the 9th c. it was one of the five boroughs of the Danelaw, and after the Norman Conquest it ranked as the fourth most important town in England. In the Middle Ages it was a seaport and an important centre of the wool trade. During the First World War the first tanks were manufactured here, and engineering is now the town's main industry.

SIGHTS. – The modern lower town forms a striking contrast with the peaceful and picturesque old upper town around the Cathedral. Starting from the *High Street*, the first church to be seen is *St Peter-at-Gowts*, which has a Saxon tower. A short distance N is *St Mary's Guildhall* (1180–90), a fine example of Norman secular architecture. In *Akrill's Passage* is a notable 15th c. half-timbered house. On the right is the church of *St Mary-le-Wigford* (Early English, with a Saxon tower). *St Mary's Conduit* was built in the 16th c. with stone from a Carmelite friary. To the left is *St Benedict's Church* (no longer used for worship), with a war

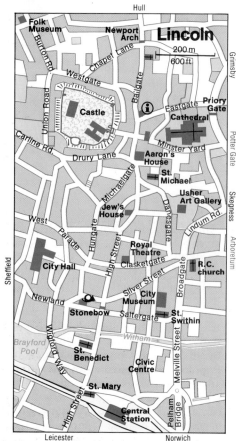

and the *Assize Court* (by Sir Robert Smirke, 1823–26).

The street called *Bailgate* was the centre of the Roman town. Circles mark the positions of the Roman columns, and in the cellar of No. 29, the Roman House, can be seen *remains of the Roman basilica. St Paul's Church* stands on the site of the church built by St Paulinus, who brought Christianity to Lincoln in 627. At the N end of Bailgate is the *Newport Arch*, one of the two best preserved Roman town gates in England. A small section of the Roman *town walls* can be seen in East Bight.

The **Cathedral** could surely claim to surpass all others in Britain in beauty, situation and the harmonious proportions of the interior and exterior; but unfortunately the stone has suffered severely from weathering, and it is a costly enterprise to preserve this great building, which Cobbett described as the "finest building in the whole world". Built in the honey-coloured local limestone, it was begun by Bishop Remigius about 1070; but of the original building only the *base of the W front* survives. After a fire in 1141 the church was rebuilt by Bishop Alexander (1123–48), and the *W doorways*, the *arcades*, and the three lowest storeys of the *W towers* probably date from this second Norman period. The carved panels on the W front were added somewhat later, in the mid 12th c.

In 1185 the Cathedral was damaged by an earthquake and thereafter was rebuilt by Hugh of Avalon (bishop 1186–1200).

memorial in front of it. From the S side of the nearby *Brayford Pool*, which is fed by the River Witham, there is a splendid view of the Cathedral. The river is spanned by the **High Bridge**, which dates from 1160. On the W side are a number of old houses and shops, the backs of which can be seen by going down the steps. From here the High Street continues N to pass under the *Stonebow*, a 15th c. town gate with the Guildhall above it, and runs into the *Strait* and then the *Steep*, or Steep Hill, which climbs to the upper town. Here are to be found the most interesting remains of the OLD TOWN, in the form of two 12th c. houses, the *Jew's House*, and, in the adjoining Jew's Court, the *House of Aaron the Jew* – rare examples of Norman secular architecture. The Jews, being prosperous, were able to build stone houses, but were expelled from England in 1290.

On Castle Hill is the entrance to the **Castle**, built by William the Conqueror in 1068. Within the precincts are the *Observatory Tower* (fine view from top), a 13th c. bastion known as *Cobb Hall*, the *keep*

Lincoln Cathedral

who was responsible for the *choir* and *transepts*, the earliest and purest examples of Early English. The *W transepts*, the *chapterhouse* and the *nave*, including the W front, were completed by Hugh of Wells (bishop 1209–35) and his successor Robert Grosseteste (1235–53). The *presbytery* was built by Richard de Gravesend (1258–79), the *cloisters* by his successor Oliver Sutton (1280–99). The lower part of the *central tower* dates from 1240–50, the upper part from 1300–20; it was originally crowned by a tall spire. The upper parts of the W towers are Decorated (*c.* 1380). Perpendicular work can be seen in the *W window* and the *chantry chapels*. The towers house nine bells, the largest of which, Great Tom, weighs over 5 tons. Particularly striking features of the exterior are the tiers of Gothic blind arcades and the carved panels on the W front. The *S doorway* is particularly beautiful (to the right a gargoyle of the devil looking out over the city).

In the INTERIOR the honey-coloured limestone is well preserved, forming an attractive contrast with the dark Purbeck marble. The *Choir* is one of the earliest examples of pure Gothic. The effect is slightly spoiled by the *organ* built above the *choir screen*. In the S choir aisle are remains of the sarcophagus of "Little St Hugh", a boy who is said to have been crucified in 1255.

The 62 *choir-stalls* (1360–80) have magnificent carving on the bench ends and the misericords. The presbytery or **Angel Choir** is of exquisite beauty, notable both for its proportions and for its details. Built in 1280, it gets its name from the 30 angels on the triforium. The style shows the transition from Early English to Decorated. At the top of the second-last pillar to the N is the famous "Lincoln Imp". To the left of the *high altar* are an *Easter sepulchre* and the tomb of Bishop Remigius, to the right the monument of Catherine Swynford (d.1403), wife of John of Gaunt. The *E window is an outstanding example of geometric tracery. Below the window is a monument to Eleanor, Edward I's queen, who died near Lincoln. Her coffin was conveyed to Westminster, and "Eleanor crosses" were set up at each of the 12 halting places on the way. In the S transept is a very beautiful *round window* (first half of 14th c.), with tracery in the form of branches; its counterpart in the N transept is a fine *rose window* with 13th c. glass.

The *Cloisters* date from the end of the 13th c., and have beautifully carved timber *roof-bosses*. The N side, from which there is one of the finest views of the Cathedral, was rebuilt by Wren in 1647, together with the library above it. The *Chapterhouse* is decagonal, with its vaulting springing from a central pier; it dates from the early 13th c. Several Parliaments met here in the reigns of Edward I and II.

The *Cathedral Close* is very picturesque, with a number of notable buildings, including the remains of the *Old Bishop's Palace*, the *Cantilupe Chantry House* and the *Vicars' Court*.

In the gardens to the S of the Cathedral is the **Usher Art Gallery**, which has a fine collection of watches, jewellery, miniatures and porcelain. The *City and County Museum* in Broadgate contains Roman material.

SURROUNDINGS. – 16 miles SW is **Newark-on-Trent** (pop. 24,300; hotel – Robin Hood, C, 20 r.), a picturesque little town which is worth a visit. In spite of its name it is not situated directly on the main course of the River Trent. Its principal features of interest are the castle of the bishop of Lincoln, in which King John died in 1216, and the Perpendicular church of St Mary Magdalene in the pretty market-place, which has been much restored but preserves a beautiful rood-screen, misericords of 1525 and a Norman crypt.

From Newark it is possible to make a round trip by continuing N along the Trent in the direction of Gainsborough, 24 miles away. A short distance before Gainsborough in *Stow*, is a fortress-like church with a beautiful Norman choir which was the mother church of Lincoln.

Gainsborough (pop. 17,500) is a town with interesting historical associations. King Alfred was married here in 868, and the Danish king Sweyn Forkbeard died here in his camp at Thonock Park in 1014. During the Civil War the town was the scene of much fighting between Royalist and Parliamentary forces. The Old Hall, part of a medieval manor-house, has a handsome roof and an old kitchen. Gainsborough was George Eliot's model for St. Ogg's in "The Mill on the Floss", and some of the places she describes can still be identified. – The return to Lincoln is either via *Caenby Corner* or *Market Rasen*.

Liverpool

Central England. – County: Merseyside.
Population: 537,000.
Telephone dialling code: 501.
ⓘ **Tourist Information Centre,**
St George's Hotel, Lime Street;
tel. 709 3631.

HOTELS. – *Holiday Inn*, Paradise Street, B, 273 r.; *Atlantic Tower Thistle*, Chapel Street, B, 226 r.; *St George's*, St John's Precinct, Lime Street, B, 155 r.; *Adelphi*, Ranelagh Place, C, 309 r.; *Crest City*, Lord Nelson Street, C, 169 r.; *Crest*, East Lancs Road, C, 50 r.; *Feathers*, 119–125 Mount Pleasant, E, 80 r.

RESTAURANTS. – *Churchill Carvery*, Tithebarn Street; *Jenny's Seafood*, Fenwick Street; *Oriel*, 16 Water Street; *Ristorante del Secolo*, 36 Stanley Street.

EVENTS. – *Grand National Steeplechase*, held at Aintree.

SPORT and RECREATION. – Sailing, rowing, golf, tennis; several theatres, concerts.

Liverpool, with one of the largest harbours in the world not dependent on tides, is a major port for transatlantic shipping. It lies on the E side of the Mersey estuary, 3 miles from the open sea. The Mersey is here $\frac{3}{4}$ mile wide, opening out inland into a basin 3 miles wide. As the place where the Beatles once worked, Liverpool attracts many tourists.

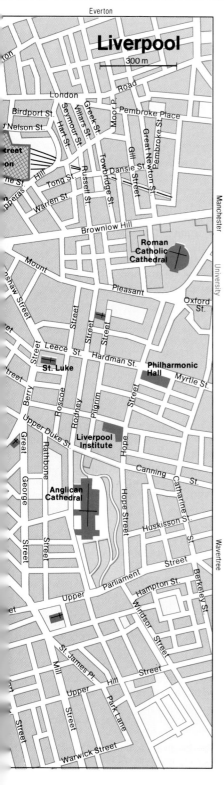

Liverpool

300 m

links Liverpool with Birkenhead, is one of the longest under-water road tunnels in the world. The port has the largest docks in Britain, extending for some 7 miles, with 29 miles of quays. The city suffered heavy damage in the last war but has been imaginatively rebuilt. The Philharmonic Hall is one of Europe's finest concert halls. The city has many handsome blocks of offices and commercial buildings and is well supplied with parks and open spaces. – Liverpool was the home of the Beatles, the legendary pop music group which achieved world fame in the 1960s.

HISTORY. – The origin of the city's name is unknown, but is traditionally connected with the mythological Liver bird (pronounced "lyver") which is represented on the towers of the Royal Liver Building on the waterfront and figures in the city's coat of arms, carrying a piece of seaweed in its beak. The name appears for the first time in a charter of 1173 granted by Henry II, who founded the town and built a castle here. The port was constructed by King John in 1207. The first dock was opened in 1715, when the town had a population of some 5000. Liverpool followed Bristol in the development of the slave trade, which formed a profitable adjunct to the local cotton industry: raw cotton was brought in from the plantations in the West Indies and North America, the finished products were mainly exported to Africa, and the ships carrying these cotton goods then conveyed cargoes of slaves to the plantations. The regular shipping services to North America which began in 1840 also contributed to the city's prosperity.

SIGHTS. – *St George's Hall (by Harvey Lonsdale Elmes, 1838–54) ranks as the finest neo-classical building in Britain. The Great Hall, with one of the world's largest organs, is used for concerts and congresses. To the rear are *St John's Gardens*, in which are statues of prominent Liverpool citizens. Looking on to the gardens is an imposing group of neo-Greek buildings, the *College of Technology* (1902) and the *Regional College*. The *Brown Library*, destroyed by bombing during the last war, was re-opened in 1961.

The large complex of the **Liverpool Museums** contains a variety of collections, covering almost every field of knowledge from archaeology to technology. Among them are an interesting collection of *ship models*, the famous *Ince Blundell Collection* of ancient marbles, the *Sassoon Collection* of ivories, and Egyptian, Babylonian and Assyrian antiquities.

Liverpool's best known museum, the *Walker Art Gallery** (1874–76), was presented to the city by a local brewer, Sir

Apart from its commercial importance, Liverpool is notable for its two cathedrals, both dating from the 20th c.; the Anglican Cathedral is one of the largest churches in Christendom. The Mersey Tunnel, which

Andrew Barclay Walker, who was Mayor in 1873. It has a rich collection of works by Italian, Dutch and French artists, and its display of English painting, particularly of the 18th–20th c., is unrivalled by any gallery outside London. The *John Moore Exhibition*, an important display of contemporary British art, is held every alternate year. Associated with the Walker Art Gallery is the *Sudley Art Gallery*, in an early 19th c. mansion on Mossley Hill, 3 miles S, notable mainly for its collection of works by English painters of the 18th and 19th c., including Gainsborough and Turner.

Liverpool's possession of two cathedrals, a Roman Catholic as well as an Anglican, reflects the high proportion of Roman Catholics of Irish origin in its population. During the great emigrations in the periods of poverty and distress in Ireland, Liverpool was the principal port of embarkation for the United States, and many of the emigrants also settled in the city. The Roman Catholic archdiocese of Liverpool was founded in 1911, and the construction of the *Roman Catholic Cathedral**, only a quarter of a mile from the Anglican Cathedral, was begun in 1928. The original design was for a neo-classical building, but only the *crypt* of this was completed. After the Second World War an architectural competition was held for the completion of the Cathedral, the successful design – much more modest than the original plan, which would have produced the second largest church in Christendom – being that of Sir

Frederick W. Gibberd, who had worked on the design of Heathrow Airport, London, but had not previously built a church.

The Cathedral, consecrated in 1967, is a massive circular structure centred on a lantern of medieval type. Round this cylindrical lantern tower is a huge "tent" 200 ft in diameter, rising sharply to a funnel-shaped drum 270 ft high. Since the Cathedral is built on a hill, it has the appearance of a huge lantern rising above the city. The principal structural materials are steel and glass – more glass than in any other cathedral. Opinions differ widely, among both local people and visitors, about the merits of the building; but whether one finds it beautiful or not, it must be conceded at any rate that it is striking.

The Cathedral can accommodate a congregation of 3000. The altar is a block of white marble from Skopje in Yugoslavia, 10 ft long and weighing 19 tons. The spaces between the 16 supporting piers are occupied by chapels, separated by blue and green *glass walls*. On the N side of the Cathedral is an *open-air altar* where services are sometimes held.

The *Anglican Cathedral**, on St James's Mount, shows a sharp contrast in style. It is neo-Gothic, modelled on the church architecture of the 12th–16th c. The design was selected by competition in 1901, the successful architect being Giles Gilbert Scott, then only 22 years old. When he died in 1960 the church was still not completed; it was finally consecrated in 1978 (the foundation stone having been laid in 1904), although services were already being held in the building in the 1920s. As completed after more than 70 years' building, the Cathedral is the fifth largest church in the world. It has only a single *tower*, 330 ft high, in place of the twin towers originally planned. The Cathedral, built of red Woolton sandstone, with a copper roof, can accommodate a congregation of some 2500. The tower contains a *carillon* of 13 bells, the largest of which weighs 4 tons.

The INTERIOR is less traditional than the exterior. It contains an abundance of fine detailing, representing the best English craftsmanship. The Willis *organ*, with 9704 pipes, is one of the largest in the world. The *Lady Chapel* is also very beautiful. The *stained glass* is by English artists.

Liverpool possesses another fine building in its *Town Hall*, built in 1754 by John Wood the Elder and enlarged in 1789. *St

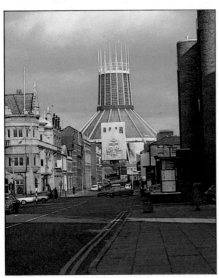
Roman Catholic Cathedral, Liverpool

John's Beacon is a 450-ft-high tower with a revolving restaurant and a viewing platform which affords wide-ranging views in all directions. The former *Bluecoat School* in Church Alley now houses an art centre. The oldest part of the *University* (founded 1903) is the School of Tropical Medicine, the earliest in the world, reflecting the far-flung Empire of the 19th c. The *Maritime Museum* is to be found in the warehouses of the Albert Dock.

Beatle City (museum with guitars, etc.) and the Cavern Walks (on the site of the Cavern Club, where the Beatles appeared; statue of the Beatles by John Doubleday) are attractions for Beatle fans (conducted tours).

SURROUNDINGS. – **Birkenhead** (pop. 110,100; hotels – Bowler Hat, D, 29 r.; Riverhill, D, 17 r.; Lincluden Guest House, D, 11 r.; Gronwen Guest Hotel, D, 7 r.) lies on the W side of the Mersey opposite Liverpool, with which it is connected by road and rail tunnels and by ferry services. It is also a busy port, with large docks, slaughterhouses and grain mills. The Williamson Art Gallery and Museum has an excellent collection of pictures and porcelain, together with much material on the history of the town. Birkenhead's only historic building is a ruined 12th c. Benedictine priory (chapterhouse, crypt, part of refectory). The town has a large and beautiful park.

Port Sunlight is of interest for the part it played in the history of British industrial development and British socialism. It was founded by Lord Leverhulme, head of Lever Brothers, as a model village for the employees of the Lever soap-works, with good schools and other amenities. The *Lady Lever Art Gallery* has an excellent collection of Art Nouveau, together with works by Turner and other British painters.

One of Liverpool's many dormitory towns is **Wallasey** (pop. 70,300), at the NE tip of the *Wirral Peninsula*.

One of the finest Tudor houses in England is *Speke Hall, 7 miles SE in *Hale* (pop. 2400), on the N side of the Mersey. This beautiful half-timbered house (1530–98) is notable for its great hall, its beautiful plasterwork and its fine furniture. The little town of Hale was described by Jane Welsh Carlyle (1801–66) as the most beautiful in the whole of England.

London

Southern England.
Administrative unit: Greater London.
Population: 7,220,000.
Telephone dialling code: 01.

Tourist Information Centre,
64 St James's Street;
tel. 499 9325.

Teletourist Service;
tel. 246 8041.

Tourist Information Centre
(Accommodation Register),
West Passageway, Victoria Station;
01–730 0791.

Harrods
Knightsbridge (4th floor);
01–730 0791.

Selfridges
Oxford Street (ground floor);
01–730 0791.

Heathrow Central (Underground Station), at Heathrow Airport.

City of London Information Service,
St Paul's Churchyard;
01–606 3030.

EMBASSIES and HIGH COMMISSIONS. –. *Australia*, Australia House, Strand, WC2; *Canada*, Canada House, Trafalgar Square, SW1; *India*, India House, Aldwych, WC2; *Ireland*, 17 Grosvenor Place, SW1; *New Zealand*, New Zealand House, Haymarket, SW1; *Pakistan*, 35 Lowndes Square, SW1; *South Africa*, South Africa House, Trafalgar Square, WC2; *Sri Lanka*, 13 Hyde Park Gardens, W2; *United States of America*, 1 Grosvenor Square, W1.

TRANSPORT. – The London **Underground** or "*Tube*", with ten principal lines and some 275 stations, provides a quick and convenient method of getting about London. The most generally useful lines are the Circle line which serves central London, the Northern line (running from N to S), the Central line (from E to W) and the Piccadilly line, which provides a connection between Heathrow international airport and central London. The Underground is the oldest of the kind in the world, dating back to 1863. The first trains were drawn by steam locomotives, electric traction being introduced in 1890. The development of the present system began in 1906–07. During the last war the Underground was extensively used to provide air raid shelters for the population.

London is also served by some 300 **bus routes**, with a total of some 8000 buses. Most of these are the familiar red double-deckers, supplemented by the limited-stop single-deck "Red Arrows" between the main-line stations. The country districts around London are served by the Green Line buses. There are night services running after midnight.

Tourists can obtain "Go as you please" tourist tickets, giving them unlimited travel on the red buses and most of the Underground system. There are also day tickets allowing unlimited travel on the buses ("Red Bus Rover") or the Underground ("Central Tube Rover").

Taxis can be hailed in the street when their "For Hire" sign is lit up. Radio taxis can be called at any time of the day or night by telephoning 01–289 1133. There are also minicabs, which are called by telephone; they are cheaper than ordinary taxis only for distances of over 2 miles.

Rail services. There are eight important main-line stations, each serving a different direction. Services to the Channel ports go from Victoria (to Dover and Folkestone) and Waterloo (to Southampton and Portsmouth). Other major stations are Charing Cross (trains to the S of London), Euston (to Birmingham, Liverpool, Manchester and Glasgow), King's Cross (to N and NE England and Edinburgh), Paddington (to the W), Liverpool Street (to the E) and St Pancras (to Sheffield and the Midlands).

London has two large **airports**. The main international airport is Heathrow, to the SW of the city centre (some 40 minutes from Piccadilly by Underground). Gatwick (reached by train from Victoria Station) is used mainly by domestic and charter flights. Smaller subsidiary airports are Luton (charter flights) and Stansted (due to be developed).

There are **boat services** on the Thames from April to September – between Westminster Pier and Tower Pier and between Charing Cross Pier, Tower Pier and Greenwich. There are much reduced services during the winter months. Hydrofoils ply between Tower Pier and Greenwich all year round.

Car parking in central London, as in most large cities, is difficult during the day and evening. Parking meters are to be found in many streets. There are also multi-storey car parks, but these are often full.

HOTELS. – MAYFAIR, OXFORD STREET, REGENT STREET, SOHO: *Hilton International*, 22 Park Lane, A, 503 r., 60 suites; *Churchill*, 30 Portman Square, A, 489 r.; *Grosvenor House*, Park Lane, A, 478 r.; *Selfridge Thistle*, 400 Grosvenor Square, A, 444 r.; *Dorchester*, Park Lane, A, 280 r.; *London Marriott*, Grosvenor Square, A, 258 r.; *Westbury*, New Bond Street, A, 256 r.; *Inn on the Park*, Hamilton Place, Park Lane, A, 228 r.; *Claridge's*, Brook Street, A, 205 r.; *Ritz*, Piccadilly, A, 139 r.; *Cumberland*, Marble Arch, A, 910 r.; *Inter-Continental*, 1 Hamilton Place, Hyde Park, A, 491 r.; *Portman Inter-Continental*, 22 Portman Square, A, 276 r.; *Montcalm*, Great Cumberland Place, A, 116 r.; *Chesterfield*, Charles Street, A, 87 r.; *Berners*, 10 Berners Street, A, 236 r.; *Mount Royal*, Bryanston Street, C, 683 r.; *Regent Crest*, Carburton Street, C, 322 r.; *Royal Angus*, Coventry Street, C, 92 r.; *St George's*, Langham Place, C, 85 r.

TRAFALGAR SQUARE, STRAND, EMBANKMENT: *Savoy*, Strand, A, 200 r.; *Howard*, 12 Temple Place, A, 136 r.; *Strand Palace*, Strand, B, 761 r.; *Royal Horseguards Thistle*, Whitehall Court, B, 274 r.; *Charing Cross*, Strand, C, 211 r.; *Shaftesbury*, 20 Monmouth Street, D, 197 r.

KNIGHTSBRIDGE, KENSINGTON: *Royal Garden*, Kensington High Street, A, 400 r.; *Hyde Park*, Knightsbridge, A, 179 r.; *Tara*, Scarsdale Place, `A, 840 r.; *Hilton International*, 179 Holland Park Avenue, A, 606 r., 35 suites; *Kensington Palace Thistle*, De Vere Gardens, A, 315 r.; *Phoenix*, Kensington Gardens Square, A, 128 r.; *Capital*, 22 Basil Street, A, 60 r.; *Kensington Close*, Wrights Lane, B, 530 r.; *Princes Lodge*, 8 Prince of Wales Terrace, B, 36 r.; *Clearlake*, 19 Prince of Wales Terrace, B, 28 r.; *London International*, 147 Cromwell Road, C, 415 r.; *Royal Kensington*, 380 Kensington High Street, C, 400 r.; *Regency*, 100 Queen's Gate, C, 195 r.; *Embassy House*, 31 Queen's Gate, C, 72 r.; *Basil Street*, Basil Street, Knightsbridge, C, 67 r.; *One-Two-Eight*, 128 Holland Road, D, 28 r.

CHELSEA, SLOANE STREET: *Sheraton Park Tower*, Knightsbridge, A, 295 r.; *Hyatt Carlton Tower*, 2

Cadogan Place, A, 228 r.; *Holiday Inn*, 17 Sloane Street, A, 206 r.; *Cadogan Thistle*, 75 Sloane Street, A, 74 r.; *Royal Court*, Sloane Square, B, 104 r.; *Executive*, 57 Pont Street, B, 29 r.; *Wilbraham*, 1 Wilbraham Place, C, 69 r.; *Diplomat*, 2 Chesham Street, E, 27 r.

WEST LONDON AIR TERMINAL, GLOUCESTER ROAD, BROMPTON ROAD: *Berkeley*, Wilton Place, A, 154 r.; *Belgravia Sheraton*, Chesham Place, A, 89 r.; *Leicester Court*, Queen's Gate, A, 67 r.; *Lexham*, Lexham Gardens, A, 64 r.; *Montana*, 67 Gloucester Road, A, 54 r.; *Lexham Lodge*, 134 Lexham Gardens, B, 25 r.; *International*, Cromwell Road, C, 415 r.; *Alexander*, 9 Sumner Place, C, 37 r.; *Fenja*, 69 Cadogan Gardens, D, 16 r.; *Tudor Court*, 58 Cromwell Road, E, 89 r.; *Apollo*, 18 Lexham Gardens, E, 58 r.; *Ashburn*, 111 Cromwell Road, E, 50 r.; *Concord*, 155 Cromwell Road, E, 40 r.

VICTORIA: *Royal Westminster*, Buckingham Palace Road, A, 135 r.; *St Ermin's*, Caxton Street, A, 244 r.; *Goring*, 15 Beeston Place, A, 100 r.; *Stanley House*, 19 Belgrave Road, B, 30 r.; *Ebury Court*, 24 Ebury Square, C, 39 r.

LONDON AIRPORT (GATWICK): *Hilton International*, Gatwick, A, 333 r., 12 suites.

LONDON AIRPORT (HEATHROW): *Posthouse*, Sipson Road, West Drayton, A, 594 r.; *Excelsior*, Bath Road, West Drayton, B, 662 r.; *Skyway*, Bath Road, Hayes, B, 445 r.; *Sheraton*, Heathrow, Colnbrook Bypass, West Drayton, B, 440 r.; *Holiday Inn*, Stockley Road, West Drayton, B, 401 r.; *Sheraton Skyline*, Bath Road, Hayes, B, 354 r.; *Crest*, Bath Road, Longford, C, 360 r.

YOUTH HOSTELS. – 36 Carter Lane, 320 b.; 4 Wellgarth Road, Hampstead, 220 b.; Holland House, Holland Walk, Kensington, 190 b.; 38 Bolton Gardens, 111 b.; 84 Highgate West Hill, Highgate, 62 b.

CAMP SITES (IN NORTH LONDON): Hackney Camping, Lea Valley Park; Sewardstone Caravan Park. (IN WEST LONDON): Tent City. (IN SOUTH LONDON): Dulwich. (IN EAST LONDON): Abbey Wood.

RESTAURANTS. – In most hotels; also: *Alonso's*, Queenstown Road; *Chelsea Room*, 2 Cadogan Place; *Grumbles*, 35 Churton Street; *Leith's*, 92 Kensington Park Road; *Le Soufflé*, 1 Hamilton Place; *Lichfield's*, 13 Lichfield Terrace, Sheen Road; *Mirabelle*, 56 Curzon Street; *Odin's*, 27 Devonshire Street; *Read's*, 152 Old Brompton Road; *Scott's*, 20 Mount Street (fish specialities); *Walton's*, 121 Walton Street.

FOREIGN RESTAURANTS. – FRENCH: *Brasserie St Quentin*, 243 Brompton Road; *Chez Moi*, 1 Addison Avenue; *Chez Nico*, 129 Queenstown Road; *Gavvers*, 61 Lower Sloane Street; *Keats*, 3 Downshire Hill; *L'Arlequin*, 123 Queenstown Road; *La Tante Claire*, 68 Royal Hospital Road; *Le Bon Bec*, 189 High Street; *Le Français*, 257 Fulham Road; *Le Gavroche*, 43 Upper Brook Street; *L'Etoile*, 30 Charlotte Street; *Ma Cuisine*, 113 Walton Street; *Oven d'Or*, 4 Crescent Way; *Porte de la Cité*, 65 Theobalds Road. – ITALIAN: *Canaletto da Leo*, 451 Edgware Road; *Cecconi's*, 5 Burlington Gardens; *City Tiberio*, 8 Lime Street; *Leonis Quo Vadis*, 26 Dean Street; *Venezia*, 21 Great Chapel Street. – GREEK: *Anemos*, 34 Charlotte Street; *Ararat*, 249 Camden High Street; *Beotys*, 79 St Martin's Lane; *Kalamaras Taverna*, 76 Inverness Mews; *White Tower*, 1 Percy Street. – INDIAN: *Bombay Brasserie*, Courtfield Close, 140 Gloucester Road;

India, 14 Wright's Lane; *Kundan*, 3 Horseferry Road; *Shezan*, 16 Cheval Place; *Star of India*, 154 Old Brompton Road. – CHINESE: *Dragon Garden*, 869 Green Lanes; *Junk Two*, 2 Thackeray Street; *Hunan*, 51 Pimlico Road; *Ken Lo's Memories of China*, 67 Ebury Street; *Mr Kai*, 65 South Audley Street; *Tiger Lee*, 251 Old Brompton Road; *Zen*, Chelsea Cloisters, Sloane Avenue. – JAPANESE: *Fuji*, 36 Brewer Street; *Masako*, 6 St Christopher's Place; *Mikado*, 110 George Street; *Shogun*, Adam's Row; *Suntory*, 72 St James's Street. – MEXICAN: *La Cucaracha*, 12 Greek Street. – TURKISH: *Ya Mustafa*, 11 High Street, Islington. – NEAR EASTERN: *Armenian*, 20 Kensington Church Street. – SCANDINAVIAN: *Kerzenstüberl*, 9 St Christopher's Place. – GERMAN: *Twin Brothers*, 51 Kensington Church Street. – VEGETARIAN: *Food for Thought*, 31 Neal Street; *Mandeer*, 21 Hanway Place. – KOSHER: *Bloom's & Son Limited*, 90 Whitechapel High Street.

EVENTS. – *Cruft's Dog Show*, Olympia (Europe's largest dog show: Feb.); *Easter Parade*, Battersea Park; *Royal Academy Summer Exhibition*, Burlington House (first Monday in May to Aug.); *Chelsea Flower Show*, Royal Hospital Grounds (May); *Trooping the Colour*, Horse Guards, Whitehall (on the Queen's official birthday, Saturday nearest 11 June); *Royal International Horse Show*, White City (July); *Battle of Britain Day* (fly-past by RAF: Saturday nearest 15 Sept.); *Commonwealth Arts Festival* (second half of Sept.); *National Brass Band Festival*, Albert Hall (Oct.); *Lord Mayor's Show* (procession to Mansion House: mid Nov.).

The Lord Mayor's State Coach

THEATRES, CONCERTS, CABARETS. – London has more than 50 **theatres**, which offer a wide range of choice from the traditional productions of the great dramatic classics to the most avant-garde and experimental productions. In addition to established and world-famous theatres such as the Old Vic (Waterloo Road, SE1), the National Theatre (three auditoriums, in the South Bank Cultural Centre), the Aldwych Theatre (former home of the Royal Shakespeare Company, in Aldwych, WC2) and the Royal Court Theatre (mainly new plays: Sloane Square, SW1), there is a great variety of smaller theatres offering experimental productions, amateur performances, theatre workshops, literary readings and political plays. A play which catches the popular fancy may run for years, such as Agatha Christie's "Mousetrap", which has played to full houses (now at St Martin's Theatre) for more than 33 years. It is advisable to book well in advance, since there is usually a great demand for tickets.

In the eyes of many people London is the **musical capital** of Europe: a reputation founded not only on the two great opera houses, the Royal Opera House in Covent Garden (Bow Street, WC2) and the English National Opera (formerly Sadler's Wells Opera) in the Coliseum (St Martin's Lane), and London's five top-class symphony orchestras (Philharmonia, London Symphony Orchestra, Royal Philharmonic Orchestra, London Philharmonic Orchestra, BBC Symphony

Shopping in London

With its enormous range of shops, from the great department stores to a multitude of boutiques, London is still an attractive shopping centre. Among items for which London shops are famous are well-cut clothing, particularly for men (suits, raincoats, leather jackets), fabrics, furs, smokers' requisites, records and books, as well as antiques, jewellery and objets d'art.

Some of the best and most attractive shops in London are to be found in Bond Street, Oxford Street, Regent Street, Sloane Street, Piccadilly and the St James's area. Certain streets are particularly noted for particular articles: thus Savile Row is famous for its men's tailors, while furriers should be looked for in Tottenham Court Road, fashion shops in Knightsbridge and Mayfair and bookshops in Charing Cross Road. Smokers will be interested in Dunhill's shop at 30 Duke Street, where individual customers can have their own particular smoking mixture made up. The great streets for boutiques are King's Road, Chelsea and Carnaby Street.

The large **department stores** include *Harrods* (Brompton Road), with telex address "Everything – London" and its own zoo, *Selfridges* (Oxford Street), *Fortnum and Mason* (Piccadilly) and *Liberty and Co*. with its Renaissance façade.

Antique shops are to be found all over London. Well-known dealers have their establishments in Kensington High Street, and the Chelsea Antique Market is famous; Chelsea is also the place to look for cast-off clothing.

The various **markets** play an essential part in London life and offer good opportunities for shoppers. The Portobello Road market (on weekdays fruit, vegetables and flowers, on Saturdays antiques) and the lively Sunday morning market in Petticoat Lane (Middlesex Street), where anything and everything is offered for sale, are among the most famous. Billingsgate Market (Lower Thames Street) is one of the largest fish markets in the world (Tuesday to Saturday; Sundays only shellfish and crustaceans). Smithfield Market (Monday to Friday) is London's largest meat market, mainly wholesale; Leadenhall Market (Gracechurch Street) also caters for retail customers.

The brochure "A Guide to London's Best Shops", obtainable from booksellers, contains details of 1000 establishments arranged according to district and what is sold, including unusual items.

Orchestra) but also on a variety of distinguished chamber orchestras (Academy of St Martin-in-the-Fields, English Chamber Orchestra, London Bach Orchestra, etc.) and choirs (Philharmonia Chorus, Ambrosian Singers, Royal Choral Society, etc.). London's leading concert hall is the Royal Festival Hall (South Bank, SE1), with seating for 3000; others are the Queen Elizabeth Hall and the Purcell Room, also on the South Bank, and the Wigmore Hall in Wigmore Street. In these and many other smaller halls, and in a number of churches as well, the concert-goer will find a wide range of choice throughout the year. A special feature of London's musical life is the series of promenade concerts (the "Proms") given every year between July and September in the Royal Albert Hall (Kensington Gore, SW7), which can accommodate an audience of 8000. Each evening during the season this huge hall is thronged with an enthusiastic audience of all ages who can enjoy at very moderate cost a series of some 50 concerts covering the whole range of music from the Baroque period to the present day. Especially popular is the "last night of the Proms", when the atmosphere is particularly relaxed and the conductor becomes a kind of compère of a traditional occasion in which the audience – good-humoured and sometimes eccentrically dressed – also has a part to play.

Lovers of the **ballet** are also well catered for in London. The world-famous Royal Ballet and the London Festival Ballet specialise in classical ballet, while the Ballet Rambert is famed for its modern productions.

Musicals and musical comedies are staged at Drury Lane Theatre (Catherine Street, WC2), and frequently also in Her Majesty's Theatre (Haymarket, SW1). Pop concerts take place at the Lyceum Theatre (Strand) and elsewhere.

Good **cabarets** are relatively few in number, and correspondingly expensive. The numerous night spots and drinking places in Soho, which charge highly for the amenities they offer, are hardly to be recommended. The "in" places vary from time to time: Carnaby Street and Soho have now given place to Chelsea (particularly King's Road), Leicester Square and a number of outlying areas. Many of London's cabarets and discotheques are private clubs, with admission for members only; but it is often possible to become a member at the entrance on payment of a modest charge, and many clubs are open to guests of members. In some clubs for young people good jazz and folk music can be heard, and in many pubs there may be music and often also improvised turns, ranging from amateur performances to strip-tease. The opening times of pubs are regulated by law (usually 1100 to 1500 and 1730 to 2300).

Information about entertainments in London can be obtained from the newspapers, or from publications such as "What's On" and "Time Out" (opening times, prices etc.).

SPORT. – Almost every kind of sport can be practised in and around London. There are more than 100 golf-courses, and tennis courts in almost every part of the capital. There are facilities for riding in Hyde Park and at many other places, and there are several race-courses in the immediately surrounding area. Boating is possible on the Thames and on lakes in several London parks. The Empire Stadium at Wembley is the venue of many important football matches, and in addition every club of any size has its own ground. There are several greyhound-racing tracks (with betting facilities).

**London, capital of the United Kingdom of Great Britain and Northern Ireland, and of the British Commonwealth, is one of the largest cities in the world, with a population of over 7 million, and one of Europe's leading commercial, financial, cultural and communication centres. It lies on both banks of the Thames some 50 miles above its mouth, in a gently undulating basin enclosed by hills some 500 ft in height, and has a port accessible to seagoing ships. The Greenwich meridian (longitude 0°) runs through the London suburb of Greenwich, and in terms of latitude London lies exactly half way between 51° and 52° N – farther N than Paris farther S than Berlin.

The Thames, which follows a winding course through London from W to E, divides the city into a northern and a southern part, with the main tourist sights lying on the northern bank. Central London – the administrative unit of Inner London – covers an area of 120 sq. miles, with a population of some 3·2 million. Greater London has an area of some 618 sq. miles. The original heart of London, the City, is almost exclusively a commercial area, with banks, the Stock Exchange, and administrative and newspaper offices. Buckingham Palace in Westminster is the London home of the monarch; in the neighbouring districts are elegant shops and department stores.

The administrative unit known as *Greater London*, established in 1963, is made up of 32 boroughs. The City of London remains as an independent local government unit, with its own Lord Mayor, its 159 Common Councilmen and its 26 aldermen. The Common Councilmen are elected by the ratepayers; the aldermen are appointed for life, and the Lord Mayor is elected annually from among their number. The Greater London Council consists of 100 councillors and 16 aldermen. The 32 London boroughs are

Barking, Barnet, Bexley, Brent, Bromley, Camden, Croydon, Ealing, Enfield, Greenwich, Hackney, Hammersmith, Haringey, Harrow, Havering, Hillingdon, Hounslow, Islington, Kensington and Chelsea, Kingston-upon-Thames, Lambeth, Lewisham, Merton, Newham, Redbridge, Richmond-upon-Thames, Southwark, Sutton, Tower Hamlets, Waltham Forest, Wandsworth and Westminster.

London is a cosmopolitan city which offers something to every visitor, whether interested in art, in museums or only in the shops, whether attracted by "swinging London" with its lively and colourful night life or by its architecture, whether he wants to hunt for bargains in the antique dealers' shops or merely to observe the busy and constantly changing pattern of London life. This great city is the melting-pot of the whole Commonwealth, in which men and women of every colour and every religion have settled.

HISTORY. – There is no unanimity among scholars about the origin of the name London. Although most of the urban area is flat, it takes in two areas of higher ground N of the Thames, and this led the 18th c. historian William Maitland to put forward the theory about 1760 that the name came from two Gaelic words, *lon* (plain) and *dyn* (hill). Thirty years later Thomas Pennent suggested another derivation which still has its supporters: on this hypothesis the Roman name **Londinium** comes from the Celtic Llyn Din, meaning "town on the lake". The philologist Henry Bradley also proposed a Celtic origin for the name, deriving the original *Londinion* from the Celtic personal name Londinos.

The origins of London go back to the Bronze and Iron Ages. Even in this prehistoric period the early settlers recognised the importance of the site as a gateway between England and the Continent. But although it is known that there were Celtic settlements here before the arrival of the Romans, the history of London began to be written only in the time of the Emperor Claudius, when Roman forces led by Aulus Plautius landed on the S coast of England and used the town's favourable situation on the Thames to further their economic and military ambitions (A.D. 43).

Roman London grew up on two low hills some 60 ft high, now occupied by Leadenhall Market in the E and St Paul's Cathedral in the W, with the Walbrook flowing into the Thames between them. The town rapidly extended westward over the Thames and towards Southwark. The first London Bridge, originally a timber structure, was in all probability built by the Romans.

The first mention of London is to be found in Tacitus's "Annals", which refer to the existence of an important trading centre here in the 1st c. Tacitus also records the capture of London by the warlike queen Boadicea (Boudica), who led her tribesmen from Norfolk and Suffolk by way of Colchester and St Albans to London, killing 30,000 of the inhabitants of these three towns. Boadicea's forces took London and drove out the Romans, but her triumph was of brief duration. The Romans recaptured the town and surrounded it with walls to provide protection against any further risings. At this period the Roman town occupied roughly the same area as the present-day City. The walls, 25 ft high and 3 miles long, enclosed some 320 acres, running from the Tower via Aldgate, Bishopsgate, London Wall, Aldersgate and Ludgate to the Thames and continuing back to the Tower. Evidence of the elegance and splendour of Roman London, with its fine public buildings, its baths, its mosaics and its luxury, can be seen in the Museum of London. Remains of Roman baths still exist in Lower Thames Street, and there are fragments of the town walls at the Tower, in Cripplegate, at London Wall, under the courtyard of the General Post Office and near the Museum of London. The principal building of the Roman period was the basilica of which remains have been found near Leadenhall Market.

London provided the Romans with a strategic base from which they could expand throughout Britain, reaching northward into Scotland. It was the starting point of their road system, and present-day Oxford Street still follows the line of a Roman road. Several main roads started from London – Watling Street South (probably the present Borough High Street and Old Kent Road) running SE to Dover, Stane Street (probably Clapham Road) SW to Chichester, a road running W to Silchester along the line of Oxford Street and Bayswater Road, Watling Street North running NW to St Albans, Wroxeter and Chester, Ermine Street (Bishopsgate and Kingsland Road) N to York and a road running NE via Aldgate and Old Ford to Colchester.

There are frequent references to London in Roman authors' writing after Tacitus: Ptolemy, for instance, mentions it three times. Around 286 the Emperor Carausius established a mint in the town – the only Roman mint in Britain.

The withdrawal of the legions to defend Rome against the Germanic tribes in 407 marked the end of Roman rule in Britain, and in 410 the Emperor Honorius gave the British towns their independence and left them to look after themselves.

From 450 onwards the Germanic Angles, Saxons and Jutes occupied Britain, having been summoned by the Celts to come to their aid against the invading Picts and Scots. London suffered a setback when the Anglo-Saxon forces of Hengist and Eric defeated the Britons at Crayford in 457, when 4000 men were killed and the rest fled back to London.

Thereafter the town became the capital of an Anglo-Saxon kingdom and increased rapidly in importance. Augustine, a Benedictine monk, was sent by Pope Gregory the Great to bring Christianity to Britain. In 796 London became a royal residence, and in 884 Alfred the Great made it the capital of his kingdom, rebuilt much of the town walls and refortified the town. Then came the Danes, and Knut (Canute) ruled over Britain. Only London was able to buy a measure of freedom, making a payment of 10,500 pounds – then a very considerable sum – as the price of an armistice.

In 1066 William of Normandy defeated the Anglo-Saxon king Harold II at Hastings (Battle) and had himself crowned in Westminster Abbey as William I, the Conqueror.

Although William granted London a charter giving the town and its citizens their previous rights and privileges, he built the White Tower in order to keep them in awe of his power. In 1215, however, King John granted further concessions in **Magna Carta**. The office of mayor had existed since 1191, and the town was governed by the mayor and council with the support of the people of London, who could express their views in a popular assembly – an early emergence of democratic rule.

The 13th and 14th c. brought further trials to the town in the form of great fires, famine and plague, which claimed thousands of victims. During the reigns of Henry VIII (1509–47) and his daughter Mary (1553–58) London saw the ruthless persecution of heretics. In the time of Elizabeth I (1558–1603) the Tower, which then stood on the fringes of the town, developed into a centre of trade and commerce. The much smaller city of Westminster lay at some distance from the area then known as London, now the City.

Between the two lay the Temple, centre of the administration of justice. The Strand, the road which ran along the bank of the Thames linking the two towns, was lined by aristocratic mansions set in beautiful gardens. During the Norman period and the Wars of the Roses most of the population lived in simple wooden houses, but the merchants and manufacturers occupied substantial and luxurious dwellings, and there were also numerous religious buildings and hospitals, while the quays and landing stages along the banks of the Thames were constantly being extended. Until the late 17th c., however, the streets were narrow, filthy and full of potholes.

The town was thrown into a state of alarm by the Gunpowder Plot of 1605, when Guy Fawkes and his Roman Catholic supporters made an unsuccessful attempt to blow up the Houses of Parliament. During the Civil War, in 1649, King Charles I was tried in Westminster Hall and executed in front of the Banqueting House in Whitehall. Thereafter Oliver Cromwell resided in Whitehall Palace as Lord Protector. In 1660, however, the monarchy was restored and Charles II returned to London.

Between 1664 and 1666 the Great Plague raged in London, and it is estimated that more than 100,000 out of a population of half a million died during this period. Almost immediately afterwards, in 1666, the Great Fire destroyed much of the central area of the town. But some good came out of these evils, for large parts of London had to be rebuilt. One of the most notable buildings erected after the fire was St Paul's Cathedral. The only major buildings which escaped destruction were Westminster Abbey and Westminster Hall, the Banqueting House, the Temple church, the Tower and a number of other churches, which were incorporated into the rebuilt town.

Many of the attractive streets and handsome buildings still to be seen in London date from the second half of the 18th c. Among them are the Mansion House, the Horse Guards and Somerset House.

During the 19th c. London developed so rapidly that it is impossible in the space available to give any full account of this building boom. Among the outstanding buildings of this period are the Mint, the Custom House, the old Waterloo Bridge, London Bridge, Buckingham Palace, Nash's Regent Street and the terraces on Regent's Park, the British Museum, Trafalgar Square, the National Gallery, the Houses of Parliament, the Embankment, the Albert Hall and the fashionable districts of Belgravia and the West End.

The first train left a London station in 1836. Towards the end of the century Tower Bridge and the Blackwall and Rotherhithe Tunnels were constructed, and work began on the Underground. Westminster Cathedral was completed in 1903. Notable buildings erected between the two world wars include Bush House, the offices of the Port of London Authority, the new Waterloo Station and two new buildings for the University of London.

During the Second World War London was the target of almost 100 German air raids, which began in August 1940 and continued until May 1941. The worst of these were described as the second Fire of London (16 April and 5 May 1941). After these raids had been beaten off London enjoyed a breathing space until June 1944, when V1 and V2 rockets began to wreak further destruction. Out of London's 2·25 million houses 1·75 million were damaged or destroyed, and more than a third of the City was demolished. Altogether 60,000 civilians were killed in Britain during the war and 86,000 were wounded, and of these no less than 54·8% were Londoners.

In 1952 London was divided into new administrative units, and in 1963 Greater London was established. In 1966 the city acquired a new landmark in the form of the Post Office Tower, then Britain's tallest building (580 ft). From 1965 onwards life in London was made more difficult by recurring strikes and by a number of bomb attacks by Irish terrorists. In 1973 Tower Bridge became a museum. In 1974 work began on the development of the new satellite town of Thamesmead, E of London, designed for a population of 80,000. In 1978 Heathrow Airport was linked with central London by an extension of the Piccadilly Underground line. In 1982 the Barbican Centre for Arts and Conferences was opened.

A selection of Museums and Principal Sights

The opening times of museums, etc., vary considerably, and no general pattern can be distinguished. Most museums are closed on Good Friday, on the Spring Bank holiday, from Christmas Eve to Boxing Day and on New Year's Day. Before visiting a museum it is advisable to check its opening times at one of the information bureaux listed on p. 141, with the hotel or by telephoning the museum concerned. London has so many museums that museum addicts should beware of trying to do too much: if time is short they should limit themselves to a small selection of the most interesting exhibitions.

Banqueting House,
Palace of Whitehall, SW1.
(Tel. 01–212 4785)

Bethnal Green Museum of Childhood,
Cambridge Heath Road, E2.
(Tel. 01–980 2415/4315)

British Museum,
Great Russell Street, WC1.
(Tel. 01–636 1555, ext. 525)

Commonwealth Institute & Art Gallery,
Kensington High Street, W8.
(Tel. 01–602 3252)

Courtauld Institute Galleries,
(move planned)
Woburn Square, WC1.
(Tel. 01–580 1015)

Cutty Sark and Gipsy Moth IV,
Greenwich Pier, SE10.
(Tel. 01–858 3445 Cutty Sark; Tel. 01–858 3445 Gipsy Moth)

Geffrye Museum,
Kingsland Road, E2.
(Tel. 01–739 8368)

Geological Museum,
Exhibition Road, SW7.
(Tel. 01–589 3444)

Guildhall,
King Street, Cheapside, EC2.
(Tel. 01–606 3030)

Guildhall Clock Museum,
King Street, Cheapside, EC2.
(Tel. 01–606 3030)

Hayward Art Gallery,
South Bank, SE11.
(Tel. 01–928 3144)

HMS *Belfast*,
Symons Wharf, Vine Lane (opposite the Tower).
(Tel. 01–407 6434)

Hogarth House,
Hogarth Lane, Great West Road, W4.
(Tel. 01–994 6757)

Horniman Museum,
London Road, Forest Hill, SE23.
(Tel. 01–699 1872/2339/4911)

Houses of Parliament,
Westminster, SW1.
(Tel. 01–219 3000)

A tour of the House of Commons is only possible by arrangement with a Member of Parliament. Sittings of the Commons take place from October to July. Debates may be listened to from Monday to Thursday from 4.15 p.m., on Friday from 10 a.m.; it is necessary to queue outside St Stephen's Hall. For entry to the House of Lords visitors must also queue in the same place, on Monday to Wednesday from 2.30 p.m., Thursday from 5 p.m., Friday from 11 a.m.

Imperial War Museum,
Lambeth Road, SE1.
(Tel. 01–735 8922)

Jewish Museum,
Woburn House, Upper Woburn Place, WC1.
(Tel. 01–387 3081)

Kensington Palace State Apartments,
Kensington Gardens, W8.
(Tel. 01–937 9561, ext. 2)

Kenwood House (Iveagh Bequest),
Hampstead Lane, NW3.
(Tel. 01–348 1286)

Lancaster House,
St James's Palace, SW1.

London Dungeon,
34 Tooley Street, SE1.
(Tel. 01–403 0606)

London Toy & Model Museum,
23 Craven Hill, W2.

Madame Tussaud's,
Marylebone Road, NW1.
(Tel. 01–935 6861)

Marble Hill House,
Marble Hill Park, Richmond Road, Twickenham.
(Tel. 01–348 1286)

Museum of London,
Barbican, London Wall, EC2.
(Tel. 01–600 3699)

Museum of Mankind,
6 Burlington Gardens, W1.
(Tel. 01–437 2224)

Musical Museum,
368 High Street, Brentford, Middlesex.
(Tel. 01–560 8108)

National Army Museum,
Royal Hospital Road, Chelsea, SW3.
(Tel. 01–730 0717)

National Gallery,
Trafalgar Square, WC2.
(Tel. 01–839 3321)

National Maritime Museum,
Romney Road, Greenwich, SE10.
(Tel. 01–858 4422)

National Portrait Gallery,
2 St Martin's Place, WC2.
(Tel. 01–930 1552)

National Postal Museum,
King Edward Street, EC1.
(Tel. 01–432 3851)

Natural History Museum,
Cromwell Road, SW7.
(Tel. 01–589 6323)

Planetarium,
Marylebone Road, NW1.
(Tel. 01–486 1121)

Queen's Gallery,
Buckingham Palace, Buckingham Palace Road, SW1.
(Tel. 01–930 3007)

RAF Museum,
Aerodrome Road, Hendon, NW9.
(Tel. 01–205 2266)

Ranger's House,
Chesterfield Walk, Blackheath, SE10.
(Tel. 01–853 0035)

Roman Bath,
Strand Lane, WC2.

Royal Academy of Arts,
Burlington House, Piccadilly, W1.
(Tel. 01–734 9052)

Royal Mews,
Buckingham Palace, SW1.
(Tel. 01–930 4832)

Royal Naval College (Painted Hall and Chapel),
Greenwich, SE10.
(Tel. 01–858 2154)

St Martin-in-the-Fields,
Trafalgar Square, WC2.

St Mary-le-Bow,
Cheapside, EC2.

St. Paul's Cathedral,
Ludgate Hill, EC4.

Science Museum,
Exhibition Road, SW7.
(Tel. 01-589 3456)

Serpentine Gallery,
Kensington Gardens, W2.
(Tel. 01-402 6075)

Soane Museum,
Lincoln's Inn Fields, WC2.

Southwark Cathedral,
London Bridge, SE1.

Stock Exchange,
Old Broad Street, EC2.
(Tel. 01-588 2355)

Tate Gallery,
Millbank, SW1.
(Tel. 01-821 1313; Recorded Information, tel. 01-821 7182)

Tower of London (and Jewel Tower),
Tower Hill, EC3.
(Tel. 01-709 0765)

Victoria and Albert Museum,
Cromwell Road, SW7.
(Tel. 01-589 6371)

Wallace Collection,
Hertford House, Manchester Square, W1.
(Tel. 01-935 0687)

Wellington Museum,
Apsley House, 149 Piccadilly, W1.
(Tel. 01-499 5676)

Westminster Abbey,
Parliament Square, SW1.

Westminster Cathedral,
Ashley Place, SW1.

Westminster Hall,
Parliament Square, SW1.
(Visits only possible by arrangement with a Member of Parliament.)

Sightseeing Tours

Coach tours. – The "ROUND LONDON SIGHTSEEING TOUR", operated by *London Transport* is a good way of getting a first impression of London and its sights. This two-hour non-stop tour runs hourly in summer from 9 a.m. to 8 p.m. and in winter from 9 a.m. to 4 p.m. (no guide, but plan with explanations: tel. 222 1234); departures from Piccadilly Circus, Victoria (Grosvenor Gardens) and Marble Arch. Other coach tours are operated by *American Express International*, 6 Haymarket, SW1, tel. 930 4411; *Evan Evan's Tours*, Metropolis House, 41 Tottenham Court Road, W1, tel. 637 4171; *Frames Tours*, Frames House, 46 Albemarle Street, W1, tel. 493 3181 and *Thomas Cook*, 45 Berkeley Street, W1, tel. 499 4000.

Guided walks. – *London Walks* (walks devoted to particular themes – architecture, pubs, history, etc.), 139 Conway Road, Southgate, N14, tel. 882 2763; *Off Beat Tours*, 66 St Michael's Street, W2, tel. 262 9572; *Streets of London* (walks through various parts of London with occasionally different themes), 32 Grovelands Road, N13, tel. 882 3414.

Trips on the Thames. – Departures from Charing Cross Pier, Westminster Pier and Tower Pier. Information from London Tourist Board, tel. 730 4812.

Canal cruises on Regent's Canal, part of the Grand Union Canal, are run by *Jason's Trip*, 60 Blomfield Road, W9, tel. 286 3428; *Jennie Wren Cruises*, 250 Camden High Street, NW1, tel. 485 4433; and *Zoo Water Bus*, Delamere Terrace, W2, tel. 286 6101.

Spanish fleet at Trafalgar in 1805. In the centre is *Nelson's Column*, topped by a statue and guarded by four bronze lions. On the N side of the square is the imposing building (by William Wilkins, 1834–37) which houses the ** **National Gallery,** with a rich collection of European paint-

Sightseeing in London

Trafalgar Square – Buckingham Palace – Whitehall

A convenient starting point for sightseeing in central London is ** **Trafalgar Square,** one of Britain's finest open spaces and one of London's busiest traffic intersections. It was laid out in the first quarter of the 19th c. to the design of John Nash and named in honour of Nelson's victory over the French and

Trafalgar Square

ing, particularly notable for its Dutch masters, including 19 Rembrandts, its 15th and 16th c. Italian masters and its representation of the various British schools. The National Gallery was established in 1824, when the government granted £60,000 for the purchase and display of 38 pictures from the famous Angerstein collection. Some 2000 pictures are now on show, with many more in reserve. Particularly notable works are Goya's "Doña Isabel Cobos de Porcel", Bellini's "Agony in the Garden" and Leonardo da Vinci's famous cartoon of the Virgin and Child with John the Baptist and St Anne.

Immediately behind the National Gallery is the *National Portrait Gallery, founded in 1856 to illustrate British social and cultural history, which contains a comprehensive collection of paintings and sculpture of leading figures in British life and history. Perhaps the most valuable item is Holbein's portrait of Henry VIII. Also of great interest is the only known portrait of Shakespeare drawn during his lifetime. The collection includes fine works by Millais, Romney and Reynolds and some 4500 royal portraits, only a selection of which are on display. Other pictures not on display can be seen on

request. A notable feature of the collection is the series of portraits of members of the Kit-Cat Club, a political and literary circle of the late 17th and early 18th c. to which many members of the nobility belonged.

At the NE corner of the square is the church of *St Martin-in-the-Fields*, originally founded in 1222, altered in the time of Henry VIII and rebuilt in 1721 to the design of James Gibbs. There is a bust of the architect in the S aisle. St Martin's is the parish church of Buckingham Palace and the Admiralty, and in the chancel are a royal and an Admiralty box-pew.

At the SW corner of the square is the *Admiralty Arch*, a triumphal arch erected in 1910 to commemorate Queen Victoria, which leads into the splendid avenue known as the **Mall**. Immediately on the left are the imposing buildings of the *Admiralty*, the oldest part of which (1725) was designed by Thomas Ripley. The domed extension was built between 1895 and 1905. Along the left-hand side of the Mall extends **St James's Park**, landscaped in the English style, with a lake in the middle. The park was once a hunting preserve of Henry VIII. It affords

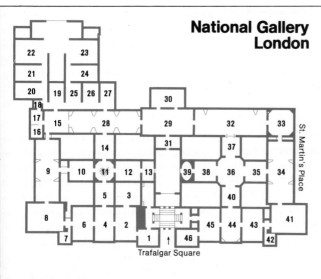

National Gallery London

16–19	17th c. Dutch school
20–22	17th c. Flemish school
23	15th and early 16th c. German school
24	Dutch school
25	16th c. Dutch school and Holbein
26–28	17th c. Dutch school
29	17th c. Italian school
30	16th c. Italian school: Brescia
31	Domenichino frescoes
32	17th c. French school
33	18th c. French school
34	British school
35	18th c. Italian school
36	19th c. French school
37	17th c. Italian school
38–39	18th c. Italian school
40	19th c. French school
41	Spanish school
42	Goya
43–46	19th c. French school

Trafalgar Square

European Painting

1–2	Early Italian school
3–6	15th c. Italian school: Florence
7	Leonardo da Vinci
8	Correggio, Michelangelo, Parmigiano, Raphael
9	16th c. Italian school: Venice
10	15th c. Italian school: Venice
11	15th c. Italian altarpieces
12	15th c. North Italian school
13	Crivelli
14	15th c. Italian school: Milan
15	16th c. Italian school

views of the various government offices in Whitehall and of Buckingham Palace.

Welsh Guards outside Clarence House

From the NE corner of St James's Park a flight of steps leads up to *Carlton House Terrace* and Waterloo Place. To the left is *Pall Mall*, a narrower street running parallel to the Mall and which contains many of the leading London clubs. These are, of course, private establishments, and visitors can secure admission only as the guest of a member. Until recently the great majority of clubs did not admit women, but for some years there has been a tendency towards less rigidity in this respect. At the far end of Pall Mall is the historic old **St James's Palace**, joined on to Clarence House and adjoined by Lancaster House. Occupying the site of an earlier leper-house dedicated to St James the Younger, this was for long the seat of the British court (from 1699 to 1837). The palace was built for Henry VIII in 1530–36 to the design of Holbein the Younger. In 1837 Queen Victoria moved the court to Buckingham Palace, but foreign ambassadors are still accredited to the Court of St James's. Only the Gatehouse survives from the original palace; the numerous courtyards and the *Chapel Royal* in which Queen Victoria was married are later additions. Much of the palace is occupied by the royal family and is not open to visitors, but the Gatehouse, Chapel Royal and Ambassadors' Court can be seen. Here too can be seen the "Beefeaters", the royal bodyguard whose main headquarters are in the Tower of London. Attached to St James's Palace is *Clarence House*, residence of the Queen Mother.

The adjoining *Lancaster House* is a notable example of early Victorian architecture, built for the Duke of York, George IV's brother, by Benjamin Wyatt. It later passed into the hands of the Duke of Sutherland and was enlarged by Sir Charles Barry in 1827. Formerly part of the London Museum, it is now used for conferences, meetings and receptions.

NE of St James's Palace, in Marlborough Road, is *Marlborough House*, which was the home of Queen Mary, George V's widow, until her death in 1953. This handsome building was erected at the beginning of the 18th c. to the design of Sir Christopher Wren, marking the culminating point of a busy career which had begun with the rebuilding of London after the Great Fire. The house was originally built for the Duke of Marlborough, and it contains magnificent wall paintings by the French artist Louis Laguerre depicting Marlborough's victories at Blenheim, Ramillies and Malplaquet. The original red-brick building was subsequently much altered and enlarged, becoming in the 19th c. the residence of the Prince of Wales, the future Edward VII.

From St James's Palace *St James's Street*, with a number of famous clubs, runs NW into the wide thoroughfare of *Piccadilly*. Here, at No. 64, are the offices of the *British Tourist Authority*, where visitors can obtain any information they require. Off the E side of St James's Street opens King Street, at No. 8 of which is the famous firm of art auctioneers, Christie's, founded in 1766. King Street runs into *St James's Square*, originally laid out in the 17th c., which still preserves a number of historic old houses. No. 32 was for 140 years the residence of the Bishops of London. At No. 31 Gen. Eisenhower planned the Allied landings in North Africa (June–Nov. 1942) and the Normandy landings (Jan.–June 1944. – From the square, Duke of York Street runs N into *Jermyn Street*, long renowned for its exclusive and specialised shops, now with many boutiques and cosmetic shops. Between Jermyn Street and Piccadilly is *St James's Church*, built by Wren between 1676 and 1684, badly damaged during the last war but since restored in the original style. It contains a fine organ, the gift of Mary II which was originally intended for Whitehall.

To the W of St James's Palace is **Green**

Park, an extension of St James's Park which borders Piccadilly and ends at Hyde Park Corner, another of London's major traffic intersections. The imposing *Wellington Arch* was erected in 1828 to commemorate Wellington's victory at Waterloo. Originally a court pleasure ground, Green Park is now open to the public, though the adjoining gardens to the S of the roadway called Constitution Hill now form the grounds of Buckingham Palace, the main front of which faces the *Queen Victoria Memorial* at the E end of Constitution Hill.

*Buckingham Palace (not open to visitors), originally built for the Duke of Buckingham, was bought by George III in 1761. It was altered for George IV by John Nash (1826–30), and in 1913 the E front was remodelled for George V by Sir Aston Webb. On the S side is the *Queen's Gallery*, open to the public, displaying a selection of pictures and other works of art from the royal collection, one of the largest private art collections in the world. Although visitors are not admitted to the palace, numbers of sightseers congregate at the entrance, particularly to watch the Changing of the Guard, performed every weekday at 11.30 with traditional ceremonial. The ceremony may occasionally be cancelled (e.g. when the Queen is absent or on account of bad weather), but this will be intimated in advance.

S of the palace, in Buckingham Gate, are the *Royal Mews*, with a magnificent *collection of coaches and carriages,

Horse Guard

including the state coach and the coronation coach.

St James's Park is bounded on the S by *Birdcage Walk*, which runs from Buckingham Palace to the government offices at the S end of Whitehall. The name is thought to be derived from the royal aviary which stood here in the time of James I. Birdcage Walk runs into Great George Street, which in turn leads into Parliament Square. To the left is **WHITEHALL**, the street which has become a synonym for the central government and administration. It is named after the old Palace of Whitehall, the only surviving remnant of which is the *Banqueting House*, half way down Whitehall on the right-hand side.

In the 13th c. the old Whitehall Palace was the residence of the archbishops of York. In the 16th c. it was occupied by the powerful Cardinal Wolsey, and after his fall (1529) it was enlarged by Henry VIII and remained a royal residence until the end of the following century, when William III chose to live in the country outside the town. After the destruction of the palace by fire in 1691 and 1698 the Banqueting House was built by Inigo Jones, incorporating some remains of the older buildings. The flat roof of the Banqueting House is surrounded by a balustrade. Later George I converted the building into a Chapel Royal. In more recent times it housed a United Services Museum, but it has now been restored and is used for its original purpose, forming a splendid setting for government banquets and receptions. The banqueting hall, in the form of a double cube, is 110 ft long by 55 ft high and broad. Its main feature is the ceiling with its nine allegorical paintings by Rubens, who was paid £3000 for the work by Charles I in 1635.

Detail of State Coach, Royal Mews

Opposite the Banqueting House, to the NW, are the buildings of the *Horse Guards*, built as a barracks by William Kent in 1751–53. Here one of London's great tourist attractions, the Changing of the Guard, takes place daily (11 a.m. on weekdays, 10 on Sundays). The guard is mounted for six hours every day by two troopers of the Household Cavalry. A distinctive feature of the Horse Guards building is the clock-tower. – Immediately N of the Banqueting House, on the same side of Whitehall, is the old War Office, now part of the Ministry of Defence. To the SW, on the opposite side of Whitehall, is the old *Treasury* (by William Kent, 1733), now mostly occupied by the Cabinet Office. Farther S, beyond the Banqueting House, is a huge modern block housing the main offices of the Ministry of Defence, which incorporates the former Admiralty, War Office and Air Ministry.

On the opposite side of Whitehall is an unpretentious little cul-de-sac with a famous name – **Downing Street**. This is the nerve centre of British government, with the residence of the Prime Minister in a house which might be that of any prosperous middle-class citizen, the famous "No. 10". The house was originally made available to Britain's first Prime Minister, Sir Robert Walpole, by George II in 1732; the façade was subsequently rebuilt. – Beyond this, in the middle of Whitehall, is the *Cenotaph*, a national memorial to the dead of the two world wars. Originally a temporary plaster structure, it was rebuilt in stone in 1920. Here the fallen are remembered every year on the second Sunday in November. – Beyond this Whitehall continues S into Parliament Square, lined on the right with a succession of government offices – the *Foreign and Commonwealth Office*, the *Home Office* and the *Ministry of Housing*.

At the opposite corner of Whitehall (here properly known as Parliament Street), on the Embankment, is *Norman Shaw House*, now occupied by government offices but formerly better known as New Scotland Yard, headquarters of the Metropolitan Police (since 1967 in Victoria Street). The building was erected in 1891, replacing earlier premises occupied by the police force established by Sir Robert Peel (hence the popular name "bobbies") in

1829. – *Parliament Square* was formerly an area of gardens belonging to the Palace of Westminster, which had to be sacrificed to the needs of traffic. In the square are statues of various distinguished figures in British and world history, including Abraham Lincoln, Benjamin Disraeli, General Smuts and Sir Winston Churchill.

From Parliament Square Bridge Street runs E past the Houses of Parliament on the right and the end of the Victoria Embankment on the left on to *Westminster Bridge* (810 ft long), built 1854–62, which crosses the Thames into Lambeth, affording impressive views on both sides. The present iron bridge replaced an earlier stone bridge, the second bridge over the Thames (after Old London Bridge).

Houses of Parliament – Westminster Abbey – Tate Gallery – Victoria Station

This itinerary brings us into the heart of the old borough of Westminster. Its most characteristic landmark is the ****Houses of Parliament** (officially known as the New Palace of Westminster). The present buildings, erected in 1834 by Sir Charles Barry after the destruction by fire of the old Palace of Westminster, are in neo-

"Big Ben", Houses of Parliament

Gothic style – a gesture of respect to their near neighbour, Westminster Abbey. Even before the 19th c. fire, however, the old palace had suffered many vicissitudes. It was originally built for Edward the Confessor about 1050, and was later enlarged by William the Conqueror and William Rufus. It was extensively rebuilt by Richard II after destruction by fire, but in 1512 it was devastated by a further fire which left only Westminster Hall and the crypt still standing. From 1547 it was the meeting place of Parliament. In 1605 it was the scene of Guy Fawkes's attempt to blow up Parliament (the Gunpowder Plot). After the 1834 fire Westminster Hall and the crypt were again the only buildings left unscathed.

*Westminster Hall, with its fine oak hammerbeam roof, has seen many great events in the course of its long history. It was the scene of many famous or notorious trials, including those of Sir Thomas More (1535) and Charles I (1649). From 1224 to 1883 the highest English courts of law met here. Later it was used for the lying in state of monarchs and other distinguished persons. – To the E of Westminster Hall are the premises occupied by the House of Commons and the House of Lords. At the northern end is the chamber of the House of Commons, restored after bomb damage during the last war. The chamber is relatively small, with the government benches on the right of the Speaker's chair and the opposition benches on the left. To the S is the chamber of the House of Lords, more elaborately decorated, with the royal throne behind the Woolsack (a reminder of the thriving English woollen industry of the 14th c.), the seat of the Lord Chancellor who presides over the House of Lords. Visitors can obtain tickets for admission to the proceedings of both Houses at the Admission Order Office in *St Stephen's Hall* (on the site of the earlier St Stephen's Chapel in which the House of Commons used to sit). The *Crypt* survived all the fires which ravaged the Houses of Parliament, and was restored in 1886. Also of interest are the *Royal Gallery*, with two large paintings by Daniel Maclise, "Death of Nelson" and "Meeting of Wellington and Blücher after Waterloo", and the *Victoria Tower*, a striking square tower 323 ft high and 75 ft across. The Union Jack flies from the tower when Parliament is sitting.

The *Clock-Tower, at the N end of the Houses of Parliament, is London's best-known landmark, the very symbol of the capital. The huge 13-ton bell known as *Big Ben* (after Sir Benjamin Hall, First Commissioner of Works when it was hung in 1859) became world-famous through its use as an interval signal by the BBC. The name Big Ben is now generally applied to the whole tower, which stands 320 ft high. The dials of the clock are 23 ft in diameter. A white light in the tower after dark indicates that Parliament is sitting.

Across the road from the Houses of Parliament is the *Jewel Tower*, a relic of the old Palace of Westminster, probably built for Edward III in 1365 to provide safe keeping for his jewels and treasure. It now contains a *museum* with items from the old palace.

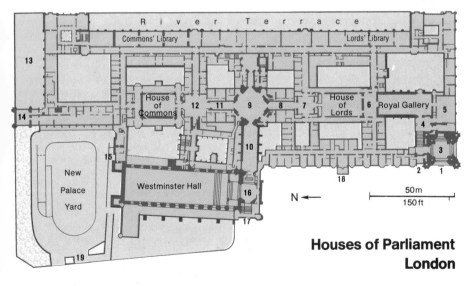

**Houses of Parliament
London**

1 Royal Entrance	6 Prince's Chamber	11 Commons' Corridor	16 St Stephen's Porch .
2 Visitors' Entrance	7 Peers' Lobby	12 Commons' Lobby	17 St Stephen's Entrance
3 Victoria Tower	8 Peers' Corridor	13 Speaker's Green	18 Peers' Entrance
4 Norman Porch	9 Central Lobby	14 Clock Tower (Big Ben)	19 Entrance to
5 Robing Room	10 St Stephen's Hall	15 Members' Entrance	Westminster Hall

Westminster Abbey　　　　　　　　　　London

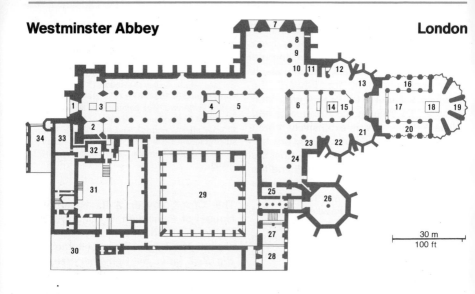

1 West doorway	9 St Michael's Chapel	16 Tomb of Elizabeth I	25 St Faith's Chapel
2 St George's Chapel	10 Chapel of St John the	17 Henry VII's Chapel	26 Chapterhouse
3 Tomb of Unknown Warrior	Evangelist	18 Tomb of Henry VII	27 Chapel of the Pyx
and memorial to Sir Winston	11 Islip Chapel	19 RAF Chapel (Battle of Britain	28 Undercroft Museum
Churchill	12 Chapel of St John the	memorial window)	29 Cloisters
4 Organ gallery	Baptist	20 Tomb of Mary Queen of Scots	30 Dean's Yard
5 Choir	13 St Paul's Chapel	21 St Nicholas's Chapel	31 Deanery (closed)
6 Sanctuary (high altar)	14 St Edward's Chapel	22 St Edmund's Chapel	32 Jericho Parlour (closed)
7 North doorway	(coronation chair)	23 St Benedict's Chapel	33 Jerusalem Chamber (closed)
8 St Andrew's Chapel	15 Henry V's Chantry	24 Poets' Corner	34 Bookshop

Immediately W of the Houses of Parliament is ****Westminster Abbey**, built between the 13th and 14th c. This unusually tall church with its distinctive fenestration and its flying buttresses shows closer affinities to French Gothic than any other English church, and seems to have been modelled on such well-known French churches as the cathedrals of Reims and Amiens. The influence of the Sainte-Chapelle in Paris can also be detected. The rebuilding of the church was begun by Henry III in 1245, but he did not live to see it completed: the nave, indeed, was not finished until after 1375. Building was continued by Henry Yevele, who followed the 13th c. plans so closely that the Abbey has all the appearance of having been completed within a single short period. The 13th c. sculpture is of high quality; perhaps the best-known figures are the angels in the transepts. Only the two W towers depart from the strict Gothic style of the rest of the church: they were designed by Wren and Hawksmoor and added as late as 1740. The site of the church was originally occupied by an abbey founded in 750: the name Westminster reflects the fact that it lay on the western edge of the town, which then occupied the area of the present City.

Since the 11th c. Westminster Abbey has been the place of coronation of the monarch; the first to be crowned here was William the Conqueror. Since the late Middle Ages it has also been the last resting place of kings and queens and distinguished figures in national life. At the W end of the nave is the *Tomb of the Unknown Warrior*, containing the remains of a soldier who fell in Flanders during the First World War. In the *Warrior's Chapel* (to the right of the main entrance) is a memorial to the dead of the two world wars. The nave contains a large number of monuments. In the N aisle of the choir ambulatory is the entrance to *Edward the Confessor's Chapel*, behind the high altar, which contains Edward's tomb. In this chapel is the *Coronation Chair*, made of English oak, which houses the Stone of Scone, brought from Scotland by Edward I in 1297. In its original position in Scone Abbey this had been the coronation seat of the kings of Scotland. – From the ambulatory a flight of steps leads up to ***Henry VII's Chapel**, which forms the eastern end of the church. Built between 1502 and 1520, it is the finest example of the English late Gothic (Perpendicular) style. It contains the splendid *Tomb of Henry VII* and his queen, Elizabeth of York. The tomb, of black and white marble and enclosed within a fine bronze grille, was the work of the Florentine sculptor Torrigiani, who was commissioned by Henry VIII in 1512 and spent six years on the task. A particularly notable feature of the chapel is the stalactitic vaulting of the roof. Above the choirstalls hang the banners of the knights of the Order of the Bath. In the N aisle of the chapel is the tomb of Elizabeth I, in the S aisle that of her great rival Mary Queen of Scots. – Other notable features of the abbey are the **Cloisters* and the **Chapter House*, in which Parliament met from the 13th c. until 1547. The Norman *Undercroft* contains wooden and wax figures of monarchs buried in the Abbey, offering a cross-section of the country's history.

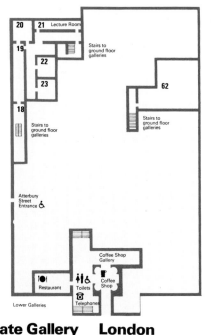

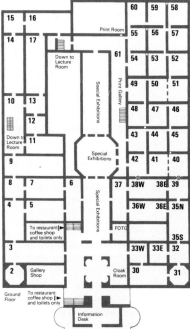

Tate Gallery London

PLAN OF THE GALLERY

BRITISH COLLECTION

Rooms
2	Hogarth
3	16th, 17th and early 18th c. painting
4, 5	Late 18th c. painting
6	Painters of the sublime and the exotic
7	William Blake and his followers
8	Late 18th c. painting
9, 10	Turner
11	Constable
12	Landscape painting 1800–50
13	Turner watercolours and drawings
14	Turner
15	19th c. landscape painting
16, 17	Later Victorian painting
18	Drawings and watercolours
19	Subject painting 1800–60
20	The Pre-Raphaelites
21	Lecture Room (Access for evening lectures and films via Atterbury Street entrance)
22, 23	Sporting art

MODERN COLLECTION

30	Impressionism and Post-Impressionism
31	Sickert, Camden Town
32	Bonnard and contemporaries
33E	Bloomsbury
33W	Whistler and contemporaries
35N	European Expressionism
35S	Matisse and the Fauves
36E, 36W	Closed for re-hanging
37	Works on paper
38	Picasso, Braque, Gris, Léger
39	Abstraction
40, 41	American Abstract Expressionism
42	Dada and Surrealism
43	Ivon Hitchens
44	Francis Bacon
45	Naum Gabo
46	Mark Rothko
47, 48	Henry Moore
49	Alberto Giacometti
50	Ben Nicholson
51	Barbara Hepworth
52	American Pop Art
53, 56	Anthony Caro
54	Jean Dubuffet
55	European Post-War Abstraction
57	Richard Long
58	British Post-War Abstraction
59, 60	British Pop Art
61	Artists' prints
62	Closed for re-hanging

Further information from the Information Desk in the entrance hall.

N of Westminster Abbey, in Victoria Street, is the *Middlesex Guildhall*, built between 1905 and 1919 on the site of the abbey sanctuary and a Norman tower. During the Second World War the maritime courts of the Allied nations met here.

W of the Guildhall, in Storey's Gate is the *Central Hall* (1912), headquarters of the Methodist Church, which played a major part in world affairs when the Preparatory General Assembly of the United Nations met here in 1946.

From Westminster Abbey going S along Abingdon Street and Millbank, we see on the left the beautiful *Victoria Tower Gardens*, in which is a bronze cast of Rodin's "*Burghers of Calais*". A short distance W of the gardens, in Smith Square, is the Baroque *St John's Church*.

Beyond *Lambeth Bridge* Millbank runs alongside the Thames. On the opposite bank is the borough of Lambeth. After passing *Queen Alexandra's Military Hospital* we come to the ****Tate Gallery**, one of London's great art collections. It concentrates on British painting, modern foreign art and modern sculpture. The gallery, opened in 1897, owed its origin to the munificence of Henry Tate, a sugar manufacturer, who inaugurated it with his own collection of British paintings. The gallery's aim is to collect all British pictures, from the 16th c. to the present day, which reflect significant trends in the development of art.

Beyond the Tate Gallery is the intersection between Millbank, its continuation Grosvenor Road, Vauxhall Bridge and Vauxhall Bridge Road. To the W of the intersection extends the residential district of PIMLICO, which is bounded on the N by the more fashionable district of Belgravia. Turning right along Vauxhall Bridge Road, we come to **Victoria Station**, London's busiest traffic junction, with the main-line station serving south-eastern England and the Channel ports. To the rear of the station, in Buckingham Palace Road, is the *British Airways Terminal*, linked with Heathrow Airport by a shuttle bus service.

Vauxhall Bridge Road, which runs from the Thames to Victoria Station, has little of interest to offer the tourist, with the possible exception of the blocks of government offices and *Lillington Gardens* near the S end of the street. At *Vauxhall Bridge*, which links the districts of Pimlico and Kennington, is the colourful *Hovis McDougall House*.

From the N end of Vauxhall Bridge Road and Victoria Station *Victoria Street* leads back to Westminster. The modern office blocks at its E end, include the *Department of Industry·and Trade* and *New Scotland Yard*, headquarters of the Metropolitan Police since 1967.

E of Victoria Station, in Ashley Place, is *Westminster Cathedral*, see of the Cardinal Archbishop of Westminster, which ranks with Liverpool Cathedral as one of the two major Roman Catholic churches in Britain. Built by J. F. Bentley between 1895 and 1903, it is in Romanesque-Byzantine style. The square campanile, 284 ft high, affords wide *views of London (lift at NW entrance).

The INTERIOR, richly decorated with marble and mosaics, is of impressive size (342 ft long, 149 ft wide, 117 ft high). It is of basilican type, with four domes.

With its aisles and side chapels, the *nave* is the widest in Britain. The walls are to be faced with coloured marbles and the domes and upper parts of the walls with additional mosaics. On the columns are carved Stations of the Cross (by Eric Gill). Near the entrance are two pillars of red Norwegian granite, symbolising the Precious Blood of Jesus to which the Cathedral is dedicated. On the left-hand pillar is a copy of the famous figure of St Peter from St Peter's in Rome. The great 30-foot-long cross, which hangs from the arch at the E end of the nave, bears painted representations of Christ (front) and the Mater Dolorosa (rear).

The *side chapels* are particularly notable for their rich decoration of marble and mosaics. The baptistery, to the right of the main entrance, is separated by a marble wall from the chapel of SS. Gregory and Augustine. The next chapel (St Patrick and the Saints of Ireland) is a memorial to the Irishmen who fell in the First World War. Beyond it is a chapel dedicated to St Andrew and the Saints of Scotland. The mosaic floor of the following chapel, dedicated to St Paul, follows a design by the Cosmati. The high altar in the *sanctuary*, flanked by two arcades, has a fine marble canopy; the altar-table is a granite slab weighing 11 tons. The archbishop's throne, to the left, is a smaller version of the Papal throne in the Lateran. To the left of the sanctuary is the Chapel of the Blessed Sacrament, with over-rich mosaic decoration by Boris Anrep. Immediately left of this is the Chapel of the Sacred Heart. At the entrance to the N transept is the Chapel of St Thomas of Canterbury, with a fine statue of Cardinal Vaughan, who was responsible, as archbishop, for the building of the Cathedral.

The *Crypt*, containing valuable relics, is entered from the Lady Chapel, to the right of the sanctuary.

N of Victoria Station, in Buckingham Gate, are *Wellington Barracks* headquarters of the Guards Division, with stucco-fronted buildings set round the parade ground. From Buckingham Gate *Petty France* runs E past the *Passport Office* to Old Queen Street and Queen Anne's Gate. In this area are some very handsome houses built around 1780, narrow-fronted but with fine façades. The rather countrified houses in Old Queen Street date from around 1700. Some of the old street lamps are still preserved in this quarter, from which it is only a few paces to Birdcage Walk.

Mayfair and Soho

Some parts of London are "good" addresses, others are not. Mayfair belongs to the former category, Soho to the latter. But in both Mayfair and Soho and in the surrounding streets there is excellent shopping, eating and entertainment to be had.

This itinerary begins at **Hyde Park Corner**, a busy traffic intersection surrounded by the *Wellington Arch*, St

George's Hospital and the Wellington Museum (Apsley House). A system of underpasses allows pedestrians to cross the street. From Hyde Park Corner two important streets, Piccadilly and Park Lane, run respectively E and N, forming the southern and western boundaries of Mayfair. Looking up Park Lane, there is a fine view of Hyde Park to the left, while immediately adjoining is the *Wellington Museum, in *Apsley House*, residence of the great Duke of Wellington, which was opened as a museum in 1952. It contains mementoes of the "Iron Duke" and works of art which belonged to him. The house, built in 1778, was acquired by the duke in 1817.

In the entrance hall and elsewhere in the house are marble busts of Wellington and his contemporaries. On the ground floor are a variety of items which belonged to the Duke. In the China Room is part of the service of Prussian porcelain presented to him after the battle of Waterloo by King Frederick William III. On the upper floor is a bust of Cicero, the only one with an ancient inscription. To the left of this is the Piccadilly Gallery, containing among much else three works by Brueghel the Elder. In the dining room is the valuable silver centrepiece presented to the Duke by the Prince Regent of Portugal in 1816. In the Waterloo Gallery are paintings captured from Joseph Bonaparte after the battle of Vitoria, including works by Rubens, Murillo and Sassoferrato. In this gallery the Duke held the famous "Waterloo Banquets" every year until his death in 1852.

In *Park Lane*, which ends at Oxford Street, are a series of large hotels, among them the tower block of the *Inn on the Park*, the *Hilton* and the fashionable *Dorchester*. To the right is Hertford Street, with the house (No. 10) in which Gen. Burgoyne lived from 1795 until his death in 1802. At 93 Park Lane is a house in which Benjamin Disraeli lived for many years. Beyond this *Curzon Street* runs into the very heart of MAYFAIR (named after an annual fair held in the month of May). At No. 19 Disraeli died in 1881. In *Worcester House* (No. 30) are the showrooms of the Worcester Royal Porcelain Company.

From Curzon Street two arched streets run S into *Shepherd Market*, a much-favoured residential area with something of a village atmosphere. N of Curzon Street, reached by way of Queen Street, is *Charles Street*, at the narrow W end of which is an unusual house with a timber-built upper storey, believed to be the work of John Phillips, a carpenter in the service of Lord Berkeley. To the E this street runs into *Berkeley Square*, originally an aristocratic square built in 1739 in the grounds of Berkeley House but now completely altered in character by the office building which has taken place during the 20th c. From the square Mount Street leads back to Park Lane. Turning right off this street into Carlos Place, we come into *Grosvenor Square*, laid out by Richard Grosvenor in 1725, the centre of a very select area. On the W side of the square is the *United States Embassy* (by Eero Saarinen, 1958). In the gardens is a *statue of Franklin D. Roosevelt*. The monumental buildings which now surround the square include offices and residences of United States embassy staff and two hotels.

From here we can take either Duke Street or Audley Street to reach *Oxford Street*, perhaps London's busiest street, with several large department stores. Along with Regent Street and New Bond Street it rivals Knightsbridge as one of London's great shopping areas. Going E, past the celebrated *Selfridges* department store, we come to *Oxford Circus*, a kind of counterpart to Piccadilly Circus. The two circuses are linked by *Regent Street* with its imposing classical-style buildings, the mile-long N–S axis of London's West End, which is continued beyond Piccadilly Circus by Lower Regent Street. The wide arc immediately N of Piccadilly Circus is known as the Quadrant. Regent Street was originally laid out by Nash about 1820 but was rebuilt in the 1920s (the Quadrant by Sir Reginald Blomfield, 1926). In the Quadrant is the *Café Royal*, once a favourite haunt of the literary world.

*Piccadilly Circus, with its famous statue of Eros in the centre, is one of London's busiest traffic intersections, endlessly circled by cars, taxis and buses. Situated at the meeting-place of a number of major streets, it is the real centre of the West End, illuminated at night by a great array of flashing neon signs. Its central feature is the *Shaftesbury Memorial*, a bronze fountain topped by a winged figure with a bow and arrow, intended to symbolise Christian charity but popularly known as Eros. From Piccadilly Circus the *Haymarket* runs SE, parallel to Lower Regent Street, towards Trafalgar Square. In this street are numbers of restaurants and snack bars and two of London's leading theatres, *Her Majesty's* and the *Haymarket Theatre*, which was built by John Nash.

Conduit Street and Maddox Street, in which are numerous elegant gentlemen's outfitters and tailors, run W from Regent Street into New Bond Street. **Bond Street**, the very Mecca of fashionable shoppers, is made up of Old Bond Street to the S and New Bond Street to the N. It was originally laid out by Sir Thomas Bond in 1686 and represents the eastern boundary of Mayfair. The art auctioneering firm of Sotheby's was established here in 1744, and has since been joined by others. Sotheby's auctions usually start at 11 a.m., books being sold on Mondays, china on Tuesdays, pictures on Wednesdays, silver and jewellery on Thursdays and furniture on Fridays. At the corner of Bruton Street is the *Time-Life Building*.

At its S end Old Bond Street runs into *Piccadilly*, London's second great E–W thoroughfare, linking Piccadilly Circus with Hyde Park Corner. The name probably comes from a mansion known as Piccadilly Hall, built in 1611, which was a great meeting-place of the fashionable world. On the N side of the street, near Piccadilly Circus, is the *Piccadilly Hotel*. A little way SW is **Burlington House**, now the home of the Royal Academy of Arts, which was built in 1655 for the third earl of Burlington. The gateway leads into a square courtyard, in the centre of which is a *statue of Sir Joshua Reynolds*, first President of the Academy.

The Royal Academy's annual summer exhibition displays contemporary painting, sculpture and architecture, mostly works which have not previously been exhibited. The private rooms of the Academy can be seen only on the personal invitation of a member. The permanent exhibition, not open to the general public, consists of diploma works by academicians. The Academy frequently organises special exhibitions during the winter.

Burlington House is also the home of the Royal Society, founded in 1660, whose membership has included such notable figures as Sir Christopher Wren, Samuel Pepys and Sir Isaac Newton. Here too other learned societies have their headquarters – the British Academy, the Chemical Society, the Geological Society, the Society of Antiquaries, the Royal Astronomical Society. Visitors can enter their premises only in the company of a member. The British Academy, founded with the support of the Royal Society, seeks to promote historical, philosophical and philological studies. The Chemical Society has one of the most comprehensive specialised libraries in the world. Another occupant of Burlington House is the Linnean Society, which is concerned with natural history and possesses the collection of the great Swedish botanist Carl von Linné (Linnaeus), who devised the accepted system of nomenclature of animals and plants.

Along the W side of Burlington House is the long *Burlington Arcade*, originally built in 1818; the entrance was remodelled in 1931 and the northern section rebuilt in 1954. The arcade, 585 ft long, contains 72 exclusive shops of different kinds, and is watched over by "beadles", ex-soldiers of the 10th Hussars. At the N end is a building erected in 1866 for London University which now houses the **Museum of Mankind**, the British Museum's department of ethnography. The exhibits are changed almost every year. The collections illustrate tribal life in various parts of the world; the material from West Africa (including Benin in particular), Oceania and America is especially notable. – At the end of Burlington Gardens is *Savile Row*, a street synonymous with high-class gentlemen's tailoring.

Returning to Piccadilly and going W, we come to Albemarle Street (on right), which runs along one side of *Clarendon House*. At the N end of this street, behind a long façade of Corinthian columns, is the *Royal Institution of Great Britain*, founded in 1799 for the "promotion, diffusion and extension of science and useful knowledge".

Farther along Piccadilly are a number of exclusive clubs and hotels, with views of the Green Park on the opposite side of the street. At No. 105 are the offices of the *Arts Council*.

Having thus completed our circuit of Mayfair, we can return to Piccadilly Circus in order to explore London's most colourful quarter, **SOHO**. The name first appears in 1632, being explained as an old hunting cry dating from the time when this was open country. Soho is bounded on the N and S by Oxford Street and Shaftesbury Avenue, on the E and W by Charing Cross Road and Regent Street. This was already a cosmopolitan part of the town in the 17th c., when French refugees settled in Bateman Street shortly after the revocation of the Edict of Nantes (1685). It is now noted for two things – its numerous restaurants offering a varied range of national cuisines and its proliferation of entertainment facilities of varying degrees of respectability. Striptease and similar establishments, are to be found in the streets of Soho, though they are perhaps less blatant and obtrusive than in the corresponding districts of other large cities throughout the world. There are also numerous pubs where Londoners can enjoy a breathing space after their day's work.

Going NE up Shaftesbury Avenue from Piccadilly Circus, we come to the junction with *Wardour Street*, the centre of the British film industry. The territory of Soho extends also a certain distance S of Shaftesbury Avenue, taking in, for example, *Gerrard Street*, which shows increasing Chinese influence. At No. 43 the poet Dryden lived until his death in 1700. In a French restaurant in this street G. K. Chesterton and Hilaire Belloc met for the first time in 1900. In Wardour Street, just N of Shaftesbury Avenue, is the tower of *St Anne's Church*, on which is a memorial to the writer William Hazlitt (1778–1830). The nave of the church, which was partly by Wren, was destroyed in 1940. Farther along Shaftesbury Avenue is the junction with *Dean Street*, which runs N through Soho. At No. 28 the sculptor *Joseph Nollekens* was born in 1737, and at No. 26 *Karl Marx* lived from 1851 to 1856; the two houses, both dating from 1734, are now a restaurant. Parallel with Dean Street is *Frith Street*, with many restaurants and clubs, and the house (No. 22) in which J. L. Baird demonstrated television for the first time in 1926.

Farther N is *Soho Square*, originally built in 1681, though it has now only one house dating as far back as the 18th c. Later it became a centre of the music trade. At No. 22, then the house of the Lord Mayor, William Beckford, *Mozart* performed in 1764. The *statue of Charles II* was the work of Cibber (1681). On the E side of the square is the Roman Catholic *St Patrick's Church* (1793), which shows Italian influence. The *French Protestant Church* was built in 1893.

Originally Soho Square was an aristocratic quarter, with a mansion belonging to the Duke of Monmouth, who used "Soho" as a watchword during the battle of Sedgemoor (1685). In the 18th c. it was surrounded by handsome town houses, much favoured by foreign ambassadors; the famous botanist Sir Joseph Banks also had a house here which drew many of his fellow scientists to the area. At the SE corner of the square is the *House of St Barnabas in Soho*, built *c.* 1750 and occupied since 1862 by a charitable organisation. It can be visited (offerings gratefully accepted). *Richard Beckford* lived here in 1754, and was probably responsible for the interior decoration with its Rococo plasterwork, carved wood and wrought-iron. The chapel dates from 1862. The setting for the fictional meeting between Dr Manette and Sidney Carton in Dickens's "Tale of Two Cities" was in the rear courtyard of the chapel. – *Greek Street*, which runs S from Soho Square, takes its name from the Greek immigrants who settled here.

Charing Cross Road, the eastern boundary of Soho, is still a great centre of the secondhand book trade, though less flourishing than in the past. There are also a number of theatres in this street, including the *Palace Theatre* (1888) in Cambridge Circus, where Anna Pavlova made her London debut.

Just before Cambridge Circus a turn to the right leads into *Old Compton Street*, a characteristic Soho street with its numerous restaurants. Crossing Wardour Street, we come into Brewer Street. The busy street market in *Berwick Street*, to the N, is well worth a visit (food, flowers, secondhand goods).

Brewer Street eventually leads into Regent Street; but by turning right before this is reached we come into *Golden Square*, for long centre of the woollen cloth trade. Among famous residents of the square have been the Austrian woman painter *Angelica Kauffman* (1741–1807) at No. 16, *Cardinal Wiseman* (1802–65) at No. 35 and *Dr John Hunter* at No. 31. All these houses have had to be rebuilt. In the centre of the square is a statue of *George II*.

NW of Golden Square, beyond Beak Street, is **Carnaby Street**, a name of special magic for the younger generation, which still vies with King's Road in Chelsea as the shopping Mecca of the fashion-conscious teenager – though nowadays other streets are challenging the predominance of these two. The most interesting part of Carnaby Street is the short stretch between Beak Street and Ganton Street. It must be said that the worldwide reputation of Carnaby Street is founded on shrewd management methods as well as on the quality of the merchandise. The neighbouring side streets, formerly of little account, now

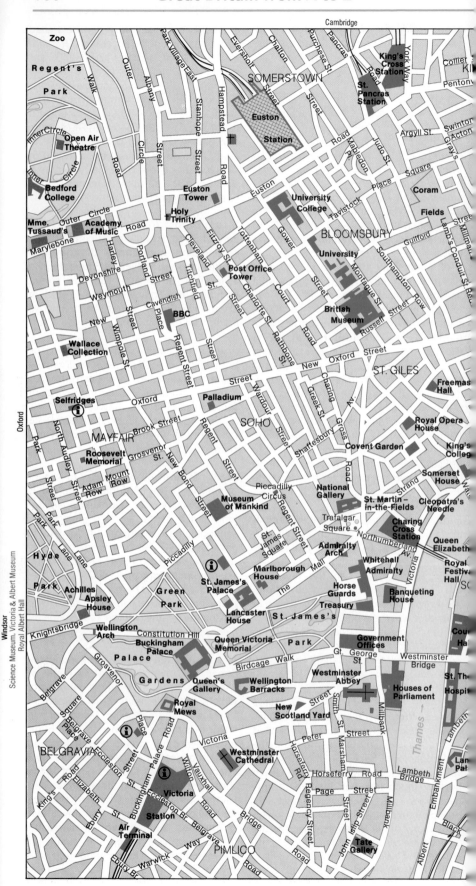

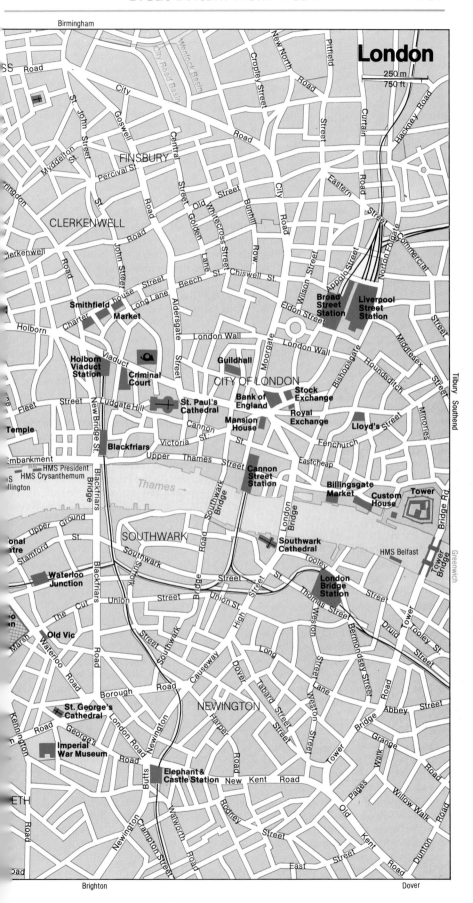

London

250 m
750 ft

Birmingham

Brighton   Dover

Tilbury Southend

Greenwich

offer a profusion of boutiques, discotheques, snack bars and pubs. – At the N
end of Carnaby Street is Great Marlborough Street. Turning left along this,
we come into Regent Street, and from
here it is only a short distance to Oxford
Circus, which is a convenient starting
point for an exploration of the northern
part of central London.

Oxford Street to Regent's Park

From Oxford Circus the northern section
of Regent Street runs into *Langham Place*,
on the left-hand side of which is the
Polytechnic of Central London, an institute founded in 1882 with the object of
promoting the mental, moral and physical
development of young people. On the
right-hand side is *All Souls Church*, with a
striking needle-like spire. The church was
built by Nash in 1823–24, and contains a
bust of the architect.

Langham Place runs into *Portland Place*,.
one of London's widest streets, on the
right-hand side of which is *Broadcasting
House*, the monumental headquarters of
the British Broadcasting Corporation.
Built in 1931 by Val Myer and Watson
Hart, it has a sculptured group by Eric Gill
("Prospero and Ariel") over the main
entrance. At 28 Portland Place is the
*Royal Institute of Public Health and
Hygiene*, and at No. 66 the *Royal Institute
of British Architects*. Also in Portland
Place are monuments to Sir George
White, the defender of Ladysmith, and
Lord Lister, the pioneer of antiseptic
surgery.

The area E of Portland Place is of less
interest. The next street, running parallel,
is Great Portland Street. Round about
here are the premises of many wholesale
textile firms. In Mortimer Street the
sculptor *Joseph Nollekens* lived for fifty
years. This street runs E to the *Middlesex
Hospital*, founded in 1755 and now an
important teaching hospital, in which
Kipling died in 1936. In Foley Street, N of
the hospital, are houses once occupied by
the painters Sir Edwin Landseer (No. 33)
and Henry Fuseli (No. 37). In Great
Tichfield Street lived the American
Samuel Morse, inventor of the telegraph,
and the artist C. R. Leslie (though the
house no longer exists). To the E of the
Middlesex Hospital is *Charlotte Street*,

with many foreign restaurants. Greek
restaurants are to be found in *Goodge
Street*. In Scala Street is *Pollock's Toy
Museum*.

From the Middlesex Hospital *Cleveland
Street* runs N to the **Post Office Tower**
(580 ft high), built in 1966, which affords
what is surely the best *view over London.
It houses a radio transmitter and receiver
as well as a television relay station, and at
the foot is a telephone exchange. There
are two lifts up to the top of the tower,
which is surmounted by a 40 ft aerial mast.
There are three superimposed viewing
platforms, from which in clear weather the
whole of London and the immediately
surrounding area can be seen.

On the W side of Regent Street and
Langham Place *Cavendish Place* leads
into *Cavendish Square*, laid out in 1717.
The pillared façades of two houses on the
N side of the square, dating from 1720, are
relics of a palace begun by the Duke of
Chandos. *Nelson* lived for a time at No. 5.

In *Holles Street*, which runs from Cavendish Square to Oxford Street, is the site of
a house (No. 21), now replaced by a
department store, in which *Lord Byron*
was born in 1788. In *Chandos Street*,
which leaves the NE corner of the square,
is a handsome house by Robert Adam
(1771), now occupied by the Royal
Society of Medicine.

From Cavendish Square *Wigmore Street*
runs W. This busy street, part of the great
shopping complex of Oxford Street and
Regent Street, with numerous restaurants
and cafés to provide relaxation from the
fatigues of a shopping expedition, leads
into *Baker Street*, a major artery running N
in the direction of Regent's Park. In
Wigmore Street is the *Wigmore Hall*, a
concert hall mainly used for the performance of chamber music. – From the SW
corner of Cavendish Square *Henrietta
Place* also runs W, parallel to Wigmore
Street. At its western end are the headquarters of the *Royal Society of Medicine*,
notable for its excellent library.

Welbeck Street, which cuts across Wigmore Street, was the home of many
figures prominent in British history, including Edward Gibbon, who published
the first volumes of his "Decline and Fall"
while living at No. 7. Half way along this
street *Queen Anne Street* goes off on the

right, with a house (No. 58) in which Berlioz lived for some months in 1851. N of Wigmore Street and E of Baker Street is *Manchester Square*, built between 1770 and 1788, which still preserves a number of handsome old houses dating from that period.

The most important building in Manchester Square, however, is *Hertford House*, on the N side, which contains the famous ****Wallace Collection**. The house originally built for the duke of Manchester, later became the residence of the marquesses of Hertford and of *Sir Richard Wallace*, son of the fourth marquess (1818–90). The collection was begun in France by the third and fourth marquesses and added to by Sir Richard. In 1871, during the Prussian siege of Paris, he made his way to London, bringing most of his collection with him. The collection was left to the nation by his widow, and is believed to be the most valuable gift any private individual has ever made to his country. The museum, opened in 1900, is notable both for the quality and the variety of its contents.

The collection, housed in 22 rooms, consists of French paintings, porcelain and furniture of the 17th and 18th c., together with arms and armour both European and Oriental, Renaissance terracottas, jewellery and pictures by English, Flemish, Spanish and Italian masters *Rooms I and II* contain Louis XVI furniture and a Beauvais tapestry after designs by Francesco Casanova. *Rooms III and IV*, devoted to the art of the Renaissance, contain a valuable collection of Italian majolica by leading masters, including the famous "Bath of the Maidens" dish by Giorgio Andreoli and three cases of 15th and 17th c. bronzes. *Rooms V–VII* display a collection of European arms and armour from the 15th c. onwards. *Room VIII* contains Oriental scenes by French painters. *Room X* has terracottas, furniture and pictures by Sassoferrato, Titian and others. Works by Spanish and Italian masters of the 17th c. are displayed in *Room XI*.

The collection continues on the upper floor. In *Room XII* are Louis XV and XVI porcelain, furniture and clocks. *Rooms XIII and XIV* contain 17th c. Dutch and Flemish paintings, including "Christ on the Cross" by Rubens and five small but very fine studies by masters of the same period. *Room XV* contains Dutch landscapes and coastal scenes, also of the 17th c. *Room XVI* has pictures by Rembrandt, Frans Hals, Van Dyck, Rubens and other masters. The French painters of the 19th c. are represented in *Room XVII*, which contains some small works by Meissonnier of insurpassable quality. *Rooms XVIII and XIX* contain works by 18th c. French painters, together with three secretaires which belonged to Marie-Antoinette.

In *Room XX* is the largest collection of Bonington's works, together with a writing-table which is believed to have belonged to Catherine the Great. *Rooms XXI and XXII* contain Sèvres porcelain, miniatures and still lifes by Desportes and others. In the *Entrance Hall* are a portrait of George IV by Lawrence, a portrait by Van Dyck and busts of Charles I (Roubiliac) and Queen Caroline (Rysbrack). – With so much to see, visitors should nevertheless spare a glance for the very elegant and decorative staircase which leads up to the first floor.

N of Manchester Square extends the old district of ST MARYLEBONE – a name derived from the old church of St Mary on the Bourne which once stood here. In *Marylebone Road*, which runs from E to W through this part of the town, is *Marylebone Church* (by Hardwick, 1813–17), in which Robert Browning was married (mementoes in the Browning Room). In a chapel on the N side of the church is a "Holy Family" by Benjamin West. An earlier church of the same name (1741), in which Byron and Nelson's daughter Horatia were baptised, stood until 1949 in Marylebone High Street, S of Marylebone Road; the site is now occupied by gardens, in which are the graves of Charles and Samuel Wesley, Allan Ramsay and George Stubbs. – The great tourist attraction in Marylebone Road is ***Madame Tussaud's**, the famous waxworks exhibition. Madame Tussaud's waxworks originally came from Paris, where her uncle Philippe Creutz opened a waxworks cabinet in 1770. *Marie Grosholz*, later Madame Tussaud (1761–1850), worked in this cabinet while still a child. In 1802 she settled in England, and in 1835 came to London.

In the "Conservatory", set in an artificial landscape of plants and palms, are life-like representations of prominent contemporaries, from the Dutch footballer Cruyff to Glenda Jackson, from Liza Minnelli to Len Murray. Then follows a series of heroic figures, with commentaries in sound and slides to explain their significance. At the entrance to the Grand Hall is a self-portrait of Madame Tussaud herself at the age of 81, and behind her are Henry VIII with his six wives and Elizabeth I in her jewelled dress. Then come figures of Queen Elizabeth II and the royal family, for which the Queen, like other contemporary figures, gave special sittings. Other figures in the hall include Sir Winston Churchill, Benjamin Franklin and George Washington. The *Chamber of Horrors*, modelled on the interior of the old French state prison, the Bastille, contains representations of the French royal family (Marie-Antoinette, Louis XVI), Robespierre, Marat and Fouquier-Tinville, all beheaded during the French Revolution and modelled immediately after their execution by Madame Tussaud, who was thus able to use the actual heads as her models. Figures of hangmen and murderers on the scaffold and an original guillotine of the French Revolutionary period add to the gruesome effect. In the room of *Tableaux* are representations of Mary Queen of Scots awaiting execution and of Madame Dubarry asleep. The battle of Trafalgar is commemorated by a reproduction of the gun-deck of Nelson's flagship *Victory*.

Adjoining Madame Tussaud's is the *London Planetarium*, in which programmes are presented regularly throughout the day. The Laserium (open only in the evening) offers an unusual spectacle called a "cosmic laser concert", in which light effects combine with the music of the spheres and normal music of different periods in a performance designed to convey to the spectators something of the timelessness and immense size of the universe.

A little way E of Madame Tussaud's is the *Royal Academy of Music*, founded in 1822; it is not open to the public. From here we turn N to reach Regent's Park, one of the many open spaces which have been preserved in spite of London's rapid growth. More than 10% of the city's area, in fact, is open space. Most of the parks were originally hunting grounds frequented by the court and the aristocracy. The entrance to Regent's Park is formed by *Park Crescent* at the E end of Marylebone Road, a particularly fine example (by John Nash, 1812–22) of the crescents which are such a feature of London's urban design. At No. 1 is the *International Students' House*, with a bust of President John F. Kennedy in front of it.

From Park Crescent we cross Park Square to enter **Regent's Park**. After completing Park Crescent, Nash laid out the area to the N as a landscaped park (*c.* 1827), surrounded by terraces of elegant houses. The park is a delightful place of recreation and relaxation, with restaurants and cafeterias in the very beautiful *Queen Mary's Gardens* and an *open-air theatre* which in summer attracts large audiences to performances of Shakespeare and pop concerts.

The park is surrounded by a carriage drive known as the *Outer Circle*, beyond which is a still wider circle running parallel, formed by Albany Street, Prince Albert Road, Park Road and Marylebone Road. The surrounding terraces, in a monumental neo-classical style, were also designed by Nash. The *Broad Walk* runs straight across the park from S to N, leading to the Zoological Gardens which occupy the northern section of the park. In the SW of the park is an artificial lake (rowing boats for hire). Most of the park is used for various forms of sport, particularly cricket. From York Gate, on the S side of the park, a path runs N into the Inner Circle which surrounds *Queen Mary's Gardens*, perhaps the most beautiful small public garden in London. To the left can be seen *Bedford College*, now part of London University, which was originally founded in 1849 to provide secular education for women.

A triangular area at the N end of Regent's Park is occupied by the ****Zoological Gardens**, founded in 1826 by Sir Stamford Raffles and Sir Humphry Davy and subsequently enlarged and extended. The Zoo, which also provides research facilities for the Zoological Society of London, is traversed by the *Regent's Canal (Grand Union Canal)* and the Outer Circle, but its unity is preserved by three bridges over the canal and two pedestrian passages under the Outer Circle. It is at present in the middle of a long-term redevelopment plan initiated by Sir Hugh Casson in 1959, involving the transfer of many animals to the spaciously planned Whipsnade Park Zoo, 30 miles NW of London, near Luton. There are three entrances to the Zoo: the main gate on the Outer Circle, the N gate in Prince Albert Road and the S gate in Broad Walk. During the summer a motorboat runs on the Regent's Canal from Little Venice (3 miles SW) to the Zoo. Among special attractions for children are the Children's Zoo (to the S), with a variety of tame animals, as well as chimpanzees and donkey and pony rides.

While in this part of the town it is worth while going a little farther N on to *Primrose Hill* (219 ft), beyond Prince Albert Road, from which there is an excellent view of London. To the W of the hill is the residential district of ST JOHN'S WOOD, much favoured by artists, which was originally laid out around 1820 but now consists largely of houses of later date.

Hyde Park – Kensington Gardens – Paddington

Hyde Park, with the adjoining Kensington Gardens, is London's largest open space. The area, originally belonging to Westminster Abbey, was taken over by Henry VIII and made into a deer park. It was thrown open to the public in 1635, thus becoming one of the earliest public parks in the country. Hyde Park and Kensington Gardens are bounded on the S by Kensington Road, on the W by Kensington Palace Gardens (a street, not a park), on the N by Bayswater Road and on the E by Park Lane. The combined parks extend for a mile and a half from E to W and for some 1000 yards from N to S. The two lakes, the Serpentine and the

Round Pond, were formed at the behest of Queen Caroline, wife of George II, about 1730. The more easterly of the two, the Serpentine, is a mile long and offers facilities for rowing, motorboating, sailing, bathing and bird-watching.

From Hyde Park Corner *Rotten Row*, a riding track, runs W though the park, and other paths run N towards Marble Arch and NW along the northern side of the Serpentine. At Hyde Park Corner is the *Achilles Statue* (by Westmacott), modelled on a figure on the Quirinal in Rome, erected in 1822 in honour of Wellington and his men. Continuing N past an attractive fountain, we come to **Speakers' Corner**, at Marble Arch – a traditional English institution where everyone has a right to have his say. It is particularly busy on Sundays. At the NE corner of the park is **Marble Arch**, a triumphal arch modelled by John Nash on the Arch of Constantine in Rome. Originally erected in front of Buckingham Palace, it was moved to its present position in 1850. It stands on a site once notorious as Tyburn, the place of execution to which criminals were brought from the Tower or Newgate Prison, passing through the City on their way to be hanged. The first execution was carried out here in 1196, the last in 1793, and until that date the gallows – popularly known as "Tyburn Tree" – stood here permanently ready. There is a commemorative tablet on the traffic island opposite the Odeon cinema. – Continuing along the N side of the park and turning S at Victoria Gate on the path known as the Ring, we come to the Serpentine and cross it on *Rennie's Bridge*, 200 yards long, from which there is a good view of a section of the London skyline. On the S side of the lake are a restaurant and a bathing area. Continuing S towards the *Alexandra Gate*, we pass the *Serpentine Gallery*, in which exhibitions are held in summer.

The Alexandra Gate leads into the busy shopping area of Kensington Road and Knightsbridge. To the left are *Knightsbridge* and *Hyde Park Barracks*. If we turn right before reaching the gate we come to the **Albert Memorial**, which stands in Kensington Gardens opposite the Royal Albert Hall, and offers an impressive view of the huge edifice. The Albert Memorial (by Sir George Gilbert Scott, 1872) commemorates Queen Victoria's consort, Prince Albert of Saxe-Coburg-Gotha (1819–61). The bronze figure of the prince depicts him holding the catalogue of the Great Exhibition of 1851. (The Great Exhibition was housed in the Crystal Palace in Hyde Park, but three years later the Crystal Palace was moved to Sydenham in the outskirts of London, where a second Great Exhibition drew 50,000 spectators; in 1936 it was destroyed by fire.) On the base of the Memorial are marble figures of 150 artists of many nationalities from antiquity to the 19th c., carved by J. B. Philip and H. H. Armstead. At the four corners are allegorical groups symbolising Agriculture, Commerce, Manufactures and Engineering and four groups representing Europe, Asia, Africa and America.

Kensington Gardens were originally the private grounds of Kensington Palace. The *Round Pond* and Broad Walk were planned by George I, but the present layout of the gardens was the work of Queen Caroline, George II's wife, between 1728 and 1731. The attractive *Flower Walk* extends W behind the Albert Memorial into the *Broad Walk*, which runs N between the Round Pond (popular in summer with model boat enthusiasts) and Kensington Palace to Bayswater Road. On the S side of Kensington Palace is a *statue of William III*, presented to Edward VII by Kaiser William II; in front of the E side is a monument to Queen Victoria.

Kensington Palace was acquired by William III in 1689 from the earl of Nottingham, and thereafter, until the death of George II (1760), it was the permanent residence of the reigning monarchs. Originally dating from 1605, the house was enlarged and modernised by Wren. The interior was redecorated by William Kent. Mary II, William III, Anne and George II all died in the palace, and Queen Victoria was born here on 24 May 1819. The State Apartments have recently been opened to visitors, but much of the palace is occupied by dependents of the court and members of aristocratic families ("grace and favour" residences). The London Museum was temporarily housed in the palace, but is now installed in its new premises on London Wall. The State Apartments, entered from the NE corner of the palace, contain paintings by various 17th and 18th c. artists. The very beautiful *Queen's Staircase*, designed by Wren, leads up to the *Queen's Gallery*. Visitors are also shown dining rooms, drawing rooms and other apartments used by queens Mary, Anne and Victoria and kings William III, George I and George II. These handsome rooms, designed by Wren, contain fine wood-carving by Grinling Gibbons. – N of the palace is a *helicopter landing pad* used by the royal family.

To the W of the palace is *Kensington Palace Gardens*, a private road popularly known as "Millionaires' Row" which forms the western boundary of Kensington Gardens. It was laid out in 1843 by Pennethorne. This is an area of palatial mansions set in large gardens.

Kensington Gardens are bounded on the N by Bayswater Road, another high-income residential area. Beyond Bayswater Road at the northern end of the Broad Walk is *Queensway*, a busy shopping street with many shops which stay open late into the evening. A little way E of this exit from the gardens, in Lancaster Gate, can be seen the spire of *Christ Church*. In front of the church is a monument to the earl of Meath. At the NW corner of Kensington Gardens is Orme Square, from which St Petersburgh Place runs N to the *North West End Synagogue* with its massive towers and *St Matthew's Church* with its steeples. In Moscow Road is the Byzantine-style Greek Orthodox *Cathedral of the Holy Wisdom*, with mosaics by Boris Anrep. Bayswater Road is continued westward by *Notting Hill Gate*, which runs past the *Czechoslovak Centre* and the very individual architecture of the *Czechoslovak Embassy* (1971). From Notting Hill Gate it is only a short distance, by way of Pembridge Road (on right), to *Portobello Road* – an exotic name which commemorates the capture of Puerto Bello in

the Caribbean by Admiral Vernon in 1739. This little street is noted for its *markets*. The main one is now the busy vegetable market; the market for antiques held on Saturday was formerly a great attraction, but in recent years its interest has tended to decline.

N of Bayswater is the district of PADDINGTON, now traversed by a motorway. From *Paddington Station* the first underground railway in the world ran to Farringdon in 1863. NW of the station is the area known as *Little Venice*, where the Grand Union Canal opens out into a basin. From here there are motor-launch trips to the Zoo in Regent's Park and on to Camden Town.

Leaving the not particularly attractive area around Paddington Station, we return towards the livelier central districts by way of *Edgware Road*. Just off this street to the left, via Harrowby Street, is *Cato Street*, noted for its association with the "Cato Street conspiracy" of 1820, aimed at murdering the whole of the Cabinet. After the failure of their plot the conspirators were arrested in Cato Street and soon afterwards hanged.

From Edgware Road *George Street* leads back to Baker Street, on the W side of which is *Portman Square*, an exclusive residential complex built about 1760. *Home House* (No. 20) is a well-preserved example of Robert Adam's domestic architecture, with beautifully decorated rooms and staircases and pictures by Zucchi, as well as a "Holy Family" by Pierino del Vaga. The house is now occupied by the *Courtauld Institute of Art*, part of London University. Visitors can be admitted to the Institute and use the *Witt Library* during university vacations or by prior arrangement. The Witt Library contains 950,000 reproductions of European paintings from the Renaissance to the present day. The house at No. 21 also belongs to the Institute, and since 1972 has been occupied by the Royal Institute of British Architects, which puts on special exhibitions of sketches and designs by well-known architects in the *Heinz Gallery* and has a library containing some 200,000 drawings by European architects.

In *Seymour Street*, which runs W from Portman Square, is a house (No. 30) once occupied by the painter and writer of

Market stall, Portobello Road

nonsense verse Edward Lear (1812–88). W of Portman Square two short streets lined with enticing little shops run N into *Montagu Square*, at the NW corner of which is the *Jews College*, an institute for the training of rabbis.

For times of opening of museums, exhibitions, churches, etc., see p. 146.

Belgravia – Chelsea – Brompton – Kensington

Kensington and Chelsea, favoured residential areas, lie to the W and S of London's West End. Brompton and Earls Court also belong to this "best" part of London, lying between Knightsbridge and the Thames, between Grosvenor Place and West Cromwell Road, the diplomatic quarters around Belgravia. Quiet and secluded as some of these areas are, they lie conveniently close to the busy main and through roads.

This part of London is reached by way of *Knightsbridge*, the second great shopping and business street of the capital, which is continued to the SW by *Brompton Road*. In this street, on the left, is *Harrods*, the world's largest department store, which displays goods from every part of the world in a nostalgically old-fashioned setting. Between the Minema cinema at the E end of Knightsbridge and Harrods extends the main shopping quarter, with its numerous boutiques, department stores and specialised shops. From Knightsbridge the long straight line of *Sloane Street* runs due S, separating Belgravia to the E from Brompton to the W. BELGRAVIA begins at the Minema cinema, where we turn S off Knightsbridge into Wilton Place to reach *Wilton Crescent*, a very handsome example (by Peter Hardwick, 1842) of a typical London crescent. Belgravia, a district of large white villas, mostly stucco-fronted, was developed by Lord Grosvenor with the help of Thomas Cubitt. Around Wilton Crescent are a number of pubs, each with a character of its own. To the W of the crescent is Kinnerton Street with its photographic studios. At its S end are the *Halkin Arcades*, mainly occupied by antique dealers and art galleries. Motcomb Street runs W to the *Pantechnicon*, fronted by Doric columns, which was built in 1830 as a store and warehouse but

now contains the Victorian showrooms of Sotheby's, the well-known firm of auctioneers whose headquarters are in Bond Street. To the E is *Belgrave Square, unquestionably one of London's most beautiful squares, built by Basevi in 1825. There are a number of embassies in the square, which has very attractive gardens.

Going SE from Belgrave Square along Upper Belgrave Street, we pass a number of handsome side streets which go off on the left into busy Grosvenor Place. Upper Belgrave Street runs into the elongated park-like *Eaton Square*. To the E of this square is *Grosvenor Gardens*, with the head office and information centre of the *London Tourist Board* at No. 26 and the headquarters of the English Tourist Board at No. 4.

At the E end of Eaton Square is *St Peter's Church*, the scene of many fashionable weddings. Along the middle of the square runs the north-easterly section of *King's Road*. The long square is flanked by two rows of rather monotonous white stucco-fronted houses, relieved by the beautiful gardens between them. The SE boundary of Belgravia is formed by Buckingham Palace Road, on the W side of which, at the back of Victoria Station, are the offices of *Pan Am*, with those of *British Airways* opposite them. Also on the W side of the road is *Victoria Coach Station*. Going SW from here, we come into Pimlico Road, to the S of which are *Chelsea Barracks*. This is another good shopping area. On the N side of the street is *St Barnabas's Church* (by Cundy and Butterfield, 1846).

From Pimlico Road Lower Sloane Street runs N into Sloane Square, in the centre of which is a beautiful fountain surrounded by plane-trees. In this square is the *Royal Court Theatre*, formerly noted for its avant-garde productions. Some of George Bernard Shaw's plays were first produced here, and John Osborne's "Look Back in Anger" also had its initial success at the Royal Court. From the square *Sloane Street* with its numerous shops continues N. On the right is Sloane Terrace, with the First Church of Christ Scientist; farther N the street is flanked by beautiful gardens. Sloane Street and others of the same name commemorate Sir Hans Sloane, a famous 18th c. President of the Royal Society whose collection, bequeathed to the nation in 1753, was the nucleus of the British

Museum. The area W of Sloane Street was long known as Hans Town.

From Sloane Square the main part of *King's Road* runs SW into the heart of **CHELSEA**, which extends for about a mile and a half from the Thames, W of Pimlico, to Fulham Road in the N. As early as the 16th c. this was a much favoured residential area, and it has always had a particular attraction for artists. King's Road, which runs across the centre of the area, was until 1829 a private road used by the royal family for the journey between Hampton Court and St James's. Along its considerable length are the *Duke of York's Headquarters*, the *Town Hall*, the *College of Science and Technology* and the *School of Art*. In recent years the King's Road has acquired wide reputation as a shopping Mecca for the younger generation. At Sloane Square begins a succession of boutiques, shops selling jeans, pubs and music shops, which, particularly on Saturdays, attract crowds of young people to meet one another as well as to buy. There are, of course, numerous restaurants, cafeterias and places of entertainment. The street is also noted for its antique shops. At the junction with Old Church Street, three-quarters of a mile from Sloane Square, the *Chelsea Antique Market* tempts antique-hunters with its varied display.

Chelsea Embankment runs alongside the Thames between *Chelsea Bridge* (built 1858, rebuilt 1937) and Battersea Bridge, offering a pleasant walk of about a mile with a variety of scenery. On the other side of the river is Battersea Park. At the E end of the Embankment are *Ranelagh Gardens*, adjoining the grounds of the **Chelsea Hospital** (officially the Royal Hospital, Chelsea). The grounds are open daily, and in May are the scene of the famous Chelsea Flower Show.

The Hospital, brick-built, was designed by Sir Christopher Wren (1682–92). It was (and is) a home for old soldiers, who wear the uniforms of Marlborough's time, red in summer and dark blue in winter. The foundation stone of the Hospital was laid by Charles II. The central part, containing the *Hall* and *Chapel*, has a Doric portico flanked by colonnades and a small tower with a cupola. In the two side wings, laid out round courtyards, are the rooms occupied by the old soldiers, the "Chelsea pensioners". At the S end is the *Governor's House*. The Chapel has been preserved in its original condition. The Hall contains a portrait of Charles II. In the eastern range of buildings is a *museum* illustrating the history of the Hospital. In the *Figure Court* is a bronze *statue of Charles II*, a

master work by Grinling Gibbons. On Founder's Day (29 May) each year the statue is decorated with oak wreaths and the pensioners receive double pay. The adjoining Ranelagh Gardens is now a popular park, but nothing is left of the famous Rotunda which stood here from 1742 to 1804.

W of the Hospital, in Royal Hospital Road, is the **National Army Museum**, opened in 1971, which illustrates the history of the British army from the 15th c. to the First World War. Previously the collection was housed in Sandhurst Military Academy. An anteroom, with the colours of many famous regiments, leads into the main hall, which shows the development of the army in chronological order. There are vivid representations of important events in British military history, and changes in methods of warfare and logistics are well illustrated. These displays are supplemented by numerous mementoes, pictures and trophies.

On the first floor is the *Uniform Gallery*, in which old uniforms are displayed in appropriate contemporary settings. Orders of the day by such leading generals as Gough, Roberts and Kitchener hang on the walls. The adjoining *picture gallery* is mainly devoted to battle pictures and portraits. The *reading room*, to which readers are admitted only by previous arrangement, contains 20,000 volumes on military science, together with the papers of many noted commanders. In the basement are displays of arms and armour.

Among prominent residents in Tite Street was *Oscar Wilde* (No. 31). To the N is Tedworth Square, with a house (No. 23) in which *Mark Twain* lived during his stay in London (commemorative tablet). – Returning to the Embankment, we continue W into *Cheyne Walk*, a row of distinctive brick-built houses with gardens enclosed by wrought-iron railings and gates. *George Eliot* lived at 4 Embankment Gardens. No. 16 was occupied by *Dante Gabriel Rossetti*, who kept a menagerie in the garden; there is a memorial to him in front of the house.

Just beyond this point we come to the *Albert Bridge*, and a few paces farther on turn right off Cheyne Walk into Cheyne Row, a quiet little street with the house in which *Thomas Carlyle* and his wife lived from 1834 until their deaths. There is a statue of Carlyle on the Embankment at the end of the street. Here he wrote his "French Revolution" and "Heroes and Hero-Worship". The house contains personal relics of the Carlyles, together with portraits, photographs and pictures connected with Carlyle's life. On the top floor can be seen the attic room in which he worked, with the double walls he had built to keep out the noise of the outside world.

Nearby, on the Embankment, is *Chelsea Old Church*, which probably dates from the 12th c. It was severely damaged by bombing during the last war but was restored by W. H. Godfrey. On the wall of the chancel is a *monument to Sir Thomas More*. In Danvers Street, which branches off Cheyne Walk before Battersea Bridge, is *Crosby Hall*, moved here from Bishopgate in 1910, which is now a hall of residence of the British Federation of University Women. *Battersea Bridge* continues the line of Beaufort Street over the Thames; the present iron structure, built in 1890, replaced an earlier wooden bridge dating from 1771. There are a number of interesting old houses in the section of Cheyne Walk beyond the bridge – e.g. No. 96, in which the writer *Mrs Gaskell* (1810–65) was born, and No. 101, in which the painter *J. McN. Whistler* lived for 12 years.

We now leave the southern part of Chelsea, going N up Beaufort Street and then turning right into *Fulham Road* to enter the district of BROMPTON. *Brompton Hospital* is passed on the left and the *Royal Marsden Hospital* on the right. Numerous small streets lead off both sides of Fulham Road into pleasant residential areas. At the end of Fulham Road are two typical London crescents – *Pelham Crescent* (left) and *Egerton Crescent* (right). Here we are at the eastern end of the **South Kensington museum area**, most of which is enclosed within the rectangle bounded by Cromwell Road, Queen's Gate, Kensington Gore and Exhibition Road. The most easterly point in this great complex of buildings is the *Brompton Oratory*, a church in Italian Baroque style built between 1854 and 1884, with a dome added at the end of the century. It is served by priests of the Oratorian order, founded by St Philip Neri in Rome in 1575 and introduced into England by Cardinal Newman, whose statue stands to the left of the entrance. The interior makes a powerful impression with the magnificence of its conception, the width of the nave and its rich decoration, with a profusion of marble and pictures. The monumental Renaissance altar in the Lady Chapel came from Brescia.

Immediately W of the Oratory is the ****Victoria and Albert Museum**. The idea of the South Kensington museum complex, together with the educational establishments which were to make it the cultural centre of London, came from Queen Victoria's consort, Prince Albert. The project was to be financed by the profits from the Great Exhibition of 1851. The foundation stone of the Victoria and Albert Museum was laid by Queen Victoria in 1899, and the museum was opened by Edward VII in 1909. It now contains one of the greatest collections of fine and applied art in the world, displayed in more than 145 rooms. To get any real idea of the treasures of the "V. & A." – including paintings, engravings, drawings, porcelain and ceramics, costume, wood-carving, period furniture and much else besides – a single visit is not enough. The intention of the Museum, which developed out of an earlier Museum of Manufactures established in 1852, was to foster artistic developments which should be of use to British manufacturers and to stimulate artists and craftsmen by the example of both ancient and modern work displayed in the Museum. Plan of Museum: see p. 170.

W of the Victoria and Albert Museum, in Cromwell Road, is the vast complex of buildings occupied by the ***Natural History Museum**. The nucleus of the museum came from the collections of Sir Hans Sloane, acquired after his death in 1753. The present building, in Romanesque style, was built between 1873 and 1880. It is 675 ft long, with two towers 192 ft high, and is faced with terracotta slabs bearing figures of animals. The Museum, which is part of the British Museum, has five departments, each with its own library and reading rooms – zoology, mineralogy, botany, entomology and palaeontology.

The *Central Hall* on the ground floor contains elephants (including an African elephant 11 ft 4 in. tall), hippopotamuses, rhinoceroses and other pachyderms. The E wing contains special displays illustrating the history of evolution: I–III, selection and adaptation of individual species; IV, connections between fossils and living species; VI, principles of distribution of organic life illustrated by lower animals and fishes; VII–X, the development of man. Behind the staircase is the *North Hall*, mainly used for special exhibitions. In the W wing is the *Bird Gallery*, with particular emphasis on British species. To the N of this gallery are sections concerned with insects, reptiles and fish, as well as a very interesting collection of starfishes. Behind this is the *Whale Hall*, with skeletons and models of various whale species, the

Victoria and Albert Museum
London

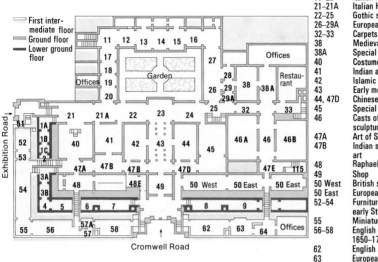

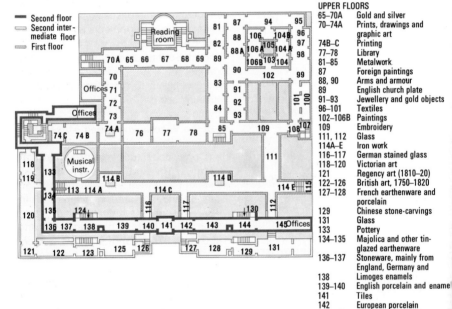

LOWER FLOORS

1A–4	European art of the 17th c.
5–7	European art of the 18th c.
11–20	Italian Renaissance
21–21A	Italian High Renaissance
22–25	Gothic sculpture
26–29A	European Renaissance
32–33	Carpets
38	Medieval tapestries
38A	Special exhibitions
40	Costume
41	Indian art
42	Islamic art
43	Early medieval art
44, 47D	Chinese and Japanese art
45	Special exhibitions
46	Casts of famous European sculpture (courtyard)
47A	Art of South-East Asia
47B	Indian sculpture and Islamic art
48	Raphael Cartoons (1515–16)
49	Shop
50 West	British sculpture
50 East	European sculpture
52–54	Furniture of the Tudor and early Stuart periods
55	Miniatures
56–58	English decorative arts, 1650–1750
62	English alabaster and ivory
63	European sculpture
64	Bronzes

UPPER FLOORS

65–70A	Gold and silver
70–74A	Prints, drawings and graphic art
74B–C	Printing
77–78	Library
81–85	Metalwork
87	Foreign paintings
88, 90	Arms and armour
89	English church plate
91–93	Jewellery and gold objects
96–101	Textiles
102–106B	Paintings
109	Embroidery
111, 112	Glass
114A–E	Iron work
116–117	German stained glass
118–120	Victorian art
121	Regency art (1810–20)
122–126	British art, 1750–1820
127–128	French earthenware and porcelain
129	Chinese stone-carvings
131	Glass
133	Pottery
134–135	Majolica and other tin-glazed earthenware
136–137	Stoneware, mainly from England, Germany and
138	Limoges enamels
139–140	English porcelain and enamel
141	Tiles
142	European porcelain
143–145	Far Eastern porcelain, pottery and enamels

star attraction being a fine blue whale. Also on the ground floor are a lecture hall and the Museum's *Library*.

The FIRST FLOOR is mainly devoted to mammals. Among particular rarities are an okapi, a platypus and a Tasmanian devil. The *Mineral Gallery* contains some 130,000 types of mineral, or 75% of the world's known minerals. The *Meteorite Pavilion* contains 1270 items, including the Cranbourne meteorite from Australia, weighing over 3 tons. On the SECOND FLOOR is the *Botanical Gallery*.

Adjoining the Natural History Museum on the N is the *Science Museum*, in a handsome building erected in 1928. The

Museum, founded in 1856, covers every aspect of science and technology, with numerous working models and machines to illustrate scientific principles and show how things work.

On the GROUND FLOOR is a Foucault pendulum illustrating the rotation of the earth. The *East Hall* shows the development of motive power. *Gallery 4* has a collection of weights and measures. *Gallery 6* is devoted to electricity. Gallery 7 leads into the *Central Block*, which houses the originals of many steam locomotives and Underground coaches. A staircase leads down to the BASEMENT, which contains a reproduction of a coal-mine and the *Children's Gallery*, with many working models.

The FIRST FLOOR is devoted to various branches of industry (steel and iron production, textile machinery, papermaking, etc.). Here too is a gallery devoted to astronomy, with an observatory on the roof.

The SECOND FLOOR has departments of biochemistry, photography and cinematography, nuclear power, mathematics and electronics, navigation and shipbuilding, etc.

The THIRD FLOOR is occupied by optics, acoustics, meteorology, geology, telegraphy, radio, television, etc. Gallery 67 is devoted to aeronautics, with models and originals of aircraft of different generations, including many historic machines, as well as hot-air balloons and a variety of curious and interesting craft.

The *Library* contains some 380,000 volumes.

Adjoining the E end of the Natural History Museum is the *Geological Museum, founded in 1837, which also houses the headquarters of the Geological Survey of Great Britain. The collections are open to the ·public, the displays being supplemented by film presentations.

The GROUND FLOOR is devoted to the geological history of the earth, illustrated by displays · of specimens. In the Main Hall is a rotating globe 6 ft high. Here too are interesting collections of precious stones and dioramas of landscapes. The FIRST FLOOR is devoted to the regional geology of Britain, the SECOND FLOOR to mineralogy. The *Library* contains 32,000 maps and over 70,000 volumes.

To the N of the museums are the large buildings occupied by the *Imperial College of Science and Technology*, which since 1907 has been part of London University. Enclosed by more modern buildings on Exhibition Road is a tall campanile-like tower (by Thomas Collcutt, 1893) built to commemorate Queen Victoria's Jubilee.

Turning left from Exhibition Road into Prince Consort Road, we come to the *Royal College of Music*, founded in 1884, which contains the Donaldson collection of old musical instruments. A bronze statue of *Prince Albert* commemorates the Great Exhibition of 1851. Close by are the *Royal College of Organists*, with fine graffito (graffito) decoration, and the *Royal College of Art*.

At the N end of the museum area is the **Royal Albert Hall**, originally planned as a centre of art and learning (1867–71). This huge circular hall, crowned by a large glass dome, can accommodate an audience of 8000, and is used for large meetings, concerts, charity balls and other events. It has a Willis organ with 10,000 pipes. During the summer the popular promenade concerts attract large audiences to the Albert Hall.

Finally we come to the district of **KENSINGTON**, W of Kensington Gardens. In the narrow *Kensington Church Street*, which runs N towards Notting Hill, is *St Mary Abbots Church*, rebuilt 1869–72. At *Kensington Palace Barracks* Holland Street turns off to the W, with some attractive early 18th c. houses. The artist Walter Crane (1845–1915) lived in No. 13, the Irish composer Sir Charles Stanford (d. 1924) in No. 50A (commemorative tablets). Holland Street runs into Campden Hill Road, in which are the *Chelsea Public Library* and the new *Town Hall*. To the N, on the left-hand side of the street, is the brick-built *Queen Elizabeth College* (1955). The writer Henry Newbolt died in No. 29; John Galsworthy lived in No. 78. Turning off to the W, we follow Aubrey Walk to *Campden Hill*, which runs N towards Notting Hill. This has been a favoured residential district since the 17th c. The pleasant road ends at the entrance to *Aubrey House*, only a short distance from Holland Hill. Close by is *Holland House*, once a fine Tudor mansion which became the "favourite resort of wits and beauties, of painters and poets, of scholars, philosophers and statesmen" (Macaulay) in the time of the third Lord Holland (1773–1840). The house was severely damaged in 1941, and now only the E wing survives, incorporated in the King George VI Memorial Youth Hostel.

Holland Park, with its beautiful trees, is a favourite place of recreation for young and old. Behind attractive flowerbeds is the *Orangery*, mainly used for concerts and exhibitions. The *Belvedere* restaurant has been restored after fire damage. Near the car park is a miniature jungle playground for children.

At the S end of Holland Park, with its entrance in Kensington High Street, is the *Commonwealth Institute*, which puts on exhibitions illustrating the life of the various Commonwealth countries, prepared by the countries themselves. The Institute (by Robert Matthew and Johnson Marshall, 1960–62) also contains a library and reading room, a cinema and a cafeteria.

From the Victoria Embankment to Euston Road

One of the most attractive promenades in central London is the Victoria Embankment, which extends for a mile and a quarter from Westminster Bridge to Blackfriars Bridge. For the greater part of the way it is lined by beautiful gardens, and it offers magnificent views of the Thames. Just E of Waterloo Bridge (rebuilt 1945) is *Somerset House*, a classical building erected in 1787 on the foundations of an older palace (1574) belonging to the duke of Somerset; it is now mainly occupied by government offices. Between Waterloo and Blackfriars Bridges, off the Temple Gardens, historic ships lie at anchor, including the *Wellington*, the *Chrysanthemum* and the *President*. The *Chrysanthemum* and *President* are used as training ships for the Royal Naval Volunteer Reserve. The *Discovery*, the polar research ship (1901–04) of Captain Scott, is at St Katherine's Dock as part of the Maritime Trust Historic Ship Collection. On the embankment opposite Embankment Gardens stands *Cleopatra's Needle*, an Egyptian obelisk (*c.* 1500 B.C.) from Heliopolis, near Cairo, which was set up here in 1878. A little way W, near Trafalgar Square, is the very busy *Charing Cross Station*, with an equally busy Underground station and heavy bus traffic. From here the *Strand*, one of London's major traffic arteries, runs NE towards the City. At the far end, in the crescent-shaped street called Aldwych, are *India House* and *Australia House*. In the Strand opposite Australia House is the church of *St Clement Danes*, built by Wren in 1681 on the site of an earlier Danish settlement and rebuilt after 1945; it is now the headquarters church of the RAF, and contains reproductions of the badges of more than 700 RAF units. Just beyond the church, at the beginning of Fleet Street, are the *Royal Courts of Justice*. Beyond these again *Chancery Lane* goes off on the left, running N towards High Holborn and passing on the way the *Patent Office* (on right) and the *London Silver Vaults*, which contain a rich collection of silver articles.

In the rectangular area enclosed by High Holborn, Chancery Lane, Aldwych and Kingsway are a number of features of interest. On the N side of *Lincoln's Inn Fields* is the **Soane Museum**, once the home of the rather eccentric architect Sir John Soane. The interior has an air of confusion, having been left as it was when Soane died in 1837, but it is well worth visiting for its contents – pictures, sculpture, antiques – as well as for its carefully preserved original interior decoration. The pictures include works by such masters as Hogarth and Watteau. – To the S of Lincoln's Inn Fields is the *Royal College of Surgeons*, with the *Hunterian Museum* (mainly items of medical interest, together with a collection of anatomical specimens prepared by the noted surgeon Dr John Hunter). Adjoining the Royal College is the nostalgic "Old Curiosity Shop", which specialises in objects dating from Dickens's time. A notice at the entrance claims that this old antique dealer's shop gave Dickens the idea of his novel.

Going W from Kingsway on Old Queen Street, we pass on the left the *Freemasons' Hall*, home of the United Grand Lodge of England, an imposing building crowned by a 200 ft high tower. Crossing Drury Lane into Long Acre and turning left into Bow Street, we see on the right, in *Covent Garden*, the **Royal Opera House**. The Opera House, which is also notable for its productions of ballet, was built by E. M. Barry in 1858 on the site of an earlier theatre which had been destroyed by fire. It is one of the largest theatres in the country, with seating for 2000. – Close by, in the former Flower and Vegetable Market, now moved to a new site S of the river, is the *London Transport Museum*. The old market area is now a modern shopping precinct.

Long Acre leads into *Leicester Square*, a busy square which was laid out about 1650 but did not become a public garden until two centuries later. In the gardens are busts of various distinguished figures including Newton, Hogarth and Reynolds. A short distance E Charing Cross Road runs N to *Cambridge Circus*, on the edge of Soho (see p. 158), and St Giles Circus, at the intersection of Oxford Street with New Oxford Street. On the corner is one of London's largest cinemas, the *Dominion*. Beyond this point *Tottenham Court Road* continues N to Euston Road. To the E of Tottenham Court Road is the district of BLOOMSBURY.

Immediately beyond St Giles Circus Great Russell Street goes off Tottenham Court Road on the right towards the

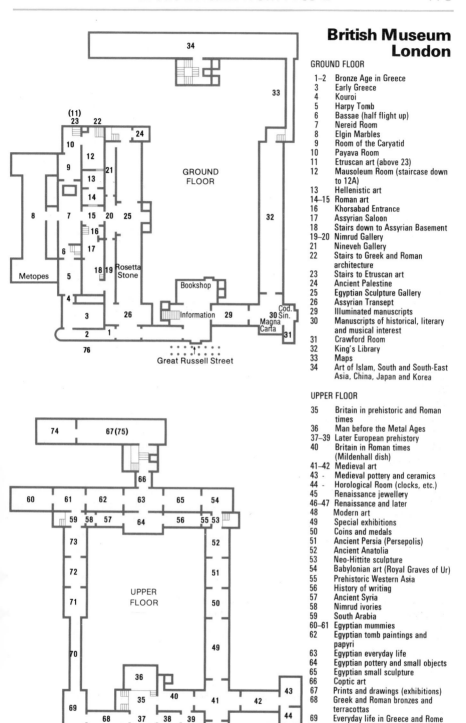

British Museum
London

GROUND FLOOR

1–2	Bronze Age in Greece
3	Early Greece
4	Kouroi
5	Harpy Tomb
6	Bassae (half flight up)
7	Nereid Room
8	Elgin Marbles
9	Room of the Caryatid
10	Payava Room
11	Etruscan art (above 23)
12	Mausoleum Room (staircase down to 12A)
13	Hellenistic art
14–15	Roman art
16	Khorsabad Entrance
17	Assyrian Saloon
18	Stairs down to Assyrian Basement
19–20	Nimrud Gallery
21	Nineveh Gallery
22	Stairs to Greek and Roman architecture
23	Stairs to Etruscan art
24	Ancient Palestine
25	Egyptian Sculpture Gallery
26	Assyrian Transept
29	Illuminated manuscripts
30	Manuscripts of historical, literary and musical interest
31	Crawford Room
32	King's Library
33	Maps
34	Art of Islam, South and South-East Asia, China, Japan and Korea

UPPER FLOOR

35	Britain in prehistoric and Roman times
36	Man before the Metal Ages
37–39	Later European prehistory
40	Britain in Roman times (Mildenhall dish)
41–42	Medieval art
43 -	Medieval pottery and ceramics
44 -	Horological Room (clocks, etc.)
45	Renaissance jewellery
46–47	Renaissance and later
48	Modern art
49	Special exhibitions
50	Coins and medals
51	Ancient Persia (Persepolis)
52	Ancient Anatolia
53	Neo-Hittite sculpture
54	Babylonian art (Royal Graves of Ur)
55	Prehistoric Western Asia
56	History of writing
57	Ancient Syria
58	Nimrud ivories
59	South Arabia
60–61	Egyptian mummies
62	Egyptian tomb paintings and papyri
63	Egyptian everyday life
64	Egyptian pottery and small objects
65	Egyptian small sculpture
66	Coptic art
67	Prints and drawings (exhibitions)
68	Greek and Roman bronzes and terracottas
69	Everyday life in Greece and Rome
70	Figure of Augustus
71	Sutton-Hoo treasure
72–73	Greek vases
74	Special exhibitions (Orient)
75	Oriental art
76	Special exhibitions

**British Museum, one of the world's largest museums, founded by Act of Parliament in 1753. The first nucleus of the museum was the collection bequeathed to the nation by Sir Hans Sloane in return for a payment of £20,000 (which had to be raised by a lottery). Another major contribution was made by the immense collection left by the antiquarian and bibliomaniac Sir Robert Cotton (d. 1631) – though the Museum did not receive this until much later. Associated

Skyline of the City of London

with the British Museum is the **British Library**, one of the largest in the world. One copy of everything published in Britain must by law be deposited in the British Library. The Museum was extended to the plans of Sir Robert Smirke between 1823 and 1850, and over the years its collections have grown steadily by both purchases and gifts. Material from all over the world and from many centuries has flowed into the Museum, while the Library, in addition to its six million books, has acquired a wide range of material from medieval manuscripts to rare old music, from the logbooks of Nelson's *Victory* to postage stamps. Many thousands of prints and drawings illustrate the history of graphic art from the 15th c. onwards. Statues, funerary stelae, mummies and architectural fragments display the cultures of the Assyrians, the Greeks, the Persians and many more.

Some *items of outstanding interest*: The *Mildenhall dish*, from a large hoard of Roman silver discovered at Mildenhall in Suffolk in 1942. It shows Bacchus, god of wine, Hercules and other figures of Roman mythology; in the centre is a bearded mask surrounded by nymphs riding on marine monsters. The mask probably represents the sea god Oceanus. The dish is thought to have been made in Rome in the 3rd c. – A *bronze head* from the old West African kingdom of *Benin*. It represents a queen mother and was found in a ruined palace and brought back to Britain by a punitive expedition in 1897, with 3000 other works of art. – The *Codex Sinaiticus*, a 4th c. Greek manuscript of the Bible, purchased from the Soviet Union in 1933 for £100,000. – The *horse of Selene* from the E pediment of the Parthenon in Athens, one of the "Elgin marbles" brought to Britain by Lord Elgin at the beginning of the 19th c. It was one of a group of horses drawing the triumphal chariot of Selene; two others are still in Athens, the fourth is lost. – A *head of*

Aphrodite, double life size, found at Satala in Armenia. Together with the left arm, which holds a fragment of clothing, it belonged to a torso which is thought to have been by Praxiteles (4th c. B.C.).

Immediately N of the British Museum is the **University of London**, founded in 1836. At first only an examining body, it became a teaching university in 1900. The university complex, including *University College* and *University College Hospital*, extends N to Euston Road. The central point of the University proper is the *Senate House*, a tower block 210 ft high which contains administrative offices and a library of almost a million volumes. It also houses the School of Slavonic and East European Studies, the Institute of Historical Research and a department of education. The University has nine faculties and a variety of specialised departments.

Within the university complex, in Woburn Square, are the **Courtauld Institute Galleries**, established in 1932 through the munificence of Viscount Lee of Fareham and Samuel Courtauld, a textile manufacturer, who bequeathed their collections to the University. The *Samuel Courtauld Collection* consists of a representative display of Impressionist and Post-Impressionist works, including a number of fine Cézannes ("Lac d'Annecy", "The Card-Players", etc.). The *Lee Collection* of old masters, displayed in rooms furnished with fine period furniture, includes a masterpiece by Rubens ("Descent from the Cross") and

foreground the Tower

works by Veronese, Gainsborough, Goya, Van Dyck and Tintoretto.

SW of the Courtauld Galleries is the *Royal Academy of Dramatic Art*, and to the N, in Gordon Square, is the *Percival David Foundation of Chinese Art*, a collection of Chinese porcelain of the 10th–18th c., mostly produced for Chinese emperors and nobles, together with a library on Chinese art. NE of Gordon Square is the *Jewish Museum*. Immediately NE of the British Museum is spacious Russell Square, from which Guilford Street runs E into the district of St Pancras. Off this to the right is *Doughty Street*, in which is the only one of the many houses occupied by *Charles Dickens* which still survives. In this house Dickens completed the "Pickwick Papers". It is now a museum, with the largest Dickens library in the world.

In Euston Road, which forms the northern boundary of BLOOMSBURY and ST PANCRAS, are three important main-line stations – *Euston*, one of the few London stations to have been modernised since the war; *St Pancras*, a handsome example of Victorian Gothic; and *King's Cross*. From these stations trains run to the Midlands and Scotland.

The City and the Tower

The **CITY**, with a resident population of only some 4500 – it is said to have more cats and dogs than people – is a place of hectic activity during the day. More than half a million Londoners work here, who in the evening rush hour set out on their homeward journey in trains and buses filled to overflowing. The City is bounded broadly by a line running from the Tower to Liverpool Street Station, London Wall, Holborn Viaduct and Chancery Lane, with the Thames forming the southern boundary. This city within a city is crowded into an area of no more than a square mile. Since the last war the skyline of the City has been transformed by the building of tower blocks like the Commercial Union building (1969, 387 ft), the Cromwell, Lauderdale and Shakespeare Towers in the Barbican complex (1971, each 419 ft), Guy's Hospital (1974, 460 ft) and the latest and tallest of them all, the National Westminster Tower (600 ft) – far exceeding in height what in the past was London's tallest building, St Paul's (365 ft).

The City is reached from the West End by way of the Strand, at the far end of which, beyond the Royal Courts of Justice, is the beginning of **Fleet Street**, the "street of ink", which has been for 150 years the home of the country's leading newspapers. Originally the little River Fleet flowed S in the area of Farringdon Road and New Bridge Street and joined the Thames. Fleet Street was the eastern boundary of this stream which was later covered over. In earlier days Fleet Street was the resort of robbers, who lay in wait for well-to-do merchants returning from the City. In Ludgate Circus, at the far end of the street, is a bronze tablet com-

St Paul's Cathedral

memorating *Edgar Wallace*, the popular novelist and journalist, "whose heart belonged to Fleet Street".

At the W end of Fleet Street, almost opposite Chancery Lane, an arched gateway leads into the extensive precincts of the **Temple**. In the 12th and 13th c. this was the English headquarters of the knightly order of the Templars, founded in Jerusalem in 1119. After the dissolution of the order in 1312 the premises were occupied by the Knights of St John (1324), but within a short period the Temple became the residence of students of the law, and ever since then it has been the great citadel of English law. The four "Inns of Court" are the bodies which admit lawyers to practise as barristers (advocates) at the English bar, and two of them have their headquarters in the Temple – the *Inner Temple* and the *Middle Temple*. The buildings were badly damaged by bombing during the last war but have since been rebuilt; they include assembly chambers (halls), libraries, teaching facilities and residential accommodation, laid out round several courts. The *Inner Temple Hall*, as rebuilt, even has a heated marble floor. The fine 12th c. * **Temple Church**, a round church modelled on the Church of the Holy Sepulchre in Jerusalem, serves both the Inner and Middle Temple as a place of meditation

and repose. The *Temple Gardens* alongside the Thames, planted with roses, are not open to the public. – Near the E end of Fleet Street is *St Bride's Church*, the "parish church of the press", first referred to in the 12th c., rebuilt by Wren, and again rebuilt after war damage in 1957, preserving Wren's style.

Fleet Street ends at Ludgate Circus, the intersection with Farringdon Street and New Bridge Street, which runs S to *Blackfriars Bridge* (1870). Straight ahead, up Ludgate Hill (on the left *Old Bailey*, with the Central Criminal Court), is St Paul's Cathedral.

** **St Paul's Cathedral** is the City's largest and most famous church. The site was originally occupied by a large Gothic cathedral, with a spire 550 ft high, which was destroyed by fire in 1561. For many years the ruins were left as they were, but about 1600 the question of rebuilding began to be considered. Inigo Jones did some work on certain parts of the church, and further restoration was carried out about 1660; but in 1666, during the Great Fire, the Cathedral was totally destroyed. In 1670 Wren put forward a first plan for rebuilding St Paul's, but this was turned down, and a further proposal in 1673 (for a church in the form of a Greek cross) was also rejected. Finally in 1675 agreement

St Paul's Cathedral

London

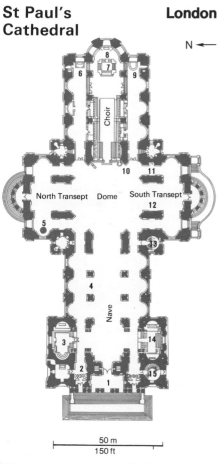

N ←—

1 West doorway
2 All Souls Chapel
3 St Dunstan's Chapel
4 Wellington monument
5 Font
6 Anglican Martyrs' Chapel
7 High altar
8 American Memorial Chapel
9 Lady Chapel
10 Pulpit
11 Entrance to Crypt
12 Nelson monument
13 Staircase to Library, Whispering Gallery and Dome
14 Chapel of St Michael and St George
15 Dean's Staircase

was reached on a third plan, a compromise between Wren's original proposals and the ideas of the church commissioners, who wanted a Latin cross plan. In the same year the foundation stone was laid; in 1708 Wren's son laid the last stone; and in 1711 the church was completed. Some years ago the stonework was cleaned, removing the grime of 250 years and revealing afresh the fine carving by Francis Bird, Edward Pierce and Grinling Gibbons. The magnificent new high altar with its oak canopy, consecrated in 1958, was the work of Dykes Bower and Godfrey Allen, following sketches by Wren. The previous high altar (1888) was badly damaged by bombing. Also new is the Jesus Chapel, dedicated to American soldiers stationed in Britain who died in the Second World War.

N of St Paul's, in Newgate Street, is the **National Postal Museum**, which must be the largest collection of stamps and other documents in the world. The Phillips collection illustrates the planning, development and issue of the first postage stamps, which are claimed as a British invention, and the history of British stamps in the 19th c. is displayed in 45 volumes. In the same building is the unique collection of the nearby General Post Office, including designs for stamps and philatelic works of art.

Off Newgate Street is King Edward Street, with the *General Post Office* (open 24 hours a day). At the W end of Newgate Street, where it runs into Holborn Viaduct, the street called *Old Bailey* runs S. Immediately on the left is the **Central Criminal Court**, also popularly known as the Old Bailey, in which all the major criminal trials take place. Until 1902 the site was occupied by Newgate Prison, and for more than 100 years (until 1868) public executions were held here. The Central Criminal Court was built between 1902 and 1907, but was damaged by bombing during the last war and rebuilt after 1945. The dome, 195 ft high, is crowned by a large figure of Justice.

NE of the General Post Office, at the corner of Aldersgate and London Wall, is the new *Museum of London, completed in 1976, which contains the collections previously housed in Kensington Palace and the Guildhall Museum. After its opening this fine modern building, splendidly laid out, quickly became one of London's major tourist attractions. It is entered by way of a spiral staircase.

The northern boundary of the City is *London Wall*, on the line of part of the old Roman walls which enclosed London. From the Museum of London it runs E to Old Broad Street, which leads N to Liverpool Street Station. In the western half of the street is the former churchyard of *St Alphege*, where remains of the old town walls can be seen. Farther N stands the new *Barbican Centre, consisting of flats and an integrated cultural and congress centre, including the Barbican Hall (home of the London Symphony Orchestra), the Barbican Theatre (London home of the Royal Shakespeare Company) and an art gallery for periodic exhibitions.

A little way S of London Wall, at the N end of King Street, is the **Guildhall**, the City's "town hall", where the Court of Common Council holds its meetings. Here too prominent visitors to the City are received by the Lord Mayor or the livery companies or guilds. (Although the companies are no longer guilds in the old sense they are still organised in the various trades. Their members are influential City businessmen.) The original Guildhall dates back to 1411, but little is left of the 15th c. building, which was a victim of the Great Fire. The Council Chamber and the roof of the Great Hall were destroyed by bombing in December 1940. Restoration began after the war, and the interior was reconstructed by Sir Giles Gilbert Scott in 1952. The *Corporation Art Gallery*, also badly damaged in 1940, contains paintings of great state occasions of the last 100 years. The *Library*, which is also sometimes used for the reception of royal visitors, contains 123,000 volumes, together with such treasures as the First and Second Folios of Shakespeare, a map of London in 1591 and the deed of purchase of a house bearing Shakespeare's signature. The *Guildhall Art Gallery* (dating in its present form from 1886 but with a history going back to 1670) has a fine permanent collection which includes drawings of London Bridge by E. W. Cook and watercolours of London scenes by Alister Macdonald.

King Street runs S into *Cheapside*, the site of an ancient market with an ancient name (from an Anglo-Saxon word meaning to barter). On the S side of the street is the church of *St Mary-le-Bow*, built by Wren on Norman foundations, with the famous "Bow bells". Restoration of the church, including the Norman crypt with its arches or "bows", was completed in 1964. – Some 300 yards E of the church, at the intersection with Queen Victoria Street (on right, running SW), stands the **Mansion House**, official residence of the Lord Mayor, built by George Dance the Elder between 1739 and 1753 and subsequently remodelled on several occasions. Visitors are admitted, on written application, to a series of 18th c. rooms and the 100 ft long Egyptian Hall, which is used for official receptions. – A short distance SW of the Mansion House, on the S side of the busy Queen Victoria Street, are the remains of a *Temple of Mithras*, of basilican type, discovered in 1954; it dates from about A.D. 80. At the end of Queen Victoria Street, on the left, is the *Mermaid Theatre*, built in 1959 – the first new theatre in the City of London since the 16th c.

Opposite the Mansion House, to the N, is the **Bank of England**, which claims to be the most secure building in the world – apart, perhaps, from Fort Knox in the United States. Although it stands at one of the busiest spots in the City it does not offer facilities for visitors.

From the intersection in front of the Bank

View from the Monument, looking north

of England **Lombard Street** (named after the Italian moneylenders from Lombardy who had their offices here in the 13th c.) runs E. Most of the buildings date from the 19th c., though many of the banks still bear heraldic emblems, a relic of the medieval period when signs were used to identify buildings to people who could not read. In this area visitors will encounter men wearing the "uniform" of the City – the bowler hat and rolled umbrella.

Facing the Bank of England on the opposite side of Threadneedle Street, to the SE, is the **Royal Exchange**, founded in 1566 by Sir Thomas Gresham, which was given its present form by Sir William Tite in 1842–44, the two previous buildings on the site having been destroyed by fire. There is a statue of Sir Thomas Gresham on the tower. From the broad flights of steps leading up to the handsome Corinthian portico royal proclamations are read out (e.g. the accession of a monarch or a declaration of war). On the arcades of the central courtyard are paintings of events in English history. There is a carillon which plays daily at 9, 12, 3 and 6.

Immediately E of the Bank of England is another major City institution, the **Stock Exchange**, in a handsome new 30-storey tower block. It has a viewing gallery from which visitors can watch the hectic activity of brokers and jobbers (dealers) in the buying and selling of shares.

A little way N of the Stock Exchange, at the corner of Throgmorton Avenue and London Wall, is the 500-year-old *Carpenters' Hall*, destroyed in the last war but later rebuilt. London Wall is continued E by Wormwood Street, which runs into *Bishopsgate*, named after an old town gate pulled down in 1760, and which runs N to *Liverpool Street Station*. In Bishopsgate is London's newest and highest tower block, the highest building in the country and the second highest office block in Europe – The National Westminster Tower (600 ft, 52 storeys). Just E of Liverpool Street Station is the narrow street officially known as Middlesex Street but more familiar to visitors as *Petticoat Lane*, in which a noisy and colourful market is held on Sunday mornings.

A mile and a half NE of Liverpool Street Station, in Cambridge Heath Road, is the *Bethnal Green Museum of Childhood*, founded in 1872. Originally established in South Kensington, it is a branch of the Victoria and Albert Museum, with one of the finest collections of toys in the country – mainly dolls, dolls' houses, children's clothing, books and games. Although the Museum lies outside the City, it can be conveniently reached from Liverpool Street Station by way of Bishopsgate and Shoreditch High Street.

Farther S along Bishopsgate are *St Ethelburga's Church*, which dates from Saxon times, and *St Helen's Church* (12th c., with later alterations), which has been called the "Westminster Abbey of the City".

At the intersection of King William Street, which runs S from the Bank of England, with Upper and Lower Thames Street, the most southerly E–W axis of the City, is *Fishmongers' Hall*, originally built in 1504, burned down in the Great Fire, damaged again in the last war and restored in 1951. From here **London Bridge** crosses the Thames to Southwark Cathedral. A succession of wooden bridges spanned the river in Roman, Anglo-Saxon and Norman times, until the first stone bridge was begun during the reign of Henry II, in 1176, and completed 30 years later, in the time of King John. Until the construction of Westminster Bridge in 1750 London Bridge was the only road crossing of the Thames. It played a central part in the life of the city in the Middle Ages; houses were built on it, and a chapel dedicated to St Thomas of Canterbury. The heads of traitors were displayed at the ends of the bridge after their execution. Finally a new bridge, a masterpiece of 19th c. civil engineering designed by John Rennie, was built between 1825 and 1831. But this in turn proved inadequate for the needs of 20th c. traffic, and since it could not be enlarged it was replaced by a new bridge completed in 1972. During reconstruction part of the foundations of a bridge built by the Romans was discovered at a depth of 30 ft. Rennie's Bridge was then transported to the United States and re-erected at Havasu City in the Arizona desert.

NE of Fishmongers' Hall, in a small square, stands the **Monument**, a 200 ft high column designed by Wren, with a carving of Charles II on the pedestal. It was erected to commemorate the Great Fire, which started 200 ft E of the column, destroying a total of 16,000 houses before

Tower of London

it burnt itself out. – From the Monument it is a short distance E along Monument Street to *Billingsgate Market*, which has a history dating back to 1660, and in Londoners' eyes is the most celebrated fish market in the world. Adjoining it on the E is the *Custom House*. A little way NE, in Byward Street, is the church of *All Hallows by the Tower*, founded in 675. Here can be seen remains of a paved Roman road and a Saxon arch under the tower. The church was rebuilt in the 13th and 15th c.; the tower, which has a new steeple added in 1959, is the only one in London to have survived the Great Fire (though it was burned out in 1940). – In Mark Lane, a short distance NW of the church, is the *Corn Exchange*, badly damaged by bombing but rebuilt in 1953.

Immediately E of All Hallows Church, on *Tower Hill*, is the ＊＊**Tower of London**, of all buildings in England the one which carries the heaviest burden of history. Here the visitor is reminded of a succession of horrors which have gone to make up the history of England. The list of those who have languished or died as prisoners in the Tower is a long one: a selection of the best known would include Henry VI, Edward V, Sir Thomas More, Anne Boleyn, Elizabeth I, the earl of Essex, James I of Scotland and, most recently, Rudolf Hess. The idea of the fortress was first conceived by William the Conqueror, who built the White Tower in 1078 to maintain control over the people of London. While restoring their former privileges, he was concerned to ensure that they recognised his authority. The building of the Tower also gave him a commanding point from which to control shipping on the Thames.

In the course of time, during the 12th, 13th and 14th c., the frowning walls of the fortress underwent further extensions and alterations; but thereafter they suffered little change until major restoration work was carried out in the 19th c. (1852–1900). The Tower is guarded by the Yeomen Warders, popularly known as Beefeaters (from the French *buffetiers*) in their picturesque Tudor uniforms. The 40 Yeomen can date their history back to 1485, when they were established as a bodyguard for Henry VII. The Yeomen on

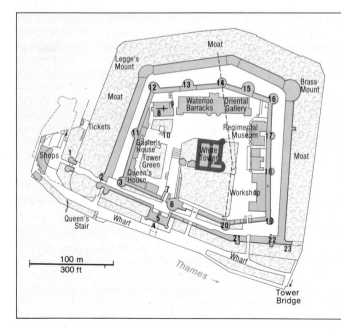

Tower of London

1 Middle Tower
2 Byward Tower
3 Bell Tower
4 Traitors' Gate
5 St Thomas's Tower
6 Wakefield Tower
7 Bloody Tower
8 Royal Chapel of
  St Peter ad Vincula
9 Jewel House
  (entrance)
10 Site of scaffold
11 Beauchamp Tower
12 Devereux Tower
13 Flint Tower
14 Bowyer Tower
  (torture chamber)
15 Brick Tower
16 Martin Tower
17 Constable Tower
18 Broad Arrow Tower
19 Salt Tower
20 Lanthorn Tower
21 Cradle Tower
22 Well Tower
23 Develin Tower

Tower Bridge

duty in the Tower are always ready to give help or information to visitors.

The area enclosed by the outer walls is roughly square, with William the Conqueror's White Tower in the middle. The walls surrounding the *Inner Ward*, with 13 towers, were built by Henry III. The *Outer Ward* is enclosed by a further wall which is believed to have been built by Edward I in the 14th c. This has six towers and two corner bastions. These massive defences were still further strengthened by a moat surrounding the whole structure. Another tower, the Lion Tower, formerly stood at the SW corner. The entrance to the *Middle Tower* is protected by two drawbridges, and beyond this is the *Byward Tower* (from "by-word", meaning watchword), housing guard-rooms and the portcullis machinery (which can still be seen). This gives access to the Outer Ward, with the *Bell Tower* (built by Richard I, 1191) straight ahead. From here Princess Elizabeth's Walk, to the left, runs along the ramparts to the *Beauchamp Tower*. Straight ahead, on the right, is the *Traitors' Gate*, which opens directly on to the Thames and was formerly used for bringing in prisoners and for throwing the bodies of executed offenders into the river.

Opposite the Traitors' Gate are the Bloody Tower and the Wakefield Tower. The *Bloody Tower*, built by Richard II, inherited its name from the numerous executions which it witnessed, but it was also used for the confinement of long-term prisoners. Among these was Sir Walter Raleigh, who wrote his "History of the World" during his 13 years' incarceration here. The *Wakefield Tower*, in the Inner Ward, was built by Henry III, and until 1968 housed the Crown Jewels. Most of the original Crown Jewels were melted down and sold during the Commonwealth, but after the Restoration in 1660 those which remained were taken into safe keeping in the Wakefield Tower. They are now kept in an underground strong-room in the *Waterloo Barracks*. Among the finest items are St Edward's Crown, of pure gold, which is still used in the coronation of British monarchs; the Imperial State Crown, set with 3000 diamonds, which is worn by the Queen on important occasions; the Imperial Crown of India, with a 34-carat emerald and 6500 diamonds; and the Queen Elizabeth Crown, named after the present Queen Mother, which is set with the world-famous Koh-i-Noor diamond of 108 carats.

Compared with the other parts of the Tower, the Inner Ward has an almost idyllic aspect. The *Gaoler's House* is in a rather countrified style, though on special occasions the Yeoman Gaoler may still appear wearing his traditional uniform and carrying the executioner's axe. Also in the Inner Ward are *Tower Green*, where the scaffold once stood; the Waterloo Barracks; the *Chapel Royal*; the Regimental Museum of the Royal Fusiliers;

and the *Beauchamp Tower*. The *White Tower* (so named from the white Caen stone of which it is built) was originally erected by three men – Gundulf, William Rufus and Ranulph Flambard – and was restored by Wren. It contains a large collection of arms and armour, etc.

The six ravens in the Tower owe their presence to a legend that the British Empire would come to an end when the ravens left the Tower. Although the British Empire now belongs to the past, the ravens are still there, with clipped wings and cared for by a raven-master. When a bird dies it is replaced by another.

From the Tower it is only a few steps to *Tower Bridge, the last of London's bridges before the Thames flows into the sea. With its very distinctive silhouette and its Gothic architecture, it is the very emblem and symbol of the river. It was erected in 1895. The massive towers stand over 200 ft high, and the roadway is carried on two heavy hydraulically operated drawbridges, which must be raised several times every day to let large vessels through; two glassed-in corridors link the twin towers at a height of 148 ft above the river.

London South of the Thames

The S bank of the Thames and the southern parts of central London – Southwark, Lambeth and Battersea – are relatively little visited by tourists. SOUTHWARK, reached by crossing Tower Bridge, occupies a rather special position. Although it has been part of the City since 1531 it takes no part either in the election of councillors or the selection of aldermen. Separated from the main part of the City by the Thames, it has its own administrative life.

W of Tower Bridge lies the cruiser *Belfast*, now a museum ship open to visitors. Tooley Street, parallel to the river, runs W to *London Bridge Station*, London's first railway station (1836), from which there are services to the SE and S.

*Southwark Cathedral lies between the railway lines and the river, close to the S end of London Bridge. Although much rebuilt and restored, it is still London's finest Gothic church after Westminster Abbey. Its official style is the Cathedral and Collegiate Church of St Saviour and St Mary Overy, Southwark. Its early history is obscure, although tradition has it that there was originally a nunnery on this site founded by a ferryman's daughter named Mary, the name of St Mary Overy being interpreted as a corruption of "St Mary of the Ferry". In 862, on the direction of St Swithin, bishop of Winchester, it became a house of Augustinian canons. The original church, of which little survives, was built in 1106. The present chancel was built by the bishop of Winchester in 1207. The transepts were rebuilt in the 15th c. Part of the nave collapsed in 1838, and was rebuilt by Sir Arthur Blomfield in 1890–96. Over the crossing rises an imposing tower, 163 ft high, in the style of the 15th c.

INTERIOR. – The Cathedral is entered through the SW doorway. At the SW corner of the nave is some 13th c. arcading. At the NW corner are original 15th c. roof bosses. Under the sixth window is the tomb of John Gower (1330–1408). A 12th c. Norman doorway which gave access to the cloisters has been preserved.

In the *N transept* are a number of monuments, including one to a quack doctor named John Lockyer (d. 1672) with a humorous inscription. On the E of the transept is the Harvard Chapel (restored in 1907), commemorating John Harvard (1607–38), founder of the famous American university, who was born in the parish and baptised in the church. During restoration work a Norman column base was brought to light to the left of the altar. The chancel, divided into two, is probably one of the earliest Gothic structures in London. The *Choir* itself dates from about 1273. On the N side of the sanctuary are the bishop's throne and stalls for the suffragan bishops. The high altar dates from 1520; the pillars are 13th c.

Beyond the choir is the *retrochoir*, with four chapels along the E end, the Chapels of St Andrew and St Christopher, the Lady chapel and the Chapel of St Francis. In the retrochoir during the Catholic restoration in the 16th c., bishops Gardiner and Bonner presided over the summary trials which sent Hooper, Rogers, Saunders and other Protestants to the stake.

The *S transept* was rebuilt in the 15th c. by Cardinal Beaufort, whose niece Joan Beaufort was married to James I of Scotland in the Cathedral.

From the Cathedral London Bridge can be reached by way of the Nancy Steps, immortalised in Dickens's "Oliver Twist".

On the S side of the Cathedral is *Borough Market*, the oldest market in London, founded by Edward VI (though there are references to a market here as early as the 13th c.). It is mainly a market for fruit and vegetables. The buildings around the market are in strong contrast to the Gothic architecture of the Cathedral. – *Borough High Street* was once the main road out of London to SE England and the Continent and was traversed by numerous pilgrims on their way to Canterbury. On the E side there were formerly a number of well-known inns. The "King's Head" opposite Southward Street was once known as the "Pope's Head". Adjoining it stood the "White Hart", immortalised by Shakespeare, in which the rebel leader Jack Cade stayed in 1450. In a courtyard at George House is the *George Inn*, the last of the old inns, now a kind of museum, with a façade dating from 1676. In summer there are performances of Shakespeare's plays in the courtyard.

A tablet in Borough High Street marks the site of the old Marshalsea Prison, first mentioned in 1377, which was closed down in 1758. A little way E of Borough High Street is **Guy's Hospital**, with a 32-storey tower block (1976). A lane called Bank End leads to *Bankside*, on which we can walk W alongside the Thames. E of Southwark Bridge are large warehouses. From Bankside there is a view of St Paul's Cathedral, and a 17th c. inscription marks the spot from which Wren liked to contemplate his creation. In *Bear Gardens* is an old 19th c. warehouse which now houses a *museum*, with old machines and representations of the Elizabethan theatre, and special exhibitions illustrating the history of this part of London, where Shakespeare worked in his early years.

In Park Street, near the Borough Market, is a brewery which belonged in the 18th c. to Henry Thrale, with a tablet on the wall marking the approximate site of the old *Globe Theatre* built by the Burbage brothers in 1599. In Emerson Street are the headquarters of the *Globe Playhouse Trust*, formed in 1971 to promote interest in Shakespeare and the theatrical history of Southwark. The World Centre for Shakespeare Studies runs a summer school here. There are long-term plans to revive the area as a theatrical centre and build a new Globe Theatre.

From here either Bankside and Upper Ground or Southwark Street and Stamford Street will bring us into the borough of LAMBETH, an old district between Southwark and Battersea, with its most interesting parts lying near the Thames. Adjoining Waterloo Bridge is the area known as the *South Bank*, a rather neglected and unattractive part of the town, with the exception of the section between the bridge and County Hall which was tidied up for the Festival of Britain in 1951.

The **Royal Festival Hall** near the S end of *Hungerford Bridge* (rail and pedestrians), opened in 1965, is a large hall, seating 3000, with two restaurants and other facilities, which offers ideal conditions for concerts of orchestral and choral music. The adjoining *Queen Elizabeth Hall* and *Purcell Room* are smaller concert halls. Nearby are the *Hayward Gallery*, used by the Arts Council for special exhibitions, and the *National Film Theatre*. NE of the Festival Hall is the **National Theatre** (by Sir Denys Lasdun, 1976), which in fact contains three theatres, one seating 1200 with an open stage, another with a normal proscenium stage seating 900, and a third with a small auditorium. To the S of the theatre is *Waterloo Station* (trains to the S coast and the SW).

E of Waterloo Station is the **Old Vic Theatre**, in the *Royal Victoria Hall*, originally built in 1817 as the Coburg Theatre, which specialised in melodrama. In the latter part of the 19th c., under new management, it put on operas and classical plays at popular prices. It was destroyed by bombing during the last war and reopened after rebuilding in 1950. Until the opening of the National Theatre it was the home of the National Theatre Company. – Some 300 yards N of the Old Vic is the 30-storey **King's Reach Tower** (1978), among the modern flats of the *Peabody Centre*.

W of Waterloo Station, on the Thames, is **London County Hall**, built between 1912 and 1933 to house the London County Council, which is now the headquarters of the Greater London Council. The Council's meetings (on alternate Tuesdays) are open to the public, and visitors can see round the main parts of County Hall on Saturdays and the Summer Bank Holiday. The *Library*, open to students, has a large collection of pictures, prints and drawings illustrating the history and topography of London. The Greater London Council was created in 1963, when 70 older administrative units were amalgamated and replaced by 32 boroughs; at the same time the boundaries of London were extended to take in the old county of Middlesex and parts of Essex and Surrey.

S of County Hall are the new buildings of *St Thomas's Hospital*, founded in 1213, which suffered severe destruction during the last war. Along the river, facing the Houses of Parliament, runs the *Albert Embankment*, leading to *Lambeth Bridge* and **Lambeth Palace**, which has been for more than 70 years the London residence of the archbishop of Canterbury. Originally built in 1219, it was frequently altered and enlarged in later centuries. It is open to visitors only by prior arrangement. Apart from the library, it has some fine portraits of archbishops of the past. The oldest part of the building is the crypt, which is believed to date from about 1200. In front of the palace is *St Mary's Church*, which dates in its present form from 1851 but has a 15th c. tower. – From Lambeth Bridge *Lambeth Road* runs E, with the *Archbishop's Park* on the left. At the intersection with *Kennington Road* is the Harmsworth Park. At Nos. 261 and 287 are houses in which Charlie Chaplin lived as a boy.

In the Harmsworth Park is the ***Imperial War Museum**, opened in the Crystal Palace in 1920 and thereafter, until 1936, housed in the Imperial Institute. It contains a large collection of material on the two world wars, in three sections – sea warfare, land warfare and air warfare.

Room 1 (sea warfare) contains a German one-man submarine, an Italian one-man torpedo, German magnetic mines, models of naval vessels and sub-marines and naval uniforms. An interesting model illustrates the landing at Walcheren in Holland, and there is also a model of the Mulberry harbour used in the Normandy landings.

Room 2 (air warfare) illustrates the development of military aircraft, with examples of Second World War planes including the Spitfire, the Heinkel 162, the Messerschmitt and the Japanese Zeke. Here too are the German V1 and V2 rockets. There are also numerous maps, plans and diagrams illustrating military operations, as well as a collection of decorations and medals.

Room 3 (land warfare) begins with a display illustrating the origins of the First World War. The gallery contains numerous mortars, field guns, anti-aircraft guns and machine guns, British and Indian uniforms, and pioneers' and paratroops' equipment.

Finally mention must be made of **Battersea Park**, on the S bank of the Thames between Chelsea Bridge and Albert Bridge, which was laid out in 1858. It was previously known as Battersea Fields, the scene of a duel between the duke of Wellington and the earl of Winchilsea. The *subtropical garden* W of the boating pond is at its best in summer.

SURROUNDINGS OF LONDON

Visitors who want to see something of the area round London are offered an embarrassingly wide choice. The rapid train services give them an extensive radius of action, bringing the south coast, Oxford, Cambridge, the romantic Cotswolds and Shakespeare's Stratford-on-Avon within day-trip range.

In addition to road and rail transport, visitors also have at their disposal a variety of interesting *trips on the Thames*. There are, for example, boats to Battersea and **Kew**, with the beautiful Kew Gardens and *Kew Palace*, which is open to the public. Nearby is

Hampton Court Palace, garden front

The *Cutty Sark*, Greenwich

a *museum* illustrating the early development of industry.

Another worthwhile trip is to **Richmond**, with wide views of the Thames valley from Richmond Hill. The trip in this direction usually ends at *Hampton Court Palace*, built by Cardinal Wolsey in 1514 and later a favourite residence of Henry VIII and Anne Boleyn. It is set in beautiful gardens, with a famous *maze*. In the Orangery is a masterpiece of European painting, Mantegna's "Triumph of Caesar".

Downstream, past the Tower, the boats reach **Greenwich**, one of the more attractive places in the outskirts of London.

Greenwich is known throughout the world for its Observatory, with the Greenwich Meridian. In Greenwich High Road, which runs through the town, are the *Old Town Hall*, with a clock-tower 165 ft high, and the *New Town Hall*.

A few paces from Greenwich High Road is *Greenwich Pier*, where the eye is caught at once by the *Cutty Sark*, the last of a long line of sailing clippers which carried tea to Britain. Built on the Clyde in 1870, it is a vessel of just under 1000 tons, and could make 17 knots on the run from the East. It is now a training centre for merchant seamen, but is open to visitors. It contains a collection of ship models, drawings and other relics of the sailing ship traffic between India and Britain. – *Gipsy Moth*, in which Sir Francis Chichester sailed alone round the world, is also on view.

From the pier King William Walk runs S into the town, in which is the **Royal Naval College**, occupying Greenwich Hospital, built by Wren. This is a historic site, once occupied by a palace belonging to Edward I (d. 1307) and later by the Placentia Palace built for the duke of Gloucester in 1426, a favourite residence

of Henry VII and other kings. Anne Boleyn's death sentence was signed here by Henry VIII.

A notable feature of the College is the *Painted Hall*, decorated by Sir James Thornhill in 1727. The *Chapel* in the SE block was designed by Wren, but was destroyed by fire and thereafter restored. Its central feature is an altarpiece 25 ft high representing St Paul's shipwreck.

From King William Walk we turn E into Romney Road to reach the **National Maritime Museum**, a comprehensive survey of British naval history. The period down to the 17th c. is covered in the Queen's House, from then down to 1815 in the W wing and the most recent period in the E wing. A special room is devoted to relics and uniforms of Nelson. The *Neptune Hall* is devoted to the history of shipbuilding.

S of the Museum in *Greenwich Park* in *Flamsteed House*, the original home of the Royal Observatory (now at Herstmonceux Castle in Sussex). The *Greenwich Meridian* runs through Flamsteed House and the park, marked by a tablet in the house and a line on the roadway. The house contains a display of old astronomical apparatus. On the turret on the roof is a time-ball which drops at 1 o'clock every day, originally installed to enable ships to set their chronometers. – Greenwich can be reached from London not only by the sightseeing boats but also by hydrofoil from Tower Pier and by train from Charing Cross Station. To protect London from possible flooding by abnormal high tides, the GLC Thames Barrier has been constructed across the river near *Woolwich*; close by is the Thames Barrier Centre for visitors.

Some 20 miles W of central London is **Windsor** (see p. 278), with **Windsor Castle, residence of the monarch for 860 years. To the S of Windsor Great Park are many fine country houses.

Ascot (see p. 279) is noted for its racecourse. Ascot Week (in June) is one of the great social events of the season.

Across the river from Windsor is the little town of **Eton**, with the most celebrated English public school, **Eton College: see p. 102.

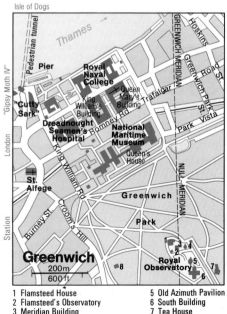

1 Flamsteed House
2 Flamsteed's Observatory
3 Meridian Building
4 Great Equatorial Building
5 Old Azimuth Pavilion
6 South Building
7 Tea House
8 Conduit House

Londonderry

Northern Ireland. – County: Londonderry.
Population: 70,000.
Telephone dialling code: 0504.

ⓘ **Tourist Information Centre,**
Water Street;
tel. 69501.
Foyle Tourism Association,
5 Guildhall Street;
tel. 265151

HOTELS. – *White Horse Inn*, 68 Clooney Road, A, 43 r.; *Everglades*, Prehen Road, A, 38 r.; *Broomhill House*, Limavady Road, B, 21 r.

RESTAURANTS. – *Inn at the Cross*, Glenshane Road; *Me Da's*, Groaty Road; *New York, New York*, Strand Road; *Steak House*, Custom House Street; *Woodburn*, Woodburn, Waterside.

SPORT and RECREATION. – Riding, fishing, rowing, golf, hockey, tennis, swimming, sailing, diving, water skiing.

Londonderry, known to its inhabitants by its Irish name of Derry, is Northern Ireland's second largest town, an important port and industrial town with a traditional textile industry (linen shirts) but also chemical and engineering plants and factories producing artificial fibres and ceramics. With its attractive surroundings, it is a popular tourist centre and a good base for trips into the Inishowen peninsula and Donegal in the Republic of Ireland, as well as the immediately surrounding area. The town itself preserves an almost complete circuit of walls and a number of interesting old buildings.

HISTORY. – The town's original name was *Derry-Calgach* ("Calgach's oak forest"). St Columba landed here and founded an abbey in 546; then 17 years later he moved to Iona and continued his missionary activities in Scotland and England. The abbey and the settlement which grew up round it were several times attacked and destroyed by Vikings. In 1618 the town and the town walls were rebuilt. – In recent years Londonderry has acquired an unhappy reputation as one of the focal points of the conflict between Roman Catholics and Protestants in Northern Ireland.

SIGHTS. – The *town walls of London-derry are the best preserved in Britain, and apart from three later gates built into them, the walls are exactly as they were in 1618. The circuit of the walls offers a pleasant walk round the OLD TOWN. The town is entered through four of the original gates – *Butcher's Gate, Ferryquay Gate, Ship-quay Gate* and *Bishop's Gate*, the finest of the four. The four principal streets of the town run from these gates to meet in the **Diamond**, as their junction (still following the medieval town plan) has been known since the 17th c. The Town Hall originally stood here, but it was destroyed during one of the many sieges of the town and rebuilt elsewhere. The centre of the square is now occupied by the *War Memorial*. The town contains numbers of Georgian houses, particularly in Shipquay Street, Magazine Street and Bishop Street. The *Deanery*, in Bishop Street, was built in 1833. *St Columb's Cathedral* (Church of Ireland) dates mainly from 1629 to 1636; the tower was added in 1802.

The *Cathedral is in late Perpendicular style. The roof vaulting is borne on corbels with the carved heads of 16 bishops of Londonderry. Eight of the 13 bells in the *tower* date from the 17th c. The *bishop's throne* incorporates the chair of Bishop Bramhall, who dedicated the church in 1633. The *chapterhouse* contains relics of the town's history and the locks and keys of the four town gates.

Magee University College, a neo-Gothic building of 1865, is beautifully situated on the River Foyle. The *Guildhall* (1912), also neo-Gothic, contains interesting relics of Irish history. The best view of the town is from the *Walker Monument* on the Royal Bastion.

SURROUNDINGS. – The handsome two-level *Craigavon Bridge* (400 yards long), built in 1933, leads over the Foyle into a new and modern suburb of Londonderry. In the grounds of Belmont House School, on the Moville road, is **St Columba's Stone**, with two depressions resembling footprints. It is said to have been the coronation stone of the O'Neills, kings of Ulster.

The royal seat of the O'Neills, the **Grianan of Aileach**, lies W of the town, in the Republic of Ireland. From the old tower, believed to be the oldest building in Ireland, there are magnificent *views of Lough Foyle, the mouth of the River Foyle, Lough Swilly and the rocky Inishowen coast in the Republic. – The two great tourist attractions which can be visited from Londonderry are the beautiful *Antrim coast* and the *Giant's Causeway*.

Dunluce Castle

Giant's Causeway

The A 2 runs E through the charming villages of *Eglinton* and *Ballykelly* to *Limavady* (18 miles; on the left the new Foyle Bridge), an old town in the Roe valley, from which the A 37 continues to **Coleraine** (pop. 18,000; hotels – Bohill Auto Inn, E, 30 r.; Lodge, E, 14 r.; Greenhill House, E, 7 r.), one of the oldest English settlements in the area. This lively town on the River *Bann* (which is navigable at this point) is noted for its salmon, its whiskey distilleries and its linen factories.

From here the A 2 runs NW to the coast, coming in 6 miles to **Portstewart** (pop. 6500; hotels – Edgewater, D, 29 r.; Strand, E, 40 r.; Windsor, E, 21 r.), which has beautiful sandy beaches and a harbour. So too has **Portrush**, 4 miles E (hotels – Skerryban, E, 43 r.; Eglinton, E, 32 r.; Carrig-Na-Rone, E, 11 r.). Offshore are the *Skerries*. From Portrush the road continues E passing the 14th c. *Dunluce Castle*, built on an isolated crag and linked with the mainland by a bridge.

8 miles farther on is one of the great tourist sights of Northern Ireland, the * **Giant's Causeway**, a geological formation consisting of a series of vertical basalt columns of prismatic form and varying width and height. Some of the columns have names, like the ''Lady's Fan'', the ''Giant's Organ'' and the ''Horseshoe''. The most imposing part, reached by the Shepherd's Path, is known as the Amphitheatre, with columns up to 80 ft high and numerous blocks of basalt resembling seats. – The coast road then continues by way of *Ballintoy* (13 miles) and *Cushendun*, surrounded by heath, to **Ballycastle** (pop. 3000; hotels – Marine, D, 33 r.; Antrim Arms, D, 19 r.; Hilsea, E, 20 r.; youth hostel at 34 North Street, 36 b.), a picturesque little harbour town surrounded by wooded country. From here a boat can be taken to the island of *Rathlin*, 6½ miles offshore, once a Viking base but perhaps better known for the cave in which the fugitive Scottish king Robert the Bruce once took refuge. – The road from Ballycastle to *Cushendall*, passing the famous Glens of Antrim, is the most beautiful coastal road in Ireland. From Cushendall it is possible to continue along the coast to Belfast (48 miles), or alternatively to return to Londonderry by the very attractive inland road via Glenariff (A 43).

Lough Erne

Northern Ireland. – County: Fermanagh.

One of the most attractive inland tourist areas in Northern Ireland is the county of Fermanagh, with its county town of Enniskillen and the beautiful scenery round * Lough Erne, which ranks as Ireland's most beautiful lough. It is some 20 miles long, with a maximum width of 6 miles. The southern part, known as Upper Lough Erne, is a maze of inlets and islands, with a shoreline which twists and turns so that it is difficult to think of it as a single lake.

The lough is a paradise for water-sports enthusiasts and anglers. In summer there are motorboat services, and motor cruisers can also be hired. At the W end, almost on the frontier with the Republic, are sluices to regulate the water level. The A 46 runs along the W side of the lough to *Enniskillen*, passing hills of some height on the right-hand side. In the lough is the island of *Inishmacsaint*, with remains of a 12th c. church.

* **Enniskillen** (pop. 12,500; hotel – Killyhevlin, D, 26 r.) is a lively and popular holiday resort, beautifully situated between the two parts of Lough Erne, with numerous rivers and streams and delightful parkland scenery, particularly the grounds of Castlecoole, a mansion built by James Wyatt. It has a fine Cathedral with a 17th c. tower. Portora Royal School, founded by James I in 1608, was attended by Oscar Wilde.

No visitor should omit the trip to the island of **Devenish**, at the S end of Lower Lough Erne, which has the remains of an abbey founded by St Molaise in the 6th c., with a * round tower over 80 ft high, tapering towards the top. There are also fragments of St Mary's Abbey and the Great Church (12th c.), with a cross some 6 ft high.

Other holiday resorts in this area are *Ballinamallard*, on the river of the same name (5 miles NE); the village of *Bellanaleck*, in the heart of the lake district (5 miles S of Enniskillen); *Kesh*, beautifully situated on Lower Lough Erne, with possible excursions to Boa Island and White Island; *Lisbellaw* on Upper Lough Erne, with wool spinning and weaving mills; and *Lisnaskea*, also on Upper Lough Erne, with a ruined castle and an angling centre.

Another place of tourist interest is **Omagh** (pop. 17,000; hotels – Royal Arms, D, 21 r.; Silverbirch, E, 32 r.), the county town of Tyrone, with excellent salmon fishing and good walking in the *Sperrin Mountains*.

Isle of Man

(i) **Tourist Information,**
13 Victoria Street, Douglas;
tel. (0624) 4323.

The * Isle of Man, situated in the Irish Sea 31 miles from England, about the same distance from Northern Ireland and 16 miles from Scotland, is a very popular holiday island, with a coastline of more than 100 miles made up partly of sandy bathing beaches and partly of steep cliffs. Most of the island, which is some 33 miles long and 12 miles wide, is undulating and hilly, with a varied scenic pattern of moorland and heath, narrow glens with waterfalls and wooded hills. In winter the temperature seldom falls below 5 °C (41 °F) in summer it barely rises above 20° (68 °F). A fresh breeze blows almost all the time.

The island has a population of some 50,000, swollen in summer by more than half a million holidaymakers. About a third of the inhabitants live in Douglas, the island's capital and principal port.

There are ferry services (carrying cars as well as passengers) from Liverpool and Heysham to Douglas throughout the year and during the summer there are additional services from other ports. There are air services operating from most airports within the United Kingdom.

HISTORY. – The Isle of Man has a very interesting past. The oldest inhabitants were a hunting and fishing people of the Mesolithic period, c. 2000 B.C. Long before the Romans came to Britain the island was occupied by Celts, to whom the Iron Age forts and the large circular timber framed huts found here are attributed. The Isle of Man was never occupied by the Romans. St Patrick (d. 463) is believed to have converted the people to Christianity long before St Augustine was sent to Canterbury. Celtic Christianity flourished until the arrival of the Vikings, whose raids began at the end of the 8th c. All these various periods have left traces on the island, which has much of interest to offer the archaeologically inclined visitor.

The Isle of Man has its own Parliament, whose lower house, the House of Keys, is the oldest in the world. The old Manx language, a Celtic idiom, has for all practical purposes died out, being preserved only in family and place-names. The tailless Manx cat, on the other hand, continues to flourish; originally the result of a mutation, it is now bred to preserve the species. There is a rich variety of bird life, and an abundant growth of flowers; the island's fuchsia hedges are particularly beautiful.

Almost all the places of any size are on the coast. **Douglas** (pop. 19,900; hotels – Palace and Casino, D, 139 r.; Rothesay Private, E, 32 r.; Woodburne, E, 12 r.) lies on a beautiful bay into which flow the little rivers Dhoo and Glass. The Promenade, 2 miles long, is crowded with visitors in summer. The town offers every variety of accommodation, from luxury hotels to the most modest guest-houses, and a great range of tourist attractions – large dance-halls, horse-trams, an indoor swimming pool, a golf-course, a gambling casino. There are a number of handsome buildings, including the Legislative Building, home of the Manx parliament.

Of particular interest is the * Manx Museum in Finch Road, which illustrates the history of the island from the earliest times, with reproductions of rooms and domestic equipment of the past and works by Manx artists. There is an important collection of material of the Celtic and Viking periods, particularly notable for the Manx crosses.

S of Douglas a beautiful panoramic road runs round Douglas Head to **Port Soderick**, a popular seaside resort, passing the churches of Braddan (1½ miles) and Onchan (2 miles), which have old crosses. The road then continues to Ballasalla (8 miles), with the ruins of a Cistercian house, **Rushen Abbey**, founded in 1134. This was the last monastery in the British Isles to be dissolved (1540). The old Monks' Bridge is very picturesque.

From Ballasalla, which lies inland, the road leads towards the coast, passing Ronaldsway Airport on the left, and comes to the Langness peninsula, which has very beautiful sandy beaches. The little resort of **Derbyhaven** is noted for an excellent golf-course and for King William's College, founded in 1668, the island's principal school. The little chapel is worth seeing.

The next place is **Castletown** (1¼ miles: Golf Links Hotel, C, 65 r.), once capital of the island. **Castle Rushen**, on the site of an earlier Viking stronghold, destroyed in 1313, has played a great part in Manx history.

The Castle, once part of a royal residence, is very well preserved. The clock in the S tower was presented by Elizabeth I in 1597, and there is also an interesting sundial with 13 dials. Within the walls of the castle Derby House was built by the seventh earl of Derby in 1644. From the tower there are wide-ranging views. Here too is one of the island's greatest treasures, a Celtic crucifix brought from the little offshore islet, the

Calf of Man. – There is also an interesting *Nautical Museum*.

The road continues round Poolvash Bay and comes to *Port St Mary* (pop. 1400), a quiet little port and seaside resort. Beyond it extends a very beautiful peninsula, off which, beyond the Calf Sound, lies the Calf of Man. The wild beauty of the scenery can best be enjoyed by walking to Calf Sound (2½ miles along the cliffs, past *Spanish Head*).

The road from Port St Mary continues to *Cregneish* (1½ miles), the most southerly place on the island. On *Mull Hill* (430 ft) is a group of six chamber tombs known as the *Mull Circle* or *Meayll Circle*. At Cregneish is the **Manx Open Air Folk Museum*, a group of thatched cottages with their original furnishings and the implements of various trades and occupations (blacksmithing, fishing, weaving), as well as a shop.

The **Calf of Man** is a bird reserve with a large population of rare seabirds, as well as seals. It can be visited outside the nesting season (boat from Port Erin). There are fine views from the highest point (360 ft).

Port Erin (pop. 1800; Hotel Belle Vue, C, 63 r.) lies at the head of a deep bay, sheltered by *Bradda Head* (400 ft). It is the terminal point of a small old-time steam railway from Douglas. The Marine Biological Station has an interesting aquarium. Port Erin, with its picturesque fishing harbour, is a very popular family resort, the second largest on the island.

For wildly beautiful scenery, a walk along the cliffs to Fleshwick Bay is recommended, continuing to the Niarbyl and Dalby (½ mile inland). In places the cliffs fall sheer down to the sea.

The road from Port Erin to Peel (14 miles) runs via *Colby*, with a picturesque gorge, *Ballabeg*, with the *Round Table* (1000 ft) and the higher *South Barrule*, Dalby and *Glen Maye*, with a beautiful waterfall.

Peel (pop. 3500), half way up the W coast of the island at the mouth of the little river Neb, is a picturesque fishing port which claims to produce the best kippers in England and is also a developing holiday resort. Outside the harbour lies the rocky *St Patrick's Isle*, linked with the

Peel Castle, Isle of Man

mainland by a causeway, on which are *Peel Castle*, a red sandstone structure surrounded by a 16th c. wall, and the *Cathedral*, dedicated to St Germanus, a disciple of St Patrick. The oldest part of the Cathedral – the smallest Church of England cathedral – is the choir (1226–47). St Patrick's Chapel probably dates from the 9th c.

From Peel a beautiful panoramic road runs high above the coast to **Kirk Michael** (6½ miles), passing *White Strand*, a fine bathing beach. Kirk Michael, the largest place in the NW of the island, is beautifully situated between the coast and hills rising to 1600 ft.

From Kirk Michael it is possible to continue along the coast, perhaps with a detour to *Point of Ayre*, but the scenery along this stretch is less attractive, although there are some sand and shingle beaches. It is more interesting to take the inland road, over the wide Ayre plain with its low hills. The road runs past the *Curragh*, an area of heath and bog, some of which has been brought into cultivation. A mile beyond Ballaugh Bridge is the *Curragh Wild Life Park*. The road then continues via *Sulby*, a pretty little place in the valley of the river of the same name (waterfall), to Ramsey.

Ramsay (pop. 6200), in a wide sandy bay, is the second largest place on the island. It is the traditional rival of Douglas, and the inhabitants were delighted when Queen Victoria landed here in 1847, heavy seas having made it impossible to enter Douglas harbour. The pier is now called the Queen's Pier. Ramsey offers a variety of pleasant walks – for example to *Kirk Maughold*, with a 13th c. church and a churchyard containing 44 old crosses.

Between Ramsey and Douglas is the little resort of **Laxey** (pop. 1340), linked with both towns by electric tram – a route of great scenic attraction. From here there is an electric mountain railway up *Snaefell*, the island's highest point (2034 ft), from which the four countries of Ireland, Scotland, England and Wales can be seen on a clear day. The town's main tourist attraction is the *Lady Isabella*, a huge water-wheel $72\frac{1}{2}$ ft in diameter, once used to pump water out of the lead-mines (now disused).

Visitors who are on the island on 5 July should not miss the Tynwald Day ceremony on the **Tynwald Hill** at *St John's*, $8\frac{1}{2}$ miles E of Peel. On this ancient artificial mound, perhaps a Bronze Age burial mound, all the laws passed during the previous year are proclaimed in Manx and English, with traditional ceremonial.

> The popular and world-famous Tourist Trophy (T.T.) motorcycle race is held annually in June.

Manchester

Northern England. – Administrative unit: Greater Manchester.
Population: 464,200.
Telephone dialling code: 061.
(i) **Magnum House,**
     Portland Street, Piccadilly;
     tel. 247 3694.
     Town Hall,
     6 Lloyd Street;
     tel. 236 1606.

HOTELS. – *Piccadilly*, 107 Piccadilly, A, 248 r.; *Midland*, Peter Street, B, 281 r.; *Portland Thistle*, 3–5 Portland Street, B, 220 r.; *Post House*, Palatine Road, B, 201 r.; *Grand*, Aytoun Street, B, 146 r.; *Britannia*, Portland Street, C, 360 r.; *Willow Bank*, 340 Wilmslow Road, Fallowfield, D, 123 r.; *Mitre*, Cathedral Gates, D, 25 r.; *Victoria Park*, 4 Park Crescent, *Victoria*, D, 19 r.; *Excelsior*, at the airport, B, 304 r.

RESTAURANTS. – *Casa España*, 100 Wilmslow Road; *Isola Bella*, 6A Booth Street; *Leen Hong*, 35 George Street; *Terrazza*, 14 Nicholas Street; *Moss Nook*, at the airport (Ringway Road).

SPORT and RECREATION. – Golf, tennis, sailing, riding.

Manchester, one of Britain's largest industrial centres, was the cradle of the cotton trade but now has a great diversity of industry. It is also the home of many insurance companies, banks and large commercial firms.

Manchester has now absorbed many neighbouring towns and villages to form the large administrative unit of Greater Manchester.

Manchester played an important part in the Industrial Revolution and the growth of the workers' movement. Friedrich Engels (1820–95) worked in his father's business in Manchester, gathering material for his "Condition of the Working Classes in England". The slums which he described have now disappeared, and the city, which suffered much destruction during the Second World War, has been rebuilt in modern style. Manchester was the first town to establish a "smokeless zone" (1951). It has an interesting Cathedral and a number of other buildings, good museums, an art gallery and a variety of other cultural and sporting facilities, being noted as the home of Manchester United and Manchester City football clubs and also of the famous Hallé Orchestra.

HISTORY. – The town was known in Roman times as *Mancunium*. Its rise to prosperity began after Flemish immigrants brought in the manufacture of wool and linen in the 14th c. The first machines came into use in 1781, and the first steam-driven spinning mill began to operate in 1798. The two earliest machines, the spinning jenny and the spinning mule, can be seen in the Textile Museum in Blackburn, N of Manchester. The $35\frac{1}{2}$-mile-long Manchester Ship Canal was constructed between 1887 and 1894, making Manchester a seaport. In 1819 St Peter's Field was the scene of the "Peterloo massacre", in which 12 people were killed in a demonstration calling for better representation in Parliament. The "Manchester Guardian", a Liberal newspaper (now known simply as the "Guardian"), was founded in 1821.

SIGHTS. – The *Cathedral, on the banks of the Irwell, is in Perpendicular style and dates mostly from 1422 to 1506. It was raised to cathedral status in 1847. The *chapels* on both sides of the nave and choir were built between 1486 and 1508, and there were further additions and alterations in almost every subsequent century. Particularly notable are the *choir-stalls*, with misericords which are among the most richly decorated in the country. The side chapels in the choir have been preserved, unlike those in the nave. *St John's Chapel* is the chapel of the Manchester Regiment. The little *Lady Chapel* has a wooden screen of about 1440. The octagonal *Chapterhouse*, built in 1465, has mural paintings by C. Weight (1962) at the entrance, including a figure of Christ in modern dress. The E end of the Cathedral was damaged in an air raid in 1940.

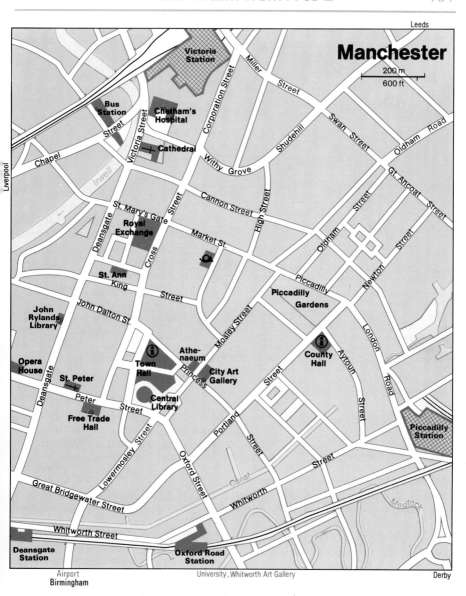

Manchester

Chetham's Hospital, just N of the Cathedral, dates in part from 1422–61. It was originally a residence for priests of a collegiate foundation, and is now occupied by a music school. Its *library*, the oldest public library in England, possesses valuable manuscripts. – In Deansgate is the ***John Rylands Library**, built in 1899, which is another treasurehouse of early printed books.

The neo-Gothic **Town Hall** (1868–77) has a *tower* 281 ft high from which there are wide-ranging views. The great hall contains an interesting series of mural paintings on the history of the town by Ford Madox Brown. The *Central Library*, a large rotunda by E. Vincent Harris (1934), houses nine specialised libraries. The *Free Trade Hall* was rebuilt in 1951.

The ***City Art Gallery** possesses one of the largest collections in Britain outside London. In addition to works by Dutch, French (Gauguin) and German (Max Ernst) painters it has examples of the work of almost every English artist of any note. The sculpture collection includes works by Rodin, Maillol and Henry Moore ("Mother and Child"). W of Deansgate lies the Castlefield Urban Heritage Park with the *Museum of Science and Industry* and the *Air and Space Museum*.

A number of other **museums** cater for a variety of special interests. *Heaton Hall* (by James Wyatt, 1772), Prestwich, has applied art, furniture, prints, etc.; *Platt Hall* (1764) has a fine collection of English costume; *Queen's Park Art Gallery*, apart from its pictures, is the museum of the Manchester Regiment; porcelain, silver and pictures are to be seen in *Wythenshawe Hall*, a 16th c. half-timbered mansion with later additions, and in the *Fletcher Moss Museum* in Didsbury, which also has a collection of pictures by English artists from Paul Sandby and Turner to the present day.

Manchester University

Manchester University was founded in 1851 as *Owens College*, with the help of a bequest of £100,000 by John Owens (1790–1846), a wealthy merchant who left the money for the establishment of a university not subject to ecclesiastical influence. The "Manchester educational precinct" is a large complex which includes a variety of institutes and halls of residence.

Manchester University can claim three Nobel prize-winners: *Lord Rutherford* (1871–1939), who put forward the theory of atomic disintegration and laid the foundations of modern atomic physics with his model of the atom (Nobel prize for chemistry, 1908); the physicist *Sir James Chadwick*, born in Manchester in 1891, who in 1932 proved the existence of the neutron (Nobel prize 1935); and *Sir John Cockcroft* (1897–1967), the leading atomic physicist, who worked for a time in Manchester (Nobel prize 1951).

Mid Wales

Counties: Powys and Dyfed.

Mid Wales takes in the former counties of Montgomery and Radnor and part of Brecknock, now forming the new county of Powys (county town Llandrindod Wells), the former county of Cardigan which is now part of Dyfed, and parts of Merioneth and Carmarthen. It covers a wide variety of scenery, from the great sweep of Cardigan Bay with its sandy beaches to the border regions which were disputed with England for so many centuries. It has great expanses of farming country, extensive sheep grazings and small towns and villages which have changed little over the centuries.

In general the hills of Mid Wales are lower and less steep than those of South Wales, most of them being gently rounded and undulating. Large reservoirs, now assimilated into the landscape, supply water to Liverpool and Birmingham. The houses are either stone-built or, particularly in the border areas, half-timbered.

The coast of Mid Wales offers two different types of scenery, sand dunes in the northern half, cliffs with small sandy beaches in the south, the latter offering long and beautiful cliff walks. On the S side of Barmouth Bay are the little seaside resorts of *Fairbourne*, with the smallest narrow-gauge railway in Wales, running along the coast to the Barmouth passenger ferry, and *Llwyngwril*, at the foot of the Cadair Idris.

Near *Rhoslefain* A 493 leaves the coast and runs inland to **Llanegryn** (2 miles), a quiet little village whose church has a finely carved roof and a Norman font. Nearby is the mansion of *Peniarth*, where the famous Peniarth manuscripts, now in the National Library in Aberystwyth, were collected. The road continues along the windings of the little River Dysynni to *Craig yr Aderyn*, the nesting-place of great numbers of sea birds, including cormorants. Beyond, at Llanfihangel y Pennant, are the picturesque remains of *Castell y Bere*, crowning the hilltop. The road then runs SE to *Abergynolwyn*, the terminus of the Talyllyn Railway from Tywyn, claimed to be Wales's oldest narrow-gauge line (opened 1865). It formerly carried slate from the Abergynolwyn quarries but is now run for the benefit of holidaymakers, who enjoy delightful views of narrow gorges and woodland, with a glimpse of the Dolgoch Falls.

Tywyn (Corbett Arms Hotel, D, 35 r.), at the other end of the line, lies on the coast and on the coastal road. It is a seaside resort with a 3-mile-long beach of sand and shingle, a golf-course, a caravan park and a variety of entertainments. The little town, with a resident population of 4000, is thronged with visitors in summer. It has an interesting Railway Museum. In *St Cadfan's Church*, which is mainly Norman, is Cadfan's Stone, 7 ft high, with the oldest inscription in the Welsh language. From here the coast road runs S to the mouth of the River Dovey and the town of **Aberdovey**, a seaside resort with a number of hotels and restaurants which offers good sailing and angling as well as bathing.

$10\frac{1}{2}$ miles up the Dovey valley is **Machynlleth** (pop. 1900; Wynnstay Hotel, D, 26 r.), an attractive little town with broad tree-lined streets, little shops and a tall clock-tower. Here, in what is now the Owain Glyndwr Institute, Glyndwr (Owen Glendower) held his first parliament in 1404. Plas Machynlleth, built in 1671, was formerly a residence of Lord Londonderry.

View of Aberystwyth

bridges, the lowest of which, believed to date from the 12th c., is known as the Devil's Bridge. Tradition has it that this bridge was built by a monk from Strata Florida Abbey, 7 miles S. 3 miles N is *Nant y Moch Lake*, well stocked with fish. Here there is a nature reserve with a number of waymarked nature trails. From Aberystwyth to Devil's Bridge there is a narrow-gauge steam railway, originally built to carry lead from the many mines in the hills, the last of which closed down 1912.

Little is left of **Strata Florida Abbey**, a Cistercian foundation of 1196 near the source of the River Teifi, although it was in its day one of the leading monastic houses in Wales and a great cultural centre. The finest surviving fragment is the W doorway, but there are also remains of the sacristy and chapterhouse as well as a number of tombstones. The medieval Welsh poet Dafydd ap Gwilym is buried here.

From Machynlleth A 487 runs SW at a distance of some 3 miles from the coast, on which are the little seaside resorts of *Ynyslas*, at the mouth of the Dovey, and *Borth*, with a beautiful 3-mile-long sandy beach. The road runs through *Tre'r Ddol* and *Tre Taliesin*, small villages which are good centres for walking in the Plynlimon range, above the flat coastal area between the Dovey valley and the Vale of Rheidol, and comes to **Talybont**, where there are many craft producers, particularly hand-weavers renowned for their tweed. 6 miles S is **Aberystwyth** (pop. 15,300), at the mouth of the rivers Ystwyth and Rheidol, which join just before reaching the coast. Aberystwyth, a university town and a shopping town for Mid Wales, is also a popular seaside resort.

The more modern buildings of the *University* (founded in 1872) are on the hills behind the town, together with the *National Library of Wales* (founded in 1907), one of the six libraries of deposit which receive a copy of every book published in Britain. It possesses some 2 million books and many thousands of manuscripts, with particular emphasis on Celtic and Welsh literature. From time to time it puts on special exhibitions displaying some of its treasures. *Theatr y Werin*, the University Theatre, has a summer season.

On a rocky crag are the remains of a castle built by Edward I. From the pier there is a good view of Cardigan Bay. The beach is rather stony. Near the University is *Pen Dinas*, the site of a powerful prehistoric hill-fort. At **Llanfarian**, 3 miles S, is *Bryn Eithyn Hall*, with a collection of Welsh furniture, dolls, ship models, etc.

From Aberystwyth there is a beautiful road along the Vale of Rheidol to *****Devil's Bridge**, which many consider to be one of Britain's most notable beauty spots. Here the River Mynach flows down through a deep gorge in a series of spectacular waterfalls, with a total drop of 300 ft, to join the Rheidol. There are three

The road to the Elan valley from Devil's Bridge leads to the pretty little country town of *Rhayader*, in the upper Wye valley, a popular tourist centre with fine Welsh craft goods to offer (hand-woven cloth, pottery). Here there are facilities for pony trekking in the surrounding hills with their picturesque little lakes. The *Elan valley* and the *Claerwen reservoir*, though serving the purposes of water supply, are of great scenic beauty.

From Rhayader we continue E by either A 470 or A 44 to reach the county town of Powys, **Llandrindod Wells** (pop. 4000; hotels – Metropole, D, 141 r.; Glen Usk, D, 80 r.; Griffin Lodge, D, 10 r.), Wales's leading spa, with magnesium, sulphur, chalybeate and other springs. In its heyday the town attracted some 80,000 visitors every year to take the cure, mainly for rheumatism and gout. From this period it has preserved a legacy of Georgian houses, wide streets with plenty of room for parking and numerous hotels. There are excellent facilities for sport and entertainment, and a Bowling Festival is held every summer in the town. The golf-course, 1100 ft above sea level, with fine views of the valley below, is one of the highest in Britain. There is good fishing in the River Ithon and the lake adjoining the Common. 2 miles N, at *Castell Collen*, are the remains of a Roman camp.

From Llandrindod Wells A 483 runs S to Builth Wells, where the Irfon flows into the Wye, passing through *Howey*, formerly a town of some consequence – with four markets in the year – near the drove road on which the cattle were driven from Wales into England, but now a quiet little village.

Builth Wells is still an important cattle market, the scene of the Welsh Agricultural Society's annual show in July, to which the best cattle in Wales are sent. The town itself was almost completely destroyed by fire in 1691. Of the castle which once stood here practically nothing is left. At *Cilmery*, $1\frac{1}{2}$ miles W, is a monument to the 13th c. Prince Llewelyn.

From Builth Wells A 470 ascends the beautiful Wye valley, passing through *Aberedw*, with a very fine 15th c. church and its famous rocks, and *Erwood*, a pretty little place on the Wye, where Henry Mayhew is said to have conceived the idea of "Punch", to the *Black Mountains* and the Welsh marches.

On the coast S of Aberystwyth are the seaside resorts of *Llanrhystyd* and *Llanon*, both with shingle beaches. Then comes **Aberaeron**, an old fishing port (pop. 1300) with many Georgian houses, at the mouth of the Aeron.

From here it is worth while making an excursion inland to *Lampeter*, a little market town in the Teifi valley, noted for the horse market in March which attracts buyers and sellers from all over Britain. *St David's College* (founded 1827), in a fine neo-Gothic building, has university status and has close associations with Oxford and Cambridge. – 10 miles NE and situated amid beautiful hills is **Tregaron**, a little market town on the Teifi, which attracts large numbers of visitors in summer. The high moorland area called the *Bog of Tregaron* is a nature reserve.

SW of Aberaeron is **New Quay** ($6\frac{1}{2}$ miles: youth hostel, The Glyn, Church Street, 50 b.), a good mackerel-fishing centre and a pleasant seaside resort with plenty of entertainments and a good beach. Beyond this is *Llangranog*, with a small bay between high cliffs. A path leads to *Ynys Lochtyn*, with the remains of an old castle. **Aberporth** is a very popular resort with a good sandy beach. *Mwnt* is a charming and secluded beach with beautiful cliff scenery which can only be reached by a steep path.

Newcastle upon Tyne

Northern England. – County: Tyne and Wear.
Population: 292,500.
Telephone dialling code: 0632.
(i) **Tyne and Wear City Information Service**,
Central Library, Princess Square;
tel. 610691.

HOTELS. – *Gosforth Park Thistle*, High Gosforth Park, B, 178 r.; *Holiday Inn*, Great North Road, Seaton Burn, B, 150 r.; *Crest*, New Bridge Street, C, 180 r.; *Imperial*, Jesmond Road, C, 130 r.; *The County Thistle*, Neville Street, C, 115 r.; *Avon*, Osborne Road, Jesmond, C, 91 r.; *Royal Turks Head*, Grey Street, C, 89 r.; *Royal Station*, Neville Street, D, 132 r.; *Swallow*, Newgate Arcade, D, 92 r.; *Stakis Airport*, at the airport, C, 100 r.

YOUTH HOSTEL. – 107 Jesmond Road, 58 b.

RESTAURANTS. – *Fisherman's Lodge*, Jesmond Dene Road; *Fisherman's Wharf*, 15 The Side; *Michelangelo*, 25 King Street.

SPORT and RECREATION. – Water sports of all kinds.

Newcastle is a county town and an important industrial city situated on the N bank of the Tyne 9 miles from its mouth. In earlier days it was a great coal shipping port, handling more coal than any other type of freight: hence the phrase "carrying coals to Newcastle" applied to any unnecessary activity. It now has much heavy industry and engineering, shipbuilding, aircraft construction, chemical industry and locomotive-building. Along with the neighbouring towns it forms the great Tyneside conurbation whose cultural and economic centre is Newcastle. In spite of its industry it is by no means an unattractive city, with a cathedral, a castle and a number of interesting streets which make it well worth a visit.

HISTORY. – In Roman times the town (*Pons Aelius*) was a fort on Hadrian's Wall. In the Saxon period it was known as *Monk Chester* on account of the large number of religious houses it contained. The present name comes from the New Castle erected in the 12th c. In 1823 George Stephenson (1781–1848) established the locomotive industry here. The University was founded in 1852 as a college of Durham University.

SIGHTS. – Approaching Newcastle from the S, the visitor sees three bridges of very different types. The oldest is the *High Level Bridge*, a two-level steel railway bridge built by Robert Stephenson in

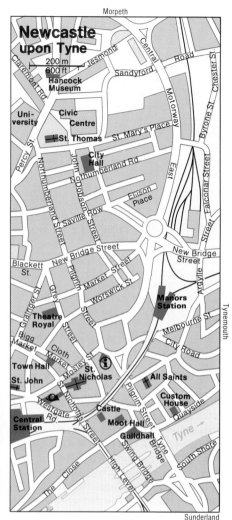

Newcastle upon Tyne

Morpeth

Jesmond
Central Road
Sandyford
Hancock Museum
Claremont Rd.
University
Civic Centre
St. Thomas
St. Mary's Place
Motorway
Byron St.
Chester St.
Percy St.
Northumberland St.
John Dobson St.
City Hall
Northumberland Rd.
East St.
Ellison Place
Falconar Street
Saville Row
Saville Street
New Bridge Street
New Bridge Street
Blackett St.
New Bridge Street
Pilgrim St.
Grey St.
Market Street
Worswick St.
Argyle Street
Manors Station
Tynemouth
Cranmer St.
Theatre Royal
Bigg Market
Cloth Market
Mosley St.
Melbourne St.
City Road
Town Hall
St. John
St. Nicholas
All Saints
Custom House
Westgate Rd.
Nicholas St.
Castle
Central Station
Pilgrim Street
Moot Hall
Quayside
Guildhall
Tyne
Swing Bridge
High Level Bridge
Tyne Bridge
South Shore
The Close
Sunderland

200 m
600 ft

and the numerous *statues*, some of them of great interest. – The *statue of Queen Victoria* in St Nicholas Square was the work of Sir Alfred Gilbert (1900).

Near the river, in St Nicholas Street, is the *Black Gate* (1247), separated from the Castle by the railway line. It now houses a unique collection of bagpipes. On the other side of the railway is the keep of the **New Castle**, built by Henry II in 1172–77 on the site of the earlier Roman fort. Its main features are the Norman *Chapel*, the *King's Chamber* and a *well*.

From the Black Gate the street named *Side* leads to *Sandhill*, with interesting old houses, the *Guildhall* (1658, rebuilt in the early 19th c.) and the *Merchants' Court*, with a chimneypiece of 1636. From Quayside we pass under the Tyne Bridge into one of the oldest parts of the town, known as the CHARES, with narrow streets and stepped lanes. Interesting buildings in this area are the *Custom House* (1766, later rebuilt), *Trinity House* (1721), *almshouses* (1787–91), a chapel and a school (1733).

In City Road is the John G. Joicey Museum (1681). From here Pilgrim and Mosley Streets lead to *Grey Street*, with a column 135 ft high (good views from top) erected in 1835 in honour of the second Earl Grey, who, as Prime Minister, carried through the Reform Bill of 1832. **Grainger Street**, one of Newcastle's best shopping streets, is named after Richard Grainger (1798–1861), a local architect who about 1830 gave Newcastle a new city centre.

The *Laing Art Gallery and Museum* in Higham Place displays old master paintings, English watercolours, antiques, china and Greek and Roman material. A notable collection of antiquities, mainly Roman but some dating from prehistoric or Anglo-Saxon times, can be seen in the *Museum of Antiquities* in the university complex; it also includes a model of Hadrian's Wall (see p. 117), which is well worth seeing before visiting the Wall itself. N of the University stands the *Hancock Museum* (Natural History and Ethnology).

In the Percy Building is the *Greek*

1845–49. The *Swing Bridge* occupies the position of the old Roman bridge. The boldest structure is the *Tyne Bridge*, which has the largest arch of any bridge in Britain (span 531 ft); it was built in 1925–28. To the W are three other bridges: the bridge carrying the new Tyne and Wear Metro, the King Edward railway bridge and the Redheugh road bridge. There is another bridge at *Scotswood* and a road tunnel at *Jarrow*.

From the Tyne Bridge *Mosley Street* leads to the *Old Town Hall* (1858–63) and the **Cathedral**, mainly built in the 14th and 15th c. as the parish church of St Nicholas and raised to cathedral status in 1882. Its *lantern tower* (1435–70) is topped by a crown spire, the earliest and finest of the kind in Britain, which is illuminated at night. Features of the interior are the canopied *font* (1500), the *organ* (1676)

Museum, with a large collection of vases, terracottas and bronzes.

Visitors interested in technological matters will want to see the *Museum of the Department of Mining Engineering*, with much material on the coal-mining industry, and the *Museum of Science and Technology* in Blandford House, with locomotives and ships, machinery and apparatus of various kinds.

*Jesmond Dene** and *Armstrong Park*, to the NE of the city, make up one of the most beautiful parks in England.

New Forest

Southern England. – County: Hampshire.

In spite of its name, the *New Forest is by no means new and is not a continuous area of forest, large parts of it being heath and moorland, with a certain amount of agricultural land as well. It extends from the coast opposite the Isle of Wight as far as Winchester and from the outskirts of Southampton to beyond Fordingbridge.

Since the time of William the Conqueror this has been a royal hunting preserve, and it is still Crown property. There is little animal life, however, apart from the half-wild New Forest ponies and some deer. Extensive reafforestation is now in progress. This area of unspoiled natural beauty, with its abundance of wild flowers in spring and the brilliant colour of the heather in autumn, attracts large numbers of visitors, offering a restful holiday and plenty of good walking.

Off the motor roads the Forest is quiet and peaceful. Possible hazards are adders – about which the Forestry Commission display warning notices – and areas of marsh and bog. Those who do not care for walking can drive through the Forest, and in this way will gain some impression of its considerable size.

A good starting point for a tour of the Forest is **Lyndhurst**, its largest town (pop. 3000; hotels – Crown, C, 46 r.; Parkhill, C, 18 r.; Lyndhurst Park, D, 64 r.), taking Cadnam Road (A 337) in the direction of *Minstead*, where Sir Arthur Conan Doyle is buried. The road passes the beautiful *Furzey Gardens*.

The *Rufus Stone* (31½ miles NW) was set up in its present position in 1745. It is said to mark the spot where King William Rufus was killed by an arrow in 1100 while out hunting.

Beyond Ringwood is *Boldrewood Arboretum*, a collection of rare trees. A narrow road runs through *Mark Ash Wood*, a nature reserve with very beautiful beeches, to *Knightwood*, with famous old oaks, some of them of very great size. Immediately opposite is the beautiful *Ornamental Drive*.

Northampton

Central England. – County: Northamptonshire.
Altitude: 300 ft. – Population: 157,200.
Telephone dialling code: 0604.
(i) **Tourist Information Centre**,
     21 St Giles's Street;
     tel. 22677.

HOTELS. – *Saxon Inn*, Silver Street, C, 140 r.; *Westone Moat House*, Weston Favell, C, 63 r.

SPORT and RECREATION. – Tennis, golf, riding.

Northampton, county town of Northamptonshire, is an important industrial town, noted particularly as a centre of the boot and shoe industry. At the end of the 17th c. the town was ravaged by a fire which destroyed many historic old buildings, including some dating from the Saxon and Norman periods. Apart from two fine churches, therefore, the town – situated on the N bank of the River Nene – has relatively few sights to offer the tourist.

HISTORY. – The dispute between Henry II and Thomas Becket in 1164 took place in Northampton Castle, the site of which is now occupied by the railway station. During the Wars of the Roses, in 1460, Lancastrian forces were defeated near the town and Henry VI was taken prisoner.

SIGHTS. – Northampton has one of England's four round churches, the **Church of the Holy Sepulchre** in Sheep Street, which is modelled on the Church of the Holy Sepulchre in Jerusalem. It originally belonged to a monastic house and was founded by Simon de Senlis, earl of Northampton (d. 1109), who had taken part in a crusade to the Holy Land.

The present *nave*, eight steps higher than the original one, is in Early English style; the apse is modern. The tower is Perpendicular. The interior is highly impressive with its massive Norman piers.

In the town centre, near the Market Square, is **All Saints Church**, built after the 1675 fire. The 14th c. *tower* survived the fire. On the front is a *statue* *of Charles II* wearing a toga and a full wig (1712).

Northampton's second major church is **St Peter's**, in Marefair, a typical example of the richly decorated Middle Norman style (c. 1160). The *Hazelrigge Mansion*, also in Marefair, survived the 1675 fire. The *County Hall*, with beautifully decorated ceilings, dates from 1682.

St Matthew's Church in Kettering Road is worth a visit for the sake of Henry Moore's Madonna and Child" (1944) and Graham Sutherland's "Crucifixion" (1946). The *Central Museum*, reflecting the town's main industry, contains a collection of footwear from Roman times to the present day.

SURROUNDINGS. – **Abington Park** (1 mile away on the Wellingborough Road), a 15th c. mansion altered in 1740 which was once the home of Lady Barnard, is now a museum.

Althorp (6 miles NW), residence of Earl Spencer, dates from 1573, with later alterations. Visitors can see an excellent collection of pictures, furniture and porcelain.

There is a beautiful road from Northampton through the Nene valley. 5 miles away is *Ecton*, a small village from which Benjamin Franklin's father emigrated to New England; some family tombs can still be seen. The road to Castle Ashby passes through *Earls Barton*, which has a church with a fine Saxon tower; the battlemented top is later.

Castle Ashby (6 miles E), seat of the marquess of Northampton, is an Elizabethan house with a façade of 1635 and an interesting stone balustrade lettered with the Latin text of Psalm 127. It has a beautiful park and a fine picture collection.

North Devon Coast

Western England. – County: Devon.

The *cliffs of North Devon are widely held to offer the finest cliff scenery in the whole of Britain. These slate formations on the Bristol Channel, differing in age and colour and often much weathered, are impressive in their grandiose beauty. This coastal area combines with the adjoining Exmoor, which rises to a height of 750 ft in Dunkery Beacon, to form a holiday region of great variety, from the lively seaside resorts on the Bristol Channel to the tiny and secluded villages in the heart of the moor.

Barnstaple (pop. 19,900; hotels – Imperial, C, 56 r.; Royal & Fortescue, D, 64 r.; North Devon Motel, D, 26 r.), on the Taw estuary, claims, on the strength of a charter granted in 830, to be the oldest town in England. With numerous hotels and guest-houses, it is a good centre from which to explore North Devon.

A 13th c. bridge spans the Taw estuary. The town, formerly a busy seaport, has the atmosphere of the 18th c., with many fine old buildings including the *Guildhall* (1826), *Horwood's Almshouses* (1674) in Church Lane, *Penrose Almshouses* (1627) in Litchdon Street and *Salem Almshouses* (1834) in Trinity Street. The parish church of *SS Peter and Paul*, unfortunately much altered during its restoration by George Gilbert Scott (1866–82), has a curious crooked spire (13th c.) and numerous 17th c. monuments. Also of interest is the *Colonnade* of the Bristol Merchant Venturers, built in 1708 as a stock exchange, with a statue of Queen Anne.

9 miles SW is **Bideford** (pop. 13,000; Riversford Hotel, D, 18 r.), another former seaport, situated on the estuary of the Torridge 3 miles from its mouth, and with many handsome houses of the 17th, 18th and early 19th c. The bridge, of 24 arches, was widened in 1925. St Mary's Church has a fine Norman font. On the picturesque quay, a relic of the time when Bideford carried on a thriving trade with America, is a statue of Charles Kingsley (1819–75), who wrote his famous novel "Westward Ho!" in a house which is now part of the Royal Hotel.

Westward Ho! (Buckleigh Grange Hotel, D, 14 r.), a seaside resort named after Kingsley's novel, lies 4 miles N on the Torridge estuary, on a road which runs through Appledore. It has a very fine sandy beach and a well known golf-course.

Lundy Island, also known as *Puffin Island*, is a windswept granite islet 11 miles off Hartland Point which can be reached by boat from Bideford. 3½ miles long and ½ mile wide, it has cliffs rising to 400 or 500 ft above the sea. It has interesting flora and fauna (bird reserves); seals rear their families on the rocky coast, and large numbers of lobsters are caught here. It has only a few buildings of any consequence – light-

Cliff scenery, Ilfracombe

houses, the remains of *Marisco Castle*, once a pirates' stronghold, Millcombe House (1836) and a church. It can also be reached from Ilfracombe and Barnstaple.

**Clovelly (pop. 450; Red Lion Hotel, E, 11 r.) is one of England's most renowned beauty spots, crowded with visitors in summer. Perched on a narrow ridge of rock which falls steeply away to the sea, it has steep and narrow streets – some of them stepped lanes – and cars are not admitted. A good view of the pretty little village can be had from the pier, or better still from a boat. The surroundings are also very beautiful. At the end of the village is Yellary Gate, the entrance to the grounds of Clovelly Court, with attractive walks through delightful scenery, a round trip of some 5 miles and a shorter trip of 3 miles along Hobby Drive.

N of Barnstaple, on the *Bristol Channel*, are a series of popular seaside resorts and much beautiful scenery. Particularly attractive is the coast road from Barnstaple to Ilfracombe, which runs past *Saunton Sands* (good bathing). To the S are *Braunton Burrows*, an area of sand-dunes with interesting fauna and flora.

Woolacombe (17 miles) is a pleasant seaside resort with a sandy beach 2 miles long. From the coast project *Baggy Point*, *Morte Point* and *Bull Point*, with striking rock formations. The little resort of **Mortehoe** has a 12th–13th c. church which has preserved some old stalls.

Ilfracombe (pop. 10,000; hotels – Langleigh Country, D, 10 r.; St Helier, E, 32 r.; Torrs, E, 14 r.) is the oldest established and most popular seaside resort on the North Devon coast, with a picturesque harbour and good bathing beaches sheltered by towering cliffs. The town, largely built in the last third of the 19th c., differs from other resorts in having been built between hills, the beaches being reached through tunnels in the rock. The old chapel of St Nicholas, on a crag above the harbour, has been converted into a lighthouse. W of the town is the attractive *Torrs Walk*.

The beautiful coast road continues E to *Watermouth Castle*, with fine subtropical gardens, and **Combe Martin** (Pack of Cards Inn, 1752), a straggling village with disused silver mines. From here A 399 turns inland on to *Exmoor*, most of which is now a National Park. Much of the area is cultivated, but there are still expanses of moorland and heath. The road passes *Parracombe* (on left), with a charming old church, and comes to **Lynton** (Lynbridge youth hostel, 38 b.) and **Lynmouth** (pop 2000; Tors Hotel, D, 38 r.). Lynmouth lies on the coast, Lynton 400 ft above sea level near the point where the East and West Lyn join before flowing into the sea. The old word *llyn* means "rushing stream" and the River Lyn certainly lived up to its name in the great flood of 1952 which destroyed much of Lynmouth, so that the town had to be almost entirely rebuilt. Lynton has largely preserved its Victorian character. Although this is a popular resort, the bathing is not particularly good. The beauty of the surrounding country, however, more than makes up for this, particularly attractive spots being the *Valley of Rocks, Woody Bay* and *Waters-meet*. Beyond this is the county boundary: the rest of the coast is in Somerset.

North Downs

Southern England. – Counties: Surrey and Kent.

The North Downs are a ridge of high ground which extends across Surrey and Kent, S of London, from Guildford in the W to Dover and Folkestone in the E. The word "downs" is related to "dunes", and the Downs do indeed sometimes resemble dunes, though they are formed of chalk rather than sand, terminating magnificently in the chalk cliffs of Dover. They were formed in the Tertiary Age, at the same time as

the Alps; but the fringes of the earth movements which thrust the Alps steeply upwards here created a series of gentle ridges running parallel to the coast. This is true of both the North and the South Downs.

To the W, near Guildford, runs the narrow ridge known as the *Hog's Back*. To the E the North Downs increase steadily in height, reaching some 900 ft on the Kent border. The North Downs are popular with walkers, especially at weekends, offering great variety of scenery – pastureland, fertile arable land, occasional areas of heath and scrub and patches of mixed forest – so that they never become monotonous. Five rivers have broken their way through this chalk barrier, and in the valleys lie trim little villages, often surrounded by fruit orchards. Many old trading and pilgrims' roads run over the Downs or along the foot of the hills, often now followed by footpaths. Only the most enthusiastic walkers will want to explore the whole length of the Downs, but it is well worth while making visits to some of the more attractive spots.

Guildford (pop. 60,000; hotels – Angel, B, 25 r.; White Horse, C, 40 r.; Quinns, D, 11 r.), in Surrey, is a good base for the western part of the North Downs. Formerly the county town, it is still a favoured residential and shopping town. The *High Street* is one of the steepest and most picturesque in England, with a number of interesting old buildings. At the top of the street is the *Grammar School*, founded by Edward VI in 1553, with fine Tudor buildings and a library containing chained books. Next comes *Abbot's Hospital*, with a large gatehouse and old furniture, founded by George Abbot, Archbishop of Canterbury, in 1619–22 for 12 men and eight women. The *Town Hall*, a brick and timber building with a famous clock, was given a new façade in 1683. *St Mary's Church*, near the foot of the hill, is mainly Late Norman (c. 1180). Little is left of the old royal castle but the keep (c. 1170). The Castle Archway is now a local museum.

Charles Lutwidge Dodgson (1832–98), the professor of mathematics who is better known as Lewis Carroll, author of "Alice in Wonderland", died in a house on Castle Hill, "The Chestnuts". The town also has a number of interesting new buildings, including the Cathedral, one of England's few new cathedrals. The foundation stone was laid in 1936, but as a result of the war the church was not completed and consecrated until 1961. It contains some fine sculpture and wood-carving. Also new are the University, on Stag Hill, and the Yvonne Arnaud Theatre on the banks of the Wey, completed in 1965.

Around Guildford are a number of very beautiful estates. 3 miles away is *Clandon Park*, a Palladian house (1731) with fine plaster decoration and valuable furniture. 8 miles NW are the Royal Horticultural Society's gardens at *Wisley*.

Some of the most beautiful parts of the North Downs are seen by taking the Leatherhead road (A 246) as far as *Merrow* and then bearing right to *Newlands Corner*, from which there is a good view of the Weald, a level expanse with pleasant scenery.

Beyond this is **Albury** (4 miles), with *Albury Park*, residence of the Duchess of Northumberland. The house, rebuilt by Pugin, contains a valuable collection of pictures and clocks, and has 64 chimneypieces, all different.

A mile or two E is the village of *Abinger Hammer*. The "Abinger Hammer" is a clock with the figure of a blacksmith, recalling the old water-driven forging mills which once worked here. From here a beautiful road runs over the Downs to *Leith Hill* (965 ft), from the top of which it is supposed to be possible to see London.

5 miles farther on is **Dorking** (pop. 23,000; hotels – White Horse, B, 70 r.; Burford Bridge, B, 53 r.), on the River Mole. Near the town is *Box Hill* (590 ft), with numerous beeches as well as the box trees from which it takes its name. In summer it draws large numbers of visitors, attracted by the beautiful view. Part of the area belongs to the National Trust, including *Flint Cottage*, in which the novelist George Meredith (1828–1909) lived for over 30 years until his death. *Juniper Hall* offered a refuge to many French refugees during the Revolution, including Mme de Stael (1766–1817). 3 miles NW is the mansion of *Polesden Lacey*, with the fine *Greville collection of pictures, tapestries and furniture. – Another good centre from which to explore the North Downs and the Weald is **Tunbridge Wells**, officially *Royal Tunbridge Wells* (pop. 44,800; hotels – Spa, C, 70 r.; Wellington, D, 55 r.; Beacon, D, 9 r.; Royal Wells Inn, E, 15 r.), whose chalybeate springs made it a much frequented spa in the 18th c. Its principal feature is the Pantiles, a colonnaded promenade where visitors drank the waters. The town is beautifully situated, and there are many places of interest within easy reach. – Another possible base is *Sevenoaks* (pop. 20,000; hotel – Seven Oaks Post House, 120 r.), also attractively situated in the Greensand Hills. Adjoining Sevenoaks School, founded in 1432, is the entrance to Knole Park.

*Knole, home of the Sackville family, is one of the largest and finest country houses in England. Begun in 1456 by Thomas Bourchier, archbishop of Canterbury, and considerably enlarged in 1603 by Thomas Sackville, first earl of Dorset, it has remained practically unaltered both externally and internally since then. The state apartments, with their magnificent furniture, pictures, tapestries, silver, etc., are open to visitors, as is the beautiful park.

From here or from Tunbridge Wells it is only a few miles to **Chiddingstone**, a pretty little place with 16th and 17th c. houses, the old Castle Inn and a fine parish church. The pseudo-medieval Chiddingstone Castle contains a variety of collections, including Stuart relics.

Hever Castle dates from the 13th–15th c., but was rebuilt in Gothic style in 1810. Anne Boleyn lived here as a girl, and her father's tomb is in the church. The Castle preserves the original drawbridge.

Ightham Mote is another old mansion, with a moat, a 15th c. gate tower, a 14th c. great hall and a 16th c. chapel. In the village of Plaxtol is *Old Soar Manor*, which incorporates part of a 13th c. knight's house.

In the pretty little town of *Penshurst* (5 miles from Tunbridge Wells) is the magnificent grey stone mansion of *Penshurst Place, seat of Viscount De l'Isle and Dudley. The main part of the house dates from about 1340, the N and W fronts and the King's Tower from 1585. The great hall with its life-size figures is particularly fine.

Also within easy reach of Tunbridge Wells is **Goudhurst** (pop. 2700; Star and Eagle Hotel, D, 11 r.; youth hostel, Twyssenden Manor, 54 b.), picturesquely situated on a hill, with a village pond with swans, and wide views over the rolling country of the Weald (many fruit orchards and hopfields). The church contains interesting monuments. 2 miles S, in *Bedgebury*, is a fine *Pinetum*, a branch of Kew Gardens.

$2\frac{1}{2}$ miles S is **Cranbrook** (pop. 4300; Willesley Hotel, D, 16 r.), an old weavers' town with one of the largest windmills in England, a church rebuilt in 1430 and a school founded in 1576.

Near Cranbrook is Sissinghurst, with *Sissinghurst Castle*, part of a Tudor mansion dating from before 1550, with beautiful gardens. – A short distance away is the pleasant little village of *Biddenden*, where Siamese twins were born about 1500. In memory of these "maids of Biddenden" cakes stamped with a representation of the twins are still eaten here on Easter Monday.

North-East Coast

Northern England. – Counties: Humberside, North Yorkshire, Cleveland, Durham, Tyne and Wear Northumberland.

The NE coast of England extends from N of the Humber to the Scottish border. With one or two exceptions, the seaside resorts here are newer and less popular than those on other stretches of coast. They are less favoured by climate than the resorts in the south of England, but they have the advantage of being less crowded, except perhaps at weekends, and some of them have preserved their original character and charm. Travelling along this coast, visitors will encounter many small resorts in addition to those mentioned here, together with camping sites, holiday villages mushrooming here and there, and many weekend houses.

Withernsea is a resort favoured by the people of Hull, with a sandy beach which extends, with interruptions, for miles along the coast. There is little to interest the tourist in the town itself, but there are two fine churches within easy reach, at *Hedon* (14 miles) and *Patrington*. The church at Hedon, with a Decorated nave, an Early English choir and transepts and a Perpendicular tower, is known as the "King of Holderness" (the rich corn-growing area on the plain E of Hull). The Patrington church, with a tall spire, is mainly Decorated; it is known as the "Queen of Holderness".

Bridlington (pop. 28,600; hotels Expanse, D, 50 r.; Monarch, D, 43 r. Langdon, E, 20 r.) is a seaside resort with a long beach which extends S for almost the whole length of Bridlington Bay. The town is a mixture of old and new: among its old buildings are the Priory Church begun in the reign of Henry I, and the Bayle Gate (1388), now a museum.

South Beach, Scarborough

Ruins of Whitby Abbey

Scarborough (pop. 43,500; hotels – Crown, C, 84 r.; Holbeck Hall, C, 30 r.; St Nicholas, D, 166 r.; Royal, D, 137 r.; Clifton, D, 70 r.; Brooklands, D, 52 r.; Mayfair, D, 19 r.; Avoncroft, E, 32 r.; Crescent, E, 25 r.; youth hostel, White House, Burniston Road, 70 b.) is the best-known resort on this stretch of coast, called the "Queen of the Yorkshire Coast" because of its beautiful sandy beaches. It has been the leading seaside resort in the north of England since 1734, and still preserves its Victorian character. It is well supplied with parks and gardens, cafés and entertainments of all kinds. On the headland between the two beaches are the *Castle*, with a 12th c. keep, and *St Mary's Church* (12th–13th c., Transitional and Early English). Anne Brontë (1820–49) is buried in the churchyard. From Oliver's Mount (500 ft) there is a good view of the town.

Whitby (pop. 13,800; hotels – Saxonville, D, 22 r.; Langley, D, 15 r.; youth hostel, East Cliff, 66 b.), an old seaport and now a popular holiday resort, has magnificent beaches of fine sand, extending to Robin Hood's Bay and beyond. The River Esk flows between the older and newer parts of the town. Whitby was formerly an important whaling station. Captain Cook served as an apprentice in a house in Grape Lane, now occupied by an antique shop. The best view of the town and the coast is to be had from the inappropriately named Khyber Pass. Above the harbour stands the old *Castle*. *Whitby Abbey*, founded in 657, was the venue of the famous Synod of Whitby (664). After being destroyed by the Danes the Abbey was rebuilt in 1078. On the edge of the cliff are the picturesque ruins of the church, mainly Early English in style.

From Whitby the coast road continues to *Sandsend*, where a long-distance swimming race to Whitby is held annually in summer, and *Saltburn-by-the-Sea*, a seaside resort favoured by rheumatic sufferers. Then follows a beautiful stretch of road, with the magnificent *Boulby Cliffs*, to **Redcar** (Newbigging Hotel, D, 28 r.), a resort with a mile-long beach, a lively promenade 3 miles in length, a racecourse and a wide range of entertainments. It also has a museum devoted to fishing and sea rescue.

The next resort of any size is **Tynemouth** (pop. 50,000; hotel – Grand, D, 39 r.), now joined up with *South Shields*, *North Shields* and *Newcastle*, a residential town which is also much frequented at weekends by the inhabitants of its industrial neighbours. There are many rocks along the coast, and on an outlying crag surrounded by water are the remains of the Castle (restored) and the ruins of the Priory Church (c. 1090), with a fine Early English choir and the completely preserved Percy Chapel (15th c.).

Whitley Bay (pop. 37,300; hotels – Ambassador, C, 28 r.; Croglin, D, 40 r.), with *Cullercoats*, has a much more attractive beach. It is a very modern resort, with excellent facilities for sport, recreation and entertainment. 3 miles N is *Seaton Sluice*, inland from which is **Seaton Delaval Hall**, seat of Lord Hastings, a gigantic Palladian house built by Vanbrugh in 1718–29 which contains an excellent collection of furniture, pictures and documents. – The road continues via *Blyth*, at the mouth of the River Blyth, one of the country's largest coal-shipping ports, and the pretty little village of *Bedlington*,

Bamburgh Castle

which gave its name to the Bedlington terrier, to the seaside resort of **Newbiggin-by-the-Sea**, with cliffs, a sandy beach and an impressive church (St Bartholomew's, 13th c.).

The next stretch of coast, 40 miles long, between Amble and *Berwick* is designated as an area of outstanding natural beauty. The little town of *Amble* is noted for its salmon and for its boatbuilding.

Warkworth (Sun Hotel, D, 15 r.) is prettily situated in a loop of the River Coquet. The Castle, founded in 1139, has a later keep which is well preserved, although roofless. St Laurence's Church is largely Norman. From here the road continues via *Lesbury*, with a medieval bridge, to **Alnmouth**, a trim seaside resort and yachting centre. $3\frac{1}{2}$ miles inland is **Alnwick** (pop. 7000; hotels – White Swan, D, 40 r.; Hotspur, D, 29 r.), a little town of medieval aspect situated high above the River Aln. Alnwick Castle, seat of the Duke of Northumberland, is a well-preserved example of a medieval fortress (1309), with many handsome rooms and a collection of Roman and British antiquities. – Also worth seeing are the remains of *Hulne Priory*, a Carmelite foundation of 1240, and the parish church, *St Michael's*, an outstanding example of Perpendicular architecture (15th c.) with fine Victorian stained glass. – The road to the fishing village and seaside resort of Seahouses runs past *Dunstanburgh Castle*, begun in 1314. Here, with luck, visitors may find some of the coloured quartz crystals known as "Dunstanburgh diamonds"

which are used in the manufacture of souvenirs.

From **Seahouses** and the neighbouring village of Bamburgh there are motorboat trips to the uninhabited *Farne Islands*, a group of some 30 dolerite islets lying between $1\frac{1}{2}$ and 5 miles offshore, now a bird reserve. More than 30 species of birds nest on the islands, which are also the home of seals. During the nesting season only a few of the islands are open to visitors. St Cuthbert spent eight years here as a hermit.

Bamburgh (Lord Crewe Arms Hotel, C, 26 r.), once capital of the kingdom of Bernicia, is a pleasant little seaside resort (pop. 700). The enormous *Castle with its Norman keep is largely the product of a thorough restoration in the 18th c. St Aidan's Church has a very fine crypt and a beautiful 13th c. choir. The popular 19th c. heroine, Grace Darling (1815–42), who rowed out with her father, the lighthouse-keeper, to save the crew of the ship-wrecked *Forfarshire*, is buried in the churchyard.

11 miles farther N is *Beal*, from which a boat can be taken to ***Lindisfarne** or **Holy Island**. At low tide it is possible to walk or drive out to the island on a causeway ($2\frac{3}{4}$ miles).

Lindisfarne is known as the Holy Island because it was one of the earliest centres of Christianity in England. St Aidan was sent from Iona to convert the people of Northumbria to the Christian faith, and built a small monastery on the island, but after a raid by the Danes the monks fled, taking with them the remains of St Cuthbert, sixth bishop here. In 1093 a Benedictine priory was founded on Lindisfarne, with a magnificent church of which remains dating from that period still survive. Most of the church is Late Norman (1140–50). The Castle, originally 16th c., was rebuilt in 1902. Part of the island is a bird reserve.

The most northerly town in England is **Berwick-upon-Tweed** (pop. 12,000; hotels – King's Arms, D, 39 r.; Turret House, D, 10 r.), an old frontier town which over a period of 300 years changed its allegiance 13 times. For a time it was Scotland's principal seaport. Three large bridges span the Tweed, on the northern bank of which the town is situated; the Old Bridge, with 15 arches, was built in 1610–34, the Royal Border Bridge by Robert Stephenson in 1847–50.

Old Bridge, Berwick-upon-Tweed

The main tourist feature of the town is the *Elizabethan ramparts, which still enclose Berwick on the E and N. In their day a model of the kind, they were built on the orders of Elizabeth I in 1558–60 to provide protection from a threatened French invasion. With their five bastions, they are unique in Britain. Most of *Berwick Castle* was demolished to make way for a railway station, and only a few fragments have survived. There is an attractive little *Town Hall* (1754–66), with a bell-tower and a peal of bells. The Barracks are the oldest in Britain (1717–21). The coastal scenery is very fine, with rocks and cliffs only occasionally interrupted by small bays and harbours. Berwick's bathing beach is in the little seaside resort of *Spittal*, to the S.

North of Scotland

Region: Highland.

This area covers the northern third of Scotland, separated from the rest of the country by Glen More, the Great Glen, a tremendous geological fault which cuts across Scotland from coast to coast, from Loch Linnhe in the W to the Moray Firth in the E. The crust of the earth has not

Fort Augustus, Caledonian Canal

finally settled down in this region, and minor tremors are still occasionally felt.

This geological structure facilitated the construction in the first half of the 19th c. of the **Caledonian Canal** (by Telford, 1803–49), designed to enable small vessels to avoid the long and sometimes dangerous voyage by way of the Pentland Firth, between the northernmost tip of the Scottish mainland and the Orkney Islands. For most of the way it was possible to use the long narrow lochs which now occupy the fault, and only a third of the total length of the canal had to be cut through land. From W to E these lochs are *Loch Linnhe*, a fjord-like arm of the sea; *Loch Lochy*; the little *Loch Oich*; and the longest (24 miles) and best known, *Loch Ness*. The Canal, which no longer serves its original purpose but is much used by pleasure boats and canoeists, has a total length of just over 60 miles; it is 16 ft deep and has 29 locks. The most difficult part of the canal-builders' task was to overcome the difference in height between Loch Linnhe, at sea level, and Loch Lochy, which lay 93 ft higher. This was achieved by a triumph of early 19th c. engineering, a series of eight locks known as Neptune's Staircase. The terminal points of the Canal are Fort William and Inverness (which are also linked by a good road).

Fort William (pop. 4300; hotels – Ladbroke, C, 61 r.; Croit Anna, D, 100 r.; Imperial, D, 38 r.; Grand, D, 33 r.; Innseagan Guest, D, 26 r.) is the main base for climbers of Ben Nevis; it is a busy town with numerous hotels and guesthouses. The fort after which the town is named has long since disappeared. A very beautiful panoramic road, the "Road to the Isles", runs from here to Mallaig (42

Ben Nevis, Britain's highest mountain

miles), from which there are ferry services to Skye.

The area's main attraction is *Ben Nevis, Britain's highest mountain (4406 ft), a bare mass of rock which is bathed in a reddish glow at sunrise and sunset. The climb is not difficult if the path from *Achintee Farm* (2½ miles) is followed; it takes about 2½ hours. Every year in September there is a race up Ben Nevis; the present record stands at 106 minutes. There is a longer and more difficult route by way of Allt a Mhuilinn and the neighbouring summit, *Carn More Dearg, affording views of breathtaking beauty.

On the summit are the remains of a weather station and a refuge hut, which many years ago was a restaurant. The top is fairly flat, and is covered with loose stones of varying shape and size. To the S it falls away gently at first and then steeply down into Glen Nevis. To the E is a grandiose ridge 1½ miles long and some 2000 ft high. The gullies on the NE side are almost always filled with snow. The **view from the summit in clear weather is of overwhelming magnificence, extending in all directions for anything up to 150 miles. Almost all the mountains of Scotland and Ireland are within sight, and stretches of coast and islands as well. Many climbers start their climb in the evening and spend the night on the top in order to see the sun rise. Unfortunately the view – and the climb – may often be spoiled by mist; and in general changes in weather conditions are a constant hazard even on this relatively simple climb. Every year climbers get into difficulty on Ben Nevis, usually because they are inadequately clad or equipped.

Some of the best and longest climbs are on the NE face, but these are for experienced climbers only. The Scottish Mountaineering Club publishes guides to the climbs. – There are a number of theories about the meaning of the name Nevis. The most probable is that it means "snow-capped" – an interpretation which is confirmed by the facts, at least on many days in the year.

The *road from Fort William to Inverness is one of the most beautiful panoramic roads in the country. The first stretch, to *Spean Bridge*, affords magnificent *views of the N face of Ben Nevis. Here large-scale engineering works have been carried out to use the water of Loch Treig for the production of hydroelectric

power. Spean Bridge is a good base for rewarding walks up Glen Roy. There are also bus services from here, but there have been no boat services on the Caledonian Canal since the last war.

On the shores of **Loch Lochy** are the two castles of *Inverlochy*, old and new, and a whisky distillery, one of the many to be seen in this part of Scotland. At the junction with the road to Gairlochy is the impressive *Commando Memorial*. To the left, beyond Gairlochy, is **Loch Arkaig**, with a cave in which Prince Charlie hid during his flight after Culloden. The road then continues along **Loch Oich**, the prettiest of the lochs in this region, with a background of steep hills and a scatter of islets on the loch. A curious monument over the *Well of the Heads* (Tobar nan

In Glen Nevis

Loch Ness, with Urquhart Castle

Nessie, the friendly monster of Loch Ness

Ceann) commemorates a bloody incident in the 17th c. when the heads of seven murderers were washed in the well before being presented to a chief of the Macdonell clan.

Invergarry (Glengarry Castle Hotel, D, 30 r.) is a popular base for walkers and anglers. From here a magnificent road (A 87) runs NW past Loch Garry and through Glen Shiel to *Kyle of Lochalsh*,

from which there is a ferry service to **Skye** (p. 119).

Fort Augustus (pop. 1000), at the beginning of Loch Ness, is also a popular tourist centre. The fort from which it takes its name was built in 1715. Much of it was incorporated in the Benedictine abbey built here in 1876, with a school of considerable reputation. From Fort Augustus there is a strenuous but very

Eilean Donan Castle, Loch Duich

rewarding walk over the *Corrieyairack pass* (2507 ft) to *Laggan*, a distance of 25 miles with no overnight accommodation on the way.

The main road to Inverness (A 82) runs along the N side of Loch Ness, with a minor road on the S side. The latter, which passes through *Foyers*, with the magnificent Falls of Foyers, offers the more attractive scenery of the two, but both roads are well wooded. Doubts about the existence of the Loch Ness monster are, of course, not permitted in this area, which draws its main tourist attraction from the monster – for there are many Highland lochs more beautiful than Loch Ness. The road on the N side runs past the ruins of the 12th c. *Urquhart Castle*, on a tongue of land projecting into the loch, and comes to Drumnadrochit, to the S of which are the *Falls of Divach*. At the NE end of Loch Ness is *Aldourie Castle*, and at Dochgarroch begins the last section of the Caledonian Canal, which 3 miles farther on flows into the Moray Firth.

Inverness (pop. 41,000; hotels – Culloden House, A, 20 r.; Ladbroke, C, 96 r.; Station, C, 65 r.; Kingsmills, C, 54 r.; Royal, C, 48 r.; Caledonian, D, 120 r.;

Inverness Castle

Drumossie, D, 81 r.) is the chief town of the Highland Region. In earlier times it was the capital of a Pictish kingdom. It is a busy and popular tourist centre in the holiday season, particularly at the time of the Inverness Highland Games in July. The imposing red sandstone buildings of Inverness Castle are occupied by local government offices; the castle of Macbeth's time probably stood farther E. Opposite Castle Hill is *St Andrew's Cathedral*. Other attractions of Inverness are the beautiful islands in the River Ness, all connected with one another and with the banks of the river by bridges; the cemetery on the hill of *Tomnahurich*; *Craig Phadrig* (550 ft), with a fine view and the remains of a prehistoric hill-fort; and the very interesting Museum. The battlefield of *Culloden* lies 6 miles E; about 30 miles farther E are the ruins of *Elgin Cathedral* (1224).

A road runs N from Inverness, following the coast for most of the way, to Scotland's most north-easterly point, *John o' Groats*, and Thurso. From Inverness it borders the Beauly Firth to **Beauly**, so called (French *beau lieu*, "beautiful place") because of the picturesque situation of a priory built here by French monks in the 13th c. The remains include the W doorway and three fine triangular windows. The road then cuts across the **Black Isle*, which is green rather than black and not an island but a peninsula, between the Beauly and Cromarty Firths. It is the best farming area in the Highlands. The largest place on the Black Isle is **Fortrose**, once a considerable port but now mainly a holiday resort with a good golf-course. The 15th c. bell in the belltower of the ruined abbey is still rung every evening. Of the small Cathedral the main surviving part is the chapterhouse. *Rosemarkie*, now part of Fortrose, is a still older foundation, the site of a 6th c. monastic school. In 1125 David I made it an episcopal see later transferred to Fortrose.

Continuing N from Beauly, A 9 passes through *Muir of Ord* and *Conon Bridge*, at the head of the Cromarty Firth, and comes to **Dingwall** (pop. 4400; hotel – National, C, 42 r.) an old town granted the status of a royal burgh in 1226, formerly the county town of Ross and Cromarty, with an excellent school. The *Town House* dates from 1730. Near the church is an obelisk commemorating the first earl of Cromarty. 5 miles NE is Foulis Castle.

Wick harbour

Dingwall is an important road and rail junction, with a very beautiful road branching off and running NW to Braemore Forest, where it divides, one branch going to *Dundonnell* and the other to *Ullapool* (see below, p. 208). – The main road continues NE via *Alness*, with the Black Rock of Novar, to *Invergordon*, once an important naval base. After leaving Ballchraggan the road passes close to the little farming town of *Fearn* (on right), with the ruins of a Premonstratensian abbey church whose roof fell in during a service in 1742, and comes to **Tain**, a former royal burgh which is now a pleasant holiday resort on the Dornoch Firth. It has a fine *Tolbooth* with a conical roof and the 14th c. *St Duthus Church*. The ruined St Duthus Chapel was once a popular place of pilgrimage. – Beyond Tain the road makes a wide sweep round the *Dornoch Firth*.

Dornoch (pop. 1100) is a pretty little town with a much restored 13th c. cathedral (arcading, fine W window). Of the old castle, formerly the bishop's palace, there remains only the tower. The town has good bathing beaches and golf-courses. 5 miles W is *Skibo Castle*, a favourite residence of the Scottish-born American steel king Andrew Carnegie (1835–1919), who gave 350 million dollars for educational, scientific and charitable purposes, founding numerous Carnegie Institutes; he built the castle in 1898.

From Dornoch the road, in places running close to the sea, continues to *Golspie* (pop. 1400), with a good beach and an interesting church, and *Dunrobin Castle*, which has a 13th c. tower and contains a

good collection of pictures. The park and gardens are very attractive.

Brora (pop. 1800), at the mouth of the river of the same name, is a popular fishing centre and seaside resort. To the W is *Loch Brora*, with the 650-ft-high *Carrol Rock* and several smaller lochs. A small coal-mine in the town, which now belongs to the miners themselves, scarcely spoils its amenity.

12 miles NE is **Helmsdale** (youth hostel, 38 b.), a fishing village with a sheltered harbour and a 15th c. castle. 7 miles short of Helmsdale, close to the road, is a very well-preserved broch (defensive tower), and there is another a short distance beyond the village. The next stretch of road, to Berriedale (10 miles), is steep and winding, but scenically interesting, with numerous hills and ravines. *Berriedale* is beautifully situated, with a ruined castle below which the Langwell and Berriedale Waters flow into the sea. Inland, some distance away, can be seen the peaks of *Morven* (2313 ft) and *Scaraben* (2055 ft). Permission to climb these mountains must be obtained in Berriedale.

Dunbeath (pop. 490), a fishing village with a fine broch and a 15th c. castle, and *Latheron*, with an old bell-tower and a prehistoric standing stone, seem lost in this hilly region, littered with ruined castles, some of them no more than shapeless heaps of stone. 2 miles N of Latheron is *Forse*, with another ruined castle and the remains of a primitive settlement dating from early in the Christian era.

The road continues through the villages of *Lybster*, *Clyth* and *Thrumster*, to **Wick** (pop. 7000; hotels – Station, C, 54 r.; Ladbroke, C, 48 r.), a herring-fishing centre with an interesting harbour, particularly during the summer fishing season. Along the rocky coast near the town are numerous castles. To the S are the ruins of the *Castle of Old Wick*, a natural rock arch known as the *Brig o' Tram* and a tower called the *Old Man of Wick*. To the N are the remains of *Castle Girnigoe* and *Castle Sinclair*, perched on the cliff-top, and *Ackergill Tower*. – From Wick the main road continues to Thurso, running inland in a north-westerly direction. However, the coast road runs N, past *Noss Head*, to Sinclair's Bay, passing through *Reiss* and *Keiss*. N of Keiss in the 16th c. *Bucholly Castle*. At **John o' Groats** we come to the most northerly place in Scotland which is accessible by road. The extreme north-easterly point is 2 miles farther on, at *Duncansby Head*. At John o' Groats itself there is little to see: the house which belonged to John o' Groats has long since been destroyed, and he himself is buried in Canisbay churchyard. – From the cliffs there is a fine view of the Orkney Islands.

Ben Loyal

Thurso

Thurso, the most northerly railway station in Britain, has beautiful views, a ruined castle and the ruins of a 13th c. bishop's palace. The town was once the centre of a flourishing trade in Caithness flagstones, but this no longer exists. The Museum is of interest for the collection of stones and fossils assembled by the local geologist Robert Dick (1811–66). From the nearby harbour of *Scrabster* there is a car ferry service to the Orkney Islands and in summer to the Faroe Islands.

There are beautiful roads along the N and W coasts; the former keeping close to the sea for most of the way, the latter running farther inland to avoid the numerous indentations of the coast. There are also very attractive roads running inland from E to W, often following the little rivers which traverse these northern Highlands and passing numerous lochs of all sizes. One of the larger of these lochs is *Loch Shin* (15 miles long by 2 miles across), which serves for the production of hydro-electric power but also offers good fishing and water sports. At the S end of the loch is **Lairg** (pop. 950), from which there are roads running N and W. To the N is *Loch Naver*, with *Altnaharra*, a good centre for hill walking and fishing, and farther N *Loch Loyal* and the massive bulk

of *Ben Loyal* with its four peaks. Nearer Lairg is *Ben Kilbreck* (3154 ft). There is also a very beautiful road NW along Loch Shin, *Loch Merkland*, *Loch More* and *Loch Stack* to *Scourie* (44 miles). All these lochs afford good fishing; Loch More and Loch Stack are splendidly situated amid mountains ranging from 2300 to 2800 ft.

One of the most popular holiday resorts in the NW Highlands is **Ullapool** (pop. 800; hotels – Ladbroke Mercury Motor Inn, C, 60 r.; Royal, D, 60 r.; Harbour Lights Motel, D, 22 r.; youth hostel in Shore Street, 88 b.), a picturesque fishing village on sheltered *Loch Broom*. From here there is a ferry service to *Stornoway* on the island of Lewis. At the mouth of Loch Broom are the beautiful *Summer Isles*. Ullapool is a good base for exploring some of the most extraordinary scenery in Britain, between Loch Broom and Loch Assynt – a landscape of bizarrely formed peaks rising sheer from the plain, interspersed with numerous lochs.

Loch Maree and Slioch

There is a good road to this area via Ledmore, but the scenery is even wilder and more beautiful on the *Inverkirkaig* road (with the Kirkaig Falls, 2 miles S). The backdrop of mountains changes all the time, as *Ben More Coigach* (2438 ft), *Cul Beag* (2523 ft) and *An Stac*, usually called *Stac Polly* (2009 ft), present themselves in different aspects. These are mountains for rock climbers rather than hill walkers. Then, beyond *Loch Lurgain* and *Loch Bad a Ghaill*, *Cul Mor* (2787 ft) and *Suilven* (2399 ft), from certain points of view resembling a huge sugarloaf, come into view. *Loch Assynt*, noted for its trout, is also surrounded by mountains. The road along the N side of this loch is one of the most beautiful in Scotland, with a magnificent backdrop of mountains and ruined castles. Round *Lochinver* there are said to be no fewer than 280 lochs, many of them having no name, which offer excellent fishing. The climate here is very mild, and subtropical plants flourish in *Inverewe Gardens* (National Trust) near *Poolewe*, 5 miles N of *Gairloch*. – From Ullapool there is a good road to **Braemore**, with the magnificent *Corrieshalloch Gorge* and the 150-ft-high *Measach Falls* (best seen from the bridge).

North Wales

North Wales, one of Britain's oldest established tourist regions, offers an abundance of holiday attractions within a relatively small area. Llandudno was one of the earliest seaside resorts to become popular, and the North Welsh coast offers a great variety of scenery, with its spacious beaches and lively bathing resorts, its rugged cliffs, its little fishing villages and secluded bays. Snowdonia, with Wales' highest mountain, Snowdon (3560 ft), has for centuries attracted climbers and walkers, and among much else that awaits discovery by visitors are the Lleyn peninsula, designated as an area of outstanding natural beauty, and many attractive towns and villages and beautiful valleys.

There is an interesting coast road which runs from the wide Dee estuary to the Menai Bridge linking Anglesey with the mainland and continues, bypassing the Lleyn peninsula, into Cardigan Bay.

Entering North Wales from Chester, the road runs alongside the Dee estuary through a heavily industrialised area to **Flint**, an old town which was granted a charter by Edward I in 1284. Edward also built the castle (now ruined), which has an unusual plan with a separate keep surrounded by a moat. The castle features in Shakespeare's "Richard II" as the scene of the king's capture by Bolingbroke.

At the *Point of Air*, at the mouth of the estuary (lighthouse), begins a stretch of coast, with sandy beaches and good bathing, which extends to beyond Llanfairfechan. Frequently the beaches are bordered by sand-dunes, and there are numerous lively resorts with ample facilities for entertainment and sport, pony and donkey rides, shops, seafront promenades and small yachting harbours. Among them are *Prestatyn*, *Rhyl*, with a promenade 3 miles long, *Kinmel Bay* and a whole series of popular resorts in the wide sweep of Colwyn Bay, including the town of *Colwyn Bay itself, with its annual fishing festival, *Rhos-on-Sea* and *Llandudno*.

From Rhyl an excursion can be made to **St Asaph** (pop. 2800; Oriel House Hotel, C, 19 r.), a little town between the rivers Clwyd and Elwy in the wide Clwyd valley. It has a charming little *Cathedral*, the smallest medieval cathedral in Britain, originally the church of Llanelwy abbey. The see was probably established by St Asaph himself (d. about 596). Although the church was burned down by Owen Glendower in 1402 and rebuilt in the 18th–19th c. it has largely preserved its Decorated style of 1284–1381. The massive square tower dates from 1715 (fine views from the top). The Cathedral contains a monument to Bishop Morgan and other bishops who translated the Bible into Welsh in the reign of Elizabeth I, and a collection of early Bibles and prayerbooks.

Llandudno (pop. 20,000; hotels – Marine, C, 79 r.; New Style Imperial, D, 142 r.; Ormescliffe, D, 65 r.; Baby Tree, D, 55 r.; Somerset, D, 37 r.; Tan Lan, D, 19 r.; Bromwell Court, D, 12 r.) is one of the most popular seaside resorts in Wales, with two sandy beaches, one on either side of the town, separated by the limestone promontory of Great Orme Head. The more easterly of the two beaches, North Shore, is bounded by

Conwy Castle

Little Orme. There is an original Victorian promenade, and in summer there is a full programme of concerts and other entertainments.

Great Orme Head can be reached by road, tramway or cable-car. The Headland rises to 679 ft but seems even higher, towering directly out of the sea. **Little Orme Head**, though lower (463 ft), offers more beautiful cliff scenery.

W of Llandudno is *Conwy Bay*, also mainly sandy. **Conwy** itself (pop. 13,000; Castle Hotel, C, 25 r.), situated at the mouth of the River Conwy, is one of the most attractive towns in Wales. It has preserved an almost complete circuit of walls, with four gates and 21 semicircular towers, and the imposing remains of *Conwy Castle, which are particularly picturesque when seen from the river. This massive fortress was built by some 2000 workmen for Edward I in 1283–88. In 1290 it was besieged by Welsh forces, but was finally relieved. It also played its part in later wars. The walls are between 12 and 15 ft thick and it has eight sturdy towers. The Great Hall, 125 ft long, is now roofless, but one of the eight arches which supported the roof has been rebuilt to show the beauty of the structure. The *King's Tower* contains a very beautiful oratory.

St Mary's Church, in the centre of the town, occupies the site of an earlier Cistercian abbey and dates mainly from the 13th c. Notable features are the W doorway, a 15th c. font and the monument of Nicholas Hookes, his father's 41st child and himself the father of 27 children. *Plas Mawr*, now occupied by the Cambrian Academy of Art, is a typical example of Elizabethan domestic architecture (1577–80), with 365 windows, 52 doors and 52 steps up to the top of the tower. The banqueting hall is particularly fine. A short distance away, also in the High Street, is the 15th c. Aberconwy House.

Up the beautiful valley of the River Conwy, at Talcafn Bridge, are the magnificent *Bodnant Gardens, laid out by Henry Pochin in 1875. Reckoned among the very finest gardens in Britain, they are particularly renowned for their rhododendrons, azaleas and camellias and for the rose-garden and rock garden.

The road continues up the valley to **Llanrwst**, a little market town of 3000 inhabitants. Here the crystal-clear River Conwy is spanned by a beautiful three-arched bridge designed by Inigo Jones (1636). Near the bridge are the remains of *Plas Isaf*, home of William Salisbury, the first translator of the Old Testament into English. Also of interest are the *North Wales Museum of Wild Life* and the parish church, with the Gwydir Chapel (1633), containing brasses and a stone coffin.

There is a very beautiful road from Conwy over the Sychnant pass to *Penmaenmawr*, a seaside resort particularly favoured by sailing enthusiasts. To the W is the Penmaenbach promontory (783 ft). Here there is an interesting history trail, with stone circles and a Stone Age axe factory.

The coast road continues from Penmaenmawr via *Llanfairfechan*, one of the quieter seaside resorts, to **Bangor** (pop. 15,000; hotels – Castle, E, 46 r.; Ty Uchaf, E, 10 r.), a university town and the starting point for a trip to the island of Anglesey. It is also a popular base for sailing in the Menai Strait (which is also one of Britain's richest fishing grounds). The small, squat *Cathedral*, which also serves as a parish church, was probably founded by Deiniol, the first bishop, in 548. Three earlier churches on the site were destroyed in 1071 by the Normans, in 1282 by Edward I and in 1404 by the Welsh rebel leader Owen Glendower (1359–c. 1416). The choir was rebuilt about 1496 and the rest of the church in the early 16th c., but the whole building was restored about 1870 by Sir George Gilbert Scott. The chapterhouse contains interesting old books and manuscripts. – The Art Gallery and Museum has a fine collection of Welsh antiquities. The new theatre, Theatr Gwynedd, concentrates on works by Welsh authors.

1 mile E is the neo-Norman *Penrhyn Castle* (1827–40), which contains a notable collection of more than a thousand dolls.

9 miles SW of Bangor is the county town of Gwynedd, **Caernarfon** (pop. 9300), beautifully situated on the Menai Strait at the mouth of the River Seiont. It is a picturesque old town of narrow streets, with old town walls and a magnificent castle. It is also a popular yachting centre and seaside resort (though the bathing here is dangerous), and it is a good base from which to explore the beauties of the Lleyn peninsula.

** **Caernarfon Castle**, the construction of which was begun by Edward I (1272–1307), is one of the most impressive and externally best-preserved medieval fortresses in Europe. It occupies the site of an earlier Norman castle, washed by the River Seiont and the Menai Strait. On the landward side it was protected by a moat. The building of the Castle took 37 years: the Eagle Tower, Queen's Tower and Chamberlain Tower were built in 1285–91, the Black Tower and Queen's Gate in 1295–1301, the rest of the structure in 1315–22. The castle has had an eventful history and has withstood many sieges; more recently, it was the scene of Prince Charles's investiture as Prince of Wales in 1969. Thirteen towers and two gates are still preserved. A large market is held on the square in front of the Castle, for Caernarfon is the shopping centre for the Lleyn peninsula. The roman *Fort Segontium*, SE of the town, has a museum containing material excavated on the site.

The **Lleyn peninsula**, one of the earliest parts of Wales to be settled, with many prehistoric remains, is one of the strongholds of the Welsh language. It is an area of great natural beauty, with a number of hills of some height, the highest being the *Rivals* (1849 ft), to the NE. Much of the coast is rocky, but there are nevertheless a number of small seaside resorts like *Trefor*, Nant Gwrtheyrn and *Nefyn*, *Porth Ysgadan*, Porth Ychen and *Porth Golmon*. *Porth Oer* has an excellent beach, known as the Whistling Sands because of the noise it makes when walked on. *Aberdaron* (pop. 500) is a fishing village which has developed into a seaside resort thanks to its 1½-mile-long beach. From here there is a very rewarding cliff-top walk (2½ miles) to *Braich-y-Pwll*. *Y Gegin Fawr*, now a café and souvenir shop, was in the 14th c. a rest-house for pilgrims travelling to *Bardsey*, the "isle of 20,000 saints", now occupied only by a few fishermen (bird reserve).

Porth Neigwl is a sandy bay 4 miles long, the largest place on which is *Llanengan*, with an interesting 15th c. church. The next little bay, *Porth Ceirad*, is also almost empty of habitation. *Abersoch*, with St Tudwal's Islands lying offshore, has two large sandy beaches and is much favoured by water-skiing enthusiasts. The next two resorts, *Llanbedrog* in sheltered Tremadog Bay and *Pwllheli*, both have excellent beaches and are crowded with visitors in summer.

The little town of **LLanystumdwy**, situated on the wide estuary formed by the rivers Dwyfor and Dwyfach, in a very attractive area which offers excellent walking, has a museum devoted to Lloyd George, who spent his early years here

Caernarfon Castle

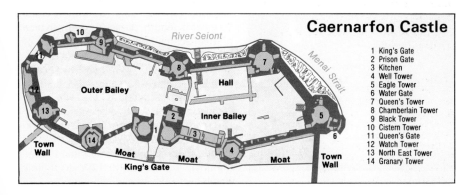

Caernarfon Castle

1 King's Gate
2 Prison Gate
3 Kitchen
4 Well Tower
5 Eagle Tower
6 Water Gate
7 Queen's Tower
8 Chamberlain Tower
9 Black Tower
10 Cistern Tower
11 Queen's Gate
12 Watch Tower
13 North East Tower
14 Granary Tower

River Seiont

Menai Strait

Outer Bailey

Hall

Inner Bailey

Town Wall

Moat

Moat

King's Gate

Moat

Town Wall

Panorama of Snowdonia

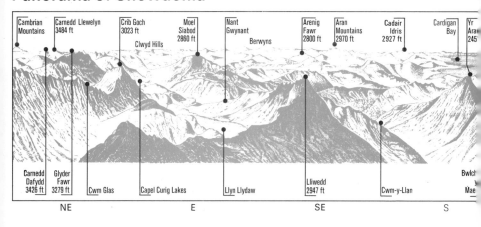

| Cambrian Mountains | Carnedd Llewelyn 3484 ft | Crib Goch 3023 ft | Moel Siabod 2860 ft | Nant Gwynant | Arenig Fawr 2800 ft | Aran Mountains 2970 ft | Cadair Idris 2927 ft | Cardigan Bay | Yr Ara 245 |

Clwyd Hills   Berwyns

| Carnedd Dafydd 3426 ft | Glyder Fawr 3279 ft | Cwm Glas | Capel Curig Lakes | Llyn Llydaw | Lliwedd 2947 ft | Cwm-y-Llan | Bwlch Mae |

NE   E   SE   S

and is buried nearby. The museum is in one of the typical local stone-built houses. – **Criccieth** is a popular seaside resort, with a small 13th c. Welsh castle from which there are very fine views.

At the mouth of the River Glaslyn are the twin towns of **Porthmadog** and **Tremadog** (pop. 3600). They are holiday resorts, with excellent facilities for sport. Here too is the oldest narrow-gauge railway in the world, built in 1836 to carry slate from Blaenau Ffestiniog to the port of Porthmadog. It now carries thousands of visitors through the beautiful *Ffestiniog valley*. From Ynys Towyn, near the harbour, there are wide views of the surrounding area. The poet Shelley (1792–1822) lived for some time in Tremadog, and Lawrence of Arabia

(1888–1935) was born there. The *Coed-Tremadoc Woods* are a nature reserve.

Also in Tremadog Bay, on a wooded peninsula between Porthmadog and Harlech, is a little town of Italian aspect, **Portmeirion**, created by the Welsh architect Clough Williams-Ellis, with reconstructions of historic buildings, flights of steps and vistas, gardens and sculpture. The whole thing, with the *Gwylt Gardens* and their rhododendrons and subtropical plants, is a charming and successful "folly".

Harlech (pop. 1200; Noddfa Hotel, E, 77 r.; youth hostel, Pen-y-Garth, 36 b.), a historic old town and former county town of Merioneth, now lies half a mile from the sea. It is dominated by a massive castle on a rocky hill, built in 1283, with massive towers like those of a story-book castle and a three-storey gatehouse. From the Castle there are magnificent views of the mountains and the sea. *Morfa Harlech*, outside the town, is an area of salt marshland and sand-dunes, with a very fine golf-course.

The road from Harlech to Barmouth, some 10 miles in length, passes through an area of great scenic beauty. Inland lies part of Snowdonia National Park, with mountains rising to 2462 ft. *Rhinog Fawr* (2362 ft) is popular with climbers; the starting point for the ascent is the village of Llanbedr on the Artro, a good trout river. The road runs along the foot of the hills, passing through *Ardudwy*, long a centre of Welsh resistance to England, and *Llanaber*, with an early 13th c. church which has survived almost intact.

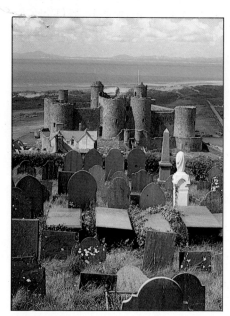
Harlech Castle

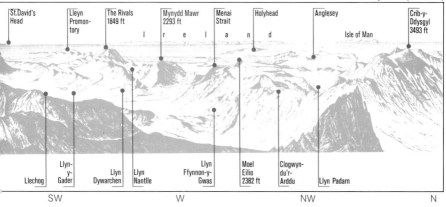

View from the main peak of Snowdon
Yr Wyddfa (3560 ft)

St.David's Head | Lleyn Promontory | The Rivals 1849 ft | Mynydd Mawr 2293 ft | Menai Strait | Holyhead | Anglesey | Crib-y-Ddysgyl 3493 ft

I r e l a n d   Isle of Man

Llechog | Llyn-y-Gader | Llyn Dywarchen | Llyn Nantlle | Llyn Ffynnon-y-Gwas | Moel Eilio 2382 ft | Clogwyn-du'r-Arddu | Llyn Padarn

SW   W   NW   N

Barmouth (pop. 2200; hotels – Cors-y-Gedol, D, 32 r.; Bryn Melyn, D, 9 r.) is a popular seaside resort situated on a narrow strip of land between the hills and the sea. The Mawddach estuary is of great scenic beauty. A road runs along its shores to **Dolgellau** (10 miles: pop. 2500; hotels – Golden Lion Royal, Lion Street, 23 r.; Royal Ship, 22 r.), a town of stone-built and slate-roofed houses beautifully sit-

Barmouth estuary from Bontddu

uated in the valley of the Wnion. With its magnificent setting, this is a favourite base for walks and climbs in the surrounding hills and on Cadair Idris. The beauty of the scenery can be enjoyed from the *Precipice Walk* to *Moel Cynwch* (1068 ft) and on to *Cymmer Abbey*, a Cistercian foundation of 1198, of which only the Norman church (restored) has been preserved.

From Dolgellau there are three routes up Cadair Idris (2927 ft), the most popular Welsh mountain after Snowdon, and offering even better views. The walk takes between $2\frac{1}{2}$ and 4 hours according to the route chosen.

Cadair Idris (Cader Idris in the Anglicised spelling), the chair of the giant Idris,

is a massive ridge 7 miles long which falls steeply down into the Mawddach valley but slopes more gently away into outlying hills on the other three sides. The rocks are of considerable geological interest. The four highest peaks – *Mynydd Moel, Pen-y-Gader*, the *Saddle* and *Tyrau Mawr* – range between 1848 and 2927 ft. From the summit there are splendid *views in all directions.

Snowdonia is the name given to the mountainous area in the county of Gwynedd, with 14 peaks over 3000 ft, culminating in Snowdon itself (3560 ft). It has several main summits – *Crib Goch* (3023 ft), *Crib-y-Ddysgl* or *Garnedd Ugain* (3493 ft), *Lliwedd* (2947 ft), *Yr Aran* (2451 ft) and *Yr Wyddfa* (Snowdon). The best view of the whole group is to be had from *Capel Curig*; the peaks can be seen from Porthmadog or the Nantlle valley.

*Snowdonia National Park is a more recent creation and covers a much wider area than the traditional Snowdonia, extending inland from the coast between Penmaenmawr and Caernarfon by way of Bethesda to Bala Lake and Llanfairfechan. Access to a beautiful part of this area, including Snowdon itself, is made easier by the Snowdon Mountain Railway, which starts from *Llanberis* (pop. 2049; hotels – Gallt-y-Glyn, 10 r.), in a magnificent setting at the beginning of the Llanberis pass. The twin lakes of Padarn and Peris have one of the largest pumping stations in Europe for the purposes of water supply. Between them is *Dolbadarn Castle*, with an early 13th c. round tower, and 2 miles S is *Bryn Bras Castle*. The area round Llanberis is disfigured by many quarries. This is the starting point of the easiest route up Snowdon, and of the even easier ascent by the little rack-and-pinion train which steams up to the summit of Snowdon at a speed of little more than 5 miles an hour by way of *Hebron, Halfway* and *Clogwyn* stations. There is a bus service, the "Snowdon Sherpa", serving *Porthmadog, Beddgelert, Llanrwst, Betws-y-Coed, Capel Curig, Caernarfon* and *Llanberis*, all good starting points for trips into Snowdonia. There are National Park information centres at Llanrwst, Llanberis, Blaenau Ffestiniog, Harlech, Bala, Conwy, Aberdovey and Dolgellau. A variety of way-marked trails, each only a few miles long, enable visitors to become acquainted with the scenery, flora and fauna and geology of the region. There are five waymarked and relatively safe and easy routes to the summit, starting from Llanberis, Pen-y-Pass, Beddgelert, Nant Gwynant and the Snowdon Ranger. The most direct route, but the least attractive, is the one from Llanberis; the best ascent is to start from Beddgelert and return to Pen-y-Pass, or vice versa.

Apart from ***Snowdon** itself (Welsh *Eryri*), from the highest peak of *Yr Wyddfa* (3560 ft) there are incomparable**views in all directions, numerous other mountains in the area are well worth climbing. All over Snowdonia there are good walks and climbs, offering wide-ranging views of beautiful mountains and valleys.

***Beddgelert** (pop. 550; hotels – Royal Goat, D, 25 r.; Bryn Eglwys, D, 10 r.), situated at the junction of the rivers Colwan and Glaslyn, is one of the most charming little places in Wales, a favourite starting point for walks and climbs at the junction of two main roads. From *Moel*

Hebog, a 2 hours' climb from here, there is a splendid panoramic view extending out into Cardigan Bay. One road from here descends to Caernarfon, another runs NE through *Nant Gwynant*, the beautiful valley of the Glaslyn. This leads to the delightful little town of **Betws-y-Coed** (pop. 700; hotels – Royal Oak, C, 26 r.; Craig-y-Dderwen Country House, D, 22 r.), situated in Gwydyr Forest at the junction of the Conwy, Lledr and Llugwy valleys. This is a very popular holiday place, crowded with visitors in summer. Pont-y-Pair is a 15th c. bridge. The immediate surroundings are very beautiful, with the *Fairy Glen* and the *Conwy Falls*.

Bethesda, 4 miles SE of Bangor in the Ogwen valley, is also a good base for exploring Snowdonia. The town itself offers little attraction apart from the huge Penrhyn Quarries, 1000 ft deep, which yield quantities of slate in many different hues – a material used over a wide surrounding area in the manufacture of souvenirs and ornaments. From here the two **Carnedds**, *Carnedd Llewelyn* (3484 ft) and *Carnedd Dafydd* (3426 ft), named after two Welsh brothers, can be climbed, with magnificent views of Snowdonia from the summits.

Llyn Ogwen is a beautiful mountain lake with a waterfall (*Benglog Falls*). Half mile S is *Llyn Idwal*, in which the son of Prince Owain Gwynedd is supposed to have been drowned by his stepfather. High in the mountains is the *Cwm Idwal* nature reserve (Alpine flora), and near here is an almost inaccessible gorge known as the **Devil's Kitchen*, 6 ft wide and 500 ft deep. Here and at one or two other spots in Snowdonia are the only habitats in Britain of the rare Snowdon lily, *Lloydia serotina*, a protected species. At the S end of Llyn Ogwen are the triple peaks of *Tryfan* (3010 ft), much favoured by climbers. From here the land falls to **Capel Curig** (youth hostel, Plas Curig 56 b.), an attractive little place in a magnificent setting, frequented by climbers as a good base for climbing in Snowdonia, and also by anglers and painters.

A popular holiday region in the interior of North Wales is *Bala Lake*, with the little market town of **Bala** (pop. 1800; Bala Lakeside Motel, D, 14 r.), at the foot of the

Snowdon from Llyn Padarn

Aran and Berwyn Mountains. The main attractions here are the 4-mile-long lake, which offers ideal conditions for sailing, and the narrow-gauge steam railway which runs along the S side.

Another very popular holiday resort is **Llangollen** (pop. 3100; hotels – Royal, C, 33 r.; Hand, D, 59 r.; Bryn Derwen, D, 14 r.; youth hostel, Tyndwr Hall, Birch Hill, 141 b.), in a beautiful setting on both banks of the Dee. The town is famed for the International Musical Eisteddfod held here every summer. The 14th c. bridge over the Dee, one of the "seven wonders of Wales", was not improved by its reconstruction in 1973. The parish church, *St Collen's*, has a fine carved roof with figures of angels, animals and flowers, probably from Valle Crucis Abbey.

Valle Crucis Abbey, 2 miles N, was founded by Prince Madog ap Gruffydd Maelor in 1202 for Cistercian monks. The remains include the W front of the church, with three beautiful 14th c. windows, a pointed arch at the E end, the sacristy, the chapterhouse, the dorter and the fish-pond. In a field a quarter of a mile away is the early 9th c. *Eliseg's Pillar* commemorating Eliseg, Prince of Powys, and his victory in the battle of Bangor, in which he lost his life. From here the road climbs to the *Horseshoe Pass* (1353 ft), with *Moel-y-Gamelin* (1897 ft).

In the most southerly part of North Wales, close to the border with England, is **Welshpool** (pop. 5000), former county town of Montgomeryshire, on the Severn. It has many Georgian houses and – unusually for Wales – most of the houses in the town are built of brick. Features of interest are *St Mary's Church* and the *Powysland Museum*, with many finds from the region. To the west of the town is another of Wales attractive narrow-gauge steam railways, the Welshpool and Llanfair Light Railway, which runs between Llanfair Caereinion and Sylfaen.

Powis Castle, 1 mile S, has been for over 500 years the seat of the Earls of Powis. Built of red sandstone, it has largely preserved the aspect of a 13th–14th c. castle in spite of its restoration in the 16th c. It contains fine plaster decoration and carved woodwork, early Georgian furniture and pictures. The terraced gardens were laid out in the early 18th c.; in the * park are some of the largest oaks in Britain.

North-West Coast

North-western England. – Counties: Cheshire, Merseyside, Lancashire and Cumbria.

The NW coast of England extends from the Welsh to the Scottish borders. It is a flat region bordered by beaches of fine sand, from which the sea recedes at low tide anything up to 2 miles. Climatically the resorts on this stretch of coast are less favoured than those farther S, but inland the scenery is often very beautiful.

On the **Wirral** peninsula between the estuaries of the Dee and the Mersey are the resorts of **West Kirby** and **Hoylake**, looking across the Dee to Wales. The Wirral was formerly a royal hunting preserve. The little *Hilbre Islands*, which can be reached on foot from West Kirby at low tide, are the refuge and nesting-place of numerous seabirds. Both West Kirby and Hoylake have long sandy beaches and promenades, and Hoylake has a first-class golf-course. West Kirby ("Church Town") takes its name from a church which stood here before the Norman Conquest.

As its name indicates, **New Brighton** was originally established in emulation of the popular Sussex resort. It lies on the S side of the Mersey, here almost a mile wide, opposite Liverpool docks, and is a very popular resort, with one of the largest swimming pools in Europe, an amusement park and a long promenade extending from Hoylake to beyond Seacombe.

N of Liverpool there are no resorts of any consequence until Southport. Near Formby, which has a good golf-course, is the large *Ainsdale* nature reserve, with sand-dunes and areas of marsh and brackish water, where rare flowers and butterflies can be found. Adjoining this reserve is the Southport wildfowl sanctuary.

Southport (pop. 86,900; hotels – Scarisbrick, D, 52 r.; Bold, D, 28 r.; Carlton, D, 25 r.), a popular seaside resort, prides itself on being England's oldest garden city. It is a town of wide tree-lined streets and beautiful parks and gardens: in the eyes of local people Lord Street ranks as one of the world's finest streets. There is a spacious beach looking out on to the Irish Sea, and the town offers every amenity to the visitor – a promenade and a long pier, a swimming pool, an amusement park, a salt-water lagoon and several excellent golf-courses.

Inland from Southport the country is flat and featureless, apart from *Rufford Old Hall* (8 miles E), a late medieval manor-house with a 17th c. and 19th c. wing. It houses the Philip Ashcroft Museum (relics of Lancashire life in the past).

Lytham St Annes (pop. 41,500; hotels – Clifton Arms, C, 49 r.; Grand Crest, C, 40 r.; Chadwick, D, 70 r.) is a family holiday resort, situated at the mouth of the River Ribble, a much quieter place than its neighbour Blackpool. The town was formed in 1875 by the amalgamation of five smaller places. It has a very beautiful beach, 6 miles long, fringed by sand-dunes, fine parks and gardens, and five good golf-courses.

Blackpool beach, with the Tower

Blackpool (pop. 147,000; hotels – Norbreck Castle, C, 348 r.; Pembroke, C, 205 r.; Savoy, D, 128 r.; Cliftonville, E, 20 r.; Sunray, E, 8 r.) is the largest holiday resort in the North of England, and is still expanding. It can accommodate approximately half a million visitors, and does in fact receive this number during the holiday season. Entertainment for every taste is provided in profusion – donkey rides, golf, zoos, a circus, dance-halls, a huge range of amusements and side-shows, theatres, cinemas, bathing pools, three piers, from which visitors can take a variety of boat trips, and the famous Blackpool Tower, 519 ft high (built 1889), with an aquarium. In autumn the whole of the Promenade is illuminated, an attraction which draws people from far and wide. Other annual events which attract many visitors are the ballroom dancing championships, musical festival and agricultural show in summer. The conference of the Trade Union Congress is usually held at Blackpool.

Fleetwood (pop. 30,300) is a busy fishing port which is developing into a holiday resort. The town, situated on the Wyre estuary, was founded in the 19th c. by the founder of Rossall School, above Morecambe Bay.

Morecambe (pop. 40,700, with Heysham; hotels – Strathmore, C, 55 r.; Midland, C, 46 r.; Elms, C, 40 r.), with a good beach and all the amenities of a large and lively seaside resort, also has beautiful scenery in its immediate hinterland. It is situated on *Morecambe Bay*, and at low tide it is possible to walk over the spacious bay on marked paths. The local fishermen catch shrimps with nets and horse-drawn carts.

From *Heysham* there are occasional day trips to the Isle of Man. The church is 12th–14th c., with some Saxon work; in the churchyard is a Viking grave with 10th c. carving.

Grange-over-Sands (pop. 3500; Graythwaite Manor, C, 28 r.; Cumbria Grand, D, 90 r.; Netherwood, D, 23 r.) is a small and elegant resort on Morecambe Bay, with beautiful public gardens and good golf-courses. It is a good base for visits to the Lakes.

Cartmel (2 miles W), an attractive little Georgian town, has a fine church, originally belonging to an Augustinian priory founded by the earl of Pembroke in 1188. The lower part of the church is Transitional, the upper part of the tower, the nave and most of the windows Perpendicular. The Renaissance stalls date from 1612 to 1613. *Holker Hall* is a 17th c. mansion with beautiful gardens and a deer park.

Seascale (pop. 2100) is a pleasant little seaside resort, another good base from which to explore the Lake District. It has a fine church with good carving and modern glass.

The most northerly seaside resort on the W coast before the Scottish border is **Silloth** (pop. 2600; hotels – Skinburness, D, 25 r.; Golf, D, 23 r.), on the Solway Firth, with a good anchorage which led to its foundation in 1855 as a port for Carlisle. This function has been taken over by *Port Carlisle*, and Silloth is now of importance only as a holiday resort. It has good golf-courses.

Norwich

Eastern England. – County: Norfolk.
Population: 121,000.
Telephone dialling code: 0603.

(i) **Tourist Information Centre,**
Augustine Steward House, 14 Tombland;
tel. 620679, 623445.

HOTELS. – *Post House*, Ipswich Road, C, 120 r.; *Norwich*, 121 Boundary Road, C, 102 r.; *Nelson*, Prince of Wales Road, C, 94 r.; *Maid's Head*, Tombland, C, 82 r.; *Lansdowne*, 116 Thorpe Road, C, 44 r.; *Castle*, Castle Meadow, D, 79 r.

YOUTH HOSTEL. – 112 Turner Road, 72 b.

RESTAURANTS. – *Marco's*, 17 Pottergate; *Savoy*, 50 Prince of Wales Road; *Oaklands*, 89 Yarmouth Road, Thorpe St Andrew.

SPORT and RECREATION. – Rowing, canoeing, walking, sailing (Norfolk Broads).

Norwich, county town of Norfolk, is ranked by those who know it as one of the most interesting towns in England. It lies on the little River Wensum within easy reach of the beautiful Norfolk Broads, and has more medieval churches (32 in all) than any other town in the country with the exception of London, as well as a beautiful Norman cathedral. Many of the streets and lanes are narrow and winding, and there are remains of the old town walls and towers.

Norwich is an important market for corn and livestock. Shoe manufacture is an important industry; other products are electrical goods, mustard, chocolate and silk. Canary-breeding is another significant local activity.

SIGHTS. – The ****Cathedral**, dedicated to the Holy Trinity, with a striking spire which is a prominent landmark, has preserved its Norman character better than any other church in England, and is

Norwich Cathedral

one of the most beautiful of English cathedrals. From *Tombland*, the ancient market-place, with some fine old buildings, the Cathedral close is entered by either *St Ethelbert's Gate* (1272; upper part restored) or the *Erpingham Gate* (1420). The building of the Cathedral was begun in 1096 by Herbert de Losinga (bishop 1091–1119), who transferred the episcopal see of Thetford to Norwich in 1092. The choir and aisles were completed in 1101, and the nave by his successor Eborard or Everard (bishop 1121–46). The spire collapsed in 1362, damaging the choir, and was rebuilt in Decorated style. In the 15th c. the nave and presbytery were re-roofed, a Perpendicular window was inserted in the W front and the spire was renewed. The spire (315 ft) is the highest in England after Salisbury.

A stone cross near the SE corner of the Cathedral marks the grave of Nurse Edith Cavell (1865–1915), who, during the German occupation of Belgium in the First World War, helped many Belgians to escape military service by smuggling them out of the country and was court-martialled and shot by the Germans.

INTERIOR. – The *nave*, of 14 bays, is mainly Norman, with short massive columns. The *windows* are Decorated and Perpendicular; the glass is mostly 19th c. Particularly notable is the fine *lierne vaulting*, with 326 bosses (out of a total of over 800 in the whole

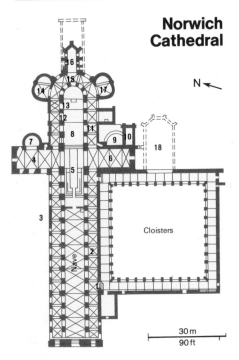

Norwich Cathedral

N ←

Cloisters

Nave

30 m
90 ft

1 Monks' Door
2 Bishop Nyx's Chapel
3 Bishop's Palace
4 North Transept
5 Choir
6 South Transept
7 Westcott Chapel
8 Presbytery
9 St Peter's Chapel
10 Vestry

11 Bishop Goldwell's monument
12 Herbert de Losinga's
     monument
13 Sir Thomas Erpingham's
     monument
14 Jesus Chapel
15 Ambulatory
16 War Memorial Chapel
17 St Luke's Chapel
18 Site of Chapterhouse

that of Bishop James Goldwell (1472–99). Behind the high altar is the old stone bishop's throne dating from the 6th or 8th c. (restored 1959).

The two-storey *Cloister*, built between 1297 and 1425, is the largest in England, with more than 400 finely carved bosses. The *Bishop's Palace*, with a doorway of about 1430, and *St John's Chapel* (1322) are now part of *Norwich School* (founded 1240).

The **Castle** was built on an artificial mound, probably about 1160 by Hugh Bigod, earl of Norfolk. It consists mainly of a *Norman keep*, which was used until 1884 as a prison and since 1894 has housed a museum. The *Museum* has a very fine collection, including numerous works of the Norwich School of painters.

The founder of the Norwich School was a young local man named *John Crome* (1768–1821), a weaver's son who was trained as a sign-painter and later devoted himself almost exclusively to painting landscapes of his native area. Among the other members of the School one of the best known and the most gifted was John Sell Cotman (1782–1842).

One of the largest markets in Norfolk is held in the spacious *Market Place*, near which are the *City Hall*, the *War Memorial* (by Lutyens, 1927), the *Guildhall* (1407), with 15th c. glass, and the new *Central Library* (1963). *Strangers' Hall* in Charing Cross is a late medieval merchant's house, containing an interesting museum of domestic life. *St Andrew's Hall*, originally the nave of a Dominican church, is now used as a concert hall and contains a number of fine portraits. *Suckling House*, adjacent to St Andrew's Church, is a handsome example of a medieval town house. The old *Bridewell* in Bridewell Alley houses a museum of local crafts and industries. The disused church of *St Peter Hungate* in Princes Street contains a display of religious arts and crafts. *Elm Hill* is a picturesque old cobbled street lined with trim little shops.

One of the most interesting of Norwich's many medieval churches is *St George Colegate*, built in 1459, with a choir dating from 1498; the interior is practically unchanged. *St Giles* has very fine decorative flint-work of the type seen in many houses in Norwich and throughout Norfolk. Of the town's medieval fortifications there still survive five towers, including the *Cow Tower*. One of the oldest bridges in the country, *Bishop*

church). The *aisles* are also Norman. Two bays of the S aisle were converted into chantry chapels by Bishop Nyx or Nykke (bishop 1501–35). Two doors, the Monks' Door and the Prior's Door, lead into the *Cloister*. The *transepts* resemble the nave, with beautiful 16th c. vaulting.

The *Choir* was rebuilt in Perpendicular style, but the original apse was preserved. The 62 *choir-stalls*, with canopies and fine misericords, date from 1420 to 1480. In the aisles are a number of *tombs*, including

Cloister, Norwich Cathedral

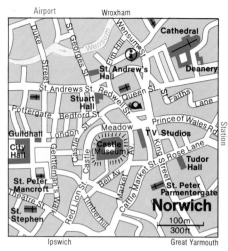

Norwich *(map)*

Nottingham

Central England. – County: Nottinghamshire.
Altitude: 420 ft. – Population: 271,100.
Telephone dialling code: 0602.
(i) **Tourist Information Centre,**
    18 Milton Street;
    tel. 40661.

HOTELS. – *Albany*, St James Street, B, 160 r.; *Stakis Victoria*, Milton Street, C, 167 r.; *Strathdorn Thistle*, Derby Road, C, 69 r.; *Bestwood Lodge*, Bestwood Lodge Drive, D, 35 r.

Two CAMPING SITES.

RESTAURANTS. – *Moulin Rouge*, 5 Trinity Square; *Flying Horse*, Rufford, 53 Melton Road.

EVENTS. – *Goose Fair* (Thurs.–Sat., first week in October).

SPORT and RECREATION. – Golf, tennis, sailing, fishing.

Nottingham, county town of Nottinghamshire, is built on a number of hills on the N bank of the River Trent, which is navigable as far as Nottingham for vessels up to about 120 tons. It is an important industrial town, noted in the past for its lace, curtains and stockings but now producing cigarettes, pharmaceuticals, bicycles and textiles. As the prosperous centre of a thriving region Nottingham likes to think of itself as the "Queen of the Midlands". It has a university founded in 1948.

The Nottinghamshire, Derbyshire and Yorkshire coalfield is the largest in England. The hosiery industry which formerly flourished in the whole county was founded in Elizabethan times by a local parson who invented the stocking-frame – a device which was soon adopted throughout the surrounding area. Nottingham is a good base for a visit to Robin Hood's Sherwood Forest (although not much of the forest is left).

HISTORY. – The town of *Snotingaham* or *Snotengaham* was occupied by the Danes in 868, and became the capital of the five boroughs of the Danelaw (the others being Derby, Leicester, Lincoln and Stamford). Nottingham was one of Britain's earliest industrial towns, and as such became a centre of the Luddite riots of 1811–16, aimed at the destruction of the new industrial machinery. William Booth, founder of the Salvation Army, was born in an outlying district of the town, and Byron went to school here, living in Newstead House, St James's Street (now marked by a tablet).

Bridge (1395), carries the road to Mousehold Heath, NE of the town; from here there is a fine general view of the Norwich skyline.

SURROUNDINGS. – 14 miles N is **Aylsham** (pop. 4800), an attractive old market town, once the residence of Benjamin Britten. 1 mile N of Aylsham is *Blickling Hall*, a large brick mansion (1616–28) with a magnificent plaster ceiling and fine furniture and pictures. In the park, well planted with trees, are a lake and an 18th c. mausoleum.

The **Norfolk Broads**, lying roughly within the triangle formed by *Yarmouth*, *Wroxham* and *Stalham*, are an expanse of lagoons and rivers, magnificently suited for boating holidays, whether sailing or rowing. In the area traversed by the River Yare and its tributaries the Ant, Thurne, Bure and Waveney there are about 200 miles of waterways. In the past there were extensive peat-cuttings here, now occupied by shallow lagoons which are usually overgrown with weeds. The windmills once used for drainage are reminiscent of similar scenery in Holland. Nature-lovers will find hosts of waterfowl, butterflies, dragonflies and rare flowers, and anglers will be attracted by the large numbers of fish (bream, rudd, roach, perch, pike).

The beauties of the Broads cannot be seen properly by road: they must be explored by boat. Sailing boats can be hired, as can motor cruisers (advance booking necessary in summer).

The largest of the Broads, and one of the most beautiful, is *Hickling Broad*. The best starting point for an exploration of this area is Potter Heigham, going upstream on the River Thurne to *Martham*, *Horsey* and *Hickling Broads* downstream to the River Bure. From there it is possible to continue SE by way of *Breydon Water* and the River Waveney to *Lowestoft* or to go W through a series of Broads to **Wroxham**.

Potter Heigham is usually less crowded with visitors than Wroxham. Other good centres from which to explore the Broads are *Ranworth* and *South Walsham*. The little villages in this area, many of them with very interesting old churches, are picturesque but have little to offer in the way of accommodation.

Council House, Nottingham

SIGHTS. – In the centre of the town is the **Old Market Square**, the largest in England, on which the famous Goose Fair was formerly held (it is now held in the Forest Recreation Ground). On the E side of the square is the neo-classical **Council House** (by Cecil Howitt, 1929), crowned by an imposing dome.

N of the town centre are the impressive **Guildhall** (1929) and the *Technical College*, both by Cecil Howitt. In the *Arboretum*, a beautiful park, there are a number of statues, and there are others in front of the *College of Art*. W of the town centre is the Roman Catholic *Cathedral*, an early work by Pugin (1842–44).

The *Castle*, on a rock 133 ft high, affords a good view of the town. Outside it are bronze statues of Robin Hood and his merry men. The old castle was destroyed in 1651 by Parliamentary forces and replaced by an Italian-style palace belonging to the duke of Newcastle. This was burned down by Reform rioters in 1831 but later rebuilt. It now houses the Nottingham *Museum and Art Gallery*, with a fine collection of pottery and

Wollaton Hall

beautiful examples of the work of the Nottingham School of alabaster sculpture (14th–15th c.).

From here *Castle Boulevard* runs W (2 miles) to **Highfields Park**, presented to the city by Lord Trent, which is now occupied by the University. Jesse Boot, who became Lord Trent, opened the first of his chain of chemist's shops in Nottingham, and the firm still has a large factory in the area.

Near the University, in a large park, is **Wollaton Hall**, an Elizabethan mansion (by Robert Smythson, 1580–87) which now houses a Natural History Museum. Close by is *Lenton Church*, which has a beautiful Norman font with rich carved decoration.

SURROUNDINGS. – 9 miles N is **Newstead Abbey**, the family home of Byron, whose tomb is in Newstead parish church. When he inherited the estate he and his mother were too poor to live here. In spite of his debts, however, he came to live in the house after leaving Cambridge, but was obliged to sell the property six years later (1817). The house was originally an Augustinian abbey founded in 1170 by Henry II. Of the original buildings there remain the W front of the church, the refectory, the chapterhouse (now a chapel) and the cloisters. Newstead now belongs to the city of Nottingham, and Byron's rooms have been preserved as they were in his lifetime, with many mementoes of the poet. The grounds contain fine old trees.

From Newstead it is 11 miles to *Hardwick*, where there is another fine Elizabethan mansion, **Hardwick Hall** – "Hardwick Hall, more glass than wall", the contemporary jingle went, for the house has 50 windows and relatively small areas of wall. It was built by Robert Smythson in 1591–97 for "Bess of Hardwick" (Elizabeth, daughter of John Hardwick), who married four times, her last husband being the sixth earl of Shrewsbury. She was widowed for the last time at the age of 70, having inherited property from all her husbands.

Hardwick Hall contains a rich collection of tapestries, furniture, embroidery and portraits. In the centre of the house is a large two-storey hall, with a magnificent staircase leading to the upper floor. From the house there are beautiful glimpses of the gardens. Close by are the remains of *Hardwick Old Hall*, with fine plasterwork. In the park, to the N, is **Ault Hucknall Church**, with the tomb of Thomas Hobbes (1588–1679), the philosopher and author of "Leviathan".

5 miles from Hardwick is **Bolsover Castle**, originally built by William Peveril in the 11th c. and restored in 1613–17 by Charles Cavendish, Bess of Hardwick's son. It is now partly ruined, but contains some fine chimneypieces.

24 miles NE is **Southwell** (pop. 6500; Saracen's Head Hotel, C, 23 r.), a market town which makes a good base for the exploration of the Robin Hood country. Charles I stayed in the Saracen's Head before

giving himself up to the Scots in 1646, thus beginning the long period of imprisonment which ended with his execution. **Southwell Minster** is one of England's east visited cathedrals. The church was begun in the 12th c., and the nave and transepts of this period have been preserved. There are three Norman towers, one over the crossing and two on the W front; the W towers still have their original roofs, in spite of rebuilding after a fire in 1711 and further alterations in 1880. The Minster, originally served by a college of secular canons, became a cathedral in 1884. The fine brass lectern was found in a lake in the grounds of Newstead Abbey, where it had probably been thrown for concealment by the monks at the time of the Dissolution of the Monasteries. The most exquisite part of the Minster is the Decorated chapterhouse (c. 1300), with a profusion of beautiful naturalistic leaves and flowers, vines and grapes, animals and human figures, carved by an unknown sculptor. The doorway is one of the finest in the whole of England.

Offa's Dyke

Eastern Wales (the Welsh Marches).

Offa's Dyke is an earth rampart built by King Offa of Mercia between 784 and 796 to provide protection against Welsh attacks. It extends from the Severn estuary to the Dee, a total distance of some 170 miles.

After defeating Caradoc, a Welsh prince, between Abergele and Rhuddlan (S of Rhyl) Offa built the wall to mark the frontier between Mercia and Wales. His palace was at Sutton Walls.

The earth rampart was reinforced by a ditch on the Welsh side. It can be followed, with many interruptions, for a distance of more than 140 miles between the Dee estuary and the Wye. A second earthwork known as *Wat's Dyke* runs parallel to Offa's Dyke, 3 miles away, for a distance of some 40 miles from the Dee to the Severn; it is probably rather later.

There are well-preserved stretches of Offa's Dyke at some places in England, for example at **Kington**, a little market town near the Welsh border, noted also for the large sheep market held annually in September.

Not far away is **Knighton** (Powys county, Wales), a little town set among wooded hills on the River Teme, with well-preserved stretches of the Dyke on either side of the town. Here too there is a large sheep and lamb market in autumn.

Another attractive little town where Offa's Dyke can be seen is **Montgomery** (pop. 1000), 10 miles S of *Welshpool*. It was formerly county town (at least in name) of Montgomeryshire, now part of the new county of Powys. The little town, which has many Elizabethan and Georgian houses, lies off the main road, and its railway station is a mile from the town. It takes its name from Roger de Montgomery, Earl of Shrewsbury (d. about 1093), who conquered Powys. The Castle, of which some remains exist above the town (good view), was built by Henry III in 1223.

This was the birthplace of the poet George Herbert (1593–1663), whose brother Lord Herbert of Cherbury (1583–1648), the philosopher, also lived here for a time. In the 13th c. parish church is a monument to their father. The church also contains an early Norman font, carved misericords and a beautiful rood-screen, probably from the ruined abbey of Chirbury (Salop).

A well-preserved stretch of the Dyke can also be seen at **Mold** (pop. 8900), county town of Clywd (Wales). The town has a charming old High Street and a beautiful late 15th c. parish church with its original glass.

The painter Richard Wilson (1714–82) is buried here. The most celebrated native of the town was the 19th c. Welsh writer Daniel Owen, who is commemorated by a statue in the town centre. 1 mile S, in Cilcain Road, a pillar marks the spot where in 430 British forces led by St Germanus, bishop of Auxerre, defeated the pagan Picts and Scots.

Offa's Dyke Path is one of the long-distance paths laid out by the Countryside Commission. The paths are waymarked and described in booklets issued by the Commission. They are for pedestrians only.

Orkney Islands

Northern Scotland. – Administrative unit: Orkney Islands.

The Orkneys are a group of 67 islands of varying size, of which 29 are inhabited. They are separated from the mainland of Scotland by the Pentland Firth, which is 6½ miles wide at its narrowest point. The group extends over some 48 miles from N to S and 35 miles from E to W. The islands, built mainly of red sandstone, are predominantly agricultural, with a fertile soil and, thanks to the Gulf Stream, enjoy a mild climate (though subject to frequent violent storms). In recent years North Sea oil has brought increased prosperity.

ACCESS. – There is a *car ferry* service between Scrabster, on the N coast of Scotland, and Stromness, on the largest island, known as Mainland. – There are daily *air services* from London, Glasgow, Aberdeen and Inverness.

HISTORY. – For centuries the Orkneys belonged to Norway, and many of the place-names are Scandinavian in origin. In 1468 King Christian I pledged the Orkneys and Shetlands as security for the dowry of his daughter Margaret on her marriage to James III of Scotland. The dowry was not paid, and the islands were thereupon annexed by Scotland in 1472.

The total population of the Orkneys is some 17,000, most of whom live on **Mainland**. The capital is **Kirkwall** (pop. 4600; Kirkwall Hotel, D, 40 r.), situated in a wide bay at the narrowest point of the island. It is a town of narrow streets, and houses built in Norwegian fashion with small windows and gables facing on to the streets. The most notable building is the large *Cathedral*, dedicated to St Magnus, its architecture reminiscent of Trondheim Cathedral in Norway. It was begun in 1137, the oldest surviving parts of the present building being the transepts and three bays of the choir. The massive Norman columns are notable for being set at irregular distances from one another. King Haco V of Norway was buried here but his remains were later transferred to Trondheim. Two skeletons found in pine chests inside two pillars in 1926 are probably the remains of St Magnus (murdered in 1114) and his nephew. Near the Cathedral are the ruins of the Bishop's Palace and the *Earl's Palace*, a fine example of 16th c. secular architecture.

From *Wideford Hill* (741 ft), 3 miles W of Kirkwall, there is a magnificent view of the whole of the Orkneys. On the NW slopes

Standing stones, Ring of Brogar

of the hill is a chambered cairn. This is bu[t] one of the numerous prehistoric remains to be found all over the Orkneys – perhaps the richest archaeological region in the British Isles, with many sites of European significance. *Skara Brae*, a Neolithic village of about 3000 B.C., gives a vivid impression of the life of Stone Age man. *Maes Howe* is the finest chamber tomb in Western Europe, dating from about 2700 B.C., with later runic inscriptions and incised drawings left by raiding Norsemen. Nearby are the *Standing Stones o[f] Stenness* and, beyond Brogar Bridge, the mysterious *Ring of Brogar*, between two lochs. Of the original 36 undressed monoliths 20 are still standing. – At the N end of the Orkney group, on the little island of *Papa Westray* (named after the hermits who once inhabited it), is Europe's oldest surviving house.

The second largest town on Mainland is **Stromness** (pop. 1670), on the W side of the island, with a harbour sheltered to the SW by the island of Hoy, the second largest in the group. Here too the streets and houses show Norwegian influence. The little town is a good base for exploring this part of Mainland. There is a very rewarding, though strenuous, walk along the rugged W coast, going N, with magnificent views. To the S is the great anchorage of *Scapa Flow*, where [a] German fleet of 70 ships was scuttled after the end of the First World War to prevent them from falling into the hands of the British. During the second world war the battleship *Royal Oak* was sunk in Scapa Flow by a German submarine, with the loss of 800 lives.

Neolithic house, Skara Brae

On the island of **Hoy**, across Scapa Flow, the scenery is more dramatic than anywhere else in the Orkneys, with cliffs rising to over 1000 ft and *Ward Hill* to 1565 ft. The *Dwarfie Stone* and the *Carbuncle*, a great mass of sandstone, feature in Scott's novel "The Pirate". The *Old Man of Hoy*, 2 miles S of St John's Head, is an isolated stack 450 ft high, pierced by a number of holes. St John's Head itself, falling sheer to the sea from a height of 1141 ft, is one of the grandest cliffs in Britain.

Each of the other islands has its own character and its own features of interest. One of the most interesting is the little island of **Egilsay**, E of Rousay, with the remains of the *church of St Magnus*, in which the saint was murdered in 1116; it has a high round tower. There are remains of a Cistercian abbey on the uninhabited island of **Eynhallow**, between Rousay and Mainland, an enchanting island which is the haunt of seals and hosts of seabirds. But the whole of Orkney is a paradise for bird-watchers, with more than 300 recorded species, including auks, petrels, the red-throated diver and numerous species of ducks and gulls. The island of Copinsay is a bird reserve, and there are extensive nesting areas on all the islands.

Rousay has very fine cliffs and many remains of the past. **South Ronaldsay** is connected with Mainland by the *Churchill Barrier*, built during the last war to protect Scapa Flow. Near the village of *St Margaret's Hope* is the Howe of Hoxa, a defensive tower of the early historical period. On **Westray** is the ruined *Noltand Castle* (16th c.).

From Mainland there are regular boat services to the other islands. The larger islands have a few small hotels or guest-houses, and accommodation can also be found in private houses. Many of the sights can be reached only on foot or by bicycle. Spectator entertainments are not to be looked for in the Orkneys, apart from the cinema on Mainland; but the islands are a paradise for nature-lovers who do not need to have their entertainment provided for them, and also for fishermen, who will find an abundance of fish both in the sea and the lochs on Mainland. (There are no rivers and few trees on the islands.)

Oxford

Central England. – County: Oxfordshire.
Population: 123,000.
Telephone dialling code: 0865.
(i) **Tourist Information Centre,**
St Aldate's Chambers,
St Aldates;
tel. 726871.
Erskine Bureaux Ltd,
Railway Station.

HOTELS. – *Randolph*, Beaumont Street, B, 109 r.; *Ladbroke Linton Lodge*, 9–13 Linton Road, B, 72 r.; *Oxford Moat House*, Wolvercote Roundabout, C, 155 r.; *Travelodge Motel*, Peartree Roundabout, C, 102 r.; *Cotswold Lodge*, 66A Banbury Road, C, 52 r.; *Eastgate*, The High, C, 38 r.; *Royal Oxford*, Park End Street, C, 25 r.; *Westwood Country*, Hinksey Hill, D, 18 r.

YOUTH HOSTEL. – Jack Straw's Lane, Marston Road, 104 b.

RESTAURANTS. – *Elizabeth*, 84 St Aldate's; *La Sorbonne*, 130A High Street (1st floor); *Le Petit Blanc*, 272 Banbury Road; *Saraceno*, 15 Magdalen Street; *Wrens*, 29 Castle Street.

EVENTS. – *Sunrise Service* (11 May); *St Giles Market* (Sept.); *Eights Week*, boat races ("bump" races), with many social events (June–July).

SPORT and RECREATION. – Rowing, fishing, riding, golf, tennis; "Gourmet's Oxford" (cookery courses by famous English cooks: 6 days, mid Aug.).

**Oxford is one of the oldest and most celebrated university towns in Europe, and among English towns second only to London in historical and architectural importance. It is also the county town of Oxfordshire – a long straggling town situated at the junction of the Thames and the Cherwell, in the centre of an area of great interest and scenic beauty. During the 20th c. it has acquired some industry, particularly car manufacture. The character of the town is determined by the picturesque old colleges, the Cathedral, the gardens and squares, and the High Street, which has been called the finest street in England.

HISTORY. – The name of the town comes either from its literal meaning, a ford for oxen, or from "Osca's ford". It first appears in the records in 912. The foundation of the University is ascribed by tradition – no doubt wrongly – to King Alfred: what is certain is that the first teaching institutions independent of monasteries and the Church came into being in the 13th and 14th c. Nevertheless the Church continued to enjoy considerable influence. In 1382, for example, John Wycliffe was expelled from the University for attacking abuses in the Church; and until liberty of teaching was achieved there was constant controversy in Oxford, and sometimes bloody clashes. During the Civil War the Royalist headquarters were in Oxford. Since then the town and University have made major contributions to the country's intellectual and cultural development: thus Oxford was the place of origin of such diverse trends as the Oxford Movement of the 19th c. and the Moral Rearmament movement of the 20th.

SIGHTS. – Although the centre of Oxford is not large, plenty of time should be allowed for a visit, since there are so many things to see. The main features, of course, are the 37 colleges, most of them venerable buildings of weathered stone which at first have a rather austere aspect but are mellowed by the fresh green lawns in the quadrangles.

The four principal streets of the town meet at the intersection known as **Carfax**, which makes a good starting point for a tour. The 13th c. tower which stands here, with figures of knights which emerge to strike the hours, is a relic of St Martin's Church.

Going S down St Aldate's Street, past the *Town Hall*, we come to *St Aldate's Church*, which dates from about 1318 but has been much altered. Beyond this is **Pembroke College**, founded in 1624 but now housed in 19th and 20th c. buildings. It contains a portrait by Reynolds of Dr Samuel Johnson, who was at Pembroke in 1728–29.

St Aldate's Street continues S to *Folly Bridge* over the Thames, passing on the way Brewer Street, with *Campion Hall*, an institution for Jesuit students founded in 1896, and Rose Place, in which is the *Old Palace* (1622–28).

Christchurch, known as "the House", is one of the largest colleges, founded in 1525 by Cardinal Wolsey and re-founded after Wolsey's fall by Henry VIII. *Tom Tower*, built by Wren (1681–82), contains the huge bell weighing over 7 tons known as *Great Tom*. Every evening at 5 minutes past 9 it peals 101 times (once for each member of the original college). In earlier days this was the signal for all the college gates to be closed.

The main quadrangle of Christ Church, **Tom Quad**, is the largest in Oxford; it was originally built as a cloister. The lower tower, which contains 12 bells, has a very fine *staircase* of 1630 with fan vaulting. It leads up to the *Hall, the largest and finest in Oxford, completed in 1529. It contains portraits of Henry VIII and distinguished members of the college, including John Locke (1632–1704), who was sent down (expelled) for sedition, and William Penn (1644–1718), founder of Pennsylvania, who was

also sent down as a Nonconformist, having defended the persecuted Quakers. There are also portraits of many Prime Ministers and of Lewis Carroll, author of "Alice in Wonderland", who under his real name of Charles Lutwidge Dodgson was professor of mathematics in Oxford.

The *Cathedral is also the chapel of Christ Church. The entrance, easily overlooked, is on the E side of Tom Quad. On the site which it now occupies there was originally a nunnery founded by S Frideswide, a Mercian princess, probably in 735. The present building, mainly in Transitional style, dates from the second half of the 12th c. The *spire* is one of the oldest in England. The W end of the nave was pulled down by Wolsey to make room for Tom Quad, making the Cathedral one of the smallest in the country, though the diocese is the largest.

INTERIOR. – The most striking feature is the double arcading of the nave. The very fine *organ* is by Bernhard Schmidt (rebuilt). On the N side of the nave is the monument of the philosopher George Berkeley (d. in Oxford 1735), after whom the town of Berkeley in California is named. Some of the *stained glass* is by Sir Edward Burne-Jones. In the S transept is a window depicting Thomas Becket's martyrdom from which the saint's head has been removed – it is said on the orders of Henry VIII.

Also very fine are the choir aisles and the *Lady Chapel* (mid 13th c.), which contains part of the shrine of S Frideswide (1289). The E window (by Burne-Jones) relates the saint's story.

The small *cloister* is Perpendicular, the entrance to the chapterhouse Late Norman. At the NE corner of Tom Quad, beyond the Deanery (in which Charles lived between 1642 and 1646), is a passage known as *Kill-Canon*, so chill it was feared that the canons would catch their death of cold. Here stands statue of Dean Fell (d. 1686), the subject of the famous lines (originally by Thomas Brown), "I do not like thee, Doctor Fell, The reason why I cannot tell". The passage leads into **Peckwater Quadrangle**, a Palladian structure designed by Dean Aldrich (1705–13) and recently completely restored. The *Library* contains a collection of manuscripts and Wolsey's hat and chair. The new *Picture Gallery* beyond it has a fine collection of Italian and other drawings and pictures, including works by Leonardo da Vinci and other old masters. – *Canterbury Quadrangle* (by James Wyatt, 1773–78) occupies the site of Canterbury Hall, where Sir Thomas More (1478–1535), the statesman and humanist, was a student. From here

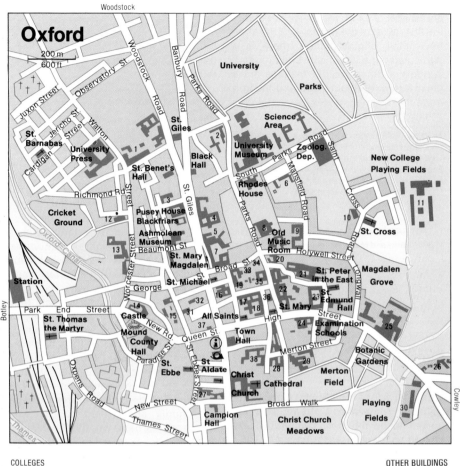

Oxford

200 m
600 ft

COLLEGES

1 Somerville	11 St. Catherine's	21 New College
2 Keble	12 Ruskin	22 All Souls
3 Regents Park	13 Worcester	23 Queen's
4 St. John's	14 Nuffield	24 University
5 Trinity	15 St. Peter's	25 Magdalen
6 Mansfield	16 Jesus	26 Wayneflete
7 Balliol	17 Lincoln	27 Pembroke
8 Wadham	18 Brasenose	28 Corpus Christi
9 Manchester	19 Exeter	29 Merton
10 St. Cross	20 Hertford	30 St. Hilda's

OTHER BUILDINGS

31 Frewin Hall
32 Union Soc Rooms
33 Sheldonian
    Theatre
34 Clarendon
    Building
35 Bodleian Library
36 Radcliffe Camera
37 St. Martin's Tower
38 Peckwater Quad

Canterbury Gate leads out into Merton Street. To the S is the beautiful *Christ Church Meadow*, with a path leading to the Thames (here called the Isis).

On the right-hand side of Merton Street is **Corpus Christi College**, founded by Richard Foxe, bishop of Winchester, in 1516. It is notable particularly for its beautiful garden front and a sundial of 1581 with a perpetual calendar.

Opposite Corpus Christi is **Oriel College**, founded by Edward II in 1326. It takes its name from a house known as La Oriole which previously stood on the site. The 15th and 16th c. buildings are very beautiful; a newer block built in 1911, with a statue of Cecil Rhodes (who was a member of Oriel), is less attractive.

The 19th c. Tractarian movement originated in Oriel. It took its name from the "Tracts for the Times" written here by John Henry Newman (1801–90), an Anglican priest who was one of the leaders of the Oxford Movement but became a Catholic in 1845 and was made a cardinal in 1870.

Near Oriel, in Bear Lane, is the *Museum of Modern Art*, established in 1966. From here we continue E along **Merton Street**, one of Oxford's most picturesque old streets.

***Merton College**, on the right, is one of the oldest of the colleges, and has some of the most interesting buildings. It was founded about 1266 at Merton in Surrey by Walter de Merton, bishop of Rochester, and moved to Oxford in 1284. Unlike other colleges, it was intended in the first place for secular students. The *Chapel* consists of a choir of 1277 and a large antechapel of 1414; the tower was added in 1451. Most of the *windows* of the choir have their original glass (there is a particularly fine Virgin and Child in the E window). Other notable features are a brass *lectern* of about 1500 and the iron *door*.

From the front range of buildings a passage leads under the *Treasury* into the attractive *"Mob Quad"* (c. 1380). The library in this quadrangle is the oldest in England still in use, with many chained books. Among much else it contains the diary of Andrew Irvine, who lost his life on Mount Everest in 1924.

Among distinguished members of Merton have been Lord Randolph Churchill (1849–94), T. S. Eliot (1888–1965) and Max Beerbohm (1872–1956).

Merton Street runs into the splendid ****High Street**, a busy street half a mile long lined with magnificent buildings. It was described by Wordsworth in a sonnet, and the American writer Nathaniel Hawthorne (1804–64) called it "the finest street in England".

On the far side of High Street, a little to the right, is ****Magdalen College**, generally agreed to be the most beautiful of the Oxford colleges. It was founded in 1458 by William of Waynflete, bishop of Winchester, on a site which was then outside the town walls.

Magdalen Tower, in late Perpendicular style, was built between 1482 and 1504. Under the *Muniment Tower* is the entrance to the *Chapel*. The chapel choir is famous, and during the University session evensong, celebrated daily (except Mondays), attracts a considerable congregation. In the *Founder's Tower* are the state apartments, with early 16th c. tapestries. The passage under this tower leads into the cloisters, with grotesque figures known as "hieroglyphs". Beyond the college stretches a deer park, the *Grove*. A bridge in the park leads over the Cherwell into the *Water Walks*, one of which is known as Addison's Walk. (Joseph Addison was a member of Magdalen, as were Oscar Wilde and King Edward VII.)

Opposite the entrance to Magdalen is the **University Botanic Garden**, one of the oldest in England, founded in 1621. The *Magdalen Rose-Garden* was a gift from the Albert and Mary Lasker Foundation of New York (1953) to commemorate the development of penicillin, in which Oxford played a considerable part. The new drug was first used in the *Radcliffe Infirmary* in Woodstock Road.

The High Street is carried over the Cherwell on *Magdalen Bridge*, built in 1772 and widened in 1883. Beyond the bridge, in Cowley Place, is *St Hilda's College* (1893). In Iffley Road are the church and mission of the Cowley Fathers and Greyfriars Hall. – Returning along the High Street, we come (on left) to the *Examination Schools* (1882), designed by Sir G. T. Jackson, an Oxford architect. Beyond this, on the right, is *St Edmund Hall*, built in 1270, the only surviving example of a medieval hall of residence, now a college in its own right; the fine existing buildings mostly date from the 17th c. It is followed by **The Queen's College**, founded in 1340 by Robert de Eglesfield and rebuilt in Palladian style between 1692 and 1730. A statue of Queen Caroline commemorates her gift of £1000 to the college. Opposite The Queen's College is **University College** (commonly abbreviated to "Univ"), whose original name was the *Great Hall of the University*. Founded in 1249, it is the oldest of the colleges. The very dark chapel has fine stained glass by Abraham van Linge (1642).

In a small domed building is a statue of Shelley, who was expelled from the college for atheism.

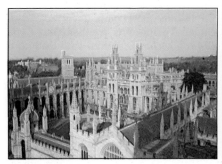
All Souls College

Beyond The Queen's College is *All Souls College*, a college for postgraduate study only, with many members prominent in public life. The college was founded in 1438, and the front range of buildings dates from this period. The chapel has preserved its original glass, and is notable also for its fan tracery and a beautiful reredos. To the N is the *Codrington Library*, with a sundial by Wren.

The University church, **St Mary the Virgin**, has a fine Decorated spire (1280–1310). The *choir* was rebuilt in 1462–66, the *nave* and *Lady Chapel* in 1490–1503. The Baroque *S doorway* with its twisted columns was added in 1637 by Dr Morgan Owen. The stalls date from 1466. From the tower there is a very fine view of the town.

NE of the church is the *Old Congregation Hall*, now a chapel. *All Saints*, at the corner of Turl and High Streets, formerly the City Church, houses the Library of Lincoln College. The *Mitre Hotel* dates from the 17th–18th c.

Radcliffe Camera

N of St Mary's is *Radcliffe Square*, surrounded by university buildings. The *Radcliffe Camera* (1737–49), a rotunda designed by James Gibbs (1682–1754), the most prominent representative of the Anglo-Italian style of architecture, originally housed the Radcliffe Library. The 16-sided room on the ground floor is now a reading room of the Bodleian Library.

The main group of university buildings is on the N side of the square. The *Old Schools Quadrangle* dates from 1613 to 1618; the site was previously occupied by earlier buildings of 1439. The tower has

columns of the five classical orders and a statue of James I. Since 1884 all these buildings have formed part of the **Bodleian Library**, the University library and the first public library in England, founded by Sir Thomas Bodley in 1598. A copy of every book published in Britain is deposited in the Bodleian, which contains almost 2 million volumes and some 40,000 manuscripts. Numerous treasures are displayed in the picture gallery and reading room.

The *Divinity School* dates from 1426 to 1480. The building adjoining the library has a fine ceiling which was restored by Wren. Charles I's Parliament met here during the Civil War.

The *Sheldonian Theatre*, Wren's second major building, was erected in 1664–69; the windows have been altered since his time. The Theatre is used on the occasion of the annual Commemoration or Encaenia in the middle of June, when benefactors of the University are honoured, honorary degrees are conferred and prize compositions are recited.

The *Clarendon Building*, on the E side, is occupied by various University offices. The *Old Ashmolean Museum*, on the W side, now houses the Museum of the History of Science. Among much else it contains the Lewis Evans and Billmeir collections of early scientific and astronomical instruments. Opposite it is the *Bodleian Library Extension* (1935–46), with a bookshop and exhibition room. Nearby, in Holywell Street, is the **Holywell Music Room** (1748), the oldest concert hall in the world.

In Catte Street, opposite the Bodleian, is *Hertford College*, on a site previously occupied by Hart Hall, founded in 1301. The "Bridge of Sighs" over New College Lane joins the old and new buildings of Hertford College; not far to the E is the fortress-like *New College*, which in spite of its name is not new, having been founded in 1379 by William of Wykeham, bishop of Winchester. Until 1854 only students from Winchester were admitted. The *Chapel* was one of the earliest examples of the Perpendicular style. The stained glass is mostly 14th c.; an exception is the large window in the antechapel, painted in 1787 from designs by Sir Joshua Reynolds. Notable features are the *statue of Lazarus* by Epstein and memorials to three German members of the college who fell in the war. The stalls have the original 14th c. misericords. Choral evensong in the chapel is an occasion not to be missed if opportunity offers. The high *Hall* has fine linenfold panelling. The cloisters, with wood vaulting, and the detached bell-tower date from the 14th c. The beautiful gardens (1711) are bounded on two sides by the old town walls.

Returning along New College Road and turning into Parks Road, we come to **Wadham College**, little changed since its foundation in 1610. The *Hall* ranks as the second finest in Oxford, the *Chapel* has good stained glass and the *gardens* are particularly beautiful. Among notable members of Wadham have been Admiral Blake (1599–1657) and Sir Christopher Wren.

In *Turl Street* is **Exeter College**, one of the largest colleges, founded by Walter de Stapledon, bishop of Exeter, in 1314. Opposite is **Jesus College**, founded by Elizabeth I in 1571, which has close connections with Wales. The rear quadrangle (1660–70) is particularly fine. Near Exeter College is **Lincoln College**, founded in 1427 by Richard Fleming, bishop of Lincoln; the N quadrangle dates from the period of the original foundation.

Lincoln College was the birthplace of Methodism. *John Wesley* was a member of the college from 1726 to 1751, and while still an undergraduate established, with his brother Charles, a group of devout Christians whose methodically organised lives earned them the nickname of "Methodists". He was much influenced by the Moravian Brethren. Thereafter he spread his doctrines widely both in Britain and the United States.

There are other interesting colleges N of Broad Street. Beyond the New Bodleian Library is **Trinity College**, founded by Sir Thomas Pope in 1555. Facing Broad Street is *Kettell Hall* (*c.* 1620). The beautiful chapel (1691–94), probably by Dean Aldrich, has fine wood-carving in the manner of Grinling Gibbons.

Adjoining Trinity College is **Balliol College**, another of the oldest and largest of the colleges, founded about 1265 by John de Balliol and his wife. The present buildings are 19th c. The library has a collection of 181 medieval manuscripts.

Balliol is traditionally preferred by Scottish students.

Among distinguished members of Balliol have been John Wycliffe, who taught here in 1361; Adam Smith (1723–90), founder of classical political economy; Robert Southey (1774–1843), Poet Laureate, who produced over 100 volumes of poems and ballads; Algernon Swinburne (1837–1909); and, more recently, Harold Macmillan, King Olav of Norway and the novelist Graham Greene.

A cross in *Broad Street* marks the spot where the reformers Latimer, Ridley and Cranmer were burned at the stake. They are also commemorated by the *Martyrs' Memorial* (by Sir George Gilbert Scott, 1841). Nicholas Ridley, bishop of London, and Hugh Latimer, bishop of Worcester, were martyred on 16 October 1555 and Thomas Cranmer, archbishop of Canterbury, on 21 March 1556. Cranmer was examined from September 1555 to February 1556 in the hall of the Divinity School.

Also in St Giles, the wide handsome street which runs N from the Martyrs' Memorial, is **St John's College**, founded in 1555 by Sir Thomas White, a wealthy merchant who was Lord Mayor of London in 1553. Part of the front range of buildings belonged to St Bernard's College, a Cistercian establishment built in 1437. The *Chapel* contains the tomb of Archbishop Laud (beheaded 1645), a member and later Master of the college. A fan-vaulted passage leads into *Canterbury Quadrangle*, mainly built by Laud (1631–36), with Italian-style colonnades. The *gardens* are among the most beautiful in Oxford.

Farther along St Giles are *Regent's Park College* (Baptist) and *St Benet's Hall* (Benedictine). To the right, in Museum Road, is **Rhodes House**, headquarters of the *Rhodes Trust*, founded under the will of the South African statesman Cecil Rhodes (1853–1902), which grants some 200 scholarships to Commonwealth and foreign students.

The *University Museum*, built 1855–60 under Ruskin's direction, contains a number of interesting collections. A pretty bridge over the Cherwell leads from Manor Road to **St Catherine's College**, built in 1960–64 on part of Holywell Great Meadow. From the end of South Parks Road there is a pleasant walk along the Cherwell past *Parsons' Pleasure* to a

Ashmolean Museum Oxford

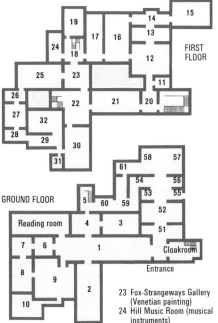

1 Randolph Gallery (classical sculpture)
2 Ruskin Gallery
3 Sunken Court (Greek antiquities)
4 Medieval Room
5 Library Lobby (Viking antiquities)
6 Petrie Room (Egyptian antiquities)
7 Chester Room (Egyptian antiquities)
8 Egyptian Dynastic Gallery
9 Griffith Gallery (Egyptian sculpture and inscriptions)
10 Marshall Room (Worcester porcelain)
11 Tradescant Room ("rarities")
12 John Evans Room (prehistoric Europe, the Etruscans)
13 Arthur Evans Room (Cretan antiquities)
14 Myres Room (Cypriot antiquities)
15 Drapers' Gallery (Near Eastern antiquities)
16 Beazley Room (Greek pottery)
17 Leeds Room (Roman and Anglo-Saxon Britain)
18 Coins and medals
19 Heberden Coin Room (coins and medals)
20 Founder's Room (portraits)
21 Fortnum Gallery (Italian painting)
22 Mallett Gallery (tapestries)

23 Fox-Strangeways Gallery (Venetian painting)
24 Hill Music Room (musical instruments)
25 Weldon Gallery (European painting)
26 Combe Room (Preraphaelites)
27 Hindley Smith Gallery (Impressionists)
28 Pissarro Room (English painting)
29 Eldon Gallery (graphic art)
30 Farrer Gallery (English silver and Italian majolica)
31 Warren Room (English stoneware)
32 McAlpine Gallery (special exhibitions)
51 Vestibule (Gandhara sculpture)
52 Ingram Gallery (Chinese ceramics)
53 Chinese ceramics
54 Asian ceramics
55 Sayce Room (Chinese ceramics)
56 Modern Chinese ceramics
57 Islamic art
58 Japanese art
59 Indian art
60 Special exhibitions
61 Oriental painting and graphic art

SECOND FLOOR

71 Chambers Hall Gallery (English painting)
72 Madan Gallery (Dutch and Flemish painting, English glass)
73 Ward Gallery (Dutch still lifes)

path called Mesopotamia which leads to Magdalen Bridge.

The **Ashmolean Museum is the most important of the four University museums and the oldest museum in the country. The neo-classical building houses a magnificent collection of art and anti-quities, including classical sculpture, Far Eastern art, Greek and Roman pottery and a valuable collection of jewellery.

Worcester College, at the end of Beaumont Street, was founded in 1714. It incorporates parts of Gloucester College, founded for Benedictine students in 1283. On the S side of the college are six 15th c. cottages, and there are three other cottages on the N side. The college *gardens*, with a lake, are among the largest in Oxford.

Almost all the women's colleges apart from St Hilda's are in this part of Oxford – *Lady Margaret Hall* in Norham Gardens, *Somerville*, *St Hugh's*, *St Anne's*. The buildings all date from the second half of the 19th and the 20th c. Women were not granted equal rights as students until 1920.

Cornmarket Street, commonly known as the "Corn", is Oxford's busiest shopping street. On the right-hand side is *St Michael's Church*, with a Saxon tower. The former *Crew Inn*, in which Shakespeare is said to have stayed on the journey between Stratford and London, now contains the offices of the Oxford Preservation Trust. The "Painted Room" on the second floor has walls dating from 1450 and 1550.

Apart from the colleges mentioned above there are a number of others of more recent foundation, among them St Peter's College, Nuffield College and Ruskin College.

SURROUNDINGS. – A favourite walk is from Folly Bridge (1½ miles S) to Iffley, which has a famous *Norman church* (1175–82) with a very beautiful W front. The high altar is Early English; many of the windows are 14th and 15th c.

Blenheim Palace

12 miles N, in the pretty little village of Rousham on the Cherwell, is *Rousham House*, a large Jacobean mansion situated above the river, with very beautiful gardens.

8 miles N, in *Woodstock* (pop. 2000; hotels – Bear, B, 44 r.; Feathers, C, 15 r.; King's Arms, D, 8 r.), is *Blenheim Palace, seat of the dukes of Marlborough, an enormous Baroque mansion built by Sir John Vanbrugh (1705). Its 200 rooms, with fine stonework and wood-carving, contain a splendid collection of furniture, pictures and porcelain, Many visitors, however, come to see the little room in which Winston Churchill was born in 1874, when his mother was staying at Blenheim for a house-party. The large park was laid out by Capability Brown and contains a lake formed by the damming of the little River Clyme.

6 miles S is **Abingdon** (pop. 22,000; hotels – Upper Reaches, B, 20 r.; Crown and Thistle, D, 23 r.), a charming town on the Thames and formerly the county town of Berkshire. It has a large number of interesting buildings and churches, including the old Market Hall (1678–82), now a local museum; the beautiful St Helen's Church (Perpendicular), with a graceful spire and double aisles; St Nicholas, with the gatehouse of a once powerful Benedictine abbey (1475); Christ's Hospital, founded 1553, and other old hospitals of various dates between 1446 and 1797. There are also some remains of a Benedictine abbey – the Checker ("Exchequer"), the Checker Hall, the Long Gallery (15th–16th c.) and fragments of the church.

10 miles NW of Oxford is **Minster Lovell** (Old Swan Hotel, C, 10 r.), an attractive village on the River Windrush. The church has a fine 14th c. central tower. There are also the ruins of a 15th c. manor-house.

Peak District

Central England. – County: Derbyshire.

The Peak District was England's first national park, created to preserve the natural beauty of this area lying between the cities of Manchester, Sheffield and Derby, and also to provide a recreation area enabling their inhabitants to get out into the open air at weekends. The people of these towns take full advantage of these tracts of wild country lying almost on their doorstep, and the roads are often busy with traffic; but on the many footpaths and on the hills, except at certain favourite picnic spots, it is still possible, even at weekends, to find peace and quietness.

The Peak District contains two quite different types of landscape. The wilder northern part, known as the *High Peak* or *Dark Peak*, takes in the southern part of the Pennine chain, with expanses of high moorland, abrupt gritstone crags and hills rising to over 2000 ft. The *Low Peak* or *White Peak* is limestone country, often with very curious rock formations, through which rivers have cut their way to form beautiful valleys. This is an area of lonely farms, fields enclosed by stone walls and patches of woodland.

The two principal holiday resorts in the Peak District are *Buxton* and *Matlock*. At a height of 1690 ft on the beautiful 4 miles of road between Macclesfield and Buxton is the Cat and Fiddle Inn, which claims to be the second highest in England.

Three main roads traverse the area, between Derby and Manchester, offering excellent opportunities to see the magnificent scenery of the Peak. The first route (A 52 and A 523) is from Derby via Leek and Macclesfield to Manchester; the 8 miles beyond Leek are particularly fine. The second (A 6) runs via Matlock and Buxton, through beautiful scenery all the way. The third (A 52, A 515 and A 6) goes via Ashbourne and Buxton.

The best way of seeing the Peak District is to make your headquarters in one of the principal resorts and explore the surrounding area by car or on foot. The Peak also offers excellent riding holidays.

Buxton (pop. 20,800; hotels – Palace, C, 120 r.; St Ann's, D, 82 r.; Buckingham, D, 30 r.; Grove, D, 21 r.), situated at a height of 1000 ft, is a good centre from which to explore the Peak District. The radioactive springs here were known in Roman times, and many centuries later Mary Queen of Scots came to Buxton to take the waters; but the town's former importance as a spa has now greatly declined. It offers a wide range of entertainments and recreational facilities, with occasional skiing in winter. In the beautifully situated *Pavilion Gardens*, through which the River Wye flows, are an opera-house and concert hall, a café and a boating pond. The fine *Crescent*, 316 ft long, was modelled on the crescents of Bath. The Devonshire Royal Hospital, originally built as a riding school, has a dome 154 ft in diameter; it is now a major centre for the treatment of rheumatic diseases. In the higher (and older) part of the town are the Town Hall and the Museum.

Buxton, like other places in the Peak District, is noted for the custom of "well-dressing", said to have originated in the nearby village of Tissington. The custom may well go back to pagan times, although now associated with Ascension Day. It involves setting up a sacred image of wood covered with clay and then coating it with a mosaic of flower-petals, leaves, moss, etc. The whole village takes part in this intricate and time-consuming work, which produces a very striking effect. The final image will last only a day or two, perhaps a week, depending on the weather.

Within easy reach of Buxton are *Arbor Low* (9 miles SE), a Neolithic stone circle of 50 stones situated at an altitude of some 1200 ft, and the *Goyt valley* (3 miles NW), with an outlook tower on Grin Low.

Castleton (12 miles NE) is beautifully situated at the W end of the Hope valley, attracting many visitors in summer. On a steep-sided crag above the village is *Peveril Castle*; the massive keep with its thick walls dates from 1176. Castleton is noted for its *caves*, which are open to visitors throughout the year. The most impressive is the *Peak Cavern*, half a mile long. Also of interest is the *Speedwell Mine*, in which visitors take a boat trip along an underground gallery half a mile long to a huge pothole where the water tumbles down into an abyss. The most attractive route to the *Blue John Mine* is by way of the *Winnats*, a steep and narrow ravine 1 mile long. This cavern is named after the bluish (sometimes also yellow-tinged) type of felspar found here, which can also be seen, in many varying shades of colour, in Treak Cliff and *Treak Cliff Cavern*.

Chatsworth (15 miles E) is one of the great country houses of Derbyshire. Little remains of the original Elizabethan house, which was replaced between 1687 and 1705 by the present Palladian mansion. A wing was added in the 19th c. by Wyatville. Chatsworth contains a magnificent collection of old masters, sculpture, tapestries, furniture and objets d'art which call for a visit of 2 or 3 hours if they are to be seen properly. The gardens, designed by Joseph Paxton from 1826 onwards, are delightful, with fountains and cascades, an orangery, a rose-garden with statues and a miniature temple decorated with carved figures of dolphins. There is also a deer park. On a hill behind the house is the Elizabethan *Hunting Tower*, from which there is a good view, and near the bridge is *Queen Mary's Bower*, said to have been a favourite spot of the imprisoned Mary Queen of Scots, who was confined at Chatsworth on several occasions between 1570 and 1581.

*Haddon Hall** (15 miles SE) has a magnificent setting on a hillside above the Wye. One of the duke of Rutland's seats, it is the very picture of a noble mansion, one of the most romantic spots in England. It was originally a Norman stronghold, and the NE tower and parts of the chapel are late Norman work. The hall is 14th c., the E wing 15th c. and the garden front 16th c. A handsome flight of steps leads down into the beautiful gardens, skilfully remodelled at the beginning of this century. The house contains fine furniture and pictures.

Bakewell (pop. 3900; Rutland Arms Hotel, C, 33 r.; youth hostel, Fly Hill, 40 b.) is another good base from which to explore the Peak District. It is a pretty little town on the Wye, here spanned by a medieval bridge, with handsome 17th and 18th c. houses. The church (12th–14th c.) contains a 13th c. font and monuments of the Vernon family.

Monsal Dale (4 miles NW) is a beautiful little valley, which can only be explored on foot.

Matlock (pop. 14,300; hotels – New Bath, C, 58 r.; Riber Hall, C, 12 r.; Temple, D, 14 r.; youth hostel in Bank Road, 44 b.) was a much-frequented spa in the 19th c. and is still a popular resort. It is made up of a number of separate parts – Matlock Bridge, at a medieval bridge over the Derwent; Matlock Bank on the hills and Matlock Bath, the most picturesque part of the town, in the narrow gorge of the Derwent.

E of Matlock Bath is *High Tor*, a limestone crag rising to a height of 400 ft above the river. Another group of rocks is known as the *Heights of Abraham*. The 19th c. *Riber Castle* is now an animal and nature reserve, with British animals and birds. Other great tourist attractions are the *Petrifying Wells* and caves.

5 miles SE, at *South Wingfield*, are the ruins of a 15th c. manor-house in which Mary Queen of Scots was imprisoned, with a tower and vaulted cellars. 6 miles SE of Matlock is the National Tramway Museum.

The highest plateau in the Peak District is **Kinder Scout** (2088 ft), best climbed from the village of Edale in the vale of the same name.

Edale is the starting point of the *Pennine Way*, a long-distance route for walkers and riders, waymarked by the National Parks Commission, which runs N for 250 miles to the borders of Scotland. Other classic walks in the area are through *Cheedale*, *Wye Dale* and *Ashwood Dale*.

Peterborough

Central England. – County: Cambridgeshire.
Population: 110,000.
Telephone dialling code: 0733.
ⓘ **Tourist Information Centre**,
Town Hall, Bridge Street;
tel. 63141
Central Library,
Broadway;
tel. 48343, ext. 23.

HOTELS. – *Saxon Inn*, Thorpe Wood, C, 98 r.; *Crest*, Great North Road, C, 97 r.

RESTAURANTS. – *Angel*, Bridge Street; *Grand*, Wentworth Street.

SPORT and RECREATION. – Rowing, fishing, tennis, walking (in the Fens).

Peterborough is an industrial town attractively situated on the N bank of the River Nene, on the outskirts of the Fen district. It has large factories producing diesel engines, and among its other products are refrigerators and agricultural machinery. The town is mainly modern, but its principal attraction for visitors is its Cathedral, one of the finest Norman churches in England. There are also a number of interesting old buildings round the marketplace.

HISTORY. – The town, "Peter's borough", grew up round the Saxon monastery of Medeshamstede, founded about 650 by the first Christian king of Mercia on the site now occupied by the Cathedral. The monastery was destroyed by the Danes in 870 and rebuilt by Ethelwold, bishop of Winchester (963–84). Thereafter it developed into one of the

Peterborough Cathedral

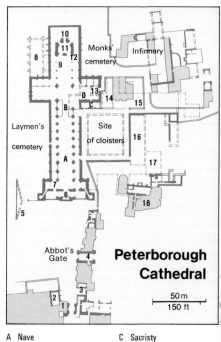

Peterborough Cathedral

50 m
150 ft

A Nave
B Choir

C Sacristy
D Saxon church

1 Outer Gate (St Nicholas Chapel above)
2 Chapel of St Thomas of Canterbury
3 Prison
4 Knight's Chamber
5 Prior's Gate
6 Trinity Chapel (now Library)
7 Portrait of Old Scarlett
8 Site of Lady Chapel (destroyed 1651)
9 Tomb of Catherine of Aragon

10 New Building
11 Monks' Stone (8th c.)
12 Burial place of Mary Queen of Scots
13 Entrance to foundations of Saxon church
14 Site of Chapterhouse
15 Site of monks' dormitory
16 Site of monks' refectory
17 Site of monks' kitchen
18 Bishop's Palace

mightiest Benedictine abbeys in the country. The Cathedral suffered much destruction at the hands of Cromwell's troops in 1643.

SIGHTS. – The *Cathedral, begun in 1117, was built of local stone, a beautiful ivory-coloured stone from quarries at Barnack in Northamptonshire, only 10 miles away. The *choir* was completed by 1140, the *transepts* and *nave* by the end of the century. The *W transepts*, in Transitional style, date from 1193 to 1200. The *W front*, one of the finest examples of Early English architecture, was added in 1200–22, with three huge arches (81 ft high) which seem disproportionately large for the rest of the structure. The central arch is narrower than the other two. Above the arches are intricate patterns of tracery, three small rose windows and a row of figures (preserved in part). The two towers flanking the W front appear small in comparison. The *central tower* was pulled down in the 14th c. and replaced by a smaller one. The

Perpendicular *porch*, above which is the library, was added in 1370.

The INTERIOR is something of a surprise after the exterior. The *nave* is very impressive, with an air of great lightness in spite of its massive Norman piers.

The very beautiful *painted ceiling* (c. 1220) is unique in England. Near the W door is an 18th c. portrait of "Old Scarlett" (d. 1594), sexton and gravedigger, who prided himself on having buried two queens in the Cathedral. In the N aisle is the *tomb of Catherine of Aragon*, in the S aisle that of *Mary Queen of Scots*, whose remains were removed to Westminster Abbey in 1612 by her son James VI of Scotland and I of England. Both tombs were destroyed by Cromwell's troops.

The 13th c. *font* is made of local marble. The transepts are the only parts of the church which preserve the original *Norman ceiling painting*, the finest example of the kind in England. Under the S transept can be seen the foundations of the second Saxon church, with a number of tombstones.

The retrochoir, also known as the *New Building*, has fan vaulting. The timber *ceiling* of the sanctuary dates from the 14th c. The elaborate brass *lectern* is 15th c. On the S side of the nave, in *Laurel Court*, are the remains of the cloisters, with a Norman *fountain* in the centre. Three old *gates* are set round the Minster Yard.

The *Museum* in Priestgate contains among much else Roman remains, articles made by French prisoners during the Napoleonic wars and what is believed to be the earliest portrait of a judge wearing his robes (16th c.).

SURROUNDINGS. – 13 miles NW is **Stamford** (pop. 16,200; George Hotel, C, 47 r.), an old market town, with four fine churches, which has preserved its original character almost intact. St Mary's Church has an Early English tower with a Decorated broach spire. All Saints Church is Early English, with a Perpendicular tower and spire, and contains some fine brasses. St John's Church (Perpendicular) has fine stained glass and woodwork, and there is also some old glass in St George's Church (rebuilt 1420). The most interesting secular building is Browne's Hospital, founded in 1480, with a Jacobean hall and chapel. The Town Hall dates from 1777, the former theatre in St Mary's Street from 1769. – During the 14th c. Stamford sought to compete with Oxford as a teaching centre, and in addition to the churches it possesses a large number of fine Elizabethan, Jacobean and Georgian houses.

On the other side of the River Welland is *Stamford Baron*, with St Martin's Church, in which William Cecil, Lord Burghley, Elizabeth I's principal minister, is buried. Close by is the entrance to *Burghley House*, seat of the Marquess of Exeter, and one of England's finest Elizabethan houses (built 1553–87), containing good ceiling paintings, furniture and pictures.

Barnack (3 miles SE) is the source of the fine building stone, ranging in colour from ivory-white to yellowish, used in so many churches and houses in this part of the country. It can be seen in the local church, built in the 11th c. and thus one of the oldest

in England; it has a Saxon tower with an Early English spire and a fine doorway, and contains a notable font.

Longthorpe (3 miles W) has a 13th–14th c. fortified house, called Longthorpe Tower, with contemporary wall paintings. – *Castor* (pop. 550) is so called because it occupies the site of a Roman camp (*Durobrivae*). The Norman church (1124) is dedicated to St Cyneburga, a Mercian princess. It has a richly decorated tower and a 14th c. painting of St Catherine.

Peakirk Waterfowl Gardens (7 miles N) belong to the Severn Wildfowl Trust, founded by Sir Peter Scott in 1946 to preserve and maintain Britain's many species of waterfowl.

Plymouth

South-western England. – County: Devon.
Altitude: 100 ft. – Population: 256,400.
Telephone dialling code: 0752.
(i) **Tourist Information Centre**,
Civic Centre, Royal Parade;
tel. 264851/264849.
Ferry Terminal,
Millbay Docks.

HOTELS. – *Holiday Inn*, Armada Way, B, 218 r.; *Mayflower Post House*, Cliff Road, The Hoe, B, 104 r.; *Duke of Cornwall*, Millbay Road, C, 67 r.; *Berni Grand*, The Hoe, D, 76 r.

YOUTH HOSTEL. – Belmont House, Devonport Road, Stoke, 80 b.

RESTAURANTS. – *Marquee*, 1 Sherwell Arcade; *Ristorante Bella Napoli*, 41/42 Southside Street, The Barbican; *Khyber*, 44 Mayflower Street; *Green Lanterns*, 31 New Street.

EVENTS. – *Navy Week* (Aug.).

SPORT and RECREATION. – Good facilities for sailing and water sports; riding, golf, tennis.

Plymouth, situated at the mouth of the River Tamar, which forms the boundary between Devon and Cornwall, is one of Britain's largest seaports and naval bases, and historically the most important. The defeat of the Spanish Armada off Plymouth marked the beginning of Britain's rise to the status of a world power.

Together with Stonehouse and Devonport, Plymouth has now become a considerable town. Bordered by a wide beach, it lies between hills which reach down to the adjoining bays, and the surrounding woodland and meadows combine with extensive parks and gardens to give the town an open and attractive aspect. The names of Sir Francis

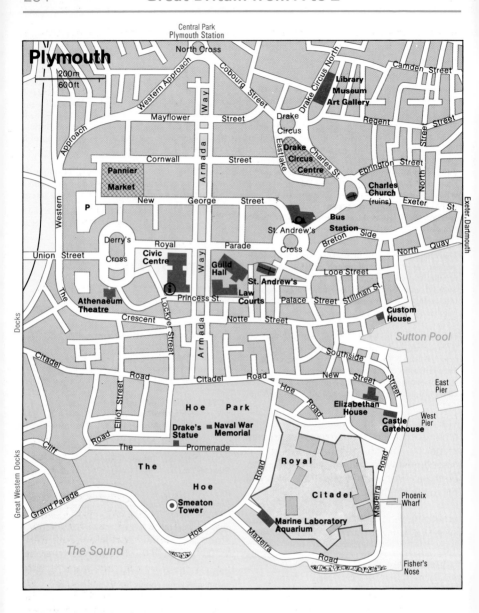

Drake and the *Mayflower* are closely associated with Plymouth.

HISTORY. – The town takes its name from the little River Plym. From here the Black Prince sailed for France in 1355, and from here too many discoverers and conquerors set out, among them Drake, Raleigh and Captain Cook. On 31 July 1588 the Spanish Armada was defeated in Plymouth Sound, and on 6 September 1620 the *Mayflower* sailed for America. In later centuries many emigrants left here on their way to the New World. As a result there are something like a dozen towns called Plymouth in the United States. – During the Second World War the town suffered heavy damage.

SIGHTS. – The finest views of the town and Plymouth Sound are to be had from the **Hoe**, a spacious park traversed by the Promenade, with a prospect extending over the Sound as far as the famous Eddystone lighthouse, 14 miles away. On the Hoe is Smeaton's Tower, the upper part of the third *Eddystone lighthouse*, which was replaced by the present one in 1878; it now houses a *Maritime Museum*. Here too are the *Armada Memorial* and a *statue of Sir Francis Drake*. Just offshore is *Drake's Island*.

The **Citadel**, E of the Hoe, was built in 1566–70. Under its walls is an *Aquarium* belonging to the Marine Biological Laboratory. From the road which runs round the Citadel there is a good view of the remains of the old town, with only a few old houses. Beyond is *Sutton Pool*, once the only harbour, now a fishing harbour. On the pier is the *Mayflower Memorial* and a tablet commemorating an American seaplane which was the first aircraft to cross the Atlantic (1919, via the Azores). On the Parade are the *Old Custom House* (1586) and the *New Custom House* (1810).

The busy activity in the narrow little streets in this quarter (New Street, Castle Street, etc.) gives some impression of what the old town must have been like in the past. Plymouth's principal church *St Andrew's* (1430–90), was severely damaged during the last war but has been rebuilt. *Prysten House* also dates from the 15th c.

The centre of Plymouth has been completely rebuilt. From the *Civic Centre with its 14-storey block of offices and restaurant there are good panoramic views of the city. The Centre was built to the plans of H. J. W. Stirling in 1958–62. The *City Museum and Art Gallery* in North Drake Circus is well worth a visit.

Stonehouse and *Devonport* contain many fine old houses, mainly Georgian and Regency. The *Royal Dockyard*, established in 1691 by William III, can be visited. In addition to various naval establishments it contains a *memorial to Captain Scott*, who was born in Devonport and died in 1912 on his expedition to the South Pole. *Gun Wharf* (by Vanbrugh, 1718–25) is a fine piece of early 18th c. architecture.

SURROUNDINGS. – Plymouth offers a variety of interesting excursions, some of them by boat. There is, for example, a ferry service to the Cornish village of Cremyll which has interesting 18th c. buildings. Here too is *Mount Edgcumbe*, a 16th c. mansion restored after war damage, with beautiful grounds.

Another attractive trip is up the River Tamar to Cotehele, passing Calstock, with the *Morwell Rocks*. **Cotehele House** is a fine grey granite Tudor mansion (1485–1539), a former seat of the earl of Mount Edgcumbe, which claims to be the least altered medieval manor-house in England. It contains fine furniture, needlework and weapons.

Saltram House (3 miles E) is a mansion in classical style by Robert Adam (1750). It is notable particularly for ten pictures by Sir Joshua Reynolds, who lived and worked for several years in Devonport and was a frequent visitor to Saltram, where he painted portraits of the family. The house also contains valuable porcelain, furniture and chinoiseries.

Antony House (5 miles W of Plymouth) is a Queen Anne mansion, partly dating from the 17th c. but mostly from 1711 to 1721, with fine panelled rooms and a beautiful landscaped park.

Buckland Abbey (11 miles N) was originally a Cistercian house, founded in 1278, which was converted into a mansion by Sir Richard Grenville in 1541. It was purchased in 1581 by Sir Francis Drake, who lived here until 1595. The house is now a museum, notable particularly for its fine models of famous old ships. It also has Drake's drum.

Portsmouth

Southern England. – County: Hampshire.
Altitude: 27 ft. – Population: 179,000.
Telephone dialling code: 0705.
ⓘ **Tourist Information Centre,**
Castle Buildings, Clarence Esplanade;
tel. 826722.
Civic Offices,
Guildhall Square;
tel. 834092/3.

HOTELS. – *Holiday Inn*, North Harbour, B, 170 r.; *Crest*, Pembroke Road, C, 169 r.; *Pendragon*, Clarence Parade, C, 58 r.

YOUTH HOSTEL. – *Wymering Manor*, Cosham, 58 b.

RESTAURANTS. – *Murrays*, 27A South Parade, Southsea; *Three Musketeers*, Hayling Island; *The Old House*, Wickham (old Georgian house, 7 miles NW on A32).

EVENTS. – *Navy Week* (Aug.).

Portsmouth, situated on the "island" of Portsea, owes its importance to its magnificent natural harbour. For centuries, from the time of the Armada onwards, it was the principal English naval base. Nelson's flagship, HMS *Victory*, on which he was mortally wounded during the battle of Trafalgar, lies in the dry dock at the entrance to the Royal Dockyard and is open to visitors. Launched in 1765, it is barely 200 ft long, with five decks and more than a hundred guns.

HISTORY. – The strategic importance of this site on the Channel was recognised by the Romans, who built a fort at Portchester, on a promontory just W of Portsmouth – the only Roman fort in Britain or northern Europe which was never destroyed, though frequently captured. The Normans took over the Roman fortress; Henry II strengthened it; and Richard II enlarged it and built a fortified palace adjoining the keep. Henry V assembled his army here before sailing for France. – During the Second World War large areas of Portsmouth were destroyed. – On 6 June 1984 an Invasion Museum was opened as a memorial to the Allied landings in Normandy in 1944 (90-ft-long tapestry).

SIGHTS. – The centre of interest in Portsmouth is the **Harbour**. On the quay, near the *Victory*, is a *Museum*, with many relics of Nelson and the battle of Trafalgar.

Round Tower and Tower House, Portsmouth

The *Round Tower* and *Square Tower* date from the 15th c. The old *Naval Academy* (1729) and *Admiralty House* are handsome Georgian buildings. In the historic *High Street* only one building survived the bombing – *Buckingham House* (No. 10), in which the duke of Buckingham was murdered in 1628. The only church of any interest is the **Cathedral**, dedicated to St Thomas. The other major buildings are mainly of functional significance. Appropriately, the great 19th c. engineer Brunel was born here.

Another native of Portsmouth was *Charles Dickens*, whose father was a clerk in the dockyard; his birthplace at 393 Commercial Road is now a museum. Sir Arthur Conan Doyle, author of the Sherlock Holmes stories, practised as a doctor in Portsmouth.

SOUTHSEA, a favoured residential area, is now part of Portsmouth. It has a 3-mile-long *Promenade* from which there are good views of the Isle of Wight and passing shipping. In *Cumberland House* are a museum and art gallery. On the Promenade stand many memorials to naval heroes. The **Guildhall** (1890) has a *clock-tower* 210 ft high.

SURROUNDINGS. – At **Titchfield** (19 miles NW), a little place on the River Meon, are the remains of a Premonstratensian abbey founded in 1238 which the earl of Southampton converted into a residence in 1537, calling it Place House. The fine gatehouse and four towers survive from the original foundation, with fine medieval tiles which are unusually well preserved. There is a portrait of the earl in the church.

Richmond

Northern England. – County: North Yorkshire.
Altitude: 500 ft. – Population: 7200.
Telephone dialling code: 0748.
ⓘ **Tourist Information Centre**,
  Friary Gardens, Queen's Road;
  tel. 3525 (May–Sept.).

HOTELS. – *King's Head*, Market Square, D, 25 r.; *Frenchgate*, 59 Frenchgate, D, 12 r.

SPORT and RECREATION. – Rowing, sailing, walking (Pennines, North Yorkshire Moors).

Richmond is a very attractive little town, described by the British Council in 1945 as "typically English". It lies on the River Swale, dominated by the imposing ruins of a Norman castle. Every morning and every evening, following an old tradition, a curfew bell is rung. Richmond is an excellent base for walks in the great open spaces of the Pennines.

HISTORY. – The name of the town comes from the castle ("Riche Mont") built about 1070 by Alan the Red, first earl of Richmond. His extensive possessions, including no fewer than 164 manors, became known as *Richmondshire*. Henry VII, who inherited the title of earl of Richmond, gave the name to his new palace in Surrey (now in Greater London), previously known as Sheen.

SIGHTS. – The best view of the town, formerly defended by walls and three gates, is to be had from the top of the Norman *keep*, a massive structure built between 1150 and 1180. The **Castle**, dating from the 11th c., was impregnable on three sides, thanks to its situation; the fourth side was protected by the keep. The great hall, known as *Scotland's Hall*, is probably the oldest in the country.

In the large cobbled market-place is the little church of *Holy Trinity*, hemmed in

View of the River Swale from Richmond Castle

between houses and shops. To the N, in Queen's Road, is *Greyfriars Tower* (*c*. 1360–70). In Friars' Wynd is a charming little Georgian theatre, the *Theatre Royal (1788), the second oldest in England (restored). It is still used, and is open to visitors. The parish church is *St Mary's*, which has 16th c. stalls from Easby Abbey.

A beautiful path along the River Swale leads to the extensive and picturesque ruins of **Easby Abbey** (1 mile), a Premonstratensian house founded in 1155. The parish church, *St Agatha's*, has a copy of the *Easby Cross* (Anglo-Saxon, *c*. 800: original in British Museum) and mid 13th c. wall paintings.

SURROUNDINGS. – *Swaledale* and *Wensleydale* are part of the most wildly beautiful area in England (see under *Yorkshire Dales*).

Rochester Cathedral

Rochester

Southern England. – County: Kent.
Population: 31,300.
Telephone dialling code: 0634.
ⓘ **Tourist Information Centre**,
Eastgate Cottage, Eastgate, High Street;
tel. 43666.

HOTELS. – *Crest*, Maidstone Road, 106 r.; *Gordon*, 91 High Street, E, 18 r.

RESTAURANT. – *Leather Bottle*, Cobham (17th c. workhouse, associated with Dickens).

SPORT and RECREATION. – Water sports of all kinds.

Rochester is a charming old town, now almost joined up with the industrial towns of Chatham and Gillingham. It lies on the Medway, just above the estuary. The Castle, standing high above the river, was mainly built by William of Corbeil, archbishop of Canterbury, about 139. From the massive keep there is a good view of the town and the Medway. On the bridge over the river is a small chapel.

Charles Dickens (1812–70) spent part of his childhood in Rochester, and the town frequently features in his novels. The houses with Dickens associations are marked by tablets.

HISTORY. – By virtue of its situation Rochester was already a place of some consequence in Roman times. In 604 St Augustine founded the third English episcopal see here, and the position of his church is now occupied by the Cathedral. Kent is the only one of the old English counties which had two cathedrals (Rochester and Canterbury).

Rochester Cathedral

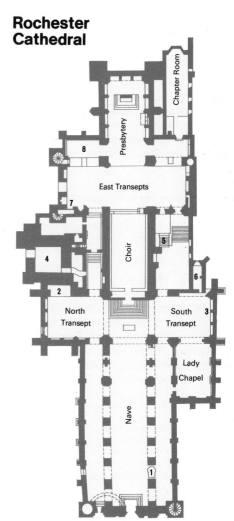

1	Font
2	Jesus Chapel
3	Watts and Dickens monuments
4	Gundulf's Tower

5	Entrance to Crypt
6	Vestry
7	Tomb of Bishop Walter de Merton
8	St John's Chapel

SIGHTS. – The *Cathedral has similarities with Canterbury. Its origins go back to the time of Ethelbert (6th c.), but the present building is largely Norman (built between the 11th and 15th c., consecrated in 1130). It was begun by Bishop Gundolf, successor to the first Norman bishop, St Justus, who also built the White Tower in London. The *choir* was rebuilt in 1201–27 after a fire. The *central tower* was completed in 1343 (restored 1904). The Norman *W doorway* (*c.* 1160) is flanked by two *statues*, probably of Solomon and the Queen of Sheba, which are the oldest of their kind in England.

The low, wide *nave* is Norman. The *transepts* (1240) and the raised *Choir* (early 13th c.) are Early English. Notable features of the Choir are the fragment of a 13th c. *wall painting* of the Wheel of Fortune and the *choir-stalls*, some of which are among the oldest in England (1227). Also very fine are the figures at the entrance to the *Chapterhouse*, representing the Church and the Synagogue, four Fathers of the Church and a soul emerging from Purgatory. The *Crypt*, one of the largest in the country, has fine Early English vaulting.

From the Cathedral, passing *Minor Canons Row*, a terrace of early Georgian houses (1723), we come to *King's School*, which claims a history going back to 604 but which was re-founded by Henry VIII.

Among the houses associated with Dickens is *Restoration House* in Maidstone Road, said to have been occupied by Charles II in 1660, which is identified as Miss Havisham's house in "Great Expectations". In the High Street is *Eastgate House*, an Elizabethan house dating from 1591, now a *museum*, with a Dickens Room. *Watts' Charity*, a hostel for "six poor travellers" founded in 1579, features in Dickens's story "The Seven Poor Travellers". Close by is the *Old Corn Exchange*, with a *clock* dating from 1706. The *Guildhall* dates from 1687.

SURROUNDINGS. – **Chatham** and **Gillingham**, immediately adjoining Rochester, are industrial and naval towns. There are associations with Dickens in Chatham, where he lived as a boy, and at *Gad's Hill*, the house where he spent his later years.

The little village of **Cobham** is familiar to readers of the "Pickwick Papers". The *Leather Bottle Inn* has Dickens relics. The church of St Mary Magdalene has no fewer than 18 brasses in the chancel, the largest collection of any church in England. Dating from the 14th–16th c., the figures of knights, ladies and ecclesiastics are a valuable source of information about the costumes and weapons of the different periods. Also of interest are the College Almshouses (1598). Cobham Park is widely famed for its beautiful

large rhododendrons. Cobham Hall (*c.* 1580–1670), now a girls' school, is a late Elizabethan brick manor-house, with four turrets. The Gilt Hall, a music room, has a fine gilded plaster ceiling.

An interesting excursion can be made from Rochester to *Maidstone* (12 miles S), passing through the pretty little village of **Aylesford**, with a 14th c. bridge over the Medway. The church has a Norman tower, and there is a Carmelite friary (reoccupied) originally founded in 1240. Near the village is a Neolithic chambered tomb (two uprights and a capstone).

Maidstone (pop. 74,400; hotels – Larkfield, C, 52 r.; Emma, D, 51 r.; Royal Star, D, 33 r.) is the county town of Kent. Around the parish church of All Saints, along the river, is a fine group of 14th c. houses. The church (1381–96) has interesting misericords. Adjoining it is a college of secular canons. The 14th c. Archbishop's Palace has a fine external staircase. Maidstone also has an interesting collection of old carriages, housed in the Archbishop's Stables, and a Museum and Art Gallery in a 16th c. manor-house.

St Albans

Central England. – County: Hertfordshire.
Population: 50,900.
Telephone dialling code: 0727.
ⓘ Town Hall,
37 Chequer Street;
tel. 64511/2.

HOTELS. – *The Noke Thistle*, Watford Road, B, 57 r.; *St Michael's Manor*, Fishpool Street, C, 22 r.; *Haven*, 234 London Road, D, 47 r.

The old market town of St Albans, situated on a hill above the left bank of the River Ver, N of London, is of interest both for its old Abbey and for the excavations of the Roman town of Verulamium.

HISTORY. – The town takes its name from St Alban, a Roman soldier converted to Christianity by St Amphibalus who was martyred about the year 304. His remains were found when King Offa of Mercia founded a Benedictine abbey here in 793. The abbey church was raised to cathedral status in 1872. – There were two battles at St Albans during the Wars of the Roses, in 1455 and 1461.

St Albans Cathedral

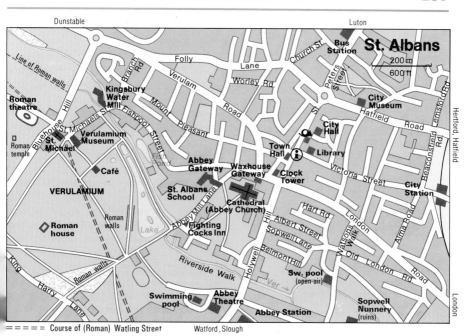

SIGHTS. – In the centre of the old town is a *Clock-Tower* erected between 1403 and 1412. Near this is the Market Place, in which is the *Town Hall* (1829). From here St Peter's Street runs N to *St Peter's Church*, with a nave and S transept dating from the 15th c. (restored).

To the S of the old town is the *Cathedral*, formerly the church of a Benedictine abbey founded by Offa, which after the dissolution of the abbey in 1539 became the parish church. Originally a Norman church (1077–88), it was later much altered and enlarged. The W end of the nave was extended in 1214–35, the monks' choir was added in 1235–60 and the Lady Chapel in 1308–26. The W front and the transept fronts were remodelled in 1879–84 by Lord Grimthorpe. The *central tower* is Norman. With a total length of 556 ft, the Cathedral is one of the largest in England, exceeded only by Winchester.

The INTERIOR shows the same range of styles as the exterior. The first few bays at the W end are Early English; the next five bays on the S side were rebuilt in 1323 after this part of the wall had collapsed. The Norman pillars on the N side of the nave have fragments of *13th–14th c. painting*, including a fine Crucifixion of about 1220.

The *lay choir*, separated from the nave by a *rood-screen* (c. 1350), has a coffered wooden ceiling. – Above the *crossing* rises the Norman tower. The ceiling of the crossing has painting (1951–52) modelled on the original medieval decoration, with red and white roses which refer to the conflict between the houses of York and Lancaster in the Wars of the Roses. – The S transept has some Saxon arches, altered in Norman times.

The *monks' choir* is roofed with ribbed timber vaulting with painted decoration of 1422–61. At the E end is an *altar screen* richly decorated with figures (1484, restored 1884–90). On both sides are small chapels; in the one to the S is the brass of Abbot Thomas de la Mare (d. 1375). – Behind the altar screen is **St Alban's Chapel** (c. 1315), with *St Alban's Shrine* (reconstructed from fragments in 1872–75), which shows scenes from his martyrdom. On the N side is a fine oak *watching loft*. In the N choir aisle is the shrine of St Amphibalus, who converted St Alban to Christianity. – Beyond the retrochoir is the 14th c. *Lady Chapel*, which was used until 1877 by the adjoining grammar school. The school still occupies the large *gatehouse* (1361) W of the Cathedral, the only relic of the monastic buildings.

From the Cathedral a path leads SW over the former abbey gardens to the *Fighting Cocks Inn*, said to be Britain's oldest inn. Beyond this a bridge crosses the River Ver to the site of Roman **Verulamium**.

The Roman town was founded about A.D. 45, and became the only *municipium* in Britain and the third largest town in the country. The ruins of the Roman city provided building material for the Norman abbey.

Roman theatre, Verulamium

Excavations in the 1930s brought to light the remains of town walls, a Roman **theatre** and a *mosaic floor* with a hypocaust (heating installation). Finds from the site can be seen in the **Verulamium Museum**.

Near the Museum, on the site of the Roman forum, is **St Michael's Church**, with the tomb of Francis Bacon, Lord Verulam, philosopher and statesman (1561–1626).

SURROUNDINGS. – 7 miles E of St Albans, outside the old market town of *Hatfield* (pop. 29,000), is *Hatfield House, an imposing early 17th c. Jacobean mansion (open to visitors), with beautiful gardens.

Salisbury

Southern England. – County: Wiltshire.
Altitude: 150 ft. – Population: 36,000.
Telephone dialling code: 0722.
(i) **Tourist Information Centre,**
   10 Endless Street;
   tel. 27676.

HOTELS. – *White Hart*, 1 St John's Street, C, 72 r.; *Rose and Crown*, Harnham Road, Harnham, C, 27 r.; *Cathedral*, 7 Milford Street, D, 32 r.; *Kings Arms*, St John's Street, D, 16 r.; *Pembroke Arms*, 200 Minster Street, Wilton, D, 8 r.

YOUTH HOSTEL. – Milford Hill, 72 b.

RESTAURANTS. – *Crane's*, 90–92 Crane Street; *Dutch Mill*, 58A Fisherton Street; *Yew Tree Inn*, Odstock (2½ miles S).

SPORT and RECREATION. – Rowing, fishing, riding.

Salisbury, the county town of Wiltshire, situated at the point where the rivers Nadder and Bourne flow into the Avon, offers two major attractions to visitors – the charm of the medieval town, with its famous Cathedral, and its convenience as a base from which to visit **Stonehenge (see p. 267), one of the largest and most important prehistoric monuments in Europe.**

HISTORY. – Before 1220 the town was situated 2 miles from the present town centre at *Old Sarum*, a hill previously occupied by a prehistoric earthwork. On this site the Romans established a fort, *Sorviodunum*, and the Saxons in turn built a town there. William the Conqueror erected a castle on this strategically important site, and in 1075 transferred the episcopal see of Sherborne to Sarum. The Castle and the Cathedral, which was consecrated in 1092, were intended to assert the dominance of the Normans. In the 13th c., probably as a result of conflict between the Church and the military authorities and because of the poor water supply at Old Sarum, the Church resolved to build a new cathedral elsewhere. In 1220 the old cathedral was abandoned, and the town moved 2 miles away to New Salisbury, where both the town and the Cathedral were magnificently rebuilt, stone and other materials from the old cathedral being used in the construction of the new one. The foundations of the old cathedral can still be seen at Old Sarum,

together with some remains of the Norman castle, enclosed within an earth rampart.

SIGHTS. – The present town of Salisbury of New Sarum was founded in 1220. The town was laid out on a grid plan, with gardens behind the houses – a masterpiece of enlightened planning.

The *Cathedral, built between 1220 and 1280, is a magnificent example of the later Early English style. The rectangular termination of the chancel became the model for later English churches, displacing the rounded Norman apse. The Decorated *tower* and *spire* over the crossing, the tallest in England (404 ft), were added by Robert of Farleigh between 1330 and 1370. In spite of this difference in style the slender and elegant spire is in perfect harmony with the rest of the structure. It delights the eye with its apparent lightness; and yet the piers of Purbeck marble are supporting a weight of 6400 tons.

Salisbury Cathedral

The INTERIOR reveals classical proportions, but appears somewhat cold and austere – a consequence of the thoroughgoing restoration carried out between 1778 and 1792 by James Wyatt, President of the Royal Academy, who removed the original stained glass and pulled down or altered the chapels, choir screen and monuments. Sir George Gilbert Scott sought in 1859 to restore the Cathedral to its original state.

The *nave* is articulated by pillars of black Purbeck marble. Of the monuments, most of which are not in their original position, the most interesting is the one to a boy-bishop – a choirboy elected on St Nicholas's Day (6 December) to bear the title of bishop, retaining it until 28 December.

Among other notable monuments is one to William Longespee, third earl of Salisbury, Henry II's natural son. There is also part of the shrine of a bishop of Old Sarum (d. 1099) brought from there to Salisbury. The monuments in the *N transept* are by Chantrey and Flaxman. The **clock** in this transept, dating from 1386, is probably the oldest clock mechanism in the world; it strikes the hours, but has no dial.

In the *S transept* is a War Memorial Chapel. The *Hungerford Chantry* has fine 15th c. ironwork. The unusual *brass* of Bishop Wyville (d. 1375) in the NE transept shows him sitting in the tower of a castle – an expression of episcopal power. In the SE transept is the *Chantry of Bishop Bridport* (bishop 1257–65), with very fine *carving*. There are numerous other monuments and tombs.

The *Lady Chapel* at the E end is the oldest part of the Cathedral (1220–26). One of the windows still has the original grisaille glass.

The *Cloisters* and the octagonal *Chapterhouse* date from 1364 to 1380. Modelled on those of Westminster Abbey, they are of great harmony and dignity. Since the Cathedral never belonged to a monastic house the cloisters served no function.

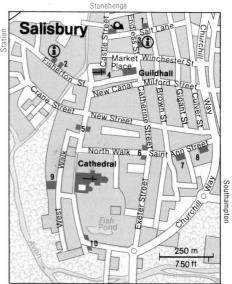

1 Shoemakers' Hall
2 Theatre
3 Bus Station
4 St. Thomas's
5 North Gate

6 St Ann's Gate
7 Museum
8 Joiners' Hall
9 King's House
10 Harnham Gate

The *Library* (1445) contains some notable treasures, including one of the four surviving original copies of Magna Carta, numerous Anglo-Saxon documents and Sir Christopher Wren's report on the Cathedral spire.

Unlike many other churches, the Cathedral does not stand amid tightly packed houses but in the middle of spacious lawns. The Close is walled, with three old *gates*, and contains a number of fine old houses dating between the 14th and 18th c., the residences of church dignitaries, the Dean and teachers of the Cathedral School. Particularly fine is *Mompesson House*, with a very elegant interior (open to visitors). The Cathedral, surrounded by tall trees, can best be seen from the NE; but the view from the River Avon – the prospect painted by Constable – is particularly charming.

The town of Salisbury, which rose to prosperity through the wool trade, has preserved its original beauty and character with notable care, and a walk through the streets will reveal a succession of fresh delights and challenges for the photographer. The spacious old **Market Place** is still used for its original purpose. In the street called New Canal is *John Halle's House* built between 1470 and 1483 by a wealthy wool merchant of that name. Other fine buildings are the *Guildhall* (1788–95), *St Thomas's Church* (15th c.)

and *Joiners' Hall*, a half-timbered building of the 16th c. In St Ann's Street is the *Salisbury and South Wiltshire Museum*.

SURROUNDINGS. – 9 miles NW of Salisbury is *Wilton House, seat of the earl of Pembroke, with a great hall which ranks as one of the finest in England. The house occupies the site of a former Benedictine abbey, of which there remain only the E tower and the "Holbein Porch", now in the garden. The present house was built in 1647 to the plans of John Webb, assisted by his uncle Inigo Jones and a French architect named Isaac de Caus. The main front of the house is so plain that the visitor is unprepared for the seven splendid rooms concealed behind it.

The INTERIOR is overwhelming in its elegance and magnificence. The Double Cube Room, 60 ft long by 30 ft wide and 30 ft high, with gilded flowers and fruit and a mythological ceiling painting, is particularly splendid. It was constructed to house ten *portraits painted by Van Dyck in 1632–34 for the fourth earl. The gilded furniture, though made a hundred years later (by William Kent), is entirely in keeping with the general effect. Scarcely less magnificent is the Single Cube Room, with ceiling paintings of scenes from Sir Philip Sidney's "Arcadia" (which was written here in 1590). The other rooms contain numbers of valuable pictures, including works by Rembrandt, Rubens, Lucas van Leyden and Sir Joshua Reynolds.

The *gardens* of Wilton House are also very beautiful. A feature frequently imitated elsewhere is the *Palladian bridge* over the Nadder, a tributary of the Wye.

The town of *Wilton* is the home of the Royal Carpet Factory and other carpet-making firms. The parish church (by T. H. Wyatt, 1843) has good glass.

Isles of Scilly

South-western England. – County: Cornwall.

The *Isles of Scilly lie some 25 miles SW of Land's End, the farthest tip of Cornwall. The group comprises between 150 and 200 islands fringed by granite rocks and sandy bays; some of them are tiny little islets, and only five are inhabited. Formerly the terror of seamen and the scene of many wrecks, they are now a holiday paradise, with a mild climate and beautiful beaches, rocks and moorland scenery. The 2400 inhabitants live partly from tourism and partly from flower-growing, favoured by the warmest climate in the British Isles.

From Penzance it is barely 3 hours by boat to **Hugh Town**, the capital, situated on the largest island, **St Mary's** (hotels – Bell Rock, C, 17 r.; Godolphin, D, 31 r.). There are also regular helicopter services. The view of the islands from the sea is particularly fine. The most notable building on St Mary's is an *Elizabethan fort*, Star Castle (1593–94), above Hugh Town. The numerous little fields of flowers, often separated by hedges, are a beautiful sight. On all the islands there are prehistoric chambered tombs. It used to be thought that the Scillies were the "Tin Islands" of antiquity, particularly since tin has long been mined in Cornwall; but this theory is still without proof.

The next largest island is **Tresco**, with *Tresco Abbey* and its beautiful subtropical gardens, laid out in terraces. Apart from the remains of the abbey, visitors can see a collection of figureheads from ships

Tresco Abbey Gardens

wrecked off the Scillies. *Cromwell's Castle* dates from the mid 16th c.

Of the other inhabited islands, known as the Off Islands, the most beautiful is **St Martin's**. On **St Agnes** is the second oldest lighthouse in the country (1680). The last of the inhabited islands is **Bryher**. Some of the uninhabited islands are nature reserves, on which visitors can land only with special permission.

Shaftesbury

Southern England. – County: Dorset.
Altitude: 700 ft. – Population: 5200.
Telephone dialling code: 0747.
ⓘ **Tourist Information Centre**,
County Library,
Bell Street;
tel. 2256.

HOTELS. – *Grosvenor*, The Commons, C, 48 r.; *Royal Chase*, Royal Chase Roundabout, D, 21 r.; *Grove House*, Ludwell, D, 12 r.

RESTAURANT. – *Lamb Inn* (17th c. Inn, 7 miles N on B 3089).

SPORT and RECREATION. – Walking, riding.

Situated on a sandstone hill, Shaftesbury is a picturesque little market town with a long history. It is a good centre from which to explore Blackmore Vale and Cranborne Chase, a peaceful countryside of fruit orchards and great expanses of pastureland. There are a number of interesting buildings in the surrounding area.

HISTORY. – Alfred the Great founded a Benedictine nunnery here in 880 for his daughter Elgiva, whom he made abbess. After her death she was canonised, and the town became a much frequented place of pilgrimage with almost a dozen churches. King Edward the Martyr was buried here.

SIGHTS. – Of the Benedictine nunnery there remain only the foundations and a few ruins, and the only one of the town's many old churches to survive is *St Peter's* (Perpendicular), which has an interesting crypt and a beautiful porch. At the top of Gold Hill, one of the steep and picturesque old cobbled lanes, is the *Museum* of Local History.

SURROUNDINGS. – 7 miles SW of Shaftesbury is **Sturminster Newton** (pop. 2110), an old market town in a loop of the River Stour. Sturminster is linked with Newton by a beautiful six-arched bridge. From here it is 9 miles W to **Sherborne** (pop. 7600; hotels – Post House, C, 60 r.; Eastbury, D, 15 r.), a little town of medieval aspect. Like Shaftesbury, it was formerly more important than it is today. In 705 it became the seat of a bishop, and for a time it was the chief town of Wessex, with an abbey, a monastic school (now an important public school) and two castles. It has preserved many remains of the past, as it declined in importance and did not grow. The Abbey Church, Sherborne School, a medieval hospital and the adjoining old houses form a striking group.

The **Abbey Church** has a fine Late Norman S doorway (c. 1170), a relic of the Benedictine abbey, Norman tower arches and an Early English Lady Chapel. The main structure, rebuilt in the 15th c., is Perpendicular. The fan vaulting is among the finest and most delicate in England. The canopied choir-stalls, with misericords, also date from the 15th c. Two Anglo-Saxon kings are said to have been buried in the church, but their tombs have not been preserved. In the tower is a bell ("Great Tom") presented by Cardinal Wolsey. Some of the monastic buildings are now incorporated in the school. The hospital or almshouse (1437) preserves the original chapel, great hall and bedrooms. The two castles are situated in a spacious park. Of the 11th c. castle of Bishop Roger of Salisbury there remain only the Norman gatehouse and keep. **Sherborne Castle** was partly built by Sir Walter Raleigh (1592–1603).

On the way to Yeovil it is worth making a detour to the little village of **Bradford Abbas** on the River Yeo, which has one of the largest churches in Dorset.

Yeovil (pop. 27,300; hotels – Manor Crest, C, 42 r.; Mermaid, D, 15 r.) is a busy market town and textile centre in a fertile farming region with many orchards and old villages. The beautiful Early Perpendicular church has a mid 15th c. brass lectern. There is a good collection of old weapons and costumes in the Wyndham Museum in King George Street.

****Montacute House** (4 miles W) is one of England's finest country houses, built by Sir Edward Phelips (probably begun in 1588, completed about 1600). Both the house and the village are constructed of the yellowish Ham Hill limestone which is quarried in the area. It is a typical Elizabethan mansion, fitted out with all that was most beautiful and precious in the period. The exterior is notable for its curved gables with their high decorative chimneys and their carved figures of dogs. Below the stone dogs, in niches between the windows, are figures of famous men, from King David to Godfrey de Bouillon. The Long Gallery, the largest room in the house, used for entertainments and dances, is 200 ft long. The beautiful *gardens are one of the few surviving examples of an early Jacobean formal garden. The house contains a collection of Tudor and Jacobean portraits. – The little village of *Montacute* has a picturesque square, the Borough, surrounded by old houses of Ham Hill stone.

From Yeovil continuing by way of *Marston Magna* and *Sparkford*, we pass **Cadbury Castle**, a large Iron Age hill-fort, and then via *Wincanton* to *Stourton* (11 miles NE of Shaftesbury), with the mansion of **Stourhead**, built by Colin Campbell for a London banker named Henry Hoare (1721). The main feature of Stourhead is the English-style *landscaped garden, one of the most beautiful in the country, a unique composition laid out between 1730 and 1780, with a lake, grottoes, statues and a temple of the sun and the nymphs. In the grounds is King Alfred's Tower, from which there are fine views of the surrounding area.

At **Fonthill Bishop** (9 miles NE) is one of the most extraordinary buildings in the country – *Fonthill Abbey*, a fantasy palace built between 1796 and 1800, by William Beckford, one of the wealthiest and most eccentric men of his day. The estate was surrounded by a high wall some 7 miles long, since Beckford loved animals and wanted to keep them from being hunted. A public road runs from Fonthill Bishop through the massive gateway to the remains of the house, continuing to the lake and through romantic artificial caves to a copse of yew-trees. Of the house nothing is left but a few walls, a tower and part of the E wing, but in its day, if contemporary accounts are to be believed, it was a place of unimaginable splendour. Beckford assembled here a large collection of pictures and objets d'art, which he later transferred to his new house in Bath; it is now dispersed, but many museums contain items from the collection. The house itself was sold by auction in 1822.

The grounds of *Longleat House (5 miles N), seat of the marquess of Bath, are another magnificent example of 18th c. landscape gardening (by Capability Brown), also with a lake and carefully disposed clumps of trees. They now contain a Safari Park, with lions and other wild animals.

Longleat House itself is a splendid Elizabethan mansion (1559–78). The façade is of magnificent symmetry, though the interior has been much altered: only the Great Hall remains in its original form. Behind the house is a cemetery for domestic animals, with tombstones and inscriptions.

Sheffield

Central England. – County: South Yorkshire.
Population: 544,200.
Telephone dialling code: 0742.
(i) **Tourist Information Centre**,
    Central Library, Surrey Street;
    tel. 734760.

HOTELS. – *Hallam Tower Post House*, Manchester Road, Broomhill, B, 135 r.; *Grosvenor House*, Charter Square, B, 111 r.; *St George*, Kenwood Road, D, 119 r.; *Royal Victoria*, Victoria Station Road, D, 65 r.

RESTAURANTS. – *Rutland*, Glossop Road; *St Andrew's*, Kenwood Road; *Glenmore*, Glen Road.

SPORT and RECREATION. – Golf, tennis.

The industrial city of Sheffield lies in a beautiful situation on the River Don, at the foot of the Derbyshire hills. It is a good base from which to explore the Peak District. The city itself has a number of beautiful parks and a green belt with pleasant residential suburbs. Its main tourist attraction is the Cathedral.

Sheffield has long been famous for the manufacture of cutlery, and as early as the 14th c. Chaucer refers in the "Canterbury Tales" to a "Sheffield thwitel", the ancestor of the modern pocket-knife. The

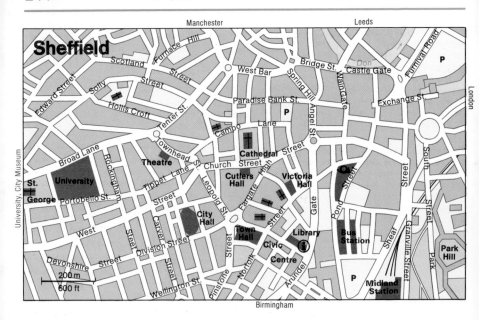

knives and other implements were formerly made in home workshops; they are
now manufactured in large factories and
exported all over the world. In more recent
times other industries have also established themselves in Sheffield, which
claims to be the cleanest industrial city in
the world.

SIGHTS. – The *Cathedral stands on the
site of a parish church built by a Norman
baron named William de Lovetot soon
after 1100. In the 15th c. a new church
was built in Perpendicular style, and parts
of this survive in the present building, in
particular the choir and the tower. The
nave was built in the late 18th c. and
restored and enlarged in 1880. When
Sheffield became the see of a bishop in
1914 it was planned to make the present
nave the transept of a new and much
larger church, but this project was a
casualty of the two world wars, leaving
the church with an unusual ground plan.
In 1966 it was further altered and restored.

The INTERIOR is entered through an open *narthex* or
porch on the S side. At the W end of the nave is a *font*
presented by the Freemasons (1884). The *Lady
Chapel* dates from before 1538. The marble tomb of
the fourth earl of Shrewsbury (d. 1538) shows him
between his two wives; the beautiful *alabaster figures*
were originally painted. A very unusual feature is the
portable *sedilia* of black oak (15th c.) in *St
Catherine's Chapel*. In the *Chapterhouse* are modern
stained-glass windows (1966) depicting the history
of the town. The *Chaucer Window* shows the miller of
Trumpington (in the Reeve's Tale) with his Sheffield
knife.

Opposite the Cathedral is *Cutlers' Hall*,
headquarters of the Company of Cutlers,

founded in 1624, which is authorised to
grant trade marks for articles reaching
appropriate standards of quality. It has a
fine *collection of silver* from 1773 to the
present day, made up of one master work
from each year.

The **Town Hall** is a picturesque neo-
Renaissance building erected in 1897 and
enlarged in 1923. The tower, 193 ft high,
is topped by a figure of Vulcan, the
blacksmith god, holding aloft the arrows
he has just forged – a symbol of Sheffield's
predominant industry. The *City Hall* (by
Vincent Harris, 1932) is used for congresses and concerts; it has seating for
2700.

The **Central Library and Art Gallery**,
built in 1934, has an excellent collection
of British art from the 18th c. to the
present day, Italian painting of the
15th–18th c. and French artists of
the 19th and 20th c. (Cézanne, Corot,
Picasso, Braque, etc.). Here too is the
Graves Art Gallery, a collection assembled
by Dr J. F. Graves, who contributed
towards the cost of the building and presented more than 1000 pictures to the city.

Castle Market and *Castle Square* are
modern shopping centres, partly underground. The *City Museum*, founded in
1874 and now housed in a building
erected in 1937, contains a unique
collection of British and European cutlery
from the 16th c. to the present, together
with a considerable collection of Bronze
Age material. The adjoining *Mappin Art*

Gallery has a good collection of 19th c. British art.

SURROUNDINGS. – 3½ miles SW is **Abbeydale Industrial Hamlet**, an 18th c. village with the old workshops and workers' houses, devoted particularly to the making of scythes, where visitors can watch the whole process of manufacture, from the raw material to the finished article.

To the E of the village is **Beauchief Abbey**, with the remains of a Premonstratensian abbey founded about 1175 and a chapel built in 1660, the two architectural styles harmonising perfectly together.

Bolsover Castle (12 miles SE) stands on a steep hill above the town of *Bolsover* (pop. 11,800). It is a Jacobean mansion on the site of a Norman castle built by William Peveril (who also built a castle at Castleton: see p. 231). In 1613–17 Sir Charles Cavendish reconstructed the Norman keep and built his new house beside it. Notable features are the elaborate marble chimneypieces. Cavendish's monument is in the church in Bolsover.

Shetland Islands

Northern Scotland. – Administrative unit: Shetland Islands.

The Shetland Islands (known locally as Shetland) – consisting of about a hundred islands in all, of which 12 are inhabited – are Britain's most northerly outpost, lying 48 miles NE of the Orkneys. Half way between the Orkneys and the Shetlands is Fair Isle, a storm-swept island between the Atlantic and the North Sea, where many ships have been wrecked. It has a bird-watching station. In recent years North Sea oil has become economically important.

The Shetland Islands (traditionally also Zetland) have a population of 17,500. They are rocky (mainly schists), with magnificent cliff scenery. Most of the larger islands are hilly, the heather- and broom-clad hills forming a contrast with the blue of the sea and the green of the areas of cultivation in the valleys. The highest point is *Ronas Hill*, a red granite mass 1486 ft above sea level, from the top of which there is a grandiose * view of the islands. Here during the midsummer nights a magnificent sunset can be seen, followed one or two hours later by the sunrise; during June and July it is never really dark in Shetland, and variations in temperature are very slight. The coasts of the islands are rugged and much indented, with sheer cliffs, long fjord-like inlets and numerous caves and "kirns" (clefts in the rock) in which the sea swirls and thunders.

The largest of the islands, 54 miles long, with jagged, irregular coasts, is known as **Mainland**. It has so many fjords and inlets that no spot on the island is more than 3 miles from the sea. The chief town is **Lerwick** (pop. 6200; hotels – Shetland, C, 64 r.; Lerwick, C, 60 r.; youth hostel, Isleburgh House, 40 b.), the most northerly town in Britain (there being only villages on the islands farther N). There are regular ferry services to Lerwick from Aberdeen (3 times weekly) and also air services from most Scottish airports.

Lerwick has attractive old streets and lanes, several hotels and a good fishing harbour. Fishing is still a major source of income for the Shetlanders, though the North Sea oil industry via the Sullom Voe oil terminal has brought an increase in prosperity in recent years. During the fishing season the little town is filled with seafarers from many nations. Among the amenities of Lerwick is a 9-hole golf-course on the island of Bressay (1 mile by motorboat). 1 mile W of the town is a well-preserved broch (a Dark Ages defensive tower).

At the southern tip of Mainland, at *Sumburgh*, are the airport, a lighthouse, a hotel and the interesting site of **Jarlshof**, with remains of buildings dating from the 5th c. B.C. and also from the 9th c. A.D. (a Viking house). – Opposite Lerwick on the W coast is the former island capital of *Scalloway* (7 miles from Lerwick), with

Jarlshof

the remains of Scalloway Castle (1600). From here there is a mailboat service to the island of *Foula*, the haunt of countless seabirds, with imposing cliffs rearing up to a height of 1220 ft.

Hillswick (30 miles from Lerwick), reached by the main road which passes via Voe and Brae, lies in a magnificent rocky setting, with *Ronas Hill* as the highest peak.

There are ferry services from here to the northern islands. St Magnus Hotel, run by the shipping company, is open in summer. W of Hillswick is the little fishing village of *Stenness*, amid impressive rock formations and caves. Particularly striking is the *Grind of the Navir* (gate of the Giants), rugged porphyry cliffs, stepped like a giant staircase, facing the open Atlantic.

A very attractive trip from Lerwick in good weather is to the island of **Bressay**, 1 mile away by motorboat across the Bressay Sound. From the easily climbed hill called the *Ward of Bressay* there is a good view of the islands. At the S end of Bressay is the *Orkneyman's Cave*, a sea-cave which can be entered by boat. The smaller island of **Noss**, to the E, is a nature reserve, with many rare plants and hosts of birds on the headland called the *Noup of Noss*. A permit is required to land on Noss. At the SE corner of Noss is a tiny islet once linked with it by a rope bridge, the **Holm of Noss**, also the haunt of thousands of seabirds.

From the archaeological point of view the most interesting of the islands is the little uninhabited island of **Mousa**, off the SE coast of Mainland, which has the best preserved of all the Scottish brochs. It can be reached by boat from Sandwick (permission necessary). The broch, known as *Mousa Castle*, has a circumference of 158 ft at the base and stands 40 ft high, tapering towards the top. The double walls, each 5 ft thick and laid without mortar, must have made the broch almost impregnable in prehistoric times. There are more than 80 such brochs, most of them much ruined, at various strategic situations in the Shetlands, on hills or beside bays.

The most beautiful of the other islands is **Unst** (mailboat service three times weekly from Lerwick), with an interesting coastline, bird reserves, archaeological

excavations and what is said to be the most northerly castle in the world, Muness Castle. The most northerly inhabited place in the British Isles is the rocky islet of *Muckle Flugga* (200 ft high), with a lighthouse which in spite of its height of 250 ft is frequently lashed by breakers.

Shrewsbury

Central England. – County: Shropshire.
Altitude: 320 ft. – Population: 87,300.
Telephone dialling code: 0743.
ⓘ **Tourist Information Centre**,
The Square;
tel. 52019.

HOTELS. – *Lion*, Wyle Cop, C, 60 r.; *Ainsworth Radbrook Hall*, Radbrook Road, C, 48 r.; *Prince Rupert*, Butcher Row, D, 64 r.; *Shelton Hall*, Shelton, D, 11 r.

YOUTH HOSTEL. – *Woodlands*, Abbey Foregate, 75 b.

RESTAURANTS. – *Santa Maria* (restaurant ship on the Severn, near Welsh Bridge); *The White Horse Inn*, Pulverbatch; *Just William*, 62/63 Mardol (15th c. half-timbered building).

CAMP SITE.

EVENTS. – *Shropshire and West Midland Agricultural Show* (May); *Flower Show* (Aug.); *National Ploughing Championships* (Oct.).

SPORT and RECREATION. – Golf, tennis, hockey, bowling, rowing, canoeing, fishing.

Shrewsbury, county town of Shropshire, lies on a kind of peninsula in a loop of the Severn, England's longest river, which is spanned by two imposing bridges, the English Bridge and the Welsh Bridge. The narrow streets and half-timbered houses give Shrewsbury – surely one of the most beautiful old Tudor towns in England – a character all its own. As the centre of a wide farming area it is a town full of life and activity, particularly on market days. The surrounding countryside is a region of lush green meadows and pastureland, with fine old trees standing by themselves adding character to the landscape.

HISTORY. – Shrewsbury was for centuries a border fortress on the frontier with Wales, and in 1403 was the scene of a battle between Henry IV and Welsh rebel forces (cf. Shakespeare's "Henry IV"). The Castle was built in 1071 by Roger de Montgomery, first earl of Shrewsbury. Edward VI founded Shrewsbury School, a famous public school whose pupils have included Charles Darwin (b. in Shrewsbury 1809) and Samuel Butler (1835–1902), author of "Erewhon", whose grandfather and namesake was headmaster of the school for nearly 40 years. The novelist Mary Webb (1881–1927), whose novels were set in Shropshire (Salop), is buried in the churchyard.

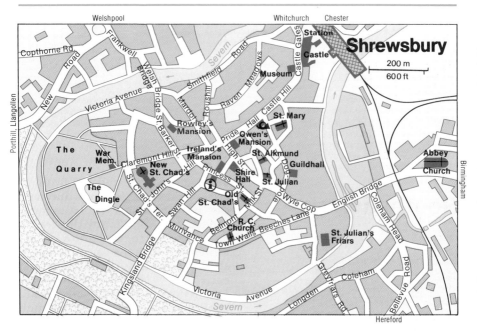

SIGHTS. – At the NE corner of Shrewsbury is the **Castle**, with two towers, which was converted into a dwelling-house by Telford at the end of the 18th c.; it affords fine views of the town. *St **Mary's Church**, a large church with a graceful spire, has fine stained glass (14th and 15th c.), some of it made in Germany. The ***Abbey Church**, which belonged to a Benedictine house founded by Roger de Montgomery in 1083, has a Norman nave. The reader's pulpit came from the old abbey, and the church contains many interesting features brought from other churches. *New St Chad's Church* is a round church built in 1792.

The town contains many well-preserved half-timbered buildings, among them the *Old Market Hall* (1596), *Owen's Mansion* (1592), *Ireland's Mansion* (1580) and *Rowley's Mansion* (1618, but much restored), which now houses a museum (prehistoric, Roman and medieval material). In Butcher Row, the town's oldest street, is another fine half-timbered building, *Abbot's House* (15th c.).

There are also many old houses in Frankwell, the street which runs N from the Welsh Bridge to Darwin's birthplace. – The old *Quarry*, from which came much of the stone used in the building of Shrewsbury, is now an attractive park, with a beautiful flower garden, the Dingle.

SURROUNDINGS. – 6 miles SE, on the Severn, is **Wroxeter**, with the interesting excavations of the Roman station of *Viroconium*. The church is also worth a visit.

20 miles E is **Tong** (pop. 261), which is well worth a visit for the sake of the church, with beautiful fan vaulting and wood-carving and a whole series of fine monuments of the Vernon family. – 3½ miles E is *Boscobel House* (16th–17th c.), where Charles II sought refuge after the battle of Worcester. It has beautiful grounds.

Picturesquely situated on the Severn, 21 miles SE, is **Bridgnorth** (pop. 10,700; hotels – Falcon, D, 16 r.; Croft, E, 7 r.), a town of medieval aspect, with a "High Town" and a "Low Town" connected by England's steepest funicular. In the High Town is a tower which formed part of the old castle; it leans farther from the vertical than the Leaning Tower of Pisa. Numerous "black and white" half-timbered houses. The Severn Valley Railway, a well-restored steam railway, runs from here to Bewdley.

13 miles S is **Church Stretton** (pop. 3350; hotels – Sandford, D, 23 r.; Mynd House, E, 12 r.), a small health resort in a beautiful setting.

Half-timbered house, Shrewsbury

22 miles S is *Stokesay Castle, built at the end of the 13th c., a fine example of a fortified manor-house of the period.

29 miles S is **Ludlow** (pop. 7500; hotels – Feathers, C, 35 r.; Overton Grange, D, 17 r.; youth hostel, Ludford Lodge, Ludford, 52 b.), much visited for its beautiful situation on the River Teme and its trim half-timbered houses. The oldest part of the Castle is the keep (*view), begun in 1086. In Broad Street is one of the old town gates. The Decorated parish church is one of the finest in Shropshire, with beautiful windows and carved choir-stalls.

Southampton

Southern England. – County: Hampshire.
Population: 204,400.
Telephone dialling code: 0703.
ⓘ **Tourist Information Centre**,
Above Bar;
tel: 23855.

HOTELS. – *Post House*, Herbert Walker Avenue, B, 132 r.; *Polygon*, Cumberland Place, B, 119 r.; *Southampton Park*, Cumberland Place, C, 77 r.; *Dolphin*, High Street, C, 72 r.; *Southampton Moat House*, Highfield Lane, Portswood, D, 70 r.; *Albany*, 2 Winn Road, D, 41 r.

YOUTH HOSTEL. – 461 Winchester Road, Bassett, 59 b.

RESTAURANTS. – *London Steak House*, Civic Centre Road; *Cotswold*, Highfield Lane; *Portswood Royal*, Cumberland Place; *Wessex*, Northlands Road.

SPORT and RECREATION. – Sailing, rowing, swimming, golf, tennis.

Southampton is one of Britain's largest seaports and was formerly the principal port for passenger services – though today this traffic has declined to a shadow of its former self with the development of air travel. The city lies on a peninsula between the mouths of the River Test to the W and the Itchen to the E. The 9 miles long estuary of the Itchen and Test has a double tide, and the largest ships are able to anchor (deep water harbour).

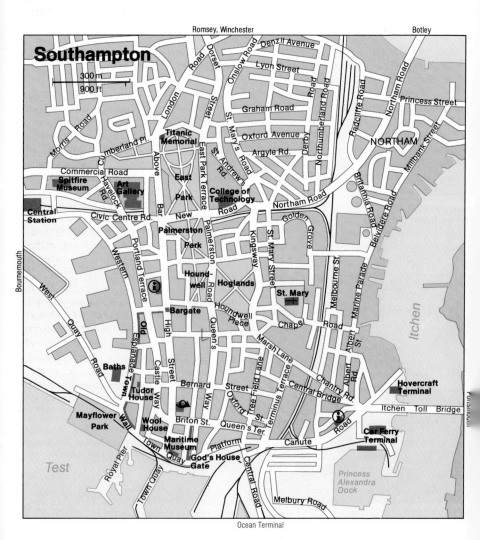

Although the town suffered much destruction during the last war, it has preserved a number of old buildings. The handsome Tudor House (1535), with its characteristic "black and white" half-timbering, is now a museum. Parts of the town walls have also survived. Southampton is a good base for touring the New Forest.

HISTORY. – There was already a harbour here in Roman times, situated a little way inland at Bitterne, on the Itchen. In 1017 Canute was chosen as king here by the Saxons. In 1189 Richard Cœur-de-Lion and his knights took ship here on their way to the third Crusade; and from here Edward III set out in 1345 and Henry V in 1415 for their campaigns in France. In 1620 the Pilgrim Fathers sailed from here before their final departure for the New World from Plymouth. This was also the port of departure for many troopships in both world wars. In 1940 and 1941 the town was severely damaged in air-raids.

SIGHTS. – Only one of Southampton's medieval churches has survived in the town centre, *St Michael's*, with some Norman work, a tall spire and a beautiful font. On the banks of the Test can be seen parts of the old *town walls*, still standing 30–40 ft high, with a number of *towers* and *gates*. Near the West Gate is the *Mayflower Memorial*; there is also a monument commemorating the loss of the *Titanic*, which sailed from here in 1912; *God's House* or the *Hospice of St Julian* was founded in the 12th c.; *God's House Tower* (15th c.) now houses the Museum of Archaeology. Near the town walls stands the Woolhouse (14th c.), now a Maritime Museum.

Apart from these few remains of the past Southampton is a modern port and industrial city. The **Civic Centre** (by Berry Webber, 1930–36) contains municipal offices, schools, law courts, a public library, etc., as well as the *Municipal Art Gallery*, with an excellent selection of modern British painting and a collection of china.

SURROUNDINGS. – At *Netley* (pop. 2300), 3 miles S, are the beautifully situated ruins of *Netley Abbey*, a Cistercian house founded in 1239. The surviving buildings are mainly Early English.

In the little market town of *Romsey* (pop. 13,200; hotels – White Horse, B, 33 r.; Dolphin, D, 9 r.), 8 miles NW of Southampton, is **Romsey Abbey**. The massive abbey, looking from a distance more like a fortress than a church, was founded in 907 in association with a convent of Benedictine nuns, and still preserves Saxon foundations. A Norman church was built about 1125, and most of the present building is pure Norman. The E window is Early English (beginning of 14th c.); the W end, with

pointed arches, was built about 1225. The N transept contains a painted wooden reredos of 1520. High above the choir arch are two figures of angels which probably formed part of a Crucifixion group. In the S choir aisle and outside the S transept are two Saxon stone crucifixes. – E of the church is King John's House (1206), now a museum. In the market-place is a statue of Lord Palmerston (1784–1865), whose country house was S of the town.

Another interesting church in the surrounding area is *Beaulieu Abbey (8 miles SE), originally a Cistercian house founded by King John in 1204. Margaret of Anjou and her son found refuge here in 1471. The large gatehouse was converted into a dwelling-house in 1538 and is now the home of Lord Montagu of Beaulieu. In the Early English refectory is a beautiful reader's pulpit. The house and grounds are now one of the country's most popular tourist attractions, with a variety of entertainments and the very interesting National Motor Museum (over 200 cars, including vintage and veteran models and racing cars).

3 miles down river is **Buckler's Hard** (Master Builder's House Hotel, D, 21 r.), a picturesque little place dating from 1750 to 1820, when ships were built here because the Southampton shipyards were overloaded. There is a small Maritime Museum.

10 miles SE of Southampton are the very beautiful *Exbury Gardens, planted by Edmond de Rothschild (d. 1942).

South Coast

Southern England. – Counties: Kent, East Sussex, West Sussex, Hampshire, Dorset, Devon and Cornwall.

The English * South Coast, separated from France by the Straits of Dover and the English Channel, is climatically one of the most favoured parts of Britain, with a long succession of popular holiday resorts. It is a coast which offers great variety of scenery. In many places chalk cliffs rear up from the sea, most strikingly at Dover; elsewhere the coast is fringed by marshland barely 12 ft above sea level, as at Romney Marsh; and opposite the Isle of Wight estuaries and fjord-like inlets cut deep into the land. The limestone of Portland and a wide surrounding area, worked in enormous quarries, has carried the name of Portland cement far beyond the boundaries of Britain and of Europe.

Ramsgate (pop. 39,600; hotels – Savoy, D, 25 r.; Abbeygail, E, 10 r.; Spencer, E, 9 r.), enjoys an exceedingly mild climate. The harbour, constructed in 1750, provides moorings for numerous yachts in summer. Ramsgate is a much favoured

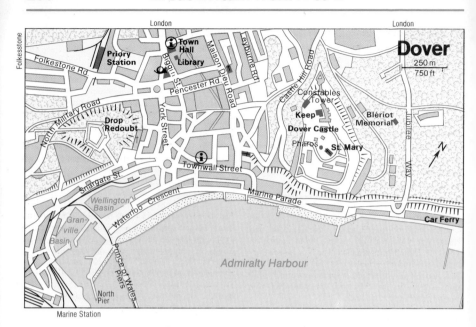

seaside resort, with good bathing and abundant entertainment facilities. The Roman Catholic *St Augustine's Church* on West Cliff is a masterpiece of neo-Gothic, built by Pugin in 1847–51 at his own expense together with an adjoining house for his own occupation. He is buried in the church.

Sandwich (pop. 4500) still lives on the memory of its glorious past. Although now 2 miles from the sea, it was once one of England's leading seaports, joined with Dover, Hastings, Romney and Hythe as one of the Cinque Ports. It was also a notorious smugglers' lair. Unfortunately the aspect of the charming old town with its narrow streets and many fine houses is being altered, (not for the better,) by street-widening and modernisation. The main features of interest are the *Barbican* and *Fisher Gate*; the *Guildhall* (1579, restored); *St Clement's Church* (Early English, with a Norman tower); *St Peter's Church* (17th c.), in Market Street; *Manwood Court* (1564) and the Old House; St Thomas's Hospital, founded, 1392, rebuilt 1864; and St Bartholomew's Hospital, with an Early English choir. In *Sandwich Bay* there are a small number of houses, good bathing and three first-class golf-courses.

1½ miles N of Sandwich is **Richborough Castle**, one of the most important Roman sites in Britain. The fort built here by the Romans, *Rutupiae*, was intended to protect the port and the entrance to the important Wantsum channel which then ran NW to Reculver.

Later, in the 3rd c., the fort became part of the defences of the "Saxon Shore". Within the fort is a huge platform which seems to have supported some massive monument. The foundations of a Roman amphitheatre and a pre-Norman chapel have been excavated; finds from the site are in a small museum.

Deal (pop. 26,100; Royal Hotel, D, 27 r.) has a long maritime tradition, in spite of its lack of any real harbour (though it has shipyards). Ships are loaded and discharged in the Downs, the roadstead between the Goodwin Sands and the coast, and the cargoes transhipped in lighters. Although now well marked, the Goodwin Sands, lying 7 miles offshore, have long been a hazard to shipping, and down the centuries many vessels have gone aground there. The lifeboat service in Deal is therefore particularly well equipped. Legend has it that the Goodwin Sands were originally the fertile island of Lomea, on which was the castle of Earl Godwin (d. 1053), and that the whole island was submerged in a great storm.

With its many old houses, its piers, promenade and golf-course, Deal is a popular holiday resort in spite of its shingle beach.

St Margaret's Bay, which also has a shingle beach, is attractively situated under wooded cliffs. It is a quiet little place, with very pleasant walks.

Dover (pop. 34,400; hotels – Holiday Inn, C, 83 r.; Dover, C, 67 r.; White Cliffs, D, 63 r.; Dover Stage, D, 42 r.; Mildmay, D, 22 r.; St James, D, 22 r.; youth hostels –

Charlton House, 306 London Road, 69 b.), whose famous white cliffs can be seen gleaming from afar, is one of Britain's principal cross-Channel ports. In earlier days it was a naval port. Above the town stands *Dover Castle*, the earliest example in Europe of a concentrically planned castle, its 12th c. walls built on prehistoric ramparts. The Pharos, within the castle precincts, was originally a Roman lighthouse.

The *church of St Mary in Castro*, which contains some Saxon work, is built with Roman bricks. Other features of the Castle are the *keep*, the deep well and the *casemates* and underground passages. In clear weather the view from the Castle extends right across the Channel to Calais, also with chalk cliffs which were originally part of a much higher chalk ridge linking what are now the two sides of the Channel. Dover, which suffered severe destruction during the last war, is not primarily a seaside resort, and most of its visitors are in transit to or from the Continent. It has a few buildings of particular interest – the *Town Hall*, the *Maison Dieu Hall*, originally built in 1203 as a hostel for pilgrims, a recently excavated *Roman house* with wall paintings. In Roman times it was called *Dubris*. For many centuries it was a bulwark against attacks from the Continent.

Folkestone (pop. 46,500; hotels – Clifton, C, 62 r.; Burlington, C, 57 r.; Wearbay, E, 12 r.) is also a cross-Channel port, but is mainly a popular seaside resort. The *Leas*, a wide grassy promenade running along the cliff-top, are claimed to be the finest seafront promenade in the country, with views which in clear weather extend over to France. The town has excellent sports and entertainment facilites. E of the harbour is the Warren, produced by a cliff fall, which offers good hunting for fossil collectors. 5 miles NNW is *Acrise Place*, an Elizabethan and Georgian manor-house, with an interesting costume collection.

From Hythe onwards the coast is fairly flat: this is the beginning of *Romney Marsh*, an area largely devoted to flower growing which is particularly beautiful in spring. **Hythe** (pop. 12,200; hotels – Imperial, B, 83 r.; Stade Court, C, 32 r.) is a quiet and attractive little town, formerly an important port. The *church* is partly Norman, with a crypt containing large numbers of human skulls and bones. The town is traversed by the *Royal Military Channel*, now used only for fishing and boating but originally constructed to provide a safe waterway to Rye at a time when there was a threat of invasion by Napoleon.
Half a mile away is *Saltwood Castle*, a

fine Norman stronghold (restored) from which Thomas Becket's murderers set out for Canterbury in 1170. It has a fine gatehouse.

***Rye** (pop. 5000; hotels – George, C, 20 r.; Mermaid Inn, D, 29 r.; Mariner's, D, 19 r.) was also once a considerable seaport. The name means "island"; and indeed the town lies on higher ground above an area of low-lying country which was from time to time invaded by the sea. It is a picturesque little town which attracts many artists. It has steep cobbled streets and many charming old houses which deserve to be seen at leisure, perhaps the most rewarding features being *Mermaid Street*, with the old Mermaid Inn and Lamb House, and the *church* with its clock-tower. From Gun Garden there are fine wide-ranging views.

Also beautifully situated on a hill is **Winchelsea**, founded by Edward I in the 13th c. after an earlier town had been destroyed by a great flood. The streets were laid out on a grid plan, with 40 "blocks" (not all of them built up) containing many delightful old houses. Three of the old gates have survived. The *church*, in early Decorated style, dates from about 1300, but lacks the nave. It contains fine modern glass and tombs of the Alard family.

All Saints Street, Hastings

The next place of any size is **Hastings**, of which *St Leonards* forms part (pop. 73,600; hotels – Beauport Park, C, 20 r.; Royal Victoria, D, 82 r.; youth hostel, Guestlings Hall, Rye Road, 64 b.). It is a popular seaside resort, famed as the site of the battle of Hastings in 1066, which in fact took place at Battle (see p. 49), 6 miles away. Its harbour, formerly important, has disappeared, leaving only the red-roofed fishermen's houses and net-lofts in the old part of the town. There is an interesting *Fisherman's Museum*. The

Grand Parade, Eastbourne

narrow High Street and All Saints Street contain many half-timbered houses. Above the town are the ruins of the Norman *castle* built to protect the harbour. Near the castle is the entrance to St Clement's Caves.

Bexhill-on-Sea (pop. 35,000; hotels – Cooden Beach, C, 32 r.; Dunselma, E, 11

r.; – golf-course.) is a trim modern resort which was the first place in Britain to have a motor-racing track, half a mile long.

Pevensey Bay, where William the Conqueror landed in 1066, is now a small seaside resort, with one of the Martello towers which were built along this coast between 1805 and 1810 as defences against a French invasion.

Pevensey has the imposing remains of a *Roman fort*, with walls still standing 20 ft high, within which the Normans built a castle. The castle has a late 11th c. keep and a 13th c. gatehouse.

Eastbourne (pop. 75,000; hotels – Grand, A, 150 r.; Cavendish, B, 115 r.; Chatsworth, C, 52 r.; Eastbourne Motel, D, 84 r.; Congress, D, 44 r.; Farrar's, D, 44 r.; Downland Private, D, 16 r.; Courtlands, D, 8 r.; Hydro, E, 102 r.; Edward, E, 12 r.; Elmscroft Private, E, 11 r.) is one of England's most elegant seaside resorts. It was originally a mere fishing village, but in the middle of the 19th c. the seventh duke of Devonshire developed it as a large bathing resort in the Victorian style. It has a promenade 3 miles long, a pier with a theatre at its seaward end and a wide

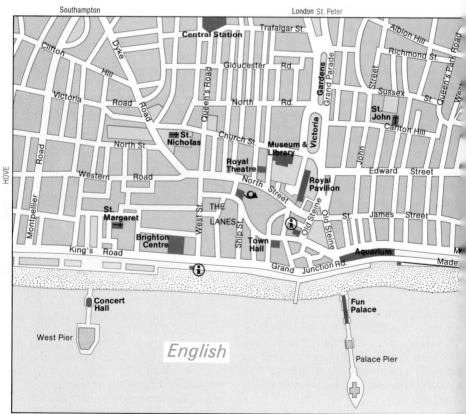

range of entertainment facilities. A major international tennis tournament is held here annually in June. In the older part of the town, away from the sea, are numerous art and antique shops. The parish church, *St Mary's*, has Norman choir arches. Eastbourne has many attractive parks and gardens, and is famous for its schools.

3 miles W of the town is *Beachy Head (575 ft high), a favourite viewpoint which marks the end of the South Downs. An attractive footpath runs along the cliffs to Beachy Head, continuing for another $3\frac{1}{2}$ miles to *Cuckmere Haven* and *Seaford*. There are a number of schools at Seaford, a quiet little place in a beautiful setting.

Newhaven, at the mouth of the River Ouse, is a cross-Channel port (services to Dieppe) and also has a large pleasure harbour. There is little to see in the town itself.

Between Newhaven and Brighton, along the cliffs, is *Peacehaven*, a sprawl of bungalows with no real centre. The beach is not particularly attractive.

Brighton (pop. 151,800; hotels – Metropole, B, 335 r.; Grand, B, 174 r.; Bedford, B, 126 r.; Old Ship, C, 153 r.; Dudley, C,

79 r.; Norfolk Continental, C, 65 r.; Alexandra, C, 60 r.; Royal Crescent, C, 51 r.; Sackville, C, 50 r.; Curzon, C, 45 r.; youth hostel, Patcham Place, 76 b.) is a large and famous seaside resort with innumerable hotels, restaurants and places of entertainment, cinemas, and theatres, a swimming pool, sports facilities and an abundance of night life – everything, in fact, that the holidaymaker or visitor could ask for, except perhaps peace and quiet.

Brighton was no more than a poor fishing village until in the middle of the 18th c. Dr Richard Russell discovered and recommended to his patients the therapeutic virtues of sea-bathing. In 1782 the Prince Regent came with the court to Brighton and laid the foundations of the town's prosperity. From this period date the many handsome Regency terraces and hotels which form a pleasing contrast with the more modern buildings and contribute to the atmosphere of the resort.

The *Royal Pavilion, built for the Prince Regent by John Nash and Henry Holland, is Brighton's principal sight, its major landmark and the very emblem of the town. This huge and fantastic palace in the Oriental style, built regardless of expense, has magnificent state apartments and is crowded with objets d'art of the Regency period. The *Dome*, originally a riding school, is now used as a congress and concert hall. Adjoining is the Art Gallery and Museum, which contains much of interest, including the Willett collection of English pottery.

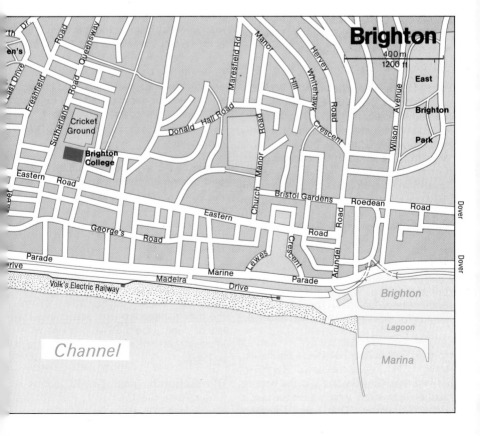

Royal Pavilion, Brighton

There is also a well-stocked *Aquarium*. Part of the old fishing village is preserved in the **Lanes** round North Street, East Street, West Street and King's Road, now given up to art shops, bookshops and antique dealers, boutiques and small cafés and pubs.

Above the beach a wide promenade extends W to Brighton's sister town of **Hove** and E to *Black Rock*, a distance of 4 miles. Between Brighton and Hove are large expanses of beautiful lawns.

W of Hove is **Shoreham** (pop. 20,900), a busy little harbour town, with the Marlipins Museum (14th c. house-front) and the church of Old Shoreham (mainly Norman, mid 12th c.). Beyond this is **Worthing** (pop. 92,100), a resort noted for its mild climate, where tomatoes flourish in glasshouses. It has a moderately good beach, a promenade, an iron pier and a theatre and concert hall. It is a good base for exploring the Downs.

Littlehampton (pop. 22,000), at the mouth of the Arun, caters particularly for younger visitors, with a wide variety of entertainment facilities. The long beach extends for miles to Bognor and beyond.

Bognor Regis (pop. 37,000; Clarehaven Hotel, D, 34 r.) owes the suffix "Regis" to the fact that King George V came here to recuperate in 1929, which gave the resort added attraction. The gently sloping beach is very suitable for children, and the town offers entertainment facilities for all ages.

Selsey Bill is a projecting spur of flat and low-lying land much exposed to wind and weather, parts of which are perpetually being washed away by the sea. *Selsey* is a growing seaside resort with many holiday homes, and these are found also in *Bracklesham Bay* and *East Wittering*. The much ramified *Chichester Harbour* and the harbours of *West Wittering* and *Itchenor* are popular sailing centres, and a new harbour was built near Birdham in 1965. The coast in this area, the nesting-place of many seabirds, is of great scenic beauty.

Southsea is a pleasant residential area of Portsmouth, with two beaches and piers and a long promenade flanked by gardens.

Portsmouth: see p. 235. – **Southampton:** see p. 248.

Lymington (pop. 11,900; Passford House Hotel, C, 50 r.) is a rapidly developing resort and a popular sailing centre. From here there are ferry services to the Isle of Wight (see p. 274). It is also within easy reach of the **New Forest** (see p. 196).

Christchurch (pop. 38,000; hotels – King's Arms Crest, C, 32 r.; Fisherman's Haunt, D, 17 r.), at the far end of the bay which bears its name and on which lie a number of seaside resorts, is a lively and interesting old town lying between the rivers Avon and Stour. Off the busy main street is the *Priory Church, founded in 1150, of dimensions appropriate to a cathedral rather than a parish church (312 ft long). The Norman nave (c. 1093) has a beautiful Early English triforium; the N porch dates from about 1300. Visitors can climb the late 15th c. tower. Notable features of the interior are the 14th c. rood-screen (restored), the reredos (not completely preserved) representing the Tree of Jesse, which is of about the same date, and the choir-stalls, with 39 misericords.

There are also remains of a Norman castle and a Norman house. Christchurch is popular with sailing enthusiasts, who like to take their boats round *Hengistbury Head*, a narrow tongue of land which was occupied by Early Neolithic settlers and has remains of prehistoric defensive works.

Bournemouth beach

Bournemouth (pop. 144,600; hotels – Carlton, A, 79 r.; Royal Bath, B, 135 r.; Bournemouth Moat, C, 113 r.; Ladbroke Savoy, C, 109 r.; Palace Court, C, 106 r.; Crest, C, 102 r.; Marsham Court, C, 94 r.; New Normandie, C, 70 r.; Cliff End, C, 40 r.; Heathlands, D, 120 r.; Queen's, D, 116 r.; Durley Dean, D, 110 r.; Durley Hall, D, 94 r.; Anglo-Swiss, D, 64 r.) is only slightly smaller than Brighton but of more recent development. Its mild climate makes it a popular resort both in summer and in winter, and it is well supplied with good shops, restaurants and sports and entertainment facilities. It also has a first-class symphony orchestra of its own. It is a

town of parks and gardens and many trees, and the beauties of the *New Forest* lie within easy reach. It has a magnificent beach of fine sand and beautiful promenades which in summer are closed to traffic. The cliffs are cut at several points by deep valleys ("chines"), such as Boscombe Chine, Durley Chine, etc. Just W of the town are the beautiful *gardens of Compton Acres. Art-lovers should not miss the *Russell-Cotes Art Gallery and Museum* (pictures by R. Wilson, Morland and painters of the Victorian age; also objets d'art from Japan and Burma). A visit is recommended to the *Rothsay Museum* which has English furniture, china and porcelain, and rooms devoted to shipping.

From *Sandbanks*, 5 miles W of the town, there is a ferry service across *Poole Harbour*, another favourite sailing area, to the *Isle of Purbeck*, a peninsula famous for the "Purbeck marble" used in innumerable English churches.

On the E side of the peninsula is **Swanage** (pop. 8100; hotels – Grosvenor, C, 105 r.; Pines, D, 51 r.; Ship Inn, D, 16 r.), a seaside resort with a beautiful beach, situated on a fine bay flanked by hills. The cliffs here are much weathered. The town is mainly modern but has a number of old stone houses, particularly near the old millpond. From the 13th c. tower of the Norman church there are wide views.

5 miles inland is *Corfe Castle, a charming little town of old houses huddled under the ruins of its castle (12th–13th c.) built to protect Poole Harbour. It occupies the site of an earlier building in which King Edward the Martyr was murdered in 978 by the thanes of his stepmother Elfrida. All that is left of the church is a 15th c. tower.

Weymouth (pop. 45,000; hotels – Treverbyn Court, E, 14 r.; Bay View, E, 10 r.), situated in a wide bay, is a modern seaside resort which originally grew up around its harbour. On the promenade is a statue of George III, who was a frequent visitor. The town has a number of handsome Georgian houses, and in Trinity Street are houses of the Tudor period completely furnished with 17th c. furniture.

George III used to stay in Gloucester House, now a hotel. A pleasant trip from Weymouth is to the *Isle of Portland*, a peninsula linked with the mainland by the *Chesil Bank*, a long spit of land with a remarkable beach on which the pebbles decrease regularly in size from E to W. The Isle of Portland is famous for its quarries, stone from which was used in the construction of St Paul's Cathedral and many other buildings. Portland Castle, built by Henry VIII, occupies the site of an earlier Saxon stronghold. At the S tip of the Isle is *Portland Bill*, with a lighthouse and bird-watching station.

From Weymouth there are regular ferry services to the *Channel Islands* and to Cherbourg. At *Abbotsbury*, 9 miles W of Weymouth, are the ruins of a Benedictine abbey. Here too is a famous swannery belonging to Lord Ilchester, which appears in the records as early as 1393 and is the home of over a thousand swans. The lagoon which extends all the way from Portland to Abbotsbury is a bird sanctuary with many species of waterfowl.

Lyme Regis (pop. 3400; hotels – Three Cups, D, 19 r.; High Cliff, D, 12 r.) lies at the mouth of the River Lyme half way along the wide sweep of *Lyme Bay*. It is a charming little town, favoured by Jane Austen, and its old stone pier, the Cobb, features in "Persuasion". The duke of Monmouth landed here in 1685. It has a steep main street and a number of handsome Georgian houses. The cliff scenery is magnificent, and inland the country is also very beautiful. The *Philpot Museum* contains interesting fossils (remains of an ichthyosaurus).

The * coast road from Lyme Regis to Exeter has many steep gradients and is very narrow in places, but offers a succession of splendid views. In 8 miles it comes to **Seaton** (pop. 5000; Hawkeshyde Motel, D, 26 r.), a seaside resort, situated at the mouth of the Axe, with excellent facilities for sport. Beyond this is the trim and attractive resort of **Sidmouth** (pop. 12,400; hotels – Salcombe Hill House, C, 33 r.; Fortfield, D, 56 r.; Royal Glen, E, 27 r.), a fashionable place in the first half of the 19th c. Its many attractions include a remarkably mild climate which allows eucalyptus trees to flourish. The town is sheltered from rough winds by reddish cliffs through which the River Sid has cut its way. There are many Regency houses, and above the beach runs a small promenade. The climate and the pretty setting, with areas of woodland just outside the town, make this an attractive place to stay in winter as well as in summer.

Budleigh Salterton (pop. 4500), 3 miles SW at the end of Lyme Bay, is similar in character. Inland is *East Budleigh*, a typical Devon village, with a pretty church and the birthplace of Sir Walter Raleigh

(1522–1618), seafarer, favourite of Elizabeth I and author of a "History of the World".

Exmouth (pop. 31,000; hotels – Imperial, B, 61 r.; Devoncourt, C, 60 r.; Royal Beacon, D, 32 r.), at the mouth of the wide estuary of the Exe, has a beautiful beach, a promenade and red cliffs. At low tide outcrops of rock are exposed along the beach. The little harbour provides moorings for many sailing boats. There is a ferry across the Exe to Starcross, where there are many pleasant walks. During the summer and at weekends the place is crowded with visitors from Exeter, only a few miles away.

Dawlish (pop. 9500; Charlton House Hotel, D, 23 r.) is a picturesque little resort on the W side of the Exe estuary, with beautiful yellow sand and fascinating red cliffs – a quiet, comfortably old-fashioned holiday place.

Teignmouth (pop. 13,100; London Hotel, D, 26 r.) lies on a tongue of land at the mouth of the River Teign, and thus enjoys a vista out to sea and over the estuary. A long bridge (560 yards) crosses the estuary to *Shaldon*, a quiet little resort with red cliffs, a beautiful sandy beach, a promenade, a pier and attractive gardens.

Torquay (pop. Torbay District 115,000; hotels – Imperial, A, 164 r.; Grand, C, 101 r.; Rainbow House, D, 93 r.; Livermead House, D, 76 r.; Palm Court, D, 72 r.; Devonshire, D, 69 r.; Livermead Cliff, D, 64 r.; Kistor, D, 52 r.; Gleneagles, D, 42 r.; Nepaul, D, 41 r.; Homers, D, 17 r.) is the principal resort in **Torbay** (the adjoining towns of *Paignton* and *Brixham* having been incorporated into it in 1968). Known to its inhabitants as "Queen of the English Riviera", Torquay has a favourable climate and offers every amenity for both summer and winter holidays. Over a million visitors come to Torquay every year.

Torquay owed its origin to the Napoleonic wars, for in anticipation of a French landing troops were stationed here and houses built for their families. There are few remains of earlier periods, apart from the ruins of Torre Abbey (gatehouse, tithe barn, foundations of church, etc.), a Premonstratensian house founded in 1196, now containing the municipal Art Gallery. Torquay's situation, sheltered by red cliffs and wooded hills, favours the growth of plants found nowhere else in Britain, and the town's parks and gardens are a feast for the eye, with palms and subtropical plants. The harbour is lively and colourful, with numbers of yachts

Torquay: view over the harbour to the town

and other craft; and from here visitors can take boat trips to a variety of destinations. A regatta is held annually in August. A contrast to the modern town of Torquay (which has nevertheless succeeded in avoiding the worst horrors of tower-block development) is provided by the old-fashioned suburb of *Cockington* with its thatched houses, a smithy and an old church.

On the E side of Torquay is *Kent's Cavern, consisting of two parallel stalactitic caves in which human remains were found, probably the oldest in Britain. Finds from here are in the Torquay museum.

The stretch of coast extending S from Brixham as far as Start Point is of great interest and beauty. From *Kingswear* there is a ferry across the River Dart to **Dartmouth** (pop. 6500; Royal Castle Hotel, D, 20 r.). Once a considerable port, Dartmouth is now a pleasant little town with many old houses. Its main feature of interest is the Butterwalk (1635–40), an arcade with carved decoration on the façade and the Town Museum.

St Saviour's Church, on a hill outside the town, dates from the 13th–15th c.; particularly notable is the ironwork on the S door. At the mouth of the Dart are St Petroc's Church (1641) and Dartmouth Castle (14th–15th c.).

The road to Start Point skirts the wide curve of *Start Bay*. The fertile region between the coast and Dartmoor is

known as the *South Hams*. The road runs via *Stoke Fleming*, the beautiful bay called *Blackpool Sands* and *Strete*, then downhill to *Slapton Sands*, a long stretch of sandbanks (largely consisting in fact of shingle) which extends for almost 7 miles to Start Point. For a mile and a half the road runs alongside *Slapton Ley*, a freshwater lagoon. It then turns W to reach *Kingsbridge*, a charming little town with old houses, from which a minor road runs S to **Salcombe** (pop. 2400), another attractive resort with a sheltered boating harbour, a sandy beach, a mild climate and subtropical vegetation. The town nestles under a steep hill, from which there is a good view of the fjord-like arms of the sea which here cut into the land.

The coast from here to Plymouth is highly picturesque but difficult of access. There are numerous beautiful bathing beaches and little forgotten villages like *Thurlestone* and *Aveton Gifford*.

Bigbury-on-Sea lies in a charming setting at the mouth of the Avon, half way along the wide arc of Bigbury Bay. A causeway leads to *Burgh Island*, on which there is a noted restaurant.

Plymouth: see p. 233. – **Cornwall:** see p. 80.

South Downs

Southern England. – Counties: West Sussex and East Sussex.

The *South Downs, like the North Downs, are a long ridge of chalk hills extending from Eastbourne in the E to beyond Winchester, running almost parallel to the coast. They are magnificent walking country, and have been designated as an area of outstanding natural beauty. Formerly this was mainly pastureland used principally for the grazing of sheep. Much of it is now arable land, producing corn.

The road which runs along the N side of the South Downs from Eastbourne to Brighton (A 27) offers a convenient way of obtaining an impression of the scenery of this area and seeing some of the principal places of interest. The first stop should be made at *Wilmington* (7 miles), with the remains of a Benedictine priory which now houses a small museum of rural life. Many people may be more interested in the *Long Man of Wilmington*, a gigantic figure cut out of the chalk hillside and standing out clearly from the grass-covered slope. It is similar to the figure at Cerne Abbas (see p. 90), but larger (more than 230 ft), with a staff held in each hand. The age and origin of the figure are unknown: it may possibly date from Saxon times (7th c.) and represent Wotan. The first reference to it occurs in 1764.

The road continues to *Alfriston*, a pretty little town with the Star Inn of 1520 and a large 14th c. church, and *Beddingham*, where a road goes off to Glynde and the famous *Glyndebourne Opera House*, founded by Mr John Christie in 1934. The performances of opera (particularly Mozart) given here in summer attract music-lovers from all over the world.

17 miles farther on is **Lewes** (pop. 14,700; hotel – White Hart, C, 33 r.), county town of East Sussex, magnificently situated on the Downs at the point where the River Ouse has cut its way through the hills. Lewes Castle was built around 1088 to defend this passage. It has a ruined keep (view) and fine flint masonry. The picturesque old town grew up round the Castle. It has steep streets

and many handsome old houses, some half-timbered, some Georgian and a number with flint walls.

In *Barbican House* is the Museum of the Sussex Archaeological Society, and associated with this is *Anne of Cleves' House*. The most interesting churches are *St Anne's* (mainly Norman) and *St Michael's*, with a round tower. The *Town Hall*, with a fine oak staircase (1593), contains the Municipal Museum. SE of the town is *Mount Caburn*, which rises steeply to 490 ft; to the W is *Mount Harry* (639 ft), above the racecourse. 4 miles farther W is the *University of Sussex*, founded in 1961. The University offices are in Stanmer House, a Palladian mansion built in 1720–27; the new buildings were designed by Sir Basil Spence.

Arundel, with Arundel Castle

Arundel (pop. 2200; Norfolk Arms Hotel, D, 35 r.), situated on the River Arun at the foot of the South Downs, is one of the most attractive towns in the south of England. The imposing *Castle*, seat of the Duke of Norfolk, which dominates the town was built in the 10th c. but completely destroyed in 1644. Since then it has been much altered and restored, most recently between 1890 and 1903. Together with the Roman Catholic church of St Philip Neri (19th c.) and the 14th c. parish church, the Castle is still an imposing sight, seen from the wide bend in the Arun. There are beautiful walks along the river. The *Great Park*, with Swanbourne Lake, is also very attractive. About 7 miles N, near Bignor, is a Roman villa with mosaics (museum).

Petworth (pop. 3000), on the northern fringe of the Downs, is a delightful little town, known to tourists for its "great house", *Petworth House*, seat of Lord Egremont. The house itself (rebuilt 1688–96) is very handsome, with a particularly fine W front, and contains one of the most important collections of pictures in England, including works by Van Dyck, Turner and Reynolds. Turner had his studio here from 1830 to 1837, and among the pictures he painted there is one of the beautiful park, a masterpiece of English landscape gardening, designed by Capability Brown. Petworth also has one of the finest collections of ancient sculpture in the country.

2½ miles S of Petworth, beyond the River Rother, is the highest point on the Sussex South Downs, *Duncton Hill* or Littleton Down (837 ft). Beyond the hill, on a side road off A 285, is **Boxgrove**, with a priory church (1120–1220) which shows the transition from Norman to Early English.

South-East Coast

See East and South-East Coasts.

Southern Uplands

Southern Scotland. – Regions: Strathclyde, Dumfries and Galloway, Borders.

The Southern Uplands are the region of hills and mountains, with coastal fringes of plain, which extends across southern Scotland from the border with England to the lowland area between Edinburgh and Glasgow formed by the Forth and Clyde valleys.

The mountains to the SW are higher, reaching 2760 ft in the Merrick, the highest peak in southern Scotland. Loch Enoch, under the Merrick, lies at 1650 ft. In the E the land rises to about 2000 ft. The scenery of the Southern Uplands is very varied: numerous valleys, large and small, cut through the hills, high moorland alternates with fertile arable land, here and there industry has established itself. The contours of the Southern Uplands are gentler than in the Highlands: this is ideal walking country.

Two famous Scottish writers have given their names to parts of the region. In the W and SW is the **Burns country**, extending from his birthplace at Alloway to Dumfries, where he died. To the E, in the Tweed valley, is the **Scott country**, the

area generally thought of as the Borderland. Throughout the whole region, however, there are many interesting and attractive towns and villages, pleasant places to stay and good centres for exploring the surrounding country. One of the most popular centres is **Ayr** (pop. 49,500), on the coast facing the Island of Arran. The River Ayr on which it stands is spanned by two bridges, the Auld Brig, dating from the 13th c., and the New Brig, built in 1788. The New Brig, fulfilling the prophecy in Burns's poem "The Brigs of Ayr", had to be rebuilt in 1877. In front of the station is a statue of Burns. The cottage in which Burns was born in 1759 can be seen at Alloway, 2 miles S of Ayr. – The Scottish Tourist Board publishes a useful leaflet on the "Burns Heritage Trail", taking in the many places in SW Scotland with Burns associations.

Some 12 miles down the coast S of Ayr is *Culzean Castle* (by Robert Adam, 1777), with beautiful gardens. A few miles SW is **Kirkoswald**, with *Souter Johnnie's House* (cf. Burns's "Tam o' Shanter"), furnished as in Burns's day. From here the road continues E, passing the ruins of *Crossraguel Abbey*, a Cluniac house founded in 1244, to *Maybole*, from which B 72 runs NE to *Tarbolton*, where Burns became a Freemason and founded the Bachelors' Club. A mile or two E is *Mauchline*, where he was married and lived for some time, with *Poosie Nancy's Tavern* which has been considerably altered since his day. The house in which he lived is now a museum; nearby is the Burns Memorial Tower.

To the S, via *Dalmellington*, a beautiful country road runs through the *Galloway Forest Park* to the attractive little town of **Newton Stewart** (pop. 2000), with a golf-course and fishing in the River Cree. 7 miles N is *Bargrennan*, from where there is a pleasant excursion through the Glen Trool Forest to **Loch Trool**, lying high among the hills. From here there are magnificent wide-ranging *views.

S of Newton Stewart is the pretty little town of **Whithorn**, where St Ninian brought Christianity to Scotland at the end of the 4th c. There are remains of a Premonstratensian priory founded in the 12th c. and a small museum with Early Christian stones.

From Newton Stewart the coast road runs SE to the tiny burgh of *Gatehouse of Fleet*, 2 miles from the head of a narrow inlet in Wigtown Bay, where Burns wrote "Scots wha ha'e". There are a number of castles in the surrounding area, including *Cardoness Castle* (1 mile SW), which has a fine 15th c. tower.

Beyond Gatehouse is **Kirkcudbright** (pop. 3400; Selkirk Arms Hotel, D, 27 r.), prettily situated at the mouth of the Dee, which here flows into Kirkcudbright Bay. John Paul Jones, founder of the United States navy, was imprisoned in the *Tolbooth* (16th–17th c.), which has a handsome tower; there are mementoes of him in the interesting *Stewartry Museum*. *Maclellan's Castle* is an imposing fortified mansion (now ruined) of the mid 16th c.

A few miles SE of Kirkcudbright are the ruins of *Dundrennan Abbey*, still conveying some impression of the former splendour of this 12th c. Cistercian foundation. The choir and transepts have been largely preserved, and there are some interesting monuments. Mary Queen of Scots is said to have spent her last night in Scotland here before seeking refuge in England. Farther along the beautiful coast road, beyond Dalbeattie, is *Sweetheart Abbey* or New Abbey, a Cistercian foundation of the 13th c. The foundress, Devorguilla, asked to be buried here together with her husband's heart: hence its romantic name. From the summit of Criffel (1866 ft), S of the abbey ruins, there is a magnificent view over the Solway Firth towards the Lake District.

Dumfries (pop. 32,000; hotels – Cairndale, C, 44 r.; Station, D, 30 r.; Waverley, E, 35 r.; Edenbank, E, 8 r.), on the banks of the River Nith, chief town of the Dumfries and Galloway region, is another place with Burns associations. Here he spent the last years of his life until his death in 1796. Visitors can see his house (now a museum), his mausoleum and the Globe Inn, one of his favourite haunts.

The town has a long history, its first charter having been granted by Robert II in 1395. The old tolbooth, the Midsteeple, which stands in the market-place was built in 1708. The Old Bridge (pedestrians only) dates from 1208. Nearby is the Bridge House Museum. 1½ miles N are the ruins of *Lincluden Abbey*, a house of Benedictine nuns.

9 miles NE is **Lochmaben**, a popular holiday town surrounded by five lochs, making it appear almost like an island. There is good fishing in the local streams. The ruined castle may have been the birthplace of Robert the Bruce (1274–1329), whose statue stands in front of the Town Hall.

On the coast road SE of Dumfries are two places which no visitor should miss – Ruthwell and Caerlaverock Castle. In Ruthwell church is an Early Christian monument of outstanding importance, the *Ruthwell Cross*, probably dating from the 8th c. The cross, 17 ft high, is carved with scenes from the life of Christ and has inscriptions in both Latin and runic script.

Caerlaverock Castle (6 miles SW) was built in the 13th c. (with a double moat and a drawbridge) and altered in the 15th. It has an unusual triangular ground-plan, with a watch-tower and two other towers at the corners. The buildings round the courtyard date mainly from the 17th c., when the castle was more a residence than a fortress. It is supposed to be the Ellangowan of Scott's "Guy Mannering".

From here the road continues over the border into England, by way of Annan and **Gretna Green**, where runaway couples from England used to be married by the local blacksmith.

There are also many places of interest and much beautiful scenery in the SE part of the Southern Uplands, the area com-

The Marriage Room, Gretna Green

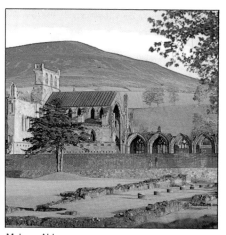

Melrose Abbey

nearby **Eildon Hills**, a three-headed hill whose highest peak is 1387 ft high. He is traditionally said to have caused the devil to split the hill into three. From the top of the Eildons there are magnificent panoramic views. Near the village of Newstead, on the N side of the hills, is a monument marking the site of the important Roman station of *Trimontium*, where excavations yielded much interesting material, now in the Museum of Antiquities in Edinburgh.

Admirers of Sir Walter Scott will want to make a pilgrimage to *Abbotsford House*, the baronial-style mansion he built for himself in 1817, a few miles W of Melrose. The house is full of mementoes of Scott, including his library, and contains a fine collection of arms and armour. Here Scott wrote many of his novels, and here he died in 1832.

Scott is buried in * **Dryburgh Abbey**, one of Scotland's most beautiful ruins, picturesquely situated amid wooded country on the banks of the Tweed. The abbey, one of the four famous Border abbeys, was founded in 1150 as a Premonstratensian house and became wealthy and powerful, but was repeatedly attacked, plundered and destroyed by English raiders. The remains, in High Gothic style, include the beautiful W doorway, the rose window at

monly known as the **Borders**. The history of the Border country begins with the foundation of four famous abbeys in the reign of David I (1124–53). In spite of frequent incursions from England the monks promoted the development of agriculture and craft industry, and the production of wool brought them prosperity.

The best preserved of the abbeys is at *Melrose*, a little town (pop. 2300) which makes a good centre for exploring the Border country and has excellent fishing in the Tweed. * **Melrose Abbey** is the most beautifully situated and the most magnificent of all the Scottish abbeys. Built of red sandstone, it was founded in 1136 as a Cistercian house but thereafter was frequently devastated and plundered, the ruins being used as a quarry of building material. In spite of these ravages the remains, mostly dating from the 15th c., are still of great splendour, if the additions of recent years are disregarded. Melrose is particularly noted for the variety and beauty of the capitals; and the windows in the transepts and the large E window are also very fine. Robert the Bruce, who restored the abbey after its destruction by Edward II, is said to be buried near the high altar. Some fine vaulting has also been preserved, and there are many architectural details which are worth careful study. The beauty of Melrose Abbey, particularly by moonlight, was celebrated by Sir Walter Scott in the 'Lay of the Last Minstrel''.

Another Scott, a 13th c. magician named Michael Scott, has associations with the

Kelso Abbey

the W end of the refectory, the chapter-house and St Modan's Chapel. (St Modan is said to have been the abbot of a 6th c. abbey on this site.)

14 miles NE is **Kelso** (pop. 4000), a pleasant town on the Tweed near its junction with the Teviot. *Kelso Abbey*, founded in 1128, the largest of the four Border abbeys, suffered the same destruction as the other three. A late Norman building of red sandstone, it now consists mainly of the transepts and the W tower, which is more reminiscent of a castle than a church.

Kelso has a handsome market square in which the curfew is rung every evening from the Court House. From the five-arched bridge (by Rennie, 1803) there is the best view of the abbey. The local school was attended by Scott. A famous ram market is held in Kelso in September, attracting buyers from many lands.

Jedburgh Abbey

To the W of the town is *Floors Castle*, seat of the duke of Roxburgh. A tree in the grounds marks the spot where King James II was killed in 1460 during the siege of Roxburgh Castle. Practically nothing is left of this castle, and the 13th c. town of *Roxburgh*, once an important royal burgh, has disappeared altogether, being now represented only by the little village of the same name, 3 miles S.

Mellerstain House, 6 miles NW, is a fine Adam mansion set in beautiful grounds.

The fourth of the Border abbeys is at **Jedburgh** (pop. 4000), one of the most attractive little towns in the Borders, which has had many famous visitors over the centuries, among them Mary Queen of

Scots. The house in which she stayed in 1566, after a long ride to see Bothwell at Hermitage Castle, is now a museum. Prince Charlie, Burns and Scott also stayed in the town.

The three-arched *bridge* dates from the 16th c. *Jedburgh Castle* was converted into a prison in 1823, and is now a museum. The main feature of the town, however, is the picturesque ruin of *Jedburgh Abbey, founded in 1118. The *church* is almost completely preserved, with Norman pillars in the choir and an Early English nave. Particularly fine are two Norman *doorway arches*; also notable is the tracery of the windows. There is a small *museum* of sculpture. Excavations to the S of the church have brought to light some of the monastic buildings.

The road S from Jedburgh into England (A 68) runs through the *Cheviot Hills*, with magnificent views from the top of the pass, the *Carter Bar*. Visitors passing that way in June will find it worth while making a detour to *Selkirk* for the "Common Riding", a traditional cavalcade around the countryside.

South Wales

Counties: Dyfed, Glamorgan and Gwent.

South Wales is a popular holiday region, with many seaside resorts along the coast and hills, and beautiful valleys farther inland. The western part, facing the Atlantic, vies in beauty with the West of England coast, and many old towns and remains of the past bear witness to a long history. But South Wales is also a land of coal and steel, and the giant steelworks at Margam, Port Talbot, is one of the largest and most modern in Europe. To the traditional coal-mining and iron and steel industry have been added a variety of other industries – chemicals, textiles, electrical goods and plastics. South Wales takes in the counties of Gwent, Glamorgan (divided into West, Mid and South Glamorgan) and the southern part of Dyfed.

South Wales is a climatically favoured region. Thanks to the Gulf Stream the winters are mild, there is little rain between January and June, and the coastal areas have many hours of sunshine. There are more than 80 bathing beaches, from wide bays to small rock-enclosed coves, many of them almost deserted, others crowded with holidaymakers in summer. Round the whole coast the water is clean and unpolluted; only

Tintern Abbey

are a Roman mosaic and the tombstone of a Roman officer. $2\frac{1}{2}$ miles NW is *Llanmelin Wood* hill-fort, probably the capital of the Silures before the foundation of Venta Silurum. – $2\frac{1}{2}$ miles S is *Caldicot Castle*, dating from the time of Edward II, with a completely preserved Norman round tower which in the quality of its masonry and details is superior to any fortification of the period in England.

Newport (pop. 133,700; hotels – Ladbroke, 125 r.; Queen's, 45 r.; Celtic Manor, 17 r.), at the mouth of the River Usk, is the third largest town in Wales, a port and industrial centre (aluminium, chemicals). There is a very considerable rise and fall of the tide here – up to 30 ft in the Bristol Channel – so that the bridges over the Usk (of which there are five in Newport) have to be high above water level. *St Woolos' Cathedral*, in a beautiful situation on Stow Hill, has a Norman nave, with a fine doorway, and a 15th c. tower. The Museum has excellent archaeological and natural history collections.

3 miles NE, up the Usk valley, is **Caerleon** (pop. 6300), the Roman *Isca Silurum*, with remains of the fortress of the Second Legion, established *c*. A.D. 70, abandoned *c*. A.D. 140. There are some well-preserved sections of walling, and the *amphitheatre* is the only one in Britain to have been completely excavated.

16 miles NE of Newport is the little town of *Raglan*, with *Raglan Castle*, originally a Norman foundation but extensively rebuilt and altered in the 15th c., which is believed to be the last example of medieval military engineering in Wales. The hexagonal tower (view) dates from the Norman period. Charles I visited the castle, and in 1646 it was defended by the Marquess of Worcester against Fairfax's forces. Cromwell caused the fortifications to be destroyed.

Cardiff: see p. 67.

the stretch between Chepstow and Newport, in the Severn estuary, is unsuitable for bathing.

Chepstow (pop. 8900; hotels – Two Rivers, C, 31 r.; George, C, 20 r.) is picturesquely situated on the Wye 3 miles above its mouth. Its situation made it a town of strategic importance, and the Normans built a large castle on a crag above the town, then known as Striguil. The present *Chepstow Castle* dates mainly from the time of Edward I, with a Norman keep of 1120–30, and is very well preserved. In the courtyard is a walnut-tree said to be 600 years old.

The narrow streets of the town are still partly enclosed by the old town walls. The old *Town Gate* (14th c.) now houses a museum.

From Chepstow there is an attractive trip up the *Wye Valley*. In 3 miles is a side road to the left, which should be followed for a quarter of a mile. From the end of the road it is a 15 minutes' walk to the top of *Wynd Cliff* (800 ft), from which there are wide views. The area is noted for the variety of its flora. – Returning to the main road and continuing N, we come to the ruins – among the most romantic in the country – of *Tintern Abbey*, on the W bank of the Wye, a Cistercian house founded by Walter de Clare in 1131. The church (Decorated, 1270–1325) is 228 ft long. The roof, central tower and N wall of the nave have disappeared, but the rest is remarkably well preserved.

Caerwent is of interest for the excavations of the best preserved Romano-British town in Wales, *Venta Silurum*, a tribal capital. It gives an excellent impression of Roman town planning, since substantial remains – walls, town gates, baths, shops, an amphitheatre, etc. – have been brought to light. In the parish church

Raglan Castle

Barry (pop. 44,700); hotels – Mount Sorrel, D, 40 r.; Water's Edge, E, 38 r.), situated on a narrow peninsula, offers a variety of attractions to visitors – a number of beaches, trim parks and gardens, a ruined castle, excellent entertainment facilities, a golf-course and a small zoo.

Whitmore Bay, Fontygary, Southern-down and *Porthcawl* are among the smaller seaside resorts which are mainly frequented by day visitors, since they have only limited accommodation. They all have sandy beaches, and usually a range of entertainments.

Aberavon, with 2 miles of sandy beach, is Wales's most recent seaside resort. It has a beautiful promenade and is a great favourite with surfers. The Afan Lido has a wide variety of sports and entertainment facilities.

Swansea, known in Welsh as *Abertawe* (pop. 173,200; hotels – Dragon, B, 118 r.; Dolphin, D, 66 r.; Osborn, D, 42 r.; Windsor Lodge, D, 18 r.; Llwyn Helyg, D, 11 r.), is Wales's second largest city, an important seaport at the mouth of the River Tawe and a major industrial town. It is also a popular seaside resort and a good base for exploring the Gower peninsula and the Mumbles. The largest market in the whole of Wales is held in Swansea, and on market days – and for that matter at other times as well – the city is a hive of activity.

After suffering heavy destruction during the last war, the city was rebuilt in a planned way, with the wide thoroughfare of *Kingsway* as its main artery. The remains of Swansea Castle are concealed behind modern buildings, with the exception of a turret and a few sections of wall to be seen in Castle Street and Castle Lane.

Swansea is a city of parks (48 in all). *Clyne Gardens* are famous for their rhododendrons and azaleas, seen at their best in late spring. *Blackpill Lido* has boating ponds and a children's playground.

The city has a lively cultural life. The great event of the musical year is the *Swansea Music Festival*, held annually in October in the *Guildhall* (which has murals by Sir Frank Brangwyn). The *Grand Theatre* in Singleton Street has its own company, and during the summer there is a full programme of variety shows, dancing, concerts and performances for children in the *Patti Pavilion* near the Guildhall. The *Maritime and Industrial Museum* has a collection of old vehicles, industrial machinery, weaving-looms and much else besides.

The beach is long and sandy, and there are excellent facilities for water-skiing. From the *Mumbles Pier* the White Funnel Fleet runs boat trips, particularly to the Mumbles.

The *Mumbles* are the favourite recreation area of the people of Swansea – a wide bay with a long promenade, piers, cafés, restaurants and a variety of entertainments. On a hill above the coast road are the very picturesque remains of *Oystermouth Castle* (*c.* 1287), including the gatehouse, great hall and chapel. On one of two rocky islands beyond *Mumbles Head* is a prominent lighthouse.

The Mumbles are the gateway to the *Gower peninsula*, a limestone massif of great scenic beauty. The romantic S coast is a nature reserve which, apart from the towns and villages, is accessible only on foot. There are a number of beaches and bays, though some of them are not entirely safe for bathing. *Langland* and *Caswell Bay* have sandy beaches which are particularly popular with surfers.

Oxwich has a sandy beach 3 miles long and large areas of dunes. There is a nature trail along the coast which offers magnificent views.

Port Eynon (youth hostel in the Old Lifeboat House, 32 b.) is a popular seaside resort, with a sandy beach and dunes and the additional interest of the *Culver Hole*, a cave occupied by prehistoric man.

W of Port Eynon is the very beautiful **Mewslade Bay**, and beyond it Rhossili Bay, with a fine sandy beach. The little seaside resort of *Rhossili* is beautifully situated under Rhosili Down, which rises to 633 ft. **Worm's Head** is a small isolated ridge of rock which can be reached on foot at low tide (about 1 mile from Rhossili). *Burry Holms* (3 miles N) is another little islet lying off the seaside resort of *Llangennith* which can be visited only when the tide is out.

E of *Whiteford Point*, still in the Gower peninsula, is *Penclawdd*, for long a well-known cockle-fishing centre. There are also cockle banks at *Llansaint*, near Kidwelly, *Ferryside* and *Llanstephan*, on the Taf estuary. There are castle ruins at Llanstephan and Kidwelly.

Round the wide curve of *Carmarthen Bay* are a number of other seaside resorts. **Cefn Sidan** has good surfing, with a beach 5 miles long backed by dunes and coniferous woodland. There are plenty of fish to be caught here, and also at

Ferryside (though the bathing is dangerous). Ferryside is popular with sailing enthusiasts.

Laugharne, on the Taf estuary, is also a cockle-fishing centre. It has many 18th c.

sailing centre of South Wales. Well-known regattas are held here. There is also good sea angling.

Tenby (pop. 5000; hotels – Fourcroft, D, 38 r.; Clarence House, E, 68 r.; Red House, E, 28 r.; Croft, E, 20 r.), still with its old town walls, is situated on a rocky peninsula at the W end of Carmarthen Bay. It has a picturesque harbour, two beautiful sandy beaches, charming old houses lining its narrow streets and the remains of a castle. Particular features of interest are the 15th c. Tudor Merchant's House, St Mary's (the largest parish church in Wales) and the Tenby Museum, on the S side of Castle Hill.

A very popular excursion from Tenby is a motorboat trip to *Caldy Island (2½ miles S), a very beautiful island which has belonged to Trappist monks since 1929. The first abbey here was founded in 1113, and there are still some buildings dating from the 14th and 15th c.

The coastal scenery in this area is particularly fine, though some stretches of coast are accessible only on foot. The Pembrokeshire Coast Path extends for a distance of 167 miles, through the Pembrokeshire Coast National Park, offering not only magnificent scenery but an abundance of wild flowers and numbers of rare birds.

Carmarthen Bay takes its name from the town of Carmarthen (pop. 15,300), lying 9 miles inland on the River Towy. It is the county town of the new county of Dyfed, which takes in the old counties of

Carmarthen, Pembroke and Cardigan. Formerly a seaport and Wales's largest town, it is now mainly an agricultural and cultural centre. The enchanter Merlin is supposed to have been born here.

The principal church, St Peter's, dates mainly from the 14th c. and has a fortified tower. There are remains of the town walls and a gateway (14th c.). The Guildhall (1766) and the County Museum are also of interest.

The distance from Carmarthen to Pembroke is some 30 miles, and there are a number of possible routes. The coast road runs via Manorbier (pop. 1170), a pretty little place with red sandstone cliffs. The *Castle is one of the most picturesque in Wales, with buildings dating from 1275 to 1325.

This was the birthplace in 1146 of Giraldus Cambrensis, one of the finest thinkers of the Middle Ages – archdeacon of Brecon, a vigorous protagonist of an independent Welsh Church, an adviser on Irish affairs and an outstanding orator. He accompanied Archbishop Baldwin of Canterbury on his tour of Wales to gain support for the Third Crusade, and this journey gave rise to his best known work, the "Itinerary of Wales", in which he describes Manorbier as the pleasantest spot in the Principality.

The more direct inland route to Pembroke passes the impressive ruins of *Carew Castle, on one of the many hills round Milford Haven. The castle was built about 1270; the beautifully carved high cross which stands near the entrance is believed to date from the 9th c. The church at Carew Cheriton is a fine example of 14th c. architecture, with a Perpendicular tower.

Pembroke (pop. 14,200; Wheeler's Old King's Arms Hotel, D, 21 r.) is a pleasant old town with remains of its 13th c. walls. Over the town towers** Pembroke Castle, one of the most imposing in Britain, built in 1090 by Arnulf, Earl of Pembroke. Henry VII was born here. From the top of the massive round keep, 75 ft high, there

Pembroke Castle

IMEX Group Ltd.

Buses, Cars and Motor Cycles are parked entirely at owner's risk and responsibility.

Car £ 2.00

Parking Ticket

are magnificent views. Adjoining the keep are the Prison Tower, the Norman Hall and the North Hall, from which a staircase leads down into the huge natural cavern known as the *Wogan*.

On the hill SW of the Castle is *Monkton Priory*, a Benedictine house founded at the same time as the Castle. 1 mile N is *Pembroke Dock*, which was planned to develop into a large naval dockyard but was closed down in 1926.

Pembroke is a good base from which to explore the beautiful scenery of the SW coast.

Milford Haven is the name both of the town (pop. 13,800) and of one of the largest natural harbours in Britain. The town was a place of some importance in the Middle Ages, and is now a considerable fishing port with large oil refineries. The harbour, 20 miles long and 1–2 miles wide, is a drowned river valley. There are many bays with good bathing in the surrounding area.

Dale is a very popular sailing harbour in a sheltered situation at the entrance to Milford Haven. Hereabouts are a number of good beaches of fine sand – *Musselwick Sands*, *Martin's Haven*, *Marloes Sands* and *Westdale Bay*. Henry VII landed here in 1485 and marched through Wales to defeat Richard III in the battle of Bosworth Field and win the English crown.

Westdale Bay, *Watwick Bay*, *Mill Bay* and *Castlebeach* are quiet and uncrowded bathing beaches on a little peninsula S of Dale. Swimming is dangerous here at low tide. – *Newgale* has a sandy beach 2½ miles long with fine views of *St Bride's Bay*, a straggling holiday resort with a camping site. When the tide is particularly low a sunken forest can be seen. 1½ miles SE is the romantic little *Roch Castle* (unoccupied), perched high on the cliffs looking down on the village below. There is heavy surf on the sea here. *Solva* is a popular boating centre and a good starting point for a visit to the St David's peninsula. The Castle with its church, wells, mills, park and orchards offers a complete picture of a Norman fortified residence.

St David's (pop. 1500), a long-drawn-out little town situated on a remote peninsula, was for centuries a place of pilgrimage. Its *Cathedral, the largest and most interesting church in Wales, is one of the earliest of the British cathedrals. In order to escape the attentions of marauders from the sea it was built in a hollow, so that from the immediately surrounding area only the tower can be seen. The precincts of the Cathedral are enclosed by a 13th c. wall.

The Cathedral is mainly Late Norman (end of 12th c.), but 14th c. rebuilding has given the exterior a Decorated aspect. As in many early churches and cathedrals the original tower collapsed in 1220 and was rebuilt in 1250. The *Lady Chapel* was added in the Early English period. The *W front* was given its present form in the 19th c. restoration by Sir George Gilbert Scott (1862–78). The general aspect of the Cathedral from outside is rather sombre and austere, and by no means imposing.

In contrast, however, the INTERIOR is of overwhelming effect. The Norman *nave* is richly articulated and shows great variety of form. The beautiful ceiling of Irish oak was added in the 15th c. The very fine *roodscreen* is also 15th c. Of the four arches supporting the tower, the one on the W side dates from before the collapse of the original tower, the other three from after 1220. The *choir-stalls*, with misericords, and the *bishop's throne* date from the second half of the 15th c. A unique feature is the stall for the reigning monarch. Bishop Vaughan's Chapel has fine fan vaulting. The transepts are partly original, partly rebuilt after the collapse of the tower in an Early Gothic style characteristic of South Wales and some churches in the West of England.

On the N side of the Cathedral are the ruins of *St Mary's College*, with a slender tower, founded in 1365. To the W is the *Bishop's Palace*, with fine arcading, built 1280–1350. The whole building stands on a vaulted *undercroft*. The great hall is impressive, with a handsome porch and rose windows. Adjoining is the chapel, with a picturesque bell-tower.

Off the St David's peninsula is *Ramsey Island*, with Woodwalton Fen and (to N) Holme Fen, a nature reserve with rare plants and insects (permit required to visit). There are remains of a Benedictine abbey on the island.

On *St David's Head*, the most westerly point in Wales, fringed with high cliffs, are remains of the prehistoric earthwork known as the Warriors' Dyke. The area from St David's to beyond Cardigan, with its rocky coasts, bleak plateaux and narrow valleys, is one of the least spoiled stretches of natural scenery in Wales: there are no seaside resorts here. It is a thinly populated region mainly devoted to sheep-farming. In Fishguard Bay are the twin towns of *Goodwick* and *Fishguard* (joint pop. 5000), terminal of the ferry service to Rosslare in Ireland. Fishguard consists of two distinct parts, the old town and the modern town. Round the beautiful harbour, known as Abergwaun, is a huddle of old houses and wharfs, known to a wider public as the setting for the film version of Dylan Thomas's "Under Milk Wood" which was made here in 1971. At the tip of the promontory are the ruins of an old fort. The newer part of the town, with the shops, is at the top of the hill. Here there are pleasant walks along the coast, with wide views. The *Pen Caer peninsula*, to the NW, has many prehistoric remains, Iron Age forts, chambered tombs, etc.

Newport (7 miles E) is an old town on the River Nevern which is now a pleasant seaside resort, with remains of a 13th c. castle, good beaches, excellent fishing and a golf-course. 3 miles SE is *Pentre Ifan*, the largest prehistoric burial chamber in Wales.

1 mile S, in the Preseli Hills, is *Carn Ingli Common*, with remains of an Early Christian settlement. From this area came 33 dolerite stones which were transported to Stonehenge (see below). In a valley on the other side of the Preseli Hills is the *Gors Fawr* stone circle. – At *Nevern*, 2 miles E, is *St Brynach's Church*, dedicated to a Celtic saint, with a richly carved Celtic cross 12½ ft high.

Cardigan (pop. 4300) is a busy little market town, formerly a seaport, on the Teifi 2½ miles above its mouth. There is a charming old bridge over the river from which there is a fine view. Close by are the remains of a castle. The River Teifi is well stocked with salmon and trout, and Cardigan is a favourite place for a fishing holiday. 3 miles S, on the southern bank of the Teifi, are the picturesque ruins of the 13th c. *Cilgerran Castle*. – Beyond this point, see under *Mid Wales*.

Near the eastern end of South Wales, high in the hills, is one of the most beautiful parts of Wales, the **Brecon Beacons National Park**. Separated from the Black Mountains along the English border opposite Hereford by the valley of the Usk, the Park extends westward to the borders of the old county of Carmarthenshire in a swathe between 10 and 15 miles

wide. To the W is an area of moorland rising to 2630 ft in *Fan Brycheiniog*. Most of the hills are over 1000 ft, many over 2000 ft. The highest peaks are in the centre of the Park – composed of red sandstone, they gleam in the sun like beacons, giving the range its name. There are numerous waterfalls in the Park, the most famous being the *Henryd Falls* near Coelbren. There are also a number of striking caves, including *Dan yr Ogof* in the Tawe valley, which is floodlit for the benefit of visitors.

The town of **Brecon** (pop. 7000) lies in a beautiful setting in the valley of the Usk at its junction with the Honddu and the Tarell. It has many Georgian houses, remains of the old town walls and a ruined castle of the 12th and 13th c. The red sandstone *Cathedral* (13th and 14th c.) is a former priory church, typically Welsh in its plain and massive construction. The *Brecknock Museum* in Glamorgan Street has a good collection of local history and folklore and natural history.

Stonehenge

Southern England. – County: Wiltshire.

****Stonehenge, on Salisbury Plain 10 miles N of Salisbury, is Britain's most important prehistoric monument; and indeed there is no monument of the same period anywhere in Europe which can compare with it. This huge megalithic structure, in all probability of religious significance, dates from between 1850 and 1400 B.C. In its original form it consisted of two concentric rings of standing stones surrounding a smaller horseshoe formation of stones.**

The outer ring, with a diameter of 97 ft, originally had 30 stones (now 17) topped by a continuous series of lintel stones. This formation of trilithons (structures formed of three stones, two uprights topped by a lintel) gave Stonehenge its name ("hanging stones"). The lintels were fitted end to end by tongue-and-groove joints and attached to the uprights by tenon-and-mortise joints. The inner ring consisted of 60 smaller stones (now 21) without lintels. Inside this ring was a

Stonehenge

horseshoe-shaped formation of massive trilithons (originally five, now three) with the open end to the N. One of the largest stones stands 22 ft high and has an estimated weight of 45 tons. Within this formation was a smaller horseshoe, originally of 19 stones (now 11).

The stones used in the structure are of different types. The outer ring and the trilithons of the main horseshoe formation are sarsen stones, sandstone erratics found locally, perhaps on the Marlborough Downs 25 miles away. The stones of the inner ring and the smaller horseshoe are bluestones (a kind of basalt), which have been shown to come from the Preseli Hills in Wales. These heavy stones, weighing up to 4 tons each, must thus have been transported over a distance of some 135 miles – probably by boat from Milford Haven by way of the Bristol Channel, the Wye and the Wiltshire Avon, being dragged on rollers over the intervening overland stretches. By any standard it was an extraordinary achievement. The Altar Stone of micaceous sandstone came from the coast N of Milford Haven. The function of this stone – as indeed of the structure as a whole – is an enigma.

Stonehenge is enclosed within a circular earthwork, with an "Avenue" leading into it from the NE. Outside the entrance is the Heel Stone or "Friar's Heel", which has an impression in the shape of a human heel. Inside the entrance is the "Slaughter Stone". Round the inner side of the circular earthwork is a ring of 56 holes, the Aubrey holes (named after the 17th c. antiquary John Aubrey who discovered them), in some of which traces of cremation burials were found. In this ring too are two "Station Stones" standing opposite one another; originally there were four, spaced equally round the circle.

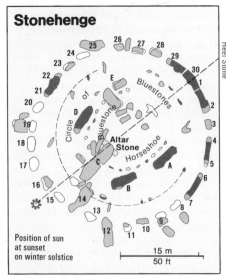

Stonehenge

Position of sun at sunset on winter solstice

15 m
50 ft

■ Lintels
▨ Standing stones
A–E Trilithons

▨ Fallen stones
○ Missing stones
1–30 Sarsen circle

The Station Stones may have been used for the purpose of astronomical surveying; and indeed one theory is that Stonehenge was a kind of astronomical observatory used in the determination of the annual calendar. At the summer solstice the sun, seen from the Altar Stone, rises directly above the Heel Stone; and this has led to the theory that Stonehenge was connected with the Druids – though the monument is in fact much older than the time of the Druids. It seems most probable that Stonehenge was a solar temple, and perhaps also associated with a cult of the dead. In the surrounding area 345 barrows (burial mounds) containing valuable utensils and jewelry have been found, some of them older than Stonehenge, some contemporary, some younger.

On some of the sarsen stones are carved symbols (daggers, axe-heads, etc.), distinguishable only in certain light conditions. It has also been established that the various rings of stones are of different dates. The oldest stones date from about 1800 B.C., the Avenue from about 1600, the most recent stones from 1400. But Stonehenge still presents many puzzles to the archaeologist, and recently has excited the interest of mathematicians and astronomers; it has always, of course, had a powerful appeal to artists and the ordinary interested visitor.

Apart from its numerous prehistoric remains Salisbury Plain also has a series of curious features of more recent origin – the **White Horses** to be found at *Cherhill, Pewsey, Alton Barnes* and elsewhere. Unlike the famous White Horse of Uffington, which probably dates from between 600 and 500 B.C., these huge figures outlined in the turf of the hillsides were cut in the 18th, 19th and even 20th c.

Stratford-upon-Avon

Central England. – County: Warwickshire.
Altitude: 120 ft. – Population: 21,200.
Telephone dialling code: 0789.

(i) **Tourist Information Centre,**
Judith Shakespeare's House, 1 High Street; tel. 293127.

HOTELS. – *Alveston Manor*, Clapton Bridge, B, 112 r.; *Welcome*, Warwick Road, B, 84 r.; *Shakespeare*, Chapel Street, B, 66 r.; *Stratford-upon-Avon Moat House*, Bridgefoot, C, 249 r.; *Falcon*, Chapel Street, C, 73 r.; *Arden*, Waterside, C, 63 r.

YOUTH HOSTEL. – *Hemingford House*, Alveston, 174 b.

CAMP SITE.

RESTAURANTS. – *Marlowe's Elizabethan Room*, 18 High Street; *Giovanni*, 8 Ely Street.

EVENTS. – *Shakespeare's Birthday*, St George's Day (23 Apr.); *Mop Fair* (12 Oct.); *Shakespeare Festival* (Apr.–Nov.).

SPORT and RECREATION. – Rowing, riding, golf, tennis.

Without Shakespeare, *Stratford would be an ordinary medium-sized town with a few pretty old houses, one or two fine churches, a 14-arched bridge over the Avon and attractive parks and gardens; its association with Shakespeare has made it a place of pilgrimage which draws thousands of visitors from all over the world. The performances of Shakespeare's plays during the summer are usually of outstanding quality.

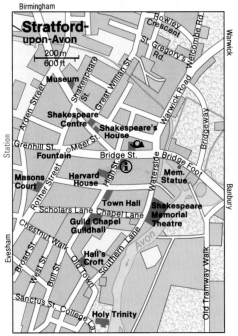

The town lives on and for Shakespeare, in spite of the fact that there are many uncertainties and problems about his life and works and that, for all the books that have been written about him, much of the Shakespeare legend is based on mere speculation.

HISTORY. – The date of Shakespeare's birth is not accurately known, but was probably 23 April 1564; it is known at any rate that he was christened in the parish church on 26 April. He was the third child and eldest son of John Shakespeare, a farmer, glover and wool dealer (d. 1601) and Mary Arden (d. 1608).

John Shakespeare was a man of some local influence, a member of the town council from 1565 to 1586. William probably attended Stratford grammar school. In 1582, at the age of 18, he married Anne Hathaway, then aged 16, and they had three children – Susanna (christened 1583, d. 1649) and twins named Hamnet and Judith (christened 1585). In 1584 or 1586 he went to London, leaving his family behind, and appears in the records in 1592 as a successful playwright and actor. In 1610 or 1611 he retired from the theatre and returned to Stratford to live in New Place, which he had bought in 1597. He died on 23 April 1616, his 52nd birthday, and was buried in Stratford parish church on 25 April.

Shakespeare's Birthplace, Stratford-upon-Avon

SIGHTS. – *Shakespeare's Birthplace, the Mecca of hundreds of thousands of visitors every year, is in Henley Street. It is a double house, the eastern half of which was bought by John Shakespeare in 1556 and used for his wool business; he probably already owned the other half.

The rooms are furnished in the fashion of middle-class houses of the period. The front room on the first floor, probably the room in which Shakespeare was born, contains many editions of his works, including the First Folio of 1623. Many famous visitors have scratched their names on the window. The E end of the house is a museum, with many mementoes, books, manuscripts and pictures.

Adjoining the Birthplace is a modern building which houses the **Shakespeare Centre** (opened 1964) and the headquarters of the Shakespeare Birthplace Trust (founded 1847), with two libraries and rooms for study.

At the corner of the High Street and Bridge Street is *Quiney's House*, which was occupied from 1616 to 1652 by Thomas Quiney, a wine-dealer, and his wife Judith, Shakespeare's younger daughter. Close by, in the High Street, is *Harvard House*, a half-timbered house built in 1696 which belonged to the mother of John Harvard, founder of Harvard University.

On the N front of the *Town Hall* (1769) is a statue of Shakespeare presented by David Garrick, the famous 18th c. actor and manager of Drury Lane Theatre in London. Beside the Town Hall is the Shakespeare Hotel, dating in part from the 15th c. Close by is *Nash's House*, which belonged to Thomas Nash, husband of a granddaughter of Shakespeare; it now contains a museum (Roman and Saxon material, mementoes of Shakespeare and Garrick). Adjoining Nash's House is the site of *New Place*, one of the finest houses in the town, which Shakespeare bought for £60 on 4 May 1597 and in which he lived from 1610 to 1611 until his death. There are very beautiful *gardens* – the Elizabethan-style *Knot Garden*, in which Shakespeare is said to have written "The Tempest", and the *Great Garden*.

The *Guild Chapel* at the corner of Chapel Lane has a fine wall painting of the Last Judgment of about 1500. Next door is the half-timbered *Guildhall*, the upper floor of which was occupied for centuries by the Grammar School which Shakespeare probably attended.

On the opposite side of Church Street is *Mason Croft*, since 1951 the Shakespeare Institute of Birmingham University.

One of the finest Tudor houses in Stratford, with fine period furniture, is **Hall's Croft**, in the street called Old Town. This was probably the home of Dr John Hall, who married Shakespeare's elder daughter Susanna. Part of the house is occupied by the Festival Club.

The parish church of **Holy Trinity**, in which Shakespeare is buried, is beautifully situated on the banks of the Avon. The tower is Early English (c. 1210), with a spire added in 1763. The nave and N aisles are also Early English, the rest of the church Decorated and Perpendicular.

Shakespeare's grave, on the N side of the chancel, bears a doggerel inscription:

> Good frend for Jesus sake forbeare
> To digg the dust encloased heare;
> Bleste be ye man y^t spares thes stones
> And curst be he y^t moves my bones.

It is a matter of controversy whether Shakespeare composed these lines himself or not. On the wall above the grave is a *monument* to Shakespeare, set up before 1623, probably by the Flemish sculptor Geraert Janssen or Johnson (restored about 1745). Close by are the *graves* of Shakespeare's wife Anne Hathaway, his daughter Susanna and her husband Dr John Hall, and the first husband of his granddaughter, Thomas Nash. The church also contains the late 15th c. *font* used in Shakespeare's christening and the *parish registers* containing the record of his baptism and burial.

Southern Lane runs along the Avon to the **Royal Shakespeare Theatre** (by Elizabeth Scott, 1920–32), which replaced the earlier Memorial Theatre (1879) after its destruction by fire. The figures on the façade (Love, Life, Death, Mirth, Faithlessness, War) are by Eric Kennington. On the upper floor is the *Picture Gallery and Museum*, which contains paintings and sculpture of Shakespeare and famous actors and actresses who have appeared in his plays, together with costumes and stage-settings. Not far to the N at "The World of Shakespeare" audio-visual shows are given, lasting 25 minutes.

SURROUNDINGS. – In Shottery, 1 mile W of the town centre, is *Anne Hathaway's Cottage*, which has been preserved almost exactly as it was when Shakespeare came wooing here. Until 1899 it was occupied by descendants of the Hathaway family, and still contains some of the original furniture.

In *Wilmcote*, 4 miles NW of Stratford, is **Mary Arden's House,** said to have been the home of Shakespeare's mother. The house, with contemporary furniture, is open to visitors.

4 miles E is **Charlecote Park,** built by the Lucy family in 1558 but much altered in 1830. According to an old tradition Shakespeare was arrested and brought before Sir Thomas Lucy in the great hall for killing a deer in the park.

Alcester (pop. 5300; Cherrytrees Motel, D, 22 r.), 8 miles W of Stratford, is an attractive little town with many handsome old buildings, including the Old Malt House (*c.* 1500) and the picturesque Town Hall. 1½ miles SW is *Ragley Hall* (1680), seat of the Marquess of Hertford. 2 miles N is **Coughton Court,** an Elizabethan manor-house which has been the home of the Throckmorton family since 1409.

14 miles S is ****Compton Wynyates**, seat of the marquess of Northampton; it is the finest Tudor mansion in England, scarcely altered since it was built in 1520. Laid out round a courtyard, it is constructed of brick, a yellowish stone and black timberwork and contains fine plaster ceilings, furniture of various periods, tapestries and pictures.

The *Stratford-on-Avon Canal,* completed in 1816, has lost its economic importance but after cleaning up and restoration in 1961–64 is now a very attractive and picturesque waterway with 35 locks and 19 Georgian bridges. The towpath offers a pleasant walk through beautiful countryside.

Wales

See Mid Wales, North Wales and South Wales

Warwick Castle

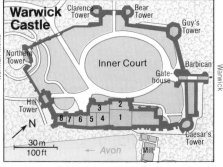

1 Great Hall	3 Chapel	5 Cedar Room	7 Bedroom
2 Dining Room	4 Red Room	6 Drawing Room	8 Boudoir

Warwick

Central England. – County: Warwickshire.
Population: 21,900 – Telephone dialling code: 0926.
ⓘ **Tourist Information Centre,**
The Court House, Jury Street;
tel. 492212.

HOTELS. – *Ladbroke,* Longbridge, B, 130 r.; *Warwick Arms,* High Street, D, 30 r.

CAMP SITE.

Warwick, situated on the Avon, is the county town of Warwickshire and possesses many fine old buildings. The town was largely rebuilt by the Smith brothers in 1694 after a fire, and the High Street and Northgate Street still bear witness to their work. The Court House, Landor House and Shire Hall date from the same period.

Two of the old town gates, the East Gate and West Gate, have been preserved. The High Street, which runs between them, contains many 17th and 18th c. houses. The best view of Warwick Castle is to be had from the bridge over the Avon. The Castle, is one of the most imposing medieval strongholds in the country.

SIGHTS. – *Warwick Castle, on a crag overlooking the Avon, is approached by a road cut in the rock which leads into the Outer Court, with *Caesar's Tower* on the left and *Guy's Tower* on the right. Although Guy's Tower looks the higher of the two, it is actually lower than Caesar's Tower. Between the two towers a gateway, with a portcullis, gives access to the Inner Court. To the right are two other towers, to the left the entrance to the state apartments. These, mostly dating from the 17th c., contain a fine collection of furniture, paintings, sculpture, porcelain, weapons and curios of all kinds.

Half-timbered houses, Warwick

In the town centre is the collegiate church of **St Mary**, rebuilt (apart from the E end) in 1694 after the great fire and completed in 1704 by Sir William Wilson with the help of Wren. The tower (which can be climbed) is 174 ft high and contains ten bells. The most splendid feature of the church is the **Beauchamp Chapel** or Lady Chapel on the S side of the choir (Perpendicular, 1443–64). The original glass has largely been preserved. The device of the Warwick family, the bear and ragged staff, features prominently in the decoration. In the centre of the chapel is the tomb of the founder, Richard Beauchamp, earl of Warwick (1381–1439); it is made of Purbeck marble, and has 14 figures of mourners. Other monuments include that of Robert Dudley, earl of Leicester, Elizabeth I's favourite. The choir, completed in 1394, has a rib-vaulted roof, sedilia and an Easter Sepulchre; the stalls date from 1449. In the centre is the tomb of Thomas Beauchamp (d. 1369). In the Norman crypt (1123) under the choir is a ducking-stool.

Nearby is the *Market House* (c. 1670), which contains the *County Museum*. *Oken's House*, in Castle Street, is occupied by the Doll Museum, with a collection of dolls and toys. At the N end of Castle Street is the *Court House*, which has a Georgian ballroom. To the W, along the High Street, is the splendid half-timbered *Lord Leycester Hospital*, a group

of houses dating from 1383 in which Robert Dudley, earl of Leicester, established a home for 12 old soldiers in 1571. It contains an interesting collection of relics of the past.

Wells

South-western England. – County: Somerset.
Population: 8400.
Telephone dialling code: 0749.
ⓘ **Tourist Information Centre,**
Town Hall, Market Place;
tel. 72552.

HOTELS. – *Red Lion*, Market Place, D, 34 r.; *Crown*, Market Place, D, 18 r.

RESTAURANTS. – *Star*, High Street (16th c.); *Gauloise*, 64 High Street; *Ancient Gate House* (14th c.).

Wells is one of the most delightful little towns in England, a place in which time seems to stand still. Most of the hotels and restaurants are several hundred years old, and although the Cathedral may not be one of the largest churches in the country it is undoubtedly one of the most beautiful. Its unique feature is the assemblage of 350 statues on the W front, figures from both sacred and secular history.

Vicars' Close is an excellently preserved street of mid 14th c. houses, still occupied by vicars' choral and theological students, and there is a picturesque Bishop's Palace, with a moat occupied by swans, which sometimes ring a bell when they want to be fed. Markets are still held in the old market-place – which is no doubt why there are so many pubs in the immediate area.

HISTORY. – Wells became an episcopal see in 909, but there are no remains of any churches of the Saxon period. The see was transferred for a time to Bath, but Bishop Jocelin (bishop 1206–42) brought it back to Wells. Since 1244 the diocese has been known as Bath and Wells.

SIGHTS. – The *Cathedral*, begun in the time of Bishop Reginald FitzJocelin (1174–91), is dedicated to St Andrew. The *transepts*, six bays at the E end of the nave and the most westerly bays are the oldest parts of the church, in Transitional style. The rest of the nave, the famous *W front* and the *N doorway* were built in Early English style by Bishop Jocelin, and the church was consecrated in 1239. To the Decorated period (c. 1290–1340)

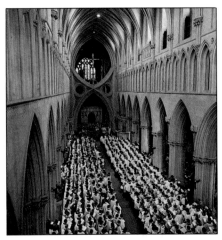

Wells Cathedral

belong the *Chapterhouse*, the *Lady Chapel*, the E end of the Choir and the *central tower*, which was rebuilt about 100 years later. The *Cloisters* are Perpendicular. Although the Cathedral suffered from ill-considered 19th c. restoration, it is notable for the exquisite harmony of the whole structure.

The Cathedral Close is entered from the Market Place by the *Penniless Porch*, where alms were distributed to the poor. This gateway, like *Browne's Gate* in Sadler Street, the *Chain Gate* (from Vicars' Close) and the *Bishop's Eye* (the entrance to the Bishop's Palace from the Market Place), was built by Bishop Thomas Beckington (1443–65). The **W front** of the Cathedral, with more than 350 statues, is of a splendour unmatched in England. The grey sandstone wall is 147 ft long; and in order to leave sufficient room for the long rows of figures the towers were not built at the end of the side aisles but were displaced to the side. The *Statues*, which were originally painted, are disposed in eight horizontal rows and represent figures and scenes from the Old and New Testaments and from both ecclesiastical and secular history – angels, saints, heroes, apostles and bishops. Particularly fine is the Coronation of the Virgin in the first row. – The N porch is a masterpiece of Early English architecture.

The INTERIOR of the Cathedral has an unusual feature of curiously modern effect, the *double pointed arch* between the nave and the crossing – an unorthodox solution devised in 1338 to prevent the central tower from collapsing.

The *capitals* are particularly fine, with stylised leaves, birds and animals. In the first chapel in the S transept is a splendid *alabaster monument* (Nottingham alabas-

ter, *c.* 1400) with panels depicting the Annunciation and the Trinity. In the N transept is a famous *astronomical clock* (*c.* 1392), with figures of mounted knights which ride into action at the hour.

The *windows* show both the early and later Decorated style, at first strictly geometrical in form but later with freer lines. One of them depicts the Tree of Jesse. The large *E window* is 14th c.

The *Choir*, *Lady Chapel* and presbytery are among the most beautiful parts of the Cathedral, notable for their harmony and unity of style. The *choir-stalls* are modern, but incorporate fine misericords of 1325.

A beautiful early Decorated *staircase* leads from the Cathedral to the *Chapterhouse*, an octagonal room (Decorated) of consummate perfection. The vaulting is borne on a single central pier, with the figure of a monk in the role of Atlas. The *Cloisters* are 15th c. The immediate surroundings of the Cathedral and the adjoining buildings have scarcely changed since the Cathedral was built. The *Bishop's Palace*, enclosed by its wall and its moat, is particularly impressive.

To the N of the Cathedral, reached by way of a bridge over the Chain Gate, is *Vicars' Close*, a remarkable row of over 40 houses dating from the middle of the 14th c.

SURROUNDINGS. – In the region around Wells there are a number of famous *caves*. The most interesting, but also the most crowded during the summer, are those in the *Cheddar Gorge* (8 miles NW). *Cheddar* is a small town (pop. 3700) once well-known for cheese making. The *Gorge*, a quarter of a mile long, is enclosed by limestone cliffs up to 450 ft high. The two largest caves, with fine stalactites and stalagmites, are Cox's Cavern and Gough's Cavern, though the special lighting effects do not always enhance their beauty. *Wookey Hole*, nearer Wells, has no stalactites or stalagmites and fewer visitors: its interest lies in the traces of prehistoric occupation found here. Tourist attractions include wax models of the heads of people who were once imprisoned in Wookey Hole.

Gough's Cavern, Cheddar Gorge

Isle of Wight

(i) **Tourist Information Office,**
21 High Street, Newport, IOW;
tel. 0983 524343.

The *Isle of Wight, lying off the S coast of England opposite Southampton and Portsmouth, is 23 miles long from E to W and 13 miles across from N to S. It was known to the Romans as *Vectis*. Poets have celebrated its beauties, monarchs and prosperous citizens have built their houses here. The island fully justifies the epithets that have been applied to it – the "Island of Flowers", the "Island of Gardens", a "diamond in the sea". The climate is mild, though occasionally there can be rough winds. Queen Victoria frequently spent the summer here with Prince Albert, who himself designed Osborne House, the royal holiday residence in East Cowes, and after Albert's death the queen often spent the whole year on the island. Something of the Isle of Wight's Victorian atmosphere has been preserved into our own day.

The good weather and long hours of sunshine still attract many holidaymakers. Other attractions are provided by the charming villages and towns, not yet spoiled by modern development. Then, too, yachtsmen and sailing enthusiasts flock to the island, and the great social occasion of the year is the fashionable "Cowes Week" in August, when the Solent, the wide channel between the Isle of Wight and the Hampshire coast, is dotted with hundreds of sails. And finally there are few areas containing such a variety of scenery in a narrow space; and it is no surprise to find that much of the island has been officially designated as an area of outstanding natural beauty.

There are ferry services (carrying cars) from Portsmouth, Southampton and Lymington, and from Southsea it is an 8 minutes' trip by hovercraft to Ryde. The finest views of the island are to be had from the sea, and during the season there are boat trips round it. There are also bus trips round the island. The best time to go to the Isle of Wight is not during the height of the summer season but in spring, when the island's numerous rhododendrons are in bloom, or in September, when it is still warm and beautiful but not so crowded. Even in winter it is a pleasant place for a holiday, though many of the hotels, restaurants and shops are closed.

The capital of the Isle of Wight, with 22,300 out of its total population of 95,000, is **Newport** (hotels – Bugle, D, 25 r.; Roach's Hotel), situated roughly in the centre of the island. It lies on the river *Medina*, which is navigable up to this point, and at the meeting-place of the principal roads. It is a lively and bustling town, particularly on market days.

Just over a mile SW of Newport, picturesquely situated on a hill, is *Carisbrooke Castle, long the seat of authority on the island. The site was previously occupied by a Roman fort. The Castle is the most interesting building on the Isle of Wight, able to stand comparison with castles much farther afield. The keep, from which there are very fine views, is Norman (early 12th c.), the rest mainly 13th c. Charles I was held prisoner in Carisbrooke in 1647–48; his 15-year-old daughter died in captivity here and she is commemorated by a monument in Newport. Visitors are shown the remains of the royal apartments. The *Governor's House* is now a museum on the history of the island. Behind the house is the deep castle well.

The village of *Carisbrooke* has a beautiful 12th c. church with a tower added in 1474.

At the mouth of the River Medina is the island's principal yachting centre, **Cowes** (pop. 18,900; hotels – Padmore House; Fountain, D, 22 r.). This world-famous sailing centre, home of the exclusive Royal Yacht Squadron, reaches the high-point of its year in the races held in Cowes Week (the first week in August). *Cowes Castle*, built by Henry VIII in 1540, is the headquarters of the Royal Yacht Squadron. Most of the town lies on the W side of the Medina estuary; in East Cowes is one of the town's major tourist attractions, **Osborne House**, in which Queen Victoria died in 1901. Visitors are shown the state apartments, the private rooms and the Swiss Cottage, specially imported from Switzerland as a play-house for the royal children, with its museum. During the First World War part of the house was taken over by the Royal Naval College, and King George VI received some of his training here.

From Cowes a road runs E via Fishbourne, at the mouth of Wootton Creek, to **Ryde** (pop. 23,200; hotels – Yelf's, C, 21 r.; Royal Esplanade, D, 63 r.), the island's most popular holiday resort.

Ryde has wide sandy beaches, a pier almost half a mile long and a wide variety of entertainments. Here too the aspect of the town is still Victorian. As a terminal of the frequent passenger ferry services from the mainland it is a hive of activity during the summer. Spring and autumn visitors are catered for by a heated open-air swimming pool. There are pleasant walks to *Quarr Abbey*, the scanty remains of a Cistercian house founded in 1132, and to *Seaview* (4 miles E), a little resort with a good beach and an iron pier over 300 yards long. Beyond Seaview the road continues via St Helen's to *Bembridge*, a trim seaside resort and sailing centre with a windmill dating from about 1700. From here there is a beautiful cliff-top walk to the *Foreland*, the most easterly point on the island, and *Culver Cliff*, where there is a statue of the first earl of Yarborough, who founded the Royal Yacht Club (later the Royal Yacht Squadron) in 1815.

Sandown (pop. 4400; hotels – Broadway Park, D, 53 r.; St Catherine's, D, 18 r., youth hostel, The Firs, Fitzroy Street, 76 b.) is a popular modern resort with a gently sloping beach which makes it very suitable for children. It has a golf-course, a small zoo housed in an old fort and a geological museum with an excellent collection of fossils.

In the same beautiful bay is **Shanklin** (pop. 7400; hotels – Luccombe Hall, D, 32 r.; Hartland, D, 25 r.; Luccombe Chine, D, 6 r.), a town much favoured by writers and artists which gains its particular charm from its situation in and around a valley. It also has a picturesque *"Old Village"* of thatched cottages with beautiful country gardens.

Shanklin has a good beach, a variety of sports facilities and entertainments and beautiful walks. Among its 19th c. visitors were two poets, Keats and Longfellow. A third poet, Swinburne, grew up in the district and is buried in the nearby village of Bonchurch, which lies on the road from Shanklin to Ventnor, a pleasant 4 miles' walk.

Ventnor (pop. 5800; hotels – Royal, C, 55 r.; Ventnor Towers, D, 30 r.; Channel View, E, 14 r.), situated on a series of natural terraces above beautiful bathing beaches, has an almost southern air. Sheltered on the N by limestone hills, it has the mildest climate on the island and is reputed as a health resort for the treatment of lung conditions. The best view of the Victorian-style architecture of the town can be had from the pier. There is a very beautiful park with a magnificent view of the *Undercliff*, a stretch of chalk and limestone plateau which extends for 6 miles to Blackgang Chine. The warm climate and subtropical vegetation of this

area of coast has earned it the name of the English Riviera.

The road to Freshwater (20 miles) runs along the Undercliff to Chale, passing houses with beautiful gardens and affording frequent glimpses of the sea, with scenery reminiscent of the Mediterranean. On *St Catherine's Point*, the southernmost tip of the island, is a powerful lighthouse. A large area round Brook, including *Brook Chine* and *Brook Down*, belongs to the National Trust.

Freshwater Bay (pop. 5000; hotels – Albion, D, 43 r.; Saunders, E, 13 r.) is a quiet seaside resort where Tennyson lived for more than 30 years. One of the finest walks on the island is from Freshwater Bay to Alum Bay, passing the Tennyson Monument on *High Down*, from which there are magnificent views of the sea and the coast. Much to be recommended also is a boat trip from Freshwater Bay, with views of Freshwater Cliffs and the pointed crags known as the Needles. The cliffs are between 400 and 500 ft high, the finest being those at *Main Bench*.

The Needles, Isle of Wight

The best route for returning to Newport from Freshwater is the coast road by way of Alum Bay (17 miles), which offers much finer scenery than the more direct inland road (10½ miles).

* **Alum Bay** is a Mecca for geologists, with almost vertical strata of sandstone in a variety of hues – red, yellow, green and grey – contrasting strikingly with the

gleaming white of the chalk. The Needles, at the extreme western tip of the Isle of Wight, rise to a height of 100 ft; on the outermost one is a lighthouse.

Yarmouth (pop. 970; hotels – Bugle, D, 10 r.; Jireh House, E, 9 r.), an ancient little town in low-lying country, is a busier place than the population figure would suggest, partly because it is the terminal of the ferry from Lymington but also because it is a popular sailing centre. It has the ruins of a castle built by Henry VIII, a little Town Hall (rebuilt 1763) and a curious statue which has the body of Louis XIV and the head of Admiral Sir Robert Holmes (d. 1692), substituted after the statue had been captured at sea. Admiral Holmes seized the Dutch possessions in North America, including New York, in 1664 and later became Governor of the Isle of Wight. – From Yarmouth the road runs inland to *Shalfleet*, with a beautiful Norman church, and then through *Parkhurst Forest* to Newport.

Winchester

Southern England. – County: Hampshire.
Altitude: 128 ft. – Population: 33,200.
Telephone dialling code: 0962.
(i) **Tourist Information Centre,**
　Guildhall, The Broadway;
　tel. 65406 or 68166.

HOTELS. – *Lainston House*, Sparsholt, B, 28 r.; *Wessex*, Paternoster Row, C, 94 r.; *Chantry Mead*, 22 Bereweeke Road, D, 20 r.; *Harestock Lodge*, Harestock Road, E, 14 r.

YOUTH HOSTEL. – *City Mill*, 1 Water Lane, 61 b.

TWO CAMP SITES.

RESTAURANTS – *Old Chesil Rectory*, 1 Chesil Street; *Elizabethan*, 18/19 Jewry Street; *Georgian*, 29 Jewry Street.

RECREATION and SPORT. – Golf, tennis.

Winchester, for centuries the capital of England, possesses one of the longest cathedrals in Europe, in which almost every style of English architecture is represented. The city has a picturesque High Street, near one end of which is the Castle Hall, the only remnant of the town's 13th c. castle. Winchester College is one of the oldest of the English public schools, and the St Cross Hospital, founded in 1136, is the most ancient almshouse, still offering bread and beer to visitors as it once did to the poor of the town.

HISTORY. – Winchester was the Roman *Venta Belgarum*, but excavations have revealed a Celtic settlement which occupied the site before the coming of the Romans. In 519 it became the capital of Wessex and in 675 the see of a bishop. Its rise began when Egbert of Wessex was crowned here as king of England in 827, and it reached its heyday during the reign of Alfred the Great (871–901). William the Conqueror had himself crowned in both Winchester and London; and it was only in the reign of Henry III (1216–72) that London finally displaced Winchester as capital. Christianity was brought to Winchester in 635 by St Birinus, first bishop of Dorchester, and the episcopal see was transferred from Dorchester to Winchester in 676.

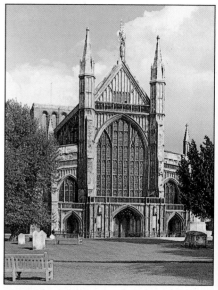

Winchester Cathedral

SIGHTS. – In spite of its great length (526 ft), the **Cathedral** is not at first sight particularly imposing. The *tower* is disproportionately low. The oldest parts of the church – which is the third to occupy the site – are the *transepts*, which are good examples of Early Norman architecture. The Perpendicular *nave* was begun by William of Edington (bishop 1346–66) and carried on by William of Wykeham (1367–1404). The E end shows a mingling of Early English Decorated and Perpendicular.

The INTERIOR makes a striking impact with the beauty and harmony of its proportions and the wealth of treasures it contains. The two *bronze statues* of James I and Charles I are by Hubert Le Sueur (1635). A notable feature of Winchester Cathedral is its fine series of *chantry chapels*: those of William of Wykeham and William of Edington are on the S side of the nave, and there are several others dedicated to later bishops of Winchester. The *grille* between the choir and transept (11th c.), once on the shrine of St Swithun (bishop in the 9th c.), is a masterpiece of wrought-iron work. Another feature of outstanding quality is the *font* of black Tournai marble in the N aisle, decorated with scenes from the life of St

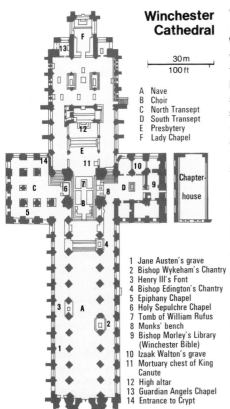

Winchester Cathedral

30m
100ft

A Nave
B Choir
C North Transept
D South Transept
E Presbytery
F Lady Chapel

Chapter-house

1 Jane Austen's grave
2 Bishop Wykeham's Chantry
3 Henry III's Font
4 Bishop Edington's Chantry
5 Epiphany Chapel
6 Holy Sepulchre Chapel
7 Tomb of William Rufus
8 Monks' bench
9 Bishop Morley's Library (Winchester Bible)
10 Izaak Walton's grave
11 Mortuary chest of King Canute
12 High altar
13 Guardian Angels Chapel
14 Entrance to Crypt

Winchester College was founded in 1382 by William of Wykeham, bishop of Winchester, and has a close association with New College, Oxford, which he founded in 1379. It is the most ambitiously planned of the early public schools. Building began in 1387 and the school was opened in 1394. Two of the original ranges of buildings, *Flint Court* and *Chamber Court*, have been preserved. The Seventh Chamber is the oldest school-room in the country. The *Chapel* preserves its fan-vaulted timber roof, original stained glass, a reredos of 1500 and old misericords. The *Hall* has 16th c. panelling and interesting old portraits. In the *Kitchen* can be seen a curious painting of the "Trusty Servant". On the pillars of the *Cloisters* generations of schoolboys have carved their names; among the most famous are those of the poet Edward Young (1683–1765), Field-Marshal Lord Wavell (who is buried in the cloister garth) and Hugh Gaitskell. The *War Memorial Cloister* (entered from Kingsgate Street) was designed by Sir Herbert Baker (1924) and is notable for the beauty of its carving.

Nicholas (*c.* 1180). Also in the N aisle is the *grave of Jane Austen*, marked by a brass tablet. In the S transept are buried Samuel Wilberforce (bishop 1869–73) and Izaak Walton (1593–1683). Among the bishops' tombs is a monument to an ordinary labourer, William Walker, who worked for years on the foundations of the Cathedral at the beginning of this century. Under the tower is a tomb reputed to be that of William Rufus. The oak *choir-stalls*, with canopies and 60 misericords dating from 1308 (in some cases 1540), are among the oldest in the country. The *E window* has very fine early 16th c. stained glass. The *Lady Chapel* has wall paintings (*c.* 1500) of scenes from the life of the Virgin. In the Chapel of the Guardian Angels, which has wall paintings of 1241, is the tomb of the first earl of Portland (d. 1636), by Le Sueur.

Among the treasures contained in the *Library* is the famous *Winchester Bible*, one of the finest of medieval manuscripts. In the 12th c. English monks were noted for their skill as illuminators.

The *King's Gate* leads out of the Cathedral close into College Street; over the gate is *St Swithun's Church* (16th c.). Nearby are two houses built by Wren, one at 26–27 St Swithun's Street for James II, the other in Kingsgate Street for the duke of Buckingham. College Street leads to the main entrance to Winchester College, passing the house (No. 8) in which Jane Austen died in 1817.

At the W end of the High Street is the imposing *Westgate* (13th c.). Near here is the **Castle Hall**, all that is left of *Winchester Castle*, built by William the Conqueror and demolished by Parliament in 1644–45. The hall, with its columns of Purbeck marble, was the scene of many great events – Edward I's first parliament, Henry VIII's reception of the Emperor Charles V, the trial of Sir Walter Raleigh for conspiring against James I. It contains the so-called Round Table of King Arthur.

The **Hospital of St Cross**, founded in 1136, is in St Cross Road, to the S of the town. It gave Trollope the setting for his novel "The Warden".

Beyond *Wolvesey Palace*, a wing of which (rebuilt by Wren) is the present bishop's palace, are the remains of *Wolvesey Castle*, built by Henry of Blois (bishop 1129–71). Beyond this again, at the E end of the High Street, reached by Soke Bridge (1813) over the River Itchen, is a *statue of King Alfred*. Across the Itchen, to the E, is *St Catherine's Hill*, on which are a hill-fort of the 3rd c. B.C., the foundations of an old chapel and a turf maze over 80 ft long, the significance of which is unknown.

Windsor Castle

Windsor

Central England. – County: Berkshire.
Population: 30,000.
Telephone dialling code: 07535.
ⓘ **Tourist Information Centre,**
Windsor Central Station;
tel. 52010 (open Easter to September).

HOTELS. – *Castle*, High Street, B, 85 r.; *Harte and Garter*, High Street, C, 48 r.

YOUTH HOSTEL. – *Edgeworth House*, Mill Lane, 76 b.

EVENTS. – *Ascot Week* (June).

SPORT and RECREATION. – Rowing, fishing, swimming, walking, golf.

The name of Windsor at once summons up the picture of Windsor Castle. Although Windsor itself is an attractive little town of old houses, beautifully situated on the S bank of the Thames, its life is centred on the Castle, which has been the principal residence of almost every monarch since William the Conqueror. Windsor Castle is one of the finest royal

residences in the world, magnificently situated, and the largest castle which is still inhabited. The royal standard flies from the Round Tower when the Queen is in residence. When she is not there the state apartments are open to visitors.

To the S of the town lies the beautiful Windsor Great Park, within which are the famous Savill Garden and the Valley Garden. Windsor has a Town Hall designed by Wren and a number of Georgian houses.

SIGHTS. – ****Windsor Castle** is the result of building or alteration by something like a dozen monarchs. The first castle on the site was built by William the Conqueror; thereafter much work was carried out by Henry I, Henry II and Henry III, and it reached something like its present layout in the reign of Edward III. Extensive restoration was done in the reigns of George IV, William IV and Victoria by Sir Jeffry Wyatville. The Castle is built round two courtyards, the *Upper* and *Lower Wards*, with the *Round Tower* between them in the *Middle Ward*. The Lower Ward, the *North Terrace* and at certain times also *St George's Chapel* are shown to visitors. The Castle is entered by *Henry VIII's gateway* (1511).

The gateway leads into the Lower Ward, on the far side of which is ***St George's Chapel**, begun by Edward IV in 1477 and completed by Henry VIII. It is one of the finest examples of Late Perpendicular architecture.

The *nave* and *choir*, which are of the same size, have beautiful *fan vaulting*. The *W window* has stained glass of 1503–09. In the choir are numerous monuments and tombs, including those of King George V and Queen Mary, and the *stalls of the Knights of the Garter*, with their banners and coats of

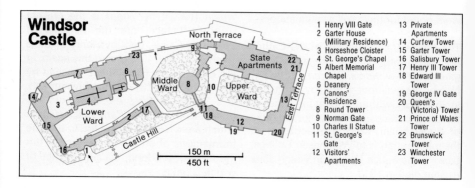

Windsor Castle

North Terrace
State Apartments
Middle Ward
Upper Ward
Lower Ward
East Terrace
Castle Hill

150 m
450 ft

1	Henry VIII Gate	13	Private
2	Garter House		Apartments
	(Military Residence)	14	Curfew Tower
3	Horseshoe Cloister	15	Garter Tower
4	St. George's Chapel	16	Salisbury Tower
5	Albert Memorial	17	Henry III Tower
	Chapel	18	Edward III
6	Deanery		Tower
7	Canons'	19	George IV Gate
	Residence	20	Queen's
8	Round Tower		(Victoria) Tower
9	Norman Gate	21	Prince of Wales
10	Charles II Statue		Tower
11	St. George's	22	Brunswick
	Gate		Tower
12	Visitors'	23	Winchester
	Apartments		Tower

arms. St George's is the chapel of the Order of the Garter, founded by Edward III. Henry VIII, Charles I and other monarchs are buried in a vault under the choir. (Most royal burials, however, are in the Royal Tomb House, built in 1240 and altered in the reign of Victoria, under the *Albert Memorial Chapel*.) A notable modern monument is that of the duke of Clarence (1864–92), eldest son of Edward VII, by Sir Alfred Gilbert. A special service is held in the chapel on St George's Day (23 April).

On the S side of the Lower Ward are the houses of the *Military Knights of Windsor*, an order originally founded by Edward III at the same time as the order of the Garter. Adjoining St George's Chapel are the *Horseshoe Cloisters* (1479–81), of brick and timber. Also very picturesque are the *Dean's Cloisters* and *Canon's Cloisters*.

On the North Terrace, from which there are wide views, is the entrance to the *State Apartments* (extensively restored by Wyatville), with *ceiling paintings* by Verrio and *wood-carving* by Grinling Gibbons, and a notable collection of pictures, furniture, weapons, tapestries and porcelain. One item which should not be missed is the *Queen's Dolls' House, a masterpiece of craftsmanship presented to Queen Mary in 1924. – From the *Round Tower*, originally built by Henry II and doubled in height by Wyatville in 1830, there are magnificent *views, said to extend over 12 counties.

The *Home Park*, with Frogmore House and Mausoleum, is not open to the public, but visitors can drive through the extensive **Windsor Great Park**, through which runs the road to Ascot.

SURROUNDINGS. – **Old Windsor** (1½ miles SE) was the residence of the Saxon kings, and excavations here have brought to light the remains of a building which may have been the palace of Edward the Confessor.

At the S end of *Windsor Great Park* is **Ascot** (pop. 7100; hotels – Berystede, B, 90 r.; Royal Foresters, D, 34 r.), which for 11 months of the year is a quiet little town but comes into its own in June with *Ascot Week, the great racing occasion which draws many thousands of visitors and is attended by the royal family, who drive through Windsor Great Park to Ascot in a splendid procession.

Windsor also offers the possibility of attractive boat trips on the River **Thames**. The Thames is a river full of variety, with its many branches and backwaters, its islands and the delightful park-like landscape through which it flows. Many of the gardens which stretch down to the river are of great beauty, and the boats and boathouses, with their flags and burgees, add variety and liveliness to the scene.

There are no boat services to London, but it is possible to take trips to Maidenhead, Henley and Oxford. The boat trip to *Oxford*, some 70 miles, takes two days, passing through beautiful scenery. The boats travel only during the day, but overnight accommodation can be found in *Wallingford* or *Henley*. Wallingford is an old town with a 17th c. Town Hall and a 14-arched bridge. William the Conqueror crossed the Thames here on his way to capture London. There are remains of a medieval castle.

River Thames Services

LAUNCH AND STEAMER SERVICES
Pleasure steamer and boat services on the River Thames fall into two types:
1. Trips of short duration viewing riverside bridges and buildings within the London area, extending from Greenwich upstream to Richmond and Hampton Court.
2. Services upstream from Staines to Windsor, Maidenhead, Henley, and Oxford which is the upper limit for large passenger craft.

Henley-on-Thames (pop. 12,000; hotels – Red Lion, D, 28 r.; Edwardian, E, 20 r.; Sydney House, E, 12 r.; youth hostel, Friends' Meeting House, 45 Northfield End, 28 b.) is a pleasant town famed for the Royal Regatta, held in the first week of July, which is one of the great social events of the London season. Another traditional ceremony is "swan-upping" in the third week in July, when the young swans are marked as a sign of royal ownership. The town lies between wooded hills and has a picturesque 18th c. bridge spanning the wide curve of the Thames and many handsome Georgian and other houses. The church contains many monuments to persons famous in their day but now largely forgotten.

3 miles SE is the meadow of **Runnymede** on which King John signed Magna Carta in 1215. There is a Magna Carta Memorial, and the place attracts large numbers of visitors. In the trees on Cooper's Hill is the Air Forces Memorial.

Maidenhead (pop. 50,000; hotels – Crest, C, 190 r.; Bear, C, 12 r.; Fredrick's, C, 30 r.; Kingswood, D, 10 r.), 6 miles NW, is a popular holiday place with many boat clubs, favoured particularly by young people. The beautiful 18th c. bridge has been relieved of heavy through traffic by the construction of the M 4 motorway.

2 miles upstream, standing high above the river, is the famous country house, *Cliveden, home of the Astor family (1851–1966), which is open to visitors. It was made over to the National Trust in 1942. It lies in the beautiful Cliveden Woods on the Buckinghamshire bank of the Thames.

NE of Maidenhead is **Burnham Beeches**, a beautiful area of woodland and heath purchased by the Corporation of London in 1879 as a place of recreation for Londoners. With the more recent addition of Dorney Wood, it forms a large expanse of good walking country which is busy at weekends but uncrowded during the rest of the week.

Stoke Poges (4 miles N) is famed for the beautiful churchyard little changed since the day when Thomas Gray (1716–71) wrote his "Elegy in a Country Churchyard". A statue by Wyatt marks the poet's grave. In the church is the famous "Bicycle Window", showing a man riding a hobby-horse.

Worcester: on right, to rear, the Cathedral

Worcester

Central England. – County: Hereford and Worcester.
Population: 74,800.
Telephone dialling code: 0905.
ⓘ **Tourist Information Centre,**
Guildhall, High Street;
tel. 23471.

HOTELS. – *Giffard*, High Street, C, 104 r.; *Diglis*, Riverside, C, 10 r.; *Star*, Foregate Street, D, 36 r.

CAMP SITE.

RESTAURANTS. – In the hotels listed, and also *King Charles II*, 29 New Street.

EVENTS. – *Three Choirs Festival* (Sept., in rotation with Gloucester and Hereford).

SPORT and RECREATION. – Rowing, fishing, golf, tennis, horse-racing.

Worcester, county town of Hereford and Worcester, lies on the E bank of the Severn, with the Cathedral which is its chief glory beautifully situated by the river away from the town centre. It has a number of streets with half-timbered houses of the Tudor period, but has lost much of its former charm as a result of the growth of industry and modern development. Its main products, apart from its famous sauce, are porcelain and gloves. The town is also known to fame as the scene of the battle of Worcester in which Charles II was finally defeated by Cromwell's forces.

HISTORY. – The town was known to the Romans as *Vigornia* and to the Saxons as *Wigorna Ceaster*. In 680 it became one of the six English episcopal sees. The Benedictine abbey was founded by Bishop Oswald

(961–92), who was canonised after his death. Worcester was the last town to surrender to Cromwell during the Civil War. It was Charles II's headquarters during the last battle in the war, which ended in his defeat on 3 September 1651 outside the walls of the town.

SIGHTS. – The best view of the *Cathedral is from the Severn, with its imposing bulk reflected in the water. The building dates from many different periods, and the exterior in particular was much altered in the restoration carried out by Sir George Gilbert Scott between 1857 and 1873. Built of red sandstone, the Cathedral is mainly Early English and Decorated, but other styles from Norman to Late Perpendicular are also represented.

S of the church founded by St Oswald, his 11th c. successor St Wulfstan built a new Norman cathedral, of which there survive the crypt, two bays of the nave and parts of the walls. The Choir and Lady Chapel were built between 1224 and 1260. The N side of the nave is Decorated, the S side Early Perpendicular. The *central tower*, completed in 1374, shows the transition from Decorated to Perpendicular.

The most striking feature of the INTERIOR, with its mingling of different styles, is the continuous range of *vaulting* 387 ft long – a feature unequalled in any other church in England. In spite of the juxtaposition of round-headed and pointed arches in the nave the general effect is harmonious. The *Choir* is in the purest Early English style. As at Salisbury, the slender pillars of Purbeck marble make an important contribution to the total effect. The *bosses* and *capitals* are exquisitely carved. The *choir-stalls* have richly decorated misericords (1379). The central feature of the choir is the *tomb of King John*, who died at Newark in 1216 and was buried here in accordance with his wish. His effigy in Purbeck marble, which dates from about 1240, is believed to be the earliest portrait of an English king. On the S side of the high altar is the richly decorated Perpendicular *Chantry of Prince Arthur*, Henry VI's eldest son, who died at Ludlow in 1502 at the age of 17.

In the *Lady Chapel* are the tombs of two bishops and a tablet commemorating Izaak Walton's second wife Anne, with a curious inscription composed by himself.

The *Crypt* (1084–92), a relic of the Norman cathedral, has 50 graceful pillars. The Perpendicular *Cloisters* have fine bosses, with representations of the Tree of Jesse and figures of angels adoring the Virgin and Child.

The *Chapterhouse* is one of the earliest examples of vaulting borne on a single central pier. The main structure is Norman, with a circular interior and a decagonal exterior; the windows are 15th c. The principal relic of the monastic buildings is the *refectory*, a large hall with a Norman crypt under it; it is now used as the hall of the **King's School** (founded 1541).

In addition to the Cathedral Worcester has seven other medieval churches. There are fine *half-timbered Tudor houses* in New Street, Fish Street and Friar Street. Particularly attractive is the **Guildhall**, built (as were some of the churches) by Thomas White, a pupil of Wren. At the entrance to the Guildhall are statues of Charles I and II, with their enemy Cromwell hanging by his ears above the door.

The most interesting of the old buildings is the ***Commandery**, a handsome Tudor house on the site of an earlier hospice founded by St Wulfstan in 1085. Charles II made it his headquarters in 1651. It is now a private house, but is open to visitors (an impressive great hall, fine woodwork, stained-glass windows). *King Charles's House* (1577), at the corner of New Street and Cornmarket, is famous as the scene of Charles II's escape from his pursuers by slipping out of the back door. The museum of the Royal Porcelain Works (founded 1750) in Severn Street has an interesting collection, with fine examples of Worcester porcelain of all periods.

SURROUNDINGS. – 16 miles SE is **Evesham** (pop. 15,300; hotels – Evesham, C, 34 r.; Northwick Arms, E, 22 r.), a pleasant town on both banks of the Avon, in a region famous for its fruit and vegetables. There are many half-timbered houses; the bell-tower (1533) and gateway of a Benedictine abbey founded in 701; and two churches within the abbey precincts, All Saints and St Lawrence, both with fan-vaulted chapels.

The road from Worcester to Evesham runs through **Pershore** (pop. 5800; hotel – Angel Inn, D, 19 r.), on the N bank of the Avon, which is spanned by a medieval stone bridge of six arches. The town has preserved a largely Georgian character. *Pershore Abbey*, originally the church of a Benedictine house, has a fine lantern-tower of about 1320, a Norman S transept and a Norman crossing. The choir is Early English, with beautiful vaulting.

8 miles SW is **Malvern** (pop. 31,000; hotels – Abbey, C, 110 r; Foley Arms, C, 26 r.; Cottage in the Wood, C, 21 r.), one of Britain's most popular health resorts. It consists of several different parts, the centre being Great Malvern. It is beautifully situated on the lower slopes of the *Malvern Hills*, a range some 9 miles long of moderate height (1000–1400 ft) which affords magnificent *views of the surrounding area: it is said that in clear weather 14 counties can be seen from here. The highest point is the *Worcestershire Beacon* (1395 ft), from which there is a very pleasant walk along the ridge to the *Herefordshire Beacon*, with remains of a British hill-fort.

In the various parts of Malvern – Malvern Link, North Malvern, Great Malvern, Malvern Wells, Little Malvern and West Malvern – there are numerous houses of the Victorian period, together with many hotels and guest-houses. In Great Malvern are a theatre and a girls' school. The Priory Church, originally belonging to a Benedictine house founded by Bishop Wulfstan in 1085, has a Perpendicular exterior (1400–1600), but the nave and some other parts of the interior are Early Norman. The beautiful tower (good view from top) is modelled on the tower of Gloucester Cathedral. The church is famous for its stained glass, mostly dating from 1480. Other notable features are the locally made tiles in the choir screen, the misericords and a number of monuments.

9 miles NW of Malvern is **Lower Brockhampton Hall**, a late 14th c. moated manor-house, half-timbered, with a separate gatehouse. 7 miles E is another moated manor, **Birtsmorton Court**.

York

Northern England. – County: North Yorkshire.
Altitude: 57 ft. – Population: 97,200.
Telephone dialling code: 0904.

(i) **De Grey Rooms**,
Exhibition Square;
tel. 21756–7.
Jorvik Viking Centre,
Coppergate;
tel. 643211.

HOTELS. – *Post House*, Tadcaster Road, B, 147 r.; *Dean Court*, Duncombe Place, B, 35 r.; *Viking*, North Street, C, 187 r.; *Royal York*, Station Road, C, 130 r.; *Ladbroke Abbey Park*, The Mount, C, 83 r.; *Friars Garden*, Station Road, C, 22 r.; *Judges Lodging*, 9 Lendal, C, 17 r.; *Newington*, 147–157 Mount Vale, D, 46 r.

YOUTH HOSTEL. – Haverford, Water End, Clifton, 140 b.

RESTAURANTS. – *Staircase*, 53 Micklegate; *Tanglewood*, Malton Road; *Ashcroft*, 294 Bishopthorpe Road; *Beechwood Close*, Shipton Road.

EVENTS. – *York Festival* (second half of June); *York Races* (Aug.).

SPORT and RECREATION. – Golf, riding, tennis, rowing, sailing, fishing.

*York is the ''secret'' capital of northern England, the counterpart of London, and was the county town of Yorkshire before it was divided in 1974 into four separate counties York is also the ecclesiastical capital of the Church of England, the archbishop of York, with the style of Primate of England, being second only to the archbishop of Canterbury. The Lord Mayor of York, too, has a special status, sharing only with the Lord Mayor of London the honorific prefix of ''Right Honourable''.

York prides itself on a number of unique tourist attractions. Its principal glory is, of course, the Minster, the largest medieval church in England and beyond question one of the most beautiful, with the largest area of medieval glass in the country (claimed, in fact, to represent more than half the total surviving quantity). York also has the only guildhall in England which has remained continuously in use since the 14th c. and the longest circuit of medieval town walls, some 3 miles in extent, which offer a pleasant walk with magnificent views of the city.

HISTORY. – In Roman times York, then known as *Eboracum* or *Eburacum*, was the headquarters of the Sixth Legion and one of the principal Roman bases in northern Britain. Later it became a *colonia*, the second most important town in Britain and a major cultural centre. Two Roman emperors died here, Severus in 211 and Constantius Chlorus in 306, and Constantius's son Constantine (the Great) was proclaimed emperor in York. Under the Saxons the town, now known as *Eoforwic*, retained its importance, becoming capital of the Anglian kingdom of Deira and the centre from which Christianity spread throughout the North of England. Under the great scholar Alcuin (735–804) the monastic school gained an international reputation, and Alcuin was summoned by Charlemagne to advise him on the establishment of schools in the Frankish kingdom. In 876 the Danes occupied York and burned down many of its fine buildings. Thereafter it became an important Danish town under the name of *Jorvik*, from which the present name is derived. Some 200 years later the Normans arrived, destroyed the town for a second time and then built it up again into a handsome and powerful city. In medieval times the area enclosed within the town walls contained some 50 churches, together with numbers of monastic houses and hospitals.

SIGHTS. – ****York Minster** is one of the largest medieval churches N of the Alps. The first church on the site was a wooden chapel built for the baptism of King Edwin of Northumbria in 627; the Minster, dating from the 13th–15th c., is the fifth. It shows a mingling of many styles. The magnificent *W front* is Decorated, with Perpendicular towers, and the *central tower* is also Perpendicular. The *SW tower* contains 12 bells; the thirteenth hangs by itself in the NW tower. This bell, *Big Peter*, weighs almost 11 tons; it is rung only at noon.

INTERIOR. – The *nave is regarded as the finest example of the Decorated style in England. The roof is of wood, painted to look like stone. The 125 ****stained-glass windows** are mostly 14th and 15th c. The large *W window* has delicate tracery and glass dating from 1338.

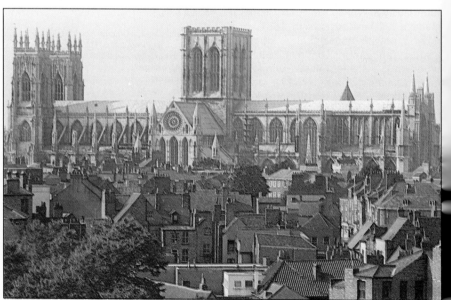

York Minster

York Minster

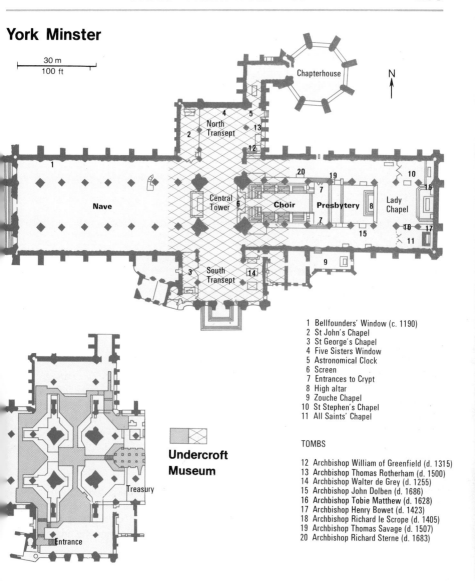

30 m
100 ft

N

Chapterhouse

4   5
North
Transept
13
2
12

1

20
19
7   10
18
Central
Tower   6   **Choir**   **Presbytery**   8   Lady
Nave   Chapel
7
15   16   17
11

3   South
Transept   14   9

**Undercroft
Museum**

Treasury

Entrance

1 Bellfounders' Window (c. 1190)
2 St John's Chapel
3 St George's Chapel
4 Five Sisters Window
5 Astronomical Clock
6 Screen
7 Entrances to Crypt
8 High altar
9 Zouche Chapel
10 St Stephen's Chapel
11 All Saints' Chapel

TOMBS

12 Archbishop William of Greenfield (d. 1315)
13 Archbishop Thomas Rotherham (d. 1500)
14 Archbishop Walter de Grey (d. 1255)
15 Archbishop John Dolben (d. 1686)
16 Archbishop Tobie Matthew (d. 1628)
17 Archbishop Henry Bowet (d. 1423)
18 Archbishop Richard le Scrope (d. 1405)
19 Archbishop Thomas Savage (d. 1507)
20 Archbishop Richard Sterne (d. 1683)

The *transepts, the oldest parts of the building, are in pure Early English style. The five narrow lancet windows, 53½ ft high by 5 ft wide, are the famous *"Five Sisters"; the grisaille glass dates from 1305 to 1325. In the S transept is a 15th c. *rose window*. The most interesting of the monuments is an *astronomical clock* commemorating airmen killed in the Second World War. In July 1984 the S transept was struck by lightning and almost completely destroyed. Rebuilding, however, is already in progress.

Excavations carried out from 1967 onwards in the course of work to strengthen the foundations of the central tower revealed extensive *Roman structures*. After the completion of the work this area was fitted up as the *Undercroft Museum, which contains not only Roman architectural fragments but also numerous items from later periods. In the *Treasury* are displayed some of the Minster's most precious possessions, including the "Horn of Ulf" (c. 1020) and valuable liturgical utensils.

The *Choir* is a splendid example of Perpendicular architecture. The *Lady Chapel* is rather earlier. The stone *rood-screen* with statues of English kings dates from the 15th c. The roof and woodwork of the choir

were destroyed in 1829 when a deranged individual set fire to the organ. The great *E window* of the choir, dating from 1405 to 1408, has the largest area of stained glass in the world.

From the N transept the vestibule of the Chapterhouse is entered. The octagonal **Chapterhouse** (Decorated, c. 1310) is acknowledged to be the finest in England. It has a timber roof with a span of 64 ft.

NE of the Minster are *St William's College*, the *Treasurer's House* and the *Minster Library*, which is housed in a chapel of the 12th–13th c. and contains many valuable books and manuscripts. On the S side of the Minster is the church of *St Michael-le-Belfry* (rebuilt 1536), which has interesting locally made *stained glass of a kind rarely found.

From the W front of the Minster Duncombe Place leads SW to the **Museum Gardens**, in which, to the right, are the

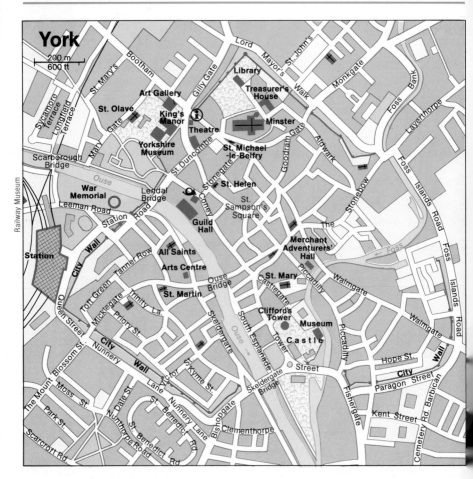

remains of *St Leonard's Hospital* and a length of *Roman wall*, with the *Multangular Tower*, the lower part of which is also Roman work. The *Yorkshire Museum* has archaeological and geological collections. Also in the Museum Gardens are the remains of **St Mary's Abbey**, founded by William Rufus in 1098. The *Hospitium* (abbey guest-house), lower down, contains one of the best collections of Roman remains in England. To the NE of the gardens is *King's Manor*, a 16th–17th c. house which, well restored, now belongs to the University. Adjoining it in Exhibition Square is the **City Art Gallery**, with a collection of 120 old masters.

Between Coney Street and the Minster is the best shopping area in the city. Here too is the Mansion House, the official residence of the Lord Mayor, designed by the earl of Burlington (1725). From here a gateway gives access to the **Guildhall** on the banks of the River Ouse (1449–59, rebuilt after war damage). The roof is supported by ten massive oak pillars; the wrought-iron *balustrade* was a present

from Münster, York's twin town in Germany. – It is well worth taking a stroll through this part of the city to see the interesting churches, streets and shops.

Many streets in York, and in some other towns in the North of England, are known by the Scandinavian term "gate" – e.g. Stonegate, Petergate, etc. The York town gates are known as "bars".

Among the finest churches in York are *St Martin-le-Grand*, in Coney Street; *St Michael's*, Spurriergate, with 12th c. arcades and fine glass; and *St Mary's*, Castlegate, which is of Saxon origin. Of particular interest is the church of *All Saints*, North Street, with the most curious stained glass windows in York (15th c.). Based on the writings of the 14th c. mystic Richard Rolle, a Yorkshire monk and hermit, they depict the Six Corporal Acts of Mercy and the Last Fifteen Days of the World in a series of pictures each of which has an appropriate line of text below it.

The narrowest and best-known street in York is the **Shambles**, formerly the butchers' quarter, now with antique shops and art shops. The *Merchant Adventurers' Hall* (1357–68) has a fine timber roof, a 15th c. chapel and an undercroft with seven sturdy oak pillars. *St Denys's Church* has a Norman S doorway and seven windows with 14th–15th c. *stained glass. St Margaret's Church* too has a Norman doorway. *St Lawrence's Church* is also of interest, with the tower and gatehouse of an earlier church in the churchyard. Under a public house in St Sampson's Square are the remains of a *Roman bath.* In *Stonegate, York's finest medieval street, are a 12th c. Norman house, *Mulberry Hall* (1434) and a whole series of other interesting old buildings. Near its W end is *St Helen's Church*, dedicated to the mother of Constantine the Great. Other churches well worth seeing are the little church of *Holy Trinity* (14th c.) in Goodramgate, with old glass and 18th c. box pews; *Holy Trinity*, Micklegate, which originally belonged to a Benedictine priory; *St Martin-cum-Gregory*, with 14th–15th c. stained glass; and *St Mary's*, Bishophill Junior, with a Saxon tower.

No visitor should omit the finest walk in York, a circuit of the old *town walls. Mostly built in the 14th c., they follow the line of the Roman walls for much of the way, and incorporate some Roman work. The walls have a total extent of some 3 miles, with six gates or "bars". Four of the old gates have been preserved – *Walmgate Bar, Monk Bar* and *Bootham Bar*, all with the original portcullis, and *Micklegate Bar*, with three figures of knights. The most interesting stretch of wall, with the best view of the Minster, is between Bootham and Monk Bars. Bootham Bar is the starting point of a handsome Georgian street, **Bootham**, with *Bootham School*, *St Peter's School* and *Ingram's Hospital* (1640).

York Castle, between Fishergate and Skeldergate Bridge over the Ouse, was founded by William Rufus. The oldest part is the 13th c. *Clifford's Tower*, built by Henry III. The Clifford Arms occupies the site of a wooden house in which 500 Jews sought refuge in 1190 from a mob seeking to kill them and were burned to death. In the adjoining square are the 18th c. Assize Courts and two other 18th c. buildings, originally prisons, which now house the **Castle Museum**. This contains the *Kirk collection* of bygones assembled by a local country doctor of

that name and is splendidly presented, with reconstructions of streets and shops, old street lights and vehicles. A short way N, in Coppergate, lies the *Jorvik Viking Centre, an underground reconstruction of a row of streets in the York of the Viking era, with simulated old craft businesses; (narrow gauge railway).

In Heslington Road is another building of historical interest, the *Retreat*, a hospital established by a Quaker named William Tuke for the care of the mentally ill – the first institution to provide humane accommodation and treatment for patients of this kind.

A museum of great interest for railway enthusiasts is the *National Railway Museum** in Leeman Road, adjoining the

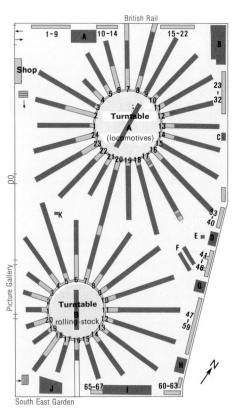

National Railway Museum   **York**

A	Weatherhill winding engine (1833)
B	Swannington winding engine (1833)
C	Kent and East Sussex horse bus
D	Dandy cart (for carrying horses)
E	Clock from Euston Station
F	LNWR coaches (quarter-scale models)
G	Belvoir Castle railway wagon (1815)
H	Peak Forest Canal Co. truck (1797)
I	Signalling equipment
J	Permanent way inspection vehicles
K	Clock from Gravesend Station

WALL CASES

1–9	Locomotive technology
10–32	Locomotive models
33–40	Bridge models
41–46	Goods wagons
47–59	Passenger carriages
60–63, 65–67	Signalling

Balcony Railway history

station. Here can be seen a fascinating collection of old locomotives, rolling-stock, equipment and other paraphernalia covering the history of steam trains, their ancestors and their successors. See plan on p. 285.

York University, founded in 1963, lies 1½ miles SE of the town in the grounds of *Heslington Hall*, originally an Elizabethan mansion which now accommodates the University offices. The new buildings include a number of halls of residence and a large assembly hall with seating for 1250.

SURROUNDINGS. – York is an excellent centre from which to explore the surrounding area, which offers a wide range of beautiful scenery and historical and artistic interest. Apart from the *Yorkshire Dales (see p. 288), which could occupy a whole holiday on their own, two circular tours are recommended – one taking in *Beverley* and *Selby* with their famous churches, the other heading towards the coast and running across either the *North York Moors* or the Yorkshire Wolds.

To Beverley and Selby. – Leaving York by Lawrence Street, we follow A 1079, the road to Hull. In 11 miles we come to **Barnby Moor** (pop. 260; hotel – Ye Olde Bell, C, 55 r.), from which a detour can be made to *Pocklington* (pop. 4180; Feathers Hotel, Market Square, 14 r.), with the beautiful gardens of Burnby Hall and a museum housing the *Stewart collection*. From here there is a road via *Nunburn-holme*, which has a fine Viking cross in the churchyard representing a seated warrior with the Virgin and Child, to **Market Weighton** (pop. 3600; hotel – Londesborough Arms, D, 10 r.), from which A 1079 runs E to Beverley (29 miles).

Beverley (pop. 17,200; Beverley Arms Hotel, B, 61 r.) is an attractive old market town on the fringes of the *East Yorkshire Wolds*. The town's rise to prosperity was based on the wool trade, for in Yorkshire in earlier days there were more sheep than people.

On the S side of the town is **Beverley Minster** (built between 1220 and 1420), which surpasses

Beverley Minster

many cathedrals in size (it is 334 ft long) and beauty. It was founded by St John of Beverley, bishop of York (d. 721). The choir and double transepts are in the purest Early English style (second quarter of 13th c.). The nave, begun in 1308, is mainly Decorated; the W front with its twin towers is Perpendicular (14th–15th c.). In spite of the mingling of styles the general effect is harmonious, thanks largely to the magnificent carving of the stonework.

The large W doorway has figures of the Evangelists (18th c.). The N doorway is early 15th c. Notable features of the nave are the triforium, the Late Norman font of Frosterley marble and the "Maiden Tomb". The main transepts have both E and W aisles. The columns at the E end of the church are of Purbeck marble.

The Choir is a magnificent example of Early English architecture, with details which deserve careful examination. The magnificent choir-stalls (1520) have the largest number of misericords in England (68). The canopied *Percy Tomb, a masterpiece of craftsmanship, between the high altar and the N transept, commemorates Eleanor Fitzalan (d. 1328), wife of the second Lord Percy. The large E window in the Lady Chapel behind the high altar contains some fine old glass (1416).

The fine Market Cross dates from 1714, the Guildhall from the 17th c. On the N side of the market-place is *St Mary's Church* (Decorated and Perpendicular), the finest parts of which are the W front (1380–1411), the choir-stalls and misericords, the painted figures of English kings and the rich sculptural decoration. Behind the church is the brick-built North Bar, the only surviving town gate, and beyond this lies a charming Georgian residential area.

Hull: see p. 125.

From Hull we return along A 63, running close to the Humber for the first part of the way, to **Howden** (pop. 3200; Bowmans Hotel, C, 13 r.), a little town with cobbled streets and a medieval church which has a very beautiful W front and a 15th c. tower 135 ft high. The ruined choir and chapterhouse are well worth examination.

From here it is 11 miles on A 63 to **Selby** (pop. 11,100; Londesborough Arms Hotel, E, 37 r.) with one of the most beautiful churches in England. The town, prettily situated on the Ouse, which is navigable for small boats up to this point, has many Georgian and early 19th c. houses. Its central feature, however, is the splendid **Abbey Church**. The first church on the site belonged to a Benedictine house founded in 1069 – the first major abbey to be established after the Norman Conquest. The present church, dedicated to St Germanus, was begun about 1100. The central tower collapsed in 1690, damaging the S transept, and both were then rebuilt. In 1906 the whole church was seriously damaged by fire. Externally, the finest parts are the W front (Late Norman) and the N doorway. The E half of the nave is Norman, the W half Transitional. The Choir (Decorated, 1280–1340) is particularly beautiful. Other notable features are the great E window, the sacristy and font, the stone rood-screen and the sedilia. – From Selby it is only 14 miles back to York.

To the coast. – This route provides an opportunity of seeing the *North York Moors* and the *Yorkshire Wolds*, which rise to a height of some 800 ft. Formerly this was a vast sheep-grazing area, with only a thin covering of poor soil over the underlying limestone.

Rievaulx Abbey: the church

Rievaulx Abbey

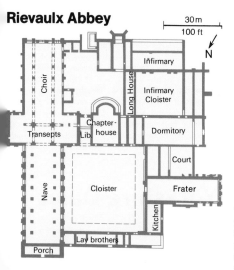

(drawings and paintings; collection of doll's-house furniture). Queen Henrietta Maria, wife of Charles I, landed here with arms bought with money obtained by selling the crown jewels but was forced to withdraw to Boynton Hall when the harbour was bombarded.

From Bridlington a beautiful *coast road runs N to Scarborough and Whitby. It can be followed all the way to *Whitby* (see p. 201) and beyond over the *North York Moors*, with occasional glimpses of the coast. One of the finest stretches is between Scarborough and *Robin Hood's Bay*. Alternatively it is possible to turn inland at *Scarborough* (see p. 201) and return to York via Pickering and Helmsley. **Pickering** (pop. 6000; Forest and Vale Hotel, D, 23.), 17 miles W of Scarborough, has a ruined castle, with the Coleman Tower (1180) and remains of other towers. The church contains the best preserved medieval wall paintings in the country (mid 15th c., over-restored in 1880). From here the road continues via *Kirbymoorside*, with a nature reserve which is particularly beautiful in spring when the wild daffodils are out, to **Helmsley** (pop. 1400; hotels – Black Swan, B, 38 r.; Feversham Arms, C, 15 r.; Feathers, D, 18 r.), with a ruined 12th c. castle, stone from which was used to build the adjoining mansion, Duncombe Park, now a girls' school.

More recently, however, the land has been improved and is now a fertile corn-growing region, a landscape variegated by white crags of rock, stone bridges, clumps of woodland and avenues of tall trees.

From York A 166 runs E to *Stamford Bridge*, a little town whose claim to fame rests on the last great victory of the Saxons, the battle in 1066 in which Harold defeated his brother Tostig and King Harold Hardrada of Norway, who had sailed up the Humber. The road then continues via *Great Driffield* (interesting church tower) and **Burton Agnes** (late Elizabethan manor-house, with pictures and fine carving) and over the Yorkshire Wolds to the popular seaside resort of **Bridlington** (see p. 200), 25 miles from York. The older part of the town, on the inland side, is attractive, with a priory church founded in the reign of Henry I. The Bayle Gate (1388) is now a museum

2½ miles NW of Helmsley are the magnificent ruins of *Rievaulx Abbey, a Cistercian house founded in 1131 by Walter l'Espec, lord of Helmsley. The remains range in date between the 12th and the mid 13th c. and are mainly in Early English style. They include the choir and transepts of the church, the infirmary, the lavatory and other monastic buildings. On a terrace above the abbey, reached by a steep and narrow path, is an 18th c. temple, from which there are fine views of the picturesque ruins and the whole valley.

Castle Howard

Returning to Helmsley, we take the road which runs S via Oswaldkirk, Ampleforth and Byland Abbey to Coxwold (10 miles). 3 miles E of *Oswaldkirk* is **Nunnington Hall**, a large house of the late 17th c. with a 16th c. W wing. At *Ampleforth* is a well-known Roman Catholic public school, founded in 1802 by English Benedictine monks returning from France. There is a fine modern church by Sir Giles Gilbert Scott. Of **Byland Abbey**, a Cistercian house founded in 1177, only a few ruins are left – the splendid W front of the church, the S transept and part of the gatehouse.

Coxwold (pop. 210) is a charming little village where Laurence Sterne was curate from 1760 until his death in 1768. In the house now called Shandy Hall he wrote the last part of "Tristram Shandy" and the whole of the "Sentimental Journey". The Georgian façade was built by him, and visitors can see his study. The church (Perpendicular) is also of interest.

Just S of Oswaldkirk, at *Gilling East*, is **Gilling Castle**, an attractive house of the 16th and 18th c. with a Norman tower and a richly decorated Great Chamber (1575–85) in Elizabethan style (heraldic windows by Bernard Dirickhoff, 1585), now occupied by a school. Visitors can also see the beautiful terraced gardens. – From here it is 10 miles SE to Malton.

About half way to Malton a road on the right leads to * Castle Howard, an immense and magnificent Palladian mansion built for the third earl of Carlisle by Vanbrugh. It was Vanbrugh's first major work, based on plans drawn by Wren. The garden front is particularly fine. The house, which is still lived in by the Howard family, is open to visitors. It has a series of splendid rooms, with fine staircases and a profusion of vases and statuary, and contains magnificent collections of pictures, carving by Grinling Gibbons, furniture and sculpture.

The grounds are on a scale to match the house, with an impressive family mausoleum on a hill, a tall obelisk, a pyramid and a graceful Temple of the Four Winds (1724–26) by Vanbrugh. To the N of the park is a large lake.

Malton (pop. 4200; hotels – Green Man, D, 25 r.; Talbot, D, 24 r.), is the last stopping-place on the tour. This little market town on the Derwent lies in the centre of a large farming area, mainly devoted to corn-growing but also noted for the breeding of racehorses. St Michael's Church is a fine Late Norman building with a Perpendicular tower. *St Mary's Church*, in Old Malton, is all that remains of a Gilbertine priory founded about 1150. A cross in nearby Orchard Field marks the site of the Roman station of *Derventio*. Finds from here can be seen in the Roman Museum in the market square. – From Malton A 64 runs SW back to York (18 miles).

The **North York Moors National Park** extends from the beautiful cliff scenery on the coast into a great expanse of country farther inland, a thinly populated region of moorland and heath, of pines and broom and a variety of wild flowers. One of the few villages is **Goathland**, a station on the North Yorkshire Moors Railway which operates between Grosmont and Pickering. Nearby are impressive remains of a Roman road. The moors are excellent walking country, with the *Cleveland Way*, a long-distance path opened in 1969, 100 miles long, following a circular route round the whole area (many small villages but little overnight accommodation).

Yorkshire Dales

Northern England. – County: North Yorkshire.

The * Yorkshire Dales in NW Yorkshire are a region of great natural beauty and variety, now forming the Yorkshire Dales National Park, which takes in Wharfedale, Upper Ribblesdale, Wensleydale, Swaledale and the S side of Teesdale, together with their side valleys.

The Dales, watered by rivers flowing down from the Pennines, are upland valleys, with land rising to an average of 600 ft and individual summits of up to 2000 ft. Common to all the dales is their scanty population but each has its own particular character. Ribblesdale is the most dramatic, with waterfalls and towering crags, interesting caves and large quarries. Swaledale is also wild, with rugged gorges and jagged rocks. Wharfedale, particularly Upper Wharfedale, is gentler valley of great beauty. Wensleydale is wider, with lush pasturage, but also with waterfalls and areas of heath.

Lead was worked in the dales in Roman times, and continued to be worked until the latter part of the 19th c., when cheap imports made the mines uneconomic. The main economic resource is now agriculture, particularly stock- and dairy-farming. There are also quarries producing some high-quality limestone, which is used for a variety of purposes.

Apart from its beautiful scenery, the main tourist attraction of *Wharfedale* is **Bolton Abbey**, a small but romantic ruin near Beamsley. The major surviving part is now used as the parish church, with an Early English and Decorated nave. A W tower was begun in 1520 but never completed. The gatehouse is incorporated in the adjoining Bolton Hall, a seat of the duke of Devonshire. Opposite the abbey a footbridge and stepping-stones cross the river: the view from here is very fine. Not far SW lies *Skipton*, with a stately castle, until 1955 the home of the Clifford family.

There is a very pleasant walk along the W bank of the river to the *Strid*, where the river surges through a gorge which at times is not much more than a yard wide. It is a dangerous spot where many people have come to grief trying to jump across the river. From here the path continues past *Pembroke Seat* (very fine view) to Barden Bridge, 3 miles from the abbey. The return is along the E bank, with a series of attractive viewpoints. – The beauties of *Upper Wharfedale can be seen by taking the road along the W bank of the river to *Barden Bridge* (1659), passing the ruins of *Barden Tower*, once the home of the 15th c. Lord Clifford who was known as the "shepherd lord".

Wharfedale, seen from Kidstone

Between *Appletreewick* and *Burnsall* is a particularly beautiful stretch of country. The road then continues past *Grassington* (bridge) to *Kilnsey*, with the formidable *Kilnsey Crag*, which presents a challenge to rock-climbers. Beyond this point a road goes off on the left to Arncliffe, in Littondale.

Beyond Kilnsey, 13 miles from Bolton Abbey, is **Kettlewell**, under Great Whernside (2310 ft). Farther on is *Buckden*, at the foot of Buckden Pike (2302 ft), where it is possible either to bear left into the uppermost reaches of Wharfedale or to keep right on the road which leads into Wensleydale.

Wensleydale is not named after a river – the stream which flows through it is the Ure or Yore – but after the little market town of Wensley. A good starting point is the attractive old-world cathedral city of **Ripon** (pop. 12,500; hotels – Ripon Spa, C, 41 r.; Unicorn, D, 28 r.).

The river is spanned by an old bridge. The main feature of the town is the *Cathedral, originally belonging to a monastery founded by Alcfrith in 657. It was raised to cathedral status in 1836. The oldest parts, the choir and transepts, date from the time of Archbishop Roger of York (1154–81). The *W front* (Early English) was built in 1220–30, the E end (Decorated) about 1300. The nave and parts of the central tower are Perpendicular.

The interior also shows a mingling of styles. The *choir* shows Transitional, Early English and Decorated work. The *triforium* is glazed – a feature unique in England. The tracery of the E window is particularly fine, as are the 34 misericords of the choir-stalls (1489 and 1494). Of great interest is the Saxon *crypt*, built by St Wilfrid in 670 as a *confessio* for the display of relics; it resembles the crypt of Hexham Priory (see p. 124).

Ripon contains numerous old buildings of different periods. The oldest is the ruined *chapel* of St Anne's Hospital (14th c.). Others are the *Thorpe Prebend House* (17th c.), the *Town Hall* (1799) and the half-timbered *Wakeman's House*, which contains a small museum. A horn is blown every night at 9 in front of the Wakeman's House, as it has been since the year 884.

4 miles SW of Ripon is **Fountains Abbey**, which has been called – with every justification – one of the most beautiful ruins in Europe. Named after the springs which emerge on the site, it was a Cistercian house, founded in 1132. The best way to approach it is through the large park of Studley Royal with its pleasure-grounds (ponds, small temples, statues) and over the Skell towards the octagonal tower. The abbey then suddenly comes into view in all its

splendour: one of the largest, most magnificent and best preserved of Britain's ruined abbeys, and an excellent illustration of the process by which the dissolved monasteries were converted into private residences.

The *walls* are almost completely preserved, creating an impressive effect, with a romantic air which is enhanced by the beauty of the setting. Even the absence of the roof does not spoil the effect. The monks acquired considerable wealth through sheep-farming and dealing in wool and were thus able to finance the splendid buildings they erected here.

The roofless *church*, with its nave and transepts, is in Transitional style (1135–47); the tower is Perpendicular. The finest feature is the Chapel of the Nine Altars, in which the pointed arch makes its first appearance in England. The extensive *monastic buildings* have largely been preserved, although the *cloister* has lost its arcading (which was probably of timber) and the *chapterhouse* its roof. The other buildings – dormitory and lavatory, refectory and kitchen, infirmary and guest-houses – cover a considerable area, most of them being provided in duplicate, for monks and lay brothers.

Fountains Hall (1595–1611), partly built with material from the abbey, contains an interesting collection of furniture.

14 miles away is another beautiful ruined abbey, also in a beautiful riverside setting. This is *Jervaulx Abbey*, the imposing ruin of a Cistercian house dating from the late 12th and early 13th c. Little is left of the church, but there are considerable remains of the monastic buildings.

The valley of the Ure is known as Wensleydale only above Jervaulx; and here too its most beautiful scenery begins, with waterfalls and a series of charming little villages on the banks of the river. One of the most beautiful of these is *Middleham* (pop. 738), with racing stables. Here too are the massive ruins of **Middleham Castle**, once a favourite residence of Richard III; the keep is one of the largest in England.

The road continues via *Wensley*, with a fine church (Flemish brass of *c.* 1360) to the well-preserved *Bolton Castle* (1379–97), home of the Scrope family until 1630, which contains a small museum. Behind the pretty little village of *West Witton* (Wensleydale Heifer Inn, 17th c.) rises *Penhill Beacon* (1792 ft). Beyond Aysgarth (23 miles from Ripon) are three waterfalls, the finest of which is *Aysgarth Force*, half a mile beyond the

bridge. On the left bank of the river are *Burton* and *Bainbridge* (where a horn is blown every night at 9). From Bainbridge a bridge crosses the river to the little village of *Askrigg*, with handsome stone houses of the 17th and 18th c. At *Hawes* (32 miles) a cheese factory making Wensleydale cheese can be visited. From here a winding hill road runs over to Muker in Swaledale, passing another fine waterfall, *Hardraw Force*, and going over the Buttertubs Pass, named after five deep holes in the rock between 50 and 100 ft deep. Beyond Hawes the road up Wensleydale continues over a pass and descends via *Sedburgh* and *Dent* to *Kendal*. About 5 miles SW of Kendal stands *Levens Hall* (16th c.) with a fine park.

Swaledale is for the most part rugged and wild. A good base from which to see it is the romantic old town of *Richmond* (see p. 236). Following the River Swale through ever-changing scenery, we come in 11 miles to *Reeth*, which was a lead-mining centre from Roman times until the end of the 19th c. 4 miles NW of the little town is the *Old Gang smelting mill. At Reeth a hilly moorland road goes off on the right into *Arkengarthdale*, passing through a number of tiny villages and hamlets, and a few miles along this road another hill road branches off and runs N to **Barnard Castle**, an old town beautifully situated on the River Tees with a ruined castle (1112–32) overlooking the river. The Town Hall was built in 1747. To the E of the town is the *Bowes Museum*, housed in an imposing building (1869–75) modelled on the Tuileries Palace in Paris, with an outstanding collection of 18th c. French works of art, including tapestries, porcelain, manuscripts, furniture and pictures, as well as a number of old masters (El Greco, Goya).

The scenery of Teesdale above Barnard Castle is of great beauty. *High Force* is a 72-ft-high waterfall. *Mickle Fell* in Upper Teesdale is famous for the variety of its flora, which includes Alpine and continental plants as well as species which normally grow farther south. In order to protect these plants nature reserves have been established at *Cow Green* and *Moor House*, and permits are required to enter them.

Practical Information

Pull's Ferry, Norwich

AA classification of tourist accommodation

The British Automobile Association's full time and highly qualified team of inspectors regularly inspects all AA-recommended tourist accommodation in Britain and Ireland.

Hotels

Hotels are classified by stars; each classification reflects the provision of facilities and services rather than comparative merit. The range of menus, service and hours of service are appropriate to the classification, although hotels often satisfy several of the requirements of a classificiation higher than that awarded.

★ Good hotels and inns, generally of small scale and with modest facilities and furnishings, frequently run by the proprietor himself. All bedrooms with hot and cold water, adequate bath and lavatory arrangements; main meals with a choice of dishes served to residents; menus for residents and meal facilities for non-residents may be limited, especially at weekends.

★★ Hotels offering a higher standard of accommodation, more baths and perhaps a few private bathrooms/showers; lavatories on all floors, wider choice of meals (but these may be restricted, especially to non-residents).

★★★ Well-appointed hotels with more spacious accommodation and at least 40% of the bedrooms with private bathrooms/showers; full meal facilities for residents every day of the week but at weekends service to non-residents may be restricted.

★★★★ Exceptionally well-appointed hotels offering a high standard of comfort and cooking with 80% of the bedrooms providing private bathrooms/showers. At weekends meal service to non-residents may be restricted.

★★★★★ Luxury hotels, offering a very high standard of accommodation, service and comfort. All bedrooms have private bathrooms/showers.

(ap) Approved hotels which do not conform to the minimum classification requirements in respect of porterage, reception facilities, and choice of dishes; facilities for non-residents are often limited.

★ The award of red stars is based on a subjective assessment to highlight hotels considered to be of outstanding merit within their normal star ratings, offering something special in the way of welcome and hospitality. The award is normally withdrawn when the hotel undergoes a change of ownership.

Country house

♨ Hotels which display many of the characteristics of a traditional country house, set in secluded rural surroundings. Reception and service facilities may be of a more informal nature than in conventional hotels of similar classification.

Rosette awards

⊛ Each year the AA presents rosette awards to hotels and restaurants where the cooking, wine and service can be particularly recommended. The award can be of one, two or, exceptionally, three rosettes.

Restaurants

✗ Restaurants are inspected by the AA who classify them by knife-and-fork symbols ranging in number from one to five, reflecting comfort, service and cooking. The basic requirements for a recommendation are a high standard of cooking, prompt and courteous service, a pleasant atmosphere and value for money.
A high standard of cooking and service is expected from restaurants throughout the British Isles, but differing national or regional tastes and styles are taken into account.

Guest-houses, farmhouses and inns

These establishments are not graded by the AA, but they are regularly inspected and have to maintain minimum standards and meet stipulated criteria.

Camping and caravanning sites

► The AA inspects camping and caravanning sites throughout the British Isles and classifies them with between one and five pennant symbols. Each classification indicates the type of site and its range of facilities.
By using the pennant scheme, members are now better able to choose a site best suited to their needs.

▽ The inverted triangle represents Venture Sites – these are simple un-developed sites in particularly attractive areas of the country.

Self-catering holiday accommodation

In the British Isles this popular form of holiday accommodation is now inspected by The Automobile Association. Basic criteria have to be met, one of which is that all units must be fully self-contained.

Picnic sites/transit picnic sites

A picnic site is one considered worthy of a visit and must be equipped with litter bins. Listed transit picnic sites are conveniently situated for breaking a journey and are equipped with litter bins, toilets, drinking water and furniture, they are not necessarily of scenic interest.

Hotels awarded red stars

England

Avon	Bath	⊛	★★★		Priory, Weston Rd, tel. (0225) 331922
	Freshford	⊛	★★★	⚲	Homewood Park, Hinton Charterhouse, tel. Limpley Stoke (022122) 3731
	Hunstrete		★★★	⚲	Hunstrete House, Chelwood, tel. Compton Dando (07618) 578
	Thornbury	⊛	★★★	⚲	Thornbury Castle, tel. (0454) 412647
Buckinghamshire	Aston Clinton	⊛	★★★		Bell Inn, tel. Aylesbury (0296) 630252
Cheshire	Chester		★★★★		Chester Grosvenor, Eastgate St, tel. (0244) 24024
Cumbria	Borrowdale		★★★★		Lodore Swiss, tel. (059684) 285
	Brampton	⊛	★★	⚲	Farlam Hall, Hallbankgate (2¾m SE A689), tel. Hallbankgate (06976) 234
	Grasmere	⊛	★★	⚲	Michael's Nook, tel. (09665) 496
		⊛	★		White Moss House, Rydal Water, tel. (09665) 295
	Pooley Bridge	⊛⊛	★★★	⚲	Sharrow Bay, Sharrow Bay (1¾m S unclass rd), tel. (08536) 301
	Watermillock		★	⚲	Old Church, tel. Pooley Bridge (08536) 204
	Windermere	⊛⊛	★★		Miller Howe, Rayrigg Rd, tel. (09662) 2536
Devon	Barnstaple		★★	⚲	Downrew House (off unclass rd 1½m SE of Bishop's Tawton A377), tel. (0271) 42497
	Chagford	⊛	★★★	⚲	Gidleigh Park, tel. (06473) 2225
	Gittisham	⊛	★★	⚲	Combe House, tel. Honiton (0404) 2756
	Heddon's Mouth		★★	⚲	Heddon's Gate, tel. Parracombe (05983) 313
	Whimple		★★	⚲	Woodhayes, tel. (0404) 822237
Dorset	Poole		★★★		Mansion House, Thames St, tel. (0202) 685666
Essex	Dedham	⊛	★★★	⚲	Maison Talbooth, Stratford Rd, tel. Colchester (0206) 322367
			★★		Dedham Vale, Stratford Rd, tel. Colchester (0206) 322273
Gloucestershire	Buckland	⊛	★★★	⚲	Buckland Manor, tel. Broadway (0386) 852626
	Cheltenham	⊛	★★★	⚲	Greenway, Shurdington, tel. (0242) 862352
Hampshire	Hurstbourne Tarrant		★★	⚲	Esseborne Manor, tel. (026476) 444
	New Milton	⊛⊛	★★★★	⚲	Chewton Glen, Christchurch Rd, tel. Highcliffe (04252) 5341
Hereford &	Abberley	⊛	★★★	⚲	Elms (on A443), tel. Great Witley (029921) 666
Worcester	Broadway		★★★★		Lygon Arms, tel. (0386) 852255
Leicestershire	Oakham	⊛⊛	★★★	⚲	Hambleton Hall (3m E off A606), tel. (0572) 56991
London Postal District	SW1		★★★★★		Berkeley, Wilton Place, Knightsbridge, tel. 01-235 6000
			★★★★		Goring, Beeston Pl, Grosvenor Gardens, tel. 01-834 8211

Lygon Arms, Broadway

London **Postal District** **(contd.)**	SW1		★	Ebury Court, 26 Ebury St, tel. 01–730 8147
	SW3	⊗	★★★★	Capital, Basil St, Knightsbridge, tel. 01–589 5171
	W1		★★★★★	Claridges, Brook St, tel. 01–629 8860
		⊗⊗	★★★★★	Connaught, Carlos Place, tel. 01–499 7070
	W1	⊗⊗	★★★★★	Dorchester, Park Lane, tel. 01–629 8888
	W1		★★★★	Athenaeum, Piccadilly, tel. 01–499 3464
			★★★★	Brown's, Dover St, Albemarle St, tel. 01–493 6020
	WC2	⊗	★★★★★	Savoy, The Strand, tel. 01–836 4343
Northumberland	Powburn	⊗	★★	Breamish House, tel. (066578) 266
Oxfordshire	Milton, Great	⊗⊗	★★★	Le Manoir aux Quat' Saisons, tel. (08446) 8881
	Kingham		★★	Mill, tel. (060871) 8188
	Woodstock	⊗	★★	Feathers, Market St, tel. (0993) 812291
Somerset	Ston Easton	⊗	★★★ 🏩	Ston Easton Park, tel. Chewton Mendip (076121) 631
	Taunton	⊗	★★★★	Castle, Castle Gdn, tel. (0823) 72671
Sussex, West	East Grinstead	⊗	★★★ 🏩	Gravetye Manor (3m SW off unclass rd joining B2110 & B2028), tel. Sharpthorne (0342) 810567
	Rushlake Green		★★★ 🏩	Priory, tel. (0435) 830553
Warwickshire	Leamington Spa	⊗⊗	★★★ 🏩	Mallory Court, Harbury Lane, Bishop's Tachbrook (2m S off A452), tel. (0926) 30214
Wiltshire	Warminster	⊗	★★★ 🏩	Bishopstrow House, Boreham Rd (2m SE A36), tel. (0985) 212312
Yorkshire	York	⊗	★★★	Middlethorpe Hall, Bishopthorpe Rd, tel. (0904) 641241

Channel Isles

Jersey	St Saviour	⊗	★★★★ 🏩	Longueville Manor (off St Helier/ Grouville rd, A3), tel. Jersey (0534) 25501

Wales

Gwynedd	Llandudno		★★★	♨	Bodysgallen Hall (off B5115), tel. Deganwy (0492) 84466
			★★		St Tudno, North Parade, tel. (0492) 74411

Scotland

Dumfries and Galloway	Portpatrick	⊛	★★	♨	Knockinaam Lodge (2m S on unclass rd), tel. (077681) 471
Grampian	Banchory		★★★	♨	Banchory Lodge, tel. (03302) 2625
Highland	Arisaig	⊛	★★★	♨	Arisaig House, Beasdale (3m E A830), tel. (06875) 622
	Fort William	⊛⊛	★★★★	♨	Inverlochy Castle (3m NE A82), tel. (0397) 2177
	Inverness	⊛	★★	♨	Dunain Park, tel. (0463) 230512
Lothian	Gullane	⊛	★★★	♨	Greywalls, Duncar Rd, tel. (0620) 842144
Strathclyde	Eriska		★★★	♨	Isle of Eriska, tel. Ledaig (063172) 371
	Kilchrenan	⊛	★★★		Ardanaiseig, tel. (08663) 333
	Port Appin	⊛	★★		Airds, tel. Appin (063173) 236
	Stewarton	⊛	★★★	♨	Chapeltoun House, tel. (0560) 82696
Tayside	Perth	⊛	★★★	♨	Balcraig House, Scone (2½m NE off A94 towards New Scone), tel. (0738) 51123

Hotels and restaurants awarded rosettes
Three rosettes ⊛⊛⊛

England

Berkshire	Bray	XXXX	Waterside, Ferry Rd, tel. Maidenhead (0628) 20691
London Postal District	W1	XXXX	Le Gavroche, 43 Upper Brook St, tel. 01-408 0881

Two rosettes ⊛⊛

England

Avon	Bristol	XX		Les Semailles, 9 Druid Hill, Stoke Bishop (2m NW), tel. (0272) 686456
Cumbria	Pooley Bridge	★★★	♨	Sharrow Bay, Sharrow Bay (1¾m S unclass rd), tel. (085 36) 301
	Windermere	★★		Miller Howe, Rayrigg Rd, tel. (09662) 2536
Hampshire	New Milton	★★★★	♨	Chewton Glen, Christchurch Rd, tel. Highcliffe (04252) 5341
Leicestershire	Oakham	★★★	♨	Hambleton Hall, Hambleton (3m E off A606), tel. (0572) 56991
London Postal Districts	EC2	XXX		Le Poulbot, 45 Cheapside, tel. 01 236 4379
	SW3	XX		Tante Claire, 68 Royal Hospital Rd, tel. 01-352 6045
	SW8	XX		L'Arlequin, 123 Queenstown Rd, tel. 01-622 0555
	W1	★★★★★		Connaught, Carlos Place, tel. 01-499 7070
	W1	★★★★★		Dorchester (Terrace Room), 53 Park Ln, tel. 01-629 8888
	WC2	XXXX		Inigo Jones, 14 Garrick St, tel. 01-836 6456
Oxfordshire	Milton, Gt	★★★	♨	Le Manoir aux Quat' Saisons (9m SE of Oxford, follow signs to Wallingford from junc A40/A329 (M40 junc 7) then second turning right), tel. (08446) 8881
Warwickshire	Leamington Spa Royal	★★★	♨	Mallory Court, Harbury Lane, Bishop's Tachbrook (2m S off A452). tel. (0926) 30214
Yorkshire, West	Ilkley	XXX		Box Tree, Church St, tel. (0943) 608484

Scotland

Highland	Fort William	★★★★★ 👤🌹	Inverlochy Castle (3m NE A82), tel. (0397) 2177

One rosette ❀

England

Avon	Bath	★★★	Priory, Weston Rd, tel. (0225) 331922
		✕	Clos du Roy, 7 Edgar Buildings, George St, tel. (0225) 64356
	Freshford	★★★ 👤🌹	Homewood Park, Hinton Charterhouse, tel. Limpley Stoke (022122) 3731
	Thornbury	★★★ 👤🌹	Thornbury Castle, tel. (0454) 412647
Bedfordshire	Turvey	★★	Laws, tel. (023064) 213
	Woburn	✕✕✕	Paris House, Woburn Park, tel. (052525) 692
Berkshire	Burghfield	✕✕	Knights Farm (dinner only), tel. Reading (0734) 52366
	Kintbury	✕✕	Dundas Arms, tel. (0488) 58263
	Maidenhead	★★★	Fredrick's, Shoppenhangers Rd, tel. (0628) 35934
	Windsor	★★★★	Oakley Court, Windsor Rd, Water Oakley (2m W A308), tel. Maidenhead (0628) 74141
Buckinghamshire	Aston Clinton	★★★	Bell Inn, tel. Aylesbury (0296) 630252
Cambridgeshire	Ely	✕	Old Fire Engine House, 25 St Mary's Street, tel. (0353) 2582
Cheshire	Handforth (Manchester Airport)	★★★★	Belfry, Stanley Rd, tel. 061–437 0511
	Nantwich	★★★ 👤🌹	Rookery Hall, Worleston (2m N B5074), tel. (0270) 626866
	Wilmslow	★★★	Stanneylands, Stanneylands Rd, tel. (0625) 525225
Cornwall	Helford	✕✕	Riverside (dinner only), tel. Manaccan (032623) 443
Cumbria	Ambleside	★★★	Rothay Manor (dinner only), Rothay Br, tel. (0966) 33605
	Brampton	★★ 👤🌹	Farlam Hall (dinner only), Hallbankgate (2¾m SE A689), tel. Hallbankgate (06976) 234
		★★	Tarn End, Talkin Tarn (2½m S off B6413), tel. (06977) 2340
	Grasmere	★★ 👤🌹	Michael's Nook (dinner only), tel. (09665) 496
		★	White Moss House (dinner only), Rydal Water, tel. (09665) 295
	Kendal	✕	Castle Dairy (dinner only), 26 Wildman St, tel. (0539) 21170
	Longtown	★ 👤🌹	March Bank (dinner only), Scotsdyke (3m N A7 Galashiels rd), tel. (0228) 791325
	Windermere	✕	Porthole Eating House (dinner only)
Derbyshire	Derby	✕✕✕	524, 524 Burton Rd, Littleover, tel. (0332) 371524
Devon	Chagford	★★★ 👤🌹	Gidleigh Park, tel. (06473) 2225
	Dartmouth	✕✕	Carved Angel, 2 South Embankment, tel. (08043) 2465
	Gittisham	★★ 👤🌹	Combe House (dinner only), tel. Honiton (0404) 2756
	Gulworthy	✕✕✕	Horn of Plenty, tel. Tavistock (0822) 832528
	Ottery St Mary	✕✕	Lodge, 17 Silver St, tel. (040481) 2356
	Plymouth	✕	Chez Nous, 13 Frankfort Gate, tel. (0752) 266793
Dorset	Bournemouth & Boscombe	✕	Provence (dinner only), 91 Belle Vue Rd, Southbourne, tel. (0202) 424421
	Poole	✕✕	Le Chateau, 13 Haven Rd, Canford Cliffs, tel. (0202) 707400
Essex	Dedham	★★★ 👤🌹	Maison Talbooth (& Le Talbooth), Stratford Rd, tel. Colchester (0206) 322367
	Dunmow, Gt	✕✕	Starr, Market Place, tel. (0371) 4321

Gloucestershire	Buckland	★★★	♨	Buckland Manor, tel. Broadway (0386) 852626
	Cheltenham	★★★	♨	Greenway, Shurdington, tel. (0242) 862352
	Chipping Campden	★		King's Arms (dinner only), The Square, tel. Evesham (0386) 840256
Hampshire	Fordingbridge	✕		Three Lions, Stuckton, tel. (0425) 52489
	Grayshott	✕		Woods, Headley Rd (1m SW B3002 off A3), tel. Hindhead (042873) 5555
	Hook	✕✕		Whitewater House (off A30, 1m NE), tel. (025672) 2436
	Liphook	✕✕		Lal Quilla, 15 The Square, tel. (0428) 722095
	Lyndhurst	★★★	♨	Parkhill House, Beaulieu Rd, tel. (042128) 2944
	Southampton	✕✕		Kohinoor, 2 The Broadway, Portswood, tel. (0703) 582770
		✕		Golden Palace, 17A Above Bar St, tel. (0703) 226636
	Winchester	✕✕		Old Chesil Rectory, 1 Chesil St, tel. (0962) 53177
	Wickham	★★		Old House, tel. (0329) 833049
Hereford & Worcester	Abberley	★★★	♨	Elms (on A443), tel. Great Witley (029921) 666
	Belbroughton	✕✕✕		Bell, Bell End, tel. (0562) 730232
	Bromsgrove	✕✕✕		Grafton Manor, Grafton Ln, tel. (0527) 31525
	Corse Lawn	✕✕✕		Corse Lawn House, tel. Tirley (045278) 479
	Ledbury	★★	♨	Hope End (dinner only), Hope End (2½m NE unclass rd), tel. (0531) 3613
	Malvern	★★		Walmer Lodge (dinner only), 49 Abbey Rd, tel. (06845) 4139
		✕✕		Croque-en-Bouche, 221 Wells Rd, Malvern Wells (3m S A449), tel. (06845) 65612
	Worcester	✕✕		Brown's, The Old Cornmill, South Quay, tel. (0905) 26263
Hertfordshire	St Albans	✕		La Province, 13 George St, tel. (0727) 52142
Isle of Wight	Seaview	★★		Seaview, High St, tel. (098371) 2711
Kent	Ashford	★★★★	♨	Eastwell Manor, Eastwell Park (3m N A251), tel. (0233) 35751
	Canterbury	✕✕		Restaurant Seventy Four, 74 Wincheap, tel. (0227) 67411
	Faversham	✕✕		Read's, Painters Forstal, tel. (0795) 535344
	Hadlow	✕		La Crémaillère, The Square, tel. (0732) 851489
	Ightham	✕✕		Town House (dinner only), tel. Borough Green (0732) 884578
Lincolnshire	Lincoln	✕		Whites, The Jews House, 15 The Strait, tel. (0522) 24851
London Postal Districts	EC1	✕		Bubb's, 329 Central Markets, tel. 01–236 2435
	N1	✕		Anna's Place, 90 Mildmay Park, tel. 01–249 9379
	NW1	✕✕		Pratt's, Camden Lock, Commercial Pl, tel. 01–485 9987
	NW3	✕✕		Keats (dinner only), 3 Downshire Hill, tel. 01–435 3544
	SW1	✕✕		Gavvers (dinner only), 16 Lower Sloane St, tel. 01–730 5983
		✕✕		Ken Lo's Memories of China, 67 Ebury St, tel. 01–730 7734
		✕✕		Mazarin (dinner only), 30 Winchester St, tel. 01–828 3366
		✕✕		Mijanou, 143 Ebury St, tel. 01–730 4099
		✕✕		Pomegranates, 94 Grosvenor Rd, tel. 01–828 6560
		✕✕		Salloos, 62–64 Kinnerton St, tel. 01–235 4444
		✕		Ciboure, 21 Eccleston St, tel. 01–730 2505
	SW3	★★★★		Capital, Basil St, Knightsbridge, tel. 01–589 5171
		✕✕✕✕		Waltons, 121 Walton St, tel. 01–584 0204
		✕✕		English Garden, 10 Lincoln St, tel. 01–584 7272
		✕✕		English House, 3 Milner St, tel. 01–584 3002

London Postal Districts (contd.)	SW3	✕		Ma Cuisine, 113 Walton St, tel. 01–584 7585
		✕		Dan's, 119 Sydney St, tel. 01–352 2718
	SW5	✕		Reads, 152 Old Brompton Rd, tel. 01–373 2445
	SW6	✕✕		Gastronome One, 311–313 New Kings Rd, tel. 01–731 6381
		✕		Perfumed Conservatory, 182 Wandsworth Bridge Rd, tel. 01–731 0732
	SW7	✕✕		Hilaire (dinner only), 68 Old Brompton Rd, tel. 01–584 8993
		✕✕		Shezan, 16–22 Cheval Pl, tel. 01–589 7918
	W1	★★★★★		Inter-Continental, 1 Hamilton Pl, Hyde Park Corner, tel. 01–409 3131
		✕✕		Au Jardin des Gourmets, 5 Greek St, tel. 01–437 1816
		✕✕		Odin's, 27 Devonshire St, tel. 01–935 7296
		✕✕		Rue St Jacques, 5 Charlotte St, tel. 01–637 0222
		✕		Yungs (dinner only), 23 Wardour St, tel. 01–437 4986
	W8	✕✕		La Ruelle, 14 Wrights Lane, tel. 01–937 8525
	WC1	✕✕		Mr Kai of Russell Square, 50 Woburn Pl, tel. 01–580 1188
	WC2	★★★★★		Savoy (Savoy Restaurant), Strand, tel. 01–836 4343
		✕✕✕		Boulestin, 25 Southampton St, tel. 01–836 7061
		✕✕		Interlude de Tabaillau, 7–8 Bow St, tel. 01–379 6473
		✕✕		Poons of Covent Garden, 41 King St, tel. 01–240 1743
		✕		Poons, 4 Leicester St, tel. 01–437 1528
London Greater	Richmond-upon Thames	✕✕		Lichfields, Lichfield Ter, Sheen Rd, tel. 01–940 5236
	Surbiton	✕✕		Chez Max, 85 Maple Rd, tel. 01–399 2365
	Sutton	✕		Partners 23, 23 Stonecot Hill, tel. 01–644 7743
Manchester, Greater	Manchester	✕		Yang Sing, 34 Princess St, tel. 061–236 2200
Norfolk	Brockdish	✕✕		Sheriff House, tel. Hoxne (037975) 316
	Grimston	★★★	🏵	Congham Hall, Lynn Rd, tel. Hillington (0485) 600250
Northamptonshire	Horton	✕✕		French Partridge, tel. Northampton (0604) 870033
	Roade	✕		Roadhouse, 16–18 High St, tel. (0604) 863372
Northumberland	Powburn	★★		Breamish House (dinner only), tel. (066578) 266
Oxfordshire	Chesterton	✕✕		Woods, tel. Bicester (0869) 241444
	North Stoke	★★★		Springs, Wallingford Rd, tel. (0491) 36687
	Oxford	✕		Le Petit Blanc, 272 Banbury Rd, Summertown, tel. (0865) 53540
	Woodstock	★★		Feathers, Market St, tel. (0993) 812291
Somerset	Axbridge	★★		Oak House, The Square, tel. (0934) 732444
	Ston Easton	★★★	🏵	Ston Easton Park, tel. Chewton Mendip (076121) 631
	Taunton	★★★★		Castle, Castle Gn, tel. (0823) 72671
	Williton	★★		White House (dinner only), Long St, tel. (0984) 32306
Staffordshire	Waterhouses	✕✕		Old Beams, Leek Rd, tel. (05386) 254
Suffolk	Fressingfield	✕		Fox and Goose, tel. (037986) 247
	Hintlesham	✕✕✕		Hintlesham Hall, tel. (047387) 268
	Ipswich	★★★		Marlborough, 73 Henley Rd, tel. (0473) 57677
Surrey	Haslemere	✕✕		Morels, 25–27 Lower St, tel. (0428) 51462
	Limpsfield	✕✕		Old Lodge, High St, tel. Oxted (08833) 2996
Sussex, East	Herstmonceux	✕✕		Sundial, tel. (0323) 832217
	Selmeston	✕		Corins, Church Farm, tel. Ripe (032183) 343
	Wadhurst	★★	🏵	Spindlewood, Wallcrouch, tel. Ticehurst (0580) 200430

Sussex, West	Chilgrove	XX		White Horse Inn, tel. East Marden (024359) 219
	East Grinstead	★★★	⬥♣	Gravetye Manor (3m SW off unclass rd adjoining B2110 & B2028), tel. Sharpthorne (0342) 810567
	Findon	X		Darlings Bistro (dinner only), The Square, tel. (090671) 3817
	Pulborough	X		Stane Street Hollow, Codmore Hill, tel. (07982) 2819
	Storrington	XXX		Manleys, Manleys Hill, tel. (09066) 2331
	Thakeham	★★★		Abingworth Hall, tel. West Chiltington (07983) 3636
Warwickshire	Billesley	★★★	⬥♣	Billesley Manor, tel. Stratford-upon-Avon (0789) 763737
	Ettington	★★	⬥♣	Chase Country House (dinner only), Banbury Rd, tel. Stratford-upon-Avon (0789) 740000
	Stratford-upon-Avon	X		Hills, 3 Greenhill St, tel. (0789) 293563
	Warwick	XX		Randolph's, Coten End, tel. (0926) 491292
West Midlands	Birmingham	XX		Chung Ying, 16/18 Wrottesley St, tel. 021–622 5669
		XX		Rajdoot, 12/22 Albert St, tel. 021–643 8805
	Oldbury	XX		Jonathan's, 16 Wolverhampton Rd, Quinton, tel. 021–429 3757
Wiltshire	Barford St Martin	XX		Michel's (dinner only), tel. Salisbury (0722) 742240
	Melksham	★★★		Beechfield House, Beanacre (1m N A350), tel. (0225) 703700
	Warminster	★★★	⬥♣	Bishopstrow House (dinner only), Boreham Rd, (2m SE A36), tel. (0985) 212312
Yorkshire, North	Ayton, Gt	★★★	⬥♣	Ayton Hall (dinner only), Low Green, tel. Middlesborough (0642) 723595
	Brampton-by-Sawdon	X		Brompton Forge, tel. Scarborough (0723) 85409
	Fadmoor	X		Plough Inn (dinner only), tel. Kirkbymoorside (0751) 31515
	Nunnington	XX		Ryedale Lodge (dinner only), tel. (04395) 246
	Staddlebridge	XX		McCoys (Tontine Inn) (dinner only), tel. East Harsley (060982) 207
	Walshford	XXX		Bridge Inn (Byron Room), Great North Road, tel. Wetherby (0937) 62345
	York	★★★		Middlethorpe Hall, Bishopthorpe Rd, tel. (0904) 641241
Yorkshire, West	Pool in Wharfedale	XXX		Pool Court (dinner only), Pool Bank, tel. Arthington (0532) 842288

Channel Islands

Guernsey	St Peter Port	★★★		La Frégate, Les Côtils, tel. Guernsey (0481) 24624
Jersey	St Brelade	★★★★		Hotel L'Horizon (Star Grill), St Brelade's Bay, tel. Jersey (0534) 43101
	St Helier	★★★★		Grand (Victoria's), The Esplanade, tel. Jersey (0534) 22301
	St Saviour	★★★★	⬥♣	Longueville Manor (off St Helier/ Grouville Rd A3), tel. Jersey (0534) 25501

Isles of Scilly

| Tresco | Old Grimsby | ★★★ | | Island, Scillonia, tel. (0720) 22883 |

Wales

Glamorgan, South	Cardiff	X		La Chaumière, Cardiff Rd, Llandaff, tel. (0222) 555319
		X		Gibsons, Romilly Cres, tel. (0222) 41264
Glamorgan, West	Swansea	XX		Drangway, 66 Wind St, tel. (0792) 461397
Gwent	Llanddewiskyrrid	X		Walnut Tree, (3m NE of Abergavenny), tel. Abergavenny (0873) 2797
	Whitebrook	★★		Crown at Whitebrook (dinner only), tel. Monmouth (0600) 860254
Gwynedd	Abersoch	★★★	⬥♣	Porth Tocyn (dinner only), Bwlch Tocyn, tel. (075881) 2966

Scotland

Region	Town	Rating	Details
Borders	Tweedsmuir	★★	Crook Inn (dinner only), tel. (08997) 272
Central	Blair Drummond	×	Broughton's Country Cottage (dinner only), Burnbank Cottages, (1m W on A873), tel. Doune (0786) 841897
	Dunblane	★★★ ♨	Cromlix House (dinner only), Kinbuck (3m NE B8033), tel. (0786) 822125
Dumfries & Galloway	Canonbie	×	Riverside (dinner only), tel. (05415) 295
	Moffat	★★	Beechwood Country House (dinner only), tel. (0683) 20210
	Newton Stewart	★★★ ♨	Kirroughtree (dinner only), Minnigaff, tel. (0671) 2141
	Portpatrick	★★ ♨	Knockinaam Lodge (dinner only), 2m S on unclass rd), tel. (077681) 471
Fife	Anstruther	××	Cellar, 24 East Green, tel. (0333) 310378
	Cupar	×	Ostlers Close, 25 Bonnygate, tel. (0334) 55574
	Peat Inn	××	Peat Inn, tel. (033484) 206
Grampian	Drybridge	××	Old Monastery (dinner only), (1m E off Deskford Rd), tel. Buckie (0542) 32660
	Kildrummy	★★★ ♨	Kildrummy Castle, tel. (03365) 288
	Newburgh	★★	Udney Arms (dinner only), Main St, tel. (03586) 444
Highland	Arisaig	★★★ ♨	Arisaig House (dinner only), Beasdale (3 m E A830), tel. (06875) 622
	Dulnain Bridge	★★ ♨	Muckrach Lodge (dinner only), tel. (047985) 257
	Harlosh	★	Harlosh (dinner only), tel. Dunvegan (047022) 367
	Inverness	★★ ♨	Dunain Park (dinner only), tel. (0463) 230512
	Isle Ornsay	★★ ♨	Kinloch Lodge (dinner only), tel. (04713) 214
	Kentallen	★★ ♨	Ardsheal House (dinner only), tel. Duror (063174) 227
	Kingussie	★	Columba House (dinner only), Manse Rd, tel. (05402) 402
		★	Osprey (dinner only), Ruthven Rd, tel. (05402) 510
	Nairn	★★	Clifton (dinner only), tel. (0667) 53119
	Newtonmore	★	Ard-Na-Coille (dinner only), Kinguissie Rd, tel. (05403) 214
	Strathpeffer	★	Holly Lodge (dinner only), tel. (0997) 21254
	Whitebridge	★★ ♨	Knockie Lodge (dinner only), tel. Gorthleck (04563) 276
Lothian	Edinburgh	★★★★	Caledonian, Princes St, tel. 031–225 2433
		×	MacKintosh's, 24A Stafford St, tel. 031–226 7530
	Gullane	★★★ ♨	Greywalls, Duncar Rd, tel. (0620) 842144
		×	La Potiniere, Main St, tel. (0620) 843214
Strathclyde	Glasgow	×××	Fountain, 2 Woodside Cres, tel. 041–332 6396
		××	The Buttery, 652 Argyle St, tel. 041–221 8188
	Kilchrenan	★★★ ♨	Ardanaiseig (dinner only), tel. (08663) 333
	Kilfinan	★★	Kilfinan (dinner only), tel. (070082) 201
	Langbank	★★★ ♨	Gleddoch House, tel. (047554) 711
	Port Appin	★★	Airds (dinner only), tel. Appin (063173) 236
	Stewarton	★★★ ♨	Chapeltoun House, tel. (0560) 82696
	Tarbert	★	West Loch (dinner only), tel. (08802) 283
	Troon	×	Campbell's Kitchen (dinner only), 3 South Beach, tel. (0292) 314421
Tayside	Auchterhouse	★★★ ♨	Old Mansion House, tel. (082626) 366
	Blairgowrie	★★ ♨	Kinloch House (dinner only), (2m W A923), tel. Essendy (025084) 237
	Killiecrankie	★★	Killiecrankie (dinner only), tel. Pitlochry (0796) 3220
	Perth	★★★ ♨	Balcraig House (dinner only), Scone (2½m NE off A94 towards New Scone), tel. (0738) 51123
		××	Coach House, 8–10 North Port, tel. (0738) 27950
Western Isles	Scarista, Isle of Harris	★★ ♨	Scarista House (dinner only), tel. (085985) 238

Country-house hotels ⚹♣

Quiet, often secluded hotels are listed below. At an AA country-house hotel you should be assured of a restful night, together with a relaxed, informal atmosphere and personal welcome. On the other hand, some of the facilities may differ from those to be found in specially-built hotels of the same star rating.
It should be noted that not all rurally situated hotels are AA country-house hotels, neither are AA country-house hotels always located in an isolated situation.

England

Avon	Bath	★★★	Combe Grove, Monkton Combe (1½m S on Exeter light traffic rd, A367, turn off at Brass Knocker Hill), tel. (0225) 834644
	Freshford	⊛ ★★★	Homewood Park, Hinton Charterhouse (between A36 & village), tel. Limpley Stoke (022122) 3731
	Hunstrete	★★★	Hunstrete House, Chelwood, tel. Compton Dando (07618) 578
	Lympsham	★★	Batch Farm Country, tel. Edingworth (093472) 371
	Rangeworthy	★	Rangeworthy Court, Wooton Rd, tel. (045422) 347
	Thornbury	★★★	Thornbury Castle, tel. (0454) 412647
Cheshire	Nantwich	⊛ ★★★	Rookery Hall, Worleston (2m N B5074), tel. (0270) 626866
	Tarporley	★★	Willington Hall (3m NW off unclass rd linking A51 & A54), tel. Kelsall (0829) 52321
Cleveland	Loftus	★★★	Grinkle Park, tel. Guisborough (0287) 40515
Cornwall	Falmouth	★★★	Penmere Manor, Mongleath Rd, tel. (0326) 314545
	Helland Bridge	★★★	Tredethy County (off B3266), tel. St Mabyn (020884) 262
	Helston	★	Nansloe Manor, Meneage Rd, tel. (0326) 574691
	Lamorna Cove	★★★	Lamorna Cove, tel. Penzance (0736) 731411
	Liskeard	★★	Country Castle, Station Rd, tel. (0579) 42694
	Mawnan Smith	★★★	Meudon, tel. Falmouth (0326) 250541
	Newquay	★★	Porth Veor Manor House, Porthway, tel. (06373) 3274 Due to change to (0637) 873274
	Penzance	★★★	Higher Faugan, Newlyn (off B3315), tel. (0736) 62076
	Portscatho	★★	Roseland House, Rosevine, tel. (087258) 644
	Ruan High Lanes	★★	Polsue Manor, tel. Truro (0872) 501270
	St Agnes	★★	Rose in Vale Country House, Rose in Vale, Mithian, tel. (087255) 2202
	St Wenn	★	Wenn Manor, tel. Roche (0726) 890240
	Talland Bay	★★★	Talland Bay, tel. Polperro (0503) 72667
Cumbria	Alston	★★	Lovelady Shield, tel. (0498) 81203
	Ambleside	★★	Nanny Brow, Clappersgate, tel. (0966) 32036
	Appleby-in-Westmoreland	★★★	Appleby Manor, Roman Rd, tel. (0930) 51571
	Bassenthwaite	★★★	Armathwaite Hall, tel. Bassenthwaite Lake (059681) 551
		★★	Overwater Hall, Ireby (2m N), tel. Bassenthwaite Lake (059681) 566
	Blawith	★★	Highfield, tel. Lowick Bridge (022985) 238
	Brampton	⊛ ★★	Farlam Hall, Hallbankgate (2¾m SE A689), tel. Hallbankgate (06976) 234

Farlam Hall, Hallbankgate, Brampton

Cumbria | Crosby on Eden | ★★ | Crosby Lodge, tel. (022873) 618
(contd.) | Grange-over-Sands | ★★ | Graythwaite Manor, Fernhill Rd,
| | | tel. (04484) 2001
| Grasmere | ⊗ ★★ | Michael's Nook, tel. (09665) 496
| Hawkshead | ★★★ | Tarn Hows, Hawkshead Hill, tel. (09666) 330
| Keswick | ★★★ | Underscar, Applethwaite (1m N off A591),
| | | tel. (0596) 72469
| | ★★ | Red House, Under Skiddaw (on A591),
| | | tel. (0596) 72211
| Levens | ★★ | Heaves (off A6, ½ from junc with A591),
| | | tel. Sedgwick (0448) 60396
| Longtown | ⊗ ★ | March Bank, Scotsdyke (3m N A7 Galashiels
| | | rd), tel. (0228) 791325
| Loweswater | ★★ | Scale Hill, tel. Lorton (090085) 232
| Pooley Bridge | ⊗ ★★★ | Sharrow Bay, Sharrow Bay (1¾m S unclass
| | | rd), tel. (08536) 301
| Thornthwaite | ★★ | Thwaite Howe,
| | | tel. Braithwaite (059682) 281
| Watermillock | ★★★ | Leeming House, Ullswater,
| | | tel. Pooley Bridge (08536) 444
| | ★ | Old Church, tel. Pooley Bridge (08536) 204
| Whitehaven | ★★ | Roseneath, Low Moresby (3m NE of A595),
| | | tel. (0946) 61572
| Windermere | ★★★ | Langdale Chase,
| | | tel. Ambleside (0966) 32201
| | ★★ | Holbeck Ghyll, Holbeck Ln,
| | | Ambleside (0966) 32375
| | ★★ | Lindeth Fell, Upper Storrs Park Rd, Bowness,
| | | tel. (09662) 3286
| | ★★ | Linthwaite, Bowness, tel. (09662) 3688
| | ★ | Quarry Garth Country House, Troutbeck,
| | | tel. (09662) 3761
| Witherslack | ★ | Old Vicarage Country House,
| | | tel. (044 852) 381
Derbyshire | Matlock | ★★★ | Riber Hall, Riber, tel. (0629) 2795
Devon | Ashburton | ★★ | Holne Chase, tel. Poundsgate (03643) 471
| Barnstaple | ★★ | Downrew House (off unclass rd 1½ SE
| | | Bishops Tawton A377),
| | | tel. (0271) 42497
| Bideford | ★★ | Yeoldon House, Durrant Ln, Northam,
| | | tel. (02372) 74400
| Bovey Tracey | ★★ | Edgemoor, Haytor Rd, tel. (0626) 832466
| | ★★ | Prestbury Country House, Brimley Ln,
| | | tel. (0626) 833246
| Buckland in the Moor | ★★ | Buckland Hall Country House,
| | | tel. Ashburton (0364) 52679
| Burrington | ★★★ | Northcote Manor (2m NW of village towards
| | | Portsmouth Arms Station & A377,
| | | tel. High Bickington (0769) 60501
| Chagford | ⊗ ★★★ | Gidleigh Park, tel. (06473) 2225
| | ★★★ | Great Tree, Sandy Park (2½ N on A382),
| | | tel. (06473) 2491
| | ★★★ | Mill End, Sandy Park (2m N on A382),
| | | tel. (06473) 2282
| | ★★★ | Teignworthy, Frenchbeer
| | | (2m S on unclass rd to Thornworthy),
| | | tel. (06473) 3355
| Clawton | ★★ | Court Barn Country House,
| | | tel. North Tamerton (040927) 219
| Combeinteignhead | ★★ | Netherton House,
| | | tel. Shaldon (062687) 3251
| Fairy Cross | ★★★ | Portledge (off A39),
| | | tel. Horns Cross (02375) 262
| Gittisham | ⊗ ★★ | Combe House, tel. Honiton (0404) 2756
| Haytor | ★★ | Bel Alp, tel. (03646) 217
| Heddon's Mouth | ★★ | Heddon's Gate, tel. Parracombe (05983) 313
| Holbeton | ★★★ | Alston Hall, Battisborough Cross,
| | | tel. (075530) 259
| Honiton | ★★★ | Deer Park, Weston (2½m W off A30),
| | | tel. (0404) 2064
| Horn's Cross | ★★★ | Foxdown Manor (signed from A39 W of
| | | village), tel. (02375) 325
| Ilfracombe | ★★ | Langleigh Country, Langleigh Rd,
| | | tel. (0271) 62629
| Kingsbridge | ★★★ | Buckland-Tout-Saints, Goveton (2½m NE on
| | | unclass rd), tel. (0548) 3055
| Lydford | ★★ | Lydford House, tel. (082282) 347
| Lynmouth | ★★ | Beacon, Countisbury Hill,
| | | tel. Lynton (0598) 53268

Kingsbridge, Devon

Devon	Lynton	★	Combe Park, Hillsford Bridge, tel. (0598) 52356
(contd.)	Martinhoe	★	Old Rectory, tel. Parracombe (05983) 368
	Mary Tavy	★★	Moorland Hall, tel. (082281) 466
	Monkleigh	★★	Beaconside, tel. Bideford (02372) 77205
	Moretonhampstead	★★	Glebe House, North Bovey (1½m SW), tel. (0647) 40544
	Newton Ferrers	★★	Court House, tel. Plymouth (0752) 872324
	North Huish	★★	Brookdale Country House, tel. Gara Bridge (054 882) 402
	Sidmouth	★★	Brownlands, Sid Rd, tel. (03955) 3053
	South Brent	★★	Glazebrook House, tel. (03647) 3322
	Stoke Gabriel	★★★	Gabriel Court, tel. (080428) 206
	Whimple	★★	Woodhayes, tel. (0404) 822237
Dorset	Bridport	★	Little Wych Country House, Burton Rd, tel. (0308) 23490
	Milton Abbas	★★	Milton Manor, tel. (0258) 880254
	Milton on Stour	★★★	Milton Lodge, tel. Gillingham (07476) 2262
	Studland	★★	Manor House, tel. (092944) 288
Essex	Dedham	⊛ ★★★	Maison Talbooth, Stratford Rd, tel. Colchester (0206) 322367
Gloucestershire	Bibury	★★	Bibury Court, tel. (028574) 337
	Buckland	⊛ ★★★	Buckland Manor, tel. Broadway (0386) 852626
	Cheltenham	⊛ ★★★	Greenway, Shurdington, tel. (0242) 862352
	Coleford	★	Lambsquay, tel. Dean (0594) 33127
	Lower Slaughter	★★★	Manor, tel. Cotswold (0451) 20456
	Stroud	★★★	Burleigh Court, Brimscombe (2½m SE off A419), tel. (0453) 883804
	Tetbury	★★★	Calcot Manor, Calcot (3m NW), tel. Leighterton (066689) 227
	Upper Slaughter	★★★	Lords of the Manor, tel. Cotswold (0451) 20243
Hampshire	Brockenhurst	★★	Whitley Ridge Restaurant and Country House, Beaulieu Rd, tel. Lymington (0590) 22354
	Burley	★★	Moorhill House, tel. (04253) 3285
	Hurstbourne Tarrant	★★	Esseborne Manor, tel. (026476) 444
	Lymington	★★★	Passford House, Mount Pleasant (2m NW on Sway rd), tel. (0590) 682398
	Lyndhurst	⊛ ★★★	Parkhill House, Beaulieu Rd, tel. (042128) 2944
	New Milton	⊛⊛ ★★★	Chewton Glen, Christchurch Rd, tel. Highcliffe (04252) 5341
	Winchester	★★★	Lainston House, Sparsholt (3m NW off A272), tel. (0962) 63588
	Woodlands	★★	Woodlands Lodge, Bartley Rd, tel. Ashurst (042129) 2257
Hereford & Worcester	Abberley	⊛ ★★★	Elms (on A443), tel. Great Witley (029921) 666
	Broadway	★★	Collin House, Collin Ln, tel. (0386) 858354
	Ledbury	⊛ ★★	Hope End Country House, Hope End (2½ NE unclass), tel. (0531) 3613
	Malvern	★★★	Cottage in the Wood, Holywell Rd, Malvern Wells (3m S A449), tel. (06845) 3487
		★★	Holdfast Cottage, Welland (4m SE on A4104), tel. Hanley Swan (0684) 310288
	Pencraig	★★	Pencraig Court, tel. Llangarron (098984) 306
Humberside	Driffield, Gt,	★★	Wold Country House, Nafferton (3m E A166), tel. (0377) 44242
	Little Weighton	★★★	Rowley Manor, tel. Hull (0482) 848248

Isle of Wight	Bembridge		★★	Elm Country, tel. (0983) 872248
	Ventnor		★★	Winterbourne, Bonchurch (1m E), tel. (0983) 852535
			★	Madeira Hall, Trinity Rd, tel. (0983) 852624
	Whippingham		★★	Padmore House, Beatrice Av, tel. Isle of Wight (0983) 293210
Kent	Ashford	⊛	★★★	Eastwell Manor, Eastwell Park (3m N A251), tel. (0233) 35751
	Cranbrook		★★	Kennel Holt, tel. (0580) 712032
Leicestershire	Oakham	⊛⊛	★★★	Hambleton Hall, Hambleton (3m E off A606), tel. (0572) 56991
Manchester, Greater	Bolton		★★★	Egerton House, Egerton (3m N A666), tel. (0204) 57171
Norfolk	Bunwell		★★	Bunwell Manor, tel. (095389) 317
	Grimston		★★★	Congham Hall, Lynn Rd, tel. Hillington (0485) 600250
	Shipdham		★★	Shipdham Place, Church Cl, tel. Dereham (0362) 820303
	Thorpe Market		★★	Elderton Lodge, tel. Southrepps (026379) 547
	Witchingham, Gt		★★	Lenwade House, tel. (0603) 872288
Northumberland	Allendale		★	The Riding, tel. (043483) 237
	Otterburn		★★	Otterburn Tower, tel. (0830) 20620
	Powburn	⊛	★★	Breamish House, tel. (066578) 266
Oxfordshire	Horton-cum-Studley		★★★	Studley Priory, tel. Stanton St John (086735) 203
	Milton, Gt	⊛⊛	★★★	Le Manoir aux Quat' Saisons (9m SE of Oxford, follow signs to Wallingford from junc A40/A329 (M40 junc 7) then 2nd turning right), tel. (08446) 8881
Shropshire	Oswestry		★★	Sweeny Hall, Morda (1m S on A483), tel. (0691) 652450
	Worfield		★★	Old Vicarage, tel. (07464) 498
Somerset	Dulverton		★★★	Carnarvon Arms, Brushford (2m S on B3222), tel. (0398) 23302
			★★	Ashwick House (3m NW off B3223), tel. (0398) 23868
			★★	Three Acres Captain's Country Brushford, tel. (0398) 23426
	Evercreech		★★	Maesmoor Glen, Shapway Ln, tel. (0749) 830369
	Holford		★★	Alfoxton Park, tel. (027874) 211
			★★	Combe House, tel. (027874) 382
	Minehead		★★	Woodcombe Lodge, Bratton Ln, tel. (0643) 2789
	Shapwick		★★	Shapwick House, Monks Dr, tel. Ashcott (0458) 210321
	Shipham		★★	Daneswood House, Cuck Hill, tel. Winscombe (093484) 3145
	Simonsbath		★★	Simonsbath House, tel. Exford (064383) 259
	Ston Easton	⊛	★★★	Ston Easton Park, tel. Chewton Mendip (076121) 631
	Wheddon Cross		★★	Raleigh Manor, tel. Timberscombe (064384) 484
	Wincanton		★★	Holbrook House, Castle Cary Rd, Holbrook, tel. (0963) 32377
	Withypool		★	Westerclose Country House, tel. Exford (064383) 302
Staffordshire	Rangemore		★★	Needwood Manor, tel. Burton-on-Trent (0283) 712932
Suffolk	Brome		★★	Oaksmere, tel. Eye (0379) 870326
	Woodbridge		★★★	Seckford Hall, tel. (03943) 5678
Surrey	Bagshot		★★★★	Pennyhill Park, College Rd, tel. (0276) 71774
	Farnham		★★	Trevena House, Alton Rd, tel. (0252) 716908
Sussex, East	Battle		★★★	Netherfield Place, Netherfield (3m NW B2096), tel. (04246) 4455
	Rushlake Green		★★★	Priory Country House, tel. (0435) 830553
	Stone Cross		★★★	Glyndley Manor, Hailsham Rd (2m NW of B2104), tel. Eastbourne (0323) 843737
	Wadhurst		★★	Spindlewood, Wallcrouch, tel. Ticehurst (0580) 200430
Sussex, West	Arundel		★	Burpham Country, Old Down, Burpham (3m NE off A27), tel. (0903) 882160

Gravetye Manor, East Grinstead, W Sussex

Sussex, West (contd.)	Climping	★★★	Bailiffscourt, tel. Littlehampton (0903) 723511
	Cuckfield	★★	Hilton Park, tel. Haywards Heath (0444) 454555
	East Grinstead	❀ ★★★	Gravetye Manor (3m SW off unclass rd joining B2110 & B2028), tel. Sharpthorne (0342) 810567
	Thakeham	❀ ★★★	Abingworth Hall, tel. West Chiltington (07983) 3636
Warwickshire	Billesley	❀ ★★★	Billesley Manor, tel. Stratford-upon-Avon (0789) 763737
	Ettington	❀ ★★	Chase Country House, Banbury Rd, tel. Stratford-upon-Avon (0789) 740000
	Leamington Spa (Royal)	❀❀ ★★★	Mallory Court, Harbury Ln, Bishop's Tachbrook (2m S off A454), tel. (0926) 30214
	Rugby	★★★	Clifton Court, Lilbourne Rd, Clifton-upon-Dunsmore, tel. (0788) 65033
	Wishaw	★★★	Moxhull Hall, Holly Ln, tel. 021-329 2056
Wiltshire	Castle Combe	★★★	Manor House, tel. (0249) 782206
	Limpley Stoke	★★★	Cliffe, tel. (022122) 3226
	Malmesbury	★★★	Whatley Manor, Easton Grey, tel. (06662) 2888
	Warminster	❀ ★★★	Bishopstrow House, Boreham Rd (2m SE A36), tel. (0985) 212312
Yorkshire, North	Arncliffe	★★	Amerdale House, tel. (075677) 250
	Ayton, Gt	❀ ★★★	Ayton Hall, Low Green, tel. Middlesborough (0642) 723595
	Crathorne	★★★★	Crathorne Hall, tel. Stokesley (0642) 700398
	Hackness	★★★	Hackness Grange, tel. Scarborough (0723) 369966
	Kirkby Fleetham	★★★	Kirkby Fleetham Hall, tel. Northallerton (0609) 748226
	Lastingham	★★	Lastingham Grange, tel. (07515) 345
	Markington	★★★	Hob Green, tel. Harrogate (0423) 770031
	Masham	★★	Jervaulx Hall, tel. Bedale (0677) 60235
	Monk Fryston	★★★	Monk Fryston Hall, tel. South Milford (0977) 682369
	Northallerton	★★★	Solberge Hal, Newby Wiske (3¼m S off A167), tel. (0609) 779191
	Scarborough	★★	Wrea Head, Scalby (3m NW off A171), tel. (0723) 378211
	Whitwellon-the-Hill	★★★	Whitwell Hall, tel. (065381) 551
Yorkshire, West	Wentbridge	★★★	Wentbridge House, tel. Pontefract (0977) 620444

Channel Islands

Jersey	Rozel Bay	★★	Château la Chaire, Rozell Valley, tel. Jersey (0534) 63354
	St Saviour	❀ ★★★	Longueville Manor (off St Helier/Grouville Rd A3), tel. Jersey (0534) 25501

Wales

Dyfed	Aberystwyth	★★★	Conrah, Chancery, Ffosrhydygaled, tel. (0970) 617941
	Crugybar	★★	Glanrannell Park, tel. Talley (05583) 230
	Eglwysfach	★★★	Ynyshir Hall, tel. Glandyfi (065474) 209
	Lamphey	★★★	Court, tel. (0646) 672273
	Llechryd	★★★	Castell Malgwyn (½m S unclass towards Boncath), tel. (023987) 382
	St David's	★★★	Warpool Court, tel. (0437) 720300
Gwynedd	Aberdovey	★★★	Plas Penhelig, tel. (065472) 676
	Abersoch	⊛ ★★★	Porth Tocyn, Bwlch Tocyn, tel. (075881) 2966
	Barmouth	★★	Plas Mynach Castle, Llanaber Rd, tel. (0341) 280252
	Beddgelert	★	Bryn Eglwys, tel. (076686) 210
	Criccieth	★★★	Bron Eifion, tel. (076671) 2385
		★★	Parciau Mawr, High St, tel. (076671) 2368
	Dolwyddelan	★★★	Plas Hall, Pont-y-Pant, tel. (06906) 206
	Llanbedr	★★	Cae Nest Hall, tel. (034123) 349
	Llandderfel	★★★	Palé Hall, tel. (06783) 285
	Llandudno	★★★	Bodysgallen Hall (off B5115), tel. Deganwy (0492) 84466
	Llanrwst	★★★	Gwesty-Plas Maenan, Maenan (3m N), tel. Dolgarrog (049269) 232
	Pennal	★★	Llugwy Hall (1m E on A483), tel. (065475) 228
	Rowen	★	Tir-y-Coed, tel. Tyn y groes (049267) 219
	Talsarnau	★★	Maes y Neuadd (2m SE on unclass rd off B4573), tel. Harlech (0766) 780200
Powys	Builth Wells	★★	Caer Beris Manor, Garth Rd, tel. (0982) 552601
	Crickhowell	★★	Gliffaes, tel. Bwlch (0874) 730371
	Llanfyllin	★★	Bodfach Hall, tel. (069184) 272
	Llangammarch Wells	★★★	Lake, tel. (05912) 202

Scotland

Borders	Chirnside	★★	Chirnside Country House, tel. (089081) 219
	Dryburgh	★★★	Dryburgh Abbey, Newton St Boswells, tel. St Boswells (0835) 22261
	Ettrick Bridge	★★	Ettrickshaws (1m W of B7009), tel. (0750) 52229
	Greenlaw	★★	Purves Hall (4m SE off A697), tel. Leitholm (089084) 558
	Kelso	★★★	Sunlaws House, Heiton (2m SW A698), tel. Roxburgh (05735) 331
	Peebles	★★	Cringletie House, tel. Eddleston (07213) 233
		★★	Venlaw Castle, Edinburgh Rd, tel. (0721) 20384
	St Boswells	★★★	Dryburgh Abbey, Newton St Boswells, tel. (0835) 22261
	Walkerburn	★★	Tweed Valley, Galashiels Rd, tel. (089687) 220
Central	Callander	★★★	Roman Camp, tel. (0877) 30003
	Dunblane	⊛ ★★★	Cromlix House, Kinbuck (3m NE B8033), tel. (0786) 822125
Dumfries &	Auchencairn	★★	Balcary Bay, tel. (055664) 217
Galloway	Borgue	★★	Senwick House, Brighouse Bay, tel. (05577) 236
	Colvend	★★	Clonyard House, tel. Rockcliffe (055663) 372
	Crossmichael	★★	Culgruff House, tel. (055667) 230
	Newton Stewart	⊛ ★★★	Kirroughtree, Minnigaff, tel. (0671) 2141
	Portpatrick	⊛ ★★	Knockinaam Lodge (2m S on unclass rd), tel. (077681) 471
	Port William	★★★	Corsemalzie House, tel. Mochrum (098886) 254
	Rockcliffe	★★★	Baron's Craig, tel. (055663) 225
	Ruthwell	★	Kirklands (1m E of Clarencefield off B724), tel. Clarencefield (038787) 284
Fife	Letham	★★★	Fernie Castle, tel. (033781) 381

Grampian	Banchory	★★★	Banchory Lodge, tel. (03302) 2625
		★★★	Raemoir, tel. (03302) 4884
	Huntly	★★★	Castle, tel. (0466) 2696
	Kildrummy	⊛ ★★★	Kildrummy Castle, tel. (03365) 288
	Rothes	★★★	Rothes Glen, tel. (03403) 254
Highland	Achnasheen	★★	Ledgowan Lodge, tel. (044588) 252
	Arisaig	⊛ ★★★	Arisaig House, Beasdale (3m E A830), tel. (06875) 622
	Drumnadrochit	★★	Polmaily House, Milton, tel. (04562) 343
	Dulnain Bridge	⊛ ★★	Muckrach Lodge, tel. (047985) 257
	Fort William	⊛⊛★★★★	Inverlochy Castle (3m NE A82), tel. (0397) 2177
	Glenborrodale	★★	Glenborrodale Castle, Acharacle, tel. (09724) 266
	Invergarry	★★	Glengarry Castle, tel. (08093) 254
	Inverness	★★★★	Culloden House, Culloden (2m E off A96), tel. (0463) 790461
		⊛ ★★	Dunain Park, tel. (0463) 230512
	Isle Ornsay (Isle of Skye)	⊛ ★★	Kinlock Lodge, tel. (04713) 214
	Kentallen	⊛ ★★	Ardsheal House, tel. Duror (063174) 227
	Leckmelm	★	Tir Aluinn, tel. Ullapool (0854) 2074
	Muir of Ord	★★	Ord House, tel. (0463) 870492
	Nairn	★★★★	Newton, Inverness Rd, tel. (0667) 53144
	Skeabost Bridge (Isle of Skye)	★★★	Skeabost House, tel. (047032) 202
	Torridon	★★	Loch Torridon, tel. (044587) 242
	Whitebridge	⊛ ★★	Knockie Lodge, tel. Gorthleck (04563) 276
Lothian	Bonnyrigg	★★★★	Dalhousie Castle, tel. Gorebridge (0875) 20153
	Gullane	⊛ ★★★	Greywalls, Duncar Rd, tel. (0620) 842144
	Uphall	★★★	Houston House, tel. Broxburn (0506) 853831
Shetland	Brae	★★★	Busta House, tel. (080622) 506
Strathclyde	Eriska	★★★	Isle of Eriska, tel. Ledaig (063172) 371
	Kilchrenan	⊛ ★★★	Ardanaiseig, tel. (08663) 333
		★★★	Taychreggan, Lochaweside
	Langbank	⊛ ★★★	Gleddoch House, tel. (047554) 711
	Skelmorlie	★★★	Manor Park, tel. Wemyss Bay (0475) 520832
	Stewarton	⊛ ★★★	Chapeltoun House, tel. (0560) 82696
Tayside	Alyth	★★	Lands of Loyal, Loyal Rd, tel. (08283) 2481
	Auchterhouse	⊛ ★★★	Old Mansion House, tel. (082626) 366
	Blairgowrie	★★	Altamount House, Coupar Angus Rd, tel. (0250) 3512
		⊛ ★★	Kinloch House (2m W A923), tel. Essendy (025084) 237
	Cleish	★★	Nivingston House, tel. Cleish Hills (05775) 216
	Clova	★★	Rottal Lodge, Glen Cova (3m SE on B955 on East bank of river), tel. (05755) 224
	Dunkeld	★★★	Dunkeld House, tel. (03502) 771
	Glenshee (Spital of)	★★	Dalmunzie, tel. (025085) 224
	Kinclaven	★★★	Ballathie House, tel. Meikleour (025083) 268
	Meigle	★★	Kings of Kinloch, tel. (08284) 273
	Perth	⊛ ★★★	Balcraig House, Scone (2¾m NE off A94 towards New Scone), tel. (0738) 51123
	Pitlochry	★★	Pine Trees, Strathview Ter, tel. (0796) 2121
	Strathtummel	★★	Port-an-Eilean, tel. Tummel Bridge (08824) 233
Western Isles	Scarista (Isle of Harris)	⊛ ★★	Scarista House, tel. (085985) 238

Guest-houses

ABERAERON, Dyfed
See Pennant

ABERDARE, Mid Glam
Cae-Coed Private Hotel, Craig St, off Monk St,
tel. (0685) 871190

ABERDEEN, Grampian
Alelanro, 272 Holburn St, tel. (0224) 575601
Broomfield Private Hotel, 15 Balmoral Place,
tel. (0224) 588758
Klibreck, 410 Great Western Rd, tel. (0224) 36115
(due to change to 316115)
Mannofield Hotel, 447 Great Western Rd,
tel. (0224) 35888 (due to change to 315888)
Open Hearth, 349 Holburn St,
tel. (0224) 596888
Strathboyne, 26 Abergeldie Ter,
tel. (0224) 593400
Tower Hotel, 36 Fonthill Rd, tel. (0224) 584050
Western, 193 Great Western Rd, tel. (0224) 56919

ABERDOVEY, Gwynedd
Cartref, tel. (065472) 273

ABERFELDY, Tayside
Balnearn Private Hotel, Crieff Rd, tel. (0887) 431
Caber-Feidh, 66 Dunkeld St, tel. (0887) 23042
Guinach House, Urlar Rd, tel. (0887) 20251
Nessbank House, Crieff Rd, tel. (0887) 20214

ABERGAVENNY, Gwent
Belchamps, 1 Holywell Rd (Guestacomm),
tel. (0873) 3204
Llanwenarth House, Govilon,
tel. Gilwern (0873) 830289
Park, 36 Hereford Rd, tel. (0873) 3715

ABERPORTH, Dyfed
Ffynonwen Country, tel. (0239) 810312

ABERSOCH, Gwynedd
Llysfor, tel. (075881) 2248

ABERYSTWYTH, Dyfed
Glan-Aber Hotel, 7–8 Union St,
tel. (0970) 617610
Glyn-Garth, South Rd, tel. (0970) 615050
Llety-Gwyn, Llanbadarn Fawr, (Im E A44),
tel. (0970) 3965
Shangrila, 36 Portland St, tel. (0970) 617659
Swn-y-Don, 40–42 North Pde, tel. (0970) 612647
Windsor Private Hotel, 41 Queen's Rd,
tel. (0970) 612134

ALDERSHOT, Hants
Cedar Court Hotel, Eggars Hill,
tel. (0252) 20931
Glencoe Hotel, 4 Eggars Hill, tel. (0252) 20801

ALNMOUTH, Northumb
Marine House Private Hotel, 1 Marine Drive,
tel. Alnwick (0665) 830349

ALNWICK, Northumb
Aln House, South Rd, tel. (0665) 602265
Aydon House, South Rd, tel. (0665) 602218
Bondgate House Hotel, Bondgate Without,
tel. (0665) 602025
Hope Rise, The Dunterns, tel. (0665) 602930

ALTRINCHAM, Gt Manchester
Bollin Hotel, 58 Manchester Rd,
tel. 061–928 2390

AMBLESIDE, Cumbria
Borrans Park Hotel, Borrans Rd,
tel. (0966) 33454
Chapel House Hotel, Kirkstone Rd,
tel. (0966) 33143
Compston House, Compston Rd,
tel. (0966) 32305
Gables Private Hotel, Church Walk,
Compston Rd, tel. (0966) 33272

Gale Crescent, Lower Gale, tel. (0966) 32284
Hillsdale Private Hotel, Church St,
tel. (0966) 33174
Horseshoe, Rothay Rd, tel. (0966) 32000
Oaklands Country House Hotel, Millans Park,
tel. (0966) 32525
Park House, Compston Rd, tel. (0966) 33542
Romney Hotel, Waterhead, tel. (0966) 32219
Rothay Garth Hotel, Rothay Rd,
tel. (0966) 32217
Smallwood Hotel, Compston Rd,
tel. (0966) 32330

ANDOVERSFORD, Glos
Old Cold Comfort, Dowdeswell (Im W A436),
tel. (0242) 820349

ANNAN, Dumfries and Galloway
Ravenswood, St John's Rd, tel. (04612) 2158

APPLEBY-IN-WESTMORLAND, Cumbria
Bongate House, tel. (0930) 51245
Howgill House, tel. (0930) 51574

ARBROATH, Tayside
Kingsley, 29 Market Gate, tel. (0241) 73933

ARDGAY, Highland
Croit Mairi, Kincardine Hill, tel. (08632) 504

ARDROSSAN, Strathclyde
Ellwood House, 6 Arran Place,
tel. (0294) 61130

ARINAGOUR
Coll Island of, Strathclyde
Details are listed under **COLL (Island of)**

ARNSIDE, Cumbria
Grosvenor Private Hotel, The Promenade,
tel. (0524) 761666

ARRAN, ISLE OF, Strathclyde
See Corrie, Lamlash, Lochranza and Sannox

ARRETON, Isle of Wight
Stickworth Hall, tel. (098377) 233

ARUNDEL, W Sussex
Arden, 4 Queens Ln, tel. (0903) 882544
Bridge House, 18 Queens St, tel. (0903) 882142

ASCOT, Berks
Highclere House, Kings Rd, Sunninghill,
tel. (0990) 25220

ASHBURTON, Devon
Gages Mill, Buckfastleigh Rd, tel. (0364) 52391

ASHFORD, Kent
Croft Hotel, Canterbury Rd, Kennington,
tel. (0233) 22140
Downsview, Willesborough Rd, Kennington,
tel. (0233) 21953

ASHURST, Hants
Barn, 112 Lyndhurst Rd, tel. (042129) 2531

ATHERSTONE, Warwicks
Chapel House, Friars Gate, tel. (08277) 66238

AVIEMORE, Highland
Aviemore Chalets Motel, Aviemore Centre,
tel. (0479) 810624
Corrour House, Inverdruie, tel. (0479) 810220
Craiglea, Grampian Rd, tel. (0479) 810210
Ravenscraig, tel. (0479) 810278

AYR, Strathclyde
Clifton Hotel, 19 Miller Rd, tel. (0292) 264521
Parkhouse, 1A Ballantine Dr, tel. (0292) 264151
Windsor Hotel, 6 Alloway Pl, tel. (0292) 264689

BACUP, Lancs
Burwood House Hotel, Todmorden Rd,
tel. Rochdale (0706) 873466

BAKEWELL, Derbys
Cliffe House Hotel, Monsal Head,
tel. Gt Longstone (062987) 376

Bala Lake

Merlin House Country Hotel, Ashford Lane, Monsal Head,
tel. Great Longstone (062987) 475

BALA, Gwynedd
Frondderw, tel. (0678) 520301
Plas Teg, Tegid St, tel. (0678) 520268

BALDOCK, Herts
Butterfield House Hotel, Hitchin St,
tel. (0462) 892701

BALLACHULISH, Highland
Lyn-Leven, White St, tel. (08552) 392

BALLATER, Grampian
Moorside, Braemar Rd, tel. (0338) 55492
Morvada, tel. (0338) 55501
Netherley, 2 Netherley Pl, tel. (0338) 55792

BALMAHA, Central
Arrochoile, tel. (036087) 231

BAMPTON, Devon
Bridge House Hotel, Luke St,
tel. (0398) 31298
Courtyard Hotel, tel. (0398) 31536

BAMPTON, Oxon
Bampton House, Bushey Row,
tel. Bampton Castle (0993) 850135

BANBURY, Oxon
Lismore Hotel & Restaurant, 61 Oxford Rd,
tel. (0295) 62105
Mill House, North Newington (3m W off B3035),
tel. Wroxton St Mary (029573) 212
Tredis, 15 Broughton Rd,
tel. (0295) 4632

BANFF, Grampian
Carmelite House Hotel, Low St,
tel. (02612) 2152
Ellerslie, 45 Low St, tel. (02612) 5888

BARMOUTH, Gwynedd
Cranbourne, 9 Marine Pde, tel. (0341) 280202
Lawrenny Lodge, tel. (0341) 28046
Morwendon, Llanaber, tel. (0341) 280566

BARNSTAPLE, Devon
Cresta, 26 Sticklepath Hill, tel. (0271) 74022
Northcliff, Hele Manor, 8 Rhododendron Avenue
off A39), tel. (0271) 42524
Yeo Dale Hotel, Pilton Bridge,
tel. (0271) 42954

BARROW-IN-FURNESS, Cumbria
Barrie House Hotel, 179 Abbey Rd,
tel. (0229) 25507
Lisdoonie Private Hotel, Abbey Rd,
tel. (0229) 27312

BARRY, S Glam
Aberthaw House Hotel, Porthkerry Rd,
tel. (0446) 737314
Maytree, 9 The Parade, tel. (0446) 734075
Sheridan, 11 The Parade, tel. (0446) 738488

BARTON-ON-SEA, Hants
Cliff House Hotel, Marine Drive West,
tel. New Milton (0425) 619333
Gainsborough Hotel, 39 Marine Drive East,
tel. New Milton (0425) 610541
Old Coastguard Hotel, 53 Marine Drive East,
tel. New Milton (0425) 612987

BASINGSTOKE, Hants
See Sherfield-on-Loddon

BASSENTHWAITE, Cumbria
Link House Hotel,
tel. Bassenthwaite Lake (059681) 291
Ravenstone Hotel,
tel. Bassenthwaite Lake (059681)240

BATH, Avon
Arden Hotel, 73 Great Pulteney St,
tel. (0225) 66601
Arney, 99 Wells Rd, tel. Bath (0225) 310020
Ashley Villa Hotel, 26 Newbridge Rd,
tel. (0225) 21683
Carfax Hotel, Great Pulteney St, tel. (0225) 62089
Charnwood House, 51 Upper Oldfield Park,
tel. (0225) 334937
Dorset Villa, 14 Newbridge Rd, tel. (0225) 25975
Edgar Hotel, 64 Great Pulteney St,
tel. (0225) 20619
Gainsborough Hotel, Weston Ln,
tel. (0225) 311380
Glenbeigh Hotel, 1 Upper Oldfield Park,
tel. (0225) 26336
Grove Lodge, 11 Lambridge, London Rd,
tel. (0225) 310860
Highways House, 143 Wells Rd,
tel. (0225) 21238
Kennard Hotel, 11 Henrietta St,
tel. (0225) 310472
Leighton House, 139 Wells Rd,
tel. (0225) 314769
Lynwood, 6 Pulteney Gdns, tel. (0225) 26410
Millers Hotel, 69 Great Pulteney St,
tel. (0225) 65798
Oldfields, 102 Wells Rd, tel. (0225) 31794
Orchard House Hotel, Warminster Rd (A36),
Bathampton, tel. (0225) 6615
Oxford Private Hotel, 5 Oxford Row,
Lansdown Rd, tel. (0225) 314039
Paradise House Hotel, Holloway,
tel. (0225) 317723
Hotel St Clair, 1 Crescent Gdns, Upper Bristol Rd,
tel. (0225) 25543
Tacoma, 159 Newbridge Hill, tel. (0225) 310197
Villa Magdala Private Hotel, Henrietta Rd,
tel. (0225) 66329
Waltons, 17 Crescent Gdns, tel. (0225) 26528
Wentworth House Hotel, 106 Bloomfield Rd,
tel. (0225) 310460

BEAMINSTER, Dorset
Hams Plot, Bridport Rd, tel. (0308) 862979

BEAULY, Highland
Chrialdon, Station Rd, tel. (0463) 782336
Heathmount, Station Rd, tel. (0463) 782411

BEAUMARIS, Gwynedd
Sea View, 10 West End, tel. (0248) 810384

BECCLES, Suffolk
Riverview House, Ballygate, tel. (0502) 713519

BEDDGELERT, Gwynedd
Sygyn Fawr Country House Hotel,
tel. (076686) 258

BEDFORD, Beds
Clarendon House Hotel, 25–27 Ampthill Rd,
tel. (0234) 66054
Hurst House Hotel, 178 Hurst Grove,
tel. (0234) 40791
Kimbolton Hotel, 78 Clapham Rd,
tel. (0234) 54854

BEER, Devon
Bay View, Fore St,
tel. Seaton (2097) 20489

BEESTON, Notts
Brackley House Hotel, 31 Elm Av,
tel. Nottingham (0602) 251787

BELL BUSK, N Yorks
Tudor, tel. Airton (07293) 301

BEPTON, nr Midhurst, W Sussex
Park House Hotel,
tel. Midhurst (070381) 2880

BERRYNARBOR, Devon
Lodge Country House,
tel. Combe Martin (027188) 3246

BETWSGARMON, Gwynedd
Bryn Gloch Farm,
tel. Waunfawr (028685) 216

BETWS-Y-COED, Gwynedd
Bryn Llewelyn, Holyhead Rd (A5),
tel. (06902) 601
Glenwood, tel. (06902) 508
Hafan, tel. (06902) 233
Henllys (Old Court) Hotel, tel. (06902) 534
Mount Garmon Hotel, tel. (06902) 335

BEXHILL-ON-SEA, E Sussex
Chantry Close Hotel, 13 Hastings Rd,
tel. (0424) 222024

BICKINGTON (nr Ashburton), Devon
Privet Cottage, tel. (062682) 319

BICKLEIGH (nr Tiverton), Devon
Bickleigh Cottage, tel. (08845) 230

BIDEFORD, Devon
Edelweiss, 2 Buttgarden St, tel. (02372) 72676
Kumba, Chudleigh Rd, East-the-Water,
tel. (02372) 72133
Mount Private Hotel, Northdown Rd,
tel. (02372) 73748
Sonnenheim Private Hotel, Heywood Rd,
Northam, tel. (02372) 74989
Tadworthy House Hotel, Tadworthy Rd, Northam
(2m N off A386), tel. (02372) 74721

BINGLEY, W Yorks
Hall Bank Private Hotel, Beck Ln,
tel. Bradford (0274) 565296

BIRMINGHAM, W Midlands
Alexander, 44 Banbury Rd, tel. 021–475 4341
Bridge House Hotel, 49 Sherbourne Rd, Acocks
Green, tel. 021–706 5900
Cape Race Hotel, 929 Chester Rd, Erdington,
tel. 021–373 3085
Hagley Court Hotel, 229 Hagley Rd, Edgbaston,
tel. 021–454 6514
Heath Lodge Hotel, Coleshill Rd, Marston Gn,
tel. 021–779 2218
Hurstwood Hotel, 775–777 Chester Rd,
Erdington, tel. 021–382 8212
Kerry House Hotel, 946 Warwick Rd, Acocks
Green, tel. 021–707 0316
Linden Lodge Hotel, 79 Sutton Rd, Erdington,
tel. 021–382 5992
Lyndhurst Hotel, 135 Kingsbury Rd, Erdington,
tel. 021–373 5695
Rollason Wood Hotel, 130 Wood End Rd,
Erdington, tel. 021–373 1230
Tr-Star Hotel, Coventry Rd, Elmdon,
tel. 021–779 2233
Welcome House, 1641 Coventry Rd, Yardley,
tel. 021–707 3232
Wentsbury Hotel, 21 Serpentine Rd, Selly Park,
tel. 021–472 1258
Wentworth Hotel, 103 Wentworth Rd, Harborne,
tel. 021–427 2839
Westbourne Lodge, 27–29 Fountain Rd,
Edgbaston, tel. 021–429 1003

BISHOP'S CLEEVE, Glos
Old Manor House, 43 Station Rd,
tel. (024267) 4127

BISHOPTON, W Glamorgan
See also Langland Bay and Mumbles
Winston Hotel, 11 Church Ln, Bishopton Valley,
tel. (044128) 2074

BLACKPOOL, Lancs
Arandora Star Private Hotel, 559 New South
Prom, tel. (0253) 41528
Arosa Hotel, 18–20 Empress Drive,
tel. (0253) 52555
Ashcroft Private Hotel, 42 King Edward Av,
tel. (0253) 51538
Berwick Private Hotel, 23 King Edward Av,
tel. (0253) 51496
Brabyns Hotel, 1–3 Shaftesbury Av,
tel. (0253) 52163
Burlees Hotel, 40 Knowle Av,
tel. (0253) 54535
Cliftonville Hotel, 14 Empress Dr, Northshore,
tel. (0253) 51052
Denely Private Hotel, 15 King Edward Avenue,
tel. (0253) 52757
Derwent Private Hotel, 8 Gynn Av,
tel. (0253) 55194
Garville Hotel, 3 Beaufort Avenue, Bispham
(2m N), tel. (0253) 51004
Lynstead Private Hotel, 40 King Edward Avenue,
tel. (0253) 51050
Mavern Private Hotel, 238 Queen's Prom,
Bispham (1m N on A584), tel. (0253) 51409
Motel Mimosa, 24A Lonsdale Rd,
tel. (0253) 41906
New Heathcot Private Hotel, 270 Queens Prom,
tel. (0253) 52083
North Mount Private Hotel, 22 King Edward Av,
tel. (0253) 55937
Sunnycliff, 98 Queen's Prom, Northshore,
tel. (0253) 51155
Sunray Private Hotel, 42 Knowle Avenue,
Queen's Prom, tel. (0253) 51937
Surrey House Hotel, 9 Northumberland Avenue,
tel. (0253) 51743

BLAENAU FFESTINIOG, Gwynedd
Don, 147 High St, tel. (0766) 830403

BLAIRGOWRIE, Tayside
Glensheiling, Hatton Rd, Rattray,
tel. (0250) 4605
Rosebank House, Balmoral Rd, tel. (0250) 2912

BLEADNEY, Somerset
Threeway Country House Hotel & Restaurant,
tel. Wells (0749) 78870

BLUE ANCHOR, Somerset
Camelot, tel. Dunster (064382) 348

BOAT OF GARTEN, Highland
Moorfield House Hotel, Deshar Rd,
tel. (047983) 646

BOGNOR REGIS, W Sussex
Lansdowne Hotel, 55–57 West St,
tel. (0243) 865552

BOLNEY, W Sussex
Bolney Grange House Hotel,
tel. Burgess Hill (04446) 45164

BONSALL, Derbys
Sycamore, 76 High St, Town Head,
tel. Wirksworth (062982) 3903
Town Head Farmhouse, 70 High St,
tel. Wirksworth (062982) 3762

BOOT, Cumbria
Brook House, tel. (09403) 288

BORROWDALE, Cumbria
Greenbank Country, tel. (059684) 215
Langstrath Hotel, tel. (059684) 239

BOSCASTLE, Cornwall
St Christophers Country House Hotel, High St
(Guestaccom), tel. (08405) 412

BOSHAM, W Sussex
White Barn, Crede Ln, tel. (0243) 573113

BOSWINGER, Cornwall
Van Ruan House, tel. Mevagissey (0726) 842425

BOUGHTON MONCHELSEA, Kent
Tanyard, Wierton, tel. Maidstone (0622) 44705

BOURNEMOUTH AND BOSCOMBE, Dorset
For additional guest-houses see Christchurch
and Poole
Alcombe Private Hotel, 37 Sea Rd, Boscombe,
tel. (0202) 36206
Alum Bay Hotel, 19 Burnaby Rd, Alum Chine,
tel. (0202) 761034
Alumcliff Hotel, 121 Alumhurst Rd, Alum Chine,
tel. (0202) 764777
Alum Grange Hotel, 1 Burnaby Rd, Alum Chine,
tel. (0202) 761195
Anfield Private Hotel, 12 Bradbourne Rd,
tel. (0202) 290749
Arlington Hotel, Exeter Park Rd,
tel. (0202) 22879
Bay Tree Hotel, 17 Burnaby Rd, Alum Chine,
tel. (0202) 763807
Blinkbonnie Heights Hotel, 26 Clifton Rd,
Southbourne, tel. (0202) 426512
Blue Cedars Hotel, Portchester Pl,
tel. (0202) 26893
Borodale Hotel, 10 St Johns Rd, Boscombe,
tel. (0202) 35285
Bracken Lodge Private Hotel, 5 Bracken Rd,
Southbourne, tel. (0202) 428777
Braemar Private Hotel, 30 Glen Rd, Boscombe,
tel. (0202) 36054
Hotel Bristol, Terrace Rd, tel. (0202) 27007
Britannia Hotel, 40 Christchurch Rd,
tel. (0202) 26700
Brun-Lea Hotel, 94 Southbourne Rd,
tel. (0202) 425956
Bursledon Hotel, 34 Gervis Rd, tel. (0202) 24622
Carisbrooke Hotel, 42 Tregonwell Rd,
tel. (0202) 290432
Charles Taylor Hotel, Knyveton Gardens, 40–44
Frances Rd, tel. (0202) 22695
Chawson House Hotel, 72 Lansdowne Rd North,
tel. (0202) 22317
Chequers Hotel, 17 West Cliff Rd,
tel. (0202) 23900
Chilterns Hotel, 44 Westby Rd, Boscombe,
tel. (0202) 36539
Chineside Private Hotel, 15 Studland Rd, Alum
Chine, tel. (0202) 761206
Cintra Hotel, 10–12 Florence Rd, Boscombe,
tel. (0202) 36103
Cliff House Hotel, 113 Alumhurst Rd,
Westbourne, tel. (0202) 763003
Clifton Court Hotel, 30 Clifton Rd,
tel. (0202) 427753
Cransley Private Hotel, 11 Knyveton Rd, East
Cliff, tel. (0202) 290067
Crescent Grange Hotel, 6–8 Crescent Grange Rd,
The Triangle, tel. (0202) 26959
Cresta Court Hotel, 3 Crescent Rd,
tel. (0202) 25217
Croham Hurst Hotel, 9 Durley Rd, Boscombe,
tel. (0202) 22353
Crossroads Hotel, 88 Belle Vue Rd, Southbourne,
tel. (0202) 426307
Dean Court Hotel, 4 Frances Rd,
tel. (0202) 28165
Derwent House, 36 Hamilton Rd, Boscombe,
tel. (0202) 309102
Dorset Westbury Hotel, 62 Lansdowne Rd,
tel. (0202) 21811
Earlham Lodge, 91 Alumhurst Rd, Alum Chine,
tel. (0202) 761943

East Cliff Cottage Private Hotel, 57 Grove Rd,
East Cliff, tel. (0202) 22788
Egerton House Private Hotel, 385 Holdenhurst
Rd, Queens Pk, tel. (0202) 34024
Eglan Court Hotel, 7 Knyveton Rd,
tel. (0202) 290093
Farlow Private Hotel, 13 Walpole Rd, Boscombe,
tel. (0202) 35865
Florida Hotel, 35 Boscombe Spa Rd,
tel. (0202) 34537
Freshfields Hotel, 55 Christchurch Rd,
tel. (0202) 34023
Gervis Court Hotel, 38 Gervis Rd,
tel. (0202) 26871
Golden Sands Hotel, 83 Alumhurst Rd,
tel. (0202) 763832
Gordons Hotel, 84 West Cliff Rd, Alum Chine,
tel. (0202) 765844
Grassmere, 5 Pine Avenue, Southbourne,
tel. (0202) 428660
Hamilton Hall Private Hotel, 1 Carysfort Rd,
Boscombe, tel. (0202) 35758
Hartford Court Hotel, 48 Christchurch Rd,
tel. (0202) 21712
Hawaiian Hotel, 4 Glen Rd, Boscombe,
tel. (0202) 33234
Heathcote Hotel, 2 Heathcote Rd, Boscombe,
tel. (0202) 36185
Heather Mount Hotel, 70 Landsdowne Rd,
tel. (0202) 24557
Highclere Hotel, 15 Burnaby Rd,
Alum Chine, tel. (0202) 761350
Highlin Private Hotel, 14 Knole Rd,
tel. (0202) 33758
High Trees Hotel, 3 Glenferness Av,
tel. (0202) 761380
Holmcroft Hotel, 5 Earle Rd, Alum Chine,
tel. (0202) 761289
Kensington Hotel, Durley Chine Rd, West Cliff,
tel. (0202) 27434
Kings Barton Hotel, 22 Hawkwood Rd,
Boscombe, tel. (0202) 37794
Kingsley Hotel, 20 Glen Rd, Boscombe,
tel. (0202) 38683
Langton Hall Hotel, 8 Durley Chine Rd, West Cliff,
tel. (0202) 25025
Linwood House Hotel, 11 Wilfred Rd,
tel. (0202) 37818
Mae-Mar Private Hotel, 91–93 West Hill Rd,
West Cliff, tel. (0202) 23167
Mariner's Hotel, 22 Clifton Rd, Southbourne,
tel. (0202) 420851
Mayfield, 46 Frances Rd,
tel. (0202) 21839
Monreith Hotel, Lower Gdns, 6 Exeter Park Rd,
tel. (0202) 290344
Mount Lodge Hotel, 19 Beaulieu Rd, Alum Chine,
tel. (0202) 761173
Mount Stuart Hotel, 31 Tregonwell Rd,
tel. (0202) 24639
Myrtle House, 41 Hawkwood Rd, Boscombe,
tel. (0202) 36579
Naseby-Nye Hotel, Byron Rd, Boscombe,
tel. (0202) 34079
Newfield Private Hotel, 29 Burnaby Rd, Alum
Chine, tel. (0202) 762724
Norland Private Hotel, 6 Westby Rd, Boscombe,
tel. (0202) 36729
Northover Private Hotel, 10 Earle Rd, Alum
Chine, tel. (0202) 767349
Oak Hall Private Hotel, 9 Wilfred Rd, Boscombe,
tel. (0202) 35062
Penmore Hotel, 17 Carysfort Rd, Boscombe,
tel. (0202) 35903
Pine Beach Hotel, 31 Boscombe Spa Rd,
Boscombe, tel. (0202) 35902
Ravenstone Hotel, 36 Burnaby Rd, Alum Chine,
tel. (0202) 761047
Hotel Restormel, Upper Terrace Rd,
tel. (0202) 25070

BOURNEMOUTH AND BOSCOMBE, Dorset (contd.)
St John's Lodge Hotel, 10 St Swithuns Rd, tel. (0202) 20677
St Wilfreds Private Hotel, 15 Walpole Rd, Boscombe, tel. (0202) 36189
Safari Hotel, 91 St Michaels Rd, West Cliff, tel. (0202) 290782
Sandelheath Hotel, 1 Knyveton Rd, East Cliff, tel. (0202) 25428
Sea-Dene, 10 Burnaby Rd, Alum Chine, tel. (0202) 761372
Sea Shells, 203–205 Holdenhurst Rd, tel. (0202) 292542
Sea View Court Hotel, 14 Boscombe Spa Rd, tel. (0202) 37197
Sherbourne Hotel, 6 Walpole Rd, Boscombe, tel. (0202) 36222
Silver Trees Hotel, 57 Wimborne Rd, tel. (0202) 26040
Hotel Sorrento, 16 Owls Rd, Boscombe, tel. (0202) 34019
Hotel Sorrento, 8 Studland Rd, Alum Chine, Westbourne, tel. (0202) 762116
Stratford Hotel, 20 Grand Avenue, Southbourne, tel. (0202) 424726
Tower House Hotel, West Cliff Gdns, tel. (0202) 290742
Tree Tops Hotel, 16 Grand Av, West Southbourne, tel. (0202) 426933
Trent Private Hotel, 12 Studland Rd, tel. (0202) 761088
Tudor Grange Hotel, 31 Gervis Rd, tel. (0202) 291472
Valberg Hotel, 1A Wollstonecraft Rd, Boscombe, tel. (0202) 34644
Vine, 22 Southern Rd, Southbourne, tel. (0202) 428309
Waldale, 37–39 Boscombe Spa Rd, tel. (0202) 37744
Wenmaur House Hotel, 14 Carysfort Rd, Boscombe, tel. (0202) 35081
West Dene Private Hotel, 117 Alumhurst Rd, Alum Chine, tel. (0202) 764843
West Leigh, 26 West Hill Rd, tel. (0202) 292195
Whitley Court Hotel, West Cliff Gdns, tel. (0202) 21302
Woodford Court Hotel, 19–21 Studland Rd, Alum Chine, tel. (0202) 764907
Wood Lodge hotel, 10 Manor Rd, East Cliff, tel. (0202) 290891
Woodside Private Hotel, 29 Southern Rd, Southbourne, tel. (0202) 427213

BOWNESS-ON-WINDERMERE, Cumbria
Guest-houses are listed under Windermere

BRADFORD, W Yorks
Belvedere Hotel, 19 North Park Rd, Manningham, tel. (0274) 492559
Maple Hill, 23 Park Drive, Heaton, tel. (0274) 44061

BRAEMAR, Grampian
Callater Lodge Hotel, tel. (03383) 275

BRANSCOMBE, Devon
The Bulstone, tel. (029780) 446

BRAUNTON, Devon
Brookdale Hotel, 62 South St, tel. (0271) 812075

BRECONS, Powys
Beacons, 16 Bridge St, tel. (0874) 3339

BREDWARDINE, Heref & Worcs
Bredwardine Hall, tel. Moccas (09817) 596

BRIDGNORTH, Salop
Croft Hotel, St Mary's Street, tel. (07462) 2416

Severn Arms Hotel, Underhill St, tel. (07462) 4616

BRIDLINGTON, Humberside
Bay Ridge Hotel, Summerfield Rd, tel. (0262) 673425
Langdon Hotel, Pembroke Ter, tel. (0262) 673065
Shirley Private Hotel, 48 South Marine Drive, tel. (0262) 672539
Southdowne Hotel, South Marine Drive tel. (0262) 673270

BRIDPORT, Dorset
Britmead House, 154 West Bay Rd, Guestaccom, tel. (0308) 22941
Roundham House Hotel, West Bay Rd, tel. (0308) 22753

BRIGHTON & HOVE, E Sussex
Adelaide Hotel, 51 Regency Sq, tel. (0273) 205286
Ascott House, 21 New Steine, Marine Pde, tel. (0273) 688085
Cavalaire House, 34 Upper Rock Gdns, Kemptown, tel. (0273) 696899
Charlotte House, 9 Charlotte St, tel. (0273) 692849
Corner Lodge Hotel, 33 Wilbury Gdns, Hove, tel. (0273) 775931
Cornerways Private Hotel, 20 Caburn Rd, Hove, tel. (0273) 731882
Croft Hotel, 24 Palmeira Av, Hove, tel. (0273) 732860
Downlands Hotel, 19 Charlotte St, tel. (0273) 601203
Langham, 16 Charlotte St, tel. (0273) (0273) 682843
Marina House Hotel, 8 Charlotte St, tel. (0273) 605349
Melford Hall Hotel, 41 Marine Pde, tel. (0273) 681435
Prince Regent Hotel, 29 Regency Square, tel. (0273) 29962
Regency Hotel, 28 Regency Sq, tel. (0273) 202690
Rowland House, 21 St George's Ter, Kemptown, tel. (0273) 603639
Sutherland Hotel, 10 Regency Sq, tel. (0273) 27055
Tatler Hotel, 26 Holland Rd, tel. (0273) 736698
Trouville, 11 New Steine, Marine Pde, tel. (0273) 697384
Twenty One, 21 Charlotte St, Marine Pde, tel. (0273) 696450
Whitehaven Hotel, 24 Wilbury Rd, Hove, tel. (0273) 778355

BRISTOL, Avon
Alandale Hotel, Tyndall's Park Rd, Clifton, tel. (0272) 735407
Alcove, 508–510 Fishponds Rd, Fishponds, tel. (0272) 653886
Birkdale Hotel, 11 Ashgrove Rd, Redland, tel. (0272) 733635
Cavendish House Hotel, 18 Cavendish Rd, Henleaze, tel. (0272) 621017
Chesterfield Hotel, 3 Westbourne Place, Clifton, tel. (0272) 734606
Glenroy Hotel, 30 Victoria Sq, Clifton, tel. (0272) 739058
Oakdene Hotel, 45 Oakfield Rd, Clifton, tel. (0272) 735900
Oakfield Hotel, 52–54 Oakfield Rd, Clifton, tel. (0272) 735556
Pembroke Hotel, 13 Arlington Villas, Clifton, tel. (0272) 735550
Rodney Hotel, 4 Rodney Place, Clifton, tel. (0272) 735422
Seeleys Hotel, 19–27 St Paul's Rd, Clifton, tel. (0272) 738544

Brixham Harbour

Washington Hotel, 11–15 St Paul's Rd, Clifton, tel. (0272) 733980
Westbury Park Hotel, 37 Westbury Rd, Westbury-on-Trym, tel. (0272) 620465

BRIXHAM, Devon
Cottage Hotel, Mount Pleasant Rd, tel. (08045) 2123
Harbour View Hotel, King St, tel. (08045) 3052
Harbour Side, 63–65 Berry Head Rd, tel. (08045) 58899
Raddicombe Lodge, 105 Kingswear Rd, tel. (08045) 2125
Ranscambe House Hotel, Ranscambe Rd, tel. (08045) 2337
Sampford House, 57–59 King St, tel. (08045) 7761

BROADFORD, Isle of Skye, Highland
Hilton, tel. (04712) 322

BROAD HAVEN (nr Haverfordwest), Dyfed
Broad Haven Hotel, tel. (043783) 366

BROAD MARSTON, Heref and Worcs
Broad Marston Manor, tel. Stratford-upon-Avon (0789) 720252

BROADSTAIRS, Kent
Bay Tree Hotel, 12 Eastern Esp, tel. Thanet (0843) 62502
Corner Ways Hotel, 49–51 Westcliff Rd, tel. Thanet (0843) 61612
Dutch House Hotel, 30 North Foreland Rd, tel. Thanet (0843) 62824
East Horndon Private Hotel, 4 Eastern Esp, tel. Thanet (0843) 68306
Keston Court Hotel, 14 Ramsgate Rd, tel. Thanet (0843) 62401
Rothsay Private Hotel, 10 Pierremont Av, tel. Thanet (0843) 62646
St Augustines Hotel, 19 Granville Rd, tel. Thanet (0843) 65017
Seapoint Private Hotel, 76 Westcliff Rd, tel. (0843) 62269

BROADWAY, Heref & Worcs
Old Rectory, Church St, tel. Evesham (0386) 853729
Olive Branch, 78–80 High St, tel. (0386) 853440

BROMLEY, Gt London
Bromley Continental Hotel, 56 Plaistow Lane, tel. 01–464 2415

BRUTON, Somerset
Fryerning, Frome Rd, Burrowfield, tel. (0749) 2343

BUCKDEN, N. Yorks
Hartrigg House, tel. Kettlewell (075676) 246

BUCKFASTLEIGH, Devon
Black Rock, Buckfast Rd, Dart Bridge (at Buckfast 1m N), tel. (0364) 42343
Furzeleigh Mill, tel. (03644) 2245

BUDE, Cornwall
Atlantic Beach, 25 Downs View, tel. (0288) 3431
Cliff Hotel, Maer Down, Crooklets, tel. (0288) 3110
Kisauni, 4 Downs View, tel. (0288) 2653
Links View, 13 Morwenna Ter, tel. (0288) 2561
Pencarrol, 21 Downs View, tel. (0288) 2478
Surf Haven, 31 Downs View, tel. (0288) 2998
Sweeney's, 35 Downs View, tel. (0288) 2073
Wayfarer Hotel, 23 Downs View, tel. (0288) 2253
Wyvern House, 7 Downs View, tel. (0288) 2205

BUDLEIGH SALTERTON, Devon
Long Range Hotel, Vale's Rd, tel. (03954) 3321
Tidwell House Country Hotel, tel. (03954) 2444
Willowmead, 12 Little Knowle, tel. (03954) 3115

BURFORD, Oxon
Corner House Hotel, High St. tel. (099382) 3151

BURNSALL, N Yorks
Manor House, tel. (075672) 231

BURNTISLAND, Fife
Forthaven, 4 South View, Lammerlaws, tel. (0592) 872600

BURROW BRIDGE, Somerset
Old Bakery, tel. (082369) 234

BURTON UPON TRENT, Staffs
Delter Hotel, 5 Derby Rd, tel. (0283) 35115

BURY ST EDMUNDS, Suffolk
Chantry, 8 Sparhawk St, tel. (0284) 2157
White Hart, 35 Southgate St, tel. (0284) 5547

BUXTON, Derbys
Fairhaven, 1 Dale Ter, tel. (0298) 4481
Griff, 2 Compton Rd, tel. (0298) 3628
Hawthorn Farm, Fairfield Rd, tel. (0298) 3230
Kingscroft, 10 Green Lane, tel. (0298) 2757
Nithen Corner, 45 Manchester Rd, tel. (0298) 2008
Old Manse, 6 Clifton Rd, Silverlands, tel. (0298) 5638
Roseleigh Private Hotel, 19 Broad Walk, tel. (0298) 4904
Templeton, 13 Compton Rd, tel. (0298) 5275
Thorn Heyes Private Hotel, 137 London Rd, tel. (0298) 3539
Westminster Hotel, 21 Broad Walk, tel. (0298) 3829

CAERNARFON, Gwynedd
Caer Menai, 15 Church St, tel. (0286) 2612
Menai View Hotel, North Rd, tel. (0286) 4602
Plas Treflan, Caethro, tel. (0286) 2542

CALDBECK, Cumbria
High Greenrigg House, tel. (06998) 430

CALLANDER, Central
Abbotsford Lodge, Stirling Rd, tel. (0877) 30066
Annfield, 18 North Church St, tel. (0877) 30204
Arden House, Bracklinn Rd, tel. (0877) 30235
Brook Linn Country House, Leny Fevs, tel. (0877) 30103
Edina, 111 Main St, tel. (0877) 30004
Greenbank, 143 Main St, tel. (0877) 30296
Highland House Hotel, South Church St, tel. (0877) 30269
Kinnell, 24 Main St, tel. (0877) 30181
Riverview House Private Hotel, Leny Rd, tel. (0877) 30635
Rock Villa, 1 Bracklinn Rd, tel. (0877) 30331

CAMBORNE, Cornwall
Pendarves Lodge, Ramsgate, tel. (0209) 712691
Regal Hotel, Church Lane, tel. (0209) 713131

CAMBRIDGE, Cambs
Antwerp, 36 Brookfields, tel. (0223) 247690
Ayeone Cleave, 95 Gilbert Rd, tel. (0223) 63387
Belle Vue, 33 Chesterton Rd, tel. (0223) 351859

CAMBRIDGE, Cambs (contd.)
Cambridge Lodge Hotel, 139 Huntingdon Rd,
tel. (0223) 352833
Fairways, 143 Cherryhinton Rd, tel. (0223) 246063
Hamilton, 88 Chesterton Rd, tel. (0223) 314866
Helen's Hotel, 167–169 Hills Rd, tel. (0223)
246465
Lensfield Hotel, 53 Lensfield Rd, tel. (0223)
355017
Suffolk House Private Hotel, 69 Milton Rd,
tel. (0223) 352016

CAMELFORD, Cornwall
Sunnyside Hotel, Victoria Rd, tel. (0840) 212250
Warmington House, 32 Market Place,
tel. (0840) 213380

CAMPBELTOWN, Strathclyde
Seafield Private Hotel, Kilkerran Rd,
tel. (0586) 54385

CANTERBURY, Kent
Abba Hotel, Station Rd West, tel. (0227) 464771
Castle Court, 8 Castle St, tel. (0227) 463441
Ebury Hotel, New Dover Rd, tel. (0227) 468434
Ersham Lodge, 12 New Dover Rd,
tel. (0227) 463174
Highfield Hotel, Summer Hill, Harbledown,
tel. (0227) 462772
Kingsbridge Villa Hotel, 15 Best Lane,
tel. (0227) 66415
Magnolia House, 36 St Dunstan's Ter,
tel. (0227) 65121
Pilgrims, 18 The Friars, tel. (0227) 464531
Pointers Hotel, 1 London Rd, tel. (0227) 456846
Red House Hotel, London Rd, Harbledown (1m W
A2), tel. (0227) 463578
St Stephens, 100 St Stephen's Rd,
tel. (0227) 462167
Victoria Hotel, 59 London Rd, tel. (0227) 459333

CARDIFF, S Glam
Ambassador Hotel, 4 Oakfield St, Roath,
tel. (0222) 491988
Balkan Hotel, 144 Newport Rd,
tel. (0222) 463673
Clayton Hotel, 65 Stacey Rd, Roath,
tel. (0222) 492345
Domus, 201 Newport Rd, tel. (0222) 495785
Dorville Hotel, 3 Ryder St, tel. (0222) 30951
Ferrier's (Alva Hotel), 130–132 Cathedral Rd,
tel. (0222) 383413
Princes, 10 Princes St, Roath, tel. (0222) 491732
Tane's Hotel, 148 Newport Rd, tel. (0222) 491755

CARDIGAN, Dyfed
Brynhfryd, Gwbert Rd, tel. (0239) 612861

CARLISLE, Cumbria
Angus Hotel, 14 Scotland Rd, tel. (0228) 23546
East View, 110 Warwick Rd, tel. (0228) 22112
Georgian House, 40–44 London Rd,
tel. (0228) 23805
Kenilworth Hotel, 24 Lazonby Ter,
tel. (0228) 26179

CARRADALE, Strathclyde
Ashbank Hotel, tel. (05833) 650
Drumfearne, tel. (05833) 232
Duncrannag, tel. (05833) 224
Dunvalanree, Portrigh, tel. (05833) 226

CARRBRIDGE, Highland
Ard-na-Coille, Station Rd, tel. (047984) 239
Mountain Thyme Country, Station Rd,
tel. (047984) 696
Old Manse Private Hotel, Duthil,
tel. (047984) 278

CASTLE DONINGTON, Leics
Delven Hotel, 12 Delven Lane,
tel. Derby (0332) 810153
Four Poster, 73 Clapgun St,
tel. Derby (0332) 810335

CATÊL (CASTEL), Guernsey, Channel Islands
La Galaad Hotel, Rue Des Francais,
tel. Guernsey (0481) 57233

CAWOOD, N Yorks
Compton Court Hotel, tel. Selby (075786) 315

CHAGFORD, Devon
Bly House, Nattadon Hill, tel. (06473) 2404
Glendaragh, tel. (06473) 3270

CHANNEL ISLANDS
Information is shown under individual place
names.

CHAPELHALL, Strathclyde
Laurel House Hotel, 101 Main St,
Tel. Airdrie (02364) 63230

CHARD, Somerset
Watermead, 83 High St, tel. (04606) 2834

CHARLTON, W Sussex
Woodstock House Hotel,
tel. Singleton (024363) 666

CHARLWOOD, Surrey
For accommodation details see under
Gatwick Airport

CHARMOUTH, Dorset
Newlands House, Stonebarrow Lane,
tel. (0297) 60212
White House, 2 Hillside, tel. (0297) 60411

CHELMSFORD, Essex
Beechcroft Private Hotel, 211 New London Rd,
tel. (0245) 352462
Boswell House Hotel, 118–120 Springfield Rd,
tel. (0245) 87587 (due to change to 287587)
Newholme Hotel, 440 Baddow Rd, Gt Baddow,
tel. (0245) 76691
Tanunda Hotel, 219 New London Rd,
tel. (0245) 354295

CHELTENHAM, Glos
See also Bishop's Cleeve
Askham Court Hotel, Pittville Circus Rd,
tel. (0242) 525547
Beaumont House, 56 Shurdington Rd,
tel. (0242) 45986
Beechworth Lanns Hotel, 133 Hales Rd,
tel. (0242) 522583
Bowler Hat Hotel, 130 London Rd,
tel. (0242) 523614
Carrs Hotel, 42 Clarence St,
tel. (0242) 524003
Central Hotel, 7–9 Portland St,
tel. (0242) 582172
Cleevelands House, 38 Evesham Rd,
tel. (0242) 518898
Cotswold Grange Hotel, Pittville Circus Rd,
tel. (0242) 515119
Hannaford's, 20 Evesham Rd, tel. (0242) 515181
Hollington House Hotel, 115 Hales Rd,
tel. (0242) 519718
Ivy Dene, 145 Hewlett Rd, tel. (0242) 521726
Lawn Hotel, 5 Pittville Lawn, tel. (0242) 526638
North Hall Hotel, Pittville Circus Rd,
tel. (0242) 520589
Regency, 50 Clarence Sq, tel. (0242) 582718
Wellington House Hotel, Wellington Sq,
tel. (0242) 521627
Willoughby, 1 Suffolk Sq, tel. (0242) 522798

CHESTER, Cheshire
Brookside Private Hotel, 12 Brook Lane, (Exec
Hotels) tel. (0244) 381943
Cavendish Hotel, 44 Hough Green,
tel. (0244) 675100
Chester Court Hotel, 48 Hoole Rd,
tel. (0244) 20779
Devonia, 33–35 Hoole Rd,
tel. (0244) 22236
Eaton Hotel, 29 City Rd,
tel. (0244) 312091

Egerton Lodge, 57 Hoole Rd,
tel. (0244) 20712
Eversley Private Hotel, 9 Eversley Park,
(Guestaccom), tel. (0244) 373744
Gables, 5 Vicarage Rd, Hoole, tel. (0244) 23969
Green Bough Hotel, 60 Hoole Rd,
tel. (0244) 26241
Hamilton Court, 5–7 Hamilton St,
tel. (0244) 45387
Malvern, 21 Victoria Rd, tel. (0244) 380865
Redland Private Hotel, 64 Hough Green,
tel. (0244) 671024
Riverside Private Hotel, 22 City Walls, off Lower
Bridge St, tel. (0244) 26580

CHICKLADE, Wilts
Old Rectory, tel. Hindon (074789) 226

CHIDEOCK, Dorset
Betchworth House Hotel, tel. (0297) 89478

CHILLINGTON, Devon
White House Hotel, tel. Kingsbridge (0548)
580580

CHIPPING SODBURY, Avon
Moda Hotel, 1 High St, tel. (0454) 312135

CHRISTCHURCH, Dorset
For additional guest-houses see Bournemouth
Belvedere Hotel, 59 Barrack Rd,
tel. (0202) 485978
Broomway Hotel, 46 Barrack Rd,
tel. (0202) 483405
Ferndale, 41 Stour Rd, tel. (0202) 482616
Laurels, 195 Barrack Rd, tel. (0202) 485530
Park House Hotel, 48 Barrack Rd,
tel. (0202) 482124
Pines Private Hotel, 39 Mudeford Rd,
tel. (0202) 475121
Sea Witch Hotel, 153–155 Barrack Rd,
tel. (0202) 482846
Shortwood House, Magdalen Lane,
tel. (0202) 485223

CHURCH STRETTON, Salop
Dudgeley Mill, All Stretton (2m N B4370)
(Guestaccom), tel. (0694) 723461
Mynd House Private Hotel, Ludlow Rd, Little
Stretton (2m S B4370), tel. (0694) 722212

CINDERFORD, Glos
Overdean, 31 St White's Rd,
tel. Dean (0594) 22136

CIRENCESTER, Glos
Raydon House Hotel, 3 The Avenue,
tel. (0285) 3485
Rivercourt, Beeches Rd, tel. (0285) 3998
La Ronde, 52–54 Ashcroft Rd, tel. (0285) 4611
Wimborne, Victoria Rd, tel. (0285) 3890

CLACTON-ON-SEA, Essex
Chudleigh Hotel, Agate Rd, tel. (0255) 425407
Sandrock Hotel, 1 Penfold Rd, tel. (0255) 428215
Stonar Private Hotel, 19 Agate Rd,
tel. (0255) 426554

CLEARWELL, Glos
Tudor, tel. Dean (0594) 33046

CLEVEDON, Avon
Amberley, 146 Old Church Rd, tel. (0272) 874402

CLIFTONVILLE, Kent
See Margate

COLL (Island of), Strathclyde
Car ferry from Oban (some services via Lochaline/
Tobermory. Also linking with Tiree)
Tigh-na-Mara, tel. (08793) 354

COLWYN BAY, Clwyd
Cabin Hill Private Hotel, College Avenue, Rhos-
on-Sea, tel. (0492) 44568
Grosvenor Hotel, 106–108 Abergele Rd,
tel. (0492) 31586

Christchurch, Dorset

Northwood Hotel, 47 Rhos Rd, Rhos-on-Sea,
tel. (0492) 49931
Southlea, 4 Upper Prom, tel. (0492) 2004
Sunny Downs Private Hotel, 66 Abbey Rd,
Rhos-on-Sea, tel. (0492) 44256

COLYTON, Devon
Old Bakehouse, Lower Church St,
tel. (0297) 52518

COMBE MARTIN, Devon
Channel Vista, tel. (027188) 3514
Firs, Woodlands, tel. (027188) 3404
Mellstock House, Woodlands,
tel. (027188) 2592
Miramar Hotel, Victoria St,
tel. (027188) 3558
Newberry Lodge Hotel, Newberry Rd,
tel. (027188) 3316
The Woodlands, Woodlands, tel. (027188) 2769

COMRIE, Tayside
Mossgiel, tel. (0764) 70567

CONWY, Gwynedd
Llys Gwilym, 3 Mountain Rd, off Cadnant Park,
tel. (049263) 2351
Sunnybanks, Llanrwst Rd, Woodlands,
tel. (049263) 3845

COPMANTHORPE, N Yorks
Duke of Connaught,
tel. Appleton Roebuck (090484) 318

CORRIE, Isle of Arran, Strathclyde
Blackrock House, tel. (077081) 282

COVENTRY, W Midlands
Croft Hotel, 23 Stoke Green (off Binley Rd),
tel. (0203) 457846
Fairlight, 14 Regent St, tel. (0203) 24215
Northanger House, 35 Westminster Rd,
tel. (0203) 26780
Spire View, 36 Park Rd, tel. (0203) 51602
Trinity House Hotel, 28 Lower Holyhead Rd,
tel. (0203) 555654

COWDENBEATH, Fife
Struan Bank Private Hotel, 74 Perth Rd,
tel. (0383) 511057

CRAIL, Fife
Calpie, 51–53 High St, tel. (0333) 50564

CRAWLEY, W Sussex
For accommodation details see under
Gatwick Airport

CRIANLARICH, Central
Glenardran, tel. (08383) 236
Mountgreenan, tel. (08383) 286

CRICCIETH, Gwynedd
Glyn-y-Coed Private Hotel, Portmadoc Rd,
tel. (076671) 2870
Kairon Hotel, Marine Ter,
tel. (076671) 2453

Coventry Cathedral

CRICCIETH, Gwynedd (contd.)
Min-y-Gaer Private Hotel, Portmadoc Rd,
tel. (076671) 2151
Moorings, Marine Ter, tel. (076671) 2802
Môr Heli Private Hotel, Marine Ter.
tel. (076671) 2878
Neptune Private Hotel, Marine Ter,
tel. (076671) 2794

CRICKHOWELL, Powys
Dragon Country House Hotel, High St,
tel. (0873) 810362

CRIEFF, Tayside
Comely Bank, 32 Burrel St, tel. (0764) 3409
Heatherville, 29–31 Burrell St, tel. (0764) 2825
Keppoch House Hotel, Perth Rd,
tel. (0764) 4341

CROESGOCH, Dyfed
Cwmwdig Water, Berea, tel. (03483) 434

CROMER, Norfolk
Brightside, 19 Macdonald Rd, tel. (0263) 513408
Chellow Dene, 23 Macdonald Rd,
tel. (0263) 513251
Morden, 20 Cliff Av, tel. (0263) 513396
Sandcliffe Private Hotel, Runton Rd,
tel. (0263) 512888
Westgate Lodge Private Hotel, 10 Macdonald Rd,
tel. (0263) 512840

CROSSGATES, Powys
Guidfa House, tel. Pennybont (059787) 241

CROYDE, Devon
Bay View Hotel, Baggy Point (1m W),
tel. (0271) 890224
Kittiwell House Hotel, (0271) 890247
Moorsands House Hotel, Moor Ln,
tel. (0271) 890781

CROYDON, Gt London
Friends, 50 Friends Rd, tel. 01-688 6215
Lonsdale Hotel, 158 Lower Addiscombe Rd,
tel. 01-654 2276
Markington Hotel, 9 Haling Park Rd, South
Croydon, tel. 01-688 6530
Oakwood Hotel, 69 Outram Rd, tel. 01-654 2835

CULLEN, Grampian
Wakes Hotel, Seafield Place, tel. (0542) 40251

CWMBACH, nr Builth Wells, Powys
Rhydfelin Farm, Builth Rd,
tel. Builth Wells (0982) 553678

CWMDUAD, Dyfed
Neuadd-Wen, tel. Cynwyl Elfed (026787) 438

DALMALLY, Strathclyde
Orchy Bank, Stronmilchan Rd, tel. (08382) 370

DARLINGTON, Co Durham
Raydale Hotel, Stanhope Rd South,
tel. (0325) 58993

DARTMOUTH, Devon
Orleans, 24 South Town, tel. (08043) 2967

DAVENTRY, Northants
Abercorn Hotel, Warwick St, tel. (0327) 703741

DAWLISH, Devon
Broxmore Private Hotel, 20 Plantation Ter,
tel. (0626) 863602
Lynbridge Private Hotel, Barton Villas,
tel. (0626) 862352
Mimosa, 11 Barton Ter, tel. (0626) 863283
Radfords Hotel, Dawlish Water,
tel. (0626) 863322

DEDHAM, Essex
Dedham Hall, tel. Colchester (0206) 323027

DENBIGH, Clwyd
Cayo, 74 Vale St, tel. (074571) 2686

DERBY, Derbys
Ascot Hotel, 724 Osmaston Rd, tel. (0332) 41916
Dalby House, 100 Radbourne St,
tel. (0332) 42353
Georgian House Hotel, 32–34 Ashbourne Rd,
tel. (0332) 49806
Kerrance Hotel, 115 London Rd,
tel. (0332) 45242
Rangemoor Hotel, 67 Macklin St,
tel. (0332) 47252

DERSINGHAM, Norfolk
Westdene House Hotel, 60 Hunstanton Rd,
tel. (0485) 40395

DEVORAN, Cornwall
Driffold Hotel, 8 Devoran Lane,
tel. (0872) 863314

DIBDEN, Hants
Dale Farm, Manor Rd,
tel. Southampton (0703) 849632

DOLGELLAU, Gwynedd
Clifton Private Hotel, Smithfield Sq,
tel. (0341) 422554

DONCASTER, S Yorks
Dartington, 30–32 Kings Rd, tel. (0302) 60956

DOUGLAS, Isle of Man
Ainsdale, 2 Empire Ter, Central Prom,
tel. (0624) 76695
Ascoat Private Hotel, 7 Empire Ter,
tel. (0624) 75081
Beachcomber, 2 Athol Ter, Queen's Prom,
tel. (0624) 75551
Gladwyn Private Hotel, Queen's Prom,
tel. (0624) 75406
Holyrood Hotel, 51 Loch Promenade,
tel. (0624) 73790
Hydro Hotel, Queen's Prom, tel. (0624) 76870
Rosslyn, 3 Empire Ter, Central Prom,
tel. (0624) 76056
Rothesay Private Hotel, 15–16 Loch Prom,
tel. (0624) 75274
Rutland Hotel, Queen's Prom, tel. (0624) 21218
Welbeck Private Hotel, Mona Dr,
tel. (0624) 75663

DOVER, Kent
Beulah House, 94 Crabble Hill, London Rd,
tel. (0304) 824615
Castle Court, 10 Castle Hill Rd,
tel. (0304) 201656
Dover Stop, 45 London Rd, River (2m NW A256),
tel. (0304) 822751
Kernow, 189 Folkestone Rd, tel. (0304) 207797
Number One, 1 Castle St, tel. (0366) 202007
St Brelade's, 82 Buckland Avenue,
tel. (0304) 206126
St Martins, 17 Castle Hill Rd, tel. (0304) 205938

DOWNHAM MARKET, Norfolk
Cross Keys Riverside Hotel, Hilgay,
tel. (0366) 387777

DOWNTON, Wilts
Warren, High St, tel. (0725) 20263

DROXFORD, Hants
Little Uplands Country Motel, Garrison Hill,
tel. (0489) 878507

DUMFRIES, Dumfries and Galloway
Fulwood Private Hotel, 30 Lovers Walk,
tel. (0387) 52262
Newall House, 22 Newall Ter, tel. (0387) 52676

DUNBAR, Lothian
Marine, 7 Marine Rd, tel. (0368) 63315
St Beys, 2 Bayswell Rd, tel. (0368) 63571
Springfield House, Edinburgh Rd,
tel. (0368) 62502

DUNOON, Strathclyde
Cedars Private Hotel, Alexandra Pde, East Bay,
tel. (0369) 2425

DUNVEGAN, Isle of Skye, Highland
Roskhill, Roskhill (3m S A863),
tel. (047022) 317

DYMCHURCH, Kent
Chantry House Hotel, Sycamore Gdns
(Guestaccom), tel. (0303) 873137
Waterside, 15 Hythe Rd, tel. (0303) 872253

EASTBOURNE, E Sussex
Alfriston Hotel, Lushington Rd, tel. (0323) 25640
Beach Rise, Beachy Head Rd, tel. (0323) 639171
Chalk Farm Hotel & Restaurant, Coopers Hill,
tel. Willingdon (2m NNE), tel. (0323) 503800
Courtlands Hotel, 68 Royal Pde,
tel. (0323) 21068
Croft Hotel, Prideaux Rd, tel. (0323) 642291
Delladale Lodge, 35 Lewes Rd, tel. (0323) 25207
Edmar, 30 Hyde Gdns, tel. (0323) 33024
Ellesmere Hotel, Wilmington Sq,
tel. (0323) 31463
Fairlands Hotel, 15–17 Lascelles Ter,
tel. (0323) 33287
Far End Hotel, 139 Royal Pde, tel. (0323) 25666
Flamingo Private Hotel, 20 Enys Rd,
tel. (0323) 21654
Hanburies Hotel, 4 Hardwick Rd,
tel. (0323) 30698
Little Crookham Private Hotel, 16 Southcliffe
Avenue, tel. (0323) 34160
Hotel Mandalay, 16 Trinity Trees,
tel. (0323) 29222
Merton Private Hotel, 49 Jevington Gdns,
tel. (0323) 21943
Mowbray Hotel, 2 Lascelles Ter,
tel. (0323) 20012
Orchard House, 10 Old Orchard Rd,
tel. (0323) 23682
Park View Hotel, Wilmington Gdns,
tel. (0323) 21242
Rosforde Private Hotel, 51 Jevington Gdns,
tel. (0323) 32503
Saffrons Hotel, 30–32 Jevington Gdns,
tel. (0323) 25539
St Clare, 70 Pevensey Rd, tel. (0323) 29483
Somerville Private Hotel, 6 Blackwater Rd,
tel. (0323) 29342
South Cliff House, 19 South Cliff Avenue,
tel. (0323) 21019
Southcroft, 15 South Cliff Avenue,
tel. (0323) 29071
Traquair Private Hotel, 25 Hyde Gdns,
tel. (0323) 25198
Wynstay Private Hotel, 13 Lewes Rd,
tel. (0323) 21550

EAST GRINSTEAD, W Sussex
Cranfield Hotel, Maypole Rd, tel. (0342) 21251

EASTLEIGH, Devon
Pines Farmhouse Hotel, tel. (0271) 860561

EAST WITTERING, W Sussex
Wittering Lodge Hotel, Shore Rd,
tel. Bracklesham Bay (0243) 673207

EBBERSTON, N Yorks
Foxholm Hotel (on B1258),
tel. Scarborough (0723) 85550

EDINBURGH, Lothian
Adam Hotel, 19 Lansdowne Cres,
tel. 031–337 1148
Adria Hotel, 11–12 Royal Ter, tel. 031–556 7875
Ben Doran Hotel, 11 Mayfield Gdns,
tel. 031–667 8488
Boisdale Hotel, 9 Coates Gdns, tel. 031–337 1134
Bonnington, 202 Ferry Rd, tel. 031–554 7610
Buchan Hotel, 3 Coates Gdns, tel. 031–337 1045
Clans Hotel, 4 Magdala Cres, tel. 031–337 6301
Dorstan Private Hotel, 7 Priestfield Rd,
tel. 031–667 6721
Dunstane House, 4 West Coates,
tel. 031–337 6169
Galloway, 22 Dean Park Cres, tel. 031–332 3672
Glendale, 5 Lady Rd, tel. 031–667 6588
Glenisia Hotel, 12 Lygon Rd, tel. 031–667 4098
Greenside Hotel, 9 Royal Ter, tel. 031–557 0022
Grosvenor, 1 Grosvenor Gdns, Haymarket,
tel. 031–337 4143
Halcyon Hotel, 8 Royal Ter, tel. 031–556 1033
Heriott Park, 256 Ferry Rd, tel. 031–552 6628
Hillview, 92 Dalkeith Rd, tel. 031–667 1523
Kariba, 10 Granville Ter, tel. 031–229 3773
Kildonan Lodge Hotel, 27 Craigmillar Park,
tel. 031–667 2793
Kingsley, 30 Craigmillar Park, Newington,
tel. 031–667 8439
Marchhall Hotel, 14–16 Marchhall Cres,
tel. 031–667 2743
Marvin, 46 Pilrig St, tel. 031–554 6605
Newington, 18 Newington Rd, tel. 031–667 3356
St Margaret's Hotel, 18 Craigmillar Park,
tel. 031–667 2202
Salisbury Hotel, 45 Salisbury Rd,
tel. 031–667 1264
Sharon, 1 Kilmaurs Ter, tel. 031–667 2002
Sherwood, 42 Minto St, tel. 031–667 1200
Southdown, 20 Craigmillar Park,
tel. 031–667 2410
Thrums Private Hotel, 14 Minto St, Newington,
tel. 031–667 5545
Tiree, 26 Craigmillar Park, tel. 031–667 7477

ELIE, Fife
Elms, Park Place, tel. (0333) 330404

ELLESMERE, Salop
Grange Hotel, Grange Rd, tel. (069171) 3495

ELY, Cambs
Castle Lodge Hotel, 50 New Barns Rd,
tel. (0353) 2276
Nyton, 7 Barton Rd, tel. (0353) 2459

EMSWORTH, Hants
Jingles, 77 Horndean Rd, tel. (02434) 3755
(due to change to (0243) 373755)
Merry Hall Hotel, 73 Horndean Rd,
tel. (02434) 2424

ETON, Berks
Christopher Hotel, High St,
tel. Windsor (07535) 52359

EVESHAM, Heref and Worcs
Waterside Family Hotel, 56–59 Waterside,
tel. (0386) 2420

EXETER, Devon
Braeside, 21 New North Rd, tel. (0392) 56875
Dunmore, 22 Blackall Rd, tel. (0392) 31643
Hotel Gledhills, 32 Alphington Rd,
tel. (0392) 71439
Park View Hotel, 8 Howell Rd, tel. (0392) 71772
Radnor Hotel, 79 St David's Hill,
tel. (0392) 72004
Regents Park Hotel, Polsloe Rd,
tel. (0392) 59749
Sunnymede, 24 New North Rd, tel. (0392) 73844

EXETER, Devon (contd.)
Sylvania House Hotel, 64 Pennsylvania Rd (Guestaccom), tel. (0392) 75583
Telstar Hotel, 77 St David's Hill, tel. (0392) 72466
Trees Mini Hotel, 2 Queen's Cres, York Rd, tel. (0392) 59531
Trenance House Hotel, 1 Queen's Cres, York Rd, tel. (0392) 73277
Westholme, 85 Heavitree Rd, tel. (0392) 71878
Willowdene Hotel, 161 Magdalen Rd, tel. (0392) 71925

EXFORD, Somerset
Exmoor House, tel. (064383) 304

EXMOUTH, Devon
Blenheim, 39 Morton Rd, tel. (0395) 264230
Carlton Lodge Hotel, Carlton Hill, tel. (0395) 3314
Clinton House, 41 Morton Rd, tel. (0395) 271969
Dawson's, 8 Morton Rd, tel. (0395) 272321

FALMOUTH, Cornwall
Bedruthan, 49 Castle Drive, Sea Front, tel. (0326) 311028
Cotswold House Private Hotel, 49 Melvill Rd, tel. (0326) 312077
Hotel Dracaena, Dracaena Avenue, tel. (0326) 314470
Evendale Private Hotel, 51 Melvill Rd, tel. (0326) 314164
Gyllyngvase House Hotel, Gyllyngvase Rd, tel. (0326) 312956
Harbour Hotel, Harbour Ter, tel. (0326) 311344
Langton Leigh, 11 Florence Place, tel. (0326) 313684
Maskee House, Spernen Wyn Rd, tel. (0326) 311783
Milton House, 33 Melvill Rd, tel. (0326) 314390
Penty Bryn Hotel, 10 Melvill Rd, tel. (0326) 314988
Rathgowry Hotel, Gyllyngvase Hill, tel. (0326) 313482
Rosemary Hotel, 22 Gyllyngvase Ter, tel. (0326) 314669
Tregenna House, 28 Melvill Rd, tel. (0326) 313881
Wickham, 21 Gyllyngvase Ter, tel. (0326) 311140

FAR SAWREY, Cumbria
West Vale, tel. Windermere (09662) 2817

FAZELEY, Staffs
Buxton House Hotel, 65 Colehill St, tel. Tamworth (0827) 284842

FELMINGHAM, Norfolk
Felmingham Hall, tel. Swanton Abbott (069269) 228

FENITON, Devon
Colestocks House, Colestocks (1m N unclass rd), tel. Honiton (0404) 850633

FERNDOWN, Dorset
Broadlands Hotel, West Moors Rd, tel. (0202) 877884

FESTINIOG, Gwynedd
Newborough House Hotel, Church Sq, tel. (076676) 2682

FILEY, N Yorks
Downcliffe Hotel, The Beach, tel. (0723) 513310
Seafield Hotel, 9–11 Rutland St, tel. Scarborough (0723) 513715

FISHGUARD, Dyfed
Glanmay Country House, Goodwick (1m NW on A40), tel. (0348) 872844

FLUSHING, Cornwall
Nankersey Hotel, St Peters Rd, tel. Falmouth (0326) 74471

FOLKESTONE, Kent
Argos Private Hotel, 6 Marine Ter, tel. (0303) 54309

Arundel Hotel, The Leas, 3 Clifton Rd, tel. (0303) 52442
Beaumont Private Hotel, 5 Marine Ter, tel. (0303) 52740
Belmonte Private Hotel, 30 Castle Hill Avenue, tel. (0303) 54470
Wearbay Hotel, 23–25 Wearbay Cres, tel. (0303) 52586
Westward Ho!, 13 Clifton Cres, tel. (0303) 52663

FONTMELL MAGNA, Dorset
Estyard House, tel. (0747) 811460

FORDINGBRIDGE, Hants
Oakfield Lodge, 1 Park Rd, tel. (0425) 52789

FORT WILLIAM, Highland
Benview, Belford Rd, tel. (0397) 2966
Guisachan, Alma Rd, tel. (0397) 3797
Hillview, Achintore Rd, tel. (0397) 4349
Innseagan, Achintore Rd, tel. (0397) 2452
Lochview, Heathercroft, off Argyll Rd, tel. (0397) 3149
Rhu Mhor, Alma Rd, tel. (0397) 2213
Stronchreggan View, Achintore Rd, tel. (0397) 4644

FOWEY, Cornwall
Ahsley House Hotel, 14 Esplanade, tel. (072683) 2310
Carnethic House, Lambs Barn, tel. (072683) 3336
Wheelhouse, 60 Esplanade, tel. (072683) 2452

FOWNHOPE, Heref and Worcs
Bowens Farmhouse, tel. (043277) 430

FRADDON, Cornwall
St Margaret's Country Hotel, tel. St Austell (0726) 860375

FRESHWATER, Isle of Wight
Blenheim House, Gate Lane, tel. (0983) 752858

FRINTON-ON-SEA, Essex
Forde, 18 Queen's Rd, tel. (02556) 4758
Montpellier Private Hotel, 2 Harold Gr, tel. (02556) 4462
Uplands, 41 Hadleigh Rd, tel. (02556) 4889

GAIRLOCH, Highland
Horisdale House, Strath, tel. (0455) 2151

GALASHIELS, Borders
Buckholmburn, Edinburgh Rd, tel. (0896) 2697

GARFORTH, W Yorks
Coach House Hotel, 58 Lidgett Lane, tel. Leeds (0532) 862303

GARGRAVE, N Yorks
Kirk Syke, 19 High St, tel. (075678) 356

GATWICK AIRPORT, LONDON, W Sussex
Barnwood Hotel, Balcombe Rd, Pound Hill, Crawley, tel. Crawley (0293) 882709
Gainsborough Lodge, 39 Massetts Rd, Horley (2m NE of airport adjacent A23), tel. Horley (0292) 783982
Gatwick Skylodge Motel, London Rd, County Oak, Crawley (2m S of airport on A23), tel. Crawley (0293) 544511
Trumbles Hotel and Restaurant, Stanhill, Charlwood (Exec Hotels), tel. Crawley (0293) 862212
Woodlands, 42 Massetts Rd, Horley, tel. Crawley (0293) 782994

GIGGLESWICK, N Yorks
Woodlands, The Mains, tel. (07292) 2576

GLASGOW, Strathclyde
Dalmeny Hotel, 62 St Andrew's Drive, Nithsdale Cross, tel. 041–427 1106
Kelvin Private Hotel, 15 Buckingham Ter, Hillhead, tel. 041–339 7143

Linwood Hotel, 356 Albert Drive, Pollokshields, tel. 041–427 1642
Marie Stuart Hotel, 46–48 Queen Mary Avenue, Cathcart, tel. 041–423 3939
Smith's Hotel, 963 Sauchiehall St, tel. 041–339 6363

GLASTONBURY, Somerset
Hawthorn Hotel, 8–10 Northload St, tel. (0458) 31255

GLENCOE, Highland
Dunire, tel. Ballachulish (08552) 318
Scorrybreac, tel. Ballachulish (08552) 354

GLENRIDDING, Cumbria
Bridge House, tel. (08532) 236

GLOSSOP, Derbys
Colliers Hotel & Restaurant, 14–14A High St East, tel. (04574) 63409
Wind in The Willows, Derbyshire Level (off A57), Sheffield Rd, tel. (04574) 3354

GLOUCESTER, Glos
Alma, 49 Kingsholm Rd, tel. (0452) 20940
Claremont, 135 Stroud Rd, tel. (0452) 29540
Lulworth, 12 Midland Rd, tel. (0452) 21881
Monteith, 127 Stroud Rd, tel. (0452) 25369
Rotherfield House Hotel, 5 Horton Rd, tel. (0452) 410500

GOLSPIE, Highland
Glenshee, Station Rd, tel. (04083) 3254

GOREY, Jersey, Channel Islands
Royal Bay Hotel, tel. (0534) 53318

GORRAN HAVEN, Cornwall
Perhaver, tel. Mevagissey (0726) 842471

GOSPORT, Hants
Bridgemary Manor Hotel, Brewers Lane, tel. Fareham (0329) 232946

GOUROCK, Strathclyde
Claremont, 34 Victoria Rd, tel. (0475) 31687

GRANDES ROCQUES, Guernsey, Channel Islands
Hotel le Saumarez, Rue de Galad, tel. Guernsey (0481) 56341

GRANGE (in Borrowdale), Cumbria
Grange, tel. Borrowdale (059684) 251

GRANGE-OVER-SANDS, Cumbria
Corner Beech, Methven Ter, Kents Bank Rd, tel. (04484) 3088
Elton Private Hotel, Windermere Rd, tel. (04484) 2838
Grayrigg Private Hotel, Kents Bank Rd, tel. (04484) 2345
Thornfield House, Kents Bank Rd, tel. (04484) 2512

GRANTOWN-ON-SPEY, Highland
Braemoray Private Hotel, Main St, tel. (0479) 2303

Dar-il-Hena, Grant Rd, tel. (0479) 2929
Dunachton, Off Grant Rd, tel. (0479) 2098
Dunalian, Woodside Avenue, tel. (0479) 2140
Kinross House, Woodside Avenue, tel. (0479) 2042
Pines Hotel, Woodside Avenue, tel. (0479) 2092
Ravenscourt, Seafield Avenue, tel. (0479) 2286
Riversdale, Grant Rd, tel. (0479) 2648
Umaria, Woodlands Ter, tel. (0479) 2104

GRASMERE, Cumbria
Beck Steps, College St, tel. (09665) 348
Bridge House Hotel, Stock Lane, tel. (09665) 425
Chesnut Villa Private Hotel, Keswick Rd, tel. (09665) 218
Dunmail, Keswick Rd, tel. (09665) 256
Lake View, Lake View Drive tel. (09665) 384
Titteringdales, Pye Lane, tel. (09665) 439

GRASSINGTON, N Yorks
Ashfield House Hotel, tel. (0756) 752584
Lodge, tel. (0756) 752518

GRAVESEND, Kent
Cromer, 194 Parrock St, tel. (0474) 61935
Overcliffe Hotel, 15–16 The Overcliffe, tel. (0474) 22131

GREAT
Place-names incorporating the word "Great", such as Gt Malvern and Gt Yarmouth will be found under the actual place-name, i.e. Malvern, Yarmouth

GRETNA, Dumfries and Galloway
Surrone House, Annan Rd, tel. (0461) 38341

GRETNA GREEN, Dumfries and Galloway
Greenlaw, tel. Gretna (0461) 38361

GUERNSEY, Channel Islands
See Câtel, Grandes Rocques, St Martin, St Peter Port, St Sampson's & St Saviour

GUILDFORD, Surrey
Blanes Court Hotel, Albury Rd, tel. (0483) 573171
Quinns Hotel, 78 Epsom Rd, tel. (0483) 60422

HALTWHISTLE, Northumb
Ashcroft, tel. (0498) 20213

HALWELL, Devon
Stanborough Hundred Hotel, tel. East Allington (054852) 236

HARROGATE, N Yorks
Abbey Lodge, 31 Ripon Rd, tel. (0423) 69712
Alexa House & Stable Cottages, 26 Ripon Rd, tel. (0423) 501988
Alphen Lodge, 2 Esplanade, tel. (0423) 502882
Ashley Hotel, 36–40 Franklin Rd, tel. (0423) 57474
Aston Hotel, Franklin Mount, tel. (0423) 69534
Aygarth, 11 Harlow Moor Dr, tel. (0423) 68705
Cavendish Hotel, 3 Valley Dr, tel. (0423) 509637
Cheltenham Lodge Hotel, Cheltenham Pde, tel. (0423) 55041
Craighleigh, 6 West Grove Rd, tel. (0423) 64064
Croft Hotel, 42–44 Franklin Rd, tel. (0423) 63326
Franklin Private Hotel, 25 Franklin Rd, tel. (0423) 69028
Gillmore Hotel, 98 King's Rd, tel. (0423) 503699
Grafton Hotel, 1–3 Franklin Mount, tel. (0423) 58491
Ingleside Hotel, 37 Valley Dr, tel. (0423) 502088
Kingsway, 36 Kings Rd, tel. (0423) 62179
Lamont House, 12 St Mary's Walk, tel. (0423) 67143
Manor Hotel, 3 Clarence Drive, tel. (0423) 503916
Moorland Private Hotel, 34 Harlow Moor Dr, tel. (0423) 64596
Norman Hotel, 41 Valley Drive, tel. (0423) 502171

Glencoe

HARROGATE, N Yorks (contd.)
Oakbrae, 3 Springfield Avenue, tel. (0423) 67682
Oakfield Hotel, 32–34 Kings Rd,
tel. (0423) 67516
Prince's Hotel, 7 Granby Rd, tel. (0423) 883469
Roan, 90 Kings Rd, tel. (0423) 503087
Rosedale, 86 Kings Rd, tel. (0423) 66630
Shelbourne, 78 Kings Rd, tel. (0423) 504390
Strayend, 56 Dragon View, Skipton Rd,tel. (0423) 61700
Wharfdale House, 28 Harlow Moor Dr,
tel. (0423) 522233
Woodhouse, 7 Spring Grove, tel. (0423) 60081

HARROW, Gt London
Hindes Hotel, 8 Hindes Rd, tel. 01–427 7468
Kempsford House Hotel, 21–23 St John's Rd,
tel. 01–427 4983
Lindal Hotel, 2 Hindes Rd, tel. 01–863 3164

HARTLAND, Devon
Fosfelle, tel. (02374) 273

HARWICH, Essex
Hotel Continental, 28–29 Marine Pde, Dovercourt Bay, tel. (0255) 503454

HASTINGS AND ST LEONARDS, E Sussex
Burlington Hotel, 2 Robertson Ter,
tel. (0424) 429656
Chimes Hotel, 1 St Mathews Gdns (Guestaccom),
tel. (0424) 434041
Eagle House, 12 Pevensey Rd, St Leonards,
tel. (0424) 430535
Gainsborough Hotel, 5 Carlisle Pde,
tel. (0424) 434010
Harbour Lights, 20 Cambridge Gdns,
tel. (0424) 423424
Waldorf Hotel, 4 Carlisle Pde, tel. (0424) 422185

HAVERFORDWEST, Dyfed
Elliots Hill Hotel, Camrose Rd, tel. (0437) 2383

HAWES, N Yorks
Rookhurst Georgian Country Hotel, West End, Gayle, tel. (09697) 454

HAWKSHEAD, Cumbria
Greenbank Hotel, tel. (09666) 497
Highfield House, Hawkshead Hill,
tel. (09666) 344
Ivy House, tel. (09666) 204
Rough Close Country House, tel. (09666) 370

HAWORTH, W Yorks
Ferncliffe, Hebden Rd, tel. (0535) 43405

HEACHAM, Norfolk
St Annes, 53 Neville Rd, tel. (0485) 70021

HEASLEY MILL, Devon
Heasley House, tel. North Molton (05984) 213

HELSBY, Cheshire
Poplars Private Hotel, 130 Chester Rd,
tel. (09282) 3433

HELSTON, Cornwall
Hillside, Godolphin Rd, tel. (03265) 4788
Wheal Tor Hotel, 29 Godolphin Rd,
tel. (03265) 61211

HEMEL HEMPSTEAD, Herts
Southlea Private Hotel, 8 Charles St,
tel. (0442) 3061
Southville Private Hotel, 9 Charles St,
tel. (0442) 51387

HENLEY-IN-ARDEN, Warwicks
Ashleigh House, Whitley Hill, tel. (05642) 2315

HENLEY-ON-THAMES, Oxon
Flohr's Hotel & Restaurant, Northfield End,
tel. (0491) 573412

HEREFORD, Heref and Worcs
Breinton Court, Lower Breinton,
tel. (0432) 268156

Ferncroft Hotel, 144 Ledbury Rd,
tel. (0432) 265538
Munstone House, Munstone, tel. (0432) 267122
White Lodge Hotel, 50 Ledbury Rd,
tel. (0432) 273382

HERNE BAY, Kent
Northdown Hotel, 14 Cecil Park (Guestaccom),
tel. (0227) 372051

HERSTMONCEUX, E Sussex
Cleavers Lyng Country Hotel (Guestaccom),
tel. (0323) 833131

HESKET NEWMARKET, Cumbria
Denton House, tel. Caldbeck (06998) 415

HEWISH, Avon
Kara, tel. Yatton (0934) 834442

HEYSHAM, Lancs
Carr-Garth, Bailey Lane, tel. (0524) 51175

HICKLING, Norfolk
Jenter House, Town St, tel. (069261) 372

HIGHAM, Suffolk
Old Vicarage, tel. (020637) 248

HIGH WYCOMBE, Bucks
Amersham Hill, 52 Amersham Hill,
tel. (0494) 20635
Clifton Lodge Private Hotel, 210 West Wycombe Rd, tel. (0494) 40095
Drake Court Hotel, London Rd,
tel. (0494) 23639

HILL HEAD, Hants
Seven Sevens Private Hotel, Hill Head Rd,
tel. Stubbington (0329) 662408

HINCKLEY, Leics
Kings Hotel & Restaurant, 13–19 Mount Rd,
tel. (0455) 637193

HOLMROOK, Cumbria
Carleton Green, Saltcoats Rd, tel. (09404) 608

HOLSWORTHY, Devon
Coles Mill, tel. (0409) 253313

HOLT, Norfolk
Lawns Private Hotel, Station Rd,
tel. (026371) 3390

HOLYHEAD, Gwynedd
Witchingham Guest House, 20 Walthew Av,
tel. (0407) 2426

HOOK, Hants
Oaklea, London Rd, tel. (025672) 2673

HONITON, Devon
Hill House Country Hotel, Combe Raleigh,
tel. (0404) 3371

HOPE COVE, Devon
Crest Hotel, tel. Kingsbridge (0548) 561304
Fern Lodge, tel. Kingsbridge (0548) 561326
Sand Pebbles Hotel,
tel. Kingsbridge (0548) 561673

HOPTON, Derbys
Henmore Grange, tel. Carsington (062985) 420

HORNSEA, Humberside
Hotel Seaforth, Esplanade,
tel. (04012) 2616

HORRABRIDGE, Devon
Overcombe Hotel (Guestaccom),
tel. Yelverton (0822) 853501

HORSHAM, W Sussex
Blatchford House, 52 Kings Rd,
tel. (0403) 65317
Horsham Wimblehurst Hotel, 6 Wimblehurst Rd,
tel. (0403) 62319
Winterpick Corner, Winterpit Ln, Manning's Heath, tel. (0403) 53882

HORSHAM ST FAITH, Norfolk
Elm Farm Chalet, Norwich Rd,
tel. Norwich (0603) 898366

HOUNSLOW, Gt London
Shalimar Hotel, 219–221 Staines Rd,
tel. 01-572 2816

HOVE, E Sussex
See Brighton

HOWEY, Powys
Corven Hall Country,
tel. Llandrindod Wells (0597) 3368

HOYLAKE, Merseyside
Sandtoft Hotel, 70 Alderley Rd,
tel. 051–632 2204

HULL, Humberside
Ashford, 125 Park Avenue,
tel. (0482) 492849
Parkwood Hotel, 113 Princes Av,
tel. (0482) 445610

HUNA, Highland
Haven Gore, tel. John o' Groats (095581) 314

HUNSTANTON, Norfolk
Caley Hall Motel, tel. (04853) 33486
Claremont, 35 Greevegate, tel. (04853) 33171
Deepdene Hotel, 29 Avenue Rd,
tel. (04853) 2460
Sunningdale, 3 Avenue Rd, tel. (04853) 2562
Sutton House Hotel, 24 Northgate,
tel. (04853) 2552
Tolcarne Private Hotel, 3 Boston Sq,
tel. (04853) 2359

HUTTON-LE-HOLE, N Yorks
Barn, tel. Lastingham (07515) 311

ICKENHAM, Gt London
Woodlands, 84 Long Lane,
tel. Ruislip (08956) 34830

ICKLESHAM, E Sussex
Snailham House, Broad St,
tel. Hastings (0424) 814556

ILFORD, Gt London
Cranbrook Hotel, 24 Coventry Rd,
tel. 01-554 6544
Park Hotel, 327 Cranbrook Rd, tel. 01-554 9616

ILFRACOMBE, Devon
Avenue Private Hotel, Greenclose Rd,
tel. (0271) 63767
Briercliffe Hotel, 9 Montpelier Ter,
tel. (0271) 63274
Bristol Merchant Hotel, 10 Hillsborough Ter,
tel. (0271) 62141
Carbis Private Hotel, 50 St Brannocks Rd,
tel. (0271) 62943
Chalfont Private Hotel, 21 Church Rd,
tel. (0271) 62224
Collingdale Hotel, Larkstone Ter,
tel. (0271) 63770
Combe Lodge Hotel, Chambercombe Park Rd,
tel. (0271) 64518
Cresta Private Hotel, Torrs Park,
tel. (0271) 63742
Dèdés Hotel, 1–3 The Promenade,
tel. (0271) 62545
Earlsdale Hotel, 51 St Brannocks Rd,
tel. (0271) 62496
Elmfield Hotel, Torrs Park, tel. (0271) 63377
Glendower, Wilder Rd, tel. (0271) 65711
Gloucester Hotel, Cross Park, Wilder Rd,
tel. (0271) 63763
Headlands Hotel, Capstone Cres,
tel. (0271) 62887
Lantern House Hotel, 62 St Brannocks Rd,
tel. (0271) 64401
Laston House Private Hotel, Hillsborough Rd,
tel. (0271) 62627

Lympstone Private Hotel, 14 Cross Park,
tel. (0271) 63038
Marlyn, 7–8 Regent Place, tel. (0271) 63785
Merlin Court Hotel, Torrs Park, tel. (0271) 62697
New Cavendish Hotel, 9–10 Larkstone Ter,
tel. (0271) 63994
Norbury, Torrs Park, tel. (0271) 63888
Queen's Court Hotel, Wilder Rd,
tel. (0271) 63789
Rosebank Hotel, 26 Watermouth Rd, Hele Bay,
tel. (0271) 66488
Seven Hills Hotel, Torrs Park, tel. (0271) 62207
Southcliffe Hotel, Torrs Park, tel. (0271) 62958
South Tor Hotel, Torrs Park, tel. (0271) 63750
Strathmore Private Hotel, 57 St Brannocks Rd,
tel. (0271) 62248
Sunny Hill, Lincombe, tel. (0271) 62953
Sunnymeade Country House Hotel, West
Down, tel. (0271) 63668
Wentworth House Private Hotel, Belmont Rd,
tel. (0271) 63048
Westwell Hall Hotel, Torrs Park, tel. (0271)
62792
Wilson, 16 Larkstone Ter, tel. (0271) 63921

ILKLEY, W Yorks
Moorview House Hotel, 104 Skipton Rd
(Guestaccom), tel. (0943) 600156

INGLETON, N Yorks
Oakroyd Private Hotel, Main St,
tel. (0468) 41258
Springfield Private Hotel, Main St,
tel. (0468) 41280

INSTOW, Devon
Anchorage Hotel, The Quay, tel. (0271) 860655

INVERGARRY, Highland
Craigard, tel. (08093) 258
Lundie View, Aberchalder, tel. (08093) 291

INVERKEITHING, Fife
Forth Craig Private Hotel, 90 Hope St,
tel. (0383) 418440

INVERNESS, Highland
Abermar, 25 Fairfield Rd, tel. (0463) 239019
Ardnacoille House, 1A Annfield Rd,
tel. (0463) 233451
Arran, 42 Union St, tel. (0463) 232115
Brae Ness Hotel, Ness Bank,
tel. (0463) 231732
Craigside, 4 Gordon Ter, tel. (0463) 231576
Four Winds, 42 Old Edinburgh Rd,
tel. (0463) 230397
Glencairn, 19 Ardross St, tel. (0463) 232965
Leinster Lodge, 27 Southside Rd,
tel. (0463) 233311
Lyndale, 2 Ballifeary Rd, tel. (0463) 231529
Moray Park Hotel, Island Bank Rd,
tel. (0463) 233528
Riverside Hotel, 8 Ness Bank, tel. (0463) 231052
St Ann's House Hotel, 37 Harrowden Rd,
tel. (0463) 236157
Whinpark, 17 Ardross St, tel. (0463) 232549

IPSWICH, Suffolk
Bentley Tower Hotel, 172 Norwich Rd,
tel. (0473) 212142
Gables Hotel, 17 Park Rd, tel. (0473) 54252

ISLE OF MAN
Places with AA-listed guest-houses/inns will
be found under individual place-names in the
gazetteer section

ISLE OF SKYE, Highland
**See Broadford, Dunvegan,
Isle Ornsay, Portree, Waterloo**

ISLE OF WIGHT
Places with AA-listed accommodation will be
found under individual place-names within
the gazetteer

Kelso

ISLE ORNSAY, Isle of Skye, Highland
Old Post Office House, tel. (04713) 201

ISLES OF SCILLY
See Scilly, Isles of

ISLEWORTH, Gt London
Kingswood Hotel, 33 Woodlands Rd,
tel. 01–560 5614

IVER HEATH, Bucks
Bridgettine Convent, Fulmer Common Rd,
tel. Fulmer (02816) 2073

JEDBURGH, Borders
Ferniehirst Mill Lodge, tel. (0835) 63279
Kenmore Bank, Oxnam Rd, tel. (0835) 62369

JERSEY, Channel Islands
See Beaumont, Gorey, La Haule, Rozel Bay,
St Aubin, St Brelade, St Clement, St Helier,
St Martin, St Peter's Valley, St Saviour,
Trinity

KELSO, Borders
Bellevue, Bowmont St, tel. (0573) 24588

KENILWORTH, Warwicks
Enderley, 20 Queens Rd, tel. (0926) 55388
Ferndale, 45 Priory Rd, tel. (0926) 53214
Hollyhurst, 47 Priory Rd, tel. (0926) 53882
Nightingales Hotel & Restaurant,
95–97 Warwick Rd, tel. (0926) 53594

KESWICK, Cumbria
Acorn House Private Hotel, Ambleside Rd,
tel. (0596) 72553
Allerdale House, 1 Eskin St, tel. (0596) 73891
Clarence House, 14 Eskin St, tel. (0596) 73186
Derwent Lodge, Portinscale, tel. (0596) 72746
Feil House, 28 Stranger St, tel. (0596) 72669
Foye House, 23 Eskin St, tel. (0596) 73288
Hazeldene Hotel, The Heads, tel. (0596) 72106
Highfield, The Heads, tel. (0596) 72508
Lynwood Private Hotel, 12 Ambleside Rd,
tel. (0596) 72081
Melbreak House, 29 Church St, tel. (0596) 73398
Ravensworth, 29 Station St, tel. (0596) 72476
Richmond House, 37–39 Eskin St,
tel. (0596) 73965
Rickerby Grange, Portinscale, tel. (0596) 72344
Silverdale Hotel, Blencathra St, tel. (0596) 72294
Squirrel Lodge, 43 Eskin St, tel. (0596) 73091
Stonegarth, 2 Eskin St, tel. (0596) 72436
Sunnyside, 25 Southey St, tel. (0596) 72446
Thornleigh, 23 Bank St, tel. (0596) 72863
Woodlands, Brundholme Rd, tel. (0596) 72399

KETTLEWELL, N Yorks
Dale House, tel. (075676) 836
Langcliffe House, tel. (075676) 243

KEYNSHAM, Avon
Grasmere Hotel, 22 Bath Rd, tel. (02756) 2662

KIDLINGTON, Oxon
Bowood House, 238 Oxford Rd, tel. (08675) 2839

KILGETTY, Dyfed
Manian Lodge, Begelly, tel. (0834) 813273

KILLIECRANKIE, Tayside
Dalnasgadh House, tel. Pitlochry (0796) 3237

KINCRAIG, Highland
March House, Lagganlia, tel. (05404) 388

KINGHAM, Oxon
Conygree Gale, Church St (Guestacomm),
tel. (060871) 389

KINGHORN, Fife
Long Boat, 107 Pettycur Rd, tel. (0592) 890625

KINGSBRIDGE, Devon
Ashleigh House, Ashleigh Rd, Westville,
tel. (0548) 2893
Hotel Kildare, Balkwill Rd, tel. (0548) 2451

KINGSDOWN, Kent
Blencathra Country, Kingsdown Hill,
tel. Deal (030345) 373725

KINGSGATE, Kent
Marylands Hotel, Marine Dr,
tel. Thanet (0843) 61259

KING'S LYNN, Norfolk
Havana, 117 Gaywood Rd, tel. (0553) 772331
Russet House Hotel, 53 Goodwins Rd,
tel. (0553) 773098

KINGSTON, Devon
Trebles Cottage Private Hotel,
tel. Bigbury-on-Sea (054881) 268 (due to change
to (0548) 810268)

KINGSTON UPON THAMES, Gt London
Hotel Antoinette, 26 Beaufort Rd,
tel. 01–546 1044

KINGUSSIE, Highland
Homewood Lodge, Newtonmore Rd,
tel. (05402) 507
Sonnhalde, East Ter, tel. (05402) 266

KIRKBEAN, Dumfries and Galloway
Cavens House, tel. (038788) 234

KIRKOSWALD, Cumbria
Prospect Hill Hotel, tel. Lazonby (076883) 500

KIRTON, Notts
Old Rectory, Main St,
tel. Mansfield (0623) 861540

LAIRG, Highland
Carnbren, tel. (0594) 2259

LAMLASH, Isle of Arran, Strathclyde
Glenisle Hotel, tel. (07706) 258
Marine House Hotel, tel. (07706) 298

LANCING, W Sussex
Beach House, 81 Brighton Rd, tel. (0903) 753368

L'ANCRESSE VALE, Guernsey, Channel Islands
Lynton Private Hotel, Hacsé Ln,
tel. Guernsey (0481) 45418

LANG HO, Lancs
Mytton Fold Farm, Whalley Rd,
tel. Blackburn (0254) 48255

LANGLAND BAY, W Glam
See also Bishopston and Mumbles
Brynteg Hotel, 1 Higher Ln,
tel. Swansea (0792) 66820
Wittemberg Hotel, 2 Rotherslade Rd,
tel. Swansea (0792) 69696

LARGS, Strathclyde
Carlton, 10 Aubery Cres, tel. (0475) 672313
Holmesdale, 74 Moorburn Rd, tel. (0475) 674793
Sunbury, 12 Aubery Cres, tel. (0475) 673086

LEAMINGTON SPA (ROYAL), Warwicks
Buckland Lodge Hotel, 35 Avenue Rd,
tel. (0926) 23843

Glendower, 8 Warwick Place, tel. (0926) 22784
Poplars Hotel, 1 Milverton Ter, tel. (0926) 28335
Westella Hotel, 26 Leam Ter, tel. (0926) 22710

LEEDS, W Yorks
Aragon Hotel, 250 Stainbeck Lane, Meanwood, tel. (0532) 759306
Ash Mount Hotel, 22 Wetherby Rd, Roundhay, tel. (0532) 658164
Budapest Private Hotel, 14 Cardigan Rd, Headingley, tel. (0532) 756637
Clock Hotel, 317 Roundhay Rd, Gipton Wood, tel. (0532) 490304
Highfield Hotel, 79 Cardigan Rd, Headingley, tel. (0532) 752193
Oak Villa Hotel, 57 Cardigan Rd, Headingley, tel. (0532) 758439
Trafford House Hotel, 18 Cardigan Rd, Headingley, tel. (0532) 752034

LEEK, Staffs
Peak Weavers Hotel, King St, tel. (0538) 383729

LEE-ON-THE-SOLENT, Hants
Ash House Private Hotel, 35 Marine Pde West, tel. (0705) 550240

LEICESTER, Leics
Alexandra Hotel, 342 London Rd, Stoneygate, tel. (0533) 703056
Burlington Hotel, Elmfield Av, tel. (0533) 705112
Daval Hotel, 292 London Rd, tel. (0533) 708234
Old Tudor Rectory, Main St, Glenfield, tel. (0533) 312214
Scotia Hotel, 10 Westcotes Dr, tel. (0533) 549200
Stanfre House Hotel, 265 London Rd, tel. (0533) 704294

LEOMINSTER, Heref & Worcs
Broadward Lodge Guesthouse & Restaurant, tel. (0568) 2914

LERWICK, Shetland
Glen Orchy, 20 Knab Rd, tel. (0595) 2031

LEWDOWN, Devon
Stowford House Hotel, tel. (056683) 415

LEWIS, ISLE OF, Western Isles
See Stornoway

LEYBURN, N Yorks
Eastfield Lodge, St Matthews Ter, tel. Wensleydale (0969) 23196

LICHFIELD, Staffs
Oakleigh House Hotel, 25 St Chads Rd, tel. (05432) 22688

LIFTON, Devon
Mayfield House, Tinhay, tel. (0566) 84401

LINCOLN, Lincs
Brierley House Hotel, 54 South Park, tel. (0522) 26945
D'Isney Place Hotel, Eastgate, tel. (0522) 38881
Loudor Hotel, 37 Newark Rd, tel. (0522) 680333
Tennyson Hotel, 7 South Park, tel. (0522) 21624

LISKEARD, Cornwall
Elnor, 1 Russell St, tel. (0579) 42472

LITTLEHAMPTON, W Sussex
Regency Hotel, 85 South Ter, tel. (0903) 717707

LITTLE HAVEN, Dyfed
Pendyffryn Private Hotel, tel. Broad Haven (043783) 337

LITTON, N Yorks
Park Bottom, tel. Arncliffe (075677) 235

LIVERPOOL, Merseyside
Aachen Hotel, 91 Mount Pleasant, tel. 051–709 3477
New Manx Hotel, 39 Catherine St, tel. 051–708 6171

LIZARD, Cornwall
Mounts Bay Hotel, Penmenner Rd, tel. (0326) 290305
Parc Brawse House, tel. (0326) 290446
Penmenner House Private Hotel, Penmenner Rd, tel. (0326) 290370

LLANBEDROG, Gwynedd
Glyn Garth Hotel, tel. (0758) 740268

LLANBERIS, Gwynedd
Lake View Hotel, Tan-y-Pant, tel. (0286) 870422

LLANDOGO, Gwent
Brown's Hotel & Restaurant, tel. Dean (0594) 530262

LLANDOVERY, Dyfed
Llwyncelyn, tel. (0550) 20566

LLANDRINDOD WELLS, Powys
Griffin Lodge Hotel, Temple St, tel. (0597) 2432

LLANDUDNO, Gwynedd
Bella Vista Private Hotel, 72 Church Walks, tel. (0492) 76855
Braemar Hotel, 5 St David's Rd, tel. (0492) 76257
Brannock Private Hotel, 36 St David's Rd, tel. (0492) 77483
Brigstock Private Hotel, 1 St David's Place, tel. (0492) 76416
Britannia Hotel, 15 Craig-y-Don Pde, tel. (0492) 77185
Bryn Rosa, 16 Abbey Rd, tel. (0492) 78215
Bryn-y-Mor Private Hotel, North Pde, tel. (0492) 76790
Buile Hill Private Hotel, 46 St Mary's Rd, tel. (0492) 76972
Capri Hotel, 70 Church Walks, tel. (0492) 79177
Carmel Private Hotel, 17 Craig-y-Don Pde, Promenade, tel. (0492) 77643
Hotel Carmen, Carmen Sylva Rd, Craig-y-Don, tel. (0492) 76361
Causeway Hotel, Lloyd St, tel. (0492) 75466
Cleave Court Private Hotel, 1 St Seiriol's Rd, tel. (0492) 77849
Cliffbury Private Hotel, 34 St David's Rd, tel. (0492) 77224
Craig Ard Private Hotel, Arvon Avenue, tel. (0492) 77318
Cumberland Hotel, North Pde, tel. (0492) 76379
Cwlach Private Hotel, Cwlach Rd, tel. (0492) 75587
Grafton Hotel, 13 Craig-y-Don Pde, tel. (0492) 76814
Granby, Deganwy Av, tel. (0492) 76095
Heath House Hotel, Central Prom, tel. (0492) 76538
Lynwood Private Hotel, Clonmel St, tel. (0492) 76613
Mayfair Private Hotel, 4 Abbey Rd, tel. (0492) 76170
Mayfield Private Hotel, 19 Curzon Rd, Craig-y-Don, tel. (0492) 77427
Minion Private Hotel, 21–23 Carmen Sylva Rd, Craig-y-Don, tel. (0492) 77740
Montclare Hotel, North Pde, tel. (0492) 77061
Nant-y-Glyn, 58 Church Walks, tel. (0492) 75915
Orotava Private Hotel, 105 Glan-y-Mor Rd, Penrhyn Bay, tel. (0492) 49780
Plas Madoc Private Hotel, 60 Church Walks, tel. (0492) 76514
Puffin Lodge Hotel, Promenade, tel. (0492) 77713
Rosaire Private Hotel, 2 St Seiriol's Rd, tel. (0492) 77677
St Davids, 32 Clifton Rd, tel. (0492) 79216
St Hilary Hotel, 16 Promenade, Craig-y-Don, tel. (0492) 75551
Sandilands Private Hotel, Dale Rd, West Shore, tel. (0492) 75555
Stratford Hotel, Promenade, Craig-y-Don, tel. (0492) 77962

LLANDUDNO, Gwynedd (contd.)
Tan-y-Marian, 87 Abbey Rd, West Shore,
tel. (0492) 77727
Tilstone Private Hotel, Carmen Sylva Rd, Craig-
y-Don, tel. (0492) 75588
Warwick Hotel, 56 Church Walks,
tel. (0492) 76823
Wilton Hotel, South Parade, tel. (0492) 76086

LLANFYLLIN, Powys
Challenge Adventure Centre, (½m E) Dollyd,
tel. (069184) 703

LLANGATTOCK, Powys
Parc Place, The Legar,
tel. Crickhowell (0873) 810562

LLANWRTYD WELLS, Powys
Carlton Court Hotel, Dolecoed Rd,
tel. (05913) 494
Lasswade House, tel. (05913) 515

LOCHINVER, Highland
Ardglas, tel. (05714) 257
Hillcrest, Badnaban, tel. (05714) 391

LOCHRANZA, Isle of Arran, Strathclyde
Kincardine Lodge, tel. (077083) 267

LOCKERBIE, Dumfries and Galloway
Rosehill, Carlisle Rd, tel. (05762) 2378

LONDON, Gt London
Places within the London postal area are listed
below in postal district order commencing East then
North, South and West with a brief indication of the
area covered. Other places within the county of
London are listed under their respective place
names.

E18 South Woodford
Grove Hill Hotel, Grove Hill, South Woodford,
tel. 01–989 3344

N8 Hornsey
Aber Hotel, 89 Crouch Hill,
tel. 01–340 2847

NW2 Cricklewood
Clearview House, 161 Fordwych Rd,
Cricklewood, tel. 01–452 9773
Garth Hotel, 70–76 Hendon Way, Cricklewood,
tel. 01–455 4742

NW3 Hampstead and Swiss Cottage
Frognall Lodge Hotel, 14 Frognal Gdns, off
Church Row, Hampstead, tel. 01–435 8238

NW6 Kilburn, West Hampstead
Dawson House Hotel, 72 Canfield Gdns,
tel. 01–624 0079

NW11 Golders Green
Central Hotel, 35 Hoop Lane, tel. 01–458 5636
Croft Court Hotel, 44–46 Ravenscroft Avenue,
Golders Green, tel. 01–458 3331

SE3 Blackheath
Bardon Lodge Hotel, 15 Stratheden Rd,
Blackheath, tel. 01–853 4051

SE9 Eltham
Yardley Court Private Hotel, 18 Court Rd,
Eltham, tel. 01–850 1850

SE19 Norwood
Crystal Palace Tower Hotel, 114 Church Rd,
tel. 01–653 0176

SE23 Forest Hill
Ritz, 16 Vancouver Rd, Forest Hill, tel. 01–699 3071

SE25 South Norwood
Toscana, 19 South Norwood Hill, tel. 01–653 3962

SW1 West End–Westminster, St James's Park,
Victoria Station
Arden House, 12 St Georges Drive,
tel. 01–834 2988

Chesham House, 64–66 Ebury St, Belgravia,
tel. 01–730 8513
Easton Hotel, 36–40 Belgrave Rd,
tel. 01–834 5938
Elizabeth Hotel, 37 Eccleston Sq, Victoria,
tel. 01–828 6812
Hanover Hotel, 30 St Georges Drive,
tel. 01–834 0134
Willet Hotel, 32 Sloane Gdns, Sloane Sq,
tel. 01–730 0634
Windermere Hotel, 142 Warwick Way, Victoria,
tel. 01–834 5163

SW3 Chelsea
Eden House Hotel, 111 Old Church St,
tel. 01–352 3403
Garden House Hotel, 44–46 Egerton Gdns,
tel. 01–584 2990
Knightsbridge, 10 Beaufort Gdns (Exec Hotels),
tel. 01–589 9271

SW19 Wimbledon
Trochee, 21 Malcolm Rd, Wimbledon,
tel. 01–946 1579 & 3924
Wimbledon Hotel, 78 Worple Rd, Wimbledon,
tel. 01–946 9265
Worcester House, 38 Alwyne Rd,
tel. 01–946 1300

W1 West End, Piccadilly Circus, St Marylebone and
Mayfair
Hotel Concorde, 50 Gt Cumberland Place,
tel. 01–402 6169
Georgian House Hotel, 87 Gloucester Place,
Baker St, tel. 01–935 2211
Hart House Hotel, 51 Gloucester Place, Portman
Sq, tel. 01–935 2288
Montagu House, 3 Montagu Pl,
tel. 01–935 4632

W2 Bayswater, Paddington
Ashley Hotel, 15 Norfolk Sq, Hyde Park,
tel. 01–723 3375
Camelot Hotel, 45 Norfolk Sq,
tel. 01–723 9118
Dylan Hotel, 14 Devonshire Ter, Lancaster Gate,
tel. 01–723 3280
Garden Court Hotel, 30–31 Kensington Gdns Sq,
tel. 01–727 8304
Nayland Hotel, 134 Sussex Gdns,
tel. 01–723 3380
Pembridge Court Hotel, 34 Pembridge Gdns,
tel. 01–229 9977
Slavia Hotel, 2 Pembridge Sq, tel. 01–727 1316

W4 Chiswick
Chiswick Hotel, 73 Chiswick High Rd,
tel. 01–994 1712

W5 Ealing
Grange Lodge, 50 Grange Rd, tel. 01–567 1049

W8 Kensington
Apollo Hotel, 18–22 Lexham Gdns, Kensington,
tel. 01–373 3236
Atlas Hotel, 24–30 Lexham Gdns, Kensington,
tel. 01–373 7873

W14 Kensington
Avonmore Hotel, 66 Avonmore Rd,
tel. 01–603 4296

WC1 Bloomsbury, Holborn
Mentone Hotel, 54–55 Cartwright Gdns,
tel. 01–387 3927

LOOE, Cornwall
Kantara, 7 Trelawney Ter, tel. (05036) 2093
Ogunquit, Portuan Rd, Hannafore,
tel. (05036) 3105
Panorama Hotel, Hannafore Rd, Hannafore,
tel. (05036) 2123
Riverside Hotel, Station Rd, tel. (05036) 2100
St Aubyns, Marine Dr, Hannafore, West Looe,
tel. (05036) 4351

LOUGHBOROUGH, Leics
De Montfort Hotel, 88 Leicester Rd,
tel. (0509) 216061
Sunnyside Hotel, The Coneries,
tel. (0509) 216217

LOWESTOFT, Suffolk
Amity, 396 London Rd South, tel. (0502) 2586
Belmont, 270 London Road South,
tel. (0502) 3867
Clarendon Hotel, 46 Kirkley Cliff,
tel. (0502) 87061
Kingsleigh, 44 Marine Pde, tel. (0502) 2513

LUDLOW, Salop
Cecil Private Hotel, Sheet Rd, tel. (0584) 2442
Croft, Dinham, tel. (0584) 2076

LULWORTH, Dorset
Gatton House Hotel,
tel. West Lulworth (092941) 252
Lulworth Hotel, Main Rd,
tel. West Lulworth (092941) 230
Shirley Hotel, tel. West Lulworth (092941) 358

LUTON, Beds
Ambassador Hotel, 31 Lansdowne Rd,
tel. (0582) 31411
Arlington Hotel, 137 New Bedford Rd,
tel. (0582) 419614
Humberstone Hotel, 616–618 Dunstable Rd,
tel. (0582) 54399
Stoneygate Hotel, 696 Dunstable Rd,
tel. (0582) 582045

LYDNEY, Glos
Parkend House Hotel, Parkend,
tel. Dean (0594) 562171

LYME REGIS, Dorset
Coverdale, Woodmead Rd, tel. (02974) 2882
Kersbrook Hotel, Pound Rd, tel. (02974) 2596
Old Monmouth Hotel, Church St,
tel. (02974) 2456
Rotherfield, View Rd, tel. (02974) 2811
White House, 47 Silver St, tel. (02974) 3420

LYNDHURST, Hants
Bench View, Southampton Rd, tel. (042128) 2502
Ormonde House Hotel, Southampton Rd,
tel. (042128) 2806
Whitemoor House Hotel, Southampton Rd,
tel. (042128) 2186

LYNMOUTH, Devon
Countisbury Lodge Hotel, Countisbury Hill,
tel. Lynton (0598) 52388
East Lyn, Watersmeet Rd, tel. Lynton (0598) 52540
Glenville Hotel, 2 Tors Rd,
tel. Lynton (0598) 52202
Heatherville, Tors Park, tel. Lynton (0598) 52327
Rock House, tel. Lynton (0598) 53508

LYNTON, Devon
Alford House, 3 Alford Ter. tel. (0598) 52359
The Croft, Lydiate Ln, tel. (0598) 52391
Gable Lodge, Lee Rd, tel. (0598) 52367
Hazeldene, 27–28 Lee Rd, tel. (0598) 52364
Horwood House, Lydiate Ln, tel. (0598) 52334
Ingleside Hotel, Lee Rd, tel. (0598) 52223
Kingford House Private Hotel, Longmead,
tel. (0598) 52361
Longmead House, 9 Longmead, tel. (0598) 52523
Lyndhurst House, Lynway, tel. (0598) 52241
Mayfair Hotel, Lynway, tel. (0598) 53227
Pine Lodge, Lynway, tel. (0598) 53230
Retreat, 1 Park Gdns, tel. (0598) 53526
Southcliffe, Lee Rd, tel. (0598) 53328
St Vincent, Castle Hill, tel. (0598) 52244
Turret, Lee Rd, tel. (0598) 53284
Valley House Hotel, Lynbridge Rd,
tel. (0598) 52285
Waterloo House Hotel, Lydiate Ln,
tel. (0598) 53391
Woodlands Hotel, Lynbridge, tel. (0598) 52324

LYTHAM ST ANNES, Lancs
Beaumont Private Hotel, 11 All Saints Rd,
St Annes, tel. (0253) 723958
'Cullerne S' Hotel, 55 Lightbourne Ave,
tel. (0253) 721753
Endsleigh Private Hotel, 315 Clifton Drive South,
tel. (0253) 725622
Ennes Court, 107 South Prom, tel. (0253) 723731
Harcourt Hotel, 21 Richmond Rd,
tel. (0253) 722299
Lyndhurst Private Hotel, 338 Clifton Drive North,
tel. (0253) 724343

MABELTHORPE, Lincs
Auralee, tel. (0251) 77660

MACHRIHANISH, Strathclyde
Ardell House, tel. (058681) 235

MAIDSTONE, Kent
Carval Hotel, 56–58 London Rd,
tel. (0622) 62100
Howard Hotel, 22–24 London Rd,
tel. (0622) 58778
Rock House Hotel, 102 Tonbridge Rd,
tel. (0622) 51616

MALHAM, N Yorks
Sparth House Hotel, tel. Airton (07293) 315

MALVERN, Heref and Worcs
Bredon House, 34 Worcester Rd,
tel. (06845) 66990
Fromefield, 147 Barnards Green Rd,
tel. (06845) 62466

MANCHESTER, Gt Manchester
Horizon Hotel, 69 Palatine Rd, West Didsbury,
tel. 061–445 4705
Kempton House Hotel, 400 Wilbraham Rd,
Chorlton-cum-Hardy, tel. 061–881 8766
New Central Hotel, 144–146 Heywood Rd,
tel. 061–205 2169
Hotel Tara, 10–12 Oswald Rd, Chorlton-cum-
Hardy, tel. 061–861 0385

MAN, ISLE OF
**Full details will be found under individual
place names in the gazetteer section. See
Douglas and Port St Mary**

MARGATE, Kent
Alice Springs Hotel, 6–8 Garfield Rd,
tel. Thanet (0843) 223543
Beachcomber Hotel, 2–3 Royal Esp, Westbrook,
tel. Thanet (0843) 221616
Charnwood Private Hotel, 20 Canterbury Rd,
tel. Thanet (0843) 224158
Galleon Lights Hotel, 12–14 Fort Cres,
Cliftonville, tel. Thanet (0843) 291703
Tyrella Private Hotel, 19 Canterbury Rd,
tel. Thanet (0843) 292746
Westbrook Bay House, 12 Royal Esp, Westbrook,
tel. Thanet (0843) 292700

MARLOW, Bucks
Glade Nook, 75 Glade Rd, tel. (06284) 4677

Bank Villa, Masham

MASHAM, N. Yorks
Bank Villa, tel. Ripon (0765) 89605

MAWGAN PORTH, Cornwall
Pandora, Tredragon Rd,
tel. St Mawgan (0637) 860412
White Lodge Hotel,
tel. St Mawgan (0637) 860512

MELKSHAM, Wilts
Longhope, 9 Beanacre Rd, tel. (0225) 706737
Regency Hotel, 10–12 Spa Rd, tel. (0225) 702971
Shaw Farm, Shaw, tel. (0225) 702836
York, Church Walk, tel. (0225) 702063

MELTON MOWBRAY, Leics
Westbourne House Hotel, 11A–15 Nottingham
Rd, tel. (0664) 69456

MERIDEN, W. Midlands
Meriden Hotel, Main Rd,
tel. Meriden (0676) 22005

MEVAGISSEY, Cornwall
Headlands Hotel, Polkirt Hill,
tel. (0726) 843453
Polhaun Hotel, Polkirt Hill, tel. (0726) 843222
Valley Park Private Hotel, Tregoney Hill,
tel. (0726) 842347

MIDDLESBROUGH, Cleveland
Chadwick Private Hotel, 27 Clairville Rd,
tel. (0642) 245340
Grey House Hotel, 79 Cambridge Rd,
tel. (0642) 817485
Longlands Hotel, 295 Marton Rd,
tel. (0642) 244900

MIDDLETON-ON-SEA, W Sussex
Ancton House Hotel, Ancton Lane,
tel. (024369) 2482

MIDHURST, W Sussex
See Bepton

MILFORD HAVEN, Dyfed
Bellhaven House Hotel, 29 Hamilton Ter,
tel. (06462) 5983

MILFORD-ON-SEA, Hants
Seaspray, 8 Hurst Rd,
tel. Lymington (0590) 42627

MILLPOOL, Cornwall
Chyraise Lodge Hotel,
tel. Penzance (0736) 763485

MINEHEAD, Somerset
Carbery, Western Lane, The Parks, tel. (0643) 2941
Dorchester Hotel, 38 The Avenue,tel. (0643) 2052
Gascony Hotel, The Avenue, tel. (0643) 5939
Glen Rock Hotel, 23 The Avenue,
tel. (0643) 2245
Mayfair Hotel, 25 The Avenue, tel. (0643) 2719

MINSTERWORTH, Glos
Severn Bank, tel. (045275) 357

MOFFAT, Dumfries and Galloway
Arden House, High St, tel. (0683) 20220
Bridge, Well Rd, tel. (0683) 20383
Buchan, 13 Beechgrove, tel. (0683) 20378
Hartfell House, Hartfell Cres, tel. (0683) 20153
Robin Hill, Beechgrove, tel. (0683) 20050
Rockhill, 14 Beechgrove, tel. (0683) 20283
St Olaf, Eastgate, off Dickson St, tel. (0683) 20001
Well View, Ballplay Rd, tel. (0683) 20184

MONTROSE, Tayside
Linksgate, 11 Dorward Rd, tel. (0674) 72273

MORECAMBE, Lancs
Ashley Private Hotel, 371 Marine Rd East,
tel. (0524) 412034
Beach Mount, 395 Marine Rd East,
tel. (0524) 420753
Ellesmere Private Hotel, 44 Westminster Rd,
tel. (0524) 411881

Glendene, 42 Westminster Rd, tel. (0524) 416358
New Hazlemere Hotel, 391 Marine Rd East,
tel. (0524) 417876
Hotel Prospect, 363 Marine Rd East,
tel. (0524) 417819
Rydal Mount Private Hotel, 361 Marine Rd East,
tel. (0524) 411858
Hotel Warwick, 394 Marine Rd East,
tel. (0524) 418151
Wimslow Private Hotel, 374 Marine Rd East,
tel. (0524) 417804

MORETONHAMPSTEAD, Devon
Crookshayes, 33 Court St, tel. (0647) 40374
Elmfield, Station Rd, tel. (0647) 40327
Wray Barton Manor, tel. (0647) 40246

MORETON-IN-MARSH, Glos
Moreton House, High St, tel. (0608) 50747

MORFA NEFYN, Gwynedd
Erw Goch, tel. Nefyn (0758) 720539

MORTEHOE, Devon
Baycliffe Hotel, Chapple Hill,
tel. Woolacombe (0271) 870393
Haven, tel. Woolacombe (0271) 870426
Sunnycliffe Hotel,
tel. Woolacombe (0271) 870597

MOUSEHOLE, Cornwall
Tavis Vor, tel. Penzance (0736) 731306

MOY, Highland
Invermoy House, Tomatin, tel. (08082) 271

MULL, ISLE OF, Strathclyde
See Salen, Tobermory

MULLION, Cornwall
Belle Vue, tel. (0326) 240483
Henscath House, Mullion Cove,
tel. (0326) 240537
Treynowyth House Private Hotel, Mullion Cove,
tel. (0326) 240486

MUMBLES, W. Glam
See also Bishopston and Langland Bay
Carlton Hotel, 654–656 Mumbles Rd,
South End, tel. Swansea (0792) 60450
Harbour Winds Private Hotel, Overland Rd,
Langland, tel. Swansea (0792) 69298
Shoreline, 648 Mumbles Rd, South End,
tel. Swansea (0792) 66322
Southend Hotel & Restaurant,
724 Mumbles Rd, tel. Swansea (0792) 66329

MUNGRISDALE, Cumbria
The Mill, tel. Threlkeld (059683) 659

MYLOR BRIDGE, Cornwall
Penmere, Rosehill, tel. Falmouth (0326) 74470

NAILSWORTH, Glos
Gables Private Hotel, Tiltups End, Bath Rd,
(Guestaccom), tel. (045383) 2265

NAIRN, Highland
Greenlawns, 13 Seafield St, tel. (0667) 52738
Sandown Farmhouse, Sandown Farm Ln,
tel. (0667) 54745
Sunny Brae, Marine Rd, tel. (0667) 52309

NARBERTH, Dyfed
Blaenmarlais, tel. (0834) 860326

NEAR SAWREY, Cumbria
High Green Gate, tel. Hawkshead (09666) 296
Sawrey House Private Hotel,
tel. Hawkshead (09666) 387

NEATISHEAD, Norfolk
Barton Angler Lodge Hotel, Irstead Rd,
tel. Horning (0692) 630740

NETLEY, Hants
La Casa Blanca, 48 Victoria Rd,
tel. Southampton (0703) 453718

NEWARK-ON-TRENT, Notts
Edgefield Hotel & Restaurant, Vicarage Ln, North Muskham,
tel. (0636) 700313

NEWBY BRIDGE, Cumbria
Furness Fells, tel. (0448) 31260

NEWCASTLE-UNDER-LYME, Staffs
Grove Court Hotel, 100 Lancaster Rd,
tel. (0782) 614406

NEWCASTLE UPON TYNE, Tyne and Wear
Avenue Hotel, 2 Manor House Rd, Jesmond,
tel. 091–281 1396
Chirton House Hotel, 46 Clifton Rd,
tel. 091–273 0407
Clifton Cottage, Dunholme Rd,
tel. 091–273 7347
Western House Hotel, 1 West Av,
tel. 091–285 6812

NEW MILTON, Hants
Ashley Court Hotel, 105 Ashley Rd,
tel. (0425) 619256

NEWPORT, Gwent
Caerleon House Hotel, Caerau Rd,
tel. (0633) 64869

NEWQUAY, Cornwall
During the currency of this guide Newquay telephone numbers are due to change. The code is to change from (06373) to (0637) and 4-figure numbers are to be prefixed by 87.
Arundell Hotel, Mount Wise, tel. (06373) 2481 (due to change to (0637) 872481)
Barrowcliff Hotel, Henver Rd, tel. (06373) 3492 (due to change to (0637) 873492)
Cherington, 7 Pentire Avenue, tel. (06373) 3363 (due to change to (0637) 873363)
Copper Beech Hotel, 70 Edgcumbe Avenue, tel. (06373) 3376 (due to change to (0637) 873376)
Fairlands, 107 Tower Rd, tel. (06373) 2917 (due to change to (0637) 872917)
Fistral Beach Hotel, Esplanade Rd, Pentire, tel. (06373) 3993 (due to change to (0637) 873993)
Gluvian Park Hotel, 12 Edgcumbe Gdns, tel. (06373) 3133 (due to change to (0637) 873133)
Hepworth Hotel, 27 Edgcumbe Avenue, tel. (06373) 3686 (due to change to (0637) 873686)
Jonel, 88–90 Crantock St, tel. (06373) 5084 (due to change to (0637) 875084)
Kelesboro Hotel, 12 Henver Rd, tel. (06373) 4620 (due to change to (0637) 874620)
Links Hotel, Headland Rd, tel. (06373) 3211 (due to change to (0637) 873211)
Mount Wise Hotel, Mount Wise, tel. (06373) 3080 (due to change to (0637) 873080)
Pendeen Hotel, Alexandra Rd, Porth, tel. (06373) 3521 (due to change to (0637) 873521)
Porth Enodoc, 4 Esplanade Rd, Pentire, tel. (06373) 2372 (due to change to (0637) 872372)
Priory Lodge Hotel, Mount Wise, tel. (06373) 4111 (due to change to (0637) 874111)
Rolling Waves, Alexandra Rd, Porth, tel. (06373) 3236 (due to change to (0637) 873236)
Rumours Hotel, 89 Henver Rd, tel. (06373) 2170 (due to change to (0637) 872170)
Wheal Treasure, 72 Edgcumbe Avenue, tel. (06373) 4136 (due to change to (0637) 874136)
Windward Hotel, Alexandra Rd, Porth, tel. (06373) 3185 (due to change to (0637) 873185)

NEW ROMNEY, Kent
Blue Dolphins Hotel & Restaurant, Dymchurch Rd, tel. (0676) 63224

NEWTON ABBOT, Devon
Lamorna, Exeter Rd, Coombe Cross, Sandygate, tel. (0626) 65627

NEWTONMORE, Highland
Alvey House Hotel, Golf Course Rd, tel. (05403) 260

Ard-na-Coille Hotel, tel. (05403) 214
Coig-na-Shee, Fort William Rd, tel. (05403) 216
Glenquoich, Glen Rd, tel. (05403) 461
Pines Hotel, Station Rd, tel. (05403) 271

NEWTON STEWART, Dumfries and Galloway
Duncree House Hotel, King St, tel. (0671) 2001

NITON, Isle of Wight
Windcliffe House Hotel, Sandrock Rd, tel. (0983) 730215

NORTHALLERTON, N Yorks
Windsor, 56 South Pde, tel. (0609) 774100

NORTHAMPTON, Northants
Poplars Hotel, Cross St, Moulton, tel. (0604) 43983

NORTH BERWICK, Lothian
Cragside Private Hotel, 16 Marine Pde, tel. (0620) 2879

NORTH MOLTON, Devon
Marsh Hall Country House Hotel, tel. South Molton (07695) 2666

NORTH WALSHAM, Norfolk
Beechwood Private Hotel, 20 Cromer Rd, tel. (0692) 403231

NORTHWOOD, Salop
Woodlands Country House Hotel, tel. Wem (0939) 33268

NORWICH, Norfolk
Grange Hotel, 230 Thorpe Rd, tel. (0603) 34734
Marlborough House Hotel, 22 Stracey Rd, Thorpe Rd, tel. (0603) 628005

NOTTINGHAM, Notts
Balmoral Hotel, 55–57 Loughborough Rd, West Bridgford, tel. (0602) 818588
Bridgford Lodge, 88–90 Radcliffe Rd, West Bridgford, tel. (0602) 814042
Crantock Hotel, 480 Mansfield Rd, tel. (0602) 623294
Grantham Commercial Hotel, 24–26 Radcliffe Rd, West Bridgford, tel. (0602) 811373
Waverley, 107 Portland Rd, Waverley St, tel. (0602) 786707
Windsor Lodge Hotel, 116 Radcliffe Rd, West Bridgford, tel. (0602) 813773

NUNEATON, Warwicks
Abbey Grange Hotel, 100 Manor Court Rd, tel. (0203) 385535
Drachenfels Hotel, 25 Attleborough Rd, tel. (0203) 383030

OBAN, Strathclyde
Ardblair, Dalriach Rd, tel. (0631) 62668
Crathie, Duncraggen Rd, tel. (0631) 62619
Foxholes Hotel, Cologin (along unclassified road from Junction with A816, 2 m S of Oban), tel. (0631) 64982
Glenburnie Private Hotel, Esplanade, tel. (0631) 62089
Heatherfield Private Hotel, Albert Rd, tel. (0631) 62681
Kenmore, Soraba Rd, tel. (0631) 63592
Roseneath, Dairiach Rd, tel. (0631) 62929
Sgeir Mhaol, Soroba Rd, tel. (0631) 62650
Thornloe, Albert Rd, tel. (0631) 62879
Wellpark Hotel, Esplanade, tel. (0631) 62948

OLD SODBURY, Avon
Dornden, Church Ln, tel. Chipping Sodbury (0454) 313325

ONICH, Highland
Glenmorven House, tel. (08553) 247
Tigh-A-Righ, tel. (08553) 255

ORKNEY
See Kirkwall, Stromness

OSWESTRY, Salop
Ashfield Country House, Llwyn-y-Maen,
Trefonen Rd, tel. (0691) 655200

OXFORD, Oxford
Bravalla, 242 Iffley Rd, tel. (0865) 241326
Brown's, 281 Iffley Rd, tel. (0865) 246822
Burren, 374 Banbury Rd, tel. (0865) 513512
Combermere, 11 Polstead Rd,
tel. (0865) 56971
Conifer, 116 The Slade, Headington,
tel. (0865) 63055
Earlmont, 322–324 Cowley Rd,
tel. (0865) 240236
Falcon, 88–90 Abingdon Rd, tel. (0865) 722995
Galaxie Private Hotel, 180 Banbury Rd,
tel. (0865) 55688
Green Gables, 326 Abingdon Rd,
tel. (0865) 725870
Micklewood, 331 Cowley Rd, tel. (0865) 247328
Pine Castle, 290 Iffley Rd, tel. (0865) 241497
Red Mullions, 23 London Rd, Headington,
tel. (0865) 64727
Tilbury Lodge, 5 Tilbury Ln, Botley,
tel. (0865) 862138
Westgate Hotel, 1 Botley Rd, tel. (0865) 726721
Westwood Country Hotel, Hinksey Hill Top,
tel. (0865) 735408
Willow Reaches Private Hotel, 1 Wytham St,
tel. (0865) 721545

OXWICH, W Glam
Oxwich Bay Hotel, Gower,
tel. Swansea (0792) 390329

PADSTOW, Cornwall
Alexandra, 30 Dennis Rd, tel. (0841) 532503
Dower House Private Hotel (formerly Nook
House), Fentonuluna Lane, tel. (0841) 532317
Tregea, High St, tel. (0841) 532455
Woodlands Hotel, Treator,
tel. (0841) 532426

PAIGNTON, Devon
Beresford, 1 Adelphi Rd, tel. (0803) 551560
Brackencroft, 3 St Andrews Rd,
tel. (0803) 556773
Cambria Hotel, Esplanade Rd, Seafront,
tel. (0803) 559256
Channel View Hotel, 8 Marine Pde,
tel. (0803) 522432
Cherra Hotel, 15 Roundham Rd,
tel. (0803) 550723
Clennon Valley Hotel, 1 Clennon Rise,
tel. (0803) 550304
Commodore Hotel, 14 Esplanade Rd,
tel. (0803) 553107
Danethorpe Hotel, 23 St Andrews Rd,
tel. (0803) 551251
Orange Tubs Hotel, 14 Manor Rd,
tel. (0803) 551541
Preston Sands Hotel, 12 Marine Pde, Preston,
tel. (0803) 558718
Radford Hotel, 28–30 Youngs Park Rd,
tel. (0803) 559671
Redcliffe Lodge Hotel, 1 Marine Drive
tel. (0803) 551394
St Weonard's Private Hotel, 12 Kernou Rd,
tel. (0803) 558842
Sattva Hotel, 29 Esplanade Rd,
tel. (0803) 557820
Sealawn Hotel, Sea Front, tel. (0803) 559031
Sea Verge Hotel, Marine Drive, Preston,
tel. (0803) 557795
Shorton House Hotel, 17 Roundham Rd,
tel. (0803) 557722
South Mount Hotel, 7 Southfield Rd,
tel. (0803) 557643
Sunnybank Private Hotel, 2 Cleveland Rd,
tel. (0803) 525540
Torbay Sands Hotel, Sea Front, 16 Marine Pde,
Preston, tel. (0803) 525568

Pembroke Castle

PATELEY BRIDGE, N Yorks
Grassfields Country House Hotel,
tel. Harrogate (0423) 711412
Roslyn, 9 King St, tel. Harrogate (0423) 711374
Whitestone House, Innerleithen Rd,
tel. (0721) 20337

PEEBLES, Borders
Lindores, Old Town, tel. (0721) 20441

PEMBROKE, Dyfed
High Noon, Lower Lamphey Rd,
tel. (0646) 683736

PENARTH, S Glam
Albany Hotel (formerly Alanleigh Hotel),
14 Victoria Rd, tel. Cardiff (0222) 701598

PENNANT, Dyfed
Bikerehyd Farm, tel. Nebo (09746) 365

PENRITH, Cumbria
Brandelhow, 1 Portland Place, tel. (0768) 64470
Pategill Villas, Carleton Rd, tel. (0768) 63153
Woodland House Hotel, Wordsworth St,
tel. (0768) 64177

PENZANCE, Cornwall
Beachfield Hotel, The Promenade,
tel. (0736) 62067
Bella-Vista Private Hotel, 7 Alexandra Ter.
Lariggan, tel. (0736) 62409
Camilla Hotel, Regent Ter, tel. (0736) 63771
Carlton Private Hotel, tel. (0736) 62081
Dunedin, Alexandra Rd, tel. (0736) 62652
Holbein House Hotel, Alexandra Rd,
tel. (0736) 65008
Kilindini Private Hotel, 13 Regent Ter,
tel. (0736) 64744
Kimberley House, 10 Morrab Rd (Guestaccom),
tel. (0736) 62727
Mount Royal Hotel, Chyandour Cliff,
tel. (0736) 62233
Old Manor House Private Hotel, Regent Ter,
tel. (0736) 63742
Penmorvah Hotel, Alexandra Rd,
tel. (0736) 63711
Pentrea Hotel, Alexandra Rd,
tel. (0736) 69576
Trenant Private Hotel, Alexandra Rd,
tel. (0736) 62005
Trevelyan Hotel, 16 Chapel St, tel. (0736) 62494
Trewella, 18 Mennaye Rd, tel. (0736) 63818
Willows, Cornwall Ter, tel. (0736) 63744

PERRANPORTH, Cornwall
Cellar Cove Hotel, Droskyn Point,
tel. Truro (0872) 572110
Fairview Hotel, Tywarnhayle Rd,
tel. Truro (0872) 572278
Lamorna Private Hotel, Tywarnhayle Rd,
tel. Truro (0872) 573398
Villa Margarita Private Hotel, Bolingey,
tel. Truro (0872) 572063

PERTH, Tayside
Clark Kimberley, 57–59 Dunkeld Rd,
tel. (0738) 37406
Clunie, 12 Pitcullen Cres, tel. (0738) 23625
Darroch, 9 Pitcullen Cres, tel. (0738) 36893
Gables, 24–26 Dunkeld Rd, tel. (0738) 24717
Pitcullen, 17 Pitcullen Cres, tel. (0738) 26506

PETERSFIELD, Hants
Concorde Hotel, 1 Weston Rd,
tel. (0730) 63442

PICKERING, N Yorks
Cottage Leas Country, Middleton,
tel. (0751) 72129

PILTON, Somerset
Long House, tel. (074989) 701

PITLOCHRY, Tayside
Adderley Private Hotel, 23 Toberargan Rd,
tel. (0796) 2433
Balrobin Private Hotel, Higher Oakfield,
tel. (0796) 2901
Duntrune, 22 East Moulin Rd, tel. (0796) 2172
Fasganeoin Hotel, Perth Rd, tel. (0796) 2387
Faskally Home Farm, tel. (0796) 2007
Torrdarach Hotel, Golf Course Rd,
tel. (0796) 2136

PLYMOUTH, Devon
Bowling Green Hotel, 9–10 Osborne Pl, Lockyer
St, The Hoe, tel. (0752) 667485
Cadleigh, 36 Queens Rd, Lipson,
tel. (0752) 665909
Carnegie Hotel, 172 Citadel Rd, The Hoe,
tel. (0752) 25158
Chester, 54 Stuart Rd, Pennycomequick,
tel. (0752) 663706
Cranbourne Hotel, 282 Citadel Rd, The Hoe,
tel. (0752) 263858
Dudley, 42 Sutherland Rd, Mutley,
tel. (0752) 668322
Gables End Hotel, 29 Sutherland Rd, Mutley,
tel. (0752) 20803
Georgian House Hotel, 51 Citadel Rd, The Hoe,
tel. (0752) 663237
Kildare, 82 North Road East, tel. (0752) 29375
Lockyer House Hotel, 2 Alfred St, The Hoe,
tel. (0752) 665755
Merville Hotel, 73 Citadel Rd, The Hoe,
tel. (0752) 667595
Riviera Hotel, 8 Elliott St, The Hoe,
tel. (0752) 667379
St James Hotel, 49 Citadel Rd, The Hoe,
tel. (0752) 661950
Smeaton's Tower, 44 Grand Pde,
tel. (0752) 21007
Trenant House, Queens Rd, Lipson,
tel. (0752) 663879
Trillium, 4 Alfred St, The Hoe (Guestaccom),
tel. (0752) 670452
Yorkshireman Hotel, 64 North Rd East,
tel. (0752) 668133

POLBATHIC, Cornwall
Old Mill, tel. St Germans (0503) 30596

POLMASSICK, Cornwall
Kilbol House, tel. Mevagissey (0726) 842481

POLPERRO, Cornwall
Kit Hill, Talland Hill, tel. (0503) 72369
Landaviddy Manor, Landaviddy Lane,
tel. (0503) 72210
Lanhael House, tel. (0503) 724278
Penryn House Hotel, The Coombes,
tel. (0503) 72157
Sleepy Hollow Private Hotel, Brentfields,
tel. (0503) 72288

POLZEATH, Cornwall
White Lodge, Old Polzeath,
tel. Trebetherick (020886) 2370

PONTLLYFNI, Gwynedd
Bron Dirion Hotel,
tel. Clynnogfawr (028686) 346

POOLE, Dorset
For additional guest-houses see Bournemouth
Avalon Hotel, 14 Pinewood Rd, Branksome Park,
tel. (0202) 760917
Blue Shutters Hotel, 109 North Rd, Parkstone,
tel. (0202) 748129
Dene Hotel, 16 Pinewood Rd, Branksome Park,
tel. (0202) 761143
Ebdon House Hotel, 21 St Clair Rd,
tel. (0202) 707286
Fairlight Hotel, 1 Golf Links Rd, Broadstone,
tel. (0202) 694316
Ormonde House Hotel, 18 Ormonde Rd,
Branksome Park, tel. (0202) 761093
Redcroft Hotel, 20 Pinewood Rd, Branksome
Park, tel. (0202) 763959
Sheldon Lodge, 22 Forest Rd, Branksome Park,
tel. (0202) 761186
Twin Cedars Hotel, 2 Pinewood Rd, Branksome
Park, tel. (0202) 761339
Westminster Cottage Hotel, 3 Westminster Rd
East, Branksome Park, tel. (0202) 765265

PORLOCK, Somerset
Gables Hotel, tel. (0643) 862552
Lorna Doone Hotel, High St, tel. (0643) 862404
Overstream, Parson St, tel. (0643) 862421

PORT ELLEN, Isle of Islay, Strathclyde
Tighcargaman, tel. Port Ellen (0496) 2345

PORTESHAM, Dorset
Millmead Country, Goose Hill,
tel. Abbotsbury (0305) 871432

PORTHCAWL, Mid Glam
Collingwood Hotel, 40 Mary St,
tel. (065671) 2899
Minerva Private Hotel, 52 Esplanade Av,
tel. (065671) 2428

PORTHCOTHAN BAY, Cornwall
Bay House, tel. Padstow (0841) 520472

PORTHCURNO, Cornwall
Mariners Lodge, tel. St Buryan (073672) 236

PORTHMADOG, Gwynedd
Oakleys, The Harbour, tel. (0766) 2482
Owen's Hotel, High St, tel. (0766) 2098

PORTHTOWAN, Cornwall
Porthtowan Beach Hotel, tel. (0209) 890228

PORT ISAAC, Cornwall
Archer Farm Hotel, Trewetha,
tel. Bodmin (0208) 880522
Bay Hotel, 1 The Terrace, tel. Bodmin (0208) 880380
Fairholme, 30 Trewetha Lane,
tel. Bodmin (0208) 880397
Trethoway Hotel, 98 Fore St,
tel. Bodmin (0208) 880214

PORTPATRICK, Dumfries and Galloway
Blinkbonnie, School Brae, tel. (077681) 282

PORTREE, Isle of Skye, Highland
Bosville, Bosville Ter, tel. (0478) 2846
Craiglockhart, Beaumont Cres, tel. (0478) 2233

PORT ST MARY, Isle of Man
Mallmore Private Hotel, The Promenade,
tel. (0624) 833179

PORTSMOUTH AND SOUTHSEA, Hants
Abbeville Hotel, 26 Nettlecombe Av, Southsea,
tel. (0705) 826209
Amberley Court, 97 Waverley Rd, Southsea,
tel. (0705) 735419
Astor House, 4 St Andrews Rd, Southsea,
tel. (0705) 755171
Beaufort Hotel, 71 Festing Rd, Southsea,
tel. (0705) 823707

PORTSMOUTH AND SOUTHSEA, Hants (contd.)
Birchwood, 44 Waverley Rd, Southsea,
tel. (0705) 811337
Bristol Hotel, 55 Clarence Pde, Southsea,
tel. (0705) 821815
Chequers Hotel, Salisbury Rd, Southsea,
tel. (0705) 735277
Gainsborough House, 9 Malvern Rd, Southsea,
tel. (0705) 822604
Goodwood House, 1 Taswell Rd, Southsea,
tel. (0705) 824734
Lyndhurst, 8 Festing Gv, Southsea,
tel. (0705) 735239
Ryde View, 9 Western Pde, Southsea,
tel. (0705) 820865
St Andrews Lodge, 65 St Andrews Rd, Southsea,
tel. (0705) 827079
Somerset Private Hotel, 16 Western Pde,
Southsea, tel. (0705) 822495
Upper Mount House Hotel, The Vale, Clarendon
Rd, Southsea, tel. (0705) 820456
White House Hotel, 26 South Parade, Southsea,
tel. (0705) 823709

POSTBRIDGE, Devon
Lydgate House Hotel,
tel. Tavistock (0822) 88209

POUNDSGATE, Devon
Leusdon Lodge, tel. (03643) 304

PRAA SANDS, Cornwall
La Connings, tel. Germoe (0736) 762380

PRESTATYN, Clwyd
Bryn Gwalia Hotel, 17 Gronant Rd,
tel. (07456) 2442
Hawarden House, 13 Victoria Rd,
tel. (07456) 4226

PRESTON, Lancs
Fulwood Park Hotel, 49 Watling Street Rd,
tel. (0772) 718067
Lauderdale Hotel, 29 Fishergate Hill,
tel. (0772) 555460
Tulketh Hotel, 209 Tulketh Rd, Ashton,
tel. (0772) 728096
Withy Trees, 175 Garstang Rd, Fullwood
tel. (0772) 717693

PRESTWICK, Strathclyde
Fernbank, 213 Main St, tel. (0292) 75027
Kincraig Private Hotel, 39 Ayr Rd,
tel. (0292) 79480
Villa Marina Hotel, 19 Links Rd,
tel. (0292) 70396

PWLLHELI, Gwynedd
Sea Haven Hotel, West End Pde,
tel. (0758) 612572

RAGLAN, Gwent
Grange, Old Abergavenny Rd, tel. (0291) 690260

RAMSGATE, Kent
Jalna Hotel, 49 Vale Sq,
tel. Thanet (0843) 593848
Piper Lodge Hotel, 26 Victoria Rd, East Cliff,
tel. Thanet (0843) 591661
St Hilary Private Hotel, 21 Crescent Rd,
tel. Thanet (0843) 591427

RASKELF, N Yorks
Old Farmhouse, tel. Easingwold (0347) 21971

RAVENGLASS, Cumbria
St Michael's Country House, Muncaster,
tel. (06577) 362

RAVENSCAR, N Yorks
Smugglers Rock Country,
tel. Scarborough (0723) 870044

READING, Berks
Aeron, 191 Kentwood Hill, Tilehurst,
tel. (0734) 24119

Private House Hotel, 98 Kendrick Rd,
tel. (0734) 874142

REDCAR, Cleveland
Claxton House Private Hotel, 196 High St,
tel. (0642) 486745

REDDITCH, Heref & Worcs
Old Rectory, Ipsley Ln, tel. (0527) 23000

REDHILL, Surrey
Ashleigh House Hotel, 39 Redstone Hill,
tel. (0737) 64763

REDRUTH, Cornwall
Aviary Court, Marys Well, Illogan (2m NW
unclass), tel. Portreath (0209) 842256

REIGATE, Surrey
Cranleigh Hotel, 41 West St,
tel. (07372) 40600
Priors Mead, Blandford Rd, tel. (07372) 48776

RHOS-ON-SEA, Clwyd
See Colwyn Bay

RHYL, Clwyd
Hafod-y-Mor, 18–20 Palace Av, tel. (0745) 2566
Pier Hotel, 23 East Pde, tel. (0745) 50280
Toomargoed Private Hotel, 31–33 John St,
tel. (0745) 4103

RINGWOOD, Hants
Little Forest Lodge, Poulner Hill,
tel. (04254) 78848
Little Moortown House Hotel, 244 Christchurch
Rd, tel. (04254) 3325

RIPLEY, Derbys
Britannia, 243 Church St, Waingroves,
tel. (0773) 43708

RIPON, N Yorks
Crescent Lodge, 42 North St, tel. (0765) 2331
Nordale, 1–2 North Pde, tel. (0765) 3557
Old Country, 1 The Crescent, tel. (0765) 2162

ROCHE, Cornwall
Greystones, Mount Pleasant, tel. (0726) 890863

ROCK, Cornwall
Roskarnon House Hotel,
tel. Trebetherick (020886) 2785

ROMFORD, Gt London
Repton Private Hotel, 18 Repton Dr, Gidea Park,
tel. (0708) 45253

ROMSEY, Hants
Adelaide House, 45 Winchester Rd,
tel. (0794) 512322
Chalet, Botley Rd, Whitenap,
tel. (0794) 514909

ROSS-ON-WYE, Heref and Worcs
Arches Country House, Walford Rd,
tel. (0989) 63348
Bridge House Hotel, Wilton, tel. (0989) 62655
Ryefield House, Gloucester Rd, tel. (0989) 63030
Sunnymount Hotel, Ryfield Rd, tel. (0989) 63880

ROTHBURY, Northumberland
Orchards, High St, tel. (0669) 20684

ROTTINGDEAN, E Sussex
Braemar House, Steyning Rd,
tel. Brighton (0273) 34263
Corner House, Steyning Rd,
tel. Brighton (0273) 34533

ROWLEY REGIS, W Midlands
Highfield House Hotel, Holly Rd,
tel. 021–559 1066

RUGBY, Warwicks
Grosvenor House Hotel, 81 Clifton Rd,
tel. (0788) 3437
Mound Hotel, 17–19 Lawford Rd,
tel. (0788) 3486

RUISLIP, Gt London
17th Century Barn Hotel, West End Rd,
tel. (08956) 36057

RUSTINGTON, W Sussex
Kenmore, Claigmar Rd, tel. (0903) 784634
Mayday Hotel, 12 Broadmark Lane,
tel. (0903) 771198

RYDAL, Cumbria
See Ambleside

RYDE, Isle of Wight
Dorset Hotel, 33 Dover St, tel. (0983) 64327
Teneriffe, 36 The Strand, tel. (0983) 63841

RYE, E Sussex
Little Saltcote, 22 Military Rd, tel. (0797) 223210
Mariner's Hotel, High St, tel. (0797) 223480
Monastery Hotel & Restaurant, 6 High St,
tel. (0797) 223272
Old Borough Arms, The Strand,
tel. (0797) 222128
Playden Oasts Hotel, Playden, tel. (0797) 223502

ST AGNES, Cornwall
Glen Hotel, Quay Rd, tel. (087255) 2590
Penkerris, Penwinnick Rd, tel. (087255) 2262

ST ALBANS, Herts
Ardmore House, 54 Lemsford Rd,
tel. (0727) 59313
Glenmore House Hotel, 16 Woodstock Road
North, tel. (0727) 53794
Melford, 24 Woodstock Road North,
tel. (0727) 53642

ST ANDREWS, Fife
Albany, 56 North St, tel. (0334) 77737
Argyle Hotel, 127 North St, tel. (0334) 73387
Arran House, 5 Murray Park, tel. (0334) 74724
Beachway House, 4–6 Murray Park,
tel. (0334) 73319
Cleveden House, 3 Murray Place,
tel. (0334) 74212
Craigmore, 3 Murray Park, tel. (0334) 72142
Kerelaw House, 5 Playfair Ter, North St,
tel. (0334) 75906
Number Ten, 10 Hope St, tel. (0334) 74601
West Park House, 5 St Mary's Place,
tel. (0334) 75933
Yorkston Hotel, 68 & 70 Argyle St,
tel. (0334) 72019

ST AUBIN, Jersey, Channel Islands
Panorama St Aubin, High St,
tel. Jersey (0534) 42429

ST AUSTELL, Cornwall
Alexandra Hotel, 52–54 Alexandra Rd,
tel. (0726) 74242
Cornerways, Penwinnick Rd, tel. (0726) 61579
Lynton House Hotel, 48 Bodmin Rd,
tel. (0726) 73787
Pen-Star, 20 Cromwell Rd, tel. (0726) 61367
Selwood House Hotel, 60 Alexandra Rd,
tel. (0726) 65707
Wimereux, 1 Trevanion Rd, tel. (0726) 72187

ST BLAZEY, Cornwall
Moorshill House Hotel, Rosehill,
tel. Par (072681) 2368

ST CATHERINE'S, Strathclyde
Thistle House, tel. Inveraray (0499) 2209

ST CLEMENT, Jersey, Channel Islands
Belle Plage Hotel, Green Island,
tel. Jersey (0534) 53750

ST DAVID'S, Dyfed
Alandale, 43 Nun St, tel. (0437) 720333
Belmont House, 12 Cross Sq, tel. (0437) 720264
Pen-y-Daith, 12 Millard Park, tel. (0437) 720720
Glennydd, 51 Nun St, tel. (0437) 720576
The Ramsey, Lower Moor, tel. (0437) 720321

ST HELIER, Jersey, Channel Islands
Almorah Hotel, La Pouquelaye,
tel. Jersey (0534) 21648
Cliff Court Hotel, St Andrews Rd, First Tower,
tel. Jersey (0534) 34919
Runnymede Court Hotel, 46–52 Roseville St,
tel. Jersey (0534) 20044

ST IVES, Cambs
The Firs Hotel, 50 Needingworth Rd,
tel. (0480) 63252

ST IVES, Cornwall
Bay View, Headland Rd, Carbis Bay,
tel. Penzance (0736) 796469
Blue Mist, The Warren,
tel. Penzance (0736) 795209
Chy-an-Creet Private Hotel, Higher Stennack,
tel. Penzance (0736) 796559
Cottage Hotel, Carbis Bay,
tel. Penzance (0736) 796351
Dean Court Hotel, Trelyon Avenue,
tel. Penzance (0736) 796023
Hollies Hotel, Talland Rd,
tel. Penzance (0736) 796605
Island View, 2 Park Avenue,
tel. Penzance (0736) 795111
Kandahar & Cortina, 26 The Warren,
tel. Penzance (0736) 796183
Longships, 2 Talland Rd,
tel. Penzance (0736) 798180
Lyonesse Hotel, 5 Talland Rd,
tel. Penzance (0736) 796315
Monowai Private Hotel, Headland Rd, Carbis
Bay, tel. Penzance (0736) 795733
Pondarosa, 10 Porthminster Ter,
tel. Penzance (0736) 795875
Primrose Valley Hotel, Primrose Valley,
tel. Penzance (0736) 794939
Rosemorran Private Hotel, The Belyars,
tel. Penzance (0736) 796359
Hotel Rotorua, Trencrom Lane, Carbis Bay,
tel. Penzance (0736) 795419
St Margarets, 3 Park Avenue,
tel. Penzance (0736) 795785
St Merryn Hotel, Trelyon,
tel. Penzance (0736) 795767
Sherwell, St Ives Rd, Carbis Bay,
tel. Penzance (0736) 796142
Shun Lee Private Hotel, Trelyon Avenue,
tel. Penzance (0736) 796284
Sunrise, 22 The Warren,
tel. Penzance (0736) 795407
'27 The Terrace', 27 The Terrace,
tel. Penzance (0736) 797450
Thurleston, St Ives Rd, Carbis Bay,
tel. Penzance (0736) 796369
Tregorran Hotel, Headland Rd, Carbis Bay,
tel. Penzance (0736) 795889
Trelissick Hotel, Bishops Rd,
tel. Penzance (0736) 795035

St David's Cathedral

ST IVES, Cornwall (contd.)
Verbena Hotel, Orange Lane,
tel. Penzance (0736) 796396
Westaway Farm Hotel, Old Coach Rd, Trink
(3m S off unclass rd between B3311 and Lelant),
tel. Penzance (0736) 797571
White House Hotel, The Valley, Carbis Bay,
tel. Penzance (0736) 797405
Windsor Hotel, The Terrace,
tel. Penzance (0736) 798174

ST JUST, Cornwall
Boscean Country Hotel (Guestaccom),
tel. Penzance (0736) 788748
Boswedden House, Cape Cornwall,
tel. Penzance (0736) 788733

ST JUST-IN-ROSELAND, Cornwall
Rose-Da-Mar Hotel,
tel. St Mawes (0326) 270450

ST KEYNE, Cornwall
Old Rectory Country House Hotel,
tel. Liskeard (0579) 42617

ST LAWRENCE, Isle of Wight
Woody Bank Hotel, Undercliff Drive,
tel. Ventnor (0983) 852610

ST MARTIN, Guernsey, Channel Islands
Triton Private Hotel, Les Hubits,
tel. Guernsey (0481) 38017

ST MARTIN, Jersey, Channel Islands
Le Relais de St Martin, tel. Jersey (0534) 53271

ST PETER PORT, Guernsey, Channel Islands
Baltimore House Hotel, Les Gravees,
tel. (0481) 23641
Midhurst House, Candie Rd,
tel. Guernsey (0481) 24391

ST PETER'S VALLEY, Jersey, Channel Islands
Midvale Private Hotel, tel. Jersey (0534) 42498

ST SAMPSON'S, Guernsey, Channel Islands
Ann-Dawn Private Hotel, Route Des Capelles,
tel. Guernsey (0481) 25606

ST SAVIOUR, Jersey, Channel Islands
La Girouette House Hotel,
tel. Guernsey (0481) 63269

SALCOMBE, Devon
Bay View Hotel, Bennett Rd, tel. (054884) 2238
Charborough House Hotel, Devon Rd,
tel. (054884) 2260
Lyndhurst Hotel, Bonaventure Rd,
tel. (054884) 2481
Trennels Private Hotel, Herbert Rd,
tel. (054884) 2500
Woodgrange Private Hotel, Devon Rd,
tel. (054884) 2439

SALEN, Isle of Mull, Strathclyde
Craig Hotel, tel. Aros (06803) 347

SALFORD, Gt Manchester
Hazeldean Hotel, 467 Bury New Rd,
tel. 061–792 6667

SALISBURY, Wilts
Byways House, 31 Fowlers Rd, tel. (0722) 28364
Hayburn Wyke, 72 Castle Rd, tel. (0722) 24141
Holmhurst, Downtown Rd, tel. (0722) 23164

SALTDEAN, E Sussex
See also Brighton & Hove
Linbrook Lodge, 74 Lenham Avenue,
tel. Brighton (0273) 33775

SANDOWN, Isle of Wight
Chester Lodge Hotel, Beechfield Rd,
tel. (0983) 402773
Cliff House Hotel, Cliff Rd, tel. (0983) 403656
Culver Lodge, Albert Rd, tel. (0983) 403819
St Catherine's Hotel, 1 Winchester Park,
tel. (0983) 402392
Trevallyn Hotel, 32 Broadway, tel. (0983) 402373

SANDPLACE, Cornwall
Polraen Country House Hotel,
tel. Looe (05036) 3956

SANNOX, Isle of Arran, Strathclyde
Cliffdene, tel. Corrie (077081) 224

SARISBURY GREEN, Hants
Dormy, tel. Locks Heath (04895) 2626

SAUNDERSFOOT, Dyfed
Claremont Hotel, St Bride's Hill,
tel. (0834) 813231
Harbour Lights Private Hotel, 2 High St,
tel. (0834) 813496
Jalna Hotel, Stammers Rd,
tel. (0834) 812282
Malin House Hotel, St Bride's Hill,
tel. (0834) 812344
Merlewood Hotel, St Bride's Hill,
tel. (0834) 812421
Rhodewood House Hotel, St Bride's Hill,
tel. (0834) 812200
Sandy Hill, Sandy Hill Rd, tel. (0834) 813165

SAWLEY, Lancs
Spread Eagle Hotel, tel. Clitheroe (0200) 41202

SCARBOROUGH, N Yorks
Avoncroft Hotel, Crown Ter, tel. (0723) 372737
Bay Hotel, 67 Esplanade, South Cliff,
tel. (0723) 373926
Burghcliffe Hotel, 28 Esplanade, South Cliff,
tel. (0723) 361524
Church Hills Private Hotel, St Martins Avenue,
South Cliff, tel. (0723) 363148
Geldenhuls Hotel, 145–147 Queens Pde,
tel. (0723) 361677
Park Hotel, 21–23 Victoria Park, Peasholm,
tel. (0723) 375580
Ridbech Private Hotel, 8 The Crescent,
tel. (0723) 361683
Sefton Hotel, 18 Prince of Wales Ter,
tel. (0723) 372310

SCILLY, ISLES OF

ST MARY'S
Brantwood, Rocky Hill, Hugh Town,
tel. Scillonia (0720) 22531
Carnwethers Country House, Carnwethers,
Pelistry Bay, tel. Scillonia (0720) 22415

SEAFORD, E Sussex
Avondale Hotel, 5 Avondale Rd,
tel. (0323) 890008

SEASCALE, Cumbria
Cottage, Black How, tel. (0940) 28416

SEATON, nr Looe; 7 m Cornwall
Blue Haven Hotel, Looe Hill,
tel. Downderry (05035) 310

SEATON, Devon
Check House, Beer Rd, tel. (0297) 21858
Eyre Hotel, Queen St, tel. (0297) 21455
Glendare, 46 Fore St, tel. (0297) 20542
Harbourside, 2 Trevelyan Rd, tel. (0297) 20085
Mariners Homestead, Esplanade, tel. (0297) 20560
St Margarets, 5 Seafield Rd, tel. (0297) 20462
Thornfield, 87 Scalwell Lane, tel. (0297) 20039

SEAVIEW, Isle of Wight
Northbank Hotel, Circular Rd,
tel. (0989371) 2227

SELBY, N Yorks
Hazeldene, 34 Brook St (A19), tel. (0757) 70480!

SENNEN, Cornwall
Sunny Bank Hotel, Sea View Hill,
tel. (073687) 278

SETTLE, N Yorks
Liverpool House, Chapel Sq, tel. (07292) 2247

SEVENOAKS, Kent
Moorings Hotel, 97 Hitchin Hatch Lane,
tel. (0732) 452589

SHALDON, Devon
See Teignmouth

SHANKLIN, Isle of Wight
Afton Hotel, Clarence Gdns, tel. (0983) 86307
Aqua Hotel, The Esplanade, tel. (0983) 863024
Avenue Hotel, 35 Victoria Av, tel. (0983) 862386
Bay House Hotel, 8 Chine Av, off Keats Green,
tel. (0983) 863180
Culham Private Hotel, 31 Landguard Manor Rd,
tel. (0983) 862880
Curraghmore Hotel, Hope Rd,
tel. (0983) 862605
Edgecliffe Hotel, Clarence Gdns,
tel. (0983) 866199
Fawley Hotel, 12 Hope Rd, tel. (0983) 862190
Leslie House Hotel, 10 Hope Rd,
tel. (0983) 862798
Luccombe Chine House Country Hotel, tel.
(0983) 862037
Meyrick Cliffs, The Esplanade,
tel. (0983) 862691
Monteagle Hotel, Priory Rd, tel. (0983) 862854
Ocean View Hotel, 38 The Esplanade,
tel. (0983) 862602
Overstrand Private Hotel, Howard Rd,
tel. (0983) 862100
Perran Lodge Private Hotel, 2 Crescent Rd,
tel. (0983) 862816
Soraba, Paddock Rd, tel. (0983) 862367
Swiss Cottage Hotel, 10 St Georges Rd,
tel. (0983) 862333

SHAP, Cumbria
Brookfield, tel. (09316) 397

SHEFFIELD, S Yorks
Lindum Hotel, 91 Montgomery Rd,
tel. (0742) 552356
Millingtons, 70 Broomgrove Rd (off A625
Eccleshall Rd), tel. (0742) 669549

SHERFIELD ON LODDON, Hants
Wessex House Hotel, tel. Basingstoke (0256) 882

SHERIFF HUTTON, N Yorks
Ranger's House, Sheriff Hutton Park,
tel. (03477) 397

SHERINGHAM, Norfolk
Beacon Hotel, Nelson Rd, tel. (0263) 822019
Beeston Hills Lodge, 64 Cliff Rd,
tel. (0263) 822615
Camberley House Hotel, 62 Cliff Rd
tel. (0263) 823101
Melrose Hotel, 9 Holway Rd, tel. (0263) 823299

SHETLAND
See Lerwick

SHIPDHAM, Norfolk
Pound Green, Pound Green Ln,
tel. Dereham (0362) 820165

SHOREHAM-BY-SEA, W Sussex
Pende-Shore Hotel, 416 Upper Shoreham Rd,
tel. (07917) 2905

SHOTTLE, Derbys
Shottle Hall Farm,
tel. Cowers Lane (077389) 276

SHREWSBURY, Salop
Cannock House Private Hotel, 182 Abbey
Foregate, tel. (0743) 56043
Sandford House Hotel, St Julians Friars,
tel. (0743) 3829
Sydney House Hotel, Coton Cres, Coton Hill,
tel. (0743) 54681

SIDMOUTH, Devon
Canterbury, Salcombe Rd, tel. (03955) 3373

Mount Pleasant Private Hotel, Salcombe Rd,
tel. (03955) 4694
Ryton House, 52–54 Winslade Rd,
tel. (03955) 3981

SITTINGBOURNE, Kent
Hillcroft Hotel, 94 London Rd, tel. (0795) 71501

SKEGNESS, Lincs
Chatsworth Hotel, North Pde, tel. (0754) 4177
Crawford Hotel, South Pde, tel. (0754) 4215

SKIPTON, N Yorks
Craven House, 56 Keighley Rd,
tel. (0756) 4657
Fairleigh, 24 Bell Vue Ter, Broughton Rd,
tel. (0756) 4153
Highfield Hotel, 58 Keighley Rd, tel. (0756) 3182
Unicorn Hotel, Keighley Rd, tel. (0756) 4146

SKIPTON-ON-SWALE, N Yorks
Skipton Hall, tel. Thirsk (0845) 567457

SKYE, ISLE OF, Highland
**See Broadford, Dunvegan, Isle Ornsay,
Portree, Waterloo**

SLEAFORD, Lincs
The Mallards, 6–8 Eastgate, tel. (0529) 303062

SLOUGH, Berks
Francis House Hotel, 21 London Rd, Langley,
tel. (0753) 22286

SOMERTON, Somerset
Church Farm, School Lane, Compton Dundon,
tel. (0458) 72927

SOUTHAMPTON, Hants
Banister House Hotel, 11 Brighton Rd, off
Banister Rd, tel. (0703) 221279
Claremont, 33 The Polygon, tel. (0703) 223112
Cliffden, 43 The Polygon, tel. (0703) 224003
Eaton Court Hotel, 32 Hill Lane,
tel. (0703) 223081
Elizabeth House Hotel, 43–44 The Avenue,
tel. (0703) 224327
Hunters Lodge Hotel, 25 Landguard Rd, Shirley,
tel. (0703) 227919
Linden, 51 The Polygon, tel. (0703) 225653
Lodge, 1 Winn Rd, The Avenue, tel. (0703) 557537
Madison House, 137 Hill Lane,
tel. (0703) 333374
Rosida Garden Hotel, 25–27 Hill Lane,
tel. (0703) 228501
St Regulus Hotel, 5 Archers Rd,
tel. (0703) 224243

SOUTHEND-ON-SEA, Essex
Argyle Hotel, 12 Clifftown Pde,
tel. (0702) 339483
Cobham Lodge Private Hotel, 2 Cobham Rd,
Westcliff-on-Sea, tel. (0702) 34638
Ferndale Hotel, 136 York Rd, tel. (0702) 68614
Gladstone Hotel, 40 Hartington Rd,
tel. (0702) 62776
Maple Leaf Private Hotel, 9–11 Trinity Avenue,
Westcliff-on-Sea, tel. (0702) 346904
Marine View, 4 Trinity Avenue, Westcliff-on-Sea,
tel. (0702) 344104
Mayfair, 52 Crownstone Avenue, Westcliff-on-
Sea, tel. (0702) 340693
Mayflower Hotel, 5–6 Royal Ter,
tel. (0702) 340489
Norfolk Hotel, 32 The Leas, Westcliff-on-Sea,
tel. (0702) 351069
Regency Hotel, 18 Royal Ter, tel. (0702) 340747
Terrace Hotel, 8 Royal Ter, tel. (0702) 348143
Tower Hotel, 146 Alexandra Rd,
tel. (0702) 348635
West Park Private Hotel, 11 Park Rd, Westcliff-
on-Sea, tel. (0702) 330729

SOUTH LAGGAN, Highland
Forest Lodge, tel. Invergarry (08093) 219

SOUTHPORT, Merseyside
Crimond Hotel, 28 Knowsley Rd,
tel. (0704) 36456
Fairway Private Hotel, 106 Leyland Rd,
tel. (0704) 42069
Fernley Private Hotel, 69 The Promenade,
tel. (0704) 35610
Franklyn Hotel, 65 The Promenade,
tel. (0704) 40290
Fulwood Private Hotel, 82 Leyland Rd,
tel. (0704) 30993
Garden Hotel, 19 Latham Rd, tel. (0704) 30244
Hollies Hotel, 7 Mornington Rd,
tel. (0704) 30054
Newholme, 51 King St, tel. (0704) 30425
Oakwood Private Hotel, 7 Portland St,
tel. (0704) 31858
Orleans Christian Hotel, 6–8 Latham Rd,
tel. (0704) 38430
Rosedale Hotel, 11 Talbot St, tel. (0704) 30604
Sidbrook Hotel, 14 Talbot St, tel. (0704) 30608
Stutelea Hotel, Alexandra Rd,
tel. (0704) 44220
Sunningdale Hotel, 85 Leyland Rd,
tel. (0704) 38673
Talbot Hotel, Portland St, tel. (0704) 33975
White Lodge Private Hotel, 12 Talbot St,
tel. (0704) 36320
Whitworth Falls Hotel, 16 Latham Rd,
tel. (0704) 30074
Windsor Lodge Hotel, 37 Saunders St,
tel. (0704) 30070

SOUTHSEA, Hants
See Portsmouth and Southsea

SOUTH SHIELDS, Tyne & Wear
Sir William Fox Private Hotel, 5 Westoe Village,
tel. (0632) 564554

SOUTHWOLD, Suffolk
Mount, North Pde, tel. (0502) 722292

SOUTH ZEAL, Devon
Poltimore, tel. Okehampton (0837) 840209

SPEAN BRIDGE, Highland
Coire Glas, tel. (039781) 272
Lesanne, tel. (039781) 231

STAFFORD, Staffs
Leonards Croft Hotel, 80 Lichfield Rd,
tel. (0785) 3676

STAINTON, Cumbria
Limes Country Hotel, Redhills,
tel. Penrith (0768) 63343

STANFORD LE HOPE, Essex
Homesteads, 216 Southend Rd,
tel. (0375) 672372

STEEPLE ASTON, Oxon
Westfield Farm Motel, The Fenway,
tel. (0869) 40591

STEPASIDE, Dyfed
Bay View House, Pleasant Valley.
tel. Saundersfoot (0834) 813417

STEVENAGE, Herts
Archways Hotel, 11 Hitchin Rd,
tel. (0438) 316640
Northfield Private Hotel, Stevenage Old Town,
tel. (0438) 314537

STEYNING, W Sussex
Down House, King's Barn Villas,
tel. (0903) 812319
Nash Hotel, Horsham Rd, tel. (0903) 814988

STIPERSTONES, Salop
Tankerville, tel. (0743) 791401

STOCKBRIDGE, Hants
Carbery, Salisbury Hill,
tel. Andover (0264) 810771

Old Three Cups Private Hotel,
tel. Andover (0264) 810527

STOCKPORT, Gt Manchester
Ascot House Hotel, 195 Wellington Rd North,
Heaton Norris, tel. 061–4322380

STOCKTON-ON-TEES, Cleveland
Court Private Hotel, 49 Yarm Rd,
tel. (0642) 604483
Grange Hotel, 91 Yarm Rd, tel. (0642) 65908

STOKE FLEMING, Devon
Endsleigh Hotel, tel. (0803) 770381

STOKEINTEIGNHEAD, Devon
Bailey's Farm, tel. Shaldon (062687) 3361

STOKE-ON-TRENT, Staffs
The White House, Stone Rd, Trent Vale,
tel. (0782) 642460

STOKE ST GREGORY, Somerset
Meare Green, tel. North Curry (0823) 490250

STONE, nr Berkeley, Glos
Elms, tel. Falfield (0454) 260279

STORNOWAY, Isle of Lewis, Western Isles
Ardlonan, 29 Francis St. tel. (0851) 3482

STOURBRIDGE, W Midlands
Limes, 260 Hagley Rd, Pedmore,
tel. Hagley (0562) 882689

STOW-ON-THE-WOLD, Glos
Limes, Evesham Rd, tel. Cotswold (0451) 30034
Grapevine Hotel, Sheep St, tel. (0451) 30344

STRATFORD-UPON-AVON, Warwicks
Ambleside, 41 Grove Rd, tel. (0789) 297239
Avon House, 8 Evesham Place,
tel. (0789) 293328
Avon View Hotel, 121 Shipston Rd,
tel. (0789) 297542
Brook Lodge, 192 Alcester Rd, tel. (0789) 295988
Coach House, 17 Warwick Rd (Guestaccom),
tel. (0789) 204109
Glenavon, Chestnut Walk, tel. (0789) 292588
Hardwick House, 1 Avenue Rd,
tel. (0789) 204307
Hunters Moon, 150 Alcester Rd,
tel. (0789) 292888
Hylands Hotel, Warwick Rd, tel. (0789) 297962
Kawartha House, 39 Grove Rd,
tel. (0789) 204469
Marlyn, 3 Chestnut Walk, tel. (0789) 293752
Melita Private Hotel, 37 Shipston Rd,
tel. (0789) 292432
Moonraker House, 40 Alcester Rd,
tel. (0789) 67115
Nando's, 18–19 Evesham Place,
tel. (0789) 204907
Penshurst, 34 Evesham Place,
tel. (0789) 205259
Sequoia House, 51 Shipston Rd,
tel. (0789) 68852
Stretton House, 38 Grove Rd, tel. (0789) 68647

Stratford-upon-Avon

Virginia Lodge, 12 Evesham Place,
tel. (0789) 292157
Woodburn House Hotel, 89 Shipston Rd,
tel. (0789) 204453

STRATHAVEN, Strathclyde
Springvale Hotel, 18 Letham Rd,
tel. (0357) 21131

STRATHPEFFER, Highland
Kilvannie Manor, Fodderty, tel. (0997) 21389

STRATHYRE, Central
Rosebank House Hotel, Main St,
tel. (08774) 208

STRETE, Devon
Highcliff, tel. Stoke Fleming (0803) 770307
Tallis Rock Private Hotel,
tel. Stoke Fleming (0803) 770370

STROUD, Glos
Downfield Private Hotel, Caincross Rd,
tel. (04536) 4496

SUDBURY, Suffolk
Hill Lodge Private Hotel, 8 Newton Rd,
tel. (0787) 77568

SURBITON, Gt London
Holmdene, 23 Cranes Drive, tel. 01-399 9992

SUTTON, Gt London
Dene Hotel, 39 Cheam Rd, tel. 01-642 3170
Eaton Court Hotel, 49 Eaton Rd, tel. 01-642 6766
Tara House, 50 Rosehill, tel. 01-641 6142
Thatched House Hotel, 135 Cheam Rd,
tel. 01-642 3131

SUTTON COLDFIELD, W Midlands
Cloverley Hotel, 17 Anchorage Rd,
tel. 021-354 5181
Standbridge Hotel, 138 Birmingham Rd,
tel. 021-354 3007

SWANAGE, Dorset
Boyne Hotel, 1 Cliff Avenue, tel. (0929) 422939
Burlington Hotel, 7 Highcliffe Rd,
tel. (0929) 422422
Byways, 5 Ulwell Rd, tel. (0929) 422322
Castleton Private Hotel, Highcliff Rd,
tel. (0929) 423972
Chines Hotel, 9 Burlington Rd, tel. (0929) 422457
Eversden Private Hotel, Victoria Rd,
tel. (0929) 423276
Firswood, 29 Kings Rd, tel. (0929) 422306
Golden Sands Private Hotel, 10 Ulwell Rd,
tel. (0929) 422093
Havenhurst Hotel, 3 Cranbourne Rd,
tel. (0929) 424224
Ingleston Private Hotel, 2 Victoria Rd,
tel. (0929) 422391
Kingsley Hall Hotel, 8 Ulwell Rd,
tel. (0929) 422872
Nethway Hotel, Gilberts Rd, tel. (0929) 423909
Oxford Hotel, 3 & 5 Park Rd, tel. (0929) 422247
St Michael Hotel, 31 Kings Rd,
tel. (0929) 422064
Tower Lodge Private Hotel, 17 Ulwell Rd,
tel. (0929) 422887

SWANSEA, W Glam
See also Bishopston, Langland Bay and Mumbles
Alexander Hotel, 3 Sketty Rd, Sketty,
tel. (0792) 470045
Channel View, 17 Bryn Rd, Brynmill,
tel. (0792) 466834
Crescent, 132 Eaton Cres, Uplands,
tel. (0792) 466814
Parkway Hotel, 253 Gower Rd, Sketty,
tel. (0792) 201632
St Davids Private Hotel, 15 Sketty Rd, Uplands,
tel. (0792) 473814
St Helen's House, St Helen's Cres,
tel. (0792) 460065

Tregare Hotel, 9 Sketty Rd, Uplands,
tel. (0792) 470608
Westlands, 34 Bryn Rd, Brynmill,
tel. (0792) 466689

SYMONDS YAT, EAST, Heref and Worcs
Garth Cottage Hotel, tel. (0600) 890364

SYMONDS YAT, WEST (nr Ross-on-Wye), Heref
and Worcs
Woodlea, tel. (0600) 890206

TADCASTER, N Yorks
Shann House, 47 Kirkgate, tel. (0937) 833931

TAPLOW, Bucks
Norfolk House, Bath Rd,
tel. Maidenhead (0628) 23687

TARPORLEY, Cheshire
Perth Hotel, High St, tel. (08293) 2514

TAUNTON, Somerset
Brookfield House, 16 Wellington Rd,
tel. (0823) 72786
Meryan House Hotel, Bishop's Hull Rd,
tel. (0823) 87445
Ruishton Lodge, Ruishton,
tel. Henlade (0823) 442298
Rumwell Hall, Rumwell, tel. (0823) 75268
White Lodge Hotel, 81 Bridgwater Rd,
tel. (0823) 73287

TAVISTOCK, Devon
Cherry Trees, 40 Plymouth Rd, tel. (0822) 4897

TEIGNMOUTH, Devon
Baveno Hotel, 40 Higher Brimley Rd,
tel. (06267) 3102
Bay Cottage Hotel, 7 Marine Pde, Shaldon,
tel. Shaldon (062687) 2394
Glen Devon, 3 Carlton Place,
tel. (06267) 2895
Hillrise, Winterbourne Rd,
tel. (06267) 3108
Hillsley, Upper Hermosa Rd, tel. (06267) 3878
Knoll Hotel, 5 Winterbourne Rd,
tel. (06267) 4241
Lyme Bay House Hotel, Den Promenade,
tel. (06267) 2953
Rathlin House Hotel, Upper Hermosa Rd,
tel. (06267) 4473
Ravensbourne Hotel, Higher Woodway Rd,
tel. (06267) 3415
Teign Holiday Inn Hotel, Teign St,
tel. (06267) 2976

TENBY, Dyfed
Hotel Doneva, The Norton, tel. (0834) 2460
Heywood Lodge, Heywood Lane,
tel. (0834) 2684
Hildebrand Hotel, Victoria St, tel. (0834) 2403
Myrtle House Hotel, St Mary's St,
tel. (0834) 2508
Penally Manor Hotel, Pennally, tel. (0834) 2668
Red House Hotel, Heywood Ln, tel. (0834) 2770
Richmond Hotel, The Croft, North Beach,
tel. (0834) 2533
Ripley St Mary's Hotel, St Mary's Street,
tel. (0834) 2837
Sea Breezes Hotel, 18 The Norton,
tel. (0834) 2753

TEWKESBURY, Glos
Ancient Grudge Hotel, 15 High St,
tel. (0684) 292204
South End House, 67 Church St,
tel. (0684) 294097

THORNTHWAITE (nr Keswick), Cumbria
Ladstock Country House Hotel,
tel. Braithwaite (059682) 210

THORNTON CLEVELEYS, Lancs
Lyndhope, 2 Stockdove Way, Cleveleys,
tel. Cleveleys (0253) 852531

THORNTON HEATH, Gt London
Dunheved Hotel, 639–641 London Rd,
tel. 01–684 2009

THORPE (Dovedale), Derbys
Hillcrest House, Thorpe Cloud, tel. (033529) 436

THORPE BAY, Essex
See Southend-on-Sea

THRESHFIELD, N Yorks
Greenways, Wharfside Av,
tel. Skipton (0756) 752598

THWAITE, N Yorks
Kearton, tel. Richmond (N Yorks) (0748) 86277

TIMSBURY, Avon
Old Malt House Hotel & Licensed Restaurant,
Radford, tel. (0761) 70106

TINTAGEL, Cornwall
Belvoir House, Tregatta,
tel. Camelford (0840) 770265
Penallick Hotel, Treknow,
tel. Camelford (0840) 770296
Trebrea Lodge, Trenale,
tel. Camelford (0840) 770410
Trevervan Hotel, Trewarmett,
tel. Camelford (0840) 770486
Trewarmett Lodge, tel. Camelford (0840) 770460
Willapark Manor Hotel, Bossiney,
tel. Camelford (0840) 770782

TINTERN, Gwent
Parva Farmhouse, tel. (02918) 411

TIVERTON, Devon
Bridge, 23 Angel Hill, tel. (0884) 252804

TOBERMORY, Isle of Mull, Strathclyde
Tobermory, 53 Main St, tel. (0688) 2091

TORBAY, Devon
See under Brixham, Paignton and Torquay

TORCROSS, Devon
Cove House, tel. Kingsbridge (0548) 580448

TORQUAY, Devon
Allandene Seapoint Hotel, 5 Clifton Gv, Old
Torwood Rd, tel. (0803) 211808
Ashwood Hotel, 2 St Margarets Rd, St
Marychurch, tel. (0803) 38173
Ashton Hotel, Belgrave Rd, tel. (0803) 22407
Avon Hotel, Torbay Rd, Livermead,
tel. (0803) 23946
Avron Hotel, 70 Windsor Rd, tel. (0803) 24182
Aylwood House Hotel, 24 Newton Rd,
tel. (0803) 23501
Beechmoor Hotel, Vansittart Rd,
tel. (0803) 22471
Blue Waters Hotel, 58 Bampfylde Rd,
tel. (0803) 26410
Braddon Hall Hotel, Braddons Hill Rd East,
tel. (0803) 23908
Brandize Hotel, 19 Avenue Rd, tel. (0803) 27798
Burley Court Hotel, Wheatbridge Lane,
Livermead, tel. (0803) 607879
Carn Brea, 21 Avenue Rd, tel. (0803) 22002
Cary Park Hotel, Palermo Rd, Babbacombe,
tel. (0803) 37843
Castle Mount Hotel, 7 Castle Rd,
tel. (0803) 22130
Castleton Private Hotel, Castle Rd,
tel. (0803) 24976
Cheltenham Hotel, Rousdown Rd,
tel. (0803) 605488
Chesterfield Private Hotel, 62 Belgrave Rd,
tel. (0803) 22318
Clairville, 1 Teignmouth Rd, Brunwick Sq, Torre,
tel. (0803) 24540
Hotel Concorde, 26 Newton Rd,
tel. (0803) 22330
Craig Court Hotel, 10 Ash Hill Rd, Castle Circus,
tel. (0803) 24400

Cranbourne Hotel, 58 Belgrave Rd,
tel. (0803) 28046
Cranmore, 89 Avenue Rd,
tel. (0803) 28488
Crewe Lodge, 83 Avenue Rd, tel. (0803) 28772
Daphne Court Hotel, Lower Warberry Rd,
tel. (0803) 212011
Devon Court Hotel, Croft Rd,
tel. (0803) 23603
El Marino Hotel, Lower Warberry Rd,
tel. (0803) 26882
Exmouth View Hotel, Bedford Rd, Babbacombe
Downs, tel. (0803) 37307
Fretherne Hotel, St Luke's Rd South,
tel. (0803) 22594
Glenorleigh Hotel, 26 Cleveland Rd,
tel. (0803) 22135
Glenwood Hotel, Rowdens Rd,
tel. (0803) 26318
Hart-Lea, 81 St Marychurch Rd,
tel. (0803) 312527
Hatherleigh Hotel, 56 St Marychurch Rd,
tel. (0803) 25762
Ingoldsby Hotel, 1 Chelston Rd,
tel. (0803) 607497
Jesmond Dene Private Hotel, 85 Abbey Rd,
tel. (0803) 23062
Kilworthy Hotel, 157 Westhill Rd, Babbacombe,
tel. (0803) 36452
Lindum Hotel, Abbey Rd, tel. (0803) 22795
Mapleton Hotel, St Luke's Rd North,
tel. (0803) 22389
Marlow Hotel, 23 Belgrave Rd, tel. (0803) 22833
Mount Nessing Hotel, St Luke's Rd North,
tel. (0803) 22970
Parkfield Hotel, Claddon Ln, Maidencombe,
tel. (0803) 38952
Pencarrow Hotel, 64 Windsor Rd,
tel. (0803) 23080
Pines Hotel, St Marychurch Rd,
tel. (0803) 38384
Porthcressa Hotel, 28 Perinville Rd, Babbacombe
tel. (0803) 37268
Rawlyn House Hotel, Rawlyn Rd, Chelston
tel. (0803) 605208
Richwood Hotel, 20 Newton Rd,
tel. (0803) 23729
Riva Lodge, Croft Td,. tel. (0803) 22614
Rosewood, Teignmouth Rd, Maidencombe,
tel. (0803) 38178
Rothesay Hotel, Scarborough Rd,
tel. (0803) 23161
St Bernard's Private Hotel, Castle Rd,
tel. (0803) 22508
Sevens Hotel, 27 Morgan Av, tel. (0803) 23523
Silverlands Hotel, 27 Newton Rd,
tel. (0803) 22013
Skerries Private Hotel, 25 Morgan Av,
tel. (0803) 23618
Southbank Hotel, 15–17 Belgrave Rd,
tel. (0803) 26701
Stephen House Hotel, 50 Ash Mill Rd,
tel. (0803) 25796
Sun Court Hotel, Rowdens Rd, tel. (0803) 27242
Torbay Rise, Old Mill Rd, tel. (0803) 605541
Torcroft Hotel, Croft Rd, tel. (0803) 28292
Tormohun Hotel, 28 Newton Rd,
tel. (0803) 23681
Trafalgar House Hotel, 30 Bridge Rd.
tel. (0803) 22486
Tregantle Hotel, 64 Bampfylde Rd,
tel. (0803) 27494
Ventnor, 85 St Mary Church Rd, tel. (0803) 3913
Villa Marina Hotel, Cockington Lane, Livermead,
tel. (0803) 605440
Westowe Hotel, Chelston Rd, tel. (0803) 60520
White Gables, Rawlyn Rd, tel. (0803) 605233

TORRINGTON, GREAT, Devon
Smytham, tel. (0805) 22110

TOTLAND BAY, Isle of Wight
Garrow Hotel, Church Hill,
tel. (0983) 753174
Hermitage Hotel, Cliff Rd,
tel. (0983) 752518
Hilton House Private Hotel, Granville Rd,
tel. (0983) 754768
Lismore Private Hotel, 23 The Avenue,
tel. (0983) 752025
Nodes Country Hotel, Alum Bay Old Rd,
tel. (0983) 752859
Sandford Lodge Private Hotel, 61 The Avenue,
tel. (0983) 753478
Westgrange Country Hotel, Alum Bay Old Rd,
tel. (0983) 752227

TOTNES, Devon
Four Seasons, 13 Bridgetown, tel. (0803) 862091
Ridgemark Hotel, Bridgetown Hill,
tel. (0803) 862011

TOTTENHILL, Norfolk
Oakwood House Private Hotel,
tel. King's Lynn (0553) 810256

TREARDDUR BAY, Gwynedd
Moranedd, tel. (0407) 860324

TREGARON, Dyfed
Aberdwr, Abergwesyn Rd, tel. (09744) 255

TREVONE, Cornwall
Coimbatore Hotel, West View,
tel. Padstow (0841) 520390
Green Waves Private Hotel, tel. (0841) 520114

TRINITY, Jersey, Channel Islands
Highfield Country Hotel, Route Du Ebenezer,
tel. Jersey (0534) 62194

TRURO, Cornwall
Colthrop, Tregolls Rd, tel. (0872) 72920
Farley Hotel, Falmouth Rd, tel. (0872) 70712
Manor Cottage, Tresillian (3m NW at Tresillian),
tel. Tresillian (087252) 212

TUNBRIDGE WELLS (ROYAL), Kent
Firwood, 89 Frant Rd, tel. (0892) 25596

TWO BRIDGES, Devon
Cherrybrook Hotel, tel. Tavistock (0822) 88260

TYWARDREATH, Cornwall
Elmswood, Tehidy Rd, Tywardreath Park,
tel. Par (072681) 4221

TYWYN, Gwynedd
Min-y-Mor Private Hotel, 7 Marine Pde,
tel. (0654) 710139
Monfa, Pier Rd, tel. (0654) 710858

UPTON UPON SEVERN, Heref and Worcs
Pool House, tel. (0686) 2151

UTTOXETER, Staffs
Hillcrest, 3 Leighton Rd, tel. (08893) 4627

VENN OTTERY, Devon
Venn Ottery Barton Country Hotel,
tel. Ottery St Mary (040481) 2733

VENTNOR, Isle of Wight
Channel View Hotel, Hambrough Rd,
tel. (0983) 852230
Hillside Private Hotel, Mitchell Avenue,
tel. (0983) 852271
Horseshoe Bay Hotel, Shore Rd, Bonchurch,
tel. (0983) 852487
Lake Hotel, Shore Rd, Bonchurch,
tel. (0983) 852613
Macrocarpa, Mitchell Avenue, tel. (0983) 852428
Picardie Hotel, Esplanade, tel. (0983) 852647
Richmond Private Hotel, Esplanade,
tel. (0983) 852496
St Maur Hotel, Castle Rd, tel. (0983) 852570
Under Rock Hotel, Shore Rd, Bonchurch (1m E),
tel. (0983) 852714

WALLASEY, Merseyside
Divonne Hotel, 71 Wellington Rd,
New Brighton,
tel. 051–639 4727
Sandpiper Private Hotel, 22 Dudley Rd,
New Brighton,
tel. 051–639 7870

WARSASH, Hants
Solent View Private Hotel, 33–35 Newton Rd
tel. Locks Heath (04895) 2300

WARWICK, Warwicks
Austin House, 96 Emscote Rd,
tel. (0926) 493583
Avon, 7 Emscote Rd, tel. (0926) 491367
Cambridge Villa Private Hotel, 20A Emscote Rd,
tel. (0926) 491169
Old Rectory,
tel. Sherbourne Barford (Warwicks) (0926) 624562

WASHFORD, Somerset
Washford House, tel. (0984) 40484

WATERLOO, Isle of Skye, Highland
Ceol-na-Mara, tel. Broadford (04712) 323

WATERLOOVILLE, Hants
Far End Private Hotel, 31 Queens Rd
tel. (07014) 3242

WATFORD, Herts
White House Hotel, 26–29 Upton Rd,
tel. (0923) 37316

WELLINGBOROUGH, Northants
Oak House Private Hotel, 9 Broad Green,
tel. (0933) 71133

WELLS, Somerset
Bekynton House, 7 St Thomas St,
tel. (0749) 72222
Tor, 20 Tor St, tel. (0749) 72322

WEST BAGBOROUGH, Somerset
Higher House,
tel. Bishops Lydeard (0823) 432996

WESTCLIFF-ON-SEA, Essex
See Southend-on-Sea

WEST KIRBY, Merseyside
Park Hotel, Westbourne Rd, tel. 051–625 9319

WEST LULWORTH, Dorset
See Lulworth

WESTON-SUPER-MARE, Avon
Baymead Hotel, Longton Grove Rd,
tel. (0934) 22951
Fourways, 2 Ashcombe Rd,
tel. (0934) 23827
Glenelg, 24 Ellenborough Park South,
tel. (0934) 20521
Kew Dee, 6 Neva Rd, tel. (0934) 29041
Lydia, 78 Locking Rd, tel. (0934) 25962
Milton Lodge, 15 Milton Rd, tel. (0934) 23161
Newton House, 79 Locking Rd, tel. (0934) 29331
Scottsdale Hotel, 3 Ellenborough Park North,
tel. (0934) 26489
Shire Elms, 71 Locking Rd, tel. (0934) 28605
Southmead, 435 Locking Rd, tel. (0934) 29351
Willow, 3 Clarence Rd East,
tel. (0934) 413736
Wychwood Hotel, 148 Milton Rd,
tel. (0934) 27793

WESTWARD HO!, Devon
Buckleigh Lodge, 135 Bayview Rd,
tel. Bideford (02372) 75988

WETHERBY, W Yorks
Prospect House, 8 Caxton St,
tel. (0937) 62428

WEYBRIDGE, Surrey
Warbeck House Hotel, 46 Queens Rd,
tel. (0932) 48764

Weymouth

WEYMOUTH, Dorset
Beechcroft Private Hotel, 128–129 The Esplanade, tel. (0305) 786608
Hotel Concorde, 131 The Esplanade, tel. (0305) 776900
Hazeldene, 16 Abbotsbury Rd, Westham, tel. (0305) 782579
Kenora, 5 Stavordale Rd, tel. (0305) 771215
Kings Acre Hotel, 140 The Esplanade, tel. (0305) 782534
Leam Hotel, 102–103 The Esplanade, tel. (0305) 784127
Richmoor Hotel, 146 The Esplanade, tel. (0305) 785087
Sou'-west Lodge Hotel, Rodwell Rd, tel. (0305) 783749
Sunningdale Private Hotel, 52 Preston Rd, Overcombe, tel. (0305) 832179
Tamarisk Hotel, 12 Stavordale Rd, Westham, tel. (0305) 786514
Treverbyn Court Hotel, 65 Dorchester Rd, tel. (0305) 786170

WHEDDON CROSS, Somerset
Higherley, tel. Timberscombe (064384) 582

WHITBY, N Yorks
Beach Cliff Hotel, North Prom, West Cliff, tel. (0947) 602886
Esklet, 22 Crescent Av, tel. (0947) 605663
Europa Private Hotel, 20 Hudson St, tel. (0947) 602251
Glendale, 16 Crescent Av, tel. (0947) 604242
Old Hall Hotel, Ruswarp, tel. (0947) 602801
Prospect Villa, 13 Prospect Hill, tel. (0947) 603118
Sandbeck Hotel, Crescent Ter, West Cliff, tel. (0947) 604012
Seacliffe Hotel, North Prom, West Cliff, tel. (0947) 603139

WHITCHURCH, Heref and Worcs
Portland, tel. Symonds Yat (0600) 890757

WHITLEY BAY, Tyne and Wear
York, 30 Park Pde, tel. 091–252 8313

WICKFORD, Essex
Wickford Lodge, 26 Ethelred Gdns, tel. (03744) 62663

WIDEGATES, Cornwall
Coombe Farm, tel. (05034) 223

WIDEMOUTH BAY, Cornwall
Beach House Hotel, tel. (028885) 256

WIGAN, Gt Manchester
Aalton Court, 23 Disconston St, tel. (0942) 322220

WIGHT, ISLE OF
Full details will be found under individual place-names within the appropriate gazetteer sections. See Arreton, Freshwater, Niton, Ryde, St Lawrence, Sandown, Seaview, Shanklin, Totland Bay and Ventnor

WILLERSEY, Glos
Old Rectory, Church St, tel. Evesham (0386) 853729

WILMINGTON, E Sussex
Crossways Hotel, tel. Polegate (03212) 2455

WIMBORNE MINSTER, Dorset
Riversdale, 33 Poole Rd, tel. (0202) 884528

WINCLE, Cheshire
Four Ways Diner Motel, Cleulow Cross (1m N of A54), tel. (02607) 228

WINDERMERE, Cumbria
Archway, College Rd, tel. (09662) 5613
Blakey Howe Villa Hotel, Craig Walk, Bowness, tel. (09662) 3988
Brooklands, Ferry View, Bowness, tel. (09662) 2344
Crag Brow Cottage Private Hotel, Helm Rd, Bowness, tel. (09662) 4080
Craig Foot Hotel, Lake Rd, tel. (09662) 3902
Cranleigh Hotel, Kendal Rd, Bowness, tel. (09662) 3293
Eastbourne Hotel, Biskey Howe Rd, tel. (09662) 3525
Elim Bank Hotel, Lake Rd, Bowness, tel. (09662) 4810
Fairfield Country House Hotel, Brantfell Rd, Bowness, tel. (09662) 3772
Glenburn, New Rd, tel. (09662) 2649
Glenville Hotel, Lake Rd, tel. (09662) 3371
Green Gables, 37 Broad St, tel. (09662) 3886
Greenrigs, 8 Upper Oak St, tel. (09662) 2265
Haisthorpe, Holly Rd, tel. (09662) 3445
Hawksmoor, Lake Rd, tel. (09662) 2110
Hilton House Hotel, New Rd, tel. (09662) 3934
Hollythwaite, Holly Rd, tel. (09662) 2219
Kenilworth, Holly Rd, tel. (09662) 4004
Lynwood, Broad St, tel. (09662) 2550
Myine Bridge Private Hotel, Brookside, Lake Rd, tel. (09662) 3314
Oakfield, 46 Oak St, tel. (09662) 5692
Oakthorpe Hotel, High St, tel. (09662) 3547
Orrest Head House, Kendal Rd, tel. (09662) 4315
Rosemount, Lake Rd, tel. (09662) 3739
St Johns Lodge, Lake Rd, tel. (09662) 3078
Thornleigh, Thornbarrow Rd, Bowness, tel. (09662) 4203
Tudor, 60 Main St, tel. (09662) 2363
Waverley Hotel, College Rd, tel. (09662) 5026
Westlake, Lake Rd, tel. (09662) 3020
White Lodge Hotel, Lake Rd, tel. (09662) 3624
Winbrook House, 30 Ellerthwaite Rd, tel. (09662) 4932

WINTERBOURNE ABBAS, Dorset
Church View, tel. Martinstown (030588) 296
Whitefriars, tel. Martinstown (030588) 206

WISBECH, Cambs
Glendon, Sutton Rd, tel. (0945) 584812

WOODHALL SPA, Lincs
Dunns, The Broadway, tel. (0526) 52969

WOODY BAY, Devon
The Red House, tel. Parracombe (05983) 255

WOOLACOMBE, Devon
Barton House Hotel, Barton Rd, tel. (0271) 870548
Castle, The Esplanade, tel. (0271) 870788
Combe Ridge Hotel, The Esplanade, tel. (0271) 870321
Holmesdale Hotel, Bay View Rd, tel. (0271) 870335
Springside Country Hotel, Mullacott Rd, tel. (0271) 870452

WORCESTER, Heref and Worcs
Barbourne, 42 Barbourne Rd, tel. (0905) 27507
Loch Ryan Hotel, 119 Sidbury, tel. (0905) 351143

WORTHING, W Sussex
Blair House, 11 St George's Rd, tel. (0903) 34071
Camelot House, 20 Gannon Rd,
tel. (0903) 204334
Meldrum House, 8 Windsor Rd, tel. (0903) 33808
Osborne, 175 Brighton Rd, tel. (0903) 35771
St Georges Lodge Hotel, Chesswood Rd,
tel. (0903) 208926
Southdene, 41 Warwick Gdns, tel. (0903) 32909
Wansfell Hotel, 49 Chesswood Rd (Guestaccom),
tel. (0903) 30612
Windsor House Hotel, 14–20 Windsor Rd,
tel. (0903) 39655
Windsor Lodge Hotel, 3 Windsor Rd,
tel. (0903) 200056
Wolsey Hotel, 179–181 Brighton Rd,
tel. (0903) 36149

YARMOUTH, GREAT, Norfolk
Frandor, 120 Lowestoft Rd, Gorleston-on-Sea (2m
S A12), tel. (0493) 662112
Georgian House Private Hotel, 16–17 North
Drive, tel. (0493) 842623
Hazelwood House, 57 Clarence Rd, Gorleston-
on-Sea, tel. (0493) 662830
Palm Court Hotel, 10 North Drive,
tel. (0493) 844568

YELVERTON, Devon
Harrabeer Country House Hotel,
Harrowbeer Ln, tel. (0822) 853302

YORK, N Yorks
Abingdon, 60 Bootham Cres, Bootham,
tel. (0904) 21761
Acomb Road, 128 Acomb Rd, tel. (0904) 792321
Adams House Hotel, 5 Main St, Fulford,
tel. (0904) 55413
Albert Hotel, The Mount, tel. (0904) 32525
Alcuin Lodge, 15 Sycamore Pl, Bootham,
tel. (0904) 32222
Alhambra Court Hotel, 31 St Mary's, Bootham,
tel. (0904) 28474
Amblesyde, 62 Bootham Crescent,
tel. (0904) 37165
Ascot House, 80 East Pde, tel. (0904) 426826
Avenue, 6 The Avenue, Clifton, tel. (0904) 20575
Beech Hotel, 6–7 Longfield Ter, Bootham,
tel. (0904) 34581
Bootham Bar Hotel, 4 High Petergate,
tel. (0904) 58516
Brönte House, 22 Grosvenor Ter, Bootham,
tel. (0904) 21066
Cavalier, 39 Monkgate, tel. (0904) 36615
Clifton Bridge Hotel, Water End,
tel. (0904) 53609
Coach House Hotel, Marygate, tel. (0904) 52780
Coppers Lodge, 15 Alma Ter, Fulford Rd,
tel. (0904) 39871
Craig-y-Don, 3 Grosvenor Ter, Bootham,
tel. (0904) 37186
Crescent, 77 Bootham, tel. (0904) 23216
Croft Hotel, 103 Mount Rd, tel. (0904) 22747
Dairy, 3 Scarcroft Rd, tel. (0904) 39367
Fairmount Hotel, 230 Tadcaster Rd, Mount Vale,
tel. (0904) 38298
Field House Hotel, 2 St George's Pl,
tel. (0904) 39572
Gables, 50 Bootham Cres, tel. (0904) 24381
Georgian, 35 Bootham, tel. (0904) 22874
Grasmead House Hotel, 1 Scarcroft Hill, The
Mount, tel. (0904) 29996
Greenside, 124 Clifton, tel. (0904) 23631
Hazelwood, 24–25 Portland St, Gillygate,
tel. (0904) 26548
Heworth, 126 East Pde, tel. (0904) 426384
Inglewood, 7 Clifton Green, tel. (0904) 53523
Linden Lodge, Nunthorpe Avenue, Scarcroft Rd,
tel. (0904) 20107
Mayfield Hotel, 75 Scarcroft Rd,
tel. (0904) 54834

Moat Hotel, Nunnery Lane, tel. (0904) 52926
Orchard Court Hotel, 4 St Peter's Gv,
tel. (0904) 53964
Priory Hotel, 126 Fulford Rd, tel. (0904) 25280
St Denys Hotel, St Denys Rd, tel. (0904) 22207
St Raphael, 44 Queen Anne's Rd, Bootham,
tel. (0904) 645028
Sycamore Hotel, 19 Sycamore Place,
tel. (0904) 24712

Guest-houses – Northern Ireland

Co Antrim
BALLYCASTLE
Atlantic, The Promenade, tel. Ballycastle 62412
Hillsea, 28 Quay Hill, tel. Ballycastle 62385

LARNE
Derrin, 2 Prince's Gdns, tel. Larne 3269

PORTRUSH
Mount Royal, 2 Mount Royal,
tel. Portrush 823342

Belfast
BELFAST
Camera, 44 Wellington Park, tel. Belfast 660026

Co Down
BANGOR
Ennislare, 9 Princetown Rd, tel. Bangor 2858
Malinmore, 11 Princetown Rd, tel. Bangor 3303

Co Fermanagh
ENNISKILLEN
Interlaken, 54 Fort Hill St, tel. Enniskillen 22274
Lack-a-Boy Farmhouse, Tempo Rd,
tel. Enniskillen 22488

Co Londonderry
PORTSTEWART
Links, 103 Strand Rd, tel. Portstewart 2580
Oregon, 118 Station Rd, tel. Portstewart 2826

Co Tyrone
COOKSTOWN
Piper's Cave, 38 Cady Rd, tel. Cookstown 63615

FIVEMILETOWN
Al-di-Gwyn Lodge, 103 Clabby Rd, tel. 298

Farmhouses

Details of AA-listed farmhouses in England, Wales
and Scotland are given below, listed in alphabetical
order of place-names. (*Note: there are no AA-listed
farmhouses within the Channel Islands, Isle of Man,
or Isles of Scilly.*) Farmhouses in Northern Ireland
follow. Details for islands are shown under
individual place-names.

ABBERLEY, Heref & Worcs
Mrs S. Neath, **Church**,
tel. Great Witley (029921) 316

ABBOTS BROMLEY, Staffs
Mr and Mrs W. R. Aitkenhead, **Fishers Pit**,
tel. Burton-on-Trent (0283) 840204
Mrs M. K. Hollins, **Marsh**,
tel. Burton-on-Trent (0283) 840323

ABEREDW, Powys
Mrs M. M. Evans, **Danycoed**,
tel. Enwood (09823) 298

ABERFELDY, Tayside
Mrs W. Kennedy, **Tom of Cluny**,
tel. (0887) 20477

ABERGAVENNY, Gwent
Mrs D. V. M. Nicholls, **Newcourt**, Mardy,
tel. (0873) 3734

ABERHOSAN, Powys
Mrs A. Lewis, **Bacheiddon**, tel. (0654) 2229

ABINGTON, Strathclyde
Mr G. Hodge, **Craighead**,
tel. Crawford (08642) 356
Mr D. Wilson, **Crawfordjohn Mill**, Crawfordjohn,
tel. Crawfordjohn (08644) 248
Mrs M. E. Hamilton, **Kirkton**,
tel. Crawford (08642) 376
Mrs J. Hyslop, **Netherton**, (on unclass rd joining
A74 & A73), tel. Crawford (08642) 321

ACHARACLE, Highland
Mrs M. Macaulay, **Dalilea House**,
tel. Salen (096785) 253

AINSTABLE, Cumbria
Miss K. Pollock, **Basco Dyke Head**, Basco Dyke,
tel. Croglin (076886) 254

ALDWARK, Derbys
J. N. Lomas, **Lydgate**,
tel. Carsington (062985) 250

ALFRISTON, E Sussex
Mrs D. Y. Savage, **Pleasant Rise**,
tel. (0323) 870545

ALKMONTON, Derbys
Mr A. Harris, **Dairy House**,
tel. Great Cubley (033523) 359

ALLENDALE, Northumberland
Mr and Mrs Fairless, **Bishopfield** (1m W),
tel. (043483) 248

ALLENSMOOR, Heref & Worcs
Mrs O. I. Griffiths, **Mawfield**,
tel. Hereford (0432) 277266

ALNWICK, Northumberland
Mrs A. Davison, **Alndyke**, tel. (0665) 602193

ALSTON, Cumbria
Mrs P. M. Dent, **Middle Bayles**, tel. (0498) 81383

ALVERDISCOTT, Devon
Mrs C. M. Treemer, **Garnacott**,
tel. Newton Tracey (027185) 282

APPLEBY-IN-WESTMORLAND, Cumbria
Mrs M. Wood, **Gale House**, tel. Appleby 51380

ARDBRECKNISH, Strathclyde
Mrs H. F. Hodge, **Rockhill**,
tel. Kilchrenan (08663) 218

ARDEN, Strathclyde
Mrs R. Keith, **Mid Ross**, tel. (038985) 655

ARDERSIER, Highland
Mrs L. E. MacBean, **Milton-of-Gollanfield**,
tel. (0667) 62207

ARDFERN, Strathclyde
Mrs M. C. Peterson, **Traighmhor**,
tel. Barbreck (08525) 228

ASHPRINGTON, Devon
Mrs T. C. Grimshaw, **Sharpham Barton**,
tel. Harbertonford (080423) 278

AUCHENCAIRN, Dumfries & Galloway
Mrs D. Cannon, **Bluehill**, tel. (055664) 228

AUSTWICK, N Yorks
Mrs M. Hird, **Rawlinshaw**,
tel. Settle (07292) 3214

AVETON GIFFORD, Devon
Mrs G. M. Balkwill, **Court Barton**,
tel. Kingsbridge (0548) 550312

AVONWICK, Devon
Mrs C. Scott, **Sopers Horsebrook**,
tel. South Brent (03647) 3235

AXBRIDGE, Somerset
Mr L. F. Dimmock, **Manor**, Cross,
tel. (0934) 732577

AXMINSTER, Devon
Mrs S. Clist, **Annings**, Wyke, tel. (0297) 33294

AYR, Strathclyde
Mr and Mrs A Stevenson, **Trees**,
tel. Joppa (0292) 570270

BABELL, Clwyd
Mrs M. L. Williams, **Bryon Glas**,
tel. Caerwys (0352) 720493

BALA, Gwynedd
Mrs E. Jones, **Eirianfa**, Sarnau (4m N on A494),
tel. Llandderfel (06783) 389
Mr D. Davies, **Tytandderwen**,
tel. (0678) 520273

BALMACLELLAN, Dumfries & Galloway
Mrs. P. Porrit, **Craig**,
tel. New Galloway (06442) 228
Mr and Mrs Shaw, **High Park**,
tel. New Galloway (06442) 298

BAMPTON, Devon
Mr and Mrs R. A. Fleming, **Holwell**,
tel. (0398) 31452
Mrs R. Cole, **Hukeley**, tel. (0398) 31267

BAMPTON, Oxon
Mrs J. Rouse, **Morar**, Weald St (½m SW off A4095),
tel. Bampton Castle (0993) 850162

BANAVIE, Highland
Mrs A. C. MacDonald, **Burnside**, Muirshearlich,
tel. (03977) 275

BARKESTON-LE-VALE, Leics
Mrs S. H. Smart, **The Paddocks**,
tel. Bottesford (0949) 42208

BARNSTAPLE, Devon
Mrs G. Hannington, **Fair Oak**, Ashford,
tel. (0271) 73698
Mrs M. Lethaby, **Home**, Lower Blakewell,
Muddiford, tel. (0271) 2955

BASSENTHWAITE, Cumbria
Mrs A. M. Trafford, **Bassenthwaite Hall (East)**,
tel. Bassenthwaite Lake (059681) 393
Mrs D Mattinson, **Bassenthwaite Hall West**,
tel. Bassenthwaite Lake (059681) 279

BATTLE, E Sussex
Mrs A. Benton, **Little Hemingford**, Telham (2¼m
SE on N side on A210), tel. (04246) 2910

BEATTOCK, Dumfries & Galloway
Mr and Mrs Bell, **Cogaie's**,
tel. Johnstone Bridge (05764) 320

BEERCROCOMBE, Somerset
Mrs C. M. Mitchem, **Whittles**,
tel. Hatch Beauchamp (0823) 480301

BEESWING, Dumfries & Galloway
Garloff, tel. Lochfoot 225

BELTON, Leics
Mrs S. L. Renner, **Old Rectory**,
tel. (057286) 279

BERKELEY, Glos
Mrs B. A. Evans, **Greenacres**, Breadstone (2m E of
A38), tel. Dursley (0453) 810348

BETHESDA, Gwynedd
Mrs D. Williams, **Maes Caradog**, Nant Ffrancon,
tel. (0248) 600266

BICKINGTON (nr Ashburton), Devon
Mr and Mrs Ross, **East Burne**, tel. (062682) 496

BINGLEY, W Yorks
Mr and Mrs G. Warin, **March Cote**, Cottingley
(2m S B6146), tel. Bradford (0274) 487433

BLORE, Staffs
M. A. Griffin, **Coldwall**, Okeover,
tel. Thorpe Cloud (033529) 249

BOGHEAD, Strathclyde
I. McInally, **Dykehead**,
tel. Lesmahagow (0555) 892226

BOLTON LE SANDS, Lancs
Mrs A. Ireland, **Thwaite End**,
tel. Carnforth (0524) 732551

BOMERE HEATH, Salop
Mrs D. M. Cooke, **Grange**, tel. (0939) 290234

BONDLEIGH, nr North Tawton, Devon
Mrs M. C. H. Patridge, **Cadditon**,
tel. North Tawton (083782) 450

BO'NESS, Central
Mrs A. Kirk, **Kinglass**, Borrowstoun Rd,
tel. (0506) 822861

BORELAND, Dumfries & Galloway
Mrs I. Maxwell, **Gall**, tel. (05766) 229

BOTALLACK, Cornwall
Mrs J. Cargeeg, **Manor**,
tel. Penzance (0736) 788525

BOVEY TRACEY, Devon
Mrs H. Roberts, **Willmead**,
tel. Lustleigh (06477) 214

BOW, Devon
Mrs V. Hill, **East Hillerton House**, Speryton,
tel. Bow (0633) 393

BRAUNTON, Devon
Mr and Mrs Barnes, **Denham Farm Holidays**,
North Buckland, tel. Croyde (0271) 890297

BRECHIN, Tayside
Mrs M. Stewart, **Blibberhill** (5m WSW off B9134),
tel. Aberlemno (030783) 225
Mrs J. Stewart, **Wood of Auldbar**,
tel. Aberlemno (030783) 218

BRENDON, Devon
Mrs C. A. South, **Farley Water**,
tel. Brendon (05987) 272

BRENT ELEIGH, Suffolk
J. P. Gage, **Street**, tel. Lavenham (0787) 247271

BRIDESTOWE, Devon
Mrs M. A. Down, **Little Bidlake**,
tel. (083786) 233
Mrs M. A. Ponsford, **Stone**, tel. (083786) 253
Mrs J. Northcott, **Town**, tel. (083786) 226
Mrs M. Hockridge, **Week**, tel. (083786) 221

BRIDGERULE, Devon
Mrs S. A. Gardener, **Buttsbeer Cross**,
tel. (028881) 210

BRIGSTEER, nr Kendal, Cumbria
Mrs E. A. Gardner, **Barrowfield**,
tel. Crosthwaite (04488) 336

BROADWINDSOR, Dorset
Mrs C. Poulton, **Hursey**,
tel. (0308) 68323

BROMPTON REGIS, Somerset
Mrs G, Payne, **Lower Holworthy**,
tel. (03987) 244

BROUGH, Cumbria
Mrs J. M. Atkinson, **Augill House**,
tel. (09304) 305

BRUTON, Somerset
Fryerning, Frome Rd, Burrowfield,
tel. (0749) 812343

BRYNGWYN, Powys
Mrs H. E. A. Nicholls, **Newhouse**,
tel. Painscastle (04975) 671

BUCKLAND BREWER, Devon
Mrs M. Brown, **Holwell**,
tel. Langtree (08055) 288

BUCKNELL, Salop
Mrs B. E. M. Davies, **Bucknell House**,
tel. (05474) 248
Mrs C. Price, **Hall**, tel. (05474) 249

BUILTH WELLS, Powys
Mrs Z. E. Hope, **Cae Pandy**, Garth Rd (1m W
A483), tel. (0982) 553793

BULKWORTHY, Devon
Mrs K. P. Hockridge, **Blakes**,
tel. Milton Damerel (040926) 249

BURGH ST PETER, Norfolk
Mrs R. M. Clarke, **Shrublands**,
tel. Aldeby (050277) 241

BUTLEIGH, Somerset
Mrs J. M. Gillam, **Dower House**,
tel. Baltonsborough (0458) 50354

BUTTERLEIGH, Devon
Mrs B. J. Hill, **Sunnyside**,
tel. Bickleigh (08845) 322

BUXTON, Derbys
Mrs C. Heathcote, **High House**, Foxlow Farm,
Harpur Hill, tel. (0298) 4219
Mrs M. A. Mackenzie, **Staden Grange**, Staden Ln
(1½m SE off A515), tel. (0298) 4965

CADNAM, Hants
Mrs A. M. Dawe, **Budds**, Winsor Rd, Winsor,
tel. Southampton (0703) 812381
Mr and Mrs R. D. L. Dawe, **Kents**, Winsor Rd,
Winsor, tel. Southampton (0703) 813497

CALDBECK, Cumbria
Mrs D. H. Coulthard, **Friar Hall Farm**,
tel. (06998) 633

CALVINE, Tayside
Mrs W. Stewart, **Clachan of Struan**,
tel. (079683) 207

CAMELFORD, Cornwall
Mrs H. MacLeod, **Melorne**, Camelford Station,
tel. (0840) 213200
Mrs R. Y. Lyes, **Pencarrow**, Advent,
tel. (0840) 213282

CAPUTH, Tayside
Mrs R. Smith, **Stralochy**,
tel. (073871) 250

CARLOPS, Borders
Mrs J. Aitken, **Carlophill** (½m SW unclass),
tel. West Linton (0968) 60340

Croyde Bay, Braunton, Devon

CARNO, Powys
P. M. Lewis, **Y Grofftydd**,
tel. (05514) 274

CARRONBRIDGE, Central
Mrs J. Morton, **Lochend**,
tel. Denny (0324) 822778

CARRUTHERSTOWN, Dumfries and Galloway
Mrs J. Brown, **Domaru**, tel. (038784) 260

CASTLE CARROCK, Cumbria
B. W. Robinson, **Gelt Hall**,
tel. Hayton (022870) 260

CATLOWDY, Cumbria
Mr and Mrs J. Sisson, **Bessiestown**,
tel. Nicholforest (022877) 219
Mr and Mrs Lawson, **Graigburn**,
tel. Nicholforest (022877) 214

CEMMAES, Powys
Mrs D. Evans-Breese, **Rhydygwiel**,
tel. Cemmaes Road (06502) 541

CERNE ABBAS, Dorset
R. and M. Paul, **Giants Head**, Old Sherborne Rd,
tel. (03003) 242

CHAPELTOWN, Strathclyde
Mr R. Hamilton, **East Drumloch**,
tel. (03573) 236
Mrs E. Taylor, **Millwell**,
tel. East Kilbride (03552) 43248

CHAPMANSLADE, Wilts
Mrs M. Hoskins, **Spinney**,
tel. (037388) 412

CHARLTON MUSGROVE, Somerset
Mrs A. Teague, **Lower Church**,
tel. Wincanton (0963) 32307

CHEDINGTON, Dorset
Lt Col and Mrs E. I. Stanford, **Lower Farm**,
tel. Corscombe (093589) 371

CHERITON FITZPAINE, Devon
Mrs D. M. Lock, **Brindiwell**, tel. (03636) 357

CHISELBOROUGH, Somerset
Mrs E. Holloway, **Manor**, tel. (093588) 203

CHURCHILL, Avon
Mrs S. Sacof, **Churchill Green**, tel. (0934) 852438

CHURCHINFORD, Somerset
M. Palmer, **Hunter Lodge**,
tel. Churchstanton (082360) 253

CHURCH STOKE, Powys
Mrs C. Richards, **Drewin**, tel. (05885) 325

CHURCH STRETTON, Salop
Mrs C. J. Hotchkiss, **Olde Hall Farm**, Wall-under-Heywood, tel. Longville (06943) 253
Mrs J. C. Inglis, **Hope Bowdler Hall**, Hope Bowdler (1m E B4371), tel. (0694) 722041

CLAVERDON, Warwicks
Mr and Mrs F. E. Bromilow, **Woodside**, Langley Rd
(¾m S of B4095), tel. (092684) 2446

CLAWDDNEWYDD, Clwyd
Mrs G. Williams, **Maestyddyw Isa**,
tel. (08245) 289

CLOVELLY, Devon
Mrs E. Symons, **Burnstone**, Higher Clovelly,
tel. (02373) 219

CLUNTON, Salop
Mrs J. Williams, **Hurst Mill**, tel. Clun (05884) 224

CLYST ST MARY, Devon
Mrs A. Freemantle, **Ivington**,
tel. Topsham (039287) 3290

CODSALL, Staffs
Mrs D. E. Moreton, **Moors**, Chillington Ln,
tel. (09074) 2330

COOMBE MARTIN, Devon
Mrs Peacock, **Longlands**, Easterclose Cross,
tel. (027188) 3522

COMRIE, Tayside
Mrs J. H. Rimmer, **West Ballindalloch**,
Glenlednock, tel. (0764) 70282

CONWY, Gwynedd
Mrs C. Roberts, **Henllys**, Llechwedd (2m W
unclass), tel. (049263) 3269
Mr and Mrs J. A. Jones, **Llechan Ucha**,
tel. (049263) 2451

COOKLEY, Suffolk
Mr and Mrs A. T. Veasy, **Green**, tel. (098685) 209

COOMBE, Cornwall
Mrs J. Scott, **Treway**,
tel. St Austell (0726) 882236

COPPLESTONE, Devon
Mrs J. A. King, **Elston Barton** (1m E on unclass
Rd), tel. (03634) 397

CORTACHY, Tayside
Mrs J. Grant, **Cullew**, tel. (05754) 242

COTHERIDGE, Heref and Worcs
Mr and Mrs V. A. Rogers, **Little Lightwood**,
tel. (090566) 236

COTLEIGH, Devon
Mrs J. Boyland, **Barn Park**,
tel. Upottery (040486) 297

COUNTISBURY (nr Lynton), Devon
Mrs R. Pile, **Coombe**,
tel. Brendon (05987) 236

COVERACK BRIDGES (nr Helston), Cornwall
Mr and Mrs E. Lawrence, **Boscadjack**,
tel. Helston (03265) 2086

CRACKINGTON HAVEN, Cornwall
Mrs M. Knight, **Manor**,
tel. St Gennys (08403) 304

CREDITON, Devon
Mr and Mrs M. Pennington, **Woolsgrove**,
Sandford, tel. Copplestone (03634) 246

CROESGOCH, Dyfed
Mr and Mrs A. Charles, **Torbant**, tel. (03483) 276
Mrs M. B. Jenkins, **Trearched**, tel. (03483) 310

CROMHALL, Avon
Mrs S. Scolding, **Varley**, Talbot End,
tel. Wickwar (045424) 292

CROOK, Cumbria
Mrs I. D. Scales, **Greenbank**,
tel. Staveley (0539) 821216

CROSCOMBE, Somerset
Mrs Keen, **Upper Thrupe**, Maesbury
(1½m NE of Croscombe unclass),
tel. Shepton Mallet (0749) 2697

CRUCKTON, Salop
Mrs M. L. Birchall, **Woodfield**,
tel. Shrewsbury (0743) 860249

CRYMYCH, Dyfed
Mr and Mrs Hazelden, **Felin Tŷgwyn**,
tel. Crosswell (023979) 603

CUBERT, Cornwall
J. and F. Whybrow, **Treworgans**,
tel. Crantock (0637) 830200

CULLODEN MOOR, Highland
Mrs E. M. C. Alexander, **Culdoich**,
tel. Inverness (0463) 790268

CULLOMPTON, Devon
Mrs A. C. Cole, **Five Bridges**, tel. (0884) 33453

CURY CROSS LANES, Cornwall
Mrs M. F. Osborne, **Polglase**,
tel. Mullion (0326) 240469

DALWOOD (nr Axminster), Devon
Mr & Mrs Cobley, **Elford,**
tel. Axminster (0297) 32415

DAVIOT, Highland
Mrs E. M. MacPherson, **Lairgandour,**
tel. (046385) 207

DEBDEN GREEN, Essex
Mrs K. M. Low, **Wychbars,**
tel. Bishops Stortford (0279) 850362

DEVIL'S BRIDGE, Dyfed
Mrs E. E. Lewis, **Erwbarfe,**
tel. Ponterwyd (097085) 251

DIDDLEBURY, Salop
Mrs E. Wilkes, **Glebe,**
tel. Munslow (058476) 221

DINDER, Somerset
Mrs P. J. Keen, **Crapnell,**
tel. Shepton Mallet (0749) 2683

DOCKLOW, Heref and Worcs
Mrs M. R. M. Brooke, **Nicholson,**
tel. Steens Bridge (056882) 269

DOLGELLAU, Gwynedd
Mrs E. W. Price, **Glyn,** tel. (0341) 422286
Mrs S. J. Lane, **Llwyn-Yr-Helm,** Brithdir,
tel. Rhydymain (034141) 254

DORNIE, Highland
Mrs M. Macrae, **Bungalow,** Ardelve,
tel. (059985) 231

DORSINGTON, Warwicks
Mrs M. J. Walters, **Church,**
tel. Stratford-upon-Avon (0789) 720471

DOVER, Kent
C. and L. Oakley, **Walletts Court,** West Cliffe,
St Margarets-at-Cliffe (1½m NE of A2/A258
junction, off B2058), tel. (0304) 852424

DRYSLWYN, Dyfed
Mrs M. Wilson, **Pant-y-Fen,** tel. (05584) 481

DULFORD, Devon
Mr and Mrs A. J. Evans, **Nap Barton,**
tel. Kentisbeare (08846) 287

DUNLOP, Strathclyde
Mr and Mrs R. B. Wilson, **Struther,**
tel. Stewarton (0560) 84946

DUNSYRE, Strathclyde
Mrs L. Armstrong, **Dunsyre Mains,**
tel. (089981) 251

DUNURE, Strathclyde
Mrs R. J. Reid, **Lagg,** tel. (029250) 647

DURSLEY, Glos
Mrs C. M. St John-Mildmay, **Drakestone House,**
Stinchcombe (2½m W off B4060)
tel. (0453) 2140
Mrs E. Pain, **Park,** Stancombe Park
tel. (0453) 45345

DYFFRYN-ARDUDWY, Gwynedd
Mrs J. Bailey, **Cors-y-Gedol Hall,** tel. (03417) 231

EARDISLAND, Heref & Worcs
Mrs F. M. Johnson, **The Elms** (Guestaccom),
tel. Pembridge (05447) 405

EAST CALDER, Lothian
Mr and Mrs D. R. Scott, **Whitecroft,** Raw
Holdings,
tel. Mid Calder (0506) 881810

EAST MEON, Hants
Mrs P. M. Berry, **Giants,** Harvesting Lane,
tel. (073087) 205

EAST MEY, Highland
Mrs M. Morrison, **Glenearn,**
tel. Barrock (084785) 608

Mr and Mrs N. Geddes, **Island View,**
tel. Barrock (084785) 254

EGLINGHAM, Northumb
A. I. Easton, **West Ditchburn,**
tel. Powburn (066578) 337

ELSDON, Northumb
Mr and Mrs T. Carruthers, **Dunns,**
tel. Rothbury (0669) 40219

ERLESTOKE, Wilts
Mrs P. Hampton, **Longwater Park,**
tel. Bratton (0380) 830095

ERWOOD, Powys
N. M. Jones, **Ty-Isaf,** tel. (09823) 607

ETTINGTON, Warwicks
Mrs B. J. Wakeham, **Whitfield,** Warwick Rd,
tel. Stratford-upon-Avon (0789) 740260

EXBOURNE, Devon
Mrs S. J. Allain, **Stapleford,** tel. (083785) 277

EXMOUTH, Devon
Mrs A. J. Skinner, **Maer,** Maer Lane,
tel. (0395) 263365
Mrs J. Reddaway, **Quentance,** Salterton Rd,
tel. Budleigh Salterton (03954) 2733

EYE, Heref & Worcs
Mrs E. M. Morris, **Park Lodge,**
tel. Leominster (0568) 5711

FALFIELD, Avon
Mr and Mrs Bryant, **Green,** tel. (0454) 260319

FARRINGTON GURNEY, Avon
Mrs J. Candy, **Cliff,** Rush Hill
(½m S over county boundary in Somerset),
tel. Chewton Mendip (076121) 274

FELINDRE, W Glam
Mr F. Jones, **Coynant,**
tel. Ammanford (0269) 2064 and 5640

FINTRY, Central
Mrs M. Mitchell, **Nether Glinns,** tel. (036086) 207

FORDEN, Powys
Mrs K. Owens, **Coed-y-Brenin,** Kingswood Ln,
tel. (093876) 510
Mr & Mrs M. C. Payne, **Heath Cottage,**
Kingswood, tel. (093876) 453

FORDOUN, Grampian
Mrs M. Anderson, **Ringswood,**
tel. Auchenblae (05612) 313

FORGANDENNY, Tayside
Mrs M. Fotheringham, **Craighall,**
tel. Bridge of Earn (0738) 812415

FOURCROSSES, Powys
Mrs J. E. Wigley, **Maerdy,** (¾m SE B4393),
tel. Guilsfield (093875) 202

FOWEY, Cornwall
M. & H. T. Dunn, **Trezare,** tel. (072683) 3485

FRAMLINGHAM, Suffolk
Mrs S. F. Stocker, **Broadwater,** Woodbridge Rd,
tel. (0728) 723645

FRESSINGFIELD, Suffolk
Mrs R. Tomson, **Hillview,**
tel. (037986) 443
Mrs R. Willis, **Priory House,** Priory Rd,
tel. (037986) 254

GALSTON, Strathclyde
Mrs J. Bone, **Auchencloigh,** tel. (0563) 820567

GARBOLDISHAM, Norfolk
Mr & Mrs Atkins, **Ingleneuk,** Hopton Rd,
tel. (095381) 541

GARSTANG, Lancs
Mrs J. Higginson, **Clay Lane Head,** Cabus (2m N
on A6), tel. (09952) 3132

GARSTANG, Lancs (contd.)
Mrs J. Fowler, **Greenhaigh Castle**, Castle Ln,
tel. (09952) 2140

GARTHMYL, Powys
Mrs P. Jones, **Trwstllewelyn**,
tel. Berriew (068685) 295

GATE HELMSLEY, N Yorks
Mrs K. M. Sykes, **Lime Field**, Scoreby,
tel. York (0904) 489224

GAYHURST, Bucks
Mrs K. Adams, **Mill**,
tel. Newport Pagnell (0908) 611489

GEDNEY HILL, Lincs
Mrs C. Cave, **Sycamore**,
tel. Holbeach (0406) 330445

GIGGLESWICK, N Yorks
Mrs B. T. Hargreaves, **Close House**,
tel. Settle (07292) 3540

GLAN-YR-AFON, Nr Corwen, Gwynedd
Mrs G. B. Jones, **Llawr-Bettws**, Bala Rd,
tel. Maerdy (049081) 224

GLASBURY, Powys
Mrs B. Eckley, **Fforddfawr**, tel. (04974) 332

GLASFRYN, Clwyd
Mrs C. Ellis, **Growine**,
tel. Cerrigydrudion (049082) 447

GLASTONBURY, Somerset
Mrs H. Tinney, **Cradlebridge**, tel. (0458) 31827

GLENMAVIS, Strathclyde
Mrs M. Dunbar, **Braidenhill**,
tel. Glenboig (0236) 872319

GORRAN, Cornwall
Mrs P. A. Atkins, **Pentargon**, High Lanes,
tel. Mevagissey (0726) 842227

GRAMPOUND, Cornwall
Mrs L. M. Wade, **Tregidgeo**,
tel. St Austell (0726) 882450

GREENHEAD, Northumb
Mrs P. Staff, **Holmhead**, tel. Gisland (06972) 402

GULVAL, Cornwall
Mrs M. E. Osborne, **Kenegie Home**,
tel. Penzance (0736) 2515

GWYSTRE, Powys
Mrs M. A. Davies, **Bryn Nicholas** (½m E on N side
of A44), tel. Penybont (059787) 447
Mrs C. Drew, **Gwystre**,
tel. Penybont (059787) 316

HALFWAY HOUSE, Salop
Mrs E. Morgan, **Willows**, tel. (074378) 233

HALSTOCK, Dorset
Mrs G. R. Swann, **Old Mill**, Higher Halstock,
tel. Corscombe (093589) 278

HALTWHISTLE, Northumb
Mrs J. Brown, **Broomshaw Hill**, Willia Rd,
tel. (0498) 20866
Mrs M. Dawson, **Park Burnfoot**, Featherstone Pk,
tel. (0498) 20378
Mrs J. I. Laidlow, **Ald White Craig**, Shield Hill
tel. (0498) 20565

HANLEY CASTLE, Heref & Worcs
Mr and Mrs Addison, **Old Parsonage**,
tel. Hanley Swan (0684) 310124

HANMER, Clwyd
C. Sumner and F. Williams-Lee, **Buck** (on A525
Whitchurch (7m)–Wrexham (9m) rd),
tel. (094874) 339

HARBERTON, Devon
Mrs I. P. Steer, **Preston**, tel. Totnes (0803) 862235
R. Rose, **Tristford**, tel. Totnes (0803) 862418

HARLECH, Gwynedd
Mrs E. A. Jones, **Tuddyn Gwynt**,
tel. (0766) 780298

HARROP FOLD, Lancs
Mr and Mrs P. Wood, **Harrop Fold**,
tel. Bolton-By-Bowland (02007) 600

HATHERSAGE, Derbys
Mrs T. C. Wain, **Highlow Hall**,
tel. Hope Valley (0433) 50393

HATTON, Warwicks
Mrs S. M. Fishwick, **Northleigh**, Five Ways Rd,
tel. Haseley Knob (092687) 203

HAUGH OF URR, Dumfries & Galloway
Mrs G. J. Macfarlane, **Markfast**, (055666) 220

HAVERFORDWEST, Dyfed
Mrs J. H. Evans, **Cuckoo Grove**, tel. (0437) 2429

HAY-ON-WYE, Powys
Mrs J. Harris, **Crossway**, Clyro
(1¼m N off A438 at Clyro),
tel. (0497) 820567

HEBRON, Dyfed
Mrs N. F. Vaughan, **Presell Farm Stud**,
tel. (09947) 425

HENFIELD, W Sussex
Mrs M. Wilkin, **Great Wapses**, Wineham (3m NE
off B2116), tel. (0273) 492544

HENSTRIDGE, Somerset
Mrs I. Pickford, **Manor**, Bowden,
tel. Templecombe (0963) 70213
Mrs P. J. Doggrell, **Toomer**, Templecombe,
tel. Milborne Port (0963) 250237

HERMITAGE, Dorset
Mrs J. Mayo, **Almshouse**,
tel. Holnest (096321) 296

HIGH CATTON, N Yorks
Mrs S. Foster, **High Catton Grange**,
tel. Stamford Bridge (0759) 71374

HITCHAM, Suffolk
Mrs B. D. Elsden, **Wetherden Hall**,
tel. Bildeston (0499) 740412

HOLBETON, Devon
Mrs J. A. Baskerville, **Keaton**, tel. (075530) 255

HOLLYBUSH, Strathclyde
Mrs A. Woodburn, **Boreland**,
tel. Patna (0292) 531228

HOLNE, Devon
S. Townsend, **Wellpritton**,
tel. Poundsgate (03643) 273

HOLSWORTHY, Devon
Mr and Mrs E. Cornish, **Leworthy**,
tel. (0409) 253488

HOLT, Clwyd
Mrs G. M. Evans, **New**, Commonwood,
tel. Farndon (0829) 270358

Leworthy Farm, Holsworthy, Devon

HOLYWELL, Clwyd
Mrs M. D. Jones, **Green Hill**, tel. (0352) 713270

HONITON, Devon
Mrs I. J. Underdown, **Roebuck**, (western end of Honiton by-pass), tel. (0404) 2225

HORNS CROSS, Devon
Mrs B. Furse, **Swanton**, tel. Clovelly (02373) 241

HORSMONDEN, Kent
Mrs S. M. Russell, **Pullens**, Lamberhurst Rd, tel. Brenchley (089272) 2241

HOWEY, nr Llandrindod Wells, Powys
Mrs C. Nixon, **Brynhir**, (1m E on unclass rd), tel. Llandrindod Wells (0597) 2425
Mrs R. Jones, **Holly**, tel. Llandrindod Wells (0597) 2402
Mr and Mrs R. Bufton, **Three Wells**, tel. Llandrindod Wells (0597) 2484

HUGHLEY, Salop
Mrs E. Bosworth, **Mill**, tel. Brockton (074636) 645

HUSTHWAITE, N Yorks
Mrs E. Smith, **Baxby Manor**, tel. Coxwold (03476) 572

IDOLE, Dyfed
Mr and Mrs A. Bowen, **Pantgwyn**, tel. Carmarthen (0267) 235859

ILAM, Staffs
Mrs S. Prince, **Beechenhill**, tel. Alstonefield (033527) 274

INGLEBY GREENHOW, N Yorks
Mrs M. Bloom, **Manor House**, tel. Great Ayton (0642) 722384

INGLETON, N Yorks
G. W. and M. Bell, **Langber**, tel. (0468) 41587

INVERGARRY, Highland
Mr and Mrs R. Wilson, **Ardgarry**, Faichem, tel. (08093) 226
Mrs L. M. Brown, **Faichem Lodge**, tel. (08093) 314

IPSTONES, Staffs
Mrs J. Brindley, **Glenwood House**, tel. (053871) 294

ISLE OF SKYE, Highland
See Portree

ISLE OF WIGHT
See Ryde

JACOBSTOWE, Devon
Mrs J. King, **Higher Cadham**, tel. Exbourne (083785) 647

KEITH, Grampian
Mrs J. Jackson, **The Haughs**, tel. (05422) 2238
Mrs E. C. Leith, **Montgrew**, tel. (05422) 2852
Mrs G. Murphy, **Tarnash House**, tel. (05422) 2728

KENDAL, Cumbria
Mrs S. Beaty, **Garnett House**, Burneside, tel. (0539) 24542
Mrs J. Ellis, **Gateside**, Windermere Rd, tel. (0539) 22036
Mrs E. M. Gardner, **Natland Mill Beck**, tel. (0539) 21122
Mrs S. K. Bell, **Oxenholme**, Oxenholme Rd, tel. (0539) 27226

KENNFORD, Devon
Mrs R. Weeks, **Holloway Barton**, tel. Exeter (0392) 832302

KENTALLEN, Highland
Mrs D. A. MacArthur, **Ardsheal Home**, tel. Duror (063174) 229

KETTLEBURGH, Suffolk
Mrs I. A. Pearce, **Rookery**, Framlingham, tel. Framlingham (0278) 723248

KEXBY, N Yorks
Mrs K. R. Daniel, **Ivy House**, tel. York (0904) 489368

KEYNSHAM, Avon
Mrs L. Sparks, **Uplands**, Wellsway, tel. (02756) 5764

KILGETTY, Dyfed
Mrs S. A. James, **Little Newton**, tel. Saundersfoot (0834) 812306

KILPECK, Heref & Worcs
Mrs I. J. Pike, **Priory**, tel. Wormbridge (098121) 366

KIMBOLTON, Heref & Worcs
M. J. & S. W. Lloyd, **Menalls**, tel. Leominster (0568) 2605

KINGSEY, Bucks
Mr N. M. D. Hooper, **Foxhill**, tel. Haddenham (0844) 291650

KINGSLAND, Heref & Worcs
Mrs F. M. Hughes, **Tremayne**, tel. (056881) 233

KINGSTONE, Heref & Worcs
Mrs G. C. Andrews, **Webton Court**, tel. Golden Valley (0981) 250220

KINGSWELLS, Grampian
Mrs M. Mann, **Bellfield**, tel. (0224) 740239

KINGTON, Heref & Worcs
Mrs E. E. Protheroe, **Bucks Head**, Upper Hergest, tel. (0544) 231063
Mrs M. Eckley, **Holme**, Lyonshall, tel. (05448) 216
J. A. Layton, **Park Gate**, Lyonshall, tel. (05448) 243

KIPPEN, Central
Mrs J. Paterson, **Powblack**, tel. (078687) 260

KIRKCONNEL, Dumfries & Galloway
Mrs E. A. Mcgarvie, **Niviston**, tel. (06593) 346

KIRKHILL, Highland
Mrs C. Munro, **Wester Moniack**, tel. Drumchardine (046383) 237

KIRKCAMBECK, Cumbria
Mrs M. Stobart, **Cracrop**, tel. Roadhead (06978) 245

KIRKWELPINGTON, Northumb
Mrs J. B. White, **Horncastle** (1m W of village off A696), tel. Otterburn (0830) 40247

KNIGHTON, Powys
R. Watkins, **Heartsease**, tel. Bucknell (05474) 220

LAIRG, Highland
Mrs M. MacKay, **Alt-Na-Sorag**, 14 Achnairn, tel. (0549) 2058
Mrs V. Mackenzie, **5 Terryside** (3½m N off A838), tel. (0549) 2332
Mrs M. Sinclair, **Woodside**, West Shinness, tel. (0549) 2072

LANLIVERY, Cornwall
Mr and Mrs J. Linfoot, **Treganoon**, tel. Bodmin (0208) 872205

LAPWORTH, W Midlands
Mr and Mrs Smart, **Mountford**, Church Ln, tel. (05643) 3283

LATHERON, Highland
Mrs C. Sinclair, **Upper Latheron**, tel. (05934) 224

LAXTON, Notts
Mrs L. S. Rose, **Moorgate**, tel. Tuxford (0777) 870274

LEAMINGTON SPA (ROYAL),
Mrs N. Ellis, **Sharmer**, Fosse Way, Radford Semele (3m E A425 then ½m S on Fosse Way), tel. Harbury (0926) 612448

LEEK, Staffs
Mrs D. Needham, **Holly Dale**, Bradnop,
tel. (0538) 383022

LEINTWARDINE, Heref & Worcs
Mrs Y. Lloyds, **Upper Buckton** (Guestaccom),
tel. (05473) 634

LEOMINSTER, Heref & Worcs
Mrs S. J. Davenport, **Stagbatch**,
tel. (0568) 2673
Mrs H. C. Davies, **Wharton Bank**, Wharton Bank,
tel. (0568) 2575

LEW, Oxon
M. J. Rouse, **University**,
tel. Bampton Castle (0993) 850297

LEWDOWN, Devon
Mrs M. E. Horn, **Venn Mill**,
tel. Bridestowe (083786) 288

LINDRIDGE, Heref & Worcs
Mrs J. M. May, **Middle Woodston**,
tel. Eardiston (058470) 244

LINLITHGOW, Lothian
Mrs A. Hay, **Belsyde House**, Lanark Rd,
tel. (0506) 842098
Mrs W. Erskine, **Woodcockdale**, Lanark Rd,
tel. (0506) 842088

LISKEARD, Cornwall
S. A. Kendall, **Tencreek**,
tel. (0579) 43379

LITTLE BREDY, Dorset
Mrs D. M. Fry, **Foxholes**,
tel. Long Bredy (03083) 395

LITTLE DEWCHURCH, Heref & Worcs
Mrs G. Lee, **CWM GRAIG**, tel. (043270) 250

LITTLE EVERSDEN, Cambs
Mrs F. Ellis, **Five Gables**, Bucks Lane,
tel. Comberton (022026) 2236

LITTLEHEMPSTON, Devon
Mrs E. P. Miller, **Buckyette**,
tel. Stavertone (080426) 638

LITTLE HEREFORD, Heref & Worcs
Mrs H. Williams, **Lower Upton**, Lower Upton (1½m
S on A456), tel. Brimfield (058472) 322

LITTLE MILL, Gwent
Mrs A. Bradley, **Pentwyn** (off A472, ½m E of
junction with A4042), tel. (049528) 249

LITTLE TORRINGTON, Devon
Mrs E. J. Watkins, **Lower Hollam**,
tel. Torrington (0805) 23253

LITTON, Derbys
Mrs A. Barnsley, **Dale House**,
tel. Tideswell (0298) 871309

LLANARTHNEY, Dyfed
Mrs M. M. Bowen, **Brynheulog**, tel. (05584) 567

LLANBOIDY, Dyfed
Mrs B. Worthing, **Maercochyrwyn**, Login
tel. Hebron (09947) 283

LLANDDEINIOLEN, Gwynedd
Mrs Kettle, **Ty'n-Rhos**, Seion
tel. Port Dinorwic (0248) 670489

LLANDELOY, Dyfed
Miss M. Jones, **Upper Vanley**,
tel. Croesgoch (03483) 418

LLANDINAM, Powys
Mrs M. C. Davis, **Trewythen**,
tel. Caersws (068684) 444. 2m SW of Caersws, on
unclass rd off B4569

LLANDRINDOD WELLS, Powys
Mrs P. Lewis, **Bailey Einon**, Cefnllys,
tel. (0597) 2449

Mrs D. Evans, **Dolberthog**, Dolberthog Ln,
tel. (0597) 2255

LLANDRINIO, Powys
Mrs G. M. Wigley, **New Hall**,
tel. Llanymynech (0691) 830384
Mrs S. M. Pritchard, **Rhos**,
tel. Llanymynech (0691) 830785

LLANELIDAN, Clwyd
Mrs M. Mosford, **Trewyn**, Rhydymeudwy,
tel. ClawddNewydd (08245) 676

LLANFACHRETH, nr Dolgellau, Gwynedd
Mrs C. Tudor-Owen, **Rhedyncochion**,
tel. Rhydymain (034141) 600

LLANFAIR DYFFRYN CLWYD, Clwyd
Mrs E. Jones, **Llanbenwch**,
tel. Ruthin (08242) 2340

LLANFIHANGEL-YNG-NGWYNFA, Powys
Mrs E. Jenkins, **Cyfie**,
tel. Llanfyllin (069184) 451

LLANFIHANGEL-Y-PENNANT
Mrs M. Jones, **Tynbryn**,
tel. Abergynolwyn (065477) 277

LLANGOLLEN, Clwyd
Mrs A. Kenrick, **Rhydonnen Ucha Rhewl**,
tel. (0978) 860153

LLANGYNOG, Dyfed
Mrs M. Thomas, **Plas**,
tel. Bancy Felin (206 782) 492

LLANRHAEADR, Clwyd
Mrs S. Evans, **Tan-yr Accar**,
tel. Llanynys (0745 78) 232

LLANRUG, Gwynedd
Mr and Mrs Mackinnon, **Plás Tirion**,
tel. Caernarfon (0286) 3190

LLANRWST, Gwynedd
Mrs M. Owen, **Bodrach**, Carmel,
tel. (0492) 640326

LLANSANTFFRAID-YM-MECHAIN, Powys
Mrs M. E. Jones, **Glanvyrnwy**,
tel. Llansantffraid (069181) 258

LLANUWCHLLYN, Gwynedd
Mrs D. D. Bugby, **Bryncaled**, tel. (06784) 270

LLANVAIR-DISCOED, Gwent
Mrs A. Barnfather, **Cribau Mill**, Cribau Mill, The
Cwm, tel. Shirenewton (02917) 528
Mr and Mrs S. Price, **Great Llanmellyn**,
tel. Shirenewton (02917) 210

LLANWARNE, Heref & Worcs
Mrs I. E. Williams, **Llanwarne Court**,
tel. Golden Valley (0981) 540385

LLANWDDYN, Powys
R. B. and H. A. Parry, **Tynymaes**, tel. (069173) 216

LLWYNDAFYDD, Dyfed
Mr M. Kelly, **Ty Hen**,
tel. New Quay (Dyfed) (0545) 560346

LOCHEYNORT' (NORTH), Isle of South Uist,
Western Isles
Mrs A. MacDonald, **Arinabane**, 8 North
Locheynort, tel. Bornish (08785) 379

LOCHGOILHEAD, Strathclyde
Mrs J. H. Jackson, **Pole**, tel. (03013) 221

LOCHWINNOCH, Strathclyde
Mrs A. Mackie, **High Belltrees**, tel. (0505) 842376

LODDISWELL, Devon
Mrs A. Pethybridge, **Reads**,
tel. Kingsbridge (0548) 550317

LODDON, Norfolk
Mrs J. Rackham, **Stubbs House**,
tel. (0508) 20231

LONGLEAT, Wilts
Mrs J. Crossman, **Stalls,**
tel. Maiden Bradley (09853) 323

LONGRIDGE, Lancs
Mr F. K. Johnson, **Falicon**, Fleet St Ln, Hothersall,
tel. Ribchester (025484) 583

LONGSDON, Staffs
Mr and Mrs M. M. Robinson, **Bank End,** Old Leek
Rd (½m SW off A53), tel. Leek (0538) 383638

LOOE, Cornwall
Mr and Mrs K. Hembrow, **Tregoed**, St Martins,
tel. (05036) 2718

LOSTWITHIEL, Cornwall
Mrs R. J. Dunn, **Pelyn Barn**, Pelyn Cross,
tel. Bodmin (0208) 872451
Mrs R. C. Dunn, **Pelyn Barn Farm Bungalow**,
Pelyn Cross, tel. Bodmin (0208) 873062

LOWER BEEDING, W Sussex
Mr J. Christian, **Brookfield**, Winterpit Ln,
Plummers Plain, tel. (040376) 568

MANATON, Devon
Mrs M. Hugo, **Langstone,**
tel. (064722) 266
Mrs B. Y. Hunt, **Neadon**, tel. (064722) 310

MAPPOWDER, Dorset
Mrs A. K. Williamson-Jones, **Boywood,**
tel. Hazelbury Bryan (02586) 416

MARK CAUSEWAY, Somerset
Mrs E. Puddy, **Croft,**
tel. Mark Moor (027864) 206

MARPLE, Cheshire
Mrs U. G. Sidebottom, **Shire Cottage Ernocroft,**
Marple Bridge, tel. Glossop (04574) 66536

MARSHGATE, Cornwall
Mrs P. Bolt, **Carleton,**
tel. Otterham Station (08406) 252

MARSTOW, Heref & Worcs
Mrs S. C. Watson, **Trebandy,**
tel. Llangarron (098984) 230

MARTIN HUSSINGTREE, Worcs
Mr and Mrs J. J. Lane, **Harlington**, Pershore Ln,
tel. Worcester (0905) 522354

MARYBANK, Highland
Mrs R. Macleod, **Easter Balloan,**
tel. Urray (09973) 211

MARY TAVY, Devon
Mrs B. Anning, **Wringworthy**, tel. (082281) 434

MATHON, Heref & Worcs
Mrs S. Williams, **Moorend Court,**
tel. Ridgeway Cross (088684) 205

MATLOCK, Derbys
Mrs M. Brailsford, **Farley**, tel. (0629) 2533
Mrs R. A. Groom, **Manor**, Dethick,
tel. Dethick (062984) 246
M. Haynes, **Packhorse**, Matlock Moor,
tel. (0629) 2781
Mrs J. Hole, **Wayside**, Matlock Moor,
tel. (0629) 2967

MATTISHALL, Norfolk
Mrs M. Faircloth, **Moat,**
tel. Dereham (0362) 850288

MENDHAM, Suffolk
Mrs J. E. Holden, **Weston House,**
tel. St Cross (098682) 206

MENHENIOT, Cornwall
Mrs S. Rowe, **Tregondale,**
tel. Liskeard (0579) 42407

MERRYMEET, Cornwall
B. Cole, **Merrymeet,**
tel. Liskeard (0579) 43231

MEVAGISSEY, Cornwall
Mrs A. Hannah, **Treleaven**, tel. (0726) 842413

MIDDLETOWN, Powys
Mrs E. J. Bebb, **Bank**, tel. Trewern (093874) 260

MILBORNE PORT, Somerset
Mrs M. J. Tizzard, **Venn**, tel. (0963) 250208

MINSTER LOVELL, Oxon
Mrs K. Brown, **Hill Grove**, tel. Witney (0993) 3120

MOLLAND, Devon
Mrs P. England, **Yeo,**
tel. Bishop's Nympton (07697) 312

MONEYDIE, Tayside
Mrs S. Walker, **Moneydie Roger,**
tel. Almondbank (073883) 239

MONKSILVER, Somerset
Mrs S. J. Watts, **Rowdon,**
tel. Stogumber (09846) 280

MONK SOHAM, Suffolk
Mrs S. E. Bagnall, **Abbey House,**
tel. Earl Soham (072882) 225

MONTROSE, Tayside
Mrs A. Ruxton, **Muirshade of Gallery,**
tel. Northwaterbridge (067484) 209

MORCHARD BISHOP, Devon
Mr and Mrs Chilcott, **Wigham,**
tel. (03637) 350

MORDIFORD, Heref & Worcs
Mrs M. J. Barrell, **Orchard,**
tel. Holme Lacy (043273) 253

MORVAH, Cornwall
Mrs J. Mann, **Merthyr,**
tel. Penzance (0736) 788464

MOUNT, Cornwall
Mrs E. J. Beglan, **Mount Pleasant,**
tel. Cardinham (020882) 342

MOYLEGROVE, Dyfed
Mrs J. I. Young, **Cwm Connell**, tel. (023986) 220
Mrs A. D. Fletcher, **Penrallt Ceibwr,**
tel. (023986) 217

MUIR OF ORD, Highland
Mrs Gilchrist, **Gilchrist**, tel. (0463) 870243

MUNGRISDALE, Cumbria
Mr and Mrs G. Wightman, **Near House,**
tel. Threlkeld (059683) 678

NANTGAREDIG, Dyfed
Mrs J. Willmott, **Cwmtwrch**, tel. (026788) 238

NARBERTH, Dyfed
Mrs I. M. Bevan, **Jacob's Park**, tel. (0834) 860525

NEATISHEAD, Norfolk
Mr and Mrs Charlton, **Allens**, Three Hammer
Common, tel. Horning (0692) 630904

NEEDHAM MARKET, Suffolk
Mrs R. M. Hackett-Jones, **Pipps Ford,**
tel. Coddenham (044979) 208

NETHER LANGWITH, Notts
Mrs J. M. Ibbotson, **Blue Barn,**
tel. Mansfield (0623) 742248

NEWBOLD ON STOUR, Warwicks
Mrs J. Kerby, **Berryfield,**
tel. Ilmington (060882) 248
Mrs J. M. Everett, **Newbold Nurseries,**
tel. Alderminster (078987) 285

NEWBOROUGH, Staffs
Mrs B. Skipper, **Chan Try View**, Moat Hill,
tel. Hoar Cross (028375) 200

NEWBRIDGE, Lothian
Mr and Mrs W. Pollock, **Easter Norton,**
tel. 031–333 1279

NEWCASTLE-UNDER-LYME, Staffs
Mrs M. J. Heath, **Home**, Keele,
tel. (0782) 627227

NEWNHAM BRIDGE, Heref & Worcs
Mrs E. J. Adams, **Lower Doddenhill**,
tel. (058479) 223

NEWQUAY, Cornwall
J. C. Wilson, **Manuels**, Lane,
tel. (06373) 3577 (Due to change to (0637)
873572

NEW QUAY, Dyfed
Mr and Mrs White, **Nanternis**, Nanternis (2m SW
off A46), tel. (0545) 560181

NEWTON, nr Vowchurch, Heref and Worcs
Mrs J. C. Powell, **Little Green**,
tel. Michaelchurch (098123) 205

NEWTON REGIS, Staffs
Mrs M. Lane, **Newton House**,
tel. Tamworth (0827) 830632

NEWTON, Powys
L. M. and G. T. Whitticase, **Highgate**,
tel. (0686) 25981
Mrs I. Jarman, **Lower Gwestydd**, Llanllwchaiarn,
tel. (0686) 26718

NORMANBY, N Yorks
D. I. Smith, **Heather View**,
tel. Whitby (0947) 880451

NORTH CADBURY, Somerset
E. J. Keen, **Hill**, tel. (0963) 40257

NORTH PETHERTON, Somerset
Mrs C. M. J. Howard, **Balls Farm**, Woolmersdon,
tel. (0278) 662320

NORTH WOOTTON, Somerset
Mrs M. White, **Barrow**,
tel. Pilton (074989) 245

NORTON, Notts
Mrs J. Palmer, **Norton Grange**,
tel. Mansfield (0623) 842666

OAKFORD, Devon
A. Boldry, **Newhouse**, tel. (03985) 347
Mr J. R. Pearce, **Westcott**, tel. (03985) 265

ODDINGLEY, Heref & Worcs
Mrs P. B. Baylis, **Pear Tree's**,
tel. Droitwich (0905) 778489

OKEHAMPTON, Devon
Mrs K. C. Heard, **Hughslade**, tel. (0837) 2883

OKEOVER, Staffs
E. J. Harrison, **Little Park**,
tel. Thorpe Cloud (033529) 341

OLD DALBY, Leics
Mrs V. Anderson, **Home Farm**, Church Lane,
tel. Melton Mowbray (0664) 822622

ONICH, Highland
Mr and Mrs A. Dewar, **Cuilcheanna House**,
tel. (08553) 226

OTTERBURN, Northumb
Mrs A. Anderson, **Blakehope Burnhaugh**,
Byrness, tel. (0830) 20267
G. F. and M. A. Stephenson, **Monkridge**,
tel. (0830) 20639

OTTERY ST MARY, Devon
Mrs S. Hansford, **Pitt Farm**, (040481) 2439

OXENHOPE, W Yorks
Mrs A. Scholes, **Lily Hall**, Uppermarsh Lane,
tel. Hawarth (0535) 43999

OXHILL, Warwicks
Mrs S. Hutsby, **Nolands**,
tel. Kineton (0926) 640309
Mrs E. A. Jones, **Pant Glas**, Pentrefoelas Rd,
tel. Pentrefoelas (06905) 248

PANTYGELLI, nr Abergavenny, Gwent
Mrs M. E. Smith, **Lower House**, Old Hereford Rd,
tel. Abergavenny (0873) 3432

PARKMILL, nr Swansea, W Glam
Mrs D. Edwards, **Parc-le-Breos House**,
tel. Penmaen (044125) 636

PARRACOMBE, Devon
Mr H. Bearryman, **Lower Dean**, Trentishoe,
tel. (05983) 215

PELYNT, Cornwall
Mrs L. Tuckett, **Trenderway**,
tel. Polperro (0503) 72214

PENMACHNO, Gwynedd
M. Jones, **Tyddyn Gethin**, tel. (06903) 392

PENRUDDOCK, Cumbria
Mrs S. M. Smith, **Highgate**,
tel. Greystoke (08533) 339

PENYBONT, Powys
Mrs S. F. Cox, **Neuadd**, Cefnllys,
tel. Llandrindod Wells (0597) 2571

PILSDON, Dorset
K. B. Brooks, **Monkwood**,
tel. Broadwindsor (0308) 68723

PLUCKLEY, Kent
Mrs F. Harris, **Elvey**, tel. (023384) 442

PONSWORTHY, Devon
Mr and Mrs Fursdon, **Old Walls**,
tel. Poundsgate (03643) 222

PONTARDULAIS, W Glam
Mr and Mrs G. Davies, **Croft**, Heol-y-Barna,
tel. (0792) 883654

PONTFAEN, Dyfed
Mrs S. Heard, **Tregynon**,
tel. Newport (0239) 820531

PONT HIRWAUN, Dyfed
Mr and Mrs J. Moine, **Penwernfach**,
tel. Newcastle Emlyn (0239) 710694

POOLEY BRIDGE, Cumbria
Mrs A. Strong, **Barton Hall**, tel. (08536) 275

PORTHCURNO, Cornwall
Mrs D. M. Jeffrey, **Corniché Trebehor**,
tel. Sennen (073687) 424

PORTHTOWAN, Cornwall
Mrs M. R. Honey, **Torvean**, Coast Rd,
tel. (0209) 890536

PORT OF MENTEITH, Central
Mrs Fotheringham, **Collymoon**,
tel. Buchlyvie (036085) 268

PORTREE, Isle of Skye, Highland
Mrs M. Bruce, **Cruachanlea**, Braes,
tel. Sligachan (047852) 233
Sylvia P. MacDonald, **Upper Ollach**, Braes,
tel. Sligachan (047852) 225

PWLLHELI, Gwynedd
Mrs M. Hughes, **Bryn Crin**, tel. (0758) 2494
Mrs J. E. Ellis, **Gwynfryn** (1m NW),
tel. (0758) 612536

REDHILL, Avon
Mrs M. J. Hawkings, **Hailstones**,
tel. Wrington (0934) 862209

REDMILE, Leics
Mr and Mrs Need, **Peacock**,
tel. Bottesford (0949) 42475

RHANDIRMWYN, Dyfed
Mrs G. A. Williams, **Galltybere**, tel. (05506) 218

RICHMOND, N Yorks
Mrs M. F. Turnbull, **Whashton Springs** (3m W on
unclass rd), tel. (0748) 2884

Rovie Farm, Rogart, Highland

RIEVAULX, N Yorks
Mrs M. E. Skilbeck, **Middle Heads,**
tel. Bilsdale (04396) 251

RODBOURNE, Nr Malmesbury, Wilts
Mrs C. M. Parfitt, **Angrove,**
tel. Malmesbury (06662) 2982

ROGART, Highland
Mrs J. S. R. Modie, **Rovie,** tel. (04084) 209

ROGATE, W Sussex
Mrs J. C. Francis, **Mizzards,** tel. (073080) 656

ROSTON, Derbys
Mrs E. K. Prince, **Roston Hall,**
tel. Ellastone (033524) 287

ROWTON, Salop
Mrs V. I. Evans, **Church,**
tel. High Ercall (0952) 770381

RUDYARD, Staffs
Mrs E. J. Lowe, **Fairboroughs,**
tel. Rushton Spencer (02606) 341

RUSHTON SPENCER, Staffs
Mrs J. Brown, **Barnswood,**
tel. (02606) 261

RUSKIE, Central
Mrs S. F. Bain, **Lower Tarr,**
tel. Thornhilll (078685) 202

RUTHIN, Clwyd
Mrs B. J. Jones, **Bryn Awel,** Bontuchel (1½m W of
Ruthin unclass rd), tel. (08242) 2481
Margaret E. Jones, **Pencoed,** Pwllglas,
tel. Clawdd Newydd (08245) 251
Mrs T. Francis, **Plas-y-Ward,** Rhewl,
tel. (08242) 3822

RYDE, Isle of Wight
Mrs S. Swan, **Aldermoor,** Upton Rd,
tel. (0983) 64743

RYE, E Sussex
Mrs P. Sullivin, **Cliff,** Iden Lock,
tel. Iden (07978) 331

ST ANDREWS, Fife
Mrs A. Duncan, **East Balrymouth,**
tel. (0334) 73475

ST BURYAN, Cornwall
Mr and Mrs W. Hoskins, **Boskenna Home,**
tel. (073672) 250
Mrs M. R. Pengelly, **Burnewhall,**
tel. (073672) 200

ST ERME, Cornwall
Mrs. F. Hicks, **Pengelly,** Trispen,
tel. Mitchell (087251) 245
Mrs B. Dymond, **Trevispian Vean,** Trispen,
tel. Truro (0872) 79514

ST EWE, Cornwall
Mrs J. G. Kent, **Lanewa,**
tel. Mevagissey (0726) 843283

ST JOHN'S IN THE VALE, Cumbria
Mrs M. E. Harrison, **Shundraw,**
tel. Threlkeld (059683) 227

ST JUST-IN-ROSELAND, Cornwall
Mrs W. Symons, **Commerrans,**
tel. Portscatho (087258) 270

ST KEYNE, Cornwall
Mr and Mrs P. Cummins, **Badham,**
tel. Liskeard (0579) 43572
Mr V. R. Arthur, **Killigorrick,**
tel. Liskeard (0579) 20559

ST MARGARET, SOUTH ELMHAM, Suffolk
Mrs H. B. Custerson, **Elm House,**
tel. St Cross (098682) 228

ST OWEN'S CROSS, Heref & Worcs
Mrs F. Davies, **Aberhall,**
tel. Harewood End (098987) 256

SAXELBY, Leics
Mrs M. A. Morris, **Manor House,**
tel. Melton Mowbray (0664) 812269

SEBERGHAM, Cumbria
Mrs E. M. Johnston, **Bustabeck,**
tel. Raughton Head (06996) 339

SHAP, Cumbria
E. and S. Hodgson, **Green Farm,**
tel. (09316) 619
S. J. Thompson, **Southfield,** tel. (09316) 282

SHAWBURY, Salop
Mrs S. J. Clarkson, **Longley,** Stanton Heath,
tel. (0939) 250289
G. C. Evans, **New,** Muckleton, tel. (0939) 250358
Mrs M. R. Griffiths, **Sowbath,** tel. (0939) 250417

SHEARSBY, Leics
Mr A. M. Knight, **Knaptoft House,**
Brungtingthorpe Rd,
tel. Peatling Magna (053758) 388
Mrs S. E. Timms, **Wheathill,** Church Ln,
tel. Peatling Magna (053758) 663

SHELFANGER, Norfolk
Mrs D. A. Butler, **Shelfanger Hall** (S of village off
B1077), tel. Diss (0379) 2094

SHIPSTON-ON-STOUR, Warwicks
Mr and Mrs Boyes, **Portabello,** tel. (0608) 61618

SHIRWELL, Devon
Mrs G. Huxtable, **Woolcott,** tel. (027182) 216

SKYE, ISLE OF, Highland
See Portree

SLAIDBURN, Lancs
Mrs P. M. Holt, **Parrock Head,** Woodhouse Lane,
tel. (02006) 614

SMEATON, GREAT, N Yorks
Mrs N. Hall, **Smeaton, East,** tel. (060981) 336

SOPWORTH, Wilts
Mrs D. M. Barker, **Manor,**
tel. Didmarton (045423) 676

SOUTH BRENT, Devon
M. E. Slade, **Great Aish,** tel. (03647) 2238

SOUTH BREWHAM, Somerset
Mrs D. Dabinett, **Holland,**
tel. Upton Noble (074985) 263

SOUTH HARTING, W Sussex
Mrs H. S. Wroe, **Foxcombe House,**
tel. Harting (073085) 357

SOUTHMOOR, Oxon
Mrs A. Crowther, **Fallowfields,** Fallow Field,
tel. Longworth (0865) 820416

SOUTH PETHERTON, Somerset
Mrs M. E. H. Vaux, **Rydon,** Compton Durville,
tel. (0460) 40468

SPARROWPIT, Derbys
Mrs E. Vernon, **Whitelee**,
tel. Chapel-en-le-Frith (0298) 812928

SPAXTON, Somerset
Mrs D. M. Porter, **Headford**, Higher Merridge,
tel. (027867) 250

SPITTAL, Dyfed
Mrs N. M. Thomas, **Lower Haythog**,
tel. Clarbeston (043782) 279

STANDLAKE, Oxon
Mr and Mrs W. J. Burton, **Church Mill**, Downs Rd
tel. (086731) 524
Mrs S. R. Pickering, **Hawthorn**, tel. (086731) 211

STAPLE FITZPAINE, Somerset
Mrs D. M. Jee, **Ruttersleigh**,
tel. Buckland St Mary (046034) 392

STAUNTON, Glos
Mrs S. Fairhead, **Upper Beaulieu** (off A4136 SW
of village), tel. Monmouth (0600) 5025

STOCKTON, Warwicks
Mrs J. Bankes-Price, **New Zealand**,
tel. Southam (092681) 4604

STOKE HOLY CROSS, Norfolk
Mr and Mrs Harrold, **Salamanca**,
tel. Framingham Earl (05086) 2322

STONE (in Oxney), Kent
Mrs E. I Hodson, **Tighe**, Tighe,
tel. Appledore (023383) 251

STON EASTON, Somerset
Mrs J. Doman, **Manor**,
tel. Chewton Mendip (076121) 266

STONEHOUSE, Glos
Mrs D. A. Hodge, **Welches**, Standish,
tel. (045382) 2018

STRAITON, Lothian
Mrs A. M. Milne, **Straiton**, Straiton Rd,
tel. 031–440 0298

STRATFORD-UPON-AVON, Warwicks
Mrs M. K. Meadows, **Monk's Barn**, Shipston Rd,
tel. (0789) 293714

STRATHAVEN, Strathclyde
E. Warnock, **Laigh Bent**, tel. (0357) 20103

STRATHPEFFER, Highland
Mrs M. Tait, **Beechwood House**, Fodderty,
tel. (0997) 21387

STURMINSTER NEWTON, Dorset
Mrs S. Wingate-Saul, **Holbrook**, Lydlinch,
tel. Hazelbury Bryan (02586) 348

STURTON BY STOW, Lincs
Mrs S. Bradshaw, **Village**,
tel. Gainsborough (0427) 788309

SUMMERCOURT, Cornwall
Mr and Mrs J. A. Mingo, **Burthy**,
tel. St Austell (0726) 860018
W. E. Lutey, **Trenithon**,
tel. St Austell (0726) 860253

SWINESHEAD, Beds
D. Marlow, **Manor**, tel. Riseley (023063) 8126

TALGARTH, Powys
Mrs B. Prosser, **Upper Genffordd**,
tel. (0874) 711360

TAVISTOCK, Devon
Mrs E. C. Blatchford, **Parswell Farm Bungalow**,
Parswell, tel. (0822) 2789

TEMPLE CLOUD, Avon
Mrs J. Harris, **Cameley Lodge**, Cameley (1m W
unclass), tel. (0761) 52423
Mr and Mrs Wyatt, **Temple Bridge**,
tel. (0761) 52377

THIRKLEBY, N Yorks
Mr and Mrs J. Knowles, **Manor**, Little Thirkleby,
tel. (0845) 401216

THIRLMERE, Cumbria
Mr and Mrs J. Hodgson, **Stybeck**,
tel. Keswick (0596) 73232

THORNHILL, Dumfries & Galloway
Mrs J. Mackie, **Waterside Mains**,
tel. (0848) 30405

THRINGSTONE, Leics
Mr F. E. White, **Talbot House**,
tel. Coalville (0530) 222233

THROWLEIGH, Devon
Mr and Mrs C. R. Mosse, **East Ash Manor**,
tel. Whiddon Down (064723) 244

THURNING, Norfolk
Mrs A. M. Fisher, **Rookery**,
tel. Melton Constable (0263) 860357

THURSBY, Cumbria
Mrs M. G. Swainson, **How End**,
tel. Wigton (0965) 42487

TIDEFORD, Cornwall
Mrs B. A. Turner, **Kilna House**,
tel. Landrake (075538) 236

TISSINGTON, Derby
Mrs B. Herridge, **Bent**,
tel. Parwich (033525) 214

TIVERTON, Devon
Mr L. Fullilove, **Lodge Hill**, Ashley,
tel. (0884) 252907
Mrs I. R. Olive, **Lower Collipriest**,
tel. (0884) 252321

TODMORDEN, W Yorks
Mrs R. Bayley, **Todmorden Edge South**, Parkin
Lane, Stourhall, tel. (070681) 3459

TOMDOUN, Highland
Mrs H. Fraser, **No 3 Greenfield**, tel. (08092) 221

TOTNES, Devon
Mrs G. J. Veale, **Broomborough House**,
tel. (0803) 863134

TRAPP, Dyfed
N. and J. Card, **Llwyndewl Farm Guesthouse**,
tel. Llandybie (0269) 850362

TRAWSFYNYDD, Gwynedd
A. Swann, **Fronoleu**, tel. (076687) 397

TREFEGLWYS, Powys
Mrs J. Williams, **Cefn-Gwyn**, tel. (05516) 648

TREFIN (TREVINE), Dyfed
Mrs B. C. Morgan, **Binchurn**,
tel. Croesgoch (03483) 264

TREFRIW, Gwynedd
Mr and Mrs D. E. Roberts, **Cae-Coch**,
tel. Llanrwst (0492) 640380

TREGARON, Dyfed
Mrs M. J. Cutter, **Neuaddlas**, tel. (09744) 380

TRENEAR, (nr Helston), Cornwall
Mrs G. Lawrance, **Longstone**,
tel. Helston (03265) 2483

TREVEIGHAN, Cornwall
Mrs M. Jory, **Treveighan**,
tel. Bodmin (0208) 850286

TROON, Cornwall
Mrs H. Tyack, **Sea View**,
tel. Praze (0209) 831260

TROUTBECK, (nr Penrith), Cumbria
Mrs R. Bird, **Askew Rigg**,
tel. Threlkeld (059683) 638
Mr P. Fellows, **Lane Head**,
tel. Threlkeld (059683) 220

UFFCULME, Devon
Mrs M. D. Farley, **Houndaller**,
tel. Craddock (0884) 40246
Mrs C. M. Baker, **Woodrow**,
tel. Craddock (0884) 40362

UFFINGTON, Salop
Mr and Mrs D. Timmis, **Preston Boats**, Preston-on-Severn, tel. Upton Magna (074377) 240

ULEY, Glos
Sam and Kay Trump, **Hodgecombe**,
tel. (0453) 860365

ULLINGSWICK, Heref & Worcs
Mrs P. A. Howland, **The Steppes**,
tel. Burley Gate (043278) 424

UPOTTERY, Devon
Mrs M. M. Reed, **Yarde**,
tel. (040486) 318

UPPER HULME, Staffs
Mrs J. Lomas, **Keekorok Lodge**, (1m NW of village), tel. Blackshaw (053834) 218

UPTON PYNE, Devon
Mrs Y. M Taverner, **Pierce's**,
tel. Stoke Canon (039284) 252

USK, Gwent
J. Arnett, **Ty Gwyn**, tel. (02913) 2878

UTTOXETER, Staffs
Mrs B. L. Noakes, **Holly Grange**, Bramshall (2m W of B5027), tel. (08893) 2405
Mrs P. J. Tunnicliffe, **Moor House**, Wood Lane,
tel. (08893) 2384
R. J. and K. P. Stockton, **Popinjay**, Stafford Rd,
tel. (08893) 66082

VOWCHURCH, Heref & Worcs
Mrs A. Williams, **The Croft**,
tel. Peterchurch (09816) 226

WALLINGTON, Northumberland
Mrs S. Robinson-Gay, **Shieldhall**,
tel. Otterburn (0830) 40387

WAREHAM, Dorset
L. S. Barnes, **Luckford Wood**, East Stoke,
tel. Bindon Abbey (0929) 463098
Mrs J. Barnes, **Redcliffe**, tel. (09295) 2225

WATERHOUSES, Staffs
Mrs K. Watson, **Weaver**,
tel. Oakamoor (0538) 702271

WATERPERRY, Oxon
Mrs S. Fonge, **Manor**, tel. Ickford (08447) 263

WATERROW, Somerset
Mr J. Bone, **Hurstone Farmhouse Hotel**,
tel. Wiveliscombe (0984) 23441

WEDMORE, Somerset
Mr and Mrs I. D. Leavy, **Overbrook**, Blackford,
tel. (0934) 712081

WEEDONLOIS, Northants
Mrs C. Raven, **Croft**, Milthorpe,
tel. Blakesley (0327) 860475

WEETON, Lancs
Mrs T. Colligan, **High Moor**, tel. (039136) 273

WELSHPOOL, Powys
Mrs E. Jones, **Gungrog House**, Rhalit,
tel. (0938) 3381
Mr and Mrs W. Jones, **Moat**,
tel. (0938) 3179
Mr and Mrs J. Emberton, **Tynllwyn**,
tel. (0938) 3175

WEST CHILTINGTON, W Sussex
A. M. Steele, **New House**, tel. (07983) 2215

WEST TAPHOUSE, Cornwall
Mrs K. V. Bolitho, **Penadlake**, Two Waters Foot,
tel. Bodmin (0208) 872271

WHAPLODE, Lincs
Mrs A. Thompson, **Guy Wells**,
tel. Holbeach (0406) 22239

WHIDDON DOWN, Devon
Mrs J. S. Robinson, **South Nethercott**,
tel. (064723) 276

WHITECROSS, nr Wadebridge, Cornwall
Mrs E. L. D. Nicholls, **Torview**,
tel. Wadebridge (020881) 2261

WHITESTONE, Devon
Mrs S. K. Lee, **Rowhorne House**,
tel. Exeter (0392) 74675

WHITHORN, Dumfries & Galloway
Mrs E. C. Forsyth, **Baitler**,
tel. Garlieston (09886) 241

WHITLAND, Dyfed
C. M. and I. A. Lewis, **Cilpost**, tel. (0994) 240280

WIDDINGTON, Essex
Mrs L. Vernon, **Thistley Hall**,
tel. Saffron Walden (0799) 40388

WIDEMOUTH BAY, Cornwall
Mr J. C. Soar, **Kennacot**, tel. (028885) 683

WIGHT, ISLE OF
See Ryde

WILBERFOSS, Humberside
Mrs J. M. Liversidge, **Cuckoo Nest**,
tel. (07595) 365

WILLAND, Devon
Mrs J. M. Granger, **Doctors**, Halberton Rd,
tel. Tiverton (0884) 820525

WIMPSTONE, Warwicks
Mrs J. E. James, **Whitchurch Farm**,
tel. Alderminster (078987) 275

WINCANTON, Somerset
Mrs J. Brunt, **Hatherleigh**, tel. (0963) 32142

WINFRITH NEWBURGH, Dorset
Mrs H. Cox, **Wynards**,
tel. Warmwell (0305) 852817

WIVELISCOMBE, Somerset
B. M. and P. E. Ferguson, **Deepleigh**, Langley Marsh,
tel. (0984) 23379
Mrs E. M. Wyatt, **Hillacre**, Crawford
tel. (0984) 23355

WIX, Essex
Mrs H. P. Mitchell, **New Farmhouse**,
tel. (025587) 365

WOOLFARDISWORTHY, Devon
R. C. and C. M. Beck, **Stroxworthy**,
tel. Clovelly (02373) 333
Mrs P. I. Westaway, **Westvilla**,
tel. Clovelly (02373) 309

WOOLSTASTON, Salop
Mrs J. A. Davies, **Rectory**,
tel. Leebotwood (06945) 306

WORMBRIDGE, Heref & Worcs
J. T. Davies, **Duffryn**, tel. (098121) 217

WOOTTON-UNDER-EDGE, Glos
Mrs K. P. Forster, **Under-the-Hill House**, Adey's Ln, tel. Dursley (0453) 842557

YEALMPTON, Devon
Mrs A. German, **Broadmoor**,
tel. Plymouth (0752) 880407

YEOVIL, Somerset
Mrs M. Tucker, **Carents**, Yeovil Marsh,
tel. (0935) 76622

YSBYTY IFAN, Gwynedd
Mrs F. G. Roberts, **Ochr Cefn Isa**,
tel. Pentrefoelas (06905) 602

Farmhouses – Northern Ireland

Co. Antrim
CUSHENDUN
Villa, Torr Rd, Ballycleagh, tel. Ballymena 252

LISBURN
Brook Lodge, 79 Ballynahinch Rd, Cargacroy, tel. Bailles Mills 454

PORTRUSH
Islay View, 36 Leeke Rd, Ballymagarry, tel. Portrush 823220
Loguestown, tel. Portrush 822742

Co. Down
BALLYWALTER
Abbey, Ballywalter Rd, Greyabbey, tel. Greyabbey 207

DOWNPATRICK
Havine, 51 Ballydonell Rd, tel. Ballykinlar 242

Co. Fermanagh
ENNISKILLEN
Lack-a-Boy, Tempo Rd, tel. Enniskillen 22488
Lake View, Drumcrow, Blaney P.O., tel. Derrygonnelly 263

Co. Londonderry
CASTLEDAWSON
Moyola Lodge, 9 Brough Rd, tel. Castledawson 68224

Inns

ABERYSTWYTH, Dyfed
Railway Hotel, Alexandra Rd, tel. (0970) 611258

ACASTER MALBIS, N Yorks
Ship, tel. York (0904) 705609

APPLEBY-IN-WESTMORLAND, Cumbria
Royal Oak, Bongate, tel. (0930) 51463

APPLEDORE, Kent
Red Lion, 15 The Street, tel. (023383) 206

ARRAN, Isle of, Strathclyde
See Blackwaterfoot

ARUNDEL, W Sussex
Swan Hotel, High St, tel. (0903) 882314

ASCOTT-UNDER-WYCHWOOD, Oxon
Wychwood Arms Hotel, tel. Skipton-under-Wychwood (0993) 830271

ASHFORD, Kent
George, High St, tel. (0233) 25512

ASHWELL, Herts
Three Tuns Hotel, 6 High St, tel. (046274) 2387

ATHERSTONE, Warwicks
Three Tuns Hotel, 95 Long St, tel. (08277) 3161

ATTLEBOROUGH, Norfolk
Griffin Hotel, Church St, tel. (0953) 452149

AXBRIDGE, Somerset
Lamb, tel. (0934) 732253

BALLANTRAE, Strathclyde
Royal Hotel, 71 Main St, tel. (046583) 204

BANTHAM, Devon
Sloop, tel. Kingsbridge (0548) 560489

BARHAM, Kent
Old Coach House, A2 Trunk Rd
tel. Canterbury (0227) 831218

BARRASFORD, Northumb
Barrasford Arms, tel. Humshaugh (043481) 237

BATH, Avon
Country Hotel, 18–19 Pulteney Rd, tel. (0225) 25003

BEAUMARIS, Gwynedd
Liverpool Arms, tel. (0248) 810362

BECKERMET, Cumbria
Royal Oak Hotel, tel. (094684) 551

BELFORD, Northumb
Black Swan, Market Sq, tel. (06683) 266

BELSTONE, Devon
Tors, tel. Okehampton (0837) 840689

BENSON, Oxon
Castle, Castle Sq, tel. Wallingford (0491) 35349

BISHOP WILTON, Humberside
Fleece, tel. (07596) 251

BLACKWATERFOOT, Isle of Arran, Strathclyde
Greannan Hotel, tel. Shiskine (077086) 200

BLACKWOOD, Gwent
Plas, Gordon Rd, tel. (0495) 224674

BLETCHINGLEY, Surrey
Whyte Harte, tel. Godstone (0883) 843231

BODEDERN, Gwynedd
Crown Hotel, tel. Valley (0407) 740734

BONTDDU, Gwynedd
Halfway House Hotel, tel. (034149) 635

BOURTON-ON-THE-WATER, Glos
Mousetrap, tel. Cotswold (0451) 20579

BRAMBER, W Sussex
Castle Hotel, The Street, tel. Steyning (0903) 812102

BREDWARDINE, Heref & Worcs
Red Lion, tel. Moccas (09817) 303

BRENCHLEY, Kent
Rose & Crown, High St, tel. (089272) 2107

BRIDGNORTH, Salop
Ball Hotel, East Castle St, tel. (07462) 2478
King's Head Hotel, Whitburn St, tel. (07462) 2141

BRIDPORT, Dorset
King Charles Tavern, 114 St Andrews Rd, tel. (0308) 22911

BROAD CHALKE, Wilts
Queens Head, tel. (072278) 344

BROMSGROVE, Heref & Worcs
Forest, 290 Birmingham Rd, tel. (0527) 72063

BRUAR, Tayside
Bruar Falls Hotel, tel. Calvine (079683) 243

BURWASH, E Sussex
Admiral Vernon, Etchingham Rd, tel. (0435) 882230
Burwash Motel, High St, tel. (0435) 882540

CAERNARFON, Gwynedd
Black Boy, Northgate St, tel. (0286) 3604

CALSTOCK, Cornwall
Boot, Fore St, tel. Tavistock (0822) 832331

CANONBIE, Dumfries and Galloway
Riverside, tel. (05415) 295

CAREY, Heref & Worcs
Cottage of Content, tel. (043270) 242

CATON, Lancs
Ship Hotel, Lancaster Rd, tel. (0524) 770265

CHAGFORD, Devon
Globe, tel. (06473) 3485

CHALE, Isle of Wight
Clarendon Hotel & Wight Mouse,
tel. (0983) 730431

CHALFONT ST PETER, Bucks
Greyhound, High St,
tel. Gerrards Cross (0753) 883404

CHARFIELD, Glos
Huntingfield Mill Hotel,
tel. Dursley (0453) 843431

CHICKERELL, Dorset
Turks Head, 6–8 East St,
tel. Weymouth (0305) 783093

CHIDDINGFOLD, Surrey
Crown, Petworth Rd,
tel. Wormley (042879) 2255

CHIRNSIDE, Borders
Mitchell's Hotel, West End, tel. (089091) 507

CINDERFORD, Glos
White Hart Hotel, St Whites Rd, Ruspidge
(B4227), tel. Dean (0594) 23139

CLEARWELL, Glos
Wyndham Arms, tel. Dean (0594) 33666

CLEOBURY MORTIMER, Salop
Talbot Hotel, High St, tel. (0299) 270382

CLITHEROE, Lancs
White Lion Hotel, Market Pl, tel. (0200) 26955

CLOVELLY, Devon
New Inn, Main St, tel. (02373) 303
Red Lion, The Quay, tel. (02373) 237

CLUN, Salop
Sun, tel. (05884) 559

COLEFORD, Devon
New Inn, tel. Copplestone (03634) 242

COLESHILL, Warwicks
George & Dragon, 154 Coventry Rd,
tel. (0675) 62249

COLLYWESTON, Northants
Cavalier, Main St, tel. Duddington (078083) 288

COMPTON, Berks
Swan Hotel, tel. (063522) 269

CONISTON, Cumbria
Crown, tel. (0966) 41243

CONSTANTINE, Cornwall
Trengilly Wartha, Nancenoy,
tel. Falmouth (0326) 40332

COSHESTON, Dyfed
Hill House, tel. Pembroke (0646) 684352

CRAFTHOLE, Cornwall
Finnygook, tel. St Germans (0503) 30338

CHEETOWN, Dumfries & Galloway
Creetown Arms Hotel, St Johns St,
tel. (067182) 282

CROYDE, Devon
Thatched Barn,
tel. Barnstaple (0271) 890349

CULROSS, Fife
Red Lion, Low Causeway,
tel. Newmills (0383) 880225

DARTINGTON, Devon
Cott, tel. Totnes (0803) 863777

DEVIZES, Wilts
Castle Hotel, New Park St,
tel. (0380) 2902

DIRLETON, Lothian
Castle, tel. (062085) 221

DODDISCOMBSLEIGH, Devon
Nobody, tel. Christow (0647) 52394

DOLWYDDELAN, Gwynedd
Gwydyr, tel. (06906) 209

DRUMNADROCHIT, Highland
Lewiston Arms, Lewiston,
tel. (04562) 225

DUNS, Borders
Black Bull Hotel, Black Bull St,
tel. (0361) 83379

DURHAM, Co Durham
Croxdale, Croxdale (3m S A167),
tel. Spennymoor (0388) 815727

DYLIFE, Powys
Star, tel. Llanbrynmair (06503) 345

EAST COWTON, N Yorks
Beeswing, tel. North Cowton (032578) 349

EGGLESTON, Co Durham
Moorcock, Hilltop,
tel. Teesdale (0833) 50395

EMPINGHAM, Leics
White Horse, High St, tel. (078086) 221

FARNHAM, Surrey
Eldon Hotel, 43 Frensham Rd, Lower Bourne,
tel. Frensham (025125) 2745

FENSTANTON, Cambs
Tudor Hotel, High St,
tel. Huntingdon (0480) 62532

FIDDLEFORD, Dorset
Fiddleford, tel. Sturminster Newton (0258) 72489

FLAX BOURTON, Avon
Jubilee, Farleigh Rd,
tel. (027583) 2741

FONTHILL BISHOP, Wilts
Kings Arms, tel. Hindon (074789) 523

FORFAR, Tayside
Queen's Hotel, 12–14 The Cross,
tel. (0307) 62533

FOVANT, Wilts
Cross Keys Hotel, tel. (072270) 284

GATEHEAD, Strathclyde
Old Rome Farmhouse,
tel. Drybridge (0563) 850265

GOLSPIE, Highland
Park House Hotel, Main St, tel. (04083) 3667

GOMSHALL, Surrey
Black Horse, tel. Shere (048641) 2242

Old Man of Coniston

GORRAN HAVEN, Cornwall
Llawnroc Hotel, tel. Mevagissey (0726) 843461

GOUDHURST, Kent
Vine, High St, tel. (0580) 211261

GRAMPOUND ROAD VILLAGE, Cornwall
Midway, tel. St Austell (0726) 882343

GRETNA, Dumfries & Galloway
Crossways, Annan Rd, tel. (04613) 465

HALFORD, Warwicks
Halford Bridge Inn,
tel. Stratford-upon-Avon (0789) 740382

HALIFAX, W Yorks
Stump Cross, tel. (0422) 66004

HAMBLEDEN, Bucks
Stag & Huntsman,
tel. Henley-on-Thames (0491) 571227

HARLECH, Gwynedd
Rum Hole Hotel, tel. (0766) 780477

HARTLAND, Devon
West Country, Bursdon Moor, tel. (02374) 475

HATHERLEIGH, Devon
Bridge, Bridge St, tel. Okehampton (0837) 810357

HAWKSHEAD, Cumbria
King's Arms Hotel, tel. (09666) 372
Queen's Head Hotel, tel. (09666) 271

HAWNBY, N Yorks
Hawnby Hotel, tel. Bilsdale (04396) 202

HAYFIELD, Derbys
Sportsman, Kinder Rd,
tel. New Mills (0663) 42118

HAZLEHEAD, S Yorks
Flouch, tel. Barnsley (0226) 762037

HEDDON'S MOUTH, Devon
Hunters, tel. Parracombe (05983) 230

HINDON, Wilts
Grosvenor Arms, High St, tel. (074789) 253

HOLMFIRTH, W Yorks
White Horse, Scholes Rd, Jackson Bridge,
tel. (0484) 683940

HOLNE, Devon
Church House, tel. Poundsgate (03643) 208

HONITON, Devon
Monkton Court, Monkton (2m E A30),
tel. (0404) 2309

HORTON, Dorset
Horton, Cranbourne Rd, tel. Witchampton (0258)
840252

HORTON-IN-RIBBLESDALE, N Yorks
Crown Hotel, tel. (07296) 209

HUBBERHOLME, N Yorks
George, Kirk Gill, tel. Kettlewell (075676) 223

HUNTINGDON, Cambs
Black Bull, Post St, Godmanchester (1m S B1043),
tel. (0480) 53310

ILFRACOMBE, Devon
Royal Britannia, The Quay, tel. (0271) 62939

INGHAM, Suffolk
Cadogan Arms, tel. Culford (028484) 226

IPSWICH, Suffolk
Station Hotel, Burrell Rd, tel. (0473) 52664

KESWICK, Cumbria
George Hotel, St Johns St (Mount Charlotte),
tel. (0596) 72076
Kings Arms Hotel, Main St, tel. (0596) 72083

KILKHAMPTON, Cornwall
London, tel. (028882) 343

KILMARTIN, Strathclyde
Kilmartin Hotel, tel. (05465) 250

KILVE, Somerset
Hood Arms, tel. Holford (027874) 210

KINGSWINFORD, W Midlands
Swan Hotel, Stream Rd, tel. (0384) 3720

KINVER, Staffs
Kinfayre Restaurant, 41 High St,
tel. (0384) 872565

KIRKCAMBECK, Cumbria
Kirkton Jeans Hotel, tel. (06556) 220
KIRTLING, Cambs
Queens Head, tel. Newmarket (0638) 730253

KNOWSTONE, Devon
Masons Arms, tel. Anstey Mills (03984) 231

LANCING, W Sussex
Sussex Pad Hotel, Old Shoreham Rd,
tel. Shoreham-by-Sea (07917) 4647

LANGDALE, GREAT, Cumbria
Three Shires, Little Langdale, tel. (09667) 215

LLANBRYNMAIR, Powys
Wynnstay Arms Hotel, tel. (06503) 431

LLANDOGO, Gwent
Sloop, tel. Dean (0594) 530291

LLANFAIR WATERDINE, Salop
Red Lion, tel. Knighton (0547) 528214

LLANGRANOG, Dyfed
Pentre Arms Hotel, tel. (023978) 299

LLANGURIG, Powys
Blue Bell, tel. (05515) 254

LONGFRAMLINGTON, Northumb
Granby, tel. (066570) 228

LOSTWITHIEL, Cornwall
Royal Oak, Duke St, tel. Bodmin (0208) 872552

LUDFORD, Lincs
White Hart, Magna Mile,
tel. Burgh-on-Bain (050781) 664

LYDFORD, Devon
Castle, tel. (082282) 242

MALDON, Essex
Swan Hotel, Maldon High St,
tel. (0621) 53170

MARSDEN, W Yorks
Coach & Horses, Standedge,
tel. Huddersfield (0484) 844241

MAYFIELD, Staffs
Queens Arms, tel. Ashbourne (03335) 42271

MELBOURNE, Derbys
Melbourne Hotel, tel. (03316) 2134

MERE, Wilts
Talbot Hotel, The Square, tel. (0747) 860427

Maldon, Essex

MINEHEAD, Somerset
Red Lion Hotel, Quay St,
tel. (0643) 6507

MOLESWORTH, Cambs
Cross Keys, tel. Bythorn (08014) 283

MONMOUTH, Gwent
Queen's Head, St James St,
tel. (0600) 2767

MORECAMBE, Lancs
York Hotel, Lancaster Rd,
tel. (0524) 418226

MORTIMER'S CROSS, Heref & Worcs
Mortimers Cross, tel. Kingsland (056881) 238

MULLION, Cornwall
The Old Inn, Church Town, tel. (0326) 240240

MUNGRISDALE, Cumbria
Mill, tel. Threlkeld (059683) 632

NESSCLIFF, Salop
Nesscliff Hotel, tel. (074381) 253

NETTLECOMBE, Dorset
Marquis of Lorne, tel. Powerstock (030885) 236

NEWBURY, Berks
Hare & Hounds Hotel, Speen (1m W on A4),
tel. (0635) 47215

NEWNHAM BRIDGE, Heref & Worcs
Talbot Hotel, tel. (058479) 355

NEWPORT, Dyfed
Golden Lion, East St, tel. (0239) 820321

NEWPORT, Isle of Wight
Shute, Clatterford Shute, Carisbrooke,
tel. (0983) 523393

NORTHALLERTON, N Yorks
Station Hotel, 2 Boroughbridge Rd,
tel. (0609) 2053

NUNNEY, Somerset
George, Church St, tel. (037384) 458

ODDINGTON, Glos
Horse & Groom, tel. Cotswold (0451) 30584

ORFORD, Suffolk
King's Head, Front St, tel. (03945) 450271

OVINGTON, Northumb
Highlander, tel. Prudhoe (0661) 32016

PENNAN, Grampian
Pennan, tel. New Aberdour (03466) 201

PORTLOE, Cornwall
Ship, tel. Truro (0872) 501356

QUEEN CAMEL, Somerset
Mildmay Arms, tel. Yeovil (0935) 850456

RAVENSTONEDALE, Cumbria
Fat Lamb Country, Cross Bank,
tel. Newbiggin on Lune (05873) 242

RHANDIRMWYN, Dyfed
Royal Oak, tel. (05506) 201

RHES-Y-CAE, Clwyd
Miners Arms, tel. Halkyn (0352) 780567

RHUALLT, Clwyd
White House, tel. St Asaph (0745) 582155

RICKINGHALL, Suffolk
Hamblyn House, The Street,
tel. Diss (0379) 898292

ST AUSTELL, Cornwall
Holmbush, 101 Holmbush Rd, tel. (0726) 73217

ST CLEARS, Dyfed
Black Lion Hotel, tel. (0994) 230700

ST MARY'S LOCH, Borders
Tibble Shiels, tel. Cappercleuch (0750) 42231

SALFORD, Beds
Red Lion Country Hotel, Wavendon Rd,
tel. Milton Keynes (0908) 583117

SALISBURY, Wilts
White Horse Hotel, Castle St,
tel. (0722) 27844

SANDWICH, Kent
Fleur de Lis, Delf St, tel. (0304) 611131

SANQUHAR, Dumfries & Galloway
Blackaddie House Hotel, Blackaddie Rd,
tel. (06592) 270

SANTON BRIDGE, Cumbria
Bridge, tel. Wasdale (09406) 221

SCOTCH CORNER, N Yorks
Vintage Hotel, tel. Richmond (0748) 4424

SEDGEFIELD, Co Durham
Dun Cow, High St, tel. (0740) 20894

SEMLEY, Wilts
Bennett Arms, tel. East Knoyle (07483) 221

SHEPTON MALLET, Somerset
Kings Arms, Leg Sq, tel. (0749) 3781
Wine Vaults & Shambles Restaurant,
tel. (0749) 2436

SHIPSTON-ON-STOUR, Warwicks
Bell, Sheep St, tel. (0608) 61443
White Bear, High St tel. (0608) 61558

SHRAWLEY, Heref & Worcs
Lenchford Hotel, tel. (0905) 620229

SKIPTON, N Yorks
Red Lion Hotel, High St, tel. (0756) 60718

SLEDMERE, Humberside
Triton, tel. Driffield (0377) 86644

SLYNE, Lancs
Slyne Lodge, tel. Hestbank (0524) 823389

SNAPE, Suffolk
Crown, tel. (072888) 324

SOUTH LUFFENHAM, Leics
Boot & Shoe, tel. (0780) 720177

SOUTH TAWTON, Devon
Seven Stars, tel. Sticklepath (083784) 292

SOUTHWOLD, Suffolk
Kings Head Hotel, 23/25 High St,
tel. (0502) 723829

SOWERBY BRIDGE, W Yorks
The Hobbit, Hob Ln, Norland,
tel. Halifax (0422) 832202

STAMFORD, Lincs
Bull & Swan, St Martins, tel. (0780) 63558

STEEPLE ASTON
Hopcrofts Holt Hotel (Inter-Hotels),
tel. (0869) 40259

SWYNNERTON, Staffs
Fitzherbert Arms, tel. (078135) 241

SYMONDS YAT, EAST, Heref & Worcs
Saracens Head, tel. (0600) 890435

TELFORD, Salop
Swan Hotel, Watling St, Wellington,
tel. (0952) 3781

TENBURY WELLS, Heref & Worcs
Crow Hotel, Teme St, tel. (0584) 810503

THRAPSTON, Northants
Court House Hotel, tel. (08012) 3618

TICEHURST, E Sussex
Bell Hotel, The Square, tel. (0580) 200234

TINTERN, Gwent
Fountain, Trellech Grange, tel. (02918) 303

TORTHORWALD, Dumfries & Galloway
Torr House Hotel,
tel. Collin (038775) 214

TOWCESTER, Northants
Brave Old Oak, Watling St,
tel. (0327) 50533

TREBARWITH, Cornwall
Mill House,
tel. Camelford (0840) 770200

TRECASTLE, Powys
Castle Hotel,
tel. Sennybridge (087482) 354

TRETOWER, Powys
Tretower Court,
tel. Bwlch (0874) 730204

UPLYME, Devon
Black Dog Hotel, Lyme Rd,
tel. Lyme Regis (02974) 2634

WADHURST, E. Sussex
Fourkeys, Station Rd,
tel. (089288) 2252

WANSFORD, Cambs
Cross Keys,
tel. Stamford (0780) 782266

WARREN STREET, nr Lenham, Kent
Harrow, tel. Maidstone (0622) 858727

WATERROW, Somerset
Rock, tel. Wiveliscombe (0984) 23293

WEST CHARLETON, Devon
Ashburton Arms,
tel. Frogmore (054853) 242

WEYMOUTH, Dorset
Golden Lion Hotel, Stedmonds St,
tel. (0305) 786778

WHITCHURCH, Heref & Worcs
Crown Hotel,
tel. Symonds Yat (0600) 890234

WHITEWEL, Lancs
The Inn at Whitewell,
tel. Dunsop Bridge (02008) 222

WHITNEY-ON-WYE, Heref & Worcs
Rhydspence, tel. Clifford (04973) 262

WICKHAM, Berks
Five Bells, tel. Boxford (048838) 242

WIGAN, Gt Manchester
Th'old Hall, 240A Warrington Rd, Lower Ince, Ince
in Makerfield, tel. (0942) 866330

WIGMORE, Heref & Worcs
Compasses Hotel, tel. (056886) 203

WITHAM, Essex
Spread Eagle, Newland St, tel. (0376) 512131

WIVELISCOMBE, Somerset
Bear, 10 North St, tel. (0984) 23537

WOOLHOPE, Heref & Worcs
Butchers Arms, tel. Fownhope (043277) 281

WOOTTON BASSETT, Wilts
Angel Hotel, 47 High St,
tel. Swindon (0793) 852314

WORKINGTON, Cumbria
Morven Hotel, Siddick, tel. (0900) 2118

WYE, Kent
New Flying Horse, Upper Bridge St,
tel. (0233) 812297

YATTON, Avon
Prince of Orange, High St, tel. (0934) 832193

YOULGRAVE, Derbys
Bulls Head, Church St, tel. (062986) 307

Caravan and Campsites

ABBEY WOOD, Gt London
See London for details

ABERCHIRDER, Grampian
► **McRobert Park**. Apply to: Director of Leisure
& Recreation, Banff & Buchan District Council,
1 Church St, Macduff, Banffshire AB4 1US,
tel. Banff (02612) 2521 ext 304

ABERCRAF, Powys
►► **Dan-Yr-Ogof Caves Caravan & Tenting
Park**, tel. (0639) 730693

ABERDEEN, Grampian
►►► **Hazelhead Caravan & Tent Site**,
Groats Rd. Apply to: Aberdeen City District Council,
St Nicholas House, Aberdeen AB1 1XJ,
tel. (0224) 642121 ext 489

ABERFELDY, Tayside
►► **Municipal Caravan Site**, Dunkeld Rd, Apply
to: Perth & Kinross District Council, Parks and
Recreation Dept, Area Office, Bank St, Aberfeldy,
Perthshire PH15 2AQ,
tel. (0887) 20662

ABERLOUR (Charlestown of Aberlour),
Grampian
►► **Aberlour Gardens Caravan Park**,
tel. (03405) 586

ABERMULE, Powys
► **Ye Old Smithy Caravan Park**,
tel. (068686) 657

ABERSOCH, Gwynedd
►►► **Bryn Cethin Bach Caravan Park**,
tel. (075881) 2719
►►► **Haulfryn Camping Site**,
tel. (075881) 2045 & 2047
► **Pant-Gwyn Cottage**, Sarn Bach,
tel. (075881) 2268

ABERYSTWYTH, Dyfed
► **"U" Tow Caravans, Aberystwyth Holiday
Village**, tel. (0970) 4211

ABOYNE, Grampian
►►► **Aboyne Loch Caravan Park**,
tel. (0339) 2244

ACASTER MALBIS, N Yorks
►►► **Chestnut Farm Caravan Site**,
tel. York (0904) 704676
►►► **Mount Pleasant Caravan Village**,
tel. York (0904) 707078
►► **Moor End Farm**,
tel. York (0904) 706727

▽ **ACASTER SELBY**, N Yorks
Hales Hill Farm,
tel. Appleton Roebuck (090484) 317

ACTON BRIDGE, Cheshire
► **Woodbine Cottage**,
tel. Weaverham (0606) 852319

ALCESTER, Warwicks
► **Hoo Hill**, tel. (0789) 762515

▽ **ALDINGBOURNE**, W Sussex
Woodland, Hook Ln,
tel. Eastergate (024368) 2467

ALFORD, Grampian
►►► **Haughton House Caravan Site**,
tel. (0336) 2107

ALLERSTON, N Yorks
►►► **Vale of Pickering Caravan Park**, Carr
House Farm, tel. Scarborough (0723) 85280

ALLERTON PARK, N Yorks
►►► **Allerton Park Caravan Site**,
tel. Green Hammerton (0901) 30569

ALPORT, Derbys
▽ **Harthill Hall Caravan Site**, Harthill Hall,
tel. Bakewell (062986) 203

ALTON, Hants
▽ **Bushey Leaze Farm**, Medstead Rd, Beech,
tel. (0420) 83760
▽ **Upper Neatham Mill**, Upper Neatham Mill Ln,
tel. (0420) 84188

ALVES, Grampian
►►►► **North Alves Caravan Park**,
tel. (034385) 223

ALVINGTON, Glos
►►► **Clanna Caravan & Camping Park**,
tel. Netherend (059452) 214 & 493

AMBLESIDE, Cumbria
►►► **Skelwith Fold Caravan Park**,
tel. (0966) 32277
►► **Low Wray National Trust Campsite**, Low
Wray, tel. (0966) 32810

AMISFIELD, Dumfries & Galloway
►► **Glen Clova Caravan Park**, Glen Clova,
tel. (0387) 710447

ANDOVER, Hants
► **Wyke Down Touring Caravans & Camping
Park**, Picket Piece,
tel. (0264) 52048

ANNAN, Dumfries & Galloway
► **Galabank Caravan & Campsite**, North St

APPLEBY, Cumbria
►►►► **Wild Rose Park**, Ormside,
tel. (0930) 51077

APPLECROSS, Highland
► **Applecross Campsite**, tel. (05204) 268

ARDGARTAN, Strathclyde
►►► **Ardgarten Campsite**,
tel. Arrochar (03012) 597

ARDMAIR, Highland
►►► **Ardmair Point Campsite**,
tel. Ullapool (0854) 2054

ARDUAINE, Strathclyde
►► **Arduaine Caravan & Camping Site**,
tel. Kilmelford (08522) 288

ARISAIG, Highland
►► **Portnadoran Caravan Site**,
tel. (06875) 267

ASHBOURNE, Derbys
►►► **Sandybrook Hall Holiday Centre**,
tel. (0335) 42679

ASHBURTON, Devon
►► **Ashburton Caravan Park**, Waterleat,
tel. (0364) 52552 or
Moretonhampstead (0647) 40543
►►► **River Dart Country Park**, Holne Park,
tel. (0364) 52511

ASHFORD IN THE WATER, Derbys
►►► **Greenhills Caravan Park**, Crow Hill Lane,
tel. Bakewell (062981) 3467 and 3052

ASHTON, Cornwall
►► **Boscreage Caravan Park**,
tel. Penzance (0736) 762231

ASHURST, Hants
►► **Ashurst Camp**, tel. Lyndhurst (042128) 3771
(Forestry Commission Office) and 2269 (Tourist
Information Centre)

ASTON CANTLOW, Warwicks
► **Island Meadow Caravan Park**, The Mill
House, tel. Great Alne (078981) 273

AUCHENBOWIE, Central
►► **Auchenbowie Caravan & Camping Site**,
tel. Denny (0324) 822141

AUCHENMALG, Dumfries & Galloway
►►► **Cock Inn Caravan Park**,
tel. (05815) 227

AVIEMORE, Highland
►►► **Aviemore Centre Caravan Park**,
tel. (0479) 810624
►►► **Dalraddy Caravan Park**,
tel. (0479) 810330
►►► **Glenmore Forest Park Campsite**, Apply
to: The Head Forester, Forestry Commission,
Glenmore, Aviemore, Inverness-shire PH22 1QU,
tel. Cairngorm (047986) 271
►►► **Speyside Caravan Park**,
tel. (0479) 810236

AYR, Strathclyde
►►► **Ayr Racecourse Site**, Whitletts Rd,
tel. (0292) 264873
►► **Crofthead Caravan Park**,
tel. (0292) 263516

AYSIDE, Cumbria
► **Oak Head Caravan Park**,
tel. Newby Bridge (0448) 31475

BACTON, Norfolk
►►► **Cable Gap Caravan Park**, Coast Rd,
tel. Walcott (0692) 650667

BAKEWELL, Derbys
▽ **Haddon Grove Farm**, Haddon Grove, Over
Haddon (3m W off B5055),
tel. (062981) 2343

BALA, Gwynedd
►►► **Pen-y-Garth Camping & Caravan Park**,
Rhos-y-Gwalia, tel. (0678) 520485
►► **Penybont Touring Park**, Llangynog Rd,
tel. (0678) 520549
► **Tytandderwen Caravan Site**,
tel. (0678) 520273
▽ **Bryn Moel**, tel. (0678) 520143

BALLATER, Grampian
►► **Ballater Caravan & Camping Site**, Apply
to: Leisure and Recreation Department, Kincardine
and Deeside District Council, Viewpoint, Arduthie
Rd, Stonehaven, Kincardineshire AB3 2DQ,
tel. Stonehaven (0569) 62001

BALLOCH, Strathclyde
►►► **Tullichewan Caravan Park**, Old Luss Rd,
tel. Alexandria (0389) 59475

BALMACARA, Highland
►► **Reraig Caravan Site**, tel. (059986) 215
▽ **Balmacara Campsite**, tel. (059986) 321

BALMAHA, Central
►►► **Cashell Caravan & Camping Site**,
tel. (036087) 234

BALMINNOCH, Dumfries and Galloway
►►►► **Three Lochs Caravan Park**,
tel. Kirkcowan (067183) 304

BAMBURGH, Northumb
►► **Glororum Caravan Park**, Glororum Farm,
tel. (06684) 205, 272 and 457

BANBURY, Oxon
▽ **Barnstones**, Great Bourton,
tel. Cropredy (029575) 289

BANFF, Grampian
►►► **Banff Links Caravan Site**, Apply to: Banff
and Buchan District Council, Director of Leisure
and Recreation, 1 Church St, Macduff, Banffshire
AB4 1US, tel. (02612) 2521 ext 304

BANGOR-ON-DEE, Clwyd
► **Camping & Caravanning Club Site**, The
Racecourse, tel. (0978) 780740

BARCALDINE, Strathclyde
►►► **Barcaldine Garden Caravan Park**,
tel. Ledaig (063172) 348

BARDON MILL, Northumb
▽ **Ashcroft Farm**, tel. (04984) 260

BARMOUTH, Gwynedd
► **Hendre Mynach Caravan Park**,
tel. (0341) 280262

BARNSTAPLE, Devon
►►► **Midland Caravan Park**, Braunton Rd,
Ashford, tel. (0271) 43691

BARRHILL, Strathclyde
►►► **Madojosa Holiday Village**,
tel. Pinwherry (046584) 227

BARROW-IN-FURNESS, Cumbria
►►► **South End Caravan Site**, Walney Island,
tel. (0229) 42823

BATH, Avon
►►►► **Newbridge Caravan Park**, Newbridge,
tel. (0225) 28778
►►►► **Newton Mill Touring Centre**, Newton
St Loe (3m NW off A4), tel. (0225) 333909

BEADNELL, Northumb
►► **Beadnell Links**, The Chimes,
tel. Chathill (066589) 241
► **Annstead Camping Site**, (Camping &
Caravanning Club Site),
tel. Seahouses (0665) 720586

BEAMISH, Co Durham
►► **Bobby Shafto Caravan Park**,
tel. Durham (0385) 701776

BEATTOCK, Dumfries & Galloway
►► **Beattock House Caravan Park**,
tel. (06833) 403

BEAULY, Highland
►►► **Cruivend Camping & Caravan Site**,
Cruivend, tel. (0463) 782367
►► **Lovat Bridge Caravan & Camping Site**,
tel. (046371) 2374

BECKFOOT, Cumbria
►► **Abbey Holme Caravan Park**,
tel. Silloth (0965) 31653

BEDDGELERT, Gwynedd
►►► **Snowdonia Forest Park Campsite**
(Forestry Commission)

BELFORD, Northumb
►►► **Waren Caravan Park**, Waren Mill,
tel. Bamburgh (06684) 366

BELTON, Norfolk
►►► **Wild Duck Caravan & Chalet Park**,
tel. Gt Yarmouth (0493) 780268

BENDERLOCH, Strathclyde
►►► **Tralee Bay Holidays**,
tel. Ledaig (063172) 255

BERE REGIS, Dorset
►► **Rowlands Walt Touring Park**, Rye Hill,
tel. (0929) 471958

BERRIEW, Powys
►► **Maes yr Afon Caravan Park**,
tel. (068685) 587

BERRYNARBOR, Devon
►►►► **Watermouth Cove**,
tel. Ilfracombe (0271) 62504
►►►► **Sandaway Holiday Park**,
tel. Combe Martin (027188) 3555
►►► **Napps Camping Site**, Old Coast Rd,
tel. Combe Martin (027188) 2557

BERWICK-UPON-TWEED, Northumb
►►► **Ord House Caravan Park**, East Ord,
tel. (0289) 305288

BETHESDA, Gwynedd
►►►► **Ogwen Bank Caravan Park &
Country Club**, tel. (0248) 600486

BETTWS EVAN, Dyfed
►►► **Pilbach Caravan Park**,
tel. Rhydlewis (023975) 434

BETWS GARMON, Gwynedd
►►► **Bryn Gloch Caravan & Camping Park**,
tel. Waunfawr (028685) 216

BEWALDETH, Cumbria
►►► **North Lakes Caravan & Camping Park**,
tel. Bassenthwaite Lake (059681) 510

BICKINTON, nr Ashburton, Devon
►►► **Lemonford Holidays**,
tel. (062682) 242

BIDDENDEN, Kent
►► **Woodlands Park**, Tenterden Rd,
tel. (0580) 291216
► **Spilland Farm Holiday Caravan & Tourer
Park**, Benenden Rd, tel. (0580) 291379

BILLINGSHURST, W Sussex
► **Limeburner's Arms**, Newbridge,
tel. (040381) 2311

BIRCHINGTON, Kent
►► **Quex Caravan & Camping Park**, Park Rd.
tel. Thanet (0843) 41273

BIRNAM, Tayside
►►►► **Erigmore House Caravan Park**,
tel. Dunkeld (03502) 236

BISHOP MONKTON, N Yorks
▽ **Church Farm**, Knaresborough Rd,
tel. Ripon (0765) 87297 and 87405

BLACKFORD, Cumbria
►► **Dandy Dinmont Caravan Site**,
tel. Rockcliffe (022874) 611

BLACKPOOL, Lancs
►► **Cropper Caravan Park**, Cropper Rd, Marton,
tel. (0253) 62051

BLACKWATER, Cornwall
►►► **Trevarth Caravan Park**,
tel. Truro (0872) 560266

BLAIR ATHOLL, Tayside
►►►► **Blair Castle Caravan Park**,
tel. (079681) 263
►►► **River Tilt Caravan Park**,
tel. (079681) 467

BLAIRLOGIE, Central
►► **Witches Craig Farm Caravan & Camping
Park**, tel. Stirling (0786) 74947

BLETCHINGDON, Oxon
►►► **Diamond Farm Caravan & Camping
Park**, Heathfield, tel. (0869) 50749
▽ **Frogsnest Farm**, Islip Rd, tel. (0869) 50389

BLUE ANCHOR, Somerset
►►►► **Beeches Holiday Site**,
tel. Washford (0984) 40391
► **Blue Anchor Bay Caravan Park**,
tel. Dunster (0643) 821360

Beddgelert, Gwynedd

BOAT OF GARTEN, Highland
►►► **Campgrounds of Scotland**,
tel. (047983) 652

BODIAM, E Sussex
►► **Park Camp**, Park Farm (off A229)
tel. Staplecross (058083) 514

BODINNICK, Cornwall
►► **Yeate Farm**, tel. Polruan (072687) 256

BODMIN, Cornwall
► **Camping & Caravanning Club Site**, Old
Callywith Rd, tel. (0208) 3834

BOLTON-LE-SANDS, Lancs
►►► **Sandside Caravan & Camping Site**, St
Michael's Lane, tel. Hest Bank (0524) 822311
►► **Bolton Holmes Farm**,
tel. Carnforth (0524) 732854
►► **Detron Gate Farm**,
tel. Carnforth (0524) 732842

BONCHESTER BRIDGE, Borders
Bonchester Bridge Caravan Park, Fernbank,
tel. (045086) 676

BOSWINGER, Cornwall
►►►► **Sea View International Caravan &
Camping Park**, tel. Mevagissey (0726) 843425

BOTHWELL, Strathclyde
►►► **Strathclyde Park Caravan Site**,
Bothwellhaugh Rd, tel. Motherwell (0698) 66155

BOURNEMOUTH, Dorset
►►► **Chesildene Touring Caravan Park**,
2 Chesildene Avenue, tel. (0202) 513238

BOUTH, Cumbria
► **Black Beck Caravan Park**,
tel. Greenodd (022986) 274

BOWNESS-ON-WINDERMERE, Cumbria
Sites are listed under Windermere

BRADFIELD, Essex
► **Strangers Home Inn**, The Street,
tel. Wix (025587) 304

BRADWELL, Norfolk
►►►► **Blue Sky Caravan Park**, Burgh Rd,
tel. Great Yarmouth (0493) 780571

BRAINTREE, Essex
Sun Lido Caravan Park, Essex Barn Restaurant,
Rayne, tel. (0376) 25445 and 25228

BRAITHWAITE, Cumbria
►► **Scotgate Caravan Site**, tel. (059682) 343

BRAMPTON, Cumbria
►► **Irthing Vale Caravan Park**, Old Church
Lane, tel. (06977) 2237

BRANSGORE, Hants
►►► **Heathfield Caravan Park**,
tel. (0425) 72397

BRAUNTON, Devon
►► **Lobb Fields Caravan & Camping Park**,
Staunton Rd, tel. (0271) 812090

BRECON, Powys
►►► **Brynich Caravan Park**, tel. (0874) 3325

BRIDESTOWE, Devon
Bridestowe Caravan Park,
tel. (083786) 261

BRIDGE OF ALLAN, Central
Allanwater Caravan Site, Blairforkie Drive,
tel. (0786) 832254

BRIDGERULE, Devon
►►► **Hedley Wood Caravan Park**,
tel. (028881) 404

BRIDLINGTON, Humberside
The Poplars Caravan Site, 45 Jewison Lane,
Sewerby, tel. (0262) 77251

BRIDPORT, Dorset
►►► **Highlands End Farm Caravan Park**,
tel. Bridport (0308) 22139
► **West Bay International Holiday Centre**
(2m S off B3157),
tel. (0308) 22424

BRIGHOUSE BAY, Dumfries & Galloway
►►►► **Brighouse Bay Holiday Park**,
tel. Borgue (05577) 267

BRIXTON, Devon
► **Brixton Camping Site**, Venn Farm,
tel. Plymouth (0752) 880378 & 880551

BROAD HAVEN, Dyfed
►► **Creampots Farm Caravan & Camping
Park** (4m W of Haverford west on B4327),
tel. (043783) 359
►► **Rosehill Caravan Park**, Portfield Gate,
tel. (043783) 245

BROADWAY, Heref & Worcs
►►► **Leedon's Park**, Childswickham Rd,
tel. (0386) 852423

BROCKENHURST, Hants
►► **Hollands Wood Camp Site**,
tel. Lyndhurst (042128) 3771 (Forestry Commission
Office) or 2269 (Tourist Information Centre)
► **Roundhill Campsite**, Beaulieu Rd,
tel. Lyndhurst (042128) 3771 (Forestry Commission
Office) or 2269 (Tourist Information Centre)
▽ **Aldridge Hill Campsite** (2m NW),
tel. Lyndhurst (042128) 3771 (Forestry Commission
Office) or 2269 (Tourist Information Centre)

BRODIE, Grampian
►►► **Old Mill Inn**,
tel. (03094) 244

BROMPTON-ON-SWALE, N Yorks
►►► **Brompton-on-Swale Caravan Site**,
tel. Richmond (0748) 4629

BROMSGROVE, Heref & Worcs
▽ **Queens Head**, Sugarbrook Ln, Stoke Pound
(2m SE), tel. (0527) 77777

BROMYARD, Heref & Worcs
►►► **Bromyard Caravan Park**, Bishell House,
Petty Bridge,
tel. (0885) 82267
►►► **Saltmarshe Castle**, tel. (0885) 83207

BRONLLYS, Powys
►►► **Anchorage Caravan Park**,
tel. Talgarth (0874) 711246

BROOME, Salop
▽ **Engine & Tender Inn**,
tel. Little Brampton (05887) 275

BRORA, Highland
► **Riverside Caravan Site**, Stonehouse Doll,
tel. (04082) 353

BROTHERS WATER, Cumbria
See Hartsop

BROUGH, Cumbria
►► **Augill House Farm Caravan Park**,
Augill House Farm, tel. (09304) 305

BROUGHTON, Humberside
►► **Briggate Lodge Caravan & Picnic Site**,
tel. Brigg (0652) 54275

BRYNCRUG, Gwynedd
►►► **Woodlands Holiday Park** (2m NE),
tel. Tywyn (0654) 710471

BRYNSIENCYN, Gwynedd
►► **Fron Farm Caravan & Camping Site**,
tel. (024873) 310

BRYNTEG, Gwynedd
►►► **Glan Gors Caravan Park**,
tel. Tynygongl (0248) 852334

BRYNTEG, Gwynedd (contd.)
►►► **Nant Newydd Caravan Park**,
tel. Tynygongl (0248) 852842
► **Garnedd Touring Site**, Garnedd,
tel. Tynygongl (0248) 853240

BUCKFASTLEIGH, Devon
►► **Buckfast Caravan Park**,
tel. (0364) 422479
▽ **Beara Farm**, Colston Rd, tel. (0364) 42234

BUDE, Cornwall
►►► **Budemeadows Touring Holiday Park**,
(3m S), tel. Widemouth Bay (028885) 646
►►► **Bude Holiday Park**, Maer Lane,
tel. (0288) 2472
►►► **Wooda Farm Camping & Caravanning
Park**, Poughill (2m E), tel. (0288) 2069

BUNGAY, Suffolk
►►► **Outney Meadow Caravan Park**,
Broad St, tel. (0986) 2388

BURGH CASTLE, Norfolk
►►► **Cherry Tree Holiday Park**, Mill Rd,
tel. Gt Yarmouth (0493) 780229

BURNHAM-ON-SEA, Somerset
►►► **Home Farm Touring Park**, Edith Mead,
tel. (0278) 783632

BURNISTON, N Yorks
►►► **Whitby Road Garage & Caravan Park**,
High St, tel. Scarborough (0723) 870326

BUTLEY, Suffolk
►► **Tangham Campsite**,
tel. Orford (03945) 707
due to change to (0394) 450707

BUXTON, Derbys
► **Dukes Drive Caravan Site**, tel. (0298) 2988

CABUS, Lancs
►►► **Robinsons Caravans**, Claylands Farm,
tel. Forton (0524) 791242

CAERNARFON, Gwynedd
►►► **Cadnant Valley Camping Site**,
Llanberis Rd, tel. (0286) 3196

CAIRNRYAN, Dumfries & Galloway
►►► **Cairnryan Caravan & Chalet Park**,
tel. (05812) 231

CAISTER-ON-SEA, Norfolk
►►► **Grasmere Caravan Park**, 7 Bultitudes
Loke, Yarmouth Rd, tel. Gt Yarmouth (0493) 720382
►► **Old Hall Caravan Park**, High St,
tel. Great Yarmouth (0493) 720400 & 721831

CALLANDER, Central
►►► **Callander Holiday Park**, Invertrossachs
Rd, tel. (0877) 30265
►►► **Gart Caravan Park**, The Gart,
tel. (0877) 30002

CALLINGTON, Cornwall
►►► **Honicombe Holiday Village**,
tel. Tavistock (0822) 832583

CAMBORNE, Cornwall
►► **Magor Farm Caravan Site**, Tehidy,
tel. (0209) 713367

CAMELFORD, Cornwall
►►►► **Juliot's Well Holiday Park**,
tel. (0840) 213302

CAMUSTIANAVAIG, Isle of Skye, Highland
► **Braes Caravan Site**

CANEWDON, Essex
►► **Riverside Trailer Park Ltd**, Creeksea Ferry
Rd, Wallasea Island, tel. (03706) 297 and 484

CANTERBURY, Kent
►►► **St Martins Touring & Camping Site**,
Bekesbourne Lane, tel. (0227) 463216

CAPERNWRAY, Lancs
►► **Old Hall Caravan Park**,
tel. Carnforth (0524) 732439 & 732975

CARGILL, Tayside
►► **Beech Hedge Restaurant & Caravan Park**,
tel. Meikleour (025083) 249

CARK-IN-CARTMEL, Cumbria
►► **Old Park Wood Caravan Site**. Apply to:
Holker Estates Co, Cark-in-Cartmel, Grange-over-Sands, Cumbria,
tel. Flookburgh (044853) 266

CARLEEN, Cornwall
►►► **Lower Polladras Farm**,
tel. Penzance (0736) 762220
► **Poldown Caravan Park**, Poldown,
tel. Helston (03265) 4560

CARLISLE, Cumbria
►►► **Orton Grange Caravan Park**, Orton
Grange, Wigton Rd,
tel. (0228) 710252

CARLYON BAY, Cornwall
►►► **Bethesda Camping & Caravan Park**,
Cypress Avenue, tel. Par (072681) 2735

CARMEL, Dyfed
►► **Marlais Caravan Park**,
tel. Cross Hands (0269) 842093

CARNFORTH, Lancs
►► **Netherbeck Caravan Site**, North Rd,
Netherbeck, tel. (0524) 733218

CARNON DOWNS (nr Truro), Cornwall
►► **Ringwell Holiday Park**, Bissoe Rd,
tel. Truro (0872) 862194

CARNOUSTIE, Tayside
►►► **Woodlands Caravan Park**, Newton Rd,
tel. (0241) 52258

CARRADALE, Strathclyde
►► **Carradale Bay Caravan Site**, The Steading,
tel. (05833) 683

CASSINGTON, Oxon
►► **Cassington Mill Caravan Park**,
Eynsham Rd, tel. Oxford (0865) 881081

CASTERTON (GREAT), Leics
►►► **Casterton Caravan & Camping Park**,
tel. Stamford (0780) 52441 & 63266

CASTLE DOUGLAS, Dumfries & Galloway
►► **Lochside Park**. Apply to: Stewartry District
Council, Environmental Health Dept,
Dunmuir Rd, Castle Douglas, Kirkcudbrightshire,
tel. (0556) 2949

CASTLESIDE, Co Durham
►►► **Allensford Park Caravan Site**. Apply to:
Derwentside District Council, Council Offices,
Consett, Co Durham DH8 5JA,
tel. Consett (0207) 509522

CASTLE SWEEN, Strathclyde
► **Castle Sween Bay Holidays**,
tel. Achnamara (054685) 223

CATON, Lancs
►► **Crook O'Lune Caravan Park**,
tel. (0524) 770216

CATSFIELD, E Sussex
► **Tellis Coppice Touring Caravan Park**,
tel. Battle (04246) 3969

CAWSTON, Norfolk
► **Haveringland Hall Caravan Park**,
Haveringland Hall Farm,
tel. Norwich (0603) 871302

CENARTH, Dyfed
►► **Aberdwylan Caravan Park**, Abercych,
tel. Boncath (023974) 476

CERNE ABBAS, Dorset
► Giant's Head Caravan & Camping Park,
Giant's Head Farm, Old Sherborne Rd,
tel. (03003) 242
► Lyons Gate Caravan Park, Lyons Gate,
tel. Buckland Newton (03005) 260

CERRIGCEINWEN, Gwynedd
►►► Tregof Caravan Park, Llangefni,
tel. Gwalchmai (0407) 720315

CHACEWATER, Cornwall
►►► Chacewater Caravan & Camping Park,
Coxhill, tel. St Day (0209) 820762
►►► Liskey Touring Park, Greenbottom,
tel. Truro (0872) 560274

CHANNEL ISLANDS
Sites are listed under individual place-names.
See under Jersey for details

CHAPEL HILL, Lincs
►►► Orchards Caravans,
tel. Coningsby (0526) 42414

CHAPMANS WELL, Cornwall
►►► Chapmanswell Caravan Park,
tel. Ashwater (040921) 382

CHARD, Somerset
►► Turnpike Woodlands Caravan Park (A30),
Exeter Rd, Howley (2¼m W), tel. (04606) 221

CHARMOUTH, Dorset
►►► Newlands Caravan & Camping Park,
2 Camping Site, tel. (0297) 60259
►►► Wood Farm Caravan Park, Axminster Rd,
tel. (0297) 60697
► Manor Farm Caravan & Camping Parks,
tel. (0297) 60226

CHEADLE, Staffs
►► Hales Hall Caravan & Camping Park,
Oakmoor Rd, tel. (0538) 753305

CHEDDAR, Somerset
►►► Broadway House Caravan &
Camping Park, tel. (0934) 742610
►►► Froglands Farm,
tel. (0934) 742058 & 743304
►► Church Farm Camping Site, Church St,
tel. (0934) 743048
► Round Oak Farm, tel. (0934) 742561

CHELTENHAM, Glos
►► Cheltenham (TRAX) Caravan Club Site,
Prestbury Park (Racecourse), tel. (0242) 523102

CHEPSTOW, Gwent
►►► Chepstow (TRAX) Caravan Club Site,
Chepstow Racecourse, St Arvans, tel. (02912) 3710
▽ Howick Farm, Howick (1¾m NW on B4293),
tel. (02912) 2590

CHERITON BISHOP, Devon
►►► Springfield Touring Park, Tedburn Rd,
tel. (064724) 242

CHESTER, Cheshire
►► Chester Southerly Caravan Park,
Balderton Ln, Marlston-cum-Lache,
tel. Farndon (0829) 270791
►► Racecourse Caravan Park,
tel. (0244) 23170 & 23211

CHICKERELL, nr Weymouth, Dorset
►►► Bagwell Farm Camping & Caravanning
Site, tel. Weymouth (0305) 782575
►►► Gloucester Farm Caravan Park,
Chickerell Rd, tel. Weymouth (0305) 783420

CHIDEOCK, Dorset
►►► Golden Cap Caravan Park, Seatown,
tel. (0297) 89341

CHILLINGTON, Devon
►► Union Inn Caravan Site,
tel. Kingsbridge (0548) 580241

CHINGFORD (E4), Gt London
See under London for details

CHITTERING, Cambs
▽ Denny Lodge,
tel. Cambridge (0223) 860223

CHIVENOR, Devon
► Chivenor Holiday Centre,
tel. Barnstaple (0271) 812217

CHRISTCHURCH, Dorset
►►►►► Hoburne Farm Caravan Park,
Highcliffe Rd,
tel. Highcliffe (04252) 3379
►►►► Grove Farm Meadow Holiday
Caravan Park, Stour Way, tel. (0202) 483597
►► Haven Caravan Park, Raven Way, Mudeford,
tel. Highcliffe (04252) 4662 & 5353

CHUDLEIGH, Devon
►►► Holmans Wood Tourist Park, Harcombe
Cross, tel. (0626) 853785
►►►► Finlake Leisure Park,
tel. (0626) 853833

CHUDLEIGH KNIGHTON, Devon
► Ford Farm,
tel. Chudleigh (0626) 853253

CHURCH STOKE, Powys
►►► Mellington Hall Caravan Park,
tel. (05885) 456

CHURT, Surrey
► Symondstone Farm

CHWILOG, Gwynedd
►► Ocean Heights Caravan Park,
tel. (076688) 519

CLACTON-ON-SEA, Essex
See St Osyth, (4m) and Weeley (6m) for details of
sites in the vicinity

CLAYTON WEST, W Yorks
► Earth's Wood Caravan Park, Bank End Ln,
Barnsley Rd (1m S off A636 unclass),
tel. Huddersfield (0484) 863211

CLIFFORD BRIDGE, Devon
►►► Clifford Bridge Caravan Park,
tel. Cheriton Bishop (064724) 226

CLIPPESBY, Norfolk
►►► Clippesby Holiday Caravan Park,
tel. Fleggburgh (049377) 367

CLYNDERWEN, Dyfed
► Derwenlas Caravan Park, Derwenlas,
tel. (09912) 324

COCKBURNSPATH, Borders
►► Chesterfield Caravan Site, Neuk Farm,
tel. (03683) 226

COCKERMOUTH, Cumbria
►►► Violet Bank Caravan Park, Simonscales
Ln, (off Lorton Rd), tel. (0900) 822169

COEDKERNEW, Gwent
►►► Tredegar House & Country Park,
tel. Newport (0633) 62275

COLCHESTER, Essex
►►► Colchester Caravan Club Site,
Cymbeline Way, Lexden, tel. (0206) 45551

COLEFORD, Glos
►► Christchurch Forest Park Camping
Ground, Braceland Drive, Berryhill,
tel. Dean (0594) 33057 (Forestry Commission
Office)
▽ Blackthorne Farm, Hillersland,
tel. Dean (0594) 32062

COLL SANDS, Lewis, Western Isles
► Broad Bay Caravan Site,
tel. Stornoway (0851) 2053

COMBE MARTIN, Devon
See also Berrynarbor
►►►► Stowford Farm Meadows,
tel. (027188) 2476

COMBERTON, Cambs
►►► Highfield Farm Camping Site, Long Rd,
tel. (022026) 2308

COMBERTON, GREAT, Heref & Worcs
▽ Shelton Farm, tel. Elmley Castle (038674) 243

COMRIE, Tayside
►►► Twenty Shilling Wood Caravan Site,
tel. (0764) 70411
►► West Lodge Caravan Site, Lawers,
tel. (0764) 70354

CONEYSTHORPE (nr Malton), N Yorks
►►► Castle Howard Caravan & Camping
Site. Apply to: Castle Howard Estates Ltd, Estate
Offices, Castle Howard, York YO6 7DD,
tel. (065384) 366

CONINGSBY, Lincs
►►►► Castle Leisure Park, Tattershall (1m SW
A153), tel. (0526) 43193

CONSTABLE BURTON, N Yorks
►►► Constable Burton Hall Caravan Park,
tel. Bedale (0677) 50428

CONWY, Gwynedd
►►► Bwlch Mawr Farm, Gyffin (1½m S on
B5106), tel. (049263) 2856
► Morfa Caravan Park, Bangor Rd (1½m W on
A55), tel. (049263) 2338

CORFE CASTLE, Dorset
►►► Woodland Camping Park, Glebe Farm,
Bucknowle, tel. (0929) 480280

CORPACH, Highland
►►►► Linnhe Caravan Park, tel. (03977) 376

COTHELSTONE, Somerset
▽ Toulton Farm,
tel. Kingston St Mary (082345) 458

COTTON, Staffs
►►► Star Caravan Park,
tel. Oakamoor (0538) 702219

COVE, Devon
►►► Orchard Caravan Park,
tel. Bampton (0398) 31563

COWES, Isle of Wight
►►► Gurnard Pines Holiday Village, Gurnard
(1m W), tel. (0983) 292395

COYLTON, Devon
►►►► Sundrum Castle Holiday Park,
tel. Ayr (0292) 261464

CRACKINGTON HAVEN, Cornwall
►►► Hentervene Farm Caravan & Camping
Park, tel. St Gennys (08403) 365

CRAIL, Fife
►►►► Sauchope Links Caravan Park. Apply to:
Largo Leisure Parks Ltd, Rankeilour House, Cupar,
Fife KY15 5RG, tel. (0333) 50460
► Balcomie Links Caravan Park, 8 Balcomie Rd,
tel. (0333) 50383

CRANTOCK, nr Newquay, Cornwall
►►►►► Travella Tourist Park,
tel. (0637) 830308
►►► Treago Farm Caravan Site,
tel. (0637) 830277

CRAOBH HAVEN, Strathclyde
►►► Craobh Haven Caravan Park,
tel. Barbreck (08525) 222 and 666

CRASTER, Northumb
►►► Dunstan Hill Camping & Caravanning
Club Site, tel. Embleton (066576) 310

Crantock, Newquay, Cornwall

CREETOWN, Dumfries & Galloway
►►► Cassencarie Holiday Park,
tel. (067182) 264

CRICCIETH, Gwynedd
►► Cae-Canol Caravan & Camping Site,
tel. (076671) 2351
►► Eisteddfa Campsite, Pentrefelin,
tel. (076671) 2104
►► Llwyn-Bugeilydd Farm, Llwyn-Bugeilydd,
tel. (076671) 2235
► Gell Farm Caravan Park, (1m N on B4411),
tel. (076671) 2781
► Muriau Bach Caravan Site, Muriau Bach
Rhoslan,
tel. Garn Dolbenmaen (076675) 642
►► Tyddyn Morthwyl,
tel. (076671) 2115

CRIEFF, Tayside
►►► Crieff Holiday Village, Turret Bank,
tel. (0764) 3513

CROCKERNWELL, Devon
►► Barley Meadow Caravan & Camping
Park, Crossways, tel. Haytor (03646) 430

CROCKETFORD, Dumfries & Galloway
►►►► Brandedleys Cara Farm,
tel. (055669) 250

CROCKEY HILL, N Yorks
▽ Wigman Hall (off unclass rd between Crockey
Hill and Wheldrake), tel. Wheldrake (090489) 221

CROESGOCH, Dyfed
►►► Torbant Caravan Park, tel. (03483) 261

CROMER, Norfolk
►►► Seacroft Camping Park, Runton Rd,
tel. (0263) 511722

CROPTON, N Yorks
►►► Spiers House Campsite (Forestry
Commission), tel. Lastingham (07515) 591

CROSSGATES, Powys
►► Park Caravan & Camping Site, Rhayader
Rd, tel. Penybont (059787) 201

CROSSWAYS, Dorset
►►►► Heathfield Caravan Site,
tel. Warmwell (0305) 852357

CROSTHWAITE, Cumbria
► Lambhowe Caravan Park, tel. (04488) 483

CROSTON, Lancs
►►► Royal Umpire Caravan Park, Moor Rd,
tel. (0772) 600257

CROWCOMBE, Somerset
►►► Quantock Orchard Caravan Park,
tel. (09848) 618

CROWDEN, Derbys
►► Camping & Caravanning Club Site.
Behind 2 Store Villas, tel. Glossop (04574) 2127

CROWHURST, E Sussex
►►► **Brakes Coppice Farm Park**,
tel. (042483) 322

CROYDE BAY, Devon
►►►► **Ruda Holiday Park**,
tel. Croyde (0271) 890671
►►► **Croyde Bay Holidays**, tel. (0271) 890351

CUBERT, Cornwall
►► **Treworgans Farm**,
tel. Crantock (0637) 830200

CULLEN, Grampian
►►► **Logie Camping & Caravan Site**,
Apply to: Moray District Council, Dept of
Recreation, 30–33 High St, Elgin IV30 1EX,
tel. Elgin (0343) 45121

CULZEAN, Strathclyde
►►► **Camping & Caravanning Club Site**,
Culzean Castle, tel. Kirkoswald (06556) 627

CUMINESTOWN, Grampian
► **A.B. Caravans**, tel. (08883) 261

CUMNOR, Oxon
▽ **Spring Farm**, Faringdon Rd,
tel. Oxford (0865) 863028

CUMWHITTON, Cumbria
► **Cairndale Caravan Park**,
tel. Croglin (076886) 280

CURDRIDGE, Hants
► **Ivy Caravan & Camping Site**, Ivy Cottage,
Wickham Rd, tel. Botley (04892) 6457

DALBEATTIE, Dumfries & Galloway
►► **Islecroft Caravan Site**, Colliston Pk, Mill St,
tel. (0556) 610012

DALSTON, Cumbria
►► **Dalston Hall Caravan Park**, Dalston Hall
Estate, tel. Carlisle (0228) 710165

DALWOOD, Devon
►►► **Andrewshayes Caravan Park**,
tel. Wilmington (040483) 225

DARTMOUTH, Devon
►► **Little Cotton Caravan Park**, Little Cotton,
tel. (08043) 2558
▽ **Bugford Farm**, Bugford (3m W off B3207),
tel. Blackawton (080421) 464

DAVIOT, Highland
►►► **Auchnahillin Caravan Park**,
tel. (046385) 223

DAWLISH, Devon
►►► **Lady's Mile Farm**, tel. (0626) 863411

DELABOLE, Cornwall
►►► **Planet Park**, tel. Camelford (0840) 213361

DENBY DALE, W Yorks
▽ **Dry Hill Farm**, tel. Huddersfield (0484) 863256

DENSOLE, Kent
► **Black Horse Farm**, 385 Canterbury Rd,
tel. Hawkinge (030389) 2665

DERBY, Derbys
►►► **Alvaston Mobile Home Park**, Meadow
Ln, tel. (0332) 72204

DEREHAM (EAST), Norfolk
►► **Dereham Touring Caravan Park**, Norwich
Rd, tel. (0362) 4619

DEVIZES, Wilts
►►► **Lakeside**, Rowde (2m NW A342),
tel. (0380) 2767

DIAL POST, W Sussex
▽ **Wincaves Park**,
tel. Partridge Green (0403) 710923

DIDDLEBURY, Salop
▽ **Glebe Farm**, tel. Munslow (058476) 221

DINAS CROSS, Dyfed
►►► **Fishguard Bay Caravan & Camping
Site**, tel. (03486) 415

DINAS DINNLE, Gwynedd
►►►► **Dinnie Caravan Park**,
tel. Llanwnda 830324

DINGESTOW, Gwent
►►► **Bridge Caravan Park & Camping Site**,
Bridge Farm,
tel. (060083) 241

DINGWALL, Highland
►►► **Camping & Caravanning Club Site**,
Jubilee Park,
tel. (0349) 62236

DITTISHAM, Devon
▽ **Little Coombe Farm**,
tel. (080422) 240

DOBWALLS, Cornwall
►►► **Pine Green Caravan Park**, Doublebois
(1m W of Dobwalls S of A38 at next crossroads),
tel. (0579) 20183

DOLGELLAU, Gwynedd
▽ **Tyddyn Farm**, Islawr Dre,
tel. (0341) 422472

DONCASTER, S Yorks
►► **Doncaster (TRAX) Caravan Club Site**,
Doncaster Racecourse,
tel. (0302) 63219

DORNEY REACH, Bucks
► **Amerden Caravan Park**, Old Marsh Ln,
tel. Maidenhead (0628) 27461

DORNOCH, Highland
►►►► **Grannie's Heilan Hame**,
tel. (0862) 810260
►►► **Royal Dornoch Links Caravan &
Camping Site**. Apply to: District Amenities Officer,
Sutherland District Council, Golspie, Sutherland
KW10 6RB, tel. (0862) 810423 (Apr–Oct) and
Golspie (04083) 3192 (Nov–Mar)

DOVER, Kent
See under Martin Mill

DOVERIDGE, Derbys
▽ **Cavendish Garage**, tel. Uttoxeter (08893) 2092

DRAYTON, Heref & Worcs
▽ **Barrow Hill**, tel. Belbroughton (0562) 730629

DRAYTON BASSETT, Staffs
▽ **Ashdene Farm**, Portleys Ln,
tel. Tamworth (0827) 284617

DRINNISHADDER, Harris, Western Isles
► **Laig House Caravan Site**, tel. (085981) 207

DULAS, Gwynedd
►►► **Tyddyn Isaf Caravan Park**, Lligwy Bay
(½m off A5025 between Benllech and Amlwch),
tel. Moelfre (024888) 203

DUMFRIES, Dumfries & Galloway
►► **Newbridge Caravan Park**, Glasgow Rd,
tel. Newbridge (0387) 720249

DUNBAR, Lothian
►► **Camping & Caravanning Club Site**, Barns
Ness, tel. (0368) 63536
►► **Kirk Park Caravan Site**. Apply to:
East Lothian DC, Leisure and Recreation Dept,
Brunton Hall, Ladywell Way, Musselburgh, East
Lothian EH21 6AE
►► **Winterfield Caravan Site**, West Prom.
Apply to: East Lothian DC, Leisure and Recreation
Dept, Brunton Hall, Ladywell Way, Musselburgh,
East Lothian EH21 6AE

DUNBEATH, Highland
► **Inver Caravan Park**, Inver Guesthouse, Inver
(½m N on A9), tel. (05933) 252

DUNDEE, Tayside
►► **Camperdown Caravan Site**, Camperdown Park. Apply to: The General Manager of Parks, Parks Dept, 353 Clepington Rd, Dundee DD3 8PL, tel. (0382) 621995

DUNKELD, Tayside
► **Inver Mill Caravan Site**

DUNKESWELL, Devon
►► **Fishponds House Campsite**, tel. Luppitt (040489) 698

DUNNET, Highland
►► **Dunnet Bay Caravan Club Site**, tel. Castletown (084782) 319

DUNOON, Strathclyde
►► **Cowal Caravan Park**, Victoria Rd, Hunters Quay, tel. (0369) 4259

DUNVEGAN, Isle of Skye
►► **Dunvegan Caravan Park**, tel. (047022) 362

DURNESS, Highland
►►► **Sango Sands Caravan Site**, Sangomore (1m E), tel. (097181) 262

EAMONT BRIDGE, Cumbria
►►► **Lowther Caravan Park**, tel. Penrith (0768) 63631

EASINGWOLD, N Yorks
▽ **Primrose Hill**, Thirsk Rd (1m NW unclass rd), tel. (0347) 21673

EAST ALLINGTON, Devon
► **Mounts Farm**, The Mounts, tel. (054852) 225

EAST ANSTEY, Devon
►►► **Zeacombe Caravan Park**, Zeacombe House, Blackerton Cross, tel. Anstey Mills (03984) 279

EAST BERGHOLT, Suffolk
►►► **Grange Caravan Park**, The Grange, tel. Colchester (0206) 298567

EASTRIGGS, Dumfries & Galloway
► **Gemmel Caravan Site**, Central Rd, tel. (04614) 304

EAST RUNTON, Norfolk
►►► **Woodhill Camping Site**, tel. West Runton (026375) 323

EAST WORLINGTON, Devon
►►► **Yeatheridge Farm Caravan Park**, tel. Tiverton (0884) 860330

EAVESTONE, N Yorks
▽ **Hill Top Farm**, tel. Sawley (076586) 662

ECCLEFECHAN, Dumfries & Galloway
►►► **Hoddam Castle Caravan Park**, Hoddam, tel. (05763) 251

ECCLESTON, GREAT, Lancs
► **Meadowcroft Caravan Park**, Garstang Rd, tel. (0995) 70266

EDALE, Derbys
►► **Coopers Caravan Site**, Newfold Farm, tel. Hope Valley (0433) 70372

EDGCUMBE, Cornwall
►►► **Retanna Country Park**, Underlane, tel. Falmouth (0326) 40643

EDGERLEY, Salop
► **Royal Hill**, tel. Nesscliffe (074381) 242

EDINBANE, Isle of Skye, Highland
►► **Loch Greshornish Caravan Site**, Borve, Arnisort, tel. (047082) 230

EDINBURGH, Lothian
See also Musselburgh
►►►► **Mortonhall Caravan Park**, 30 Frogston Road East, tel. 031–664 1533

►►► **Little France Caravan Park**, 219 Dalkeith Rd

EDMONTON (N9), Gt London
See under London for details

ELGIN, Grampian
►►► **Riverside Caravan Park**, West Rd, tel. (0343) 2813
► **Spynie Hall Caravan Site**, Spynie, tel. (0343) 45344

ELVASTON, Derbys
►► **Elvaston Castle Caravan Club Site**, Borrowash Rd, tel. Derby (0332) 73735

ELVINGTON, N Yorks
▽ **Lake Cottage**, tel. (090485) 255

ELY, Cambs
▽ **Ely Rugby Club**, Downham Rd, tel. (0353) 2156

ESKDALE, Cumbria
►► **Fisherground Farm Campsite**, tel. (09403) 319

ETTRICK VALLEY, Borders
►► **Angecroft Caravan Park**, Ettrick Valley (1m S on B709), tel. Ettrick Valley (0750) 62251 and 62310

EVERSHOT, Dorset
► **Clay Pigeon Tourist Park**, Wardon Hill (A37), tel. (093583) 492

EVESHAM, Heref & Worcs
►►► **Wier Meadow Holiday Park**, Lower Leys, tel. (0386) 2417

EWHURSTGREEN, E Sussex
► **Lordine Court Caravan Park**, tel. Staplecross (058083) 209

EXFORD, Somerset
► **Westermill**, tel. (064383) 238

EYNSHAM, Oxon
►►► **Swinford Farm Campsite**, Swinford Farm, tel. Oxford (0865) 881368

EYTON, Clwyd
►►►► **Plassey Touring Caravan Park**, tel. Bangor-on-Dee (0978) 780277

FAIRWOOD, W Glam
►► **Blackhills Caravan Park**, Blackhills Rd, Fairwood Common, tel. Swansea (0792) 207065

FAKENHAM, Norfolk
►►► **Crossways Caravan Park**, Holt Rd, Little Snoring, tel. Thursford (032877) 335
►► **Fakenham (TRAX) Caravan Club Site**, Fakenham Racecourse, tel. (0328) 2388

FALMOUTH, Cornwall
►►►► **Maen Valley Caravan Park**, tel. (0326) 312190
►►► **Golden Bank Caravans** (No. 1 Site), Swanpool Rd, tel. (0326) 312103
►►► **Tremorvah**, Swanpool, tel. (0326) 312103

FANGFOSS, Humberside
►►► **Fangfoss Old Station Caravan Park**, Old Station House, tel. Wilberfoss (07595) 491

FAR FOREST, Heref & Worcs
► **Acre Farm Caravan Park**, tel. Rock (0299) 266458

FAVERSHAM, Kent
►►► **Painters Farm Caravan & Camping Site**, Painters Forstal, tel. (0795) 532995

FAZELEY, Staffs
► **Drayton Manor Park**, tel. Tamworth (0827) 287979

FENNY BENTLEY, Derbys
►►► **Highfield Caravan Park**, Highfield Farm, tel. Thorpe Cloud (033529) 228
► **Bank Top Farm**, tel. Thorpe Cloud (033529) 250

FILEY, N Yorks
►►► **Filey Brigg Touring Caravan Site**, Arndale. Apply to: Department of Tourism and Amenities, Londesborough Lodge, The Crescent, Scarborough, N Yorks, tel. Scarborough (0723) 366212

FINCHAMPSTEAD, Berks
►► **California Country Park**, Finchampstead Rd, tel. Eversley (0734) 730028

FINDHORN, Grampian
►► **Findhorn Sands Caravan Park**, tel. (0309) 30324

FINDOCHTY, Grampian
► **Findochty Caravan Site**, tel. Elgin (0343) 45121

FISHGUARD, Dyfed
►► **Tregroes Touring Park**, Tregroes, tel. (0348) 872316

FLEET, Dorset
►►► **Sea Barn Farm Camping Site**, tel. Weymouth (0305) 782218
►►► **West Fleet Holiday Farm**, tel. Weymouth (0305) 782218

FLEET HARGATE, Lincs
►►► **Matopos Caravan & Campsite**, Main St, tel. Holbeach (0406) 22910

FLEETWOOD, Lancs
► **Broadwater Holiday Centre**, Fleetwood Rd, tel. (03917) 2796

FLOOKBURGH, Cumbria
►►► **Lakeland Caravan Park**, Moor Ln, tel. (044853) 235

FOCHABERS, Grampian
►►► **Burnside Caravan Site**, Keith Rd, tel. (0343) 820362

FOLKESTONE, Kent
►►► **Camping & Caravanning Club Site**, The Warren, tel. (0303) 55093
►► **Little Switzerland Camping & Caravan Site**, The Warren, tel. (0303) 52168

FOLKINGHAM, Lincs
►►► **Low Farm Touring Park**, Spring Ln, tel. (05297) 322

FONTWELL, W Sussex
►► **Fontwell Park Racecourse (TRAX) Caravan Club Site**, tel. Eastergate (024368) 2497

FORDINGBRIDGE, Hants
►►► **Sandy Balls Holiday Centre**, Godshill, tel. (0425) 53042

FORFAR, Tayside
►► **Lochside Caravan Park**, tel. (0307) 62528

FORT WILLIAM, Highland
►►► **Glen Nevis Caravan & Camping Park**, Glen Nevis, tel. (0397) 2191
►►► **Lochy Caravan & Camping Park**, Camaghael, tel. (0397) 3446

FRASERBURGH, Grampian
►► **Kessock Road Caravan Site**, Esplanade, Kessock Rd. Apply to: Banff and Buchan District Council, Leisure and Recreation Dept, 1 Church St, Macduff, Banffshire AB4 1US. tel. Banff (02612) 2521 ext 304
► **Esplanade Caravan Site**, Harbour Rd. Apply to: Banff and Buchan District Council, Leisure and Recreation Dept, 1 Church St, Macduff, Banffshire AB4 1US, tel. Banff (02612) 2521 ext 304

FRITHAM, Hants
► **Longbeech Campsite**, tel. Lyndhurst (042128) 3771 (Forestry Commission Office) & 2269 (Tourist Information Centre)

FYLINGDALES ("FLASK" INN), N Yorks
►►► **Grouse Hill Caravan Park**, Flask Bungalow Farm, tel. Whitby (0947) 880543

GAIRLOCH, Highland
►► **Sands Holiday Centre**, Melvaig Rd, tel. (0445) 2152

GAIRLOCHY, Highland
► **Gairlochy Caravan Park**, tel. (039782) 229

GARSTANG, Lancs
►►► **Bridge House Marina & Caravan Park**, Nateby Crossing Ln, Nateby (1m W on unclass rd), tel. (09952) 3207

GARTMORE, Central
►► **Cobeland Campsite**, tel. Aberfoyle (08772) 392

GATEHOUSE OF FLEET, Dumfries & Galloway
►►► **Anwoth Caravan Site**, tel. Gatehouse (05574) 333
►►► **Cardoness Holiday Park**, Cardoness Estate, tel. Mossyard (055724) 288

GILCRUX, Cumbria
►►► **Beeches Caravan Park**, tel. Aspatria (0965) 21555

GISBURN, Lancs
►►► **Todber Caravan Park**, tel. (02005) 322

GISLEHAM, Suffolk
► **Chestnut Farm Touring Park**, tel. Lowestoft (0502) 740227
► **White House Farm Caravans**, White House Farm, tel. Lowestoft (0502) 740248

GLAN-YR AFON, nr Corwen, Clwyd
►► **Llawr-Betws Farm Caravan & Camping Park**, tel. Maerdy (049081) 224

GLENCOE, Highland
►►► **Glencoe Caravan Club Site**, tel. Ballachulish (08552) 397
►► **Invercoe Caravan Site**, tel. Ballachulish (08552) 210

GLENDARUEL, Strathclyde
►►► **Glendaruel Caravan Park**, tel. (036982) 267

GLENLUCE, Dumfries & Galloway
►►► **Glenluce Caravan Site**, tel. (05813) 412

GLEN TROOL, Dumfries & Galloway
►►► **Caldens Campsite**. Apply to: Forestry Commission, Newton Stewart, Wigtownshire, tel. Newton Stewart (0671) 2420
►► **Merrick Caravan Park**, tel. Bargrennan (067184) 280

GLYN CEIRIOG, Clwyd
► **Glan Llyn Caravan Park**, Glan Llyn, tel. (069172) 320

GOODWOOD, W Sussex
►► **Goodwood Racecourse (TRAX) Caravan Club Site**, tel. Chichester (0243) 774486

GOONHAVERN, Cornwall
►►►► **Silverbow Park**, Perranwell, tel. Perranporth (087257) 2347
►► **Rosehill Farm Tourist Park**, tel. Truro (0872) 572448

GORRAN, Cornwall
►►► **Tregarton Farm Caravan & Camping Park**, tel. Mevagissey (0726) 843666

GRAFHAM, Cambs
►►► **Old Manor Caravan Park**, Church Lane, tel. Huntingdon (0480) 810264

GRAMPOUND, Cornwall
►►► **Lynwood Camping & Caravan Park**,
Mill Ln, tel. St Austell (0726) 882458

GRANTOWN-ON-SPEY, Highland
►►► **Grantown-on-Spey Camping &
Caravan Site**, Seafield Avenue,
tel. Grantown (0479) 2474

GREAT
Place-names incorporating the word "Great"
such as Gt Malvern and Gt Yarmouth will be
found under the actual place-names, e.g.
Yarmouth

GRETNA GREEN (A74 Service Area,
Northbound), Dumfries and Galloway
►► **Canny Scots Caravan Park**, Northbound
Service Area,
tel. Gretna (0461) 37598

GREWELTHORPE, N Yorks
►► **Newholme Caravan Site**,
tel. Kirkby Malzeard (076583) 225

GRISTHORPE BAY, N Yorks
►►►► **Blue Dolphin Holiday Park**,
tel. Scarborough (0723) 512348

GUARDBRIDGE (nr St Andrews), Fife
►►►► **Clayton Caravan Park**,
tel. Balmullo (0334) 870242

GUISBOROUGH, Cleveland
►►► **Tockett's Mill Caravan Park**, Skelton Rd,
tel. (0287) 35161

GULWORTHY, Devon
►►► **Woodovis Caravan Park**,
tel. Tavistock (0822) 832968

HADDINGTON, Lothian
►►► **Monksmuir Caravan Park**,
tel. East Linton (0620) 860340

HALDON RACECOURSE, Devon
►►► **Exeter (TRAX) Caravan Club Site**,
tel. Kennford (0392) 832107

HALE, Cumbria
►►► **Fell End Caravan Park**, Slackhead Rd,
tel. Milnthorpe (04482) 2122
►► **Hallmore Farm Caravan Park**,
tel. Milnthorpe (04482) 2375

HALTWHISTLE, Northumb
►►► **Burnfoot Campsite**, Bellister Estate,
Featherstone, tel. (0498) 20106
► **Yont The Cleugh**, Coanwood,
tel. (0498) 20274

HARGRAVE, Northants
▽ **Nags Head**, tel. Wellingborough (0933) 622368

HARLECH, Gwynedd
See Talsarnau

HAROME, N Yorks
►►► **Foxholme Caravan Park**,
tel. Helmsley (0439) 70416 & 71696

HARRIS (ISLE OF), Western Isles
See Drinnishadder

HARROGATE, N Yorks
►►► **High Moor Farm Park**, Skipton Rd,
tel. (0423) 63637 & 64995
►►► **Rudding Caravan Park**, Rudding Park,
Follifoot, tel. (0423) 870439
►► **Shaws Trailer Park**, Knaresborough Rd,
tel. (0423) 884432

HARTINGTON, Derbys
► **Barracks Farm Caravan Site**, Beresford Dale,
tel. (029884) 261

HARTSOP, Cumbria
►►► **Skyeside Camping Site**,
tel. Glenridding (08532) 239

HARWOOD, GT, Lancs
► **Harwood Bar Caravan Park**, Mill Lane,
tel. (0254) 884853

HASGUARD CROSS, Dyfed
►►► **Hasguard Cross Caravan Park**,
tel. Broad Haven (043783) 443
►►► **Redlands Touring Caravan Site**,
tel. Broad Haven (043783) 301

HASTINGS AND ST LEONARDS, E Sussex
See also Three Oaks
►►►► **Shearbarn Holiday Park**, Barley Lane,
tel. (0424) 423583

HATFIELD, S Yorks
►► **Hatfield Marina Caravan & Campsite**,
tel. Doncaster (0302) 841572

HAUGHTON, Salop
▽ **Camping & Caravanning Club Site**, Ring
Bank, Ebury Hill,
tel. Upton Magna (074377) 334

HAVERTHWAITE, Cumbria
►►► **Bigland Hall Caravan Park**,
tel. Newby Bridge (0448) 31702

HAWES, N Yorks
►► **Bainbridge Ings Caravan & Camping Site**,
tel. (09697) 354

HAWICK, Borders
►►► **Riverside Caravan Park**,
tel. (0450) 73785

HAWKCHURCH, Devon
► **Scouse Farm Caravan Park**, Scouse Farm,
tel. (02977) 402

HAWKSHEAD, Cumbria
►► **Camping & Caravanning Club Site**,
Grizedale Hall, tel. Satterthwaite (022984) 257

HAYFIELD, Derbys
►► **Camping & Caravanning Club Site**,
Kinder Rd, tel. New Mills (0663) 45394

HAYLE, Cornwall
► **St Ives Bay Chalet & Caravan Park**,
73 Loggans Rd, Upton Towans, tel. (0736) 752274

HAYLING ISLAND, Hants
►► **Fleet Farm Caravan & Camping Site**,
Yew Tree Rd, tel. (0705) 463684

HAY-ON-WYE, Powys
► **Hollybush Inn**, tel. Glasbury (04974) 371

HEATHFIELD, E Sussex
►►► **Greenview Caravan Fields**, Broad Oak,
tel. (04352) 3531

HEDGE END, Hants
►► **Grange Caravan Park**, Shamblehurst Lane,
tel. Botley (04892) 3895

HELMSLEY, N Yorks
See Harome, Nawton & Oswaldkirk

Hartington, Derbyshire

HELSTON, Cornwall
►►► **Glenhaven Camping & Touring Park**, Clodgey Lane, tel. (03265) 2734
►►► **Trelowarren Chateau Camping**, Trelowarren, Mawgan (3m S off B3292 to St Keverne), tel. Mawgan (032622) 224 and 637

HEMINGFORD ABBOTS, Cambs
►►► **Quiet Waters Caravan Park**, tel. St Ives (0480) 63405

HEREFORD, Heref & Worcs
►► **Hereford (TRAX) Caravan Club Site**, Hereford Racecourse, tel. (0432) 272364

HERMITAGE, Dorset
▽ **Almshouse Farm**, tel. Holnest (096321) 296

HERNE BAY, Kent
► **Hillborough Park**, Reculver Rd, tel. (0227) 374618
► **Westbrook Farm Caravan Park**, Sea St, tel. (0227) 375586

HEWAS WATER, Cornwall
►►► **Trencreek Farm Caravan Park**, tel. St Austell (0726) 882540

HEXHAM, Northumb
►►► **Causey Hill Caravan Park**, Benson's Fell Farm, tel. (0434) 602834
►► **Hexham Racecourse (TRAX) Caravan Club Site**, tel. (0434) 606847
►► **Lowgate Caravan Site**, tel. (0434) 602827

HIGH BENTHAM, N Yorks
►► **Riverside Caravan Park**, Wenning Avenue, tel. Bentham (0468) 61272

HIGHBRIDGE, Somerset
► **Edithmead Dairy Trailer Park**, tel. Burnham-on-Sea (0278) 783475

HILBERRY (nr Douglas), Isle of Man
►► **Glen Dhoo International Farm Camping Site**, tel. Douglas (0624) 21254

HOATH, Kent
►► **South View**, Maypole Lane, tel. Chislet (022786) 280

HODDESDON, Herts
►► **Dobbs Weir Caravan Park**, Essex Rd, tel. (0992) 462090

HOLLYBUSH, Strathclyde
►► **Skeldon Caravan Park**, tel. Dalrymple (029256) 202

HOLMROOK, Cumbria
►►► **Seven Acres Caravan Park**, Seven Acres (1m S of Gosforth, on A595), tel. Gosforth (09405) 480

HOLMSLEY, Hants
►►► **Holmsley Campsite**, Holmsley Old Aerodrome, Hinton, tel. Lyndhurst (042128) 3771 (Forestry Commission Office) or 2269 (Tourist Information Centre)

HOLTON HEATH, Dorset
►►►► **Sandford Park Caravans**, tel. Lytchett Minster (0202) 622513

HOLYWELL BAY, Cornwall
► **Trevornick Caravan & Camping Park**, tel. Crantock (0637) 830531

HONEYBOURNE, Heref & Worcs
►►► **Ranch Caravan Park**, tel. Evesham (0386) 830744

HONITON, Devon
► **Otter Valley Park**, Northcote, tel. (0404) 2917

HOPE, Derbys
►► **Laneside Caravan Park**, Laneside Farm, tel. Hope Valley (0433) 20214 and 20215

HORNS CROSS, Devon
►►► **Steart Farm**, tel. Clovelly (02373) 239

HOUGHTON, Cambs
►► **Houghton Mill Caravan & Camping Park**, Mill St, tel. St Ives (0480) 62413

HOWEY, Powys
► **Dalmore Camping Site**, tel. Llandrindod Wells (0597) 2483

HUBBERT'S BRIDGE, Lincs
►►► **Orchards Caravan Park**, tel. (020579) 328

HUGHLEY, Salop
►►► **Mill Farm Caravan Site**, tel. Brockton (074636) 208

HULME END, Staffs
▽ **Endon Cottage**, tel. Hartington (029884) 617

HUNSTANTON, Norfolk
►►► **Searles Camping Ground**, South Beach, tel. (04853) 34211

HUNTINGDON, Cambs
►►► **Park Lane Touring Park**, Godmanchester, tel. (0480) 53740
►► **Anchor Cottage Riverside Caravan & Camping Site**, Church Lane, Hartford, tel. (0480) 55642

HURN, Dorset
►►► **Tall Trees**, Matcham Ln, tel. Christchurch (0202) 477144

HUTTON ROOF, Cumbria
►►► **Thanet Well Caravan Park**, tel. Skelton (08534) 262

ILFRACOMBE, Devon
► **Big Meadow Camping Site**, Lydford Farm, tel. Ilfracombe (0271) 62282

INCHTURE, Tayside
► **Inchmartine Caravan Park & Nurseries**, Dundee Rd, tel. Rait (08217) 212

INKBERROW, Heref & Worcs
▽ **Broad Close Farm**, Stonepit Ln, tel. (0386) 792266

INSTOW, Devon
► **Lagoon Holiday Park**, tel. (0271) 860423

INVERARAY, Strathclyde
►►► **Battlefield Caravan Park**, tel. (0499) 2285

INVERGARRY, Highland
► **Faichem Park**, Ardgarry, Faichem, tel. (08093) 226

INVERMORISTON, Highland
►► **Loch Ness Caravan & Camping Park**, Easter Port Clair, tel. Glenmoriston (0320) 51207

INVERNESS, Highland
►►► **Bught Caravan & Camping Site.** Apply to: Inverness District Council, Parks Superintendent, Town House, Inverness IV1 1JJ, tel. (0463) 236920
►►► **Torvean Caravan Park**, Glenurquhart Rd, tel. (0463) 220582 and Edderton (086282) 252
►► **Dochgarroch Caravan Site**, Dochgarroch, tel. Dochgarroch (046386) 218

INVERUGLAS, Strathclyde
►► **Loch Lomond Holiday Park**, tel. (03014) 224

IPSWICH, Suffolk
See Nacton

ISLE OF MAN
See under Hillberry, Laxey and Peel

ISLE OF WHITHORN, Dumfries & Galloway
►►►► **Burrow Head Holiday Farm**, tel. Whithorn (09885) 252

ISLE OF WIGHT
Full details of sites will be found under
individual place-names within the gazetteer
section

ISLES OF SCILLY
No sites on the islands hold AA classification

JEDBURGH, Borders
►►►►► **Lilliardsedge Park**, Ancrum
tel. Ancrum (08353) 271
►►► **Elliot Park Camping & Caravanning
Club Site**, Edinburgh Rd, tel. (0835) 63393

JERSEY, Channel Islands
See St Brelade, St Martin and St Ouen

JOHN O' GROATS, Highland
►► **John O' Groats Caravan Site**,
tel. (095581) 250 and 329
► **Stroma View Site**, Huna, tel. (095581) 313

KEITH, Grampian
►► **Keith Caravan Site**, tel. Elgin (0343) 45121

KELSO, Borders
►►► **Springwood Caravan Park**,
tel. (0573) 24596

KEMPSEY, Heref & Worcs
► **Court Meadow Caravan Park**,
tel. Worcester (0905) 820295
▽ **Eastfield Farm**, tel. Worcester (0905) 820584

KENDAL, Cumbria
►► **Millcrest Caravan Park**, tel. (0539) 21075

KENMORE, Tayside
►►► **Kenmore Caravan & Camping Park**,
tel. (08873) 226

KENNACK SANDS, Cornwall
►►► **Chy Carne Caravan Site**,
tel. The Lizard (0326) 290541
►►► **Sea Acres Caravan Park**,
tel. The Lizard (0326) 290665
►►► **Silver Sands Holiday Park**,
tel. The Lizard (0326) 290631

KENNFORD, Devon
►►►► **Kennford International Caravan
Park**,
tel. Exeter (0392) 833046

KENTISBEARE, Devon
►►►► **Forest Glade Holiday Park**,
tel. Broadhembury (040484) 381

KESSINGLAND, Suffolk
►► **Denes Holiday Village**,
tel. Lowestoft (0502) 740636
►► **Heathland Beach Caravan Park**,
London Rd, tel. Lowestoft (0502) 740337

KESWICK, Cumbria
►►► **Camping & Caravanning Club Site**,
Derwentwater, tel. (0596) 72392

KIELDER, Northumb
►► **Kielder Camp Site**,
tel. Bellingham (0660) 20242

KILBERRY, Strathclyde
►► **Port Ban Park**, tel. Ormsary (08803) 224

KILKERRAN, Strathclyde
►► **Camping & Caravanning Club Site**,
The Gardens, tel. Crosshill (Ayrshire) (06554) 323

KILKHAMPTON, Cornwall
►►► **Easthorne Caravan & Camping Park**,
tel. (028882) 235

KILLIN, Central
►► **High Creagan**, Morenish (3m NE A827),
tel. (05672) 449

KILMARNOCK, Strathclyde
► **Cunningham Head Estate Caravan Park**,
Cunningham Head, tel. Torranyard (029485) 238

KILMARTIN, Strathclyde
► **Laggan Camping Site**, tel. (05465) 223

KILNINVER, Strathclyde
►►► **Glen Gallain Caravan Park**,
tel. (08526) 200

KILTARLITY, Highland
► **Glaichbea Caravan & Camping Site**,
The Filling Station, Glaichbea,
tel. (046374) 496

KINGHORN, Fife
►►►► **Pettycur Bay Caravan Park**,
tel. (0592) 890321

KINGSBRIDGE, Devon
► **Island Lodge Farm**, Slade Cross, Ledstone
(1½m N off A381)
► **Parkland**, Sorley Green Cross, tel. (0548) 2723
▽ **Beachcroft**, Churchstow (2m NW A379),
tel. (0548) 2003

KINGSBURY, Warwicks
► **Camping & Caravanning Club Site**,
Kingsbury Water Park, Bodymoor Heath (off unclass
rd joining A4097 and A4091),
tel. Tamworth (0827) 872660
▽ **Tame View**, Cliff (1m N A51),
tel. Tamworth (0827) 873853

KINGS CAPLE, Heref & Worcs
▽ **Lower Ruxton Farm**, tel. Carey (043270) 223

KINGSNORTH, Kent
►►► **Broad Hembury Farm**, Steeds Lane,
tel. Ashford (0233) 20859

KINNERLEY, Salop
►►► **Cranberry Moss Caravan & Camping
Park**, tel. Nesscliffe (074381) 444

KINROSS, Tayside
►►► **Loch Leven Caravan Site**, Sandport,
tel. (0577) 63560

KINTORE, Grampian
►►► **Hillhead Caravan Park**, tel. (0467) 32809

KIPPFORD, Dumfries & Galloway
►►► **Kippford Caravan Site**, tel. (055662) 636

KIRKBY-IN-FURNESS, Cumbria
►► **Longlands Caravan Park**, tel. (022989) 342

KIRKBY LONSDALE, Cumbria
►► **Woodclose Caravan Park**, Crossway,
tel. Kirkby Lonsdale (0468) 71403

KIRKBY THORE, Cumbria
► **Low Moor Caravan Site**, tel. (0930) 61231

KIRKCALDY, Fife
►►► **Dunnikier Caravan Site**, Dunnikier Rd,
tel. (0592) 267563

KIRKCUDBRIGHT, Dumfries & Galloway
►►► **Seaward Caravan Park**, Dhoon Bay (2m
SW off B727 Borgue Rd), tel. Borgue (05577) 267
►► **Silvercraigs Caravan & Camping Site**,
Silvercraigs Rd. Apply to: Stewartry District Council,
Director of Administration, Council Offices,
Kirkcudbright DG6 4PJ, tel. (0557) 30291

KIRKFIELDBANK, Strathclyde
►► **Clyde Valley Caravan Park**,
tel. Lanark (0555) 3951

KIRKGUNZEON, Dumfries & Galloway
►►► **Mossband Caravan Park**,
tel. (038776) 280

KIRKHAM, Lancs
►►►► **Ribby Hall Park**, The Leisure Village,
Wrea Green (½m W of Kirkham B5259),
tel. (0772) 685356

KIRKPATRICK FLEMING, Dumfries & Galloway
►► **Bruce's Cave & Caravan Site**,
tel. (04618) 285

KIRRIEMUIR, Tayside
►►► Drumshademuir Caravan Park,
Roundyhill, tel. (0575) 73284

KNIVETON, Derbys
►►► The Closes Caravan Park, Ostrich Ln,
tel. Ashbourne (0335) 43191

KNOCK, Cumbria
► Silver Band Caravan Park,
tel. Kirkby Thore (0930) 61218

LACOCK, Wilts
►► Piccadilly Caravan Site, Folly Ln,
tel. (024973) 260

LADRAM BAY, Devon
► Ladram Bay Caravan Site,
tel. Colaton Raleigh (0395) 68398

LAIRG, Highland
► Woodend Caravan & Camping Site,
tel. (0549) 2248

LALEHAM, Surrey
►► Laleham Park Camping Site, Thameside,
tel. Chertsey (09328) 64149

LAMORNA, Cornwall
► Boleigh Farm Campsite,
tel. St Buryan (073672) 305

LAMPLUGH, Cumbria
►►► Inglenook Caravan Park, Fitzbridge,
tel. (0946) 861240

LANDRAKE, Cornwall
►►► Dolbeare Caravan Park, St Ive Rd,
tel. (075538) 332

LANDSHIPPING, Dyfed
►►► New Park Caravan Site,
tel. Martletwy (083485) 284

LANIVET, Cornwall
►► Reperry Tourist Park, Reperry Manor,
tel. Lanivet (0208) 831863

LANLIVERY, Cornwall
►►► Powderham Castle Caravan & Tourist
Park, tel. (0208) 872277

LAUDER, Borders
►► Thirlestane Castle Caravan Site,
Thirlestane Castle, tel. (05782) 542

LAUGHARNE, Dyfed
►►► Ants Hill Caravan Park, tel. (099421) 293

LAUNCELLS, Cornwall
►► Red Post Holiday Park,
tel. Bridgerule (02881) 305

LAUNCESTON, Cornwall
► Travadlock Hall Holiday Park,
tel. Coads Green (056682) 392

LAXEY, Isle of Man
► Laxey Commissioners Campsite,
tel. (0624) 781241

LEBBERSTON, N Yorks
►►► Flower of May Holiday Park,
tel. Scarborough (0723) 582324 and 584311
►►► Lebberston Caravan Park, Home Farm,
tel. Scarborough (0723) 582254

LEEDSTOWN (nr Hayle), Cornwall
►►► Calloose Caravan Park,
tel. (0736) 850431

LEISTON, Suffolk
►►► Cakes & Ale, Abbey Ln, tel. (0728) 831655

LELANT DOWNS, Cornwall
►► Sunny Meadow Caravan Park,
tel. Hayle (0736) 752243

LETHAM FEUS, Fife
►►► Letham Feus Caravan Park,
tel. Kennoway (0333) 350323

LEVENS, Cumbria
►► Sampool Caravan Site,
tel. Witherslack (044852) 265

LEWIS, ISLE OF, Western Isles
See Coll Sands

LITTLE HAVEN, Dyfed
See Hasguard Cross

LITTLE TORRINGTON, Devon
►►► Smytham Caravan & Campsite,
tel. (0805) 22110

LLANBEDRGOCH, Gwynedd
►►► Ty Newydd Caravan Park & Country
Club, tel. Pentraeth (024870) 677

LLANBEDROG, Gwynedd
►► Crugan Caravan Site,
tel. Abersoch (075881) 2045 and 2047

LLANDANWG, Gwynedd
▽ Ymwlch Farm,
tel. Llanbedr (034123) 320

LLANDRE, Dyfed
►►► Riverside Caravan Park, Llanfraid,
tel. Aberystwyth (0970) 820070

LLANDRILLO, Clwyd
►►► Henwr Farm Site,
tel. (049084) 210 and 252

LLANEGRYN, Gwynedd
►► Waen Fach Caravan Site, Waen Fach,
tel. Tywyn (0654) 710375

LLANFIHANGEL-Y-PENNANT, Gwynedd
▽ Tynybryn Farm,
tel. Abergynolwyn (065477) 277

LLANGADOG, Dyfed
►► Abermarlais Caravan Park,
tel. (0550) 777868

LLANGOLLEN, Clwyd
►►► Ty-Ucha Farm, Maesmawr Rd,
tel. (0978) 860677

LLANGORSE, Powys
►►► Lakeside Caravan Park,
tel. (087484) 226

LLANGWNNADL, Gwynedd
▽ Ty Cam, tel. Pwllheli (0758) 87627

LLANGYNIEW, Powys
►►► Henllan Caravan Park,
tel. Llanfair Caereinion (0938) 810343

LLANIDLOES, Powys
► Dol-Llys Site, Dol-Llys Farm,
tel. (05512) 2694

LLANON, Dyfed
►►► Woodlands Caravan Park,
tel. (09748) 342

LLANRHYSTUD, Dyfed
►►► Pengarreg Caravan Park,
tel. Llanon (09748) 247

LLANRUG, Gwynedd
►►► Bryn Teg Caravan Park,
tel. Llanberis (0286) 871374
►► Tyn-y-Coed Camping Site,
tel. Caernarfon (0286) 3565

LLANRWST, Gwynedd
►► Bodnant Caravan Site, Nebo Rd,
tel. (0492) 640248
► Kerry's Orchard Camping Site, School Bank
Rd, tel. (0492) 640248 and 640683
► Maenan Abbey Caravan Park,
tel. Dolgarrog (049269) 630

LLANTWIT MAJOR, S Glam
►► Rosedew Farm Camping Site,
tel. (04465) 3331 and 2227

LLWYNGWRIL, Gwynedd
►► **Gwril Caravan Site**,
tel. Fairbourne (0341) 250431
► **Hendra Wall**, tel. (0341) 250391

LOCH ECK, Strathclyde
►►► **Stratheck International Caravan Park**
(at Inverchapel at end of Loch),
tel. Kilmun (036984) 472

LOCHGILPHEAD, Strathclyde
►► **Lochgilphead Caravan Site**,
tel. (0546) 2003

LOCHMABEN, Dumfries & Galloway
►► **Halleaths Caravan Site**, tel. (038781) 321
►► **Kirkloch Brae Caravan Site**. Apply to:
Annandale and Eskdale District Council, Council
Chambers, Annan, Dumfriesshire DG12 6AQ

LOCHNAW, Dumfries & Galloway
►►►► **Drumlochart Caravan Park**,
tel. Leswalt (077687) 232

LOCKERBIE, Dumfries & Galloway
►► **Glasgow Road Caravan Site**. Apply to:
Annandale and Eskdale District Council, Council
Chambers, Annan, Dumfriesshire DG12 6AQ

LONDON (GREATER)
Details of sites within the London Postal area
are listed below. For details of other sites in
the vicinity of London, see also Hoddesdon
(23m), Laleham (19m), West Drayton (15m)

ABBEY WOOD, SE2
►►► **Co-operative Wood Caravan Club Site**,
Federation Rd, tel. 01-310 2233

CHINGFORD, E4
►►► **Sewardstone Caravan Park**,
Sewardstone Rd, tel. 01-529 5689

EDMONTON, N9
►► **Picketts Lock Centre**, tel. 01-803 4756

LONG DOWNS, Cornwall
► **Calamankey Farm**,
tel. Stithians (0209) 860314

LONGNOR, Staffs
▽ **Dowall Hall**, Glutton Bridge,
tel. (029883) 272

LONGRIDGE, Lancs
►►► **Beacon Fell View Caravan Park**,
110 Higher Rd, tel. (077478) 5434

LONGTOWN, Cumbria
► **Rangiora Caravan Park**, Sandysikes,
tel. (0228) 791248

LOOE, Cornwall
►►►►► **"Treble B" Holiday Centre**, Polperro
Rd, tel. (05036) 2425
►►► **Polborder House**,
tel. Widegates (05034) 265
►►► **Tencreek Caravan & Camping Park**,
tel. (05036) 2447
►►► **Tregoad Caravan & Camping Park**,
St Martin, tel. (05036) 2718
► **Holimarine Caravan Park**, St Martins,
tel. Sedgley (09073) 77111

LOSSIEMOUTH, Grampian
►►► **Silver Sands Leisure Park**, Covesea, West
Beach (2m W B9040), tel. (034381) 3262

LOSTWITHIEL, Cornwall
► **Downend Campsite**,
tel. Bodmin (0208) 872363

LOTHERSDALE, N Yorks
►► **Springs Caravan Park**, Springs Farm,
tel. Cross Hills (0535) 32533

LOWESTOFT, Suffolk
► **North Denes Caravan Site**, North Denes,
tel. (0502) 3197

LUDCHURCH, Dyfed
►►► **Little Kings Caravan Site**,
tel. Llanteg (083483) 340
►►► **Woodland Vale Caravan Park**,
tel. Llanteg (083483) 319

LUIB, Central
►►► **Glen Dochart Caravan Park**,
tel. Killin (05672) 637

LUNDIN LINKS, Fife
►► **Woodland Gardens**, Blindwell Rd,
tel. Upper Largo (03336) 319

LUSS, Strathclyde
►► **Luss Camping Ground** (Camping &
Caravaning Club),
tel. (043686) 658

LYDFORD, Devon
►► **Pulborough Farm Caravan & Camping
Park**, The Croft,
tel. (082282) 275

LYNHURST, Hants
▽ **Denny Wood Campsite** (2m E off B3056),
tel. (042128) 3771 (Forestry Commission Office)
and 2269 (Tourist Information Centre)
▽ **Holidays Hill Campsite** (2m SW off A35),
tel. (042128) 3771 (Forestry Commission Office)
and 2269 (Tourist Information Centre)
▽ **Matley Wood Campsite** (2m E off B3056),
tel. (042128) 3771 (Forestry Commission Office)
and 2269 (Tourist Information Centre)

LYNEAL (nr Ellesmere), Salop
►►► **Fernwood Caravan Park**,
tel. Bettisfield (094875) 221

LYNTON, Devon
►►► **Channel View Caravan Park**, Manor
Farm, tel. (0598) 53349
►►► **Sunny Lyn Caravan Site**, Lynbridge,
tel. (05985) 3384
►► **Six Acre Caravan Park**, Six Acre Farm,
tel. (05985) 3224
▽ **The Meadow**, Longmead, tel. (05985) 2633

LYTCHETT MINSTER, Dorset
►►► **Beacon Hill Touring Park**, Blandford Rd
North (off A350, NW of junc A35),
tel. (0202) 631631
►►► **South Lytchett Manor Caravan Park**,
tel. (0202) 622577

LYTHAM ST ANNES, Lancs
►►►► **Eastham Hall Caravan Site**,
Saltcotes Rd, tel. Lytham (0253) 737907

MABLETHORPE, Lincs
►►►► **Golden Sands Estates**, Quebec Rd,
tel. (0521) 72671
►► **Mermaid Caravan & Tenting Site**,
Seaholme Rd, tel. (05213) 3273
► **Camping & Caravanning Club Site**,
120 Church Lane, tel. (05213) 2374

Springs Caravan Park, Lothersdale, N Yorks

MACCLESFIELD, Cheshire
►► **Capesthorne Hall**,
tel. Chelford (0625) 861221 and 861439

MACDUFF, Grampian
►►► **Myrus Caravan Site**,
tel. Banff (02612) 2845

MACHRIHANISH, Strathclyde
►► **Camping & Caravanning Club Site**, East
Trodigal, tel. (058681) 366

MACHYNLLETH, Powys
▽ **Rhiw-gam**, Aberhosan, tel. (0654) 2521

MALVERN, Heref & Worcs
► **Three Counties Show**, The Showground
(3m W off B4209), tel. (06845) 2751

MAN, ISLE OF
See under Hillberry, Laxey and Peel

MANSTON, Kent
► **Manston Caravan & Camping Park**, Manston
Court Rd, tel. (084389) 442

MARKET RASEN, Lincs
►►► **Walesby Woodlands Caravan Park**,
Walesby Grange, tel. (0673) 843285
►► **Market Rasen (TRAX) Caravan Club Site**,
Market Rasen Racecourse, Legsby Rd,
tel. (0673) 842307

MARTIN MILL, Kent
►►► **Hawthorn Caravan & Camping Site**,
tel. Dover (0304) 852658 and 852940

MARYCULTER, Grampian
►► **Lower Deeside Caravan Park**,
tel. Aberdeen (0224) 733860

MATLOCK, Derbys
►► **Packhorse Farm**, Matlock Moor,
tel. (0629) 2781
▽ **Canada Farm**, High Ln, Tansley (2m E off
A615), tel. Dethick (062984) 385

MAWGAN PORTH, Cornwall
►►► **Gluvian Caravan & Camping Site**,
tel. St Mawgan (06374) 373
►►► **Trevarrian Holiday Park**,
tel. St Mawgan (06374) 381
►► **The Marver**,
tel. St Mawgan (0637) 860493

MEALSGATE, Cumbria
►►►► **Larches Caravan Park**,
tel. Low Ireby (09657) 379

MELROSE, Borders
►► **Gibson Park Caravan Club Site**,
tel. (089682) 2969
▽ **Broad Oak Farm**, tel. Aldington (023372) 344

MERTHYR MAWR, Mid Glam
►► **Candleston Campsite**,
tel. Bridgend (0656) 2038

MIDDLETON, nr Morecambe, Lancs
►►► **Hawthorn Camping Site**, Carr Lane,
tel. Heysham (0524) 52074
►► **Melbreak Camp Site**, Carr Lane,
tel. Heysham (0524) 52430

MIDDLETOWN, Powys
►► **Bank Farm Caravan Park**,
tel. Trewern (093874) 260

MIDDLEWICH, Cheshire
▽ **Briar Pool Farm**, Cledford Ln, Kinderton
(2m SE on unclass rd off A533), tel. (060684) 2134

MILLBROOK, Devon
►►► **Whitsand Bay Holiday Camp**,
tel. Plymouth (0752) 822597

MINEHEAD, Somerset
►►► **Camping & Caravanning Club Site**, Hill
Rd, North Hill, tel. (0643) 4138

Minehead & Exmoor Caravan Site,
Porlock Rd (1m W, adj to A39), tel. (0643) 3074

MINSTER ON SEA (Isle of Sheppey), Kent
►►► **Ashcroft Caravan Park**, Plough Rd,
tel. Eastchurch (079588) 324

MINTLAW, Grampian
►► **Aden Country Park Caravan Site**. Apply to:
Director of Leisure and Recreation, Banff & Buchan
District Council, 1 Church St, Macduff, Banffshire
AB4 1US,
tel. Banff (02612) 2521 ext 304

MITCHEL TROY, Gwent
►► **Glen Trothy Caravan & Camping Site**,
tel. Monmouth (0600) 2295

MODBURY, Devon
►►► **Broad Park Caravan Site**, Higher East
Leigh Farm, tel. (0548) 830256
►►► **Camping & Caravanning Club Site**,
California Cross, tel. Gara Bridge (054882) 297
►►► **Pennymoor Camping & Caravan Park**,
tel. (0548) 830269 and 830542
►►► **South Leigh Caravan Park**,
tel. (0548) 830346

MOFFAT, Dumfries & Galloway
►►► **Camping & Caravanning Club Site**,
Hammerland's Farm, tel. (0683) 20436

MOLLAND, Devon
►►► **Molland Caravan Park**, Black Cock Hotel,
tel. Bishops Nympton (07697) 297

MONIAIVE, Dumfries & Galloway
►► **Woodlea Hotel**, tel. (08482) 209

MONIFIETH, Tayside
►►► **Riverview Caravan Park**. Apply to:
General Manager of Parks, Parks Dept, 353
Clepington Rd, Dundee DD3 8PL, tel. Dundee
(0382) 532837

MONTROSE, Tayside
►►► **South Links Site**, Traill Drive. Apply to:
Director of Parks and Cemeteries, Angus District
Council, Town House, Montrose, Angus DD10
8QW, tel. (0674) 72044

MORECAMBE, Lancs
►►►► **Regent Caravan Park**, Westgate,
tel. (0524) 413940
►►►► **Venture Caravan Park**, Westgate,
tel. (0524) 412986
► **Summerville Caravan Park**, 82 Acre Moss Ln,
tel. (0524) 414249

MORFA BYCHAN, Gwynedd
►►► **Cardigan View Caravan Park**,
tel. Porthmadog (0766) 2032

MORTEHOE, Devon
►►► **Easewell Farm**,
tel. Woolacombe (0271) 870225
►►► **Twitchen House & Mortehoe Caravan
Park**, tel. Woolacombe (0271) 870476
► **North Morte Farm Caravan & Camping
Site**, North Morte, tel. Woolacombe (0271) 870381

MOUSWALD, Dumfries & Galloway
►► **Mouswald Caravan Park**,
tel. (038783) 226

MUCH WENLOCK, Salop
▽ **Bourton Westwood Farm**,
tel. Telford (0952) 727393

MULLACOTT CROSS, Devon
►►►► **Mullacott Cross Caravan Park**,
tel. Ilfracombe (0271) 62212

MULLION, Cornwall
►►►► **Mullion Holiday Park**, Penhale Cross,
tel. (0326) 240428
►►► **Franchis**, Cury Cross Lanes,
tel. (0326) 240301

MULLION, Cornwall (contd.)
►► **Criggan Mill Caravans**, Mullion Cove,
tel. (0326) 240496
► **Teneriffe Farm Caravan Site**,
tel. (0326) 240293

MUSSELBURGH, Lothian
►►►► **Drum Mohr Caravan Park**, Levenhall,
tel. 031–665 6867

NACTON, Suffolk
►► **Priory Park**, tel. Ipswich (0473) 77393

NAIRN, Highland
►►► **East Beach Caravan Park**, East Beach,
tel. (0667) 53764
►►►►**Delnies Woods Caravan Park**,
tel. (0667) 54752

NARBERTH, Dyfed
►►►► **Redford Caravan Park**, Princes Gate,
tel. (0834) 860251
► **Noble Court Caravan Site**, Redstone Rd,
tel. (0834) 861191

NARBOROUGH, Norfolk
►►► **Pentney Park**, Gayton Rd,
tel. (0760) 337479

NAWTON, N Yorks
►► **Wrens of Ryedale Caravan Site**,
tel. Helmsley (0439) 71260

NETHER KELLET, Lancs
►►► **The Hawthorns**,
tel. Carnforth (0524) 732079

NEWBRIDGE, Isle of Wight
►►►► **Orchards Holiday Caravan Park**,
tel. Calbourne (098378) 331

NEWCASTLE EMLYN, Dyfed
►►► **Afon Teifi Caravan & Camping Site**,
Pentrecagal (2m E A484),
tel. Velindre (0559) 370532
►► **Dolbryn Farm**, Capel Ifan Rd,
tel. (0239) 710683

NEWCASTLE-UPON-TYNE, Tyne and Wear
►►► **Newcastle (TRAX) Caravan Club Site**,
Gosforth Park Racecourse,
tel. Wideopen (0632) 363258

NEWCHURCH, Isle of Wight
►►► **Southland Camping Park**,
tel. Arreton (098377) 385

NEW FOREST
The New Forest covers 144 square miles and is
composed of broadleaf and coniferous woodland,
open commonland and heath. This unique area was
originally a royal hunting forest and there are long-
established rights of access. It is not a "Forest Park"
but similar facilities for visitors are maintained by the
Forestry Commission; these include caravan and
camp sites, picnic sites, car parks, way-marked
walks and ornamental drives.

The campsites are open from the Friday before
Easter until the end of September (two sites remain
open in October). Information and camping leaflet
available from the Forestry Commission, Queen's
House, Lyndhurst, Hants SO4 7NH. Telephone
Lyndhurst (042128) 3771. Information also
available from the Tourist Information Caravan at
Lyndhurst Car Park (April–October). Telephone
Lyndhurst (042128) 2269.
**See Ashurst, Brockenhurst, Fritham and
Holmsley for AA pennant classified sites.**
AA "Venture" sites are listed under the following
locations: Brockenhurst, Lyndhurst, Nomansland
(Wiltshire) and Sway.

NEWGALE, Dyfed
► **Chapel Farm Caravan Park & Touring Site**,
tel. Camrose (0437) 710485 &
St Davids (0437) 721786

NEWHAVEN, Derbys
►►►► **Newhaven Holiday Camping &
Caravan Park**,
tel. Hartington (029884) 300

NEWMARKET, Suffolk
►►► **Newmarket (TRAX) Caravan Club Site**,
Rowley Mile Racecourse,
tel. (0638) 663235

NEW MILTON, Hants
►►►►► **Bashley Park**, Sway Rd,
tel. (0425) 612340

NEWQUAY, Cornwall
During the currency of this guide Newquay
telephone numbers are due to change. The code is
to change from (06373) to (0637) and 4-figure
numbers are to be prefixed by 87.
►►►►► **Hendra Tourist Park**, Lane (2m SE),
tel. (06373) 5778 (due to change to (0637) 875778)
►►►► **Newquay Tourist Park**, St Columb
Minor (3m E off A3059),
tel. (06373) 71111 (due to change to (0637) 871111)
►►►► **Tencreek Farm Holiday Park**, Tencreek,
tel. (06373) 4210 (due to change to (0637) 874210)
►►►► **Rosecliston Touring Park**, Trevemper
(2m S on A3075), tel. Crantock (0637) 830326
►►►► **Trevelgue Caravan Park**,
tel. (06373) 3475 & 5905 (due to change to (0637)
873475 & 875905)
►►► **Gwills Caravan Park**, Lane (2m SE),
tel. (06373) 3617 (due to change to (0637) 873617)
►►► **Porth Beach Tourist Park**, Porth (1m NE),
tel. (06373) 6531 (due to change to (0637) 876531)
►►► **Treloy Tourist Park**,
tel. (06373) 2063 (due to change to (0637) 872063)
►►► **Trenance Caravan & Chalet Park**,
Edgcumbe Avenue,
tel. (06373) 3447 (due to change to (0637) 873447)

NEWQUAY, Dyfed
►►► **Camping & Caravanning Club Site**,
Llwynhelyg, Cross Inn (3m S off A486 at Cross Inn),
tel. (0545) 560029

NEWTON ABBOT, Devon
►►►► **Dornafield**, Dornafield Farm, Two Mile
Bar, tel. Ipplepen (0803) 812732
►►►► **Stover International Caravan Park**,
Lower Staple Hill (3m N off A38),
tel. Bickington (062682) 446
►► **Country Touring Caravan Centre**, Two
Mile Oak, tel. Ipplepen (0803) 812628

NEWTONMORE, Highland
►► **Invernahaven Caravan Park**, Glentruim,
tel. (05403) 534 and 221

NEWTON STEWART, Dumfries & Galloway
►►► **Creebridge Caravan Park**,
tel. (0671) 2324
▽ **Talnotry Campsite**, Palnure (7m NE off A712).
For bookings: Forestry Commission, Forest Office,
Creebridge, Newton Stewart, Wigtownshire DG8
6AJ, tel. (0671) 2420

NOMANSLAND, Wilts
▽ **Pipers Wait** (1m SW towards B3078),
tel. Lyndhurst (042128) 3771 (Forestry Commission
Office) & 2269 (Tourist Information Centre)

NORTH BERWICK, Lothian
►►► **Rhodes Caravan Site**

NORTH KILWORTH, Leics
► **Kilworth Caravan Park**,
tel. (0858) 880385 & 880597

NORTH SOMERCOTES, Lincs
►►►► **Lakeside Holiday Park**,
tel. (050785) 315

NORTH STAINLEY, N Yorks
►►► **Sleningford Water Mill**,
tel. Ripon (0765) 85201

NORTH WOOTTON, Somerset
►► **Greenacres Camping**, Barrow Ln,
tel. Pilton (074989) 497

NOSTELL, W Yorks
►► **Nostell Priory Holiday Homes**, Top Park
Wood, tel. Wakefield (0924) 863938

NOTTER BRIDGE, Cornwall
►►► **Notter Bridge Caravan & Camping
Park**, tel. Saltash (07555) 2318

OLD CLIPSTONE, Notts
►►► **Sherwood Forest Caravan Park**,
tel. Mansfield (0623) 823132

OLDE LEAKE, Lincs
►►► **White Cat Park**, Shaw Ln,
tel. Boston (0205) 870121

ORGANFORD, Dorset
►►► **Pear Tree Farm Caravans & Camping**,
tel. Lytchett Minster (0202) 622434
► **Organford Manor**,
tel. Lytchet Minster (0202) 622202

ORLETON, Heref & Worcs
►► **Orleton Rise Caravan Park**, Green Ln,
tel. Richards Castle (058474) 617

ORMSKIRK, Lancs
►►► **Abbey Farm Caravan Site**, Blyth Ln,
tel. (0695) 72686

OSMINGTON MILLS, Dorset
►► **Osmington Mills Holidays**,
tel. Weymouth (0305) 832311

OSMOTHERLEY, N Yorks
► **Cote Ghyll Caravan Park**,
tel. (060983) 425)

OSWALDKIRK, N Yorks
►►► **Golden Square Touring Caravan Park**,
tel. Ampleforth (04393) 269

OWER, Hants
► **Green Pastures Farm**,
tel. Southampton (0703) 814444

OWERMOIGNE, Dorset
►►► **Sandy Holme Caravan Park**, Moreton Rd,
tel. Warmwell (0305) 852677

OXFORD, Oxon
►►► **Oxford Camping International**,
426 Abingdon Rd, tel. (0865) 246551

PADSTOW, Cornwall
► **Dennis Cove Leisure Park**, Denis Cove,
tel. (0841) 532349

PAIGNTON, Devon
►►►►► **Beverley Parks Caravan &
Camping Site**, Goodrington Rd,
tel. (0803) 843887
►►►►► **Grange Court Holiday Centre**,
Grange Rd, tel. (0803) 550141 and 558010
►►►► **Paignton International**,
tel. (0803) 521684
►►► **Holly Gruit Camp**, Brixham Rd,
tel. (0803) 550763
►►► **Lower Yalberton Farm Caravan &
Camping Park**, Long Rd, tel. (0803) 558127
►►► **Marine Park Holiday Centre**, Grange Rd,
tel. (0803) 843887
►►► **Whitehill Farm Caravan & Camping
Site**, Stoke Gabriel Rd,
tel. Stoke Gabriel (080428) 338
►►► **Widend Camping Park**, Berry Pomeroy
Rd, Marldon, tel. (0803) 550116
▽ **Wildwoods Farm**, Marldon,
tel. (0803) 556253

PALNACKIE, Dumfries & Galloway
►►► **Barlochan Caravan Park**,
tel. (055660) 256, and for advance bookings
Borgue (05577) 267

PAR, Cornwall
►►► **Mount Holiday Park**, The Mount,
tel. (072681) 2616

PARTON, Dumfries & Galloway
►►► **Loch Ken Holiday Centre**,
tel. (06447) 282

PATHFINDER VILLAGE, Devon
►►►►► **Pathfinder Touring Caravan Park**,
tel. Tedburn St Mary (06476) 239 and 710

PEEBLES, Borders
►►►► **Rosetta Caravan & Camping Park**,
tel. (0721) 20770
►►► **Crossburn Caravan Park**, Edinburgh Rd,
tel. (0721) 20501

PEEL, Isle of Man
► **Peel Camping Park**, Derby Rd,
tel. (062484) 2341

PELYNT, Cornwall
►►► **Camping Caradon**, Trelawne,
tel. Polperro (0503) 72388
►►► **Trelawne Holiday Estate**,
tel. Polperro (0503) 72151
► **Trelay Farm**, tel. Lanreath (0503) 20256

PENMAENMAWR, Gwynedd
► **Tyddyn Du Farm**, Conway Old Rd,
tel. (0492) 622300 and 623395

PENPONT, Dumfries & Galloway
►► **Penpont Caravan & Camping Site**,
tel. Thornhill (0848) 30470

PENRHYNDEUDRAETH, Gwynedd
► **Bwlch Bryn Caravan Park**,
tel. (0766) 770365

PENRITH, Cumbria
►►► **Thacka Lea Caravan Site**, Thacka Lane,
tel. (0768) 63319

PENRUDDOCK, Cumbria
►►► **Beckses Caravan Site**,
tel. Greystoke (08533) 224

PENTEWAN, Cornwall
►►►► **Sun Valley Caravan Park**, Nansladron
House, Pantewan Rd,
tel. Mevagissey (0726) 843266
►►► **Penhaven Tourist Park**,
tel. Mevagissey (0726) 843687
►►► **Pentewan Sands Holiday Park**,
tel. Mevagissey (0726) 843485

PENTRAETH, Gwynedd
► **Rhos Caravan Park**, tel. (024870) 214

PENTREBEIRDD, Powys
►► **Valley View Caravan Park**,
tel. Meifod (093884) 265 & 545

PENYBONTFAWR, Powys
►► **Parc Farm**, tel. Pennant (069174) 204

PENYCWM, Dyfed
►► **Park Hall Caravan Park**, Maerdy Farm,
tel. St Davids (0437) 721282

PENZANCE, Cornwall
►► **Bone Valley Caravan Park**, Heamoor,
tel. (0736) 60313

PERRANARWORTHAL, Cornwall
►►► **Cosawes Caravan Park**,
tel. Truro (0872) 863724 & 863717

PERRANPORTH, Cornwall
During the currency of this guide Perranporth
telephone numbers are due to change. All numbers
are to be prefixed by 57 and the exchange name
changed to Truro (0872).
►►►► **Perranporth Camping & Touring
Site**, Budnick Rd,
tel. (087257) 2174 (due to change to
Truro (0872) 572174)

PERRANPORTH, Cornwall (contd.)
►►►► **Perran Sands Camping & Touring Park**, tel. (087257) 3551 (due to change to Truro (0872) 573551)

PERROTT'S BROOK, Glos
►► **Mayfield Park**, Mayfield
tel. North Cerney (028583) 301

PERTH, Tayside
►►►►► **Camping Club Site**, Scone
Racecourse, tel. (0738) 52323
►► **Windsor Caravan Park**, Windsor Ter,
tel. (0738) 23721

PETERCHURCH, Heref & Worcs
►► **Poston Caravan & Camping Park**,
tel. (09816) 225

PETT, E Sussex
► **Carters Farm**, Elm Ln,
tel. Hastings (0424) 813206

PITLOCHRY, Tayside
►►► **Faskally Home Farm**,
tel. (0796) 2007 & 3202
►►► **Milton of Fonab Caravan Site**,
tel. (0796) 2882

PITTENWEEM, Fife
►►► **Grangemuir Caravan Site** (1m NW
unclass), tel. Anstruther (0333) 311213

PLUMPTON, Cumbria
►►► **Greenacres Caravan Park**,
tel. (076884) 206

PLUMPTON, W Sussex
► **Gallops Farm**, Streat Ln, Streat, Hassocks,
tel. (0273) 890387

PLUMPTON RACECOURSE, E Sussex
►► **Plumpton Racecourse (TRAX) Caravan Club Site**, Plumpton Green, tel. (0273) 890522

PLYMOUTH, Devon
►►►► **Riverside Caravan Park**, Longbridge
Rd, Marsh Mills, Plympton (3m E off A38),
tel. (0752) 334122

POLPERRO, Cornwall
►►► **Killigarth Manor Holiday Estate**,
tel. (0503) 72216

PONTLYFNI, Gwynedd
► **Llyn-y-Gele Farm & Caravan Park**,
tel. Clynnogfawr (028686) 283

PONT-RUG, Gwynedd
► **Riverside Camping**, Caer Glyddyn,
tel. Caernarfon (0286) 2524

POOLEWE, Highland
►►► **Inverewe Stage House**,
tel. (044586) 249

POOLEY BRIDGE, Cumbria
► **Hillcroft Caravan & Camping Site**,
tel. (08536) 363

PORLOCK, Somerset
►►► **Porlock Caravan Park**,
tel. (0643) 862269

PORTHTOWAN, Cornwall
►► **Porthtowan Caravan & Camping Park**,
Hilltop Cottage, Mile Hill, tel. (0209) 890256
►► **Rose Hill Park**, Rose Hill,
tel. (0209) 890802

PORTPATRICK, Dumfries & Galloway
►►► **Galloway Point Holiday Park**, Portree
Farm, tel. (077681) 561

PORTSOY, Grampian
►► **Portsoy Links Site**. Apply to: Director of
Leisure and Recreation, Banff & Buchan District
Council, 1 Church St, Macduff, Banffshire
AB4 1US, tel. Banff (0262) 2521 ext 304

Perth, Tayside

POTTERNE, Wilts
►►► **Potterne Caravan Park**, Potterne Wick,
tel. Devizes (0380) 3277

POUNDSTOCK, Cornwall
►► **Cornish Coasts Caravan & Camping Site**,
tel. Widemouth Bay (028885) 380

POWFOOT, Dumfries & Galloway
►►► **Queensberry Bay Caravan Park**,
tel. Cummertrees (04617) 205

PRAA SANDS, Cornwall
►►► **Pengersick Caravan & Camping Site**,
tel. Penzance (0736) 76220
►►► **Praa Sands Caravan Park**,
tel. St Austell (0726) 66551

PRESTATYN, Clwyd
►►►► **Presthaven Sands Holiday Park**,
tel. (07456) 6471

PRESTEIGNE, Powys
►► **Rock Bridge, Caravan & Camping Park**,
tel. Whitton (05476) 300

PRESTON PATRICK, Cumbria
►► **Milness Hill Camping Site**,
tel. Crooklands (04487) 306

PRIDDY, Somerset
►► **Mendip Heights Caravan & Camping
Park**, Townsend, tel. Wells (0749) 870241

QUATT, nr Bridgnorth, Salop
▽ **Coton Hall**, Coton (2m SE off A442)

RADFORD, Heref & Worcs
▽ **Wheelbarrow Castle**,
tel. Inkberrow (0386) 792207

RATTERY, Devon
►►► **Edeswell Caravan & Camping Park**,
Edeswell Farm, tel. South Brent (03647) 2177

RAVENGLASS, Cumbria
►► **Walls Caravan Park**, tel. (06577) 250

RAVENSTRUTHER, Strathclyde
►► **Newhouse Farm**, tel. Carstairs (0555)
870228

REAY, Highland
► **Dunvegan Euro Campsite**,
tel. (084781) 405

REDHILL, Avon
►► **Brook Lodge Caravan Park**,
tel. Wrington (0934) 862311

RED ROSES, Dyfed
►► **Old Vicarage Caravan Park**,
tel. Llanteg (083483) 637

REDRUTH, Cornwall
►►► **Cambrose Farm Camp Site**, Portreath Rd,
tel. Porthtowan (0209) 890747
►►► **Lanyon Farm Caravan Park**, Four Lanes,
tel. (0209) 216447

►►► **Tehidy Caravan Park**, Harms Mill, Illogan (2m NW off B3300 on N side of A30), tel. (0209) 216489

REJERRAH, Cornwall
►►►►► **Newperran Tourist Site**, Hendra Croft, tel. Perranporth (087257) 2407 (due to change to Truro (0872) 572407) and Crantock (0637) 830308
►►►► **Monkey Tree Farm Tourist Park**, tel. Perranporth (087257) 2032 (due to change to Truro (0872) 572032)
►►►► **Castaways Holiday Park**, tel. Perranporth (087257) 2561 (due to change to Truro (0872) 572561)

RELUBBUS, Cornwall
►►► **River Valley Caravan Park**, tel. Penzance (0736) 763398

RESIPOL (Loch Sunart), Highland
►► **Resipole Farm**, tel. Salen (096785) 235

REYNALTON, Dyfed
►►► **Croft Caravan Park**, tel. Narberth (0834) 860315

RHOSGOCH, Powys
►► **Rhosgoch Holiday Park**, tel. Painscastle (04975) 253

RHOSNEIGR, Gwynedd
► **Bodfan Farm**, tel. (0407) 810563

RICHMOND, N Yorks
►► **Swale View Caravan Site**, Reeth Rd, tel. (0748) 3106

RINGWOOD, Hants
►►► **Copper Kettle**, 266 Christchurch Rd, tel. (04254) 3904

RIPLEY, N Yorks
►►► **Ripley Caravan Park**, Knaresborough Rd. Apply to: Ripley Caravan Park, 9 Cavendish Av, Harrogate, HG2 8HX, tel. Harrogate (0423) 770050

RIPON, N Yorks
►►► **Ure Bank Caravan Park**, Ure Bank Top, tel. (0765) 2964
▽ **North Sutton Farm**, Sutton Grange (3m NW unclass rd), tel. (0765) 4037

RIXTON, Cheshire
►► **Holly Bank Caravan Park**, Warburton Bridge Rd, tel. 061–775 2842

ROBESTON WATHEN, Dyfed
► **Dyrham Caravan Park**, tel. Narberth (0834) 860367

ROCHESTER, Kent
► **Woolmans Wood Caravan Park**, Bridgewood (3¼m S of Rochester), tel. Medway (0634) 67685

ROCKBEARE, Devon
►►► **Bidgood Arms Caravan Site**, tel. Whimple (0404) 822262

RODNEY STOKE, Somerset
►►► **Bucklegrove Caravan & Camping Park**, tel. Wells (0749) 870261

ROSEHEARTY, Grampiantel.
►► **Rosehearty Caravan Site**. Apply to: Director of Leisure and Recreation, Banff & Buchan District Council, 1 Church St, Macduff, Banffshire AB4 1US, tel. Banff (02612) 2521 ext 304

ROSUDGEON, Cornwall
►► **Kenneggy Cove Holiday Park**, Higher Kenneggy, tel. Penzance (0736) 763453

ROTHBURY, Northumb
►► **Coquetdale Caravan Park**, Whitton, tel. (0669) 20549

ROUSDON, Devon
►►► **West Hayes Caravan Park**, tel. Seaton (0297) 23456
►► **Shrubbery Caravan Park**, tel. Lyme Regis (02974) 2227

ROWLANDS GILL, Tyne & Wear
►► **Derwent Park Caravan Site**, tel. (0207) 543383

ROY BRIDGE, Highland
► **Bunroy Caravan Park**, tel. Spean Bridge (039781) 332
► **Stronreigh**, tel. Spean Bridge (039781) 275

RUABON, Clwyd
►► **James Farm**, tel. (0978) 820148

RUDSTON, Humberside
►►► **Thorpe Hall Caravan & Camping Site**, Thorpe Hall, tel. Kilham (026282) 393 and 394

RUGELEY, Staffs
► **Silver Trees Caravan & Chalet Park**, Penkridge Bank, tel. (08894) 2185

RUMFORD, Cornwall
►►►► **Music Water Touring Site**, tel. (08414) 257

RUTHERNBRIDGE, Cornwall
►►► **Ruthern Valley Holidays**, tel. Lanivet (0208) 831395

RUTHIN, Clwyd
►►► **Three Pigeons Inn**, Craigfechan, tel. (08242) 3178

ST AGNES, Cornwall
►► **Presingoll Farm**, tel. (087255) 2333

ST ANDREWS, Fife
►►►►► **Craigtoun Meadows Holiday Park**, Mount Melville, tel. (0334) 75959
►►► **Kinkell Braes Caravan Park**, tel. (0334) 74250

ST AUSTELL, Cornwall
►►► **Trewhiddle Holiday Estate**, tel. (0726) 67011

ST BRELADE, Jersey
►► **Rose Farm**, Route des Genets, tel. Jersey (0534) 41231

ST BURYAN, Cornwall
►►► **Lower Treave Caravan Park**, Crows-an-Wra, tel. (073672) 559
►►► **Tower Farm Caravan & Camping Park**, tel. (073672) 286
►►► **Treveren Camping & Touring Site**, Treveren Farm, tel. (073672) 221

ST COLUMB MAJOR, Cornwall
►►► **Tregatillian Caravan Park**, Tregatillian, tel. St Columb (0637) 880482
►►► **Trekenning Manor Tourist Park**, Trekenning, tel. (0637) 880462

ST DAVID'S, Dyfed
►► **Caerfai Bay Caravan & Camping Park**, tel. (0437) 720274
►► **Dwr Cwmwdig Caravan Park**, Berea, tel. Croesgoch (03483) 376
►► **Hendre Eynon Site**, tel. (0437) 720474

ST DAY, Cornwall
►►► **Tresaddern Caravan Park**, tel. (0209) 820459

ST EWE, Cornwall
►► **Pengrugla Caravan & Campsite**, tel. Mevagissey (0726) 843485

ST HELENS, Isle of Wight
►►► **Nodes Point Holiday Village**, Nodes Rd, tel. (0983) 872401

ST HILARY, Cornwall
►►► **Wayfarers Camping Site**,
tel. Penzance (0736) 763326

ST ISSEY, Cornwall
►►► **Trewince Farm Holiday Park**,
tel. Wadebridge (020881) 2830

ST IVES, Cornwall
►►► **Ayr Holiday Park**,
tel. Penzance (0736) 795855
►► **Polmanter Farm Campsite**, Halsetown,
tel. Penzance (0736) 795640
► **Higher Penderleith Site**, Towednack,
tel. Penzance (0736) 796576

ST JUST, Cornwall
►►► **Trevaylor Caravan Park**, Truthwall,
tel. Penzance (0736) 787016
►► **Bosavern House Caravan Park**,
tel. Penzance (0736) 788301
►► **Kelynack Caravan Park**,
tel. St Buryan (073672) 465

ST JUST-IN-ROSELAND, Cornwall
►►► **Trethem Mill Caravan Site**,
tel. Portscatho (087258) 504 and
St Mawes (0326) 270427

ST LAWRENCE, Isle of Wight
▽ **The Orchard**,
tel. (0983) 730381

ST LEONARDS, Dorset
►►►► **Camping International**, Athol Lodge,
tel. Ferndown (0202) 872817
►►►► **Redcote Holiday Park**, Boundary Ln,
tel. Ferndown (0202) 872742
►►►► **Shamba Holiday Park**,
tel. Ferndown (0202) 873302

ST MABYN, Cornwall
►►►► **St Mabyn Holiday Park**,
tel. (020884) 236

ST MARTIN, Jersey
►►► **Beuvelande Camping Site**,
tel. Jersey (0534) 53575
►►► **Rozel Camping Park**, Summerville Farm,
tel. Jersey (0534) 51989

ST MERRYN, Padstow, Cornwall
►►► **Tregidier Caravan Park**, Trevean Ln,
tel. Padstow (0841) 520264
► **Carnevas Caravan & Camping Site**,
Carnevas Farm,
tel. Padstow (0841) 520230

ST MINVER, Cornwall
►►► **St Minver House Holiday Estate**,
tel. Trebetherick (020886) 2305 or for advance
bookings Hemel Hempstead (0442) 51242

ST MONANS, Fife
► **St Monans Caravan Site**, tel. (03337) 778

ST NICHOLAS-AT-WADE, Kent
► **St Nicholas-at-Wade Camping Site**, Court
Rd, tel. Thanet (0843) 47245

ST OSYTH, Essex
►► **Hutleys West Caravan Park**, St Osyth
Beach, tel. Clacton-on-Sea (0255) 820712

ST OUEN, Jersey
►►► **Summer Lodge Campsite**, Leoville,
tel. Jersey (0534) 81921

SALCOMBE, Devon
►►► **Alston Farm Camping & Caravanning
Site**, Malborough, Kingsbridge (1½m W of town off
A381 towards Malborough),
tel. Kingsbridge (0548) 561260

SALISBURY, Wilts
►►► **Coombe Nurseries Touring Park**, Race
Plain, Netherhampton (2m SW off A3094),
tel. (0722) 28451

SAMPFORD COURTENAY, Devon
►►► **Culverhayes Campsite**,
tel. North Tawton (083782) 431
►►► **Moorcroft Caravan Park**, Belstone
Corner, Crediton Rd,
tel. North Tawton (083782) 293

SANDEND, Grampian
►►► **Sandend Caravan & Camping Park**, The
Old School House, tel. Portsay (0261) 42660

SANDFORD-ON-THAMES, Oxfordshire
►► **Templars Court Country Club**, Henley Rd,
tel. Oxford (0865) 779359

SANDHEAD, Dumfries & Galloway
►► **Sands of Luce Caravan Park**,
tel. (077683) 456

SANQUHAR, Dumfries and Galloway
►► **Castle View Caravan Park**,
tel. (06592) 291

SARACEN'S HEAD (nr Holbeach), Lincs
►►► **Whaplode Manor Caravan Park**,
Whaplode Manor, tel. Holbeach (0406) 22837

SARN, Gwynedd
▽ **Talcen Eiddew**, tel. Botwnnog (075883) 619

SARNAU, Dyfed
► **Brynawelon Caravan Park**,
tel. Llangranog (023978) 584

SAUNDERSFOOT, Dyfed
►►► **Saundersvale Caravan Park**, Valley Rd,
tel. (0834) 812310

SAWLEY, N Yorks
▽ **Hallgates Farm**, tel. (076586) 275

SCANIPORT, Highland
► **Scaniport Caravan Site**,
tel. Dores (046375) 351

SCARBOROUGH, N Yorks
See also Burniston
►►►► **Scalby Manor Caravan & Camping
Site**. Apply to: Department of Tourism and
Amenities, Londesborough Lodge, The Crescent,
Scarborough YO11 2PW, tel. (0723) 366212
►►► **Burniston Road Caravan Site**. Apply to:
Department of Tourism and Amenities,
Londesborough Lodge, The Crescent, Scarborough
YO11 2PW, tel. (0723) 366212

SCILLY ISLES
No sites on the island hold AA classification

SCOLE, Norfolk
►►► **The Willows Camping & Caravan Park**,
tel. Diss (0379) 740271

SCOTCH CORNER, N Yorks
►►► **Scotch Corner Caravan Park**,
tel. Richmond (0748) 4424

SCOURIE, Highland
►►► **Scourie Caravan & Camping Park**,
tel. (0971) 2217

SCRATBY, Norfolk
►►► **Scratby Hall Caravan Park**,
tel. Gt Yarmouth (0493) 730283

SEATON, Devon
► **Manor Farm Camping**, tel. (0297) 21524

SEDBERGH, Cumbria
►►► **Pinfold Caravan Park**, tel. (0587) 20576

SEDGEFIELD, Co Durham
►► **Sedgefield (TRAX) Caravan Club Site**,
Sedgefield Racecourse, tel. (0740) 21925

SELKIRK, Borders
►► **Victoria Park Caravan Park**, Buccleuch Rd.
Apply to: Ettrick & Lauderdale District Council, and
Park Superintendent, Paton St, Galashiels,
Selkirkshire

SEVERN BEACH, Avon
►► **Salthouse Farm Caravan Site**, tel. Pilning (04545) 2274
► **Villa Caravan Park**, tel. Pilning (04545) 2540

SHANKLIN, Isle of Wight
►►►►► **Lower Hyde Leisure Park**, Lower Hyde Rd, tel. (0983) 866131
Landguard Holidays, Landguard Manor Rd, tel. (0983) 863100
►►► **Ninham Camping & Caravanning Park** (off Whitecross Ln), tel. (0983) 862049 and 864243

SHARDLOW, Derbys
►►► **Shardlow Marina Caravan Park**, London Rd, tel. Derby (0332) 792832

SHELFORD, GREAT, Cambs
►►► **Camping & Caravanning Club Site** (to the rear of Cambridge Rd), tel. Cambridge (0223) 841185

SHEPTON MALLET, Somerset
► **Manleaze Caravan Park**, Cannards Grave, tel. (0749) 2404

SHERINGHAM, Norfolk
►► **Woodlands Caravan Park**, Holt Rd, Upper Sheringham, tel. (0263) 823802

SHIEL BRIDGE, Highland
► **Shiel Bridge Caravan Site**, Dochgarroch, tel. Glenshiel (059981) 221

SHOTTISHAM, Suffolk
► **St Margaret's Guest House**, tel. (0394) 411247

SHRAWLEY, Heref & Worcs
►► **Lenchford Caravan Park**, tel. Worcester (0905) 620246

SIDCOT, Avon
► **Netherdale Caravan & Camping Ground**, Bridgwater Rd, tel. Winscombe (093484) 3481

SIDMOUTH, Devon
►►► **Kings Down Tail Caravan & Camping Site**, Kings Down Tail Farm (off A3052, 3m E of junc with A375), tel. Branscombe (029780) 313
►►► **Oakdown Touring Caravan Park** (off A3052, 2½m E of junc with A375), tel. (03955) 3731
►► **Salcombe Regis Caravan & Camping Site**, Salcombe Regis (off A3052, 3m E of junc with A375), tel. (03955) 4303

SILECROFT, Cumbria
►► **Silecroft Caravan Site**, tel. Millom (0657) 2659

SILLOTH, Cumbria
►►►► **Stanwix Park Holiday Centre** (1m SW on B5300), tel. (0965) 31671
►►► **Tanglewood Caravan Park**, Causewayhead, tel. (0965) 31253

SILPHO, N Yorks
▽ **Edgemoor**, tel. Scarborough (0723) 82300

SILSDEN, W Yorks
► **Dales Bank Holiday Park**, Low Lane (1m NW on unclass rd), tel. Steeton (0535) 53321

SILVERDALE, Lancs
►►► **Holgate's Caravan Park**, Cove Rd, tel. (0524) 701508

SKEGNESS, Lincs
►►► **Richmond Drive Carapark**, tel. (0754) 2097

SKIPSEA, Humberside
►►► **Far Grange Park**, Windhook, Hornsea Rd, tel. (026286) 248 and 293
►►► **Low Skirlington Caravan Site**, tel. (026286) 213

SKIPTON, N Yorks
►►► **Overdale Trailer Park**, Harrogate Rd, tel. (0756) 3480

SKYE, ISLE OF, Highland
See **Cumustianavaig, Dunvegan, Edinbane** and **Staffin**

SLAPTON, Devon
►► **Camping & Caravanning Club Site**, Middle Grounds, tel. Kingsbridge (0548) 580538

SLIMBRIDGE, Glos
►►► **Tudor Arms Caravan Site**, Shepherds Patch, tel. Cambridge (Glos) (045389) 483

SLINGSBY, N Yorks
► **Camping & Caravanning Club Site**, Railway Street, tel. Hovingham (065382) 335
►► **Green Dyke Camping Site & Robin Hood Caravan Park**, Green Dyke Ln, tel. Hovingham (065382) 391

SMITHALEIGH, Devon
►►► **Smithaleigh Caravan & Camping Park**, tel. Plymouth (0752) 342000 and 893194

SNAINTON, N Yorks
►► **Jasmin Site**, Low Rd, tel. Scarborough (0723) 85240

SNAPE, N Yorks
▽ **Castle Arms**, tel. Bedale (0677) 70270

SNETTISHAM, Norfolk
►►► **Diglea Caravan & Camping Park**, Beach Rd, tel. Dersingham (0485) 41367

SOLVA, Dyfed
► **Mount Farm**, tel. St Davids (0437) 721301

SOURTON DOWN, Devon
►►► **Griggs Prewley Caravan Site**, tel. Bridestowe (083786) 349

SOUTHBOURNE, W Sussex
► **Inlands House Campsite**, Inlands House, 343 Main Rd, tel. Emsworth (02434) 3202

SOUTH BRENT, Devon
►►► **Great Palstone Caravan Park**, tel. (03647) 2227

SOUTH CAVE, Humberside
► **Waudby's Caravan Site**, Brough Rd, tel. North Cave (04302) 2523

SOUTH CERNEY, Glos
►►►►► **Cotswold Caravan Park**, Broadway Ln, tel. Cirencester (0285) 860216

SOUTHERNESS, Dumfries & Galloway
►►► **Southerness Holiday Village**, tel. Kirkbean (038788) 256

SOUTH SHIELDS, Tyne & Wear
► **Lizard Lane Caravan & Camping Site**. Apply to: South Tyneside Borough Council, Cultural and Leisure Activities, Central Library Building, Catherine St, South Shields, Tyne & Wear, tel. (0632) 553405 (nightly bookings) and (0632) 557411 (for weekly bookings)

SOUTHWELL, Notts
►► **Trax Campsite**, Southwell Racecourse (at Rolleston 2½m SE unclass rd), tel. (0636) 812081

STAFFIN, Isle of Skye, Highland
►► **Staffin Caravan & Camping Site**, tel. (047062) 213

STAINFORTH, N Yorks
►►► **Knight Stainforth Hall Caravan & Campsite**, tel. Settle (07292) 2200

STAMFORD BRIDGE, Humberside
►►► **Weir Caravan Park**, tel. (0759) 71377

STANDLAKE, Oxon
▶▶▶ **Hardwick Parks**, Hardwick,
tel. (086731) 501
▶▶ **Standlake Caravans**, Lincoln Farm, High St,
tel. (086731) 239

STANSTED, Kent
▶ **Thriftwood Camping Site**, Plaxdale Green Rd,
tel. Fairseat (0732) 822261

STARCROSS, Devon
▶▶▶ **Cofton Farm Caravan Park**,
tel. (0626) 890358

STAVELEY, Cumbria
▶▶▶▶ **Ashes Lane Caravan & Camping Park**,
Ashes Ln, tel. (0539) 821119

STICKER, Cornwall
▶▶ **Glenleigh Caravan Park**,
tel. St Austell (0726) 65633

STICKLEPATH, Devon
▶▶ **Olditch Farm Caravan Park**,
tel. Okehampton (0837) 840734

STIRLING, Central
▶▶▶ **Cornton Caravan Park**, Cornton Rd,
tel. (0786) 4503

STOKE FLEMING, Devon
▶▶▶ **Deer Park Holiday Estate**,
tel. (0803) 770253

STOKE GABRIEL, Devon
▶▶▶ **Ramslade Holiday Park**, Stoke Rd,
tel. (080428) 575

STONEHAVEN, Grampian
▶▶▶ **Queen Elizabeth Caravan Site.** Apply to:
Kincardine and Deeside District Council, Leisure and
Recreation Dept, Viewmount, Arduthie Rd,
Stonehaven, Kincardineshire AB3 2DQ,
tel. (0569) 62001

STOWBRIDGE, Norfolk
▶▶▶ **Woodlakes Caravan & Camping Park**,
Holme Rd,
tel. King's Lynn (0553) 810414

STRACHAN, Grampian
▶▶ **Feughside Caravan Site**,
tel. Feughside (033045) 669

STRACHUR, Strathclyde
▶▶ **Strathlachlan Caravan Park**,
tel. (036986) 300

STRAGGLETHORPE, Notts
▶▶▶ **Thornton's Holt Camping Site**,
tel. Radcliffe-on-Trent (06073) 2125

STRANRAER, Dumfries & Galloway
▶▶▶▶ **Aird Donald Caravan Park**,
tel. (0776) 2025

STRATHAVEN, Strathclyde
▶▶ **Gallowhill Caravan Park**, Lesmahagow Rd,
tel. (0357) 21267

SUDBURY, Suffolk
▶▶▶ **Willowmere Caravan Park**, Bures Rd,
tel. (0787) 75559

SUTTON, Kent
▶▶▶ **Sutton Vale Caravan Park**,
tel. Deal (0304) 374155

SWAINBY, N. Yorks
▶ **Blacksmith's Arms**,
tel. Stokesley (0642) 700303

SWANAGE, Dorset
▶▶▶ **Ulwell Cottage Caravan Park**, Ulwell
Cottage, Ulwell (1½m N on Studland Rd),
tel. (0929) 422823

SWARLAND, Northumb
▽ **Swarland Wood Caravan Site**,
tel. Rothbury (0669) 20569

SWAY, Hants
▽ **Setthorns** (2m NW towards Burley),
tel. Lyndhurst (042128) 3771 (Forestry Commission
Office) and 2269 (Tourist Information Centre)

TAIN, Highland
▶▶▶ **Meikle Ferry Caravan & Camping Park**,
tel. (0862) 2292

TALGARTH, Powys
▶▶▶▶ **Riverside International Caravan &
Camping Park**, tel. (0874) 711320

TALSARNAU, Gwynedd
▶ **Barcdy Touring Caravan & Camping Site**,
tel. Penrhyndeudraeth (0766) 770736
▽ **Llechollwyn**, Ynys, tel. Harlech (0766) 780414

TAL-Y-BONT, nr Barmouth, Gwynedd
▶▶▶ **Islaw R'ffordd Caravan Site**,
tel. Dyffryn (03417) 269
▶ **Tynterfyn Touring Caravan Park**,
tel. Dolgarrog (049269) 525

TALYLLYN, Gwynedd
▽ **Tyn-y-Maes**, tel. Corris (065473) 288

TARLAND, Grampian
▶▶▶ **Drummie Hill Caravan Park**,
tel. (033981) 388

TAUNTON, Somerset
▶▶▶ **St Quintin Hotel Caravan & Camping
Park**, Bridgwater Rd, Bathpool, tel. (0823) 73016

TAVISTOCK, Devon
▶▶▶ **Harford Bridge Holiday Park**,
tel. Mary Tavy (082281) 349
▶▶▶ **Higher Longford Farm Caravan Site**,
tel. (0822) 3360
▶ **Langstone Manor Country Club & Caravan
Park**, Moortown, tel. (0822) 3371

TAYINLOAN, Strathclyde
▶▶▶ **Point Sands Caravan Park**, Point Sands,
tel. (05834) 263

TAYPORT, Fife
▶▶ **East Common Caravan Park**,
tel. (0382) 552334

TEBAY, Cumbria
▶▶▶ **Tebay Caravan Park**, Orton,
tel. Orton (05874) 351 and 482

TEIGNRACE, Devon
▶ **Compass Caravans Touring Park**, Higher
Brocks Plantation, tel. Bovey Tracey (0626) 832792

TENBY, Dyfed
▶▶▶▶▶ **Kiln Park Caravan Park**, Kiln Park,
Marsh Rd, tel. (0834) 4121
▶▶▶▶ **Rowston Caravan & Tent Park**, New
Hedges, tel. (0834) 2198 and 4880
▶▶▶ **New Minerton Leisure Park**, Devonshire
Dr, St Florence, tel. Carew (06467) 461
▶▶▶ **Well Park Caravan Camping Site**, New
Hedges, tel. (0834) 2179
▶▶ **Wood Park Caravans**, New Hedges,
tel. (0834) 3414
▶▶ **Lodge Farm Caravan Site**, New Hedges,
tel. (0834) 2468

THETFORD, Norfolk
▽ **Thorpe Woodlands Campsite**, Shadwell,
tel. (0842) 61248

THIRSK, N Yorks
▶▶ **Thirsk (TRAX) Caravan Club Site**, Thirsk
Racecourse, tel. (0845) 25266

THORNESS BAY, Isle of Wight
▶▶▶ **Thorness Bay Holiday Village**,
tel. (0983) 523109

THORNTON CLEVELEYS, Lancs
▶▶▶▶ **Kneps Farm**, River Rd,
tel. Cleveleys (0253) 823632

THORPE CULVERT, Lincs
►►► **Swan Lake Leisure Caravan Park**,
Culvert Rd, tel. Skegness (0754) 880469

THRAPSTON, Northants
► **Mill Marina Caravan & Boat Park**,
tel. (08012) 2850

THREE BURROWS, Cornwall
►►► **Hillview Tourist Park**,
tel. Truro (0872) 560315

THREE OAKS, E Sussex
►►► **Old Coghurst Farm Caravan &
Camping Park**, Rock Lane,
tel. Hastings (0424) 753622

THRESHFIELD, N Yorks
►►► **Long Ashes Caravan Park**,
tel. Grassington (0756) 752261
►► **Wood Nook Caravan Park**, Skirethorns,
tel. Grassington (0756) 752412

THURSO, Highland
►► **Thurso Burgh Caravan Site**, Scrabster Rd

TILSHEAD, Wilts
►► **Brades Acre**, The Bungalow,
tel. Shrewton (0980) 620402

TINTAGEL, Cornwall
► **Headland Caravan & Camping Site**,
tel. Camelford (0840) 770239

TIPTREE, Essex
▽ **Villa Farm**, West End Rd,
tel. Maldon (0621) 815217

TORRINGTON, GT, Devon
►►► **Greenways Valley Holiday Park**,
tel. (0805) 22153

TORVER, Cumbria
▽ **Hoathwaite Farm**,
tel. Coniston (0966) 41349

TOWYN, nr Abergele, Clwyd
►►►► **Ty Mawr Holiday Park**, Towyn Rd,
tel. Rhyl (0745) 822079

TREFRIW, Gwynedd
►► **Plas Meirion Caravan Park**, Gower Rd,
tel. Llanrwst (0492) 640247

TREGURRIAN, Cornwall
► **Camping & Caravanning Club Site**,
tel. St Mawgan (0637) 860448

TRENTHAM, Staffs
►►►► **Tretham Gardens Caravan & Leisure
Park**, Trentham Estate,
tel. Stoke-on-Trent (0782) 657341

TRESAITH, Dyfed
►► **Gwalia Falls Caravan Park**,
tel. Aberporth (0239) 810361

TRIMINGHAM, Norfolk
►►► **Woodlands Caravan Park**,
tel. Southrepps (026379) 301

TROUTBECK, nr Penrith, Cumbria
►►► **Troutbeck Head Caravan Park**,
Troutbeck Head,
tel. Greystoke (08533) 521 and 375
► **Hutton Moor End**, tel. Threlkeld (059683)

TRURO, Cornwall
►►►► **Leverton Place**, Greenbottom,
Chacewater, tel. (0872) 560462
►► **Carnon Downs Caravan & Camping Park**,
Carnon Downs (3m off A39),
tel. Truro (0872) 862283
► **Summer Valley**, Allet, Shortlanesend,
tel. (0872) 77877

TUMMEL BRIDGE, Tayside
►►► **Tummel Valley Holiday Park**,
tel. (08824) 221

TURRIFF, Grampian
►► **Turriff Caravan Site**,
tel. Banff (02612) 2521 ext 304
► **Kinnaird House**, Banff Rd,
tel. (0888) 62550

TUSHIELAW, Borders
► **Honey Cottage Caravan Site**, Ettrick Valley,
tel. Ettrick Valley (0750) 62246

TUXFORD, Notts
►► **Greenacres**, Lincoln Rd,
tel. (0777) 870264

TYN-Y-GROES, Gwynedd
▽ **Garthmor**, tel. (049267) 570

UGTHORPE, N Yorks
►►► **Burnt House Caravan Park**,
tel. Whitby (0947) 840448

ULLAPOOL, Highland
►► **Broomfield Holiday Park**, West Shore St,
tel. (0854) 2020 and 2664

ULLESKELF, N Yorks
►► **White Cote Caravan Park**, Ryther Rd,
tel. Tadcaster (0937) 835231

ULVERSTON, Cumbria
►► **Bardsea Leisure Park**, Priory Rd,
tel. (0229) 54712

UMBERLEIGH, Devon
►► **Overweir Caravan & Camping Park**,
Overweir,
tel. High Bickington (0769) 60387

UPLYME, Devon
►►► **Hook Farm Camping & Caravan Park**,
tel. Lyme Regis (02974) 2801

UPPER ELKSTONE, Staffs
▽ **Mount Pleasant Farm**,
tel. Blackshaw (053834) 380

UTTOXETER, Staffs
►► **Uttoxeter (TRAX) Caravan Club Site**,
Uttoxeter Racecourse, tel. (08893) 2561

VERYAN, Cornwall
►►► **Tretheake Manor Tourist Site**,
tel. Truro (0872) 50213

WADEBRIDGE, Cornwall
►►► **Little Bodieve Holiday Park**,
tel. (020881) 2323

WALDRINGFIELD, Suffolk
►►► **Moon & Sixpence**, tel. (047336) 650

WALL, Cornwall
►►► **Parbola Caravan Park**,
tel. Praze (0209) 831503

WALLINGFORD, Oxon
►► **Riverside Caravan & Camping Site**. Apply
to: South Oxfordshire District Council, PO Box 21,
Council Offices, Crowmarsh, Wallingford, Oxon
OX10 8HQ, tel. (0491) 35351 ext 3640

WARDEN POINT, Kent
► **Warden Spring Caravan Park**,
tel. Eastchurch (079588) 216

WAREHAM, Dorset
►►► **Hunter's Moon Caravan & Camping
Site**, Cold Harbour, tel. (09295) 6605
►►► **Lookout Park**, Corfe Rd, Stoborough,
tel. (09295) 2546
►►► **Manor Farm Caravan Park**,
Manor Farm Cottage, East Stoke,
tel. Bindon Abbey (0929) 462870

WARWASH, Hants
►► **Dibles Park**, Dibles Rd. Apply to:
Fareham Borough Council, Civic Offices,
PO Box 18, High Street, Fareham, Hants PO16 7PS,
tel. Locks Heath (04895) 5232

WARSILL, N Yorks
►►► **Warren House Caravan Site**,
tel. Sawley (076586) 683

WARWICK, Warwicks
►►► **Warwick (TRAX) Caravan Club Site**,
Warwick Racecourse, tel. (0926) 495448

WATCHET, Somerset
►►►► **Doniford Holiday Village**,
tel. Williton (0984) 32423 and for advance
bookings, tel. St Austell (0726) 65551
►►► **Warren Bay Caravan Park**,
tel. (0984) 31460
► **Sunny Bank Caravan Park**, Doniford,
tel. Williton (0984) 32237

WATERBECK, Dumfries & Galloway
►► **Fallford Lodge Caravan Site**,
tel. (04616) 275

WATERGATE BAY, Cornwall
►►► **Watergate Bay Tourist Park**, Tregurrian,
tel. St Mawgan (0637) 860387

WATERLOO CROSS, Devon
►► **Old Well Caravan Park**, Old Well
Roadhouse (junc A38/B3181 ½m E of M5 junc 27),
tel. Craddock (0884) 40873

WATERMILLOCK, Cumbria
►►► **Quiet Site**, tel. Pooley Bridge (08536) 337
►►► **Ullswater Caravan & Camping Park**,
tel. Pooley Bridge (08536) 666
►► **Cove Caravan & Camping Park**,
tel. Pooley Bridge (08536) 549

WEELEY, Essex
►►► **Weeley Bridge Caravan Park**,
tel. (0255) 830403

WEETON, Lancs
► **High Moor Farm Caravan Park**,
tel. (039136) 273

WELLS, Somerset
►►► **Homestead Caravan & Camping Park**,
Wookey Hole, tel. (0749) 73022

WEM, Salop
►►► **Lower Lacon Caravan Park**,
tel. (0939) 32376

WENTNOR, Salop
►► **Green Camping & Caravanning Site**,
The Green, tel. Linley (058861) 605

WEST COKER, Somerset
►► **Partway Lane Caravan Park**,
tel. (093586) 2863

WEST DRAYTON, Gt London
► **Riverside Caravans**, Thorney Mill Rd,
tel. (0895) 446520

WESTENHANGER, Kent
►► **Folkestone (TRAX) Caravan Club Site**,
tel. Folkestone (0303) 68449

WESTHAM, E Sussex
►►► **Fairfields Farm Caravan & Camping
Site**, Eastbourne Rd, tel. (0326) 763165

WESTON-SUPER-MARE, Avon
►►► **Country View Caravan Park**, Sand Rd,
Sand Bay, tel. (0934) 27595
►►► **West End Farm Touring Park**, Locking
(3m E off A371), tel. Banwell (0934) 822529
►►► **Weston Gateway Caravan Site**, West
Wick, tel. (0934) 510344
►► **Manor Farm Caravan Park**, Grange Rd,
Uphill, tel. (0934) 29731
► **Ardnave Caravan & Chalet Park**, Crooks
Lane, Kewstoke, tel. (0934) 22319

WESTWARD, Cumbria
►►► **Clea Hall Holiday Park**,
tel. Wigton (0965) 42880

WEST WITTERING, W Sussex
►► **Wicks Farm Caravan Park**, Redlands Ln,
tel. Birdham (0243) 513116

WETHERBY, W Yorks
►► **Wetherby (TRAX) Caravan Club Site**,
Wetherby Racecourse,
tel. (0937) 61618

WEYBOURNE, Norfolk
► **Kelling Heath Caravan Park**,
tel. (026370) 224

WEYMOUTH, Dorset
**See also Fleet, Dorset and Chickerell for
details of other sites in the vicinity.**
►► **Littlesea Holiday Park**, Lynch Lane,
tel. (0305) 74414 and for advance bookings
Hemel Hempstead (0442) 51244

WHALEY BRIDGE, Derbys
►► **Peaks Caravan Park**, Tunstead Milton,
tel. Wolverhampton (0902) 790630
►► **Ringstones Caravan Park**, Yeardsley Lane,
Furness Vale,
tel. (06633) 2152

WHATSTANDWELL, Derbys
►►► **Haytop Farm Caravanserai**,
tel. Ambergate (077385) 2154 and 2063
► **Mere Brooke Caravan & Camping Park**,
tel. Ambergate (077385) 2154 and 3100

WHIDDON DOWN, Devon
►►► **Dartmoor View Caravan & Camping
Park**, tel. (064723) 545

WHITBY, N Yorks
►►► **Whitby Holiday Village**, Saltwick Bay,
tel. (0947) 602664

WHITECLIFF BAY, Isle of Wight
►►►► **Whitecliff Bay Holiday Park**,
tel. (0983) 872671

WHITECROSS, Cornwall
►►► **Three Acres Holiday Park**,
tel. St Austell (0726) 860220

WHITLEY BAY, Tyne & Wear
►►► **Whitley Bay Holiday Centre Caravan
Site**, tel. Tyneside (091) 2531214

WHITSTABLE, Kent
►►► **Blue Waters Touring Harbour**,
St John's Rd

WHITSTONE, Cornwall
►►► **Keywood Caravan Park**, tel. Week St
Mary (028884) 338 and Plymouth (0752) 772285

WIDEMOUTH BAY, Cornwall
► **Widemouth Bay Caravan Park**,
tel. (028885) 208

WIGHT, ISLE OF
**Details of places with AA-classified caravan
and campsites will be found under individual
place-names**

WILLINGHAM, Cambs
►► **Roseberry Tourist Park**, Earith Rd,
tel. Swavesey (0954) 30754
► **Alwyn Camping & Caravan Site**, Over Rd,
tel. (0954) 60977

WIMBORNE MINSTER, Dorset
►►►► **Merley Court Touring Park**, Merley
(1m S A349), tel. (0202) 881488
►►► **Wilksworth Farm Caravan Park**,
Cranborne Rd,
tel. Wimborne (0202) 883769 or 886467
►► **Charris Caravan Park**, Candy's Ln, Corfe
Mullen (2m W off A31), tel. (0202) 885970

WINCANTON, Somerset
►► **Wincanton Racecourse (TRAX) Caravan
Club Site**

Windermere, Cumbria

WINCHESTER, Hants
►► **Morn Hill Caravan Site**, Morn Hill,
tel. (0962) 69877
►► **Winchester Recreation Centre**, Gordon
Rd, tel. (0962) 69525

WINDERMERE, Cumbria
►►►► **White Cross Bay Caravan Park**,
Troutbeck Bridge, tel. (09662) 3937
►►► **Park Cliffe Farm Caravan & Camping
Site**, Tower Wood,
tel. Newby Bridge (0448) 31344
►► **Braithwaite Fold Caravan Club Site**,
Glebe Rd, tel. (09662) 2177

WINKFIELD, Berks
► **Sunnybend Farm Caravan Park**, Parkers Lane,
Maidens Gdns,
tel. Winkfield Row (0344) 882846

WINKSLEY, N Yorks
►►► **Woodhouse Farm Caravan & Camping
Park**, tel. Kirkby Malzeard (076583) 309

WINSTON, Co Durham
►►► **Winston Caravan Park**,
tel. Darlington (0325) 730228

WOLVEY, Warwicks
►►► **Wolvey Villa Farm Caravan & Camping
Site**, tel. Hinckley (0455) 220493 and 220630

WOODBURY, Devon
►►► **Castle Brake Caravan Park**, Castle Ln,
tel. (0395) 32431
►► **Webbers Farm Caravan & Camping Site**,
Webbers Farm, Castle Ln, tel. (0395) 32276

WOODHALL SPA, Lincs
►►►► **Bainland Park**, Horncastle Rd,
tel. (0526) 52903

WOOL, Dorset
►►► **Whitemead Caravan Park**, East Burton
Rd, tel. Bindon Abbey (0929) 462241

WOOLACOMBE, Devon
►►►►► **Golden Coast Holiday Village**,
Station Rd, tel. (0271) 870343

WOOLER, Northumb
►►► **Bridge End Caravan Site**, Bridge End,
tel. (0668) 81447

WORKINGTON, Cumbria
►► **Oldside Caravan Club Site**, tel. (0900) 2125

WORSBROUGH, S Yorks
► **Greensprings Holiday Park**, Rockley Lane,
tel. Barnsley (0226) 288298

WORTWELL, Norfolk
► **Little Lakeland Caravan Park**,
tel. Homersfield (098686) 646
► **Lone Pine Camping Site**, Low Rd,
tel. Homersfield (098686) 596 and
Harleston (0379) 852423

WOTTON-UNDER-EDGE, Glos
►►► **Cotswold Gate Caravan Park**,
tel. Dursley (0453) 843128

WROXALL, Isle of Wight
►►►► **Appuldurcombe Gardens Caravan &
Camping Park**, Appuldurcombe Rd,
tel. (0983) 852597

WYCLIFFE, nr Barnard Castle, Co Durham
►► **Thorpe Hall** (off unclass rd between
Whorlton and A66 Greta Bridge), tel. Teesdale
(0833) 27230

WYKEHAM, N Yorks
►►►► **St Helens Caravan Park**,
tel. Scarborough (0723) 862771

WYTHALL, W Midlands
►► **Caravan Club Site**, Chapel Ln,
tel. (0564) 826483

YARMOUTH, GT, Norfolk
►►►► **Vauxhall Holiday Park**,
tel. (0493) 857231

YETHOLM, Borders
►► **Kirkfield Caravan & Camping Site**,
tel. (057382) 346

YNYS, Gwynedd
▽ **Ynys Grainog**, tel. Criccieth (076671) 234

YORK, N Yorks
►►►► **Rawcliffe Manor Caravan Site**, Manor
Ln, Shipton Rd, tel. (0904) 24422

Camping and Caravanning Sites – Northern Ireland

Co Antrim
BALLYCASTLE
►► **Moyle View Caravan Park**,
tel. Ballycastle 62550

CUSHENDALL
►► **Cushendall Caravan Camp**. Apply to:
Moyle District Council, 61 Castle St, Ballycastle,
Co Antrim, tel. Cushendall 333

CUSHENDUN
►►► **Cushendun Caravan Park**, 14 Glendun
Rd, tel. Cushendun 254

LARNE
►►► **Curran Caravan Park**, 131 Curran Rd,
tel. Larne 3797

PORTBALLINTRAE
►► **Ballintrae Holiday Caravan Camp**,
tel. Bushmills 31478

PORTRUSH
►► **Golf Links Caravan Park**, Bushmills Rd,
tel. Portrush 82288

Co Down
CASTLEWELLAN
►►► **Castlewellan Forest Park**. Apply to:
Ministry of Agriculture, Forest Division,
Castlewellan, tel. Castlewellan 664

CLOUGHEY
►► **Silver Bay Caravan Park**, Ballyspurge,
tel. Portavogie 71321

KILKEEL
►► **Leestone Caravan Park**, Leestone Rd,
tel. Kilkeel 62567

MILLISLE
►► **Seaview Caravan Park**, Ballycopeland, tel. Millisle 861248

NEWCASTLE
►► **Newcastle Caravan Trailer Park**, Tullybrannigan Rd, tel. Newcastle 22351
►►► **Tollymore Forest Park**, tel. Newcastle 22428

Co Fermanagh
CASTLE ARCHDALE
►► **Castle Archdale Caravan Park**, tel. Irvinestown 333

Co Londonderry
BALLYREAGH
►►►► **Carrick-Dhu Caravan Park**, 12 Ballyreagh Rd, tel. Portrush 823712

CASTLEROCK
►►► **Castlerock Caravan Park**, tel. Castlerock 848381

Picnic Sites

All AA-listed Picnic Sites have been visited by an AA inspector and recommended as worthy of listing because they are sufficiently attractive and/or provide useful "park and walk" access to the countryside. A Transit Picnic Site may, though well equipped, be utilitarian in character but will be suitable for breaking long journeys for rest and refreshment.

England
AVON
Tog Hill *(A420)*
8m E of Bristol, ½m E of junction with A46
Chew Valley Lake *(off B3114)*
8m S of Bristol centre on NE side of lake, on unclass rd from B3114

BEDFORDSHIRE
In Stockgrove Country Park *(off A418)*
On unclass rd, ½m W of A418, 3m NW of Leighton Buzzard
Brogborough Hill *(A5140)*
On W side of A5140, 3½m NE of Woburn Sands. Hilltop site
Totternhoe Knolls *(B489)*
2m W of Dunstable, on E side of unclass rd off B489. Signposted in advance and at entrance. In village of Totternhoe
Whipsnade Heath and Green *(off B4540)*
Off B4540 adjacent to Whipsnade Zoo. Open grass area. 10 acres. Extensive parking. Toilets
Dunstable Downs *(B4541)*
W side of B4541, 2m SW of Dunstable. Signposted in advance and at entrance. Overlooking the Vale of Aylesbury

BERKSHIRE
Childe Beale Trust *(A329)*
2m NW of Pangbourne on A329
Bracknell/Bagshot rd Transit Picnic Site *(A332)*
½m S of Hartford on S side of A556
Alexandra Gardens *(off A332 in Windsor)*
Access via car park in River St or Barry Avenue on S side of Thames
Marlow–Bisham Bypass (East) *(A404)*
On E side of Marlow–Bisham Bypass, 2¾m S of Marlow

Winter Hill, nr Marlow *(off A404)*
First turn left on S side of Marlow Bridge. After approx 2m on unclass Marlow/Cookham rd, fork left

BUCKINGHAMSHIRE
Burnham Beeches *(off A355)*
On unclass rd. ¼m W of A355 at Farnham Common
Chilterns Picnic Place (Hodgemoor Wood) *(off A355)*
¼m E of A355 via Bottrells Lane; Amersham, Beaconsfield 3m
Wendover Forest *(off A4011)*
SE of A4011 on unclass rd, signposted St Leonards, 2m NE of Wendover, 3m SW of Tring

CAMBRIDGESHIRE
Grafham Water (Three Picnic Sites) *(off A1)*
On B661 3½m from Buckden. ¾m along unclass rd to Grafham off B661 2m from Buckden
Brandon Creek *(A10)*
2¼m N of Littleport Bridge on A10
Eaton Ford Picnic Area *(A45)*
Western outskirts of St Neots
Wansford *(off A47)*
Uppingham–Peterborough rd near A1 junction
Huntingdon *(A141)*
SE side Huntingdon ring rd
Houghton Mill *(A1123)*
1¼m out of Wyton towards Houghton, in Mill St

CHESHIRE
Teggs Nose *(off A537)*
2m E of Macclesfield, N of Langley
Hartford Transit Picnic Site *(A556)*
½m S of Hartford on S side of A556
Lostock Transit Picnic Site *(A556)*
½m W of Lostock Green on N side A556
Hapsford Transit Picnic Site *(A5117)*
Near junction with M56
Delamere Forest *(off B5152)*
1m N of Delamere off B5152
Parkgate (Parkgate Village)
On edge of village

CORNWALL
Mitchell *(A30)*
½m E of junction with A3076
Tregadillet Transit Picnic Site *(A30)*
2m W of Launceston on A30
Treliever *(A394)*
1¼m W of Penryn
Trebarwith Strand *(off B3263)*
W of B3263 on outskirts of Trebarwith Strand

CUMBRIA
Edmond Castle Transit Picnic Site *(off A69)*
Mid-way between Carlisle and Brampton
Brockhole *(A591)*
2¼m N of Windermere, 2¼m S of Ambleside. ½ acre. Parking 20
Waterhead Transit Picnic Site *(A5075/A591)*
½m SE of Ambleside
Aira Force *(A5091/A592)*
6m SW of Pooley Bridge
Stock Lane Transit Picnic Site *(B5287)*
300yd Grasmere village
Whinlatter *(B5292)*
1m from Braithwaite
Allonby and Beckfoot *(B5300)*
On B5300, on the coast, within the parish of Allonby
Greenwood Picnic Area
1m S of Greenwood

DERBYSHIRE
White Lodge *(A6)*
On W side of A6, 4m W of Bakewell
Alsop en le Dale Station *(A515)*
On Ashbourn–Buxton rd 5½m N of Ashbourne

Hurdlow *(off A515)*
¼m W of A515, Monyash–Longnor rd
Parsley Hay *(off A515)*
200yd on W side of A515 8¼m S of Buxton
Tissington *(off A515)*
SE corner of Tissington village ½m E of A515
Ashover (Eddlestow) *(off A632)*
Off A632 (SP Uppertown) 2½m NE of Matlock
Staunton Harrold Reservoir *(off B587)*
1m SW of Melbourne. Turn W off B587 along Calke
Lane
Middleton Top *(off B5023)*
S of Rise End, W of B5023 via unclass rd under old
railway bridge. 1m NW of Wirksworth
Black Rocks *(off B5036)*
E of B5036, 7½m S of Cromford
Hartington *(off B5054)*
1½m NE of Hartington
Ogston Reservoir (North) *(off B6014)*
2m SW of Clay Cross on N side of B6014, on
unclass rd at Woolley
Ogston Reservoir (West) *(off B6014)*
S side of B6014 at N end of reservoir

DEVON
Honiton Clyst *(A30)*
½m E of Honiton Clyst
Tamar Bridge Transit Picnic Site *(A38)*
At E end of bridge on A38
Trimstone Cross *(off A361)*
1m SW of Mullacott Cross
Eggesford Forest *(A377)*
1m S of Eggesford railway station
Stover *(A382)*
In Country Park 3m NW Newton Abbott on A382
near junction with A38
Morwellham *(off A390)*
In Tamar Valley 4m SW of Tavistock, 1m S of A390
Little Haldon *(B3192)*
Exeter–Teignmouth rd opposite Teignmouth Golf
Course
Bellever *(off B3212)*
¼m S of B3212 at Postbridge
Newbridge, Holne *(B3357)*
4m W of Ashburton
Fernworthy Reservoir *(unclass rd)*
Approach via unclass rds. 3¾m SW of Chagford

DORSET
Henstridge Transit Picnic Site *(off A30)*
N and S sides of A30 between Shaftesbury and
Henstridge
Thorncombe Wood *(off A35)*
½m E of Dorchester on unclass rd signposted to
Higher/Lower Bockhampton
Bulbarrow Hill *(off A354)*
6m S Sturminster Newton on unclass rd off A354
signposted from Bulbarrow crossroads
Matchams View *(A358)*
4m NE Bournemouth on E side of unclass rd
Buckham Down *(off A3066)*
2m N of Beaminster
Gallows Hill *(unclass rd)*
Adjacent to Army Training Area, from A352
Dorchester–Wareham rd on unclass rd N of wood to
Bere Regis rd approx 3m on W side
Oberton Hill *(unclass rd)*
4m S of Sturminster Newton/Blandford A357 on
unclass rd through Okeford Fitzpaine
Okeford Hill *(unclass rd)*
On unclass rd between Turnworth and Okeford
Fitzpaine
Steeple *(unclass rd)*
Off unclass rds N of Steeple village
Tyneham *(unclass rd)*
Unclass rd from E Lulworth to Steeple, signed to
Tyneham Church
White Way *(unclass rd)*
On MOD rd off rd between E Lulworth and
Povington Hill

Avon Forest Park – North Park
2m W of Ringwood
Avon Forest Park – South Park
Access via A31 and left at roundabout into
Boundary Lane

DURHAM
Middleton-One-Row *(off A67)*
5m SE of Darlington off A67
Whorlton *(off A67)*
3½m SE of Barnard Castle off A67
Collier Wood *(A68)*
½m N of junction with A689 midway between Crook
and Towlaw

ESSEX
One Tree Hill *(A13/B1420)*
2m SW of Basildon, N of A13 near junction with
B1420
Weald Park *(off A128)*
On unclass rd off A128 at Pilgrims Hatch. 2m NW of
Brentwood
Danbury Park Lake *(off A414)*
Adjoins Well Lane SW side of Danbury Bridge, off
A414

GLOUCESTERSHIRE
Robinswood Hill *(off A38)*
In Robinswood Hill Country Park 2m S of
Gloucester, enter from Reservoir Rd, off ring rd
Edge End *(A4136)*
On A4136, 2½m E of Coleford
Coaley Park Picnic Site *(off B4066)*
2½m N of Uley
Beechenhurst *(B4226)*
N side of rd. 2½m E Coleford. ½m W of Speech House
Cannop Ponds *(B4226)*
Off B4226 (S side of rd) 2m E Coleford 1m W of
Speech House
Speech House *(B4226)*
On N side of rd 3½m E of Coleford on outskirts of
Speech House village
Lambsquay *(B4228)*
1m S of Coleford

HAMPSHIRE
Danebury Ring *(off A30)*
2½m NW of Stockbridge on unclass rd
Hawley Common *(A30)*
On S side of A30, 4m SW of Camberley
Bolderwood Ornamental Drive *(A31)*
3m NW of Emery Down on the Ornamental Drive
between the A31 and A35
Stoney Cross *(A31)*
In New Forest 2m W of Cadnam off A31
Old Winchester Hill *(off A32)*
From Warnford or West Meon
Southampton Common *(A33)*
On A33 London rd, 1½m from city centre
Beacon Hill Transit Picnic Site *(A34)*
2½m N of Lichfield
The Bench *(A35)*
On A35 on E side of Lyndhurst
Rhinefield, Putter Bridge, Whitfield Moor *(A35)*
2m W of Brockenhurst on unclass rd adjacent to
A35
Portsdown *(A333)*
Nr Portsmouth
Crab Wood *(off A3090)*
2m W of Winchester on unclass rd off A3090
Abbotstone Down *(B3046)*
On the B3046 2m N of Alresford
Avington Park *(off B3047)*
1m S of Itchen Abbas next to Avington House
Mayflower Park *(Southampton)*
At Royal Pier

Wye Valley

HEREFORD AND WORCESTER
Goodrich Castle *(A40)*
Ross–Monmouth rd 3½m from Ross
Symonds Yat West Garders Restaurant *(off A40)*
6m from Ross on B4161 off A40
Symonds Yat Rock East *(off A40)*
5½m from Ross
Fish Hill *(A44)*
1m S Broadway
Bromyard Downs *(off A44)*
Between A44 and B4203 NE of Bromyard
Dinmore Hill *(A49)*
At Queens Wood on Leominster–Hereford rd
Riverside, Ross-on-Wye *(off A49)*
Ross-on-Wye
Riverside, Evesham *(A435)*
Abbey Rd, Evesham
Twyford Farm *(A435)*
2m N of Evesham
Lower Malvern Common *(A449)*
Situated N of rd entering from Worcester
Riverside, Stourport on Severn *(off A451)*
Off A451 ¼m W of Stourport town centre
Wyre Forest *(A456)*
2½m from Bewdley to Leominster
Walton Hill *(off A456)*
On unclass rd 2m SSW of Halesowen off A456
signposted Kidderminster
Clent Hills *(A491)*
On unclass rd off A491 SW of Hagley
Avoncroft Museum of Buildings Picnic Site *(off A4024)*
Just off the A4024, 2m S of Bromsgrove
Hartlebury Common *(A4025)*
Access from either A4025 or B4193
Beacon Hill *(B4096)*
Monument lane off B4096 4m NE of Bromsgrove
Hartlebury Castle *(B4193)*
Nr Hartlebury village
Castlemorton Common *(B4208)*
On B4208, Malvern–Gloucester rd, 1m S of Welland
Wyche Cutting *(B4232)*
3m SW of Great Malvern on B4243
Malvern Hills *(B4232)*
On B4232 between A449 and A4105
Old Hills *(B4424)*
1m S of Callow End on B4424
Windmill and Waseley Hills *(B4551)*
SW of Birmingham, 1m NW of Rubery
Ravenshill Nature Reserve and Picnic Site *(unclass rd)*
1m N of Alfrick

HERTFORDSHIRE
Stanborough Park *(off A6129)*
Off A6129 E of junction with A1 at Welwyn Garden City

HUMBERSIDE
Raventhorpe Farm *(A18)*
N side of junction with B1398, access for eastbound traffic

ISLE OF WIGHT
Parkhurst Forest *(A3054)*
1m W of Newport
Afton Down *(A3055)*
On A3055, ½m E of Freshwater Bay. Signposted in advance and at entrance. National Trust land overlooking Freshwater Bay. 1 acre. Parking 30
Brading Down *(A3055)*
Overlooking Sandown and Shanklin. 10 acres. Parking 100
Blackgang Viewpoint *(A3055)*
1m W of Niton
Bembridge Down *(off B3395)*
On unclass rd off B3395, 2½m W of Bembridge
Brighstone Forest *(off B3401)*
On unclass rd between Calbourne and Brighstone

KENT
Shepherds Gate Transit Picnic Site *(A2)*
At B2009 interchange, 3½m W of Rochester
Hothfield Common Transit Picnic Site *(A20)*
Both sides of A20. Ashford 4m. Charing 3¾m
Dryhill Quarry Transit Picnic Site *(off A25)*
E side of Dryhill Lane ½m S of A25 (W side A25/A21 interchange) SE of Sundridge
Groveferry, Upstreet *(off A28)*
S side of railway level crossing along Grove Ferry Rd, ½m SE of its junction with the A28
Camer Park *(off A227)*
S side of Green Lane (B2009) off A227 ¼m N of Meopham
Langdon Cliff *(off A258)*
At bend on unclass Dover–St Margaret's-at-Cliff rd, 1m E of junction with A258 at Dover Castle
Bedgebury Pinetum *(B2079)*
E side of B2079, 2m S of Goudhurst

LANCASHIRE
Spring Wood *(A671)*
½m from Whalley
Bull Beck *(A683)*
3m E of M6 junction
Condor Green *(off A588)*
On unclass rd, ¼m W of Condor Green
Scorton *(unclass rd)*
1½m N of Scorton village
Becon Fell
8m N of Preston, 3m E of M6
Witton Park
On W outskirts of Blackburn
Wycoller
SE of Colne

LEICESTERSHIRE
Burbage Common *(A47)*
Between A47 and A5070. 1m W of Hinckley
Tugby Picnic Site *(A47)*
½m SE Tugby
Bosworth Park *(B585)*
On B585 ½m from centre of Market Bosworth
Beacon Hill *(B591)*
1¼m W of Woodhouse Eaves, N side of B591
Broombrigs Farm *(B591)*
Beacon Rd W of Woodhouse Eaves
Nanpantan Outwood *(off B591)*
Turn off B591 on to unclass Woodhouse Eaves–Nanpantan rd. 1½m from Woodhouse Eaves
Bradgate Park and Swithland Woods *(B5327)*
7m NW of Leicester, on B5327 at Newton Linford
Borough Hill *(unclass rd)*
Bosworth Battlefield *(unclass rd)*
2m S of Market Bosworth, between Sutton Cheney and Shenton
Foxton Locks *(unclass rd)*
3m NW of Market Harborough

Rutland Water sites:
Barnsdale *(off A606)*
3m E of Oakham
Normanton *(off A606 and A6003)*
¼m NE of Edith Weston
Sykes Lane *(off A606)*
½m W of Empingham
Whitwell *(off A606)*
1½m W of Empingham

LINCOLNSHIRE
Cater Plot Transit Picnic Site *(A17)*
1¾m E of Heckington, S side of A17
Chapel Point *(off A52)*
1m N of Chapel St Leonards
Huttoft Bank *(A52)*
E of A52, 3m S of Sutton-on-Sea
Hubbard's Hill *(off A153)*
¼m W of A153, 1½m SW Louth
Tattershall *(A153)*
On NW side of A153 ¾m SW of Tattershall
North Reston *(A157)*
W side of A157, 1m SE of Legbourne
Woodhall Spa *(off B1191)*
½m from centre of Woodhall Spa off Stixwould rd

LONDON (GR)
Richmond Park *(A3/A308)*
Farthing Downs *(A23/B2030)*
Adjacent to unclass Coulsdon–Chaldon rd, 1½m S of
junction of A23/B2030
Trent Park *(off A111)*
½m N of Cockfosters, 3m S of Potters Bar
Addington Park *(A212/B268)*
½m W of Addington village
North Cray Transit Picnic Site *(A223)*
A223 North Cray rd. 1m N of Ruxley Corner (A20).
1½m S of Bexley
Bushy Park *(off A308)*
½m W of Kingston upon Thames
Hainault Forest *(A1112)*
E and SE of Chigwell Row
Mad Bess Wood *(B455)*
Adjacent to Ruislip–Northwood rd, 1½m N of Ruislip
Bayhurst Wood *(off B455)*
On unclass Harefield–Ruislip rd, off B455
Coulsdon Common *(B2030)*
1½m NW of Caterham, on North Downs approx 600ft
above sea level

MERSEYSIDE
Eastham Woods *(off A41)*
Off A41 at Eastham
Thursastan *(unclass rd)*
At Thursastan railway station
Croxteth Park
6m NE of Liverpool
The Wirral
Between West Kirby and Parkgate, near Dee estuary

MIDLANDS (WEST)
Sandwell Valley *(off A41)*
Park Lane (between A41 and A4041) West
Bromwich 1¾m ENE opposite football ground
Sutton Park *(A453)*
1m from centre of Sutton Coldfield
Shenstone Woods *(A458)*
½m NE of Halesowen
Recreation Park, Lickey Hills *(B4096)*
1½m NE of Bromsgrove, NW side B4096
Cofton Common *(B4096)*
Lowhill Lane, Rednal, 3m NE of Bromsgrove
Warren Lane, Lickey Hills *(B4096)*
1½m NE of Bromsgrove on E side of B4096

NORFOLK
Lynford *(A134)*
1m SE of Mundford
Grimes Graves *(A134)*
On the Thetford–Mundford rd, 6m from Thetford

Two Mile Bottom *(A134)*
3m NW of Thetford
Life Woods *(A149)*
On A149 1m S of Ingoldisthorpe
Emily's Wood *(A1065)*
On the Mundford–Brandon rd, 2m S of Mundford
Bridgham Lane *(off A1066)*
On unclass rd 6m E of Thetford
Hockham *(A1075)*
1m W of Great Hockham
Hole Lanes *(B1149)*
S of Holt
Sandringham Woods *(B1440)*
Opposite main gates of the Royal Fruit Farm
overlooking the gates of Sandringham House
Punchbowl *(unclass rd)*
3½m N of Thetford on unclass rd (1m N of Croxton)

NORTHAMPTONSHIRE
Wakerley Great Wood *(off A43)*
Unclass rd off A43, 2½m SW of Duddington
Harlestone Heath *(A428)*
1m SE of Harlestone, A428 Northampton–Rugby rd
Pitsford Reservoir *(off A508)*
On unclass rd, ½m E of A508, 5½m N of Northampton
Barnwell *(A605)*
½m S of Oundle, W side of A605
Salcey Forest *(off B526)*
On unclass Quinton–Hartwell rd, off B526 1m from
Hartwell

NORTHUMBERLAND
Breamish Valley *(A697)*
8½m S of Wooler, following signs to Ingram
Blanchland *(B6306)*
In the village
Brocolita *(B6318)*
3m NW of Chollerford
Housesteads *(B6318)*
9m E of Greenhead
Twice Brewed Car Park Transit Picnic Site
(B6318)
11m W of Chollerford
Winshields Crag *(B6318)*
5m E of Greenhead

NOTTINGHAMSHIRE
Newstead Abbey Gardens *(A60)*
4½m S of Mansfield and W of A60
Major Oak, Sherwood Forest *(off A614)*
N of Edwinstowe
Clumber Park *(A6005)*
5m SE of Worksop. Access off A6005 Worksop–
Ollerton rd

OXFORDSHIRE
Cowleaze Wood *(off A40)*
On unclass rd at Christmas Common off A40, 2m W
of Stokenchurch, 4m SE of Watlington
Oxford Transit Picnic Site *(A40)*
1½m SE of ring road
Windrush Valley Park *(A40/A4047)*
3m from Burford near Asthall
Abbey Meadow *(off A415)*
Adjacent to Abingdon town centre
Sinodun Hills (Wittenham Clumps)
(off A4130)
On unclass rd between Brightwell and Little
Wittenham, 4m NW of Wallingford
White Horse Hill, nr Uffington *(off B4507)*
Off B4507 3m E of Ashbury

SHROPSHIRE
Ercall Wood *(off A5)*
1m SSW of Wellington off unclass rd from Haygate
on A5 to Shrewsbury
Whitlington Castle *(A5)*
Just N of Whitlington
Brown Moss *(off A41)*
1½m SE of Whitchurch
Corbett Wood *(off A49)*
3m S of Wem

Long Mynd *(off A49)*
Unclass rd 2m from Church Stretton
Whitcliffe Common *(off A49)*
On unclass rd off A49, 2m W of Ludlow
Severn Park, Bridgnorth *(A442)*
Edge of Bridgnorth Low Town, alongside A442
Bridgnorth–Telford rd
The Mere, Ellesmere *(A495)*
On A495 SE of town, ½m from town centre
Colemere *(off A528)*
Off A528 to Colemere village then follow sign to
Lyneal for ½m
Swimming Pool, Market Drayton *(off A529)*
Off A529 to Hinstock approx 400yd from town
centre
Cardingmill Valley *(off B4370)*
On edge of Church Stretton village
Old Racecourse, Oswestry *(B4580)*
2m NW of Oswestry on B4580
Antique Centre (Iron Bridge) *(B4830)*
On outskirts of Ironbridge

SOMERSET
Brent Knoll (East & West) Transit Picnic Site
(M5)
North and southbound carriageways 2m N of
junction 22, 5m S of junction 21, 25m S of Bristol
County Gate Transit Picnic Site *(A39)*
7m W of Porlock 4½m E of Lynton
Pittcombe Head *(off A39)*
3¼m W of Porlock
Chatworthy Reservoir *(unclass rd)*
½m W of Chatworthy village

STAFFORDSHIRE
Froghall *(off A52)*
On edge of Froghall village
Highgate Common *(off A458)*
Off unclass rds and adjacent to Enville golf course,
2m N of Enville
Cannock Chase *(A513/A34)*
4m ESE of Stafford at Millford village adjacent to
common
Hanchurch Hills *(off A519)*
3m S of Newcastle-under-Lyme
Churnet Picnic Area *(B5417)*
Cheadle Rd, Oakamoor 3m E of Cheadle
The Bratch *(unclass rd)*
1m NW of Wombourne
Central Forest Park
In centre of Stoke-on-Trent

SUFFOLK
Haughley *(A45)*
4m NW of Stowmarket
Mildenhall Woods Transit Picnic Site
(A1065/A11)
Barton Mills roundabout E side of A1065 ¾m N
Barton Mills
Knettishall Heath *(off A1088)*
On unclass rd from Euston, 3m from Hopton
Rampart Field *(off A1101)*
1m S of Icklingham on unclass rd to West Stow
The King's Picnic Place *(B1106)*
E side of B1106, 7m N of Bury St Edmunds

SURREY
Gibbet Hill, Devil's Punch Bowl *(A3)*
½m N of junction with A287 at Hindhead
Tilburstow Hill Viewpoint *(off A22)*
1½m S of Godstone
Box Hill *(off A24)*
On unclass rd 1m NE of Dorking, 1m E of A24
Leith Hill *(off A25)*
5m SW of Dorking on unclass rd off A25
Newlands Corner *(A25)*
On A25 at its junction with A247 3m E of Gomshall
Ranmore Common *(off A25)*
Unclass rd off A25, 2m NW of Dorking
Virginia Water *(A30)*
On A30, 2m NE of Sunningdale

Puttenham Common *(A31)*
1½ SW of Puttenham
Frensham Common *(A287)*
4m S of Farnham
Epsom Downs *(B290)*
1½m SE of Epsom

SUSSEX (EAST)
Broadstone (Ashdown Forest) *(A22/A275)*
N side of unclass Wych Cross–Coleman's Hatch rd,
1m E of Wych Cross
Hindleap (Ashdown Forest) *(A22/A275)*
S side of unclass Sharpthorne–Wych Cross rd, 1m W
of Wych Cross
Vine Hall Forest Trail *(B2089)*
S side of B2089 between A21 and A229, 3m SE of
Robertsbridge
Piltdown Pond *(B2102)*
4m from Uckfield via A22 and B2102
Beachy Head *(off B2103)*
3m SW of Eastbourne
Ditchling Beacon *(off B2112)*
On unclass rd between Brighton (6m) and Ditchling
(2m)

SUSSEX (WEST)
Devil's Dyke *(A23/A281)*
5½m NW of Brighton
Fairmile Bottom Transit Picnic Site *(A29)*
½m NE Whiteways Lodge. NW of Arundel
Whiteways Lodge *(A29)*
A29 at its junction with A284 3m N of Arundel
Cowdray Hill (Benbow Pond) *(A272)*
Situated N side of A272 at east end of Cowdray
Park, Midhurst 2m, Petworth 4¾m
Duncton Hill *(A285)*
1m S of Duncton
Marden Forest *(off B2146)*
On unclass rd 1m NE of Stoughton

WARWICKSHIRE
Burton Hills *(off A41)*
1m from A41 near Avon Dassett, approx 8m N of
Banbury
Burton Dassert *(off A41)*
9¾m N of Banbury
Yarningdale Common *(B4095)*
½m NW of Claverdon unclass rd off B4095 5m W
Warwick

WILTSHIRE
Postern Hill (Savernake Forest) *(off A4)*
1m S of Marlborough
Pepperbox Hill *(A36)*
On NE side of A36 5m SE of Salisbury, ¾m NW of
AA Box. Rough single track approach
Steeple Langford *(A36)*
8m N of Salisbury
Hat Gate *(A338)*
3m SE Marlborough
Inglesham/Lechlade *(off A361)*
½m S of Lechlade off A361 on W side adjoining
Lechlade bridge
Kingston Langley Transit Picnic Sites, East and
West *(A429)*
2m N of Chippenham
King Alfred's Tower *(off B3092)*
2½m NW of Stourton 2½m SW of Kilmington on
unclass rd off B3092

YORKSHIRE (NORTH)
Sheep Wash *(off A19)*
On unclass rd, signposted Osmotherley and
Swainby, off A19 11m N of Thirsk
Staxton Hill *(A64)*
1m from junction ½m from Staxton village
Sil Howe *(off A169)*
Off A169 7m S of Whitby
Cockmoor Hill, Troutsdale *(off A170)*
On unclass Snainton–Hackness rd. Snainton 3m
Sutton Bank *(A170)*
A170 6m E of Thirsk

Bickley Gate *(off A171)*
On unclass rd 6m W of A171 at Scalby
Reasty Hill Top *(off A171)*
On unclass rd to Harwood Dale 4m W of A171 at Scalby
Skelder Top *(A171)*
S side of A171 4m W of Whitby
Sledgates, Fylingdales *(off A171)*
½m along unclass rd off A171. Signposted Fyling Thorpe
Hardrow Scaur *(off A684)*
2m N of A684 from Hawes on unclass rd to Hardrow
River Swale *(A6108)*
1m W of Richmond
Clay Bank *(B1257)*
3m S of Broughton
Ingleby Bank *(off B1257)*
½m E of Ingleby Greenhow on unclass rd from Broughton
Falling Foss *(off B1416)*
Off unclass rd to Ruswarp off B1416
Bolton Abbey (Cavendish Pavilion) *(off B6160)*
On unclass rd 1m W of Bolton Abbey
Burnsall village *(B6160)*
In centre of Burnsall village
Brimham Rocks *(B6165)*
In Country Park 3m E of Pateley Bridge, N of B6165 and S of B6265, signposted from both

YORKSHIRE (SOUTH)
Cannon Hall *(off A635)*
In Country Park off A635, 4½m NW of Barnsley ½m N of Cawthorne

Wales

CLWYD
Loggerheads *(A494)*
2m W Mold
Moel Famau *(A494)*
Off Mold–Ruthin rd on unclass rd ¾m N of Llanferres
Bod Petrual *(B5105)*
In Clocaenog Forest on B5105, Llanfihangel Glyn Myfyr 3½m
Erdigg
4m SW Wrexham
Moel Arthur
5m equidistant from Mold, Ruthin, Denbigh and Holywell

DYFED
Fishguard Harbour Transit Picnic Site *(A40)*
Between Fishguard and Goodwick 1m from Fishguard town centre
Port Abraham Transit Picnic Site *(A45)*
At Junction 49 on A45 adjacent to M4
Coed Deufor *(A474)*
S side A474 ¾m W Cenarth
Picnic Site *(A478/A40)*
½m N of Narberth

ishguard Harbour

Black Mountains *(A4069)*
4m N of Brynamman
Carew Mill *(off A4075)*
On unclass rd 400yd from A4075 at Carew
Abergorlech *(B4310)*
At Abergorlech village 12m N of Llandeilo between Brechfa and Llansawel
Ffynnon Byrgwm, Brechfa *(B4310)*
Between Brechfaad and Abegoroch, 2m NE Brechfa
River Tywi *(B4310)*
1m E of junction with B4310 6m E of Carmarthen
Coed-Craig-yr-Ogof *(off B4340)*
½m E of B4340 on unclass rd from Llanafan Bridge to Pontrhydygroes
Pwllpeiran *(off B4574)*
On unclass rd off B4574 2½m SE of Devil's Bridge
The Arch *(4974)*
2m S of Devil's Bridge
Llyn Brianne Dam *(unclass rd)*
Access N from A40 at Llandovery, via 12 miles of well signed unclass rds

GLAMORGAN (MID)
Garwnant Forest Centre *(off A470)*
5m N of Merthyr Tydfil, ½m W A470
Taf Fechan Reservoir *(unclass rd)*
Near Merthyr Tydfil on Talybont rd, 1m N of Pontsticill

GWENT
Nine Wells *(off A48)*
6m SE of Usk on unclass rd between A449 and A48 in Wentwood Forest
Cardira Beeches *(off A48)*
5m SE of Usk 6½m NW Chepstow on unclass rd between A449 and A48
Mitchell Troy Transit Area Transit Picnic Site *(A449)*
On dual carriageway linking M4/M5, 1m S of Monmouth on N carriageway
Whitehall Picnic Area Transit Picnic Site *(A449)*
Both sides A449 Coldra Usk rd 3m N of M4 Junction 24
Tintern Railway Station Picnic Area *(A466)*
A seasonal site open 10.30am–6pm. Right-hand side of rd N from Tintern
Prysgau Bach *(B4235)*
3m W of Chepstow
Barnets Wood *(B4235)*
2m W of Chepstow
Wentwood Lodge *(unclass rd)*
5½m E Usk. 6½m NW Chepstow
Wentwood Reservoir *(unclass rd)*
6m Usk 9m Chepstow. On unclass rd between A48 and A449
Whitestone *(unclass rd)*
1½m W Llandogo 1½m SE Trelleck on unclass rd between A466 and B4293

GWYNEDD
Cae'n-y-Coed *(A5)*
1½m N of Betws-y-Coed
Aberhirnant Valley *(off A470)*
Along unclass rd approx 1m S of Ganllwyd
Bont Newydd *(A470)*
1m SE of Ffestiniog
Tan-y-Coed *(off A470)*
Alongside River Mawddach off A470 1m S of Ganllwyd
Dolgyfeiliau Bridge *(off A487)*
Alongside River Eden approx 1½m N of Ganllwyd
Tyn-y-Groes Transit Picnic Site *(off A487)*
Alongside River Mawddach off A470 1m S of Ganllwyd
Crogenan Lakes *(off A493)*
In Snowdonia Forest Park 6m SW of Dolgellau. 5 gates along approach
Bala Lake *(A494)*
½m SW of Bala

Cwm Nantcol *(A496)*
2m E of Llanbedr (A496) on unclass rd
Pont-Caer Gors *(A4085)*
2m N of Beddgelert
Celyn Lake *(A4212)*
6m NW of Bala
Bala Lake Foreshore *(B4403)*
Alongside B4403 approx 3½m W of Bala near
Llangower
Llyn Geironydd (Gwydyr Forest) *(off B5106)*
Via narrow access rd and lake, 3¾m
Newborough Forest *(unclass rd)*
2m from Newboróugh village
Pennllyn, Rhoss-y-Gwalla *(unclass rd)*
2½m SE of Bala on unclass rd to Lake Vyrnwy

POWYS
Ffawydday *(off A40 and A465)*
At head of Grwyne Fawr valley approx 11m N of
Abergavenny via unclass rds from A40 and A465
Hafren Road *(off A470)*
7m from Llanidloes off A470
Sugar Loaf *(A483)*
4m SW of Llanwrtyd Wells adjacent AA box 429
Rock Park *(off A681)*
Near town centre Llandrindod Wells, near Tourist
Information Centre
Brecon Beacons Mountain Centre *(off A4215)*
Off A4215 6m SW of Brecon
Llyn Clywedog *(B4518)*
On B4518 4m NW of Llanidloes

Scotland

BORDERS
Glentress Forest *(A72)*
2m E of Peebles Meiklaw Harelaw Picnic Area (A697)
on Coldstream to Carefraemill Road 3½m NW of
Greenlaw
Cambridge Picnic Site *(A697)*
A697 Lauder 3½m, at junction with unclass rd to
Spottiswoode
St Mary's Loch *(A708)*
Mid-way between Silkirk and Moffat
Glenmayne Haugh *(off A6091)*
2m S of Galashiels on unclass rd between A6091
and A7
Rankleburn *(off B709)*
¾m SE of Tushielaw on B711 of B709
Cardrona Forest Walks *(B7062)*
3m from Peebles
Meldons Picnic Areas *(unclass rd)*
Three separate areas within ½m on unclass rd linking
A72 and A703, through the Meldon Hills
Mayfield Riverside Walk *(Kelso)*
Abbotsford Grove on river bank by Kelso Abbey

CENTRAL
Loch Lubhair *(A83)*
3m from Crianlarich
Strathyre *(A84)*
Outside Strathyre village
Picnic Site *(A85)*
3½m W of Lochearnhead village,
Lochearnhead–Crianlarich rd
Queens View *(A809)*
On A809 4m S of Drymen
David Marshall Lodge (Carnegie Building)
(A821)
¾m E of Aberfoyle
Wilmimog *(A821)*
Close to River Leny 400yds from Junction with A84
Gallochy *(continuation of B837)*
On unclass rd approx 2½m S of Rowardennan
Mealldhuinne *(continuation of B837)*
On unclass rd approx 1m S of Rowardennan on E
side of loch
Milarrochy *(B837)*
1m N of Balmaha

Rowardennan *(continuation of B837)*
On unclass rd adjacent to village

DUMFRIES AND GALLOWAY
Opposite Glenairlie Bridge *(A76)*
On W side 4½m S of Sanquhar
Portpatrick Harbour *(A77)*
A77, N side of harbour
Grey Mare's Tail *(A708)*
10m NE of Moffat
St Medan, Monreith *(A747)*
1m SE of Monreith village

FIFE
Craigmead, Lomond Hills *(unclass)*
Between Leslie and Falkland

GRAMPIAN
Picnic Site *(A93)*
2m W of Aboyne
Broddie Castle *(A96)*
4½m W of Forres
Huntly Transit Picnic Site *(A97)*
On outskirts of Huntly between town and by-pass
roundabout
Picnic Site *(A97)*
1m N Kildrummy Castle
Pittodrie, Bennachie Walks *(A98)*
2m S of A98
Speymouth *(A98)*
½m E of Fochabers
Well of Lecht *(A939)*
5m SE of Tomintoul
Picnic Site *(A975)*
2m N of Newburgh by Ythan Estuary
Potarch Green *(B933)*
Off B933 near Potarch Bridge
Oyne, Back O' Bennachie *(off B9002)*
1½m SW of Oyne
Banchory Forest
Unclass rd between Potarch Bridge B993 and
Feughside B976

HIGHLAND
Daviot Wood *(A9)*
3m S of Inverness
Foulis Ferry *(A9)*
1m SW Evanton
Landmark Visitors' Centre, Carrbridge
(off A9)
Off A9 Carrbridge
Redburn *(A9)*
2m SE Eddelton
Loch Linnhe *(A82)*
3m S of Fort William
Loch Oich *(A82)*
2m S of Invergarry
Golspie, Big Burn Waterfall *(off A91)*
½m off unclass rd off A91, 1m N of Golspie
Glenn Finnan Transit Picnic Site *(A830)*
At the head of Loch Shiel between Fort William and
Mallaig
Gludie Picnic Site *(A832)*
W end of Loch Luichare 5m W of Garve
Loch Maree *(A832)*
2½m NW of Kinlochewe
Talladale, Slatterdale *(A832)*
2m W of Talladale (Loch Maree Hotel)
Talladale, Victoria Falls *(A832)*
1½m W of Talladale
Braemore Junction *(A835)*
2m W of Braemore Junction
Coldbackie Sands *(A836)*
3m NE of Tongue
Sangomore *(A838)*
At Durness
Ardery, Salen *(A861)*
E of Salen

Kylesku Bridge *(A894)*
Near Kylesku Bridge, ½m from Kylesku
Dalcraig *(B852)*
1m SW Foyers
Invershin (Falls of Shin) *(B864)*
3m from Invershin Hotel
Ralia Transit Picnic Site *(B9105)*
At junction with A9 2m S of Newtonmore
Rosehall, Ravens Rock *(unclass rd)*
2m E of Rosehill off A837
Staffin, Isle of Skye, Loch Mealt Falls Picnic Area
1½m S of Staffin

LOTHIAN
Bilsdean Transit Picnic Site *(A1)*
N of Cockburnspath
Pencraig Picnic Place *(A1)*
N side of A1 4m E Haddington 1m East Linton

STRATHCLYDE
Cauldshore *(A77)*
At Girvan
Finnarts Bay *(A77)*
3m N of Cairnyran
Duck Bay *(A82)*
1m N of Balloch
Garelochhead *(A814)*
1m N of Garelochhead
St Columb's Bay *(A828)*
10m NE of Oban
Jubilee Picnic Site *(A8003)*
2m N of Tighnabruaich

TAYSIDE
Tummel Forest–Faskally Walk *(A9)*
2m N of Pitlochry
Picnic Site, East Haven Beach *(A92)*
1½m SE of Muirdrum 1½m NE of Carnoustie
Montrose Links *(off A92)*
1m off A92 E of Montrose
Birks O' Aberfeldy *(A826)*
At Aberfeldy
Dalerb *(A827)*
On N shore at E end of Loch Tay, ¾m from Kenmore
Allean–Tummel Forest *(B8019)*
7m NW of Pitlochry ½m W Queens View
Queens View Tourist Park *(B8019)*
a On B8019
b 500yd W of above
Picnic Site *(off B951)*
Glen Isla
Cullow Market *(B955)*
¾m N of Dyke Head
Picnic Site *(off B955)*
At Ogliry Arms Hotel, Clova Village
Picnic Site *(B955)*
8¼m N of River Esk
Picnic Site *(B955)*
At Glecca Bridge 4m N of Dyke Head

Loch Maree, Highland

Northern Ireland

(Unclassified roads vary in condition from A class roads to small country lanes with passing places.)

Co ANTRIM
Ballycastle, Seafront *(A2)*
In Ballycastle
Ballygalley *(A2)*
5m N of Larne
Ballypatrick Forest *(A2)*
6½m SE of Ballycastle
Carnlough Harbour *(A2)*
On A2 near harbour
Carrick-a-Rede *(A2)*
5m W of Ballycastle
Carrickfergus Fishermans Quay *(A2)*
Scotch Quarter
Carrickfergus Marine Gardens *(A2)*
Marine Highway
Cushendall *(A2)*
On A2 at Cushendall adjacent to caravan site
Drains Bay *(A2)*
2½m N of Larne
Garron Point *(A2)*
4¼m N of Carnlough
Glenarm *(A2)*
In Glenarm
Jordanstown Loughshore Park *(A2)*
Shore Rd, White Abbey
Magheracross *(A2)*
3m from Portrush left side of rd to Bushmills
Picnic Site *(A2)*
3m from Portrush on left of Portrush–Bushmills rd
Red Bay *(A2)*
1½m SE of Glenariffe
Slieveanorra Forest *(A2/unclass)*
Off A2 5m W of Cushendall
White Rocks *(A2)*
2m from Portrush left side of rd to Bushmills
Whitehead *(A2)*
Blackpath Path on unclass rd from car park
Moira Demesne Park *(A3)*
Main St, Moira
Cranfield *(off A6)*
Cranfield Rd, Shaffordstown
Massarene Park *(A6)*
Randalstown Rd, Antrim
Paradise Walk Car Park *(A6)*
Off Paradise Walk, Templepatrick
Kirbys Lane *(off A26)*
Kirbys Lane, Dublin Rd
Lough Shore *(off A26)*
Lough Rd, Antrim
Knockstacken *(A42)*
2m SW of Carnlough
Portglenone Forest *(A42)*
1m S of Portglenone
Slemish *(off A42)*
Carnstroan Lane, Buckna
Glenariffe Glen *(A43)*
¾m SW of Waterfoot
Parkmore *(A43)*
4¾m SW of Waterfoot
Ballintoy Harbour *(B15)*
In Ballintoy
Ballycastle Forest *(B15/unclass)*
Off Ballycastle–Armoy via Glenshesk rd
Newferry *(off B52)*
Off Port Glenone–Randalstown rd. 5¼m S of Portglenone
Carnearny *(off B59)*
Carnearny Rd/Tardree Rd, Tardree
Tardree Forest *(B59)*
3½m E of Kells
Brown's Bay *(B90)*
On Island Magee on B90 from Ballycarry
Knockagh Monument *(off B90)*
Upper Rd, Greenisland

Tildarg *(B94)*
5m N of Ballyclare
Dreen Cullybackey *(off B96)*
President Chester Allans ancestral home
Portballintrae East Strand *(off B145)*
Off B145 which is off A2: adjacent to Beach Hotel
In Belfast
1 Sir Thomas and Lady Dixon Park, Upper
   Malone Rd
2 Shaws Bridge (Barnett Park), Mill Town Rd
3 Castle Estate, Antrim Rd

Co ARMAGH
Annaghmore Gardens *(off A3)*
Signposted from Roundabout
Craigavon Lakes *(A3)*
a Road from Roundabout 3
b Road from Roundabout 2
Lurgan Park *(A3)*
Lurgan–Moira rd
Fews Forest *(A29/B31)*
3m NW of Newtownhamilton
Gosford Forest Park *(off A29/B31)*
Adjacent to Market Hill entrance of forest
The Fews Forest, Carrickatuke, Deadmans Hill
(B31/B78)
Off B31/B78 4m N of Newtownhamilton
The Fews Forest Carnagh *(B32)*
On B32 Keady–Castleblayney rd
Oxford Island *(off B76)*
Unclass rd signposted from Lurgan Roundabout on
M1
Fathom Wood *(B79)*
4m S of Newry
Slieve Gullion *(B134)*
2m from Forkhill
Bartins Bay *(off B156)*
From Aghagallon on rd signposted Lough Neagh

Co DOWN
Large Park *(A1)*
In Hillsborough on A1
Loughbrickland Park *(A1)*
In Loughbrickland Village
Ballyhalbert *(A2)*
Ballyhalbert
Ballyhaskin Picnic Area *(A2)*
Ballywalter Rd, Millisle
Ballymenock Park *(A2)*
Bangor Rd, Holywood
Ballywalter Beach *(A2)*
Ballywalter
Ballywalter Harbour and Sea Front *(A2)*
Ballywalter
Bloodybridge *(A2)*
2¾m S of Newcastle
Castle Park *(A2)*
Opposite Bangor Railway Station
Cloughey Car Park *(A2)*
In Cloughey
Dormans Isle *(A2)*
Harbour Rd, Donaghadee
North Breakwater (New Pier) Long Hole
Bangor *(A2)*
Junction of Quay St and Seacliffe Rd
Groomsport Harbour *(A2)*
Groomsport
Harbour Car Park *(off A2)*
At Portavogie Harbour ¼m E of Portavogie on
unclass rd
Harbour Car Park *(A2)*
In Ballyhalbert
Killard Road *(A2)*
On Ballyhornan–Strangford rd
Lemon's Wharfe *(A2)*
The Parade, Donaghadee

Millisle Car Park *(A2)*
In Millisle
North Down Coastal Path Area *(A2)*
Hollywood–Bangor including Helens Bay
Portavogie Harbour *(A2)*
Springfield Rd, Portavogie
Seapark *(A2)*
Seapark Rd, Hollywood
Shore Street *(A2)*
Shore St, Donaghadee
Sliddery Ford Bridge *(A2)*
2¼m N of Newcastle on A2
Springfield Road Picnic Area *(A2)*
Portavogie
The Commons *(A2)*
Millisle Rd, Donaghadee
The Warren *(A2)*
Main Rd, Cloughey Beach
Ward Park *(A2)*
Hamilton Rd, Bangor
Ballyfrench Car Park *(A20)*
Near junction on Ballyhalbert rd
Grey Abbey Picnic Area *(A20)*
Kircubbin Shorefront *(A20)*
Kircubbin
Londonderry Public Park *(A20)*
Portaferry Rd, Newtownards
Windmill Hill *(off A20)*
Portaferry
Island Hill *(off A21)*
Signposted at Newtownards to Comber Rd
Quoile Low Road *(off A22)*
1m N of Downpatrick near Quoile Bridge
Whiterock Picnic Area *(off A22)*
Whiterock
Clough Village *(A24)*
Seaforde Demesne *(A24)*
¾m N of Seaforde Village on A24
Castlewellan Forest *(A25)*
In Castlewellan Forest
Creegduff *(A25)*
1m NE of Clough
Katesbridge Picnic Area *(A50)*
Main Bainbridge–Castlewellan Rd at Katesbridge
Belvoir Park *(A55)*
Off A55 Belfast Rd
Scarva Park *(B3)*
In Scarva Village
Crawfordsburn Country Park *(off B20)*
Marine Gardens *(off B20)*
Seafront, Bangor
Ballyholme Park, Lukes Point *(B21)*
Junction Seacliffe Rd and Ballyholme Rd
Rostrevor Forest *(B25)*
Adjacent to Rostrevor Village
Crocknafeola Forest *(B27)*
5½m N of Kilkeel
Cairnwood *(B170)*
Woodland Walks

Co FERMANAGH
At Enniskillen
a **Brook Park** *(A4)*
b **Lakeland Forum** *(A4)*
c **Race Course Lough** *(A32)*
d **Sligo Road** *(A4)*
e **Old Rossorry** *(off A4)*
Belcoo *(A4)*
In village
Cavanleck (1) *(A4)*
1¾m SW Fivemiletown
Cavanleck (2) *(A4)*
1¾m SW Fivemiletown
Cornamucklagh *(A4)*
1¼m NE Brookeborough
Fardross Forest *(off A4)*
Signposted from Clogher–Fivemiletown rd. 3m SE
Fivemiletown
Glencunny *(A4)*
1m NE Letterbreen

Parkanaur *(off A4)*
Near Castle Caulfield
Ring *(off A4)*
Unclass rd. 2m SW Enniskillen
Tamlaght *(A4)*
3m SE of Enniskillen
Templeneffrin *(off A4)*
Trory (Devenish) *(off A32)*
Unclass rd. 4m N Enniskillen
Carrickawick *(off A34)*
Unclass rd. 3¾m E Lisnaskea
Lough Barry *(off A34)*
Unclass rd. 5m NW Lisnaskea
Muckross *(off A35)*
Unclass rd. 1m NW Kesh
Belleek *(A46)*
In village
Camagh Bay *(off A46)*
Unclass rd. Outskirts of Blaney
Carrickreagh Ely Lodge Forest *(A46)*
6m NW Enniskillen
Leggs *(A46)*
5m NW of Tully
Lough Aleen *(A46)*
1½m S of Tully
Shean, Magho *(A46)*
3m NW Tully
Slawin (1) *(A46)*
1½m E Rosscor
Slawin (2) *(A46)*
1½m E Rosscor
Tully Castle *(off A46)*
Unclass rd from Tully
Castle Caldwell *(A47)*
5m E of Belleek
Drumgrenaghan (Boa Island) *(A47)*
5m W Kesh
Rossharbour *(A47)*
8m NE Belleek
Stonefort *(A47)*
8m E Belleek
Tawnyoran *(A47)*
3m E of Belleek
Bellanaleck *(A509)*
In village
Corradillar *(off A509/B127)*
2½m SE Derrylin
Derryallen Lough *(A509)*
6m NW Derrylin
Geaglum *(off A509)*
3½m SE Derrylin
Knockninny *(off A509)*
2m NE Derrylin
Tiraroe *(off A509)*
2m NE Derrylin
Killyfole *(B36)*
7m W Rosslea
Garrison (1) *(B52)*
Garrison (2) *(B52)*
Lough Nauar Forest *(off B81)*
5m NW Derrygonnelly
Castle Archdale Country Park *(B82)*
1m W Lisnarrick
Rossigh *(off B82)*
3m SW Lisnarrick
Derryadd *(off B127)*
4m SW Lisnaskea
Shanaghy (Smiths Strand) *(off B127)*
3m SW Lisnaskea
Carrybridge *(off B514)*
5m NW Lisnaskea
Mullanascarty Caravan Park *(B514)*
2½m NW Lisnaskea
Marlbank *(off C437)*
Unclass rd. 2½m S Belcoo

Co LONDONDERRY

Agherton *(A2)*
½m from Portstewart on Coleraine–Portrush rd

Ballysally *(A2)*
½m on right Coleraine–Portstewart rd below. New
University of Ulster
Binevenagh Forest *(A2/unclass)*
On Bishops Rd 4¾m SW of Downhill
Bishop's Gate *(A2)*
1m E of Downhill on right of rd to Coleraine
Carrakeel *(A2)*
5m NE of Londonderry
Carrickhue *(A2)*
2m W Ballykelly
Castleroe *(A2)*
Coastal Path *(A2)*
Near Portstewart on left of Portrush–Portstewart rd
Downhill *(A2)*
On A2 Coleraine–Downhill rd, 1½m from rd
Freehall *(A2)*
1½m from Downhill on right of Downhill–Coleraine
rd
Gortmore *(off A2)*
4m SW of Downhill on unclass rd
Quilly *(A2)*
2m W of Coleraine on both sides of rd to
Castlerock
Brackfield *(A6)*
7m SE of Londonderry
Carricknakielt *(A6)*
On Maghera by-pass NW of Castledawson
Craigadick *(A6)*
1m S of Maghera on Maghera by-pass at junction
with A29
Curran Bridge *(A6)*
On Maghera by-pass 4m NW of Castledawson
Ness Wood *(off A6)*
9m SE of Londonderry
Owenbeg *(A6)*
1½m from Dungiven on Dungiven–Derry rd
Ranaghan *(A6)*
4m NW of Maghera
Beagh *(A29)*
Maghera–Swatragh rd
Carndaisy Forest *(A29/unclass)*
4m NW of Moneymore
Dunderg *(A29)*
1m from A37 both sides of Coleraine–Garragh rd
Grillagh *(A29)*
Maghera–Swatragh rd
Iniscarn Forest *(A29/unclass)*
6m NW of Moneymore
Tirkeeran *(A29)*
Outside Garragh on Maghera rd
Tobermore *(A29)*
Tobermore–Desertmartin rd
Dunbeg *(A37)*
6m from Coleraine beside rd to Londonderry
Keady Mountain *(A37)*
3m NE Limrady along A37
Macosquin *(A37)*
2m from Coleraine on right of rd to Londonderry
Camus *(A54)*
To left of Coleraine–Kilvea rd overlooking River
Bann
Castleroe Wood *(A54)*
3m S of Coleraine
Glenone *(A54)*
Ballycombe Rd near Port Glenone
Banagher–Learmount Wood *(B44)*
1m W of Park Village on B44
Loughermore *(B69)*
At Loughermore Bridge 8m SW of Limavady
Feeny *(B74)*
1m from Feeny on Dungiven rd
Hillhead *(B182)*
Hillhead–Bellaghy rd
Roe Valley Country Park *(off B192)*
Adjacent to Limavady
Largantea *(B201)*
5½m E of Limavady
Newbridge *(C560)*
Toomebridge–Magherafelt rd

Mullagh *(unclass)*
UR54 on Mullagh rd
New Ferry *(unclass)*
UR94 off the A54 Bellaghy–Portglenone rd
Tirgan *(unclass)*
UR155 off UR161 Tirgan rd

Co TYRONE
Findermore *(A4)*
1¾m SW Clogher
Killymaddy *(A4)*
1m W Dungannon
Martray *(A4)*
1m NE Ballygawley
The Grange Park *(A5)*
Mountjoy Rd, Omagh
Favour Royal Forest *(A28)*
3m NW Aughnacloy
Drumcairne Forest *(off A29)*
2m SE Stewartstown. Unclass rd
Moy *(A29)*
Davagh Forest *(A505/unclass)*
Signposted from Cookstown–Omagh rd
Drum Manor Forest *(A505)*
3m W Cookstown
Lovers Retreat *(A505)*
Cookstown Rd, Omagh
Ballyronan *(B18)*
At Marina 6m NE Moneymore
Goles Forest *(B47)*
7m W Draperstown
Gortin Forest Park *(B48)*
7½m N of Omagh, 2½m S of Gortin on unclass rd off B48
Gortin Lakes Road *(B48)*
9m N of Omagh and 1m S of Gortin on unclass rd off B46 and B48
Lough Bradan Forest Tully Hill *(B50/unclass)*
5m W of Drumquin
Killeter Forest *(B72/unclass)*
Signposted from Castlederg
Lough Bradan Forest, Scraghey *(B72)*
4m N of Ederny
Coagh *(B73)*
6m from Cookstown. Off street parking
Newport Tench *(B73)*
4¾m SE Coagh
Seskinore Forest Park *(B83)*
Seskinore
Verners Bridge *(B131)*
½m from junction 14 M1/B131
Ballybriest *(B162)*
6½m NW Cookstown at Lough Fea

National Parks and Lakes

Details of National Parks Information Centres are given in the text. Most information centres are only open during the summer season (normally Easter to October) so it is advisable to telephone first before making a special journey.
* Correspondence should only be sent to those places marked with an asterisk.

England

DARTMOOR
945 sq. km (365 sq. m) of high moorland. Includes nature reserves. Details from *Information Office, "Parke", Haytor Rd, Bovey Tracey, Newton Abbot,

tel. Bovey Tracey 832093, or Information Centres at:
Newbridge (Caravan)
Postbridge Steps Bridge
Tavistock Bedford Square

EXMOOR
686 sq. km (265 sq. m) of heatherclad moorland plateau, down to coast. Details from *Information Officer, Exmoor National Park Department, Exmoor House, Dulverton, Somerset, tel. Dulverton 23665/6, or Information Centres at:
Combe Martin (Caravan) Beach Car Park, tel. Combe Martin 3319
County Gate A39 between Porlock and Lynmouth, tel. Brendon 321
Lynmouth Parish Hall, Watersmeet Rd, tel. Lynton 2509
Minehead Market House, The Parade, tel. Minehead 2984

LAKE DISTRICT
2,243 sq. km (866 sq. m) of mountain and lake scenery, including England's three highest mountains and largest lake. Details from *Information Officer, National Park Offices, Busher Walk, Kendal, Cumbria, tel. Kendal 24555, or Information Centres at:
Ambleside Old Court House, Church St, tel. Ambleside 3084 (closed Nov–Mar)
Bowness Bowness Bay, Glebe Rd, tel. Windermere 2895 (closed Jan–Mar)
Coniston (Caravan) Village Car Park, tel. Coniston 533
Glenridding (Caravan) Car Park, tel. Glenridding 414
Hawkshead (Caravan) Main Car Park, tel. Hawkshead 525
Keswick Moot Hall, tel. Keswick 72803 (closed Jan–Mar)
Pooley Bridge (Caravan) Car Park, tel. Pooley Bridge 530
Seatoller adjacent village Car Park, tel. Borrowdale 294
Waterhead (Caravan) Car Park at head of lake
Windermere National Park Centre, Brockhole, tel. Windermere 2231 (closed Dec–Mar)
Caravan Advisory Service, tel. Windermere 555/5515
Weather Information Service, tel. Windermere 5151/2/3/4

NORTHUMBERLAND
1,031 sq. km (398 sq. m) of hills and moorland. Stretches from Hadrian's Wall in the south to the Cheviot Hills on the Scottish border. Details from *Information Officer, Northumberland National Park, Eastburn, South Park, Hexham, tel. Hexham 5555, or Information Centres at:
Byrness 9 Otterburn Green, tel. Otterburn 20622
Ingram Old School House, tel. Powburn 248
Once Brewed Military Rd, Hexham, tel. Bardon Mill 396
Rothbury Church House, Church St, tel. Rothbury 20887

NORTH YORK MOORS
1,432 sq. km (553 sq. m) of hills, moors and coast. Details from *Information Officer, North York Moors National Park, North Yorkshire County Council, The Old Vicarage, Bondgate, Helmsley, North Yorkshire YO6 5BP, tel. Helmsley (04392) 657/658, or Information Centres at:
Danby National Park Centre, Danby Lodge, nr Whitby, tel. Castleton 654
Pickering Station, tel. Pickering 73791
Sutton Bank Information Centre, top of Sutton Bank by the A170 – personal callers only, tel. Sutton 426

Helmsley, North Yorkshire

PEAK DISTRICT

1,404 sq. km (542 sq. m) of country varying from limestone uplands in the south and east, to wild moorland in the north. Details from *Information Officer, Peak District National Park, Aldern House, Baslow Rd, Bakewell, Derbyshire DE41 1AE, tel. Bakewell 2881 (closed weekends) or Information Centres at:
Bakewell Market Hall, Bridge St, tel. Bakewell 3227 (closed Wednesday and Thursday in winter)
Castleton Castle St, tel. Hope Valley 20679 (closed Monday, Tuesday, Thursday and Friday in winter)
Dovestones Information Point, Dovestones Reservoir, nr Greenfield (Sunday only)
Edale Field Head, tel. Hope Valley 70207/70216
Goyt Valley Information Point, Derbyshire Bridge (Sunday only)
Hartington Information Point, Old Station (Saturday and Sunday only)
Tideswell Dale Information Point, Car Park (Sunday only)

YORKSHIRE DALES

1,761 sq. km (680 sq. m) of wide, sweeping upland moors and deep pastoral valleys. Details from *Information Officer, Yorkshire Dales National Park, "Colvend", Hebden Rd, Grassington, tel. Grassington 752748
Aysgarth Falls Car Park, tel. Aysgarth 424
Clapham Reading Room, tel. Clapham 419
Hawes (Caravan) Station Yard, tel. Hawes 450
Malham Car Park, tel. Airton 363
Sedbergh 72 Main St, tel. Sedbergh 20125
Weather Information Service, tel. Horton-in-Ribblesdale 333 (weekends only)

Wales

BRECON BEACONS

1,344 sq. km (519 sq. m) of mountain moorland including three nature reserves. Details from *Information Officer, Brecon Beacons National Park, Glamorgan St, Brecon, Powys LD3 7DW, tel. Brecon 4437. Open Easter–October (closed Sunday)
Aberclydach nr Talybont-on-Usk, open mainly summer weekends (managed by Welsh Water Authority)
Abergavenny Monk St, tel. Abergavenny 3254 (closed Sunday)
Craig-y-nos Country Park Pen-y-cae, tel. Abercrave 395
Libanus Mountain Centre, tel. Brecon 3366
Llandovery 8 Broad St, tel. Llandovery 20693

PEMBROKESHIRE COAST

583 sq. km (225 sq. m) of spectacular cliffs, secluded bays, and sandy coves. Details from *Information Officer, Pembrokeshire Coast National Park, Dyfed County Council, County Offices,

Haverfordwest, tel. Haverfordwest 3131, or Information Centres at:
Broad Haven Pembrokeshire Countryside Unit, Car Park, tel. Broad Haven 412
Fishguard Town Hall, tel. Fishguard 873484
Haverfordwest 40 High St, tel. Haverfordwest 66161
Kilgetty Kingsmoor Common, tel. Saundersfoot 813672/3
Pembroke Castle Ter, tel. Pembroke 2148
St David's City Hall, tel. St David's 392
Tenby The Norton, tel. Tenby 3510

SNOWDONIA

2,171 sq. km (838 sq. m) of mountains and woodlands in North Wales including the Snowdonia Forest Park. Details from National Park Officer, Yr Hen Ysgol, Maentwrog, tel. Maentwrog 274, or Information Centres at:
Aberdovey The Wharf, tel. Aberdovey 321
Bala Old British High School, High St, tel. Bala 367
Blaenau Ffestiniog Caerblaidd Office, Queen's Bridge, tel. Blaenau Ffestiniog 360
Conwy Castle St, tel. Conwy 2248
Dolgellau Beechwood House, tel. Dolgellau 422888
Harlech Gwyddfor House, High St, tel. Harlech 658
Llanberis Community Centre, tel. Llanberis 765
Llanrwst Glan-y-Borth, tel. Llanrwst 640604 (closed Thursday pm and weekends in winter)
Plas Tan y Bwlch (Caravan)

A small selection of Caves open to the Public

CASTLETON, Derbys
Blue John Cavern. Partly artificial; crystal formations and rock concretions
Peak Cavern. Underground river

CHEDDAR, Somerset
Gough's Caves. Rock concretions

CLAPHAM, N Yorks
Ingleborough Cave. Stalactites and stalagmites

CRAIG-Y-NOS, Powys
Cathedral Cave. Stalactites and stalagmites; rock concretions
Dan Yr Ogof. Stalactites and stalagmites; rock concretions

INGLETON, N Yorks
White Scar Cave. Underground river; stalactites and stalagmites; fossils

TORBAY, Devon
Kent's Cavern. Stalactites and stalagmites

WOOKEY, Somerset
Wookey Hole. Underground river; stalactites and stalagmites

Long-distance Footpaths

England

CLEVELAND WAY, 93m (150km). Open throughout length. Route entirely in North Yorkshire, from Helmsley to a point near Filey.

NORTH DOWNS WAY, 141m (227km). The route is open, with temporary links in some sections, between Farnham and Dover and follows the crest of the North Downs; in a few places coinciding with the medieval Pilgrims' Way. The main route skirts Folkestone, but there is an alternative link from Boughton Lees (north-east of Ashford, Kent), via Canterbury to Dover. Proposals are under consideration to extend the path to Winchester.

PENNINE WAY 250m (402km). Open throughout length. Strenuous route from Edale, Derbyshire to Kirk Yetholm in Scotland.

RIDGEWAY PATH 85m (137km). Open throughout length. Route is from Overton Hill near Avebury, Wiltshire to Ivinghoe Beacon in Buckinghamshire.

SOUTH DOWNS WAY 80m (129km). Open throughout length. Bridleway from outskirts of Eastbourne to Harting. A 26m extension from Harting to the outskirts of Winchester is proposed.

SOUTH WEST PENINSULA COAST PATH Somerset and North Devon 82m (132km). Cornwall 268m (431km. South Devon 93m (150km). Dorset 72m (116km). No rights of way in some sections. The route, totalling some 515m, extends from Minehead to Studland, near Poole.

WOLDS WAY 72m (115km). The latest long-distance footpath to be approved, work has commenced on its implementation but it will be some time before it can be officially opened. This path will eventually extend from near Hull to Filey and will link with Cleveland Way.

Wales

OFFA'S DYKE PATH 168m (270km). Open throughout length. Route runs north to south the entire length of Wales, from Prestatyn to Chepstow.

PEMBROKESHIRE COAST PATH 167m (269km). Open throughout length. Route follows the coastline from Amroth to St Dogmaels.

Scotland

The following long-distance paths have been approved, but except for the West Highland Way, it may be some years before they are fully implemented and established.

WEST HIGHLAND WAY 98m (158km). Milngavie to Fort William. Officially opened October 1980.

SOUTHERN UPLAND WAY 204m (328km). Portpatrick to Cocksburnpath. Not open.

SPEYSIDE WAY 60m (96km). Glenmore (Cairngorms) to Spey Bay. Not open.

Country Parks
England
AVON
Ashton Park
1m S of Bristol, entrance from A369 and B3128

BEDFORDSHIRE
Stewartby Lake
5m SW of Bedford on A5140
Stockgrove Country Park, Heath and Reach
2½m N of Leighton Buzzard
BERKSHIRE
Dinton Pastures
¾m along B3030 to Twyford from junction with A329
Snelsmore Common
3m N of Newbury on B4494

BUCKINGHAMSHIRE
Black Park
Access via Black Park Rd (unclass) N from A412 3m NE of Slough
Emberton Country Park
On W side of A509 at Emberton 1m S of Olney
Langley Country Park
Access via Billet Lane (unclass) S from A412 3m N of Slough

CAMBRIDGESHIRE
Burghley Park
SE of Stamford
Elton Park (Private Country Park)
A505 5m NE of Oundle
Ferry Meadows
2m W of Peterborough City Centre on A605 and A57
Thorney
A47 7m NE of Peterborough
Wandlebury Estate
Cambridge, 5m S of City off A604

CHESHIRE
Eastham Country Park
Nr junction of M53 and A41 S of Eastham signposted from Eastham town centre
Little Budworth Common
W of Winsford
Lyme Park
Nr Disley, SE of Stockport
Marbury Park
2m N of Northwich
Styal Country Park
From Wilmslow B5166 to Styal Village
Teggs Nose
N of Langley, 2m E of Macclesfield off A537
Wirral Countryside Park – see Merseyside

CORNWALL
Mount Edgcumbe House and Country Park
Off B3247 to Cremyll

CUMBRIA
Bardsea Country Park
Morecambe Bay. 2m S of Ulverston on A5087
Fell Foot
Nr Newby Bridge on E shore of Lake Windermere
Lowther Park
Off A6 4m S of Penrith
Talkin Tarn
11m S of Brampton E of Carlisle on B6413

DERBYSHIRE
Elvaston Castle
6m SE of Derby off B5010
Hardwick Hall
Doe Lea, 6½m SE of Chesterfield
Longshaw Estate
4m NW of Mansfield, 9m SW Sheffield in Peak National Park
Pools Cavern
Green Lane off A515 Buxton
Shipley
8m NE Derby. Off A608 at Heanor

DEVON
Berry Head
E of Brixham
Farway Countryside Park
Holnest Farm 4m S of Honiton
Grand Western Canal Country Park
Tiverton Basin car park A373 Tiverton
River Dart Country Park
1m from Ashburton on B3357
Stover Country Park
3m NW Newton Abbott on A382 near junction with A38

DORSET
Durlston
1½m S of Swanage on rd to Anvil Point Lighthouse

Upton Park
S side of A35. 1m W Fleetbridge intersection
entrance off slip road to Upton

DURHAM
Derwent Walk
Access point from B6310. Derwent Valley between
Swadwell and Consett
Hardwick Hall
Sedgefield, 10m S of Durham on A177
Pow Hill
Between Derwent Reservoir and B6306
Edmundbyers/Blanchland
Waldridge Fell
1m SW of Chester-le-Street

ESSEX
Cudmore Grove
East Mersea, Mersea Island approached from
Bromans Lane
Danbury Park
5m E of Chelmsford approached from the A414 on
A130 through Sanden Village or Well Lane Danbury
Hatfield Forest
On A120 4m E of Bishop's Stortford
Langdon Hills West
S of Basildon
Naze Point
N of Walton-on-the-Naze
Upper Mardyke Valley
E of S Ockendon between Mollands Lane, Buckles
Lane and the Mardyke River
Thorndon Country Park
Brentwood. Off A128 or B186
Weald Park
2m NW of Brentwood
Westley Heights
1m S of Basildon off B1007

GLOUCESTERSHIRE
Crickley Hill Country Park
Off B4070 near junction with A417 and A436. 3m S
of Cheltenham
Keynes Park (Cotswold Water Park)
Ashton Keynes. 4m S of Cirencester. Access (a) off
A419 2½m NW of Cricklade (b) off A417 1m E of
Fairford 3m W of Lechlade
Robinswood Hill
2m S of Gloucester, via Reservoir Rd off the Ring Rd

HAMPSHIRE
Farley Mount
W of Winchester on unclass rd
Lepe and Calshot Foreshores
2m S of Fawley on Solent
Queen Elizabeth Park
Butser, nr Petersfield. (Access from A3) 10m N
Portsmouth
Paulton's Country Park
½m W of Ower, off junction 2, M27
Royal Victoria Country Park
3m S along unclass rd from A27 at Windhover
Roundabout
Wellington Country Park
Stratfield Saye Estate, Heckfield. 8m NE of
Basingstoke at junction of A33 and A32
Yateley Common
N of A30 to W of Blackwater

HEREFORD AND WORCESTER
Broadway Tower
2m S of Broadway
Clent Hills
S of Halesowen, 8m W of Birmingham off A456
Kingsford
3m N of Kidderminster, W of A449
Lickey Hills
B4096 2½m NE of Bromsgrove. 8m S of Birmingham
Windmill and Waseley Hills
SW of Birmingham, 1m NW of Rubery

HERTFORDSHIRE
Aldenham Reservoir
Off A411 NW of Elstree
Great Wood, Northaw
4m SE of Hatfield on B157
Knebworth
1½m SW of Stevenage W of A1 (M) (Access from
B197 or B656)

HUMBERSIDE
Burton Constable
Sproatley, 8m NE of Hull
Normanby Hall
2m N of Scunthorpe

ISLE OF WIGHT
Fort Victoria
West of Yarmouth
Robin Hill
2m E of Newport

KENT
Camer Park, Meopham
Between Sole Street and Meopham
Eastcourt Meadows
Lower Rainham Rd, Gillingham
Manor Park
E of A228 (St Leonards St) S of West Malling
Trosley Towers Country Park
Off and E of A227 S of Vigo Village. N of Wrotham

LANCASHIRE
Beacon Country Park
E of Skelmersdale New Town, close to M6/M58
junction
Beacon Hill
8m N of Preston, 3m E of M6
Cuerdon Valley Country Park
S of Preston near Barber Bridge on the A49
Lever Park
Between Chorley, Horwich, Adington and adjacent
to Rivington Reservoir
Witton Park
On western outskirts of Blackburn
Wycoller
SE of Colne

LEICESTERSHIRE
Bradgate Park and Swithland Woods
5m NW of Leicester
Wanlip Park
5m NE of Leicester

LINCOLNSHIRE
Hartesholme
2m SW of Lincoln

LONDON (GT)
Bayhurst Wood
In Colne Valley, 2m N of Uxbridge, 1m W of Ruislip
Lido
Hainault Forest
E of Chigwell
Trent Park
W of Enfield

MANCHESTER (GT)
Chadkirk
S of Romily on A627
Daisy Nook
3m S Oldham
Etherow Park
Off B6104 at Compstall
Haigh Hall
2m NE Wigan
Hollingworth Lake
3m NE of Rochdale on B6225
Jumbles Reservoir
4m N of Bolton
Tandle Hill
Off A627 at Royton

Fritton Lake, Norfolk

MERSEYSIDE
Croxteth Park
6m NE of Liverpool
Eastham Woods
Off A41 at Eastham
The Wirral
Between West Kirby and Parkgate nr Dee estuary.
Access from A540 Chester–Hoylake rd at Croft
Drive, Caldy; Station Rd, Thurstaston; Parkgate
Baths, The Parade, Parkgate; Hadlow Rd, Willaston

NORFOLK
Fritton Lake Country Park
Off A143 Fritton–Great Yarmouth rd
Holt Lanes
On B1149 S of Holt
Sandringham
8m NE of King's Lynn

NORTHAMPTONSHIRE
Barnwell
S of Oundle on Barnwell Rd A605
Little Irchester
S of Wellingborough

NORTHUMBERLAND
Bolam Lake
Belsey, nr Morpeth
Cragside
12m SW of Alnwick at Rothbury
Plessey Woods
1½m SW of Bedlington on A1068
Wansbeck
½m S of Ashington

NOTTINGHAMSHIRE
Burnstump
3m N of Nottingham off A60
Colwick
1½m E Nottingham
Clumber Park
2¼m SE of Worksop
Holme Pierrepoint
2m W of Radcliffe, N of A52
Leen Valley Country Park
4m N of city centre
Major Oak, Sherwood Forest
N of Edwinstowe off A614
Rufford Park
3m S of Ollerton on A614

SOMERSET
Ham Hill
S of Stoke-sub-Hamdon, 6m W of Yeovil off A3088

STAFFORDSHIRE
Cannock Chase
N of Hednesford
Deep Hayes Country Park
3m SW of Leek on S edge of Longsdon village
Greenway Bank
Knypersley off A527, 4m N Stoke-on-Trent

Highgate Common
S of Wolverhampton
Himley Country Park
Off B4176 Wombourne–Dudley rd
Ilam
6m NW of Ashbourne
Parkhall
Weston Coyne, E of Stoke
Tittesworth Reservoir
3m N of Leek, 1m from A53

SUFFOLK
Brandon Park
1m S of Brandon on B1106
Clare Castle and Bailey
Between Clare village and River Stour
Easton Farm Park
W of Easton
Knettishall Heath
4m SE of Thetford, Norfolk (nr Euston Park)

SURREY
Box Hill
1½m NE of Dorking
Frensham Common
3m S of Farnham on A287
Horton
NW of Epsom
Lightwater
W of Lightwater Village Inn S of Bagshot

SUSSEX (EAST)
Ditchling Common
E of Burgess Hill, 2m N of Ditchling
Forest Way
9 mile linear park along the route of the former
railway line from Ashurst Junction to East Grinstead
Hastings Country Park
Located between Hastings and Fairlight, access via
entrance close to Fairlight Church
Seven Sisters
5m W of Eastbourne between A259 and the coast

SUSSEX (WEST)
Goodwood Estate
6m N of Chichester
Weald and Downland Open Air Museum
½m SW of Singleton

WARWICKSHIRE
Burton Dassett Hills
4m NE of Kineton
Coombe Abbey
4m E of Coventry city centre on A427
Hartshill Hayes
4m NW of Nuneaton off B4114 (formerly A47)
Kingsbury
12m NE of Birmingham, W of Kingsbury. Approach
from A4091 or A4097

WEST MIDLANDS
Lickey Hills
8m S of Birmingham

WILTSHIRE
Barbury Castle
5m S of Swindon access from M4 (Junction 15)
and Swindon via A345 or A361 then B4005 from
Wroughton
Barton Farm
Bradford-on-Avon access from A363 in town centre
Highwood and Hazel Wood Woodland Park
Brokerswood, nr Westbury
Stourhead
3½m NW of mere in Stourton village

YORKSHIRE (NORTH)
Brimham Rocks
3½m NW of Ripley off B6165
Church Cliff
Filey

YORKSHIRE (SOUTH)

Cannon Hall Park
4½m W of Barnsley
Cusworth Country Park
2m W of Doncaster, nr Sprotborough
Howell Wood
1¼m SE of South Kirby
Worsborough Mill
S of Worsborough off A61

YORKSHIRE (WEST)

Peniston Hill
Keighley

Wales

CLWYD

Erddig Park
1m SW Wrexham
Loggerheads
2m W of Mold on A494
Moel Arthur
5m equidistant from Mold, Ruthin, Denbigh and Holywell
Moel Famau
6m W of Mold

GLAMORGAN (SOUTH)

Cefn Onn
3m N of Cardiff
Porthkerry Park
Between Barry and Rhoose

GLAMORGAN (WEST)

Afan Argoed
5m NE of Port Talbot on A4107
Margam Park
Access 2m NW of Pyle on A48

GWENT

Caldicot Castle
Nr Caldicot town centre
Pen-y-Fan Pond
Access via new industrial estate rd off the B4251 Blackwood–Crumlin rd
Tredegar House (Urban Fringe Country Park)
Off A48 2m W of Newport, on unclass rd

GWYNEDD

Llyn Padarn
E of Llanberis

POWYS

Craig-y-Nos
6m N of Ystradgynlais on the A4067. Swansea–Sennybridge rd

Scotland

CENTRAL

Gartmoru Dam
E of Sauchie, 2m NE of Alloa, access off A908
Mugdock Country Park
1½m from Milngavie

FIFE

Craigtown Country Park
2½m SW of St Andrews. Off unclass rd from B939 in St Andrews to Pitscottie

GRAMPIAN

Aden Estate
6m W of Peterhead, S side of A950 W of Mintlaw
Balmedie
8m N of Aberdeen, 1m E of Balmedie village off A92(T)
Haddo Country Park
20m N Aberdeen off B9005

LOTHIAN

Almondell and Calderwood Country Park
10m W Edinburgh, 2m S Broxburn in Almond Valley, access from Mid and East Calder

Beecraigs Country Park
2m S of Linlithgow
Bonally
From Colinton via Bonally Rd under city by-pass taking minor rd past Bonally Towers
Hillend
S of Edinburgh from A702(T) to Biggar
John Muir Country Park
W of Dunbar, access from A1087 via three car parks; Linkfield, Shore Rd, Belhaven and Castle Park, Dunbar
Vogrie
10m S of Edinburgh on A68

STRATHCLYDE

Balloch Castle Country Park
Off B854 in Balloch
Brodick Castle, Isle of Arran
Off W side A841 Brodick to Lochranza, 1m N of Brodick
Calder Glen
From A726, SE to Strathaven from East Kilbride
Castle Semple Water Park
Signposted from Loch Winnoch
Cornalees Bridge Centre
Beside moorland rd from Greenock to Inverkip at the head of Shielhill Glen
Culzean
Between Maidens and Dunure on A719
Dean Castle
Access from North Lodge, Dean Rd, off B7038
Gleniffer Braes
S of Paisley, off Gleniffer Rd
Muirshiel Country Park
Signposted from Loch Winnoch, access by rd through Clader Glen
Palacerigg
2m SE of Cumbernauld
Strathclyde Country Park
N and S of M74 between Hamilton and Motherwell. Access from A725 at M74 Junction 5

TAYSIDE

Camperdown and Templeton, Dundee
Off A923

Forest Parks

Border Forest Park
145,000 acres of woodland hills and farms in Northumberland and Cumbria in England, Dumfries and Galloway and Borders in Scotland

Dean Forest Park
Covering 35,000 acres in Gloucestershire, Hereford and Worcester, and Gwent, including 30 miles of signposted walking routes, five nature trails, and a scenic motor drive

Snowdonia Forest Park
23,400 acres of woodland, moorland and lakes in NW Wales

Argyll Forest Park
Over 60,000 acres of rugged hills and lochs extending to Loch Goil and the Holy Loch near Dunoon

Galloway Forest Park
150,000 acres in the Galloway Highlands including Loch Trool and much of the Rhinns of Kells

Glenmore Forest Park
12,500 acres in the Cairngorms, including some of Scotland's best ski-ing grounds, and Loch Morlich with its sandy shores and pine trees

In Argyll Forest Park (Scotland)

Queen Elizabeth Forest Park
Over 40,000 acres of mountain, loch, moor and forest scenery. Over 60m of signposted walking routes

Northern Ireland
Co ANTRIM
Glenariff Forest Park
This park is situated in the world-famous Glens of Antrim

Co ARMAGH
Gosford Forest Park
Not as mountainous as the others in Ulster, this park includes some fine panoramic views over South Armagh

Co DOWN
Castlewhellan Forest Park
This park has one of the finest arboreta in the British Isles and includes a lake and mountain viewpoints
Tollymore Forest Park
In the Mourne Mountains

Co TYRONE
Davagh Forest Park
On the N slope of Beleevnamore Mountain on E edge of Sperrin Mountains 12m W of Cookstown
Drum Manor Forest Park
Small forest park
Gortin Glen Forest Park
Around the rugged Sperrin Mountains

Nature Trails, Forest Drives and Long-distance Motor Trails

The list which follows is not a comprehensive list of trails in Great Britain, and few town trails are included, but it does give a wide selection of the more important Nature Trails throughout the country. These are divided into three sections – England, Wales and Scotland – then listed by counties.

In the more mountainous or wild regions, stout footwear and protective clothing should be worn. It is wise to take heed of the prevailing weather conditions, for a day's outing can be marred by rain or poor visibility, and in some terrain walking can become hazardous in bad weather.

Nature Trails

England
AVON
Bristol
Ashton Court Estate, Bower Ashton, Avon Gorge. Starts at Leigh Woods just W of Bristol city off A369

BERKSHIRE
Bracknell
South Hill Park. On A3095 1m S of town

BUCKINGHAMSHIRE
Beaconsfield
Hodgemoor Wood Walks. 4¾m NE of Beaconsfield off A355
Brill
Boarstall Duck Decoy and Nature Reserve. Starts 2m SW of Brill off B4011
Buckingham
Stowe Nature Trail. Starts 3m NW of Buckingham off A422
High Wycombe
Keep Hill Woods. Starts 1m SE of High Wycombe on A40
Olney
Emberton. Starts on A509 ¼m S of Olney
Wendover
Halton Wood. Starts at Halton Woods, Chiltern Forest, 1½m NE of Wendover, S of A4011

CAMBRIDGESHIRE
Cambridge
Coe Fen. Starts within the city
Cambridge
Paradise Island. Starts within the city
Cambridge
Wandlebury. 4m S of Cambridge
Ely
Roswell Pits. Starts ¼m E of Cathedral and from the Cathedral
Peterborough
Holme Fen. Starts 7m S of Peterborough off B660
Peterborough
Southey Wood Walks. A47 7m W of Peterborough then unclass rd northwards towards Helpston
Soham
Wicken Fen. 4½m SW of Soham, S of A1123 in Wicken village

CHESHIRE
Disley (6½m SE Stockport)
Lyme Park. Starts at Disley
Kelsall
Delamare Forest Trail. Starts in Delamare Forest 2m N of Kelsall off B5152
Macclesfield
Tegg's Nose. Starts 2m E of Macclesfield on unclass rd off A537
Neston
Wirral Country Park Rock Cutting. Commences ¼m E of Neston, in Lees Lane

CORNWALL
Bodmin
Cardinham Woods. From Bodmin follow Liskeard rd (A389). At roundabout join A38, ¼m farther turn left (unclass) along the Cardinham rd. After sharp bend (600yd) turn left
Bude
Coombe Valley. 5m N of Bude via A39 and Stibb

Launceston
Halvana. 8m SW of Launceston. Leave A30 at Five Lanes (signposted Tregirls)
Looe
Deer Park. Off B3359 7½m NW of Looe (unclass rd to Herodsfoot)
Ruan Minor (3m NE of Lizard)
Poltesco. Starts ½m NE of village
Truro
St Clement Woods. 2m N of Truro, nr Idless village

CUMBRIA
Ambleside
Loughrigg Fell. Starts in Car Park off Keswick rd in Ambleside
Ambleside
White Moss Common. Starts 2m N of Ambleside town off A591
Appleby
Holme Wood Woodland Trail. On River Eden 200yd downstream from A66
Arnside
Arnside Knott. 1m SW of Arnside
Grange-over-Sands
Hampsfell Nature Trail. Starts into woods W side of B5271
Hawkshead
Millwood Forest Trail, Grizedale Forest. 3m S of Hawkshead
Hawkshead
Tarn Hows. 2m NW of Hawkshead off B5285 between Hawkshead and Coniston
Kendal
Serpentine Wood. Starts W side of Kendal town, Serpentine Rd
Keswick
Friars Crag. Starts off A591 through Keswick
Keswick
Swirls Forest Trail. 6½m SW of Keswick off A591 on W side of Thirlmere
Ravenglass
Muncaster Castle Tree Trail. Starts 1m E on A595
Seatoller
Johnny's Wood on B5289 7m SW of Keswick
Ulverston
Bardsea Country Park. Starts within park 2m S of Ulverston on A5087
Windermere
Brockhole Nature Trail. Starts 2m NW of Windermere town on A591

DERBYSHIRE
Buxton
Errwood Hall. 4m NW of Buxton off A5002 beside Errwood Reservoir
Derby
Elvaston Castle Country Park. Starts 4m E of Derby off B5010
Derby
Shipley Hill Woodland Trail. 9m NE of Derby and 2m S of Heanor. In Shipley Country Park
Hathersage
Padley Gorge Nature Walk. Starts 3m SE of Hathersage on B6521 just off A625
Hayfield (4½m S of Glossop)
Sett Valley Trail
Mansfield (Nottinghamshire)
Hardwick Hall. Starts in park 6m NW of Mansfield. Also approached from M1 Junction 29
Tideswell (8½m NE of Buxton)
Tideswell Dale National Park Trail between Tideswell and Millers Dale
Wirksworth
Black Rock. 1m N of Wirksworth, off B5036

DEVON
Barnstaple
Arlington Court. 6m NE of Barnstaple. Circular walk through Park

Bideford
Melbury Woods. 6½m SE of Bideford
Bovey Tracey
Yarner Wood Nature Trail. Starts 2m W of Bovey Tracey on B3344
Bovey Tracey
Yarner Wood Woodland Walk. Starts 2m W of Bovey Tracey on B3344
Dunsford
Dunsford and Meadhay Down Nature Trail. Starting point: Steps Bridge (B3212)
Eggesford
Eggesford Woods – Two walks; on A377 just S of Eggesford; and Haywood Walk, NW of Eggesford
Exeter
Stoke Woods. Starts at Stoke Woods – Exeter Forest 3m N of Exeter on A396
Hartland
Summerwell Trail. 4m SE of Hartland. Off A39 at Bursdon Moor
Holsworthy
Holsworthy Woods. 1¾m S of Holsworthy
Lydford
Lydford Woods. 1½m SW of Lydford
Lynton
Heddon Valley. Starts 4m W of Lynton off A39
Okehampton
Abbeyford Woods. 1¼m N of Okehampton off B3217
Parracombe
Cowley Cleave Nature Trail. Starts 1½m W of Parracombe off A399 and A39
Postbridge
Bellever Forest Walk. Starts at Bellever Forest – Dartmoor Forest – just S of Postbridge
Sidmouth
Salcombe Hill Nature Trail. E of Sidmouth
Tavistock
Morwellham Blue Trail. Starts 4m SW of Tavistock. 2m S of the A390
Torcross
Slapton Ley Footpath. Starts 2m N of Torcross off A379
Torcross
Slapton Sands Footpath. Starts in N end of Torcross on A379

DORSET
Christchurch
Hengistbury Head. Starts 2½m SE of Christchurch off A35
Dorchester
Thorncombe and Blackheath Trails. 3½m NE of Dorchester off A35
Poole
Brownsea Island. Access by boat from Poole Quay or Sandbanks
Puddletown
Puddletown Forest Wall. Starts at Wareham Forest 2m S of Puddletown

Hardwick Hall, Mansfield

Swanage
Sand Dune Nature Trail. Starts 3m N of Swanage off B3351 beyond Studland village
Swanage
Woodland Trail. Starts 3m N of Swanage off B3351 beyond Studland village
Wareham
Northport Forest Walk. Starts at Wareham Forest 1m NW of Wareham on unclass rd

DURHAM
Consett
Derwent Walk. Starts in Derwent Walk Country Park 6m NE of Consett on A694
Darlington
River Tees Nature Trail. Starts 3m SW of Darlington on A67
Darlington
South Park Nature Trail. Starts in Parkside off A66
Edmondbyers
Pow Hill. Starts 1m N of Edmondbyers off B6306 at S side of Derwent Reservoir
Hamsterley
Hamsterley Forest Park. Starts 1m W of Hamsterley village off A68 between West Auckland and Tow Law
Sedgefield
Hardwick Hall. Starts W of Sedgefield at Hardwick Hall Country Park
Tow Law
Collier Wood Nature Trail. Starts 2m S of Tow Law at Collier Wood Picnic Area W of A68

ESSEX
Basildon
Langdon Hills East. Starts 3½m S of Basildon in Langdon Hills East Country Park off A176
Basildon
Langdon Hills West. Starts 3½m S of Basildon in Langdon Hills West Country Park off B1007
Bishop's Stortford (Herts)
Hatfield Forest Walk. Starts 3m E of Bishop's Stortford off A120 at Shell House
Colchester
Fingringhoe Wick Nature Reserve – The Blue Trail. Starts 6m SE of Colchester off B1025 beyond Fingringhoe village
Danbury
The Backwarden. Starts just S of Danbury at Backwarden Car Park, Danbury Common off A414 from Chelmsford
Danbury
Scrubs Woods. Starts ½m N of Danbury off A414 from Chelmsford
Harlow
The Harlow Trail. Farm trail and urban walk. Starts at Museum ½m from town centre on Third Avenue
Walton-on-the-Naze
The Naze Nature Trail. Starts 2m N of Walton-on-the-Naze at car park along Hall Lane

GLOUCESTERSHIRE
Blakeney
Wenchford Trail. On B4431 (Blakeney–Coleford rd) 1½m NW of Blakeney
Cheltenham
Coopers Hill Local Nature Reserve. 6m SW of Cheltenham off A46
Christchurch
Biblins Adventure Trail. Starts within the Forest of Dean ¼m W of Christchurch off B4228
Christchurch
Symonds Yat Forest Walk. Starts within the Forest of Dean 1½m N of Christchurch on B4432
Cinderford
Boys Grave and Cannop Forest Trail. Starts on unclass rd ½m S of Speech House Hotel (B4226), 3m W of Cinderford

Cinderford
Speech House Trail. Starts within the Forest of Dean 3m from Cinderford on B4226 ¼m from Speech House Hotel
Gloucester
Robinswood Hill. Starts at S edge of Gloucester in Robinswood Hill Country Park

HAMPSHIRE
Alton
Gibbet Trail. Chawton Park, 4½m SW of Alton leaving A31 northwards from Four Marks
Basingstoke
Wellington Country Park. 8m NE of Basingstoke on A32 ½m S of Riseley
Beaulieu
Woodland Walk and Farm Trail. Starts at Information Centre, National Motor Museum
Beaulieu
Riverside Walk. Starts at Visitor Centre, Bucklers Hard, 2½m SE of Beaulieu on unclass rd
Bucks Horn Oak (4m SW of Farnham)
Alice Holt Forest. ½m SE of Bucks Horn Oak
Lyndhurst
Bolderwood Woodland Walks. Starts in New Forest 5m W of Lyndhurst at car Park on by-road from Lyndhurst via Emery Down N fo A31 Romsey–Ringwood rd
Lyndhurst
Rhinefield Woodland Walks. Starts in New Forest 4m SW of Lyndhurst off A35 Southampton–Bournemouth rd
Petersfield
Butser Hill. Starts in Queen Elizabeth Country Park, Queen Elizabeth Forest, 4m S of Petersfield, ¾m W of A3
Petersfield
Holt Forest Trail. Queen Elisabeth Country Park, off A3 4m S of Petersfield. Also several miles of forest paths within the Park
Warnford
Old Winchester Hill. Starts 2m SE of Warnford on unclass rd

HEREFORD AND WORCESTER
Alfrick
Ravenshill Woodland Reserve. 1m NW of Alfrick, 2m S of A44 Bromyard–Worcester rd
Bewdley
Wyre Forest Trails. Starts 3m W of Bewdley on A456
Broadway
Broadway Tower. Starts in Broadway Tower Country Park 2m SW of Broadway off A44
Dymock
Queen's Wood Walk. From Dymock take B4215 for 2m to Kempley then take unclass rd SE for 1m to start of walk
Hereford
Haugh Wood Walk. 4m SE of Hereford off B4224, 1½m beyond Mordiford
Kidderminster
Kingsford. Starts in Kingsford Country Park 3m N of Kidderminster E of A442
Rubery (SW of Birmingham)
Windmill and Waseley Hills Country Park. Starts 1m NW of Rubery

HERTFORDSHIRE
Hemel Hempstead
Gade Valley Trail. Starts at St Mary's Church, High Street
St Albans
Verulam Park Nature Trail. Starts at Verulamium Museum on A414
Watford
Cassiobury Park Nature Trail. Starts at entrance to Cassiobury Park, Gade Avenue, N of A412 Watford–Rickmansworth rd
Wheathampstead
Nomansland Nature Trail. Starts 1m S of Wheathampstead at common on B651

HUMBERSIDE
Bridlington
Danes Dyke Nature Trail. Starts 3½m NE of Bridlington on minor road to S of B1255
Hull
Burton Constable. Starts at Burton Constable Country Park 8m NE of Hull
Kilnsea
Spurn Peninsula. Starts to the S of Kilnsea, nr Warren Cottage
Scunthorpe
Normanby Hall. Starts at Normanby Hall Country Park 3m N of Scunthorpe on B1430

ISLE OF WIGHT
Ordnance Survey 1:50 000 sheet number 196 covers the whole of this island
Carisbrooke
Carisbrooke Walk Nature Trail. Starts at car park S of Carisbrooke Castle
Carisbrooke
Shepherds Trail. Starts at St Dominics Priory SE of Carisbrooke Castle nr B3401
Newport
Brighstone Forest Jubilee Walk. Starts 5m SW of Newport at National Trust Car Park on Brighstone–Calbourne rd
Newport
Parkhurst Forest Walk. Starts 1m NW of Newport on A3054
Newport
River Medina Trail (East Bank). Starts at Newport Quay
Newport
Robin Hill. Starts at Robin Hill Country Park 2m E of Newport
Ryde
Firestone Forest Walks 4m SW of Ryde. On by-road between Wootton Bridge and Havenstreet
Ryde
Nunwell Trail. Starts at St John's Railway Station, Ryde
Sandown
Riverside Walk Nature Trail. Starts 2m NW of Sandown by old mill off A3056
Ventnor
Blackgang Nature Trail. Starts 6m W of Ventnor at car park above Blackgang
Ventnor
Stenbury Trail. Starts at Whitwell Rd 1m N of Ventnor town centre
Yarmouth
Brooke Nature Trail. Starts 6m SE of Yarmouth off A3055
Yarmouth
Hamstead Trail. Starts 6m SE of Yarmouth on A3055 W of Brooke
Yarmouth
Riverside Walk Nature Trail (West Wight). Starts at car park in Yarmouth town centre

KENT
Ashford
Faggs Wood. 5m S of Ashford off B2070
Canterbury
Clowes Wood. 3¾m N of Canterbury on by-road to Whitstable
Canterbury
West Wood (Lyminge Forest). 9m S of Canterbury off B2068, by-road for Lyminge
Challock (6m N of Ashford)
King's Wood Forest Trail. Starts at Challock Forest m S of Challock crossroads
Chilham
Chilham Castle. Starts in castle grounds
Hawkhurst
Bedgebury. Starts at National Pinetum Bedgebury Forest 5m NW of Hawkhurst on B2079

Sevenoaks
Kemsing Youth Hostel Walk. Starts 3m NE of Sevenoaks from Kemsing Youth Hostel
Tonbridge
Dene Park Forest Walks. 3m NNE of Tonbridge off A227

LANCASHIRE
Blackburn
Witton Park. Starts in Witton Country Park 2½m W of Blackburn
Colne
Wycoller. Starts in Wycoller Country Park 2½m E of Colne
Harwood, Great
Great Harwood ½m N of town centre. Leave by Cliffe Lane. Starting point Allsprings Lodge
Lytham St Annes
Witchford Forest. Starts at Skew Bridge, Blackpool Rd B5261
Preston
Beacon Fell. Starts in Beacon Fell Country Park, 12m N of Preston. Approach from A6 nr Bilsborrow (6½m N of Preston) thence unclass rd eastwards
Silverdale
Eaves Wood. Approach from Elmslack Lane
Whalley
Spring Wood. Off A671 ½m E of Whalley

LEICESTERSHIRE
Leicester
Bradgate Park. Starts in Bradgate Country Park 3m NW of Leicester on B5327

LINCOLNSHIRE
Bourne
Callan's Lane Wood. 6½m N of Bourne via A15 and unclass rd thence via Kirkby Underwood
Colsterworth (8m S of Grantham)
Twyford Wood Walk. On A151, ½m E of junction A1 nr Colsterworth
Grantham
Ropsley Rise Wood Trail. 3m SE of Grantham (A52 and B1176) thence 1m NE of Old Somerby
Market Rasen
Willingham Forest Walks on A631, 2m E of Market Rasen
Stamford
Monkery Wood Trail. 12m NW of Stamford 1m E of A1 junction/Castle Bytham rd
Woodhall Spa
Ostlers Plantation Walks. 2m E of Woodhall Spa via B1191 and unclass rd towards Kirkby on Bain
Wragby (11½m NE of Lincoln)
Chambers Wood Walks. 3m S of Wragby via B1202 thence E unclass

LONDON (GT)
Bromley
High Elms Woodland Walk. Starts at Cuckoo Wood Car Park, High Elms Rd, nr Downe
Croydon
Coulsdon Downs Nature Trail No. 1. Starts at Welcome Tea Rooms at southern end of Farthing Downs off A23
Croydon
Coulsdon Downs Nature Trail No. 2. Starts at Happy Valley Car Park on Fox Lane off B2030
Croydon
Downland Rambles. Starts at N end of Farthing Downs
Croydon
Woodland Rambles. Starts at Conduit Lane, off Coombe Rd A212
Enfield
Trent Park. Starts near Fishpond, Cockfosters Rd entrance to Trent Park
Enfield
Trent Park Trail for the Blind. Starts at Trent Park, Cockfosters Rd

South Woodford
Epping Forest Nature Trail. Start at junction of Oak Hill and A104, ¾m N of A406 roundabout on N Circular Rd

MANCHESTER (GT)
Bolton
Jumbles Reservoir. Starts 4m N of Bolton at Jumbles Reservoir Country Park
Bolton
Nob End Nature Trail. Boscow Rd, Little Lever
Bolton
Smithills Hall. Dean Rd
Cheadle Hulme
Cheadle Hulme Trail. Farnham Close
Middleton
Hopwood Clough. Off A664, nr entrance to De La Salle College
Stockport
Bramhall Park Trail. Bramhall Hall Park
Stockport
Etherow Park. Starts 3m E of Stockport in Etherow Country Park off B6104

MERSEYSIDE
Eastham
Eastham Woods. Starts at Eastham Country Park off A41 N of Eastham
Thurstaston (4m SE of Hoylake)
Thurstaston Environmental Trail

NORFOLK
Brancaster
Scolt Head Island Nature Trail. Starts 2½m E of Brancaster by boat from Brancaster Staithe N of A149
Cromer
Felbrigg Hall. Starts 2m SW of Cromer at Felbrigg Hall off A148 and B1436
Hickling
Hickling Broad Water Trail. Starts at Pleasure Boat Inn, Hickling, E of A149 via Sutton, Hickling Green and Stubb
Hunstanton
Holme Nature Reserve. Starts 2m NE of Hunstanton at the Warden's House, The Firs (on Reserve)
North Walsham
Bacton Wood. Starts at Wensum Forest 2m E of North Walsham on unclass rd S of the B1150 North Walsham–Bacton rd
Norwich
Mousehold Heath. Starts 1m NE of city centre at car park on Gurney Rd
Sandringham
Sandringham Nature Trail. On a Royal estate. Starts at car park – signposted off B1440
Thetford
East Wretham Heath. Starts 5m NE of Thetford at East Wretham on A1075
Thetford
Lynford Forest Trail. Starts at Thetford Forest 8m NW of Thetford off A134
Wroxham
Hoveton Great Broad Nature Trail. Starts 2½m downstream from Wroxham on N bank of River Bure, accessible only by boat hired from Wroxham or Horning

NORTHAMPTONSHIRE
Northampton
Salcey Forest Walk. Starts at Salcey Forest 8m S of Northampton off A508 via Roade and Hartwell villages or from B526
Silverstone
Bucknell Wood Forest Trail. Starts on unclass rd 1m NW of Silverstone
Stamford (Lincs)
Wakerley Forest Trail. Starts 7m SW of Stamford W of A43 towards Wakerley village

Seahouses, Northumberland

Wellingborough
Irchester. Starts at Irchester Country Park 2m SE of Wellingborough off A509

NORTHUMBERLAND
Bedlington
Plessey Woods. Starts at Plessey Wood Country Park 1½m SW of Bedlington on A1068
Bellingham
Falstone Forest – Sidwood Trail. 6m NW of Bellingham, via Greenhaugh
Holystone (7m W of Rothbury)
Holystone Forest Walks. Approached from the Rothbury–Otterburn rd, B6341
Kielder
Duchess Drive Walk. Starts at Kielder Castle
Morpeth
Bolam Lake. Starts at Bolam Lake Country Park 8m SW of Morpeth, nr Belsay. Car park
Rothbury
Simonside (Rothbury Forest) Trail. Starts at Rothbury Forest 3m SW of Rothbury at car park nr Great Tosson
Seahouses
Inner Farne (Farne Islands). Reached by boat from Seahouses
Wark (11m NW of Hexham)
Wark Forest. Starts in Wark Forest, 6m W of Wark off B6320 at Stonehaugh
Whittingham (7½m W of Alnwick)
Thrunton Wood Walks. Starts at Rothbury Forest 2m S of Whittingham ½m W of A696
Wooler
Hepburn Wood. 7¾m SE of Wooler, off A697, or from A1 at North Charlton (6¾m). Overlooks Chillingham Park

NOTTINGHAMSHIRE
Nottingham
Burnstump. Starts at Burnstump Country Park 7m N of Nottingham off A60
Ollerton
Rufford Abbey. Starts at Rufford Abbey Country Park 3m S of Ollerton on A614
Southwell
Southwell Trail. Starts ¾m NE of Southwell off A612

OXFORDSHIRE
Aston Rowant
Aston Rowant National Nature Reserve. Starts 1½m S of Aston Rowant at Beacon Hill, signposted from A40 between Stokenchurch and Postcombe
Watlington
Cowleaze Wood Walk. Located on by-road 1½m N of Christmas Common (2m SE of Watlington)

SALOP

Church Stretton
Old Rectory Wood. Starts ½m up Burway Rd at
reservoir in Townbrook Hollow
Ludlow
Whitecliffe Wood. Starts 1m SE of Ludlow at
Forestry Commission Museum on Burrington Rd off
A49
Shrewsbury
Corbet Wood Trail. 7m N of Shrewsbury, off A49,
eastern side of summit of Grinshill

SOMERSET

Broadway
Castle Neroche. Starts within Neroche Forest 3m W
of Broadway on unclass rd to N of A303
Cheddar
Black Rock. Starts 1½m NE of Cheddar at upper end
of Cheddar Gorge
Cheddar
Longwood Nature Trail. Starts 1½m NE of Cheddar,
above upper end of Cheddar Gorge
Cloutsham
Cloutsham Nature Trail. 2m S of A39 (Porlock–
Minehead rd)
Minehead
North Hill Nature Trail. Starts northern end of
Minehead Sea Front
Nether Stowey (A39 Minehead–Bridgdwater rd)
Seven Wells Nature Trail. 2m SW of village
(signposted)
Wookey Hole
Ebbor Gorge National Nature Reserve. 1m NW of
Wookey Hole. Length ½m and 1½m

STAFFORDSHIRE

Ilam (5m NW of Ashbourne)
Ilam Nature Walk. In grounds of Ilam Hall (Country
Park
Oakamoor
Hawksmoor Nature Reserve. 1m SW of village off
B5417
Rugeley
Cannock Chase Forest Walks. Starts 2m SW of
Rugeley nr forest centre
Rugeley
Haywood Warren (Cannock Chase). 3m NW of
Rugeley off A513 nr Weetman's Bridge
Rugeley
Seven Springs Outdoor Trail. Starts 2m W of
Rugeley off unclass Rugeley–Penkridge rd
Stafford
Shorbrook Valley Outdoor Trail. Starts 3m SE of
Stafford at Milford Common on A513
Tamworth
Alvecote Pools. Starts 3m E of Tamworth on minor
rd N from B5000

SUFFOLK

Brandon
Brandon Park. Starts in Brandon Country Park 1m S
of Brandon on B1106
Bury St Edmunds
King's Forest Walk. Starts 5m NW of Bury St
Edmunds nr West Stow off A1101
Thetford (Norfolk/Suffolk borders)
Santon Downham Forest Walks. Starts 5m NW of
Thetford at Santon Downham church, between
B1107 and A134
Woodbridge
Easton Farm Park Nature Trail. Starts 8m N of
Woodbridge signposted from Easton

SURREY

Banstead
Perrotts Wood. Starts 1m SE of Banstead behind
Park Farm
Dorking
Abinger Highridge Forest Walk. 3½m SE of Dorking
off Dorking–Newdigate rd

Dorking
Ranmore. Starts from National Trust Car Park 2½m W
of Dorking on unclass rd to East Horsley
Epsom
Horton. Starts NW of Epsom in Horton Country Park
Farnham
Rowhill Nature Reserve. Starts 2½m NE of Farnham
at junction of A325 and B3008
Guildford
Guildford Nature Trail. Starts nr Canoe Club on
A281 ½m S of town centre
Haslemere
Witley Holmen's Grove. 2½m N of Haslemere on
A286
Hindhead
Gibbet Hill Trail. Off A3, ½m E of Hindhead cross-
roads (junc A3/A287)
Leatherhead
Abinger Mountain Wood Walk. Starts ½m E of East
Horlsey (5½m SW of Leatherhead) at car park at
Greendene
Leatherhead
Abinger East Horsley Forest Walk. Same start as
above, following Abinger Mountain Wood Walk for
a short distance

SUSSEX (EAST)

Brighton
Stanmer Park Nature Trail. Starts 4½m NE of Brighton
½m inside gates of Stanmer Park
Ditchling
Ditchling Common. Starts 2m N of Ditchling on
B2112 in Ditchling Common Country Park
Eastbourne
Beachy Head Nature Trail. Starts 3m SW of
Eastbourne at Beachy Head, signposted from B2103
Eastbourne
Wilmington–Abbots Wood Forest Walk. 8½m NW of
Eastbourne. Approach from Eastbourne–Lewes rd
A27 turning northwards along unclass rd to
Arlington. (Or from A22, 7m N of Eastbourne, turn
eastwards along unclass rd to Arlington.)
Friston
Friston Forest. Starts at West Dean picnic area 2¾m
NW of Friston off A259
Hastings
Footlands Wood Forest Walk. 8m N of Hastings via
A21, then eastwards B2089
Hastings
Warren Glen. Starts 3m E of Hastings off minor rd off
A259
Horam
Horam Quiet Corner. Starts at Horam village, off
A267
Seaford
Friston Forest Walk. 2½m E of Seaford on A259, turn
N along unclass rd to Litlington
Seaford
Seven Sisters Country Park Nature Trail. Starts
opposite Exceat Farm off A259

SUSSEX (WEST)

Arundel
Fairmile Bottom. Starts 2m NW of Arundel at
Fairmile café, 1m SW of A29 and A284 junction
Chichester
Goodwood. Starts in Goodwood Country Park, 6m
N of Chichester
Chichester
Selhurst Park. 7m NE of Chichester ½m W of A285
Chichester
Stoughton Down. 8m NW of Chichester. Approach
via B2178 and B2176 and unclass rd through
Walderton or via A286 and B2141 and unclass rd via
East Marden
Chichester
Weald and Downland Open Air Museum. Starts
6m N of Chichester signposted off A286 at
Singleton

Eartham
Eartham Wood. Starts at Arundel Forest, Eartham Wood ½m E of A285 (Petworth–Chichester rd)
East Grinstead
Forest Way Trail. Starts on A22 SE side of town, in Forest Way Country Park, between East Grinstead and Groombridge
East Grinstead
Gravetye Woods. 3m SW of East Grinstead via B2110 thence along Vowel Lane unclass
Shoreham
Mill Hill Nature Trail. Starts 1m N of Shoreham at car park on Mill Hill
West Wittering (7m SW of Chichester)
East Head Nature Walks. Promontory at entrance to Chichester Harbour

TYNE AND WEAR
Newcastle-upon-Tyne
Derwent Walk. Starts 10m SW of Newcastle-upon-Tyne at Swalwell Old Station off A694 beyond Rowlands Gill

WARWICKSHIRE
Alcester
Oversley Wood. Starts 2m E of Alcester to S of A422
Alcester
Ragley Country Trail. Starts 2m S of Alcester at forecourt of Ragley Hall on A435
Warwick
Stratford-upon-Avon Canal Trail. 8m NW of Warwick via A41/B4439 to Kingswood (Lapworth). Starts at canal depot
Whichford (6m N of Chipping Norton)
Whichford Woods. Starts 1¼m W of Whichford village

WEST MIDLANDS
Birmingham
Earlswood. Starts 8m S of Birmingham at New Fallings Coppice off B4102
Coventry
Coombe Abbey Nature Trail. Starts 8m E of Coventry on A427
Dudley
Wrens Nest National Nature Reserve. Starts at Caves Public House between A459 and A457
Walsall
Hay Head Nature Trail. Starts 2m E of Walsall at Longwood Lane off A454

WILTSHIRE
Devizes
Roundway Hill Covert Countryside Trail. 2m N of Devizes via A361 and unclass rd to Roundway village
Marlborough
Postern Hill Walk. Starts at Savernake Forest on A346 1m SE of Marlborough
Westbury
Woodland Park. Starts 2m NW of Westbury off B3099

YORKSHIRE (NORTH)
Pickering
Bridestones Moor Nature Walk. Starts 7m NE of Pickering off A169. Access via Dalby Forest Drive
Pickering
Dalby Forest Walk. Several walks starting in Dalby Forest 6m NE of Pickering (follow Scarborough rd A170, to Thornton Dale and take unclass rd northwards to Low Dalby)
Pickering
Cropton Forest Walks 7m N of Pickering. Several trails starting in forest drive
Ravenscar
Ravenscar Geology Trail. Starts at Ravenscar
Scarborough
Silpho (Langdale) Forest Trail. 7m NW of Scarborough via A171 and unclass rd N of Scalby

Scarborough
Wykeham. Starts at Wykeham Forest 5m W of Scarborough (A170). NW of Wykeham village
Selby
Bishop Wood. Starts at York Forest 5½m W of Selby on B1222
Selby
Skipwith Common Nature Trail. Starts 5m N of Selby off A19
Settle
Reginald Farrer Nature Trail. Starts 6m NW of Settle at National Park Information Centre, Ingleborough, off B6480 or A65
Thirsk
Sutton Bank Nature Trail. Starts 3m E of Thirsk at car park on A170
Whitby
Falling Foss. 5m S of Whitby of B1416
York
Moorlands Nature Trail. Starts 5m N of York off B1363 on unclass rd to Shipton

YORKSHIRE (SOUTH)
Barnsley
Worsborough. Starts in Worsborough Mill Country Park 2m S of Barnsley on A61
Doncaster
Melton Wood Walk. Leave Doncaster by Sprotbrough rd (unclass), 1¼m beyond Sprotbrough turn right
Sheffield
Graves Park Nature Trail. Starts 3m S of Sheffield off A61 S of B6068 junction
Sheffield
Rivelin Nature Trail. Starts 3m W of Sheffield E of A57 and A6101 junction
South Kirkby (West Yorkshire)
Howell Wood. Starts in Howell Wood Country Park 1m SE of South Kirkby

YORKSHIRE (WEST)
Halifax
North Dean Nature Trail. Starts 3m SE of Halifax off B6113 at Clay House
Hebden Bridge
Slurring Rock Nature Trail. Starts 1m NE of Hebden Bridge off A6033 at the Lodge, Hebden Valley
Huddersfield
Beaumont Park Nature Trail. Starts at Meltham Rd, Huddersfield. Length 1¼m. Open all year
Ilkley
Ilkley Moor Nature Trail. Starts ¼m S of Ilkley in Wells Rd
Ilkley
Middleton Woods. Starts 1m NE of Ilkley off A65
Ilkley
River Wharf. Starts at Ilkley New Bridge off A65
Keighley
Penistone Hill. Starts in Penistone Hill Country Park W of Haworth (3m S of Keighley)
Pontefract
Brockdale Nature Park. Starts 5m SE of Pontefract E of A1

Forest Drives

England

DURHAM
Bishop Auckland
Hamsterley Forest Drive 10m W of Bishop Auckland via A688, West Auckland A68, thence unclass rd via Hamsterley

NORTHUMBERLAND
Kielder
Kielder to Byrness (A68) Forest Drive. Starts from
North Kielder Forest at Kielder Castle or from
Blakehopeburnhaugh off A68, 8½m NW of
Otterburn

YORKSHIRE (NORTH)
Pickering
Cropton Forest Drive 7m N of Pickering. Follow the
Scarborough rd A169 for 5m then turn left unclass
through Levisham. (Entrance/exit (SE796944) also
on minor rd between Pickering and Egton Bridge)
Pickering
Dalby Forest Drive. Starts 1½m N of Thornton Dale
on unclass rd off Scarborough–Pickering rd (A170).
Can also be reached from Scarborough via A171
and unclass rd at Scalby, thence via Hackness
(entrance SE911910)

Nature Trails

Wales

CLWYD
Colwyn Bay
Bryn Euryn Scenic Trail. Starts 1m W of Colwyn Bay
between Rhos-on-Sea and Mochdre on A546
Holywell
Holywell Nature Trail. Starts from Pen-y-Maes
estate off A5026
Llangollen
Pontcysyllte Trail. Commences at Pontcysyllte
(B5434), 4m E of Llangollen
Llangollen
World's End Nature Trail. Starts 5m N from A542 at
Llangollen
Mold
The Leete Nature Trail. Starts 2½m NW of Mold on
A541 (at Rhydymwyn)
Mold
Loggerheads Nature Trail. Starts 3m W of Mold at
Loggerheads Inn on A494
Mold
Loggerheads Country Park Nature Trail. 3m W of
Mold on A494, several walks
Mold
Moel Famau Nature Trail. Starts 5m SW of Mold at
Coed Clwyd car park on unclass rd off A494
Prestatyn
Bishopswood Nature Trail. Starts 2m S of Prestatyn
off A547
Queensferry
Ewole Castle Nature Trail. Starts 2m SW of
Queensferry, ½m NW of Ewole roundabout
Wrexham
Bersham Industrial Trail. Starts 3m W of Wrexham
on A525
Wrexham
Geological Trail. Starts 7m W of Wrexham on A525
at Bwlchgwyn
Wrexham
Vaun-y-Llyn Country Park. 6½m NW of Wrexham

DYFED
Aberystwyth
Constitution Hill Nature Trail. Starts at foot of
Constitution Hill off B4346
Aberystwyth
Cwmrheidol Nature Trail. Starts 5m E of
Aberystwyth at Power Station Reception Centre off
A44
Aberystwyth
Rheidol Forest Walk. Starts 3m NW of Aberystwyth
off A4159

Devil's Bridge, Dyfed

Aberystwyth
Tynbedw Forest Trail. Starts 10m SE of Aberystwyth
on by-road linking B4340 with Pontrhydygroes
Borth
Ynyslas Nature Trail. Starts 3m N of Borth off B4572
Dale (13m SW of Haverfordwest)
Dale Peninsula Path. Starts at Griffin Inn, Dale, on
B4327
Devil's Bridge
Arch Forest Trail. Starts 2m SE of Devil's Bridge at
car park at The Arch off B4574
Devil's Bridge
Devil's Bridge Nature Trail. Starts off A4120 at
junction with B4574 at Devil's Bridge
Fishguard
Dinas Island Walk. Starts 4m E of Fishguard off
A487 at Dinas. Length 3m
Haverfordwest
Llys-y-Frân Reservoir. 8m NE of Haverfordwest, in
Llys-y-Frân Country Park
Lampeter
Estate Walk. Starts 8m SE of Lampeter on A482 ¼m
NW of Pumpsaint
Lampeter
Dolaucothi Nature Trails. Starts 8m SE of Lampeter,
½m E of Pumpsaint off A582
Llandovery
Dinas Nature Trail. Starts 8m N of Llandovery at
Warden's Information Centre at car park 3m N of
Rhandirmwyn off unclass rd
Llandovery
Llyn Brianne Walks on the borders of Dyfed and
Powys, 15m NW of Llandovery on unclass rd via
Rhandirmwyn. Various walks not waymarked
Llandovery
Sugar Loaf Walk. 7m NW of Llandovery off A483
Machynlleth (Powys)
Taliesin Forest Walk. Starts 7m SW of Machynlleth
1m E of Furnace off A487
Marloes
Marloes Sands Nature Trail. Starts 1m W of Marloes
on unclass rd off B4327

Marloes
Skomer Island Nature Trail. Starts 2m W of Marloes boat embarkation point at Martin's Haven on unclass rd off B4327. Trail starts at North Haven on Island

Narberth
Slebech Forest Trail. Starts 3m W of Narberth, ¾m SW of junction A40 and A4075

Tenby
Lydstep Headland Nature Trail. Starts 3½m W of Tenby at Lydstep Head car park on A4139

Tenby
Penally Nature Trail. Starts 2m SW of Tenby at Crown Inn, Penally on A4139

GLAMORGAN (MID)
Aberdare
Walks in the Dare Valley Country Park. Starts W side of Aberdare by A4059 or B4277

Caerphilly
Caerphilly Common Nature Trail. Starts 1m NW of car park on Caerphilly Common on A469

Caerphilly
Rudry Forest Walk. Starts 2½m E of Caerphilly on minor rd off A469 in Caerphilly

Merthyr Tydfil
Garwnant Forest Trails (Coed Taff Forest). 5m N of Merthyr Tydfil off A470

Merthyr Tydfil
Old Glamorgan Canal Walk. Starts 1m S of Merthyr Tydfil at Technical College car park, Abercanaid, off A470

Merthyr Tydfil
Talybont Forest Walk (Powys). Starts 8m N of Merthyr on minor rd between Merthyr Tydfil and Talybont-on-Usk off A465

Porthcawl
Kenfig Burrows Walk. Starts 3m N of Porthcawl at car park in Kenfig village on A48

Pontypridd
Walks on Mynydd Eglwysilan. Starts ½m E of Pontypridd opposite hospital on A470

Rhondda
Blaen Rhondda Walk. Starts 5m NW of Rhondda at car park 3m NW of Treherbert on A4061

GLAMORGAN (SOUTH)
Barry
Porthkerry Country Park. Starts 2m W of Barry on Minor rd W from A4050 at Barry

Cardiff
Bute Park Nature Trail. Starts at west entrance of Cardiff Castle on A48

Cardiff
Canton to Llandaf Walk. Starts at Victoria Park on A48

Cardiff
Cefn-Onn Walk, Llanisen. Starts at NE edge of Cardiff 1m E on minor rd off A469

Cardiff
Glamorgan Canal Wharf. Starts 2m N of Cardiff off A4054

Cardiff
Great Garth Walk. Starts 5m NW of Cardiff on minor rd W from A470 N of Tongwynglais

Cardiff
Nant Fawr Walk. Starts 1m NW of Cardiff on Waterloo Rd, Roath on A48

Cardiff
Rhymney Walk. Starts on E outskirts of Cardiff on A48

Cardiff
Taff Valley Walk. Starts at Castle grounds North Gate

Cardiff
Wenallt Nature Trails. Starts 1m SW of Travellers Rest Inn on A469

Cowbridge
Hensol Forest Walks (Tair Onen Forest). Starts 3m NE of Cowbridge at car park ½m N of Welsh St Donat's on minor rd from A4222 or A48

GLAMORGAN (WEST)
Oxwich
Oxwich Sand Trail. Starts at car park, Oxwich, on minor rd of A4118

Port Eynon
Port Eynon Point Walk. Starts at Port Eynon car park at end of A4118

Port Talbot
Afan Argoed Country Park Walks. Starts 5m NE of Port Talbot on A4107

Port Talbot
Walks in Margam Park. Starts 1m E of Port Talbot nr Margam Parish Church off A48

Rhossili
Gower Coast Nature Trail. Starts at Rhossili car park on B4247, off A4118, at Scurlage

GWENT
Abercarn
Cwm Gwyddon Walk in Ebbw Forest. Starts at car park 1½m E of A467 at Abercarn

Abergavenny
Thirty walks in the Gwent section of the Brecon Beacons National Park, starting at various points in the vicinity of Abergavenny

Abergavenny
Mynydd Du Forest Walk. Starts 8m N of Abergavenny at car park, Grywyne Fawr Valley on minor rd N from A465 at Abergavenny

Abergavenny
St Mary's Vale Nature Trail. Starts 1½m NW of Abergavenny on unclass rd N of A40

Chepstow
Wyndcliff Nature Trail. Starts 2m N of Chepstow at car park, Wyndcliff on A466

Monmouth
Wye Valley Walk (Chepstow to Symonds Yat). Starts at Kingsmark School, Chepstow to Symonds Yat station

Newport
Gray Hill Countryside Trail. Starts at Wentwood Reservoir picnic site N of Penhow on A48

Newport
Walks in Wentwood Forest 9¾m NE of Newport, reached via A48, turning north nr Penhow (7¾m) on unclass rd

Pontypool
Llandegfedd Reservoir Walks. Starts 3m SE of Pontypool at Eastern picnic area. Brook picnic area reaced by unclass rd off A4042

Tintern
Barbadoes Hill Forest Walk. Starts at car park, Tintern on A466

Tintern
Chapel Hill Forest Walk. Starts at car park, Tintern on A466

GWYNEDD
Amlwch
Wylfa Nature Trail. Starts 5m W of Amlwch at car park at power station 1m W of Cemaes Bay on A5025

Beddgelert (13m SE Caernarfon)
Beddgelert Forest Trail. Starts 1m NW of Beddgelert on A4085

Beddgelert (13m SE Caernarfon)
Beddgelert Forest Walks (Pont Cae'r Gors) 2m NW of Beddgelert off A4085

Beddgelert (13m SE Caernarfon)
Cae Dafydd Forest Walk. Starts 3m SE of Beddgelert off A4085

Beddgelert (13m SE Caernarfon)
Nant Gwynant Walk off A498 3m NE of Beddgelert

Bethesda
Cwm Idwal Nature Trail. Starts 4m SE of Bethesda at entrance to Llyn Idwal Reserve 4½m W of Capel Curig on A5

Betws-y-Coed
Caen-y-Coed Arboretum and Walk (Gwydyr Forest).
Starts 2m W of Betws-y-Coed on A5 nr Swallow
Falls
Betws-y-Coed
Gwydyr Forest Trail. Starts 2½m W of Betws-y-Coed
at Ty Hyll (Ugly House) on A5
Betws-y-Coed
Gwydyr Forest Walks. Starts at car park S of A5
Dolgellau
Dolgefeiliau Forest Trail. Starts 5m N of Dolgellau
off A470 at Ganllwyd
Dolgellau
Precipice Walk. Starts 2¾m N of Dolgellau on minor
rd N from A494 or E from A470
Dolgellau
Ty'n-y-Groes Forest Trail. Starts 5m N of Dolgellau
at Forest picnic site, Ganllwyd, off A470
Harlech
Cwm Nantcol Nature Trail. Starts 4m SE of Harlech
at picnic site off A496 at Llanbedr
Holyead
Penrhos Nature Trail. Starts 2m SE of Holyhead
100yd along rd joining A5 nr Old Toll House on
Stanley Embankment
Holyhead
South Stack Lighthouse Walk. Starts 3m W of
Holyhead at steps leading down to South Stack
Lighthouse on minor rd from A5 at Holyhead
Llanberis
Llyn Padarn Country Park. Starts E of Llanberis in
Llyn Padarn Country Park
Llanberis
The Miners Track. Starts 5m SE of Llanberis at
Pen-y-Pass car park on A4068
Llanfairfechan
Coedydd Aber Nature Trail. 2m W of Llanfairfechan
along A55 thence S at Aber
Llanfairfechan
Llanfairfechan History Trail. Starts 1m SE of
Llanfairfechan (which is 7m W of Conwy) at Three
Streams car park and picnic site Valley Rd, on A55
Llandudno
Great Orme Nature Trail. Starts in Llandudno at
Happy Valley Café, nr the pier
Llanrwst
Lady Mary's Walk. Starts at drive of Forestry
Commission offices at Gwydyr Uchaf, Llanrwst on
B5106
Llanrwst
Llyn Geriónnydd Forest Trail. Starts 3m W of
Llanrwst at car park at SW end of Llyn Geriónnydd
on minor rd from B5106 or from A5
Llithfaen (9m N of Pwllheli)
Ty Canol Walk, ¾m N of Llithfaen
Maentwrog (10m E of Porthmadog)
Coed Llyn Mair Nature Trail. Starts 1m NW of
Maentwrog at car park on B4410
Newborough
Hendai Forest Trail. Starts at Newborough Forest car
park off A4080 at Newborough
Newborough
Newborough Warren. Starts at Newborough village
on A4080
Penmaenmawr
History Trail. Starts ½m S of Penmaenmawr of A55
Trawsfynydd
Trawsfynydd Nature Trail. Starts at car park,
Trawsfynydd Power Station off A470

POWYS
Brecon
Some short walks round Brecon. Starts in the centre
of Brecon close to A40/A4062
Knighton
Radnorshire Trail No. 1 (Bleddfa). 8m SW of
Knighton off A488
Llanidloes
Llafren Forest Walks. 7m W of Llanidloes via
Llan-y-nant

Llanidloes
Llyn Clywedog Scenic Trail. Starts 4m W of
Llanidloes on S shore of Clywedog Reservoir off
B4518
Llanwrtyd Wells
Cwym Irfon Forest Walks (Abergwesyn). 2¼m NW of
Llanwrtyd Wells on unclass rd to Abergwesyn
Machynlleth
Tan-y-Coed Forest Walk. Starts in Dyfi Forest at
Tan-y-Coed picnic site 4m N of Machynlleth off
A487

Forest Drives

Wales
GWENT
Cwmcarn
Ebbw Forest Scenic Drive. Starts in Ebbw Forest, 1m
from Cwmcarn off A467

Nature Trails

Scotland
BORDERS
Hawick
Craik Forest Trail. Starts at Craik Forest 12½m SW of
Hawick on minor rd from B711 at Roberton
Melrose
Eildon Walk. Starts at the Square, Melrose on A68
Peebles
Cardrona Nature Trails. Starts in Glentress Forest 4m
SW of Peebles on B7062, S of the River Tweed
Peebles
Glentress Forest Trails. Starts 2m E of Peebles on
A72

CENTRAL
Aberfoyle
Silver Ring Walk (Loch Ard Forest). Starts nr
junction A821/B829; cross River Forth on to
unclass rd
Aberfoyle
Waterfall Trail (Achray Forest). Commences at David
Marshall Lodge ¾m NW of Aberfoyle
Callander
Invertrossachs Nature Reserve. Starts 6m W of
Callander off A892 SW of Callander
Callander
Ben Shian Walk (Strathyre Forest). Commences in
Strathyre Village, 8½m NW of Callander. Cross
footbridge over River Balvaig
Callander
Strathyre Forest Trail. Commences in Strathyre, 8½m
NW of Callander
Drymen
Balmaha Forest Walks (Buchanan Forest, Queen
Elizabeth Forest Park). Starts 6½m NW of Drymen at
Balmaha on B837 from A811 at Drymen
Drymen
Sallochy Trail (Buchanan Forest, Queen Elizabeth
Forest Park). Starts 10½m NW Drymen at Sallochy
beyond Balmaha on minor rd off B837
Stirling
Mill Glen Nature Trail. Starts 8m E of Stirling at
Tillicoutry on A91

DUMFRIES AND GALLOWAY
Dalbeattie
Dalbeattie Trails. Starts in Solway Forest 1m S of Dalbeattie on A710
Dumfries
Ae Forest Walks. Starts 8m N of Dumfries near Ae village NW of A701
Dumfries
Heron Walk (Forest of AE). Starts 7½m N of Dumfries at car park in Forest of Ae, beyond Ae village W of A701
Dumfries
Mabie Forest Trails. Starts 3m S of Dumfries, 1m NW of A710 on by-road nr Mabie Lodge gates
Gatehouse of Fleet
Fleet Forest Trails. Starts ½m E of Gatehouse of Fleet on by-road to Cally Hotel off A75
Glen Trool (Galloway Forest Park), (14m N of Newton Stewart)
Loch Trool (Galloway Forest Park). Starts at Caldon's Camp Site, Glen Trool on SW shore of Loch Trool
Glen Trool (Galloway Forest Park), (14m N of Newton Stewart)
Stroan Forest Walk. Starts 1m E of Glen Trool off A714
Newton Stewart
Larg Hill and Bruntis Trails. Starts 4m SE of Newton Stewart at Forest Nursery on minor rd N of A75 at Palnure
Newton Stewart
Talnotry Trail (Galloway Forest Park). Starts 7m NE of Newton Stewart at camp site on A712
Thornhill
Drumlanrig Castle. Starts 3m NW of Thornhill on minor rd N of A702 at Burnhead
Wigtown
Kilsture Forest Trail. Starts in Bareagle Forest 4m S of Wigtown off A746 nr Sorbie

FIFE
Cupar
Craighall Den Nature Trail. Starts 3m S of Cupar ½m W of Ceres on minor rd to Largo
Dunfermline
Pittencrieff Glen. Starts at Pittencrieff Park at Bridge St, just off A994
Kirkcaldy
Dunnikier Park Nature Trail. Starts ½m N of Kirkcaldy off B926
Kirkcaldy
Ravenscraig Park Nature Trail. Starts ½m NE of Kirkcaldy town centre off A955
Leven
Letham Glen Nature Trail. Starts at Letham Glen Park, Leven, off A915

GRAMPIAN
Aberdeen
Forest Lodge Walks (Kirkhill Forest). 5m W of Aberdeen between A93 and A944. Several walks in area
Aberdeen
Hazlehead Nature Trail. Starts 4m W of Aberdeen at Hazlehead Park off A944 on W outskirts of Aberdeen
Alford (19m W of Inverurie)
Haughton House Nature Trail. Starts ¾m N of Alford on minor rd off A944
Alford (19m W of Inverurie)
Murray Park Nature Trail. Starts ¾m N of Alford on minor rd
Banchory
Banchory Forest Walks (Shooting Greens). Starts 5m W of Banchory at car park in Forest on minor rd between B976 and A93
Banchory
Crathes Castle Woodlands Nature Trail. Starts 3m E of Banchory on A93

Elgin
Laigh of Moray Forest Walks. Starts 4m SW of Elgin on minor rd off B9010. (Signposted Pluscarden)
Inverurie
Bennachie Forest Walks. 8m W of Inverurie via A96 (Huntly rd) thence B9002 and Oyne village turning S, ½m W of Oyne. Or leaving Inverurie via B993 to Monymusk, then unclass rd northwards for 3½m

HIGHLAND
Aviemore
Glenmore Forest Park. 6m E of Aviemore nr Glenmore Caravan Sites. On Cairngorm ski rd from junction B970/A951
Aviemore
Loch an Eilein Nature Trail. Starts 3m S of Aviemore at Information Centre on minor rd S of A971 at N end of Loch an Eilein
Bonar Bridge
Kyle of Sutherland Forest Walks. Start in Shin Forest 5m NW of Bonar Bridge, on minor rd to Culrain from A9 at Bonar Bridge Station
Cannich (28m SW of Inverness)
Dog Falls Trail (Affric Forest). From Cannich follow unclass rd to Fasnakyle Power Station and turn along Glen Affric
Drumnadrochit (14¾m SW of Inverness)
Falls of Divach (Glenurquhart Forest). From Drumnadrochit follow A82 southwards for ½m and turn right unclass and follow signs
Elphin (12m N of Ullapool)
Knockan Cliff Nature Trail. Starts 3m SW of Elphin on A835
Fort Augustus
Inchnacardoch Trail. Starts 1m W of Fort Augustus off A82. Linking two picnic areas
Fort William
Archriabhach (Leanachan Forest) Walk. 5m SSE of Fort William; unclass rd through Glen Nevis
Fort William
Corrychurrachan (Lochaber Forest). 6m SW of Fort William off A82
Gairloch
Slattadale Forest Walks and Tollie Path. Starts 7m SE of Gairloch off A832 at car park on W side of Loch Maree
Glencoe
Lochan Forest Trail. Starts off A82 across Bridge of Coe through Glencoe village
Glencoe
Signal Rock. Starts off A82 3m SE of Glencoe via National Trust for Scotland Information Centre or from Clachaig Inn on unclass rd to Glencoe village
Inverfarigaig
Farigaig Forest Walk. Starts nr Inverfarigaig off B852
Inverness
Craig Phadrig Forest Walk. A9 northwards from Inverness for 1m and turn left at Muirtown Basin unclass
Inverness
Culloden Forest Trail. Starts 3m E of Inverness on by-road reached off A96 and B9006
Inverness
Culloden Battlefield Trail. 5½m E of Inverness off B9006 Culloden Moor rd
Kinlochewe
Loch Maree and Glas Leitire Nature Trail. Starts at car park in forest on A832 SE end of Loch Maree
Rhum, Isle of
Kinloch Glen and South Side Nature Trails. Starts at jetty on E coast of island for passenger ferry service from Mallaig
Strathpeffer
Torrachilty Forest Walk. Starts 3m SW of Strathpeffer off A834 at Contin
Strontian
Strontian Glen Nature Trail. Starts 1¼m N of Strontian, E of minor rd off A861

Hopetoun House, Queensferry, Lothian

Tain
Morangie Forest Walk. Starts 3m W of Tain on A9
Tongue (A836), Thurso (45m) – Durness (30½m)
Borgie Forest Walk (Naver Forest). 6½m E of Tongue
off A836, S of A836 nr Borgie Bridge

LOTHIAN
Broxburn (10m W of Edinburgh)
Almondell and Calderwood Country Park. N
entrance: 2m S of Broxburn along unclass rd from
junction A899 in Broxburn, or A89 junction ½m S of
Broxburn. S entrance from Edinburgh–Ayr rd A71, nr
East Calder
Dalkeith
Dalkeith Park Nature Trail. Starts just N of Dalkeith
High St, off A68
Dunbar
Barns Ness Nature Trail. Starts 3m SE of Dunbar, ½m
N of A1 at lighthouse at Barns Ness
Dunbar
Pressmennan Forest Trail. Starts 5m SW of Dunbar
at car park on minor rd 1m S of Stenton off B6370
North Berwick
Yellowcraig Nature Trail. Starts 2m W of North
Berwick on minor rd N of B1345 (from A198) at
Dirleton
Queensferry (South)
Hopetoun House. Starts 2m W of South Queensferry
off A904
Queensferry (South)
House of the Binns Woodland Walk. Starts 5m W of
South Queensferry on track at junction of A904 and
B9109

STRATHCLYDE
Ayr
Enterkine Wood Nature Trail. Starts 7m E of Ayr off
B744 2m NE of Annbank
Ayr
Rozelle Nature Trail. Starts 1½m S of Rozelle Estate,
Monument Rd. ½m off B7024
Balloch
Balloch Nature Trail. Starts at main gate of Loch
Lomond Park on B854
Carradale
Carradale Forest Walks. Starts 1m W of Carradale on
B879
Dunoon
Kilmun Arboretum and Benmore Forest (Pucks
Glen) Walks. Starts 7m N of Dunoon at Benmore
Forest on A880, 1m S of A815 junction
Glasgow
Dawsholm Park Nature Trail. Starts at main gate of
Dawsholm Park between A809 and A81
Glasgow
Kelvin Walkway. Starts N of city centre at Botanic
Gardens on A82
Glasgow
Kelvingrove Park Nature Trail. Starts in city centre at
Kelvingrove Museum and Art Gallery, between A82
and A814

Glasgow
Linn Park Nature Trail (Cathcart). Starts on S edge
of Glasgow at Mansion House off A727 (Clarkston
Rd)
Glasgow
Pollok Park Nature Trail. Starts S of Glasgow at
Pollok House off A736 at Pollockshaws
Glasgow
Rosshall Park Nature Trail. Starts at Nature Kiosk,
Rosshall Park on A754, Crookston Rd
Glasgow
Springburn Park Nature Trail. Starts at NE side of
Glasgow at Information Centre, Springburn Park on
A803
Glasgow
Tollcross Park Nature Trail. Starts in E part of
Glasgow at Mansion House on A721 Tollcross Rd,
nr Braidfauld
Greenock
Cornalees Bridge Trail. 6m SW of Greenock off
A742, leave main rd 4m from Greenock, following
minor rd to S
Inverliever Forest (22m SW of Oban)
Inverliever Forest Trail and Walks. Starts at
Inverinan car park on west side of Loch Awe on
unclass rd linking B845 from Taynuilt and B840
at Ford
Lanark
Corehoue Nature Reserve. Starts 2m S of Lanark on
minor rd S of A72
Lochwinnoch
Muirshiel Country Park. Country Trail and Habitat
Trail. 4½m NW of Lochwinnoch on minor rd
NE from B786
Motherwell
Orbiston Glen Nature Trail. On minor rd approached
from A721 1¾m N of Motherwell or nr junction
M74/A725
Oban
Barcaldine Forest Walks, 7m NE of Oban off A828.
Several walks: Beinn Lora Walks 2½m N of Connel
Bridge; Glen Dubh Walks 7m N of Connel Bridge;
East na Circe Walk 10½m N of Connel Bridge, nr
northern end of Loch Geran
Paisley
Paisley Glen Nature Trail. Starts at Glenfield Rd,
Paisley off B774
Rothesay, Isle of Bute
Bull Loch Farm. Starts 8m NW of Rothesay at
Rhubodach Ferry nr end of A886
Rothesay, Isle of Bute
Ettrick Bay Kilmichael Trail. Starts 5m W of Rothesay
at Ettrick Bay
Rothesay, Isle of Bute
Kilchattan Trail. Starts at Kilchattan Pier on B881,
8m S of Rothesay off A844
Rothesay, Isle of Bute
Kingarth Trail. Starts 7m S of Rothesay at Kingarth
churchyard on A844
Rothesay, Isle of Bute
Loch Ascog Trail. Starts 3m S of Rothesay at Ascog
Bay on A844
Rothesay, Isle of Bute
Loch Fad Trail. Starts at Bute Museum in Rothesay
Rutherglen
Cathkin Braes. Starts 2½m S of Rutherglen on B759
Tighnabruaich
Caladh Castle Trail (Glendaruel Forest). Starts 3m N
of Tighnabruaich on A8003

TAYSIDE
Aberfeldy
Birks of Aberfeldy Nature Trail. Starts ¼m S of
Aberfeldy off A826
Aberfeldy
The Mains Walks, Drummond Hill. ¼m N of Kenmore
(5¾m W of Aberfeldy). Just off A827
Arbroath
Arbroath Cliffs Nature Trail. Starts in Arbroath at end
of esplanade

Crieff
Crieff Nature Trail. Starts at Culcrieff Farm on outskirts of Crieff on A85
Dundee
Camperdown Park Nature Trail. Starts 3m NW of Dundee off junction A923/A972
Dunkeld
Hermitage Forest Woodland Trail. Starts 1m W of Dunkeld on B898
Killin
Ben Lawyers Nature Trail. Starts 7m NE of Killin off A827
Kinross
Loch Leven, Vane Farm Nature Trail. Starts 6m SE of Kinross at Vane Farm off B9097, E of Junction 5 (M90 Motorway) also E of B996 from Kinross
Meigle
Belmont Estate Nature Trail. Starts ½m S of Meigle off A927 nr Belmont Castle
Perth
Kinnoull Hill. Starts 1m E of Perth on minor rd off A93
Pitlochry
Kindrogan Field Centre Hill Trail. Starts at Kindrogan House, Kindrogan Wood on A924 10m NE of Pitlochry
Pitlochry
Tummel Forest Walks. Starts 7m W of Pitlochry off B8019

Forest Drives

Scotland
CENTRAL
Aberfoyle
Achray Forest Drive. Starts 2m N of Aberfoyle on A821

DUMFRIES AND GALLOWAY
Clatteringshaws
Raiders Rd (Galloway Forest Park). Starts ¾m S of Clatteringshaws on A712 and on A762

Long-distance Motor Trails

Scotland
STRATHCLYDE
Bute, Isle of
Motorists: A drive round the island. Length 30–35m.

TAYSIDE
Blair Atholl
Atholl Way Motor Trail. Starts from Blair Atholl

Nature Trails

Northern Ireland
ANTRIM
Ballycastle
Ballycastle. Starts in town centre, follows close Ballycastle railway
Ballycastle
Ballycastle Forest. Starts at entrance gate to forest drive. Diamond, Ballycastle. Access from Fairhill Street and track of former narrow-gauge railway
Giant's Causeway
Starts from car park on B146 E of Portrush
Portrush
Portrush Nature Reserve
Antrim
Shanes Castle. Starts 1m from Antrim on A6 at entrance to Shanes Castle Nature Reserve and Railway at Antrim Gate Lodge
Connor
Tardree Forest
Ballintoy
Whitepark Bay. Starts from car park 1¼m W of Ballintoy

ARMAGH
Markethill
Gosford Forest Park. Starts ½m from Markethill from bypass rd B3
Oxford Island
Access from M1 Motorway signposted to Oxford Island

DOWN
Bangor
Castle Park. Entrance from Main Street, Bangor via Castle Park Avenue opposite railway station
Newcastle
Murlough Nature Reserve. Starts 2m NW of Newcastle at Twelve Arches public car park
Newcastle
Tollymore Forest Park. Starts 2m from Newcastle on B180 Bryansford rd

FERMANAGH
Belleek
Castlecaldwell Forest. Starts 5m E of Belleek on main Belleek–Kesh rd
Derrygonnelly
Correl Glen Forest. Starts 4m from Derrygonnelly opposite entrance to Lough Navar Forest

Calendar of Events

(A selection of major events)

February

London (Earls Court)	Cruft's Dog Show
London (Royal Albert Hall)	Folk Festival
London (Royal Horticultural Halls)	STAMPEX – National Stamp Exhibition

March

Downpatrick, Northern Ireland	Horse-racing: Ulster Harp National
London (Old Town Hall, Chelsea)	Chelsea Antiques Fair
London (Earls Court)	Daily Mail Ideal Home Exhibition
Cheltenham	Horse-racing: Cheltenham Gold Cup
Edinburgh	Edinburgh Folk Festival

April

Liverpool (Aintree Racecourse, Aintree)	Horse-racing: Grand National Steeplechase
Badminton	Badminton Horse Trials
Harrogate	Harrogate International Youth Music
Belfast (Start and Finish)	Circuit of Ireland International Rally
London	Easter Parade
London (Regent's Park)	Harness Horse Parade
Birmingham (National Exhibition Centre)	Birmingham International Show Jumping Championships
St Andrews	St Andrews Golf Week

April–January

Stratford-upon-Avon	Shakespeare Theatre Season

May

London (Wembley)	Rugby League: State Express Challenge Cup Final
London (Olympia)	Photo World Exhibition

Folk-dancers in Northern Ireland

Brighton	Brighton Festival
Spalding	Spalding Flower Parade
London (Wembley)	Football Association Cup Final
Windsor	Royal Windsor Horse Show
London (South Bank)	English Bach Festival
Malvern	Malvern Festival
London (Royal Hospital, Chelsea)	Chelsea Flower Show
Perth	Perth Festival of Arts
Leeds	Leeds Musical Festival
Edinburgh	International Gathering Scotland

May–June

Bath	Bath Festival

May–August

Glyndebourne	Glyndebourne Festival Opera Season

May–September

Chichester	Chichester Festival Theatre Season

May–October

Pitlochry	Pitlochry Festival Theatre Season

June

	Golf: British Amateur Championship
Epsom	Horse-racing: The Derby
Shepton Mallet (The Showground)	Royal Bath and West Show
London (Olympia)	Fine Art and Antiques Fair
Isle of Man	International T.T. Motorcycle Races
Appleby	Appleby Horse Fair
London (Europa Hotel)	Antiquarian Book Fair
Albeburgh	Aldeburgh Festival
London	Trooping the Colour
Ascot	Horse-racing: Royal Ascot
Ingliston, Edinburgh	Royal Highland Agricultural Show

June–July

Wimbledon	Lawn Tennis Championships
Cheltenham	Cheltenham International Festival of Music

July

Henley-on-Thames	Henley Royal Regatta
Stoneleigh (National Agricultural Centre)	Royal Agricultural Show
Llangollen	International Music Eisteddfod
London (Earls Court)	Royal Tournament
	Golf: British Open Championship
Silverstone Circuit	Motor Racing: British Grand Prix
Builth Wells (Hanelwedd)	Royal Welsh Show

London (Wembley)	Royal International Horse Show
King's Lynn	King's Lynn Festival
London (Lord's Cricket Ground)	Cricket: Benson and Hedges Cup Final
Goodwood	Horse-racing: Goodwood Week

July–August

Harrogate	Harrogate International Festival

August

Machynlleth	Royal National Eisteddfod
Cowes, Isle of Wight	Sailing: Cowes Week
Worcester/Hereford/Gloucester (alternating)	Three Choirs Festival
Oban	Argyllshire Highland Gathering
Dunoon	Dunoon and Cowal Highland Gathering

August–September

Edinburgh	Edinburgh Military Tattoo
Edinburgh	Edinburgh International Festival

September

London (Lord's)	Cricket: National Westminster Cup Final
Braemar	Royal Highland Gathering
Leeds	Leeds International Pianoforte Competition
London (Chelsea)	Chelsea Autumn Antiques Fair
Burghley	Burghley Horse Trials
Doncaster	Horse-racing: St Leger Stakes

October

London (Wembley)	Horse of the Year Show
Nottingham	Nottingham Goose Fair

November

London (Start)	London to Brighton Veteran Car Run
Belfast	Belfast Festival of the Arts at Queens
London (City)	Lord Mayor's Procession and Show

December

London (Earls Court)	Royal Smithfield Show and Agricultural Machinery Exhibition

Official Tourist Offices

British Tourist Authority
Thames Tower
Black's Road
Hammersmith
London W6 9EL

National Tourist Information Centre
Victoria Station Forecourt
London SW1
tel. 01–730 3488

Scottish Tourist Board
23 Ravelston Ter
Edinburgh EH4 3EU
tel. 031–332 2433

Wales Tourist Board
PO Box 1
Cardiff CF1 2XN
tel. (0222) 27281

Isle of Man Tourist Board
13 Victoria St
Douglas
Isle of Man
tel. Douglas (0624) 4323

Northern Ireland Tourist Board
River House
48 High St
Belfast BT1 2DS
tel. (0232) 231221

AA Breakdown Service

AA centres telephone numbers are listed below.

AA Members needing Breakdown Service should normally ring the nearest centre listed below. In case of difficulty, any other centre will be able to take the details and pass them on to the appropriate office.

Please note that all calls to 24-hr Breakdown Service Centres are answered in turn. If the ringing tone is heard, DO NOT RING OFF.

England

Alconbury Weston, Cambs
tel. Cambridge (0223) 312302
24-hr service

Ashton-under-Lyne, Gt Manchester
tel. 061–485 6299

Barnstaple, Devon
tel. Barnstaple (0271) 45691
24-hr service

Barrow-in-Furness, Cumbria
tel. Barrow (0229) 20665
24-hr service

Barton Mills, Suffolk
tel. Mildenhall (0638) 712928
24-hr service

Basingstoke, Hants
tel. Basingstoke (0256) 56565
24-hr service

Bath, Avon
tel. Bath (0225) 24731
24-hr service

Bedford, Beds
tel. Bedford (0234) 218888
24-hr service

Bexhill, E. Sussex
tel. Bexhill (0424) 214014
24-hr service

Birkenhead, Merseyside
tel. 051–709 7252
24-hr service

Birmingham, W. Midlands
tel. 021–550 4858
24-hr service

Blackburn, Lancs
tel. Blackburn (0254) 51369
24-hr service

Blackpool, Lancs
tel. Blackpool (0253) 44947
24-hr service

Bolton, Gt Manchester
tel. 061–485 6299
24-hr service

Boston, Lincs
tel. Boston (0205) 63905
24-hr service

Bournemouth, Dorset
tel. Bournemouth (0202) 25751
24-hr service

Bradford, W Yorks
tel. Bradford (0274) 724703
24-hr service

Brighton, E Sussex
tel. Brighton (0273) 695231
24-hr service

Bristol, Avon
tel. Bristol (0272) 298531
24-hr service

Cambridge, Cambs
tel. Cambridge (0223) 312302
24-hr service

Carlisle, Cumbria
tel. Carlisle (0228) 24274
24-hr service

Carnforth, Lancs
tel. Carnforth (0524) 732036
24-hr service

Chelmsford, Essex
tel. Chelmsford (0245) 261711
24-hr service

Chester, Cheshire
tel. Chester (0244) 20438
07.00–23.00

Chichester, W Sussex
tel. Chichester (0243) 783111
24-hr service

Colchester, Essex
tel. Colchester (0206) 66769
24-hr service

Coventry, W Midlands
tel. 021–550 4858
24-hr service

Crawley, W Sussex
tel. Crawley (0293) 25685
24-hr service

Darlington, Co Durham
tel. Stockton (0642) 607215
24-hr service

Doncaster, S Yorks
tel. Doncaster (0302) 60733
09.00–17.00

Dorchester, Dorset
tel. Dorchester (0305) 62330
24-hr service

Dunstable, Beds
tel. Dunstable (0582) 607218
24-hr service

Durham, Co Durham
tel. Durham (0385) 62894
24-hr service

Eastbourne, E Sussex
tel. Polegate (03212) 3312
24-hr service

Epping, Essex
tel. Theydon Bois (037881) 4121
24-hr service

Esher, Surrey
tel. 01–398 5374
09.00–17.00

Exeter, Devon
tel. Exeter (0392) 32121
24-hr service

Faversham, Kent
tel. Faversham (0795) 532536
24-hr service

Gailey, Staffs
tel. 021–550 4858
24-hr service

Gallows Corner, Gt London
tel. Ingrebourne (04023) 42310
24-hr service

Gatwick, W Sussex
tel. Crawley (0293) 26842
24-hr service

Gloucester, Glos
tel. Gloucester (0452) 23278
24-hr service

Gravesend, Kent
tel. Gravesend (0474) 52814
24-hr service

Grimsby, Humberside
tel. Grimsby (0472) 41393
09.00–17.00

Guildford, Surrey
tel. Guildford (0483) 572841
24-hr service

Halifax, W Yorks
tel. Halifax (0422) 57810
09.00–17.00

Harrogate, N Yorks
tel. Harrogate (0423) 69545
09.00–17.00

Hartlepool, Cleveland
tel. Hartlepool (0429) 62786
09.00–17.00

Hatfield, Herts
tel. Hatfield (07072) 62852
24-hr service

Heathrow Airport, Gt London
tel. 01–897 8842
09.00–17.00

Hillingdon, Gt London
tel. Uxbridge (0895) 34884
09.00–17.00

Hounslow, Gt London
tel. 01–759 0107
09.00–17.00

Huddersfield, W Yorks
tel. Huddersfield (0484) 20039
09.00–17.00

Hull, Humberside
tel. Hull (0482) 28580
24-hr service

Ipswich, Suffolk
tel. Ipswich (0473) 214942
24-hr service

Kendal, Cumbria
tel. Kendal (0539) 27652
09.00–17.00

Keswick, Cumbria
tel. Keswick (0596) 73458
09.00–17.00

King's Lynn, Norfolk
tel. King's Lynn (0553) 773731
24-hr service

Lamberhurst, Kent
tel. Lamberhurst (0892) 890248
24-hr service

Leamington Spa, Warwicks
tel. 021–550 4858
24-hr service

Leatherhead, Surrey
tel. Leatherhead (0372) 372085
24-hr service

Leeds, W Yorks
tel. Leeds (0532) 438161
24-hr service

Leicester, Leics
tel. Leicester (0533) 20491
24-hr service

Lincoln, Lincs
tel. Lincoln (0522) 42363
24-hr service

Liverpool, Merseyside
tel. 051–709 7252
24-hr service

London
tel. 01–954 7373
24-hr service

Luton, Bedfordshire
tel. Luton (0582) 419549
24-hr service

Maidstone, Kent
tel. Maidstone (0622) 55353
24-hr service

Manchester, Gt Manchester
tel. 061–485 6299
24-hr service

Middlesbrough, Cleveland
tel. Middlesbrough (0642) 246832
24-hr service

Milton Keynes, Bucks
tel. Milton Keynes (0908) 665188
24-hr service

Newcastle-upon-Tyne, Tyne and Wear
tel. Newcastle-upon-Tyne (0632) 610111
24-hr service

Northampton, Northants
tel. Northampton (0604) 66241
24-hr service

Norwich, Norfolk
tel. Norwich (0603) 629401
24-hr service

Nottingham, Notts
tel. Nottingham (0602) 787751
24-hr service

Oldham, Gt Manchester
tel. 061–485 6299
24-hr service

Ollerton, Notts
tel. Nottingham (0602) 787751
24-hr service

Oxford, Oxon
tel. Oxford (0865) 240286
24-hr service

Pampisford, Cambs
tel. Cambridge (0223) 312302
24-hr service

Peterborough, Cambs
tel. Cambridge (0223) 312302
24-hr service

Plymouth, Devon
tel. Plymouth (0752) 669989
24-hr service

Pontefract, W Yorks
tel. Pontefract (0977) 706923
09.00–17.00

Portsmouth, Hants
tel. Portsmouth (0705) 667012
24-hr service

Raynes Park, Gt London
tel. 01–543 3565
09.00–17.00

Reading, Berks
tel. Reading (0734) 581122
24-hr service

Rotherham, S Yorks
tel. Sheffield (0742) 28861
24-hr service

St Austell, Cornwall
tel. Truro (0872) 76455
24-hr service

St Helens, Merseyside
tel. St Helens (0744) 34189
07.00–23.00

St Nicholas at Wade (Margate), Kent
tel. Thanet (0843) 47226
24-hr service

Salisbury, Wilts
tel. Salisbury (0722) 22246
24-hr service

Scarborough, N Yorks
tel. Scarborough (0723) 60344
24-hr service

Sheffield, S Yorks
tel. Sheffield (0742) 28861
24-hr service

Shrewsbury, Salop
tel. Shrewsbury (0743) 53003
24-hr service

Skipton, N Yorks
tel. Skipton (0756) 3354
09.00–17.00

Slough, Berks
tel. Slough (0753) 75588
24-hr service

Southampton, Hants
tel. Southamton (0703) 36811
24-hr service

Southport, Merseyside
tel. Southport (0704) 36431
09.00–17.00

South Woodford, Gt London
tel. 01–989 6567
09.00–17.00

Stockport, Gt Manchester
tel. 061–485 6299
24-hr service

Stockton-on-Tees, Cleveland
tel. Stockton (0642) 607215
24-hr service

Stoke-on-Trent, Staffs
tel. Stoke-on-Trent (0782) 25881
24-hr service

Stratford-upon-Avon, Warwicks
tel. 021–550 4858
24-hr service

Sunderland, Tyne and Wear
tel. Sunderland (0783) 659018
24-hr service

Sutton Scotney, Hants
tel. Winchester (0962) 760630
24-hr service

Swindon, Wilts
tel. Swindon (0793) 21446
24-hr service

Taunton, Somerset
tel. Taunton (0823) 73363
24-hr service

Torquay, Devon
tel. Torquay (0803) 25903
24-hr service

Truro, Cornwall
tel. Truro (0872) 76455
24-hr service

Wakefield, W Yorks
tel. Wakefield (0924) 377957
24-hr service

Washington, Tyne and Wear
tel. Newcastle (0632) 610111
24-hr service

Wolverhampton, W Midlands
tel. 021–550 4858
24-hr service

Worcester, Heref and Worcs
tel. Worcester (0905) 51070
24-hr service

Wrotham, Kent
tel. Borough Green (0732) 882103
24-hr service

Yarmouth (Great), Norfolk
tel. Norwich (0603) 629401
24-hr service

Yeovil, Somerset
tel. Yeovil (0935) 27744
24-hr service

York, N Yorks
tel. York (0904) 27698
24-hr service

Channel Islands

Guernsey
tel. Guernsey (0481) 22984
08.00–19.00

Jersey
tel. Jersey (0534) 23344
08.00–19.00

Isle of Man

Douglas
tel. Douglas (0624) 5826
09.00–17.00
051–709 7252 all other times incl weekends

Isle of Wight

Newport
tel. Newport (0983) 522653
24-hr service

Wales

Aberystwyth, Dyfed
tel. Aberystwyth (0970) 4801
24-hr service

Brecon, Powys
tel. Brecon (0874) 2015
24-hr service

Caernarfon, Gwynedd
tel. Caernarfon (0286) 3935
24-hr service

Cardiff, S Glam
tel. Cardiff (0222) 394111
24-hr service

Llandudno, Gwynedd
tel. Llandudno (0492) 79066
24-hr service

Newport, Gwent
tel. Newport (Gwent) (0633) 62559
24-hr service

Newtown, Powys
tel. Newtown (0686) 26103
24-hr service

Pont Abraham, W Glam
tel. Swansea (0792) 55598
24-hr service

Swansea, W Glam
tel. Swansea (0792) 55598
24-hr service

Scotland

Aberdeen, Grampian
tel. Aberdeen (0224) 639231
24-hr service

Aviemore, Highland
tel. Aviemore (0479) 810300
07.00–19.00

Dalkeith, Lothian
tel. 031–225 8464
24-hr service

Dumfries, Dumfries and Galloway
tel. Dumfries (0387) 69257
24-hr service

Dundee, Tayside
tel. Dundee (0382) 25585
24-hr service

Dunfermline, Fife
tel. Dunfermline (0383) 32125
08.00–20.00

Edinburgh, Lothian
tel. 031–225 8464
24-hr service

Elgin, Grampian
tel. Elgin (0343) 46450
07.00–19.00

Falkirk, Central
tel. Falkirk (0324) 25454
08.00–20.00

Fort William, Highland
tel. Fort William (0397) 2099
07.00–19.00

Galashiels, Borders
tel. Galashiels (0896) 55615
08.00–20.00

Glasgow, Strathclyde
tel. 041–812 0101
24-hr service

Gretna, Dumfries and Galloway
tel. Gretna (0461) 38242
24-hr service

Inverness, Highland
tel. Inverness (0463) 233213
07.00–19.00

Kilmarnock, Strathclyde
tel. Kilmarnock (0563) 25240
09.00–17.00

Kirkcaldy, Fife
tel. Kirkcaldy (0592) 262371
09.00–17.00

Motherwell, Strathclyde
tel. 041–812 0101
24-hr service

Oban, Strathclyde
tel. Oban (0631) 62854
09.00–17.00

Perth, Tayside
tel. Perth (0738) 23551
08.00–20.00

Prestwick, Strathclyde
tel. Prestwick (0292) 77789
24-hr service

St Andrews, Fife
tel. St Andrews (0334) 76407
08.00–20.00

Stirling, Central
tel. Stirling (0786) 64072
09.00–17.00

Stranraer, Dumfries and Galloway
tel. Stranraer (0776) 2659
09.00–17.00

Northern Ireland and Republic of Ireland

Belfast, Co Antrim (NI)
tel. Belfast (0232) 244538
24-hr service

Coleraine, Co Londonderry (NI)
tel. Coleraine (0265) 2596
09.00–17.00

Cork, Co Cork (RoI)
tel. Cork (021) 505155
08.00–24.00 Mon–Fri
09.00–24.00 Sat, Sun & Bank Hol

Craigavon, Co Armagh (NI)
tel. Craigavon (0762) 41576
09.00–17.00

Dublin, Co Dublin (RoI)
tel. Dublin (01) 779481
08.00–01.00 Mon–Sat
09.00–01.00 Sun & Bank Hol

Dundalk, Co Louth (RoI)
tel. Dundalk (042) 32955
09.00–17.00

Enniskillen, Co Fermanagh (NI)
tel. Enniskillen (0365) 22589
09.00–17.00

Galway, Co Galway (RoI)
tel. Galway (091) 64438
09.00–17.00

Larne, Co Antrim (NI)
tel. Larne (0574) 3958
09.00–17.00

Limerick, Co Limerick (RoI)
tel. Limerick (061) 48241
09.00–17.00

Londonderry, Co Londonderry (NI)
tel. Londonderry (0504) 43467
24-hr service

Port Laoise, Co Laoise (RoI)
tel. Port Laoise (0502) 21692
09.00–17.00

Sligo, Co Sligo (RoI)
tel. Sligo (071) 62065
09.00–17.00

Waterford, Co Waterford (RoI)
tel. Waterford (051) 73765
09.00–17.00

NB. Area codes shown against telephone numbers in the Republic of Ireland are applicable within the Republic. To dial from the UK, consult your local Dialling Code book.

AA Centres

All Centres listed below have reception facilities and deal with telephone enquiries on the numbers shown. Office hours are normally 9 a.m.–5 p.m. from Monday to Friday; on Tuesday mornings offices open half an hour later at 9.30 a.m. to allow training to take place. Some offices are open on Saturdays. Local variations of opening and closing times will occur to take account of early-closing arrangements and other factors; you should check these before calling.

London

Telephone enquiries
General, home travel information and 24-hr breakdown service
tel. 01-954 7373*
Legal, technical, insurance, overseas travel and other specialised subjects
tel. 01-954 7355

City Centre, Regis House, King William St, London EC4R 9AN
Members' Services, tel. 01-954 7373

Croydon Centre, 104 North End, Croydon, Surrey CR0 1UD
Members' Services, tel. 01-954 7373

Ealing Centre, 22 New Broadway, Ealing, London W5 2XA
Members' Services, tel. 01-954 7373

Hammersmith Centre, 24 King St, Hammersmith, London W6 0QW
Members' Services, tel. 01-954 7373

Kingston-upon-Thames Centre, 32 Market Place, Kingston-upon-Thames, Surrey KT1 1JH
Members' Services, tel. 01-954 7373

Leicester Square Centre, Fanum House, 5 New Coventry St, London W1V 8HT
Members' Services, tel. 01-954 7373

Romford Centre, 119 South St, Romford, Essex RM1 1NX
Members' Services, tel. 01-954 7373

Stanmore Centre, Fanum House, The Broadway, Stanmore, Middlesex HA7 4DF
Members' Services, tel. 01-954 7373

Twickenham Centre, 13 London Rd, Twickenham TW1 3ST
Members' Services, tel. 01-954 7373

Wood Green Centre, 105 High Rd, Wood Green, London N22 6BB
Members' Services, tel. 01-954 7373

Southern Britain

Basingstoke Centre, Fanum House, Basingstoke, Hants RG21 2EA
Members' Services, tel. (0256) 20123

Bedford Centre, 73 High St, Bedford MK40 1NE
Members' Services, tel. (0234) 218888

Bournemouth Centre, Fanum House, 47 Richmond Hill, Bournemouth BH2 6LU
Members' Services, tel. (0202) 25751

Brighton Centre, 10 Churchill Sq, Brighton BN1 2EY
Members' Services, tel. (0273) 695231

Cambridge Centre, Janus House, 46–48 St Andrews St, Cambridge CB2 3BH
Members' Services, tel. (0223) 312302

Chelmsford Centre, 205 Moulsham St, Chelmsford CM2 0LP
Members' Services, tel. (0245) 261711

Colchester Centre, 10–11 Trinity Sq, Colchester CO1 1JR
Members' Services, tel. (0206) 66769

Dover Port Service Centre, Eastern Dock Terminal, Dover, Kent CT16 1JA
Port Services, tel. (0304) 208122
Hire Services Unit, Snargate St, Dover, Kent CT17 9XA, tel. (0304) 203655

Exeter Centre, Fanum House, Bedford St, Exeter EX1 1LD
Members' Services, tel. (0392) 32121

Folkestone Port Service Centre, Folkestone Harbour, Folkestone CT20 1QG
tel. (0303) 58111

Guernsey Port Service Centre, The White Rock, St Peter Port, Guernsey, Channel Islands
tel. (0481) 22984

Guildford Centre, 22 Friary St, Guildford, Surrey GU1 4EH
Members' Services, tel. (0483) 572841

Harwich Port Service Centre, Car Ferry Terminal, Parkeston Quay, Harwich, Essex CO12 4SH
tel. (0255) 503331

Ipswich Centre, 41 Upper Brook St, Ipswich IP4 1HT
Members' Services, tel. (0473) 214942

Jersey Centre, 11 Esplanade, St Helier, Jersey, Channel Islands
Members' Services, tel. (0534) 23344

Luton Centre, 45 George St, Luton LU1 2AQ
Members' Services, tel. (0582) 419549

Maidstone Centre, 8 Colman Parade, King St, Maidstone, Kent ME14 1DL
Members' Services, tel. (0622) 55353

Newhaven Port Service Centre, Car Ferry Terminal, Newhaven Harbour, Newhaven, East Sussex BN9 0DB
tel. (0273) 514245

Northampton Centre, 67 Abington St, Northampton NN1 2BH
Members' Services, tel. (0604) 66241

Norwich Centre, Fanum House,
126 Thorpe Rd, Norwich NR1 1RL
Members' Services, tel. (0603) 629401

Oxford Centre, 133–134 High St,
Oxford OX1 4DN
Members' Services, tel. (0865) 240286

Plymouth Centre, 10 Old Town St,
Plymouth PL1 1DE
Members' Services, tel. (0752) 669989

Plymouth Port Service Centre, Millbay Docks,
Plymouth PL1 3DS
tel. (0752) 665437

Portsmouth Port Service Centre, Wharf Rd,
(Rudmore Roundabout), Portsmouth PO2 8HB
tel. (0705) 698854

Ramsgate Port Service Centre, Port Sally,
Western Terminal, Ramsgate Harbour,
Ramsgate, Kent CT11 8RP
tel. (0843) 592940

Reading Centre, 45 Oxford Rd,
Reading RG1 7QL
Members' Services, tel. (0734) 581122

Slough Centre, 222–224 High St,
Slough SL1 1JS
Members' Services, tel. (0753) 75588

Southend-on-Sea Centre, The Air Ferry Terminal,
Southend-on-Sea, Essex SS2 6YH
tel. (0702) 544790

Southampton Centre, 126 Above Bar St,
Southampton SO9 1GY
Members' Services, tel. (0703) 36811

Swindon Centre, 22 Canal Walk, Brunel Centre,
Swindon SN1 1LD
Members' Services, tel. (0793) 21446

Truro Centre, 10 River St, Truro,
Cornwall TR1 2SQ
Members' Services, tel. (0872) 76455

Weymouth Port Service Centre, Weymouth
Quay, Weymouth, Dorset, DT4 6DX
tel. (0305) 786057

Central Britain

Birmingham Centre, 134 New St,
Birmingham B2 4NP
Members' Services, tel. 021–550 4858

Bradford Centre, 101 Godwin St,
Bradford, West Yorkshire BD1 3PP
Members' Services, tel. (0274) 724703

Cardiff Centre, Fanum House, 140 Queen St,
Cardiff CF1 4EP
Members' Services, tel. (0222) 394111

Chester Centre, 36–38 Frodsham St,
Chester CH1 3JB
Members' Services, tel. (0244) 20438

Coventry Centre, 39–40 Hertford St,
Coventry CV1 1LF
Members' Services, tel. 021–550 4858

Derby Centre, 22 East St,
Derby DE1 2AF
Members' Services, tel. (0602) 787751

Hull Centre, 28 Paragon St,
Hull HU1 3NE
Members' Services, tel. (0482) 28580

Leeds Centre, 95 The Headrow,
Leeds LS1 6LU
Members' Services, tel. (0532) 438161

Leicester Centre, 132 Charles St,
Leicester LE1 1NA
Members' Services, tel. (0533) 20491

Liverpool Centre, Derby Sq,
Liverpool L2 1UF
Members' Services, tel. 051–709 7252

Llandudno Centre, Gwynedd, 2 Trinity Sq,
Llandudno LL30 2PY
Members' Services, tel. (0492) 79066

Manchester Centre, St Ann's House,
St Ann's Place, Manchester M2 7LP
Members' Services, tel. 061–485 6299

Nottingham Centre, Fanum House,
484 Derby Rd, Nottingham NG7 2GT
Members' Services, tel. (0602) 787751

Preston Centre, 3–4 Cheapside,
Preston PR1 2AP
Members' Services, tel. (0772) 201134

Sheffield Centre, 5 St James Row,
Sheffield
Members' Services, tel. (0742) 28861

Stoke-on-Trent Centre, 32–38 Stafford St,
Hanley, Stoke-on-Trent ST1 1JP
Members' Services, tel. (0782) 25881

Swansea Centre, 20 Union St,
Swansea SA1 3EH
Members' Services, tel. (0792) 465018

Wolverhampton Centre, 19 The Gallery,
Mander Centre, Wolverhampton WV1 3NG
Members' Services, tel. 021–550 4858

York Centre, 6 Church St,
York YO1 2BG
Members' Services, tel. (0904) 27698

Northern Britain

Aberdeen Centre, Fanum House, 19 Golden Sq,
Aberdeen AB9 1JN
Members' Services, tel. (0224) 639231

Belfast Centre, Fanum House,
108–110 Great Victoria St, Belfast BT2 7AT
Members' Services, tel. (0232) 244538

Douglas Centre, 12B Walpole Av,
Douglas, Isle of Man
Members' Services, tel. (0624) 75826

Dundee Centre, 124 Overgate,
Dundee DD1 1DX
Members' Services, tel. (0382) 25585

Edinburgh Centre, Fanum House,
18/22 Melville St, Edinburgh EH3 7PD
Members' Services, tel. 031–225 8464

Glasgow Centre, 269 Argyle St,
Glasgow G2 8DW
Members' Services, tel. 041–204 0711

Middlesbrough Centre, 17 Corporation Rd,
Middlesbrough, Cleveland TS1 1LS
Members' Services, tel. (0642) 246832

Newcastle Centre, 13 Princess Sq,
Newcastle-upon-Tyne NE1 8EX
Members' Services, tel. 091–261 0111